The Broadview Anthology of

VICTORIAN
POETRY

AND POETIC THEORY

CONCISE EDITION

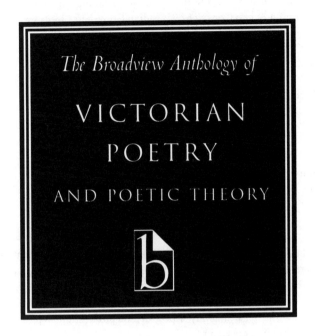

The Broadview Anthology of

VICTORIAN POETRY

AND POETIC THEORY

CONCISE EDITION

EDITED BY

THOMAS J. COLLINS

& VIVIENNE J. RUNDLE

ASSISTANT EDITORS: WAI YING LEE & KIRSTEN MUNRO

BROADVIEW ANTHOLOGIES OF ENGLISH LITERATURE

broadview press

NATIONAL LIBRARY OF CANADA CATALOGUING IN PUBLICATION

The Broadview Anthology of Victorian poetry and poetic theory

Concise ed.
ISBN 1-55111-366-X

1. English poetry — 19th Century. 2. English poetry — 19th century —
History and criticism — Theory, etc. I. Collins, Thomas J., 1936–. II. Rundle, Vivienne Jill.

PR1223.B68   2000   821'.808   C00-930259-X

Broadview Press, Ltd. is an independent, international publishing house, incorporated in 1985. Broadview believes in shared ownership, both with its employees and with the general public; since the year 2000 Broadview shares have traded publicly on the Toronto Venture Exchange under the symbol BDP.

We welcome comments and suggestions regarding any aspect of our publications—please feel free to contact us at the addresses below or at broadview@broadviewpress.com.

North America
PO Box 1243,
Peterborough, Ontario
Canada K9J 7H5
P.O. Box 1015,
3576 California Road,
Orchard Park, NY, USA 14127
Tel: (705) 743-8990;
Fax: (705) 743-8353
email: customerservice@broadviewpress.com

UK, Ireland, and continental Europe
NBN Plymbridge
Estover Road
Plymouth
UK PL6 7PY
Tel: +44 (0) 1752 202301;
Fax: +44 (0) 1752 202331;
Fax Order Line: +44 (0) 1752 202333;
Cust Ser: cservs@nbnplymbridge.com
Orders: orders@nbnplymbridge.com

Australia and New Zealand
UNIREPS,
University of New South Wales
Sydney, NSW, 2052
Australia
Tel: 61 2 9664 0999;
Fax: 61 2 9664 5420
email: info.press@unsw.edu.au

www. broadviewpress.com

Broadview Press gratefully acknowledges the financial support of the Government of Canada through the Book Publishing Industry Development Program for our publishing activities.

Cover design by George Kirkpatrick

PRINTED IN CANADA

Editorial Preface

In preparing *The Broadview Anthology of Victorian Poetry and Poetic Theory*, we were guided by four criteria: the desire to include as full a representation of lesser-known poets as possible; the desire also to provide the widest possible range of selections from poets long established in the canon of Victorian English literature; the desire to recognize the ways in which the perceived canon has changed over time and is continuing to change; and, finally, the desire to include a substantial selection of theoretical commentary.

At the outset we decided that we would avoid, insofar as possible, using brief excerpts from longer works. The long poem is such a central part of Victorian poetry that we were determined to give such works an appropriate amount of space. Readers will, therefore, find the whole of Alfred Tennyson's *In Memoriam,* for example, and two complete books from Elizabeth Barrett Browning's *Aurora Leigh.* In order to accommodate these longer works, and others, as well as a generous selection of theoretical prose, the publisher has adopted a two-column format, thereby allowing the inclusion of considerably more material than would have otherwise been possible.

The selection process was influenced by several factors. We determined that our interpretation of the term "Victorian" would not be restrictive. To define one's selective limits as Queen Victoria's reign (1837–1901) imposes arbitrary historical limitations on choice, and the notion of historical periodicity is, at best, questionable. Readers will, therefore, find poetry which is pre-1837 (Felicia Hemans, the early Tennyson, for example), and post-1901 (Charlotte Mew and Alice Meynell, for example). The selection process was also significantly shaped by the editors' perception of the aesthetic quality of particular poems, the topical nature of some poems, and the contemporary importance and influence of theoretical essays. We endeavoured to take into account, and to have the anthology reflect, the extensive amount of critical work undertaken over the past generation. In addition, we have included some poems widely read and/or influential in their times, even though they might not be held in such high esteem today.

Another influential factor in our decisions about what to print was the response of scholars from various parts of the world to our request for reactions to the initial, very tentative, table of contents that we published on the Victoria Research Web almost five years ago. The table of contents in this volume differs markedly from the original one, and we want to thank all those colleagues (too many to name individually) who responded so generously to our call for assistance and suggestions. Many of the good things about this anthology (but none of the faults) are a result of that Internet interchange.

Gender issues have been the subject of some of the most interesting and controversial discussions in the study of Victorian poetry for the past decade or more. It will be evident to readers that the selection process was informed significantly by these discussions. Perhaps even more so than in other areas of English literature, recent anthologizing in Victorian literature has focused on providing—at last—a fuller representation of the work of women poets beyond the standard choices from Elizabeth Barrett Browning and Christina Rossetti. The publication of large anthologies devoted entirely to Victorian women poets has been of enormous value to students, to the profession, and particularly to us.

The Broadview Anthology of Victorian Poetry and Poetic Theory attempts to achieve a balance which includes the voices of both men and women poets and theorists. This should not be taken to imply any criticism of those efforts by other scholars to collect and to discuss solely the work of women poets. Indeed, as suggested above, compiling an anthology such as this would have been much more difficult had it not been for the work of recovery and reassessment carried out by such scholars as Isobel Armstrong, in *Victorian Poetry: Poetry, poetics, and politics* (Routledge, 1993), Angela Leighton, in *Victorian Women Poets: Writing Against the Heart* (Harvester Wheatsheaf, 1992), and Angela Leighton and Margaret Reynolds, editors of *Victorian Women Poets: An Anthology* (Blackwell, 1995) to name but a few. In her excellent introduction to *Victorian Women Poets*, Margaret Reynolds makes an interesting observation about the Victorian "conversation," particularly among women poets: "There are numerous poems addressed by one poet to another as if carrying on a conversation with one another" (xxx). This idea of conversation can, we believe, be profitably expanded to include the somewhat more wide-ranging notion of direct and indirect dialogue among poets, theorists, and the Victorian (and modern) communities of writers and readers.

Some critics have suggested in recent years that prose fiction was the prevailing Victorian genre. Its importance is unarguable. But as we worked on this anthology we were struck more acutely than ever before (even after decades of teaching), by the sheer volume of poetry published in annuals, periodicals, and collections by both men and women, a good deal of which, for both sexes, has only recently been recovered. In that poetry, and related theory, we perceived an intense dialogue of writers interacting with one another, and their predecessors, directly and indirectly, on all manner of topics important in their time, and still important in ours. "Intertextuality" was not in the vocabulary of the Victorians, but it was certainly in their practice. For a discussion of this subject, framed in slightly different terms, see, for example, Isobel Armstrong's incisive analysis of the poetic and intellectual currents and countercurrents involving Arthur Henry Hallam, Tennyson, William J. Fox, Browning, male and female feminists, and John Stuart Mill in Chapter 1, "Two Systems of Concentric Circles" of her *Victorian Poetry*. We hope that this work will provide readers with a more comprehensive sense than hitherto possible, drawing from material available in a single anthology, of the extent of this interactive dialogue in poetry, in theory, and between poetry and theory.

This concise edition of *The Broadview Anthology of Victorian Poetry and Theory* is intended particularly for university courses covering Victorian literature as a whole. While less than half the length of the full anthology, it preserves the main principles of the larger work. A number of longer poems are included in their entirety; there are generous selections from the work of all major poets, and a representative selection of other work; the work of Victorian women poets features very prominently; and a substantial selection of poetic theory is included to round out the volume.

EDITORIAL NOTE

Readers will find moderate annotation, for our desire has been to remain as unobtrusive as possible. Annotation is restricted, almost without exception, to the explanatory, and our guiding principle has been brevity and clarity.

In the Poetry section, we have used the normal practice of ordering chronologically by the birth dates of the poets; poems are arranged chronologically for each poet by publication date, with a few exceptions (for example, Matthew Arnold and Thomas Hardy). Dates of first publication are given when known, and dates of composition, if known, are given in brackets—both at the end of poems. In the Theory section, we have arranged the essays by date of publication, primarily because many of the essays interact with one another and with their contemporary intellectual and cultural circumstances.

Finally, we would like to thank all those individuals who have so helpfully responded to our seemingly endless series of questions about matters of content and form. In addition to our Internet advisors, they are: David Bentley, George Bornstein, Chris Brown, Wolfram Burghardt, Nigel Crowther, Doug Gerber, Jim Good, Don Hair, Jim Hatch, Bruce Howe, Adrienne Kertzer, Margot Louis, Lorne Macdonald, Brenda MacEachern, Anne McWhir, Ninian Mellamphy, Elizabeth Murray, Victor Neufeldt, David Oakleaf, Tilottama Rajan, Marjorie Ratcliffe, R.J. Shroyer, Patricia Srebrnik, Lisa Surridge, Jane Toswell, and Mary Louise Young. We received great help from our graduate student assistants: Susan Birkwood at the beginning of the project and Natalie Sliscovic in its final stages. Wai Ying Lee and Kirsten Munro, also graduate students, have contributed so much to this anthology, in quality and quantity, that the least we could do is give them title-page recognition as Assistant Editors. And, as always and in everything, the members of the English Department office staff at the University of Western Ontario (Pat Dibsdale, Teresa MacDonald, Anne McFarland, and Beth McIntosh) have been immensely helpful. At Broadview Press, Don LePan has been forbearing and kind, Eileen Eckert has nobly endured the exhausting job of proofreading, and Kathryn Brownsey (the actual "maker" of this book) has exhibited estimable skill, saintly patience, and the endurance of an Ironman triathlete.

TJC
VJR

Contents

POETRY

POETIC THEORY

INDEXES

POETRY

෴

Felicia Hemans
1793 – 1835

Felicia Hemans, although by dates a late-Romantic poet, is also regarded as the initiator of a tradition of Victorian women's poetry. She was one of six children born to George Browne and Felicity Wagner. The family was deserted by her father when she was fourteen, about the time she published her first volume of verse. In 1812 Felicia married Captain Alfred Hemans, who left his family in 1818 after fathering five children; it is little wonder that her poetry concerns women's domestic responsibilities in relation to the unreliable behaviour of men. The fourteen volumes of verse published between 1818 and her death in 1835 reflect these themes, as well as those of heroic suicide, the conflict between public and private spheres of activity, and the relationship between love and creativity.

☙❧

The Suliote Mother

[[It] is related, in a French life of Ali Pasha,[1] that several of the Suliote women, on the advance of the Turkish troops into the mountain fastnesses, assembled on a lofty summit, and, after chanting a wild song, precipitated themselves with their children, into the chasm below, to avoid becoming the slaves of the enemy.]

She stood upon the loftiest peak,
  Amidst the clear blue sky;
A bitter smile was on her cheek,
  And a dark flash in her eye.

5 "Dost thou see them, boy?—through the dusky
    pines
Dost thou see where the foeman's armor shines?
Hast thou caught the gleam of the conqueror's
    crest?
My babe, that I cradled on my breast!
Wouldst thou spring from thy mother's arms with
    joy?
10 —That sight hath cost thee a father, boy!"

  For in the rocky strait beneath,
    Lay Suliote sire and son:

They had heaped high the piles of death
  Before the pass was won.

15 "They have crossed the torrent, and on they come:
Woe for the mountain hearth and home!
There, where the hunter laid by his spear,
There, where the lyre hath been sweet to hear,
There, where I sang thee, fair babe! to sleep,
20 Naught but the blood-stain our trace shall keep!

  And now the horn's loud blast was heard,
    And now the cymbal's clang,
  Till even the upper air was stirred,
    As cliff and hollow rang.

25 "Hark! they bring music, my joyous child!
What saith the trumpet to Suli's wild?
Doth it light thine eye with so quick a fire,
As if at a glance of thine armèd sire?
Still!—be thou still!—there are brave men low:
30 Thou wouldst not smile couldst thou see him
    now!"

  But nearer came the clash of steel,
    And louder swelled the horn,
  And farther yet the tambour's peal
    Through the dark pass was borne.

---

[1] Turkish pasha of Janina (1741–1822).

35 "Hear'st thou the sound of their savage mirth?
Boy! thou wert free when I gave thee birth,—
Free, and how cherished, my warrior's son!
He too hath blessed thee, as I have done!
Ay, and unchained must his loved ones be—
40 Freedom, young Suliote! for thee and me!"

And from the arrowy peak she sprung,
    And fast the fair child bore:—
A veil upon the wind was flung,
    A cry—and all was o'er!

—1825

The Lady of The Castle

From the "Portrait Gallery," an unfinished poem.

"If there be but one spot on thy name,
One eye thou fearest to meet, one human voice
Whose tones thou shrinkest from—Woman! veil
    thy face,
And bow thy head—and die!"

5 Thou seest her pictured with her shining hair,
    (Famed were those tresses in Provençal song,)
Half braided, half o'er cheek and bosom fair
    Let loose, and pouring sunny waves along
Her gorgeous vest. A child's light hand is roving
10 Midst the rich curls; and, oh! how meekly loving
Its earnest looks are lifted to the face
Which bends to meet its lip in laughing grace!
Yet that bright lady's eye, methinks, hath less
Of deep, and still, and pensive tenderness,
15 Than might beseem a mother's; on her brow
    Something too much there sits of native scorn,
And her smile kindles with a conscious glow,
    As from the thought of sovereign beauty born.
These may be dreams—but how shall woman tell
20 Of woman's shame, and not with tears? She fell!
That mother left that child!—went hurrying by

Its cradle—haply not without a sigh,
Haply one moment o'er its rest serene
She hung. But no! it could not thus have been,
25 For *she went on!*—forsook her home, her hearth,
All pure affection, all sweet household mirth,
To live a gaudy and dishonored thing,
Sharing in guilt the splendors of a king.

Her lord, in very weariness of life,
30 Girt on his sword for scenes of distant strife.
He recked no more of glory: grief and shame
Crushed out his fiery nature, and his name
Died silently. A shadow o'er his halls
Crept year by year: the minstrel passed their walls;
35 The warder's horn hung mute. Meantime the child
On whose first flowering thoughts no parent
    smiled,
A gentle girl, and yet deep-hearted, grew
Into sad youth; for well, too well, she knew
Her mother's tale! Its memory made the sky
40 Seem all too joyous for her shrinking eye;
Checked on her lip the flow of song, which fain
Would there have lingered; flushed her cheek to
    pain,
If met by sudden glance; and gave a tone
Of sorrow, as for something lovely gone,
45 E'en to the spring's glad voice. Her own was low
And plaintive. Oh! there lie such depths of woe
In a *young* blighted spirit! Manhood rears
A haughty brow, and age has done with tears;
But youth bows down to misery, in amaze
50 At the dark cloud o'ermantling its fresh days;—
And thus it was with her. A mournful sight
    In one so fair—for she indeed was fair;
Not with her mother's dazzling eyes of light—
    Hers were more shadowy, full of thought and
        prayer,
55 And with long lashes o'er a white-rose cheek
Drooping in gloom, yet tender still and meek,
Still that fond child's—and oh! the brow above
So pale and pure! so formed for holy love

To gaze upon in silence!—But she felt
60 That love was not for her, though hearts would melt
Where'er she moved, and reverence mutely given
Went with her; and low prayers, that called on
    heaven
To bless the young Isaure.

               One sunny morn
With alms before her castle gate she stood,
65 Midst peasant groups: when, breathless and
    o'erworn,
And shrouded in long weeds of widowhood,
A stranger through them broke. The orphan maid,
With her sweet voice and proffered hand of aid,
Turned to give welcome; but a wild sad look
70 Met hers—a gaze that all her spirit shook;
And that pale woman, suddenly subdued
By some strong passion, in its gushing mood,
Knelt at her feet, and bathed them with such tears
As rain the hoarded agonies of years
75 From the heart's urn; and with her white lips
    pressed
The ground they trod; then, burying in her vest
Her brow's deep flush, sobbed out—"Oh
    undefiled!
I am thy mother—spurn me not, my child!"

Isaure had prayed for that lost mother; wept
80 O'er her stained memory, while the happy slept
In the hushed midnight; stood with mournful gaze
Before yon picture's smile of other days,
But never breathed in human ear the name
Which weighed her being to the earth with shame.
85 What marvel if the anguish, the surprise,
The dark remembrances, the altered guise,
Awhile o'erpowered her? From the weeper's touch
She shrank—'twas but a moment—yet too much
For that all-humbled one; its mortal stroke
90 Came down like lightning, and her full heart broke
At once in silence. Heavily and prone
She sank, while o'er her castle's threshold stone,

Those long fair tresses—*they* still brightly wore
Their early pride, though bound with pearls no
    more—
95 Bursting their fillet,[1] in sad beauty rolled,
And swept the dust with coils of wavy gold.

Her child bent o'er her—called her: 'twas too late
Dead lay the wanderer at her own proud gate!
The joy of courts, the star of knight and bard—
100 How didst thou fall, O bright-haired Ermengarde!
    —1826

To Wordsworth

Thine is a strain to read among the hills,
    The old and full of voices,—by the source
Of some free stream, whose gladdening presence
    fills
    The solitude with sound; for in its course
5 Even such is thy deep song, that seems a part
Of those high scenes, a fountain from their heart.

Or its calm spirit fitly may be taken
    To the still breast in sunny garden bowers,
Where vernal winds each tree's low tones awaken,
10   And bud and bell with changes mark the hours.
There let thy thoughts be with me, while the day
Sinks with a golden and serene decay.

Or by some hearth where happy faces meet,
    When night hath hushed the woods, with all
    their birds,
15 There, from some gentle voice, that lay were sweet
    As antique music, linked with household words;
While in pleased murmurs woman's lip might
    move,
And the raised eye of childhood shine in love.

---

[1] ribbon.

Or where the shadows of dark solemn yews
20   Brood silently o'er some lone burial-ground,
Thy verse hath power that brightly might diffuse
    A breath, a kindling, as of spring, around;
From its own glow of hope and courage high,
And steadfast faith's victorious constancy.

25 True bards and holy!—thou art e'en as one
    Who, by some secret gift of soul or eye,
In every spot beneath the smiling sun,
    Sees where the springs of living waters lie:
Unseen awhile they sleep—till, touched by thee,
30 Bright healthful waves flow forth, to each glad
    wanderer free.
—1826

Casabianca [1]

The boy stood on the burning deck
    Whence all but he had fled;
The flame that lit the battle's wreck,
    Shone round him o'er the dead.

5 Yet beautiful and bright he stood,
    As born to rule the storm;
A creature of heroic blood,
    A proud, though child-like form.

The flames roll'd on—he would not go
10   Without his Father's word;
That Father, faint in death below,
    His voice no longer heard.

He call'd aloud:—"Say, Father, say
    If yet my task is done?"

15 He knew not that the chieftain lay
    Unconscious of his son.

"Speak, Father!" once again he cried,
    "If I may yet be gone!"
And but the booming shots replied,
20   And fast the flames roll'd on.

Upon his brow he felt their breath,
    And in his waving hair,
And look'd from that lone post of death,
    In still, yet brave despair.

25 And shouted but once more aloud,
    "My Father! must I stay?"
While o'er him fast, through sail and shroud,
    The wreathing fires made way.

They wrapt the ship in splendour wild,
30   They caught the flag on high,
And stream'd above the gallant child,
    Like banners in the sky.

There came a burst of thunder sound—
    The boy—oh! where was he?
35 Ask of the winds that far around
    With fragments strew'd the sea!—

With mast, and helm, and pennon fair,
    That well had borne their part—
But the noblest thing which perish'd there
40   Was that young faithful heart!
—1826

[1] "Young Casabianca, a boy about thirteen years old, son to the Admiral of Orient, remained at his post (in the Battle of the Nile) after the ship had taken fire, and all the guns has been abandoned; and perished in the explosion of the vessel, when the flames had reached the powder." (Hemans's note.)

The Grave of a Poetess [1]

"Ne me plaignez pas—si vous saviez
Combien de peines ce tombeau m'a épargnées!" [2]

I stood beside thy lowly grave;
   Spring odors breathed around,
And music, in the river wave,
   Passed with a lulling sound.

5   All happy things that love the sun
   In the bright air glanced by,
And a glad murmur seemed to run
   Through the soft azure sky.

Fresh leaves were on the ivy bough
10   That fringed the ruins near;
Young voices were abroad—but thou
   Their sweetness couldst not hear.

And mournful grew my heart for thee!
   Thou in whose woman's mind
15   The ray that brightens earth and sea,
   The light of song, was shrined.

Mournful, that thou wert slumbering low,
   With a dread curtain drawn
Between thee and the golden glow
20   Of this world's vernal [3] dawn.

Parted from all the song and bloom
   Thou wouldst have loved so well,
To thee the sunshine round thy tomb
   Was but a broken spell.

25   The bird, the insect on the wing,
   In their bright reckless play,
Might feel the flush and life of spring—
   And thou wert passed away.

But then, e'en then, a nobler thought
30   O'er my vain sadness came;
The immortal spirit woke, and wrought
   Within my thrilling frame.

Surely on lovelier things, I said,
   Thou must have looked ere now,
35   Than all that round our pathway shed
   Odors and hues below.

The shadows of the tomb are here,
   Yet beautiful is earth!
What see'st thou, then, where no dim fear,
40   No haunting dream hath birth?

Here a vain love to passing flowers
   Thou gavest; but where thou art,
The sway is not with changeful hours—
   There love and death must part.

45   Thou hast left sorrow in thy song,
   A voice not loud but deep
The glorious bowers of earth among,
   How often didst thou weep?

Where couldst thou fix on mortal ground
50   Thy tender thoughts and high?—
Now peace the woman's heart hath found,
   And joy the poet's eye.
—1828

[1] "Extrinsic interest has lately attached to the fine scenery of Woodstock, near Kilkenny, on account of its having been the last residence of the author of *Psyche*. Her grave is one of many in the churchyard of the village. The river runs smoothly by. The ruins of an ancient abbey, that have been partially converted into a church, reverently throw their mantle of tender shadow over it.—*Tales by the O'Hara Family*." (Hemans's note.)

[2] "Do not grieve—if you knew how much pain this grave has spared me!"

[3] spring.

The Image In Lava [1]

Thou thing of years departed!
  What ages have gone by
Since here the mournful seal was set
  By love and agony.

5 Temple and tower have mouldered,
  Empires from earth have passed,
And woman's heart hath left a trace
  Those glories to outlast!

And childhood's fragile image,
10   Thus fearfully enshrined,
Survives the proud memorials reared
  By conquerors of mankind.

Babe! wert thou brightly slumbering
  Upon thy mother's breast
15 When suddenly the fiery tomb
  Shut round each gentle guest?

A strange, dark fate o'ertook you,
  Fair babe and loving heart!
One moment of a thousand pangs—
20   Yet better than to part!

Haply of that fond bosom
  On ashes here impressed,
Thou wert the only treasure, child!
  Whereon a hope might rest.

25 Perchance all vainly lavished
  Its other love had been,
And where it trusted, naught remained
  But thorns on which to lean.

Far better, then, to perish,
30   Thy form within its clasp,
Than live and lose thee, precious one
  From that impassioned grasp.

Oh! I could pass all relics
  Left by the pomps of old,
35 To gaze on this rude monument
  Cast in affection's mould.

Love! human love! what art thou?
  Thy print upon the dust
Outlives the cities of renown
40   Wherein the mighty trust!

Immortal, oh! immortal
  Thou art, whose earthly glow
Hath given these ashes holiness—
  It must, it *must* be so!
  —1828

The Indian With His Dead Child [2]

In the silence of the midnight
  I journey with my dead;
In the darkness of the forest-boughs
  A lonely path I tread.

5 But my heart is high and fearless,
  As by mighty wings upborne;
The mountain eagle hath not plumes
  So strong as love and scorn.

---

[1] "The impression of a woman's form, with an infant clasped to the bosom, found at the uncovering of Herculaneum." (Hemans's note.)

[2] "An Indian, who had established himself in a township of Maine, feeling indignantly the want of sympathy evinced towards him by the white inhabitants, particularly on the death of his only child, gave up his farm soon afterwards, dug up the body of his child, and carried it with him two hundred miles through the forests to join the Canadian Indians.—See Tudor's *Letters on the Eastern States of America.*" (Hemans's note.)

I have raised thee from the grave-sod,
10   By the white man's path defiled;
On to the ancestral wilderness
    I bear thy dust, my child!

I have asked the ancient deserts
    To give my dead a place,
15 Where the stately footsteps of the free
    Alone should leave a trace.

And the tossing pines made answer—
    "Go, bring us back thine own!"
And the streams from all the hunters' hills
20   Rushed with an echoing tone.

Thou shalt rest by sounding waters
    That yet untamed may roll;
The voices of that chainless host
    With joy shall fill thy soul.

25 In the silence of the midnight
    I journey with the dead,
Where the arrows of my father's bow
    Their falcon flight have sped.

I have left the spoilers' dwellings
30   For evermore behind;
Unmingled with their household sounds,
    For me shall sweep the wind.

Alone, amidst their hearth-fires,
    I watched my child's decay;
35 Uncheered, I saw the spirit-light
    From his young eyes fade away.

When his head sank on my bosom,
    When the death-sleep o'er him fell,
Was there one to say, "A friend is near?"
40   There was none!—pale race, fare-well!

To the forests, to the cedars,
    To the warrior and his bow,
Back, back!—I bore thee laughing thence,
    I bear thee slumbering now!

45 I bear thee unto burial
    With the mighty hunters gone;
I shall hear thee in the forest-breeze,
    Thou wilt speak of joy, my son!

In the silence of the midnight
50   I journey with the dead;
But my heart is strong, my step is fleet,
    My father's path I tread.
—1830

The Rock of Cader Idris

[*It is an old tradition of the Welsh bards, that on the summit of the mountain Cader Idris is an excavation resembling a couch; and that whoever should pass a night in that hollow, would be found in the morning either dead, in a frenzy, or endowed with the highest poetical inspiration.*]

I lay on that rock where the storms have their
        dwelling,
    The birthplace of phantoms, the home of the
        cloud;
Around it forever deep music is swelling,
    The voice of the mountain-wind, solemn and
        loud.
5 'Twas a midnight of shadows all fitfully streaming,
    Of wild waves and breezes, that mingled their
        moan;
Of dim shrouded stars, as from gulfs faintly
        gleaming;
    And I met the dread gloom of its grandeur
        alone.

9

I lay there in silence—a spirit came o'er me;
10   Man's tongue hath no language to speak what I
      saw;
Things glorious, unearthly, passed floating before
    me,
    And my heart almost fainted with rapture and
      awe.
I viewed the dread beings around us that hover,
    Though veiled by the mists of mortality's
      breath;
15 And I called upon darkness the vision to cover,
    For a strife was within me of madness and
      death.

I saw them—the powers of the wind and the ocean,
    The rush of whose pinions bears onward the
      storms;
Like the sweep of the white rolling wave was their
    motion—
20   I *felt* their dim presence, but knew not their
      forms!

I saw them—the mighty of ages departed—
    The dead were around me that night on the hi.
From their eyes, as they passed, a cold radiance
    they darted,—
    There was light on my soul, but my heart's
      blood was chill.

25 I saw what man looks on, and dies—but my spirit
    Was strong, and triumphantly lived through
      that hour;
And, as from the grave, I awoke to inherit
    A flame all immortal, a voice, and a power!
Day burst on that rock with the purple cloud
    crested,
30   And high Cader Idris rejoiced in the sun;—
But oh! what new glory all nature invested,
    When the sense which gives soul to her beauty
      was won!

—1834

Letitia E. Landon
L.E.L.
1802 – 1838

Letitia Elizabeth Landon, the poet and novelist well known in her own time as L.E.L., was born in Chelsea. She wrote to support her family, producing, tirelessly, five volumes of poetry in seven years: *The Fate of Adelaide* (1821), *The Improvisatrice* (1824), *The Troubadour* (1825), *The Golden Violet* (1827), and *The Venetian Bracelet, the Lost Pleiad, A History of the Lyre, and Other Poems* (1828). Landon embraces the Romantic aesthetic of spontaneity, yet tends to elaborate typically Victorian topics (indulging at times in excesses of Victorian sentimentality). As well as poetry, she published four novels between 1831 and 1838. She married George Maclean, the colonial governor of Cape Coast Castle in Ghana, and accompanied him back to the Gold Coast despite rumours that Maclean was a bigamist. Four months later, L.E.L. was found dead in her room with a bottle of prussic acid in her hand.

❧❧❧

from *The Improvisatrice*

Advertisement

Poetry needs no Preface: if it do not speak for itself, no comment can render it explicit. I have only, therefore, to state that *The Improvisatrice* is an attempt to illustrate that species of inspiration common in Italy, where the mind is warmed from earliest childhood by all that is beautiful in nature and glorious in art. The character depicted is entirely Italian,—a young female with all the loveliness, vivid feeling, and genius of her own impassioned land. She is supposed to relate her own history; with which are intermixed the tales and episodes which various circumstances call forth.

L.E.L.

I am a daughter of that land,
Where the poet's lip and the painter's hand
Are most divine,—where the earth and sky,
Are picture both and poetry—
5   I am of Florence. 'Mid the chill
Of hope and feeling, oh! I still
Am proud to think to where I owe
My birth, though but the dawn of woe!

My childhood passed 'mid radiant things,
10   Glorious as Hope's imaginings;
Statues but known from shapes of the earth,
By being too lovely for mortal birth;
Paintings whose colours of life were caught
From the fairy tints in the rainbow wrought;
15   Music whose sighs had a spell like those
That float on the sea at the evening's close;
Language so silvery, that every word
Was like the lute's awakening chord;
Skies half sunshine, and half starlight;
20   Flowers whose lives were a breath of delight;
Leaves whose green pomp knew no withering;
Fountains bright as the skies of our spring;
And songs whose wild and passionate line
Suited a soul of romance like mine.

25   My power was but a woman's power;
Yet, in that great and glorious dower
Which Genius gives, I had my part:
I poured my full and burning heart
In song, and on the canvass made
30   My dreams of beauty visible;
I knew not which I loved the most—
Pencil or lute,—both loved so well.

Oh, yet my pulse throbs to recall,
When first upon the gallery's wall
35 Picture of mine was placed, to share
Wonder and praise from each one there!
Sad were my shades; methinks they had
    Almost a tone of prophecy—
I ever had, from earliest youth,
40   A feeling what my fate would be.

    My first was of a gorgeous hall,
Lighted up for festival;
Braided tresses, and cheeks of bloom,
Diamond agraff,[1] and foam-white plume;
45 Censers of roses, vases of light,
Like what the moon sheds on a summer night.
Youths and maidens with linked hands,
Joined in the graceful sarabands,[2]
Smiled on the canvass; but apart
50   Was one who leant in silent mood
As revelry to sick heart
    Were worse than veriest solitude.
Pale, dark-eyed, beautiful, and young,
    Such as he had shone o'er my slumbers,
55 When I had only slept to dream
    Over again his magic numbers.

    Divinest Petrarch! he whose lyre,
Like morning light, half dew, half fire,
To Laura and to love was vowed—
60 He looked on one, who with the crowd
Mingled, but mixed not; on whose cheek
    There was a blush, as if she knew
Whose look was fixed on hers. Her eye,
    Of a spring-sky's delicious blue,
65 Had not the language of that bloom,
But mingling tears, and light, and gloom,
Was raised abstractedly to Heaven:—
No sign was to her lover given.
I painted her with golden tresses,

70 Such as float on the wind's caresses,
When the laburnums wildly fling
Their sunny blossoms to the spring,
A cheek which had the crimson hue
    Upon the sun touched nectarine;
75 A lip of perfume and of dew;
    A brow like twilight's darkened line.
I strove to catch each charm that long
Has lived,—thanks to her lover's song!
Each grace he numbered one by one,
80 That shone in her of Avignon.[3]

    I ever thought that poet's fate
Utterly lone and desolate.
It is the spirit's bitterest pain
To love, to be beloved again;
85 And yet between a gulf which ever
The hearts that burn to meet must sever.
And he was vowed to one sweet star,
Bright yet to him, but bright afar.

    O'er some, Love's shadow may but pass
90 As passes the breath-stain o'er glass;
And pleasures, cares, and pride combined,
Fill up the blank Love leaves behind.
But there are some whose love is high,
Entire, and sole idolatry;
95 Who, turning from a heartless world,
    Ask some dear thing, which may renew
Affection's severed links, and be
    As true as they themselves are true.
But Love's bright fount is never pure;
100 And all his pilgrims must endure
All passion's mighty suffering
Ere they may reach the blessed spring.
And some who waste their lives to find
    A prize which they may never win:
105 Like those who search for Irem's[4] groves,
    Which found, they may not enter in.

---

[1] a kind of hook used as a clasp.

[2] a slow, elegant Spanish dance in triple time.

[3] a southern French city which served as the papal seat in 1309–77.

[4] a paradise named in the Koran.

Where is the sorrow but appears
In Love's long catalogue of tears?
And some there are who leave the path
110   In agony and fierce disdain;
But bear upon each cankered breast
     The scar that never heals again.

My next was of a minstrel too,
Who proved that woman's hand might do,
115 When, true to the heart pulse, it woke
     The harp. Her head was bending down,
As if in weariness, and near,
     But unworn, was a laurel crown.
She was not beautiful, if bloom
120 And smiles form beauty; for, like death,
Her brow was ghastly; and her lip
Was parched, as fever were its breath.
There was a shade upon her dark,
Large, floating eyes, as if each spark
125 Of minstrel ecstasy was fled,
Yet leaving them no tears to shed;
Fixed in their hopelessness of care,
And reckless in their great despair.
She sat beneath a cypress tree,
130   A little fountain ran beside,
And, in the distance, one dark rock
     Threw its long shadow o'er the tide;
And to the west, where the nightfall
Was darkening day's gemm'd coronal,[1]
135 Its white shafts crimsoning in the sky,
Arose the sun-god's sanctuary.
I deemed, that of lyre, life, and love
     She was a long, last farewell taking;—
That, from her pale and parched lips,
140   Her latest, wildest song was breaking.

SAPPHO'S SONG [2]

Farewell, my lute!—and would that I
     Had never waked thy burning chords!
Poison has been upon thy sigh,
     And fever has breathed in thy words.

5 Yet wherefore, wherefore should I blame
     Thy power, thy spell, my gentlest lute?
I should have been the wretch I am,
     Had every chord of thine been mute.

It was my evil star above,
10   Not my sweet lute, that wrought me wrong:
It was not song that taught me love,
     But it was love that taught me song.

If song be past, and hope undone,
     And pulse, and head, and heart, are flame;
15 It is thy work, thou faithless one!
     But, no!—I will not name thy name!

Sun-god! lute, wreath are vowed to thee!
     Long be their light upon my grave—
My glorious grave—yon deep blue sea:
20   I shall sleep calm beneath its wave!

FLORENCE! with what idolatry
     I've lingered in thy radiant halls,
Worshipping, till my dizzy eye
     Grew dim with gazing on those walls,
25 Where Time had spared each glorious gift
By Genius unto Memory left!
And when seen by the pale moonlight,
More pure, more perfect, though less bright,
What dreams of song flashed on my brain,
30 Till each shade seemed to live again;
And then the beautiful, the grand,
The glorious of my native land,

_____
[1] a crown or coronet.

_____
[2] Sappho was a Greek lyric poet, born on the island of Lesbos (?–650 BC).

In every flower that threw its veil
Aside, when wooed by the spring gale;
35 In every vineyard, where the sun,
His task of summer ripening done,
Shone on their clusters, and a song
Came lightly from the peasant throng;—
In the dim loveliness of night,
40 In fountains with their diamond light,
In aged temple, ruined shrine,
And its green wreath of ivy twine;—
In every change of earth and sky,
Breathed the deep soul of poesy.

45   As yet I loved not;—but each wild,
High thought I nourished raised a pyre
For love to light; and lighted once
By love, it would be like the fire
The burning lava floods that dwell
50 In Etna's[1] cave unquenchable.

.   .   .   .   .

—1824

"Preface" to *The Venetian Bracelet,*
The Lost Pleiad, A History of the Lyre,
and Other Poems

Diffidence of their own abilities, and fear, which
heightens the anxiety for public favour, are pleas
usually urged by the youthful writer: may I, while
venturing for the first time to speak of myself, be
permitted to say they far more truly belong to one
who has had experience of both praise and censure.
The feelings which attended the publication of the
"Improvisatrice," are very different from those that
accompany the present volume. I believe I *then* felt
little beyond hope, vague as the timidity which
subdued it, and that excitement which every author
must know: *now* mine is a "farther looking hope;"
and the timidity which apprehended the verdict of

others, is now deepened by distrust of my own
powers. Or, to claim my poetical privilege, and
express my meaning by a simile, I should say, I am no
longer one who springs forward in the mere energy of
exercise and enjoyment; but rather like the Olympian
racer, who strains his utmost vigour, with the distant
goal and crown in view. I have devoted my whole life
to one object: in society I have but sought the mate-
rial for solitude. I can imagine but one interest in
existence,—that which has filled my past, and haunts
my future,—the perhaps vain desire, when I am
nothing, of leaving one of those memories at once a
good and a glory. Believing, as I do, in the great and
excellent influence of poetry, may I hazard the
expression of what I have myself sometimes trusted to
do? A highly cultivated state of society must ever have
for concomitant evils, that selfishness, the result of
indolent indulgence; and that heartlessness attendant
on refinement, which too often hardens while it
polishes. Aware that to elevate I must first soften, and
that if I wished to purify I must first touch, I have
ever endeavoured to bring forward grief, disappoint-
ment, the fallen leaf, the faded flower, the broken
heart, and the early grave. Surely we must be less
worldly, less interested, from this sympathy with the
sorrow in which our unselfish feelings alone can take
part. And now a few words on a subject, where the
variety of the opinions offered have left me somewhat
in the situation of the prince in the fairy tale, who,
when in the vicinity of the magic fountain, found
himself so distracted by the multitude of voices that
directed his way, as to be quite incapable of deciding
which was the right path. I allude to the blame and
eulogy which have been equally bestowed on my
frequent choice of love as my source of song. I can
only say, that for a woman, whose influence and
whose sphere must be in the affections, what subject
can be more fitting than one which it is her peculiar
province to refine, spiritualize, and exalt? I have
always sought to paint it self-denying, devoted, and
making an almost religion of its truth; and I must

[1] volcanic mountain in eastern Sicily.

add, that such as I would wish to draw her, woman actuated by an attachment as intense as it is true, as pure as it is deep, is not only more admirable as a heroine, but also in actual life, than one whose idea of love is that of light amusement, or at worst of vain mortification. With regard to the frequent application of my works to myself, considering that I sometimes pourtrayed love unrequited, then betrayed, and again destroyed by death—may I hint the conclusions are not quite logically drawn, as assuredly the same mind cannot have suffered such varied modes of misery. However, if I must have an unhappy passion, I can only console myself with my own perfect unconsciousness of so great a misfortune. I now leave the following poems to their fate: they must speak for themselves. I could but express my anxiety, an anxiety only increased by a popularity beyond my most sanguine dreams.

With regard to those whose former praise encouraged, their best recompense is the happiness they bestowed. And to those whose differing opinion expressed itself in censure, I own, after the first chagrin was past, I never laid down a criticism by which I did not benefit, or trust to benefit. I will conclude by apostrophizing the hopes and fears they excited, in the words of the Mexican king—"Ye have been the feathers of my wings."

—1829

The Nameless Grave

A nameless grave,—there is no stone
  To sanctify the dead:
O'er it the willow droops alone,
  With only wild flowers spread.

5 "Oh, there is nought to interest here,
  No record of a name,
A trumpet call upon the ear,
  High on the roll of fame.

"I will not pause beside a tomb
10   Where nothing calls to mind
Aught that can brighten mortal gloom,
  Or elevate mankind;—

"No glorious memory to efface
  The stay of meaner clay;
15 No intellect whose heavenly trace
  Redeem'd our earth:—away!"

Ah, these are thoughts that well may rise
  On youth's ambitious pride;
But I will sit and moralize
20   This lowly stone beside.

Here thousands might have slept, whose name
  Had been to thee a spell,
To light thy flashing eyes with flame,—
  To bid thy young heart swell.

25 Here might have been a warrior's rest,
  Some chief who bravely bled,
With waving banner, sculptured crest,
  And laurel on his head.

That laurel must have had its blood,
30   That blood have caused its tear,—
Look on the lovely solitude—
  What! wish for warfare here!

A poet might have slept,—what! he
  Whose restless heart first wakes
35 Its lifepulse into melody,
  Then o'er it pines and breaks?—

He who hath sung of passionate love,
  His life a feverish tale:—
Oh! not the nightingale, the dove
40   Would suit its quiet vale.

See, I have named your favourite two,—
    Each had been glad to crave
Rest 'neath this turf's unbroken dew,
    And such a nameless grave!
—1829

The Factory

'Tis an accursed thing!

There rests a shade above yon town,
    A dark funeral shroud:
'Tis not the tempest hurrying down,
    'Tis not a summer cloud.

5   The smoke that rises on the air
    Is as a type and sign;
A shadow flung by the despair
    Within those streets of thine.

That smoke shuts out the cheerful day
10   The sunset's purple hues,
The moonlight's pure and tranquil ray,
    The morning's pearly dews.

Such is the moral atmosphere
    Around thy daily life;
15   Heavy with care, and pale with fear,
    With future tumult rife.

There rises on the morning wind
    A low appealing cry,
A thousand children are resign'd
20   To sicken and to die!

We read of Moloch's[1] sacrifice,
    We sicken at the name,
And seem to hear the infant cries—
    And yet we do the same;—

25   And worse—'twas but a moment's pain
    The heathen altar gave,
But we give years,—our idol, Gain,
    Demands a living grave!

How precious is the little one,
30   Before his mother's sight,
With bright hair dancing in the sun,
    And eyes of azure light!

He sleeps as rosy as the south,
    For summer days are long;
35   A prayer upon the little mouth,
    Lull'd by his nurse's song.

Love is around him, and his hours
    Are innocent and free;
His mind essays its early powers
40   Beside his mother's knee.

When afteryears of trouble come,
    Such as await man's prime,
How will he think of that dear home,
    And childhood's lovely time!

45   And such should childhood ever be,
    The fairy well; to bring
To life's worn, weary memory
    The freshness of its spring.

But here the order is reversed,
50   And infancy, like age,
Knows of existence but its worst,
    One dull and darken'd page;—

Written with tears and stamp'd with toil,
    Crush'd from the earliest hour,
55   Weeds darkening on the bitter soil
    That never knew a flower.

---

[1] the god of the ancient Phoenicians and Ammonites to whom children were sacrificed by burning.

Look on yon child, it droops the head,
    Its knees are bow'd with pain;
It mutters from its wretched bed,
60   "O, let me sleep again!"

Alas! 'tis time, the mother's eyes
    Turn mournfully away;
Alas! 'tis time, the child must rise,
    And yet it is not day.

65 The lantern's lit—she hurries forth,
    The spare cloak's scanty fold
Scarce screens her from the snowy north,
    The child is pale and cold.

And wearily the little hands
70   Their task accustom'd ply;
While daily, some 'mid those pale bands,
    Droop, sicken, pine, and die.

Good God! to think upon a child
    That has no childish days,
75 No careless play, no frolics wild,
    No words of prayer and praise!

Man from the cradle—'tis too soon
    To earn their daily bread,
And heap the heat and toil of noon
80   Upon an infant's head.

To labour ere their strength be come,
    Or starve,—is such the doom
That makes of many an English home
    One long and living tomb?

85 Is there no pity from above,—
    No mercy in those skies;
Hath then the heart of man no love,
    To spare such sacrifice?

O, England! though thy tribute waves
90   Proclaim thee great and free,
While those small children pine like slaves,
    There is a curse on thee!
—1835

Carthage [1]

"Early on the morning following, I walked to the site of the great Carthage,—of that town, at the sound of whose name mighty Rome herself had so often trembled,—of Carthage, the mistress of powerful and brave armies, of numerous fleets, and of the world's commerce, and to whom Africa, Spain, Sardinia, Corsica, Sicily, and Italy herself bowed in submission as to their sovereign—in short,— '*Carthago, dives opum, studiisque asperrima belli:*' [2] I was prepared to see but few vestiges of its former grandeur, it had so often suffered from the devastating effects of war, that I knew many could not exist; but my heart sunk within me when ascending one of its hills, (from whose summit the eye embraces a view of the whole surrounding country to the edge of the sea,) I beheld nothing more than a few scattered and shapeless masses of masonry. The scene that once was animated by the presence of nearly a million of warlike inhabitants is now buried in the silence of the grave; no living soul appearing, if we occasionally except a soldier going or returning from the fort, or the solitary and motionless figure of an Arab, watching his flocks from the summit of the fragment of some former palace or temple."—Sir G. Temple's *Excursions in the Mediterranean.*

Low it lieth—earth to earth—
All to which that earth gave birth—

-----

[1] an ancient city and state in northern Africa, founded by the Phoenicians near present-day Tunis, and destroyed by the Romans in 146 BC.

[2] "Carthage, rich in resources, most fierce in the arts of war."

Palace, market-street, and fane;[1]
Dust that never asks in vain,
5 Hath reclaim'd its own again.
       Dust, the wide world's king.
Where are now the glorious hours
Of a nation's gather'd powers?
Like the setting of a star,
10 In the fathomless afar;
       Time's eternal wing
Hath around those ruins cast
The dark presence of the past.

Mind, what art thou? dost thou not
15 Hold the vast earth for thy lot?
In thy toil, how glorious.
What dost thou achieve for us,
Over all victorious!
       Godlike thou dost seem.
20 But the perishing still lurks
In thy most immortal works;
Thou dost build thy home on sand,
And the palace-girdled strand
       Fadeth like a dream.
25 Thy great victories only show
All is nothingness below.
       —1837

Felicia Hemans

No more, no more—oh, never more returning,
   Will thy beloved presence gladden earth;
No more wilt thou with sad, yet anxious, yearning
   Cling to those hopes which have no mortal birth.
5 Thou art gone from us, and with thee departed,
   How many lovely things have vanished too:
Deep thoughts that at thy will to being started,
   And feelings, teaching us our own were true.
Thou hast been round us, like a viewless spirit,
10   Known only by the music on the air;

The leaf or flowers which thou hast named inherit
   A beauty known but from thy breathing there:
For thou didst on them fling thy strong emotion.
   The likeness from itself the fond heart gave;
15 As planets from afar look down on ocean,
   And give their own sweet image to the wave.

And thou didst bring from foreign lands their
       treasures,
   As floats thy various melody along;
We know the softness of Italian measures,
20   And the grave cadence of Castilian song.
A general bond of union is the poet,
   By its immortal verse is language known,
And for the sake of song do others know it—
   One glorious poet makes the world his own.
25 And thou—how far thy gentle sway extended!
   The heart's sweet empire over land and sea;
Many a stranger and far flower was blended
   In the soft wreath that glory bound for thee.
The echoes of the Susquehanna's[2] waters
30   Paused in the pine-woods words of thine to hear;
And to the wide Atlantic's younger daughters
   Thy name was lovely, and thy song was dear.

Was not this purchased all too dearly?—never
   Can fame atone for all that fame hath cost.
35 We see the goal, but know not the endeavour
   Nor what fond hopes have on the way been lost.
What do we know of the unquiet pillow,
   By the worn check and tearful eyelid prest,
When thoughts chase thoughts, like the tumultuous
       billow,
40   Whose very light and foam reveals unrest?
We say, the song is sorrowful, but know not
   What may have left that sorrow on the song:
However mournful words may be, they show not
   The whole extent of wretchedness and wrong.
45 They cannot paint the long sad hours, passed only

[1] temple or church.

[2] river flowing through New York, Pennsylvania, and Maryland into Chesapeake Bay.

In vain regrets o'er what we feel we are.
Alas! The kingdom of the lute is lonely—
    Cold is the worship coming from afar.

50 Yet what is mind in woman but revealing
    In sweet clear light the hidden world below,
By quicker fancies and a keener feeling
    Than those around, the cold and careless, know?
What is to feed such feeling, but to culture
    A soil whence pain will never more depart?
55 The fable of Prometheus and the vulture,[1]
    Reveals the poet's and the woman's heart.
Unkindly are they judged—unkindly treated—
    By careless tongues and by ungenerous words;
While cruel sneer, and hard reproach, repeated,
60   Jar the fine music of the spirit's chords.
Wert thou not weary—thou whose soothing
        numbers
    Gave other lips the joy thine own had not.
Didst thou not welcome thankfully the slumbers
    Which closed around thy mourning human lot?

65 What on this earth could answer thy requiring,
    For earnest faith—for love, the deep and true,
The beautiful, which was thy soul's desiring,
    But only from thyself its being drew.
How is the warm and loving heart requited
70   In this harsh world, where it awhile must dwell.
Its best affections wronged, betrayed, and slighted—
    Such is the doom of those who love too well.
Better the weary dove should close its pinion,
    Fold up its golden wings and be at peace,
75 Enter, O ladye, that serene dominion,
    Where earthy cares and earthy sorrows cease.
Fame's troubled hour has cleared, and now replying,
    A thousand hearts their music ask of thine.

---

[1] Prometheus stole fire from heaven and bestowed it upon humanity,
subsequently earning the wrath of Zeus. Prometheus's punishment was
to be chained to a rock where a vulture arrived each day to devour his
liver, which always grew back after the encounter.

Sleep with a light the lovely and undying
80   Around thy grave—a grave which is a shrine.
    —1838

Rydal Water and Grasmere Lake

The Residence of Wordsworth

Not for the glory on their heads
    Those stately hill-tops wear,
Although the summer sunset sheds
    Its constant crimson there.
5 Not for the gleaming lights that break
    The purple of the twilight lake,
Half dusky and half fair,
    Does that sweet valley seem to be
A sacred place on earth to me.

10 The influence of a moral spell
    Is found around the scene,
Giving new shadows to the dell,
    New verdure to the green.
With every mountain-top is wrought
15   The presence of associate thought,
A music that has been;
    Calling that loveliness to life
With which the inward world is rife.

His home—our English poet's home—
20   Amid these hills is made;
Here, with the morning, hath he come,
    There, with the night delay'd.
On all things is his memory cast,
    For every place wherein he past
25 Is with his mind array'd,
    That, wandering in a summer hour,
Ask'd wisdom of the leaf and flower.

Great poet, if I dare to throw
    My homage at thy feet,
30 'Tis thankfulness for hours which thou

Hast made serene and sweet;
As wayfarers have incense thrown
  Upon some mighty altar-stone,
Unworthy, and yet meet,
35   The human spirit longs to prove
The truth of its uplooking love.

Until thy hand unlock'd its store,
  What glorious music slept!
Music that can be hush'd no more
40   Was from our knowledge kept.
But the great Mother gave to thee
  The poet's universal key,
And forth the fountains swept—
  A gushing melody forever,
45 The witness of thy high endeavours.

Rough is the road which we are sent,
  Rough with long toils and pain;
And when upon the steep ascent,
  A little way we gain,
50 Vex'd with our own perpetual care,
  Little we heed what sweet things are
Around our pathway blent;
  With anxious steps we hurry on,
The very sense of pleasure gone.

55 But thou dost in this feverish dream
  Awake a better mood,
With voices from the mountain stream,
  With voices from the wood.
And with their music dost impart
60   Their freshness to the world-worn heart,
Whose fever is subdued
  By memories sweet with other years,
By gentle hopes, and soothing tears.

A solemn creed is thine, and high,
65   Yet simple as a child,
Who looketh hopeful to yon sky
  With eyes yet undefiled.
By all the glitter and the glare

This life's deceit and follies wear,
70 Exalted, and yet mild,
  Conscious of those diviner powers
Brought from a better world than ours.

Thou hast not chosen to rehearse
  The old heroic themes;
75 Thou hast not given to thy verse
  The heart's impassion'd dreams.
Forth flows thy song as waters flow
  So bright above—so clam below,
Wherein the heaven seems
80   Eternal as the golden shade
Its sunshine on the stream hath laid.

The glory which thy spirit hath,
  Is round life's common things,
And flingeth round our common path,
85   As from an angel's wings,
A light that is not of our sphere,
  Yet lovelier for being here,
Beneath whose presence springs
  A beauty never mark'd before,
90 Yet once known, vanishing no more.

How often with the present sad,
  And weary with the past,
A sunny respite have we had,
  By but a chance look cast
95 Upon some word of thine that made
  The sullenness forsake the shade,
Till shade itself was past:
  For Hope divine, serene, and strong,
Perpetual lives within thy song.

100 Eternal as the hills thy name,
  Eternal as thy strain;
So long as ministers of Fame
  Shall Love and Hope remain.
The crowded city in its streets,
105   The valley, in its green retreats,

Alike thy words retain.
    What need hast thou of sculptured stone?—
Thy temple, is thy name alone.
—1838

Infanticide in Madagascar [1]

A luxury of summer green
    Is on the southern plain,
And water-flags, with dewy screen,
    Protect the ripening grain.
5 Upon the sky is not a cloud
    To mar the golden glow,
Only the palm-tree is allow'd
    To fling its shade below.

And silvery, 'mid its fertile brakes,
10   The winding river glides,
And every ray in heaven makes
    Its mirror of its tides.
And yet it is a place of death—
    A place of sacrifice;
15 Heavy with childhood's parting breath
    Weary with childhood's cries.

The mother takes her little child—
    Its face is like her own;
The cradle of her choice is wild—
20   Why is it left alone?
The trampling of the buffalo
    Is heard among the reeds,
And sweeps around the carrion crow
    That amid carnage feeds.

25 O! outrage upon mother Earth
    To yonder azure sky;
A destined victim from its birth,
    The child is left to die.
We shudder that such crimes disgrace

30 E'en yonder savage strand;
Alas! and hath such crime no trace
    Within our English land?

Pause, ere we blame the savage code
    That such strange horror keeps;
35 Perhaps within her sad abode
    The mother sits and weeps,
And thinks how oft those eyelids smiled,
    Whose close she may not see,
And says, "O, would to God, my child,
40   I might have died for thee!"

Such law of bloodshed to annul
    Should be the Christian's toil;
May not such law be merciful,
    To that upon our soil?
45 Better the infant eyes should close
    Upon the first sweet breath,
That weary for their last repose,
    A living life in death!

Look on the children of our poor
50   On many an English child:
Better that it had died secure
    By yonder river wild.
Flung careless on the waves of life,
    From childhood's earliest time,
55 They struggle, one perpetual strife,
    With hunger and with crime.

Look on the crowded prison-gate—
    Instructive love and care
In early life had saved the fate
60   That waits on many there.
Cold, selfish, shunning care and cost,
    The poor are left unknown;
I say, for every soul thus lost,
    We answer with our own.
—1838

[1] island off the southeastern coast of Africa, colonized by the French.

Elizabeth Barrett Browning
1806 – 1861

Long before she met and married Robert Browning, Elizabeth Barrett Browning's popularity and reputation as a major Victorian poet was well established. The eldest of eleven children, Barrett was a confined invalid by twenty-two, dominated by her patriarchal father, Edward. Her literary activity, however, could not be contained so easily: after teaching herself Latin and Greek, Elizabeth Barrett anonymously published *The Battle of Marathon* (1820), at the age of fourteen, *An Essay on Mind, with Other Poems* (1826), when she was twenty, and a translation of *Prometheus Bound* in 1838. Her reputation was established with *The Seraphim and Other Poems* (1838), which was her first signed volume, and *Poems* (1844), which features the famous plea to the social consciences of

Victorian middle classes, "The Cry of the Children." Elizabeth Barrett and Robert Browning began corresponding in January, 1845, but he did not visit her until 21 May. They secretly married in 1846 and settled in Italy, where their son, Robert (Pen) Weidemann, was born. Barrett Browning published the well-known sequence, *Sonnets from the Portuguese*, in the 1850 volume, *Poems*, and her productivity continued with *Casa Guidi Windows* (1851), and *Poems Before Congress* (1860). Her most important and impressive work, however, is the verse novel, *Aurora Leigh* (1857), which considers and discusses, against a melodramatic Victorian backdrop, the role of poetry, the female as both writer and heroine, and the circumscribed role of women.

გუღ

The Cry of the Children

"Φεῦ, φεῦ, τί προσδέρκεσθέ μ' ὄμμασιν, τέκνα;" [1]
—Medea.

I

Do ye hear the children weeping, O my
    brothers,
  Ere the sorrow comes with years?
They are leaning their young heads against their
    mothers,
  And *that* cannot stop their tears.
5 The young lambs are bleating in the meadows,
    The young birds are chirping in the nest,
The young fawns are playing with the shadows,
    The young flowers are blowing toward the
      west—
But the young, young children, O my brothers,
10   They are weeping bitterly!

They are weeping in the playtime of the others,
  In the country of the free.

II

Do you question the young children in the sorrow
  Why their tears are falling so?
15 The old man may weep for his to-morrow
    Which is lost in Long Ago;
The old tree is leafless in the forest,
  The old year is ending in the frost,
The old wound, if stricken, is the sorest,
20   The old hope is hardest to be lost:
But the young, young children, O my brothers,
    Do you ask them why they stand
Weeping sore before the bosoms of their mothers,
    In our happy Fatherland?

III

25 They look up with their pale and sunken faces,
    And their looks are sad to see,
For the man's hoary anguish draws and presses
    Down the cheeks of infancy;

---

[1] Euripedes, *Medea*, l. 1040: "Oh! What is the meaning of your glance at me, children."

"Your old earth," they say, "is very dreary,
   Our young feet," they say, "are very weak;
30 Few paces have we taken, yet are weary—
   Our grave-rest is very far to seek:
Ask the aged why they weep, and not the children,
   For the outside earth is cold,
35 And we young ones stand without, in our
      bewildering,
   And the graves are for the old.

IV

"True," say the children, "it may happen
   That we die before our time:
Little Alice died last year, her grave is shapen
40   Like a snowball, in the rime.
We looked into the pit prepared to take her:
   Was no room for any work in the close clay!
From the sleep wherein she lieth none will wake her,
   Crying, 'Get up, little Alice! it is day.'
45 If you listen by that grave, in sun and shower,
   With your ear down, little Alice never cries;
Could we see her face, be sure we should not know
      her,
   For the smile has time for growing in her eyes:
And merry go her moments, lulled and stilled in
50   The shroud by the kirk-chime.
It is good when it happens," say the children,
   "That we die before our time."

V

Alas, alas, the children! they are seeking
   Death in life, as best to have:
55 They are binding up their hearts away from
      breaking,
   With a cerement from the grave.
Go out, children, from the mine and from the city,
   Sing out, children, as the little thrushes do;
Pluck your handfuls of the meadow-cowslips pretty,
60   Laugh aloud, to feel your fingers let them
      through!
But they answer, "Are your cowslips of the meadows
   Like our weeds anear the mine?

Leave us quiet in the dark of the coal-shadows,
   From your pleasures fair and fine!

VI

65 "For oh," say the children, "we are weary,
   And we cannot run or leap;
If we cared for any meadows, it were merely
   To drop down in them and sleep.
Our knees tremble sorely in the stooping,
70   We fall upon our faces, trying to go;
And, underneath our heavy eyelids drooping
   The reddest flower would look as pale as snow.
For, all day, we drag our burden tiring
   Through the coal-dark, underground;
75 Or, all day, we drive the wheels of iron
   In the factories, round and round.

VII

"For all day the wheels are droning, turning;
   Their wind comes in our faces,
Till our hearts turn, our heads with pulses burning,
80   And the walls turn in their places:
Turns the sky in the high window, blank and reeling,
   Turns the long light that drops adown the wall,
Turn the black flies that crawl along the ceiling:
   All are turning, all the day, and we with all.
85 And all day the iron wheels are droning,
   And sometimes we could pray,
'O ye wheels' (breaking out in a mad moaning),
   'Stop! be silent for to-day!'"

VIII

Ay, be silent! Let them hear each other breathing
90   For a moment, mouth to mouth!
Let them touch each other's hands, in a fresh
      wreathing
   Of their tender human youth!
Let them feel that this cold metallic motion
   Is not all the life God fashions or reveals:
95 Let them prove their living souls against the notion
   That they live in you, or under you, O wheels!
Still, all day, the iron wheels go onward,

Grinding life down from its mark;
And the children's souls which God is calling sunward,
    Spin on blindly in the dark.

₁₀₀

IX

Now tell the poor young children, O my brothers,
    To look up to Him and pray;
So the blessed One who blesseth all the others,
    Will bless them another day.
₁₀₅ They answer, "Who is God that He should hear us,
    While the rushing of the iron wheels is stirred?
When we sob aloud, the human creatures near us
    Pass by, hearing not, or answer not a word.
And *we* hear not (for the wheels in their resounding)
₁₁₀   Strangers speaking at the door:
Is it likely God, with angels singing round Him,
    Hears our weeping any more?

X

"Two words, indeed, of praying we remember,
    And at midnight's hour of harm,
₁₁₅ 'Our Father,' looking upward in the chamber,
    We say softly for a charm.
We know no other words except 'Our Father,'
    And we think that, in some pause of angels' song,
God may pluck them with the silence sweet to gather,
₁₂₀   And hold both within His right hand which is strong.
'Our Father!' If He heard us, He would surely
    (For they call Him good and mild)
Answer, smiling down the steep world very purely,
    'Come and rest with me, my child.'"

XI

₁₂₅ "But, no!" say the children, weeping faster,
    "He is speechless as a stone:
And they tell us, of His image is the master
    Who commands us to work on.
Go to! say the children,—"up in Heaven,

₁₃₀ Dark, wheel-like, turning clouds are all we find.
Do not mock us; grief has made us unbelieving:
    We look up for God, but tears have made us blind."
Do you hear the children weeping and disproving,
    O my brothers, what ye preach?
₁₃₅ For God's possible is taught by His world's loving,
    And the children doubt of each.

XII

And well may the children weep before you!
    They are weary ere they run;
They have never seen the sunshine, nor the glory
₁₄₀   Which is brighter than the sun.
They know the grief of man, without its wisdom;
    They sink in man's despair, without its calm;
Are slaves, without the liberty in Christdom,
    Are martyrs, by the pang without the palm;
₁₄₅ Are worn as if with age, yet unretrievingly
    The harvest of its memories cannot reap,—
Are orphans of the earthly love and heavenly.
    Let them weep! let them weep!

XIII

They look up with their pale and sunken faces,
₁₅₀   And their look is dread to see,
For they mind you of their angels in high places,
    With eyes turned on Deity.
"How long," they say, "how long, O cruel nation,
    Will you stand, to move the world, on a child's heart,—
₁₅₅ Stifle down with a mailed heel its palpitation,
    And tread onward to your throne amid the mart?
Our blood splashes upward, O gold-heaper,
    And your purple shows your path!
But the child's sob in the silence curses deeper
₁₆₀   Than the strong man in his wrath."
—1844

Sonnets From the Portuguese [1]

III

Unlike are we, unlike, O princely Heart!
Unlike our uses and our destinies.
Our ministering two angels look surprise
On one another, as they strike athwart
5   Their wings in passing. Thou, bethink thee, art
A guest for queens to social pageantries,
With gages [2] from a hundred brighter eyes
Than tears even can make mine, to play thy part
Of chief musician. What hast *thou* to do
10 With looking from the lattice-lights at me,
A poor, tired, wandering singer, singing through
The dark, and leaning up a cypress tree?
The chrism [3] is on thine head,—on mine, the dew,—
And Death must dig the level where these agree.

XXII

When our two souls stand up erect and strong,
Face to face, silent, drawing nigh and nigher,
Until the lengthening wings break into fire
At either curvèd point,—what bitter wrong
5   Can the earth do to us, that we should not long
Be here contented? Think. In mounting higher,
The angels would press on us and aspire
To drop some golden orb of perfect song
Into our deep, dear silence. Let us stay
10 Rather on earth, Belovèd,—where the unfit
Contrarious moods of men recoil away
And isolate pure spirits, and permit
A place to stand and love in for a day,
With darkness and the death-hour rounding it.

XXIX

I think of thee!—my thoughts do twine and bud
About thee, as wild vines, about a tree,
Put out broad leaves, and soon there's nought to see
Except the straggling green which hides the wood.
5   Yet, O my palm-tree, be it understood
I will not have my thoughts instead of thee
Who art dearer, better! Rather, instantly
Renew thy presence; as a strong tree should,
Rustle thy boughs and set thy trunk all bare,
10 And let these bands of greenery which insphere thee
Drop heavily down,—burst, shattered, everywhere!
Because, in this deep joy to see and hear thee
And breathe within thy shadow a new air,
I do not think of thee—I am too near thee.

XLIII

How do I love thee? Let me count the ways.
I love thee to the depth and breadth and height
My soul can reach, when feeling out of sight
For the ends of Being and ideal Grace.
5   I love thee to the level of everyday's
Most quiet need, by sun and candle-light.
I love thee freely, as men strive for Right;
I love thee purely, as they turn from Praise.
I love thee with the passion put to use
10 In my old griefs, and with my childhood's faith.
I love thee with a love I seemed to lose
With my lost saints—I love thee with the breath,
Smiles, tears, of all my life!—and, if God choose,
I shall but love thee better after death.
—1850 (1845–47)

The Runaway Slave at Pilgrim's Point

I

I stand on the mark beside the shore
Of the first white pilgrim's bended knee,
Where exile turned to ancestor,
    And God was thanked for liberty.

---

[1]   Presented as translations from the Portuguese language, the sequence consists of forty-four sonnets.

[2]   pledges.

[3]   consecrated oil.

5 I have run through the night, my skin is as dark,
  I bend my knee down on this mark:
   I look on the sky and the sea.

II

 O pilgrim-souls, I speak to you!
  I see you come proud and slow
10 From the land of the spirits pale as dew
  And round me and round me ye go.
 O pilgrims, I have gasped and run
 All night long from the whips of one
  Who in your names works sin and woe!

III

15 And thus I thought that I would come
  And kneel here where ye knelt before,
 And feel your souls around me hum
  In undertone to the ocean's roar;
 And lift my black face, my black hand,
20 Here, in your names, to curse this land
  Ye blessed in freedom's, evermore.

IV

 I am black, I am black,
  And yet God made me, they say:
 But if He did so, smiling back
25 He must have cast His work away
 Under the feet of His white creatures,
 With a look of scorn, that the dusky features
  Might be trodden again to clay.

V

 And yet He has made dark things
30 To be glad and merry as light:
 There's a little dark bird sits and sings,
  There's a dark stream ripples out of sight,
 And the dark frogs chant in the safe morass,
 And the sweetest stars are made to pass
35 O'er the face of the darkest night.

VI

 But *we* who are dark, we are dark!
  Ah God, we have no stars!
 About our souls in care and cark
  Our blackness shuts like prison-bars:
40 The poor souls crouch so far behind
 That never a comfort can they find
  By reaching through the prison-bars.

VII

 Indeed we live beneath the sky,
  That great smooth Hand of God stretched out
45 On all His children fatherly,
  To save them from the dread and doubt
 Which would be if, from this low place,
 All opened straight up to His face
  Into the grand eternity.

VIII

50 And still God's sunshine and His frost,
  They make us hot, they make us cold,
 As if we were not black and lost;
  And the beasts and birds, in wood and fold,
 Do fear and take us for very men:
55 Could the whip-poor-will or the cat of the glen
  Look into my eyes and be bold?

IX

 I am black, I am black!
  But, once, I laughed in girlish glee,
 For one of my colour stood in the track
60 Where the drivers drove, and looked at me,
 And tender and full was the look he gave—
 Could a slave look *so* at another slave?—
  I look at the sky and sea.

X

 And from that hour our spirits grew
65 As free as if unsold, unbought:
 Oh, strong enough, since we were two,
  To conquer the world, we thought.

The drivers drove us day by day;
We did not mind, we went one way,
70   And no better a freedom sought.

XI

In the sunny ground between the canes,
      He said "I love you" as he passed;
When the shingle-roof rang sharp with the rains,
      I heard how he vowed it fast:
75 While others shook he smiled in the hut,
As he carved me a bowl of the cocoa-nut
      Through the roar of the hurricanes.

XII

I sang his name instead of a song,
      Over and over I sang his name,
80 Upward and downward I drew it along
      My various notes,—the same, the same!
I sang it low, that the slave-girls near
Might never guess, from aught they could hear,
      It was only a name—a name.

XIII

85 I look on the sky and the sea.
      We were two to love, and two to pray:
Yes, two, O God, who cried to Thee,
      Though nothing didst Thou say!
Coldly Thou sat'st behind the sun:
90 And now I cry who am but one,
      Thou wilt not speak to-day.

XIV

We were black, we were black,
      We had no claim to love and bliss,
What marvel if each went to wrack?
95   They wrung my cold hands out of his
They dragged him—where? I crawled to touch
His blood's mark in the dust...not much,
      Ye pilgrim-souls, though plain as *this!*

XV

Wrong, followed by a deeper wrong!
100   Mere grief's too good for such as I:
So the white men brought the shame ere long
      To strangle the sob of my agony.
They would not leave me for my dull
Wet eyes!—it was too merciful
105   To let me weep pure tears and die.

XVI

I am black, I am black!
      I wore a child upon my breast,
An amulet that hung too slack,
      And, in my unrest, could not rest:
110 Thus we went moaning, child and mother,
One to another, one to another,
      Until all ended for the best.

XVII

For hark! I will tell you low, low,
      I am black, you see,—
115 And the babe who lay on my bosom so,
      Was far too white, too white for me;
As white as the ladies who scorned to pray
Beside me at church but yesterday,
      Though my tears had washed a place for my
      knee.

XVIII

120 My own, own child! I could not bear
      To look in his face, it was so white;
I covered him up with a kerchief there,
      I covered his face in close and tight:
And he moaned and struggled, as well might be,
125 For the white child wanted his liberty—
      Ha, ha! he wanted the master-right.

XIX

He moaned and beat with his head and feet,
      His little feet that never grew;
He struck them out, as it was meet,

130 Against my heart to break it through:
I might have sung and made him mild,
But I dared not sing to the white-faced child
   The only song I knew.

XX

I pulled the kerchief very close:
135   He could not see the sun, I swear,
More, then, alive, than now he does
   From between the roots of the mango…where?
I know where. Close! A child and mother
Do wrong to look at one another
140   When one is black and one is fair.

XXI

Why, in that single glance I had
   Of my child's face,…I tell you all,
I saw a look that made me mad!
   The *master's* look, that used to fall
145 On my soul like his lash…or worse!
And so, to save it from my curse,
   I twisted it round in my shawl.

XXII

And he moaned and trembled from foot to head,
   He shivered from head to foot;
150 Till after a time, he lay instead
   Too suddenly still and mute.
I felt, beside, a stiffening cold:
I dared to lift up just a fold,
   As in lifting a leaf of the mango-fruit.

XXIII

155 But *my* fruit…ha, ha!—there, had been
   (I laugh to think on't at this hour!)
Your fine white angels (who have seen
   Nearest the secret of God's power)
And plucked my fruit to make them wine,
160 And sucked the soul of that child of mine
   As the humming-bird sucks the soul of the
      flower.

XXIV

Ha, ha, the trick of the angels white!
   They freed the white child's spirit so.
I said not a word, but day and night
165   I carried the body to and fro,
And it lay on my heart like a stone, as chill.
—The sun may shine out as much as he will:
   I am cold, though it happened a month ago.

XXV

From the white man's house, and the black man's
      hut,
170   I carried the little body on;
The forest's arms did round us shut,
   And silence through the trees did run:
They asked no question as I went,
They stood too high for astonishment,
175   They could see God sit on His throne.

XXVI

My little body, kerchiefed fast,
   I bore it on through the forest, on;
And when I felt it was tired at last,
   I scooped a hole beneath the moon:
180 Through the forest-tops the angels far,
With a white sharp finger from every star,
   Did point and mock at what was done.

XXVII

Yet when it was all done aright,—
   Earth, 'twixt me and my baby, strewed,—
185 All, changed to black earth,—nothing white,—
   A dark child in the dark!—ensued
Some comfort, and my heart grew young;
I sate down smiling there and sung
   The song I learnt in my maidenhood.

XXVIII

190 And thus we two were reconciled,
   The white child and black mother, thus;
For as I sang it soft and wild,

The same song, more melodious,
Rose from the grave whereon I sate:
195 It was the dead child singing that,
To join the souls of both of us.

XXIX

I look on the sea and the sky.
Where the pilgrims' ships first anchored lay
The free sun rideth gloriously,
200 But the pilgrim-ghosts have slid away
Through the earliest streaks of the morn:
My face is black, but it glares with a scorn
Which they dare not meet by day.

XXX

Ha!—in their stead, their hunter sons!
205 Ha, ha! they are on me—they hunt in a ring!
Keep off! I brave you all at once,
I throw off your eyes like snakes that sting!
You have killed the black eagle at nest, I think:
Did you ever stand still in your triumph, and shrink
210 From the stroke of her wounded wing?

XXXI

(Man, drop that stone you dared to lift!—)
I wish you who stand there five abreast,
Each, for his own wife's joy and gift,
A little corpse as safely at rest
215 As mine in the mangoes! Yes, but *she*
May keep live babies on her knee,
And sing the song she likes the best.

XXXII

I am not mad: I am black.
I see you staring in my face—
220 I know you staring, shrinking back,
Ye are born of the Washington-race,
And this land is the free America,
And this mark on my wrist—(I prove what I say)
Ropes tied me up here to the flogging-place.

XXXIII

225 You think I shrieked then? Not a sound!
I hung, as a gourd hangs in the sun;
I only cursed them all around
As softly as I might have done
My very own child: from these sands
230 Up to the mountains, lift your hands,
O slaves, and end what I begun!

XXXIV

Whips, curses; these must answer those!
For in this UNION you have set
Two kinds of men in adverse rows,
235 Each loathing each; and all forget
The seven wounds in Christ's body fair,
While HE sees gaping everywhere
Our countless wounds that pay no debt.

XXXV

Our wounds are different. Your white men
240 Are, after all, not gods indeed,
Nor able to make Christs again
Do good with bleeding. *We* who bleed
(Stand off!) we help not in our loss!
We are too heavy for our cross,
245 And fall and crush you and your seed.

XXXVI

I fall, I swoon! I look at the sky.
The clouds are breaking on my brain;
I am floated along, as if I should die
Of liberty's exquisite pain.
250 In the name of the white child waiting for me
In the death-dark where we may kiss and agree,
White men, I leave you all curse-free
In my broken heart's disdain!
—1850

29

Aurora Leigh

FIRST BOOK

Of writing many books there is no end;[1]
And I who have written much in prose and
  verse
For others' uses, will write now for mine,—
Will write my story for my better self,[2]
5 As when you paint your portrait for a friend,
Who keeps it in a drawer and looks at it
Long after he has ceased to love you, just
To hold together what he was and is.
I, writing thus, am still what men call young;
10 I have not so far left the coasts of life
To travel inward, that I cannot hear
That murmur of the outer Infinite[3]
Which unweaned babies smile at in their sleep
When wondered at for smiling; not so far,
15 But still I catch my mother at her post
Beside the nursery door, with finger up,
"Hush, hush—here's too much noise!" while her
  sweet eyes
Leap forward, taking part against her word
In the child's riot. Still I sit and feel
20 My father's slow hand, when she had left us both,
Stroke out my childish curls across his knee,
And hear Assunta's[4] daily jest (she knew
He liked it better than a better jest)
Inquire how many golden scudi[5] went
25 To make such ringlets. O my father's hand,
Stroke heavily, heavily the poor hair down,

Draw, press the child's head closer to thy knee!
I'm still too young, too young, to sit alone.

I write. My mother was a Florentine,
30 Whose rare blue eyes were shut from seeing me
When scarcely I was four years old, my life
A poor spark snatched up from a failing lamp
Which went out therefore. She was weak and frail;
She could not bear the joy of giving life,
35 The mother's rapture slew her. If her kiss
Had left a longer weight upon my lips
It might have steadied the uneasy breath,
And reconciled and fraternised my soul
With the new order. As it was, indeed,
40 I felt a mother-want about the world,
And still went seeking, like a bleating lamb
Left out at night in shutting up the fold,—
As restless as a nest-deserted bird
Grown chill through something being away,
  though what
45 It knows not. I, Aurora Leigh, was born
To make my father sadder, and myself
Not overjoyous, truly. Women know
The way to rear up children (to be just),
They know a simple, merry, tender knack
50 Of tying sashes, fitting baby-shoes,
And stringing pretty words that make no sense,
And kissing full sense into empty words,
Which things are corals[6] to cut life upon,
Although such trifles: children learn by such,
55 Love's holy earnest in a pretty play
And get not over-early solemnised,
But seeing, as in a rose-bush, Love's Divine
Which burns and hurts not,[7]—not a single
  bloom,—
Become aware and unafraid of Love.
60 Such good do mothers. Fathers love as well

---

[1] See Ecclesiastes 12:12.

[2] Aurora, age 26 or 27, is writing her life story retrospectively.

[3] Cf. William Wordsworth's "Ode: Intimations of Immortality from Recollections of Early Childhood" (1807).

[4] common nineteenth-century Italian name meaning "Our Lady, received into Heaven."

[5] a former coin of Italy and Sicily.

[6] a toy made of polished coral, given to infants to assist teething (*OED*).

[7] See Exodus 3:2.

—Mine did, I know,—but still with heavier brains,
And wills more consciously responsible,
And not as wisely, since less foolishly;
So mothers have God's license to be missed.

65 My father was an austere Englishman,
Who, after a dry lifetime spent at home
In college-learning, law, and parish talk,
Was flooded with a passion unaware,
His whole provisioned and complacent past
70 Drowned out from him that moment. As he stood
In Florence, where he had come to spend a month
And note the secret of Da Vinci's[1] drains,
He musing somewhat absently perhaps
Some English question…whether men should pay
75 The unpopular but necessary tax
With left or right hand—in the alien sun
In that great square of the Santissima[2]
There drifted past him (scarcely marked enough
To move his comfortable island scorn)
80 A train of priestly banners, cross and psalm,
The white-veiled rose-crowned maidens holding up
Tall tapers, weighty for such wrists, aslant
To the blue luminous tremor of the air,
And letting drop the white wax as they went
85 To eat the bishop's wafer at the church;
From which long trail of chanting priests and girls,
A face flashed like a cymbal on his face
And shook with silent clangour brain and heart,
Transfiguring him to music. Thus, even thus,
90 He too received his sacramental gift
With eucharistic meanings; for he loved.

And thus beloved, she died. I've heard it said
That but to see him in the first surprise
Of widower and father, nursing me,
95 Unmothered little child of four years old,
His large man's hands afraid to touch my curls,

As if the gold would tarnish,—his grave lips
Contriving such a miserable smile
As if he knew needs must, or I should die,
100 And yet 'twas hard,—would almost make the stones
Cry out for pity.[3] There's a verse he set
In Santa Croce[4] to her memory,—
"Weep for an infant too young to weep much
When death removed this mother"—stops the mirth
105 To-day on women's faces when they walk
With rosy children hanging on their gowns,
Under the cloister to escape the sun
That scorches in the piazza. After which
He left our Florence and made haste to hide
110 Himself, his prattling child, and silent grief,
Among the mountains above Pelago;
Because unmothered babes, he thought, had need
Of mother nature more than others use,
And Pan's[5] white goats, with udders warm and full
115 Of mystic contemplations, come to feed
Poor milkless lips of orphans like his own—
Such scholar-scraps he talked, I've heard from
      friends,
For even prosaic men who wear grief long
Will get to wear it as a hat aside
120 With a flower stuck in't. Father, then, and child,
We lived among the mountains many years,
God's silence on the outside of the house,
And we who did not speak too loud within,
And old Assunta to make up the fire,
125 Crossing herself whene'er a sudden flame
Which lightened from the firewood, made alive
That picture of my mother on the wall.

The painter drew it after she was dead,
And when the face was finished, throat and hands,

---

[1] Leonardo da Vinci (1452–1519), Florentine artist, celebrated as a painter, sculptor, architect, engineer, and scientist.

[2] the church of the Santissima Annunziata in Florence.

[3] See Luke 19:40.

[4] a church in Florence.

[5] the god of woods, fields, and flocks, having a human body with goat's legs, horns, and ears.

130 Her cameriera[1] carried him, in hate
Of the English-fashioned shroud, the last brocade
She dressed in at the Pitti;[2] "he should paint
No sadder thing than that," she swore, "to wrong
Her poor signora."[3] Therefore very strange
135 The effect was. I, a little child, would crouch
For hours upon the floor with knees drawn up,
And gaze across them, half in terror, half
In adoration, at the picture there,—
That swan-like supernatural white life
140 Just sailing upward from the red stiff silk
Which seemed to have no part in it nor power
To keep it from quite breaking out of bounds.
For hours I sat and stared. Assunta's awe
And my poor father's melancholy eyes
145 Still pointed that way. That way went my thoughts
When wandering beyond sight. And as I grew
In years, I mixed, confused, unconsciously,
Whatever I last read or heard or dreamed,
Abhorrent, admirable, beautiful,
150 Pathetical, or ghastly, or grotesque,
With still that face…which did not therefore change,
But kept the mystic level of all forms,
Hates, fears, and admirations, was by turns
Ghost, fiend, and angel, fairy, witch, and sprite,
155 A dauntless Muse[4] who eyes a dreadful Fate,[5]
A loving Psyche who loses sight of Love,[6]

A still Medusa[7] with mild milky brows
All curdled and all clothed upon with snakes
Whose slime falls fast as sweat will; or anon
160 Our Lady of the Passion, stabbed with swords
Where the Babe sucked;[8] or Lamia[9] in her first
Moonlighted pallor, ere she shrunk and blinked
And shuddering wriggled down to the unclean;
Or my own mother, leaving her last smile
165 In her last kiss upon the baby-mouth
My father pushed down on the bed for that,—
Or my dead mother, without smile or kiss,
Buried at Florence. All which images,
Concentred on the picture, glassed themselves
170 Before my meditative childhood, as
The incoherencies of change and death
Are represented fully, mixed and merged,
In the smooth fair mystery of perpetual Life.
And while I stared away my childish wits
175 Upon my mother's picture (ah, poor child!),
My father, who through love had suddenly
Thrown off the old conventions, broken loose
From chin-bands[10] of the soul, like Lazarus,[11]
Yet had no time to learn to talk and walk
180 Or grow anew familiar with the sun,—
Who had reached to freedom, not to action, lived,
But lived as one entranced, with thoughts, not
  aims,—
Whom love had unmade from a common man
But not completed to an uncommon man,—
185 My father taught me what he had learnt the best
Before he died and left me,—grief and love.
And, seeing we had books among the hills,

---

[1] Italian waiting woman.

[2] The Pitti Palace was the official residence of the grand dukes of Tuscany in the nineteenth century.

[3] lady.

[4] In Greek mythology, the nine Muses, the offspring of Zeus and Mnemosyne, presided over the arts; the nine are Calliope, Clio, Thalia, Melpomene, Euterpe, Terpsichore, Erato, Polyhymnia, and Urania.

[5] The three Fates, daughters of Erebus and Night, were Clotho ("the spinner"), Lachesis ("the measurer"), and Atropos ("she who cannot be avoided").

[6] The marriage of Eros, or Cupid, with Psyche was ruined when she disobeyed his orders and attempted to view him unawares.

---

[7] the Gorgon, loved by Poseidon and mother of Chrysaor and Pegasus. Medusa was transformed by Athene into a snake-haired monster whose glance turned men into stone; she was eventually beheaded by Perseus.

[8] See Luke 2:35.

[9] In Greek mythology, Lamia's children were killed by Hera, jealous of the mortal's relationship with Zeus. Thereafter, Lamia sought out and killed the children of others in revenge; see also Keats's "Lamia."

[10] a shroud; winding-cloth.

[11] See John 11:1–53.

Strong words of counselling souls confederate
With vocal pines and waters,—out of books
190 He taught me all the ignorance of men,
And how God laughs in heaven when any man
Says "Here I'm learned; this, I understand;
In that, I am never caught at fault or doubt."
He sent the schools to school, demonstrating
195 A fool will pass for such through one mistake,
While a philosopher will pass for such,
Through said mistakes being ventured in the gross
And heaped up to a system.
                                    I am like,
They tell me, my dear father. Broader brows
200 Howbeit, upon a slenderer undergrowth
Of delicate features,—paler, near as grave;
But then my mother's smile breaks up the whole,
And makes it better sometimes than itself.
So, nine full years, our days were hid with God
205 Among his mountains: I was just thirteen,
Still growing like the plants from unseen roots
In tongue-tied Springs,—and suddenly awoke
To full life and life's needs and agonies
With an intense, strong, struggling heart beside
210 A stone-dead father. Life, struck sharp on death,
Makes awful lightning. His last word was "Love—"
"Love, my child, love, love!"—(then he had done
    with grief)
"Love, my child." Ere I answered he was gone,
And none was left to love in all the world.

215 There, ended childhood. What succeeded next
I recollect as, after fevers, men
Thread back the passage of delirium,
Missing the turn still, baffled by the door;
Smooth endless days, notched here and there with
    knives,
220 A weary, wormy darkness, spurred i' the flank
With flame, that it should eat and end itself
Like some tormented scorpion. Then at last
I do remember clearly how there came
A stranger with authority, not right

225 (I thought not), who commanded, caught me up
From old Assunta's neck; how, with a shriek,
She let me go,—while I, with ears too full
Of my father's silence to shriek back a word,
In all a child's astonishment at grief
230 Stared at the wharf-edge where she stood and
    moaned,
My poor Assunta, where she stood and moaned!
The white walls, the blue hills, my Italy,
Drawn backward from the shuddering steamer-deck,
Like one in anger drawing back her skirts
235 Which suppliants catch at. Then the bitter sea
Inexorably pushed between us both
And, sweeping up the ship with my despair,
Threw us out as a pasture to the stars.

Ten nights and days we voyaged on the deep;
240 Ten nights and days without the common face
Of any day or night; the moon and sun
Cut off from the green reconciling earth,
To starve into a blind ferocity
And glare unnatural; the very sky
245 (Dropping its bell-net down upon the sea,
As if no human heart should 'scape alive)
Bedraggled with the desolating salt,
Until it seemed no more that holy heaven
To which my father went. All new and strange;
250 The universe turned stranger, for a child.

Then, land!—then, England! oh, the frosty cliffs
Looked cold upon me. Could I find a home
Among those mean red houses through the fog?
And when I heard my father's language first
255 From alien lips which had no kiss for mine
I wept aloud, then laughed, then wept, then wept,
And some one near me said the child was mad
Through much sea-sickness. The train swept us on:
Was this my father's England? the great isle?
260 The ground seemed cut up from the fellowship
Of verdure, field from field, as man from man;
The skies themselves looked low and positive,

As almost you could touch them with a hand,
And dared to do it they were so far off
265 From God's celestial crystals; all things blurred
And dull and vague. Did Shakespeare and his mates
Absorb the light here?—not a hill or stone
With heart to strike a radiant colour up
Or active outline on the indifferent air.

270 I think I see my father's sister stand
Upon the hall-step of her country-house
To give me welcome. She stood straight and calm,
Her somewhat narrow forehead braided tight
As if for taming accidental thoughts
275 From possible pulses; brown hair pricked with gray
By frigid use of life (she was not old,
Although my father's elder by a year),
A nose drawn sharply, yet in delicate lines;
A close mild mouth, a little soured about
280 The ends, through speaking unrequited loves
Or peradventure niggardly half-truths;
Eyes of no colour,—once they might have smiled,
But never, never have forgot themselves
In smiling; cheeks, in which was yet a rose
285 Of perished summers, like a rose in a book,
Kept more for ruth than pleasure,—if past bloom,
Past fading also.
                    She had lived, we'll say,
A harmless life, she called a virtuous life,
A quiet life, which was not life at all
290 (But that, she had not lived enough to know),
Between the vicar and the county squires,
The lord-lieutenant[1] looking down sometimes
From the empyrean[2] to assure their souls
Against chance vulgarisms, and, in the abyss,
295 The apothecary, looked on once a year
To prove their soundness of humility.
The poor-club[3] exercised her Christian gifts

---

[1] the official, though mostly ceremonial, governor of a county.

[2] i.e., heaven.

[3] a charitable club collecting clothes or funds for the poor.

Of knitting stockings, stitching petticoats,
Because we are of one flesh, after all,
300 And need one flannel (with a proper sense
Of difference in the quality)—and still
The book-club, guarded from your modern trick
Of shaking dangerous questions from the crease,
Preserved her intellectual. She had lived
305 A sort of cage-bird life, born in a cage,
Accounting that to leap from perch to perch
Was act and joy enough for any bird.
Dear heaven, how silly are the things that live
In thickets, and eat berries!
                              I, alas,
310 A wild bird scarcely fledged, was brought to her
    cage,
And she was there to meet me. Very kind.
Bring the clean water, give out the fresh seed.

She stood upon the steps to welcome me,
Calm, in black garb. I clung about her neck,—
315 Young babes, who catch at every shred of wool
To draw the new light closer, catch and cling
Less blindly. In my ears my father's word
Hummed ignorantly, as the sea in shells,
"Love, love, my child." She, black there with my
    grief,
320 Might feel my love—she was his sister once—
I clung to her. A moment she seemed moved,
Kissed me with cold lips, suffered me to cling,
And drew me feebly through the hall into
The room she sat in.
                      There, with some strange spasm
325 Of pain and passion, she wrung loose my hands
Imperiously, and held me at arm's length,
And with two grey-steel naked-bladed eyes
Searched through my face,—ay, stabbed it through
    and through,
Through brows and cheeks and chin, as if to find
330 A wicked murderer in my innocent face,
If not here, there perhaps. Then, drawing breath,
She struggled for her ordinary calm—

And missed it rather,—told me not to shrink,
As if she had told me not to lie or swear,—
335 "She loved my father and would love me too
As long as I deserved it." Very kind.

I understood her meaning afterward;
She thought to find my mother in my face,
And questioned it for that. For she, my aunt,
340 Had loved my father truly, as she could,
And hated, with the gall of gentle souls,
My Tuscan mother who had fooled away
A wise man from wise courses, a good man
From obvious duties, and, depriving her,
345 His sister, of the household precedence,
Had wronged his tenants, robbed his native land,
And made him mad, alike by life and death,
In love and sorrow. She had pored for years
What sort of woman could be suitable
350 To her sort of hate, to entertain it with,
And so, her very curiosity
Became hate too, and all the idealism
She ever used in life was used for hate,
Till hate, so nourished, did exceed at last
355 The love from which it grew, in strength and heat,
And wrinkled her smooth conscience with a sense
Of disputable virtue (say not, sin)
When Christian doctrine was enforced at church.

And thus my father's sister was to me
360 My mother's hater. From that day she did
Her duty to me (I appreciate it
In her own word as spoken to herself),
Her duty, in large measure, well pressed out[1]
But measured always. She was generous, bland,
365 More courteous than was tender, gave me still
The first place,—as if fearful that God's saints
Would look down suddenly and say "Herein
You missed a point, I think, through lack of love."
Alas, a mother never is afraid

370 Of speaking angrily[2] to any child,
Since love, she knows, is justified of love.

And I, I was a good child on the whole,
A meek and manageable child. Why not?
I did not live, to have the faults of life:
375 There seemed more true life in my father's grave
Than in all England. Since *that* threw me off
Who fain would cleave (his latest will, they say,
Consigned me to his land), I only thought
Of lying quiet there where I was thrown
380 Like sea-weed on the rocks, and suffering her
To prick me to a pattern with her pin,
Fibre from fibre, delicate leaf from leaf,
And dry out from my drowned anatomy
The last sea-salt left in me.
                                    So it was.
385 I broke the copious curls upon my head
In braids, because she liked smooth-ordered hair.
I left off saying my sweet Tuscan words
Which still at any stirring of the heart
Came up to float across the English phrase
390 As lilies (*Bene* or *Che che*),[3] because
She liked my father's child to speak his tongue.
I learnt the collects and the catechism,[4]
The creeds, from Athanasius[5] back to Nice,
The Articles, the Tracts *against* the times[6]
395 (By no means Buonaventure's "Prick of Love"),[7]
And various popular synopses of

---

[1] See Luke 6:38.

[2] i.e., angrily.

[3] "good" or "well, well."

[4] the manual of Christian doctrine arranged in the form of question and answer, intended for instructing those to be confirmed.

[5] The Athanasian creed forms part of the basic tenets of faith in the liturgy of the Church of England.

[6] In 1833 and 1841, *Tracts for the Times* was published by the Oxford High Church warning against the secularization of the church, and calling for a strengthened reliance on Catholic principles.

[7] *Stimulus Divini Amoris* (The Prick, or Goad, of Love), incorrectly attributed to St. Buonaventure, is a devotional work which emphasizes an emotional, rather than logical, approach to the mysteries.

Inhuman doctrines never taught by John,
Because she liked instructed piety.
I learnt my complement of classic French
400 (Kept pure of Balzac and neologism)
And German also, since she liked a range
Of liberal education,—tongues, not books.
I learnt a little algebra, a little
Of the mathematics,—brushed with extreme flounce
405 The circle of the sciences, because
She misliked women who are frivolous.
I learnt the royal genealogies
Of Oviedo, the internal laws
Of the Burmese empire,—by how many feet
410 Mount Chimborazo outsoars Teneriffe.
What navigable river joins itself
To Lara, and what census of the year five
Was taken at Klagenfurt,—because she liked
A general insight into useful facts.
415 I learnt much music,—such as would have been
As quite impossible in Johnson's day
As still it might be wished—fine sleights of hand
And unimagined fingering, shuffling off
The hearer's soul through hurricanes of notes
420 To a noisy Tophet; and I drew…costumes
From French engravings, nereids neatly draped
(With smirks of simmering godship): I washed in
Landscapes from nature (rather say, washed out).
I danced the polka and Cellarius,
425 Spun glass, stuffed birds, and modelled flowers in
    wax,
Because she liked accomplishments in girls.
I read a score of books on womanhood
To prove, if women do not think at all,
They may teach thinking (to a maiden aunt
430 Or else the author),—books that boldly assert
Their right of comprehending husband's talk
When not too deep, and even of answering
With pretty "may it please you," or "so it is,"—
Their rapid insight and fine aptitude,
435 Particular worth and general missionariness,
As long as they keep quiet by the fire

And never say "no" when the world says "ay,"
For that is fatal,—their angelic reach
Of virtue, chiefly used to sit and darn,
440 And fatten household sinners,—their, in brief,
Potential faculty in everything
Of abdicating power in it: she owned
She liked a woman to be womanly,
And English women, she thanked God and sighed
445 (Some people always sigh in thanking God)
Were models to the universe. And last
I learnt cross-stitch, because she did not like
To see me wear the night with empty hands
A-doing nothing. So, my shepherdess
450 Was something after all (the pastoral saints
Be praised for't), leaning lovelorn with pink eyes
To match her shoes, when I mistook the silks;
Her head uncrushed by that round weight of hat
So strangely similar to the tortoise-shell
455 Which slew the tragic poet.
                              By the way,
The works of women are symbolical.
We sew, sew, prick our fingers, dull our sight,
Producing what? A pair of slippers, sir,
To put on when you're weary—or a stool
460 To stumble over and vex you…"curse that stool!"
Or else at best, a cushion, where you lean
And sleep, and dream of something we are not
But would be for your sake. Alas, alas!
This hurts most, this—that, after all, we are paid
465 The worth of our work, perhaps.
                              In looking down
Those years of education (to return)
I wonder if Brinvilliers suffered more
In the water-torture…flood succeeding flood
To drench the incapable throat and split the veins…
470 Than I did. Certain of your feebler souls
Go out in such a process; many pine
To a sick, inodorous light; my own endured:
I had relations in the Unseen, and drew
The elemental nutriment and heat
475 From nature, as earth feels the sun at nights,

Or as a babe sucks surely in the dark.
I kept the life thrust on me, on the outside
Of the inner life with all its ample room
For heart and lungs, for will and intellect,
480 Inviolable by conventions. God,
I thank thee for that grace of thine!
                                        At first
I felt no life which was not patience,—did
The thing she bade me, without heed to a thing
Beyond it, sat in just the chair she placed,
485 With back against the window, to exclude
The sight of the great lime-tree on the lawn,
Which seemed to have come on purpose from the
        woods
To bring the house a message,—ay, and walked
Demurely in her carpeted low rooms,
490 As if I should not, hearkening my own steps,
Misdoubt I was alive. I read her books,
Was civil to her cousin, Romney Leigh,
Gave ear to her vicar, tea to her visitors,
And heard them whisper, when I changed a cup
495 (I blushed for joy at that),—"The Italian child,
For all her blue eyes and her quiet ways,
Thrives ill in England: she is paler yet
Than when we came the last time; she will die."

"Will die." My cousin, Romney Leigh, blushed too,
500 With sudden anger, and approaching me
Said low between his teeth, "You're wicked now?
You wish to die and leave the world a-dusk
For others, with your naughty light blown out?"
I looked into his face defyingly;
505 He might have known that, being what I was,
'Twas natural to like to get away
As far as dead folk can: and then indeed
Some people make no trouble when they die.
He turned and went abruptly, slammed the door,
510 And shut his dog out.
                        Romney, Romney Leigh.
I have not named my cousin hitherto,
And yet I used him as a sort of friend;

My elder by few years, but cold and shy
And absent…tender, when he thought of it,
515 Which scarcely was imperative, grave betimes,
As well as early master of Leigh Hall,
Whereof the nightmare sat upon his youth,
Repressing all its seasonable delights,
And agonising with a ghastly sense
520 Of universal hideous want and wrong
To incriminate possession. When he came
From college to the country, very oft
He crossed the hill on visits to my aunt,
With gifts of blue grapes from the hothouses,
525 A book in one hand,—mere statistics (if
I chanced to lift the cover), count of all
The goats whose beards grow sprouting down
        toward hell
Against God's separative judgment-hour.
And she, she almost loved him,—even allowed
530 That sometimes he should seem to sigh my way;
It made him easier to be pitiful,
And sighing was his gift. So, undisturbed,
At whiles she let him shut my music up
And push my needles down, and lead me out
535 To see in that south angle of the house
The figs grow black as if by a Tuscan rock,
On some light pretext. She would turn her head
At other moments, go to fetch a thing,
And leave me breath enough to speak with him,
540 For his sake; it was simple.
                                Sometimes too
He would have saved me utterly, it seemed,
He stood and looked so.
                        Once, he stood so near,
He dropped a sudden hand upon my hand
Bent down on woman's work, as soft as rain—
545 But then I rose and shook it off as fire,
The stranger's touch that took my father's place
Yet dared seem soft.
                        I used him for a friend
Before I ever knew him for a friend.
'Twas better, 'twas worse also, afterward:

550 We came so close, we saw our differences
Too intimately. Always Romney Leigh
Was looking for the worms, I for the gods.
A godlike nature his; the gods look down,
Incurious of themselves; and certainly
555 'Tis well I should remember, how, those days,
I was a worm too, and he looked on me.

A little by his act perhaps, yet more
By something in me, surely not my will,
I did not die. But slowly, as one in swoon,
560 To whom life creeps back in the form of death,
With a sense of separation, a blind pain
Of blank obstruction, and a roar i' the ears
Of visionary chariots which retreat
As earth grows clearer...slowly, by degrees;
565 I woke, rose up...where was I? in the world;
For uses therefore I must count worth while.

I had a little chamber in the house,
As green as any privet-hedge a bird
Might choose to build in, though the nest itself
570 Could show but dead-brown sticks and straws; the
    walls
Were green, the carpet was pure green, the straight
Small bed was curtained greenly, and the folds
Hung green about the window which let in
The out-door world with all its greenery.
575 You could not push your head out and escape
A dash of dawn-dew from the honeysuckle,
But so you were baptized into the grace
And privilege of seeing...
                    First, the lime
(I had enough there, of the lime, be sure,—
580 My morning-dream was often hummed away
By the bees in it); past the lime, the lawn,
Which, after sweeping broadly round the house,
Went trickling through the shrubberies in a stream
Of tender turf, and wore and lost itself
585 Among the acacias, over which you saw
The irregular line of elms by the deep lane

Which stopped the grounds and dammed the
    overflow
Of arbutus and laurel. Out of sight
The lane was; sunk so deep, no foreign tramp
590 Nor drover of wild ponies out of Wales
Could guess if lady's hall or tenant's lodge
Dispensed such odours,—though his stick well-
    crooked
Might reach the lowest trail of blossoming briar
Which dipped upon the wall. Behind the elms,
595 And through their tops, you saw the folded hills
Striped up and down with hedges (burly oaks
Projecting from the line to show themselves),
Through which my cousin Romney's chimneys
    smoked
As still as when a silent mouth in frost
600 Breathes, showing where the woodlands hid Leigh
    Hall;
While, far above, a jut of table-land,
A promontory without water, stretched,—
You could not catch it if the days were thick,
Or took it for a cloud; but, otherwise,
605 The vigorous sun would catch it up at eve
And use it for an anvil till he had filled
The shelves of heaven with burning thunder-bolts,
Protesting against night and darkness:—then,
When all his setting trouble was resolved
610 To a trance of passive glory, you might see
In apparition on the golden sky
(Alas, my Giotto's background!) the sheep run
Along the fine clear outline, small as mice
That run along a witch's scarlet thread.

615 Not a grand nature. Not my chestnut-woods
Of Vallombrosa, cleaving by the spurs
To the precipices. Not my headlong leaps
Of waters, that cry out for joy or fear
In leaping through the palpitating pines,
620 Like a white soul tossed out to eternity
With thrills of time upon it. Not indeed
My multitudinous mountains, sitting in

The magic circle, with the mutual touch
Electric, panting from their full deep hearts
625 Beneath the influent heavens, and waiting for
Communion and commission. Italy
Is one thing, England one.
                                        On English ground
You understand the letter,—ere the fall
How Adam lived in a garden. All the fields
630 Are tied up fast with hedges, nosegay-like;
The hills are crumpled plains, the plains parterres,
The trees, round, woolly, ready to be clipped,
And if you seek for any wilderness
You find, at best, a park. A nature tamed
635 And grown domestic like a barn-door fowl,
Which does not awe you with its claws and beak,
Nor tempt you to an eyrie too high up,
But which, in cackling, sets you thinking of
Your eggs to-morrow at breakfast, in the pause
640 Of finer meditation.
                                        Rather say,
A sweet familiar nature, stealing in
As a dog might, or child, to touch your hand
Or pluck your gown, and humbly mind you so
Of presence and affection, excellent
645 For inner uses, from the things without.

I could not be unthankful, I who was
Entreated thus and holpen. In the room
I speak of, ere the house was well awake,
And also after it was well asleep,
650 I sat alone, and drew the blessing in
Of all that nature. With a gradual step,
A stir among the leaves, a breath, a ray,
It came in softly, while the angels made
A place for it beside me. The moon came,
655 And swept my chamber clean of foolish thoughts.
The sun came, saying, "Shall I lift this light
Against the lime-tree, and you will not look?
I make the birds sing—listen! but, for you,
God never hears your voice, excepting when
660 You lie upon the bed at nights and weep."

Then, something moved me. Then, I wakened up
More slowly than I verily write now,
But wholly, at last, I wakened, opened wide
The window and my soul, and let the airs
665 And out-door sights sweep gradual gospels in,
Regenerating what I was. O, Life,
How oft we throw it off and think,—"Enough,
Enough of life in so much!—here's a cause
For rupture;—herein we must break with Life,
670 Or be ourselves unworthy; here we are wronged,
Maimed, spoiled for aspiration: farewell, Life!"
And so, as froward babes, we hide our eyes
And think all ended.—Then, Life calls to us
In some transformed, apocalyptic voice,
675 Above us, or below us, or around:
Perhaps we name it Nature's voice, or Love's,
Tricking ourselves, because we are more ashamed
To own our compensations than our griefs:
Still, Life's voice!—still, we make our peace with
    Life.

680 And I, so young then, was not sullen. Soon
I used to get up early, just to sit
And watch the morning quicken in the gray,
And hear the silence open like a flower
Leaf after leaf,—and stroke with listless hand
685 The woodbine through the window, till at last
I came to do it with a sort of love,
At foolish unaware: whereat I smiled,—
A melancholy smile, to catch myself
Smiling for joy.
                                        Capacity for joy
690 Admits temptation. It seemed, next, worth while
To dodge the sharp sword set against my life;
To slip down stairs through all the sleepy house,
As mute as any dream there, and escape
As a soul from the body, out of doors,
695 Glide through the shrubberies, drop into the lane,
And wander on the hills an hour or two,
Then back again before the house should stir.

Or else I sat on in my chamber green,
And lived my life, and thought my thoughts, and
    prayed
700 My prayers without the vicar; read my books
Without considering whether they were fit
To do me good. Mark, there. We get no good
By being ungenerous, even to a book,
And calculating profits,—so much help
705 By so much reading. It is rather when
We gloriously forget ourselves and plunge
Soul-forward, headlong, into a book's profound,
Impassioned for its beauty and salt of truth—
'Tis then we get the right good from a book.

710 I read much. What my father taught before
From many a volume, Love re-emphasised
Upon the self-same pages: Theophrast
Grew tender with the memory of his eyes,
And Ælian made mine wet. The trick of Greek
715 And Latin he had taught me, as he would
Have taught me wrestling or the game of fives
If such he had known,—most like a shipwrecked
    man
Who heaps his single platter with goats' cheese
And scarlet berries; or like any man
720 Who loves but one, and so gives all at once,
Because he has it, rather than because
He counts it worthy. Thus, my father gave;
And thus, as did the women formerly
By young Achilles, when they pinned a veil
725 Across the boy's audacious front, and swept
With tuneful laughs the silver-fretted rocks,
He wrapt his little daughter in his large
Man's doublet, careless did it fit or no.

But, after I had read for memory,
730 I read for hope. The path my father's foot
Had trod me out (which suddenly broke off
What time he dropped the wallet of the flesh
And passed), alone I carried on, and set
My child-heart 'gainst the thorny underwood,

735 To reach the grassy shelter of the trees.
Ah babe i' the wood, without a brother-babe!
My own self-pity, like the red-breast bird,
Flies back to cover all that past with leaves.

Sublimest danger, over which none weeps,
740 When any young wayfaring soul goes forth
Alone, unconscious of the perilous road,
The day-sun dazzling in his limpid eyes,
To thrust his own way, he an alien, through
The world of books! Ah, you!—you think it fine,
745 You clap hands—"A fair day!"—you cheer him on,
As if the worst, could happen, were to rest
Too long beside a fountain. Yet, behold,
Behold!—the world of books is still the world,
And worldlings in it are less merciful
750 And more puissant. For the wicked there
Are winged like angels; every knife that strikes
Is edged from elemental fire to assail
A spiritual life; the beautiful seems right
By force of beauty, and the feeble wrong
755 Because of weakness; power is justified
Though armed against Saint Michael; many a crown
Covers bald foreheads. In the book-world, true,
There's no lack, neither, of God's saints and kings,
That shake the ashes of the grave aside
760 From their calm locks and undiscomfited
Look steadfast truths against Time's changing mask.
True, many a prophet teaches in the roads;
True, many a seer pulls down the flaming heavens
Upon his own head in strong martyrdom
765 In order to light men a moment's space.
But stay!—who judges?—who distinguishes
'Twixt Saul and Nahash justly, at first sight,
And leaves king Saul precisely at the sin,
To serve king David? who discerns at once
770 The sound of the trumpets, when the trumpets blow
For Alaric as well as Charlemagne?
Who judges wizards, and can tell true seers
From conjurers? the child, there? Would you leave
That child to wander in a battle-field

775 And push his innocent smile against the guns;
Or even in a catacomb,—his torch
Grown ragged in the fluttering air, and all
The dark a-mutter round him? not a child.

I read books bad and good—some bad and good
780 At once (good aims not always make good books:
Well-tempered spades turn up ill-smelling soils
In digging vineyards even); books that prove
God's being so definitely, that man's doubt
Grows self-defined the other side the line,
785 Made atheist by suggestion; moral books,
Exasperating to license; genial books,
Discounting from the human dignity;
And merry books, which set you weeping when
The sun shines,—ay, and melancholy books,
790 Which make you laugh that any one should weep
In this disjointed life for one wrong more.

The world of books is still the world, I write,
And both worlds have God's providence, thank God,
To keep and hearten: with some struggle, indeed,
795 Among the breakers, some hard swimming through
The deeps—I lost breath in my soul sometimes
And cried "God save me if there's any God,"
But, even so, God saved me; and, being dashed
From error on to error, every turn
800 Still brought me nearer to the central truth.

I thought so. All this anguish in the thick
Of men's opinions…press and counter-press,
Now up, now down, now underfoot, and now
Emergent…all the best of it, perhaps,
805 But throws you back upon a noble trust
And use of your own instinct,—merely proves
Pure reason stronger than bare inference
At strongest. Try it,—fix against heaven's wall
The scaling-ladders of school logic—mount
810 Step by step!—sight goes faster; that still ray
Which strikes out from you, how, you cannot tell,
And why, you know not (did you eliminate,

That such as you indeed should analyse?)
Goes straight and fast as light, and high as God.

815 The cygnet finds the water, but the man
Is born in ignorance of his element
And feels out blind at first, disorganised
By sin i' the blood,—his spirit-insight dulled
And crossed by his sensations. Presently
820 He feels it quicken in the dark sometimes,
When, mark, be reverent, be obedient,
For such dumb motions of imperfect life
Are oracles of vital Deity
Attesting the Hereafter. Let who says
825 "The soul's a clean white paper," rather say,
A palimpsest, a prophet's holograph
Defiled, erased and covered by a monk's,—
The apocalypse, by a Longus! poring on
Which obscene text, we may discern perhaps
830 Some fair, fine trace of what was written once,
Some upstroke of an alpha and omega
Expressing the old scripture.

Books, books, books!
I had found the secret of a garret-room
Piled high with cases in my father's name,
835 Piled high, packed large,—where, creeping in and
out
Against the giant fossils of my past,
Like some small nimble mouse between the ribs
Of a mastodon, I nibbled here and there
At this or that box, pulling through the gap,
840 In heats of terror, haste, victorious joy,
The first book first. And how I felt it beat
Under my pillow, in the morning's dark,
An hour before the sun would let me read!
My books! At last because the time was ripe,
845 I chanced upon the poets.

As the earth
Plunges in fury, when the internal fires
Have reached and pricked her heart, and, throwing
flat
The marts and temples, the triumphal gates

And towers of observation, clears herself
850 To elemental freedom—thus, my soul,
At poetry's divine first finger-touch,
Let go conventions and sprang up surprised,
Convicted of the great eternities
Before two worlds.
                    What's this, Aurora Leigh,
855 You write so of the poets, and not laugh?
Those virtuous liars, dreamers after dark,
Exaggerators of the sun and moon,
And soothsayers in a tea-cup?
                              I write so
Of the only truth-tellers now left to God,
860 The only speakers of essential truth,
Opposed to relative, comparative,
And temporal truths; the only holders by
His sun-skirts, through conventional gray glooms;
The only teachers who instruct mankind
865 From just a shadow on a charnel-wall
To find man's veritable stature out
Erect, sublime,—the measure of a man,
And that's the measure of an angel, says
The apostle. Ay, and while your common men
870 Lay telegraphs, gauge railroads, reign, reap, dine,
And dust the flaunty carpets of the world
For kings to walk on, or our president,
The poet suddenly will catch them up
With his voice like a thunder,—"This is soul,
875 This is life, this word is being said in heaven,
Here's God down on us! what are you about?"
How all those workers start amid their work,
Look round, look up, and feel, a moment's space,
That carpet-dusting, though a pretty trade,
880 Is not the imperative labour after all.

My own best poets, am I one with you,
That thus I love you,—or but one through love?
Does all this smell of thyme about my feet
Conclude my visit to your holy hill
885 In personal presence, or but testify
The rustling of your vesture through my dreams

With influent odours? When my joy and pain,
My thought and aspiration like the stops
Of pipe or flute, are absolutely dumb
890 Unless melodious, do you play on me
My pipers,—and if, sooth, you did not blow,
Would no sound come? or is the music mine,
As a man's voice or breath is called his own,
Inbreathed by the Life-breather? There's a doubt
895 For cloudy seasons!
                      But the sun was high
When first I felt my pulses set themselves
For concord; when the rhythmic turbulence
Of blood and brain swept outward upon words,
As wind upon the alders, blanching them
900 By turning up their under-natures till
They trembled in dilation. O delight
And triumphs of the poet, who would say
A man's mere "yes," a woman's common "no,"
A little human hope of that or this,
905 And says the word so that it burns you through
With a special revelation, shakes the heart
Of all the men and women in the world,
As if one came back from the dead and spoke,
With eyes too happy, a familiar thing
910 Become divine i' the utterance! while for him
The poet, speaker, he expands with joy;
The palpitating angel in his flesh
Thrills inly with consenting fellowship
To those innumerous spirits who sun themselves
915 Outside of time.
                  O life, O poetry,
—Which means life in life! cognisant of life
Beyond this blood-beat, passionate for truth
Beyond these senses!—poetry, my life,
My eagle, with both grappling feet still hot
920 From Zeus's thunder, who hast ravished me
Away from all the shepherds, sheep, and dogs,
And set me in the Olympian roar and round
Of luminous faces for a cup-bearer,
To keep the mouths of all the godheads moist
925 For everlasting laughters,—I myself

Half drunk across the beaker with their eyes!
How those gods look!
                    Enough so, Ganymede,
We shall not bear above a round or two.
We drop the golden cup at Heré's foot
930 And swoon back to the earth,—and find ourselves
Face-down among the pine-cones, cold with dew,
While the dogs bark, and many a shepherd scoffs,
"What's come now to the youth?" Such ups and
        downs
Have poets.
                    Am I such indeed? The name
935 Is royal, and to sign it like a queen
Is what I dare not,—though some royal blood
Would seem to tingle in me now and then,
With sense of power and ache,—with imposthumes
And manias usual to the race. Howbeit
940 I dare not: 'tis too easy to go mad
And ape a Bourbon in a crown of straws;
The thing's too common.
                    Many fervent souls
Strike rhyme on rhyme, who would strike steel on
        steel
If steel had offered, in a restless heat
945 Of doing something. Many tender souls
Have strung their losses on a rhyming thread,
As children cowslips: the more pains they take,
The work more withers. Young men, ay, and maids,
Too often sow their wild oats in tame verse,
950 Before they sit down under their own vine
And live for use. Alas, near all the birds
Will sing at dawn,—and yet we do not take
The chaffering swallow for the holy lark.
In those days, though, I never analysed,
955 Not even myself. Analysis comes late.
You catch a sight of Nature, earliest,
In full front sun-face, and your eyelids wink
And drop before the wonder of 't; you miss
The form, through seeing the light. I lived, those
        days,
960 And wrote because I lived—unlicensed else;

My heart beat in my brain. Life's violent flood
Abolished bounds,—and, which my neighbour's
        field,
Which mine, what mattered? it is thus in youth!
We play at leap-frog over the god Term;
965 The love within us and the love without
Are mixed, confounded; if we are loved or love,
We scarce distinguish: thus, with other power;
Being acted on and acting seem the same:
In that first onrush of life's chariot-wheels,
970 We know not if the forests move or we.

And so, like most young poets, in a flush
Of individual life I poured myself
Along the veins of others, and achieved
Mere lifeless imitations of live verse,
975 And made the living answer for the dead,
Profaning nature. "Touch not, do not taste,
Nor handle,"—we're too legal, who write young:
We beat the phorminx till we hurt our thumbs,
As if still ignorant of counterpoint;
980 We call the Muse,—"O Muse, benignant Muse,"—
As if we had seen her purple-braided head,
With the eyes in it, start between the boughs
As often as a stag's. What make-believe,
With so much earnest! what effete results
985 From virile efforts! what cold wire-drawn odes
From such white heats!—bucolics, where the cows
Would scare the writer if they splashed the mud
In lashing off the flies,—didactics, driven
Against the heels of what the master said;
990 And counterfeiting epics, shrill with trumps
A babe might blow between two straining cheeks
Of bubbled rose, to make his mother laugh;
And elegiac griefs, and songs of love,
Like cast-off nosegays picked up on the road,
995 The worse for being warm: all these things, writ
On happy mornings, with a morning heart,
That leaps for love, is active for resolve,
Weak for art only. Oft, the ancient forms
Will thrill, indeed, in carrying the young blood.

1000 The wine-skins, now and then, a little warped,
Will crack even, as the new wine gurgles in.
Spare the old bottles!—spill not the new wine.

By Keats's soul, the man who never stepped
In gradual progress like another man,
1005 But, turning grandly on his central self,
Ensphered himself in twenty perfect years
And died, not young (the life of a long life
Distilled to a mere drop, falling like a tear
Upon the world's cold cheek to make it burn
1010 For ever); by that strong excepted soul,
I count it strange and hard to understand
That nearly all young poets should write old,
That Pope was sexagenary at sixteen,
And beardless Byron academical,
1015 And so with others. It may be perhaps
Such have not settled long and deep enough
In trance, to attain to clairvoyance,—and still
The memory mixes with the vision, spoils,
And works it turbid.
                                  Or perhaps, again,
1020 In order to discover the Muse-Sphinx,
The melancholy desert must sweep round,
Behind you as before.—
                                  For me, I wrote
False poems, like the rest, and thought them true
Because myself was true in writing them.
1025 I peradventure have writ true ones since
With less complacence.
                                  But I could not hide
My quickening inner life from those at watch.
They saw a light at a window, now and then,
They had not set there: who had set it there?
1030 My father's sister started when she caught
My soul agaze in my eyes. She could not say
I had no business with a sort of soul,
But plainly she objected,—and demurred
That souls were dangerous things to carry straight
1035 Through all the spilt saltpetre of the world.
She said sometimes "Aurora, have you done

Your task this morning? have you read that book?
And are you ready for the crochet here?"—
As if she said "I know there's something wrong;
1040 I know I have not ground you down enough
To flatten and bake you to a wholesome crust
For household uses and proprieties,
Before the rain has got into my barn
And set the grains a-sprouting. What, you're green
1045 With out-door impudence? you almost grow?"
To which I answered, "Would she hear my task,
And verify my abstract of the book?
Or should I sit down to the crochet work?
Was such her pleasure?" Then I sat and teased
1050 The patient needle till it split the thread,
Which oozed off from it in meandering lace
From hour to hour. I was not, therefore, sad;
My soul was singing at a work apart
Behind the wall of sense, as safe from harm
1055 As sings the lark when sucked up out of sight
In vortices of glory and blue air.

And so, through forced work and spontaneous work,
The inner life informed the outer life,
Reduced the irregular blood to a settled rhythm,
1060 Made cool the forehead with fresh-sprinkling
          dreams,
And, rounding to the spheric soul the thin,
Pined body, struck a colour up the cheeks
Though somewhat faint. I clenched my brows
          across
My blue eyes greatening in the looking-glass,
1065 And said "We'll live, Aurora! we'll be strong.
The dogs are on us—but we will not die."

Whoever lives true life will love true love.
I learnt to love that England. Very oft,
Before the day was born, or otherwise
1070 Through secret windings of the afternoons,
I threw my hunters off and plunged myself
Among the deep hills, as a hunted stag
Will take the waters, shivering with the fear

And passion of the course. And when at last
1075 Escaped, so many a green slope built on slope
Betwixt me and the enemy's house behind,
I dared to rest, or wander, in a rest
Made sweeter for the step upon the grass,
And view the ground's most gentle dimplement
1080 (As if God's finger touched but did not press
In making England), such an up and down
Of verdure,—nothing too much up or down,
A ripple of land; such little hills, the sky
Can stoop to tenderly and the wheatfields climb;
1085 Such nooks of valleys lined with orchises,
Fed full of noises by invisible streams;
And open pastures where you scarcely tell
White daisies from white dew,—at intervals
The mythic oaks and elm-trees standing out
1090 Self-poised upon their prodigy of shade,—
I thought my father's land was worthy too
Of being my Shakespeare's.

                    Very oft alone,
Unlicensed; not unfrequently with leave
To walk the third with Romney and his friend
1095 The rising painter, Vincent Carrington,
Whom men judge hardly as bee-bonneted,
Because he holds that, paint a body well,
You paint a soul by implication, like
The grand first Master. Pleasant walks! for if
1100 He said "When I was last in Italy,"
It sounded as an instrument that's played
Too far off for the tune—and yet it's fine
To listen.

          Often we walked only two
If cousin Romney pleased to walk with me.
1105 We read, or talked, or quarrelled, as it chanced.
We were not lovers, nor even friends well-matched:
Say rather, scholars upon different tracks,
And thinkers disagreed: he, overfull
Of what is, and I, haply, overbold
1110 For what might be.

                    But then the thrushes sang,
And shook my pulses and the elms' new leaves:

At which I turned, and held my finger up,
And bade him mark that, howsoe'er the world
Went ill, as he related, certainly
1115 The thrushes still sang in it. At the word
His brow would soften,—and he bore with me
In melancholy patience, not unkind,
While breaking into voluble ecstasy
I flattered all the beauteous country round,
1120 As poets use, the skies, the clouds, the fields,
The happy violets hiding from the roads
The primroses run down to, carrying gold;
The tangled hedgerows, where the cows push out
Impatient horns and tolerant churning mouths
1125 'Twixt dripping ash-boughs,—hedgerows all alive
With birds and gnats and large white butterflies
While look as if the May-flower had caught life
And palpitated forth upon the wind;
Hills, vales, woods, netted in a silver mist,
1130 Farms, granges, doubled up among the hills;
And cattle grazing in the watered vales,
And cottage-chimneys smoking from the woods,
And cottage-gardens smelling everywhere,
Confused with smell of orchards. "See," I said,
1135 "And see! is God not with us on the earth?
And shall we put Him down by aught we do?
Who says there's nothing for the poor and vile
Save poverty and wickedness? behold!"
And ankle-deep in English grass I leaped
1140 And clapped my hands, and called all very fair.

In the beginning when God called all good,
Even then was evil near us, it is writ;
But we indeed who call things good and fair,
The evil is upon us while we speak;
1145 Deliver us from evil, let us pray.

SECOND BOOK

Times followed one another. Came a morn
I stood upon the brink of twenty years,

45

And looked before and after, as I stood
Woman and artist,—either incomplete,
5 Both credulous of completion. There I held
The whole creation in my little cup,
And smiled with thirsty lips before I drank
"Good health to you and me, sweet neighbour mine,
And all these peoples."
                            I was glad, that day;
10 The June was in me, with its multitudes
Of nightingales all singing in the dark,
And rosebuds reddening where the calyx split.
I felt so young, so strong, so sure of God!
So glad, I could not choose be very wise!
15 And, old at twenty, was inclined to pull
My childhood backward in a childish jest
To see the face of 't once more, and farewell!
In which fantastic mood I bounded forth
At early morning,—would not wait so long
20 As even to snatch my bonnet by the strings,
But, brushing a green trail across the lawn
With my gown in the dew, took will and away
Among the acacias of the shrubberies,
To fly my fancies in the open air
25 And keep my birthday, till my aunt awoke
To stop good dreams. Meanwhile I murmured on
As honeyed bees keep humming to themselves,
"The worthiest poets have remained uncrowned
Till death has bleached their foreheads to the bone;
30 And so with me it must be unless I prove
Unworthy of the grand adversity,
And certainly I would not fail so much.
What, therefore, if I crown myself to-day
In sport, not pride, to learn the feel of it,
35 Before my brows be numbed as Dante's own
To all the tender pricking of such leaves?
Such leaves! what leaves?"
                            I pulled the branches down
To choose from.
                "Not the bay! I choose no bay
(The fates deny us if we are overbold),
40 Nor myrtle—which means chiefly love; and love

Is something awful which one dares not touch
So early o' mornings. This verbena strains
The point of passionate fragrance; and hard by,
This guelder-rose, at far too slight a beck
45 Of the wind, will toss about her flower-apples.
Ah—there's my choice,—that ivy on the wall,
That headlong ivy! not a leaf will grow
But thinking of a wreath. Large leaves, smooth
   leaves,
Serrated like my vines, and half as green.
50 I like such ivy, bold to leap a height
'Twas strong to climb; as good to grow on graves
As twist about a thyrsus; pretty too
(And that's not ill) when twisted round a comb."
Thus speaking to myself, half singing it,
55 Because some thoughts are fashioned like a bell
To ring with once being touched, I drew a wreath
Drenched, blinding me with dew, across my brow,
And fastening it behind so, turning faced
…My public!—cousin Romney—with a mouth
60 Twice graver than his eyes.
                            I stood there fixed,—
My arms up, like the caryatid, sole
Of some abolished temple, helplessly
Persistent in a gesture which derides
A former purpose. Yet my blush was flame,
65 As if from flax, not stone.
                            "Aurora Leigh,
The earliest of Auroras!"
                            Hand stretched out
I clasped, as shipwrecked men will clasp a hand,
Indifferent to the sort of palm. The tide
Had caught me at my pastime, writing down
70 My foolish name too near upon the sea
Which drowned me with a blush as foolish. "You,
My cousin!"
            The smile died out in his eyes
And dropped upon his lips, a cold dead weight,
For just a moment, "Here's a book I found!
75 No name writ on it—poems, by the form;
Some Greek upon the margin,—lady's Greek

Without the accents. Read it? Not a word.
I saw at once the thing had witchcraft in't,
Whereof the reading calls up dangerous spirits:
80 I rather bring it to the witch."

              "My book.
You found it"…
           "In the hollow by the stream
That beech leans down into—of which you said
The Oread in it has a Naiad's heart
And pines for waters."
        "Thank you."
             "Thanks to *you*
85 My cousin! that I have seen you not too much
Witch, scholar, poet, dreamer, and the rest,
To be a woman also."
         With a glance
The smile rose in his eyes again and touched
The ivy on my forehead, light as air.
90 I answered gravely "Poets needs must be
Or men or women—more's the pity."
            "Ah,
But men, and still less women, happily,
Scarce need be poets. Keep to the green wreath,
Since even dreaming of the stone and bronze
95 Brings headaches, pretty cousin, and defiles
The clean white morning dresses."
          "So you judge!
Because I love the beautiful I must
Love pleasure chiefly, and be overcharged
For ease and whiteness! well, you know the world,
100 And only miss your cousin, 'tis not much.
But learn this; I would rather take my part
With God's Dead, who afford to walk in white
Yet spread His glory, than keep quiet here
And gather up my feet from even a step
105 For fear to soil my gown in so much dust.
I choose to walk at all risks.—Here, if heads
That hold a rhythmic thought, much ache perforce,
For my part I choose headaches,—and to-day's
My birthday."
      "Dear Aurora, choose instead

110 To cure them. You have balsams."
            "I perceive.
The headache is too noble for my sex.
You think the heartache would sound decenter,
Since that's the woman's special, proper ache,
And altogether tolerable, except
115 To a woman."
        Saying which, I loosed my wreath,
And swinging it beside me as I walked,
Half-petulant, half-playful, as we walked,
I sent a sidelong look to find his thought,—
As falcon set on falconer's finger may,
120 With sidelong head, and startled, braving eye,
Which means, "You'll see—you'll see! I'll soon take
    flight,
You shall not hinder." He, as shaking out
His hand and answering "Fly then," did not speak,
Except by such a gesture. Silently
125 We paced, until, just coming into sight
Of the house-windows, he abruptly caught
At one end of the swinging wreath, and said
"Aurora!" There I stopped short, breath and all.

"Aurora, let's be serious, and throw by
130 This game of head and heart. Life means, be sure,
Both heart and head,—both active, both complete,
And both in earnest. Men and women make
The world, as head and heart make human life.
Work man, work woman, since there's work to do
135 In this beleaguered earth, for head and heart,
And thought can never do the work of love:
But work for ends, I mean for uses, not
For such sleek fringes (do you call them ends,
Still less God's glory?) as we sew ourselves
140 Upon the velvet of those baldaquins[1]
Held 'twixt us and the sun. That book of yours,
I have not read a page of; but I toss
A rose up—it falls calyx down, you see!
The chances are that, being a woman, young
145 And pure, with such a pair of large, calm eyes,

---

[1] a ceremonial canopy for a doorway, altar, or throne.

47

You write as well…and ill…upon the whole,
As other women. If as well, what then?
If even a little better,…still, what then?
We want the Best in art now, or no art.
150 The time is done for facile settings up
Of minnow gods, nymphs here and tritons there;
The polytheists have gone out in God,
That unity of Bests. No best, no God!
And so with art, we say. Give art's divine,
155 Direct, indubitable, real as grief,
Or leave us to the grief we grow ourselves
Divine by overcoming with mere hope
And most prosaic patience. You, you are young
As Eve with nature's daybreak on her face,
160 But this same world you are come to, dearest coz,
Has done with keeping birthdays, saves her wreaths
To hang upon her ruins,—and forgets
To rhyme the cry with which she still beats back
Those savage, hungry dogs that hunt her down
165 To the empty grave of Christ. The world's hard
      pressed;
The sweat of labour in the early curse
Has (turning acrid in six thousand years)
Become the sweat of torture. Who has time,
An hour's time…think!—to sit upon a bank
170 And hear the cymbal tinkle in white hands?
When Egypt's slain, I say, let Miriam sing!—
Before—where's Moses?"
                              "Ah, exactly that.
Where's Moses?—is a Moses to be found?
You'll seek him vainly in the bulrushes,
175 While I in vain touch cymbals. Yet concede,
Such sounding brass has done some actual good
(The application in a woman's hand,
If that were credible, being scarcely spoilt,)
In colonising beehives."
                              "There it is!—
180 You play beside a death-bed like a child,
Yet measure to yourself a prophet's place
To teach the living. None of all these things
Can women understand. You generalise

Oh, nothing,—not even grief! Your quick-breathed
      hearts,
185 So sympathetic to the personal pang,
Close on each separate knife-stroke, yielding up
A whole life at each wound, incapable
Of deepening, widening a large lap of life
To hold the world-full woe. The human race
190 To you means, such a child, or such a man,
You saw one morning waiting in the cold,
Beside that gate, perhaps. You gather up
A few such cases, and when strong sometimes
Will write of factories and of slaves, as if
195 Your father were a negro, and your son
A spinner in the mills. All's yours and you,
All, coloured with your blood, or otherwise
Just nothing to you. Why, I call you hard
To general suffering. Here's the world half-blind
200 With intellectual light, half-brutalised
With civilisation, having caught the plague
In silks from Tarsus, shrieking east and west
Along a thousand railroads, mad with pain
And sin too!…does one woman of you all
205 (You who weep easily) grow pale to see
This tiger shake his cage?—does one of you
Stand still from dancing, stop from stringing pearls,
And pine and die because of the great sum
Of universal anguish?—Show me a tear
210 Wet as Cordelia's, in eyes bright as yours,
Because the world is mad. You cannot count,
That you should weep for this account, not you!
You weep for what you know. A red-haired child
Sick in a fever, if you touch him once,
215 Though but so little as with a finger-tip,
Will set you weeping; but a million sick…
You could as soon weep for the rule of three
Or compound fractions. Therefore, this same world,
Uncomprehended by you, must remain
220 Uninfluenced by you.—Women as you are,
Mere women, personal and passionate,
You give us doating mothers, and perfect wives,
Sublime Madonnas, and enduring saints!

We get no Christ from you,—and verily
225 We shall not get a poet, in my mind."

"With which conclusion you conclude!"…
                                        "But this,
That you, Aurora, with the large live brow
And steady eyelids, cannot condescend
To play at art, as children play at swords,
230 To show a pretty spirit, chiefly admired
Because true action is impossible.
You never can be satisfied with praise
Which men give women when they judge a book
Not as mere work but as mere woman's work,
235 Expressing the comparative respect
Which means the absolute scorn. 'Oh, excellent,
What grace, what facile turns, what fluent sweeps,
What delicate discernment…almost thought!
The book does honour to the sex, we hold.
240 Among our female authors we make room
For this fair writer, and congratulate
The country that produces in these times
Such women, competent to…spell.'"
                                    "Stop there,"
I answered, burning through his thread of talk
245 With a quick flame of emotion,—"You have read
My soul, if not my book, and argue well
I would not condescend…we will not say
To such a kind of praise (a worthless end
Is praise of all kinds), but to such a use
250 Of holy art and golden life. I am young,
And peradventure weak—you tell me so—
Through being a woman. And, for all the rest,
Take thanks for justice. I would rather dance
At fairs on tight-rope, till the babies dropped
255 Their gingerbread for joy,—than shift the types
For tolerable verse, intolerable
To men who act and suffer. Better far
Pursue a frivolous trade by serious means,
Than a sublime art frivolously."
                                  "You,
260 Choose nobler work than either, O moist eyes

And hurrying lips and heaving heart! We are young,
Aurora, you and I. The world,—look round,—
The world, we're come to late, is swollen hard
With perished generations and their sins:
265 The civiliser's spade grinds horribly
On dead men's bones, and cannot turn up soil
That's otherwise than fetid. All success
Proves partial failure; all advance implies
What's left behind; all triumph, something crushed
270 At the chariot-wheels; all government, some wrong
And rich men make the poor, who curse the rich,
Who agonise together, rich and poor,
Under and over, in the social spasm
And crisis of the ages. Here's an age
275 That makes its own vocation! here we have stepped
Across the bounds of time! here's nought to see,
But just the rich man and just Lazarus,
And both in torments, with a mediate gulf,
Though not a hint of Abraham's bosom. Who
280 Being man, Aurora, can stand calmly by
And view these things, and never tease his soul
For some great cure? No physic for this grief,
In all the earth and heavens too?"
                                   "You believe
In God, for your part?—ay? that He who makes
285 Can make good things from ill things, best from worst,
As men plant tulips upon dunghills when
They wish them finest?"
                        "True. A death-heat is
The same as life-heat, to be accurate,
And in all nature is no death at all,
290 As men account of death, so long as God
Stands witnessing for life perpetually,
By being just God. That's abstract truth, I know,
Philosophy, or sympathy with God:
But I, I sympathise with man, not God
295 (I think I was a man for chiefly this),
And when I stand beside a dying bed,
'Tis death to me. Observe,—it had not much
Consoled the race of mastodons to know,
Before they went to fossil, that anon

300 Their place would quicken with the elephant.
They were not elephants but mastodons;
And I, a man, as men are now and not
As men may be hereafter, feel with men
In the agonising present."

                                    "Is it so,"
305 I said, "my cousin? is the world so bad,
While I hear nothing of it through the trees?
The world was always evil,—but so bad?"

"So bad, Aurora. Dear, my soul is grey
With poring over the long sum of ill;
310 So much for vice, so much for discontent,
So much for the necessities of power,
So much for the connivances of fear,
Coherent in statistical despairs
With such a total of distracted life,…
315 To see it down in figures on a page,
Plain, silent, clear, as God sees through the earth
The sense of all the graves,—that's terrible
For one who is not God, and cannot right
The wrong he looks on. May I choose indeed,
320 But vow away my years, my means, my aims,
Among the helpers, if there's any help
In such a social strait? The common blood
That swings along my veins is strong enough
To draw me to this duty."

                                    Then I spoke.
325 "I have not stood long on the strand of life,
And these salt waters have had scarcely time
To creep so high up as to wet my feet:
I cannot judge these tides—I shall, perhaps.
A woman's always younger than a man
330 At equal years, because she is disallowed
Maturing by the outdoor sun and air,
And kept in long-clothes past the age to walk.
Ah well, I know you men judge otherwise!
You think a woman ripens, as a peach,
335 In the cheeks chiefly. Pass it to me now;
I'm young in age, and younger still, I think,
As a woman. But a child may say amen

To a bishop's prayer and feel the way it goes,
And I, incapable to loose the knot
340 Of social questions, can approve, applaud
August compassion, Christian thoughts that shoot
Beyond the vulgar white of personal aims.
Accept my reverence."

                            There he glowed on me
With all his face and eyes. "No other help?"
345 Said he—"no more than so?"

                                    "What help?" I asked.
"You'd scorn my help,—as Nature's self, you say,
Has scorned to put her music in my mouth
Because a woman's. Do you now turn round
And ask for what a woman cannot give?"

350 "For what she only can, I turn and ask,"
He answered, catching up my hands in his,
And dropping on me from his high-eaved brow
The full weight of his soul,—"I ask for love,
And that, she can; for life in fellowship
355 Through bitter duties—that, I know she can;
For wifehood—will she?"

                                "Now," I said, "may God
Be witness 'twixt us two!" and with the word,
Meseemed I floated into a sudden light
Above his stature,—"am I proved too weak
360 To stand alone, yet strong enough to bear
Such leaners on my shoulder? poor to think,
Yet rich enough to sympathise with thought?
Incompetent to sing, as blackbirds can,
Yet competent to love, like HIM?"

                                        I paused;
365 Perhaps I darkened, as the lighthouse will
That turns upon the sea. "It's always so.
Anything does for a wife."

                                "Aurora, dear,
And dearly honoured,"—he pressed in at once
With eager utterance,—"you translate me ill.
370 I do not contradict my thought of you
Which is most reverent, with another thought
Found less so. If your sex is weak for art

50

(And I, who said so, did but honour you
By using truth in courtship), it is strong
375 For life and duty. Place your fecund heart
In mine, and let us blossom for the world
That wants love's colour in the grey of time.
My talk, meanwhile, is arid to you, ay,
Since all my talk can only set you where
380 You look down coldly on the arena-heaps
Of headless bodies, shapeless, indistinct!
The Judgment-Angel scarce would find his way
Through such a heap of generalised distress
To the individual man with lips and eyes,
385 Much less Aurora. Ah, my sweet, come down,
And hand in hand we'll go where yours shall touch
These victims, one by one! till, one by one,
The formless, nameless trunk of every man
Shall seem to wear a head with hair you know,
390 And every woman catch your mother's face
To melt you into passion."
                              "I am a girl,"
I answered slowly; "you do well to name
My mother's face. Though far too early, alas,
God's hand did interpose 'twixt it and me,
395 I know so much of love as used to shine
In that face and another. Just so much;
No more indeed at all. I have not seen
So much love since, I pray you pardon me,
As answers even to make a marriage with
400 In this cold land of England. What you love
Is not a woman, Romney, but a cause:
You want a helpmate, not a mistress, sir,
A wife to help your ends,—in her no end.
Your cause is noble, your ends excellent,
405 But I, being most unworthy of these and that,
Do otherwise conceive of love. Farewell."

"Farewell, Aurora? you reject me thus?"
He said.
          "Sir, you were married long ago.
You have a wife already whom you love,
410 Your social theory. Bless you both, I say.

For my part, I am scarcely meek enough
To be the handmaid of a lawful spouse.
Do I look a Hagar,[1] think you?"
                                    "So you jest."

"Nay, so, I speak in earnest," I replied.
415 "You treat of marriage too much like, at least,
A chief apostle: you would bear with you
A wife…a sister…shall we speak it out?
A sister of charity."
                       "Then, must it be
Indeed farewell? And was I so far wrong
420 In hope and in illusion, when I took
The woman to be nobler than the man,
Yourself the noblest woman, in the use
And comprehension of what love is,—love,
That generates the likeness of itself
425 Through all heroic duties? so far wrong,
In saying bluntly, venturing truth on love,
'Come, human creature, love and work with me,'—
Instead of 'Lady, thou art wondrous fair,
And, where the Graces walk before, the Muse
430 Will follow at the lightning of their eyes,
And where the Muse walks, lovers need to creep:
Turn round and love me, or I die of love.'"

With quiet indignation I broke in.
"You misconceive the question like a man,
435 Who sees a woman as the complement
Of his sex merely. You forget too much
That every creature, female as the male,
Stands single in responsible act and thought
As also in birth and death. Whoever says
440 To a loyal woman, 'Love and work with me,'
Will get fair answers if the work and love,
Being good themselves, are good for her—the best
She was born for. Women of a softer mood,
Surprised by men when scarcely awake to life,
445 Will sometimes only hear the first word, love,
And catch up with it any kind of work,

---

[1] the mother of Ishmael by Abraham.

Indifferent, so that dear love go with it.
I do not blame such women, though, for love,
They pick much oakum; earth's fanatics make
450 Too frequently heaven's saints. But *me* your work
Is not the best for,—nor your love the best,
Nor able to commend the kind of work
For love's sake merely. Ah, you force me, sir,
To be overbold in speaking of myself:
455 I too have my vocation,—work to do,
The heavens and earth have set me since I changed
My father's face for theirs, and, though your world
Were twice as wretched as you represent,
Most serious work, most necessary work
460 As any of the economists.' Reform,
Make trade a Christian possibility,
And individual right no general wrong;
Wipe out earth's furrows of the Thine and Mine,
And leave one green for men to play at bowls,
465 With innings for them all!…What then, indeed,
If mortals are not greater by the head
Than any of their prosperities? what then,
Unless the artist keep up open roads
Betwixt the seen and unseen,—bursting through
470 The best of your conventions with his best,
The speakable, imaginable best
God bids him speak, to prove what lies beyond
Both speech and imagination? A starved man
Exceeds a fat beast: we'll not barter, sir,
475 The beautiful for barley.—And, even so,
I hold you will not compass your poor ends
Of barley-feeding and material ease,
Without a poet's individualism
To work your universal. It takes a soul,
480 To move a body: it takes a high-souled man,
To move the masses, even to a cleaner stye:
It takes the ideal, to blow a hair's-breadth off
The dust of the actual.—Ah, your Fouriers[1] failed,
Because not poets enough to understand
485 That life develops from within.—For me,
Perhaps I am not worthy, as you say,

Of work like this: perhaps a woman's soul
Aspires, and not creates: yet we aspire,
And yet I'll try out your perhapses, sir,
490 And if I fail…why, burn me up my straw
Like other false works—I'll not ask for grace;
Your scorn is better, cousin Romney. I
Who love my art, would never wish it lower
To suit my stature. I may love my art.
495 You'll grant that even a woman may love art,
Seeing that to waste true love on anything
Is womanly, past question."

              I retain
The very last word which I said that day,
As you the creaking of the door, years past,
500 Which let upon you such disabling news
You ever after have been graver. He,
His eyes, the motions in his silent mouth,
Were fiery points on which my words were caught,
Transfixed for ever in my memory
505 For his sake, not their own. And yet I know
I did not love him…nor he me…that's sure…
And what I said is unrepented of,
As truth is always. Yet…a princely man!—
If hard to me, heroic for himself!
510 He bears down on me through the slanting years,
The stronger for the distance. If he had loved,
Ay, loved me, with that retributive face,…
I might have been a common woman now
And happier, less known and less left alone,
515 Perhaps a better woman after all,
With chubby children hanging on my neck
To keep me low and wise. Ah me, the vines
That bear such fruit are proud to stoop with it.
The palm stands upright in a realm of sand.

520 And I, who spoke the truth then, stand upright,
Still worthy of having spoken out the truth,
By being content I spoke it though it set
Him there, me here.—O woman's vile remorse,
To hanker after a mere name, a show,
525 A supposition, a potential love!

---

[1] Charles Fourier (1772–1837), French social theorist.

Does every man who names love in our lives
Become a power for that? is love's true thing
So much best to us, that what personates love
Is next best? A potential love, forsooth!
530 I'm not so vile. No, no—he cleaves, I think,
This man, this image,—chiefly for the wrong
And shock he gave my life, in finding me
Precisely where the devil of my youth
Had set me, on those mountain-peaks of hope
535 All glittering with the dawn-dew, all erect
And famished for the noon,—exclaiming, while
I looked for empire and much tribute, "Come,
I have some worthy work for thee below.
Come, sweep my barns and keep my hospitals,
540 And I will pay thee with a current coin
Which men give women."
                                    As we spoke, the grass
Was trod in haste beside us, and my aunt,
With smile distorted by the sun,—face, voice
As much at issue with the summer-day
545 As if you brought a candle out of doors,
Broke in with "Romney, here!—My child, entreat
Your cousin to the house, and have your talk,
If girls must talk upon their birthdays. Come."

He answered for me calmly, with pale lips
550 That seemed to motion for a smile in vain,
"The talk is ended, madam, where we stand.
Your brother's daughter has dismissed me here;
And all my answer can be better said
Beneath the trees, than wrong by such a word
555 Your house's hospitalities. Farewell."

With that he vanished. I could hear his heel
Ring bluntly in the lane, as down he leapt
The short way from us.—Then a measured speech
Withdrew me. "What means this, Aurora Leigh?
560 My brother's daughter has dismissed my guests?"

The lion in me felt the keeper's voice
Through all its quivering dewlaps; I was quelled

Before her,—meekened to the child she knew:
I prayed her pardon, said "I had little thought
565 To give dismissal to a guest of hers,
In letting go a friend of mine who came
To take me into service as a wife,—
No more than that, indeed."
                                    "No more, no more?
Pray Heaven," she answered, "that I was not mad.
570 I could not mean to tell her to her face
That Romney Leigh had asked me for a wife,
And I refused him?"
                                    "Did he ask?" I said;
"I think he rather stooped to take me up
For certain uses which he found to do
575 For something called a wife. He never asked."

"What stuff!" she answered; "are they queens, these
        girls?
They must have mantles, stitched with twenty silks,
Spread out upon the ground, before they'll step
One footstep for the noblest lover born."

580 "But I am born," I said with firmness, "I,
To walk another way than his, dear aunt."

"You walk, you walk! A babe at thirteen months
Will walk as well as you," she cried in haste,
"Without a steadying finger. Why, you child,
585 God help you, you are groping in the dark,
For all this sunlight. You suppose, perhaps,
That you, sole offspring of an opulent man,
Are rich and free to choose a way to walk?
You think, and it's a reasonable thought,
590 That I, beside, being well to do in life,
Will leave my handful in my niece's hand
When death shall paralyse these fingers? Pray,
Pray, child, albeit I know you love me not,
As if you loved me, that I may not die!
595 For when I die and leave you, out you go
(Unless I make room for you in my grave),
Unhoused, unfed, my dear poor brother's lamb

(Ah heaven!—that pains!)—without a right to crop
A single blade of grass beneath these trees,
600 Or cast a lamb's small shadow on the lawn,
Unfed, unfolded! Ah, my brother, here's
The fruit you planted in your foreign loves!—
Ay, there's the fruit he planted! never look
Astonished at me with your mother's eyes,
605 For it was they who set you where you are,
An undowered orphan. Child, your father's choice
Of that said mother disinherited
His daughter, his and hers. Men do not think
Of sons and daughters, when they fall in love,
610 So much more than of sisters; otherwise
He would have paused to ponder what he did,
And shrunk before the clause in the entail
Excluding offspring by a foreign wife
(The clause set up a hundred years ago
615 By a Leigh who wedded a French dancing-girl
And had his heart danced over in return);
But this man shrank at nothing, never thought
Of you, Aurora, any more than me—
Your mother must have been a pretty thing,
620 For all the coarse Italian blacks and browns,
To make a good man, which my brother was,
Unchary of the duties to his house;
But so it fell indeed. Our cousin Vane,
Vane Leigh, the father of this Romney, wrote
625 Directly on your birth, to Italy,
'I ask your baby daughter for my son,
In whom the entail now merges by the law.
Betroth her to us out of love, instead
Of colder reasons, and she shall not lose
630 By love or law from henceforth'—so he wrote;
A generous cousin was my cousin Vane.
Remember how he drew you to his knee
The year you came here, just before he died,
And hollowed out his hands to hold your cheeks,
635 And wished them redder,—you remember Vane.
And now his son, who represents our house,
And holds the fiefs and manors in his place,
To whom reverts my pittance when I die

(Except a few books and a pair of shawls),
640 The boy is generous like him, and prepared
To carry out his kindest word and thought
To you, Aurora. Yes, a fine young man
Is Romney Leigh; although the sun of youth
Has shone too straight upon his brain, I know,
645 And fevered him with dreams of doing good
To good-for-nothing people. But a wife
Will put all right, and stroke his temples cool
With healthy touches."…
                              I broke in at that.
I could not lift my heavy heart to breathe
650 Till then, but then I raised it, and it fell
In broken words like these—"No need to wait:
The dream of doing good to…me, at least,
Is ended, without waiting for a wife
To cool the fever for him. We've escaped
655 That danger,—thank Heaven for it."
                              "You," she cried,
"Have got a fever. What, I talk and talk
An hour long to you,—I instruct you how
You cannot eat or drink or stand or sit
Or even die, like any decent wretch
660 In all this unroofed and unfurnished world,
Without your cousin,—and you still maintain
There's room 'twixt him and you for flirting fans
And running knots in eyebrows? You must have
A pattern lover sighing on his knee?
665 You do not count enough, a noble heart
(Above book-patterns) which this very morn
Unclosed itself in two dear fathers' names
To embrace your orphaned life? Fie, fie! But stay,
I write a word, and counteract this sin."

670 She would have turned to leave me, but I clung.
"O sweet my father's sister, hear my word
Before you write yours. Cousin Vane did well,
And cousin Romney well,—and I well too,
In casting back with all my strength and will
675 The good they meant me. O my God, my God!
God meant me good, too, when He hindered me

From saying 'yes' this morning. If you write
A word, it shall be 'no.' I say no, no!
I tie up 'no' upon His altar-horns,
680 Quite out of reach of perjury! At least
My soul is not a pauper; I can live
At least my soul's life, without alms from men;
And if it must be in heaven instead of earth,
Let heaven look to it,—I am not afraid."

685 She seized my hands with both hers, strained them
        fast,
And drew her probing and unscrupulous eyes
Right through me, body and heart. "Yet, foolish
        Sweet,
You love this man. I've watched you when he came,
And when he went, and when we've talked of him:
690 I am not old for nothing; I can tell
The weather-signs of love: you love this man."

Girls blush sometimes because they are alive,
Half wishing they were dead to save the shame.
The sudden blush devours them, neck and brow;
695 They have drawn too near the fire of life, like gnats,
And flare up bodily, wings and all. What then?
Who's sorry for a gnat…or girl?
                                        I blushed.
I feel the brand upon my forehead now
Strike hot, sear deep, as guiltless men may feel
700 The felon's iron, say, and scorn the mark
Of what they are not. Most illogical
Irrational nature of our womanhood,
That blushes one way, feels another way,
And prays, perhaps another! After all,
705 We cannot be the equal of the male
Who rules his blood a little.
                                For although
I blushed indeed, as if I loved the man,
And her incisive smile, accrediting
That treason of false witness in my blush,
710 Did bow me downward like a swathe of grass
Below its level that struck me,—I attest

The conscious skies and all their daily suns,
I think I loved him not,—nor then, nor since,
Nor ever. Do we love the schoolmaster,
715 Being busy in the woods? much less, being poor,
The overseer of the parish? Do we keep
Our love to pay our debts with?
                                White and cold
I grew next moment. As my blood recoiled
From that imputed ignominy, I made
720 My heart great with it. Then, at last, I spoke,
Spoke veritable words but passionate,
Too passionate perhaps…ground up with sobs
To shapeless endings. She let fall my hands
And took her smile off, in sedate disgust,
725 As peradventure she had touched a snake,—
A dead snake, mind!—and, turning round, replied,
"We'll leave Italian manners, if you please.
I think you had an English father, child,
And ought to find it possible to speak
730 A quiet 'yes' or 'no,' like English girls,
Without convulsions. In another month
We'll take another answer—no, or yes."
With that, she left me in the garden-walk.

I had a father! yes, but long ago—
735 How long it seemed that moment. Oh, how far,
How far and safe, God, dost thou keep thy saints
When once gone from us! We may call against
The lighted windows of thy fair June-heaven
Where all the souls are happy,—and not one,
740 Not even my father, look from work or play
To ask, "Who is it that cries after us,
Below there, in the dusk?" Yet formerly
He turned his face upon me quick enough,
If I said "Father." Now I might cry loud;
745 The little lark reached higher with his song
Than I with crying. Oh, alone, alone,—
Not troubling any in heaven, nor any on earth,
I stood there in the garden, and looked up
The deaf blue sky that brings the roses out
750 On such June mornings.

You who keep account
Of crisis and transition in this life,
Set down the first time Nature says plain "no"
To some "yes" in you, and walks over you
In gorgeous sweeps of scorn. We all begin
By singing with the birds, and running fast
With June-days, hand in hand: but once, for all,
The birds must sing against us, and the sun
Strike down upon us like a friend's sword caught
By an enemy to slay us, while we read
The dear name on the blade which bites at us!—
That's bitter and convincing: after that,
We seldom doubt that something in the large
Smooth order of creation, though no more
Than haply a man's footstep, has gone wrong.
Some tears fell down my cheeks, and then I smiled,
As those smile who have no face in the world
To smile back to them. I had lost a friend
In Romney Leigh; the thing was sure—a friend,
Who had looked at me most gently now and then,
And spoken of my favourite books, "our books,"
With such a voice! Well, voice and look were now
More utterly shut out from me I felt,
Than even my father's. Romney now was turned
To a benefactor, to a generous man,
Who had tied himself to marry…me, instead
Of such a woman, with low timorous lids
He lifted with a sudden word one day,
And left, perhaps, for my sake.—Ah, self-tied
By a contract, male Iphigenia[1] bound
At a fatal Aulis for the winds to change
(But loose him, they'll not change), he well might seem
A little cold and dominant in love!
He had a right to be dogmatical,
This poor, good Romney. Love, to him, was made
A simple law-clause. If I married him,
I should not dare to call my soul my own
Which so he had bought and paid for: every thought
And every heart-beat down there in the bill;

Not one found honestly deductible
From any use that pleased him! He might cut
My body into coins to give away
Among his other paupers; change my sons,
While I stood dumb as Griseld,[2] for black babes
Or piteous foundlings; might unquestioned set
My right hand teaching in the Ragged Schools,
My left hand washing in the Public Baths,
What time my angel of the Ideal stretched
Both his to me in vain. I could not claim
The poor right of a mouse in a trap, to squeal,
And take so much as pity from myself.

Farewell, good Romney! if I loved you even
I could but ill afford to let you be
So generous to me. Farewell, friend, since friend
Betwixt us two, forsooth, must be a word
So heavily overladen. And, since help
Must come to me from those who love me not,
Farewell, all helpers—I must help myself,
And am alone from henceforth.—Then I stooped
And lifted the soiled garland from the earth,
And set it on my head as bitterly
As when the Spanish monarch crowned the bones
Of his dead love. So be it. I preserve
That crown still,—in the drawer there! twas the first.
The rest are like it;—those Olympian crowns,
We run for, till we lose sight of the sun
In the dust of the racing chariots!
                              After that,
Before the evening fell, I had a note,
Which ran,—"Aurora, sweet Chaldean, you read
My meaning backward like your eastern books,
While I am from the west, dear. Read me now
A little plainer. Did you hate me quite
But yesterday? I loved you for my part;
I love you. If I spoke untenderly

[1] the daughter of Agamemnon who was sacrificed at Aulis when the Greek fleet was stranded during its voyage to Troy.

[2] the patient wife who survives the trials and tortures by her husband as he tests the limits of her devotion and obedience; a popular literary figure, there are different versions provided by Boccaccio, Petrarch, and Chaucer.

This morning, my beloved, pardon it;
825 And comprehend me that I loved you so
I set you on the level of my soul,
And overwashed you with the bitter brine
Of some habitual thoughts. Henceforth, my flower,
Be planted out of reach of any such,
830 And lean the side you please, with all your leaves!
Write woman's verses and dream woman's dreams;
But let me feel your perfume in my home
To make my sabbath after working-days.
Bloom out your youth beside me,—be my wife."

835 I wrote in answer—"We Chaldeans discern
Still farther than we read. I know your heart,
And shut it like the holy book it is,
Reserved for mild-eyed saints to pore upon
Betwixt their prayers at vespers. Well, you're right,
840 I did not surely hate you yesterday;
And yet I do not love you enough to-day
To wed you, cousin Romney. Take this word,
And let it stop you as a generous man
From speaking farther. You may tease, indeed,
845 And blow about my feelings or my leaves,
And here's my aunt will help you with east winds
And break a stalk, perhaps, tormenting me;
But certain flowers grow near as deep as trees,
And, cousin, you'll not move my root, not you,
850 With all your confluent storms. Then let me grow
Within my wayside hedge, and pass your way!
This flower has never as much to say to you
As the antique tomb which said to travellers, 'Pause,
Siste, viator.'" Ending thus, I sighed.

855 The next week passed in silence, so the next,
And several after: Romney did not come
Nor my aunt chide me. I lived on and on,
As if my heart were kept beneath a glass,
And everybody stood, all eyes and ears,
860 To see and hear it tick. I could not sit,
Nor walk, nor take a book, nor lay it down,
Nor sew on steadily, nor drop a stitch,

And a sigh with it, but I felt her looks
Still cleaving to me, like the sucking asp
865 To Cleopatra's breast, persistently
Through the intermittent pantings. Being observed,
When observation is not sympathy,
Is just being tortured. If she said a word,
A "thank you," or an "if it please you, dear,"
870 She meant a commination,[1] or, at best,
An exorcism against the devildom
Which plainly held me. So with all the house.
Susannah could not stand and twist my hair
Without such glancing at the looking-glass
875 To see my face there, that she missed the plait.
And John,—I never sent my plate for soup,
Or did not send it, but the foolish John
Resolved the problem, 'twixt his napkined thumbs,
Of what was signified by taking soup
880 Or choosing mackerel. Neighbours who dropped in
On morning visits, feeling a joint wrong,
Smiled admonition, sat uneasily,
And talked, with measured, emphasised reserve,
Of parish news, like doctors to the sick,
885 When not called in,—as if, with leave to speak,
They might say something. Nay, the very dog
Would watch me from his sun-patch on the floor,
In alternation with the large black fly
Not yet in reach of snapping. So I lived.

890 A Roman died so; smeared with honey, teased
By insects, stared to torture by the moon:
And many patients souls 'neath English roofs
Have died like Romans. I, in looking back,
Wish only, now, I had borne the plague of all
895 With meeker spirits than were rife at Rome.

For, on the sixth week, the dead sea broke up,
Dashed suddenly through beneath the heel of Him
Who stands upon the sea and earth and swears
Time shall be nevermore. The clock struck nine

[1] a threat of divine vengeance.

57

900 That morning too,—no lark was out of tune,
The hidden farms among the hills breathed straight
Their smoke toward heaven, the lime-tree scarcely
    stirred
Beneath the blue weight of the cloudless sky,
Though still the July air came floating through
905 The woodbine at my window, in and out,
With touches of the out-door country news
For a bending forehead. There I sat, and wished
That morning-truce of God would last till eve,
Or longer. "Sleep," I thought, "late sleepers,—sleep,
910 And spare me yet the burden of your eyes."

Then, suddenly, a single ghastly shriek
Tore upward from the bottom of the house.
Like one who wakens in a grave and shrieks,
The still house seemed to shriek itself alive,
915 And shudder through its passages and stairs
With slam of doors and clash of bells.—I sprang,
I stood up in the middle of the room,
And there confronted at my chamber-door
A white face,—shivering, ineffectual lips.

920 "Come, come," they tried to utter, and I went:
As if a ghost had drawn me at the point
Of a fiery finger through the uneven dark,
I went with reeling footsteps down the stair,
Nor asked a question.
                    There she sat, my aunt,—
925 Bolt upright in the chair beside her bed,
Whose pillow had no dint! she had used no bed
For that night's sleeping, yet slept well. My God,
The dumb derision of that grey, peaked face
Concluded something grave against the sun,
930 Which filled the chamber with its July burst
When Susan drew the curtains ignorant
Of who sat open-eyed behind her. There
She sat…it sat…we said "she" yesterday…
And held a letter with unbroken seal
935 As Susan gave it to her hand last night:
All night she had held it. If its news referred

To duchies or to dunghills, not an inch
She'd budge, 'twas obvious, for such worthless odds:
Nor, though the stars were suns and overburned
940 Their spheric limitations, swallowing up
Like wax the azure spaces, could they force
Those open eyes to wink once. What last sight
Had left them blank and flat so,—drawing out
The faculty of vision from the roots,
945 As nothing more, worth seeing, remained behind?

Were those the eyes that watched me, worried me?
That dogged me up and down the hours and days,
A beaten, breathless, miserable soul?
And did I pray, a half-hour back, but so,
950 To escape the burden of those eyes…those eyes?
"Sleep late" I said?—
                    Why, now, indeed, they sleep.
God answers sharp and sudden on some prayers,
And thrusts the thing we have prayed for in our face,
A gauntlet with a gift in't. Every wish
955 Is like a prayer, with God.
                    I had my wish
To read and meditate the thing I would,
To fashion all my life upon my thought,
And marry or not marry. Henceforth none
Could disapprove me, vex me, hamper me.
960 Full ground-room, in this desert newly made,
For Babylon or Baalbec,—when the breath,
Now choked with sand, returns for building towns.

The heir came over on the funeral day,
And we two cousins met before the dead,
965 With two pale faces. Was it death or life
That moved us? When the will was read and done,
The official guests and witnesses withdrawn,
We rose up in a silence almost hard,
And looked at one another. Then I said,
970 "Farewell, my cousin."
                    But he touched, just touched
My hatstrings, tied for going (at the door
The carriage stood to take me), and said low,

58

His sister a little unsteady through his smile,
"Siste, viator."
             "Is there time," I asked,
975 "In these last days of railroads, to stop short
Like Cæsar's chariot (weighing half a ton)
On the Appian road, for morals?"
                      "There is time,"
He answered grave, "for necessary words,
Inclusive, trust me, of no epitaph
980 On man or act, my cousin. We have read
A will, which gives you all the personal goods
And funded moneys of your aunt."
                   "I thank
Her memory for it. With three hundred pounds
We buy, in England even, clear standing-room
985 To stand and work in. Only two hours since,
I fancied I was poor."
             "And, cousin, still
You're richer than you fancy. The will says,
Three hundred pounds, and any other sum
Of which the said testatrix dies possessed.
990 I say she died possessed of other sums."

"Dear Romney, need we chronicle the pence?
I'm richer than I thought—that's evident.
Enough so."
          "Listen rather. You've to do
With business and a cousin," he resumed,
995 "And both, I fear, need patience. Here's the fact.
The other sum (there *is* another sum,
Unspecified in any will which dates
After possession, yet bequeathed as much
And clearly as those said three hundred pounds)
1000 Is thirty thousand. You will have it paid
When?…where? My duty troubles you with words."

He struck the iron when the bar was hot;
No wonder if my eyes sent out some sparks.
"Pause there! I thank you. You are delicate
1005 In glosing gifts;—but I, who share your blood,

Am rather made for giving, like yourself,
Than taking, like your pensioners. Farewell."

He stopped me with a gesture of calm pride.
"A Leigh," he said, "gives largesse and gives love,
1010 But gloses never: if a Leigh could glose,
He would not do it, moreover, to a Leigh,
With blood trained up along nine centuries
To hound and hate a lie from eyes like yours.
And now we'll make the rest as clear: Your aunt
1015 Possessed these moneys."
               "You will make it clear,
My cousin, as the honour of us both,
Or one of us speaks vainly! that's not I.
My aunt possessed this sum,—inherited
From whom, and when? bring documents, prove
    dates."

1020 "Why now indeed you throw your bonnet off
As if you had time left for a logarithm!
The faith's the want. Dear cousin, give me faith,
And you shall walk this road with silken shoes,
As clean as any lady of our house
1025 Supposed the proudest. Oh, I comprehend
The whole position from your point of sight.
I oust you from your father's halls and lands
And make you poor by getting rich—that's law;
Considering which, in common circumstance,
1030 You would not scruple to accept from me
Some compensation, some sufficiency
Of income—that were justice; but, alas,
I love you,—that's mere nature; you reject
My love,—that's nature also; and at once,
1035 You cannot, from a suitor disallowed,
A hand thrown back as mine is, into yours
Receive a doit, a farthing,—not for the world!
That's woman's etiquette, and obviously
Exceeds the claim of nature, law, and right,
1040 Unanswerable to all. I grant, you see,
The case as you conceive it,—leave you room
To sweep your ample skirts of womanhood,

59

While, standing humbly squeezed against the wall,
I own myself excluded from being just,
1045 Restrained from paying indubitable debts,
Because denied from giving you my soul.
That's my misfortune!—I submit to it
As if, in some more reasonable age,
'Twould not be less inevitable. Enough.
1050 You'll trust me, cousin, as a gentleman,
To keep your honour, as you count it, pure,
Your scruples (just as if I thought them wise)
Safe and inviolate from gifts of mine."
I answered mild but earnest. "I believe
1055 In no one's honour which another keeps,
Nor man's nor woman's. As I keep, myself,
My truth and my religion, I depute
No father, though I had one this side death,
Nor brother, though I had twenty, much less you,
1060 Though twice my cousin, and once Romney Leigh,
To keep my honour pure. You face, to-day,
A man who wants instruction, mark me, not
A woman who wants protection. As to a man,
Show manhood, speak out plainly, be precise
1065 With facts and dates. My aunt inherited
This sum, you say—"
                              "I said she died possessed
Of this, dear cousin."
                              "Not by heritage.
Thank you: we're getting to the facts at last.
Perhaps she played at commerce with a ship
1070 Which came in heavy with Australian gold?
Or touched a lottery with her finger-end,
Which tumbled on a sudden into her lap
Some old Rhine tower or principality?
Perhaps she had to do with a marine
1075 Sub-transatlantic railroad, which pre-pays
As well as pre-supposes? or perhaps
Some stale ancestral debt was after-paid
By a hundred years, and took her by surprise?—
You shake your head, my cousin; I guess ill."

1080 "You need not guess, Aurora, nor deride;
The truth is not afraid of hurting you.
You'll find no cause, in all your scruples, why
Your aunt should cavil at a deed of gift
'Twixt her and me."
                              "I thought so—ah! a gift."

1085 "You naturally thought so," he resumed.
"A very natural gift."
                              "A gift, a gift!
Her individual life being stranded high
Above all want, approaching opulence,
Too haughty was she to accept a gift
1090 Without some ultimate aim: ah, ah, I see,—
A gift intended plainly for her heirs,
And so accepted…if accepted…ah,
Indeed that might be; I am snared perhaps
Just so. But, cousin, shall I pardon you,
1095 If thus you have caught me with a cruel springe?"

He answered gently, "Need you tremble and pant
Like a netted lioness? is't my fault, mine,
That you're a grand wild creature of the woods
And hate the stall built for you? Any way,
1100 Though triply netted, need you glare at me?
I do not hold the cords of such a net;
You're free from me, Aurora!"
                              "Now may God
Deliver me from this strait! This gift of yours
Was tendered…when? accepted…when?" I asked.
1105 "A month…a fortnight since? Six weeks ago
It was not tendered; by a word she dropped
I know it was not tendered nor received.
When was it? bring your dates."
                              "What matters when?
A half-hour ere she died, or a half-year,
1110 Secured the gift, maintains the heritage
Inviolable with law. As easy pluck
The golden stars from heaven's embroidered stole
To pin them on the grey side of this earth,
As make you poor again, thank God."

"Not poor
1115 Nor clean again from henceforth, you thank God?
Well, sir—I ask you—I insist at need,—
Vouchsafe the special date, the special date."

"The day before her death-day," he replied,
"The gift was in her hands. We'll find that deed,
1120 And certify that date to you."
As one
Who has climbed a mountain-height and carried up
His own heart climbing, panting in his throat
With the toil of the ascent, takes breath at last,
Looks back in triumph—so I stood and looked.
1125 "Dear cousin Romney, we have reached the top
Of this steep question, and may rest, I think.
But first,—I pray you pardon, that the shock
And surge of natural feeling and event
Has made me oblivious of acquainting you
1130 That this, this letter (unread, mark, still sealed),
Was found enfolded in the poor dead hand:
That spirit of hers had gone beyond the address,
Which could not find her though you wrote it
clear,—
I know your writing, Romney,—recognise
1135 The open-hearted A, the liberal sweep
Of the G. Now listen,—let us understand:
You will not find that famous deed of gift,
Unless you find it in the letter here,
Which, not being mine, I give you back.—Refuse
1140 To take the letter? well then—you and I,
As writer and as heiress, open it
Together, by your leave.—Exactly so:
The words in which the noble offering's made
Are nobler still, my cousin; and, I own,
1145 The proudest and most delicate heart alive,
Distracted from the measure of the gift
By such a grace in giving, might accept
Your largesse without thinking any more
Of the burthen of it, than King Solomon
1150 Considered, when he wore his holy ring
Charactered over with the ineffable spell,

How many carats of fine gold made up
Its money-value: so, Leigh gives to Leigh!
Or rather, might have given, observe,—for that's
1155 The point we come to. Here's a proof of gift,
But here's no proof, sir, of acceptancy,
But, rather, disproof. Death's black dust, being
blown,
Infiltrated through every secret fold
Of this sealed letter by a puff of fate,
1160 Dried up for ever the fresh-written ink,
Annulled the gift, disutilized the grace,
And left these fragments."
As I spoke, I tore
The paper up and down, and down and up
And crosswise, till it fluttered from my hands,
1165 As forest-leaves, stripped suddenly and rapt
By a whirlwind on Valdarno, drop again,
Drop slow, and strew the melancholy ground
Before the amazèd hills...why, so, indeed,
I'm writing like a poet, somewhat large
1170 In the type of the image, and exaggerate
A small thing with a great thing, topping it:—
But then I'm thinking how his eyes looked, his,
With what despondent and surprised reproach!
I think the tears were in them as he looked;
1175 I think the manly mouth just trembled. Then
He broke the silence.
"I may ask, perhaps,
Although no stranger...only Romney Leigh,
Which means still less...than Vincent Carrington,
Your plans in going hence, and where you go.
1180 This cannot be a secret."
"All my life
Is open to you, cousin. I go hence
To London, to the gathering-place of souls,
To live mine straight out, vocally, in books;
Harmoniously for others, if indeed
1185 A woman's soul, like man's, be wide enough
To carry the whole octave (that's to prove),
Or, if I fail, still purely for myself.
Pray God be with me, Romney."

"Ah, poor child,
Who fight against the mother's 'tiring hand,
1190 And choose the headsman's! May God change His
    world
For your sake, sweet, and make it mild as heaven,
And juster than I have found you."
                              But I paused.
"And you, my cousin?"—
                              "I," he said,—"you ask?
You care to ask? Well, girls have curious minds
1195 And fain would know the end of everything,
Of cousins therefore with the rest. For me,
Aurora, I've my work; you know my work;
And, having missed this year some personal hope,
I must beware the rather that I miss
1200 No reasonable duty. While you sing
Your happy pastorals of the meads and trees,
Bethink you that I go to impress and prove
On stifled brains and deafened ears, stunned deaf,
Crushed dull with grief, that nature sings itself,
1205 And needs no mediate poet, lute or voice,
To make it vocal. While you ask of men
Your audience, I may get their leave perhaps
For hungry orphans to say audibly
'We're hungry, see,'—for beaten and bullied wives
1210 To hold their unweaned babies up in sight,
Whom orphanage would better, and for all
To speak and claim their portion…by no means
Of the soil,…but of the sweat in tilling it;
Since this is nowadays turned privilege,
1215 To have only God's curse on us, and not man's.
Such work I have for doing, elbow-deep
In social problems,—as you tie your rhymes,
To draw my uses to cohere with needs
And bring the uneven world back to its round,
1220 Or, failing so much, fill up, bridge at least
To smoother issues some abysmal cracks
And feuds of earth, intestine heats have made
To keep men separate,—using sorry shifts
Of hospitals, almshouses, infant schools,
1225 And other practical stuff of partial good

You lovers of the beautiful and whole
Despise by system."
                              "I despise? The scorn
Is yours, my cousin. Poets become such
Through scorning nothing. You decry them for
1230 The good of beauty sung and taught by them,
While they respect your practical partial good
As being a part of beauty's self. Adieu!
When God helps all the workers for His world,
The singers shall have help of Him, not last."

1235 He smiled as men smile when they will not speak
Because of something bitter in the thought;
And still I feel his melancholy eyes
Look judgment on me. It is seven years since:
I know not if 'twas pity or 'twas scorn
1240 Has made them so far-reaching: judge it ye
Who have had to do with pity more than love
And scorn than hatred. I am used, since then,
To other ways, from equal men. But so,
Even so, we let go hands, my cousin and I,
1245 And in between us rushed the torrent-world
To blanch our faces like divided rocks,
And bar for ever mutual sight and touch
Except through swirl of spray and all that roar.

FIFTH BOOK

Aurora Leigh, be humble. Shall I hope
To speak my poems in mysterious tune
With man and nature?—with the lava-lymph
That trickles from successive galaxies
5 Still drop by drop adown the finger of God
In still new worlds?—with summer-days in this
That scarce dare breathe they are so beautiful?
With spring's delicious trouble in the ground,
Tormented by the quickened blood of roots,
10 And softly pricked by golden crocus-sheaves
In token of the harvest-time of flowers?
With winters and with autumns,—and beyond

With the human heart's large seasons, when it
    hopes
And fears, joys, grieves, and loves?—with all that
    strain
15 Of sexual passion, which devours the flesh
In a sacrament of souls? with mother's breasts
Which, round the new-made creatures hanging
    there,
Throb luminous and harmonious like pure
    spheres?—
With multitudinous life, and finally
20 With the great escapings of ecstatic souls,
Who, in a rush of too long prisoned flame,
Their radiant faces upward, burn away
This dark of the body, issuing on a world
Beyond our mortal?—can I speak my verse
25 So plainly in tune to these things and the rest
That men shall feel it catch them on the quick
As having the same warrant over them
To hold and move them if they will or no,
Alike imperious as the primal rhythm
30 Of that theurgic[1] nature?—I must fail,
Who fail at the beginning to hold and move
One man,—and he my cousin, and he my friend,
And he born tender, made intelligent,
Inclined to ponder the precipitous sides
35 Of difficult questions; yet, obtuse to *me*,
Of *me*, incurious! likes me very well,
And wishes me a paradise of good,
Good looks, good means, and good digestion,—ay,
But otherwise evades me, puts me off
40 With kindness, with a tolerant gentleness,—
Too light a book for a grave man's reading! Go,
Aurora Leigh: be humble.
               There it is,
We women are too apt to look to one,
Which proves a certain impotence in art.
45 We strain our natures at doing something great,
Far less because it's something great to do,

Than haply that we, so, commend ourselves
As being not small, and more appreciable
To some one friend. We must have mediators
50 Betwixt our highest conscience and the judge;
Some sweet saint's blood must quicken in our palms,
Or all the like in heaven seems slow and cold:
Good only being perceived as the end of good,
And God alone pleased,—that's too poor, we think,
55 And not enough for us by any means.
Ay—Romney, I remember, told me once
We miss the abstract when we comprehend.
We miss it most when we aspire,—and fail.

Yet, so, I will not.—This vile woman's way
60 Of trailing garments shall not trip me up:
I'll have no traffic with the personal thought
In Art's pure temple. Must I work in vain,
Without the approbation of a man?
It cannot be; it shall not. Fame itself,
65 That approbation of the general race,
Presents a poor end (though the arrow speed
Shot straight with vigorous finger to the white),
And the highest fame was never reached except
By what was aimed above it. Art for art,
70 And good for God Himself, the essential Good!
We'll keep our aims sublime, our eyes erect,
Although our woman-hands should shake and fail;
And if we fail…But must we?—
                    Shall I fail?
The Greeks said grandly in their tragic phrase,
75 "Let no one be called happy till his death."
To which I add,—Let no one till his death
Be called unhappy. Measure not the work
Until the day's out and the labour done,
Then bring your gauges. If the day's work's scant,
80 Why, call it scant; affect no compromise;
And, in that we have nobly striven at least,
Deal with us nobly, women though we be,
And honour us with truth if not with praise.
    .   .   .   .   .   .

---

[1] supernatural or divine force.

The critics say that epics have died out
140 With Agamemnon and the goat-nursed gods;
I'll not believe it. I could never deem,
As Payne Knight did (the mythic mountaineer
Who travelled higher than he was born to live,
And showed sometimes the goitre in his throat
145 Discoursing of an image seen through fog),
That Homer's heroes measured twelve feet high.
They were but men:—his Helen's hair turned grey
Like any plain Miss Smith's who wears a front;
And Hector's infant whimpered at a plume
150 As yours last Friday at a turkey-cock.
All actual heroes are essential men,
And all men possible heroes: every age,
Heroic in proportions, double-faced,
Looks backward and before, expects a morn
155 And claims an epos.
                                    Ay, but every age
Appears to souls who live in't (ask Carlyle)
Most unheroic. Ours, for instance, ours:
The thinkers scout it, and the poets abound
Who scorn to touch it with a finger-tip:
160 A pewter age,—mixed metal, silver-washed;
An age of scum, spooned off the richer past,
An age of patches for old gaberdines,
An age of mere transition, meaning nought
Except that what succeeds must shame it quite
165 If God please. That's wrong thinking, to my mind,
And wrong thoughts make poor poems.
                                                        Every age,
Through being beheld too close, is ill-discerned
By those who have not lived past it. We'll suppose
Mount Athos carved, as Alexander schemed,
170 To some colossal statue of a man.
The peasants, gathering brushwood in his ear,
Had guessed as little as the browsing goats
Of form or feature of humanity
Up there,—in fact, had travelled five miles off
175 Or ere the giant image broke on them,
Full human profile, nose and chin distinct,
Mouth, muttering rhythms of silence up the sky

And fed at evening with the blood of suns;
Grand torso,—hand, that flung perpetually
180 The largesse of a silver river down
To all the country pastures. 'Tis even thus
With times we live in,—evermore too great
To be apprehended near.
                                    But poets should
Exert a double vision; should have eyes
185 To see near things as comprehensively
As if afar they took their point of sight,
And distant things as intimately deep
As if they touched them. Let us strive for this.
I do distrust the poet who discerns
190 No character or glory in his times,
And trundles back his soul five hundred years,
Past moat and drawbridge, into a castle-court,
To sing,—oh, not of lizard or of toad
Alive i' the ditch there,—'twere excusable,
195 But of some black chief, half knight, half sheep-lifter,
Some beauteous dame, half chattel and half queen,
As dead as must be, for the greater part,
The poems made on their chivalric bones;
And that's no wonder: death inherits death.

200 Nay, if there's room for poets in this world
A little overgrown (I think there is),
Their sole work is to represent the age,
Their age, not Charlemagne's,—this live,
    throbbing age,
That brawls, cheats, maddens, calculates, aspires,
205 And spends more passion, more heroic heat,
Betwixt the mirrors of its drawing-rooms,
Than Roland with his knights at Roncesvalles.
To flinch from Modern varnish, coat or flounce,
Cry out for togas and the picturesque,
210 Is fatal,—foolish too. King Arthur's self
Was commonplace to Lady Guenever;
And Camelot to minstrels seemed as flat
As Fleet Street to our poets.
                                    Never flinch,
But still, unscrupulously epic, catch

215 Upon the burning lava of a song
The full-veined, heaving, double-breasted Age:
That, when the next shall come, the men of that
May touch the impress with reverent hand, and say
"Behold,—behold the paps we have all sucked!
220 This bosom seems to beat still, or at least
It sets ours beating: this is living art,
Which thus presents and thus records true life."

What form is best for poems? Let me think
Of forms less, and the external. Trust the spirit,
225 As sovran nature does, to make the form;
For otherwise we only imprison spirit
And not embody. Inward evermore
To outward,—so in life, and so in art
Which still is life.
                                    Five acts to make a play.
230 And why not fifteen? why not ten? or seven?
What matter for the number of the leaves,
Supposing the tree lives and grows? exact
The literal unities of time and place,
When 'tis the essence of passion to ignore
235 Both time and place? Absurd. Keep up the fire,
And leave the generous flames to shape themselves.

'Tis true the stage requires obsequiousness
To this or that convention; "exit" here
And "enter" there; the points for clapping, fixed,
240 Like Jacob's white-peeled rods before the rams,
And all the close-curled imagery clipped
In manner of their fleece at shearing-time.
Forget to prick the galleries to the heart
Precisely at the fourth act,—culminate
245 Our five pyramidal acts with one act more,
We're lost so: Shakespeare's ghost could scarcely
          plead
Against our just damnation. Stand aside;
We'll muse for comfort that, last century,
On this same tragic stage on which we have failed,
250 A wigless Hamlet would have failed the same.

And whosoever writes good poetry,
Looks just to art. He does not write for you
Or me,—for London or for Edinburgh;
He will not suffer the best critic known
255 To step into his sunshine of free thought
And self-absorbed conception and exact
An inch-long swerving of the holy lines.
If virtue done for popularity
Defiles like vice, can art, for praise or hire,
260 Still keep its splendour and remain pure art?
Eshew such serfdom. What the poet writes,
He writes: mankind accepts it if it suits,
And that's success: if not, the poem's passed
From hand to hand, and yet from hand to hand,
265 Until the unborn snatch it, crying out
In pity on their fathers' being so dull,
And that's success too.
                                    I will write no plays;
Because the drama, less sublime in this,
Makes lower appeals, submits more menially,
270 Adopts the standard of the public taste
To chalk its height on, wears a dog-chain round
Its regal neck, and learns to carry and fetch
The fashions of the day to please the day,
Fawns close on pit and boxes, who clap hands
275 Commending chiefly its docility
And humour in stage-tricks,—or else indeed
Gets hissed at, howled at, stamped at like a dog,
Or worse, we'll say. For dogs, unjustly kicked,
Yell, bite at need; but if your dramatist
280 (Being wronged by some five hundred nobodies
Because their grosser brains most naturally
Misjudge the fineness of his subtle wit)
Shows teeth an almond's breadth, protests the
          length
Of a modest phrase,—"My gentle countrymen,
285 "There's something in it haply of your fault,"—
Why then, besides five hundred nobodies,
He'll have five thousand and five thousand more
Against him,—the whole public,—and all the hoofs
Of King Saul's father's asses, in full drove,

290 And obviously deserve it. He appealed
To these,—and why say more if they condemn,
Than if they praise him?—Weep, my Æschylus,
But low and far, upon Sicilian shores!
For since 'twas Athens (so I read the myth)
295 Who gave commission to that fatal weight
The tortoise, cold and hard, to drop on thee
And crush thee,—better cover thy bald head;
She'll hear the softest hum of Hyblan bee
Before thy loudest protestation!
                                        Then
300 The risk's still worse upon the modern stage.
I could not, for so little, accept success,
Nor would I risk so much, in ease and calm,
For manifester gains: let those who prize,
Pursue them: I stand off. And yet, forbid,
305 That any irreverent fancy or conceit
Should litter in the Drama's throne-room where
The rulers of our art, in whose full veins
Dynastic glories mingle, sit in strength
And do their kingly work,—conceive, command,
310 And, from the imagination's crucial heat,
Catch up their men and women all a-flame
For action, all alive and forced to prove
Their life by living out heart, brain, and nerve,
Until mankind makes witness, "These be men
315 As we are," and vouchsafes the greeting due
To Imogen and Juliet—sweetest kind
On art's side.
                        'Tis that, honouring to its worth
The drama, I would fear to keep it down
To the level of the footlights. Dies no more
320 The sacrificial goat, for Bacchus slain,
His filmed eyes fluttered by the whirling white
Of choral vestures,—troubled in his blood,
While tragic voices that clanged keen as swords,
Leapt high together with the altar-flame
325 And made the blue air wink. The waxen mask,
Which set the grand still front of Themis' son
Upon the puckered visage of a player,—
The buskin, which he rose upon and moved,

As some tall ship first conscious of the wind
330 Sweeps slowly past the piers,—the mouthpiece,
    where
The mere man's voice with all its breaths and
    breaks
Went sheathed in brass, and clashed on even
    heights
Its phrasèd thunders,—these things are no more,
Which once were. And concluding, which is clear,
335 The growing drama has outgrown such toys
Of simulated stature, face, and speech,
It also peradventure may outgrow
The simulation of the painted scene,
Boards, actors, prompters, gaslight, and costume,
340 And take for a worthier stage the soul itself,
Its shifting fancies and celestial lights,
With all its grand orchestral silences
To keep the pauses of its rhythmic sounds.

Alas, I still see something to be done,
345 And what I do falls short of what I see,
Though I waste myself on doing. Long green days,
Worn bare of grass and sunshine,—long calm
    nights,
From which the silken sleeps were fretted out,
Be witness for me, with no amateur's
350 Irreverent haste and busy idleness
I set myself to art! What then? what's done?
What's done, at last?
                        Behold, at last, a book.
If life-blood's necessary, which it is,—
(By that blue vein athrob on Mahomet's brow,
355 Each prophet-poet's book must show man's blood!)
If life-blood's fertilising, I wrung mine
On every leaf of this,—unless the drops
Slid heavily on one side and left it dry.
That chances often: many a fervid man
360 Writes books as cold and flat as graveyard stones
From which the lichen's scraped; and if Saint Preux
Had written his own letters, as he might,
We had never wept to think of the little mole

'Neath Julie's¹ drooping eyelid. Passion is
365 But something suffered, after all.
                                                    While Art
Sets action on the top of suffering:
The artist's part is both to be and do,
Transfixing with a special, central power
The flat experience of the common man,
370 And turning outward, with a sudden wrench,
Half agony, half ecstasy, the thing
He feels the inmost,—never felt the less
Because he sings it. Does a torch less burn
For burning next reflectors of blue steel,
375 That *he* should be the colder for his place
'Twixt two incessant fires,—his personal life's,
And that intense refraction which burns back
Perpetually against him from the round
Of crystal conscience he was born into
380 If artist-born? O sorrowful great gift
Conferred on poets, of a twofold life,
When one life has been found enough for pain!
We, staggering 'neath our burden as mere men,
Being called to stand up straight as demi-gods,
385 Support the intolerable strain and stress
Of the universal, and send clearly up
With voices broken by the human sob,
Our poems to find rhymes among the stars!

But soft,—a "poet" is a word soon said,
390 A book's a thing soon written. Nay, indeed,
The more the poet shall be questionable,
The more unquestionably comes his book.
And this of mine—well, granting to myself
Some passion in it,—furrowing up the flats,
395 Mere passion will not prove a volume worth
Its gall and rags even. Bubbles round a keel
Mean nought, excepting that the vessel moves.
There's more than passion goes to make a man
Or book, which is a man too.
                                                    I am sad.

400 I wonder if Pygmalion had these doubts
And, feeling the hard marble first relent,
Grow supple to the straining of his arms,
And tingle through its cold to his burning lip,
Supposed his senses mocked, supposed the toil
405 Of stretching past the known and seen to reach
The archetypal Beauty out of sight,
Had made his heart beat fast enough for two,
And with his own life dazed and blinded him!
Not so; Pygmalion loved,—and whoso loves
410 Believes the impossible.
                                                    But I am sad:
I cannot thoroughly love a work of mine,
Since none seems worthy of my thought and hope
More highly mated. He has shot them down,
My Phœbus Apollo, soul within my soul,
415 Who judges, by the attempted, what's attained,
And with the silver arrow from his height
Has struck down all my works before my face
While I said nothing. Is there aught to say?
I called the artist but a greatened man.
420 He may be childless also, like a man.

I laboured on alone. The wind and dust
And sun of the world beat blistering in my face;
And hope, now for me, now against me, dragged
My spirits onward, as some fallen balloon,
425 Which, whether caught by blossoming tree or bare,
Is torn alike. I sometimes touched my aim,
Or seemed,—and generous souls cried out "Be
      strong,
Take courage; now you're on our level,—now!
The next step saves you!" I was flushed with praise,
430 But, pausing just a moment to draw breath,
I could not choose but murmur to myself
"Is this all? all that's done? and all that's gained?
If this then be success, 'tis dismaller
Than any failure."
                                        O my God, my God,
435 O supreme Artist, who as sole return
For all the cosmic wonder of Thy work,

---

¹ characters from Rousseau's *La Nouvelle Héloïse* (1761), an adaptation
of the tale of Abelard and Eloisa.

Demandest of us just a word…a name,
"My Father!" thou hast knowledge, only thou,
How dreary 'tis for women to sit still,
440 On winter nights by solitary fires,
And hear the nations praising them far off,
Too far! ay, praising our quick sense of love,
Our very heart of passionate womanhood,
Which could not beat so in the verse without
445 Being present also in the unkissed lips
And eyes undried because there's none to ask
The reason they grew moist.
                                        To sit alone
And think for comfort how, that very night,
Affianced lovers, leaning face to face
450 With sweet half-listenings for each other's breath,
Are reading haply from a page of ours,
To pause from a thrill (as if their cheeks had
        touched)
When such a stanza, level to their mood,
Seems floating their own thought out—"So I feel
455 For thee,"—"And I, for thee: this poet knows
What everlasting love is!"—how, that night,
Some father, issuing from the misty roads
Upon the luminous round of lamp and hearth
And happy children, having caught up first
460 The youngest there until it shrink and shriek
To feel the cold chin prick its dimples through
With winter from the hills, may throw i' the lap
Of the eldest (who has learnt to drop her lids
To hide some sweetness newer than last year's)
465 Our book and cry,…"Ah you, you care for rhymes;
So here be rhymes to pore on under trees,
When April comes to let you! I've been told
They are not idle as so many are,
But set hearts beating pure as well as fast.
470 'Tis yours, the book; I'll write your name in it,
That so you may not lose, however lost
In poet's lore and charming reverie,
The thought of how your father thought of *you*
In riding from the town."
                                        To have our books

475 Appraised by love, associated with love,
While *we* sit loveless! is it hard, you think?
At least 'tis mournful. Fame, indeed, 'twas said,
Means simply love. It was a man said that:
And then, there's love and love: the love of all
480 (To risk in turn a woman's paradox)
Is but a small thing to the love of one.
You bid a hungry child be satisfied
With a heritage of many corn-fields: nay,
He says he's hungry,—he would rather have
485 That little barley-cake you keep from him
While reckoning up his harvests. So with us
(Here, Romney, too, we fail to generalise):
We're hungry.
                                Hungry! but it's pitiful
To wail like unweaned babes and suck our thumbs
490 Because we're hungry. Who, in all this world
(Wherein we are haply set to pray and fast
And learn what good is by its opposite),
Has never hungered? Woe to him who has found
The meal enough! if Ugolino's[1] full,
495 His teeth have crunched some foul unnatural thing,
For here satiety proves penury
More utterly irremediable. And since
We needs must hunger,—better, for man's love,
Than God's truth! better, for companions sweet,
500 Than great convictions! let us bear our weights,
Preferring dreary hearths to desert souls.
Well, well! they say we're envious, we who rhyme;
But I, because I am a woman perhaps
And so rhyme ill, am ill at envying.
505 I never envied Graham his breadth of style,
Which gives you, with a random smutch or two,
(Near sighted critics analyse to smutch)
Such delicate perspectives of full life:
Nor Belmore, for the unity of aim
510 To which he cuts his cedarn poems, fine
As sketchers do their pencils: nor Mark Gage,
For that caressing colour and trancing tone

---

[1] Count Ugolino Della Gherardesca (d. 1289), despot ruler of Pisa (1284–88).

Whereby you're swept away and melted in
The sensual element, which with a back wave
515 Restores you to the level of pure souls
And leaves you with Plotinus.[1] None of these,
For native gifts or popular applause,
I've envied; but for this,—that when by chance
Says some one,—"There goes Belmore, a great man!
520 He leaves clean work behind him, and requires
No sweeper up of the chips,"…a girl I know,
Who answers nothing, save with her brown eyes,
Smiles unaware as if a guardian saint
Smiled in her:—for this, too,—that Gage comes
home
525 And lays his last book's prodigal review
Upon his mother's knee, where, years ago,
He laid his childish spelling-book and learned
To chirp and peck the letters from her mouth,
As young birds must. "Well done," she murmured
then;
530 She will not say it now more wonderingly:
And yet the last "Well done" will touch him more,
As catching up to-day and yesterday
In a perfect chord of love: and so, Mark Gage,
I envy you your mother!—and you, Graham,
535 Because you have a wife who loves you so,
She half forgets, at moments, to be proud
Of being Graham's wife, until a friend observes,
"The boy here, has his father's massive brow,
Done small in wax…if we push back the curls."
540 Who loves me? Dearest father,—mother sweet,—
I speak the names out sometimes by myself,
And make the silence shiver. They sound strange,
As Hindostanee to an Ind-born man
Accustomed many years to English speech;
545 Or lovely poet-words grown obsolete,
Which will not leave off singing. Up in heaven
I have my father,—with my mother's face
Beside him in a blotch of heavenly light;
No more for earth's familiar, household use,

550 No more. The best verse written by this hand,
Can never reach them where they sit, to seem
Well-done to *them*. Death quite unfellows us,
Sets dreadful odds betwixt the live and dead,
And makes us part as those at Babel did
555 Through sudden ignorance of a common tongue.
A living Cæsar would not dare to play
At bowls with such as my dead father is.

And yet this may be less so than appears,
This change and separation. Sparrows five
560 For just two farthings, and God cares for each.
If God is not too great for little cares,
Is any creature, because gone to God?
I've seen some men, veracious, nowise mad,
Who have thought or dreamed, declared and
testified,
565 They heard the Dead a-ticking like a clock
Which strikes the hours of the eternities,
Beside them, with their natural ears,—and known
That human spirits feel the human way
And hate the unreasoning awe which waves them
off
570 From possible communion. It may be.
At least, earth separates as well as heaven.
For instance, I have not seen Romney Leigh
Full eighteen months…add six, you get two years.
They say he's very busy with good works,—
575 Has parted Leigh Hall into almshouses.
He made one day an almshouse of his heart,
Which ever since is loose upon the latch
For those who pull the string.—I never did.

It always makes me sad to go abroad,
580 And now I'm sadder that I went to-night,
Among the lights and talkers at Lord Howe's.
His wife is gracious, with her glossy braids,
And even voice, and gorgeous eyeballs, calm
As her other jewels. If she's somewhat cold,
585 Who wonders, when her blood has stood so long
In the ducal reservoir she calls her line

---

[1] Neoplatonist philosopher (c. 205–70).

By no means arrogantly? she's not proud;
Not prouder than the swan is of the lake
He has always swum in;—'tis her element;
590 And so she takes it with a natural grace,
Ignoring tadpoles. She just knows perhaps
There *are* who travel without outriders,
Which isn't her fault. Ah, to watch her face,
When good Lord Howe expounds his theories
595 Of social justice and equality!
'Tis curious, what a tender, tolerant bend
Her neck takes: for she loves him, likes his talk,
"Such clever talk—that dear, odd Algernon!"
She listens on, exactly as if he talked
600 Some Scandinavian myth of Lemures,
Too pretty to dispute, and too absurd.
She's gracious to me as her husband's friend,
And would be gracious, were I not a Leigh,
Being used to smile just so, without her eyes,
605 On Joseph Strangways the Leeds mesmerist,
And Delia Dobbs the lecturer from "the States"
Upon the "Woman's question." Then, for him,
I like him; he's my friend. And all the rooms
Were full of crinkling silks that swept about
610 The fine dust of most subtle courtesies.
What then?—why then, we come home to be sad.

How lovely, One I love not looked to-night!
She's very pretty, Lady Waldemar.
Her maid must use both hands to twist that coil
615 Of tresses, then be careful lest the rich
Bronze rounds should slip:—she missed, though, a
        grey hair,
A single one,—I saw it; otherwise
The woman looked immortal. How they told,
Those alabaster shoulders and bare breasts,
620 On which the pearls, drowned out of sight in milk,
Were lost, excepting for the ruby-clasp!
They split the amaranth velvet-bodice down
To the waist or nearly, with the audacious press
Of full-breathed beauty. If the heart within
625 Were half as white!—but, if it were, perhaps

The breast were closer covered and the sight
Less aspectable, by half, too.
                                    I heard
The young man with the German student's look—
A sharp face, like a knife in a cleft stick,
630 Which shot up straight against the parting line
So equally dividing the long hair,—
Say softly to his neighbour, (thirty-five
And mediæval) "Look that way, Sir Blaise.
She's Lady Waldemar—to the left—in red—
635 Whom Romney Leigh, our ablest man just now,
Is soon about to marry."
                            Then replied
Sir Blaise Delorme, with quiet, priestlike voice,
Too used to syllable damnations round
To make a natural emphasis worth while:
640 "Is Leigh your ablest man? the same, I think,
Once jilted by a recreant pretty maid
Adopted from the people? Now, in change,
He seems to have plucked a flower from the other
        side
Of the social hedge."
                        "A flower, a flower," exclaimed
645 My German student,—his own eyes full-blown
Bent on her. He was twenty, certainly.

Sir Blaise resumed with gentle arrogance,
As if he had dropped his alms into a hat
And gained the right to counsel,—"My young
        friend,
650 I doubt your ablest man's ability
To get the least good or help meet for him,
For pagan phalanstery[1] or Christian home,
From such a flowery creature."
                                "Beautiful!"
My student murmured rapt,—"Mark how she stirs!
655 Just waves her head, as if a flower indeed,
Touched far off by the vain breath of our talk."

_____

1 a community of people living together, free of external regulation and
holding property in common. The term was used by Fourier in his
socialist scheme for the reorganization of society.

At which that bilious Grimwald (he who writes
For the Renovator), who had seemed absorbed
Upon the table-book of autographs
660 (I dare say mentally he crunched the bones
Of all those writers, wishing them alive
To feel his tooth in earnest), turned short round
With low carnivorous laugh,—"A flower, of course!
She neither sews nor spins,—and takes no thought
665 Of her garments…falling off."
                                    The student flinched;
Sir Blaise, the same; then both, drawing back their
    chairs
As if they spied black-beetles on the floor,
Pursued their talk, without a word being thrown
To the critic.
                    Good Sir Blaise's brow is high
670 And noticeably narrow: a strong wind,
You fancy, might unroof him suddenly,
And blow that great top attic off his head
So piled with feudal relics. You admire
His nose in profile, though you miss his chin;
675 But, though you miss his chin, you seldom miss
His ebon cross worn innermostly (carved
For penance by a saintly Styrian monk
Whose flesh was too much with him), slipping
    through
Some unaware unbuttoned casualty
680 Of the under-waistcoat. With an absent air
Sir Blaise sat fingering it and speaking low,
While I, upon the sofa, heard it all.

"My dear young friend, if we could bear our eyes,
Like blessedest Saint Lucy, on a plate,
685 They would not trick us into choosing wives,
As doublets, by the colour. Otherwise
Our fathers chose,—and therefore, when they had
    hung
Their household keys about a lady's waist,
The sense of duty gave her dignity;
690 She kept her bosom holy to her babes,
And, if a moralist reproved her dress,

'Twas, 'Too much starch!'—and not, 'Too little
    lawn!'"

"Now, pshaw!" returned the other in a heat,
A little fretted by being called "young friend,"
695 Or so I took it,—"for Saint Lucy's sake,
If she's the saint to swear by, let us leave
Our fathers,—plagued enough about our sons!"
(He stroked his beardless chin) "yes, plagued, sir,
    plagued:
The future generations lie on us
700 As heavy as the nightmare of a seer;
Our meat and drink grow painful prophecy:
I ask you,—have we leisure, if we liked,
To hollow out our weary hands to keep
Your intermittent rushlight of the past
705 From draughts in lobbies? Prejudice of sex
And marriage-law…the socket drops them through
While we two speak,—however may protest
Some over-delicate nostrils like your own,
'Gainst odours thence arising."
                                    "You are young,"
710 Sir Blaise objected.
                            "If I am," he said
With fire,—"though somewhat less so than I seem,
The young run on before, and see the thing
That's coming. Reverence for the young, I cry.
In that new church for which the world's near ripe,
715 You'll have the younger in the Elder's chair,
Presiding with his ivory front of hope
O'er foreheads clawed by cruel carrion-birds
Of life's experience."
                            "Pray your blessing, sir,"
Sir Blaise replied good-humouredly,—"I plucked
720 A silver hair this morning from my beard,
Which left me your inferior. Would I were
Eighteen and worthy to admonish you!
If young men of your order run before
To see such sights as sexual prejudice
725 And marriage-law dissolved,—in plainer words,
A general concubinage expressed

In a universal pruriency,—the thing
Is scarce worth running fast for, and you'd gain
By loitering with your elders."

              "Ah," he said,

730 "Who, getting to the top of Pisgah-hill,[1]
Can talk with one at bottom of the view,
To make it comprehensible? Why, Leigh
Himself, although our ablest man, I said,
Is scarce advanced to see as far as this,

735 Which some are: he takes up imperfectly
The social question—by one handle—leaves
The rest to trail. A Christian socialist
Is Romney Leigh, you understand."

              "Not I.

I disbelieve in Christian-pagans, much

740 As you in women-fishes. If we mix
Two colours, we lose both, and make a third
Distinct from either. Mark you! to mistake
A colour is the sign of a sick brain,
And mine, I thank the saints, is clear and cool:

745 A neutral tint is here impossible.
The church—and by the church, I mean, of course
The catholic, apostolic, mother-church,—
Draws lines as plain and straight as her own walls;
Inside of which are Christians obviously

750 And outside…dogs."[2]

              "We thank you. Well I know
The ancient mother-church would fain still bite,
For all her toothless gums,—as Leigh himself
Would fain be a Christian still, for all his wit.
Pass that; you two may settle it, for me.

755 You're slow in England. In a month I learnt
At Göttingen[3] enough philosophy
To stock your English schools for fifty years;
Pass that, too. Here alone, I stop you short,
— Supposing a true man like Leigh could stand

760 Unequal in the stature of his life
To the height of his opinions. Choose a wife
Because of a smooth skin?—not he, not he!
He'd rail at Venus' self for creaking shoes,
Unless she walked his way of righteousness:

765 And if he takes a Venus Meretrix[4]
(No imputation on the lady there),
Be sure that, by some sleight of Christian art,
He has metamorphosed and converted her
To a Blessed Virgin."

              "Soft!" Sir Blaise drew breath

770 As if it hurt him—"Soft! no blasphemy,
I pray you!"

              "The first Christians did the thing:
Why not the last?" asked he of Göttingen,
With just that shade of sneering on the lip,
Compensates for the lagging of the beard,—

775 "And so the case is. If that fairest fair
Is talked of as the future wife of Leigh,
She's talked of too, at least as certainly,
As Leigh's disciple. You may find her name
On all his missions and commissions, schools,

780 Asylums, hospitals,—he had her down,
With other ladies whom her starry lead
Persuaded from their spheres, to his country-place
In Shropshire, to the famed phalanstery
At Leigh Hall, christianised from Fourier's[5] own

785 (In which he has planted out his sapling stocks
Of knowledge into social nurseries),
And there, they say, she has tarried half a week,
And milked the cows, and churned, and pressed the
    curd,
And said 'my sister' to the lowest drab

790 Of all the assembled castaways; such girls!
Ay, sided with them at the washing-tub—
Conceive, Sir Blaise, those naked perfect arms,
Round glittering arms, plunged elbow-deep in suds,
Like wild swans hid in lilies all a-shake."

---

1 the summit from which Moses saw the promised land: Deuteronomy 3:27 and 34:1–4.

2 Revelation 22:14.

3 German university founded in 1734.

4 a prostitute.

5 Charles Fourier (d. 1837), French socialist.

795 Lord Howe came up. "What, talking poetry
So near the image of the unfavouring Muse?
That's you, Miss Leigh: I've watched you half an
      hour,
Precisely as I watched the statue called
A Pallas in the Vatican;[1]—you mind
800 The face, Sir Blaise?—intensely calm and sad,
As wisdom cut it off from fellowship,—
But *that* spoke louder. Not a word from *you*!
And these two gentlemen were bold, I marked,
And unabashed by even your silence."

                                    "Ah,"
805 Said I, "my dear Lord Howe, you shall not speak
To a printing woman who has lost her place
(The sweet safe corner of the household fire
Behind the heads of children), compliments,
As if she were a woman. We who have clipt
810 The curls before our eyes may see at least
As plain as men do. Speak out, man to man;
No compliments, beseech you."

                          "Friend to friend,
Let that be. We are sad to-night, I saw,
(—Good night, Sir Blaise! ah, Smith—he has
      slipped away),
815 I saw you across the room, and stayed, Miss Leigh,
To keep a crowd of lion-hunters off,
With faces toward your jungle. There were three;
A spacious lady, five feet ten and fat,
Who has the devil in her (and there's room)
820 For walking to and fro upon the earth,
From Chipewa to China; she requires
Your autograph upon a tinted leaf
'Twixt Queen Pomare's and Emperor
      Soulouque's.[2]
Pray give it; she has energies, though fat:
825 For me, I'd rather see a rick on fire

---

[1] The statue is also called Minerva Medica and La Dea Salus, standing in the "Braccio Nuovo" of the Vatican Museum.

[2] Queen Pomare IV of Tahiti (1813–77); Faustin-Elie Soulouque (c. 1782–1867), president of Haiti in 1847 who declared himself Emperor Faustin I of Haiti in 1849.

Than such a woman angry. Then a youth
Fresh from the backwoods, green as the underboughs,
Asks modestly, Miss Leigh, to kiss your shoe,
And adds, he has an epic in twelve parts,
830 Which when you've read, you'll do it for his boot:
All which I saved you, and absorb next week
Both manuscript and man,—because a lord
Is still more potent than a poetess
With any extreme republican. Ah, ah,
835 You smile, at last, then."

                          "Thank you."

                                    "Leave the smile,
I'll lose the thanks for't,—ay, and throw you in
My transatlantic girl, with golden eyes,
That draw you to her splendid whiteness as
The pistil of a water-lily draws,
840 Adust with gold. Those girls across the sea
Are tyrannously pretty,—and I swore
(She seemed to me an innocent, frank girl)
To bring her to you for a woman's kiss,
Not now, but on some other day or week:
845 —We'll call it perjury; I give her up."

"No, bring her."

                "Now," said he, "you make it hard
To touch such goodness with a grimy palm.
I thought to tease you well, and fret you cross,
And steel myself, when rightly vexed with you,
850 For telling you a thing to tease you more."

"Of Romney?"

                "No, no; nothing worse," he cried,
"Of Romney Leigh than what is buzzed about,—
That *he* is taken in an eye-trap too,
Like many half as wise. The thing I mean
855 Refers to you, not him."

                          "Refers to me."

He echoed,—"Me! You sound it like a stone
Dropped down a dry well very listlessly
By one who never thinks about the toad
Alive at the bottom. Presently perhaps

860   You'll sound your 'me' more proudly—till I
      shrink."

"Lord Howe's the toad, then, in this question?"
                                 "Brief,
We'll take it graver. Give me sofa-room,
And quiet hearing. You know Eglinton,
John Eglinton, of Eglinton in Kent?"

865   "Is *he* the toad?—he's rather like the snail,
Known chiefly for the house upon his back:
Divide the man and house—you kill the man;
That's Eglinton of Eglinton, Lord Howe."

He answered grave. "A reputable man,
870   An excellent landlord of the olden stamp,
If somewhat slack in new philanthropies,
Who keeps his birthdays with a tenants' dance,
Is hard upon them when they miss the church
Or hold their children back from catechism,
875   But not ungentle when the agèd poor
Pick sticks at hedge-sides: nay, I've heard him say,
'The old dame has a twinge because she stoops;
'That's punishment enough for felony.'"

"O tender-hearted landlord! may I take
880   My long lease with him, when the time arrives
For gathering winter-faggots!"
                          "He likes art,
Buys books and pictures…of a certain kind;
Neglects no patent duty; a good son"…

"To a most obedient mother. Born to wear
885   His father's shoes, he wears her husband's too:
Indeed I've heard it's touching. Dear Lord Howe,
You shall not praise *me* so against your heart,
When I'm at worst for praise and faggots."
                                 "Be
Less bitter with me, for…in short," he said,
890   "I have a letter, which he urged me so
To bring you…I could scarcely choose but yield;

Insisting that a new love, passing through
The hand of an old friendship, caught from it
Some reconciling odour."
                            "Love, you say?
895   My lord, I cannot love: I only find
The rhyme for love,—and that's not love, my lord.
Take back your letter."
                      "Pause: you'll read it first?"

"I will not read it: it is stereotyped;[1]
The same he wrote to,—anybody's name,
900   Anne Blythe the actress, when she died so true
A duchess fainted in a private box:
Pauline the dancer, after the great *pas*[2]
In which her little feet winked overhead
Like other fire-flies, and amazed the pit:
905   Or Baldinacci, when her F in alt[3]
Had touched the silver tops of heaven itself
With such a pungent spirit-dart, the Queen
Laid softly, each to each, her white-gloved palms,
And sighed for joy: or else (I thank your friend)
910   Aurora Leigh,—when some indifferent rhymes,
Like those the boys sang round the holy ox
On Memphis-highway, chance perhaps to set
Our Apis-public lowing. Oh, he wants,
Instead of any worthy wife at home,
915   A star upon his stage of Eglinton?
Advise him that he is not overshrewd
In being so little modest: a dropped star
Makes bitter waters, says a Book I've read,[4]—
And there's his unread letter."
                            "My dear friend,"
920   Lord Howe began…

---

[1] a printing process where a relief printing plate is cast in a mould made from composed type or an original plate; a widely held but fixed and oversimplified image or idea.

[2] the virtuoso set piece of a ballet; more commonly, the phrase is used to describe the *pas de deux* of two dancers.

[3] a high note in the upper register in music.

[4] Revelation 8:10–11.

In haste I tore the phrase.
"You mean your friend of Eglinton, or me?"

"I mean you, you," he answered with some fire.
"A happy life means prudent compromise;
The tare runs through the farmer's garnered sheaves,
925 And though the gleaner's apron holds pure wheat
We count her poorer. Tare with wheat, we cry,
And good with drawbacks. You, you love your art,
And, certain of vocation, set your soul
On utterance. Only, in this world we have made
930 (They say God made it first, but if He did
'Twas so long since, and, since, we have spoiled it
       so,
He scarce would know it, if He looked this way,
From hells we preach of, with the flames blown
       out),
—In this bad, twisted, topsy-turvy world
935 Where all the heaviest wrongs get uppermost,—
In this uneven, unfostering England here,
Where ledger-strokes and sword-strokes count
       indeed,
But soul-strokes merely tell upon the flesh
They strike from,—it is hard to stand for art,
940 Unless some golden tripod from the sea
Be fished up, by Apollo's divine chance,
To throne such feet as yours, my prophetess,
At Delphi.[1] Think,—the god comes down as fierce
As twenty bloodhounds, shakes you, strangles you,
945 Until the oracular shriek shall ooze in froth!
At best 'tis not all ease,—at worst too hard:
A place to stand on is a 'vantage gained,
And here's your tripod. To be plain, dear friend,
You're poor, except in what you richly give;
950 You labour for your own bread painfully
Or ere you pour our wine. For art's sake, pause."

I answered slow,—as some wayfaring man,
Who feels himself at night too far from home,
Makes steadfast face against the bitter wind.
955 "Is art so less a thing than virtue is,
That artists first must cater for their ease
Or ever they make issue past themselves
To generous use? Alas, and is it so,
That we, who would be somewhat clean, must
       sweep
960 Our ways as well as walk them, and no friend
Confirm us nobly,—'Leave results to God,
But you, be clean?' What! 'prudent compromise
Makes acceptable life,' you say instead,
You, you, Lord Howe?—in things indifferent, well.
965 For instance, compromise the wheaten bread
For rye, the meat for lentils, silk for serge,
And sleep on down, if needs, for sleep on straw;
But there, end compromise. I will not bate
One artist-dream on straw or down, my lord,
970 Nor pinch my liberal soul, though I be poor,
Nor cease to love high, though I live thus low."

So speaking, with less anger in my voice
Than sorrow, I rose quickly to depart;
While he, thrown back upon the noble shame
975 Of such high-stumbling natures, murmured words,
The right words after wrong ones. Ah, the man
Is worthy, but so given to entertain
Impossible plans of superhuman life,—
He sets his virtues on so raised a shelf,
980 To keep them at the grand millennial height,
He has to mount a stool to get at them;
And, meantime, lives on quite the common way,
With everybody's morals.
                              As we passed,
Lord Howe insisting that his friendly arm
985 Should oar me across the sparkling brawling stream
Which swept from room to room,—we fell at once
On Lady Waldemar. "Miss Leigh," she said,
And gave me such a smile, so cold and bright,

---

[1] a religious sanctuary of ancient Greece, dedicated to Apollo and situated on Mount Parnassus; thought of as the navel of the earth, it was the seat of the Pythia, the priestess of Apollo, who delivered her riddling responses there. The tripod is the bronze altar on which the priestess sits.

As if she tried it in a 'tiring glass[1]
990 And liked it; "all to-night I've strained at you
As babes at baubles held up out of reach
By spiteful nurses ('Never snatch,' they say),
And there you sat, most perfectly shut in
By good Sir Blaise and clever Mister Smith
995 And then our dear Lord Howe! at last indeed
I almost snatched. I have a world to speak
About your cousin's place in Shropshire, where
I've been to see his work…our work,—you heard
I went?…and of a letter yesterday,
1000 In which if I should read a page or two
You might feel interest, though you're locked of
    course
In literary toil.—You'll like to hear
Your last book lies at the phalanstery,
As judged innocuous for the elder girls
1005 And younger women who care for books.
We all must read, you see, before we live,
Till slowly the ineffable light comes up
And, as it deepens, drowns the written word,—
So said your cousin, while we stood and felt
1010 A sunset from his favourite beech-tree seat.
He might have been a poet if he would,
But then he saw the higher thing at once
And climbed to it. I think he looks well now,
Has quite got over that unfortunate…
1015 Ah, ah…I know it moved you. Tender-heart!
You took a liking to the wretched girl.
Perhaps you thought the marriage suitable,
Who knows? a poet hankers for romance,
And so on. As for Romney Leigh, 'tis sure
1020 He never loved her,—never. By the way,
You have not heard of *her*…? quite out of sight,
And out of saving? lost in every sense?"

She might have gone on talking half an hour
And I stood still, and cold, and pale, I think,
1025 As a garden-statue a child pelts with snow

For pretty-pastime. Every now and then
I put in "yes" or "no," I scarce knew why;
The blind man walks wherever the dog pulls,
And so I answered. Till Lord Howe broke in:
1030 "What penance takes the wretch who interrupts
The talk of charming women? I, at last,
Must brave it. Pardon, Lady Waldemar!
The lady on my arm is tired, unwell,
And loyally I've promised she shall say
1035 No harder word this evening, than…good-night;
The rest her face speaks for her."—Then we went.

And I breathe large at home. I drop my cloak
Unclasp my girdle, loose the band that ties
My hair…now could I but unloose my soul!
1040 We are sepulchred alive in this close world,
And want more room.
                    The charming woman there—
This reckoning up and writing down her talk
Affects me singularly. How she talked
To pain me! woman's spite.—You wear steel-mail:
1045 A woman takes a housewife[2] from her breast
And plucks the delicatest needle out
As 'twere a rose, and pricks you carefully
'Neath nails, 'neath eyelids, in your nostrils,—say,
A beast would roar so tortured,—but a man,
1050 A human creature, must not, shall not flinch,
No, not for shame.
                  What vexes, after all,
Is just that such as she, with such as I,
Knows how to vex. Sweet heaven, she takes me up
As if she had fingered me and dog-eared me
1055 And spelled me by the fireside half a life!
She knows my turns, my feeble points.—What
    then?
The knowledge of a thing implies the thing;
Of course, she found *that* in me, she saw *that*,
Her pencil underscored *this* for a fault,
1060 And I, still ignorant. Shut the book up,—close!

---

[1] a mirror.

[2] a small case for needles, etc. (*OED*).

And crush that beetle in the leaves.
                                        O heart,
At last we shall grow hard too, like the rest,
And call it self-defence because we are soft.

And after all, now…why should I be pained
1065 That Romney Leigh, my cousin, should espouse
This Lady Waldemar? And, say, she held
Her newly-blossomed gladness in my face,…
'Twas natural surely, if not generous,
Considering how, when winter held her fast,
1070 I helped the frost with mine, and pained her more
Than she pains me. Pains me!—but wherefore
        pained?
'Tis clear my cousin Romney wants a wife,—
So, good!—The man's need of the woman, here,
Is greater than the woman's of the man,
1075 And easier served; for where the man discerns
A sex (ah, ah, the man can generalise,
Said he), we see but one, ideally
And really: where we yearn to lose ourselves
And melt like white pearls in another's wine,
1080 He seeks to double himself by what he loves,
And make his drink more costly by our pearls.
At board, at bed, at work and holiday,
It is not good for man to be alone,
And that's his way of thinking, first and last,
1085 And thus my cousin Romney wants a wife.
But then my cousin sets his dignity
On personal virtue. If he understands
By love, like others, self-aggrandisement,
It is that he may verily be great
1090 By doing rightly and kindly. Once he thought,
For charitable ends set duly forth
In Heaven's white judgment-book, to marry…ah,
We'll call her name Aurora Leigh, although
She's changed since then!—and once, for social
        ends,
1095 Poor Marian Erle, my sister Marian Erle,
My woodland sister, sweet maid Marian,
Whose memory moans on in me like the wind

Through ill-shut casements, making me more sad
Than ever I find reasons for. Alas,
1100 Poor pretty plaintive face, embodied ghost!
He finds it easy then, to clap thee off
From pulling at his sleeve and book and pen,—
He locks thee out at night into the cold
Away from butting with thy horny eyes
1105 Against his crystal dreams, that now he's strong
To love anew? that Lady Waldemar
Succeeds my Marian?
                        After all, why not?
He loved not Marian, more than once he loved
Aurora. If loves at last that Third,
1110 Albeit she prove as slippery as spilt oil
On marble floors, I will not augur him
Ill-luck for that. Good love, howe'er ill-placed,
Is better for a man's soul in the end,
Than if he loved ill what deserves love well.
1115 A pagan, kissing for a step of Pan
The wild-goat's hoof-print on the loamy down,
Exceeds our modern thinker who turns back
The strata…granite, limestone, coal, and clay,
Concluding coldly with, "Here's law! where's
        God?"

1120 And then at worst,—if Romney loves her not,—
At worst,—if he's incapable of love,
Which may be—then indeed, for such a man
Incapable of love, she's good enough;
For she, at worst too, is a woman still
1125 And loves him…as the sort of woman can.

My loose long hair began to burn and creep,
Alive to the very ends, about my knees:
I swept it backward as the wind sweeps flame,
With the passion of my hands. Ah, Romney laughed
1130 One day…(how full the memories come up!)
"—Your Florence fire-flies live on in your hair,"
He said, "it gleams so." Well, I wrung them out,
My fire-flies; made a knot as hard as life
Of those loose, soft, impracticable curls.

1135 And then sat down and thought…"She shall not
    think
Her thought of me,"—and drew my desk and
    wrote.

"Dear Lady Waldemar, I could not speak
With people round me, nor can sleep to-night
And not speak, after the great news I heard
1140 Of you and of my cousin. May you be
Most happy; and the good he meant the world,
Replenish his own life. Say what I say,
And let my word be sweeter for your mouth,
As you are *you*…I only Aurora Leigh."
1145 That's quiet, guarded: though she hold it up
Against the light, she'll not see through it more
Than lies there to be seen. So much for pride;
And now for peace, a little. Let me stop
All writing back…"Sweet thanks, my sweetest friend,
1150 You've made more joyful my great joy itself."
—No, that's too simple! she would twist it thus,
"My joy would still be as sweet as thyme in drawers,
"However shut up in the dark and dry;
"But violets, aired and dewed by love like yours,
1155 "Out-smell all thyme: we keep that in our clothes,
"But drop the other down our bosoms till
"They smell like"…ah, I see her writing back
Just so. She'll make a nosegay of her words,
And tie it with blue ribbons at the end
1160 To suit a poet;—pshaw!
                And then we'll have
The call to church, the broken, sad, bad dream
Dreamed out at last, the marriage-vow complete
With the marriage-breakfast; praying in white
    gloves,
Drawn off in haste for drinking pagan toasts
1165 In somewhat stronger wine than any sipped
By gods since Bacchus had his way with grapes.

A postscript stops all that and rescues me.
"You need not write. I have been overworked,
And think of leaving London, England even,

1170 And hastening to get nearer the sun
Where men sleep better. So, adieu."—I fold
And seal,—and now I'm out of all the coil;
I breathe now, I spring upward like a branch
The ten-years school-boy with a crooked stick
1175 May pull down to his level in search of nuts,
But cannot hold a moment. How we twang
Back on the blue sky, and assert our height,
While he stares after! Now, the wonder seems
That I could wrong myself by such a doubt.
1180 We poets always have uneasy hearts,
Because our hearts, large-rounded as the globe,
Can turn but one side to the sun at once.
We are used to dip our artist-hands in gall
And potash, trying potentialities
1185 Of alternated colour, till at last
We get confused, and wonder for our skin
How nature tinged it first. Well—here's the true
Good flesh-colour; I recognise my hand,—
Which Romney Leigh may clasp as just a friend's,
1190 And keep his clean.
                And now, my Italy.
Alas, if we could ride with naked souls
And make no noise and pay no price at all,
I would have seen thee sooner, Italy,
For still I have heard thee crying through my life,
1195 Thou piercing silence of ecstatic graves,
Men call that name!

                But even a witch to-day
Must melt down golden pieces in the nard
Wherewith to anoint her broomstick ere she rides;
And poets evermore are scant of gold,
1200 And if they find a piece behind the door
It turns by sunset to a withered leaf.
The Devil himself scarce trusts his patented
Gold-making art to any who make rhymes,
But culls his Faustus from philosophers[1]

---

[1] See Marlowe's *The Tragical History of Doctor Faustus* (1604), and Goethe's drama, *Faust* (1808 and 1832). Faust is a philosopher and alchemist who sells his soul to the devil in return for the secret of

1205 And not from poets. "Leave my Job," said God;[1]
And so the Devil leaves him without pence,
And poverty proves plainly special grace.
In these new, just, administrative times
Men clamour for an order of merit: why?
1210 Here's black bread on the table and no wine!

At least I am a poet in being poor,
Thank God. I wonder if the manuscript
Of my long poem, if 'twere sold outright,
Would fetch enough to buy me shoes to go
1215 A-foot (thrown in, the necessary patch
For the other side the Alps)? It cannot be.
I fear that I must sell this residue
Of my father's books, although the Elzevirs[2]
Have fly-leaves over-written by his hand
1220 In faded notes as thick and fine and brown
As cobwebs on a tawny monument
Of the old Greeks—*conferenda hæc cum his*—
Corruptè citat—lege potiùs,[3]
And so on, in the scholar's regal way
1225 Of giving judgment on the parts of speech,
As if he sat on all twelve thrones up-piled,
Arraigning Israel.[4] Ay, but books and notes
Must go together. And this Proclus too,
In these dear quaint contracted Grecian types,
1230 Fantastically crumpled like his thoughts
Which would not seem too plain; you go round
    twice
For one step forward, then you take it back
Because you're somewhat giddy; there's the rule
For Proclus.[5] Ah, I stained this middle leaf

1235 With pressing in't my Florence iris-bell,
Long stalk and all: my father chided me
For that stain of blue blood,—I recollect
The peevish turn his voice took,—"Silly girls,
Who plant their flowers in our philosophy
1240 To make it fine, and only spoil the book!
No more of it, Aurora." Yes—no more!
Ah, blame of love, that's sweeter than all praise
Of those who love not! 'tis so lost to me,
I cannot, in such beggared life, afford
1245 To lose my Proclus,—not for Florence even.

The kissing Judas, Wolff,[6] shall go instead,
Who builds us such a royal book as this
To honour a chief-poet, folio-built,
And writes above, "The house of Nobody!"
1250 Who floats in cream, as rich as any sucked
From Juno's breasts,[7] the broad Homeric lines,
And, while with their spondaic prodigious mouths
They lap the lucent margins as babe-gods,
Proclaims them bastards. Wolff's an atheist:
1255 And if the Iliad fell out, as he says,
By mere fortuitous concourse of old songs,
Conclude as much too for the universe.

That Wolff, those Platos: sweep the upper shelves
As clean as this, and so I am almost rich,
1260 Which means, not forced to think of being poor
In sight of ends. To-morrow: no delay.
I'll wait in Paris till good Carrington
Dispose of such and, having chaffered for[8]
My book's price with the publisher, direct
1265 All proceeds to me. Just a line to ask
His help.

---

alchemy, wealth, and power.

[1] Cf. Job 42:10.

[2] a family of printers, working in Amsterdam, Leyden, and the Hague (1592–1680); the printers were famous for their editions of the classics.

[3] "Compare this with that. Corruptly or incorrectly cited."

[4] Cf. Matthew 19:28.

[5] Proclus of Byzantium (c. 411–85); the last major writer of the Neo-platonic school.

---

[6] Friedrich Augustus Wolf—EBB's spelling is incorrect—(1759–1824); his *Prolegomena to Homer* (1795) argues that the *Iliad* and *Odyssey* are not works by a single, identifiable poet, but works composed by a number of authors.

[7] The Milky Way was said to originate from Juno's flowing milk—from Hyginus's *Poetica Astronomica* 2:43.

[8] haggled over.

And now I come, my Italy,
My own hills! Are you 'ware of me, my hills,
How I burn toward you? do you feel to-night
The urgency and yearning of my soul,
1270   As sleeping mothers feel the sucking babe
And smile?—Nay, not so much as when in heat
Vain lightnings catch at your inviolate tops
And tremble while ye are steadfast. Still ye go
Your own determined, calm, indifferent way
1275   Toward sunrise, shade by shade, and light by light,
Of all the grand progression nought left out,
As if God verily made you for yourselves
And would not interrupt your life with ours.
—1857

A Curse for a Nation

PROLOGUE

I heard an angel speak last night,
        And he said "Write!
Write a Nation's curse for me,
And send it over the Western Sea."

5   I faltered, taking up the word:
        "Not so, my lord!
If curses must be, choose another
To send thy curse against my brother.

"For I am bound by gratitude,
10   By love and blood,
To brothers of mine across the sea,
Who stretch out kindly hands to me."

"Therefore," the voice said, "shalt thou write
        My curse to-night.
15   From the summits of love a curse is driven,
As lightning is from the tops of heaven."

"Not so," I answered. "Evermore
        My heart is sore
For my own land's sins: for little feet
20   Of children bleeding along the street:

"For parked-up honours that gainsay
        The right of way:
For almsgiving through a door that is
Not open enough for two friends to kiss:

25   "For love of freedom which abates
        Beyond the Straits:
For patriot virtue starved to vice on
Self-praise, self-interest, and suspicion:

"For an oligarchic parliament,
30   And bribes well-meant.
What curse to another land assign,
When heavy-souled for the sins of mine?"

"Therefore," the voice said, "shalt thou write
        My curse to-night.
35   Because thou hast strength to see and hate
A foul thing done *within* thy gate."

"Not so," I answered once again.
        "To curse, choose men.
For I, a woman, have only known
40   How the heart melts and the tears run down."

"Therefore," the voice said, "shalt thou write
        My curse to-night.
Some women weep and curse, I say
(And no one marvels), night and day.

45   "And thou shalt take their part to-night,
        Weep and write.
A curse from the depths of womanhood
Is very salt, and bitter, and good."

So thus I wrote, and mourned indeed,
50   What all may read.
And thus, as was enjoined on me,
I send it over the Western Sea.
—1860

A Musical Instrument

I

What was he doing, the great god Pan,[1]
   Down in the reeds by the river?
Spreading ruin and scattering ban,[2]
Splashing and paddling with hoofs of a goat,
5   And breaking the golden lilies afloat
      With the dragon-fly on the river.

II

He tore out a reed, the great god Pan,
   From the deep cool bed of the river:
The limpid water turbidly ran,
10   And the broken lilies a-dying lay,
And the dragon-fly had fled away,
      Ere he brought it out of the river.

III

High on the shore sat the great god Pan
   While turbidly flowed the river;
15   And hacked and hewed as a great god can,
With his hard bleak steel at the patient reed,
Till there was not a sign of the leaf indeed
      To prove it fresh from the river.

IV

He cut it short, did the great god Pan,
20   (How tall it stood in the river!)
Then drew the pith,[3] like the heart of a man,
Steadily from the outside ring,
And notched the poor dry empty thing
      In holes, as he sat by the river.

V

25   "This is the way," laughed the great god Pan
      (Laughed while he sat by the river),
"The only way, since gods began
To make sweet music, they could succeed."
Then, dropping his mouth to a hole in the reed,
30   He blew in power by the river.

VI

Sweet, sweet, sweet, O Pan!
   Piercing sweet by the river!
Blinding sweet, O great god Pan!
The sun on the hill forgot to die,
35   And the lilies revived, and the dragon-fly
      Came back to dream on the river.

VII

Yet half a beast is the great god Pan,
   To laugh as he sits by the river,
Making a poet out of a man:
40   The true gods sigh for the cost and pain,—
For the reed which grows nevermore again
      As a reed with the reeds in the river.
—1862

[1] the god of woods, fields, and flocks, having a human body with goat's legs, horns, and ears. According to Greek myth, the nymph Syrinx, in attempting to escape Pan's pursuit of her, was metamorphosed into a reed in a stream. Pan turned the reed into a shepherd's pipe.

[2] curses; condemnation.

[3] the central tissue.

Caroline Norton
1808 – 1877

Caroline Norton was the daughter of the Scottish novelist Henrietta Callander, granddaughter of the dramatist and politician Richard Brinsley Sheridan, and great-granddaughter of the novelist Frances Sheridan. Caroline married George Norton in 1827 and soon discovered, as her first American editor delicately wrote, that he was "a man of a lower range of feelings" than she. The marriage was an unhappy one emotionally, intellectually, and even politically (Norton was a Whig and her husband was a Tory MP). After her husband's death in 1875,

Norton married a long-time friend, but died shortly thereafter. Norton was ardently engaged in contemporary debates on married women's rights and on child labour, which she vigorously opposed and which forms the subject of "A Voice from the Factories" (1836). From the publication of her first collection, *The Sorrows of Rosalie* (1829), her poetry was well-received by her peers, and Hartley Coleridge, famously remarking that she was "the Byron of modern poetesses," identified her in 1840 as the foremost woman poet writing in England.

ᕮᔕᕮᔦ

From *Voice From the Factories*

I

When fallen man from Paradise was driven
  Forth to a world of labour, death, and
      care;
Still, of his native Eden, bounteous Heaven
Resolved one brief memorial to spare,
5 And gave his offspring an imperfect share
Of that lost happiness, amid decay;
Making their first *approach* to life seem fair,
And giving, for the Eden past away,
CHILDHOOD, the weary life's long happy holyday.

IX

Ever a toiling *child* doth make us sad:
'T is an unnatural and mournful sight,
75 Because we feel their smiles should be so glad,
Because we know their eyes should be so bright.
What is it, then, when, tasked beyond their
      might,
They labour all day long for others' gain,—
Nay, trespass on the still and pleasant night,
80 While uncompleted hours of toil remain?
Poor little FACTORY SLAVES—for YOU these lines
complain!

X

Beyond all sorrow which the wanderer knows,
Is that these little pent-up wretches feel;
Where the air thick and close and stagnant
      grows,
85 And the low whirring of the incessant wheel
Dizzies the head, and makes the senses reel:
There, shut for ever from the gladdening sky,
Vice premature and Care's corroding seal
Stamp on each sallow cheek their hateful die,
90 Line the smooth open brow, and sink the
      saddened eye.

XI

For them the fervid summer only brings
A double curse of stifling withering heat;
For them no flowers spring up, no wild bird
      sings,
No moss-grown walks refresh their weary
      feet;—
95 No river's murmuring sound;—no wood-walk,
      sweet
With many a flower the learned slight and
      pass;—
Nor meadow, with pale cowslips thickly set

Amid the soft leaves of its tufted grass,—
Lure *them* a childish stock of treasures to amass.

XIV

Mark the result. Unnaturally debarred
All nature's fresh and innocent delights,
120 While yet each germing energy strives hard,
And pristine good with pristine evil fights;
When every passing dream the heart excites,
And makes even *guarded* virtue insecure;
Untaught, unchecked, they yield as vice invites:
125 With all around them cramped, confined,
      impure,
Fast spreads the moral plague which nothing new
   shall cure.

XV

Yes, this reproach is added; (infamous
In realms which own a Christian monarch's
   sway!)
Not suffering *only* is their portion, thus
130 Compelled to toil their youthful lives away:
Excessive labour works the SOUL's decay—
Quenches the intellectual light within—
Crushes with iron weight the mind's free play—
Steals from us LEISURE purer thoughts to
   win—
135 And leaves us sunk and lost in dull and native sin.

XVI

Yet in the British Senate men rise up,
(The freeborn and the fathers of our land!)
And while these drink the dregs of Sorrow's cup,
Deny the sufferings of the pining band.
140 With nice-drawn calculations at command,
They prove—rebut—explain—and reason long;
Proud of each shallow argument they stand,
And prostitute their utmost powers of tongue
Feebly to justify this great and glaring wrong.

XVII

145 So rose, with such a plausible defence
Of the unalienable RIGHT OF GAIN,
Those who against Truth's brightest eloquence
Upheld the cause of torture and of pain:
And fear of Property's Decrease made vain,
150 For years, the hope of Christian Charity
To lift the curse from SLAVERY's dark domain,
And send across the wide Atlantic sea
The watchword of brave men—the thrilling
   shout, "BE FREE!"

XVIII

What is to be a slave? Is 't not to spend
155 A life bowed down beneath a grinding ill?—
To labour on to serve another's end,—
To give up leisure, health, and strength, and
   skill—
And give up each of these *against your will?*
Hark to the angry answer:—"Theirs is not
160 A life of slavery; if they labour,—still
We *pay* their toil. Free service is their lot;
And what their labour yields, by us is fairly got."

XIX

Oh, Men! blaspheme not Freedom! Are they
   free
Who toil until the body's strength gives way?
165 Who may not set a term for Liberty,
Who have no time for food, or rest, or play,
But struggle through the long unwelcome day
Without the leisure to be good or glad?
Such is their service—call it what you may.
170 Poor little creatures, overtasked and sad,
Your Slavery hath no name,—yet is its Curse
   as bad!

XX

Again an answer. "'Tis their parents' choice.
By *some* employ the poor man's child must earn
Its daily bread; and infants have no voice

175 In what the allotted task shall be: they learn
What answers best, or suits the parents' turn."
Mournful reply! Do not your hearts inquire
Who tempts the parents' penury? They yearn
Toward their offspring with a strong desire,
180 But those who starve *will* sell, even what they
most require.

XXI

We grant their class must labour—young and
old;
We grant the child the needy parents' tool:
But still our hearts a better plan behold;
No bright Utopia of some dreaming fool,
185 But rationally just, and good by rule.
Not against TOIL, but TOIL's EXCESS we pray,
(Else were we nursed in Folly's simplest school);
That so our country's hardy children may
Learn not to loathe, but bless, the well apportioned
day.

XXII

190 One more reply! The *last* reply—the great
Answer to all that sense or feeling shows,
To which all others are subordinate:—
"The Masters of the Factories must lose
By the abridgment of these infant woes.
195 Show us the remedy which shall combine
Our equal gain with their increased repose—
Which shall not make our trading class repine,
But to the proffered boon its strong effects
confine."

XXIII

Oh! shall it then be said that TYRANT acts
200 Are those which cause our country's looms to
thrive?
That Merchant England's prosperous trade
exacts
This bitter sacrifice, e'er she derive
That profit due, for which the feeble strive?

Is her commercial avarice so keen,
205 That in her busy multitudinous hive
Hundreds must die like insects, scarcely seen,
While the thick-thronged survivors work where
they have been?

XXIV

Forbid it, Spirit of the glorious Past
Which gained our Isle the surname of 'The
Free,'
210 And made our shores a refuge at the last
To all who would not bend the servile knee,
The vainly-vanquished sons of Liberty!
Here ever came the injured, the opprest,
Compelled from the Oppressor's face to flee—
215 And found a home of shelter and of rest
In the warm generous heart that beat in England's
breast.

XLIV

Examine and decide. Watch through his day
One of these little ones. The sun hath shone
390 An hour, and by the ruddy morning's ray,
The last and least, he saunters on alone.
See where, still pausing on the threshold stone,
He stands, as loth to lose the bracing wind;
With wistful wandering glances backward
thrown
395 On all the light and glory left behind,
And sighs to think that HE must darkly be
confined!

XLV

Enter with him. The stranger who surveys
The little natives of that dreary place
(Where squalid suffering meets his shrinking
gaze),
400 Used to the glory of a young child's face,
Its changeful light, its coloured sparkling grace,
(Gleams of Heaven's sunshine on our shadowed
earth!)

84

Starts at each visage wan, and bold, and base,
Whose smiles have neither innocence nor
    mirth,—
405 And comprehends the Sin original from birth.

XLVI

There the pale Orphan, whose unequal strength
Loathes the incessant toil it *must* pursue,
Pines for the cool sweet evening's twilight
    length,
The sunny play-hour, and the morning's dew:
410 Worn with its cheerless life's monotonous hue,
Bowed down, and faint, and stupified it stands;
Each half-seen object reeling in its view—
While its hot, trembling, languid little hands
Mechanically heed the Task-master's commands.

XLVII

415 There, sounds of wailing grief and painful
    blows
Offend the ear, and startle it from rest;
(While the lungs gasp what air the place
    bestows;)
Or misery's joyless vice, the ribald jest,
Breaks the sick silence: staring at the guest
420 Who comes to view their labour, they beguile
The unwatched moment; whispers half supprest
And mutterings low, their faded lips defile,—
While gleams from face to face a strange and sullen
    smile.

XLVIII

These then are his Companions: he, too young
425 To share their base and saddening merriment,
Sits by: his little head in silence hung;
His limbs cramped up; his body weakly bent;
Toiling obedient, till long hours so spent
Produce Exhaustion's slumber, dull and deep.
430 The Watcher's stroke,—bold—sudden—
    violent,—
Urges him from that lethargy of sleep,

And bids him wake to Life,—to labour and to
    weep!

XLIX

But the day hath its End. Forth then he hies
With jaded, faltering step, and brow of pain;
435 Creeps to that shed,—his HOME,—where
    happy lies
The sleeping babe that cannot toil for Gain;
Where his remorseful Mother tempts in vain
With the best portion of their frugal fare:
Too sick to eat—too weary to complain—
440 He turns him idly from the untasted share,
Slumbering sinks down unfed, and mocks her
    useless care.

L

Weeping she lifts, and lays his heavy head
(With all a woman's grieving tenderness)
On the hard surface of his narrow bed;
445 Bends down to give a sad unfelt caress,
And turns away;—willing her God to bless,
That, weary as he is, he need not fight
Against that long-enduring bitterness,
The VOLUNTARY LABOUR of the Night,
450 But sweetly slumber on till day's returning light.

LI

Vain hope! Alas! unable to forget
The anxious task's long, heavy agonies,
In broken sleep the victim labours yet!
Waiting the boding stroke that bids him rise,
455 He marks in restless fear each hour that flies—
Anticipates the unwelcome morning prime—
And murmuring feebly, with unwakened eyes,
"Mother! Oh Mother! is it yet THE TIME?"—
Starts at the moon's pale ray—or clock's far
    distant chime.

LII

460 Such is *his* day and night! Now then return
Where your OWN slumber in protected ease;
They whom no blast may pierce, no sun may
burn;
The lovely, on whose cheeks the wandering
breeze
Hath left the rose's hue. Ah! not like these
465 Does the pale infant-labourer ask to be:
He craves no tempting food—no toys to
please—
Not Idleness,—but less of agony;
Not Wealth,—but comfort, rest, CONTENTED
POVERTY.

LIII

There is, among all men, in every clime,
470 A difference instinctive and unschooled:
God made the MIND unequal. From all time
By fierceness conquered, or by cunning fooled,
The World hath had its Rulers and its Ruled:—
Yea—uncompelled—men abdicate free choice,
475 Fear their own rashness, and, by thinking cooled,
Follow the counsel of some trusted voice;—
A self-elected sway, wherein their souls rejoice.

LIV

Thus, for the most part, willing to obey,
Men rarely set Authority at naught:
480 Albeit a weaker or a worse than they
May hold the rule with such importance fraught:
And thus the peasant, from his cradle taught
That some must *own*, while some must *till* the
land,
Rebels not—murmurs not—even in his thought.
485 Born to his lot, he bows to high command,
And guides the furrowing plough with a contented
hand.

LV

But, if the weight which habit renders light
Is made to gall the Serf who bends below—
The dog that watched and fawned, prepares to
bite!
490 Too rashly strained, the cord snaps from the
bow—
Too tightly curbed, the steeds their riders
throw—
And so, (at first contented his fair state
Of customary servitude to know,)
Too harshly ruled, the poor man learns to hate
495 And curse the oppressive law that bids him serve
the Great.

LVI

THEN first he asks his gloomy soul the CAUSE
Of his discomfort; suddenly compares—
Reflects—and with an angry Spirit draws
The envious line between his lot and theirs,
500 Questioning the JUSTICE of the unequal shares.
And from the gathering of this discontent,
Where there is strength, REVOLT his standard
rears;
Where there is weakness, evermore finds vent
The sharp annoying cry of sorrowful complaint.

LVII

505 Therefore should Mercy, gently and serene,
Sit by the Ruler's side, and share his Throne:—
Watch with unerring eye the passing scene,
And bend her ear to mark the feeblest groan;
Lest due Authority be overthrown,
510 And they that ruled perceive (too late confest!)
Permitted Power might still have been their own,
Had they but watched that none should be
opprest—
No just complaint despised—no WRONG left
unredrest.
—1836

The Creole Girl

Elle etait de ce monde, ou les plus belles choses
    Ont le pire destin;
Et Rose, elle a vecu ce que vivent les Roses,
    L'espace d'un matin! [1]

She came to England from the island clime
    Which lies beyond the far Atlantic wave;
She died in early youth—before her time—
    "Peace to her broken heart, and virgin grave!"

5 She was the child of Passion, and of Shame,
    English her father, and of noble birth;
Though too obscure for good or evil fame,
    Her unknown mother faded from the earth.

And what that fair West Indian did betide,
10   None knew but he, who least of all might tell,—
But that she lived, and loved, and lonely died,
    And sent this orphan child with him to dwell.

Oh! that a fair, an innocent young face
    Should have a poison in its looks alone,
15 To raise up thoughts of sorrow and disgrace
    And shame most bitter, although not his own:

Cruel were they who flung that heavy shade
    Across the life whose days did but begin;
Cruel were they who crush'd her heart, and made
20   *Her* youth pay penance for *his* youth's wild sin:

Yet so it was;—among her father's friends
    A cold compassion made contempt seem light,
But in "the world," no justice e'er defends
    The victims of their tortuous wrong and
        right:—

25 And "moral England," striking down the weak,
    And smiling at the vices of the strong,
On her, poor child! her parent's guilt would wreak,
    And that which was her grievance, made her
        wrong.

The world she understood not; nor did they
30   Who made that world,—her, either, understand;
The very glory of her features' play
    Seem'd like the language of a foreign land;

The shadowy feelings, rich and wild and warm,
    That glow'd and mantled in her lovely face,—
35 The slight full beauty of her youthful form,
    Its gentle majesty, its pliant grace,—

The languid lustre of her speaking eye,
    The indolent smile of that bewitching mouth,
(Which more than all betray'd her natal sky,
40   And left us dreaming of the sunny South,)—

The passionate variation of her blood,
    Which rose and sank, as rise and sink the waves,
With every change of her most changeful mood,
    Shock'd sickly Fashion's pale and guarded slaves.

45 And so in this fair world she stood alone,
    An alien 'mid the ever-moving crowd,
A wandering stranger, nameless and unknown
    Her claim to human kindness disallow'd.

But oft would Passion's bold and burning gaze,
50   And Curiosity's set frozen stare,
Fix on her beauty in those early days,
    And coarsely thus her loveliness declare!

Which she would shrink from, as the gentle plant,
    Fern-leaved Mimosa[2] folds itself away;

---

[1] "She was of this world where the most beautiful things have the worst fate. She lived like the rose in the space of a morning."

[2] plant with yellow flowers and sensitive leaflets which droop when touched.

55 Suffering and sad;—for easy 'twas to daunt
     One who on earth had no protecting stay.

   And often to her eye's transparent lid
     The unshed tears would rise with sudden start,
   And sink again, as though by Reason chid,
60   Back to their gentle home, her wounded heart,

   Even as some gushing fountain idly wells
     Up to the prison of its marble side,
   Whose power the mounting wave forever quells,—
     So rose her tears—so stemm'd by virgin pride.

65 And so more lonely each succeeding day,
     As she her lot did better understand,
   She lived a life which had in it decay,
     A flower transplanted to too cold a land,—

   Which for a while gives out a hope of bloom,
70   Then fades and pines, because it may not feel
   The freedom and the warmth which gave it room
     The beauty of its nature to reveal.

   For vainly would the heart accept its lot,
     And rouse its strength to bear avow'd contempt,
75 Scorn *will* be felt as scorn—deserved or not—
     And from its bitter spell none stand exempt

   There is a basilisk[1] power in human eyes
     When they would look a fellow-creature down,
   Neath which the faint soul fascinated lies,
80   Struck by the cold sneer and the with'ring
       frown.

   But one there was among the cruel crowd,
     Whose nature *half* rebell'd against the chain,
   Which fashion flung around him; though too proud
     To own that slavery's weariness and pain.

85 Too proud; perhaps too weak; for Custom still
     Curbs with an iron bit the souls born free;
   They start and chafe, yet bend them to the will
     Of this most nameless ruler,—so did he.

   And even unto *him* the worldly brand
90   Which rested on her, half her charm effaced;
   Vainly all pure and radiant did she stand,—
     Even unto *him* she was a thing disgraced.

   Had she been early doom'd a cloister'd nun,
     To Heaven devoted by an holy vow—
95 His union with that poor deserted one
     Had seem'd not *more* impossible than now.

   He *could* have loved her—fervently and well;
     But still the cold world with its false allure,
   Bound his free liking in an icy spell,
100   And made its whole foundation insecure.

   But not like meaner souls, would he, to prove
     A vulgar admiration, her pursue;
   For though his glance after her would rove,
     As something beautiful, and strange, and new.

105 They were withdrawn if but her eye met his,
     Or, for an instant if their light remain'd,
   They soften'd into gentlest tenderness,
     As asking pardon that his look had pain'd.

   And she was nothing unto him,—nor he
110   Aught unto her; but each of each did dream
   In the still hours of thought, when we are free
     To quit the real world for things which seem.

   When in his heart Love's folded wings would stir,
     And bid his youth choose out a fitting mate,
115 *Against his will* his thoughts roam'd back to her,
     And all around seem'd blank and desolate.

---

[1] a fatal glance; derived from the legend of a mythical lizard-like creature with a lethal look and glance.

When, in his worldly haunts, a smother'd sigh
    Told he had won some lady of the land,
The dreaming glances of *his* earnest eye
120   Beheld far off the Creole orphan stand;

And to the beauty by his side he froze,
    As though she were not fair, nor he so young,
And turn'd on her such looks of cold repose
    As check'd the trembling accents of her tongue,

125 And bid her heart's dim passion seek to hide
    Its gathering strength, although the task be
        pain,
Lest she become that mock to woman's pride—
    A wretch that loves unwoo'd, and loves in vain.

So in his heart she dwelt,—as one may dwell
130   Upon the verge of a forbidden ground;
And oft he struggled hard to break the spell
    And banish her, but vain the effort found;

For still along the winding way which led
    Into his inmost soul, unbidden came
135 Her haunting form,—and he was visited
    By echoes soft of her unspoken name,

Through the long night, when those we love *seem*
        near,
    However cold, however far away,
Borne on the wings of floating dreams, which cheer
140   And give us strength to meet the struggling day.

And when in twilight hours *she* roved apart,
    Feeding her love-sick soul with visions fair,
The shadow of *his* eyes was on her heart,
    And the smooth masses of his shining hair

145 Rose in the glory of the evening light,
    And, where she wander'd glided, evermore,
A star which beam'd upon her world's lone night
    Where nothing glad had ever shone before.

But vague and girlish was that love,—no hope,
150   Even of familiar greeting, ever cross'd
Its innocent, but, oh! most boundless scope;
    She loved him,—and she knew her love was
        lost.

She gazed on him, as one from out a bark,
    Bound onward to a cold and distant strand,
155 Some lovely bay, some haven fair may mark,
    Stretching far inward to a sunnier land;

Who, knowing he must still sail on turns back
    To watch with dreaming and most mournful
        eyes
The ruffling foam which follows in his track,
160   Or the deep starlight of the shoreless skies.

Oh! many a hopeless love like this may be,—
    For love will live that never looks to win
Gems rashly lost in Passion's stormy sea,
    Not to be lifted forth when once cast in!

PART II

So time roll'd on, till suddenly that child
    Of southron clime and feelings, droop'd and
        pined;
Her cheek wax'd paler, and her eye grew wild,
    And from her youthful form all strength
        declined.

5 Twas then I knew her; late and vainly call'd
    To "minister unto a mind diseased,"—
When on her heart's faint sickness all things pall'd
    And the deep inward pain was never eased:

Her step was always gentle, but at last
10   It fell as lightly as a wither'd leaf
In autumn hours; and wheresoe'er she pass'd
    Smiles died away, she look'd so full of grief.

And more than ever from that world, where still
    Her father hoped to place her, she would shrink;

15 Loving to be alone, her thirst to fill
    From the sweet fountain where the dreamers
      drink.

One eve, beneath the acacia's waving bough,
    Wrapt in these lonely thoughts she sate and
      read;
Her dark hair parted from her sunny brow,
20   Her graceful arm beneath her languid head;

And droopingly and sad she hung above
    The open page, whereon her eyes were bent,
With looks of fond regret and pining love;
    Nor heard my step, so deep was she intent.

25 And when she me perceived, she did not start,
    But lifted up those soft dark eyes to mine,
And smiled, (that mournful smile which breaks the
      heart!)
    Then glanced again upon the printed line.

"What readest thou?" I ask'd. With fervent gaze,
30   As though she would have scann'd my inmost
      soul,
She turn'd to me, and, as a child obeys
    The accustom'd question of revered control,

She pointed to the title of that book,
    (Which, bending down, I saw was "Coralie,"
35 Then gave me one imploring piteous look,
    And tears, too long restrain'd, gush'd fast and
      free.

It was a tale of one, whose fate had been
    Too like her own to make that weeping strange;
Like her, transplanted from a sunnier scene;
40   Like her, all dull'd and blighted by the change.

No further word was breathed between us two;—
    No confidence was made to keep or break;—
But since that day, which pierced my soul quite
      thro',
    My hand the dying girl would faintly take,

45 And murmur, as its grasp (ah! piteous end!)
    Return'd the feeble pressure of her own,
"Be with me to the last,—for thou, dear friend,
    Hast all my struggles, all my sorrow known!"

She died!—The pulse of that untrammell'd heart
50   Fainted to stillness. Those most glorious eyes
Closed on the world where she had dwelt apart
    And her cold bosom heaved no further sighs.

She died!—and no one mourn'd except her sire,
    Who for a while look'd out with eyes more dim;
55 Lone was her place beside his household fire,
    Vanish'd the face that ever smiled on him.

And no one said to him—"Why mournest thou?"
    Because she was the unknown child of shame;
(Albeit her mother better kept the vow
60   Of faithful love, than some who keep their
      fame.)

Poor mother, and poor child!—unvalued lives!
    Wan leaves that perish'd in obscurest shade!
While round me still the proud world stirs and
      strives,
    Say, Shall I weep that ye are lowly laid?

65 Shall *I* mourn for ye? No!—and least for thee,
    Young dreamer, whose pure heart gave way
      before
Thy bark was launch'd upon Love's stormy sea,
    Or treachery wreck'd it on the farther shore.

Least, least of all for thee! Thou art gone hence?
70   Thee never more shall scornful looks oppress,
Thee the world wrings not with some vain pretence,
    Nor chills thy tears, nor mocks at thy distress.

From man's unjustice, from the cold award
    Of the unfeeling thou hast pass'd away;

75 Thou 'rt at the gates of light where angels guard
    Thy path to realms of bright eternal day.

There shall thy soul its chains of slavery burst,
    There, meekly standing before God's high
        throne,
Thou'lt find the judgments of our earth reversed,
80   And answer for no errors but thine own.
    —1840

The Poet's Choice

'Twas in youth, that hour of dreaming;
  Round me, visions fair were beaming,
Golden fancies, brightly gleaming,
      Such as start to birth
5 When the wandering restless mind,
Drunk with beauty, thinks to find
Creatures of a fairy kind
      Realized on Earth!

Then, for me, in every dell
10 Hamadryads[1] seem'd to dwell
(They who die, as Poet's tell,
      Each with her own tree);
And sweet mermaids, low reclining,
Dim light through their grottos shining,
15 Green weeds round their soft limbs twining,
      Peopled the deep Sea.

Then, when moon and stars were fair,
Nymph-like visions fill'd the air,
With blue wings and golden hair
20   Bending from the skies;
And each cave by echo haunted
In its depth of shadow granted,

Brightly, the Egeria[2] wanted,
      To my eager eyes.

25 But those glories pass'd away;
Earth seem'd left to dull decay,
And my heart in sadness lay,
      Desolate, uncheer'd;
Like one wrapt in painful sleeping,
30 Pining, thirsting, waking, weeping,
Watch thro' Life's dark midnight keeping,
      Till THY form appear'd!

THEN my soul, whose erring measure
Knew not where to find true pleasure,
35 Woke and seized the golden treasure
      Of thy human love;
And looking on thy radiant brow,
My lips in gladness breathed the vow
Which angels, not more fair than thou,
40   Have register'd above.

And now I take my quiet rest,
With my head upon thy breast,
I will make no further quest
      In Fancy's realms of light;
45 Fay, nor nymph, nor winged spirit,
Shall my store of love inherit;
More thy mortal charm doth merit
      Than dream, however bright.

And my soul, like some sweet bird
50 Whose song at summer eve is heard,
When the breeze, so lightly stirr'd,
      Leaves the branch unbent,—
Sits and all triumphant sings,
Folding up her brooding wings,
55 And gazing out on earthly things
      With a calm content.
    —1840

[1] a wood nymph whose life was intertwined with that of the tree she lived in.

[2] a nymph who advised and dictated laws to Numa, the second king of Rome.

Edward FitzGerald
1809 – 1883

Edward FitzGerald, poet and translator, graduated from Trinity College, Cambridge, in 1830. He is best known for his adaptation and translation of the *Rubáiyát* of *Omar Khayyám* (1859), which initiated Robert Browning's reply in "Rabbi Ben Ezra" (1864).

❧❧❧

Rubáiyát of Omar Khayyám [1]

1

Wake! For the Sun, who scattered into flight
    The Stars before him from the Field of Night,
Drives Night along with them from Heav'n
        and strikes
The Sultán's Turret with a Shaft of Light.

2

5 Before the phantom of False morning[2] died,
Methought a Voice within the Tavern cried,
    "When all the Temple is prepared within,
Why nod the drowsy Worshiper outside?"

3

And, as the Cock crew, those who stood before
10 The Tavern shouted—"Open, then, the Door!
    You know how little while we have to stay,
And, once departed, may return no more."

4

Now the New Year[3] reviving old Desires,
The thoughtful Soul to Solitude retires,

15 Where the WHITE HAND OF MOSES on the
        Bough[4]
Puts out, and Jesus from the Ground suspires.[5]

5

Iram[6] indeed is gone with all his Rose,
And Jamshyd's[7] Sevn'-ringed Cup where no one
        knows;
    But still a Ruby kindles in the Vine,
20 And many a Garden by the Water blows.

6

And David's lips are locked; but in divine
High-piping Pehlevi,[8] with "Wine! Wine! Wine!
    Red Wine!"—the Nightingale cries to the Rose
That sallow cheek of hers to incarnadine.

7

25 Come, fill the Cup, and in the fire of Spring
Your Winter-garment of Repentance fling;
    The Bird of Time has but a little way
To flutter—and the Bird is on the Wing.

---

[1] Omar Khayyám, or Omar the Tent-maker, was a Persian poet and astronomer of the eleventh century. *Rubáiyát* is the plural form of *rubai*, or quatrain.

[2] "A transient light on the Horizon about an hour before the…True Dawn; a well-known phenomenon in the East." (FitzGerald's note.)

[3] The Persian New Year begins with the vernal equinox.

---

[4] See Exodus 4:6.

[5] The Persians believed that the healing power of Jesus resided in his breath.

[6] "A royal Garden now sunk somewhere in the Sands of Arabia." (FitzGerald's note.)

[7] a legendary king of Persia; his seven-ringed cup symbolized the seven heavens, the seven planets, the seven seas, etc.

[8] David the holy singer; Pehlevi is the ancient literary language of Persia.

8

Whether at Naishápur[1] or Babylon,
Whether the Cup with sweet or bitter run,
　　The Wine of Life keeps oozing drop by drop,
The Leaves of Life keep falling one by one.

9

Each Morn a thousand Roses brings, you say;
Yes, but where leaves the Rose of Yesterday?
　　And this first Summer month that brings the Rose
Shall take Jamshyd and Kaikobad[2] away.

10

Well, let it take them! What have we to do
With Kaikobád the Great, or Kaikhosru?[3]
　　Let Zál and Rustum[4] bluster as they will,
Or Hátim[5] call to Supper—heed not you.

11

With me along the strip of Herbage strown
That just divides the desert from the sown,
　　Where name of Slave and Sultán is forgot—
And Peace to Mahmúd[6] on his golden Throne!

12

A Book of Verses underneath the Bough,
A Jug of Wine, a Loaf of Bread—and Thou
　　Beside me singing in the Wilderness—
Oh, Wilderness were Paradise enow!

13

Some for the glories of This World; and some
Sigh for the Prophet's[7] Paradise to come;
　　Ah, take the Cash, and let the Credit go,
Nor heed the rumble of a distant Drum![8]

14

Look to the blowing Rose about us—"Lo,
Laughing," she says, "into the world I blow,
　　At once the silken tassel of my Purse
Tear, and its Treasure[9] on the Garden throw."

15

And those who husbanded the Golden Grain,
And those who flung it to the winds like Rain,
　　Alike to no such aureate Earth are turned
As, buried once, Men want dug up again.

16

The Worldly Hope men set their Hearts upon
Turns Ashes—or it prospers; and anon,
　　Like Snow upon the Desert's dusty Face,
Lighting a little hour or two—is gone.

17

Think, in this battered Caravanserai[10]
Whose Portals are alternate Night and Day,
　　How Sultán after Sultán with his Pomp
Abode his destined Hour, and went his way.

18

They say the Lion and the Lizard keep
The Courts where Jamshyd gloried and drank deep;

[1] the village in Persia where Omar was born.

[2] the founder of a celebrated dynasty.

[3] King.

[4] son and father who were warriors.

[5] according to FitzGerald, "a type of oriental generosity."

[6] a sultan who conquered India.

[7] Muhammad's.

[8] "A Drum—beaten outside a Palace." (FitzGerald's note.)

[9] "The Rose's Golden Centre." (FitzGerald's note.)

[10] an Oriental inn.

And Bahrám,[1] that great Hunter—the Wild
    Ass
Stamps o'er his Head, but cannot break his Sleep.

19

I sometimes think that never blows so red
The Rose as where some buried Caesar[2] bled;
75   That every Hyacinth[3] the Garden wears
Dropped in her Lap from some once lovely Head.

20

And this reviving Herb whose tender Green
Fledges the River-Lip on which we lean—
    Ah, lean upon it lightly! for who knows
80 From what once lovely Lip it springs unseen!

21

Ah my Belovèd, fill the Cup that clears
TODAY of past Regrets and future Fears:
    Tomorrow!—Why, Tomorrow I may be
Myself with Yesterday's Sev'n thousand Years.

22

85 For some we loved, the loveliest and the best
That from his Vintage rolling Time hath pressed,
    Have drunk their Cup a Round or two before,
And one by one crept silently to rest.

23

And we, that now make merry in the Room
90 They left, and Summer dresses in new bloom,
    Ourselves must we beneath the Couch of Earth
Descend—ourselves to make a Couch—for whom?

24

Ah, make the most of what we yet may spend,
Before we too into the Dust descend;
95   Dust into Dust, and under Dust to lie,
Sans Wine, sans Song, sans Singer, and—sans End!

25

Alike for those who for TODAY prepare,
And those that after some TOMORROW stare,
    A Muezzín[4] from the Tower of Darkness cries,
100 "Fools, your Reward is neither Here nor There."

26

Why, all the Saints and Sages who discussed
Of the Two Worlds so wisely—they are thrust
    Like foolish Prophets forth; their Words to Scorn
Are scattered, and their Mouths are stopped with
    Dust.[5]

27

105 Myself when young did eagerly frequent
Doctor and Saint, and heard great argument
    About it and about; but evermore
Came out by the same door where in I went.

28

With them the seed of Wisdom did I sow,
110 And with mine own hand wrought to make it
    grow;
    And this was all the Harvest that I reaped—
"I came like Water, and like Wind I go."

29

Into this Universe, and *Why* not knowing
Nor *Whence*, like Water willy-nilly flowing;
115   And out of it, as Wind along the Waste,
I know not *Whither*, willy-nilly blowing.

---

[1] a Persian ruler who died in a swamp while pursuing a wild ass.

[2] Roman general and dictator (102?–44 BC).

[3] Hyacinthus, in Greek mythology, was a youth accidentally killed by his friend Apollo; the hyacinth flower sprang up where Hyacinthus's blood had flowed.

---

[4] the officer who calls the faithful to prayer from a tower of the Mosque.

[5] The Muslims threw dust into the air to confound enemies of the faith.

30

What, without asking, hither hurried *Whence?*
And, without asking, *Whither* hurried hence!
 Oh, many a Cup of this forbidden Wine[1]
Must drown the memory of that insolence!

31

Up from the Earth's Center through the Seventh
 Gate
I rose, and on the Throne of Saturn[2] sate,
 And many a Knot unraveled by the Road;
But not the Master-knot of Human Fate.

32

There was the Door to which I found no Key;
There was the Veil through which I might not see;
 Some little talk awhile of ME and THEE[3]
There was—and then no more of THEE and ME.

33

Earth could not answer; nor the Seas that mourn
In flowring Purple, of their Lord forlorn;
 Nor rolling Heaven, with all his Signs[4] revealed
And hidden by the sleeve of Night and Morn.

34

Then of the THEE IN ME who works behind
The Veil, I lifted up my hands to find
 A lamp amid the Darkness; and I heard,
As from Without—"THE ME WITHIN THEE
 BLIND!"

35

Then to the Lip of this poor earthen Urn
I leaned, the Secret of my Life to learn;

And Lip to Lip it murmured—"While you live,
Drink!—for, once dead, you never shall return."

36

I think the Vessel, that with fugitive
Articulation answered, once did live,
 And drink; and Ah! the passive Lip I kissed,
And many Kisses might it take—and give!

37

For I remember stopping by the way
To watch a Potter thumping his wet Clay;[5]
 And with its all-obliterated Tongue
It murmured—"Gently, Brother, gently, pray!"

38

And has not such a Story from of Old
Down Man's successive generations rolled
 Of such a clod of saturated Earth
Cast by the Maker into Human mold?

39

And not a drop that from our Cups we throw
For Earth to drink of,[6] but may steal below
 To quench the fire of Anguish in some Eye
There hidden—far beneath, and long ago.

40

As then the Tulip, for her morning sup
Of Heav'nly Vintage, from the soil looks up,
 Do you devoutly do the like, till Heav'n
To Earth invert you—like an empty Cup.

41

Perplexed no more with Human or Divine,
Tomorrow's tangle to the winds resign,

---

[1] Alcohol is forbidden to faithful Moslems.

[2] the seat of knowledge. According to the ancients, Saturn was lord of the seventh of the concentric spheres or heavens surrounding the earth.

[3] "Some dividual [sic] Existence or Personality distinct from the whole." (FitzGerald's note.)

[4] of the zodiac.

[5] Compare Robert Browning's "Rabbi ben Ezra," ll. 26–27.

[6] the custom of pouring some wine on the ground before drinking. "The precious Liquor is not lost, but sinks into the ground to refresh the dust of some poor Wine-worshipper foregone." (FitzGerald's note.)

And lose your fingers in the tresses of
The Cypress-slender Minister of Wine.[1]

42

165 And if the Wine you drink, the Lip you press,
End in what All begins and ends in—Yes;
    Think then you are TODAY what YESTERDAY
You were—TOMORROW you shall not be less.

43

So when that Angel of the darker Drink
170 At last shall find you by the river brink,
    And offering his Cup, invite your Soul
Forth to your Lips to quaff—you shall not shrink.

44

Why, if the Soul can fling the Dust aside,
And naked on the Air of Heaven ride,
175   Were 't not a Shame—were 't not a Shame for
        him
In this clay carcass crippled to abide?

45

'Tis but a Tent where takes his one day's rest
A Sultán to the realm of Death addressed;
    The Sultán rises, and the dark Ferrásh[2]
180 Strikes, and prepares it for another Guest.

46

And fear not lest Existence closing your
Account, and mine, should know the like no more;
    The Eternal Sáki from that Bowl has poured
Millions of Bubbles like us, and will pour.

47

185 When You and I behind the Veil are past,
Oh, but the long, long while the World shall last,
    Which of our Coming and Departure heeds
As the Sea's self should heed a pebble-cast.

48

A Moment's Halt—a momentary taste
190 Of BEING from the Well amid the Waste—
    And Lo!—the phantom Caravan has reached
The NOTHING it set out from—Oh, make haste!

49

Would you that spangle of Existence spend
About THE SECRET—quick about it, Friend!
195   A Hair perhaps divides the False and True—
And upon what, prithee, may life depend?

50

A Hair perhaps divides the False and True—
Yes; and a single Alif[3] were the clue—
    Could you but find it—to the Treasure-house,
200 And peradventure to THE MASTER too;

51

Whose secret Presence, through Creation's veins
Running Quicksilver-like, eludes your pains;
    Taking all shapes from Máh to Máhi,[4] and
They change and perish all—but He remains;

52

205 A moment guessed—then back behind the Fold
Immersed of Darkness round the Drama rolled
    Which, for the Pastime of Eternity,
He doth Himself contrive, enact, behold.

53

But if in vain, down on the stubborn floor
210 Of Earth, and up to Heav'n's unopening Door,
    You gaze TODAY, while You are You—how
        then
TOMORROW, You when shall be You no more?

---

[1] woman servant who passes the wine.

[2] servant who takes down the tent.

---

[3] a simple vertical line, the first letter of the Arabic alphabet.

[4] "From Fish to Moon." (FitzGerald's note.)

54

Waste not your Hour, nor in the vain pursuit
Of This and That endeavor and dispute;
215   Better be jocund with the fruitful Grape
Than sadden after none, or bitter, Fruit.

55

You know, my Friends, with what a brave Carouse
I made a Second Marriage in my house;
    Divorced old barren Reason from my Bed,
220 And took the Daughter of the Vine to Spouse.

56

For "IS" and "IS-NOT" though with Rule and Line,
And "UP-AND-DOWN" by Logic, I define,
    Of all that one should care to fathom, I
Was never deep in anything but—Wine.

57

225 Ah, but my Computations, People say
Reduced the Year to better reckoning?[1]—Nay,
    'Twas only striking from the Calendar
Unborn Tomorrow, and dead Yesterday.

58

And lately, by the Tavern Door agape,
230 Came shining through the Dusk an Angel Shape
    Bearing a Vessel on his Shoulder; and
He bid me taste of it; and 'twas—the Grape!

59

The Grape that can with Logic absolute
The Two-and-Seventy jarring Sects,[2] confute;
235   The sovereign Alchemist that in a trice
Life's leaden metal into Gold transmute;

60

The mighty Mahmúd, Allah-breathing Lord,
That all the misbelieving and black Horde[3]
    Of Fears and Sorrows that infest the Soul
240 Scatters before him with his whirlwind Sword.

61

Why, be this Juice the growth of God, who dare
Blaspheme the twisted tendril as a Snare?
    A Blessing, we should use it, should we not?
And if a Curse—why, then, Who set it there?

62

245 I must abjure the Balm of Life, I must,
Scared by some After-reckoning ta'en on trust
    Or lured with Hope of some Diviner Drink,
To fill the Cup—when crumbled into Dust!

63

Oh threats of Hell and Hopes of Paradise!
250 One thing at least is certain—*This* Life flies;
    One thing is certain and the rest is Lies—
The Flower that once has blown forever dies.

64

Strange, is it not? that of the myriads who
Before us passed the door of Darkness through,
255   Not one returns to tell us of the Road,
Which to discover we must travel too.

65

The Revelations of Devout and Learn'd
Who rose before us, and as Prophets burned,[4]
    Are all but Stories, which, awoke from Sleep,
260 They told their comrades, and to Sleep returned.

---

[1] a mathematician, Omar devised a reformed calendar.

[2] "The 72 religions supposed to divide the world." (FitzGerald's note.)

[3] "Alluding to Sultan Mahmud's Conquest of India and its dark people." (FitzGerald's note.)

[4] burning zeal to spread the prophecies.

66

I sent my Soul through the Invisible,
Some letter of that After-life to spell;
      And by and by my Soul returned to me,
And answered, "I Myself am Heav'n and Hell"—

67

265 Heaven but the Vision of fulfilled Desire,
And Hell the Shadow from a Soul on fire
      Cast on the Darkness into which Ourselves,
So late emerged from, shall so soon expire.

68

We are no other than a moving row
270 Of Magic Shadow-shapes that come and go
      Round with the Sun-illumined Lantern held
In Midnight by the Master of the Show;

69

But helpless Pieces of the Game He plays
Upon this Checkerboard of Nights and Days;
275   Hither and thither moves, and checks, and slays,
And one by one back in the Closet lays.

70

The Ball no question makes of Ayes and Noes,
But Here or There as strikes the Player[1] goes;
      And He that tossed you down into the Field,
280 *He* knows about it all—HE knows—HE knows!

71

The Moving Finger writes, and, having writ,
Moves on; nor all your Piety nor Wit
      Shall lure it back to cancel half a Line,
Nor all your Tears wash out a Word of it.

72

285 And that inverted Bowl they call the Sky,
Whereunder crawling cooped we live and die,

Lift not your hands to *It* for help—for It
As impotently moves as you or I.

73

With Earth's first Clay They did the Last Man
      knead,
290 And there of the Last Harvest sowed the Seed;
      And the first Morning of Creation wrote
What the Last Dawn of Reckoning shall read.

74

YESTERDAY *This* Day's Madness did prepare;
TOMORROW'S Silence, Triumph, or Despair.
295   Drink! for you know not whence you came, nor
      why;
Drink, for you know not why you go, nor where.

75

I tell you this—When, started from the Goal,
Over the flaming shoulders of the Foal
      Of Heav'n Parwín and Mustarí they flung,
300 In my predestined Plot of Dust and Soul.[2]

76

The Vine had struck a fiber; which about
If clings my Being—let the Dervish[3] flout;
      Of my Base metal may be filed a Key.
That shall unlock the Door he howls without.

77

305 And this I know: whether the one True Light
Kindle to Love, or Wrath—consume me quite.
      One Flash of It within the Tavern caught
Better than in the Temple lost outright.

---

[1] polo player.

---

[2] The speaker's fate was predestined, and related to the relationship of
the stars and planets, the Pleiades (Parwin) and Jupiter (Mushtari), which
were "flung" by the Gods.

[3] an ascetic who would despise alcohol as a means of perceiving truth.

78

What! out of senseless Nothing to provoke
310 A conscious Something to resent the yoke
    Of unpermitted Pleasure, under pain
Of Everlasting Penalties, if broke!

79

What! from his helpless Creature be repaid
Pure Gold for what he lent him dross-allayed—
315   Sue for a Debt he never did contract,
And cannot answer—Oh, the sorry trade!

80

O Thou, who didst with pitfall and with gin[1]
Beset the Road I was to wander in,
    Thou wilt not with Predestined Evil round
320 Enmesh, and then impute my Fall to Sin!

81

O Thou, who Man of Baser Earth didst make.
And ev'n with Paradise devise the Snake,
    For all the Sin wherewith the Face of Man
Is blackened—Man's forgiveness give—and take!

82

325 As under cover of departing Day
Slunk hunger-stricken Ramazán[2] away,
    Once more within the Potter's house alone
I stood, surrounded by the Shapes of Clay—

83

Shapes of all Sorts and Sizes, great and small
330 That stood along the floor and by the wall;
    And some loquacious Vessels were; and some
Listened perhaps, but never talked at all.

84

Said one among them—"Surely not in vain
My substance of the common Earth was ta'en
335   And to this Figure molded, to be broke,
Or trampled back to shapeless Earth again."

85

Then said a Second—"Ne'er a peevish Boy
Would break the Bowl from which he drank in joy;
    And He that with his hand the Vessel made
340 Will surely not in after Wrath destroy."

86

After a momentary silence spake
Some Vessel of a more ungainly Make:
    "They sneer at me for leaning all awry;
What! did the Hand, then, of the Potter shake?"

87

345 Whereat someone of the loquacious Lot—
I think a Súfi[3] pipkin—waxing hot—
    "All this of Pot and Potter—Tell me then,
Who is the Potter, pray, and who the Pot?"

88

"Why," said another, "Some there are who tell
350 Of one who threatens he will toss to Hell
    The luckless Pots he marred in making—Pish!
He's a Good Fellow, and 'twill all be well."

89

"Well," murmured one, "Let whoso make or buy,
My Clay with long Oblivion is gone dry;
355   But fill me with the old familiar Juice,
Methinks I might recover by and by."

[1] trap.

[2] the month of fasting between sunrise and sunset.

[3] Persian mystic.

90

So while the Vessels one by one were speaking
The little Moon looked in that all were seeking;[1]
    And then they jogged each other, "Brother!
    Brother!
360 Now for the Porter's shoulder-knot[2] a-creaking!"

————

91

Ah, with the Grape my fading Life provide,
And wash the Body whence the Life has died,
    And lay me, shrouded in the living Leaf,
By some not unfrequented Garden-side—

92

365 That ev'n my buried Ashes such a snare
Of Vintage shall fling up into the Air
    As not a True-believer passing by
But shall be overtaken unaware.

93

Indeed the Idols I have loved so long
370 Have done my credit in this World much wrong,
    Have drowned my Glory in a shallow Cup,
And sold my Reputation for a Song.

94

Indeed, indeed, Repentance oft before
I swore—but was I sober when I swore?
375   And then and then came Spring, and Rose-in-
        hand
My threadbare Penitence apieces tore.

95

And much as Wine has played the Infidel,
And robbed me of my Robe of Honor—Well,
    I wonder often what the Vintners buy
380 One-half so precious as the stuff they sell.

————

[1] "At the close of the Fasting Month, Ramazán...the first Glimpse of the new Moon...is looked for with the utmost Anxiety and hailed with all Acclamation." (FitzGerald's note.)

[2] straps on which the wine jars were carried by the porter.

96

Yet Ah, that Spring should vanish with the Rose!
That Youth's sweet-scented manuscript should close!
    The Nightingale that in the branches sang,
Ah whence, and whither flown again, who knows!

97

385 Would but the Desert of the Fountain yield
One glimpse—if dimly, yet indeed, revealed,
    To which the fainting Traveler might spring,
As springs the trampled herbage of the field.

98

Would but some wingèd Angel ere too late
390 Arrest the yet unfolded Roll of Fate,
    And make the stern Recorder otherwise
Enregister, or quite obliterate!

99

Ah, Love! could you and I with Him conspire
To grasp this sorry Scheme of Things entire,
395   Would not we shatter it to bits—and then
Remold it nearer to the Heart's Desire!

————

100

Yon rising Moon that looks for us again—
How oft hereafter will she wax and wane;
    How oft hereafter rising look for us
400 Through this same Garden—and for *one* in vain!

101

And when like her, O Sákí, you shall pass
Among the Guests Star-scattered on the Grass,
    And in your joyous errand reach the spot
Where I made One—turn down an empty Glass!

TAMÁM[3]

—1859, 1889 (1857)

[3] "It is ended."

Alfred Tennyson
1809–1892

Alfred Tennyson was the most popular and prolific of Victorian poets. While Robert Browning was struggling to find his poetic voice, and an audience, as late as 1850, Tennyson in that year became Poet Laureate. Born into a large family marked by poverty and madness, Tennyson survived a difficult childhood and entered Trinity College, Cambridge, in 1827. There he met and befriended Arthur Henry Hallam, whose death in 1833 occasioned Tennyson's most important poem, *In Memoriam A.H.H.* (1850). With Hallam, Tennyson was a member of the informal debating and discussion group, the Cambridge Apostles. There is no doubt that discussions in this group influenced *Poems, Chiefly Lyrical* (1830), and *Poems* (1832). Stung by hostile critical reaction, and suffering from Hallam's loss, Tennyson spent the years from 1833 to 1850 writing *In Memoriam*, revising his early poetry and writing a number of new poems, all for inclusion in the two volumes published as *Poems* in 1842. His poetic productivity, including *Idylls of the King* (1859–74), continued until his death.

❦

Mariana [1]

With blackest moss the flower-plots
    Were thickly crusted, one and all:
The rusted nails fell from the knots
    That held the pear to the gable-wall.
5 The broken sheds looked sad and strange:
    Unlifted was the clinking latch;
    Weeded and worn the ancient thatch
Upon the lonely moated grange.
        She only said, "My life is dreary,
10   He cometh not," she said;
        She said, "I am aweary, aweary,
          I would that I were dead!"

Her tears fell with the dews at even;
    Her tears fell ere the dews were dried;
15 She could not look on the sweet heaven,
    Either at morn or eventide.
After the flitting of the bats,
    When thickest dark did trance[2] the sky,
    She drew her casement-curtain by,

20 And glanced athwart the glooming flats.
        She only said, "The night is dreary,
          He cometh not," she said;
        She said, "I am aweary, aweary,
          I would that I were dead!"

25 Upon the middle of the night,
    Waking she heard the night-fowl crow:
The cock sung out an hour ere light:
    From the dark fen the oxen's low
Came to her: without hope of change,
30   In sleep she seemed to walk forlorn,
    Till cold winds woke the gray-eyed morn
About the lonely moated grange.
        She only said, "The day is dreary,
          He cometh not," she said;
35   She said, "I am aweary, aweary,
          I would that I were dead!"

About a stone-cast from the wall
    A sluice with blackened waters slept,
And o'er it many, round and small,
40   The clustered marish-mosses crept.
Hard by a poplar shook alway,
    All silver-green with gnarlèd bark:
    For leagues no other tree did mark
The level waste, the rounding gray.

---

[1] For a detailed presentation of materials related to Tennyson's poems, sources, annotations, textural variants, etc., see *The Poems of Tennyson*, ed. Christopher Ricks, 2nd ed., 3 vols.(Berkeley: University of California Press, 1987).

[2] to throw into a trance.

45 She only said, "My life is dreary,
      He cometh not," she said;
   She said, "I am aweary, aweary,
      I would that I were dead!"

   And ever when the moon was low;
50   And the shrill winds were up and away,
   In the white curtain, to and fro,
      She saw the gusty shadow sway.
   But when the moon was very low,
      And wild winds bound within their cell,
55   The shadow of the poplar fell
   Upon her bed, across her brow.
      She only said, "The night is dreary,
         He cometh not," she said;
      She said, "I am aweary, aweary.
60   I would that I were dead!"

   All day within the dreamy house,
      The doors upon their hinges creaked;
   The blue fly sung in the pane; the mouse
      Behind the mouldering wainscot shrieked,
65   Or from the crevice peered about.
      Old faces glimmered through the doors,
      Old footsteps trod the upper floors,
   Old voices called her from without.
      She only said, "My life is dreary,
70   He cometh not," she said;
      She said, "I am aweary, aweary,
      I would that I were dead!"

   The sparrow's chirrup on the roof,
      The slow clock ticking, and the sound
75 Which to the wooing wind aloof
      The poplar made, did all confound
   Her sense; but most she loathed the hour
      When the thick-moted sunbeam lay
   Athwart the chambers, and the day
80 Was sloping toward his western bower.
      Then, said she, "I am very dreary,
         He will not come," she said;

      She wept, "I am aweary, aweary,
         Oh God, that I were dead!"
—1830

Supposed Confessions of a Second-Rate Sensitive Mind [1]

O God! my God! have mercy now.
  I faint, I fall. Men say that Thou
Didst die for me, for such as *me*,
Patient of ill, and death, and scorn,
5 And that my sin was as a thorn
Among the thorns that girt Thy brow,
Wounding Thy soul.—That even now,
In this extremest misery
Of ignorance, I should require
10 A sign! and if a bolt of fire
Would rive the slumbrous summer noon
While I do pray to Thee alone,
Think my belief would stronger grow!
Is not my human pride brought low?
15 The boastings of my spirit still?
The joy I had in my freewill
All cold, and dead, and corpse-like grown?
And what is left to me, but Thou,
And faith in Thee? Men pass me by;
20 Christians with happy countenances—
And children all seem full of Thee!
And women smile with saint-like glances
Like Thine own mother's when she bowed
Above Thee, on that happy morn
25 When angels spake to men aloud,
And Thou and peace to earth were born.
Goodwill to me as well as all—
I one of them: my brothers they:
Brothers in Christ—a world of peace
30 And confidence, day after day;
And trust and hope till things should cease,
And then one Heaven receive us all.

---

[1] published in 1830 with the longer title "...Mind Not In Unity With Itself"; not reprinted until restored in 1884.

How sweet to have a common faith!
To hold a common scorn of death!
35 And at a burial to hear
The creaking cords which wound and eat
Into my human heart, whene'er
Earth goes to earth, with grief, not fear,
With hopeful grief, were passing sweet!

40 Thrice happy state again to be
The trustful infant on the knee!
Who lets his rosy fingers play
About his mother's neck, and knows
Nothing beyond his mother's eyes.
45 They comfort him by night and day;
They light his little life alway;
He hath no thought of coming woes;
He hath no care of life or death;
Scarce outward signs of joy arise,
50 Because the Spirit of happiness
And perfect rest so inward is;
And loveth so his innocent heart,
Her temple and her place of birth,
Where she would ever wish to dwell,
55 Life of the fountain there, beneath
Its salient springs, and far apart,
Hating to wander out on earth,
Or breathe into the hollow air,
Whose chillness would make visible
60 Her subtil, warm, and golden breath,
Which mixing with the infant's blood,
Fulfils him with beatitude.
Oh! sure it is a special care
Of God, to fortify from doubt,
65 To arm in proof,[1] and guard about
With triple-mailèd trust, and clear
Delight, the infant's dawning year.

Would that my gloomèd fancy were
As thine, my mother, when with brows
70 Propt on thy knees, my hands upheld

In thine, I listened to thy vows,
For me outpoured in holiest prayer—
For me unworthy!—and beheld
Thy mild deep eyes upraised, that knew
75 The beauty and repose of faith,
And the clear spirit shining through.
Oh! wherefore do we grow awry
From roots which strike so deep? why dare
Paths in the desert? Could not I
80 Bow myself down, where thou hast knelt,
To the earth—until the ice would melt
Here, and I feel as thou hast felt?
What Devil had the heart to scathe
Flowers thou hadst reared—to brush the dew
85 From thine own lily, when thy grave
Was deep, my mother, in the clay?
Myself? Is it thus? Myself? Had I
So little love for thee? But why
Prevailed not thy pure prayers? Why pray
90 To one who heeds not, who can save
But will not? Great in faith, and strong
Against the grief of circumstance
Wert thou, and yet unheard. What if
Thou pleadest still, and seest me drive
95 Through utter dark a full-sailed skiff,
Unpiloted i' the echoing dance
Of reboant[2] whirlwinds, stooping low
Unto the death, not sunk! I know
At matins and at evensong,
100 That thou, if thou wert yet alive,
In deep and daily prayers wouldst strive
To reconcile me with thy God.
Albeit, my hope is gray, and cold
At heart, thou wouldest murmur still—
105 "Bring this lamb back into Thy fold,
My Lord, if so it be Thy will."
Wouldst tell me I must brook the rod
And chastisement of human pride;
That pride, the sin of devils, stood

---

[1] armour.

[2] re-bellowing.

110 Betwixt me and the light of God!
That hitherto I had defied
And had rejected God—that grace
Would drop from his o'er-brimming love,
As manna on my wilderness,
115 If I would pray—that God would move
And strike the hard, hard rock,[1] and thence,
Sweet in their utmost bitterness,
Would issue tears of penitence
Which would keep green hope's life. Alas!
120 I think that pride hath now no place
Nor sojourn in me. I am void,
Dark, formless, utterly destroyed.
Why not believe then? Why not yet
Anchor thy frailty there, where man
125 Hath moored and rested? Ask the sea
At midnight, when the crisp slope[2] waves
After a tempest, rib and fret
The broad-imbasèd beach, why he
Slumbers not like a mountain tarn?
130 Wherefore his ridges are not curls
And ripples of an inland mere?
Wherefore he moaneth thus, nor can
Draw down into his vexèd pools
All that blue heaven which hues and paves
135 The other? I am too forlorn,
Too shaken: my own weakness fools
My judgment, and my spirit whirls,
Moved from beneath with doubt and fear.

"Yet," said I, in my morn of youth,
140 The unsunned freshness of my strength,
When I went forth in quest of truth,
"It is man's privilege to doubt,
If so be that from doubt at length,
Truth may stand forth unmoved of change,
145 An image with profulgent brows,
And perfect limbs, as from the storm

Of running fires and fluid range
Of lawless airs, at last stood out
This excellence and solid form
150 Of constant beauty. For the Ox
Feeds in the herb, and sleeps, or fills
The horned valleys all about,
And hollows of the fringed hills
In summer heats, with placid lows
155 Unfearing, till his own blood flows
About his hoof. And in the flocks
The lamb rejoiceth in the year,
And raceth freely with his fere,[3]
And answers to his mother's calls
160 From the flowered furrow. In a time,
Of which he wots not, run short pains
Through his warm heart; and then, from whence
He knows not, on his light there falls
A shadow; and his native slope,
165 Where he was wont to leap and climb,
Floats from his sick and filmed eyes,
And something in the darkness draws
His forehead earthward, and he dies.
Shall man live thus, in joy and hope
170 As a young lamb, who cannot dream,
Living, but that he shall live on?
Shall we not look into the laws
Of life and death, and things that seem,
And things that be, and analyse
175 Our double nature, and compare
All creeds till we have found the one,
If one there be?" Ay me! I fear
All may not doubt, but everywhere
Some must clasp Idols. Yet, my God,
180 Whom call I Idol? Let Thy dove
Shadow me over,[4] and my sins
Be unremembered, and Thy love
Enlighten me. Oh teach me yet
Somewhat before the heavy clod

---

[1] Numbers 20:2.

[2] sloping.

[3] companion.

[4] to protect with wings.

185 Weighs on me, and the busy fret
Of that sharp-headed worm begins
In the gross blackness underneath.

O weary life! O weary death!
O spirit and heart made desolate!
190 O damned vacillating state!
—1830

The Poet

The poet in a golden clime was born,
With golden stars above;
Dowered with the hate of hate, the scorn of scorn,
The love of love.

5 He saw through life and death, through good and
ill,
He saw through his own soul.
The marvel of the everlasting will,
An open scroll,

Before him lay: with echoing feet he threaded
10 The secretest walks of fame:
The viewless arrows of his thoughts were headed
And winged with flame,

Like Indian reeds blown[1] from his silver tongue,
And of so fierce a flight,
15 From Calpè unto Caucasus[2] they sung,
Filling with light

And vagrant melodies the winds which bore
Them earthward till they lit;
Then, like the arrow-seeds of the field flower,[3]
20 The fruitful wit

Cleaving, took root, and springing forth anew
Where'er they fell, behold,
Like to the mother plant in semblance, grew
A flower all gold,

25 And bravely furnished all abroad to fling
The wingèd shafts of truth,
To throng with stately blooms the breathing spring
Of Hope and Youth.

So many minds did gird their orbs with beams,
30 Though one did fling the fire.
Heaven flowed upon the soul in many dreams
Of high desire.

Thus truth was multiplied on truth, the world
Like one great garden showed,
35 And through the wreaths of floating dark upcurled,
Rare sunrise flowed.

And Freedom reared in that august sunrise
Her beautiful bold brow,
When rites and forms[4] before his burning eyes
40 Melted like snow.

There was no blood upon her maiden robes
Sunned by those orient skies;
But round about the circles of the globes
Of her keen eyes

45 And in her raiment's hem was traced in flame
WISDOM, a name to shake
All evil dreams of power—a sacred name.
And when she spake,

Her words did gather thunder as they ran,
50 And as the lightning to the thunder
Which follows it, riving the spirit of man,
Making earth wonder,

---

[1] arrows shot from blowpipes.

[2] from Gibraltar, Europe's western limit, to the Caucasus Mountains in
the east.

[3] the dandelion.

[4] traditional forms of church and state.

So was their meaning to her words. No sword
    Of wrath her right arm whirled,
55 But one poor poet's scroll, and with *his* word
    She shook the world.
—1830

The Poet's Mind

I

Vex not thou the poet's mind
    With thy shallow wit:
Vex not thou the poet's mind;
    For thou canst not fathom it.
5 Clear and bright it should be ever,
Flowing like a crystal river;
Bright as light, and clear as wind.

II

Dark-browed sophist, come not anear;
    All the place is holy ground;
10   Hollow smile and frozen sneer
        Come not here.
Holy water will I pour[1]
Into every spicy flower
Of the laurel-shrubs that hedge it around.
15 The flowers would faint at your cruel cheer.
    In your eye there is death,
    There is frost in your breath
    Which would blight the plants.
        Where you stand you cannot hear
20   From the groves within
           The wild-bird's din.
In the heart of the garden the merry bird chants.
It would fall to the ground if you came in.
    In the middle leaps a fountain
25   Like sheet lightning,
        Ever brightening
With a low melodious thunder;
All day and all night it is ever drawn

From the brain of the purple mountain
30   Which stands in the distance yonder:
It springs on a level of bowery lawn,
And the mountain draws it from Heaven above,
And it sings a song of undying love;
And yet, though its voice be so clear and full,
35 You never would hear it; your ears are so dull;
So keep where you are: you are foul with sin;
It would shrink to the earth if you came in.
—1830

The Mystic [2]

Angels have talked with him, and showed him
    thrones:
Ye knew him not: he was not one of ye,
Ye scorned him with an undiscerning scorn:
Ye could not read the marvel in his eye,
5 The still serene abstraction: he hath felt
The vanities of after and before;
Albeit, his spirit and his secret heart
The stern experiences of converse lives,
The linkèd woes of many a fiery change
10 Had purified, and chastened, and made free.
Always there stood before him, night and day,
Of wayward varycolored circumstance
The imperishable presences serene
Colossal, without form, or sense, or sound,
15 Dim shadows but unwaning presences
Fourfacèd to four corners of the sky:
And yet again, three shadows, fronting one,
One forward, one respectant,[3] three but one;
And yet again, again and evermore,
20 For the two first were not, but only seemed,
One shadow in the midst of a great light,
One reflex from eternity on time,
One mighty countenance of perfect calm,

---

[1] exorcism.

[2] Published in 1830, the only blank verse poem in the volume, *Poems, Chiefly Lyrical*, it was not reprinted in subsequent editions.

[3] looking backward.

Awful with most invariable eyes.
25 For him the silent congregated hours,
Daughters of time, divinely tall, beneath
Severe and youthful brows, with shining eyes
Smiling a godlike smile (the innocent light
Of earliest youth pierced through and through with
    all
30 Keen knowledges of low-embowèd eld)
Upheld, and ever hold aloft the cloud
Which droops lowhung on either gate of life,
Both birth and death: he in the centre fixt,
Saw far on each side through the grated gates
35 Most pale and clear and lovely distances.
He often lying broad awake, and yet
Remaining from the body, and apart
In intellect and power and will, hath heard
Time flowing in the middle of the night,
40 And all things creeping to a day of doom.
How could ye know him? Ye were yet within
The narrower circle; he had wellnigh reached
The last, which with a region of white flame,
Pure without heat, into a larger air
45 Upburning, and an ether of black blue,
Investeth and ingirds all other lives.
—1830

The Kraken [1]

Below the thunders of the upper deep,
  Far, far beneath in the abysmal sea,
His ancient, dreamless, uninvaded sleep
The Kraken sleepeth: faintest sunlights flee
5 About his shadowy sides: above him swell
Huge sponges of millennial growth and height;
And far away into the sickly light,
From many a wondrous grot and secret cell
Unnumbered and enormous polypi
10 Winnow with giant arms the slumbering green.
There hath he lain for ages and will lie

Battening upon huge seaworms in his sleep,
Until the latter fire shall heat the deep;
Then once by man and angels to be seen,
15 In roaring he shall rise and on the surface die.
—1830

The Lady of Shalott

PART I

On either side the river lie
  Long fields of barley and of rye,
That clothe the wold and meet the sky;
And through the field the road runs by
5   To many-towered Camelot;[2]
And up and down the people go,
Gazing where the lilies blow
Round an island there below,
  The island of Shalott.

10 Willows whiten, aspens quiver,
Little breezes dusk and shiver
Through the wave that runs for ever
By the island in the river
  Flowing down to Camelot.
15 Four gray walls, and four gray towers,
Overlook a space of flowers,
And the silent isle imbowers
  The Lady of Shalott.

By the margin, willow-veiled,
20 Slide the heavy barges trailed
By slow horses; and unhailed
The shallop flitteth silken-sailed
  Skimming down to Camelot:
But who hath seen her wave her hand?
25 Or at the casement seen her stand?
Or is she known in all the land,
  The Lady of Shalott?

---

[1] although published in 1830, not reprinted until 1872.

[2] seat of King Arthur's Court.

Only reapers, reaping early
In among the bearded barley,
30   Hear a song that echoes cheerly
From the river winding clearly,
    Down to towered Camelot:
And by the moon the reaper weary,
Piling sheaves in uplands airy,
35   Listening, whispers "'Tis the fairy
    Lady of Shalott."

PART II

There she weaves by night and day
A magic web with colours gay.
She has heard a whisper say,
40   A curse is on her if she stay
    To look down to Camelot.
She knows not what the curse may be,
And so she weaveth steadily,
And little other care hath she,
45   The Lady of Shalott.

And moving through a mirror clear
That hangs before her all the year,
Shadows of the world appear.
There she sees the highway near
50   Winding down to Camelot:
There the river eddy whirls,
And there the surly village-churls,
And the red cloaks of market girls,
    Pass onward from Shalott.

55   Sometimes a troop of damsels glad,
An abbot on an ambling pad,
Sometimes a curly shepherd-lad,
Or long-haired page in crimson clad,
    Goes by to towered Camelot;
60   And sometimes through the mirror blue
The knights come riding two and two:
She hath no loyal knight and true,
    The Lady of Shalott.

But in her web she still delights
65   To weave the mirror's magic sights,
For often through the silent nights
A funeral, with plumes and lights
    And music, went to Camelot:
Or when the moon was overhead,
70   Came two young lovers lately wed;
"I am half sick of shadows," said
    The Lady of Shalott.

PART III

A bow-shot from her bower-eaves,
He rode between the barley-sheaves,
75   The sun came dazzling through the leaves,
And flamed upon the brazen greaves
    Of bold Sir Lancelot.
A red-cross knight for ever kneeled
To a lady in his shield,
80   That sparkled on the yellow field,
    Beside remote Shalott.

The gemmy bridle glittered free,
Like to some branch of stars we see
Hung in the golden Galaxy.
85   The bridle bells rang merrily
    As he rode down to Camelot:
And from his blazoned baldric slung
A mighty silver bugle hung,
And as he rode his armour rung,
90   Beside remote Shalott.

All in the blue unclouded weather
Thick-jewelled shone the saddle-leather,
The helmet and the helmet-feather
Burned like one burning flame together,
95   As he rode down to Camelot.
As often through the purple night,
Below the starry clusters bright,
Some bearded meteor, trailing light,
    Moves over still Shalott.

100 His broad clear brow in sunlight glowed;
     On burnished hooves his war-horse trode;
     From underneath his helmet flowed
     His coal-black curls as on he rode,
          As he rode down to Camelot.
105 From the bank and from the river
     He flashed into the crystal mirror,
     "Tirra lirra," by the river
          Sang Sir Lancelot.

     She left the web, she left the loom,
110 She made three paces through the room,
     She saw the water-lily bloom,
     She saw the helmet and the plume,
          She looked down to Camelot.
     Out flew the web and floated wide;
115 The mirror cracked from side to side;
     "The curse is come upon me," cried
          The Lady of Shalott.

          PART IV

     In the stormy east-wind straining,
     The pale yellow woods were waning,
120 The broad stream in his banks complaining,
     Heavily the low sky raining
          Over towered Camelot;
     Down she came and found a boat
     Beneath a willow left afloat,
125 And round about the prow she wrote
          The Lady of Shalott.

     And down the river's dim expanse
     Like some bold seër in a trance,
     Seeing all his own mischance—
130 With a glassy countenance
          Did she look to Camelot.
     And at the closing of the day
     She loosed the chain, and down she lay;
     The broad stream bore her far away,
135   The Lady of Shalott.

     Lying, robed in snowy white
     That loosely flew to left and right—
     The leaves upon her falling light—
     Through the noises of the night
140   She floated down to Camelot:
     And as the boat-head wound along
     The willowy hills and fields among,
     They heard her singing her last song,
          The Lady of Shalott.

145 Heard a carol, mournful, holy,
     Chanted loudly, chanted lowly,
     Till her blood was frozen slowly,
     And her eyes were darkened wholly,
          Turned to towered Camelot.
150 For ere she reached upon the tide
     The first house by the water-side,
     Singing in her song she died,
          The Lady of Shalott.

     Under tower and balcony,
155 By garden-wall and gallery,
     A gleaming shape she floated by,
     Dead-pale between the houses high,
          Silent into Camelot.
     Out upon the wharfs they came,
160 Knight and burgher, lord and dame,
     And round the prow they read her name,
          The Lady of Shalott.

     Who is this? and what is here?
     And in the lighted palace near
165 Died the sound of royal cheer;
     And they crossed themselves for fear,
          All the knights at Camelot:
     But Lancelot mused a little space;
     He said, "She has a lovely face;
170 God in his mercy lend her grace,
          The Lady of Shalott."
          —1832

To —.[1] With the Following Poem
[The Palace of Art]

I send you here a sort of allegory,
  (For you will understand it) of a soul,
A sinful soul possessed of many gifts,
A spacious garden full of flowering weeds,
5 A glorious Devil, large in heart and brain,
That did love Beauty only, (Beauty seen
In all varieties of mould and mind)
And Knowledge for its beauty; or if Good,
Good only for its beauty, seeing not
10 That Beauty, Good, and Knowledge, are three sisters
That doat upon each other, friends to man,
Living together under the same roof,
And never can be sundered without tears.
And he that shuts Love out, in turn shall be
15 Shut out from Love, and on her threshold lie
Howling in outer darkness. Not for this
Was common clay ta'en from the common earth
Moulded by God, and tempered with the tears
Of angels to the perfect shape of man.
—1832

The Palace of Art

I built my soul a lordly pleasure-house,
  Wherein at ease for aye to dwell.
I said, "O Soul, make merry and carouse,
  Dear soul, for all is well."

5 A huge crag-platform, smooth as burnished brass
  I chose. The rangèd ramparts bright
From level meadow-bases of deep grass
  Suddenly scaled the light.

Thereon I built it firm. Of ledge or shelf
10   The rock rose clear, or winding stair.
My soul would live alone unto herself
  In her high palace there.

And "while the world runs round and round," I
  said,
  "Reign thou apart, a quiet king,
15 Still as, while Saturn whirls, his stedfast shade
  Sleeps on his luminous ring."[2]

To which my soul made answer readily:
  "Trust me, in bliss I shall abide
In this great mansion, that is built for me,
20   So royal-rich and wide."

    *   *   *   *

Four courts I made, East, West and South and
  North,
  In each a squarèd lawn, wherefrom
The golden gorge of dragons spouted forth
  A flood of fountain-foam.

25 And round the cool green courts there ran a row
  Of cloisters, branched like mighty woods,
Echoing all night to that sonorous flow
  Of spouted fountain-floods.

And round the roofs a gilded gallery
30   That lent broad verge to distant lands,
Far as the wild swan wings, to where the sky
  Dipt down to sea and sands.

From those four jets four currents in one swell
  Across the mountain streamed below
35 In misty folds, that floating as they fell
  Lit up a torrent-bow.

And high on every peak a statue seemed
  To hang on tiptoe, tossing up

---

[1] probably addressed to R.C. Trench, a member of the Cambridge Apostles. Tennyson remarked that Trench "said, when we were at Trinity together, 'Tennyson, we cannot live in Art.' This poem is the embodiment of my own belief that the Godlike life is with man and for man."

[2] the shadow of the whirling Saturn.

A cloud of incense of all odour steamed
40   From out a golden cup.

So that she thought, "And who shall gaze upon
        My palace with unblinded eyes,
While this great bow will waver in the sun,
        And that sweet incense rise?"

45   For that sweet incense rose and never failed,
        And, while day sank or mounted higher,
The light aërial gallery, golden-railed,
        Burnt like a fringe of fire.

Likewise the deep-set windows, stained and traced,
50   Would seem slow-flaming crimson fires
From shadowed grots of arches interlaced,
        And tipt with frost-like spires.

        *   *   *   *

Full of long-sounding corridors it was,
        That over-vaulted grateful gloom,
55   Through which the livelong day my soul did pass,
        Well-pleased, from room to room.

Full of great rooms and small the palace stood,
        All various, each a perfect whole
From living Nature, fit for every mood
60   And change of my still soul.

For some were hung with arras green and blue,
        Showing a gaudy summer-morn,
Where with puffed cheek the belted hunter blew
        His wreathèd bugle-horn.

65   One seemed all dark and red—a tract of sand,
        And some one pacing there alone,
Who paced for ever in a glimmering land,
        Lit with a low large moon.

One showed an iron coast and angry waves.
70   You seemed to hear them climb and fall

And roar rock-thwarted under bellowing caves,
        Beneath the windy wall.

And one, a full-fed river winding slow
        By herds upon an endless plain,
75   The ragged rims of thunder brooding low,
        With shadow-streaks of rain.

And one, the reapers at their sultry toil.
        In front they bound the sheaves. Behind
Were realms of upland, prodigal in oil,
80   And hoary to the wind.[1]

And one a foreground black with stones and slags,
        Beyond, a line of heights, and higher
All barred with long white cloud the scornful crags,
        And highest, snow and fire.

85   And one, an English home—gray twilight poured
        On dewy pastures, dewy trees,
Softer than sleep—all things in order stored,
        A haunt of ancient Peace.

Nor these alone, but every landscape fair,
90   As fit for every mood of mind,
Or gay, or grave, or sweet, or stern, was there
        Not less than truth designed.

        *   *   *   *

Or the maid-mother by a crucifix,
        In tracts of pasture sunny-warm,
95   Beneath branch-work of costly sardonyx
        Sat smiling, babe in arm.

Or in a clear-walled city on the sea,
        Near gilded organ-pipes, her hair
Wound with white roses, slept St Cecily;[2]
100   An angel looked at her.

---

[1]   the white underside of the olive leaf.

[2]   the patron saint of music.

Or thronging all one porch of Paradise
    A group of Houris bowed to see
The dying Islamite, with hands and eyes
    That said, We wait for thee.

105 Or mythic Uther's deeply-wounded son[1]
    In some fair space of sloping greens
Lay, dozing in the vale of Avalon,
    And watched by weeping queens.[2]

Or hollowing one hand against his ear,
110   To list a foot-fall, ere he saw
The wood-nymph, stayed the Ausonian king to hear
    Of wisdom and of law.

Or over hills with peaky tops engrailed,[3]
    And many a tract of palm and rice
115 The throne of Indian Cama[4] slowly sailed
    A summer fanned with spice.

Or sweet Europa's mantle blew unclasped,
    From off her shoulder backward borne:
From one hand drooped a crocus: one hand
        grasped
120   The mild bull's golden horn.

Or else flushed Ganymede,[5] his rosy thigh
    Half-buried in the Eagle's down,
Sole as a flying star shot through the sky
    Above the pillared town.

125 Nor these alone: but every legend fair
    Which the supreme Caucasian[6] mind

Carved out of Nature for itself, was there,
    Not less than life, designed.

    *   *   *   *

Then in the towers I placed great bells that swung,
130   Moved of themselves, with silver sound;
And with choice paintings of wise men I hung
    The royal dais round.

For there was Milton like a seraph strong,
    Beside him Shakespeare bland and mild;
135 And there the world-worn Dante grasped his song,
    And somewhat grimly smiled.

And there the Ionian father of the rest;[7]
    A million wrinkles carved his skin;
A hundred winters snowed upon his breast,
140   From cheek and throat and chin.

Above, the fair hall-ceiling stately-set
    Many an arch high up did lift,
And angels rising and descending met
    With interchange of gift.

145 Below was all mosaic choicely planned
    With cycles of the human tale
Of this wide world, the times of every land
    So wrought, they will not fail.

The people here, a beast of burden slow,
150   Toiled onward, pricked with goads and stings;
Here played, a tiger, rolling to and fro
    The heads and crowns of kings;

Here rose, an athlete, strong to break or bind
    All force in bonds that might endure,
155 And here once more like some sick man declined,
    And trusted any cure.

---

[1] King Arthur.

[2] Avalon, the Celtic isle to which the dead Arthur was borne by the weeping queens.

[3] serrated.

[4] the Hindu God of young love.

[5] Trojan boy carried off to Olympus by Zeus in the form of a bird.

[6] Indo-European.

[7] Homer.

But over these she trod: and those great bells
    Began to chime. She took her throne:
She sat betwixt the shining Oriels,
160   To sing her songs alone.

And through the topmost Oriels' coloured flame
    Two godlike faces gazed below;
Plato the wise, and large-browed Verulam,[1]
        The first of those who know.

165 And all those names, that in their motion were
    Full-welling fountain-heads of change,
Betwixt the slender shafts were blazoned fair
        In diverse raiment strange:

Through which the lights, rose, amber, emerald,
    blue,
170   Flushed in her temples and her eyes,
And from her lips, as morn from Memnon,[2] drew
        Rivers of melodies.

No nightingale delighteth to prolong
    Her low preamble all alone,
175 More than my soul to hear her echoed song
        Throb through the ribbèd stone;

Singing and murmuring in her feastful mirth,
    Joying to feel herself alive,
Lord over Nature, Lord of the visible earth,
180   Lord of the senses five;

Communing with herself: "All these are mine,
    And let the world have peace or wars,
'Tis one to me." She—when young night divine
        Crowned dying day with stars,

185 Making sweet close of his delicious toils—
    Lit light in wreaths and anadems,[3]
And pure quintessences of precious oils
        In hollowed moons of gems,

To mimic heaven; and clapt her hands and cried,
190   "I marvel if my still delight
In this great house so royal-rich, and wide,
        Be flattered to the height.

"O all things fair to sate my various eyes!
    O shapes and hues that please me well!
195 O silent faces of the Great and Wise,
        My Gods, with whom I dwell!

"O God-like isolation which art mine,
    I can but count thee perfect gain,
What time I watch the darkening droves of swine
200   That range on yonder plain.

"In filthy sloughs they roll a prurient skin,
    They graze and wallow, breed and sleep;
And oft some brainless devil enters in,
        And drives them to the deep."

205 Then of the moral instinct would she prate
    And of the rising from the dead,
As hers by right of full-accomplished Fate;
        And at the last she said:

"I take possession of man's mind and deed.
210   I care not what the sects may brawl.
I sit as God holding no form of creed,
        But contemplating all."

      *   *   *   *

Full oft the riddle of the painful earth
    Flashed through her as she sat alone,
215 Yet not the less held she her solemn mirth,
        And intellectual throne.

---

[1] Francis Bacon (Lord Verulam).

[2] a statue near Thebes that made music when touched by the sun.

[3] crowns.

And so she throve and prospered: so three years
    She prospered: on the fourth she fell,
Like Herod, when the shout was in his ears,
220   Struck through with pangs of hell.

Lest she should fail and perish utterly,
    God, before whom ever lie bare
The abysmal deeps of Personality,
    Plagued her with sore despair.

225 When she would think, where'er she turned her
        sight
    The airy hand confusion wrought,
Wrote, "Mene, mene,"[1] and divided quite
    The kingdom of her thought.

Deep dread and loathing of her solitude
230   Fell on her, from which mood was born
Scorn of herself; again, from out that mood
    Laughter at her self-scorn.

"What! is not this my place of strength," she said,
    "My spacious mansion built for me,
235 Whereof the strong foundation-stones were laid
    Since my first memory?"

But in dark corners of her palace stood
    Uncertain shapes; and unawares
On white-eyed phantasms weeping tears of blood,
240   And horrible nightmares,

And hollow shades enclosing hearts of flame,
    And, with dim fretted[2] foreheads all,
On corpses three-months-old at noon she came,
    That stood against the wall.

245 A spot of dull stagnation, without light
    Or power of movement, seemed my soul,

'Mid onward-sloping motions infinite
    Making for one sure goal.

A still salt pool, locked in with bars of sand,
250   Left on the shore; that hears all night
The plunging seas draw backward from the land
    Their moon-led waters white.

A star that with the choral starry dance
    Joined not, but stood, and standing saw
255 The hollow orb of moving Circumstance[3]
    Rolled round by one fixed law.

Back on herself her serpent pride had curled.
    "No voice," she shrieked in that lone hall,
"No voice breaks through the stillness of this world:
260   One deep, deep silence all!"

She, mouldering with the dull earth's mouldering
        sod,
    Inwrapt tenfold in slothful shame,
Lay there exilèd from eternal God,
    Lost to her place and name;

265 And death and life she hated equally,
    And nothing saw, for her despair,
But dreadful time, dreadful eternity,
    No comfort anywhere;

Remaining utterly confused with fears,
270   And ever worse with growing time,
And ever unrelieved by dismal tears,
    And all alone in crime:

Shut up as in a crumbling tomb, girt round
    With blackness as a solid wall,
275 Far off she seemed to hear the dully sound
    Of human footsteps fall.

---

[1] from Daniel 5:23–27: "MENE; God hath numbered thy kingdom, and finished it."

[2] worm-fretted.

[3] Tennyson's comment: "Some old writer calls the Heavens 'The Circumstance.'"

As in strange lands a traveller walking slow,
　　In doubt and great perplexity,
A little before moon-rise hears the low
280　　　　Moan of an unknown sea;

And knows not if it be thunder, or a sound
　　Of rocks thrown down, or one deep cry
Of great wild beasts; then thinketh, "I have found
　　　　A new land, but I die."

285 She howled aloud, "I am on fire within.
　　There comes no murmur of reply.
What is it that will take away my sin,
　　　　And save me lest I die?"

So when four years were wholly finished,
290　　She threw her royal robes away.
"Make me a cottage in the vale," she said,
　　　　"Where I may mourn and pray.

"Yet pull not down my palace towers, that are
　　So lightly, beautifully built:
295 Perchance I may return with others there
　　　　When I have purged my guilt."
　　—1832

The Hesperides [1]

The Northwind fallen, in the newstarrèd night
Zidonian Hanno, voyaging beyond
The hoary promontory of Soloë
Past Thymiaterion, in calmèd bays,
5 Between the southern and the western Horn,
Heard neither warbling of the nightingale,
Nor melody o' the Libyan lotusflute
Blown seaward from the shore; but from a slope
That ran bloombright into the Atlantic blue,
10 Beneath a highland leaning down a weight

---

[1] The daughters of Hesperus, who lived in the west where the sun sets, guarded the golden apples given by Earth to Hera; Hercules slew the guardian dragon and stole the apples.

Of cliffs, and zoned below with cedarshade,
Came voices, like the voices in a dream,
Continuous, till he reached the outer sea.

SONG

I

The golden apple, the golden apple, the hallowed
　fruit,
15 Guard it well, guard it warily,
Singing airily,
Standing about the charmèd root.
Round about all is mute,
As the snowfield on the mountain-peaks,
20 As the sandfield at the mountain-foot.
Crocodiles in briny creeks
Sleep and stir not: all is mute.
If ye sing not, if ye make false measure,
We shall lose eternal pleasure,
25 Worth eternal want of rest.
Laugh not loudly: watch the treasure
Of the wisdom of the west.
In a corner wisdom whispers. Five and three
(Let it not be preached abroad) make an awful
　mystery.
30 For the blossom unto threefold music bloweth;
Evermore it is born anew;
And the sap to threefold music floweth,
From the root
Drawn in the dark,
35 Up to the fruit,
Creeping under the fragrant bark,
Liquid gold, honeysweet, through and through.
Keen-eyed Sisters, singing airily,
Looking warily
40 Every way,
Guard the apple night and day,
Lest one from the East come and take it away.

II

Father Hesper,[1] Father Hesper, watch, watch, ever
   and aye,
Looking under silver hair with a silver eye.
45 Father, twinkle not thy stedfast sight;
Kingdoms lapse, and climates change, and races die;
Honour comes with mystery;
Hoarded wisdom brings delight.
Number, tell them over and number
50 How many the mystic fruittree holds,
Lest the redcombed dragon slumber
Rolled together in purple folds.
Look to him, father, lest he wink, and the golden
   apple be stolen away,
For his ancient heart is drunk with overwatchings
   night and day,
55 Round about the hallowed fruittree curled—
Sing away, sing aloud evermore in the wind,
   without stop,
Lest his scalèd eyelid drop,
For he is older than the world.
If he waken, we waken,
60 Rapidly levelling eager eyes.
If he sleep, we sleep,
Dropping the eyelid over the eyes.
If the golden apple be taken
The world will be overwise.
65 Five links, a golden chain, are we,
Hesper, the dragon, and sisters three,
Bound about the golden tree.

III

Father Hesper, Father Hesper, watch, watch, night
   and day,
Lest the old wound of the world be healèd,
70 The glory unsealèd,
The golden apple stolen away,
And the ancient secret revealèd.
Look from west to east along:

Father, old Himala[2] weakens, Caucasus[3] is bold
   and strong.
75 Wandering waters unto wandering waters call;
Let them clash together, foam and fall.
Out of watchings, out of wiles,
Comes the bliss of secret smiles.
All things are not told to all.
80 Half-round the mantling night is drawn,
Purplefringèd with even and dawn.
Hesper hateth Phosphor,[4] evening hateth morn.
Every flower and every fruit the redolent breath
Of this warm seawind ripeneth,
85 Arching the billow in his sleep;
But the landwind wandereth,
Broken by the highland-steep,
Two streams upon the violet deep:
For the western sun and the western star,
90 And the low west wind, breathing afar,
The end of day and beginning of night
Make the apple holy and bright;
Holy and bright, round and full, bright and blest,
Mellowed in a land of rest;
95 Watch it warily day and night;
All good things are in the west.
Till midnoon the cool east light
Is shut out by the round of the tall hillbrow;
But when the fullfaced sunset yellowly
100 Stays on the flowering arch of the bough,
The luscious fruitage clustereth mellowly,
Goldenkernelled, goldencored,
Sunset-ripened above on the tree.
The world is wasted with fire and sword,
105 But the apple of gold hangs over the sea.
Five links, a golden chain, are we,
Hesper, the dragon, and sisters three,
Daughters three,
Bound about

---

[1] Hesperus as the evening star.

[2] the Himalayas in India.

[3] the Caucasus mountains in the east.

[4] the morning star.

110 All round about
The gnarlèd bole of the charmèd tree.
The golden apple, the golden apple, the hallowed
        fruit,
Guard it well, guard it warily,
Watch it warily,
115 Singing airily,
Standing about the charmèd root.
—1832

The Lotos-Eaters

"Courage!" he said,[1] and pointed toward
        the land,
"This mounting wave will roll us shoreward soon."
In the afternoon they came unto a land
In which it seemèd always afternoon.
5 All round the coast the languid air did swoon,
Breathing like one that hath a weary dream.
Full-faced above the valley stood the moon;
And like a downward smoke, the slender stream
Along the cliff to fall and pause and fall did seem.

10 A land of streams! some, like a downward smoke,
Slow-dropping veils of thinnest lawn, did go;
And some through wavering lights and shadows
        broke,
Rolling a slumbrous sheet of foam below.
They saw the gleaming river seaward flow
15 From the inner land: far off, three mountain-tops,
Three silent pinnacles of agèd snow,
Stood sunset-flushed: and, dewed with showery
        drops,
Up-clomb the shadowy pine above the woven
        copse.

The charmèd sunset lingered low adown
20 In the red West: through mountain clefts the dale
Was seen far inland, and the yellow down

Bordered with palm, and many a winding vale
And meadow, set with slender galingale;[2]
A land where all things always seemed the same!
25 And round about the keel with faces pale,
Dark faces pale against that rosy flame,
The mild-eyed melancholy Lotos-eaters came.

Branches they bore of that enchanted stem,
Laden with flower and fruit, whereof they gave
30 To each, but whoso did receive of them,
And taste, to him the gushing of the wave
Far far away did seem to mourn and rave
On alien shores; and if his fellow spake,
His voice was thin, as voices from the grave;
35 And deep-asleep he seemed, yet all awake,
And music in his ears his beating heart did make.

They sat them down upon the yellow sand,
Between the sun and moon upon the shore;
And sweet it was to dream of Fatherland,
40 Of child, and wife, and slave; but evermore
Most weary seemed the sea, weary the oar,
Weary the wandering fields of barren foam.
Then some one said, "We will return no more;"
And all at once they sang, "Our island home
45 Is far beyond the wave; we will no longer roam."

CHORIC SONG
I

There is sweet music here that softer falls
Than petals from blown roses on the grass,
Or night-dews on still waters between walls
Of shadowy granite, in a gleaming pass;
50 Music that gentlier on the spirit lies,
Than tired eyelids upon tired eyes;
Music that brings sweet sleep down from the
        blissful skies.
Here are cool mosses deep,
And through the moss the ivies creep,
55 And in the stream the long-leaved flowers weep,

---

[1] Odysseus urging his men to continue their journey homeward.

[2] aromatic herb.

And from the craggy ledge the poppy hangs in sleep.

II

Why are we weighed upon with heaviness,
And utterly consumed with sharp distress,
While all things else have rest from weariness?
60 All things have rest: why should we toil alone,
We only toil, who are the first of things,
And make perpetual moan,
Still from one sorrow to another thrown:
Nor ever fold our wings,
65 And cease from wanderings,
Nor steep our brows in slumber's holy balm;
Nor harken what the inner spirit sings,
"There is no joy but calm!"
Why should we only toil, the roof and crown of
      things?

III

70 Lo! in the middle of the wood,
The folded leaf is wooed from out the bud
With winds upon the branch, and there
Grows green and broad, and takes no care,
Sun-steeped at noon, and in the moon
75 Nightly dew-fed; and turning yellow
Falls, and floats adown the air.
Lo! sweetened with the summer light,
The full-juiced apple, waxing over-mellow,
Drops in a silent autumn night.
80 All its allotted length of days,
The flower ripens in its place,
Ripens and fades, and falls, and hath no toil,
Fast-rooted in the fruitful soil.

IV

Hateful is the dark-blue sky,
85 Vaulted o'er the dark-blue sea.
Death is the end of life; ah, why
Should life all labour be?
Let us alone. Time driveth onward fast,
And in a little while our lips are dumb.

90 Let us alone. What is it that will last?
All things are taken from us, and become
Portions and parcels of the dreadful Past.
Let us alone. What pleasure can we have
To war with evil? Is there any peace
95 In ever climbing up the climbing wave?
All things have rest, and ripen toward the grave
In silence; ripen, fall and cease:
Give us long rest or death, dark death, or dreamful
      ease.

V

How sweet it were, hearing the downward stream,
100 With half-shut eyes ever to seem
Falling asleep in a half-dream!
To dream and dream, like yonder amber light,
Which will not leave the myrrh-bush on the height;
To hear each other's whispered speech;
105 Eating the Lotos day by day,
To watch the crisping ripples on the beach,
And tender curving lines of creamy spray;
To lend our hearts and spirits wholly
To the influence of mild-minded melancholy;
110 To muse and brood and live again in memory,
With those old faces of our infancy
Heaped over with a mound of grass,
Two handfuls of white dust, shut in an urn of brass!

VI

Dear is the memory of our wedded lives,
115 And dear the last embraces of our wives
And their warm tears: but all hath suffered change:
For surely now our household hearths are cold:
Our sons inherit us: our looks are strange:
And we should come like ghosts to trouble joy.
120 Or else the island princes over-bold
Have eat our substance, and the minstrel sings
Before them of the ten years' war in Troy,
And our great deeds, as half-forgotten things.
Is there confusion in the little isle?
125 Let what is broken so remain.

The Gods are hard to reconcile:
'Tis hard to settle order once again.
There *is* confusion worse than death,
Trouble on trouble, pain on pain,
130 Long labour unto agèd breath,
Sore task to hearts worn out by many wars
And eyes grown dim with gazing on the pilot-stars.

VII

But, propt on beds of amaranth[1] and moly,[2]
How sweet (while warm airs lull us, blowing lowly)
135 With half-dropt eyelid still,
Beneath a heaven dark and holy,
To watch the long bright river drawing slowly
His waters from the purple hill—
To hear the dewy echoes calling
140 From cave to cave through the thick-twinèd vine—
To watch the emerald-coloured water falling
Through many a woven acanthus[3]-wreath divine!
Only to hear and see the far-off sparkling brine,
Only to hear were sweet, stretched out beneath the
pine.

VIII

145 The Lotos blooms below the barren peak:
The Lotos blows by every winding creek:
All day the wind breathes low with mellower tone:
Through every hollow cave and alley lone
Round and round the spicy downs the yellow
Lotos-dust is blown.
150 We have had enough of action, and of motion we,
Rolled to starboard, rolled to larboard, when the
surge was seething free,
Where the wallowing monster spouted his foam-
fountains in the sea.
Let us swear an oath, and keep it with an equal
mind,

In the hollow Lotos-land to live and lie reclined
155 On the hills like Gods together, careless of mankind.
For they lie beside their nectar, and the bolts are
hurled
Far below them in the valleys, and the clouds are
lightly curled
Round their golden houses, girdled with the
gleaming world:
Where they smile in secret, looking over wasted
lands,
160 Blight and famine, plague and earthquake, roaring
deeps and fiery sands,
Clanging fights, and flaming towns, and sinking
ships, and praying hands.
But they smile, they find a music centred in a
doleful song
Steaming up, a lamentation and an ancient tale of
wrong,
Like a tale of little meaning though the words are
strong;
165 Chanted from an ill-used race of men that cleave
the soil,
Sow the seed, and reap the harvest with enduring
toil,
Storing yearly little dues of wheat, and wine and oil;
Till they perish and they suffer—some, 'tis
whispered—down in hell
Suffer endless anguish, others in Elysian valleys
dwell,
170 Resting weary limbs at last on beds of asphodel.
Surely, surely, slumber is more sweet than toil, the
shore
Than labour in the deep mid-ocean, wind and
wave and oar;
Oh rest ye, brother mariners, we will not wander
more.
—1832

---

[1] an immortal flower.

[2] an herb with magical powers.

[3] a sacred plant.

The Two Voices [1]

A still small voice spake unto me,
"Thou art so full of misery,
Were it not better not to be?"

Then to the still small voice I said;
5 "Let me not cast in endless shade
What is so wonderfully made."[2]

To which the voice did urge reply;
"Today I saw the dragon-fly
Come from the wells where he did lie.

10 "An inner impulse rent the veil
Of his old husk: from head to tail
Came out clear plates of sapphire mail.

"He dried his wings: like gauze they grew;
Through crofts and pastures wet with dew
15 A living flash of light he flew."

I said, "When first the world began,
Young Nature through five cycles ran,
And in the sixth she moulded man.

"She gave him mind, the lordliest
20 Proportion, and, above the rest,
Dominion in the head and breast."[3]

Thereto the silent voice replied;
"Self-blinded are you by your pride:
Look up through night: the world is wide.

25 "This truth within thy mind rehearse,
That in a boundless universe
Is boundless better, boundless worse.

"Think you this mould of hopes and fears
Could find no statelier than his peers
30 In yonder hundred million spheres?"

It spake, moreover, in my mind:
"Though thou wert scattered to the wind,
Yet is there plenty of the kind."

Then did my response clearer fall:
35 "No compound of this earthly ball
Is like another, all in all."

To which he answered scoffingly;
"Good soul! suppose I grant it thee,
Who'll weep for thy deficiency?

40 "Or will one beam be less intense,
When thy peculiar difference
Is cancelled in the world of sense?"

I would have said, "Thou canst not know,"
But my full heart, that worked below,
45 Rained through my sight its overflow.

Again the voice spake unto me:
"Thou art so steeped in misery,
Surely 'twere better not to be.

"Thine anguish will not let thee sleep,
50 Nor any train of reason keep:
Thou canst not think, but thou wilt weep."

I said, "The years with change advance:
If I make dark my countenance,[4]
I shut my life from happier chance.

---

[1] published in 1842, but dated "1833." Tennyson's son, Hallam, describes it as "begun under the cloud of his overwhelming sorrow after the death of Arthur Hallam," which Tennyson learned about on 1 October 1833. But correspondence shows that a version of the poem was in existence as early as June of that year.

[2] Psalm 139:11–14.

[3] Psalm 8:6.

[4] Job 14:20.

55 "Some turn this sickness yet might take,
Even yet." But he: "What drug can make
A withered palsy cease to shake?"

I wept, "Though I should die, I know
That all about the thorn will blow
60 In tufts of rosy-tinted snow;

"And men, through novel spheres of thought
Still moving after truth long sought,
Will learn new things when I am not."

"Yet," said the secret voice, "some time,
65 Sooner or later, will gray prime
Make thy grass hoar with early rime.

"Not less swift souls that yearn for light,
Rapt after heaven's starry flight,
Would sweep the tracts of day and night.

70 "Not less the bee would range her cells,
The furzy prickle fire the dells,
The foxglove cluster dappled bells."

I said that "all the years invent;
Each month is various to present
75 The world with some development.

"Were this not well, to bide mine hour,
Though watching from a ruined tower
How grows the day of human power?"

"The highest-mounted mind," he said,
80 "Still sees the sacred morning spread
The silent summit overhead.

"Will thirty seasons render plain
Those lonely lights that still remain,
Just breaking over land and main?

85 "Or make that morn, from his cold crown
And crystal silence creeping down,
Flood with full daylight glebe and town?

"Forerun thy peers, thy time, and let
Thy feet, millenniums hence, be set
90 In midst of knowledge, dreamed not yet.

"Thou hast not gained a real height,
Nor art thou nearer to the light,
Because the scale is infinite.

"'Twere better not to breathe or speak,
95 Than cry for strength, remaining weak,
And seem to find, but still to seek.

"Moreover, but to seem to find
Asks what thou lackest, thought resigned,
A healthy frame, a quiet mind."

100 I said, "When I am gone away,
'He dared not tarry,' men will say,
Doing dishonour to my clay."

"This is more vile," he made reply,
"To breathe and loathe, to live and sigh,
105 Than once from dread of pain to die.

"Sick art thou—a divided will
Still heaping on the fear of ill
The fear of men, a coward still.

"Do men love thee? Art thou so bound
110 To men, that how thy name may sound
Will vex thee lying underground?

"The memory of the withered leaf
In endless time is scarce more brief
Than of the garnered Autumn-sheaf.

"Go, vexèd Spirit, sleep in trust;
The right ear, that is filled with dust,
Hears little of the false or just."

"Hard task, to pluck resolve," I cried,
"From emptiness and the waste wide
Of that abyss, or scornful pride![1]

"Nay—rather yet that I could raise
One hope that warmed me in the days
While still I yearned for human praise.

"When, wide in soul and bold of tongue,
Among the tents I paused and sung,
The distant battle flashed and rung.

"I sung the joyful Pæan clear,
And, sitting, burnished without fear
The brand, the buckler, and the spear—

"Waiting to strive a happy strife,
To war with falsehood to the knife,
And not to lose the good of life—

"Some hidden principle to move,
To put together, part and prove,
And mete the bounds of hate and love—

"As far as might be, to carve out
Free space for every human doubt,
That the whole mind might orb about—

"To search through all I felt or saw,
The springs of life, the depths of awe,
And reach the law within the law:

"At least, not rotting like a weed,
But, having sown some generous seed,
Fruitful of further thought and deed,

"To pass, when Life her light withdraws,
Not void of righteous self-applause,
Nor in a merely selfish cause—

"In some good cause, not in mine own,
To perish, wept for, honoured, known,
And like a warrior overthrown;

"Whose eyes are dim with glorious tears,
When, soiled with noble dust, he hears
His country's war-song thrill his ears:

"Then dying of a mortal stroke,
What time the foeman's line is broke,
And all the war is rolled in smoke."

"Yea!" said the voice, "thy dream was good,
While thou abodest in the bud.
It was the stirring of the blood.

"If Nature put not forth her power
About the opening of the flower,
Who is it that could live an hour?

"Then comes the check, the change, the fall,
Pain rises up, old pleasures pall.
There is one remedy for all.

"Yet hadst thou, through enduring pain,
Linked month to month with such a chain
Of knitted purport, all were vain.

"Thou hadst not between death and birth
Dissolved the riddle of the earth.
So were thy labour little-worth.

"That men with knowledge merely played,
I told thee—hardly nigher made,
Though scaling slow from grade to grade;

---

[1] *Paradise Lost* 10.282–83.

175 "Much less this dreamer, deaf and blind,
Named man, may hope some truth to find,
That bears relation to the mind.

"For every worm beneath the moon
Draws different threads, and late and soon
180 Spins, toiling out his own cocoon.

"Cry, faint not: either Truth is born
Beyond the polar gleam forlorn,
Or in the gateways of the morn.

"Cry, faint not, climb: the summits slope
185 Beyond the furthest flights of hope,
Wrapt in dense cloud from base to cope.

"Sometimes a little corner shines,
As over rainy mist inclines
A gleaming crag with belts of pines.

190 "I will go forward, sayest thou,
I shall not fail to find her now.
Look up, the fold[1] is on her brow.

"If straight thy track, or if oblique,
Thou know'st not. Shadows thou dost strike,
195 Embracing cloud, Ixion-like;[2]

"And owning but a little more
Than beasts, abidest lame and poor,
Calling thyself a little lower

"Than angels. Cease to wail and brawl![3]
200 Why inch by inch to darkness crawl?
There is one remedy for all."

"O dull, one-sided voice," said I,
"Wilt thou make everything a lie,
To flatter me that I may die?

205 "I know that age to age succeeds,
Blowing a noise of tongues and deeds,
A dust of systems and of creeds.

"I cannot hide that some have striven,
Achieving calm, to whom was given
210 The joy that mixes man with Heaven:

"Who, rowing hard against the stream,
Saw distant gates of Eden gleam,
And did not dream it was a dream;

"But heard, by secret transport led,
215 Even in the charnels of the dead,
The murmur of the fountain-head—

"Which did accomplish their desire,
Bore and forbore, and did not tire,
Like Stephen, an unquenchèd fire.

220 "He heeded not reviling tones,
Nor sold his heart to idle moans,
Though cursed and scorned, and bruised with
        stones:

"But looking upward, full of grace,
He prayed, and from a happy place
225 God's glory smote him on the face."[4]

The sullen answer slid betwixt:
"Not that the grounds of hope were fixed,
The elements were kindlier mixed."

I said, "I toil beneath the curse,
230 But, knowing not the universe,
I fear to slide from bad to worse.

---

[1] "cloud." (Tennyson's note.)

[2] "Ixion embraced a cloud, hoping to embrace a goddess." (Tennyson's note.)

[3] ll. 196–99: Ecclesiastes 3:19 and Psalm 8:4–5.

[4] ll. 222–25: Acts 7:55.

"And that, in seeking to undo
One riddle, and to find the true,
I knit a hundred others new:

235 "Or that this anguish fleeting hence,
Unmanacled from bonds of sense,
Be fixed and frozen to permanence:

"For I go, weak from suffering here:
Naked I go, and void of cheer:[1]
240 What is it that I may not fear?"

"Consider well," the voice replied,
"His face, that two hours since hath died;
Wilt thou find passion, pain or pride?

"Will he obey when one commands?
245 Or answer should one press his hands?
He answers not, nor understands.

"His palms are folded on his breast:
There is no other thing expressed
But long disquiet merged in rest.

250 "His lips are very mild and meek:
Though one should smite him on the cheek,
And on the mouth, he will not speak.

"His little daughter, whose sweet face
He kissed, taking his last embrace,
255 Becomes dishonour to her race—

"His sons grow up that bear his name,
Some grow to honour, some to shame,—[2]
But he is chill to praise or blame.

"He will not hear the north-wind rave,
260 Nor, moaning, household shelter crave
From winter rains that beat his grave.

"High up the vapours fold and swim:
About him broods the twilight dim:
The place he knew forgetteth him."[3]

265 "If all be dark, vague voice," I said,
"These things are wrapt in doubt and dread,
Nor canst thou show the dead are dead.

"The sap dries up: the plant declines.
A deeper tale my heart divines.
270 Know I not Death? the outward signs?

"I found him when my years were few;
A shadow on the graves I knew,
And darkness in the village yew.

"From grave to grave the shadow crept:
275 In her still place the morning wept:
Touched by his feet the daisy slept.

"The simple senses crowned his head:
'Omega! thou art Lord,' they said,
'We find no motion in the dead.'

280 "Why, if man rot in dreamless ease,[4]
Should that plain fact, as taught by these,
Not make him sure that he shall cease?

"Who forged that other influence,
That heat of inward evidence,
285 By which he doubts against the sense?

---

[1] Ecclesiastes 5:15.

[2] Job 14:21.

[3] Psalm 103:16, Job 7:10.

[4] *Hamlet* 1.5.32–33.

"He owns the fatal gift of eyes,
That read his spirit blindly wise,
Not simple as a thing that dies.

"Here sits he shaping wings to fly:
290 His heart forebodes a mystery:
He names the name Eternity.

"That type of Perfect in his mind
In Nature can he nowhere find.
He sows himself on every wind.

295 "He seems to hear a Heavenly Friend,
And through thick veils to apprehend
A labour working to an end.

"The end and the beginning vex
His reason: many things perplex,
300 With motions, checks, and counterchecks.

"He knows a baseness in his blood
At such strange war with something good,
He may not do the thing he would.[1]

"Heaven opens inward, chasms yawn,
305 Vast images in glimmering dawn,
Half shown, are broken and withdrawn.

"Ah! sure within him and without,
Could his dark wisdom find it out,
There must be answer to his doubt,

310 "But thou canst answer not again.
With thine own weapon art thou slain,
Or thou wilt answer but in vain.

"The doubt would rest, I dare not solve.
In the same circle we revolve.
315 Assurance only breeds resolve."

As when a billow, blown against,
Falls back, the voice with which I fenced
A little ceased, but recommenced.

"Where wert thou when thy father played
320 In his free field, and pastime made,
A merry boy in sun and shade?

"A merry boy they called him then,
He sat upon the knees of men
In days that never come again.

325 "Before the little ducts began
To feed thy bones with lime, and ran
Their course, till thou wert also man:

"Who took a wife, who reared his race,
Whose wrinkles gathered on his face,
330 Whose troubles number with his days:

"A life of nothings, nothing-worth,
From that first nothing ere his birth
To that last nothing under earth!"

"These words," I said, "are like the rest:
335 No certain clearness, but at best
A vague suspicion of the breast:

"But if I grant, thou mightst defend
The thesis which thy words intend—
That to begin implies to end;

340 "Yet how should I for certain hold,
Because my memory is so cold,
That I first was in human mould?

"I cannot make this matter plain,
But I would shoot, howe'er in vain,
345 A random arrow from the brain.

---

[1] ll. 301–03: Romans 7:18–19 and Galatians 5:17.

"It may be that no life is found,
Which only to one engine bound
Falls off, but cycles always round.

"As old mythologies relate,[1]
350 Some draught of Lethe might await
The slipping through from state to state.

"As here we find in trances, men
Forget the dream that happens then,
Until they fall in trance again.

355 "So might we, if our state were such
As one before, remember much,
For those two likes might meet and touch.

"But, if I lapsed from nobler place,
Some legend of a fallen race
360 Alone might hint of my disgrace;

"Some vague emotion of delight
In gazing up an Alpine height,
Some yearning toward the lamps of night;

"Or if through lower lives I came—
365 Though all experience past became
Consolidate in mind and frame—

"I might forget my weaker lot;
For is not our first year forgot?
The haunts of memory echo not.

370 "And men, whose reason long was blind,
From cells of madness unconfined,
Oft lose whole years of darker mind.

"Much more, if first I floated free,
As naked essence, must I be
375 Incompetent of memory:

"For memory dealing but with time,
And he with matter, could she climb
Beyond her own material prime?

"Moreover, something is or seems,
380 That touches me with mystic gleams,
Like glimpses of forgotten dreams—

"Of something felt, like something here;
Of something done, I know not where;
Such as no language may declare."

385 The still voice laughed. "I talk," said he,
"Not with thy dreams. Suffice it thee
Thy pain is a reality."

"But thou," said I, "hast missed thy mark,
Who sought'st to wreck my mortal ark,
390 By making all the horizon dark.

"Why not set forth, if I should do
This rashness, that which might ensue
With this old soul in organs new?

"Whatever crazy sorrow saith,
395 No life that breathes with human breath
Has ever truly longed for death.[2]

"'Tis life, whereof our nerves are scant,
Oh life, not death, for which we pant;
More life, and fuller, that I want."[3]

400 I ceased, and sat as one forlorn.
Then said the voice, in quiet scorn,
"Behold, it is the Sabbath morn."

---

[1] Pythagoras's metempsychosis, and Plato's myth of Er: *Republic* 10.

[2] Job 3:20–21.

[3] John 10:10.

And I arose, and I released
The casement, and the light increased
405 With freshness in the dawning east.

Like softened airs that blowing steal,
When meres begin to uncongeal,
The sweet church bells began to peal.

On to God's house the people prest:
410 Passing the place where each must rest,
Each entered like a welcome guest.

One walked between his wife and child,
With measured footfall firm and mild,
And now and then he gravely smiled.

415 The prudent partner of his blood
Leaned on him, faithful, gentle, good,
Wearing the rose of womanhood.

And in their double love secure,
The little maiden walked demure,
420 Pacing with downward eyelids pure.

These three made unity so sweet,
My frozen heart began to beat,
Remembering its ancient heat.

I blest them, and they wandered on:
425 I spoke, but answer came there none:
The dull and bitter voice was gone.

A second voice was at mine ear,
A little whisper silver-clear,
A murmur, "Be of better cheer."

430 As from some blissful neighbourhood,
A notice faintly understood,
"I see the end, and know the good."

A little hint to solace woe,
A hint, a whisper breathing low,
435 "I may not speak of what I know."

Like an Æolian harp that wakes
No certain air, but overtakes
Far thought with music that it makes:

Such seemed the whisper at my side:
440 "What is it thou knowest, sweet voice?" I cried.
"A hidden hope," the voice replied:

So heavenly-toned, that in that hour
From out my sullen heart a power
Broke, like the rainbow from the shower,

445 To feel, although no tongue can prove,
That every cloud, that spreads above
And veileth love, itself is love.

And forth into the fields I went,
And Nature's living motion lent
450 The pulse of hope to discontent.

I wondered at the bounteous hours,
The slow result of winter showers:
You scarce could see the grass for flowers.

I wondered, while I paced along:
455 The woods were filled so full with song,
There seemed no room for sense of wrong;

And all so variously wrought,
I marvelled how the mind was brought
To anchor by one gloomy thought;

460 And wherefore rather I made choice
To commune with that barren voice,
Than him that said, "Rejoice! Rejoice!"
—1842

St Simeon Stylites [1]

Although I be the basest of mankind,
From scalp to sole one slough and crust of sin,
Unfit for earth, unfit for heaven, scarce meet
For troops of devils, mad with blasphemy,
5 I will not cease to grasp the hope I hold
Of saintdom, and to clamour, mourn and sob,
Battering the gates of heaven with storms of prayer,
Have mercy, Lord, and take away my sin.

   Let this avail, just, dreadful, mighty God,
10 This not be all in vain, that thrice ten years,
Thrice multiplied by superhuman pangs,
In hungers and in thirsts, fevers and cold,
In coughs, aches, stitches, ulcerous throes and
     cramps,
A sign betwixt the meadow and the cloud,
15 Patient on this tall pillar I have borne
Rain, wind, frost, heat, hail, damp, and sleet, and
     snow;
And I had hoped that ere this period closed
Thou wouldst have caught me up into thy rest,
Denying not these weather-beaten limbs
20 The meed of saints, the white robe and the palm. [2]

   O take the meaning, Lord: I do not breathe,
Not whisper, any murmur of complaint.
Pain heaped ten-hundred-fold to this, were still
Less burthen, by ten-hundred-fold, to bear,
25 Than were those lead-like tons of sin that crushed
My spirit flat before thee.
                              O Lord, Lord,
Thou knowest I bore this better at the first,
For I was strong and hale of body then;
And though my teeth, which now are dropt away,
30 Would chatter with the cold, and all my beard
Was tagged with icy fringes in the moon,

I drowned the whoopings of the owl with sound
Of pious hymns and psalms, and sometimes saw
An angel stand and watch me, as I sang.
35 Now am I feeble grown; my end draws nigh;
I hope my end draws nigh: half deaf I am,
So that I scarce can hear the people hum
About the column's base, and almost blind,
And scarce can recognise the fields I know;
40 And both my thighs are rotted with the dew;
Yet cease I not to clamour and to cry,
While my stiff spine can hold my weary head,
Till all my limbs drop piecemeal from the stone,
Have mercy, mercy: take away my sin.

45 O Jesus, if thou wilt not save my soul,
Who may be saved? who is it may be saved? [3]
Who may be made a saint, if I fail here?
Show me the man hath suffered more than I.
For did not all thy martyrs die one death?
50 For either they were stoned, or crucified,
Or burned in fire, or boiled in oil, or sawn
In twain beneath the ribs; but I die here
Today, and whole years long, a life of death.
Bear witness, if I could have found a way
55 (And heedfully I sifted all my thought)
More slowly-painful to subdue this home
Of sin, my flesh, which I despise and hate,
I had not stinted practice, O my God.

   For not alone this pillar-punishment,
60 Not this alone I bore: but while I lived
In the white convent down the valley there,
For many weeks about my loins I wore
The rope that haled the buckets from the well,
Twisted as tight as I could knot the noose;
65 And spake not of it to a single soul,
Until the ulcer, eating through my skin,
Betrayed my secret penance, so that all

---

[1] although published in 1842, written in 1833.

[2] Revelation 7:9.

[3] Matthew 19:25.

My brethren marvelled greatly. More than this
I bore, whereof, O God, thou knowest all.

70   Three winters, that my soul might grow to thee,
I lived up there on yonder mountain side.
My right leg chained into the crag, I lay
Pent in a roofless close of ragged stones;
Inswathed sometimes in wandering mist, and twice
75 Blacked with thy branding thunder, and sometimes
Sucking the damps for drink, and eating not,
Except the spare chance-gift of those that came
To touch my body and be healed, and live:
And they say then that I worked miracles,
80 Whereof my fame is loud amongst mankind,
Cured lameness, palsies, cancers.[1] Thou, O God,
Knowest alone whether this was or no.
Have mercy, mercy! cover all my sin.[2]

    Then, that I might be more alone with thee,
85 Three years I lived upon a pillar, high
Six cubits, and three years on one of twelve;
And twice three years I crouched on one that rose
Twenty by measure; last of all, I grew
Twice ten long weary weary years to this,
90 That numbers forty cubits from the soil.

    I think that I have borne as much as this—
Or else I dream—and for so long a time,
If I may measure time by yon slow light,
And this high dial, which my sorrow crowns—
95 So much—even so.
              And yet I know not well,
For that the evil ones come here, and say,
"Fall down, O Simeon: thou hast suffered long
For ages and for ages!" then they prate
Of penances I cannot have gone through,
100 Perplexing me with lies; and oft I fall,

Maybe for months, in such blind lethargies
That Heaven, and Earth, and Time are choked.
                      But yet
Bethink thee, Lord, while thou and all the saints
Enjoy themselves in heaven, and men on earth
105 House in the shade of comfortable roofs,
Sit with their wives by fires, eat wholesome food,
And wear warm clothes, and even beasts have stalls,
I, 'tween the spring and downfall of the light,
Bow down one thousand and two hundred times,
110 To Christ, the Virgin Mother, and the saints;
Or in the night, after a little sleep,
I wake: the chill stars sparkle; I am wet
With drenching dews, or stiff with crackling frost.
I wear an undressed goatskin on my back;
115 A grazing iron collar grinds my neck;
And in my weak, lean arms I lift the cross,
And strive and wrestle with thee till I die:
O mercy, mercy! wash away my sin.

    O Lord, thou knowest what a man I am;
120 A sinful man, conceived and born in sin:[3]
'Tis their own doing; this is none of mine;
Lay it not to me. Am I to blame for this,
That here come those that worship me? Ha! ha!
They think that I am somewhat. What am I?
125 The silly people take me for a saint,
And bring me offerings of fruit and flowers:
And I, in truth (thou wilt bear witness here)
Have all in all endured as much, and more
Than many just and holy men, whose names
130 Are registered and calendared for saints.

    Good people, you do ill to kneel to me.
What is it I can have done to merit this?
I am a sinner viler than you all.
It may be I have wrought some miracles,
135 And cured some halt and maimed; but what of that?
It may be, no one, even among the saints,

---

[1] Acts 8:7.

[2] Psalm 85:2.

[3] Psalm 51: 5.

May match his pains with mine; but what of that?
Yet do not rise; for you may look on me,
And in your looking you may kneel to God.
140 Speak! is there any of you halt or maimed?
I think you know I have some power with Heaven
From my long penance: let him speak his wish.

    Yes, I can heal him. Power goes forth from me.
They say that they are healed. Ah, hark! they shout
145 "St Simeon Stylites." Why, if so,
God reaps a harvest in me. O my soul,
God reaps a harvest in thee. If this be,
Can I work miracles and not be saved?
This is not told of any. They were saints.
150 It cannot be but that I shall be saved;
Yea, crowned a saint. They shout, "Behold a saint!"
And lower voices saint me from above.
Courage, St Simeon! This dull chrysalis
Cracks into shining wings, and hope ere death
155 Spreads more and more and more, that God hath
      now
Sponged and made blank of crimeful record all
My mortal archives.
             O my sons, my sons,
I, Simeon of the pillar, by surname
Stylites, among men; I, Simeon,
160 The watcher on the column till the end;
I, Simeon, whose brain the sunshine bakes;
I, whose bald brows in silent hours become
Unnaturally hoar with rime, do now
From my high nest of penance here proclaim
165 That Pontius and Iscariot by my side
Showed like fair seraphs. On the coals I lay,
A vessel full of sin: all hell beneath
Made me boil over. Devils plucked my sleeve,
Abaddon and Asmodeus caught at me.
170 I smote them with the cross; they swarmed again.
In bed like monstrous apes they crushed my chest:
They flapped my light out as I read: I saw
Their faces grow between me and my book;

With colt-like whinny and with hoggish whine[1]
175 They burst my prayer. Yet this way was left,
And by this way I 'scaped them. Mortify
Your flesh, like me, with scourges and with thorns;
Smite, shrink not, spare not. If it may be, fast
Whole Lents, and pray. I hardly, with slow steps,
180 With slow, faint steps, and much exceeding pain,
Have scrambled past those pits of fire, that still
Sing in mine ears. But yield not me the praise:
God only through his bounty hath thought fit,
Among the powers and princes of this world,
185 To make me an example to mankind,
Which few can reach to. Yet I do not say
But that a time may come—yea, even now,
Now, now, his footsteps smite the threshold stairs
Of life—I say, that time is at the doors
190 When you may worship me without reproach;
For I will leave my relics in your land,
And you may carve a shrine about my dust,
And burn a fragrant lamp before my bones,
When I am gathered to the glorious saints.

195   While I spake then, a sting of shrewdest pain
Ran shrivelling through me, and a cloudlike change,
In passing, with a grosser film made thick
These heavy, horny eyes. The end! the end!
Surely the end! What's here? a shape, a shade,
200 A flash of light. Is that the angel there
That holds a crown? Come, blessèd brother, come.
I know thy glittering face. I waited long;
My brows are ready. What! deny it now?
Nay, draw, draw, draw nigh. So I clutch it. Christ!
205 'Tis gone: 'tis here again; the crown! the crown![2]
So now 'tis fitted on and grows to me,
And from it melt the dews of Paradise,
Sweet! sweet! spikenard, and balm, and frankincense.
Ah! let me not be fooled, sweet saints: I trust
210 That I am whole, and clean, and meet for Heaven.

---

[1] Cf. *The Tempest* 2.2.8–10.

[2] Revelation 1:7–10.

Speak, if there be a priest, a man of God,
Among you there, and let him presently
Approach, and lean a ladder on the shaft,
And climbing up into my airy home,
215 Deliver me the blessèd sacrament;
For by the warning of the Holy Ghost,
I prophesy that I shall die tonight,
A quarter before twelve.
               But thou, O Lord,
Aid all this foolish people;[1] let them take
220 Example, pattern: lead them to thy light.
—1842

Ulysses [2]

It little profits that an idle king,[3]
By this still hearth, among these barren crags,
Matched with an agèd wife, I mete and dole
Unequal laws unto a savage race,
5 That hoard, and sleep, and feed, and know not me.

I cannot rest from travel: I will drink
Life to the lees: all times I have enjoyed
Greatly, have suffered greatly, both with those
That loved me, and alone; on shore, and when
10 Through scudding drifts the rainy Hyades[4]
Vext the dim sea: I am become a name;
For always roaming with a hungry heart
Much have I seen and known; cities of men
And manners, climates, councils, governments,
15 Myself not least, but honoured of them all;
And drunk delight of battle with my peers,
Far on the ringing plains of windy Troy.
I am a part of all that I have met;
Yet all experience is an arch wherethrough
20 Gleams that untravelled world, whose margin fades
For ever and for ever when I move.
How dull it is to pause, to make an end,
To rust unburnished, not to shine in use!
As though to breathe were life. Life piled on life
25 Were all too little, and of one to me
Little remains: but every hour is saved
From that eternal silence, something more,
A bringer of new things; and vile it were
For some three suns to store and hoard myself,
30 And this gray spirit yearning in desire
To follow knowledge like a sinking star,
Beyond the utmost bound of human thought.

This is my son, mine own Telemachus,
To whom I leave the sceptre and the isle—
35 Well-loved of me, discerning to fulfil
This labour, by slow prudence to make mild
A rugged people, and through soft degrees
Subdue them to the useful and the good.
Most blameless is he, centred in the sphere
40 Of common duties, decent not to fail
In offices of tenderness, and pay
Meet adoration to my household gods,
When I am gone. He works his work, I mine.

There lies the port; the vessel puffs her sail:
45 There gloom the dark broad seas. My mariners
Souls that have toiled, and wrought, and thought
    with me—
That ever with a frolic welcome took
The thunder and the sunshine, and opposed
Free hearts, free foreheads—you and I are old;
50 Old age hath yet his honour and his toil;
Death closes all: but something ere the end,
Some work of noble note, may yet be done,
Not unbecoming men that strove with Gods.
The lights begin to twinkle from the rocks:

---

[1] Psalm 74:18.

[2] Tennyson's comment on the poem: "The poem was written soon after Arthur Hallam's death, and it gives the feeling about the need of going forward and braving the struggle of life perhaps more simply than anything in *In Memoriam*."

[3] Ulysses, King of Ithaca, has returned to his island from Troy, after ten years of wandering. He now prepares to set sail for his legendary final voyage: *Odyssey* 11.

[4] clouds believed to bring storms.

55 The long day wanes: the slow moon climbs: the deep
Moans round with many voices. Come, my friends,
'Tis not too late to seek a newer world.
Push off, and sitting well in order smite
The sounding furrows; for my purpose holds
60 To sail beyond the sunset, and the baths
Of all the western stars, until I die.
It may be that the gulfs will wash us down:
It may be we shall touch the Happy Isles,[1]
And see the great Achilles, whom we knew.
65 Though much is taken, much abides; and though
We are not now that strength which in old days
Moved earth and heaven; that which we are, we are;
One equal temper of heroic hearts,
Made weak by time and fate, but strong in will
70 To strive, to seek, to find, and not to yield.
    —1842

Tiresias [2]

I wish I were as in the years of old,
While yet the blessèd daylight made itself
Ruddy through both the roofs of sight, and woke
These eyes, now dull, but then so keen to seek
5 The meanings ambushed under all they saw,
The flight of birds, the flame of sacrifice,
What omens may foreshadow fate to man
And woman, and the secret of the Gods.
    My son, the Gods, despite of human prayer,
10 Are slower to forgive than human kings.
The great God, Arês, burns in anger still
Against the guiltless heirs of him from Tyre,
Our Cadmus, out of whom thou art, who found
Beside the springs of Dircê, smote, and stilled
15 Through all its folds the multitudinous beast,
The dragon, which our trembling fathers called
The God's own son.

---

[1] the Isles of the Blest.

[2] Although the poem was published in 1885, Hallam Tennyson notes that it was "partly written at the same time" as "Ulysses" (1833).

    A tale, that told to me,
When but thine age, by age as winter-white
As mine is now, amazed, but made me yearn
20 For larger glimpses of that more than man
Which rolls the heavens, and lifts, and lays the deep,
Yet loves and hates with mortal hates and loves,
And moves unseen among the ways of men.
    Then, in my wanderings all the lands that lie
25 Subjected to the Heliconian ridge
Have heard this footstep fall, although my wont
Was more to scale the highest of the heights
With some strange hope to see the nearer God.
    One naked peak—the sister of the sun
30 Would climb from out the dark, and linger there
To silver all the valleys with her shafts—
There once, but long ago, five-fold thy term
Of years, I lay; the winds were dead for heat;
The noonday crag made the hand burn; and sick
35 For shadow—not one bush was near—I rose
Following a torrent till its myriad falls
Found silence in the hollows underneath.
    There in a secret olive-glade I saw
Pallas Athene climbing from the bath
40 In anger; yet one glittering foot disturbed
The lucid well; one snowy knee was prest
Against the margin flowers; a dreadful light
Came from her golden hair, her golden helm
And all her golden armour on the grass,
45 And from her virgin breast, and virgin eyes
Remaining fixt on mine, till mine grew dark
For ever, and I heard a voice that said
"Henceforth be blind, for thou hast seen too much,
And speak the truth that no man may believe."
50   Son, in the hidden world of sight, that lives
Behind this darkness, I behold her still,
Beyond all work of those who carve the stone,
Beyond all dreams of Godlike womanhood,
Ineffable beauty, out of whom, at a glance,
55 And as it were, perforce, upon me flashed
The power of prophesying—but to me
No power—so chained and coupled with the curse

Of blindness and their unbelief, who heard
And heard not, when I spake of famine, plague,
60 Shrine-shattering earthquake, fire, flood,
      thunderbolt,
And angers of the Gods for evil done
And expiation lacked—no power on Fate,
Theirs, or mine own! for when the crowd would roar
For blood, for war, whose issue was their doom,
65 To cast wise words among the multitude
Was flinging fruit to lions; nor, in hours
Of civil outbreak, when I knew the twain
Would each waste each, and bring on both the yoke
Of stronger states, was mine the voice to curb
70 The madness of our cities and their kings.
      Who ever turned upon his heel to hear
My warning that the tyranny of one
Was prelude to the tyranny of all?
My counsel that the tyranny of all
75 Led backward to the tyranny of one?
      This power hath worked no good to aught that
         lives,
And these blind hands were useless in their wars.
O therefore that the unfulfilled desire,
The grief for ever born from griefs to be,
80 The boundless yearning of the Prophet's heart—
Could *that* stand forth, and like a statue, reared
To some great citizen, win all praise from all
Who past it, saying, "That was he!"
                           In vain!
Virtue must shape itself in deed, and those
85 Whom weakness or necessity have cramped
Within themselves, immerging, each, his urn
In his own well, draw solace as he may.
      Menœceus, thou hast eyes, and I can hear
Too plainly what full tides of onset sap
90 Our seven high gates, and what a weight of war
Rides on those ringing axles! jingle of bits,
Shouts, arrows, tramp of the hornfooted horse
That grind the glebe to powder! Stony showers
Of that ear-stunning hail of Arês crash
95 Along the sounding walls. Above, below,

Shock after shock, the song-built[1] towers and gates
Reel, bruised and butted with the shuddering
War-thunder of iron rams; and from within
The city comes a murmur void of joy,
100 Lest she be taken captive—maidens, wives,
And mothers with their babblers of the dawn,
And oldest age in shadow from the night,
Falling about their shrines before their Gods,
And wailing "Save us."
                        And they wail to thee!
105 These eyeless eyes, that cannot see thine own,
See this, that only in thy virtue lies
The saving of our Thebes; for, yesternight,
To me, the great God Arês, whose one bliss
Is war, and human sacrifice—himself
110 Blood-red from battle, spear and helmet tipt
With stormy light as on a mast at sea,
Stood out before a darkness, crying "Thebes,
Thy Thebes shall fall and perish, for I loathe
The seed of Cadmus—yet if one of these
115 By his own hand—if one of these—"
                                    My son,
No sound is breathed so potent to coerce,
And to conciliate, as their names who dare
For that sweet mother land which gave them birth
Nobly to do, nobly to die. Their names,
120 Graven on memorial columns, are a song
Heard in the future; few, but more than wall
And rampart, their examples reach a hand
Far through all years, and everywhere they meet
And kindle generous purpose, and the strength
125 To mould it into action pure as theirs.
      Fairer thy fate than mine, if life's best end
Be to end well! and thou refusing this,
Unvenerable will thy memory be
While men shall move the lips: but if thou dare—
130 Thou, one of these, the race of Cadmus—then
No stone is fitted in yon marble girth
Whose echo shall not tongue thy glorious doom,

---

[1] Thebes was built to the music of Amphion.

Nor in this pavement but shall ring thy name
To every hoof that clangs it, and the springs
135 Of Dircê laving yonder battle-plain,
Heard from the roofs by night, will murmur thee
To thine own Thebes, while Thebes through thee
    shall stand
Firm-based with all her Gods.
                    The Dragon's cave
Half hid, they tell me, now in flowing vines—
140 Where once he dwelt and whence he rolled himself
At dead of night—thou knowest, and that smooth
    rock
Before it, altar-fashioned, where of late
The woman-breasted Sphinx,[1] with wings drawn
    back,
Folded her lion paws, and looked to Thebes.
145 There blanch the bones of whom she slew, and these
Mixt with her own, because the fierce beast found
A wiser than herself, and dashed herself
Dead in her rage: but thou art wise enough,
Though young, to love thy wiser, blunt the curse
150 Of Pallas, hear, and though I speak the truth
Believe I speak it, let thine own hand strike
Thy youthful pulses into rest and quench
The red God's anger, fearing not to plunge
Thy torch of life in darkness, rather—thou
155 Rejoicing that the sun, the moon, the stars
Send no such light upon the ways of men
As one great deed.
                Thither, my son, and there
Thou, that hast never known the embrace of love,
Offer thy maiden life.
                  This useless hand!
160 I felt one warm tear fall upon it. Gone!
He will achieve his greatness.
                      But for me,
I would that I were gathered to my rest,
And mingled with the famous kings of old,
On whom about their ocean-islets flash

165 The faces of the Gods—the wise man's word,
Here trampled by the populace underfoot,
There crowned with worship—and these eyes will
    find
The men I knew, and watch the chariot whirl
About the goal again, and hunters race
170 The shadowy lion, and the warrior-kings,
In height and prowess more than human, strive
Again for glory, while the golden lyre
Is ever sounding in heroic ears
Heroic hymns, and every way the vales
175 Wind, clouded with the grateful incense-fume
Of those who mix all odour to the Gods
On one far height in one far-shining fire.
    —1885

The Epic [Morte d'Arthur] [2]

At Francis Allen's on the Christmas-eve,—
The game of forfeits done—the girls all kissed
Beneath the sacred bush and past away—
The parson Holmes, the poet Everard Hall,
5 The host, and I sat round the wassail-bowl,
Then half-way ebbed: and there we held a talk,
How all the old honour had from Christmas gone,
Or gone, or dwindled down to some odd games
In some odd nooks like this; till I, tired out
10 With cutting eights that day upon the pond,
Where, three times slipping from the outer edge,
I bumped the ice into three several stars,
Fell in a doze; and half-awake I heard
The parson taking wide and wider sweeps,
15 Now harping on the church-commissioners,[3]
Now hawking at Geology and schism;
Until I woke, and found him settled down

---

[1] The story of the Sphinx is from *Phoenissae*.

[2] Although published in 1842, the frames for *Morte d'Arthur* (both the introduction and conclusion—see l. 273ff.) were written some time after 1835.

[3] the Ecclesiastical Commission established in 1835 to administer the revenues of the Church of England.

Upon the general decay of faith
Right through the world, "at home was little left,
20 And none abroad: there was no anchor, none,
To hold by." Francis, laughing, clapt his hand
On Everard's shoulder, with "I hold by him."
"And I," quoth Everard, "by the wassail-bowl."
"Why yes," I said, "we knew your gift that way
25 At college: but another which you had,
I mean of verse (for so we held it then),
What came of that?" "You know," said Frank, "he
  burnt
His epic, his King Arthur, some twelve books"—
And then to me demanding why? "Oh, sir,
30 He thought that nothing new was said, or else
Something so said 'twas nothing—that a truth
Looks freshest in the fashion of the day:
God knows: he has a mint of reasons: ask.
It pleased *me* well enough." "Nay, nay," said Hall,
35 "Why take the style of those heroic times?
For nature brings not back the Mastodon,
Nor we those times; and why should any man
Remodel models? these twelve books of mine
Were faint Homeric echoes, nothing-worth,
40 Mere chaff and draff, much better burnt." "But I,"
Said Francis, "picked the eleventh from this hearth
And have it: keep a thing, its use will come.
I hoard it as a sugar-plum for Holmes."
He laughed, and I, though sleepy, like a horse
45 That hears the corn-bin open, pricked my ears;
For I remembered Everard's college fame
When we were Freshmen: then at my request
He brought it; and the poet little urged,
But with some prelude of disparagement,
50 Read, mouthing out his hollow oes and aes,
Deep-chested music,[1] and to this result.

---

[1] as Tennyson himself was said to have read.

MORTE D'ARTHUR [2]

So all day long the noise of battle rolled
Among the mountains by the winter sea;
Until King Arthur's table, man by man,
Had fallen in Lyonnesse[3] about their Lord,
5 King Arthur: then, because his wound was deep,
The bold Sir Bedivere uplifted him,
Sir Bedivere, the last of all his knights,
And bore him to a chapel nigh the field,
A broken chancel with a broken cross,
10 That stood on a dark strait of barren land.
On one side lay the Ocean, and on one
Lay a great water, and the moon was full.

Then spake King Arthur to Sir Bedivere:
"The sequel of today unsolders all
15 The goodliest fellowship of famous knights
Whereof this world holds record. Such a sleep
They sleep—the men I loved. I think that we
Shall never more, at any future time,
Delight our souls with talk of knightly deeds,
20 Walking about the gardens of the halls
Of Camelot,[4] as in the days that were.
I perish by this people which I made,—
Though Merlin[5] sware that I should come again
To rule once more—but let what will be, be,
25 I am so deeply smitten through the helm
That without help I cannot last till morn.
Thou therefore take my brand Excalibur,[6]
Which was my pride: for thou rememberest how
In those old days, one summer noon, an arm

---

[2] written in 1833–34 under the shock of Arthur Hallam's death; later incorporated in the *Idylls of the King* as *The Passing of Arthur* (1869) where it was preceded by 169 lines and followed by 29 lines. Based largely on Malory's *Morte d'Arthur* 21.4–5.

[3] the legendary country that lay between Cornwall and the Scilly Islands.

[4] the city of Arthur's court.

[5] the magician and prophet of Arthurian romance.

[6] Arthur's sword, given to him by the Lady of the Lake.

30 Rose up from out the bosom of the lake,
Clothed in white samite,[1] mystic, wonderful,
Holding the sword—and how I rowed across
And took it, and have worn it, like a king:
And, wheresoever I am sung or told
35 In aftertime, this also shall be known:
But now delay not: take Excalibur,
And fling him far into the middle mere:
Watch what thou seëst, and lightly bring me
      word."

To him replied the bold Sir Bedivere:
40 "It is not meet, Sir King, to leave thee thus,
Aidless, alone, and smitten through the helm.
A little thing may harm a wounded man.
Yet I thy hest will all perform at full,
Watch what I see, and lightly bring thee word."

45   So saying, from the ruined shrine he stept
And in the moon athwart the place of tombs,
Where lay the mighty bones of ancient men,
Old knights, and over them the sea-wind sang
Shrill, chill, with flakes of foam. He, stepping down
50 By zig-zag paths, and juts of pointed rock,
Came on the shining levels of the lake.

There drew he forth the brand Excalibur,
And o'er him, drawing it, the winter moon,
Brightening the skirts of a long cloud, ran forth
55 And sparkled keen with frost against the hilt:
For all the haft twinkled with diamond sparks,
Myriads of topaz-lights, and jacinth-work
Of subtlest jewellery. He gazed so long
That both his eyes were dazzled, as he stood,
60 This way and that dividing the swift mind,
In act to throw: but at the last it seemed
Better to leave Excalibur concealed
There in the many-knotted waterflags,

---

[1] a rich silk material.

That whistled stiff and dry about the marge.
65 So strode he back slow to the wounded King.

Then spake King Arthur to Sir Bedivere:
"Hast thou performed my mission which I gave?
What is it thou hast seen? or what hast heard?"

And answer made the bold Sir Bedivere:
70 "I heard the ripple washing in the reeds,
And the wild water lapping on the crag."

To whom replied King Arthur, faint and pale:
"Thou hast betrayed thy nature and thy name,
Not rendering true answer, as beseemed
75 Thy fëalty, nor like a noble knight:
For surer sign had followed, either hand,
Or voice, or else a motion of the mere.
This is a shameful thing for men to lie.
Yet now, I charge thee, quickly go again
80 As thou art lief and dear, and do the thing
I bad thee, watch, and lightly bring me word."

Then went Sir Bedivere the second time
Across the ridge, and paced beside the mere,
Counting the dewy pebbles, fixed in thought;
85 But when he saw the wonder of the hilt,
How curiously and strangely chased, he smote
His palms together, and he cried aloud,

"And if indeed I cast the brand away,
Surely a precious thing, one worthy note,
90 Should thus be lost for ever from the earth,
Which might have pleased the eyes of many men.
What good should follow this, if this were done?
What harm, undone? deep harm to disobey,
Seeing obedience is the bond of rule.
95 Were it well to obey then, if a king demand
An act unprofitable, against himself?
The King is sick, and knows not what he does.
What record, or what relic of my lord
Should be to aftertime, but empty breath

100 And rumours of a doubt? but were this kept,
Stored in some treasure-house of mighty kings,
Some one might show it at a joust of arms,
Saying, 'King Arthur's sword, Excalibur,
Wrought by the lonely maiden of the Lake.
105 Nine years she wrought it, sitting in the deeps
Upon the hidden bases of the hills.'
So might some old man speak in the aftertime
To all the people, winning reverence.
But now much honour and much fame were lost."

110 So spake he, clouded with his own conceit,
And hid Excalibur the second time,
And so strode back slow to the wounded King.

Then spoke King Arthur, breathing heavily:
"What is it thou hast seen? or what hast heard?"
115 And answer made the bold Sir Bedivere:
"I heard the water lapping on the crag,
And the long ripple washing in the reeds."

To whom replied King Arthur, much in wrath:
"Ah, miserable and unkind, untrue,
120 Unknightly, traitor-hearted! Woe is me!
Authority forgets a dying king,
Laid widowed of the power in his eye
That bowed the will. I see thee what thou art,
For thou, the latest-left of all my knights,
125 In whom should meet the offices of all,
Thou wouldst betray me for the precious hilt;
Either from lust of gold, or like a girl
Valuing the giddy pleasure of the eyes.
Yet, for a man may fail in duty twice,
130 And the third time may prosper, get thee hence:
But, if thou spare to fling Excalibur,
I will arise and slay thee with my hands."

Then quickly rose Sir Bedivere, and ran,
And, leaping down the ridges lightly, plunged
135 Among the bulrush-beds, and clutched the sword,
And strongly wheeled and threw it. The great brand
Made lightnings in the splendour of the moon,
And flashing round and round, and whirled in an
arch,
Shot like a streamer of the northern morn,
140 Seen where the moving isles of winter shock[1]
By night, with noises of the northern sea.
So flashed and fell the brand Excalibur:
But ere he dipt the surface, rose an arm
Clothed in white samite, mystic, wonderful,
145 And caught him by the hilt, and brandished him
Three times, and drew him under in the mere.
And lightly went the other to the King.

Then spoke King Arthur, drawing thicker breath:
"Now see I by thine eyes that this is done.
150 Speak out: what is it thou hast heard, or seen?"

And answer made the bold Sir Bedivere:
"Sir King, I closed mine eyelids, lest the gems
Should blind my purpose, for I never saw,
Nor shall see, here or elsewhere, till I die,
155 Not though I live three lives of mortal men,
So great a miracle as yonder hilt.
Then with both hands I flung him, wheeling him;
But when I looked again, behold an arm,
Clothed in white samite, mystic, wonderful,
160 That caught him by the hilt, and brandished him
Three times, and drew him under in the mere."

And answer made King Arthur, breathing hard:
"My end draws nigh; 'tis time that I were gone.
Make broad thy shoulders to receive my weight,
165 And bear me to the margin; yet I fear
My wound hath taken cold, and I shall die."

So saying, from the pavement he half rose,
Slowly, with pain, reclining on his arm,
And looking wistfully with wide blue eyes
170 As in a picture. Him Sir Bedivere

---

[1] icebergs.

Remorsefully regarded through his tears,
And would have spoken, but he found not words,
Then took with care, and kneeling on one knee,
O'er both his shoulders drew the languid hands,
175 And rising bore him through the place of tombs.

But, as he walked, King Arthur panted hard,
Like one that feels a nightmare on his bed
When all the house is mute. So sighed the King,
Muttering and murmuring at his ear, "Quick, quick!
180 I fear it is too late, and I shall die."
But the other swiftly strode from ridge to ridge,
Clothed with his breath, and looking, as he walked,
Larger than human on the frozen hills.
He heard the deep behind him, and a cry
185 Before. His own thought drove him, like a goad.
Dry clashed his harness in the icy caves
And barren chasms, and all to left and right
The bare black cliff clanged round him, as he based
His feet on juts of slippery crag that rang
190 Sharp-smitten with the dint of armèd heels—
And on a sudden, lo! the level lake,
And the long glories of the winter moon.
Then saw they how there hove a dusky barge,
Dark as a funeral scarf from stem to stern,
195 Beneath them; and descending they were ware
That all the decks were dense with stately forms
Black-stoled, black-hooded, like a dream—by these
Three Queens with crowns of gold—and from
    them rose
A cry that shivered to the tingling stars,
200 And, as it were one voice, an agony
Of lamentation, like a wind, that shrills
All night in a waste land, where no one comes,
Or hath come, since the making of the world.

Then murmured Arthur, "Place me in the
    barge,"
205 And to the barge they came. There those three
    Queens
Put forth their hands, and took the King, and wept.

But she, that rose the tallest of them all
And fairest, laid his head upon her lap,
And loosed the shattered casque, and chafed his
    hands,
210 And called him by his name, complaining loud,
And dropping bitter tears against his brow
Striped with dark blood: for all his face was white
And colourless, and like the withered moon
Smote by the fresh beam of the springing east;
215 And all his greaves and cuisses dashed with drops
Of onset;[1] and the light and lustrous curls—
That made his forehead like a rising sun
High from the daïs-throne—were parched with
    dust;
Or, clotted into points and hanging loose,
220 Mixed with the knightly growth that fringed his lips.
So like a shattered column lay the King;
Not like that Arthur who, with lance in rest,
From spur to plume a star of tournament,
Shot through the lists at Camelot, and charged
225 Before the eyes of ladies and of kings.

Then loudly cried the bold Sir Bedivere,
"Ah! my Lord Arthur, whither shall I go?
Where shall I hide my forehead and my eyes?
For now I see the true old times are dead,
230 When every morning brought a noble chance,
And every chance brought out a noble knight.
Such times have been not since the light that led
The holy Elders with the gift of myrrh.
But now the whole ROUND TABLE is dissolved
235 Which was an image of the mighty world;
And I, the last, go forth companionless,
And the days darken round me, and the years,
Among new men, strange faces, other minds."

And slowly answered Arthur from the barge:
240 "The old order changeth, yielding place to new,
And God fulfils Himself in many ways,

---

[1] armor for shin and thigh dashed with drops of blood from battle.

Lest one good custom should corrupt the world.
Comfort thyself: what comfort is in me?
I have lived my life, and that which I have done
245 May He within Himself make pure! but thou,
If thou shouldst never see my face again,
Pray for my soul. More things are wrought by prayer
Than this world dreams of. Wherefore, let thy voice
Rise like a fountain for me night and day.
250 For what are men better than sheep or goats
That nourish a blind life within the brain,
If, knowing God, they lift not hands of prayer
Both for themselves and those who call them friend?
For so the whole round earth is every way
255 Bound by gold chains about the feet of God.
But now farewell. I am going a long way
With these thou seëst—if indeed I go—
(For all my mind is clouded with a doubt)
To the island-valley of Avilion;[1]
260 Where falls not hail, or rain, or any snow,
Nor ever wind blows loudly; but it lies
Deep-meadowed, happy, fair with orchard-lawns
And bowery hollows crowned with summer sea,
Where I will heal me of my grievous wound."

265   So said he, and the barge with oar and sail
Moved from the brink, like some full-breasted swan
That, fluting a wild carol ere her death,
Ruffles her pure cold plume, and takes the flood
With swarthy webs. Long stood Sir Bedivere
270 Revolving many memories, till the hull
Looked one black dot against the verge of dawn,
And on the mere the wailing died away.

[THE EPIC]

Here ended Hall, and our last light, that long
Had winked and threatened darkness, flared and fell:
275 At which the Parson, sent to sleep with sound,
And waked with silence, grunted "Good!" but we
Sat rapt: it was the tone with which he read—

Perhaps some modern touches here and there
Redeemed it from the charge of nothingness—
280 Or else we loved the man, and prized his work;
I know not: but we sitting, as I said,
The cock crew loud; as at that time of year
The lusty bird takes every hour for dawn:
Then Francis, muttering, like a man ill-used,
285 "There now—that's nothing!" drew a little back,
And drove his heel into the smouldering log,
That sent a blast of sparkles up the flue:
And so to bed; where yet in sleep I seemed
To sail with Arthur under looming shores,
290 Point after point; till on to dawn, when dreams
Begin to feel the truth and stir of day,
To me, methought, who waited with a crowd,
There came a bark that, blowing forward, bore
King Arthur, like a modern gentleman
295 Of stateliest port; and all the people cried,
"Arthur is come again: he cannot die."
Then those that stood upon the hills behind
Repeated—"Come again, and thrice as fair;"
And, further inland, voices echoed—"Come
300 With all good things, and war shall be no more."
At this a hundred bells began to peal,
That with the sound I woke, and heard indeed
The clear church-bells ring in the Christmas-morn.
—1842

"Break, break, break"

Break, break, break,
On thy cold gray stones, O Sea!
And I would that my tongue could utter
    The thoughts that arise in me.

5 O well for the fisherman's boy,
    That he shouts with his sister at play!
O well for the sailor lad,
    That he sings in his boat on the bay!

---

[1] the Isle of the Blest.

And the stately ships go on
10   To their haven under the hill;
But O for the touch of a vanished hand,
      And the sound of a voice that is still!

Break, break, break,
      At the foot of thy crags, O Sea!
15   But the tender grace of a day that is dead
      Will never come back to me.
                                    —1842

Locksley Hall

Comrades, leave me here a little, while as yet 'tis
      early morn:
Leave me here, and when you want me, sound
      upon the bugle-horn.

'Tis the place, and all around it, as of old, the
      curlews call,
Dreary gleams about the moorland flying over
      Locksley Hall;[1]

5   Locksley Hall, that in the distance overlooks the
      sandy tracts,
And the hollow ocean-ridges roaring into cataracts.

Many a night from yonder ivied casement, ere I
      went to rest,
Did I look on great Orion sloping slowly to the
      West.

Many a night I saw the Pleiads, rising through the
      mellow shade,
10   Glitter like a swarm of fire-flies tangled in a silver
      braid.

Here about the beach I wandered, nourishing a
      youth sublime

With the fairy tales of science, and the long result
      of Time;

When the centuries behind me like a fruitful land
      reposed;
When I clung to all the present for the promise
      that it closed:

15   When I dipt into the future far as human eye could
      see;
Saw the Vision of the world, and all the wonder
      that would be.—

In the Spring a fuller crimson comes upon the
      robin's breast;
In the Spring the wanton lapwing gets himself
      another crest;

In the Spring a livelier iris changes on the
      burnished dove;
20   In the Spring a young man's fancy lightly turns to
      thoughts of love.

Then her cheek was pale and thinner than should
      be for one so young,
And her eyes on all my motions with a mute
      observance hung.

And I said, "My cousin Amy, speak, and speak the
      truth to me,
Trust me, cousin, all the current of my being sets
      to thee."

25   On her pallid cheek and forehead came a colour
      and a light,
As I have seen the rosy red flushing in the northern
      night.

And she turned—her bosom shaken with a sudden
      storm of sighs—
All the spirit deeply dawning in the dark of hazel
      eyes—

---

[1]   meant, said Tennyson, "to express the flying gleams of light across a
dreary moorland."

Saying, "I have hid my feelings, fearing they should
    do me wrong;"
30 Saying, "Dost thou love me, cousin?" weeping, "I
    have loved thee long."

Love took up the glass of Time, and turned it in his
    glowing hands;
Every moment, lightly shaken, ran itself in golden
    sands.

Love took up the harp of Life, and smote on all the
    chords with might;
Smote the chord of Self, that, trembling, passed in
    music out of sight.

35 Many a morning on the moorland did we hear the
    copses ring,
And her whisper thronged my pulses with the
    fulness of the Spring.

Many an evening by the waters did we watch the
    stately ships,
And our spirits rushed together at the touching of
    the lips.

O my cousin, shallow-hearted! O my Amy, mine
    no more!
40 O the dreary, dreary moorland! O the barren,
    barren shore!

Falser than all fancy fathoms, falser than all songs
    have sung,
Puppet to a father's threat, and servile to a shrewish
    tongue!

Is it well to wish thee happy?—having known
    me—to decline
On a range of lower feelings and a narrower heart
    than mine!

45 Yet it shall be: thou shalt lower to his level day by
    day,

What is fine within thee growing coarse to
    sympathise with clay.

As the husband is, the wife is: thou art mated with
    a clown,
And the grossness of his nature will have weight to
    drag thee down.

He will hold thee, when his passion shall have
    spent its novel force,
50 Something better than his dog, a little dearer than
    his horse.

What is this? his eyes are heavy: think not they are
    glazed with wine.
Go to him: it is thy duty: kiss him: take his hand in
    thine.

It may be my lord is weary, that his brain is
    overwrought:
Soothe him with thy finer fancies, touch him with
    thy lighter thought.

55 He will answer to the purpose, easy things to
    understand—
Better thou wert dead before me, though I slew
    thee with my hand!

Better thou and I were lying, hidden from the
    heart's disgrace,
Rolled in one another's arms, and silent in a last
    embrace.

Cursèd be the social wants that sin against the
    strength of youth!
60 Cursèd be the social lies that warp us from the
    living truth!

Cursèd be the sickly forms that err from honest
    Nature's rule!
Cursèd be the gold that gilds the straitened
    forehead of the fool!

Well—'tis well that I should bluster!—Hadst thou
    less unworthy proved—
Would to God—for I have loved thee more
    than ever wife was loved.

65 Am I mad, that I should cherish that which bears
    but bitter fruit?
I will pluck it from my bosom, though my heart be
    at the root.

Never, though my mortal summers to such length
    of years should come
As the many-wintered crow that leads the clanging
    rookery home.

Where is comfort? in division of the records of the
    mind?
70 Can I part her from herself, and love her, as I knew
    her, kind?

I remember one that perished: sweetly did she
    speak and move:
Such a one do I remember, whom to look at was to
    love.

Can I think of her as dead, and love her for the
    love she bore?
No—she never loved me truly: love is love for
    evermore.

75 Comfort? comfort scorned of devils! this is truth
    the poet sings,
That a sorrow's crown of sorrow is remembering
    happier things.

Drug thy memories, lest thou learn it, lest thy heart
    be put to proof,
In the dead unhappy night, and when the rain is on
    the roof.

Like a dog, he hunts in dreams, and thou art
    staring at the wall,
80 Where the dying night-lamp flickers, and the
    shadows rise and fall.

Then a hand shall pass before thee, pointing to his
    drunken sleep,
To thy widowed marriage-pillows, to the tears that
    thou wilt weep.

Thou shalt hear the "Never, never," whispered by
    the phantom years,
And a song from out the distance in the ringing of
    thine ears;

85 And an eye shall vex thee, looking ancient kindness
    on thy pain.
Turn thee, turn thee on thy pillow: get thee to thy
    rest again.

Nay, but Nature brings thee solace; for a tender
    voice will cry.
'Tis a purer life than thine; a lip to drain thy
    trouble dry.

Baby lips will laugh me down: my latest rival brings
    thee rest.
90 Baby fingers, waxen touches, press me from the
    mother's breast.

O, the child too clothes the father with a dearness
    not his due.
Half is thine and half is his: it will be worthy of the
    two.

O, I see thee old and formal, fitted to thy petty part,
With a little hoard of maxims preaching down a
    daughter's heart.

95 "They were dangerous guides the feelings—she
    herself was not exempt—

Truly, she herself had suffered"—Perish in thy self-
     contempt!

Overlive it—lower yet—be happy! wherefore
     should I care?
I myself must mix with action, lest I wither by
     despair.

What is that which I should turn to, lighting upon
     days like these?
100 Every door is barred with gold, and opens but to
     golden keys.

Every gate is thronged with suitors, all the markets
     overflow.
I have but an angry fancy: what is that which I
     should do?

I had been content to perish, falling on the
     foeman's ground,
When the ranks are rolled in vapour, and the winds
     are laid with sound.

105 But the jingling of the guinea helps the hurt that
     Honour feels,
And the nations do but murmur, snarling at each
     other's heels.

Can I but relive in sadness? I will turn that earlier
     page.
Hide me from my deep emotion, O thou
     wondrous Mother-Age!

Make me feel the wild pulsation that I felt before
     the strife,
110 When I heard my days before me, and the tumult
     of my life;

Yearning for the large excitement that the coming
     years would yield,

Eager-hearted as a boy when first he leaves his
     father's field,

And at night along the dusky highway near and
     nearer drawn,
Sees in heaven the light of London flaring like a
     dreary dawn;

115 And his spirit leaps within him to be gone before
     him then,
Underneath the light he looks at, in among the
     throngs of men:

Men, my brothers, men the workers, ever reaping
     something new:
That which they have done but earnest of the
     things that they shall do:

For I dipt into the future, far as human eye could
     see,
120 Saw the Vision of the world, and all the wonder
     that would be;

Saw the heavens fill with commerce, argosies of
     magic sails,
Pilots of the purple twilight, dropping down with
     costly bales;

Heard the heavens fill with shouting, and there
     rained a ghastly dew
From the nations' airy navies grappling in the
     central blue;

125 Far along the world-wide whisper of the south-
     wind rushing warm,
With the standards of the peoples plunging
     through the thunder-storm;

Till the war-drum throbbed no longer, and the
     battle-flags were furled
In the Parliament of man, the Federation of the
     world.

There the common sense of most shall hold a
    fretful realm in awe,
130 And the kindly earth shall slumber, lapt in
    universal law.

So I triumphed ere my passion sweeping through
    me left me dry,
Left me with the palsied heart, and left me with the
    jaundiced eye;

Eye, to which all order festers, all things here are
    out of joint:
Science moves, but slowly slowly, creeping on from
    point to point:

135 Slowly comes a hungry people, as a lion creeping
    nigher,
Glares at one that nods and winks behind a slowly-
    dying fire.

Yet I doubt not through the ages one increasing
    purpose runs,
And the thoughts of men are widened with the
    process of the suns.

What is that to him that reaps not harvest of his
    youthful joys,
140 Though the deep heart of existence beat for ever
    like a boy's?

Knowledge comes, but wisdom lingers, and I linger
    on the shore,
And the individual withers, and the world is more
    and more.

Knowledge comes, but wisdom lingers, and he
    bears a laden breast,
Full of sad experience, moving toward the stillness
    of his rest.

145 Hark, my merry comrades call me, sounding on the
    bugle-horn,

They to whom my foolish passion were a target for
    their scorn:

Shall it not be scorn to me to harp on such a
    mouldered string?
I am shamed through all my nature to have loved
    so slight a thing.

Weakness to be wroth with weakness! woman's
    pleasure, woman's pain—
150 Nature made them blinder motions bounded in a
    shallower brain:

Woman is the lesser man, and all thy passions,
    matched with mine,
Are as moonlight unto sunlight, and as water unto
    wine—

Here at least, where nature sickens, nothing. Ah,
    for some retreat
Deep in yonder shining Orient, where my life
    began to beat;

155 Where in wild Mahratta-battle[1] fell my father
    evil-starred;—
I was left a trampled orphan, and a selfish uncle's
    ward.

Or to burst all links of habit—there to wander far
    away,
On from island unto island at the gateways of the
    day.

Larger constellations burning, mellow moons and
    happy skies,
160 Breadths of tropic shade and palms in cluster,
    knots of Paradise.

Never comes the trader, never floats an European
    flag,

---

[1] soldiers of Bombay who were conquered in 1818.

Slides the bird o'er lustrous woodland, swings the
trailer from the crag;

Droops the heavy-blossomed bower, hangs the
heavy-fruited tree—
Summer isles of Eden lying in dark-purple spheres
of sea.

165 There methinks would be enjoyment more than in
this march of mind,
In the steamship, in the railway, in the thoughts
that shake mankind.

There the passions cramped no longer shall have
scope and breathing space;
I will take some savage woman, she shall rear my
dusky race.

Iron jointed, supple-sinewed, they shall dive, and
they shall run,
170 Catch the wild goat by the hair, and hurl their
lances in the sun;

Whistle back the parrot's call, and leap the
rainbows of the brooks,
Not with blinded eyesight poring over miserable
books—

Fool, again the dream, the fancy! but I *know* my
words are wild,
But I count the gray barbarian lower than the
Christian child.

175 I, to herd with narrow foreheads, vacant of our
glorious gains,
Like a beast with lower pleasures, like a beast with
lower pains!

Mated with a squalid savage—what to me were sun
or clime?

I the heir of all the ages, in the foremost files of
time—

I that rather held it better men should perish one
by one,
180 Than that earth should stand at gaze like Joshua's
moon in Ajalon![1]

Not in vain the distance beacons. Forward, forward
let us range,
Let the great world spin for ever down the ringing
grooves of change.

Through the shadow of the globe we sweep into
the younger day:
Better fifty years of Europe than a cycle of Cathay.

185 Mother-Age (for mine I knew not) help me as
when life begun:
Rift the hills, and roll the waters, flash the
lightnings, weigh the Sun.

O, I see the crescent promise of my spirit hath not
set.
Ancient founts of inspiration well through all my
fancy yet.

Howsoever these things be, a long farewell to
Locksley Hall!
190 Now for me the woods may wither, now for me the
roof-tree fall.

Comes a vapour from the margin, blackening over
heath and holt,
Cramming all the blast before it, in its breast a
thunderbolt.

Let it fall on Locksley Hall, with rain or hail, or fire
or snow;

---

[1] Joshua commanded the moon to remain stationary in the vale of
Ajalon.

For the mighty wind arises, roaring seaward, and I
   go.
—1842

The Vision of Sin

I

I had a vision when the night was late:
A youth came riding toward a palace-gate.
He rode a horse with wings, that would have
   flown,
But that his heavy rider kept him down.
5   And from the palace came a child of sin,
And took him by the curls, and led him in,
Where sat a company with heated eyes,
Expecting when a fountain should arise:
A sleepy light upon their brows and lips—
10   As when the sun, a crescent of eclipse,
Dreams over lake and lawn, and isles and capes—
Suffused them, sitting, lying, languid shapes,
By heaps of gourds, and skins of wine, and piles of
   grapes.

II

Then methought I heard a mellow sound,
15   Gathering up from all the lower ground;
Narrowing in to where they sat assembled
Low voluptuous music winding trembled,
Woven in circles: they that heard it sighed,
Panted hand-in-hand with faces pale,
20   Swung themselves, and in low tones replied;
Till the fountain spouted, showering wide
Sleet of diamond-drift and pearly hail;
Then the music touched the gates and died;
Rose again from where it seemed to fail,
25   Stormed in orbs of song, a growing gale;
Till thronging in and in, to where they waited,
As 'twere a hundred-throated nightingale,
The strong tempestuous treble throbbed and
   palpitated;
Ran into its giddiest whirl of sound,

30   Caught the sparkles, and in circles,
Purple gauzes, golden hazes, liquid mazes,
Flung the torrent rainbow round:
Then they started from their places,
Moved with violence, changed in hue,
35   Caught each other with wild grimaces,
Half-invisible to the view,
Wheeling with precipitate paces
To the melody, till they flew,
Hair, and eyes, and limbs, and faces,
40   Twisted hard in fierce embraces,
Like to Furies, like to Graces,
Dashed together in blinding dew:[1]
Till, killed with some luxurious agony,
The nerve-dissolving melody
45   Fluttered headlong from the sky.

III

And then I looked up toward a mountain-tract,
That girt the region with high cliff and lawn:
I saw that every morning, far withdrawn
Beyond the darkness and the cataract,
50   God made Himself an awful rose of dawn,
Unheeded: and detaching, fold by fold,
From those still heights, and, slowly drawing near,
A vapour heavy, hueless, formless, cold,
Came floating on for many a month and year,
55   Unheeded: and I thought I would have spoken,
And warned that madman ere it grew too late:
But, as in dreams, I could not. Mine was broken,
When that cold vapour touched the palace gate,
And linked again. I saw within my head
60   A gray and gap-toothed man as lean as death,
Who slowly rode across a withered heath,
And lighted at a ruined inn, and said:

IV

"Wrinkled ostler, grim and thin!
   Here is custom come your way;

---

[1] mist.

65 Take my brute, and lead him in,
    Stuff his ribs with mouldy hay.

"Bitter barmaid, waning fast!
    See that sheets are on my bed;
What! the flower of life is past:
70   It is long before you wed.

"Slip-shod waiter, lank and sour,
    At the Dragon on the heath!
Let us have a quiet hour,
    Let us hob-and-nob with Death.

75 "I am old, but let me drink;
    Bring me spices, bring me wine;
I remember, when I think,
    That my youth was half divine.

"Wine is good for shrivelled lips,
80   When a blanket wraps the day,
When the rotten woodland drips,
    And the leaf is stamped in clay.

"Sit thee down, and have no shame,
    Cheek by jowl, and knee by knee:
85 What care I for any name?
    What for order or degree?

"Let me screw thee up a peg:
    Let me loose thy tongue with wine:
Callest thou that thing a leg?
90   Which is thinnest? thine or mine?

"Thou shalt not be saved by works:
    Thou hast been a sinner too:
Ruined trunks on withered forks,
    Empty scarecrows, I and you!

95 "Fill the cup, and fill the can:
    Have a rouse[1] before the morn:
Every moment dies a man,
    Every moment one is born.

"We are men of ruined blood;
100   Therefore comes it we are wise.
Fish are we that love the mud,
    Rising to no fancy-flies.

"Name and fame! to fly sublime
    Through the courts, the camps, the schools,
105 Is to be the ball of Time,
    Bandied by the hands of fools.

"Friendship!—to be two in one—
    Let the canting liar pack!
Well I know, when I am gone,
110   How she mouths behind my back.

"Virtue!—to be good and just—
    Every heart, when sifted well,
Is a clot of warmer dust,
    Mixed with cunning sparks of hell.

115 "O! we two as well can look
    Whited thought and cleanly life
As the priest, above his book
    Leering at his neighbour's wife.

"Fill the cup, and fill the can:
120   Have a rouse before the morn:
Every moment dies a man,
    Every moment one is born.

"Drink, and let the parties rave:
    They are filled with idle spleen;
125 Rising, falling, like a wave,
    For they know not what they mean.

---

[1] carouse.

147

"He that roars for liberty
   Faster binds a tyrant's power;
And the tyrant's cruel glee
130   Forces on the freer hour.

"Fill the can, and fill the cup:
   All the windy ways of men
Are but dust that rises up,
   And is lightly laid again.

135 "Greet her with applausive breath,
   Freedom, gaily doth she tread;
In her right a civic wreath,
   In her left a human head.

"No, I love not what is new;
140   She is of an ancient house:
And I think we know the hue
   Of that cap¹ upon her brows.

"Let her go! her thirst she slakes
   Where the bloody conduit runs,
145 Then her sweetest meal she makes
   On the first-born of her sons.

"Drink to lofty hopes that cool—
   Visions of a perfect State:
Drink we, last, the public fool,
150   Frantic love and frantic hate.

"Chant me now some wicked stave,
   Till thy drooping courage rise,
And the glow-worm of the grave
   Glimmer in thy rheumy eyes.

155 "Fear not thou to loose thy tongue;
   Set thy hoary fancies free;
What is loathsome to the young
   Savours well to thee and me.

"Change, reverting to the years,
160   When thy nerves could understand
What there is in loving tears,
   And the warmth of hand in hand.

"Tell me tales of thy first love—
   April hopes, the fools of chance;
165 Till the graves begin to move,
   And the dead begin to dance.

"Fill the can, and fill the cup:
   All the windy ways of men
Are but dust that rises up,
170   And is lightly laid again.

"Trooping from their mouldy dens
   The chap-fallen² circle spreads:
Welcome, fellow-citizens,
   Hollow hearts and empty heads!

175 "You are bones, and what of that?
   Every face, however full,
Padded round with flesh and fat,
   Is but modelled on a skull.

"Death is king, and Vivat Rex!
180   Tread a measure on the stones,
Madam—if I know your sex,
   From the fashion of your bones.

"No, I cannot praise the fire
   In your eye—nor yet your lip:
185 All the more do I admire
   Joints of cunning workmanship.

"Lo! God's likeness—the ground-plan—
   Neither modelled, glazed, nor framed:
Buss me, thou rough sketch of man,
190   Far too naked to be shamed!

---

¹ red cap of the French revolutionists.

² gaping jaw of a skeleton.

"Drink to Fortune, drink to Chance,
    While we keep a little breath!
Drink to heavy Ignorance!
    Hob-and-nob with brother Death!

195 "Thou art mazed, the night is long,
    And the longer night is near:
What! I am not all as wrong
    As a bitter jest is dear.

"Youthful hopes, by scores, to all,
200   When the locks are crisp and curled;
Unto me my maudlin gall
    And my mockeries of the world.

"Fill the cup, and fill the can:
    Mingle madness, mingle scorn!
205 Dregs of life, and lees of man:
    Yet we will not die forlorn."

V

The voice grew faint: there came a further change:
Once more uprose the mystic mountain-range:
Below were men and horses pierced with worms,
210 And slowly quickening into lower forms;
By shards and scurf of salt, and scum of dross,
Old plash[1] of rains, and refuse patched with moss.
Then some one spake: "Behold! it was a crime
Of sense avenged by sense that wore with time."[2]
215 Another said: "The crime of sense became
The crime of malice, and is equal blame."
And one: "He had not wholly quenched his power;
A little grain of conscience made him sour."
At last I heard a voice upon the slope
220 Cry to the summit, "Is there any hope?"
To which an answer pealed from that high land,
But in a tongue no man could understand;
And on the glimmering limit far withdrawn
God made Himself an awful rose of dawn.
—1842

---

[1] puddle.

[2] "The sensualist becomes worn out by his senses." (Tennyson's note.)

In Memoriam A.H.H. [3]

OBIT MDCCCXXXIII

[PROLOGUE]

Strong Son of God, immortal Love,
    Whom we, that have not seen thy face,
    By faith, and faith alone, embrace,
Believing where we cannot prove;

5 Thine are these orbs of light and shade;
    Thou madest Life in man and brute;
    Thou madest Death; and lo, thy foot
Is on the skull which thou hast made.

Thou wilt not leave us in the dust:
10   Thou madest man, he knows not why,
    He thinks he was not made to die;
And thou hast made him: thou art just.

Thou seemest human and divine,
    The highest, holiest manhood, thou:
15   Our wills are ours, we know not how;
Our wills are ours, to make them thine.

---

[3] Tennyson's close friend, Arthur Henry Hallam, died at Vienna on 15 September 1833. As Christopher Ricks notes in his outstanding edition of Tennyson: "No event in Tennyson's life was of greater importance" (*The Poems of Tennyson*, 305). In Hallam Tennyson's *Memoir*, Tennyson is reported as saying: "It must be remembered that this is a poem, *not* an actual biography. It is founded on our friendship, on the engagement of Arthur Hallam to my sister, on his sudden death at Vienna, just before the time fixed for their marriage, and on his burial at Clevedon Church. The poem concludes with the marriage of my youngest sister Cecilia. It was meant to be a kind of *Divina Commedia*, ending with happiness. The sections were written at many different places, and as the phases of our intercourse came to my memory and suggested them. I did not write them with any view of weaving them into a whole, or for publication, until I found that I had written so many. The different moods of sorrow as in a drama are dramatically given, and my conviction that fear, doubts, and suffering will find answer and relief only through Faith in a God of Love. 'I' is not always the author speaking of himself, but the voice of the human race speaking through him. After the death of A.H.H., the divisions of the poem are made by First Xmas Eve (Section xxviii), Second Xmas (lxxviii), Third Xmas Eve (civ and cv etc.)."

Our little systems[1] have their day;
  They have their day and cease to be:
  They are but broken lights of thee,
20 And thou, O Lord, art more than they.

We have but faith: we cannot know;
  For knowledge is of things we see;
  And yet we trust it comes from thee,
A beam in darkness: let it grow.

25 Let knowledge grow from more to more,
  But more of reverence in us dwell;
  That mind and soul, according well,
May make one music as before,[2]

But vaster. We are fools and slight;
30   We mock thee when we do not fear:
  But help thy foolish ones to bear;
Help thy vain worlds to bear thy light.

Forgive what seemed my sin in me;
  What seemed my worth since I began;
35   For merit lives from man to man,
And not from man, O Lord, to thee.

Forgive my grief for one removed,
  Thy creature, whom I found so fair.
  I trust he lives in thee, and there
40 I find him worthier to be loved.

Forgive these wild and wandering cries,
  Confusions of a wasted youth;
  Forgive them where they fail in truth,
And in thy wisdom make me wise.
  —1850 (1849)

I

I held it truth, with him[3] who sings
  To one clear harp in divers tones,
  That men may rise on stepping-stones
Of their dead selves to higher things.

5 But who shall so forecast the years
  And find in loss a gain to match?
  Or reach a hand through time to catch
The far-off interest of tears?

Let Love clasp Grief lest both be drowned,
10   Let darkness keep her raven gloss:
  Ah, sweeter to be drunk with loss,
To dance with death, to beat the ground,

Than that the victor Hours should scorn
  The long result of love, and boast,
15   "Behold the man that loved and lost,
But all he was is overworn."

II

Old Yew, which graspest at the stones
  That name the under-lying dead,
  Thy fibres net the dreamless head,
Thy roots are wrapt about the bones.

5 The seasons bring the flower again,
  And bring the firstling to the flock;
  And in the dust of thee, the clock
Beats out the little lives of men.

O not for thee the glow, the bloom,
10   Who changest not in any gale,
  Nor branding summer suns avail
To touch thy thousand years of gloom:

And gazing on thee, sullen tree,
  Sick for thy stubborn hardihood,

---

[1] philosophy and theology.

[2] Tennyson's comment: "As in the ages of faith."

[3] Goethe.

15 I seem to fail from out my blood
And grow incorporate into thee.

III

O Sorrow, cruel fellowship,
    O Priestess in the vaults of Death,
    O sweet and bitter in a breath,
What whispers from thy lying lip?

5 "The stars," she whispers, "blindly run;
    A web is woven across the sky;
    From out waste places comes a cry,
And murmurs from the dying sun:

"And all the phantom, Nature, stands—
10   With all the music in her tone,
    A hollow echo of my own,—
A hollow form with empty hands."

And shall I take a thing so blind,
    Embrace her as my natural good;
15   Or crush her, like a vice of blood,
Upon the threshold of the mind?

IV

To Sleep I give my powers away;
    My will is bondsman to the dark;
    I sit within a helmless bark,
And with my heart I muse and say:

5 O heart, how fares it with thee now,
    That thou should'st fail from thy desire,
    Who scarcely darest to inquire,
"What is it makes me beat so low?"

Something it is which thou hast lost,
10   Some pleasure from thine early years.
    Break, thou deep vase of chilling tears,
That grief hath shaken into frost!

Such clouds of nameless trouble cross
    All night below the darkened eyes;
15   With morning wakes the will, and cries,
"Thou shalt not be the fool of loss."

V

I sometimes hold it half a sin
    To put in words the grief I feel;
    For words, like Nature, half reveal
And half conceal the Soul within.

5 But, for the unquiet heart and brain,
    A use in measured language lies;
    The sad mechanic exercise,
Like dull narcotics, numbing pain.

In words, like weeds,[1] I'll wrap me o'er,
10   Like coarsest clothes against the cold:
    But that large grief which these enfold
Is given in outline and no more.

VI

One writes, that "Other friends remain,"
    That "Loss is common to the race"—
    And common is the commonplace,
And vacant chaff well meant for grain.

5 That loss is common would not make
    My own less bitter, rather more:
    Too common! Never morning wore
To evening, but some heart did break.

O father, wheresoe'er thou be,
10   Who pledgest now thy gallant son;
    A shot, ere half thy draught be done,
Hath stilled the life that beat from thee.

O mother, praying God will save
    Thy sailor,—while thy head is bowed,

---

[1] garments related to mourning.

151

15   His heavy-shotted hammock-shroud
Drops in his vast and wandering grave.

Ye know no more than I who wrought
    At that last hour to please him well;
    Who mused on all I had to tell,
20 And something written, something thought;

Expecting still his advent home;
    And ever met him on his way
    With wishes, thinking, "here today,"
Or "here tomorrow will he come."

25 O somewhere, meek, unconscious dove,
    That sittest ranging¹ golden hair;
    And glad to find thyself so fair,
Poor child, that waitest for thy love!

For now her father's chimney glows
30   In expectation of a guest;
    And thinking "this will please him best,"
She takes a riband or a rose;

For he will see them on tonight;
    And with the thought her colour burns;
35   And, having left the glass, she turns
Once more to set a ringlet right;

And, even when she turned, the curse
    Had fallen, and her future Lord
    Was drowned in passing through the ford,
40 Or killed in falling from his horse.

O what to her shall be the end?
    And what to me remains of good?
    To her, perpetual maidenhood,
And unto me no second friend.

---

¹ arranging.

VII

Dark house,² by which once more I stand
    Here in the long unlovely street,
    Doors, where my heart was used to beat
So quickly, waiting for a hand,

5 A hand that can be clasped no more—
    Behold me, for I cannot sleep,
    And like a guilty thing I creep
At earliest morning to the door.

He is not here; but far away
10   The noise of life begins again,
    And ghastly through the drizzling rain
On the bald street breaks the blank day.

VIII

A happy lover who has come
    To look on her that loves him well,
    Who 'lights and rings the gateway bell,
And learns her gone and far from home;

5 He saddens, all the magic light
    Dies off at once from bower and hall,
    And all the place is dark, and all
The chambers emptied of delight:

So find I every pleasant spot
10   In which we two were wont to meet,
    The field, the chamber and the street,
For all is dark where thou art not.

Yet as that other, wandering there
    In those deserted walks, may find
15   A flower beat with rain and wind,
Which once she fostered up with care;

So seems it in my deep regret,
    O my forsaken heart, with thee

---

² the house where Hallam lived on Wimpole St.

And this poor flower of poesy
20 Which little cared for fades not yet.

But since it pleased a vanished eye,
    I go to plant it on his tomb,
    That if it can it there may bloom,
Or dying, there at least may die.

IX

Fair ship,[1] that from the Italian shore
    Sailest the placid ocean-plains
    With my lost Arthur's loved remains,
Spread thy full wings, and waft him o'er.

5 So draw him home to those that mourn
    In vain; a favourable speed
    Ruffle thy mirrored mast, and lead
Through prosperous floods his holy urn.

All night no ruder air perplex
10   Thy sliding keel, till Phosphor,[2] bright
     As our pure love, through early light
Shall glimmer on the dewy decks.

Sphere all your lights around, above;
    Sleep, gentle heavens, before the prow;
15   Sleep, gentle winds, as he sleeps now,
My friend, the brother of my love;

My Arthur, whom I shall not see
    Till all my widowed race be run;
    Dear as the mother to the son,
20   More than my brothers are to me.

X

I hear the noise about thy keel;
    I hear the bell struck in the night:

I see the cabin-window bright;
I see the sailor at the wheel.

5 Thou bring'st the sailor to his wife,
    And travelled men from foreign lands;
    And letters unto trembling hands;
And, thy dark freight, a vanished life.

So bring him: we have idle dreams:
10   This look of quiet flatters thus
     Our home-bred fancies: O to us,
The fools of habit, sweeter seems

To rest beneath the clover sod,
    That takes the sunshine and the rains,
15   Or where the kneeling hamlet drains
The chalice of the grapes of God;

Than if with thee the roaring wells
    Should gulf him fathom-deep in brine;
    And hands so often clasped in mine,
20   Should toss with tangle and with shells.

XI

Calm is the morn without a sound,
    Calm as to suit a calmer grief,
    And only through the faded leaf
The chestnut pattering to the ground:

5 Calm and deep peace on this high wold,
    And on these dews that drench the furze,
    And all the silvery gossamers
That twinkle into green and gold:

Calm and still light on yon great plain
10   That sweeps with all its autumn bowers,
     And crowded farms and lessening towers,
To mingle with the bounding main:

Calm and deep peace in this wide air,
    These leaves that redden to the fall;

---

[1] bearing Hallam's body from Trieste to England.

[2] star of dawn.

15 And in my heart, if calm at all,
If any calm, a calm despair:

Calm on the seas, and silver sleep,
   And waves that sway themselves in rest,
   And dead calm in that noble breast
20 Which heaves but with the heaving deep.

XII

Lo, as a dove when up she springs
   To bear through Heaven a tale of woe,
   Some dolorous message knit below
The wild pulsation of her wings;

5 Like her I go; I cannot stay;
   I leave this mortal ark behind,
   A weight of nerves without a mind,
And leave the cliffs, and haste away

O'er ocean-mirrors rounded large,[1]
10   And reach the glow of southern skies,
   And see the sails at distance rise,
And linger weeping on the marge,

And saying; "Comes he thus, my friend?
   Is this the end of all my care?"
15   And circle moaning in the air:
"Is this the end? Is this the end?"

And forward dart again, and play
   About the prow, and back return
   To where the body sits, and learn
20 That I have been an hour away.

XIII

Tears of the widower, when he sees
   A late-lost form that sleep reveals,
   And moves his doubtful arms, and feels
Her place is empty, fall like these;

---

[1] circular fields of vision.

5 Which weep a loss for ever new,
   A void where heart on heart reposed;
   And, where warm hands have prest and closed,
Silence, till I be silent too.

Which weep the comrade of my choice,
10   An awful thought, a life removed,
   The human-hearted man I loved,
A Spirit, not a breathing voice.

Come Time, and teach me, many years,
   I do not suffer in a dream;
15   For now so strange do these things seem,
Mine eyes have leisure for their tears;

My fancies time to rise on wing,
   And glance about the approaching sails,
   As though they brought but merchants' bales,
20 And not the burthen that they bring.

XIV

If one should bring me this report,
   That thou hadst touched the land today,
   And I went down unto the quay,
And found thee lying in the port;

5 And standing, muffled round with woe,
   Should see thy passengers in rank
   Come stepping lightly down the plank,
And beckoning unto those they know;

10 And if along with these should come
   The man I held as half-divine;
   Should strike a sudden hand in mine,
And ask a thousand things of home;

And I should tell him all my pain,
15   And how my life had drooped of late,
   And he should sorrow o'er my state
And marvel what possessed my brain;

And I perceived no touch of change,
    No hint of death in all his frame,
20   But found him all in all the same,
I should not feel it to be strange.

XV

Tonight the winds begin to rise
    And roar from yonder dropping day:
    The last red leaf is whirled away,
The rooks are blown about the skies;

5   The forest cracked, the waters curled,
    The cattle huddled on the lea;
    And wildly dashed on tower and tree
The sunbeam strikes along the world:

And but for fancies, which aver
10   That all thy motions gently pass
    Athwart a plane of molten glass,
I scarce could brook the strain and stir

That makes the barren branches loud;
    And but for fear it is not so,
15   The wild unrest that lives in woe
Would dote and pore on yonder cloud

That rises upward always higher,
    And onward drags a labouring breast,
    And topples round the dreary west,
20   A looming bastion fringed with fire.

XVI

What words are these have fallen from me?
    Can calm despair and wild unrest
    Be tenants of a single breast
Or sorrow such a changeling be?

5   Or doth she only seem to take
    The touch of change in calm or storm;
    But knows no more of transient form
In her deep self, than some dead lake

That holds the shadow of a lark
10   Hung in the shadow of a heaven?
    Or has the shock, so harshly given,
Confused me like the unhappy bark

That strikes by night a craggy shelf,
    And staggers blindly ere she sink?
15   And stunned me from my power to think
And all my knowledge of myself;

And make me that delirious man
    Whose fancy fuses old and new,
    And flashes into false and true,
20   And mingled all without a plan?

XVII

Thou comest, much wept for: such a breeze
    Compelled thy canvas, and my prayer
    Was as the whisper of an air
To breathe thee over lonely seas.

5   For I in spirit see thee move
    Through circles of the bounding sky,
    Week after week: the days go by:
Come quick, thou bringest all I love.

Henceforth, wherever thou mayst roam,
10   My blessing, like a line of light,
    Is on the waters day and night,
And like a beacon guards thee home.

So may whatever tempest mars
    Mid-ocean, spare thee, sacred bark;
15   And balmy drops in summer dark
Slide from the bosom of the stars.

So kind an office hath been done,
    Such precious relics brought by thee;
    The dust of him I shall not see
20   Till all my widowed race be run.

XVIII

'Tis well; 'tis something; we may stand
    Where he in English earth is laid,
    And from his ashes may be made
The violet of his native land.

5 'Tis little; but it looks in truth
    As if the quiet bones were blest
    Among familiar names to rest
And in the places of his youth.

Come then, pure hands, and bear the head
10   That sleeps or wears the mask of sleep,
    And come, whatever loves to weep,
And hear the ritual of the dead.

Ah yet, even yet, if this might be,
    I, falling on his faithful heart,
15   Would breathing through his lips impart
The life that almost dies in me;

That dies not, but endures with pain,
    And slowly forms the firmer mind,
    Treasuring the look it cannot find,
20 The words that are not heard again.

XIX

The Danube to the Severn[1] gave
    The darkened heart that beat no more;
    They laid him by the pleasant shore,
And in the hearing of the wave.

5 There twice a day the Severn fills;
    The salt sea-water passes by,
    And hushes half the babbling Wye,
And makes a silence in the hills.

The Wye is hushed nor moved along,
10   And hushed my deepest grief of all,

When filled with tears that cannot fall,
I brim with sorrow drowning song.

The tide flows down, the wave again
    Is vocal in its wooded walls;
15   My deeper anguish also falls,
And I can speak a little then.

XX

The lesser griefs that may be said,
    That breathe a thousand tender vows,
    Are but as servants in a house
Where lies the master newly dead;

5 Who speak their feeling as it is,
    And weep the fulness from the mind:
    "It will be hard," they say, "to find
Another service such as this."

My lighter moods are like to these,
10   That out of words a comfort win;
    But there are other griefs within,
And tears that at their fountain freeze;

For by the hearth the children sit
    Cold in that atmosphere of Death,
15   And scarce endure to draw the breath,
Or like to noiseless phantoms flit:

But open converse is there none,
    So much the vital spirits sink
    To see the vacant chair, and think,
20 "How good! how kind! and he is gone."

XXI

I sing to him that rests below,
    And, since the grasses round me wave,
    I take the grasses of the grave,
And make them pipes whereon to blow.

---

[1] Hallam died at Vienna on the Danube and was buried at Clevedon on the Severn.

5 The traveller hears me now and then,
 And sometimes harshly will he speak:
 "This fellow would make weakness weak,
And melt the waxen hearts of men."

Another answers, "Let him be,
10 He loves to make parade of pain,
 That with his piping he may gain
The praise that comes to constancy."

A third is wroth: "Is this an hour
 For private sorrow's barren song,
15 When more and more the people throng
The chairs and thrones of civil power?

"A time to sicken and to swoon,
 When Science reaches forth her arms
 To feel from world to world, and charms
20 Her secret from the latest moon?"

Behold, ye speak an idle thing:
 Ye never knew the sacred dust:
 I do but sing because I must,
And pipe but as the linnets sing:

25 And one is glad; her note is gay,
 For now her little ones have ranged;
 And one is sad: her note is changed,
Because her brood is stolen away.

XXII

The path by which we twain did go,
 Which led by tracts that pleased us well,
 Through four sweet years arose and fell,
From flower to flower, from snow to snow:

5 And we with singing cheered the way,
 And, crowned with all the season lent,
 From April on to April went,
And glad at heart from May to May:

But where the path we walked began
10 To slant the fifth autumnal slope,
 As we descended following Hope,
There sat the Shadow feared of man;

Who broke our fair companionship,
 And spread his mantle dark and cold,
15 And wrapt thee formless in the fold,
And dulled the murmur on thy lip,

And bore thee where I could not see
 Nor follow, though I walk in haste,
 And think, that somewhere in the waste
20 The Shadow sits and waits for me.

XXIII

Now, sometimes in my sorrow shut,
 Or breaking into song by fits,
 Alone, alone, to where he sits,
The Shadow[1] cloaked from head to foot,

5 Who keeps the keys of all the creeds,
 I wander, often falling lame,
 And looking back to whence I came,
Or on to where the pathway leads;

And crying, How changed from where it ran
10 Through lands where not a leaf was dumb;
 But all the lavish hills would hum
The murmur of a happy Pan:[2]

When each by turns was guide to each,
 And Fancy light from Fancy caught,
15 And Thought leapt out to wed with Thought
Ere Thought could wed itself with Speech;

And all we met was fair and good,
 And all was good that Time could bring,

---

[1] death.

[2] god of the fields and woods.

And all the secret of the Spring
20   Moved in the chambers of the blood;

And many an old philosophy
On Argive heights divinely sang,
And round us all the thicket rang
To many a flute of Arcady.

XXIV

And was the day of my delight
As pure and perfect as I say?
The very source and fount of Day
Is dashed with wandering isles of night.[1]

5   If all was good and fair we met,
This earth had been the Paradise
It never looked to human eyes
Since our first Sun arose and set.

And is it that the haze of grief
10   Makes former gladness loom so great?
The lowness of the present state,
That sets the past in this relief?

Or that the past will always win
A glory from its being far;
15   And orb into the perfect star
We saw not, when we moved therein?

XXV

I know that this was Life,—the track
Whereon with equal feet we fared;
And then, as now, the day prepared
The daily burden for the back.

5   But this it was that made me move
As light as carrier-birds in air;
I loved the weight I had to bear,
Because it needed help of Love:

Nor could I weary, heart or limb,
10   When mighty Love would cleave in twain
The lading of a single pain,
And part it, giving half to him.

XXVI

Still onward winds the dreary way;
I with it; for I long to prove
No lapse of moons can canker Love,
Whatever fickle tongues may say.

5   And if that eye which watches guilt
And goodness, and hath power to see
Within the green the mouldered tree,
And towers fallen as soon as built—

Oh, if indeed that eye foresee
10   Or see (in Him is no before)
In more of life true life no more
And Love the indifference to be,

Then might I find, ere yet the morn
Breaks hither over Indian seas,
15   That Shadow waiting with the keys,
To shroud me from my proper scorn.[2]

XXVII

I envy not in any moods
The captive void of noble rage,
The linnet born within the cage,
That never knew the summer woods:

5   I envy not the beast that takes
His license in the field of time,[3]
Unfettered by the sense of crime,
To whom a conscience never wakes;

_____

[1] sun-spots.

[2] scorn of myself.

[3] lacking restraint in earthly life.

Nor, what may count itself as blest,
10   The heart that never plighted troth
       But stagnates in the weeds of sloth;
Nor any want-begotten rest.

I hold it true, whate'er befall;
       I feel it, when I sorrow most;
15   'Tis better to have loved and lost
Than never to have loved at all.

XXVIII

The time draws near the birth of Christ:
       The moon is hid; the night is still;
       The Christmas bells from hill to hill
Answer each other in the mist.

5   Four voices of four hamlets round,
       From far and near, on mead and moor,
       Swell out and fail, as if a door
Were shut between me and the sound:

Each voice four changes on the wind,
10   That now dilate, and now decrease,
       Peace and goodwill, goodwill and peace,
Peace and goodwill, to all mankind.

This year I slept and woke with pain,
       I almost wished no more to wake,
15   And that my hold on life would break
Before I heard those bells again:

But they my troubled spirit rule,
       For they controlled me when a boy;
       They bring me sorrow touched with joy,
20 The merry merry bells of Yule.

XXIX

With such compelling cause to grieve
       As daily vexes household peace,
       And chains regret to his decrease,
How dare we keep our Christmas-eve;

5 Which brings no more a welcome guest
       To enrich the threshold of the night
       With showered largess of delight
In dance and song and game and jest?

Yet go, and while the holly boughs
10   Entwine the cold baptismal font,
       Make one wreath more for Use and Wont,
That guard the portals of the house;

Old sisters of a day gone by,
       Gray nurses, loving nothing new;
15   Why should they miss their yearly due
Before their time? They too will die.

XXX

With trembling fingers did we weave
       The holly round the Christmas hearth;
       A rainy cloud possessed the earth,
And sadly fell our Christmas-eve.

5 At our old pastimes in the hall
       We gambolled, making vain pretence
       Of gladness, with an awful sense
Of one mute Shadow watching all.

We paused: the winds were in the beech:
10   We heard them sweep the winter land;
       And in a circle hand-in-hand
Sat silent, looking each at each.

Then echo-like our voices rang;
       We sung, though every eye was dim,
15   A merry song we sang with him
Last year: impetuously we sang:

We ceased: a gentler feeling crept
       Upon us: surely rest is meet:
       "They rest," we said, "their sleep is sweet,"
20 And silence followed, and we wept.

Our voices took a higher range;
    Once more we sang: "They do not die
    Nor lose their mortal sympathy,
Nor change to us, although they change;

25 "Rapt from the fickle and the frail
    With gathered power, yet the same,
    Pierces the keen seraphic flame
From orb to orb, from veil to veil."

Rise, happy morn, rise, holy morn,
30   Draw forth the cheerful day from night:
    O Father, touch the east, and light
The light that shone when Hope was born.

XXXI

When Lazarus left his charnel-cave,
    And home to Mary's house returned,
    Was this demanded—if he yearned
To hear her weeping by his grave?

5 "Where wert thou, brother, those four days?"
    There lives no record of reply,
    Which telling what it is to die
Had surely added praise to praise.

From every house the neighbours met,
10   The streets were filled with joyful sound,
    A solemn gladness even crowned
The purple brows of Olivet.[1]

Behold a man raised up by Christ!
    The rest remaineth unrevealed;
15   He told it not; or something sealed
The lips of that Evangelist.[2]

XXXII

Her[3] eyes are homes of silent prayer,
    Nor other thought her mind admits
    But, he was dead, and there he sits,
And he that brought him back is there.

5 Then one deep love doth supersede
    All other, when her ardent gaze
    Roves from the living brother's face,
And rests upon the Life indeed.

All subtle thought, all curious fears,
10   Borne down by gladness so complete,
    She bows, she bathes the Saviour's feet
With costly spikenard and with tears.

Thrice blest whose lives are faithful prayers,
    Whose loves in higher love endure;
15   What souls possess themselves so pure,
Or is there blessedness like theirs?

XXXIII

O thou that after toil and storm
    Mayst seem to have reached a purer air,
    Whose faith has centre everywhere,
Nor cares to fix itself to form,

5 Leave thou thy sister when she prays,
    Her early Heaven,[4] her happy views;
    Nor thou with shadowed hint confuse
A life that leads melodious days.

Her faith through form is pure as thine,
10   Her hands are quicker unto good:
    Oh, sacred be the flesh and blood
To which she links a truth divine!

---

[1] Mt. Olivet near Jerusalem.

[2] St. John.

[3] Mary, sister of Lazarus.

[4] ideas learned in childhood.

See thou, that countest reason ripe
  In holding by the law within,
15   Thou fail not in a world of sin,
And even for want of such a type.

XXXIV

My own dim life should teach me this,
  That life shall live for evermore,
  Else earth is darkness at the core,
And dust and ashes all that is;

5 This round of green, this orb of flame,
  Fantastic beauty; such as lurks
  In some wild Poet, when he works
Without a conscience or an aim.

What then were God to such as I?
10 'Twere hardly worth my while to choose
  Of things all mortal, or to use
A little patience ere I die;

'Twere best at once to sink to peace,
  Like birds the charming serpent draws,
15 To drop head-foremost in the jaws
Of vacant darkness and to cease.

XXXV

Yet if some voice that man could trust
  Should murmur from the narrow house,
  "The cheeks drop in; the body bows;
Man dies: nor is there hope in dust:"

5 Might I not say? "Yet even here,
  But for one hour, O Love, I strive
  To keep so sweet a thing alive:"
But I should turn mine ears and hear

The moanings of the homeless sea,
10 The sound of streams that swift or slow

Draw down Æonian[1] hills, and sow
The dust of continents to be;

And Love would answer with a sigh,
  "The sound of that forgetful shore[2]
15 Will change my sweetness more and more,
Half-dead to know that I shall die."

O me, what profits it to put
  An idle case? If Death were seen
  At first as Death, Love had not been,
20 Or been in narrowest working shut,

Mere fellowship of sluggish moods,
  Or in his coarsest Satyr[3]-shape
  Had bruised the herb and crushed the grape,
And basked and battened[4] in the woods.

XXXVI

Though truths in manhood darkly join,
  Deep-seated in our mystic frame,
  We yield all blessing to the name
Of Him that made them current coin;

5 For Wisdom dealt with mortal powers,
  Where truth in closest words shall fail,
  When truth embodied in a tale
Shall enter in at lowly doors.

And so the Word had breath, and wrought
10 With human hands the creed of creeds
  In loveliness of perfect deeds,
More strong than all poetic thought;

Which he may read that binds the sheaf,
  Or builds the house, or digs the grave,

---

[1] ancient, aeons old.

[2] the land where all things are forgotten.

[3] sensual form.

[4] to feed grossly.

15   And those wild eyes that watch the wave
In roarings round the coral reef.[1]

XXXVII

Urania speaks with darkened brow:
    "Thou pratest here where thou art least;
    This faith has many a purer priest,
And many an abler voice than thou.

5   "Go down beside thy native rill,
    On thy Parnassus[2] set thy feet,
    And hear thy laurel whisper sweet
About the ledges of the hill."

And my Melpomene[3] replies,
10   A touch of shame upon her cheek:
    "I am not worthy even to speak
Of thy prevailing mysteries;

"For I am but an earthly Muse,
    And owning but a little art
15   To lull with song an aching heart,
And render human love his dues;

"But brooding on the dear one dead,
    And all he said of things divine,
    (And dear to me as sacred wine
20   To dying lips is all he said),

"I murmured, as I came along,
    Of comfort clasped in truth revealed;
    And loitered in the master's field,
And darkened sanctities with song."

XXXVIII

With weary steps I loiter on,
    Though always under altered skies

The purple from the distance dies,
    My prospect and horizon gone.

5   No joy the blowing season gives,
    The herald melodies of spring,
    But in the songs I love to sing
A doubtful gleam of solace lives.

If any care for what is here
10   Survive in spirits rendered free,
    Then are these songs I sing of thee
Not all ungrateful to thine ear.

XXXIX

Old warder of these buried bones,
    And answering now my random stroke
    With fruitful cloud and living smoke,[4]
Dark yew, that graspest at the stones

5   And dippest toward the dreamless head,
    To thee too comes the golden hour
    When flower is feeling after flower;
But Sorrow—fixt upon the dead,

And darkening the dark graves of men,—
10   What whispered from her lying lips?
    Thy gloom is kindled at the tips,
And passes into gloom again.

XL

Could we forget the widowed hour
    And look on Spirits breathed away,
    As on a maiden in the day
When first she wears her orange-flower!

5   When crowned with blessing she doth rise
    To take her latest leave of home,
    And hopes and light regrets that come
Make April of her tender eyes;

---

[1] Pacific Islanders.

[2] sacred hill of Apollo.

[3] the Muse of elegy.

[4] Tennyson's comment: "The yew, when flowering, in a wind or if struck sends up its pollen like smoke."

And doubtful joys the father move,
10   And tears are on the mother's face,
   As parting with a long embrace
She enters other realms of love;

Her office there to rear, to teach,
   Becoming as is meet and fit
15   A link among the days, to knit
The generations each with each;

And, doubtless, unto thee is given
   A life that bears immortal fruit
   In those great offices that suit
20 The full-grown energies of heaven.

Ay me, the difference I discern!
   How often shall her old fireside
   Be cheered with tidings of the bride,
How often she herself return,

25 And tell them all they would have told,
   And bring her babe, and make her boast,
   Till even those that missed her most
Shall count new things as dear as old:

But thou and I have shaken hands,
30   Till growing winters lay me low;
   My paths are in the fields I know,
And thine in undiscovered lands.

XLI

Thy spirit ere our fatal loss
   Did ever rise from high to higher;
   As mounts the heavenward altar-fire,
As flies the lighter through the gross.

5 But thou art turned to something strange,
   And I have lost the links that bound
   Thy changes; here upon the ground,
No more partaker of thy change.

Deep folly! yet that this could be—
10   That I could wing my will with might
   To leap the grades of life and light,
And flash at once, my friend, to thee.

For though my nature rarely yields
   To that vague fear implied in death;
15   Nor shudders at the gulfs beneath,
The howlings from forgotten fields;

Yet oft when sundown skirts the moor
   An inner trouble I behold,
   A spectral doubt which makes me cold,
20 That I shall be thy mate no more,

Though following with an upward mind
   The wonders that have come to thee,
   Through all the secular to-be,[1]
But evermore a life behind.

XLII

I vex my heart with fancies dim:
   He still outstript me in the race;
   It was but unity of place
That made me dream I ranked with him.

5 And so may Place retain us still,
   And he the much-beloved again,
   A lord of large experience, train
To riper growth the mind and will:

And what delights can equal those
10   That stir the spirit's inner deeps,
   When one that loves but knows not, reaps
A truth from one that loves and knows?

XLIII

If Sleep and Death be truly one,
   And every spirit's folded bloom

---

[1] aeons of the future.

Through all its intervital[1] gloom
In some long trance should slumber on;

5 Unconscious of the sliding hour,
    Bare of the body, might it last,
    And silent traces of the past
Be all the colour of the flower:

So then were nothing lost to man;
10   So that still garden of the souls
    In many a figured leaf enrolls
The total world since life began;

And love will last as pure and whole
    As when he loved me here in Time,
15   And at the spiritual prime[2]
Rewaken with the dawning soul.

XLIV

How fares it with the happy dead?
    For here the man is more and more;
    But he forgets the days before
God shut the doorways of his head.[3]

5 The days have vanished, tone and tint,
    And yet perhaps the hoarding sense
    Gives out at times (he knows not whence)
A little flash, a mystic hint;

And in the long harmonious years
10   (If Death so taste Lethean springs),[4]
    May some dim touch of earthly things
Surprise thee ranging with thy peers.

If such a dreamy touch should fall,
    O turn thee round, resolve the doubt;

15 My guardian angel will speak out
In that high place, and tell thee all.

XLV

The baby new to earth and sky,
    What time his tender palm is prest
    Against the circle of the breast,
Has never thought that "this is I:"

5 But as he grows he gathers much,
    And learns the use of "I," and "me,"
    And finds "I am not what I see,
And other than the things I touch."

So rounds he to a separate mind
10   From whence clear memory may begin,
    As through the frame that binds him in
His isolation grows defined.

This use may lie in blood and breath,
    Which else were fruitless of their due,
15   Had man to learn himself anew
Beyond the second birth of Death.

XLVI

We ranging down this lower track,
    The path we came by, thorn and flower,
    Is shadowed by the growing hour,
Lest life should fail in looking back.

5 So be it: there no shade can last
    In that deep dawn behind the tomb,
    But clear from marge to marge shall bloom
The eternal landscape of the past;

A lifelong tract of time revealed;
10   The fruitful hours of still increase;
    Days ordered in a wealthy peace,
And those five years its richest field.

[1] between lives.

[2] daybreak.

[3] Tennyson's comment: "Closing of the skull after babyhood."

[4] waters of forgetfulness.

O Love, thy province were not large,
    A bounded field, nor stretching far;
15   Look also, Love, a brooding star,
A rosy warmth from marge to marge.

XLVII

That each, who seems a separate whole,
    Should move his rounds, and fusing all
    The skirts of self again, should fall
Remerging in the general Soul,

5 Is faith as vague as all unsweet:
    Eternal form shall still divide
    The eternal soul from all beside;
And I shall know him when we meet:

And we shall sit at endless feast,
10   Enjoying each the other's good:
    What vaster dream can hit the mood
Of Love on earth? He seeks at least

Upon the last and sharpest height,
    Before the spirits fade away,
15   Some landing-place, to clasp and say,
"Farewell! We lose ourselves in light."

XLVIII

If these brief lays, of Sorrow born,
    Were taken to be such as closed
    Grave doubts and answers here proposed,
Then these were such as men might scorn:

5 Her care is not to part[1] and prove;
    She takes, when harsher moods remit,
    What slender shade of doubt may flit,
And makes it vassal unto love:

And hence, indeed, she sports with words,
10   But better serves a wholesome law,

And holds it sin and shame to draw
The deepest measure from the chords:

Nor dare she trust a larger lay,
    But rather loosens from the lip
15   Short swallow-flights of song, that dip
Their wings in tears, and skim away.

XLIX

From art, from nature, from the schools,[2]
    Let random influences glance,
    Like light in many a shivered lance
That breaks about the dappled pools:

5 The lightest wave of thought shall lisp,
    The fancy's tenderest eddy wreathe,
    The slightest air of song shall breathe
To make the sullen surface crisp.

And look thy look, and go thy way,
10   But blame not thou the winds that make
    The seeming-wanton ripple break,
The tender-pencilled shadow play.

Beneath all fancied hopes and fears
    Ay me, the sorrow deepens down,
15   Whose muffled motions blindly drown
The bases of my life in tears.

L

Be near me when my light is low,
    When the blood creeps, and the nerves prick
    And tingle; and the heart is sick,
And all the wheels of Being slow.

5 Be near me when the sensuous frame
    Is racked with pangs that conquer trust;
    And Time, a maniac scattering dust,
And Life, a Fury slinging flame.

---

[1] sort out.

[2] philosophy and theology.

Be near me when my faith is dry,
10   And men the flies of latter spring,
   That lay their eggs, and sting and sing
And weave their petty cells and die.

Be near me when I fade away,
   To point the term of human strife,
15   And on the low dark verge of life
The twilight of eternal day.

LI

Do we indeed desire the dead
   Should still be near us at our side?
   Is there no baseness we would hide?
No inner vileness that we dread?

5 Shall he for whose applause I strove,
   I had such reverence for his blame,
   See with clear eye some hidden shame
And I be lessened in his love?

I wrong the grave with fears untrue:
10   Shall love be blamed for want of faith?
   There must be wisdom with great Death:
The dead shall look me through and through.

Be near us when we climb or fall:
   Ye watch, like God, the rolling hours
15   With larger other eyes than ours,
To make allowance for us all.

LII

I cannot love thee as I ought,
   For love reflects the thing beloved;
   My words are only words, and moved
Upon the topmost froth of thought.

5 "Yet blame not thou thy plaintive song,"
   The Spirit of true love replied;
   "Thou canst not move me from thy side,
Nor human frailty do me wrong.

"What keeps a spirit wholly true
10   To that ideal which he bears?
   What record? not the sinless years
That breathed beneath the Syrian blue:

"So fret not, like an idle girl,
   That life is dashed with flecks of sin.
15   Abide: thy wealth is gathered in,
When Time hath sundered shell from pearl."

LIII

How many a father have I seen,
   A sober man, among his boys,
   Whose youth was full of foolish noise,
Who wears his manhood hale and green:

5 And dare we to this fancy give,
   That had the wild oat not been sown,
   The soil, left barren, scarce had grown
The grain by which a man may live?

Or, if we held the doctrine sound
10   For life outliving heats of youth,
   Yet who would preach it as a truth
To those that eddy round and round?

Hold thou the good: define it well:
   For fear divine Philosophy
15   Should push beyond her mark, and be
Procuress to the Lords of Hell.

LIV

Oh yet we trust that somehow good
   Will be the final goal of ill,
   To pangs of nature, sins of will,
Defects of doubt, and taints of blood;

5 That nothing walks with aimless feet;
   That not one life shall be destroyed,
   Or cast as rubbish to the void,
When God hath made the pile complete;

That not a worm is cloven in vain;
    That not a moth with vain desire
10   Is shrivelled in a fruitless fire,
Or but subserves another's gain.

Behold, we know not anything;
    I can but trust that good shall fall
15   At last—far off—at last, to all,
And every winter change to spring.

So runs my dream: but what am I?
    An infant crying in the night:
    An infant crying for the light:
20 And with no language but a cry.

LV

The wish, that of the living whole
    No life may fail beyond the grave,
    Derives it not from what we have
The likest God within the soul?

5 Are God and Nature then at strife,
    That Nature lends such evil dreams?
    So careful of the type[1] she seems,
So careless of the single life;

That I, considering everywhere
10   Her secret meaning in her deeds,
    And finding that of fifty seeds
She often brings but one to bear,

I falter where I firmly trod,
    And falling with my weight of cares
15   Upon the great world's altar-stairs
That slope through darkness up to God,

I stretch lame hands of faith, and grope,
    And gather dust and chaff, and call
    To what I feel is Lord of all,
20 And faintly trust the larger hope.

---

[1] species.

LVI

"So careful of the type?" but no.
    From scarpèd cliff and quarried stone
    She cries, "A thousand types are gone:
I care for nothing, all shall go.

5 "Thou makest thine appeal to me:
    I bring to life, I bring to death:
    The spirit does but mean the breath:
I know no more." And he, shall he,

Man, her last work, who seemed so fair,
10   Such splendid purpose in his eyes,
    Who rolled the psalm to wintry skies,
Who built him fanes of fruitless prayer,

Who trusted God was love indeed
    And love Creation's final law—
15   Though Nature, red in tooth and claw
With ravine, shrieked against his creed—

Who loved, who suffered countless ills,
    Who battled for the True, the Just,
    Be blown about the desert dust,
20 Or sealed within the iron hills?

No more? A monster then, a dream,
    A discord. Dragons of the prime,
    That tare each other in their slime,
Were mellow music matched with him.

25 O life as futile, then, as frail!
    O for thy voice to soothe and bless!
    What hope of answer, or redress?
Behind the veil, behind the veil.

LVII

Peace; come away: the song of woe
    Is after all an earthly song:
    Peace; come away: we do him wrong
To sing so wildly: let us go.

5 Come; let us go: your cheeks are pale;
       But half my life I leave behind:
       Methinks my friend is richly shrined;
   But I shall pass; my work will fail.

   Yet in these ears, till hearing dies,
10   One set slow bell will seem to toll
       The passing of the sweetest soul
   That ever looked with human eyes.

   I hear it now, and o'er and o'er,
       Eternal greetings to the dead;
15   And "Ave, Ave, Ave," said,
   "Adieu, adieu" for evermore.

LVIII

   In those sad words I took farewell:
       Like echoes in sepulchral halls,
       As drop by drop the water falls
   In vaults and catacombs, they fell;

5 And, falling, idly broke the peace
       Of hearts that beat from day to day,
       Half-conscious of their dying clay,
   And those cold crypts where they shall cease.

   The high Muse[1] answered: "Wherefore grieve
10   Thy brethren with a fruitless tear?
       Abide a little longer here,
   And thou shalt take a nobler leave."

LIX

   O Sorrow, wilt thou live with me
       No casual mistress, but a wife,
       My bosom-friend and half of life;
   As I confess it needs must be;

5 O Sorrow, wilt thou rule my blood,
       Be sometimes lovely like a bride,

   And put thy harsher moods aside,
   If thou wilt have me wise and good.

   My centred passion cannot move,
10   Nor will it lessen from today;
       But I'll have leave at times to play
   As with the creature of my love;

   And set thee forth, for thou art mine,
       With so much hope for years to come,
15   That, howso'er I know thee, some
   Could hardly tell what name were thine.

LX

   He past; a soul of nobler tone:
       My spirit loved and loves him yet,
       Like some poor girl whose heart is set
   On one whose rank exceeds her own.

5 He mixing with his proper sphere,
       She finds the baseness of her lot,
       Half jealous of she knows not what,
   And envying all that meet him there.

   The little village looks forlorn;
10   She sighs amid her narrow days,
       Moving about the household ways,
   In that dark house where she was born.

   The foolish neighbours come and go,
       And tease her till the day draws by:
15   At night she weeps, "How vain am I!
   How should he love a thing so low?"

LXI

   If, in thy second state sublime,
       Thy ransomed reason change replies
       With all the circle of the wise,
   The perfect flower of human time;

---

[1] Urania.

5 And if thou cast thine eyes below,
      How dimly charactered and slight,
      How dwarfed a growth of cold and night,
   How blanched with darkness must I grow!

   Yet turn thee to the doubtful shore,
10   Where thy first form was made a man;
      I loved thee, Spirit, and love, nor can
   The soul of Shakspeare love thee more.

LXII

   Though if an eye that's downward cast
      Could make thee somewhat blench or fail,
      Then be my love an idle tale,
   And fading legend of the past;

5 And thou, as one that once declined,
      When he was little more than boy,
      On some unworthy heart with joy,
   But lives to wed an equal mind;

   And breathes a novel world, the while
10   His other passion wholly dies,
      Or in the light of deeper eyes
   Is matter for a flying smile.

LXIII

   Yet pity for a horse o'er-driven,
      And love in which my hound has part,
      Can hang no weight upon my heart
   In its assumptions up to heaven;

5 And I am so much more than these,
      As thou, perchance, art more than I,
      And yet I spare them sympathy,
   And I would set their pains at ease.

   So mayst thou watch me where I weep,
10   As, unto vaster motions bound,
      The circuits of thine orbit round
   A higher height, a deeper deep.

LXIV

   Dost thou look back on what hath been,
      As some divinely gifted man,
      Whose life in low estate began
   And on a simple village green;

5 Who breaks his birth's invidious bar,
      And grasps the skirts of happy chance,
      And breasts the blows of circumstance,
   And grapples with his evil star;

   Who makes by force his merit known
10   And lives to clutch the golden keys,[1]
      To mould a mighty state's decrees,
   And shape the whisper of the throne;

   And moving up from high to higher,
      Becomes on Fortune's crowning slope
15   The pillar of a people's hope,
   The centre of a world's desire;

   Yet feels, as in a pensive dream,
      When all his active powers are still,
      A distant dearness in the hill,
20 A secret sweetness in the stream,

   The limit of his narrower fate,
      While yet beside its vocal springs
      He played at counsellors and kings,
   With one that was his earliest mate;

25 Who ploughs with pain his native lea
      And reaps the labour of his hands,
      Or in the furrow musing stands;
   "Does my old friend remember me?"

LXV

   Sweet soul, do with me as thou wilt;
      I lull a fancy trouble-tost

---

[1] symbols of civil office.

With "Love's too precious to be lost,
A little grain shall not be spilt."

5 And in that solace can I sing,
    Till out of painful phases wrought
    There flutters up a happy thought,
Self-balanced on a lightsome wing:

Since we deserved the name of friends,
10   And thine effect so lives in me,
    A part of mine may live in thee
And move thee on to noble ends.

LXVI

You[1] thought my heart too far diseased;
    You wonder when my fancies play
    To find me gay among the gay,
Like one with any trifle pleased.

5 The shade by which my life was crost,
    Which makes a desert in the mind,
    Has made me kindly with my kind,
And like to him whose sight is lost;

Whose feet are guided through the land,
10   Whose jest among his friends is free,
    Who takes the children on his knee,
And winds their curls about his hand:

He plays with threads, he beats his chair
    For pastime, dreaming of the sky;
15   His inner day can never die,
His night of loss is always there.

LXVII

When on my bed the moonlight falls,
    I know that in thy place of rest
    By that broad water of the west,
There comes a glory on the walls;

---

[1] Tennyson's comment: "the auditor."

5 Thy marble bright in dark appears,
    As slowly steals a silver flame
    Along the letters of thy name,
And o'er the number of thy years.

The mystic glory swims away;
10   From off my bed the moonlight dies;
    And closing eaves of wearied eyes
I sleep till dusk is dipt in gray:

And then I know the mist is drawn
    A lucid veil from coast to coast,
15   And in the dark church like a ghost
Thy tablet glimmers to the dawn.

LXVIII

When in the down I sink my head,
    Sleep, Death's twin-brother, times my breath;
    Sleep, Death's twin-brother, knows not Death,
Nor can I dream of thee as dead:

5 I walk as ere I walked forlorn,
    When all our path was fresh with dew,
    And all the bugle breezes blew
Reveillée to the breaking morn.

But what is this? I turn about,
10   I find a trouble in thine eye,
    Which makes me sad I know not why,
Nor can my dream resolve the doubt:

But ere the lark hath left the lea
    I wake, and I discern the truth;
15   It is the trouble of my youth
That foolish sleep transfers to thee.

LXIX

I dreamed there would be Spring no more,
    That Nature's ancient power was lost:
    The streets were black with smoke and frost,
They chattered trifles at the door:

Alfred Tennyson

5 I wandered from the noisy town,
    I found a wood with thorny boughs:
    I took the thorns to bind my brows,
I wore them like a civic crown:

I met with scoffs, I met with scorns
10   From youth and babe and hoary hairs:
    They called me in the public squares
The fool that wears a crown of thorns:[1]

They called me fool, they called me child:
    I found an angel of the night;[2]
15   The voice was low, the look was bright;
He looked upon my crown and smiled:

He reached the glory of a hand,
    That seemed to touch it into leaf:
    The voice was not the voice of grief,
20 The words were hard to understand.

LXX

I cannot see the features right,
    When on the gloom I strive to paint
    The face I know; the hues are faint
And mix with hollow masks of night;

5 Cloud-towers by ghostly masons wrought,
    A gulf that ever shuts and gapes,
    A hand that points, and pallèd shapes
In shadowy thoroughfares of thought;

And crowds that stream from yawning doors,
10   And shoals of puckered faces drive;
    Dark bulks that tumble half alive,
And lazy lengths on boundless shores;

Till all at once beyond the will
    I hear a wizard music roll,
15   And through a lattice on the soul
Looks thy fair face and makes it still.

LXXI

Sleep, kinsman thou to death and trance
    And madness, thou hast forged at last
    A night-long Present of the Past
In which we went through summer France.[3]

5 Hadst thou such credit with the soul?
    Then bring an opiate trebly strong,
    Drug down the blindfold sense of wrong
That so my pleasure may be whole;

While now we talk as once we talked
10   Of men and minds, the dust of change,
    The days that grow to something strange,
In walking as of old we walked

Beside the river's wooded reach,
    The fortress, and the mountain ridge,
15   The cataract flashing from the bridge,
The breaker breaking on the beach.

LXXII

Risest thou thus, dim dawn, again,[4]
    And howlest, issuing out of night,
    With blasts that blow the poplar white,
And lash with storm the streaming pane?

5 Day, when my crowned estate begun
    To pine in that reverse of doom,
    Which sickened every living bloom,
And blurred the splendour of the sun;

[1] Tennyson's comment: "To write poems about death and grief is 'to wear a crown of thorns,' which the people say ought to be laid aside." "I tried to make my grief into a crown of these poems—but it is not to be taken too closely—To write verses about sorrow grief & death is to wear a crown of thorns which ought to be put by—as people say."

[2] Tennyson's comment: "But the Divine Thing in the gloom brought comfort."

[3] a reference to a journey to the south of France with Hallam in 1830.

[4] the first anniversary of Hallam's death.

Who usherest in the dolorous hour
10   With thy quick tears that make the rose
    Pull sideways, and the daisy close
Her crimson fringes to the shower;

Who might'st have heaved a windless flame
    Up the deep East, or, whispering, played
15   A chequer-work of beam and shade
Along the hills, yet looked the same,

As wan, as chill, as wild as now;
    Day, marked as with some hideous crime,
    When the dark hand struck down through time,
20 And cancelled nature's best: but thou,

Lift as thou mayst thy burthened brows
    Through clouds that drench the morning star,
    And whirl the ungarnered sheaf afar,
And sow the sky with flying boughs,

25 And up thy vault with roaring sound
    Climb thy thick noon, disastrous day;
    Touch thy dull goal of joyless gray,
And hide thy shame beneath the ground.

LXXIII

So many worlds, so much to do,
    So little done, such things to be,
    How know I what had need of thee,
For thou wert strong as thou wert true?

5 The fame is quenched that I foresaw,
    The head hath missed an earthly wreath:
    I curse not nature, no, nor death;
For nothing is that errs from law.

We pass; the path that each man trod
10   Is dim, or will be dim, with weeds:
    What fame is left for human deeds
In endless age? It rests with God.

O hollow wraith of dying fame,
    Fade wholly, while the soul exults,
15   And self-infolds the large results
Of force that would have forged a name.

LXXIV

As sometimes in a dead man's face,
    To those that watch it more and more,
    A likeness, hardly seen before,
Comes out—to some one of his race:

5 So, dearest, now thy brows are cold,
    I see thee what thou art, and know
    Thy likeness to the wise below,
Thy kindred with the great of old.

But there is more than I can see,
10   And what I see I leave unsaid,
    Nor speak it, knowing Death has made
His darkness beautiful with thee.

LXXV

I leave thy praises unexpressed
    In verse that brings myself relief,
    And by the measure of my grief
I leave thy greatness to be guessed;

5 What practice howso'er expert
    In fitting aptest words to things,
    Or voice the richest-toned that sings,
Hath power to give thee as thou wert?

I care not in these fading days
10   To raise a cry that lasts not long,
    And round thee with the breeze of song
To stir a little dust of praise.

Thy leaf has perished in the green,
    And, while we breathe beneath the sun,
15   The world which credits what is done
Is cold to all that might have been.

So here shall silence guard thy fame;
 But somewhere, out of human view,
 Whate'er thy hands are set to do
20 Is wrought with tumult of acclaim.

LXXVI

Take wings of fancy, and ascend,
 And in a moment set thy face
 Where all the starry heavens of space
Are sharpened to a needle's end;

5 Take wings of foresight; lighten through
 The secular abyss to come,
 And lo, thy deepest lays are dumb
Before the mouldering of a yew;

And if the matin songs, that woke
10 The darkness of our planet, last,
 Thine own shall wither in the vast,
Ere half the lifetime of an oak.

Ere these have clothed their branchy bowers
 With fifty Mays, thy songs are vain;
15 And what are they when these remain
The ruined shells of hollow towers?

LXXVII

What hope is here for modern rhyme
 To him, who turns a musing eye
 On songs, and deeds, and lives, that lie
Foreshortened in the tract of time?

5 These mortal lullabies of pain
 May bind a book, may line a box,
 May serve to curl a maiden's locks;
Or when a thousand moons shall wane

A man upon a stall may find,
10 And, passing, turn the page that tells
 A grief, then changed to something else,
Sung by a long-forgotten mind.

But what of that? My darkened ways
 Shall ring with music all the same;
15 To breathe my loss is more than fame,
To utter love more sweet than praise.

LXXVIII

Again at Christmas did we weave
 The holly round the Christmas hearth;
 The silent snow possessed the earth,
And calmly fell our Christmas-eve:

5 The yule-clog[1] sparkled keen with frost,
 No wing of wind the region swept,
 But over all things brooding slept
The quiet sense of something lost.

As in the winters left behind,
10 Again our ancient games had place,
 The mimic picture's breathing grace,[2]
And dance and song and hoodman-blind.[3]

Who showed a token of distress?
 No single tear, no mark of pain:
15 O sorrow, then can sorrow wane?
O grief, can grief be changed to less?

O last regret, regret can die!
 No—mixt with all this mystic frame,
 Her deep relations are the same,
20 But with long use her tears are dry.

LXXIX

"More than any brothers are to me,"—
 Let this not vex thee, noble heart!
 I know thee of what force thou art
To hold the costliest love in fee.

---

[1] the yule-log placed on the fire on Christmas eve.

[2] tableaux of famous paintings.

[3] blindman's bluff.

5 But thou and I are one in kind,
    As moulded like in Nature's mint;
    And hill and wood and field did print
The same sweet forms in either mind.

For us the same cold streamlet curled
10   Through all his eddying coves; the same
    All winds that roam the twilight came
In whispers of the beauteous world.

At one dear knee we proffered vows,
    One lesson from one book we learned,
15   Ere childhood's flaxen ringlet turned
To black and brown on kindred brows.

And so my wealth resembles thine,
    But he was rich where I was poor,
    And he supplied my want the more
20 As his unlikeness fitted mine.

LXXX

If any vague desire should rise,
    That holy Death ere Arthur died
    Had moved me kindly from his side,
And dropt the dust on tearless eyes;

5 Then fancy shapes, as fancy can,
    The grief my loss in him had wrought,
    A grief as deep as life or thought,
But stayed[1] in peace with God and man.

I make a picture in the brain;
10   I hear the sentence that he speaks;
    He bears the burthen of the weeks
But turns his burthen into gain.

His credit thus shall set me free;
    And, influence-rich to soothe and save,
15   Unused example from the grave
Reach out dead hands to comfort me.

---

[1] endured.

LXXXI

Could I have said while he was here,
    "My love shall now no further range;
    There cannot come a mellower change,
For now is love mature in ear."

5 Love, then, had hope of richer store:
    What end is here to my complaint?
    This haunting whisper makes me faint,
"More years had made me love thee more."

But Death returns an answer sweet:
10   "My sudden frost was sudden gain,
    And gave all ripeness to the grain,
It might have drawn from after-heat."

LXXXII

I wage not any feud with Death
    For changes wrought on form and face;
    No lower life that earth's embrace
May breed with him, can fright my faith.

5 Eternal process moving on,
    From state to state the spirit walks;
    And these are but the shattered stalks,
Or ruined chrysalis of one.

Nor blame I Death, because he bare
10   The use of virtue out of earth:
    I know transplanted human worth
Will bloom to profit, otherwhere.

For this alone on Death I wreak
    The wrath that garners in my heart;
15   He put our lives so far apart
We cannot hear each other speak.

LXXXIII

Dip down upon the northern shore,
    O sweet new-year delaying long;

Thou doest expectant nature wrong;
Delaying long, delay no more.

5   What stays thee from the clouded noons,
Thy sweetness from its proper place?
Can trouble live with April days,
Or sadness in the summer moons?

Bring orchis, bring the foxglove spire,
10   The little speedwell's darling blue,
Deep tulips dashed with fiery dew,
Laburnums, dropping-wells of fire.

O thou, new-year, delaying long,
Delayest the sorrow in my blood,
15   That longs to burst a frozen bud
And flood a fresher throat with song.

LXXXIV

When I contemplate all alone
The life that had been thine below,
And fix my thoughts on all the glow
To which thy crescent would have grown;

5   I see thee sitting crowned with good,
A central warmth diffusing bliss
In glance and smile, and clasp and kiss,
On all the branches of thy blood;

Thy blood, my friend, and partly mine;
10   For now the day was drawing on,
When thou shouldst link thy life with one
Of mine own house, and boys of thine

Had babbled "Uncle" on my knee;[1]
But that remorseless iron hour
15   Made cypress of her orange flower,
Despair of Hope, and earth of thee.

I seem to meet their least desire,
To clap their cheeks, to call them mine.
I see their unborn faces shine
20   Beside the never-lighted fire.

I see myself an honoured guest,
Thy partner in the flowery walk
Of letters, genial table-talk,
Or deep dispute, and graceful jest;

25   While now thy prosperous labour fills
The lips of men with honest praise,
And sun by sun the happy days
Descend below the golden hills

With promise of a morn as fair;
30   And all the train of bounteous hours
Conduct by paths of growing powers,
To reverence and the silver hair;

Till slowly worn her earthly robe,
Her lavish mission richly wrought,
35   Leaving great legacies of thought,
Thy spirit should fail from off the globe;

What time mine own might also flee,
As linked with thine in love and fate,
And, hovering o'er the dolorous strait
40   To the other shore, involved in thee,

Arrive at last the blessèd goal,
And He that died in Holy Land
Would reach us out the shining hand,
And take us as a single soul.

45   What reed was that on which I leant?
Ah, backward fancy, wherefore wake
The old bitterness again, and break
The low beginnings of content.

---

[1] Hallam was engaged to the poet's sister Emily.

LXXXV

This truth came borne with bier and pall,
    I felt it, when I sorrowed most,
    'Tis better to have loved and lost,
Than never to have loved at all—

5   O true in word, and tried in deed,
    Demanding, so to bring relief
    To this which is our common grief,
What kind of life is that I lead;

And whether trust in things above
10   Be dimmed of sorrow, or sustained;
    And whether love for him have drained
My capabilities of love;

Your words have virtue such as draws
    A faithful answer from the breast,
15   Through light reproaches, half exprest,
And loyal unto kindly laws.

My blood an even tenor kept,
    Till on mine ear this message falls,
    That in Vienna's fatal wall
20   God's finger touched him, and he slept.

The great Intelligences fair
    That range above our mortal state,
    In circle round the blessèd gate,
Received and gave him welcome there;

25   And led him through the blissful climes,
    And showed him in the fountain fresh
    All knowledge that the sons of flesh
Shall gather in the cycled times.[1]

But I remained, whose hopes were dim,
30   Whose life, whose thoughts were little worth,
    To wander on a darkened earth,
Where all things round me breathed of him.

---

[1] times to come.

O friendship, equal-poised control,
    O heart, with kindliest motion warm,
35   O sacred essence, other form,
O solemn ghost, O crownèd soul!

Yet none could better know than I,
    How much of act at human hands
    The sense of human will demands
40   By which we dare to live or die.

Whatever way my days decline,
    I felt and feel, though left alone,
    His being working in mine own,
The footsteps of his life in mine;

45   A life that all the Muses decked
    With gifts of grace, that might express
    All-comprehensive tenderness,
All-subtilising intellect:

And so my passion hath not swerved
50   To works of weakness, but I find
    An image comforting the mind,
And in my grief a strength reserved.

Likewise the imaginative woe,
    That loved to handle spiritual strife,
55   Diffused the shock through all my life,
But in the present broke the blow.

My pulses therefore beat again
    For other friends that once I met;
    Nor can it suit me to forget
60   The mighty hopes that make us men.

I woo your love: I count it crime
    To mourn for any overmuch;
    I, the divided half of such
A friendship as had mastered Time;

65 Which masters Time indeed, and is
Eternal, separate from fears:
The all-assuming¹ months and years
Can take no part away from this:

But Summer on the steaming floods,
70 And Spring that swells the narrow brooks,
And Autumn, with a noise of rooks,
That gather in the waning woods,

And every pulse of wind and wave
Recalls, in change of light or gloom,
75 My old affection of the tomb,
And my prime passion in the grave:

My old affection of the tomb,
A part of stillness, yearns to speak:
"Arise, and get thee forth and seek
80 A friendship for the years to come.

"I watch thee from the quiet shore;
Thy spirit up to mine can reach;
But in dear words of human speech
We two communicate no more."

85 And I, "Can clouds of nature stain
The starry clearness of the free?²
How is it? Canst thou feel for me
Some painless sympathy with pain?"

And lightly does the whisper fall;
90 "'Tis hard for thee to fathom this;
I triumph in conclusive bliss,
And that serene result of all."

So hold I commerce with the dead;
Or so methinks the dead would say;

95 Or so shall grief with symbols play
And pining life be fancy-fed.

Now looking to some settled end,
That these things pass, and I shall prove
A meeting somewhere, love with love,
100 I crave your pardon, O my friend;

If not so fresh, with love as true,
I, clasping brother-hands, aver
I could not, if I would, transfer
The whole I felt for him to you.

105 For which be they that hold apart
The promise of the golden hours?
First love, first friendship, equal powers,
That marry with the virgin heart.

Still mine, that cannot but deplore,
110 That beats within a lonely place,
That yet remembers his embrace,
But at his footstep leaps no more,

My heart, though widowed, may not rest
Quite in the love of what is gone,
115 But seeks to beat in time with one
That warms another living breast.

Ah, take the imperfect gift I bring,
Knowing the primrose yet is dear,
The primrose of the later year,
120 As not unlike to that of Spring.

LXXXVI
Sweet after showers, ambrosial air,
That rollest from the gorgeous gloom
Of evening over brake and bloom
And meadow, slowly breathing bare

5 The round of space, and rapt below
Through all the dewy-tasselled wood,

---

¹ all-consuming.

² the dead.

And shadowing down the hornèd flood[1]
In ripples, fan my brows and blow

The fever from my cheek, and sigh
10   The full new life that feeds thy breath
    Throughout my frame, till Doubt and Death,
Ill brethren, let the fancy fly

From belt to belt of crimson seas
    On leagues of odour streaming far,
15   To where in yonder orient star
A hundred spirits whisper "Peace."[2]

LXXXVII

I past beside the reverend walls
    In which of old I wore the gown;[3]
    I roved at random through the town,
And saw the tumult of the halls;

5 And heard once more in college fanes
    The storm their high-built organs make,
    And thunder-music, rolling, shake
The prophet blazoned on the panes;

And caught once more the distant shout,
10   The measured pulse of racing oars
    Among the willows; paced the shores
And many a bridge, and all about

The same gray flats again, and felt
    The same, but not the same; and last
15   Up that long walk of limes I past
To see the rooms in which he dwelt.

Another name was on the door:
    I lingered; all within was noise

Of songs, and clapping hands, and boys
20 That crashed the glass and beat the floor;

Where once we held debate, a band
    Of youthful friends,[4] on mind and art,
    And labour, and the changing mart,
And all the framework of the land;

25 When one would aim an arrow fair,
    But send it slackly from the string;
    And one would pierce an outer ring,
And one an inner, here and there;

And last the master-bowman, he,
30   Would cleave the mark. A willing ear
    We lent him. Who, but hung to hear
The rapt oration flowing free

From point to point, with power and grace
    And music in the bounds of law,
35   To those conclusions when we saw
The God within him light his face,

And seem to lift the form, and glow
    In azure orbits heavenly-wise;
    And over those ethereal eyes
40 The bar of Michael Angelo.[5]

LXXXVIII

Wild bird,[6] whose warble, liquid sweet,
    Rings Eden through the budded quicks,[7]

---

[1] Tennyson's comment: "between two promontories."

[2] Tennyson's comment on the final stanza: "The west wind rolling to the Eastern seas till it meets the evening star."

[3] a reference to Trinity College, Cambridge, which Tennyson and Hallam attended.

[4] the "Cambridge Apostles," a discussion group attended by Hallam and Tennyson.

[5] Tennyson's comment: "the broad bar of frontal bone over the eyes of Michael Angelo." "These lines I wrote from what Arthur Hallam said after reading of the prominent ridge of bone over the eyes of Michael Angelo: 'Alfred, look over my eyes; surely I have the bar of Michael Angelo!'"

[6] the nightingale.

[7] quickset thorn.

O tell me where the senses mix,
　　O tell me where the passions meet,

5　Whence radiate: fierce extremes employ
　　Thy spirits in the darkening leaf,
　　And in the midmost heart of grief
Thy passion clasps a secret joy:

And I—my harp would prelude woe—
10　　I cannot all command the strings;
　　The glory of the sum of things
Will flash along the chords and go.

LXXXIX

Witch-elms that counterchange[1] the floor
　　Of this flat lawn with dusk and bright;
　　And thou, with all thy breadth and height
Of foliage, towering sycamore;

5　How often, hither wandering down,
　　My Arthur found your shadows fair,
　　And shook to all the liberal air
The dust and din and steam of town:

He brought an eye for all he saw;
10　　He mixt in all our simple sports;
　　They pleased him, fresh from brawling courts
And dusty purlieus of the law.

O joy to him in this retreat,
　　Immantled in ambrosial dark,
15　　To drink the cooler air, and mark
The landscape winking through the heat:

O sound to rout the brood of cares,
　　The sweep of scythe in morning dew,
　　The gust that round the garden flew,
20　And tumbled half the mellowing pears!

O bliss, when all in circle drawn
　　About him, heart and ear were fed
　　To hear him, as he lay and read
The Tuscan[2] poets on the lawn:

25　Or in the all-golden afternoon
　　A guest, or happy sister, sung,
　　Or here she brought the harp and flung
A ballad to the brightening moon:

Nor less it pleased in livelier moods,
30　　Beyond the bounding hill to stray,
　　And break the livelong summer day
With banquet in the distant woods;

Whereat we glanced from theme to theme,
　　Discussed the books to love or hate,
35　　Or touched the changes of the state,
Or threaded some Socratic dream;

But if I praised the busy town,
　　He loved to rail against it still,
　　For "ground in yonder social mill
40　We rub each other's angles down,

"And merge" he said "in form and gloss
　　The picturesque of man and man."
　　We talked: the stream beneath us ran.
The wine-flask lying couched in moss,

45　Or cooled within the glooming wave;
　　And last, returning from afar,
　　Before the crimson-circled star[3]
Had fallen into her father's grave,

And brushing ankle-deep in flowers,
50　　We heard behind the woodbine veil

---

[1] checker.

[2] Dante and Petrarch.

[3] Tennyson's comment: "Before Venus, the evening star, had dipt into the sunset. The planets, according to Laplace, were evolved from the sun."

The milk that bubbled in the pail,
And buzzings of the honied hours

XC

He tasted love with half his mind,
   Nor ever drank the inviolate spring
   Where nighest heaven, who first could fling
This bitter seed among mankind;

5 That could the dead, whose dying eyes
   Were closed with wail, resume their life,
   They would but find in child and wife
An iron welcome when they rise:

'Twas well, indeed, when warm with wine,
10 To pledge them with a kindly tear,
   To talk them o'er, to wish them here,
To count their memories half divine;

But if they came who past away,
   Behold their brides in other hands;
15 The hard heir strides about their lands,
And will not yield them for a day.

Yea, though their sons were none of these,
   Not less the yet-loved sire would make
   Confusion worse than death, and shake
20 The pillars of domestic peace.

Ah dear, but come thou back to me:
   Whatever change the years have wrought,
   I find not yet one lonely thought
That cries against my wish for thee.

XCI

When rosy plumelets tuft the larch,
   And rarely pipes the mounted thrush;
   Or underneath the barren bush
Flits by the sea-blue bird of March;[1]

---
[1] the kingfisher.

5 Come, wear the form by which I know
   Thy spirit in time among thy peers;
   The hope of unaccomplished years
Be large and lucid round thy brow.

When summer's hourly-mellowing change
10 May breathe, with many roses sweet,
   Upon the thousand waves of wheat,
That ripple round the lonely grange;

Come: not in watches of the night,
   But where the sunbeam broodeth warm,
15 Come, beauteous in thine after form,
And like a finer light in light.

XCII

If any vision should reveal
   Thy likeness, I might count it vain
   As but the canker of the brain;
Yea, though it spake and made appeal

5 To chances where our lots were cast
   Together in the days behind,
   I might but say, I hear a wind
Of memory murmuring the past.

Yea, though it spake and bared to view
10 A fact within the coming year;
   And though the months, revolving near,
Should prove the phantom-warning true,

They might not seem thy prophecies,
   But spiritual presentiments,
15 And such refraction of events
As often rises ere they rise.

XCIII

I shall not see thee. Dare I say
   No spirit ever brake the band
   That stays him from the native land
Where first he walked when claspt in clay?

5　No visual shade of some one lost,
　　　　But he, the Spirit himself, may come
　　　　Where all the nerve of sense is numb;
　　Spirit to Spirit, Ghost to Ghost.

　　O, therefore from thy sightless[1] range
10　　　With gods in unconjectured bliss,
　　　　O, from the distance of the abyss
　　Of tenfold-complicated change,

　　Descend, and touch, and enter; hear
　　　　The wish too strong for words to name;
15　　　That in this blindness of the frame
　　My Ghost may feel that thine is near.

　　　　　　XCIV

　　How pure at heart and sound in head,
　　　　With what divine affections bold
　　　　Should be the man whose thought would hold
　　An hour's communion with the dead.

5　In vain shalt thou, or any, call
　　　　The spirits from their golden day,
　　　　Except, like them, thou too canst say,
　　My spirit is at peace with all.

　　They haunt the silence of the breast,
10　　　Imaginations calm and fair,
　　　　The memory like a cloudless air,
　　The conscience as a sea at rest:

　　But when the heart is full of din,
　　　　And doubt beside the portal waits,
15　　　They can but listen at the gates,
　　And hear the household jar within.

　　　　　　XCV

　　By night we lingered on the lawn,
　　　　For underfoot the herb was dry;

　　　　And genial warmth; and o'er the sky
　　The silvery haze of summer drawn;

5　And calm that let the tapers burn
　　　　Unwavering: not a cricket chirred:
　　　　The brook alone far-off was heard,
　　And on the board the fluttering urn:[2]

　　And bats went round in fragrant skies,
10　　　And wheeled or lit the filmy shapes
　　　　That haunt the dusk, with ermine capes
　　And woolly breasts and beaded eyes;[3]

　　While now we sang old songs that pealed
　　　　From knoll to knoll, where, couched at ease,
15　　　The white kine glimmered, and the trees
　　Laid their dark arms about the field.

　　But when those others, one by one,
　　　　Withdrew themselves from me and night,
　　　　And in the house light after light
20　Went out, and I was all alone,

　　A hunger seized my heart; I read
　　　　Of that glad year which once had been,
　　　　In those fallen leaves which kept their green,
　　The noble letters of the dead:

25　And strangely on the silence broke
　　　　The silent-speaking words, and strange
　　　　Was love's dumb cry defying change
　　To test his worth; and strangely spoke

　　The faith, the vigour, bold to dwell
30　　　On doubts that drive the coward back,
　　　　And keen through wordy snares to track
　　Suggestion to her inmost cell.

---

[1] invisible.

[2] a tea-urn shaking slightly because of the boiling water.

[3] moths.

So word by word, and line by line,
　　The dead man touched me from the past,
35　　And all at once it seemed at last
The living soul was flashed on mine,

And mine in this was wound, and whirled
　　About empyreal heights of thought,
　　And came on that which is, and caught
40　The deep pulsations of the world,

Æonian[1] music measuring out
　　The steps of Time—the shocks of Chance—
　　The blows of Death. At length my trance
Was cancelled, stricken through with doubt.

45　Vague words! but ah, how hard to frame
　　In matter-moulded forms of speech,
　　Or even for intellect to reach
Through memory that which I became:

Till now the doubtful dusk revealed
50　　The knolls once more where, couched at ease,
　　The white kine glimmered, and the trees
Laid their dark arms about the field:

And sucked from out the distant gloom
　　A breeze began to tremble o'er
55　　The large leaves of the sycamore,
And fluctuate all the still perfume,

And gathering freshlier overhead,
　　Rocked the full-foliaged elms, and swung
　　The heavy-folded rose, and flung
60　The lilies to and fro, and said

"The dawn, the dawn," and died away;
　　And East and West, without a breath,
　　Mixt their dim lights, like life and death,
To broaden into boundless day.

---

[1] lasting through aeons.

XCVI

You[2] say, but with no touch of scorn,
　　Sweet-hearted, you, whose light-blue eyes
　　Are tender over drowning flies,
You tell me, doubt is Devil-born.

5　I know not: one[3] indeed I knew
　　In many a subtle question versed,
　　Who touched a jarring lyre at first,
But ever strove to make it true:

Perplext in faith, but pure in deeds,
10　　At last he beat his music out.
　　There lives more faith in honest doubt,
Believe me, than in half the creeds.

He fought his doubts and gathered strength,
　　He would not make his judgment blind,
15　　He faced the spectres of the mind
And laid them: thus he came at length

To find a stronger faith his own;
　　And Power was with him in the night,
　　Which makes the darkness and the light,
20　And dwells not in the light alone,

But in the darkness and the cloud,
　　As over Sinaï's peaks of old,
　　While Israel made their gods of gold,
Although the trumpet blew so loud.

XCVII

My love has talked with rocks and trees;
　　He finds on misty mountain-ground
　　His own vast shadow glory-crowned;
He sees himself in all he sees.

---

[2] probably Emily Sellwood, to whom Tennyson was engaged.

[3] Arthur Hallam.

5 Two partners of a married life—
  I looked on these and thought of thee
  In vastness and in mystery,
And of my spirit as of a wife.

  These two—they dwelt with eye on eye,
10 Their hearts of old have beat in tune,
  Their meetings made December June,
Their every parting was to die.

  Their love has never past away;
  The days she never can forget
15 Are earnest[1] that he loves her yet,
Whate'er the faithless people say.

  Her life is lone, he sits apart,
  He loves her yet, she will not weep,
  Though rapt in matters dark and deep
20 He seems to slight her simple heart.

  He thrids the labyrinth of the mind,
  He reads the secret of the star,
  He seems so near and yet so far,
He looks so cold: she thinks him kind.

25 She keeps the gift of years before,
  A withered violet is her bliss:
  She knows not what his greatness is,
For that, for all, she loves him more.

  For him she plays, to him she sings
30 Of early faith and plighted vows;
  She knows but matters of the house,
And he, he knows a thousand things.

  Her faith is fixt and cannot move,
  She darkly feels him great and wise,
35 She dwells on him with faithful eyes,
"I cannot understand: I love."

_____
[1] assurance.

XCVIII
You leave us: you will see the Rhine,
  And those fair hills I sailed below,
  When I was there with him; and go
By summer belts of wheat and vine

5 To where he breathed his latest breath,
  That City.[2] All her splendour seems
  No livelier than the wisp that gleams
On Lethe in the eyes of Death.

  Let her great Danube rolling fair
10 Enwind her isles, unmarked of me:
  I have not seen, I will not see
Vienna; rather dream that there,

  A treble darkness, Evil haunts
  The birth, the bridal; friend from friend
15 Is oftener parted, fathers bend
Above more graves, a thousand wants

  Gnarr[3] at the heels of men, and prey
  By each cold hearth, and sadness flings
  Her shadow on the blaze of kings:
20 And yet myself have heard him[4] say,

  That not in any mother town[5]
  With statelier progress to and fro
  The double tides of chariots flow
By park and suburb under brown

25 Of lustier leaves; nor more content,
  He told me, lives in any crowd,
  When all is gay with lamps, and loud
With sport and song, in booth and tent,

_____
[2] Vienna.

[3] snarl.

[4] Hallam.

[5] metropolis.

Imperial halls, or open plain;
30   And wheels the circled dance, and breaks
    The rocket molten into flakes
Of crimson or in emerald rain.

XCIX

Risest thou thus, dim dawn, again,
    So loud with voices of the birds,
    So thick with lowings of the herds,
Day, when I lost the flower of men;

5   Who tremblest through thy darkling red
    On yon swollen brook that bubbles fast
    By meadows breathing of the past,
And woodlands holy to the dead;

Who murmurest in the foliaged eaves
10   A song that slights the coming care,
    And Autumn laying here and there
A fiery finger on the leaves;

Who wakenest with thy balmy breath
    To myriads on the genial earth,
15   Memories of bridal, or of birth,
And unto myriads more, of death.

O wheresoever those may be,
    Betwixt the slumber of the poles,
    Today they count as kindred souls;
20   They know me not, but mourn with me.

C

I climb the hill: from end to end
    Of all the landscape underneath,
    I find no place that does not breathe
Some gracious memory of my friend;

5   No gray old grange, or lonely fold,
    Or low morass and whispering reed,
    Or simple stile from mead to mead,
Or sheepwalk up the windy wold;

Nor hoary knoll of ash and haw
10   That hears the latest linnet trill,
    Nor quarry trenched along the hill
And haunted by the wrangling daw;

Nor runlet tinkling from the rock;
    Nor pastoral rivulet that swerves
15   To left and right through meadowy curves,
That feed the mothers of the flock;

But each has pleased a kindred eye,
    And each reflects a kindlier day;
    And, leaving these, to pass away,
20   I think once more he seems to die.

CI

Unwatched, the garden bough shall sway,
    The tender blossom flutter down,
    Unloved, that beech will gather brown,
This maple burn itself away;

5   Unloved, the sun-flower, shining fair,
    Ray round with flames her disk of seed,
    And many a rose-carnation feed
With summer spice the humming air;

10   Unloved, by many a sandy bar,
    The brook shall babble down the plain,
    At noon or when the lesser wain[1]
Is twisting round the polar star;

Uncared for, gird the windy grove,
15   And flood the haunts of hern and crake;[2]
    Or into silver arrows break
The sailing moon in creek and cove;

Till from the garden and the wild
    A fresh association blow,

---

[1] the Little Dipper (Ursa Minor).

[2] heron and corn crake.

20   And year by year the landscape grow
Familiar to the stranger's child;

As year by year the labourer tills
    His wonted glebe, or lops the glades;
    And year by year our memory fades
25 From all the circle of the hills.

CII

We leave the well-belovèd place
    Where first we gazed upon the sky;
    The roofs, that heard our earliest cry,
Will shelter one of stranger race.

5 We go, but ere we go from home,
    As down the garden-walks I move,
    Two spirits[1] of a diverse love
Contend for loving masterdom.

One whispers, "Here thy boyhood sung
10   Long since its matin song, and heard
    The low love-language of the bird
In native hazels tassel-hung."

The other answers, "Yea, but here
    Thy feet have strayed in after hours
15   With thy lost friend among the bowers,
And this hath made them trebly dear."

These two have striven half the day,
    And each prefers his separate claim,
    Poor rivals in a losing game,
20 That will not yield each other way.

I turn to go: my feet are set
    To leave the pleasant fields and farms;
    They mix in one another's arms
To one pure image of regret.

[1] Tennyson's comment: "First, the love of the native place; second, this enhanced by the memory of A.H.H."

CIII

On that last night before we went
    From out the doors where I was bred,
    I dreamed a vision of the dead,
Which left my after-morn content.

5 Methought I dwelt within a hall,
    And maidens[2] with me: distant hills
    From hidden summits fed with rills
A river[3] sliding by the wall.

The hall with harp and carol rang.
10   They sang of what is wise and good
    And graceful. In the centre stood
A statue veiled, to which they sang;

And which, though veiled, was known to me,
    The shape of him I loved, and love
15   For ever: then flew in a dove
And brought a summons from the sea:[4]

And when they learnt that I must go
    They wept and wailed, but led the way
    To where a little shallop lay
20 At anchor in the flood below;

And on by many a level mead,
    And shadowing bluff that made the banks,
    We glided winding under ranks
Of iris, and the golden reed;

25 And still as vaster grew the shore[5]
    And rolled the floods in grander space,
    The maidens gathered strength and grace
And presence, lordlier than before;

[2] Tennyson's comment: "They are the Muses, poetry, arts—all that made life beautiful here, which we hope will pass with us beyond the grave."

[3] life on earth.

[4] eternity.

[5] the progress of the Age.

And I myself, who sat apart
30   And watched them, waxed in every limb;
   I felt the thews of Anakim,[1]
The pulses of a Titan's heart;

As one would sing the death of war,
   And one would chant the history
35   Of that great race, which is to be,[2]
And one the shaping of a star;

Until the forward-creeping tides
   Began to foam, and we to draw
   From deep to deep, to where we saw
40 A great ship lift her shining sides.

The man we loved was there on deck,
   But thrice as large as man he bent
   To greet us. Up the side I went,
And fell in silence on his neck:

45 Whereat those maidens with one mind
   Bewailed their lot; I did them wrong:
   "We served thee here," they said, "so long,
And wilt thou leave us now behind?"

So rapt I was, they could not win
50   An answer from my lips, but he
   Replying, "Enter likewise ye
And go with us:" they entered in.

And while the wind began to sweep
   A music out of sheet and shroud,
55   We steered her toward a crimson cloud
That landlike slept along the deep.

CIV

The time draws near the birth of Christ;
   The moon is hid, the night is still;

A single church below the hill
Is pealing, folded in the mist.

5 A single peal of bells below,
   That wakens at this hour of rest
   A single murmur in the breast,
That these are not the bells I know.

Like strangers' voices here they sound,
10   In lands where not a memory strays,
   Nor landmark breathes of other days,
But all is new unhallowed ground.

CV

Tonight ungathered let us leave
   This laurel, let this holly stand:
   We live within the stranger's land,
And strangely falls our Christmas-eve.

5 Our father's dust is left alone
   And silent under other snows:
   There in due time the woodbine blows,
The violet comes, but we are gone.

No more shall wayward grief abuse
10   The genial hour with mask and mime;
   For change of place, like growth of time,
Has broke the bond of dying use.

Let cares that petty shadows cast,
   By which our lives are chiefly proved,
15   A little spare the night I loved,
And hold it solemn to the past.

But let no footstep beat the floor,
   Nor bowl of wassail mantle warm;[3]
   For who would keep an ancient form
20 Through which the spirit breathes no more?

[1] the giants of Deuteronomy.

[2] Tennyson's comment: "The great hopes of humanity and science."

[3] warm frothing wine.

Be neither song, nor game, nor feast;
   Nor harp be touched, nor flute be blown;
   No dance, no motion, save alone
What lightens in the lucid east

25 Of rising worlds by yonder wood.
   Long sleeps the summer in the seed;
   Run out your measured arcs, and lead
The closing cycle rich in good.

CVI

Ring out, wild bells, to the wild sky,
   The flying cloud, the frosty light:
   The year is dying in the night;
Ring out, wild bells, and let him die.

5 Ring out the old, ring in the new,
   Ring, happy bells, across the snow:
   The year is going, let him go;
Ring out the false, ring in the true.

Ring out the grief that saps the mind,
10   For those that here we see no more;
   Ring out the feud of rich and poor,
Ring in redress to all mankind.

Ring out a slowly dying cause,
   And ancient forms of party strife;
15   Ring in the nobler modes of life,
With sweeter manners, purer laws.

Ring out the want, the care, the sin,
   The faithless coldness of the times;
   Ring out, ring out my mournful rhymes,
20 But ring the fuller minstrel in.

Ring out false pride in place and blood,
   The civic slander and the spite;
   Ring in the love of truth and right,
Ring in the common love of good.

25 Ring out old shapes of foul disease;
   Ring out the narrowing lust of gold;
   Ring out the thousand wars of old,
Ring in the thousand years of peace.

Ring in the valiant man and free,
30   The larger heart, the kindlier hand;
   Ring out the darkness of the land,
Ring in the Christ that is to be.

CVII

It is the day when he was born,
   A bitter day that early sank
   Behind a purple-frosty bank
Of vapour, leaving night forlorn.

5 The time admits not flowers or leaves
   To deck the banquet. Fiercely flies
   The blast of North and East, and ice
Makes daggers at the sharpened eaves,

And bristles all the brakes and thorns
10   To yon hard crescent,[1] as she hangs
   Above the wood which grides[2] and clangs
Its leafless ribs and iron horns

Together, in the drifts that pass
   To darken on the rolling brine
15   That breaks the coast. But fetch the wine,
Arrange the board and brim the glass;

Bring in great logs and let them lie,
   To make a solid core of heat;
   Be cheerful-minded, talk and treat
20 Of all things even as he were by;

We keep the day. With festal cheer,
   With books and music, surely we

---

[1] moon.

[2] crashes.

Will drink to him, whate'er he be,
And sing the songs he loved to hear.

CVIII

I will not shut me from my kind,
    And, lest I stiffen into stone,
    I will not eat my heart alone,
Nor feed with sighs a passing wind:

5 What profit lies in barren faith,
    And vacant yearning, though with might
    To scale the heaven's highest height,
Or dive below the wells of Death?

What find I in the highest place,
10   But mine own phantom chanting hymns?
    And on the depths of death there swims
The reflex of a human face.

I'll rather take what fruit may be
    Of sorrow under human skies:
15   'Tis held that sorrow makes us wise,
Whatever wisdom sleep with thee.

CIX

Heart-affluence in discursive talk
    From household fountains never dry;
    The critic clearness of an eye,
That saw through all the Muses' walk;[1]

5 Seraphic intellect and force
    To seize and throw the doubts of man;
    Impassioned logic, which outran
The hearer in its fiery course;

High nature amorous of the good,
10   But touched with no ascetic gloom;
    And passion pure in snowy bloom
Through all the years of April blood;

A love of freedom rarely felt,
    Of freedom in her regal seat
15   Of England; not the schoolboy heat,
The blind hysterics of the Celt;

And manhood fused with female grace
    In such a sort, the child would twine
    A trustful hand, unasked, in thine,
20 And find his comfort in thy face;

All these have been, and thee mine eyes
    Have looked on: if they looked in vain,
    My shame is greater who remain,
Nor let thy wisdom make me wise.

CX

Thy converse drew us with delight,
    The men of rathe[2] and riper years:
    The feeble soul, a haunt of fears,
Forgot his weakness in thy sight.

5 On thee the loyal-hearted hung,
    The proud was half disarmed of pride,
    Nor cared the serpent at thy side
To flicker with his double tongue.

The stern were mild when thou wert by,
10   The flippant put himself to school
    And heard thee, and the brazen fool
Was softened, and he knew not why;

While I, thy nearest, sat apart,
    And felt thy triumph was as mine;
15   And loved them more, that they were thine,
The graceful tact, the Christian art;

Nor mine the sweetness or the skill,
    But mine the love that will not tire,
    And, born of love, the vague desire
20 That spurs an imitative will.

---

[1] where the Muses gather.

[2] early.

CXI

The churl in spirit, up or down
    Along the scale of ranks, through all,
    To him who grasps a golden ball,[1]
By blood a king, at heart a clown;

5 The churl in spirit, howe'er he veil
    His want in forms for fashion's sake,
    Will let his coltish nature break
At seasons through the gilded pale:[2]

For who can always act? but he,
10   To whom a thousand memories call,
    Not being less but more than all
The gentleness he seemed to be,

Best seemed the thing he was, and joined
    Each office of the social hour
15   To noble manners, as the flower
And native growth of noble mind;

Nor ever narrowness or spite,
    Or villain fancy fleeting by,
    Drew in the expression of an eye,
20 Where God and Nature met in light;

And thus he bore without abuse
    The grand old name of gentleman,
    Defamed by every charlatan,
And soiled with all ignoble use.

CXII

High wisdom holds my wisdom less,
    That I, who gaze with temperate eyes
    On glorious insufficiencies,
Set light by narrower perfectness.

5 But thou, that fillest all the room
    Of all my love, art reason why
    I seem to cast a careless eye
On souls, the lesser lords of doom.

For what wert thou? some novel power
10   Sprang up for ever at a touch,
    And hope could never hope too much,
In watching thee from hour to hour,

Large elements in order brought,
    And tracts of calm from tempest made,
15   And world-wide fluctuation swayed
In vassal tides that followed thought.

CXIII

'Tis held that sorrow makes us wise;
    Yet how much wisdom sleeps with thee
    Which not alone had guided me,
But served the seasons that may rise;

5 For can I doubt, who knew thee keen
    In intellect, with force and skill
    To strive, to fashion, to fulfil—
I doubt not what thou wouldst have been:

A life in civic action warm,
10   A soul on highest mission sent,
    A potent voice of Parliament,
A pillar steadfast in the storm,

Should licensed boldness gather force,
    Becoming, when the time has birth,
15   A lever to uplift the earth
And roll it in another course,

With thousand shocks that come and go,
    With agonies, with energies,
    With overthrowings, and with cries,
20 And undulations to and fro.

---

[1] symbol of kingship.

[2] barriers.

CXIV

Who loves not Knowledge? Who shall rail
    Against her beauty? May she mix
    With men and prosper! Who shall fix
Her pillars?[1] Let her work prevail.

5   But on her forehead sits a fire:
    She sets her forward countenance
    And leaps into the future chance,
Submitting all things to desire.

Half-grown as yet, a child, and vain—
10   She cannot fight the fear of death.
    What is she, cut from love and faith,
But some wild Pallas from the brain

Of Demons? fiery-hot to burst
    All barriers in her onward race
15   For power. Let her know her place;
She is the second, not the first.

A higher hand must make her mild,
    If all be not in vain; and guide
    Her footsteps, moving side by side
20 With wisdom, like the younger child:

For she is earthly of the mind,
    But Wisdom heavenly of the soul.
    O, friend, who camest to thy goal
So early, leaving me behind,

25 I would the great world grew like thee,
    Who grewest not alone in power
    And knowledge, but by year and hour
In reverence and in charity.

CXV

Now fades the last long streak of snow,
    Now burgeons every maze of quick[2]
    About the flowering squares, and thick
By ashen roots the violets blow.

5   Now rings the woodland loud and long,
    The distance takes a lovelier hue,
    And drowned in yonder living blue
The lark becomes a sightless song.

Now dance the lights on lawn and lea,
10   The flocks are whiter down the vale,
    And milkier every milky sail
On winding stream or distant sea;

Where now the seamew pipes, or dives
    In yonder greening gleam, and fly
15   The happy birds, that change their sky
To build and brood; that live their lives

From land to land; and in my breast
    Spring wakens too; and my regret
    Becomes an April violet,
20 And buds and blossoms like the rest.

CXVI

Is it, then, regret for buried time
    That keenlier in sweet April wakes,
    And meets the year, and gives and takes
The colours of the crescent prime?

5   Not all: the songs, the stirring air,
    The life re-orient out of dust,
    Cry through the sense to hearten trust
In that which made the world so fair.

Not all regret: the face will shine
10   Upon me, while I muse alone;

---

[1] limits.

[2] quickset thorn hedge-row.

And that dear voice, I once have known,
Still speak to me of me and mine:

Yet less of sorrow lives in me
   For days of happy commune dead;
15   Less yearning for the friendship fled,
Than some strong bond which is to be.

CXVII

O days and hours, your work is this
   To hold me from my proper place,
   A little while from his embrace,
For fuller gain of after bliss:

5   That out of distance might ensue
   Desire of nearness doubly sweet;
   And unto meeting when we meet,
Delight a hundredfold accrue,

For every grain of sand that runs,
10   And every span of shade that steals,
   And every kiss of toothèd wheels,[1]
And all the courses of the suns.

CXVIII

Contemplate all this work of Time,
   The giant labouring in his youth;
   Nor dream of human love and truth,
As dying Nature's earth and lime;

5   But trust that those we call the dead
   Are breathers of an ampler day
   For ever nobler ends. They say,
The solid earth whereon we tread

In tracts of fluent heat began,
10   And grew to seeming-random forms,

The seeming prey of cyclic storms,[2]
Till at the last arose the man;

Who throve and branched from clime to clime,
   The herald of a higher race,
15   And of himself in higher place,
If so he type this work of time

Within himself, from more to more;
   Or, crowned with attributes of woe
   Like glories, move his course, and show
20 That life is not as idle ore,

But iron dug from central gloom,
   And heated hot with burning fears,
   And dipt in baths of hissing tears,
And battered with the shocks of doom

25 To shape and use. Arise and fly
   The reeling Faun, the sensual feast;
   Move upward, working out the beast,
And let the ape and tiger die.

CXIX

Doors, where my heart was used to beat
   So quickly, not as one that weeps
   I come once more; the city sleeps;
I smell the meadow in the street;

5   I hear a chirp of birds; I see
   Betwixt the black fronts long-withdrawn
   A light-blue lane of early dawn,
And think of early days and thee,

And bless thee, for thy lips are bland,
10   And bright the friendship of thine eye;
   And in my thoughts with scarce a sigh
I take the pressure of thine hand.

---

[1] wheels of a clock.

[2] periodic cataclysms.

CXX

I trust I have not wasted breath:
　　I think we are not wholly brain,
　　Magnetic mockeries; not in vain,
Like Paul with beasts, I fought with Death;

5　Not only cunning casts in clay:
　　Let Science prove we are, and then
　　What matters Science unto men,
At least to me? I would not stay.

Let him, the wiser man[1] who springs
10　Hereafter, up from childhood shape
　　His action like the greater ape,
But I was *born* to other things.

CXXI

Sad Hesper o'er the buried sun
　　And ready, thou, to die with him,
　　Thou watchest all things ever dim
And dimmer, and a glory done:

5　The team is loosened from the wain,[2]
　　The boat is drawn upon the shore;
　　Thou listenest to the closing door,
And life is darkened in the brain.

Bright Phosphor, fresher for the night,
10　By thee the world's great work is heard
　　Beginning, and the wakeful bird;
Behind thee comes the greater light:

The market boat is on the stream,
　　And voices hail it from the brink;
15　　Thou hear'st the village hammer clink,
And see'st the moving of the team.

Sweet Hesper-Phosphor, double name
　　For what is one, the first, the last,
　　Thou, like my present and my past,
20　Thy place is changed; thou art the same.

CXXII

Oh, wast thou with me, dearest, then,
　　While I rose up against my doom,
　　And yearned to burst the folded gloom,
To bare the eternal Heavens again,

5　To feel once more, in placid awe,
　　The strong imagination roll
　　A sphere of stars about my soul,
In all her motion one with law;

If thou wert with me, and the grave
10　Divide us not, be with me now,
　　And enter in at breast and brow,
Till all my blood, a fuller wave,

Be quickened with a livelier breath,
　　And like an inconsiderate boy,
15　As in the former flash of joy,
I slip the thoughts of life and death;

And all the breeze of Fancy blows,
　　And every dew-drop paints a bow,[3]
　　The wizard lightnings deeply glow,
20　And every thought breaks out a rose.

CXXIII

There rolls the deep where grew the tree.
　　O earth, what changes hast thou seen!
　　There where the long street roars, hath been
The stillness of the central sea.

5　The hills are shadows, and they flow
　　From form to form, and nothing stands;

---

[1] ironic—one made wise by science.

[2] wagon.

---

[3] Tennyson's comment: "Every dew-drop turns into a miniature rainbow."

They melt like mist, the solid lands,
Like clouds they shape themselves and go.

But in my spirit will I dwell,
10   And dream my dream, and hold it true;
For though my lips may breathe adieu,
I cannot think the thing farewell.

CXXIV

That which we dare invoke to bless;
Our dearest faith; our ghastliest doubt;
He, They, One, All; within, without;
The Power in darkness whom we guess;

5   I found Him not in world or sun,
Or eagle's wing, or insect's eye;
Nor through the questions men may try,
The petty cobwebs we have spun:

If e'er when faith had fallen asleep,
10   I heard a voice "believe no more"
And heard an ever-breaking shore
That tumbled in the Godless deep;

A warmth within the breast would melt
The freezing reason's colder part,
15   And like a man in wrath the heart
Stood up and answered "I have felt."

No, like a child in doubt and fear:
But that blind clamour made me wise;
Then was I as a child that cries,
20   But, crying, knows his father near;

And what I am beheld again
What is, and no man understands;
And out of darkness came the hands
That reach through nature, moulding men.

CXXV

Whatever I have said or sung,
Some bitter notes my harp would give,
Yea, though there often seemed to live
A contradiction on the tongue,

5   Yet Hope had never lost her youth;
She did but look through dimmer eyes;
Or Love but played with gracious lies,
Because he felt so fixed in truth:

And if the song were full of care,
10   He[1] breathed the spirit of the song;
And if the words were sweet and strong
He set his royal signet there;

Abiding with me till I sail
To seek thee on the mystic deeps,
15   And this electric force, that keeps
A thousand pulses dancing, fail.

CXXVI

Love is and was my Lord and King,
And in his presence I attend
To hear the tidings of my friend,
Which every hour his couriers bring.

5   Love is and was my King and Lord,
And will be, though as yet I keep
Within his court on earth, and sleep
Encompassed by his faithful guard,

And hear at times a sentinel
10   Who moves about from place to place,
And whispers to the worlds of space,
In the deep night, that all is well.

CXXVII

And all is well, though faith and form
Be sundered in the night of fear;

_____

[1] love.

Well roars the storm to those that hear
A deeper voice across the storm,

5   Proclaiming social truth shall spread,
And justice, even though thrice again
The red fool-fury of the Seine
Should pile her barricades with dead.[1]

But ill for him that wears a crown,
10   And him, the lazar, in his rags:
They tremble, the sustaining crags;
The spires of ice are toppled down,

And molten up, and roar in flood;
The fortress crashes from on high,
15   The brute earth lightens to the sky,
And the great Æon[2] sinks in blood,

And compassed by the fires of Hell;
While thou, dear spirit, happy star,
O'erlook'st the tumult from afar,
20   And smilest, knowing all is well.

CXXVIII

The love that rose on stronger wings,
Unpalsied when he met with Death,
Is comrade of the lesser faith
That sees the course of human things.

5   No doubt vast eddies in the flood
Of onward time shall yet be made,
And thronèd races may degrade;
Yet O ye mysteries of good,

Wild Hours that fly with Hope and Fear,
10   If all your office had to do
With old results that look like new;
If this were all your mission here,

---

[1] the French Revolution.

[2] great age.

To draw, to sheathe a useless sword,
To fool the crowd with glorious lies,
15   To cleave a creed in sects and cries,
To change the bearing of a word,

To shift an arbitrary power,
To cramp the student at his desk,
To make old bareness picturesque
20   And tuft with grass a feudal tower;

Why then my scorn might well descend
On you and yours. I see in part
That all, as in some piece of art,
Is toil coöperant to an end.

CXXIX

Dear friend, far off, my lost desire,
So far, so near in woe and weal;
O loved the most, when most I feel
There is a lower and a higher;

5   Known and unknown; human, divine;
Sweet human hand and lips and eye;
Dear heavenly friend that canst not die,
Mine, mine, for ever, ever mine;

Strange friend, past, present, and to be;
10   Loved deeplier, darklier understood;
Behold, I dream a dream of good,
And mingle all the world with thee.

CXXX

Thy voice is on the rolling air;
I hear thee where the waters run;
Thou standest in the rising sun,
And in the setting thou art fair.

5   What art thou then? I cannot guess;
But though I seem in star and flower
To feel thee some diffusive power,
I do not therefore love thee less:

My love involves the love before;
    My love is vaster passion now;
10 Though mixed with God and Nature thou,
I seem to love thee more and more.

Far off thou art, but ever nigh;
    I have thee still, and I rejoice;
15 I prosper, circled with thy voice;
I shall not lose thee though I die.

CXXXI

O living will that shalt endure[1]
    When all that seems shall suffer shock,
    Rise in the spiritual rock,
Flow through our deeds and make them pure,

5   That we may lift from out of dust
    A voice as unto him that hears,
    A cry above the conquered years
To one that with us works, and trust,

With faith that comes of self-control,
10 The truths that never can be proved
    Until we close with all we loved,
And all we flow from, soul in soul.

———————

[EPILOGUE]

O true and tried, so well and long,
    Demand not thou a marriage lay;
    In that it is thy marriage day
Is music more than any song.

5   Nor have I felt so much of bliss
    Since first he told me that he loved
    A daughter of our house; nor proved
Since that dark day a day like this;

Though I since then have numbered o'er
10 Some thrice three years: they went and came,
    Remade the blood and changed the frame,
And yet is love not less, but more;

No longer caring to embalm
    In dying songs a dead regret,
15 But like a statue solid-set,
And moulded in colossal calm.

Regret is dead, but love is more
    Than in the summers that are flown,
    For I myself with these have grown
20 To something greater than before;

Which makes appear the songs I made
    As echoes out of weaker times,
    As half but idle brawling rhymes,
The sport of random sun and shade.

25 But where is she, the bridal flower,
    That must be made a wife ere noon?
    She enters, glowing like the moon
Of Eden on its bridal bower:

On me she bends her blissful eyes
30 And then on thee; they meet thy look
    And brighten like the star that shook
Betwixt the palms of paradise.

O when her life was yet in bud,
    He too foretold the perfect rose.
35 For thee she grew, for thee she grows
For ever, and as fair as good.

And thou art worthy; full of power;
    As gentle; liberal-minded, great,
    Consistent; wearing all that weight
40 Of learning lightly like a flower.

———————

[1] Tennyson's comment: "That which we know as Free-will in man."

But now set out: the noon is near,
    And I must give away the bride;
    She fears not, or with thee beside
And me behind her, will not fear.

45   For I that danced her on my knee,
    That watched her on her nurse's arm,
    That shielded all her life from harm
At last must part with her to thee;

Now waiting to be made a wife,
50   Her feet, my darling, on the dead;
    Their pensive tablets round her head,
And the most living words of life

Breathed in her ear. The ring is on,
    The "wilt thou" answered, and again
55   The "wilt thou" asked, till out of twain
Her sweet "I will" has made you one.

Now sign your names, which shall be read,
    Mute symbols of a joyful morn,
    By village eyes as yet unborn;
60   The names are signed, and overhead

Begins the clash and clang that tells
    The joy to every wandering breeze;
    The blind wall rocks, and on the trees
The dead leaf trembles to the bells.

65   O happy hour, and happier hours
    Await them. Many a merry face
    Salutes them—maidens of the place,
That pelt us in the porch with flowers.

O happy hour, behold the bride
70   With him to whom her hand I gave.
    They leave the porch, they pass the grave
That has today its sunny side.

Today the grave is bright for me,
    For them the light of life increased,
75   Who stay to share the morning feast,
Who rest tonight beside the sea.

Let all my genial spirits advance
    To meet and greet a whiter sun;
    My drooping memory will not shun
80   The foaming grape of eastern France.[1]

It circles round, and fancy plays,
    And hearts are warmed and faces bloom,
    As drinking health to bride and groom
We wish them store of happy days.

85   Nor count me all to blame if I
    Conjecture of a stiller guest,
    Perchance, perchance, among the rest,
And, though in silence, wishing joy.

But they must go, the time draws on,
90   And those white-favoured horses wait;
    They rise, but linger; it is late;
Farewell, we kiss, and they are gone.

A shade falls on us like the dark
    From little cloudlets on the grass,
95   But sweeps away as out we pass
To range the woods, to roam the park,

Discussing how their courtship grew,
    And talk of others that are wed,
    And how she looked, and what he said,
100 And back we come at fall of dew.

Again the feast, the speech, the glee,
    The shade of passing thought, the wealth
    Of words and wit, the double health,
The crowning cup, the three-times-three,

---

[1] champagne.

105 And last the dance;—till I retire:
    Dumb is that tower which spake so loud,
    And high in heaven the streaming cloud,
And on the downs a rising fire:

And rise, O moon, from yonder down,
110   Till over down and over dale
    All night the shining vapour sail
And pass the silent-lighted town,

The white-faced halls, the glancing rills,
    And catch at every mountain head,
115   And o'er the friths[1] that branch and spread
Their sleeping silver through the hills;

And touch with shade the bridal doors,
    With tender gloom the roof, the wall;
    And breaking let the splendour fall
120 To spangle all the happy shores

By which they rest, and ocean sounds,
    And, star and system rolling past,
    A soul shall draw from out the vast
And strike his being into bounds,

125 And, moved through life of lower phase,
    Result in man, be born and think,
    And act and love, a closer link
Betwixt us and the crowning race

Of those that, eye to eye, shall look
130   On knowledge; under whose command
    Is Earth and Earth's, and in their hand
Is Nature like an open book;

No longer half-akin to brute,
    For all we thought and loved and did,
135   And hoped, and suffered, is but seed
Of what in them is flower and fruit;

Whereof the man, that with me trod
    This planet, was a noble type
    Appearing ere the times were ripe,
140 That friend of mine who lives in God,

That God, which ever lives and loves,
    One God, one law, one element,
    And one far-off divine event,
To which the whole creation moves.
—1850

The Charge of the Light Brigade [2]

I

Half a league, half a league,
  Half a league onward,
All in the valley of Death
    Rode the six hundred.
5 "Forward, the Light Brigade!
Charge for the guns!" he said:
Into the valley of Death
    Rode the six hundred.

II

"Forward, the Light Brigade!"
10 Was there a man dismayed?
Not though the soldier knew
    Some one had blundered:
Their's not to make reply,
Their's not to reason why,
15 Their's but to do and die:
Into the valley of Death
    Rode the six hundred.

III

Cannon to right of them,
Cannon to left of them,
20 Cannon in front of them

---

[1] narrow sea inlets.

[2] in the Crimean war. The charge took place on 25 October 1854 and Tennyson published the poem in *The Examiner* on 9 December 1854.

Volleyed and thundered;
Stormed at with shot and shell,
Boldly they rode and well,
Into the jaws of Death,
25   Into the mouth of Hell
     Rode the six hundred.

IV

Flashed all their sabres bare,
Flashed as they turned in air
Sabring the gunners there,
30   Charging an army, while
     All the world wondered:
Plunged in the battery-smoke
Right through the line they broke;
Cossack and Russian
35   Reeled from the sabre-stroke
     Shattered and sundered.
Then they rode back, but not
     Not the six hundred.

V

Cannon to right of them,
40   Cannon to left of them,
Cannon behind them
     Volleyed and thundered;
Stormed at with shot and shell,
While horse and hero fell,
45   They that had fought so well
Came through the jaws of Death,
Back from the mouth of Hell,
All that was left of them,
     Left of six hundred.

VI

50   When can their glory fade?
O the wild charge they made!
     All the world wondered.
Honour the charge they made!
Honour the Light Brigade,
55   Noble six hundred!
    —1854

Maud[1]

A MONODRAMA

PART I

I

I

I hate the dreadful hollow behind the little wood,
Its lips in the field above are dabbled with blood-
   red heath,[2]
The red-ribbed ledges drip with a silent horror of
   blood,
And Echo there, whatever is asked her, answers
   "Death."

II

5 For there in the ghastly pit long since a body was
   found,
His who had given me life—O father! O God! was
   it well?—
Mangled, and flattened, and crushed, and dinted
   into the ground:
There yet lies the rock that fell with him when he
   fell.

III

Did he fling himself down? who knows? for a vast
   speculation had failed,

---

[1] Tennyson comments on the poem as follows: "This poem of *Maud or the Madness* [A.T.'s original title] is a little *Hamlet*, the history of a morbid, poetic soul, under the blighting influence of a recklessly speculative age. He is the heir of madness, an egoist with the makings of a cynic, raised to a pure and holy love which elevates his whole nature, passing from the height of triumph to the lowest depth of misery, driven into madness by the loss of her whom he has loved, and, when he has at length passed through the fiery furnace, and has recovered his reason, giving himself up to work for the good of mankind through the unselfishness born of a great passion. The peculiarity of this poem is that different phases of passion in one person take the place of different characters."

[2] Hallam Tennyson notes, in his *Memoir*, that "My father would say that in calling heath 'blood'-red the hero showed his extravagant fancy, which is already on the road to madness."

10 And ever he muttered and maddened, and ever
    wanned with despair,
And out he walked when the wind like a broken
    worldling wailed,
And the flying gold of the ruined woodlands drove
    through the air.

IV

I remember the time, for the roots of my hair were
    stirred
By a shuffled step, by a dead weight trailed, by a
    whispered fright,
15 And my pulses closed their gates with a shock on
    my heart as I heard
The shrill-edged shriek of a mother divide the
    shuddering night.

V

Villainy somewhere! whose? One says, we are
    villains all.
Not he: his honest fame should at least by me be
    maintained:
But that old man, now lord of the broad estate and
    the Hall,
20 Dropt off gorged from a scheme that had left us
    flaccid and drained.

VI

Why do they prate of the blessings of Peace? we
    have made them a curse,
Pickpockets, each hand lusting for all that is not its
    own;
And lust of gain, in the spirit of Cain, is it better or
    worse
Than the heart of the citizen hissing in war on his
    own hearthstone?

VII

25 But these are the days of advance, the words of the
    men of mind,

When who but a fool would have faith in a
    tradesman's ware or his word?
Is it peace or war? Civil war, as I think, and that of
    a kind
The viler, as underhand, not openly bearing the
    sword.

VIII

Sooner or later I too may passively take the print
30 Of the golden age—why not? I have neither hope
    nor trust;
May make my heart as a millstone, set my face as a
    flint,
Cheat and be cheated, and die: who knows? we are
    ashes and dust.

IX

Peace sitting under her olive, and slurring the days
    gone by,
When the poor are hovelled and hustled together,
    each sex, like swine,
35 When only the ledger lives, and when only not all
    men lie;
Peace in her vineyard—yes!—but a company forges
    the wine.

X

And the vitriol madness flushes up in the ruffian's
    head,
Till the filthy by-lane rings to the yell of the
    trampled wife,
And chalk and alum and plaster are sold to the
    poor for bread,[1]
40 And the spirit of murder works in the very means
    of life,

XI

And Sleep must lie down armed, for the villainous
    centre-bits[2]

---

[1] a notorious scandal concerning the adulteration of food.

[2] burglar's tools.

Grind on the wakeful ear in the hush of the
    moonless nights,
While another is cheating the sick of a few last
    gasps, as he sits
To pestle a poisoned poison behind his crimson
    lights.

XII

45   When a Mammonite[1] mother kills her babe for a
      burial fee,
And Timour[2]-Mammon grins on a pile of
    children's bones,
Is it peace or war? better, war! loud war by land and
    by sea,
War with a thousand battles, and shaking a
    hundred thrones.

XIII

For I trust if an enemy's fleet came yonder round
    by the hill,
50   And the rushing battle-bolt sang from the three-
      decker out of the foam,
That the smooth-faced snubnosed rogue would
    leap from his counter and till,
And strike, if he could, were it but with his
    cheating yardwand, home.—

XIV

What! am I raging alone as my father raged in his
    mood?
Must *I* too creep to the hollow and dash myself
    down and die
55   Rather than hold by the law that I made,
      nevermore to brood
On a horror of shattered limbs and a wretched
    swindler's lie?

XV

Would there be sorrow for *me*? there was *love* in the
    passionate shriek,
Love for the silent thing that had made false haste
    to the grave—
Wrapt in a cloak, as I saw him, and thought he
    would rise and speak
60   And rave at the lie and the liar, ah God, as he used
    to rave.

XVI

I am sick of the Hall and the hill, I am sick of the
    moor and the main.
Why should I stay? can a sweeter chance ever come
    to me here?
O, having the nerves of motion as well as the
    nerves of pain,
Were it not wise if I fled from the place and the pit
    and the fear?

XVII

65   Workmen up at the Hall!—they are coming back
      from abroad;
The dark old place will be gilt by the touch of a
    millionaire:
I have heard, I know not whence, of the singular
    beauty of Maud;
I played with the girl when a child; she promised
    then to be fair.

XVIII

Maud with her venturous climbings and tumbles
    and childish escapes,
70   Maud the delight of the village, the ringing joy of
      the Hall,
Maud with her sweet purse-mouth when my father
    dangled the grapes,
Maud the beloved of my mother, the moon-faced
    darling of all,—

---

[1] a worshipper of Mammon, god of wealth.

[2] Tamerlane, the Mongol conqueror, guilty of atrocities against
children.

XIX

What is she now? My dreams are bad. She may
  bring me a curse.
No, there is fatter game on the moor; she will let
  me alone.
75 Thanks, for the fiend best knows whether woman
  or man be the worse.
I will bury myself in myself, and the Devil may
  pipe to his own.

II

Long have I sighed for a calm: God grant I may
  find it at last!
It will never be broken by Maud, she has neither
  savour nor salt,
But a cold and clear-cut face, as I found when her
  carriage past,
80 Perfectly beautiful: let it be granted her: where is
  the fault?
All that I saw (for her eyes were downcast, not to
  be seen)
Faultily faultless, icily regular, splendidly null,
Dead perfection, no more; nothing more, if it had
  not been
For a chance of travel, a paleness, an hour's defect
  of the rose,
85 Or an underlip, you may call it a little too ripe, too
  full,
Or the least little delicate aquiline curve in a
  sensitive nose,
From which I escaped heart-free, with the least
  little touch of spleen.

III

Cold and clear-cut face, why come you so cruelly
  meek,
Breaking a slumber in which all spleenful folly was
  drowned,
90 Pale with the golden beam of an eyelash dead on
  the cheek,

Passionless, pale, cold face, star-sweet on a gloom
  profound;
Womanlike, taking revenge too deep for a transient
  wrong
Done but in thought to your beauty, and ever as
  pale as before
Growing and fading and growing upon me without
  a sound,
95 Luminous, gemlike, ghostlike, deathlike, half the
  night long
Growing and fading and growing, till I could bear
  it no more,
But arose, and all by myself in my own dark garden
  ground,
Listening now to the tide in its broad-flung
  shipwrecking roar,
Now to the scream of a maddened beach dragged
  down by the wave,
100 Walked in a wintry wind by a ghastly glimmer, and
  found
The shining daffodil dead, and Orion low in his
  grave.

IV

I

A million emeralds break from the ruby-budded
  lime
In the little grove where I sit—ah, wherefore
  cannot I be
Like things of the season gay, like the bountiful
  season bland,
105 When the far-off sail is blown by the breeze of a
  softer clime,
Half-lost in the liquid azure bloom of a crescent of
  sea,
The silent sapphire-spangled marriage ring of the
  land?

II

Below me, there, is the village, and looks how quiet
  and small!

And yet bubbles o'er like a city, with gossip,
scandal, and spite;
110 And Jack on his ale-house bench has as many lies as
a Czar;[1]
And here on the landward side, by a red rock,
glimmers the Hall;
And up in the high Hall-garden I see her pass like a
light;
But sorrow seize me if ever that light be my leading
star!

III

When have I bowed to her father, the wrinkled
head of the race?
115 I met her today with her brother, but not to her
brother I bowed:
I bowed to his lady-sister as she rode by on the
moor;
But the fire of a foolish pride flashed over her
beautiful face.
O child, you wrong your beauty, believe it, in
being so proud;
Your father has wealth well-gotten, and I am
nameless and poor.

IV

120 I keep but a man and a maid, ever ready to slander
and steal;
I know it, and smile a hard-set smile, like a stoic, or
like
A wiser epicurean, and let the world have its way:
For nature is one with rapine, a harm no preacher
can heal;
The Mayfly is torn by the swallow, the sparrow
speared by the shrike,[2]
125 And the whole little wood where I sit is a world of
plunder and prey.

V

We are puppets, Man in his pride, and Beauty fair
in her flower;
Do we move ourselves, or are moved by an unseen
hand at a game
That pushes us off from the board, and others ever
succeed?
Ah yet, we cannot be kind to each other here for an
hour;
130 We whisper, and hint, and chuckle, and grin at a
brother's shame;
However we brave it out, we men are a little breed.

VI

A monstrous eft[3] was of old the Lord and Master of
Earth,
For him did his high sun flame, and his river
billowing ran,
And he felt himself in his force to be Nature's
crowning race.
135 As nine months go to the shaping an infant ripe for
his birth,
So many a million of ages have gone to the making
of man:
He now is first, but is he the last? is he not too
base?

VII

The man of science himself is fonder of glory, and
vain,
An eye well-practised in nature, a spirit bounded
and poor;
140 The passionate heart of the poet is whirled into
folly and vice.
I would not marvel at either, but keep a temperate
brain;
For not to desire or admire, if a man could learn it,
were more
Than to walk all day like the sultan of old in a
garden of spice.

---

[1] Nicholas I and the Crimean war.

[2] small predatory bird.

[3] "The great old lizards of geology." (Tennyson's note.)

VIII

For the drift of the Maker is dark, an Isis[1] hid by
    the veil.
145 Who knows the ways of the world, how God will
    bring them about?
Our planet is one, the suns are many, the world is
    wide.
Shall I weep if a Poland fall? shall I shriek if a
    Hungary fail?
Or an infant civilisation be ruled with rod or with
    knout?
I have not made the world, and He that made it
    will guide.

IX

150 Be mine a philosopher's life in the quiet woodland
    ways,
Where if I cannot be gay let a passionless peace be
    my lot,
Far-off from the clamour of liars belied in the
    hubbub of lies;
From the long-necked geese of the world that are
    ever hissing dispraise
Because their natures are little, and, whether he
    heed it or not,
155 Where each man walks with his head in a cloud of
    poisonous flies.

X

And most of all would I flee from the cruel
    madness of love,
The honey of poison-flowers and all the
    measureless ill.
Ah Maud, you milkwhite fawn, you are all unmeet
    for a wife.
Your mother is mute in her grave as her image in
    marble above;
160 Your father is ever in London, you wander about at
    your will;

You have but fed on the roses and lain in the lilies
    of life.

V

I

A voice by the cedar tree
In the meadow under the Hall!
She is singing an air that is known to me,
165 A passionate ballad gallant and gay,
A martial song like a trumpet's call!
Singing alone in the morning of life,
In the happy morning of life and of May,
Singing of men that in battle array,
170 Ready in heart and ready in hand,
March with banner and bugle and fife
To the death, for their native land.

II

Maud with her exquisite face,
And wild voice pealing up to the sunny sky,
175 And feet like sunny gems on an English green,
Maud in the light of her youth and her grace,
Singing of Death, and of Honour that cannot die,
Till I well could weep for a time so sordid and mean,
And myself so languid and base.

III

180 Silence, beautiful voice!
Be still, for you only trouble the mind
With a joy in which I cannot rejoice,
A glory I shall not find.
Still! I will hear you no more,
185 For your sweetness hardly leaves me a choice
But to move to the meadow and fall before
Her feet on the meadow grass, and adore,
Not her, who is neither courtly nor kind,
Not her, not her, but a voice.

---

[1] "The great Goddess of the Egyptians." (Tennyson's note.)

VI

I

190 Morning arises stormy and pale,
No sun, but a wannish glare
In fold upon fold of hueless cloud,
And the budded peaks of the wood are bowed
Caught and cuffed by the gale:
195 I had fancied it would be fair.

II

Whom but Maud should I meet
Last night, when the sunset burned
On the blossomed gable-ends
At the head of the village street,
200 Whom but Maud should I meet?
And she touched my hand with a smile so sweet,
She made me divine amends
For a courtesy not returned.

III

And thus a delicate spark
205 Of glowing and growing light
Through the livelong hours of the dark
Kept itself warm in the heart of my dreams,
Ready to burst in a coloured flame;
Till at last when the morning came
210 In a cloud, it faded, and seems
But an ashen-gray delight.

IV

What if with her sunny hair
And smile as sunny as cold,
She meant to weave me a snare
215 Of some coquettish deceit,
Cleopatra-like as of old
To entangle me when we met,
To have her lion roll in a silken net
And fawn at a victor's feet.

V

220 Ah, what shall I be at fifty
Should Nature keep me alive,
If I find the world so bitter
When I am but twenty-five?
Yet, if she were not a cheat,
225 If Maud were all that she seemed,
And her smile were all that I dreamed,
Then the world were not so bitter
But a smile could make it sweet.

VI

What if though her eye seemed full
230 Of a kind intent to me,
What if that dandy-despot, he,
That jewelled mass of millinery,
That oiled and curled Assyrian Bull[1]
Smelling of musk and of insolence,
235 Her brother, from whom I keep aloof,
Who wants the finer politic sense
To mask, though but in his own behoof,
With a glassy smile his brutal scorn—
What if he had told her yestermorn
240 How prettily for his own sweet sake
A face of tenderness might be feigned,
And a moist mirage in desert eyes,
That so, when the rotten hustings shake
In another month to his brazen lies,
245 A wretched vote may be gained.

VII

For a raven ever croaks, at my side,
Keep watch and ward, keep watch and ward,
Or thou wilt prove their tool.
Yea, too, myself from myself I guard,
250 For often a man's own angry pride
Is cap and bells for a fool.

---

[1] "With hair curled like that of the bulls on Assyrian sculpture."
(Tennyson's note.)

VIII

Perhaps the smile and tender tone
Came out of her pitying womanhood,
For am I not, am I not, here alone
255 So many a summer since she died,
My mother, who was so gentle and good?
Living alone in an empty house,
Here half-hid in the gleaming wood,
Where I hear the dead at midday moan,
260 And the shrieking rush of the wainscot mouse,
And my own sad name in corners cried,
When the shiver of dancing leaves is thrown
About its echoing chambers wide,
Till a morbid hate and horror have grown
265 Of a world in which I have hardly mixt,
And a morbid eating lichen fixt
On a heart half-turned to stone.

IX

O heart of stone, are you flesh, and caught
By that you swore to withstand?
270 For what was it else within me wrought
But, I fear, the new strong wine of love,
That made my tongue so stammer and trip
When I saw the treasured splendour, her hand,
Come sliding out of her sacred glove,
275 And the sunlight broke from her lip?

X

I have played with her when a child;
She remembers it now we meet.
Ah well, well, well I *may* be beguiled
By some coquettish deceit.
280 Yet, if she were not a cheat,
If Maud were all that she seemed,
And her smile had all that I dreamed,
Then the world were not so bitter
But a smile could make it sweet.

VII

I

285 Did I hear it half in a doze
Long since, I know not where?
Did I dream it an hour ago,
When asleep in this arm-chair?

II

Men were drinking together,
290 Drinking and talking of me;
"Well, if it prove a girl, the boy
Will have plenty: so let it be."

III

Is it an echo of something
Read with a boy's delight,
295 Viziers nodding together
In some Arabian night?

IV

Strange, that I hear two men,
Somewhere, talking of me;
"Well, if it prove a girl, my boy
300 Will have plenty: so let it be."

VIII

She came to the village church,
And sat by a pillar alone;
An angel watching an urn
Wept over her, carved in stone;
305 And once, but once, she lifted her eyes,
And suddenly, sweetly, strangely blushed
To find they were met by my own;
And suddenly, sweetly, my heart beat stronger
And thicker, until I heard no longer
310 The snowy-banded, dilettante,
Delicate-handed priest intone;
And thought, is it pride, and mused and sighed
"No surely, now it cannot be pride."

IX

I was walking a mile,
315 More than a mile from the shore,
The sun looked out with a smile
Betwixt the cloud and the moor,
And riding at set of day
Over the dark moor land,
320 Rapidly riding far away,
She waved to me with her hand.
There were two at her side,
Something flashed in the sun,
Down by the hill I saw them ride,
325 In a moment they were gone:
Like a sudden spark
Struck vainly in the night,
Then returns the dark
With no more hope of light.

X

I

330 Sick, am I sick of a jealous dread?
Was not one of the two at her side
This new-made lord, whose splendour plucks
The slavish hat from the villager's head?
Whose old grandfather has lately died,
335 Gone to a blacker pit, for whom
Grimy nakedness dragging his trucks
And laying his trams in a poisoned gloom
Wrought, till he crept from a gutted mine
Master of half a servile shire,
340 And left his coal all turned into gold
To a grandson, first of his noble line,
Rich in the grace all women desire,
Strong in the power that all men adore,
And simper and set their voices lower,
345 And soften as if to a girl, and hold
Awe-stricken breaths at a work divine,
Seeing his gewgaw castle shine,
New as his title, built last year,
There amid perky larches and pine,

350 And over the sullen-purple moor
(Look at it) pricking a cockney ear.

II

What, has he found my jewel out?
For one of the two that rode at her side
Bound for the Hall, I am sure was he:
355 Bound for the Hall, and I think for a bride.
Blithe would her brother's acceptance be.
Maud could be gracious too, no doubt
To a lord, a captain, a padded shape,
A bought commission, a waxen face,
360 A rabbit mouth that is ever agape—
Bought? what is it he cannot buy?
And therefore splenetic, personal, base,
A wounded thing with a rancorous cry,
At war with myself and a wretched race,
365 Sick, sick to the heart of life, am I.

III

Last week came one to the county town,
To preach our poor little army down,
And play the game of the despot kings,
Though the state has done it and thrice as well:
370 This broad-brimmed hawker of holy things,
Whose ear is crammed with his cotton, and rings
Even in dreams to the chink of his pence,
This huckster put down war! can he tell
Whether war be a cause or a consequence?
375 Put down the passions that make earth Hell!
Down with ambition, avarice, pride,
Jealousy, down! cut off from the mind
The bitter springs of anger and fear;
Down too, down at your own fireside,
380 With the evil tongue and the evil ear,
For each is at war with mankind.

IV

I wish I could hear again
The chivalrous battle-song
That she warbled alone in her joy!

385 I might persuade myself then
She would not do herself this great wrong,
To take a wanton dissolute boy
For a man and leader of men.

V

Ah God, for a man with heart, head, hand,
390 Like some of the simple great ones gone
For ever and ever by,
One still strong man in a blatant land,
Whatever they call him, what care I,
Aristocrat, democrat, autocrat—one
395 Who can rule and dare not lie.

VI

And ah for a man to arise in me,
That the man I am may cease to be!

XI
I

O let the solid ground
Not fail beneath my feet
400 Before my life has found
What some have found so sweet;
Then let come what come may,
What matter if I go mad,
I shall have had my day.

II

405 Let the sweet heavens endure,
Not close and darken above me
Before I am quite quite sure
That there is one to love me;
Then let come what come may
410 To a life that has been so sad,
I shall have had my day.

XII
I

Birds in the high Hall-garden
When twilight was falling,

Maud, Maud, Maud, Maud,
415 They were crying and calling.

II

Where was Maud? in our wood;
And I, who else, was with her,
Gathering woodland lilies,
Myriads blow together.

III

420 Birds in our wood sang
Ringing through the valleys,
Maud is here, here, here
In among the lilies.

IV

I kissed her slender hand,
425 She took the kiss sedately;
Maud is not seventeen,
But she is tall and stately.

V

I to cry out on pride
Who have won her favour!
430 O Maud were sure of Heaven
If lowliness could save her.

VI

I know the way she went
Home with her maiden posy,
For her feet have touched the meadows
435 And left the daisies rosy.[1]

VII

Birds in the high Hall-garden
Were crying and calling to her,
Where is Maud, Maud, Maud?
One is come to woo her.

---

[1] Tennyson's comment: "Because if you tread on the daisy, it turns up a rosy underside."

VIII

440 Look, a horse at the door,
    And little King Charley[1] snarling,
Go back, my lord, across the moor,
    You are not her darling.

XIII
I

Scorned, to be scorned by one that I scorn,
445 Is that a matter to make me fret?
That a calamity hard to be borne?
Well, he may live to hate me yet.
Fool that I am to be vext with his pride!
I past him, I was crossing his lands;
450 He stood on the path a little aside;
His face, as I grant, in spite of spite,
Has a broad-blown comeliness, red and white,
And six feet two, as I think, he stands;
But his essences turned the live air sick,
455 And barbarous opulence jewel-thick
Sunned itself on his breast and his hands.

II

Who shall call me ungentle, unfair,
I longed so heartily then and there
To give him the grasp of fellowship;
460 But while I past he was humming an air,
Stopt, and then with a riding-whip
Leisurely tapping a glossy boot,
And curving a contumelious lip,
Gorgonised[2] me from head to foot
465 With a stony British stare.

III

Why sits he here in his father's chair?
That old man never comes to his place:
Shall I believe him ashamed to be seen?
For only once, in the village street,
470 Last year, I caught a glimpse of his face,

---

[1] a spaniel.

[2] turned the beholder to stone, a power of the mythical Gorgons.

A gray old wolf and a lean.
Scarcely, now, would I call him a cheat;
For then, perhaps, as a child of deceit,
She might by a true descent be untrue;
475 And Maud is as true as Maud is sweet:
Though I fancy her sweetness only due
To the sweeter blood by the other side;
Her mother has been a thing complete,
However she came to be so allied.
480 And fair without, faithful within,
Maud to him is nothing akin:
Some peculiar mystic grace
Made her only the child of her mother,
And heaped the whole inherited sin
485 On the huge scapegoat of the race,
All, all upon the brother.

IV

Peace, angry spirit, and let him be!
Has not his sister smiled on me?

XIV
I

Maud has a garden of roses
490 And lilies fair on a lawn;
There she walks in her state
And tends upon bed and bower,
And thither I climbed at dawn
And stood by her garden-gate;
495 A lion ramps at the top,
He is claspt by a passion-flower.

II

Maud's own little oak-room
(Which Maud, like a precious stone
Set in the heart of the carven gloom,
500 Lights with herself, when alone
She sits by her music and books
And her brother lingers late
With a roystering company) looks
Upon Maud's own garden-gate:

505 And I thought as I stood, if a hand, as white
As ocean-foam in the moon, were laid
On the hasp of the window, and my Delight
Had a sudden desire, like a glorious ghost, to glide,
Like a beam of the seventh Heaven, down to my
        side,
510 There were but a step to be made.

III

The fancy flattered my mind,
And again seemed overbold;
Now I thought that she cared for me,
Now I thought she was kind
515 Only because she was cold.

IV

I heard no sound where I stood
But the rivulet on from the lawn
Running down to my own dark wood;
Or the voice of the long sea-wave as it swelled
520 Now and then in the dim-gray dawn;
But I looked, and round, all round the house I
        beheld
The death-white curtains drawn;
Felt a horror over me creep,
Prickle my skin and catch my breath,
525 Knew that the death-white curtain meant but sleep,
Yet I shuddered and thought like a fool of the sleep
        of death.

XV

So dark a mind within me dwells,
        And I make myself such evil cheer,
That if *I* be dear to some one else,
530   Then some one else may have much to fear;
But if *I* be dear to some one else,
        Then I should be to myself more dear.
Shall I not take care of all that I think,
Yea even of wretched meat and drink,
535 If I be dear,
If I be dear to some one else.

XVI

I

This lump of earth has left his estate
The lighter by the loss of his weight;
And so that he find what he went to seek,
540 And fulsome Pleasure clog him, and drown
His heart in the gross mud-honey of town,
He may stay for a year who has gone for a week:
But this is the day when I must speak,
And I see my Oread[1] coming down,
545 O this is the day!
O beautiful creature, what am I
That I dare to look her way;
Think I may hold dominion sweet,
Lord of the pulse that is lord of her breast,
550 And dream of her beauty with tender dread,
From the delicate Arab arch of her feet[2]
To the grace that, bright and light as the crest
Of a peacock, sits on her shining head,
And she knows it not: O, if she knew it,
555 To know her beauty might half undo it.
I know it the one bright thing to save
My yet young life in the wilds of Time,
Perhaps from madness, perhaps from crime,
Perhaps from a selfish grave.

II

560 What, if she be fastened to this fool lord,
Dare I bid her abide by her word?
Should I love her so well if she
Had given her word to a thing so low?
Shall I love her as well if she
565 Can break her word were it even for me?
I trust that it is not so.

III

Catch not my breath, O clamorous heart,
Let not my tongue be a thrall to my eye,

---

1 mountain nymph.

2 curved like the neck of an Arabian horse.

For I must tell her before we part,
570 I must tell her, or die.

XVII

Go not, happy day,
  From the shining fields,
Go not, happy day,
  Till the maiden yields.
575 Rosy is the West,
  Rosy is the South,
Roses are her cheeks,
  And a rose her mouth.
When the happy Yes
580   Falters from her lips,
Pass and blush the news
  Over glowing ships;
Over blowing seas,
  Over seas at rest,
585 Pass the happy news,
  Blush it through the West;
Till the red man dance
  By his red cedar-tree,
And the red man's babe
590   Leap, beyond the sea.
Blush from West to East,
  Blush from East to West,
Till the West is East,
  Blush it through the West.
595 Rosy is the West,
  Rosy is the South,
Roses are her cheeks,
  And a rose her mouth.

XVIII

I

I have led her home, my love, my only friend.
600 There is none like her, none.
And never yet so warmly ran my blood
And sweetly, on and on
Calming itself to the long-wished-for end,
Full to the banks, close on the promised good.

II

605 None like her, none.
Just now the dry-tongued laurels' pattering talk
Seemed her light foot along the garden walk,
And shook my heart to think she comes once more;
But even then I heard her close the door,
610 The gates of Heaven are closed, and she is gone.

III

There is none like her, none.
Nor will be when our summers have decreased.
O, art thou sighing for Lebanon
In the long breeze that streams to thy delicious
  East,
615 Sighing for Lebanon,
Dark cedar, though thy limbs have here increased,
Upon a pastoral slope as fair,
And looking to the South, and fed
With honeyed rain and delicate air,
620 And haunted by the starry head
Of her whose gentle will has changed my fate,
And made my life a perfumed altar-flame;
And over whom thy darkness must have spread
With such delight as theirs of old, thy great
625 Forefathers of the thornless garden, there
Shadowing the snow-limbed Eve from whom she
  came.

IV

Here will I lie, while these long branches sway,
And you fair stars that crown a happy day
Go in and out as if at merry play,
630 Who am no more so all forlorn,
As when it seemed far better to be born
To labour and the mattock-hardened hand,
Than nursed at ease and brought to understand
A sad astrology,[1] the boundless plan

---

[1] Tennyson's comment: "The *sad astrology* is modern astronomy, for of old astrology was thought to sympathise with and rule man's fate. The stars are 'cold fires,' for though they emit light of the highest intensity, no perceptible warmth reaches us. His newer astrology describes them [l. 677] as 'soft splendours.'"

635 That makes you tyrants in your iron skies,
Innumerable, pitiless, passionless eyes,
Cold fires, yet with power to burn and brand
His nothingness into man.

V

But now shine on, and what care I,
640 Who in this stormy gulf have found a pearl
The countercharm of space and hollow sky,
And do accept my madness, and would die
To save from some slight shame one simple girl.

VI

Would die; for sullen-seeming Death may give
645 More life to Love than is or ever was
In our low world, where yet 'tis sweet to live.
Let no one ask me how it came to pass;
It seems that I am happy, that to me
A livelier emerald twinkles in the grass,
650 A purer sapphire melts into the sea.

VII

Not die; but live a life of truest breath,[1]
And teach true life to fight with mortal wrongs.
O, why should Love, like men in drinking-songs,
Spice his fair banquet with the dust of death?
655 Make answer, Maud my bliss,
Maud made my Maud by that long loving kiss,
Life of my life, wilt thou not answer this?
"The dusky strand of Death inwoven here
With dear Love's tie, makes Love himself more
        dear."

VIII

660 Is that enchanted moan only the swell
Of the long waves that roll in yonder bay?
And hark the clock within, the silver knell
Of twelve sweet hours that past in bridal white,
And died to live, long as my pulses play;

---

[1] Tennyson's comment: "This is the central idea—the holy power of
Love."

665 But now by this my love has closed her sight
And given false death her hand, and stolen away
To dreamful wastes where footless fancies dwell
Among the fragments of the golden day.
May nothing there her maiden grace affright!
670 Dear heart, I feel with thee the drowsy spell.
My bride to be, my evermore delight,
My own heart's heart, my ownest own, farewell;
It is but for a little space I go:
And ye meanwhile far over moor and fell
675 Beat to the noiseless music of the night!
Has our whole earth gone nearer to the glow
Of your soft splendours that you look so bright?
I have climbed nearer out of lonely Hell.
Beat, happy stars, timing with things below,
680 Beat with my heart more blest than heart can tell,
Blest, but for some dark undercurrent woe
That seems to draw—but it shall not be so:
Let all be well, be well.

XIX

I

Her brother is coming back tonight,
685 Breaking up my dream of delight.

II

My dream? do I dream of bliss?
I have walked awake with Truth.
O when did a morning shine
So rich in atonement as this
690 For my dark-dawning youth,
Darkened watching a mother decline
And that dead man at her heart and mine:
For who was left to watch her but I?
Yet so did I let my freshness die.

III

695 I trust that I did not talk
To gentle Maud in our walk
(For often in lonely wanderings
I have cursed him even to lifeless things)

But I trust that I did not talk,
700 Not touch on her father's sin:
I am sure I did but speak
Of my mother's faded cheek
When it slowly grew so thin,
That I felt she was slowly dying
705 Vext with lawyers and harassed with debt:
For how often I caught her with eyes all wet,
Shaking her head at her son and sighing
A world of trouble within!

IV
And Maud too, Maud was moved
710 To speak of the mother she loved
As one scarce less forlorn,
Dying abroad and it seems apart
From him who had ceased to share her heart,
And ever mourning over the feud,
715 The household Fury sprinkled with blood
By which our houses are torn:
How strange was what she said,
When only Maud and the brother
Hung over her dying bed—
720 That Maud's dark father and mine
Had bound us one to the other,
Betrothed us over their wine,
On the day when Maud was born;
Sealed her mine from her first sweet breath.
725 Mine, mine by a right, from birth till death.
Mine, mine—our fathers have sworn.

V
But the true blood spilt had in it a heat
To dissolve the precious seal on a bond,
That, if left uncancelled, had been so sweet;
730 And none of us thought of a something beyond,
A desire that awoke in the heart of the child,
As it were a duty done to the tomb,
To be friends for her sake, to be reconciled;
And I was cursing them and my doom,
735 And letting a dangerous thought run wild

While often abroad in the fragrant gloom
Of foreign churches—I see her there,
Bright English lily, breathing a prayer
To be friends, to be reconciled!

VI
740 But then what a flint is he!
Abroad, at Florence, at Rome,
I find whenever she touched on me
This brother had laughed her down,
And at last, when each came home,
745 He had darkened into a frown,
Chid her, and forbid her to speak
To me, her friend of the years before;
And this was what had reddened her cheek
When I bowed to her on the moor.

VII
750 Yet Maud, although not blind
To the faults of his heart and mind,
I see she cannot but love him,
And says he is rough but kind,
And wishes me to approve him,
755 And tells me, when she lay
Sick once, with a fear of worse,
That he left his wine and horses and play,
Sat with her, read to her, night and day,
And tended her like a nurse.

VIII
760 Kind? but the deathbed desire
Spurned by this heir of the liar—
Rough by kind? yet I know
He has plotted against me in this,
That he plots against me still.
765 Kind to Maud? that were not amiss.
Well, rough but kind; why let it be so:
For shall not Maud have her will?

IX

For, Maud, so tender and true,
As long as my life endures
770 I feel I shall owe you a debt,
That I never can hope to pay;
And if ever I should forget
That I owe this debt to you
And for your sweet sake to yours;
775 O then, what then shall I say?—
If ever I *should* forget,
May God make me more wretched
Than ever I have been yet!

X

So now I have sworn to bury
780 All this dead body of hate,
I feel so free and so clear
By the loss of that dead weight,
That I should grow light-headed, I fear,
Fantastically merry;
785 But that her brother comes, like a blight
On my fresh hope, to the Hall tonight.

XX

I

Strange, that I felt so gay,
Strange, that *I* tried today
To beguile her melancholy;
790 The Sultan, as we name him,—
She did not wish to blame him—
But he vext her and perplext her
With his worldly talk and folly:
Was it gentle to reprove her
795 For stealing out of view
From a little lazy lover
Who but claims her as his due?
Or for chilling his caresses
By the coldness of her manners,
800 Nay, the plainness of her dresses?
Now I know her but in two,
Nor can pronounce upon it

If one should ask me whether
The habit, hat, and feather,
805 Or the frock and gipsy bonnet
Be the neater and completer;
For nothing can be sweeter
Than maiden Maud in either.

II

But tomorrow, if we live,
810 Our ponderous squire will give
A grand political dinner
To half the squirelings near;
And Maud will wear her jewels,
And the bird of prey will hover,
815 And the titmouse hope to win her
With his chirrup at her ear.

III

A grand political dinner
To the men of many acres,
A gathering of the Tory,
820 A dinner and then a dance
For the maids and marriage-makers,
And every eye but mine will glance
At Maud in all her glory.

IV

For I am not invited,
825 But, with the Sultan's pardon,
I am all as well delighted,
For I know her own rose-garden,
And mean to linger in it
Till the dancing will be over;
830 And then, oh then, come out to me
For a minute, but for a minute,
Come out to your own true lover,
That your true lover may see
Your glory also, and render
835 All homage to his own darling,
Queen Maud in all her splendour.

XXI

Rivulet crossing my ground,
And bringing me down from the Hall
This garden-rose that I found,
840 Forgetful of Maud and me,
And lost in trouble and moving round
Here at the head of a tinkling fall,
And trying to pass to the sea;
O Rivulet, born at the Hall,
845 My Maud has sent it by thee
(If I read her sweet will right)
On a blushing mission to me,
Saying in odour and colour, "Ah, be
Among the roses tonight."

XXII

I

850 Come into the garden, Maud,
   For the black bat, night, has flown,
Come into the garden, Maud,
   I am here at the gate alone;
And the woodbine spices are wafted abroad,
855   And the musk of the rose is blown.

II

For a breeze of morning moves,
   And the planet of Love is on high,
Beginning to faint in the light that she loves
   On a bed of daffodil sky,
860 To faint in the light of the sun she loves,
   To faint in his light, and to die.

III

All night have the roses heard
   The flute, violin, bassoon;
All night has the casement jessamine stirred
865   To the dancers dancing in tune;
Till a silence fell with the waking bird,
   And a hush with the setting moon.

IV

I said to the lily, "There is but one
   With whom she has heart to be gay.
870 When will the dancers leave her alone?
   She is weary of dance and play."
Now half to the setting moon are gone,
   And half to the rising day;
Low on the sand and loud on the stone
875   The last wheel echoes away.

V

I said to the rose, "The brief night goes
   In babble and revel and wine.
O young lord-lover, what sighs are those,
   For one that will never be thine?
880 But mine, but mine," so I sware to the rose,
   "For ever and ever, mine."

VI

And the soul of the rose went into my blood,
   As the music clashed in the hall;
And long by the garden lake I stood,
885   For I heard your rivulet fall
From the lake to the meadow and on to the wood,
   Our wood, that is dearer than all;

VII

From the meadow your walks have left so sweet
   That whenever a March-wind sighs
890 He sets the jewel-print of your feet
   In violets blue as your eyes,
To the woody hollows in which we meet
   And the valleys of Paradise.

VIII

The slender acacia would not shake
895   One long milk-bloom on the tree;
The white lake-blossom fell into the lake
   As the pimpernel dozed on the lea;
But the rose was awake all night for your sake,
   Knowing your promise to me;

900 The lilies and roses were all awake,
　　They sighed for the dawn and thee.

IX

Queen rose of the rosebud garden of girls,
　　Come hither, the dances are done,
In gloss of satin and glimmer of pearls,
905　　Queen lily and rose in one;
Shine out, little head, sunning over with curls,
　　To the flowers, and be their sun.

X

There has fallen a splendid tear
　　From the passion-flower at the gate.
910 She is coming, my dove, my dear;
　　She is coming, my life, my fate;
The red rose cries, "She is near, she is near;"
　　And the white rose weeps, "She is late;"
The larkspur listens, "I hear, I hear;"
915　　And the lily whispers, "I wait."

XI

She is coming, my own, my sweet;
　　Were it ever so airy a tread,
My heart would hear her and beat,
　　Were it earth in an earthy bed;
920 My dust would hear her and beat,
　　Had I lain for a century dead;
Would start and tremble under her feet,
　　And blossom in purple and red.

PART II
I
I

"The fault was mine, the fault was mine"—
Why am I sitting here so stunned and still,
Plucking the harmless wild-flower on the hill?—
It is this guilty hand!—
5 And there rises ever a passionate cry
From underneath in the darkening land—

What is it, that has been done?
O dawn of Eden bright over earth and sky,
The fires of Hell brake out of thy rising sun,
10 The fires of Hell and of Hate;
For she, sweet soul, had hardly spoken a word,
When her brother ran in his rage to the gate,
He came with the babe-faced lord;
Heaped on her terms of disgrace,
15 And while she wept, and I strove to be cool,
He fiercely gave me the lie,
Till I with as fierce an anger spoke,
And he struck me, madman, over the face,
Struck me before the languid fool,
20 Who was gaping and grinning by:
Struck for himself an evil stroke;
Wrought for his house an irredeemable woe;
For front to front in an hour we stood,
And a million horrible bellowing echoes broke
25 From the red-ribbed hollow behind the wood,
And thundered up into Heaven the Christless
　　code,[1]
That must have life for a blow.
Ever and ever afresh they seemed to grow.
Was it he lay there with a fading eye?
30 "The fault was mine," he whispered, "fly!"
Then glided out of the joyous wood
The ghastly Wraith of one that I know;
And there rang on a sudden a passionate cry,
A cry for a brother's blood:
35 It will ring in my heart and my ears, till I die, till I
　　die.

II

Is it gone? my pulses beat—
What was it? a lying trick of the brain?
Yet I thought I saw her stand,
A shadow there at my feet,
40 High over the shadowy land.
It is gone; and the heavens fall in a gentle rain,

------
[1] of duelling.

215

When they should burst and drown with deluging
    storms
The feeble vassals of wine and anger and lust,
The little hearts that know not how to forgive:
45 Arise, my God, and strike, for we hold Thee just,
Strike dead the whole weak race of venomous worms,
That sting each other here in the dust;
We are not worthy to live.

II

I

See what a lovely shell,[1]
50 Small and pure as a pearl,
Lying close to my foot,
Frail, but a work divine,
Made so fairly well
With delicate spire and whorl,
55 How exquisitely minute,
A miracle of design!

II

What is it? a learned man
Could give it a clumsy name.
Let him name it who can,
60 The beauty would be the same.

III

The tiny cell is forlorn,
Void of the little living will
That made it stir on the shore.
Did he stand at the diamond door
65 Of his house in a rainbow frill?
Did he push, when he was uncurled,
A golden foot or a fairy horn
Through his dim water-world?

---

1 Tennyson's comment: "In Brittany. The shell undestroyed amid the
storm perhaps symbolises to him his own first and highest nature
preserved amid the storms of passion."

IV

Slight, to be crushed with a tap
70 Of my finger-nail on the sand,
Small, but a work divine,
Frail, but of force to withstand,
Year upon year, the shock
Of cataract seas that snap
75 The three decker's oaken spine
Athwart the ledges of rock,
Here on the Breton strand!

V

Breton, not Briton; here
Like a shipwrecked man on a coast
80 Of ancient fable and fear—
Plagued with a flitting to and fro,
A disease, a hard mechanic ghost
That never came from on high
Nor ever arose from below,
85 But only moves with the moving eye,
Flying along the land and the main—
Why should it look like Maud?
Am I to be overawed
By what I cannot but know
90 Is a juggle born of the brain?

VI

Back from the Breton coast,
Sick of a nameless fear,
Back to the dark sea-line
Looking, thinking of all I have lost;
95 An old song vexes my ear;
But that of Lamech is mine.

VII

For years, a measureless ill,
For years, for ever, to part—
But she, she would love me still;
100 And as long, O God, as she
Have a grain of love for me,
So long, no doubt, no doubt,

Shall I nurse in my dark heart,
However weary, a spark of will
105 Not to be trampled out.

VIII

Strange, that the mind, when fraught
With a passion so intense
One would think that it well
Might drown all life in the eye,—
110 That it should, by being so overwrought,
Suddenly strike on a sharper sense
For a shell, or a flower, little things
Which else would have been past by!
And now I remember, I,
115 When he lay dying there,
I noticed one of his many rings
(For he had many, poor worm) and thought
It is his mother's hair.

IX

Who knows if he be dead?
120 Whether I need have fled?
Am I guilty of blood?
However this may be,
Comfort her, comfort her, all things good,
While I am over the sea!
125 Let me and my passionate love go by,
But speak to her all things holy and high,
Whatever happen to me!
Me and my harmful love go by;
But come to her waking, find her asleep,
130 Powers of the height, Powers of the deep,
And comfort her though I die.

III

Courage, poor heart of stone!
I will not ask thee why
Thou canst not understand
135 That thou art left for ever alone:
Courage, poor stupid heart of stone.—
Or if I ask thee why,

Care not thou to reply:
She is but dead, and the time is at hand
140 When thou shalt more than die.

IV[1]

I

O that 'twere possible
After long grief and pain
To find the arms of my true love
Round me once again!

II

145 When I was wont to meet her
In the silent woody places
By the home that gave me birth,
We stood tranced in long embraces
Mixt with kisses sweeter sweeter
150 Than anything on earth.

III

A shadow flits before me,
Not thou, but like to thee:
Ah Christ, that it were possible
For one short hour to see
155 The souls we loved, that they might tell us
What and where they be.

IV

It leads me forth at evening,
It lightly winds and steals
In a cold white robe before me,
160 When all my spirit reels
At the shouts, the leagues of lights,
And the roaring of the wheels.

V

Half the night I waste in sighs,
Half in dreams I sorrow after
165 The delight of early skies;

---

[1] This section (ll. 141–238) was written in 1833–34 and published in 1837.

In a wakeful doze I sorrow
For the hand, the lips, the eyes,
For the meeting of the morrow,
The delight of happy laughter,
170 The delight of low replies.

VI

'Tis a morning pure and sweet,
And a dewy splendour falls
On the little flower that clings
To the turrets and the walls;
175 'Tis a morning pure and sweet,
And the light and shadow fleet;
She is walking in the meadow,
And the woodland echo rings;
In a moment we shall meet;
180 She is singing in the meadow
And the rivulet at her feet
Ripples on in light and shadow
To the ballad that she sings.

VII

Do I hear her sing as of old,
185 My bird with the shining head,
My own dove with the tender eye?
But there rings on a sudden a passionate cry,
There is some one dying or dead,
And a sullen thunder is rolled;
190 For a tumult shakes the city,
And I wake, my dream is fled;
In the shuddering dawn, behold,
Without knowledge, without pity,
By the curtains of my bed
195 That abiding phantom cold.

VIII

Get thee hence, nor come again,
Mix not memory with doubt,
Pass, thou deathlike type of pain,
Pass and cease to move about!

200 'Tis the blot upon the brain
That *will* show itself without.

IX

Then I rise, the eavedrops fall,
And the yellow vapours choke
The great city sounding wide;
205 The day comes, a dull red ball
Wrapt in drifts of lurid smoke
On the misty river-tide.

X

Through the hubbub of the market
I steal, a wasted frame,
210 It crosses here, it crosses there,
Through all that crowd confused and loud,
The shadow still the same;
And on my heavy eyelids
My anguish hangs like shame.

XI

215 Alas for her that met me,
That heard me softly call,
Came glimmering through the laurels
At the quiet evenfall,
In the garden by the turrets
220 Of the old manorial hall.

XII

Would the happy spirit descend,
From the realms of light and song,
In the chamber or the street,
As she looks among the blest,
225 Should I fear to greet my friend
Or to say "Forgive the wrong,"
Or to ask her, "Take me, sweet,
To the regions of thy rest"?

XIII

But the broad light glares and beats,
230 And the shadow flits and fleets

And will not let me be;
And I loathe the squares and streets,
And the faces that one meets,
Hearts with no love for me:
235 Always I long to creep
Into some still cavern deep,
There to weep, and weep, and weep
My whole soul out to thee.

V

I

Dead, long dead,
240 Long dead!
And my heart is a handful of dust,
And the wheels go over my head,
And my bones are shaken with pain,
For into a shallow grave they are thrust,
245 Only a yard beneath the street,
And the hoofs of the horses beat, beat,
The hoofs of the horses beat,
Beat into my scalp and my brain,
With never an end to the stream of passing feet,
250 Driving, hurrying, marrying, burying,
Clamour and rumble, and ringing and clatter,
And here beneath it is all as bad,
For I thought the dead had peace, but it is not so;
To have no peace in the grave, is that not sad?
255 But up and down and to and fro,
Ever about me the dead men go;
And then to hear a dead man chatter
Is enough to drive one mad.

II

Wretchedest age, since Time began,
260 They cannot even bury a man;
And though we paid our tithes in the days that are
gone,
Not a bell was rung, not a prayer was read;
It is that which makes us loud in the world of the
dead;
There is none that does his work, not one;

265 A touch of their office might have sufficed,
But the churchmen fain would kill their church,
As the churches have killed their Christ.

III

See, there is one of us sobbing,
No limit to his distress;
270 And another, a lord of all things, praying
To his own great self, as I guess;
And another, a statesman there, betraying
His party-secret, fool, to the press;
And yonder a vile physician, blabbing
275 The case of his patient—all for what?
To tickle the maggot born in an empty head,
And wheedle a world that loves him not,
For it is but a world of the dead.

IV

Nothing but idiot gabble!
280 For the prophecy given of old
And then not understood,
Has come to pass as foretold;
Not let any man think for the public good,
But babble, merely for babble.
285 For I never whispered a private affair
Within the hearing of cat or mouse,
No, not to myself in the closet alone,
But I heard it shouted at once from the top of the
house;
Everything came to be known.
290 Who told *him* we were there?

V

Not that gray old wolf,[1] for he came not back
From the wilderness, full of wolves, where he used
to lie;
He has gathered the bones for his o'ergrown whelp
to crack;
Crack them now for yourself, and howl, and die.

---

[1] Maud's father.

VI

295 Prophet, curse me the blabbing lip,
And curse me the British vermin, the rat;
I know not whether he came in the Hanover ship,[1]
But I know that he lies and listens mute
In an ancient mansion's crannies and holes:
300 Arsenic, arsenic, sure, would do it,
Except that now we poison our babes, poor souls!
It is all used up for that.

VII

Tell him now: she is standing here at my head;
Not beautiful now, not even kind;
305 He may take her now; for she never speaks her mind,
But is ever the one thing silent here.
She is not *of* us, as I divine;
She comes from another stiller world of the dead,
Stiller, not fairer than mine.

VIII

310 But I know where a garden grows,
Fairer than aught in the world beside,
All made up of the lily and rose
That blow by night, when the season is good,
To the sound of dancing music and flutes:
315 It is only flowers, they had no fruits,
And I almost fear they are not roses, but blood;
For the keeper was one, so full of pride,
He linkt a dead man there to a spectral bride;
For he, if he had not been a Sultan of brutes,
320 Would he have that hole in his side?

IX

But what will the old man[2] say?
He laid a cruel snare in a pit
To catch a friend of mine one stormy day;
Yet now I could even weep to think of it;

325 For what will the old man say
When he comes to the second corpse[3] in the pit?

X

Friend, to be struck by the public foe,
Then to strike him and lay him low,
That were a public merit, far,
330 Whatever the Quaker holds, from sin;
But the red life spilt for a private blow—
I swear to you, lawful and lawless war
Are scarcely even akin.

XI

O me, why have they not buried me deep enough?
335 Is it kind to have made me a grave so rough,
Me, that was never a quiet sleeper?
Maybe still I am but half-dead;
Then I cannot be wholly dumb;
I will cry to the steps above my head
340 And somebody, surely, some kind heart will come
To bury me, bury me
Deeper, ever so little deeper.

PART III
VI
I

My life has crept so long on a broken wing
Through cells of madness, haunts of horror and fear,
That I come to be grateful at last for a little thing:
My mood is changed, for it fell at a time of year
5 When the face of night is fair on the dewy downs,
And the shining daffodil dies, and the Charioteer
And starry Gemini hang like glorious crowns
Over Orion's grave low down in the west,
That like a silent lightning under the stars
10 She seemed to divide in a dream from a band of the blest,
And spoke of a hope for the world in the coming wars—

---

[1] The Norwegian rat came to England in the ships of George I, House of Hanover, in 1714.

[2] Maud's father.

[3] Maud's brother.

"And in that hope, dear soul, let trouble have rest,
Knowing I tarry for thee," and pointed to Mars
As he glowed like a ruddy shield on the Lion's[1]
    breast.

II

15 And it was but a dream, yet it yielded a dear delight
To have looked, though but in a dream, upon eyes
    so fair,
That had been in a weary world my one thing bright;
And it was but a dream, yet it lightened my despair
When I thought that a war would arise in defence
    of the right,
20 That an iron tyranny now should bend or cease,
The glory of manhood stand on his ancient height,
Nor Britain's one sole God be the millionaire:
No more shall commerce be all in all, and Peace
Pipe on her pastoral hillock a languid note,
25 And watch her harvest ripen, her herd increase,
Nor the cannon-bullet rust on a slothful shore,
And the cobweb woven across the cannon's throat
Shall shake its threaded tears in the wind no more.

III

And as months ran on and rumour of battle grew,
30 "It is time, it is time, O passionate heart," said I
(For I cleaved to a cause that I felt to be pure and true),
"It is time, O passionate heart and morbid eye,
That old hysterical mock-disease should die."
And I stood on a giant deck and mixed my breath
35 With a loyal people shouting a battle cry,
Till I saw the dreary phantom arise and fly
Far into the North, and battle, and seas of death.

IV

Let it go or stay, so I wake to the higher aims
Of a land that has lost for a little her lust of gold,
40 And love of a peace that was full of wrongs and
    shames,
Horrible, hateful, monstrous, not to be told;

And hail once more to the banner of battle unrolled!
Though many a light shall darken, and many shall
    weep
For those that are crushed in the clash of jarring
    claims,
45 Yet God's just wrath shall be wreaked on a giant
    liar;[2]
And many a darkness into the light shall leap,
And shine in the sudden making of splendid names,
And noble thought be freër under the sun,
And the heart of a people beat with one desire;
50 For the peace, that I deemed no peace, is over and
    done,
And now by the side of the Black and the Baltic deep,
And deathful-grinning mouths of the fortress, flames
The blood-red blossom of war with a heart of fire.

V

Let it flame or fade, and the war roll down like a
    wind,
55 We have proved we have hearts in a cause, we are
    noble still,
And myself have awaked, as it seems, to the better
    mind;
It is better to fight for the good than to rail at the ill;
I have felt with my native land, I am one with my
    kind,
I embrace the purpose of God, and the doom
    assigned.
—1855

---

[1] Mars, in the constellation Leo, which is the symbol of Britain.

[2] the Czar.

Tithonus [1]

The woods decay, the woods decay and fall,
   The vapours weep their burthen to the ground,
Man comes and tills the field and lies beneath,
And after many a summer dies the swan.
5 Me only cruel immortality
Consumes: I wither slowly in thine arms,
Here at the quiet limit of the world,
A white-haired shadow roaming like a dream
The ever-silent spaces of the East,
10 Far-folded mists, and gleaming halls of morn.

   Alas! for this gray shadow, once a man—
So glorious in his beauty and thy choice,
Who madest him thy chosen, that he seemed
To his great heart none other than a God!
15 I asked thee, "Give me immortality."
Then didst thou grant mine asking with a smile,
Like wealthy men who care not how they give.
But thy strong Hours indignant worked their wills,
And beat me down and marred and wasted me,
20 And though they could not end me, left me maimed
To dwell in presence of immortal youth,
Immortal age beside immortal youth,
And all I was, in ashes. Can thy love,
Thy beauty, make amends, though even now,
25 Close over us, the silver star,[2] thy guide,
Shines in those tremulous eyes that fill with tears
To hear me? Let me go: take back thy gift:
Why should a man desire in any way
To vary from the kindly race of men,
30 Or pass beyond the goal of ordinance[3]
Where all should pause, as is most meet for all?

   A soft air fans the cloud apart; there comes
A glimpse of that dark world where I was born.
Once more the old mysterious glimmer steals
35 From thy pure brows, and from thy shoulders pure,
And bosom beating with a heart renewed.
Thy cheek begins to redden through the gloom,
Thy sweet eyes brighten slowly close to mine,
Ere yet they blind the stars, and the wild team[4]
40 Which love thee, yearning for thy yoke, arise,
And shake the darkness from their loosened manes,
And beat the twilight into flakes of fire.

   Lo! ever thus thou growest beautiful
In silence, then before thine answer given
45 Departest, and thy tears are on my cheek.

   Why wilt thou ever scare me with thy tears,
And make me tremble lest a saying learnt,
In days far-off, on that dark earth, be true?
"The Gods themselves cannot recall their gifts."
50 Ay me! ay me! with what another heart
In days far-off, and with what other eyes
I used to watch—if I be he that watched—
The lucid outline forming round thee; saw
The dim curls kindle into sunny rings;
55 Changed with thy mystic change, and felt my blood
Glow with the glow that slowly crimsoned all
Thy presence and thy portals, while I lay,
Mouth, forehead, eyelids, growing dewy-warm
With kisses balmier than half-opening buds
60 Of April, and could hear the lips that kissed
Whispering I knew not what of wild and sweet,
Like that strange song I heard Apollo sing,
While Ilion like a mist rose into towers.[5]

---

[1] Although not published until 1860, this poem was written much earlier. Tennyson says: "My friend Thackeray and his publishers had been so urgent with me to send them something, that I ferreted among my old books and found this *Tithonus*, written upwards of a quarter of a century ago.... It was originally a pendent to the *Ulysses* in my former volumes." Tithonus, as Tennyson remarks, was " beloved by Aurora [goddess of the dawn], who gave him eternal life but not eternal youth. He grew old and infirm, and as he could not die, according to the legend, was turned into a grasshopper."

[2] Venus.

[3] appointed limit.

[4] the horses which draw the chariot of dawn.

[5] Troy was built to the music of Apollo's lyre.

Yet hold me not for ever in thine East:
65 How can my nature longer mix with thine?
Coldly thy rosy shadows bathe me, cold
Are all thy lights, and cold my wrinkled feet
Upon thy glimmering thresholds, when the steam
Floats up from those dim fields about the homes
70 Of happy men that have the power to die,
And grassy barrows of the happier dead.
Release me, and restore me to the ground;
Thou seëst all things, thou wilt see my grave:
Thou wilt renew thy beauty morn by morn;
75 I earth in earth forget these empty courts,
And thee returning on thy silver wheels.
—1860

Crossing the Bar [1]

Sunset and evening star,
    And one clear call for me!
And may there be no moaning of the bar,
    When I put out to sea,

5 But such a tide as moving seems asleep,
    Too full for sound and foam,
When that which drew from out the boundless deep
    Turns again home.

Twilight and evening bell,
10   And after that the dark!
And may there be no sadness of farewell,
    When I embark;

For though from out our bourne of Time and Place
    The flood may bear me far,
15 I hope to see my Pilot [2] face to face
    When I have crost the bar.
—1889

---

[1] Before he died, Tennyson instructed: "Mind you put my 'Crossing the Bar' at the end of all editions of my poems."

[2] Tennyson said that the Pilot is "that Divine and Unseen Who is always guiding us."

Robert Browning
1812 – 1889

Robert Browning is recognized for his poetic achievement in the dramatic monologue, especially those poems in the volumes published in 1855, *Men and Women*, and in 1864, *Dramatis Personae*. Browning received little formal education—six years of schooling from the ages of nine to fourteen, and part of one year at London University. His home education was the result of his immersion in his bank-clerk father's large and esoteric library, and the influence of his nonconformist mother's religion and her interest in nature and music. Browning's depth of learning and interest in poetic experimentation is evident in his early work—*Pauline* (1833), *Paracelsus* (1835), and *Sordello* (1840), as well as in the series *Bells and Pomegranates* (1841–46). This series also contained *Dramatic Lyrics* (1842), and *Dramatic Romances and Lyrics* (1845), the former of which included his famous "My Last Duchess," and the latter his first blank-verse dramatic monologue, "The Bishop Orders His Tomb at St. Praxed's Church." Browning met Elizabeth Barrett, whose contemporary reputation as a poet exceeded his, in 1845, and they married on 12 May, 1846, after which they immediately took up residence in Italy. Browning returned to England in 1861 after Elizabeth's death, and worked on his complex multinarrative poem *The Ring and the Book* (1868–69). His poetic experimentation continued until his death in 1889.

❧❧❧

My Last Duchess [1]

FERRARA [2]

That's my last Duchess painted on the wall,
Looking as if she were alive. I call
That piece a wonder, now: Frà Pandolf's[3] hands
Worked busily a day, and there she stands.
5 Will't please you sit and look at her? I said
"Frà Pandolf" by design, for never read
Strangers like you that pictured countenance,
The depth and passion of its earnest glance,
But to myself they turned (since none puts by
10 The curtain I have drawn for you, but I)
And seemed as they would ask me, if they durst,
How such a glance came there; so, not the first
Are you to turn and ask thus. Sir, 'twas not
Her husband's presence only, called that spot
15 Of joy into the Duchess' cheek: perhaps
Frà Pandolf chanced to say "Her mantle laps
Over my lady's wrist too much," or "Paint
Must never hope to reproduce the faint
Half-flush that dies along her throat:" such stuff
20 Was courtesy, she thought, and cause enough
For calling up that spot of joy. She had
A heart—how shall I say?—too soon made glad,
Too easily impressed; she liked whate'er
She looked on, and her looks went everywhere.
25 Sir, 'twas all one! My favour at her breast,
The dropping of the daylight in the West,
The bough of cherries some officious fool
Broke in the orchard for her, the white mule
She rode with round the terrace—all and each
30 Would draw from her alike the approving speech,
Or blush, at least. She thanked men,—good! but thanked
Somehow—I know not how—as if she ranked
My gift of a nine-hundred-years-old name
With anybody's gift. Who'd stoop to blame

---

[1] For a detailed presentation of materials related to Browning's poems, sources, annotations, textual variants, etc., see *Browning: The Poems*, ed. J. Pettigrew and T.J. Collins, 3rd ed., 2 vols. (London: Penguin, 1996).

[2] The Duke is modelled on Alfonso II, fifth Duke of Ferrara. Alfonso (b.1533) married Lucrezia de Medici, then fourteen, in 1558. She died in 1561, and poison was suspected. In 1565 the Duke married the daughter of Ferdinand I, Count of Tyrol.

[3] an imaginary painter of an imaginary painting.

35 This sort of trifling? Even had you skill
In speech—(which I have not)—to make your will
Quite clear to such an one, and say, "Just this
Or that in you disgusts me; here you miss,
Or there exceed the mark"—and if she let
40 Herself be lessoned so, nor plainly set
Her wits to yours, forsooth, and made excuse,
—E'en then would be some stooping; and I choose
Never to stoop. Oh sir, she smiled, no doubt,
Whene'er I passed her; but who passed without
45 Much the same smile? This grew; I gave commands;
Then all smiles stopped together. There she stands
As if alive. Will't please you rise? We'll meet
The company below, then. I repeat,
The Count your master's known munificence
50 Is ample warrant that no just pretence
Of mine for dowry will be disallowed;
Though his fair daughter's self, as I avowed
At starting, is my object. Nay, we'll go
Together down, sir. Notice Neptune, though,
55 Taming a sea-horse, thought a rarity,
Which Claus of Innsbruck[1] cast in bronze for me!
—1842

Soliloquy of the Spanish Cloister

I

Gr-r-r—there go, my heart's abhorrence!
Water your damned flower-pots, do!
If hate killed men, Brother Lawrence,
God's blood, would not mine kill you!
5 What? your myrtle-bush wants trimming?
Oh, that rose has prior claims—
Needs its leaden vase filled brimming?
Hell dry you up with its flames!

II

At the meal we sit together:
10 *Salve tibi!*[2] I must hear
Wise talk of the kind of weather,
Sort of season, time of year:
*Not a plenteous cork-crop: scarcely
Dare we hope oak-galls,[3] I doubt:*
15 *What's the Latin name for "parsley"?*
What's the Greek name for Swine's Snout?

III

Whew! We'll have our platter burnished,
Laid with care on our own shelf!
With a fire-new spoon we're furnished,
20 And a goblet for ourself,
Rinsed like something sacrificial
Ere 'tis fit to touch our chaps—[4]
Marked with L. for our initial!
(He-he! There his lily snaps!)

IV

25 *Saint*, forsooth! While brown Dolores
Squats outside the Convent bank
With Sanchicha, telling stories,
Steeping tresses in the tank,
Blue-black, lustrous, thick like horsehairs,
30 —Can't I see his dead eye glow,
Bright as 'twere a Barbary corsair's?[5]
(That is, if he'd let it show!)

V

When he finishes refection,[6]
Knife and fork he never lays
35 Cross-wise, to my recollection,
As do I, in Jesu's praise.

---

[1] probably Browning's invention, although the Austrian city was a centre for bronze sculpting in the sixteenth century.

[2] "Hail to thee!"

[3] growths on diseased oak-leaves.

[4] "chops": cheeks.

[5] pirate from the north-west coast of Africa.

[6] a light meal.

I the Trinity illustrate,
    Drinking watered orange-pulp—
In three sips the Arian[1] frustrate;
40   While he drains his at one gulp.

VI

Oh, those melons? If he's able
    We're to have a feast! so nice!
One goes to the Abbot's table,
    All of us get each a slice.
45 How go on your flowers? None double?
    Not one fruit-sort can you spy?
Strange!—And I, too, at such trouble,
    Keep them close-nipped on the sly!

VII

There's a great text in Galatians,[2]
50   Once you trip on it, entails
Twenty-nine distinct damnations,
    One sure, if another fails:
If I trip him just a-dying,
    Sure of heaven as sure can be,
55 Spin him round and send him flying
    Off to hell, a Manichee?[3]

VIII

Or, my scrofulous French novel
    On grey paper with blunt type!
Simply glance at it, you grovel
60   Hand and foot in Belial's gripe:[4]
If I double down its pages
    At the woeful sixteenth print,
When he gathers his greengages,
    Ope a sieve and slip it in't?

IX

65 Or, there's Satan!—one might venture
    Pledge one's soul to him, yet leave
Such a flaw in the indenture
    As he'd miss till, past retrieve,
Blasted lay that rose-acacia
70   We're so proud of! *Hy, Zy, Hine*…[5]
'St, there's Vespers![6] *Plena gratiâ*
    Ave, Virgo![7] Gr-r-r—you swine!
—1842

Johannes Agricola in Meditation [8]

There's heaven above, and night by night
  I look right through its gorgeous roof;
No suns and moons though e'er so bright
    Avail to stop me; splendour-proof
5   I keep the broods of stars aloof:
For I intend to get to God,
    For 'tis to God I speed so fast,
For in God's breast, my own abode,
    Those shoals of dazzling glory passed,
10   I lay my spirit down at last.
I lie where I have always lain,
    God smiles as he has always smiled;
Ere suns and moons could wax and wane,
    Ere stars were thundergirt, or piled
15   The heavens, God thought on me his child;
Ordained a life for me, arrayed
    Its circumstances every one
To the minutest; ay, God said
    This head this hand should rest upon
20   Thus, ere he fashioned star or sun.

---

[1] heretical follower of the fourth-century Arius, who denied the doctrine of the Trinity.

[2] an imaginary text.

[3] a heretic who believes that the Universe reflects a constant fight between Good and Evil.

[4] the Devil's grip.

[5] nonsense words (?).

[6] evening prayer.

[7] "Full of grace, Hail Virgin."

[8] First published, entitled "Johannes Agricola," in the *Monthly Repository*, New Series 10, January 1836, pp. 45–46, immediately following "Porphyria," each poem signed "Z." Slightly revised, it was reprinted in *Dramatic Lyrics* in 1842, grouped with its earlier companion under the title "Madhouse Cells."

And having thus created me,
  Thus rooted me, he bade me grow,
Guiltless for ever, like a tree
  That buds and blooms, nor seeks to know
25 The law by which it prospers so:
But sure that thought and word and deed
  All go to swell his love for me,
Me, made because that love had need
  Of something irreversibly
30 Pledged solely its content to be.
Yes, yes, a tree which must ascend,
  No poison-gourd foredoomed to stoop!
I have God's warrant, could I blend
  All hideous sins, as in a cup,
35 To drink the mingled venoms up;
Secure my nature will convert
  The draught to blossoming gladness fast:
While sweet dews turn to the gourd's hurt,
  And bloat, and while they bloat it, blast,
40 As from the first its lot was cast.
For as I lie, smiled on, full-fed
  By unexhausted power to bless,
I gaze below on hell's fierce bed,
  And those its waves of flame oppress,
45 Swarming in ghastly wretchedness;
Whose life on earth aspired to be
  One altar-smoke, so pure!—to win
If not love like God's love for me,
  At least to keep his anger in;
50 And all their striving turned to sin.
Priest, doctor, hermit, monk grown white
  With prayer, the broken-hearted nun,
The martyr, the wan acolyte,
  The incense-swinging child,—undone
55 Before God fashioned star or sun!
God, whom I praise; how could I praise,
  If such as I might understand,
Make out and reckon on his ways,
  And bargain for his love, and stand,
60 Paying a price, at his right hand?
—1836

Porphyria's Lover

The rain set early in tonight,
  The sullen wind was soon awake,
It tore the elm-tops down for spite,
  And did its worst to vex the lake:
5 I listened with heart fit to break.
When glided in Porphyria; straight
  She shut the cold out and the storm,
And kneeled and made the cheerless grate
  Blaze up, and all the cottage warm;
10 Which done, she rose, and from her form
Withdrew the dripping cloak and shawl,
  And laid her soiled gloves by, untied
Her hat and let the damp hair fall,
  And, last, she sat down by my side
15 And called me. When no voice replied,
She put my arm about her waist,
  And made her smooth white shoulder bare,
And all her yellow hair displaced,
  And, stooping, made my cheek lie there,
20 And spread, o'er all, her yellow hair,
Murmuring how she loved me—she
  Too weak, for all her heart's endeavour,
To set its struggling passion free
  From pride, and vainer ties dissever,
25 And give herself to me for ever.
But passion sometimes would prevail,
  Nor could tonight's gay feast restrain
A sudden thought of one so pale
  For love of her, and all in vain:
30 So, she was come through wind and rain.
Be sure I looked up at her eyes
  Happy and proud; at last I knew
Porphyria worshipped me; surprise
  Made my heart swell, and still it grew
35 While I debated what to do.
That moment she was mine, mine, fair,
  Perfectly pure and good: I found
A thing to do, and all her hair
  In one long yellow string I wound

40   Three times her little throat around,
And strangled her. No pain felt she;
    I am quite sure she felt no pain.
As a shut bud that holds a bee,
    I warily oped her lids: again
45   Laughed the blue eyes without a stain.
And I untightened next the tress
    About her neck; her cheek once more
Blushed bright beneath my burning kiss:
    I propped her head up as before,
50   Only, this time my shoulder bore
Her head, which droops upon it still:
    The smiling rosy little head,
So glad it has its utmost will,
    That all it scorned at once is fled,
55   And I, its love, am gained instead!
Porphyria's love: she guessed not how
    Her darling one wish would be heard.
And thus we sit together now,
    And all night long we have not stirred,
60   And yet God has not said a word!
    —1836

Pictor Ignotus [1]

FLORENCE, 15–

I could have painted pictures like that youth's[2]
  Ye praise so. How my soul springs up! No bar
Stayed me—ah, thought which saddens while it
    soothes!
    —Never did fate forbid me, star by star,
5 To outburst on your night with all my gift
    Of fires from God: nor would my flesh have
      shrunk
From seconding my soul, with eyes uplift
    And wide to heaven, or, straight like thunder,
      sunk

To the centre, of an instant; or around
10   Turned calmly and inquisitive, to scan
The licence and the limit, space and bound,
    Allowed to truth made visible in man.
And, like that youth ye praise so, all I saw,
    Over the canvas could my hand have flung,
15 Each face obedient to its passion's law,
    Each passion clear proclaimed without a tongue;
Whether Hope rose at once in all the blood,
    A-tiptoe for the blessing of embrace,
Or Rapture drooped the eyes, as when her brood
20   Pull down the nesting dove's heart to its place;
Or Confidence lit swift the forehead up,
    And locked the mouth fast, like a castle
      braved,—[3]
O human faces, hath it spilt, my cup?
    What did ye give me that I have not saved?
25 Nor will I say I have not dreamed (how well!)
    Of going—I, in each new picture,—forth,
As, making new hearts beat and bosoms swell,
    To Pope or Kaiser, East, West, South, or North,
Bound for the calmly-satisfied great State,
30   Or glad aspiring little burgh, it went,
Flowers cast upon the car[4] which bore the freight,
    Through old streets named afresh from the event,
Till it reached home, where learned age should greet
    My face, and youth, the star not yet distinct
35 Above his hair, lie learning at my feet!—
    Oh, thus to live, I and my picture, linked
With love about, and praise, till life should end,
    And then not go to heaven, but linger here,
Here on my earth, earth's every man my friend,—
40   The thought grew frightful, 'twas so wildly dear!
But a voice changed it. Glimpses of such sights
    Have scared me, like the revels through a door
Of some strange house of idols at its rites!
    This world seemed not the world it was before:
45 Mixed with my loving trusting ones, there trooped

---

[1] The designation "Pictor Ignotus" (Latin, "painter unknown") is used in many art museums. "Ignotus" also means "obscure."

[2] probably Raphael (1483–1520).

[3] threatened.

[4] chariot.

…Who summoned those cold faces that begun
To press on me and judge me? Though I stooped
    Shrinking, as from the soldiery a nun,
They drew me forth, and spite of me…enough!
50   These buy and sell our pictures, take and give,
Count them for garniture and household-stuff,
    And where they live needs must our pictures live
And see their faces, listen to their prate,
    Partakers of their daily pettiness,
55   Discussed of,—"This I love, or this I hate,
    This likes me more, and this affects me less!"
Wherefore I chose my portion. If at whiles
    My heart sinks, as monotonous I paint
These endless cloisters and eternal aisles
60   With the same series, Virgin, Babe and Saint,
With the same cold calm beautiful regard,—
    At least no merchant traffics in my heart;
The sanctuary's gloom at least shall ward
    Vain tongues from where my pictures stand apart:
65   Only prayer breaks the silence of the shrine
    While, blackening in the daily candle-smoke,
They moulder on the damp wall's travertine,[1]
    'Mid echoes the light footstep never woke.
So, die my pictures! surely, gently die!
70   O youth, men praise so,—holds their praise its worth?
Blown harshly, keeps the trump its golden cry?
    Tastes sweet the water with such specks of earth?
—1845

The Lost Leader [2]

I

Just for a handful of silver he left us,[3]
    Just for a riband to stick in his coat—
Found the one gift of which fortune bereft us,
    Lost all the others she lets us devote;

[1] limestone.

[2] The figure is modelled on Wordsworth.

[3] Judas's thirty pieces of silver and Wordsworth's pension and Laureateship.

5   They, with the gold to give, doled him out silver,
    So much was theirs who so little allowed:
How all our copper had gone for his service!
    Rags—were they purple, his heart had been proud!
We that had loved him so, followed him, honoured him,
10   Lived in his mild and magnificent eye,
Learned his great language, caught his clear accents,
    Made him our pattern to live and to die!
Shakespeare was of us, Milton was for us,
    Burns, Shelley, were with us,—they watch from their graves!
15   He alone breaks from the van and the freeman,
    —He alone sinks to the rear and the slaves!

II

We shall march prospering,—not through his presence;
    Songs may inspirit us,—not from his lyre;
Deeds will be done,—while he boasts his quiescence,
20   Still bidding crouch whom the rest bade aspire:
Blot out his name, then, record one lost soul more,
    One task more declined, one more footpath untrod,
One more devils'-triumph and sorrow for angels,
    One wrong more to man, one more insult to God!
25   Life's night begins: let him never come back to us!
    There would be doubt, hesitation and pain,
Forced praise on our part—the glimmer of twilight,
    Never glad confident morning again!
Best fight on well, for we taught him—strike gallantly,
30   Menace our heart ere we master his own;
Then let him receive the new knowledge and wait us,
    Pardoned in heaven, the first by the throne!
—1845

The Bishop Orders His Tomb
at Saint Praxed's Church

ROME, 15–

Vanity, saith the preacher, vanity![1]
Draw round my bed: is Anselm keeping back?
Nephews—sons mine…ah God, I know not! Well—
She, men would have to be your mother once,
5   Old Gandolf envied me, so fair she was!
What's done is done, and she is dead beside,
Dead long ago, and I am Bishop since,
And as she died so must we die ourselves,
And thence ye may perceive the world's a dream.
10 Life, how and what is it? As here I lie
In this state-chamber, dying by degrees,
Hours and long hours in the dead night, I ask
"Do I live, am I dead?" Peace, peace seems all.
Saint Praxed's ever was the church for peace;
15 And so, about this tomb of mine. I fought
With tooth and nail to save my niche, ye know:
—Old Gandolf cozened[2] me, despite my care;
Shrewd was that snatch from out the corner South
He graced his carrion with, God curse the same!
20 Yet still my niche is not so cramped but thence
One sees the pulpit o' the epistle-side,[3]
And somewhat of the choir, those silent seats,
And up into the airy dome where live
The angels, and a sunbeam's sure to lurk:
25 And I shall fill my slab of basalt[4] there,
And 'neath my tabernacle[5] take my rest,
With those nine columns round me, two and two,
The odd one at my feet where Anselm stands:
Peach-blossom marble all, the rare, the ripe
30 As fresh-poured red wine of a mighty pulse.

—Old Gandolf with his paltry onion-stone,[6]
Put me where I may look at him! True peach,
Rosy and flawless: how I earned the prize!
Draw close: that conflagration of my church
35 —What then? So much was saved if aught were
    missed!
My sons, ye would not be my death? Go dig
The white-grape vineyard where the oil-press stood,
Drop water gently till the surface sink,
And if ye find…Ah God, I know not, I!…
40 Bedded in store of rotten fig-leaves soft,
And corded up in a tight olive-frail,[7]
Some lump, ah God, of *lapis lazuli*,[8]
Big as a Jew's head cut off at the nape,
Blue as a vein o'er the Madonna's breast…
45 Sons, all have I bequeathed you, villas, all,
That brave Frascati[9] villa with its bath,
So, let the blue lump poise between my knees,
Like God the Father's globe on both his hands
Ye worship in the Jesu Church so gay,
50 For Gandolf shall not choose but see and burst!
Swift as a weaver's shuttle fleet our years:[10]
Man goeth to the grave, and where is he?[11]
Did I say basalt for my slab, sons? Black—
'Twas ever antique-black I meant! How else
55 Shall ye contrast my frieze to come beneath?
The bas-relief in bronze ye promised me,
Those Pans[12] and Nymphs ye wot[13] of, and
    perchance

---

[1] a version of Ecclesiates 1:2.

[2] tricked.

[3] the right side.

[4] a black stone.

[5] canopy over a tomb.

[6] a cheap marble.

[7] basket.

[8] semi-precious blue stone.

[9] town near Rome.

[10] a version of Job 7:6.

[11] a version of Job 7:9 and 14:10.

[12] god of fields and forests.

[13] know.

Some tripod,[1] thyrsus,[2] with a vase or so,
The Saviour at his sermon on the mount,
60 Saint Praxed in a glory,[3] and one Pan
Ready to twitch the Nymph's last garment off,
And Moses with the tables[4]…but I know
Ye mark me not! What do they whisper thee,
Child of my bowels, Anselm? Ah, ye hope
65 To revel down[5] my villas while I gasp
Bricked o'er with beggar's mouldy travertine[6]
Which Gandolf from his tomb-top chuckles at!
Nay, boys, ye love me—all of jasper,[7] then!
'Tis jasper ye stand pledged to, lest I grieve
70 My bath must needs be left behind, alas!
One block, pure green as a pistachio-nut,
There's plenty jasper somewhere in the world—
And have I not Saint Praxed's ear to pray
Horses for ye, and brown Greek manuscripts,
75 And mistresses with great smooth marbly limbs?
—That's if ye carve my epitaph aright,
Choice Latin, picked phrase, Tully's[8] every word,
No gaudy ware like Gandolf's second line—
Tully, my masters? Ulpian[9] serves his need!
80 And then how I shall lie through centuries,
And hear the blessed mutter of the mass,
And see God made and eaten all day long,
And feel the steady candle-flame, and taste
Good strong thick stupefying incense-smoke!
85 For as I lie here, hours of the dead night,
Dying in state and by such slow degrees,

I fold my arms as if they clasped a crook,[10]
And stretch my feet forth straight as stone can point,
And let the bedclothes, for a mortcloth,[11] drop
90 Into great laps and folds of sculptor's-work:
And as yon tapers dwindle, and strange thoughts
Grow, with a certain humming in my ears,
About the life before I lived this life,
And this life too, popes, cardinals and priests,
95 Saint Praxed at his sermon on the mount,
Your tall pale mother with her talking eyes,
And new-found agate urns as fresh as day,
And marble's language, Latin pure, discreet,
—Aha, ELUCESCEBAT[12] quoth our friend?
100 No Tully, said I, Ulpian at the best!
Evil and brief hath been my pilgrimage.
All *lapis*, all, sons! Else I give the Pope
My villas! Will ye ever eat my heart?
Ever your eyes were as a lizard's quick,
105 They glitter like your mother's for my soul,
Or ye would heighten my impoverished frieze,
Piece out its starved design, and fill my vase
With grapes, and add a vizor and a Term,[13]
And to the tripod ye would tie a lynx
110 That in his struggle throws the thyrsus down,
To comfort me on my entablature[14]
Whereon I am to lie till I must ask
"Do I live, am I dead?" There, leave me, there!
For ye have stabbed me with ingratitude
115 To death—ye wish it—God, ye wish it! Stone—
Gritstone,[15] a-crumble! Clammy squares which sweat
As if the corpse they keep were oozing through—
And no more *lapis* to delight the world!
Well go! I bless ye. Fewer tapers there,
120 But in a row: and, going, turn your backs

[1] three-legged stool associated with the priestesses of Apollo.

[2] staff of Bacchus, god of wine.

[3] halo.

[4] tablets.

[5] squander.

[6] limestone.

[7] kind of quartz.

[8] Marcus Tullius Cicero (106–43 BC).

[9] Domitius Uelpianus (170–228), an inferior writer.

[10] Bishop's staff.

[11] pall.

[12] "He was illustrious."

[13] mask and pedestal bust.

[14] entablement (platform for a statue).

[15] cheap sandstone.

—Ay, like departing altar-ministrants,
And leave me in my church, the church for peace,
That I may watch at leisure if he leers—
Old Gandolf, at me, from his onion-stone,
125 As still he envied me, so fair she was!
—1845

The Laboratory

ANCIEN RÉGIME [1]

I

Now that I, tying thy glass mask tightly,
   May gaze through these faint smokes curling
      whitely,
As thou pliest thy trade in this devil's-smithy—
Which is the poison to poison her, prithee?

II

5 He is with her, and they know that I know
Where they are, what they do: they believe my tears
      flow
While they laugh, laugh at me, at me fled to the drear
Empty church, to pray God in, for them!—I am
      here.

III

Grind away, moisten and mash up thy paste,
10 Pound at thy powder,—I am not in haste!
Better sit thus, and observe thy strange things,
Then go where men wait me and dance at the
      King's.

IV

That in the mortar—you call it a gum?
Ah, the brave tree whence such gold oozings come!
15 And yonder soft phial, the exquisite blue,
Sure to taste sweetly,—is that poison too?

V

Had I but all of them, thee and thy treasures,
What a wild crowd of invisible pleasures!
To carry pure death in an ear-ring, a casket,
20 A signet, a fan-mount, a filigree basket!

VI

Soon, at the King's, a mere lozenge to give,
And Pauline should have just thirty minutes to live!
But to light a pastile,[2] and Elise, with her head
And her breast and her arms and her hands, should
      drop dead!

VII

25 Quick—is it finished? The colour's too grim!
Why not soft like the phial's, enticing and dim?
Let it brighten her drink, let her turn it and stir,
And try it and taste, ere she fix and prefer!

VIII

What a drop! She's not little, no minion[3] like me!
30 That's why she ensnared him: this never will free
The soul from those masculine eyes,—say, "no!"
To that pulse's magnificent come-and-go.

IX

For only last night, as they whispered, I brought
My own eyes to bear on her so, that I thought
35 Could I keep them one half minute fixed, she
      would fall
Shrivelled; she fell not; yet this does it all!

X

Not that I bid you spare her the pain;
Let death be felt and the proof remain:
Brand, burn up, bite into its grace-
40 He is sure to remember her dying face!

---

[1] the "Old Order" in pre-Revolution France.

[2] roll of paste, burned for perfume.

[3] delicate person.

XI

Is it done? Take my mask off! Nay, be not morose;
It kills her, and this prevents seeing it close:
The delicate droplet, my whole fortune's fee!
If it hurts her, beside, can it ever hurt me?

XII

45   Now, take all my jewels, gorge gold to your fill,
You may kiss me, old man, on my mouth if you will!
But brush this dust off me, lest horror it brings
Ere I know it—next moment I dance at the King's!
—1844

Love Among the Ruins

I

Where the quiet-coloured end of evening
    smiles,
  Miles and miles
On the solitary pastures where our sheep
  Half-asleep
5   Tinkle homeward through the twilight, stray or stop
    As they crop—
Was the site once of a city great and gay,
  (So they say)
Of our country's very capital, its prince
10   Ages since
Held his court in, gathered councils, wielding far
    Peace or war.

II

Now,—the country does not even boast a tree,
  As you see,
15   To distinguish slopes of verdure, certain rills
    From the hills
Intersect and give a name to, (else they run
    Into one)
Where the domed and daring palace shot its spires
20   Up like fires

O'er the hundred-gated circuit of a wall[1]
  Bounding all,
Made of marble, men might march on nor be
    pressed,
  Twelve abreast.

III

25   And such plenty and perfection, see, of grass
    Never was!
Such a carpet as, this summer-time, o'erspreads
    And embeds
Every vestige of the city, guessed alone,
30   Stock or stone—
Where a multitude of men breathed joy and woe
    Long ago;
Lust of glory pricked their hearts up, dread of shame
    Struck them tame;
35   And that glory and that shame alike, the gold
    Bought and sold.

IV

Now,—the single little turret that remains
    On the plains,
By the caper over-rooted, by the gourd
40   Overscored,
While the patching houseleek's[2] head of blossom
    winks
    Through the chinks—
Marks the basement whence a tower in ancient time
    Sprang sublime,
45   And a burning ring, all round, the chariots traced
    As they raced,
And the monarch and his minions and his dames
    Viewed the games.

V

And I know, while thus the quiet-coloured eve
50   Smiles to leave

---

[1] Babylon and the Egyptian Thebes were reputed to have a hundred
gates.

[2] a flowering plant.

To their folding, all our many-tinkling fleece
    In such peace,
And the slopes and rills in undistinguished grey
    Melt away—
55 That a girl with eager eyes and yellow hair
    Waits me there
In the turret whence the charioteers caught soul
    For the goal,
When the king looked, where she looks now,
    breathless, dumb
60 Till I come.

VI

But he looked upon the city, every side,
    Far and wide,
All the mountains topped with temples, all the
    glades'
    Colonnades,
65 All the causeys,[1] bridges, aqueducts,—and then,
    All the men!
When I do come, she will speak not, she will stand,
    Either hand
On my shoulder, give her eyes the first embrace
70   Of my face,
Ere we rush, ere we extinguish sight and speech
    Each on each.

VII

In one year they sent a million fighters forth
    South and North,
75 And they build their gods a brazen pillar high
    As the sky,
Yet reserved a thousand chariots in full force—
    Gold, of course.
Oh heart! oh blood that freezes, blood that burns!
80   Earth's returns
For whole centuries of folly, noise and sin!
    Shut them in,
With their triumphs and their glories and the rest!
    Love is best.
  —1855

[1] causeways.

Fra Lippo Lippi [2]

I am poor brother Lippo, by your leave!
  You need not clap your torches to my face.
Zooks,[3] what's to blame? you think you see a monk!
What, 'tis past midnight, and you go the rounds,
5 And here you catch me at an alley's end
Where sportive ladies leave their doors ajar?
The Carmine's my cloister: hunt it up,
Do,—harry out, if you must show your zeal,
Whatever rat, there, haps on his wrong hole,
10 And nip each softling of a wee white mouse,
Weke, weke, that's crept to keep him company!
Aha, you know your betters! Then, you'll take
Your hand away that's fiddling on my throat,
And please to know me likewise. Who am I?
15 Why, one, sir, who is lodging with a friend
Three streets off—he's a certain…how d'ye call?
Master—a…Cosimo of the Medici,[4]
I' the house that caps the corner. Boh! you were best!
Remember and tell me, the day you're hanged,
20 How you affected such a gullet's-gripe!
But you, sir, it concerns you that your knaves
Pick up a manner nor discredit you:
Zooks, are we pilchards,[5] that they sweep the streets
And count fair prize what comes into their net?
25 He's Judas to a tittle, that man is!
Just such a face! Why, sir, you make amends.
Lord, I'm not angry! Bid your hangdogs go
Drink out this quarter-florin to the health
Of the munificent House that harbours me
30 (And many more beside, lads! more beside!)
And all's come square again. I'd like his face—
His, elbowing on his comrade in the door
With the pike and lantern,—for the slave that holds

[2] Fra Lippo Lippi (c.1406–69), Carmelite painter and friar. His artistic creed shares much with that of Browning.

[3] "Gadzooks," a mild oath.

[4] the Florentine ruler and patron of the arts.

[5] small fish.

John Baptist's head a-dangle by the hair
35 With one hand ("Look you, now," as who should say)
And his weapon in the other, yet unwiped!
It's not your chance to have a bit of chalk,
A wood-coal or the like? or you should see!
Yes, I'm the painter, since you style me so.
40 What, brother Lippo's doings, up and down,
You know them and they take[1] you? like enough!
I saw the proper twinkle in your eye—
'Tell you, I liked your looks at very first.
Let's sit and set things straight now, hip to haunch.
45 Here's spring come, and the nights one makes up
          bands
To roam the town and sing out carnival,
And I've been three weeks shut within my mew,[2]
A-painting for the great man, saints and saints
And saints again. I could not paint all night—
50 Ouf! I leaned out of window for fresh air.
There came a hurry of feet and little feet,
A sweep of lute-strings, laughs, and whifts of song,—
Flower o' the broom,
Take away love, and our earth is a tomb!
55 *Flower o' the quince,*
I let Lisa go, and what good in life since?
Flower o' the thyme—and so on. Round they went.
Scarce had they turned the corner when a titter
Like the skipping of rabbits by moonlight,—three
          slim shapes,
60 And a face that looked up...zooks, sir, flesh and
          blood,
That's all I'm made of! Into shreds it went,
Curtain and counterpane and coverlet,
All the bed-furniture—a dozen knots,
There was a ladder! Down I let myself,
65 Hands and feet, scrambling somehow, and so
          dropped,
And after them. I came up with the fun

Hard by Saint Laurence,[3] hail fellow, well met,—
Flower o' the rose,
If I've been merry, what matter who knows?
70 And so as I was stealing back again
To get to bed and have a bit of sleep
Ere I rise up tomorrow and go work
On Jerome[4] knocking at his poor old breast
With his great round stone to subdue the flesh,
75 You snap[5] me of the sudden. Ah, I see!
Though your eye twinkles still, you shake your
          head—
Mine's shaved—a monk, you say—the sting's in
          that!
If Master Cosimo announced himself,
Mum's the word naturally; but a monk!
80 Come, what am I a beast for? tell us, now!
I was a baby when my mother died
And father died and left me in the street.
I starved there, God knows how, a year or two
On fig-skins, melon-parings, rinds and shucks,
85 Refuse and rubbish. One fine frosty day,
My stomach being empty as your hat,
The wind doubled me up and down I went.
Old Aunt Lapaccia trussed me with one hand,
(Its fellow was a stinger as I knew)
90 And so along the wall, over the bridge,
By the straight cut to the convent. Six words there,
While I stood munching my first bread that month:
"So, boy, you're minded," quoth the good fat father
Wiping his own mouth, 'twas refection-time,—
95 "To quit this very miserable world?
Will you renounce"..."the mouthful of bread?"
          thought I;
By no means! Brief, they made a monk of me;
I did renounce the world, its pride and greed,
Palace, farm, villa, shop and banking-house,
100 Trash, such as these poor devils of Medici

[1] catch the fancy of.

[2] cage.

[3] the church of San Lorenzo.

[4] St. Jerome (340–420), the highly ascetic saint Lippo is painting.

[5] seize.

Have given their hearts to—all at eight years old.
Well, sir, I found in time, you may be sure,
'Twas not for nothing—the good bellyful,
The warm serge and the rope that goes all round,
105 And day-long blessed idleness beside!
"Let's see what the urchin's fit for"—that came next.
Not overmuch their way, I must confess.
Such a to-do! They tried me with their books:
Lord, they'd have taught me Latin in pure waste!
110 *Flower o' the clove,*
All the Latin I construe is, "amo" I love!
But, mind you, when a boy starves in the streets
Eight years together, as my fortune was,
Watching folk's faces to know who will fling
115 The bit of half-stripped grape-bunch he desires,
And who will curse or kick him for his pains,—
Which gentleman processional and fine,
Holding a candle to the Sacrament,
Will wink and let him lift a plate and catch
120 The droppings of the wax to sell again,
Or holla for the Eight[1] and have him whipped,—
How say I?—nay, which dog bites, which lets drop
His bone from the heap of offal in the street,—
Why, soul and sense of him grow sharp alike,
125 He learns the look of things, and none the less
For admonition from the hunger-pinch.
I had a store of such remarks, be sure,
Which, after I found leisure, turned to use.
I drew men's faces on my copy-books,
130 Scrawled them within the antiphonary's marge,[2]
Joined legs and arms to the long music-notes,
Found eyes and nose and chin for A's and B's,
And made a string of pictures of the world
Betwixt the ins and outs of verb and noun,
135 On the wall, the bench, the door. The monks
        looked black.
"Nay," quoth the Prior, "turn him out, d'ye say?
In no wise. Lose a crow and catch a lark.

What if at last we get our man of parts,
We Carmelites, like those Camaldolese[3]
140 And Preaching Friars, to do our church up fine
And put the front on it that ought to be!"
And hereupon he bade me daub away.
Thank you! my head being crammed, the walls a
        blank,
Never was such prompt disemburdening.
145 First, every sort of monk, the black and white,
I drew them, fat and lean: then, folk at church,
From good old gossips waiting to confess
Their cribs[4] of barrel-droppings, candle-ends,—
To the breathless fellow at the altar-foot,
150 Fresh from his murder, safe and sitting there
With the little children round him in a row
Of admiration, half for his beard and half
For that white anger of his victim's son
Shaking a fist at him with one fierce arm,
155 Signing himself with the other because of Christ
(Whose sad face on the cross sees only this
After the passion of a thousand years)
Till some poor girl, her apron o'er her head,
(Which the intense eyes looked through) came at eve
160 On tiptoe, said a word, dropped in a loaf,
Her pair of earrings and a bunch of flowers
(The brute took growling), prayed, and so was gone.
I painted all, then cried "'Tis ask and have;
Choose, for more's ready!"—laid the ladder flat,
165 And showed my covered bit of cloister-wall.
The monks closed in a circle and praised loud
Till checked, taught what to see and not to see,
Being simple bodies,—"That's the very man!
Look at the boy who stoops to pat the dog!
170 That woman's like the Prior's niece[5] who comes
To care about his asthma: it's the life!"

---

[1] the eight magistrates of Florence.

[2] the margin of a book with choral music.

[3] rival religious orders. The Camaldolese are Dominicans.

[4] petty thefts.

[5] not a relation, but with whom he has relations.

But there my triumph's straw-fire flared and
    funked;[1]
Their betters took their turn to see and say:
The Prior and the learned pulled a face
175 And stopped all that in no time. "How? what's here?
Quite from the mark of painting, bless us all!
Faces, arms, legs and bodies like the true
As much as pea and pea! it's devil's-game!
Your business is not to catch men with show,
180 With homage to the perishable clay,
But lift them over it, ignore it all,
Make them forget there's such a thing as flesh.
Your business is to paint the souls of men—
Man's soul, and it's a fire, smoke…no, it's not…
185 It's vapour done up like a new-born babe—
(In that shape when you die it leaves your mouth)[2]
It's…well, what matters talking, it's the soul!
Give us no more of body than shows soul!
Here's Giotto,[3] with his Saint a-praising God,
190 That sets us praising,—why not stop with him?
Why put all thoughts of praise out of our head
With wonder at lines, colours, and what not?
Paint the soul, never mind the legs and arms!
Rub all out, try at it a second time.
195 Oh, that white smallish female with the breasts,
She's just my niece…Herodias,[4] I would say,—
Who went and danced and got men's heads cut off!
Have it all out!" Now, is this sense, I ask?
A fine way to paint soul, by painting body
200 So ill, the eye can't stop there, must go further
And can't fare worse! Thus, yellow does for white
When what you put for yellow's simply black,
And any sort of meaning looks intense
When all beside itself means and looks naught.

205 Why can't a painter lift each foot in turn,
Left foot and right foot, go a double step,
Make his flesh liker and his soul more like,
Both in their order? Take the prettiest face,
The Prior's niece…patron-saint—is it so pretty
210 You can't discover if it means hope, fear,
Sorrow or joy? won't beauty go with these?
Suppose I've made her eyes all right and blue,
Can't I take breath and try to add life's flash,
And then add soul and heighten them threefold?
215 Or say there's beauty with no soul at all—
(I never saw it—put the case the same—)
If you get simple beauty and naught else,
You get about the best thing God invents:
That's somewhat: and you'll find the soul you have
    missed,
220 Within yourself, when you return him thanks.
"Rub all out!" Well, well, there's my life, in short,
And so the thing has gone on ever since.
I'm grown a man no doubt, I've broken bounds:
You should not take a fellow eight years old
225 And make him swear to never kiss the girls.
I'm my own master, paint now as I please—
Having a friend, you see, in the Corner-house!
Lord, it's fast holding by the rings in front—
Those great rings serve more purposes than just
230 To plant a flag in, or tie up a horse!
And yet the old schooling sticks, the old grave eyes
Are peeping o'er my shoulder as I work,
The heads shake still—"It's art's decline, my son!
You're not of the true painters, great and old;
235 Brother Angelico's[5] the man, you'll find;
Brother Lorenzo[6] stands his single peer:
Fag on at flesh, you'll never make the third!"
Flower o' the pine,
You keep your mistr…manners, and I'll stick to mine!
240 I'm not the third, then: bless us, they must know!
Don't you think they're the likeliest to know,

---

[1] expired in smoke.

[2] a reference to the old doctrine that the soul leaves the body with the last breath in the form of vapour.

[3] Florentine painter and architect (1267–1337).

[4] The Prior is confused. It was Salome, daughter of Herodias, who, after dancing for Herod, asked him for the head of John the Baptist.

[5] Fra Angelico (1387–1455), an ethereal painter.

[6] Lorenzo Monaco (c.1370–c.1425), painter.

They with their Latin? So, I swallow my rage,
Clench my teeth, suck my lips in tight, and paint
To please them—sometimes do and sometimes don't;
245　For, doing most, there's pretty sure to come
A turn, some warm eve finds me at my saints—
A laugh, a cry, the business of the world—
(*Flower o' the peach,*
Death for us all, and his own life for each!)
250　And my whole soul revolves, the cup runs over,
The world and life's too big to pass for a dream,
And I do these wild things in sheer despite,
And play the fooleries you catch me at,
In pure rage! The old mill-horse, out at grass
255　After hard years, throws up his stiff heels so,
Although the miller does not preach to him
The only good of grass is to make chaff.
What would men have? Do they like grass or no—
May they or mayn't they? all I want's the thing
260　Settled for ever one way. As it is,
You tell too many lies and hurt yourself:
You don't like what you only like too much,
You do like what, if given you at your word,
You find abundantly detestable.
265　For me, I think I speak as I was taught;
I always see the garden and God there
A-making man's wife: and, my lesson learned,
The value and significance of flesh,
I can't unlearn ten minutes afterwards.

270　　You understand me: I'm a beast, I know.
But see, now—why, I see as certainly
As that the morning-star's about to shine,
What will hap some day. We've a youngster here
Comes to our convent, studies what I do,
275　Slouches and stares and lets no atom drop:
His name is Guidi[1]—he'll not mind the monks—
They call him Hulking Tom, he lets them talk—
He picks my practice up—he'll paint apace,
I hope so—though I never live so long,

I know what's sure to follow. You be judge!
You speak no Latin more than I, belike;
However, you're my man, you've seen the world
—The beauty and the wonder and the power,
The shapes of things, their colours, lights and shades,
285　Changes, surprises,—and God made it all!
—For what? Do you feel thankful, ay or no,
For this fair town's face, yonder river's line,
The mountain round it and the sky above,
Much more the figures of man, woman, child,
290　These are the frame to? What's it all about?
To be passed over, despised? or dwelt upon,
Wondered at? oh, this last of course!—you say.
But why not do as well as say,—paint these
Just as they are, careless what comes of it?
295　God's works—paint anyone, and count it crime
To let a truth slip. Don't object, "His works
Are here already; nature is complete:
Suppose you reproduce her"—(which you can't)
"There's no advantage! you must beat her, then."
300　For, don't you mark? we're made so that we love
First when we see them painted, things we have
　　passed
Perhaps a hundred times nor cared to see;
And so they are better, painted—better to us,
Which is the same thing. Art was given for that;
305　God uses us to help each other so,
Lending our minds out. Have you noticed, now,
Your cullion's hanging face? A bit of chalk,
And trust me but you should, though! How much
　　more,
If I drew higher things with the same truth!
310　That were to take the Prior's pulpit-place,
Interpret God to all of you! Oh, oh,
It makes me mad to see what men shall do
And we in our graves! This world's no blot for us,
Nor blank; it means intensely, and means good:
315　To find its meaning is my meat and drink.
"Ay, but you don't so instigate to prayer!"
Strikes in the Prior: "when your meaning's plain
It does not say to folk—remember matins,

---

[1] Tomasso Guidi (1401–28?). In fact, Lippo's teacher, not his pupil.

Or, mind you fast next Friday!" Why, for this
320 What need of art at all? A skull and bones,
Two bits of stick nailed crosswise, or, what's best,
A bell to chime the hour with, does as well.
I painted a Saint Laurence[1] six months since
At Prato, splashed the fresco in fine style:
325 "How looks my painting, now the scaffold's down?"
I ask a brother: "Hugely," he returns—
"Already not one phiz[2] of your three slaves
Who turn the Deacon off his toasted side,
But's scratched and prodded to our heart's content,
330 The pious people have so eased their own
With coming to say prayers there in a rage:
We get on fast to see the bricks beneath.
Expect another job this time next year,
For pity and religion grow i' the crowd—
335 Your painting serves its purpose!" Hang the fools!

—That is—you'll not mistake an idle word
Spoke in a huff by a poor monk, Got wot,
Tasting the air this spicy night which turns
The unaccustomed head like Chianti wine!
340 Oh, the church knows! don't misreport me, now!
It's natural a poor monk out of bounds
Should have his apt word to excuse himself:
And hearken how I plot to make amends.
I have bethought me: I shall paint a piece
345 …There's for you! Give me six months, then go, see
Something in Sant' Ambrogio's![3] Bless the nuns!
They want a cast o' my office.[4] I shall paint
God in the midst, Madonna and her babe,
Ringed by a bowery flowery angel-brood,
350 Lilies and vestments and white faces, sweet
As puff on puff of grated orris-root[5]
When ladies crowd to Church at midsummer.

And then i' the front, of course a saint or two—
Saint John,[6] because he saves the Florentines,
355 Saint Ambrose, who puts down in black and white
The convent's friends and gives them a long day,
And Job, I must have him there past mistake,
The man of Uz (and Us without the z,
Painters who need his patience). Well, all these
360 Secured at their devotion, up shall come
Out of a corner when you least expect,
As one by a dark stair into a great light,
Music and talking, who but Lippo! I!—
Mazed,[7] motionless and moonstruck—I'm the man!
365 Back I shrink—what is this I see and hear?
I, caught up with my monk's-things by mistake,
My old serge gown and rope that goes all round,
I, in this presence, this pure company!
Where's a hole, where's a corner for escape?
370 Then steps a sweet angelic slip of a thing
Forward, puts out a soft palm—"Not so fast!"
—Addresses the celestial presence, "nay—
He made you and devised you, after all,
Though he's none of you! Could Saint John there
        draw—
375 His camel-hair[8] make up a painting-brush?
We come to brother Lippo for all that,
Iste perfecit opus![9] So, all smile—
I shuffle sideways with my blushing face
Under the cover of a hundred wings
380 Thrown like a spread of kirtles[10] when you're gay
And play hot cockles,[11] all the doors being shut,
Till, wholly unexpected, in there pops
The hothead husband! Thus I scuttle off
To some safe bench behind, not letting go
385 The palm of her, the little lily thing

---

[1] The saint was roasted to death in 258.

[2] face.

[3] a convent in Florence.

[4] example of my work.

[5] iris root, used in perfume.

[6] patron saint of Florence.

[7] bewildered.

[8] St. John wore camel hair.

[9] "This man did the work."

[10] skirts.

[11] a rustic game (here a euphemism for amorous activity).

That spoke the good word for me in the nick,
Like the Prior's niece…Saint Lucy,[1] I would say.
And so all's saved for me, and for the church
A pretty picture gained. Go, six months hence!
390 Your hand, sir, and good-bye: no lights, no lights!
The street's hushed, and I know my own way back,
Don't fear me! There's the grey beginning. Zooks!
—1855

A Toccata of Galuppi's [2]

I

Oh Galuppi, Baldassaro,[3] this is very sad to find!
I can hardly misconceive you; it would prove me deaf and blind;
But although I take your meaning, 'tis with such a heavy mind!

II

Here you come with your old music, and here's all the good it brings.
5 What, they lived once thus at Venice[4] where the merchants were the kings,
Where Saint Mark's is, where the Doges used to wed the sea with rings?[5]

III

Ay, because the sea's the street there; and 'tis arched by…what you call
…Shylock's bridge[6] with houses on it, where they kept the carnival:
I was never out of England—it's as if I saw it all.

IV

10 Did young people take their pleasure when the sea was warm in May?
Balls and masks begun at midnight, burning ever to midday,
When they made up fresh adventures for the morrow, do you say?

V

Was a lady such a lady, cheeks so round and lips so red,—
On her neck the small face buoyant, like a bell-flower on its bed,
15 O'er the breast's superb abundance where a man might base his head?

VI

Well, and it was graceful of them—they'd break talk off and afford
—She, to bite her mask's black velvet—he, to finger on his sword,
While you sat and played Toccatas, stately at the clavichord?[7]

VII

What? Those lesser thirds[8] so plaintive, sixths diminished,[9] sigh on sigh,
20 Told them something? Those suspensions,[10] those solutions[11]—"Must we die?"
Those commiserating sevenths[12]—"Life might last! we can but try!"

---

[1] The martyr was a virgin, unlike the Prior's "niece."

[2] from *toccare*, "to touch" in Italian, a fast-moving keyboard piece.

[3] Baldassaro Galuppi (1706–85), the Venetian composer.

[4] the Cathedral of Venice.

[5] The Dukes of Venice annually celebrated the relationship of the city to the sea in a ceremony in which a ring was cast into the sea.

[6] the Rialto.

[7] a stringed keyboard instrument.

[8] "Lesser" means "minor"; a "third" is a chord of two notes four semitones apart.

[9] A "sixth" is a chord made up of two notes nine semitones apart; "diminished" (by two semitones), it becomes a chord of two notes seven semitones apart.

[10] A suspension is a note held from one chord to another, first producing a discord, and then resolving concordantly.

[11] resolutions, a technical term indicating a concord following a discord.

[12] chords of two notes eleven semitones apart, producing mild dissonances.

VIII

"Were you happy?"—"Yes."—"And are you still as
    happy?"—"Yes. And you?"
—"Then, more kisses!"—"Did *I* stop them, when a
    million seemed so few?"
Hark, the dominant's[1] persistence till it must be
    answered to!

IX

25 So, an octave[2] struck the answer. Oh, they praised
    you, I dare say!
"Brave Galuppi! that was music! good alike at grave
    and gay!
I can always leave off talking when I hear a master
    play!"

X

Then they left you for their pleasure: till in due
    time, one by one,
Some with lives that came to nothing, some with
    deeds as well undone,
30 Death stepped tacitly and took them where they
    never see the sun.

XI

But when I sit down to reason, think to take my
    stand nor swerve,
While I triumph o'er a secret wrung from nature's
    close reserve,
In you come with your cold music till I creep
    through every nerve.

XII

Yes, you, like a ghostly cricket, creaking where a
    house was burned:

35 "Dust and ashes, dead and done with, Venice spent
    what Venice earned.
The soul, doubtless, is immortal—where a soul can
    be discerned.

XIII

"Yours for instance: you know physics, something
    of geology,
Mathematics are your pastime; souls shall rise in
    their degree;
Butterflies may dread extinction,—you'll not die, it
    cannot be!

XIV

40 "As for Venice and her people, merely born to
    bloom and drop,
Here on earth they bore their fruitage, mirth and
    folly were the crop:
What of soul was left, I wonder, when the kissing
    had to stop?

XV

"Dust and ashes!" So you creak it, and I want the
    heart to scold.
Dear dead women, with such hair, too—what's
    become of all the gold
45 Used to hang and brush their bosoms? I feel chilly
    and grown old.
—1855

By the Fire-Side[3]

I

How well I know what I mean to do
    When the long dark autumn-evenings come,
And where, my soul, is thy pleasant hue?
With the music of all thy voices, dumb
5 In life's November too!

---

[1] A "dominant" is "the note…which, in traditional harmonic proce-dures, most urgently demands resolution upon the tonic" (Grove): it is the fifth note above the tonic or key-note.

[2] The octave, being a perfect consonance, gives the "answer" to (resolves) the dominant.

[3] one of Browning's rare personal poems; the portrait of "Leonor" is one of Mrs. Browning.

II

I shall be found by the fire, suppose,
O'er a great wise book as beseemeth age,
While the shutters flap as the cross-wind blows
And I turn the page, and I turn the page,
10   Not verse now, only prose!

III

Till the young ones whisper, finger on lip,
"There he is at it, deep in Greek:
Now then, or never, out we slip
To cut from the hazels by the creek
15   A mainmast for our ship!"

IV

I shall be at it indeed, my friends:
Greek puts already on either side
Such a branch-work forth as soon extends
To a vista opening far and wide,
20   And I pass out where it ends.

V

The outside-frame, like your hazel-trees:
But the inside-archway widens fast,
And a rarer sort succeeds to these,
And we slope to Italy at last
25   And youth, by green degrees.

VI

I follow wherever I am led,
Knowing so well the leader's hand:
Oh woman-country, wooed not wed,
Loved all the more by earth's male-lands,
30   Laid to their hearts instead!

VII

Look at the ruined chapel again
Half-way up in the Alpine gorge!
Is that a tower, I point you plain,
Or is it a mill, or an iron-forge
35   Breaks solitude in vain?

VIII

A turn, and we stand in the heart of things;
The woods are round us, heaped and dim;
From slab to slab how it slips and springs,
The thread of water single and slim,
40   Through the ravage some torrent brings!

IX

Does it feed the little lake below?
That speck of white just on its marge
Is Pella;[1] see, in the evening-glow,
How sharp the silver spear-heads charge
45   When Alp[2] meets heaven in snow!

X

On our other side is the straight-up rock;
And a path is kept 'twixt the gorge and it
By boulder-stones where lichens mock
The marks on a moth, and small ferns fit
50   Their teeth to the polished block.

XI

Oh the sense of the yellow mountain-flowers,
And thorny balls, each three in one,
The chestnuts throw on our path in showers!
For the drop of the woodland fruit's begun,
55   These early November hours,

XII

That crimson the creeper's leaf across
Like a splash of blood, intense, abrupt,
O'er a shield else gold from rim to boss,[3]
And lay it for show on the fairy-cupped
60   Elf-needled mat of moss,

[1] village in north-west Italy.

[2] probably Monte Rosa, which can be seen from the hills around Lago d'Orta, where the poem is set.

[3] the protuberance at the centre of a shield.

XIII

By the rose-flesh mushrooms, undivulged
Last evening—nay, in today's first dew
Yon sudden coral nipple bulged,
Where a freaked[1] fawn-coloured flaky crew
65 Of toadstools peep indulged.

XIV

And yonder, at foot of the fronting ridge
That takes the turn to a range beyond,
Is the chapel reached by the one-arched bridge
Where the water is stopped in a stagnant pond
70 Danced over by the midge.

XV

The chapel and bridge are of stone alike,
Blackish-grey and mostly wet;
Cut hemp-stalks steep in the narrow dike.
See here again, how the lichens fret[2]
75 And the roots of the ivy strike!

XVI

Poor little place, where its one priest comes
On a festa-day, if he comes at all,
To the dozen folk from their scattered homes,
Gathered within that precinct small
80 By the dozen ways one roams—

XVII

To drop from the charcoal-burners' huts,
Or climb from the hemp-dressers' low shed,
Leave the grange where the woodman stores his nuts,
Or the wattled cote[3] where the fowlers spread
85 Their gear on the rock's bare juts.

XVIII

It has some pretension too, this front,
With its bit of fresco half-moon-wise
Set over the porch, Art's early wont:
'Tis John in the Desert, I surmise,
90 But has borne the weather's brunt—

XIX

Not from the fault of the builder, though,
For a pent-house[4] properly projects
Where three carved beams make a certain show,
Dating—good thought of our architect's—
95 'Five, six, nine,[5] he lets you know.

XX

And all day long a bird sings there,
And a stray sheep drinks at the pond at times;
The place is silent and aware;
It has had its scenes, its joys and crimes,
100 But that is its own affair.

XXI

My perfect wife, my Leonor,
Oh heart, my own, oh eyes, mine too,
Whom else could I dare look backward for,
With whom beside should I dare pursue
105 The path grey heads abhor?

XXII

For it leads to a crag's sheer edge with them;
Youth, flowery all the way, there stops-
Not they; age threatens and they contemn,
Till they reach the gulf wherein youth drops,
110 One inch from life's safe hem!

XXIII

With me, youth led...I will speak now,
No longer watch you as you sit
Reading by fire-light, that great brow
And the spirit-small hand propping it,[6]
115 Mutely, my heart knows how—

---

[1] streaked.

[2] eat into.

[3] rough shelter of woven sticks.

[4] projecting cover.

[5] 1569.

[6] a characteristic pose of Elizabeth Barret Browning..

XXIV

When, if I think but deep enough,
You are wont to answer, prompt as rhyme;
And you, too, find without rebuff
Response your soul seeks many a time
120   Piercing its fine flesh-stuff.

XXV

My own, confirm me! If I tread
This path back, is it not in pride
To think how little I dreamed it led
To an age so blest that, by its side,
125   Youth seems the waste instead?

XXVI

My own, see where the years conduct!
At first, 'twas something our two souls
Should mix as mists do; each is sucked
In each now: on, the new stream rolls,
130   Whatever rocks obstruct.

XXVII

Think, when our one soul understands
The great Word which makes all things new,
When earth breaks up and heaven expands,
How will the change strike me and you
135   In the house not made with hands?[1]

XXVIII

Oh I must feel your brain prompt mine,
Your heart anticipate my heart,
You must be just before, in fine,
See and make me see, for your part,
140   New depths of the divine!

XXIX

But who could have expected this
When we two drew together first
Just for the obvious human bliss,

To satisfy life's daily thirst
145   With a thing men seldom miss?

XXX

Come back with me to the first of all,
Let us lean and love it over again,
Let us now forget and now recall,
Break the rosary in a pearly rain,
150   And gather what we let fall!

XXXI

What did I say?—that a small bird sings
All day long, save when a brown pair
Of hawks from the wood float with wide wings
Strained to a bell: 'gainst noon-day glare
155   You count the streaks and rings.

XXXII

But at afternoon or almost eve
'Tis better; then the silence grows
To that degree, you half believe
It must get rid of what it knows,
160   Its bosom does so heave.

XXXIII

Hither we walked then, side by side,
Arm in arm and cheek to cheek,
And still I questioned or replied,
While my heart, convulsed to really speak,
165   Lay choking in its pride.

XXXIV

Silent the crumbling bridge we cross,
And pity and praise the chapel sweet,
And care about the fresco's loss,
And wish for our souls a like retreat,
170   And wonder at the moss.

---

[1]   2 Corinthians 5:1.

XXXV

Stoop and kneel on the settle[1] under,
Look through the window's grated square:
Nothing to see! For fear of plunder,
The cross is down and the altar bare,
175   As if thieves don't fear thunder.

XXXVI

We stoop and look in through the grate,
See the little porch and rustic door,
Read duly the dead builder's date;
Then cross the bridge that we crossed before,
180   Take the path again—but wait!

XXXVII

Oh moment, one and infinite!
The water slips o'er stock[2] and stone;
The West is tender, hardly bright:
How grey at once is the evening grown—
185   One star, its chrysolite![3]

XXXVIII

We two stood there with never a third,
But each by each, as each knew well:
The sights we saw and the sounds we heard,
The lights and the shades made up a spell
190   Till the trouble grew and stirred.

XXXIX

Oh, the little more, and how much it is!
And the little less, and what worlds away!
How a sound shall quicken content to bliss,
Or a breath suspend the blood's best play,
195   And life be a proof of this!

XL

Had she willed it, still had stood the screen
So slight, so sure, 'twixt my love and her:

I could fix her face with a guard between,
And find her soul as when friends confer,
200   Friends—lovers that might have been.

XLI

For my heart had a touch of the woodland-time,
Wanting to sleep now over its best.
Shake the whole tree in the summer-prime,
But bring to the last leaf no such test!
205   "Hold the last fast!" runs the rhyme.

XLII

For a chance to make your little much,
To gain a lover and lose a friend,
Venture the tree and a myriad such,
When nothing you mar but the year can mend:
210   But a last leaf—fear to touch!

XLIII

Yet should it unfasten itself and fall
Eddying down till it find your face
At some slight wind—best chance of all!
Be your heart henceforth its dwelling-place
215   You trembled to forestall!

XLIV

Worth how well, those dark grey eyes,
That hair so dark and dear, how worth
That a man should strive and agonize,
And taste a veriest hell on earth
220   For the hope of such a prize!

XLV

You might have turned and tried a man,
Set him a space to weary and wear,
And prove which suited more your plan,
His best of hope or his worst despair,
225   Yet end as he began.

---

[1] bench.

[2] stump.

[3] semi-precious stone.

XLVI

But you spared me this, like the heart you are,
And filled my empty heart at a word.
If two lives join, there is oft a scar,
They are one and one, with a shadowy third;
230   One near one is too far.

XLVII

A moment after, and hands unseen
Were hanging the night around us fast;
But we knew that a bar was broken between
Life and life: we were mixed at last
235   In spite of the mortal screen.

XLVIII

The forests had done it; there they stood;
We caught for a moment the powers at play:
They had mingled us so, for once and good,
Their work was done—we might go or stay,
240   They relapsed to their ancient mood.

XLIX

How the world is made for each of us!
How all we perceive and know in it
Tends to some moment's product thus,
When a soul declares itself—to wit,
245   By its fruit, the thing it does!

L

Be hate that fruit or love that fruit,
It forwards the general deed of man,
And each of the Many helps to recruit
The life of the race by a general plan;
250   Each living his own, to boot.

LI

I am named and known by that moment's feat;
There took my station and degree;
So grew my own small life complete,
As nature obtained her best of me—
255   One born to love you, sweet!

LII

And to watch you sink by the fire-side now
Back again, as you mutely sit
Musing by fire-light, that great brow
And the spirit-small hand propping it,
260   Yonder, my heart knows how!

LIII

So, earth has gained by one man the more,
And the gain of earth must be heaven's gain too;
And the whole is well worth thinking o'er
When autumn comes: which I mean to do
265   One day, as I said before.
      —1855

An Epistle Containing the Strange Medical Experience of Karshish, the Arab Physician [1]

Karshish,[2] the picker-up of learning's crumbs,
The not-incurious in God's handiwork
(This man's-flesh he hath admirably made,
Blown like a bubble, kneaded like a paste,
5   To coop up and keep down on earth a space
That puff of vapour from his mouth , man's soul)[3]
—To Abib, all-sagacious in our art,
Breeder in me of what poor skill I boast,
Like me inquisitive how pricks and cracks
10   Befall the flesh through too much stress and strain,
Whereby the wily vapour fain would slip
Back and rejoin its source before the term,—
And aptest in contrivance (under God)
To baffle it by deftly stopping such:—
15   The vagrant Scholar to his Sage at home
Sends greeting (health and knowledge, fame with
      peace)

---

[1] Karshish and his master Abib are Browning's inventions. The story of Christ raising Lazarus from the dead is from John 11:1–44.

[2] Arabic for "one who gathers."

[3] a reference to the old doctrine that the soul leaves the body with the last breath in the form of vapour. As in "Fra Lippo Lippi," l. 186.

Three samples of true snakestone[1]—rarer still,
One of the other sort, the melon-shaped,
(But fitter, pounded fine, for charms than drugs)
20 And writeth now the twenty-second time.

My journeyings were brought to Jericho:[2]
Thus I resume. Who studious in our art
Shall count a little labour unrepaid?
I have shed sweat enough, left flesh and bone
25 On many a flinty furlong of this land.
Also, the country-side is all on fire
With rumours of a marching hitherward:
Some say Vespasian[3] cometh, some, his son.
A black lynx snarled and pricked a tufted ear;
30 Lust of my blood inflamed his yellow balls:[4]
I cried and threw my staff and he was gone.
Twice have the robbers stripped and beaten me,
And once a town declared me for a spy;
But at the end, I reach Jerusalem,
35 Since this poor covert where I pass the night,
This Bethany,[5] lies scarce the distance thence
A man with plague-sores at the third degree
Runs till he drops down dead. Thou laughest here!
'Sooth, it elates me, thus reposed and safe,
40 To void the stuffing of my travel-scrip[6]
And share with thee whatever Jewry yields.
A viscid choler[7] is observable
In tertians,[8] I was nearly bold to say;
And falling-sickness[9] hath a happier cure
45 Than our school wots of: there's a spider here

Weaves no web, watches on the ledge of tombs,
Sprinkled with mottles on an ash-grey back;
Take five and drop them...but who knows his mind,
The Syrian runagate[10] I trust this to?
50 His service payeth me a sublimate[11]
Blown up his nose to help the ailing eye.
Best wait: I reach Jerusalem at morn,
There set in order my experiences,
Gather what most deserves, and give thee all—
55 Or I might add, Judea's gum-tragacanth[12]
Scales off in purer flakes, shines clearer-grained,
Cracks 'twixt the pestle and the porphyry,[13]
In fine exceeds our produce. Scalp-disease
Confounds me, crossing so with leprosy—
60 Thou hadst admired one sort I gained at Zoar—[14]
But zeal outruns discretion. Here I end.

Yet stay: my Syrian blinketh gratefully,
Protesteth his devotion is my price—
Suppose I write what harms not, though he steal?
65 I half resolve to tell thee, yet I blush,
What set me off a-writing first of all.
An itch I had, a sting to write, a tang![15]
For, be it this town's barrenness—or else
The Man had something in the look of him—
70 His case has struck me far more than 'tis worth.
So, pardon if—(lest presently I lose
In the great press of novelty at hand
The care and pains this somehow stole from me)
I bid thee take the thing while fresh in mind,
75 Almost in sight—for, wilt thou have the truth?
The very man is gone from me but now,
Whose ailment is the subject of discourse.
Thus then, and let thy better wit help all!

---

[1] a stone used in treating snake bites.

[2] the city east of Jerusalem.

[3] Roman Emperor (70–79). He invaded Palestine in 66; his son, Titus, did the same in 70.

[4] eyeballs.

[5] a small village near Jerusalem, the home of Lazarus.

[6] A "scrip" is a small bag.

[7] sticky bile.

[8] fevers recurring every other day.

[9] epilepsy.

[10] vagabond.

[11] product of a refining process.

[12] a salve.

[13] a hard rock.

[14] town north of the Dead Sea.

[15] sting.

'Tis but a case of mania—subinduced[1]
80 By epilepsy, at the turning-point
Of trance prolonged unduly some three days:[2]
When by the exhibition[3] of some drug
Or spell, exorcization, stroke of art
Unknown to me and which 'twere well to know,
85 The evil thing out-breaking all at once
Left the man whole and sound of body indeed,—
But, flinging (so to speak) life's gates too wide,
Making a clear house of it too suddenly,
The first conceit[4] that entered might inscribe
90 Whatever it was minded on the wall
So plainly at that vantage, as it were,
(First come, first served) that nothing subsequent
Attaineth to erase those fancy-scrawls
The just-returned and new-established soul
95 Hath gotten now so thoroughly by heart
That henceforth she will read or these or none.
And first—the man's own firm conviction rests
That he was dead (in fact they buried him)
—That he was dead and then restored to life
100 By a Nazarene physician of his tribe:
—'Sayeth, the same bade "Rise," and he did rise.
"Such cases are diurnal," thou wilt cry.
Not so this figment!—not, that such a fume,[5]
Instead of giving way to time and health,
105 Should eat itself into the life of life,
As saffron tingeth flesh, blood, bones and all!
For see, how he takes up the after-life.
The man—it is one Lazarus a Jew,
Sanguine,[6] proportioned, fifty years of age,[7]

110 The body's habit wholly laudable,[8]
As much, indeed, beyond the common health
As he were made and put aside to show.
Think, could we penetrate by any drug
And bathe the wearied soul and worried flesh,
115 And bring it clear and fair, by three days' sleep!
Whence has the man the balm that brightens all?
This grown man eyes the world now like a child.
Some elders of his tribe, I should premise,
Led in their friend, obedient as a sheep,
120 To bear my inquisition. While they spoke,
Now sharply, now with sorrow,-told the case,—
He listened not except I spoke to him,
But folded his two hands and let them talk,
Watching the flies that buzzed: and yet no fool.
125 And that's a sample how his years must go.
Look, if a beggar, in fixed middle-life,
Should find a treasure,—can he use the same
With straitened habits and with tastes starved small,
And take at once to his impoverished brain
130 The sudden element that changes things,
That sets the undreamed-of rapture at his hand
And puts the cheap old joy in the scorned dust?
Is he not such an one as moves to mirth—
Warily parsimonious, when no need,
135 Wasteful as drunkenness at undue times?
All prudent counsel as to what befits
The golden mean, is lost on such an one:
The man's fantastic will is the man's law.
So here—we call the treasure knowledge, say,
140 Increased beyond the fleshly faculty—
Heaven opened to a soul while yet on earth,
Earth forced on a soul's use while seeing heaven:
The man is witless of the size, the sum,
The value in proportion of all things,
145 Or whether it be little or be much.
Discourse to him of prodigious armaments
Assembled to besiege his city now,
And of the passing of a mule with gourds—

---

[1] brought about as a result of something else.

[2] actually four days: John 11:17, 39; an incorrect "fact."

[3] administration.

[4] fancy.

[5] hallucination.

[6] robust.

[7] Karshish's "facts" are often wrong: Lazarus would have been well over sixty.

---

[8] healthy.

'Tis one! Then take it on the other side,
150 Speak of some trifling fact,—he will gaze rapt
With stupor at its very littleness,
(Far as I see) as if in that indeed
He caught prodigious import, whole results;
And so will turn to us the bystanders
155 In ever the same stupor (note this point)
That we too see not with his opened eyes.
Wonder and doubt come wrongly into play,
Preposterously, at cross-purposes.
Should his child sicken unto death,—why, look
160 For scarce abatement of his cheerfulness,
Or pretermission[1] of the daily craft!
While a word, gesture, glance from that same child
At play or in the school or laid asleep,
Will startle him to an agony of fear,
165 Exasperation, just as like. Demand
The reason why—" 'tis but a word," object—
"A gesture"—he regards thee as our lord
Who lived there in the pyramid alone,
Looked at us (dost thou mind?) when, being young,
170 We both would unadvisedly recite
Some charm's beginning, from that book of his,
Able to bid the sun throb wide and burst
All into stars, as suns grown old are wont.
Thou and the child have each a veil alike
175 Thrown o'er your heads, from under which ye both
Stretch your blind hands and trifle with a match
Over a mine of Greek fire,[2] did ye know!
He holds on firmly to some thread of life—
(It is the life to lead perforcedly)
180 Which runs across some vast distracting orb
Of glory on either side that meagre thread,
Which, conscious of, he must not enter yet—
The spiritual life around the earthly life:
The law of that is known to him as this,
185 His heart and brain move there, his feet stay here.
So is the man perplext with impulses

Sudden to start off crosswise, not straight on,
Proclaiming what is right and wrong across,
And not along, this black thread through the blaze—
190 "It should be" balked by "here it cannot be."
And oft the man's soul springs into his face
As if he saw again and heard again
His sage that bade him "Rise" and he did rise.
Something, a word, a tick[3] o' the blood within
195 Admonishes: then back he sinks at once
To ashes, who was very fire before,
In sedulous recurrence to his trade
Whereby he earneth him the daily bread;
And studiously the humbler for that pride,
200 Professedly the faultier that he knows
God's secret, while he holds the thread of life.
Indeed the especial marking of the man
Is prone submission to the heavenly will—
Seeing it, what it is, and why it is.
205 'Sayeth, he will wait patient to the last
For that same death which must restore his being
To equilibrium, body loosening soul
Divorced even now by premature full growth:
He will live, nay, it pleaseth him to live
210 So long as God please, and just how God please.
He even seeketh not to please God more
(Which meaneth, otherwise) than as God please.
Hence, I preceive not he affects to preach
The doctrine of his sect whate'er it be,
215 Make proselytes as madmen thirst to do:
How can he give his neighbour the real ground,
His own conviction? Ardent as he is—
Call his great truth a lie, why, still the old
"Be it as God please" reassureth him.
220 I probed the sore as thy disciple should:
"How, beast," said I, "this stolid carelessness
Sufficeth[4] thee, when Rome is on her march
To stamp out like a little spark thy town,
Thy tribe, thy crazy tale and thee at once?"

---

[1] neglecting.

[2] an incendiary mixture, but not used until the seventh century.

[3] pulse-beat.

[4] may it satisfy.

225 He merely looked with his large eyes on me.
The man is apathetic, you deduce?
Contrariwise, he loves both old and young,
Able and weak, affects[1] the very brutes
And birds—how say I? flowers of the field—
230 As a wise workman recognizes tools
In a master's workshop, loving what they make.
Thus is the man, as harmless as a lamb:
Only impatient, let him do his best,
At ignorance and carelessness and sin—
235 An indignation which is promptly curbed:
As when in certain travels I have feigned
To be an ignoramus in our art
According to some preconceived design,
And happed to hear the land's practitioners
240 Steeped in conceit sublimed[2] by ignorance,
Prattle fantastically on disease,
Its cause and cure—and I must hold my peace!

      Thou wilt object—Why have I not ere this
Sought out the sage himself, the Nazarene
245 Who wrought this cure, inquiring at the source,
Conferring with the frankness that befits?
Alas! it grieveth me, the learned leech
Perished in a tumult many years ago,
Accused,—our learning's fate,—of wizardry,
250 Rebellion, to the setting up a rule
And creed prodigious[3] as described to me.
His death, which happened when the earthquake fell
(Prefiguring, as soon appeared, the loss
To occult learning in our lord the sage
255 Who lived there in the pyramid alone)
Was wrought by the mad people—that's their wont!
On vain recourse, as I conjecture it,
To his tried virtue, for miraculous help—
How could he stop the earthquake? That's their way!
260 The other imputations must be lies:

But take one, though I loathe to give it thee,
In mere respect for any good man's fame.
(And after all, our patient Lazarus
Is stark mad; should we count on what he says?
265 Perhaps not: though in writing to a leech
'Tis well to keep back nothing of a case.)
This man so cured regards the curer, then,
As—God forgive me! who but God himself,
Creator and sustainer of the world,
270 That came and dwelt in flesh on it awhile!
—'Sayeth that such as one was born and lived,
Taught, healed the sick, broke bread at his own house,
Then died, with Lazarus by, for aught I know,
And yet was…what I said nor choose repeat,
275 And must have so avouched himself, in fact,
In hearing of this very Lazarus
Who saith—but why all this of what he saith?
Why write of trivial matters, things of price
Calling at every moment for remark?
280 I noticed on the margin of a pool
Blue-flowering borage,[4] the Aleppo[5] sort,
Aboundeth, very nitrous. It is strange!

      Thy pardon for this long and tedious case,
Which, now that I review it, needs must seem
285 Unduly dwelt on, prolixly set forth!
Nor I myself discern in what is writ
Good cause for the peculiar interest
And awe indeed this man has touched me with.
Perhaps the journey's end, the weariness
290 Had wrought upon me first. I met him thus:
I crossed a ridge of short sharp broken hills
Like an old lion's cheek teeth. Out there came
A moon made like a face with certain spots
Multiform, manifold and menacing:
295 Then a wind rose behind me. So we met
In this old sleepy town at unaware,
The man and I. I send thee what is writ.

---

[1] his affection for.

[2] fancy refined by.

[3] monstrous.

[4] herb, used medicinally.

[5] town in northern Syria.

Regard it as a chance, a matter risked
To this ambiguous Syrian—he may lose,
300 Or steal, or give it thee with equal good.
Jerusalem's repose shall make amends
For time this letter wastes, thy time and mine;
Till when, once more thy pardon and farewell!

The very God! think, Abib; dost thou think?
305 So, the All-Great, were the All-Loving too—
So, through the thunder comes a human voice
Saying, "O heart I made, a heart beats here!
Face, my hands fashioned, see it in myself!
Thou hast no power nor mayst conceive of mine,
310 But love I gave thee, with myself to love,
And thou must love me who have died for thee!"
The madman saith He[1] said so: it is strange.
—1855

"Childe Roland to the Dark Tower Came"[2]

(See Edgar's song in *Lear*)

I

My first thought was, he lied in every word,
    That hoary cripple, with malicious eye
Askance to watch the working of his lie
On mine, and mouth scarce able to afford
5 Suppression of the glee, that pursed and scored
    Its edge, at one more victim gained thereby.

II

What else should he be set for, with his staff?
    What, save to waylay with his lies, ensnare

All travellers who might find him posted there,
10 And ask the road? I guessed what skull-like laugh
Would break, what crutch 'gin write my epitaph
    For pastime in the dusty thoroughfare,

III

If at his counsel I should turn aside
    Into that ominous tract which, all agree,
15   Hides the Dark Tower. Yet acquiescingly
I did turn as he pointed: neither pride
Nor hope rekindling at the end descried,
    So much as gladness that some end might be.

IV

For, what with my whole world-wide wandering,
20   What with my search drawn out through years,
        my hope
    Dwindled into a ghost not fit to cope
With that obstreperous joy success would bring,—
I hardly tried now to rebuke the spring
    My heart made, finding failure in its scope.

V

25 As when a sick man very near to death[3]
    Seems dead indeed, and feels begin and end
    The tears and takes the farewell of each friend,
And hears one bid the other go, draw breath
Freelier outside, ("since all is o'er," he saith,
30   "And the blow fallen no grieving can amend";)

VI

While some discuss if near the other graves
    Be room enough for this, and when a day
    Suits best for carrying the corpse away,
With care about the banners, scarves and staves:
35 And still the man hears all, and only craves
    He may not shame such tender love and stay.

---

[1] The capital "H" could suggest that Karshish does not (like Cleon) reject the new religion.

[2] The title quotes Edgar (playing the role of the madman, Poor Tom) in *King Lear* 3.4.186. A childe is a candidate for knighthood. Frequently questioned about the poem, Browning said that it came upon him "as a kind of dream" that had to be written, that he did not know what it meant, that he was "very fond" of it, that it was "only fantasy" with "no allegorical intention." Asked if it meant that "he that endureth to the end shall be saved," Browning replied, "Just about that." The poem and its meaning and sources, have been extensively debated.

---

[3] See John Donne, "A Valediction: Forbidding Mourning," ll. 1–4.

VII

Thus, I had so long suffered in this quest,
    Heard failure prophesied so oft, been writ
    So many times among "The Band"—to wit,
40 The knights who to the Dark Tower's search
      addressed
Their steps—that just to fail as they, seemed best,
And all the doubt was now—should I be fit?

VIII

So, quiet as despair, I turned from him,
    That hateful cripple, out of his highway
45   Into the path he pointed. All the day
Had been a dreary one at best, and dim
Was settling to its close, yet shot one grim
    Red leer to see the plain catch its estray.[1]

IX

For mark! no sooner was I fairly found
50   Pledged to the plain, after a pace or two,
    Than, pausing to throw backward a last view
O'er the safe road, 'twas gone; grey plain all round:
Nothing but plain to the horizon's bound.
    I might go on; naught else remained to do.

X

55 So, on I went. I think I never saw
    Such starved ignoble nature; nothing throve:
    For flowers—as well expect a cedar grove!
But cockle, spurge,[2] according to their law
Might propagate their kind, with none to awe,
60   You'd think; a burr had been a treasure-trove.

XI

No! penury, inertness and grimace,
    In some strange sort, were the land's portion. "See
    Or shut your eyes," said Nature peevishly,

---

1 stray animal.

2 weeds.

"It nothing skills:[3] I cannot help my case:
65 'Tis the Last Judgement's fire must cure this place,
    Calcine[4] its clods and set my prisoners free."

XII

If there pushed any ragged thistle-stalk
    Above its mates, the head was chopped; the
      bents[5]
    Were jealous else. What made those holes and
      rents
70 In the dock's harsh swarth leaves, bruised as to balk
All hope of greenness? 'tis a brute must walk
    Pashing[6] their life out, with a brute's intents.

XIII

As for the grass, it grew as scant as hair
    In leprosy; thin dry blades pricked the mud
75   Which underneath looked kneaded up with blood.
One stiff blind horse, his every bone a-stare,
Stood stupefied, however he came there:
    Thrust out past service from the devil's stud!

XIV

Alive? he might be dead for aught I know,
80   With that red gaunt and colloped[7] neck a-strain,
    And shut eyes underneath the rusty mane;
Seldom went such grotesqueness with such woe;
I never saw a brute I hated so;
    He must be wicked to deserve such pain.

XV

85 I shut my eyes and turned them on my heart.
    As a man calls for wine before he fights,
    I asked one draught of earlier, happier sights,
Ere fitly I could hope to play my part.

---

3 is no use.

4 burn to ashes.

5 coarse grasses.

6 trampling.

7 folds of the skin.

Think first, fight afterwards—the soldier's art:
90   One taste of the old time sets all to rights.

XVI

Not it! I fancied Cuthbert's reddening face
    Beneath its garniture of curly gold,
    Dear fellow, till I almost felt him fold
An arm in mine to fix me to the place,
95 That way he used. Alas, one night's disgrace!
    Out went my heart's new fire and left it cold.

XVII

Giles then, the soul of honour—there he stands
    Frank as ten years ago when knighted first.
    What honest man should dare (he said) he durst.
100 Good—but the scene shifts—faugh! what
       hangman-hands
Pin to his breast a parchment? His own bands
    Read it. Poor traitor, spit upon and curst!

XVIII

Better this present than a past like that;
    Back therefore to my darkening path again!
105   No sound, no sight as far as eye could strain.
Will the night send a howlet[1] or a bat?
I asked: when something on the dismal flat
    Came to arrest my thoughts and change their
       train.

XIX

A sudden little river crossed my path
110   As unexpected as a serpent comes.
    No sluggish tide congenial to the glooms;
This, as it frothed by, might have been a bath
For the fiend's glowing hoof—to see the wrath
    Of its black eddy bespate with flakes and
       spumes.

XX

115 So petty yet so spiteful! All along,
    Low scrubby alders kneeled down over it;
    Drenched willows flung them headlong in a fit
Of mute despair, a suicidal throng:
The river which had done them all the wrong,
120   Whate'er that was, rolled by, deterred no whit.

XXI

Which, while I forded,—good saints, how I feared
    To set my foot upon a dead man's cheek,
    Each step, or feel the spear I thrust to seek
For hollows, tangled in his hair or beard!
125 —It may have been a water-rat I speared,
    But, ugh! it sounded like a baby's shriek.

XXII

Glad was I when I reached the other bank.
    Now for a better country. Vain presage!
    Who were the strugglers, what war did they wage,
130 Whose savage trample thus could pad[2] the dank
Soil to a plash[3]? Toads in a poisoned tank,
    Or wild cats in a red-hot iron cage—

XXIII

The fight must so have seemed in that fell cirque.[4]
    What penned them there, with all the plain to
       choose?
135   No foot-print leading to that horrid mews,[5]
None out of it. Mad brewage set to work
Their brains, no doubt, like galley-slaves the Turk
    Pits for his pastime, Christians against Jews.

XXIV

And more than that—a furlong on—why, there!
140   What bad use was that engine for, that wheel,

---

[1] owl.

[2] tread down.

[3] puddle.

[4] circus or circular space.

[5] meaning a stable, but here a place of confinement.

Or brake,[1] not wheel—that harrow fit to reel
Men's bodies out like silk? with all the air
Of Tophet's[2] tool, on earth left unaware,
    Or brought to sharpen its rusty teeth of steel.

XXV

145 Then came a bit of stubbed ground, once a wood,
    Next a marsh, it would seem, and now mere earth
    Desperate and done with; (so a fool finds mirth,
Makes a thing and then mars it, till his mood
Changes and off he goes!) within a rood—[3]
150   Bog, clay and rubble, sand and stark black
        dearth.

XXVI

Now blotches rankling, coloured gay and grim,
    Now patches where some leanness of the soil's
    Broke into moss or substances like boils;
Then came some palsied oak, a cleft in him
155 Like a distorted mouth that splits its rim
    Gaping at death, and dies while it recoils.

XXVII

And just as far as ever from the end!
    Naught in the distance but the evening, naught
    To point my footstep further! At the thought,
160 A great black bird, Apollyon's[4] bosom-friend,
Sailed past, nor beat his wide wing dragon-penned[5]
    That brushed my cap—perchance the guide I
        sought.

XXVIII

For, looking up, aware I somehow grew,
    'Spite of the dusk, the plain had given place
165   All round to mountains—with such name to grace

Mere ugly heights and heaps now stolen in view.
How thus they had surprised me,—solve it, you!
    How to get from them was no clearer case.

XXIX

Yet half I seemed to recognize some trick
170   Of mischief happened to me, God knows when—
    In a bad dream perhaps. Here ended, then,
Progress this way. When, in the very nick
Of giving up, one time more, came a click
    As when a trap shuts—you're inside the den!

XXX

175 Burningly it came on me all at once,
    This was the place! those two hills on the right,
    Crouched like two bulls locked horn in horn in
        fight;
While to the left, a tall scalped mountain...Dunce,
Dotard, a-dozing at the very nonce,
180   After a life spent training for the sight!

XXXI

What in the midst lay but the Tower itself?
    The round squat turret, blind as the fool's heart,
    Built of brown stone, without a counterpart
In the whole world. The tempest's mocking elf
185 Points to the shipman thus the unseen shelf
    He strikes on, only when the timbers start.

XXXII

Not see? because of night perhaps?—why, day
    Came back again for that! before it left,
    The dying sunset kindled through a cleft:
190 The hills, like giants at a hunting, lay,
Chin upon hand, to see the game at bay,—
    "Now stab and end the creature—to the heft!"

XXXIII

Not hear? when noise was everywhere! it tolled
    Increasingly like a bell. Names in my ears
195   Of all the lost adventurers my peers,—

---

[1] heavy harrow for crushing clods.

[2] hell.

[3] a quarter of an acre.

[4] the Devil.

[5] winged.

How such a one was strong, and such was bold,
And such was fortunate, yet each of old
　　Lost, lost! one moment knelled the woe of years.

　　　　　　XXXIV
There they stood, ranged along the hill-sides, met
200　　To view the last of me, a living frame
　　For one more picture! in a sheet of flame
I saw them and I knew them all. And yet
Dauntless the slug-horn[1] to my lips I set,
　　And blew. *"Childe Roland to the Dark Tower
　　　　came."*
—1855

The Statue and the Bust[2]

There's a palace in Florence, the world knows
　　well,
And a statue watches it from the square,
And this story of both do our townsmen tell.

Ages ago, a lady there,
5　　At the farthest window facing the East
Asked, "Who rides by with the royal air?"

The bridesmaids' prattle around her ceased;
She leaned forth, one on either hand;
They saw how the blush of the bride increased—

10　They felt by its beats her heart expand—
As one at each ear and both in a breath
Whispered, "The Great-Duke Ferdinand."

That self-same instant, underneath,
The Duke rode past in his idle way,
15　Empty and fine like a swordless sheath.

Gay he rode, with a friend as gay,
Till he threw his head back—"Who is she?"
—"A bride the Riccardi[3] brings home today."

Hair in heaps lay heavily
20　Over a pale brow spirit-pure—
Carved like the heart of the coal-black tree,[4]

Crisped like a war-steed's encolure—[5]
And vainly sought to dissemble[6] her eyes
Of the blackest black our eyes endure.

25　And lo, a blade for a knight's emprise[7]
Filled the fine empty sheath of a man,—
The Duke grew straightway brave and wise.

He looked at her, as a lover can;
She looked at him, as one who awakes:
30　The past was a sleep, and her life began.

Now, love so ordered for both their sakes,
A feast was held that selfsame night
In the pile which the mighty shadow makes.

(For Via Larga is three-parts light,
35　But the palace overshadows one,
Because of a crime[8] which may God requite!

To Florence and God the wrong was done,
Through the first republic's murder there
By Cosimo and his cursèd son.)[9]

---

[1] trumpet.

[2] The equestrian statue of Ferdinand de Medici (1549–1608), who became Grand-Duke of Florence in 1587, dominates the Piazza Annunziata in Florence. It is the work of John of Douay (l. 202), better known as Giovanni da Bologna (1524–1608). The bust is fictional.

[3] a leading Florentine family.

[4] ebony.

[5] mane.

[6] simulate by imitation (obsolete usage).

[7] enterprise.

[8] the suppression of Florentine liberty following the return of Cosimo de Medici in 1434.

[9] named Piero.

40 The Duke (with the statue's face in the square)
Turned in the midst of his multitude
At the bright approach of the bridal pair.

Face to face the lovers stood
A single minute and no more,
45 While the bridegroom bent as a man subdued—

Bowed till his bonnet brushed the floor—
For the Duke on the lady a kiss conferred,
As the courtly custom was of yore.

In a minute can lovers exchange a word?
50 In a word did pass, which I do not think,
Only one out of the thousand heard.

That was the bridegroom. At day's brink
He and his bride were alone at last
In a bedchamber by a taper's blink.

55 Calmly he said that her lot was cast,
That the door she had passed was shut on her
Till the final catafalque¹ repassed.

The world meanwhile, its noise and stir,
Through a certain window facing the East,
60 She could watch like a convent's chronicler.

Since passing the door might lead to a feast,
And a feast might lead to so much beside,
He, of many evils, chose the least.

"Freely I choose too," said the bride—
65 "Your window and its world suffice,"
Replied the tongue, while the heart replied—

"If I spend the night with that devil twice,
May his window serve as my loop² of hell
Whence a damned soul looks on paradise!

70 "I fly to the Duke who loves me well,
Sit by his side and laugh at sorrow
Ere I count another ave-bell.³

"'Tis only the coat of a page to borrow,
And tie my hair in a horse-boy's trim,
75 And I save my soul—but not tomorrow"—

(She checked herself and her eye grew dim)
"My father tarries to bless my state:
I must keep it one day more for him.

"Is one day more so long to wait?
80 Moreover the Duke rides past, I know;
We shall see each other, sure as fate."

She turned on her side and slept. Just so!
So we resolve on a thing and sleep:
So did the lady, ages ago.

85 That night the Duke said, "Dear or cheap
As the cost of this cup of bliss may prove
To body our soul, I will drain it deep."

And on the morrow, bold with love,
He beckoned the bridegroom (close on call,
90 As his duty bade, by the Duke's alcove)

And smiled "'Twas a very funeral,
Your lady will think, this feast of ours,—
A shame to efface, whate'er befall!

---

¹ structure supporting a coffin.

² loop-hole.

³ the bell calling to evening prayer.

"What if we break from the Arno[1] bowers,
95 And try if Petraja,[2] cool and green,
Cure last night's fault with this morning's flowers?"

The bridegroom, not a thought to be seen
On his steady brow and quiet mouth,
Said, "Too much favour for me so mean!

100 "But, alas! my lady leaves[3] the South;
Each wind that comes from the Apennine
Is a menace to her tender youth:

"Nor a way exists, the wise opine,
If she quits her palace twice this year,
105 To avert the flower of life's decline."

Quoth the Duke, "A sage and a kindly fear.
Moreover Petraja is cold this spring:
Be our feast tonight as usual here!"

And then to himself—"Which night shall bring
110 Thy bride to her lover's embraces, fool—
Or I am the fool, and thou art the king!

"Yet my passion must wait a night, nor cool—
For tonight the Envoy arrives from France
Whose heart I unlock with thyself, my tool.

115 "I need thee still and might miss perchance.
Today is not wholly lost, beside,
With its hope of my lady's countenance:

"For I ride—what should I do but ride?
And passing her palace, if I list,
120 May glance at its window—well betide!"

So said, so done: nor the lady missed
One ray that broke from the ardent brow,
Nor a curl of the lips where the spirit kissed.

Be sure that each renewed the vow,
125 No morrow's sun should arise and set
And leave them then as it left them now.

But next day passed, and next day yet,
With still fresh cause to wait one day more
Ere each leaped over the parapet.

130 And still, as love's brief morning wore,
With a gentle start, half smile, half sigh,
They found love not as it seemed before.

They thought it would work infallibly,
But not in despite of heaven and earth:
135 The rose would blow when the storm passed by.

Meantime they could profit in winter's dearth
By store of fruits that supplant the rose:
The world and its ways have a certain worth:

And to press a point while these oppose
140 Were simple policy; better wait:
We lose no friends and we gain no foes.

Meantime, worse fates than a lover's fate,
Who daily may ride and pass and look
Where his lady watches behind the grate!

145 And she—she watched the square like a book
Holding one picture and only one,
Which daily to find she undertook:

When the picture was reached the book was done,
And she turned from the picture at night to scheme
150 Of tearing it out for herself next sun.

---

[1] the river that runs through Florence.

[2] just north of Florence, where Ferdinand had a villa.

[3] comes from.

So weeks grew months, years; gleam by gleam
The glory dropped from their youth and love,
And both perceived they had dreamed a dream;

Which hovered as dreams do, still above:
155 But who can take a dream for a truth?
Oh, hide our eyes from the next remove!

One day as the lady saw her youth
Depart, and the silver thread that streaked
Her hair, and, worn by the serpent's tooth,

160 The brow so puckered, the chin so peaked,—
And wondered who the woman was,
Hollow-eyed and haggard-cheeked,

Fronting[1] her silent in the glass—
"Summon here," she suddenly said,
165 "Before the rest of my old self pass,

"Him, the Carver, a hand to aid,
Who fashions the clay no love will change,
And fixes a beauty never to fade.

"Let Robbia's[2] craft so apt and strange
170 Arrest the remains of young and fair,
And rivet them while the seasons range.

"Make me a face on the window there,
Waiting as ever, mute the while,
My love to pass below in the square!

175 "And let me think that it may beguile
Dreary days which the dead must spend
Down in their darkness under the aisle,

"To say, 'What matters it at the end?
I did no more while my heart was warm
180 Than does that image, my pale-faced friend.'

"Where is the use of the lip's red charm,
The heaven of hair, the pride of the brow,
And the blood that blues the inside arm—

"Unless we turn, as the soul knows how,
185 The earthly gift to an end divine?
A lady of clay is as good, I trow."

But long ere Robbia's cornice, fine,
With flowers and fruits which leaves enlace,
Was set where now is the empty shrine—

190 (And, leaning out of a bright blue space,
As a ghost might lean from a chink of sky,
The passionate pale lady's face—

Eyeing ever, with earnest eye
And quick-turned neck at its breathless stretch,
195 Some one who ever is passing by—)

The Duke had sighed like the simplest wretch
In Florence, "Youth—my dream escapes!
Will its record stay?" And he bade them fetch

Some subtle moulder of brazen shapes—
200 "Can the soul, the will, die out of a man
Ere his body find the grave that gapes?

"John of Douay shall effect my plan,
Set me on horseback here aloft,
Alive, as the crafty sculptor can,

205 "In the very square I have crossed so oft:
That men may admire, when future suns
Shall touch the eyes to a purpose soft,

---

[1] confronting.

[2] name of a family of Florentine sculptors.

"While the mouth and the brow stay brave in
    bronze—
Admire and say, "When he was alive
210 How he would take his pleasure once!"

"And it shall go hard but I contrive
To listen the while, and laugh in my tomb
At idleness which aspires to strive."

————————

So! While these wait the trump of doom,
215 How do their spirits pass, I wonder,
Nights and days in the narrow room?

Still, I suppose, they sit and ponder
What a gift life was, ages ago,
Six steps out of the chapel yonder.

220 Only they see not God, I know,
Nor all that chivalry[1] of his,
The soldier-saints who, row on row,

Burn upward each to his point of bliss—
Since, the end of life being manifest,
225 He had burned his way through the world to this.

I hear you reproach, "But delay was best,
For their end was a crime."—Oh, a crime will do
As well, I reply, to serve for a test,

As a virtue golden through and through,
230 Sufficient to vindicate itself
And prove its worth at a moment's view!

Must a game be played for the sake of pelf?
Where a button goes, 'twere an epigram
To offer the stamp of the very Guelph.[2]

235 The true has no value beyond the sham:
As well the counter as coin, I submit,
When your table's a hat,[3] and your prize a dram.[4]

Stake your counter as boldly every whit,
Venture as warily, use the same skill,
240 Do your best, whether winning or losing it,

If you choose to play!—is my principle.
Let a man contend to the uttermost
For his life's set prize, be it what it will!

The counter our lovers staked was lost
245 As surely as if it were lawful coin:
And the sin I impute to each frustrate ghost

Is—the unlit lamp and the ungirt loin,
Though the end in sight was a vice, I say.
You of the virtue (we issue join)
250 How strive you? *De te, fabula.*[5]
    —1855

How It Strikes a Contemporary [6]

I only knew one poet in my life:
And this, or something like it, was his way.

You saw go up and down Valladolid,[7]
A man of mark, to know next time you saw.
5 His very serviceable suit of black
Was courtly once and conscientious still,
And many might have worn it, though none did:
The cloak, that somewhat shone and showed the
    threads,

————————

1 band of knights.

2 A *Guelpho* was a fourteenth-century Florentine coin.

————————

3 for rolling dice on?

4 a trifling stake.

5 "The story is about you."

6 The poem is an important poetic statement about the nature of Browning's art.

7 town about 100 miles north-west of Madrid.

Had purpose, and the ruff, significance.
10 He walked and tapped the pavement with his cane,
Scenting the world, looking it full in face,
An old dog, bald and blindish, at his heels.
They turned up, now, the alley by the church,
That leads nowhither; now, they breathed
themselves
15 On the main promenade just at the wrong time:
You'd come upon his scrutinizing hat,
Making a peaked shade blacker than itself
Against the single window spared some house
Intact yet with its mouldered Moorish work,—
20 Or else surprise the ferrel of his stick
Trying the mortar's temper 'tween the chinks
Of some new shop a-building, French and fine.
He stood and watched the cobbler at his trade,
The man who slices lemons into drink,
25 The coffee-roaster's brazier, and the boys
That volunteer to help him turn its winch.
He glanced o'er books on stalls with half an eye,
And fly-leaf[1] ballads on the vendor's string,
And broad-edge bold-print posters by the wall.
30 He took such cognizance of men and things,
If any beat a horse, you felt he saw;
If any cursed a woman, he took note;
Yet stared at nobody,—you stared at him,
And found, less to your pleasure than surprise,
35 He seemed to know you and expect as much.
So, next time that a neighbour's tongue was loosed,
It marked the shameful and notorious fact,
We had among us, not so much a spy,[2]
As a recording chief-inquisitor,
40 The town's true master if the town but knew!
We merely kept a governor for form,
While this man walked about and took account
Of all thought, said and acted, then went home,
And wrote it fully to our Lord the King
45 Who has an itch to know things, he knows why,

And reads them in his bedroom of a night.
Oh, you might smile! there wanted not a touch,
A tang[3] of…well, it was not wholly ease
As back into your mind the man's look came.
50 Stricken in years a little,—such a brow
His eyes had to live under!—clear as flint
On either side the formidable nose
Curved, cut and coloured like an eagle's claw.
Had he to do with A.'s surprising fate?
55 When altogether old B. disappeared
And young C. got his mistress,—was't our friend,
His letter to the King, that did it all?
What paid the bloodless man for so much pains?
Our Lord the King has favourites manifold,
60 And shifts his ministry some once a month;
Our city gets new governors at whiles,—
But never word or sign, that I could hear,
Notified to this man about the streets
The King's approval of those letters conned
65 The last thing duly at the dead of night.
Did the man love his office? Frowned our Lord,
Exhorting when none heard—"Beseech me not!
Too far above my people,—beneath me!
I set the watch,—how should the people know?
70 Forget them, keep me all the more in mind!"
Was some such understanding 'twixt the two?

I found no truth in one report at least—
That if you tracked him to his home, down lanes
Beyond the Jewry, and as clean to pace,
75 You found he ate his supper in a room
Blazing with lights, four Titians[4] on the wall,
And twenty naked girls to change his plate!
Poor man, he lived another kind of life
In that new stuccoed third house by the bridge,
80 Fresh-painted, rather smart than otherwise!
The whole street might o'erlook him as he sat,
Leg crossing leg, on foot on the dog's back,
Playing a decent cribbage with his maid

---

[1] printed on one sheet.

[2] See *King Lear* 5.3.17.

[3] sting.

[4] paintings by Titian, the Venetian artist (c. 1485–1577).

(Jacynth, you're sure her name was) o'er the cheese
85 And fruit, three red halves of starved winter-pears,
Or treat of radishes in April. Nine,
Ten, struck the church clock, straight to bed went
    he.

My father, like the man of sense he was,
Would point him out to me a dozen times;
90 "'St—'St," he'd whisper, "the Corregidor!"[1]
I had been used to think that personage
Was one with lacquered breeches, lustrous belt,
And feathers like a forest in his hat,
Who blew a trumpet and proclaimed the news,
95 Announced the bull-fights, gave each church its
    turn,
And memorized[2] the miracle in vogue!
He had a great observance from us boys;
We were in error; that was not the man.

I'd like now, yet had haply been afraid,
100 To have just looked, when this man came to die,
And seen who lined the clean gay garret-sides
And stood about the neat low truckle-bed,
With the heavenly manner of relieving guard.
Here had been, mark, the general-in-chief,
105 Through a whole campaign of the world's life and
    death,
Doing the King's work all the dim day long,
In his old coat and up to knees in mud,
Smoked like a herring, dining on a crust,—
And, now the day was won, relieved at once!
110 No further show or need for that old coat,
You are sure, for one thing! Bless us, all the while
How sprucely we are dressed out, you and I!
A second, and the angles alter that.
Well, I could never write a verse,—could you?
115 Let's to the Prado[3] and make the most of time.
    —1855

---

[1] Chief Magistrate.

[2] memorialized.

[3] promenade.

The Last Ride Together [4]

I

I said—Then, dearest, since 'tis so,
Since now at length my fate I know,
Since nothing all my love avails,
Since all, my life seemed meant for, fails,
5   Since this was written and needs must be—
My whole heart rises up to bless
Your name in pride and thankfulness!
Take back the hope you gave,—I claim
Only a memory of the same,
10 —And this beside, if you will not blame,
    Your leave for one more last ride with me.

II

My mistress bent that brow of hers;
Those deep dark eyes where pride demurs
When pity would be softening through,
15 Fixed me a breathing—while or two
    With life or death in the balance: right!
The blood replenished me again;
My last thought was at least not vain:
I and my mistress, side by side
20 Shall be together, breathe and ride,
So, one day more am I deified.
    Who knows but the world may end tonight?

III

Hush! if you saw some western cloud
All billowy-bosomed, over-bowed
25 By many benedictions—sun's
And moon's and evening-star's at once—
    And so, you, looking and loving best,
Conscious grew, your passion drew
Cloud, sunset, moonrise, star-shine too,
30 Down on you, near and yet more near,
Till flesh must fade for heaven was here!—

---

[4] The poem is one of Browning's most admired lyrics.

Thus leant she and lingered—joy and fear!
Thus lay she a moment on my breast.

IV

Then we began to ride. My soul
35 Smoothed itself out, a long-cramped scroll
Freshening and fluttering in the wind.
Fast hopes already lay behind.
　　What need to strive with a life awry?
Had I said that, had I done this,
40 So might I gain, so might I miss.
Might she have loved me? just as well
She might have hated, who can tell!
Where had I been now if the worst befell?
　　And here we are riding, she and I.

V

45 Fail I alone, in words and deeds?
Why, all men strive and who succeeds?
We rode; it seemed my spirit flew,
Saw other regions, cities new,
　　As the world rushed by on either side.
50 I thought,—All labour, yet no less
Bear up beneath their unsuccess.
Look at the end of work, contrast
The petty done, the undone vast,
This present of theirs with the hopeful past!
55 　　I hoped she would love me; here we ride.

VI

What hand and brain went ever paired?
What heart alike conceived and dared?
What act proved all its thought had been?
What will but felt the fleshly screen?
60 　　We ride and I see her bosom heave.
There's many a crown for who can reach.
Ten lines, a statesman's life in each!
The flag stuck on a heap of bones,
A soldier's doing! what atones?

65 They scratch his name on the Abbey-stones.[1]
　　My riding is better, by their leave.

VII

What does it all mean, poet? Well,
Your brains beat into rhythm, you tell
What we felt only; you expressed
70 You hold things beautiful the best,
　　And pace them in rhyme so, side by side.
'Tis something, nay 'tis much: but then,
Have you yourself what's best for men?
Are you—poor, sick, old ere your time—
75 Nearer one whit your own sublime
Than we who never have turned a rhyme?
　　Sing, riding's a joy! For me, I ride.

VIII

And you, great sculptor—so, you gave
A score of years to Art, her slave,
80 And that's your Venus, whence we turn
To yonder girl that fords the burn!
　　You acquiesce, and shall I repine?
What, man of music, you grown grey
With notes and nothing else to say,
85 Is this your sole praise from a friend,
"Greatly his opera's strains intend,
But in music we know how fashions end!"
　　I gave my youth; but we ride, in fine.

IX

Who knows what's fit for us? Had fate
90 Proposed bliss here should sublimate
My being—had I signed the bond—
Still one must lead some life beyond,
　　Have a bliss to die with, dim-descried.
This foot once planted on the goal,
95 This glory-garland round my soul,
Could I descry such? Try and test!
　　I sink back shuddering from the quest.

---

[1] They honour him with burial in Westminster Abbey.

Earth being so good, would heaven seem best?
  Now, heaven and she are beyond this ride.

x

100 And yet—she has not spoke so long!
What if heaven be that, fair and strong
At life's best, with our eyes upturned
Whither life's flower is first discerned,
  We, fixed so, ever should so abide?
105 What if we still ride on, we two
With life for ever old yet new,
Changed not in kind but in degree,
The instant made eternity,—
And heaven just prove that I and she
110   Ride, ride together, for ever ride?
  —1855

Bishop Blougram's Apology [1]

No more wine? then we'll push back chairs and talk.
A final glass for me, though: cool, i' faith!
We ought to have our Abbey[2] back, you see.

It's different, preaching in basilicas,
5 And doing duty in some masterpiece
Like this of brother Pugin's,[3] bless his heart!
I doubt if they're half baked, those chalk rosettes,
Ciphers and stucco-twiddlings everywhere;
It's just like breathing in a lime-kiln: eh?
10 These hot long ceremonies of our church
Cost us a little—oh, they pay the price,
You take me—amply pay it! Now, we'll talk.

So, you despise me, Mr Gigadibs.
No deprecation,—nay, I beg you, sir!
15 Beside 'tis our engagement: don't you know,
I promised, if you'd watch a dinner out,
We'd see truth dawn together?—truth that peeps
Over the glasses' edge when dinner's done,
And body gets its sop and holds its noise
20 And leaves soul free a little. Now's the time:
Truth's break of day! You do despise me then.
And if I say, "despise me,"—never fear!
I know you do not in a certain sense—
Not in my arm-chair, for example: here,
25 I well imagine you respect my place
(*Status, entourage*, worldly circumstance)
Quite to its value—very much indeed:
—Are up to the protesting eyes of you
In pride at being seated here for once—
30 You'll turn it to such capital account!
When somebody, through years and years to come,
Hints of the bishop,—names me—that's enough:
"Blougram? I knew him"—(into it you slide)
"Dined with him once, a Corpus Christi Day,[4]
35 All alone, we two; he's a clever man:
And after dinner,—why, the wine you know,—
Oh, there was wine, and good!—what with the wine...
'Faith, we began upon all sorts of talk!
He's no bad fellow, Blougram; he had seen
40 Something of mine he relished, some review:

[1] According to Browning, Cardinal Wiseman (1801–65) served as a model for Blougram. Wiseman became Roman Catholic Archbishop of Westminster and head of the Roman Catholic Church in England in 1850; the appointment created much controversy. Elements of John Henry Newman also went into Browning's fictional Bishop. Unlike many of Browning's poems, this poem is firmly set in its contemporary time and place by a wealth of topical allusion. The names of protagonist and antagonist are suggestive. "Blougram" may refer to Lord Brougham (1778–1868), a leading nineteenth-century figure who might also have contributed to Browning's portrait. Like the Bishop in the poem, Brougham was a skilled orator and debater, as well as being arrogant and eccentric. The heavy, closed and normally four-wheeled carriage is named after him, while a "gig" is a light, open, two-wheeled carriage.

The word "Apology" in the title is probably deliberately ambiguous, meaning both a "statement of regret for error" and "justification." Among the many interpretations of the poem, the two poles are represented by one which sees the Bishop as a vulgar, fashionable priest justifying his own cowardice, and another, more widely accepted view, which presents the Bishop as an extremely clever rhetorician whose argument in the poem is dictated by the vulgar nature of his petty opponent.

[2] Before being taken over by Henry VIII, Westminster Abbey was Catholic.

[3] A.W.N. Pugin (1812–52), a convert to Catholicism and an architect.

[4] the Thursday after Trinity Sunday, commemorating the celebration of the Eucharist.

He's quite above their humbug in his heart,
Half-said as much, indeed—the thing's his trade.
I warrant, Blougram's sceptical at times:
How otherwise? I liked him, I confess!"
45 *Che che,*[1] my dear sir, as we say at Rome,
Don't you protest now! It's fair give and take;
You have had your turn and spoken your home-
    truths:
The hand's mine now, and here you follow suit.

Thus much conceded, still the first fact stays—
50 You do despise me; your ideal of life
Is not the bishop's: you would not be I.
You would like better to be Goethe, now,
Or Buonaparte, or, bless me, lower still,
Count D'Orsay,[2]—so you did what you preferred,
55 Spoke as you thought, and, as you cannot help,
Believed or disbelieved, no matter what,
So long as on that point, whate'er it was,
You loosed your mind, were whole and sole yourself.
—That, my ideal never can include,
60 Upon that element of truth and worth
Never be based! for say they make me Pope—
(They can't—suppose it for our argument!)
Why, there I'm at my tether's end, I've reached
My height, and not a height which pleases you:
65 An unbelieving Pope won't do, you say.
It's like those eerie stories nurses tell,
Of how some actor on a stage played Death,
With pasteboard crown, sham orb and tinselled dart,
And called himself the monarch of the world;
70 Then, going in the tire-room[3] afterward,
Because the play was done, to shift himself,
Got touched upon the sleeve familiarly,
The moment he had shut the closet door,
By Death himself. Thus God might touch a Pope
75 At unawares, ask what his baubles mean,

And whose part he presumed to play just now.
Best be yourself, imperial, plain and true!

So, drawing comfortable breath again,
You weigh and find, whatever more or less
80 I boast of my ideal realized
Is nothing in the balance when opposed
To your ideal, your grand simple life,
Of which you will not realize one jot.
I am much, you are nothing; you would be all,
85 I would be merely much: you beat me there.

No, friend, you do not beat me: hearken why!
The common problem, yours, mine, every one's,
Is—not to fancy what were fair in life
Provided it could be,—but, finding first
90 What may be, then find how to make it fair
Up to our means: a very different thing!
No abstract intellectual plan of life
Quite irrespective of life's plainest laws,
But one, a man, who is man and nothing more,
95 May lead within a world which (by your leave)
Is Rome or London, not Fool's-paradise.
Embellish Rome, idealize away,
Make paradise of London if you can,
You're welcome, nay, you're wise.

A simile!
100 We mortals cross the ocean of this world
Each in his average cabin of a life;
The best's not big, the worst yields elbow-room.
Now for our six months' voyage—how prepare?
You come on shipboard with a landsman's list
105 Of things he calls convenient: so they are!
An India screen is pretty furniture,
A piano-forte is a fine resource,
All Balzac's novels occupy one shelf,
The new edition fifty volumes long;
110 And little Greek books, with the funny type

---

[1] "come, come."

[2] Count D'Orsay (1801–52), famous Victorian dandy.

[3] dressing room.

They get up well at Leipsic,[1] fill the next:
Go on! slabbed marble, what a bath it makes!
And Parma's pride, the Jerome,[2] let us add!
'Twere pleasant could Correggio's[3] fleeting glow
115 Hang full in face of one where'er one roams,
Since he more than the others brings with him
Italy's self,—the marvellous Modenese!—
Yet was not on your list before, perhaps.
—Alas, friend, here's the agent…is't the name?
120 The captain, or whoever's master here—
You see him screw his face up; what's his cry
Ere you set foot on shipboard? "Six feet square!"
If you won't understand what six feet mean,
Computer and purchase stores accordingly—
125 And if, in pique because he overhauls[4]
Your Jerome, piano, bath, you come on board
Bare—why, you cut a figure at the first
While sympathetic landsmen see you off;
Not afterward, when long ere half seas over,
130 You peep up from your utterly naked boards
Into some snug and well-appointed berth,
Like mine for instance (try the cooler jug—
Put back the other, but don't jog the ice!)
And mortified you mutter "Well and good;
135 He sits enjoying his sea-furniture;
'Tis stout and proper, and there's store of it:
Though I've the better notion, all agree,
Of fitting rooms up. Hang the carpenter,
Neat ship-shape fixings and contrivances—
140 I would have brought my Jerome, frame and all!"
And meantime you bring nothing: never mind—
You've proved your artist-nature: what you don't
You might bring, so despise me, as I say.

Now come, let's backward to the starting-place.
145 See my way: we're two college friends, suppose.

Prepare together for our voyage, then;
Each note and check the other in his work,—
Here's mine, a bishop's outfit; criticize!
What's wrong? why won't you be a bishop too?

150 Why first, you don't believe, you don't and can't,
(Not statedly, that is, and fixedly
And absolutely and exclusively)
In any revelation called divine.
No dogmas nail your faith; and what remains
155 But say so, like the honest man you are?
First, therefore, overhaul theology!
Nay, I too, not a fool, you please to think,
Must find believing every whit as hard:
And if I do not frankly say as much,
160 The ugly consequence is clear enough.

Now wait, my friend: well, I do not believe—
If you'll accept no faith that is not fixed,
Absolute and exclusive, as you say.
You're wrong,—I mean to prove it in due time.
165 Meanwhile, I know where difficulties lie
I could not, cannot solve, nor ever shall,
So give up hope accordingly to solve—
(To you, and over the wine). Our dogmas then
With both of us, though in unlike degree,
170 Missing full credence—overboard with them!
I mean to meet you on your own premise:
Good, there go mine in company with yours!

And now what are we? unbelievers both,
Calm and complete, determinately fixed
175 Today, tomorrow and for ever, pray?
You'll guarantee me that? Not so, I think!
In no wise! all we've gained is, that belief,
As unbelief before, shakes us by fits,
Confounds us like its predecessor. Where's
180 The gain? how can we guard our unbelief,
Make it bear fruit to us?—the problem here.
Just when we are safest, there's a sunset-touch,
A fancy from a flower-bell, some one's death,

---

[1] a reference to the Teubner series of classical works which began to appear in 1849.

[2] The picture of St. Jerome is in the Ducal Academy in Parma.

[3] the Italian painter (c. 1489–1534), who studied in Modena (l. 117).

[4] throws overboard.

A chorus-ending from Euripides,—[1]
185 And that's enough for fifty hopes and fears
As old and new at once as nature's self,
To rap and knock and enter in our soul,
Take hands and dance there, a fantastic ring,
Round the ancient idol, on his base again,—
190 The grand Perhaps![2] We look on helplessly.
There the old misgivings, crooked questions are—
This good God,—what he could do, if he would,
Would, if he could—then must have done long
    since:
If so, when, where and how? some way must be,—
195 Once feel about, and soon or late you hit
Some sense, in which it might be, after all.
Why not, "The Way, the Truth, the Life?"

                —That way
Over the mountain, which who stands upon
Is apt to doubt if it be meant for a road;
200 While, if he views it from the waste itself,
Up goes the line there, plain from base to brow,
Not vague, mistakable! what's a break or two
Seen from the unbroken desert either side?
And then (to bring in fresh philosophy)
205 What if the breaks themselves should prove at last
The most consummate of contrivances
To train a man's eye, teach him what is faith?
And so we stumble at truth's very test!
All we have gained then by our unbelief
210 Is a life of doubt diversified by faith,
For one of faith diversified by doubt:
We called the chess-board white,—we call it black.

    "Well," you rejoin, "the end's no worse, at least;
We've reason for both colours on the board:
215 Why not confess then, where I drop the faith
And you the doubt, that I'm as right as you?"

Because, friend, in the next place, this being so,
And both things even,—faith and unbelief
Left to a man's choice,—we'll proceed a step,
220 Returning to our image, which I like.

    A man's choice, yes—but a cabin-passenger's—
The man made for the special life o' the world—
Do you forget him? I remember though!
Consult our ship's conditions and you find
225 One and but one choice suitable to all;
The choice, that you unluckily prefer,
Turning things topsy-turvy—they or it
Going to the ground. Belief or unbelief
Bears upon life, determines its whole course,
230 Begins at its beginning. See the world
Such as it is,—you made it not, nor I;
I mean to take it as it is,—and you,
Not so you'll take it,—though you get naught else.
I know the special kind of life I like,
235 What suits the most my idiosyncrasy,
Brings out the best of me and bears me fruit
In power, peace, pleasantness and length of days.
I find that positive belief does this
For me, and unbelief, no whit of this.
240 —For you, it does, however?—that, we'll try!
'Tis clear, I cannot lead my life, at least,
Induce the world to let me peaceably,
Without declaring at the outset, "Friends,
I absolutely and peremptorily
245 Believe!"—I say, faith is my waking life:
One sleeps, indeed, and dreams at intervals,
We know, but waking's the main point with us
And my provision's for life's waking part.
Accordingly, I use heart, head and hand
250 All day, I build, scheme, study, and make friends;
And when night overtakes me, down I lie,
Sleep, dream a little, and get done with it,
The sooner the better, to begin afresh.
What's midnight doubt before the dayspring's faith?
255 You, the philosopher, that disbelieve,
That recognize the night, give dreams their weight—

---

[1] Browning's favourite Greek dramatist.

[2] "I go to seek a grand perhaps," attributed to Rabelais on his death-bed.

To be consistent you should keep your bed,
Abstain from healthy acts that prove you man,
For fear you drowse perhaps at unawares!
260 And certainly at night you'll sleep and dream,
Live through the day and bustle as you please.
And so you live to sleep as I to wake,
To unbelieve as I to still believe?
Well, and the common sense o' the world calls you
265 Bed-ridden,—and its good things come to me.
Its estimation, which is half the fight,
That's the first-cabin comfort I secure:
The next...but you perceive with half an eye!
Come, come, it's best believing, if we may;
270 You can't but own that!

                    Next, concede again,
If once we choose belief, on all accounts
We can't be too decisive in our faith,
Conclusive and exclusive in its terms,
To suit the world which gives us the good things.
275 In every man's career are certain points
Whereon he dares not be indifferent;
The world detects him clearly, if he dare,
As baffled at the game, and losing life.
He may care little or he may care much
280 For riches, honour, pleasure, work, repose,
Since various theories of life and life's
Success are extant which might easily
Comport[1] with either estimate of these;
And whoso chooses wealth or poverty,
285 Labour or quiet, is not judged a fool
Because his fellow would choose otherwise:
We let him choose upon his own account
So long as he's consistent with his choice.
But certain points, left wholly to himself,
290 When once a man has arbitrated on,
We say he must succeed there or go hang.
Thus, he should wed the woman he loves most
Or needs most, whatsoe'er the love or need—

For he can't wed twice. Then, he must avouch,
295 Or follow, at the least, sufficiently,
The form of faith his conscience holds the best,
Whate'er the process of conviction was:
For nothing can compensate his mistake
On such a point, the man himself being judge:
300 He cannot wed twice, nor twice lose his soul.

      Well now, there's one great form of Christian
        faith
I happened to be born in—which to teach
Was given me as I grew up, on all hands,
As best and readiest means of living by;
305 The same on examination being proved
The most pronounced moreover, fixed, precise
And absolute form of faith in the whole world—
Accordingly, most potent of all forms
For working on the world. Observe, my friend!
310 Such as you know me, I am free to say,
In these hard latter days which hamper one,
Myself—by no immoderate exercise
Of intellect and learning, but the tact
To let external forces work for me,
315 —Bid the street's stones be bread and they are bread;
Bid Peter's creed, or rather, Hildebrand's,[2]
Exalt me o'er my fellows in the world
And make my life an ease and joy and pride;
It does so,—which for me's a great point gained,
320 Who have a soul and body that exact
A comfortable care in many ways.
There's power in me and will to dominate
Which I must exercise, they hurt me else:
In many ways I need mankind's respect,
325 Obedience, and the love that's born of fear:
While at the same time, there's a taste I have,
A toy of soul, a titillating thing,
Refuses to digest these dainties crude.
The naked life is gross till clothed upon:
330 I must take what men offer, with a grace

---

[1] accord.

[2] St. Peter was the first Pope; Hildebrand (Gregory VII, Pope 1073–85) fought for papal temporal power.

As though I would not, could I help it, take!
An uniform I wear though over-rich—
Something imposed on me, no choice of mine;
No fancy-dress worn for pure fancy's sake
335 And despicable therefore! now folk kneel
And kiss my hand—of course the Church's hand.
Thus I am made, thus life is best for me,
And thus that it should be I have procured;
And thus it could not be another way,
340 I venture to imagine.

You'll reply,
So far my choice, no doubt, is a success;
But were I made of better elements,
With nobler instincts, purer tastes, like you,
I hardly would account the thing success
345 Though it did all for me I say.

But, friend,
We speak of what is; not of what might be,
And how 'twere better if 'twere otherwise.
I am the man you see here plain enough:
Grant I'm a beast, why, beasts must lead beasts'
lives!
350 Suppose I own at once to tail and claws;
The tailless man exceeds me: but being tailed
I'll lash out lion fashion, and leave apes
To dock their stump and dress their haunches up.
My business is not to remake myself,
355 But make the absolute best of what God made.
Or—our first simile—though you prove me doomed
To a viler berth still, to the steerage-hole,
The sheep-pen or the pig-sty, I should strive
To make what use of each were possible;
360 And as this cabin gets upholstery,
That hutch should rustle with sufficient straw.

But, friend, I don't acknowledge quite so fast
I fail of all your manhood's lofty tastes
Enumerated so complacently,
365 On the mere ground that you forsooth can find

In this particular life I choose to lead
No fit provision for them. Can you not?
Say you, my fault is I address myself
To grosser estimators than should judge?
370 And that's no way of holding up the soul,
Which, nobler, needs men's praise perhaps, yet
knows
One wise man's verdict outweighs all the fools'—
Would like the two, but, forced to choose, takes
that.
I pine among my million imbeciles
375 (You think) aware some dozen men of sense
Eye me and know me, whether I believe
In the last winking Virgin,[1] as I vow,
And am a fool, or disbelieve in her
And am a knave,—approve in neither case,
380 Withhold their voices though I look their way:
Like Verdi[2] when, at his worst opera's end
(The thing they gave at Florence,—what's its name?)
While the mad houseful's plaudits near out-bang
His orchestra of salt-box, tongs and bones,
385 He looks through all the roaring and the wreaths
Where sits Rossini[3] patient in his stall.

Nay, friend, I meet you with an answer here—
That even your prime men[4] who appraise their kind
Are men still, catch a wheel within a wheel,
390 See more in a truth than the truth's simple self,
Confuse themselves. You see lads walk the street
Sixty the minute; what's to note in that?
You see one lad o'erstride a chimney-stack;
Him you must watch—he's sure to fall, yet stands!
395 Our interest's on the dangerous edge of things.
The honest thief, the tender murderer,

---

[1] Newman defended the belief that the Virgin's eyes move in some pictures.

[2] probably an allusion to the *Macbeth* of Verdi (1813–1901), first produced at Florence in 1847.

[3] The composer (1792–1868) was in Florence in 1847.

[4] journalists.

The superstitious atheist, demirep[1]
That loves and saves her soul in new French books—
We watch while these in equilibrium keep
400 The giddy line midway: one step aside,
They're classed and done with. I, then, keep the line
Before your sages,—just the men to shrink
From the gross weights, coarse scales and labels
    broad
You offer their refinement. Fool or knave?
405 Why needs a bishop be a fool or knave
When there's a thousand diamond weights between?
So, I enlist them. Your picked twelve, you'll find,
Profess themselves indignant, scandalized
At thus being held unable to explain
410 How a superior man who disbelieves
May not believe as well: that's Schelling's[2] way!
It's through my coming in the tail of time,
Nicking the minute with a happy tact.
Had I been born three hundred years ago
415 They'd say, "What's strange? Blougram of course
    believes";
And, seventy years since, "disbelieves of course."
But now, "He may believe; and yet, and yet
How can he?" All eyes turn with interest.
Whereas, step off the line on either side—
420 You, for example, clever to a fault,
The rough and ready man who write apace,
Read somewhat seldomer, think perhaps even less—
You disbelieve! Who wonders and who cares?
Lord So-and-so—his coat bedropped with wax,
425 All Peter's chains[3] about his waist, his back
Brave[4] with the needlework of Noodledom—[5]
Believes! Again, who wonders and who cares?
But I, the man of sense and learning too,

The able to think yet act, the this, the that,
430 I, to believe at this late time of day!
Enough; you see, I need not fear contempt.

    —Except it's yours! Admire me as these may,
You don't. But whom at least do you admire?
Present your own perfection, your ideal,
435 Your pattern man for a minute—oh, make haste,
Is it Napoleon you would have us grow?
Concede the means; allow his head and hand,
(A large concession, clever as you are)
Good! In our common primal element
440 Of unbelief (we can't believe, you know—
We're still at that admission, recollect!)
Where do you find—apart from, towering o'er
The secondary temporary aims
Which satisfy the gross taste you despise—
445 Where do you find his star?—his crazy trust
God knows through what or in what? it's alive
And shines and leads him, and that's all we want.
Have we aught in our sober night shall point
Such ends as his were, and direct the means
450 Of working out our purpose straight as his,
Nor bring a moment's trouble on success
With after-care to justify the same?
—Be a Napoleon, and yet disbelieve—
Why, the man's mad, friend, take his light away!
455 What's the vague good o' the world, for which you
    dare
With comfort to yourself blow millions up?
We neither of us see it! we do see
The blown-up millions—spatter of their brains
And writhing of their bowels and so forth,
460 In that bewildering entanglement
Of horrible eventualities
Past calculation to the end of time!
Can I mistake for some clear word of God
(Which were my ample warrant for it all)
465 His puff of hazy instinct, idle talk,

---

[1] woman of doubtful reputation.

[2] the German Idealist philosopher (1775–1845), who stressed the ultimate compatibility of apparently incompatible ideas.

[3] St. Peter's chains were miraculously removed by an angel: Acts 12:7.

[4] splendid.

[5] foolish women.

"The State, that's I,"[1] quack-nonsense about crowns,
And (when one beats the man to his last hold)
A vague idea of setting things to rights,
Policing people efficaciously,
470 More to their profit, more of all to his own;
The whole to end that dismallest of ends
By an Austrian marriage,[2] cant to us the Church,
And resurrection of the old *régime*?
Would I, who hope to live a dozen years,
475 Fight Austerlitz[3] for reasons such and such?
No: for, concede me but the merest chance
Doubt may be wrong—there's judgement, life to
    come!
With just that chance, I dare not. Doubt proves
    right?
This present life is all?—you offer me
480 Its dozen noisy years, without a chance
That wedding an archduchess, wearing lace,
And getting called by divers new-coined names,
Will drive off ugly thoughts and let me dine,
Sleep, read and chat in quiet as I like!
485 Therefore I will not.

                    Take another case;
Fit up the cabin yet another way.
What say you to the poets? shall we write
Hamlet, Othello—make the world our own,
Without a risk to run of either sort?
490 I can't—to put the strongest reason first.
"But try," you urge, "the trying shall suffice;
The aim, if reached or not, makes great the life:
Try to be Shakespeare, leave the rest to fate!"
Spare my self-knowledge—there's no fooling me!
495 If I prefer remaining my poor self,
I say so not in self-dispraise but praise.
If I'm a Shakespeare, let the well alone;
Why should I try to be what now I am?

If I'm no Shakespeare, as too probable,—
500 His power and consciousness and self-delight
And all we want in common, shall I find—
Trying for ever? while on points of taste
Wherewith, to speak it humbly, he and I
Are dowered alike—I'll ask you, I or he,
505 Which in our two lives realizes most?
Much, he imagined—somewhat, I possess.
He had the imagination; stick to that!
Let him say, "In the face of my soul's works
Your world is worthless and I touch it not
510 Lest I should wrong them"—I'll withdraw my plea.
But does he say so? look upon his life!
Himself, who only can, gives judgement there.
He leaves his towers and gorgeous palaces
To build the trimmest house in Stratford town;
515 Saves money, spends it, owns the worth of things,
Giulio Romano's[4] pictures, Dowland's[5] lute;
Enjoys a show, respects the puppets, too,
And none more, had he seen its entry once,
Than "Pandulph, of fair Milan cardinal."[6]
520 Why then should I who play that personage,
The very Pandulph Shakespeare's fancy made,
Be told that had the poet chanced to start
From where I stand now (some degree like mine
Being just the goal he ran his race to reach)
525 He would have run the whole race back, forsooth,
And left being Pandulph, to begin write plays?
Ah, the earth's best can be but the earth's best!
Did Shakespeare live, he could but sit at home
And get himself in dreams the Vatican,
530 Greek busts, Venetian paintings, Roman walls,
And English books, none equal to his own,
Which I read, bound in gold (he never did).

---

1 "L'État, c'est moi" was said by Louis XIV, not Napoleon.

2 Napoleon married Marie Louise of Austria in 1810.

3 Napoleon's victory of 1805 over the Russians and Austrians.

4 Italian painter (c. 1492–1546).

5 English lutanist and composer (1536–1626).

6 a quotation from Shakespeare's Pandulph, powerful spokesman for expediency, in *King John* 3.1.138.

—Terni's[1] fall, Naples' bay and Gothard's top—[2]
Eh, friend? I could not fancy one of these;
535 But, as I pour this claret, there they are:
I've gained them—crossed Saint Gothard last July
With ten mules to the carriage and a bed
Slung inside; is my hap[3] the worse for that?
We want the same things, Shakespeare and myself,
540 And what I want, I have: he, gifted more,
Could fancy he too had them when he liked,
But not so thoroughly that, if fate allowed,
He would not have them also in my sense.
We play one game; I send the ball aloft
545 No less adroitly that of fifty strokes
Scarce five go o'er the wall so wide and high
Which sends them back to me: I wish and get.
He struck balls higher and with better skill,
But at a poor fence level with his head,
550 And hit—his Stratford house, a coat of arms,
Successful dealings in his grain and wool,—
While I receive heaven's incense in my nose
And style myself the cousin of Queen Bess.[4]
Ask him, if this life's all, who wins the game?

555   Believe—and our whole argument breaks up.
Enthusiasm's the best thing, I repeat;
Only, we can't command it; fire and life
Are all, dead matter's nothing, we agree:
And be it a mad dream or God's very breath,
560 The fact's the same,—belief's fire, once in us,
Makes of all else mere stuff to show itself:
We penetrate our life with such a glow
As fire lends wood and iron—this turns steel,
That burns to ash—all's one, fire proves its power
565 For good or ill, since men call flare success.
But paint a fire, it will not therefore burn.
Light one in me, I'll find it food enough!

Why, to be Luther—that's a life to lead,
Incomparably better than my own.
570 He comes, reclaims God's earth for God, he says,
Sets up God's rule again by simple means,
Re-opens a shut book,[5] and all is done.
He flared out in the flaring of mankind;
Such Luther's luck was: how shall such be mine?
575 If he succeeded, nothing's left to do:
And if he did not altogether—well,
Strauss[6] is the next advance. All Strauss should be
I might be also. But to what result?
He looks upon no future: Luther did.
580 What can I gain on the denying side?
Ice makes no conflagration. State the facts,
Read the text right, emancipate the world—
The emancipated world enjoys itself
With scarce a thank-you: Blougram told it first
585 It could not owe a farthing,—not to him
More than Saint Paul! 'twould press its pay, you
think?
Then add there's still that plaguy hundredth chance
Strauss may be wrong. And so risk is run—
For what gain? not for Luther's, who secured
590 A real heaven in his heart throughout his life,
Supposing death a little altered things.

     "Ay, but since really you lack faith," you cry,
"You run the same risk really on all sides,
In cool indifference as bold unbelief.
595 As well be Strauss as swing 'twixt Paul and him.
It's not worth having, such imperfect faith,
No more available to do faith's work
Than unbelief like mine. Whole faith, or none!"

     Softly, my friend! I must dispute that point.
600 Once own the use of faith, I'll find you faith.
We're back on Christian ground. You call for faith:
I show you doubt, to prove that faith exists.

---

[1] a waterfall north of Rome.

[2] St. Gothard, the major pass between Switzerland and Italy.

[3] fate.

[4] close acquaintance of Queen Elizabeth I.

[5] has the Bible translated.

[6] David Friedrich Strauss (1808–74), the author of the *Life of Jesus* (1835), which undermined the literal translation of the Bible.

The more of doubt, the stronger faith, I say,
If faith o'ercomes doubt. How I know it does?
605 By life and man's free will, God gave for that!
To mould life as we choose it, shows our choice:
That's our one act, the previous work's his own.
You criticize the soil? it reared this tree—
This broad life and whatever fruit it bears!
610 What matter though I doubt at every pore,
Head-doubts, heart-doubts, doubts at any fingers'
ends,
Doubts in the trivial work of every day,
Doubts at the very bases of my soul
In the grand moments when she probes herself—
615 If finally I have a life to show,
The thing I did, brought out in evidence
Against the thing done to me underground
By hell and all its brood, for aught I know?
I say, whence sprang this? shows it faith or
doubt?
620 All's doubt in me; where's break of faith in this?
It is the idea, the feeling and the love,
God means mankind should strive for and show
forth
Whatever be the process to that end,—
And not historic knowledge, logic sound,
625 And metaphysical acumen, sure!
"What think ye of Christ," friend? when all's done
and said,
Like you this Christianity or not?
It may be false, but will you wish it true?
Has it your vote to be so if it can?
630 Trust you an instinct silenced long ago
That will break silence and enjoin you love
What mortified philosophy is hoarse,
And all in vain, with bidding you despise?
If you desire faith—then you've faith enough:
635 What else seeks God—nay, what else seek ourselves?
You form a notion of me, we'll suppose,
On hearsay; it's a favourable one:
"But still" (you add), "there was no such good man,
Because of contradiction in the facts.

640 One proves, for instance, he was born in Rome,
This Blougram; yet throughout the tales of him
I see he figures as an Englishman."
Well, the two things are reconcilable.
But would I rather you discovered that,
645 Subjoining—"Still, what matter though they be?
Blougram concerns me naught, born here or
there."

Pure faith indeed—you know not what you ask!
Naked belief in God the Omnipotent,
Omniscient, Omnipresent, sears too much
650 The sense of conscious creatures to be borne.
It were the seeing him, no flesh shall dare.
Some think, Creation's meant to show him forth:
I say it's meant to hide him all it can,
And that's what all the blessèd evil's for.
655 Its use in Time is to environ us,
Our breath, our drop of dew, with shield enough
Against that sight till we can bear its stress.
Under a vertical sun, the exposed brain
And lidless eye and disimprisoned heart
660 Less certainly would wither up at once
Than mind, confronted with the truth of him.
But time and earth case-harden us to live;
The feeblest sense is trusted most; the child
Feels God a moment, ichors[1] o'er the place,
665 Plays on and grows to be a man like us.
With me, faith means perpetual unbelief
Kept quiet like the snake 'neath Michael's foot[2]
Who stands calm just because he feels it writhe.
Or, if that's too ambitious,—here's my box—[3]
670 I need the excitation of a pinch
Threatening the torpor of the inside-nose
Nigh on the imminent sneeze that never comes.
"Leave it in peace" advise the simple folk:

---

[1] liquids issuing from wounds to help healing.

[2] The Archangel who threw Satan out of heaven is usually depicted stamping on the snake.

[3] snuff box.

Make it aware of peace by itching-fits,
675 Say I—let doubt occasion still more faith!

You'll say, once all believed, man, woman, child,
In that dear middle-age these noodles praise.
How you'd exult if I could put you back
Six hundred years, blot out cosmogony,
680 Geology, ethnology, what not,
(Greek endings, each the little passing-bell
That signifies some faith's about to die),
And set you square with Genesis again,—
When such a traveller told you his last news,
685 He saw the ark a-top of Ararat[1]
But did not climb there since 'twas getting dusk
And robber-bands infest the mountain's foot!
How should you feel, I ask, in such an age,
How act? As other people felt and did;
690 With soul more blank than this decanter's knob,
Believe—and yet lie, kill, rob, fornicate
Full in belief's face, like the beast you'd be!

No, when the fight begins within himself,
A man's worth something. God stoops o'er his head,
695 Satan looks up between his feet—both tug—
He's left, himself, i' the middle: the soul wakes
And grows. Prolong that battle through his life!
Never leave growing till the life to come!
Here, we've got callous to the Virgin's winks
700 That used to puzzle people wholesomely:
Men have outgrown the shame of being fools.
What are the laws of nature, not to bend
If the Church bid them?—brother Newman[2] asks.
Up with the Immaculate Conception,[3] then—
705 On to the rack with faith!—is my advice.
Will not that hurry us upon our knees,
Knocking our breasts, "It can't be—yet it shall!

Who am I, the worm, to argue with my Pope?
Low things confound the high things!" and so forth.
710 That's better than acquitting God with grace
As some folk do. He's tried—no case is proved,
Philosophy is lenient—he may go!

You'll say, the old system's not so obsolete
But men believe still: ay, but who and where?
715 King Bomba's[4] lazzaroni foster yet
The sacred flame, so Antonelli[5] writes;
But even of these, what ragamuffin saint
Believes God watches him continually,
As he believes in fire that it will burn,
720 Or rain that it will drench him? Break fire's law,
Sin against rain, although the penalty
Be just a singe or soaking? "No," he smiles;
"Those laws are laws that can enforce themselves."

The sum of all is—yes, my doubt is great,
725 My faith's still greater, then my faith's enough.
I have read much, thought much, experienced
        much,
Yet would die rather than avow my fear
The Naples' liquefaction[6] may be false,
When set to happen by the palace-clock
730 According to the clouds or dinner-time.
I hear you recommend, I might at least
Eliminate, decrassify[7] my faith
Since I adopt it; keeping what I must
And leaving what I can—such points as this.
735 I won't—that is, I can't throw one away.
Supposing there's no truth in what I hold
About the need of trial to man's faith,
Still, when you bid me purify the same,

---

[1] the mountain in Turkey where Noah's ark landed: Genesis 8:4.

[2] John Henry Newman, who had become a Roman Catholic in 1845, spoke strongly in favour of miracles.

[3] The Doctrine, proclaimed by the Pope in 1854, that the Virgin Mary was free from original sin when conceived.

---

[4] derisive nickname of Ferdinand II (1810–59), King of the Two Sicilies.

[5] Cardinal Antonelli, secretary to Pius IX.

[6] the belief that some of the crystallized blood of Saint Januarius, patron saint of Naples, liquefies regularly.

[7] purify.

To such a process I discern no end.
740 Clearing off one excrescence to see two,
There's ever a next in size, now grown as big,
That meets the knife: I cut and cut again!
First cut the Liquefaction, what comes last
But Fichte's clever cut[1] at God himself?
745 Experimentalize on sacred things!
I trust not hand nor eye nor heart nor brain
To stop betimes: they all get drunk alike.
The first step, I am master not to take.

You'd find the cutting-process to your taste
750 As much as leaving growths of lies unpruned,
Nor see more danger in it,—you retort.
Your taste's worth mine; but my taste proves more
        wise
When we consider that the steadfast hold
On the extreme end of the chain of faith
755 Gives all the advantage, makes the difference
With the rough purblind mass we seek to rule:
We are their lords, or they are free of us,
Just as we tighten or relax our hold.
So, other matters equal, we'll revert
760 To the first problem—which, if solved my way
And thrown into the balance, turns the scale—
How we may lead a comfortable life,
How suit our luggage to the cabin's size.

Of course you are remarking all this time
765 How narrowly and grossly I view life,
Respect the creature-comforts, care to rule
The masses, and regard complacently
"The cabin," in our old phrase. Well, I do.
I act for, talk for, live for this world now,
770 As this world prizes action, life and talk:
No prejudice to what next world may prove,
Whose new laws and requirements, my best pledge
To observe then, is that I observe these now,
Shall do hereafter what I do meanwhile.

775 Let us concede (gratuitously though)
Next life relieves the soul of body, yields
Pure spiritual enjoyment: well, my friend,
Why lose this life i' the meantime, since its use
May be to make the next life more intense?

780 Do you know, I have often had a dream
(Work it up in your next month's article)
Of man's poor spirit in its progress, still
Losing true life for ever and a day
Through ever trying to be and ever being—
785 In the evolution of successive spheres—
Before its actual sphere and place of life,
Halfway into the next, which having reached,
It shoots with corresponding foolery
Halfway into the next still, on and off!
790 As when a traveller, bound from North to South,
Scouts[2] fur in Russia: what's its use in France?
In France spurns flannel: where's its need in Spain?
In Spain drops cloth, too cumbrous for Algiers!
Linen goes next, and last the skin itself,
795 A superfluity at Timbuctoo.
When, through his journey, was the fool at ease?
I'm at ease now, friend; worldly in this world,
I take and like its way of life; I think
My brothers, who administer the means,
800 Live better for my comfort—that's good too;
And God, if he pronounce upon such life,
Approves my service, which is better still.
If he keep silence,—why, for you or me
Or that brute beast pulled-up in today's "Times,"
805 What odds is't, save to ourselves, what life we lead?

You meet me at this issue: you declare,—
All special-pleading done with—truth is truth,
And justifies itself by undreamed ways.
You don't fear but it's better, if we doubt,
810 To say so, act up to our truth perceived
However feebly. Do then,—act away!

---

[1] The German philosopher (1762–1814) thought God an idea created
by man.

[2] mocks at.

'Tis there I'm on the watch for you. How one acts
Is, both of us agree, our chief concern:
And how you'll act is what I fain would see
815 If, like the candid person you appear,
You dare to make the most of your life's scheme
As I of mine, live up to its full law
Since there's no higher law that counterchecks.
Put natural religion to the test
820 You've just demolished the revealed with—quick,
Down to the root of all that checks your will,
All prohibition to lie, kill and thieve,
Or even to be an atheistic priest!
Suppose a pricking to incontinence—
825 Philosophers deduce you chastity
Or shame, from just the fact that at the first
Whoso embraced a woman in the field,
Threw club down and forewent his brains beside,
So, stood a ready victim in the reach
830 Of any brother savage, club in hand;
Hence saw the use of going out of sight
In wood or cave to prosecute his loves:
I read this in a French book t'other day.
Does law so analysed coerce you much?
835 Oh, men spin clouds of fuzz where matters end,
But you who reach where the first thread begins,
You'll soon cut that!—which means you can, but
    won't,
Through certain instincts, blind, unreasoned-out,
You dare not set aside, you can't tell why,
840 But there they are, and so you let them rule.
Then, friend, you seem as much a slave as I,
A liar, conscious coward and hypocrite,
Without the good the slave expects to get,
In case he has a master after all!
845 You own your instincts? why, what else do I,
Who want, am made for, and must have a God
Ere I can be aught, do aught?—no mere name
Want, but the true thing with what proves its truth,
To wit, a relation from that thing to me,
850 Touching from head to foot—which touch I feel,

And with it take the rest, this life of ours!
I live my life here; yours you dare not live.

—Not as I state it, who (you please subjoin)
Disfigure such a life and call it names,
855 While, to your mind, remains another way
For simple men: knowledge and power have rights,
But ignorance and weakness have rights too.
There needs no crucial effort to find truth
If here or there or anywhere about:
860 We ought to turn each side, try hard and see,
And if we can't, be glad we've earned at least
The right, by one laborious proof the more,
To graze in peace earth's pleasant pasturage.
Men are not angels, neither are they brutes:
865 Something we may see, all we cannot see.
What need of lying? I say, I see all,
And swear to each detail the most minute
In what I think a Pan's face—you, mere cloud:
I swear I hear him speak and see him wink,
870 For fear, if once I drop the emphasis,
Mankind may doubt there's any cloud at all.
You take the simple life—ready to see,
Willing to see (for no cloud's worth a face)—
And leaving quiet what no strength can move,
875 And which, who bids you move? who has the right?
I bid you; but you are God's sheep, not mine:
"*Pastor est tui Dominus.*"[1] You find
In this the pleasant pasture of our life
Much you may eat without the least offence,
880 Much you don't eat because your maw objects,
Much you would eat but that your fellow-flock
Open great eyes at you and even butt,
And thereupon you like your mates so well
You cannot please yourself, offending them;
885 Though when they seem exorbitantly sheep,
You weigh your pleasure with their butts and bleats
And strike the balance. Sometimes certain fears
Restrain you, real checks since you find them so;

---

[1] "The Lord is your shepherd," from "The Lord is my shepherd": Psalm 23:1.

Sometimes you please yourself and nothing checks:
890 And thus you graze through life with not one lie,
And like it best.

But do you, in truth's name?
If so, you beat—which means you are not I—
Who needs must make earth mine and feed my fill
Not simply unbutted at, unbickered with,
895 But motioned to the velvet of the sward
By those obsequious wethers' very selves.
Look at me, sir; my age is double yours:
At yours, I knew beforehand, so enjoyed,
What now I should be—as, permit the word,
900 I pretty well imagine your whole range
And stretch of tether twenty years to come.
We both have minds and bodies much alike:
In truth's name, don't you want my bishopric,
My daily bread, my influence and my state?
905 You're young. I'm old; you must be old one day;
Will you find then, as I do hour by hour,
Women their lovers kneel to, who cut curls
From your fat lap-dog's ear to grace a brooch—
Dukes, who petition just to kiss your ring—
910 With much beside you know or may conceive?
Suppose we die tonight: well, here am I,
Such were my gains, life bore this fruit to me,
While writing all the same my articles
On music, poetry, the fictile[1] vase
915 Found at Albano,[2] chess, Anacreon's Greek.[3]
But you—the highest honour in your life,
The thing you'll crown yourself with, all your days,
Is—dining here and drinking this last glass
I pour you out in sign of amity
920 Before we part for ever. Of your power
And social influence, worldly worth in short,
Judge what's my estimation by the fact,
I do not condescend to enjoin, beseech,

Hint secrecy on one of all these words!
925 You're shrewd and know that should you publish
        one
The world would brand the lie—my enemies first,
Who'd sneer—"the bishop's an arch-hypocrite
And knave perhaps, but not so frank a fool."
Whereas I should not dare for both my ears
930 Breathe one such syllable, smile one such smile,
Before the chaplain who reflects myself—
My shade's so much more potent than your flesh.
What's your reward, self-abnegating friend?
Stood you confessed of those exceptional
935 And privileged great natures that dwarf mine—
A zealot with a mad ideal in reach,
A poet just about to print his ode,
A statesman with a scheme to stop this war,[4]
An artist whose religion is his art—
940 I should have nothing to object: such men
Carry the fire, all things grow warm to them,
Their drugget's[5] worth my purple, they beat me.
But you,—you're just as little those as I—
You, Gigadibs, who, thirty years of age,
945 Write stately for Blackwood's Magazine,[6]
Believe you see two points in Hamlet's soul
Unseized by the Germans yet[7]—which view you'll
        print—
Meantime the best you have to show being still
That lively lightsome article we took
950 Almost for the true Dickens,—what's its name?
"The Slum and Cellar, or Whitechapel[8] life
Limned after dark!" it made me laugh, I know,
And pleased a month, and brought you in ten
        pounds.
—Success I recognize and compliment,

---

[1] moulded.

[2] site of Roman ruins a few miles south-east of Rome.

[3] Greek lyric poet of the sixth century BC.

[4] The Crimean War began in March 1854.

[5] coarse material.

[6] an important and powerful magazine.

[7] German criticism of Shakespeare was dominant in the nineteenth century.

[8] district in eastern London.

955 And therefore give you, if you choose, three words
(The card and pencil-scratch is quite enough)
Which whether here, in Dublin or New York,
Will get you, prompt as at my eyebrow's wink,
Such terms as never you aspired to get
960 In all our own reviews and some not ours.
Go write your lively sketches! be the first
"Blougram, or The Eccentric Confidence"—
Or better simply say, "The Outward-bound."
Why, men as soon would throw it in my teeth
965 As copy and quote the infamy chalked broad
About me on the church-door opposite.
You will not wait for that experience though,
I fancy, howsoever you decide,
To discontinue—not detesting, not
970 Defaming, but at least—despising me!

———————

Over his wine so smiled and talked his hour
Sylvester Blougram, styled *in partibus*
Episcopus, nec non—(the deuce knows what
975 It's changed to by our novel hierarchy)
With Gigadibs the literary man,
Who played with spoons, explored his plate's design,
And ranged the olive-stones about its edge,
While the great bishop rolled him out a mind
980 Long crumpled, till creased consciousness lay
smooth.

980 For Blougram, he believed, say, half he spoke.
The other portion, as he shaped it thus
For argumentatory purposes,
He felt his foe was foolish to dispute.
Some arbitrary accidental thoughts
985 That crossed his mind, amusing because new,
He chose to represent as fixtures there,
Invariable convictions (such they seemed
Beside his interlocutor's loose cards
Flung daily down, and not the same way twice)
990 While certain hell-deep instincts, man's weak tongue
Is never bold to utter in their truth

Because styled hell-deep ('tis an old mistake
To place hell at the bottom of the earth)
He ignored these,—not having in readiness
995 Their nomenclature and philosophy:
He said true things, but called them by wrong names.
"On the whole," he thought, "I justify myself
On every point where cavillers like this
Oppugn my life: he tries one kind of fence,[1]
1000 I close, he's worsted, that's enough for him.
He's on the ground: if ground should break away
I take my stand on, there's a firmer yet
Beneath it, both of us may sink and reach.
His ground was over mine and broke the first:
1005 So, let him sit with me this many a year!"

He did not sit five minutes. Just a week
Sufficed his sudden healthy vehemence.
Something had struck him in the "Outward-bound"
Another way than Blougram's purpose was:
1010 And having bought, not cabin-furniture
But settler's-implements (enough for three)
And started for Australia—there, I hope,
By this time he has tested his first plough,
And studied his last chapter of Saint John.[2]
—1855

Andrea del Sarto [3]

(Called "The Faultless Painter")

But do not let us quarrel any more,
No, my Lucrezia; bear with me for once:
Sit down and all shall happen as you wish.

———————

[1] swordsmanship.

[2] a much debated line. One popular view is that Gigadibs has given up his shallow journalism and has travelled to Australia to start a new life and to study the gospels.

[3] Andrea d'Angelo di Francesca (1486–1531), called "del Sarto" because his father was a tailor, and "The Faultless Painter" because of his technique. As with "Fra Lippo Lippi," Browning's main source for the poem was Vasari's *Lives of the Artists*, which gives most of the facts and supports the general tenor of Browning's poem.

You turn your face, but does it bring your heart?
5 I'll work then for your friend's friend, never fear,
Treat his own subject after his own way,
Fix his own time, accept too his own price,
And shut the money into this small hand
When next it takes mine. Will it? tenderly?
10 Oh, I'll content him,—but tomorrow, Love!
I often am much wearier than you think,
This evening more than usual, and it seems
As if—forgive now—should you let me sit
Here by the window with your hand in mine
15 And look a half-hour forth on Fiesole,[1]
Both of one mind, as married people use,
Quietly, quietly the evening through,
I might get up tomorrow to my work
Cheerful and fresh as ever. Let us try.
20 Tomorrow, how you shall be glad for this!
Your soft hand is a woman of itself,
And mine the man's bared breast she curls inside.
Don't count the time lost, neither; you must serve
For each of the five pictures we require:
25 It saves a model. So! keep looking so—
My serpentining beauty, rounds on rounds!
—How could you ever prick those perfect ears,
Even to put the pearl there! oh, so sweet—
My face, my moon, my everybody's moon,
30 Which everybody looks on and calls his,
And, I suppose, is looked on by in turn,
While she looks—no one's: very dear, no less.
You smile? why, there's my picture ready made,
There's what we painters call our harmony!
35 A common greyness silvers everything,—
All in a twilight, you and I alike
—You, at the point of your first pride in me
(That's gone you know),—but I, at every point;
My youth, my hope, my art, being all toned down
40 To yonder sober pleasant Fiesole.
There's the bell clinking from the chapel-top;
That length of convent-wall across the way

Holds the trees safer, huddled more inside;
The last monk leaves the garden; days decrease,
45 And autumn grows, autumn in everything.
Eh? the whole seems to fall into a shape
As if I saw alike my work and self
And all that I was born to be and do,
A twilight-piece. Love, we are in God's hand.
50 How strange now, looks the life he makes us lead;
So free we seem, so fettered fast we are!
I feel he laid the fetter: let it lie!
This chamber for example—turn your head—
All that's behind us! You don't understand
55 Nor care to understand about my art,
But you can hear at least when people speak:
And that cartoon,[2] the second from the door
—It is the thing, Love! so such things should be—
Behold Madonna!—I am bold to say.
60 I can do with my pencil what I know,
What I see, what at bottom of my heart
I wish for, if I ever wish so deep—
Do easily, too—when I say, perfectly,
I do not boast, perhaps: yourself are judge,
65 Who listened to the Legate's talk last week,
And just as much they used to say in France.
At any rate 'tis easy, all of it!
No sketches first, no studies, that's long past:
I do what many dream of, all their lives,
70 —Dream? strive to do, and agonize to do,
And fail in doing. I could count twenty such
On twice your fingers, and not leave this town,
Who strive—you don't know how the others strive
To paint a little thing like that you smeared
75 Carelessly passing with your robes afloat,—
Yet do much less, so much less, Someone[3] says,
(I know his name, no matter)—so much less!
Well, less is more, Lucrezia: I am judged.
There burns a truer light of God in them,
80 In their vexed beating stuffed and stopped-up brain,

[1] the hill-town just north-east of Florence.

[2] sketch for a painting.

[3] Michelangelo.

Heart, or whate'er else, than goes on to prompt
This low-pulsed forthright craftsman's hand of mine.
Their works drop groundward, but themselves, I
   know,
Reach many a time a heaven that's shut to me,
85 Enter and take their place there sure enough,
Though they come back and cannot tell the world.
My works are nearer heaven, but I sit here.
The sudden blood of these men! at a word—
Praise them, it boils, or blame them, it boils too.
90 I, painting from myself and to myself,
Know what I do, am unmoved by men's blame
Or their praise either. Somebody remarks
Morello's¹ outline there is wrongly traced,
His hue mistaken; what of that? or else,
95 Rightly traced and well ordered; what of that?
Speak as they please, what does the mountain care?
Ah, but a man's reach should exceed his grasp,
Or what's a heaven for? All is silver-grey
Placid and perfect with my art: the worse!
100 I know both what I want and what might gain,
And yet how profitless to know, to sigh
"Had I been two, another and myself,
Our head would have o'erlooked the world!" No
   doubt.
Yonder's a work now, of that famous youth
105 The Urbinate² who died five years ago.
('Tis copied, George Vasari³ sent it me.)
Well, I can fancy how he did it all,
Pouring his soul, with kings and popes to see,
Reaching, that heaven might so replenish him,
110 Above and through his art—for it gives way;
That arm is wrongly put—and there again—
A fault to pardon in the drawing's lines,
Its body, so to speak: its soul is right,
He means right—that, a child may understand.

115 Still, what an arm! and I could alter it:
But all the play, the insight and the stretch—
Out of me, out of me! And wherefore out?
Had you enjoined them on me, given me soul,
We might have risen to Rafael, I and you!
120 Nay, Love, you did give all I asked, I think—
More than I merit, yes, by many times.
But had you—oh, with the same perfect brow,
And perfect eyes, and more than perfect mouth,
And the low voice my soul hears, as a bird
125 The fowler's pipe, and follows to the snare—
Had you, with these the same, but brought a mind!
Some women do so. Had the mouth there urged
"God and the glory! never care for gain.
The present by the future, what is that?
130 Live for fame, side by side with Agnolo!⁴
Rafael is waiting: up to God, all three!"
I might have done it for you. So it seems:
Perhaps not. All is as God over-rules.
Beside, incentives come from the soul's self;
135 The rest avail not. Why do I need you?
What wife had Rafael, or has Agnolo?
In this world, who can do a thing, will not;
And who would do it, cannot, I perceive:
Yet the will's somewhat—somewhat, too, the
   power—
140 And thus we half-men struggle. At the end,
God, I conclude, compensates, punishes.
'Tis safer for me, if the award be strict,
That I am something underrated here,
Poor this long while, despised, to speak the truth.
145 I dared not, do you know, leave home all day,
For fear of chancing on the Paris lords.
The best is when they pass and look aside;
But they speak sometimes; I must bear it all.
Well may they speak! That Francis, that first time,
150 And that long festal year at Fontainebleau!⁵

---

¹ mountain north of Florence.

² Raphael (1483–1520), born at Urbino.

³ Giorgio Vasari (1512–74), the main source for Browning's poem, was introduced to Andrea by Michelangelo.

---

⁴ Michelangelo.

⁵ the town south-east of Paris where Francis I built the royal palace. Tradition suggests that Andrea was given money by the King to buy paintings but instead used it to build a house for himself and his wife.

I surely then could sometimes leave the ground,
Put on the glory, Rafael's daily wear,
In that humane great monarch's golden look,—
One finger in his beard or twisted curl
155 Over his mouth's good mark that made the smile,
One arm about my shoulder, round my neck,
The jingle of his gold chain in my ear,
I painting proudly with his breath on me,
All his court round him, seeing with his eyes,
160 Such frank French eyes, and such a fire of souls
Profuse, my hand kept plying by those hearts,—
And, best of all, this, this, this face beyond,
This in the background, waiting on my work,
To crown the issue with a last reward!
165 A good time, was it not, my kingly days?
And had you not grown restless...but I know—
'Tis done and past; 'twas right, my instinct said;
Too live the life grew, golden and not grey,
And I'm the weak-eyed bat no sun should tempt
170 Out of the grange whose four walls make his world.
How could it end in any other way?
You called me, and I came home to your heart.
The triumph was—to reach and stay there; since
I reached it ere the triumph, what is lost?
175 Let my hands frame your face in your hair's gold,
You beautiful Lucrezia that are mine!
"Rafael did this, Andrea painted that;
The Roman's[1] is the better when you pray,
But still the other's Virgin was his wife—"
180 Men will excuse me. I am glad to judge
Both pictures in your presence; clearer grows
My better fortune, I resolve to think.
For, do you know, Lucrezia, as God lives,
Said one day Agnolo, his very self,
185 To Rafael...I have known it all these years...
(When the young man was flaming out his thoughts
Upon a palace-wall for Rome to see,
Too lifted up in heart because of it)
"Friend, there's a certain sorry little scrub

190 Goes up and down our Florence, none cares how,
Who, were he set to plan and execute
As you are, pricked on by your popes and kings,
Would bring the sweat into that brow of yours!"
To Rafael's!—And indeed the arm is wrong.
195 I hardly dare...yet, only you to see,
Give the chalk here—quick, thus the line should go!
Ay, but the soul! he's Rafael! rub it out!
Still, all I care for, if he spoke the truth,
(What he? why, who but Michel Agnolo?
200 Do you forget already words like those?)
If really there was such a chance, so lost,—
Is, whether you're—not grateful—but more pleased.
Well, let me think so. And you smile indeed!
This hour has been an hour! Another smile?
205 If you would sit thus by me every night
I should work better, do you comprehend?
I mean that I should earn more, give you more.
See, it is settled dusk now; there's a star;
Morello's gone, the watch-lights show the wall,
210 The cue-owls speak the name we call them by.
Come from the window, love,—come in, at last,
Inside the melancholy little house
We built to be so gay with. God is just.
King Francis may forgive me: oft at nights
215 When I look up from painting, eyes tired out,
The walls become illumined, brick from brick
Distinct, instead of mortar, fierce bright gold,
That gold of his I did cement them with!
Let us but love each other. Must you go?
220 That Cousin[2] here again? he waits outside?
Must see you—you, and not with me? Those loans?
More gaming debts to pay? you smiled for that?
Well, let smiles buy me! have you more to spend?
While hand and eye and something of a heart
225 Are left me, work's my ware, and what's it worth?
I'll pay my fancy. Only let me sit
The grey remainder of the evening out,
Idle, you call it, and muse perfectly

---

[1] Raphael worked in Rome for the last twelve years of his life.

[2] Lucrezia's lover.

How I could paint, were I but back in France,
230 One picture, just one more—the Virgin's face,
Not yours this time! I want you at my side
To hear them—that is, Michel Agnolo—
Judge all I do and tell you of its worth.
Will you? Tomorrow, satisfy your friend.
235 I take the subjects for his corridor,
Finish the portrait out of hand—there, there,
And throw him in another thing or two
If he demurs; the whole should prove enough
To pay for this same Cousin's freak. Beside,
240 What's better and what's all I care about,
Get you the thirteen scudi[1] for the ruff!
Love, does that please you? Ah, but what does he,
The Cousin! what does he to please you more?

I am grown peaceful as old age tonight.
245 I regret little, I would change still less.
Since there my past life lies, why alter it?
The very wrong to Francis!—it is true
I took his coin, was tempted and complied,
And built this house and sinned, and all is said.
250 My father and my mother died of want.[2]
Well, had I riches of my own? you see
How one gets rich! Let each one bear his lot.
They were born poor, lived poor, and poor they
    died:
And I have laboured somewhat in my time
255 And not been paid profusely. Some good son
Paint my two hundred pictures—let him try!
No doubt, there's something strikes a balance. Yes,
You loved me quite enough, it seems tonight.
This must suffice me here. What would one have?
260 In heaven, perhaps, new chances, one more chance—
Four great walls in the New Jerusalem,
Meted on each side by the angel's reed,

For Leonard,[3] Rafael, Agnolo and me
To cover—the three first without a wife,
265 While I have mine! So—still they overcome
Because there's still Lucrezia,—as I choose.

Again the Cousin's whistle! Go, my Love.
—1855

Saul [4]

I

Said Abner,[5] "At last thou art come! Ere I tell,
    ere thou speak,
Kiss my cheek, wish me well!" Then I wished it,
    and did kiss his cheek.
And he, "Since the King, O my friend, for thy
    countenance sent,
Neither drunken nor eaten have we; nor until from
    his tent
5 Thou return with the joyful assurance the King
    liveth yet,
Shall our lip with the honey be bright, with the
    water be wet.
For out of the black mid-tent's silence, a space of
    three days,
Not a sound hath escaped to thy servants, of prayer
    nor of praise,
To betoken that Saul and the Spirit have ended
    their strife,

---

[1] Roman coins.

[2] Vasari says that Andrea abandoned his own parents for Lucrezia's relatives.

[3] Leonardo da Vinci (1452–1519).

[4] The first nine stanzas of "Saul" were first published in 1845 in *Dramatic Romances and Lyrics*. The completed poem, with an additional ten stanzas, was published in *Men and Women* in 1855. Browning could not complete the poem in 1845 because he had not at that time clearly formulated his religious/aesthetic theory. Parts of his 1845 correspondence with Miss Barrett, and his "Essay on Shelley" (1851), reflect the concerns which, once resolved, enabled him to complete the poem. The Biblical source for "Saul" is 1 Samuel 16.14–23. Smart's *Song to David* led Browning in 1845 to other of Smart's work, including the preface in which Smart writes of the "fine subject" suggested to him of "David's playing to King Saul when he was troubled with the evil spirit."

[5] the captain of Saul's "host": 1 Samuel 26:5, Saul's cousin.

10 And that, faint in his triumph, the monarch sinks
    back upon life.

II

"Yet now my heart leaps, O beloved! God's child
    with his dew
On thy gracious gold hair, and those lilies still
    living and blue
Just broken to twine round thy harp-strings, as if
    no wild heat
Were now raging to torture the desert!"

III

                                Then I, as was
    meet,
Knelt down to the God of my fathers, and rose on
    my feet,
And ran o'er the sand burnt to powder. The tent
    was unlooped;
I pulled up the spear that obstructed, and under I
    stooped;
Hands and knees on the slippery grass-patch, all
    withered and gone,
That extends to the second enclosure, I groped my
    way on
20 Till I felt where the foldskirts fly open. Then once
    more I prayed,
And opened the foldskirts and entered, and was not
    afraid
But spoke, "Here is David, thy servant!" And no
    voice replied.
At the first I saw naught but the blackness; but
    soon I descried
A something more black than the blackness—the
    vast, the upright
25 Main prop which sustains the pavilion: and slow
    into sight
Grew a figure against it, gigantic and blackest of all.
Then a sunbeam, that burst through the tent-roof,
    showed Saul.

IV

He stood as erect as that tent-prop, both arms
    stretched out wide
On the great cross-support in the centre, that goes
    to each side;
30 He relaxed not a muscle, but hung there as, caught
    in his pangs
And waiting his change, the king-serpent all heavily
    hangs,
Far away from his kind, in the pine, till deliverance
    come
With the spring-time,—so agonized Saul, drear
    and stark, blind and dumb.

V

Then I turned my harp,—took off the lilies we
    twine round its chords
35 Lest they snap 'neath the stress of the noontide—
    those sunbeams like swords!
And I first played the tune all our sheep know, as,
    one after one,
So docile they come to the pen-door till folding be
    done.
They are white and untorn by the bushes, for lo,
    they have fed
Where the long grasses stifle the water within the
    stream's bed;
40 And now one after one seeks its lodging, as star
    follows star
Into eve and the blue far above us,—so blue and so
    far!

VI

—Then the tune, for which quails on the cornland
    will each leave his mate
To fly after the player; then, what makes the
    crickets elate
Till for boldness they fight one another: and then,
    what has weight

45 To set the quick jerboa[1] a-musing outside his sand
house—
There are none such as he for a wonder, half bird
and half mouse!
God made all the creatures and gave them our love
and our fear,
To give sign, we and they are his children, one
family here.

VII

Then I played the help-tune of our reapers, their
wine-song, when hand
50 Grasps at hand, eye lights eye in good friendship,
and great hearts expand
And grow one in the sense of this world's life.—
And then, the last song
When the dead man is praised on his journey—
"Bear, bear him along
With his few faults shut up like dead flowerets! Are
balm-seeds not here
To console us? The land has none left such as he
on the bier.
55 Oh, would we might keep thee, my brother!"
—And then, the glad chaunt
Of the marriage,—first go the young maidens,
next, she whom we vaunt
As the beauty, the pride of our dwelling.—And
60 then, the great march
Wherein man runs to man to assist him and
buttress an arch
Naught can break; who shall harm them, our
friends?—Then, the chorus intoned
60 As the Levites[2] go up to the altar in glory enthroned.
But I stopped here: for here in the darkness Saul
groaned.

VIII

And I paused, held my breath in such silence, and
listened apart;
And the tent shook, for mighty Saul shuddered:
and sparkles 'gan dart
From the jewels that woke in his turban, at once
with a start,
65 All its lordly male[3]-sapphires, and rubies
courageous[4] at heart.
So the head: but the body still moved not, still
hung there erect.
And I bent once again to my playing, pursued it
unchecked,
As I sang,—

IX

"Oh, our manhood's prime vigour! No
spirit feels waste,
Not a muscle is stopped in its playing nor sinew
unbraced.
70 Oh, the wild joys of living! the leaping from rock
up to rock,
The strong rending of boughs from the fir-tree, the
cool silver shock
Of the plunge in a pool's living water, the hunt of
the bear,
And the sultriness showing the lion is couched in
his lair.
And the meal, the rich dates yellowed over with
gold dust divine,
75 And the locust-flesh steeped in the pitcher, the full
draught of wine,
And the sleep in the dried river-channel where
bulrushes tell
That the water was wont to go warbling so softly
and well.
How good is man's life, the mere living! how fit to
employ

[1] a rodent with long back legs for leaping.

[2] Those assisting the priests in the Temple were traditionally chosen
from the tribe of Levi.

[3] very blue.

[4] lively.

All the heart and the soul and the senses for ever in joy!

80 Hast thou loved the white locks of thy father, whose sword thou didst guard

When he trusted thee forth with the armies, for glorious reward?

Didst thou see the thin hands of thy mother, held up as men sung

The low song of the nearly-departed, and hear her faint tongue

Joining in while it could to the witness, 'Let one more attest,

85 I have lived, seen God's hand through a lifetime, and all was for best'?

Then they sung through their tears in strong triumph, not much, but the rest.

And thy brothers, the help and the contest, the working whence grew

Such results as, from seething grape-bundles, the spirits strained true:

And the friends of thy boyhood—that boyhood of wonder and hope,

90 Present promise and wealth of the future beyond the eye's scope,—

Till lo, thou art grown to a monarch; a people is thine;

And all gifts, which the world offers singly, on one head combine!

On one head, all the beauty and strength, love and rage (like the throe

That, a-work in the rock, helps its labour and lets the gold go)

95 High ambition and deeds which surpass it, fame crowning them,—all

Brought to blaze on the head of one creature— King Saul!"

x

And lo, with that leap of my spirit,—heart, hand, harp and voice,

Each lifting Saul's name out of sorrow, each bidding rejoice

Saul's fame in the light it was made for—as when, dare I say,

100 The Lord's army, in rapture of service, strains[1] through its array,

And upsoareth the cherubim-chariot—"Saul!" cried I, and stopped,

And waited the thing that should follow. Then Saul, who hung propped

By the tent's cross-support in the centre, was struck by his name.

Have ye seen when Spring's arrowy summons goes right to the aim,

105 And some mountain, the last to withstand her, that held (he alone,

While the vale laughed in freedom and flowers) on a broad bust of stone

A year's snow bound about for a breastplate,— leaves grasp of the sheet?

Fold on fold all at once it crowds thunderously down to his feet,

And there fronts you, stark, black, but alive yet, your mountain of old,

110 With his rents, the successive bequeathings of ages untold—

Yea, each harm got in fighting your battles, each furrow and scar

Of his head thrust 'twixt you and the tempest— all hail, there they are!

—Now again to be softened with verdure, again hold the nest

Of the dove, tempt the goat and its young to the green on his crest

115 For their food in the ardours of summer. One long shudder thrilled

All the tent till the very air tingled, then sank and was stilled

---

[1] feels high tension.

At the King's self left standing before me, released
    and aware.
What was gone, what remained? All to traverse,
    'twixt hope and despair;
Death was past, life not come: so he waited. Awhile
    his right hand
120 Held the brow, helped the eyes left too vacant
    forthwith to remand
To their place what new objects should enter: 'twas
    Saul as before.
I looked up and dared gaze at those eyes, nor was
    hurt any more
Than by slow pallid sunsets in autumn, ye watch
    from the shore,
At their sad level gaze o'er the ocean—a sun's
    slow decline
125 Over hills which, resolved in stern silence, o'erlap
    and entwine
Base with base to knit strength more intensely: so,
    arm folded arm
O'er the chest whose slow heavings subsided.

XI

                      What
spell or what charm,
(For, awhile there was trouble within me) what
    next should I urge
To sustain him where song had restored him?
    —Song filled to the verge
130 His cup with the wine of this life, pressing all that
    it yields
Of mere fruitage, the strength and the beauty:
    beyond, on what fields,
Glean a vintage more potent and perfect to
    brighten the eye
And bring blood to the lip, and commend them
    the cup they put by?
He saith, "It is good"; still he drinks not: he lets me
    praise life,
135 Gives assent, yet would die for his own part.

XII

                      Then
fancies grew rife
Which had come long ago on the pasture, when
    round me the sheep
Fed in silence—above, the one eagle wheeled slow
    as in sleep;
And I lay in my hollow and mused on the world
    that might lie
'Neath his ken, though I saw but the strip 'twixt
    the hill and the sky:
140 And I laughed—"Since my days are ordained to be
    passed with my flocks,
Let me people at least, with my fancies, the plains
    and the rocks,
Dream the life I am never to mix with, and image
    the show
Of mankind as they live in those fashions I hardly
    shall know!
Schemes of life, its best rules and right uses, the
    courage that gains,
145 And the prudence that keeps what men strive for."
    And now these old trains
Of vague thought came again; I grew surer; so,
    once more the string
Of my harp made response to my spirit,
    as thus—

XIII

                  "Yea, my King,"
I began—"thou dost well in rejecting mere
    comforts that spring
From the mere mortal life held in common by man
    and by brute:
150 In our flesh grows the branch of this life, in our
    soul it bears fruit.
Thou hast marked the slow rise of the tree,—how
    its stem trembled first
Till it passed the kid's lip, the stag's antler; then
    safely outburst

The fan-branches all round; and thou mindest
   when these too, in turn
Broke a-bloom and the palm-tree seemed perfect:
   yet more was to learn,
155 E'en the good that comes in with the palm-fruit.
   Our dates shall we slight,
When their juice brings a cure for all sorrow? or
   care for the plight
Of the palm's self whose slow growth produced
   them? Not so! stem and branch
Shall decay, nor be known in their place, while the
   palm-wine shall staunch
Every wound of man's spirit in winter. I pour thee
   such wine.
160 Leave the flesh to the fate it was fit for! the spirit
   be thine!
By the spirit, when age shall o'ercome thee, thou
   still shalt enjoy
More indeed, than at first when inconscious,[1] the
   life of a boy.
Crush that life, and behold its wine running! Each
   deed thou hast done
Dies, revives, goes to work in the world; until e'en
   as the sun
165 Looking down on the earth, though clouds spoil
   him, though tempests efface,
Can find nothing his own deed produced not,
   must everywhere trace
The results of his past summer-prime,—so, each
   ray of thy will,
Every flash of thy passion and prowess, long over,
   shall thrill
Thy whole people, the countless, with ardour, till
   they too give forth
170 A like cheer to their sons, who in turn, fill the
   South and the North
With the radiance thy deed was the germ of.
   Carouse in the past!
But the license of age has its limit; thou diest at last:

As the lion when age dims his eyeball, the rose at
   her height
So with man—so his power and his beauty for
   ever take flight.
175 No! Again a long draught of my soul-wine! Look
   forth o'er the years!
Thou hast done now with eyes for the actual; begin
   with the seer's!
Is Saul dead? In the depth of the vale make his
   tomb—bid arise
A grey mountain of marble heaped four-square, till,
   built to the skies,
Let it mark where the great First King[2] slumbers:
   whose fame would ye know?
180 Up above see the rock's naked face, where the
   record shall go
In great characters cut by the scribe,—Such was
   Saul, so he did;
With the sages directing the work, by the populace
   chid,—
For not half, they'll affirm, is comprised there!
   Which fault to amend,
In the grove with his kind grows the cedar,
   whereon they shall spend
185 (See, in tablets 'tis level before them) their praise,
   and record
With the gold of the graver, Saul's story,—the
   statesman's great word
Side by side with the poet's sweet comment. The
   river's a-wave
With smooth paper-reeds[3] grazing each other when
   prophet-winds rave:
So the pen gives unborn generations their due and
   their part
190 In thy being! Then, first of the mighty, thank God
   that thou art!"

---

[1] unconscious.

[2] Saul was the first king of Israel.

[3] plants from which papyrus is made.

XIV

And behold while I sang…but O Thou who didst
    grant me that day,
And before it not seldom hast granted thy help to
    essay,
Carry on and complete an adventure,—my shield
    and my sword
In that act where my soul was thy servant, thy word
    was my word,—
195 Still be with me, who then at the summit of human
    endeavour
And scaling the highest, man's thought could,
    gazed hopeless as ever
On the new stretch of heaven above me—till,
    mighty to save,
Just one lift of thy hand cleared that distance—
    God's throne from man's grave!
Let me tell out my tale to its ending—my voice to
    my heart
200 Which can scarce dare believe in what marvels last
    night I took part,
As this morning I gather the fragments, alone with
    my sheep,
And still fear lest the terrible glory evanish like
    sleep!
For I wake in the grey dewy covert, while Hebron[1]
    upheaves
The dawn struggling with night on his shoulder,
    and Kidron[2] retrieves
205 Slow the damage of yesterday's sunshine.

XV

                      I say then,—
    my song
While I sang thus, assuring the monarch, and ever
    more strong
Made a proffer of good to console him—he slowly
    resumed

His old motions and habitudes kingly. The right-
    hand replumed
His black locks to their wonted composure,
    adjusted the swathes
210 Of his turban, and see—the huge sweat that his
    countenance bathes,
He wipes off with the robe; and he girds now his
    loins as of yore,
And feels slow for the armlets of price, with the
    clasp set before.
He is Saul, ye remember in glory,—ere error[3] had
    bent
The broad brow from the daily communion; and
    still, though much spent
215 Be the life and the bearing that front you, the same,
    God did choose,
To receive what a man may waste, desecrate, never
    quite lose.
So sank he along by the tent-prop till, stayed by the
    pile
Of his armour and war-cloak and garments, he
    leaned there awhile,
And sat out my singing,—one arm round the tent-
    prop, to raise
220 His bent head, and the other hung slack—till I
    touched on the praise
I foresaw from all men in all time, to the man
    patient there;
And thus ended, the harp falling forward. Then
    first I was 'ware
That he sat, as I say, with my head just above his
    vast knees
Which were thrust out on each side around me,
    like oak-roots which please
225 To encircle a lamb when it slumbers. I looked up
    to know
If the best I could do had brought solace: he spoke
    not, but slow

---

[1] mountain and city south of Jerusalem, the home of David.

[2] brook or gully near Jerusalem.

[3] Saul has disobeyed God: 1 Samuel 15.

Lifted up the hand slack at his side, till he laid it
  with care
Soft and grave, but in mild settled will, on my
  brow: through my hair
The large fingers were pushed, and he bent back
  my head, with kind power—
230 All my face back, intent to peruse it, as men do a
  flower.
Thus held he me there with his great eyes that
  scrutinized mine—
And oh, all my heart how it loved him! but where
  was the sign?
I yearned—"Could I help thee, my father,
  inventing a bliss,
I would add, to that life of the past, both the future
  and this;
235 I would give thee new life altogether, as good, ages
  hence,
As this moment,—had love but the warrant, love's
  heart to dispense!"

XVI

Then the truth came upon me. No harp more—
  no song more! outbroke—

XVII

"I have gone the whole round of creation: I saw and
  I spoke:
I, a work of God's hand for that purpose, received
  in my brain
240 And pronounced on the rest of his handwork—
  returned him again
His creation's approval or censure: I spoke as I saw:
I report, as a man may of God's work—all's love,
  yet all's law.
Now I lay down the judgeship he lent me. Each
  faculty tasked
To perceive him, has gained an abyss, where a dew-
  drop was asked.
245 Have I knowledge? confounded it shrivels at
  Wisdom laid bare.

Have I forethought? how purblind, how blank, to
  the Infinite Care!
Do I task any faculty highest, to image success?
I but open my eyes,—and perfection, no more and
  no less,
In the kind I imagined, full-fronts me, and God is
  seen God
250 In the star, in the stone, in the flesh, in the soul and
  the clod.
And thus looking within and around me, I ever
  renew
(With that stoop of the soul which in bending
  upraises it too)
The submission of man's nothing-perfect to God's
  all-complete,
As by each new obeisance in spirit, I climb to his
  feet.
255 Yet with all this abounding experience, this deity
  known,
I shall dare to discover some province, some gift of
  my own.
There's a faculty pleasant to exercise, hard to hood-
  wink,
I am fain to keep still in abeyance, (I laugh as I
  think)
Lest, insisting to claim and parade in it, wot ye, I
  worst
260 E'en the Giver in one gift.—Behold, I could love
  if I durst!
But I sink the pretension as fearing a man may
  o'ertake
God's own speed in the one way of love: I abstain
  for love's sake.
—What, my soul? see thus far and no farther?
  when doors great and small,
Nine-and-ninety flew ope at our touch, should the
  hundredth appal?
265 In the least things have faith, yet distrust in the
  greatest of all?
Do I find love so full in my nature, God's ultimate
  gift,

That I doubt his own love can compete with it?
    Here, the parts shift?
Here, the creatures surpass the Creator,—the end,
    what Began?
Would I fain in my impotent yearning do all for
    this man,
270 And dare doubt he alone shall not help him, who
    yet alone can?
Would it ever have entered my mind, the bare will,
    much less power,
To bestow on this Saul what I sang of, the
    marvellous dower
Of the life he was gifted and filled with? to make
    such a soul,
Such a body, and then such an earth for insphering
    the whole?
275 And doth it not enter my mind (as my warm tears
    attest)
These good things being given, to go on, and give
    one more, the best?
Ay, to save and redeem and restore him, maintain
    at the height
This perfection,—succeed with life's dayspring,
    death's minute of night?
Interpose at the difficult minute, snatch Saul the
    mistake,
280 Saul the failure, the ruin he seems now,—and bid
    him awake
From the dream, the probation, the prelude, to
    find himself set
Clear and safe in new light and new life,—a new
    harmony yet
To be run, and continued, and ended—who
    knows?—or endure!
The man taught enough, be life's dream, of the rest
    to make sure;
285 By the pain-throb, triumphantly winning
    intensified bliss,
And the next world's reward and repose, by the
    struggles in this.

XVIII

"I believe it! 'Tis thou, God, that givest, 'tis I who
    receive:
In the first is the last, in thy will is my power to
    believe.
All's one gift: thou canst grant it moreover, as
    prompt to my prayer
290 As I breathe out this breath, as I open these arms to
    the air.
From thy will, stream the worlds, life and nature,
    thy dread Sabaoth:[1]
I will?—the mere atoms despise me! Why am I not
    loth
To look that, even that in the face too? Why is it I
    dare
Think but lightly of such impuissance? What stops
    my despair?
295 This;—'tis not what man Does which exalts him,
    but what man Would do!
See the King—I would help him but cannot, the
    wishes fall through.
Could I wrestle to raise him from sorrow, grow
    poor to enrich,
To fill up his life, starve my own out, I would—
    knowing which,
I know that my service is perfect. Oh, speak
    through me now!
300 Would I suffer for him that I love? So wouldst
    thou—so wilt thou!
So shall crown thee the topmost, ineffablest,
    uttermost crown—
And thy love fill infinitude wholly, nor leave up
    nor down
One spot for the creature to stand in! It is by no
    breath,
Turn of eye, wave of hand, that salvation joins
    issue with death!
305 As thy Love is discovered almighty, almighty be
    proved

---

[1] hosts or armies.

Thy power, that exists with and for it, of being
    Beloved!
He who did most, shall bear most; the strongest
    shall stand the most weak.
'Tis the weakness in strength, that I cry for! my
    flesh, that I seek
In the Godhead! I seek and I find it. O Saul, it shall
    be
310 A Face like my face that receives thee; a Man like to
    me,
Thou shalt love and be loved by, for ever: a Hand
    like this hand
Shall throw open the gates of new life to thee! See
    the Christ stand!"

XIX

I know not too well how I found my way home in
    the night.
There were witness, cohorts about me, to left and
    to right,
315 Angels, powers, the unuttered, unseen, the alive,
    the aware:
I repressed, I got through them as hardly, as
    strugglingly there,
As a runner beset by the populace famished for
    news—
Life or death. The whole earth was awakened, hell
    loosed with her crews;
And the stars of night beat with emotion, and
    tingled and shot
320 Out in fire the strong pain of pent knowledge: but
    I fainted not,
For the Hand still impelled me at once and
    supported, suppressed
All the tumult, and quenched it with quiet, and
    holy behest,
Till the rapture was shut in itself, and the earth
    sank to rest.
Anon at the dawn, all that trouble had withered
    from earth—

325 Not so much, but I saw it die out in the day's
    tender birth;
In the gathered intensity brought to the grey of the
    hills;
In the shuddering forests' held breath; in the
    sudden wind-thrills;
In the startled wild beasts that bore off, each with
    eye sidling still
Though averted with wonder and dread; in the
    birds stiff and chill
330 That rose heavily, as I approached them, made
    stupid with awe:
E'en the serpent that slid away silent,—he felt the
    new law.
The same stared in the white humid faces upturned
    by the flowers;
The same worked in the heart of the cedar and
    moved the vine-bowers:
And the little brooks witnessing murmured,
    persistent and low,
335 With their obstinate, all but hushed voices—"E'en
    so, it is so!"
—1845 (STANZAS 1–9; COMPLETE POEM: 1855)

Cleon [1]

"As certain also of your own poets have said"—[2]

Cleon the poet (from the sprinkled isles,[3]
    Lily on lily, that o'erlace the sea,
And laugh their pride when the light wave lisps
    "Greece")—
To Protus in his Tyranny:[4] much health!

---

[1] The poem is a companion to "An Epistle...of Karshish," and was perhaps written after it.

[2] The epigraph comes from Acts 17.28: "For in him we live, and move, and have our being; as certain also of your own poets have said, For we are his offspring."

[3] The Sporades: scattered islands in the Aegean Sea.

[4] a kind of rule, but without its modern implications.

5   They give thy letter to me, even now:
I read and seem as if I heard thee speak.
The master of thy galley still unlades
Gift after gift; they block my court at last
And pile themselves along its portico
10 Royal with sunset, like a thought of thee:
And one white she-slave from the group dispersed
Of black and white slaves (like the chequer-work
Pavement, at once my nation's work and gift,
Now covered with this settle-down[1] of doves),
15 One lyric woman, in her crocus vest
Woven of sea-wools,[2] with her two white hands
Commends to me the strainer and the cup
Thy lip hath bettered ere it blesses mine.

    Well-counselled, king, in thy munificence!
20 For so shall men remark, in such an act
Of love for him whose song gives life its joy,
Thy recognition of the use of life;
Nor call thy spirit barely adequate
To help on life in straight ways, broad enough
25 For vulgar souls, by ruling and the rest.
Thou, in the daily building of thy tower,—
Whence in fierce and sudden spasms of toil,
Or through dim lulls of unapparent growth,
Or when the general work 'mid good acclaim
30 Climbed with the eye to cheer the architect,—
Didst ne'er engage in work for mere work's sake—
Had'st ever in thy heart the luring hope
Of some eventual rest a-top of it,
Whence, all the tumult of the building hushed,
35 Thou first of men mightst look out to the East:
The vulgar saw thy tower, thou sawest the sun.
For this, I promise on thy festival
To pour libation, looking o'er the sea,
Making this slave narrate thy fortunes, speak
40 Thy great words, and describe thy royal face—

Wishing thee wholly where Zeus lives the most,
Within the eventual element of calm.

    Thy letter's first requirement meets me here.
It is as thou hast heard: in one short life
45 I, Cleon, have effected all those things
Thou wonderingly dost enumerate.
That epos on thy hundred plates of gold[3]
Is mine,—and also mine the little chant,
So sure to rise from every fishing-bark
50 When, lights at prow, the seamen haul their net.
The image of the sun-god on the phare,[4]
Men turn from the sun's self to see, is mine;
The Poecile,[5] o'er-storied its whole length,
As thou didst hear, with painting, is mine too.
55 I know the true proportions of a man
And woman also, not observed before;
And I have written three books on the soul,
Proving absurd all written hitherto,
And putting us to ignorance again.
60 For music,—why, I have combined the moods,[6]
Inventing one. In brief, all arts are mine;
Thus much the people know and recognize,
Throughout our seventeen islands. Marvel not.
We of these latter days, with greater mind
65 Than our forerunners, since more composite,
Look not so great, beside their simple way,
To a judge who only sees one way at once,
One mind-point and no other at a time,—
Compares the small part of a man of us
70 With some whole man of the heroic age,
Great in his way—not ours, nor meant for ours.
And ours is greater, had we skill to know:
For, what we call this life of men on earth,
This sequence of the soul's achievements here
75 Being, as I find much reason to conceive,

---

[1] flock setting down.

[2] wools dyed with sea-purple.

[3] an epic poem engraved on tablets of gold.

[4] statue of Apollo on the lighthouse.

[5] the painted Portico at Athens.

[6] modes (types of musical scale).

Intended to be viewed eventually
As a great whole, not analysed to parts,
But each part having reference to all,—
How shall a certain part, pronounced complete,
80 Endure effacement by another part?
Was the thing done?—then, what's to do again?
See, in the chequered pavement opposite,
Suppose the artist made a perfect rhomb,[1]
And next a lozenge,[2] then a trapezoid—[3]
85 He did not overlay them, superimpose
The new upon the old and blot it out,
But laid them on a level in his work,
Making at last a picture; there it lies.
So, first the perfect separate forms were made,
90 The portions of mankind; and after, so,
Occurred the combination of the same.
For where had been a progress, otherwise?
Mankind, made up of all the single men,—
In such a synthesis the labour ends.
95 Now mark me! those divine men of old time
Have reached, thou sayest well, each at one point
The outside verge that rounds our faculty;
And where they reached, who can do more than
        reach?
It takes but little water just to touch
100 At some one point the inside of a sphere,
And, as we turn the sphere, touch all the rest
In due succession: but the finer air
Which not so palpably nor obviously,
Though no less universally, can touch
105 The whole circumference of that emptied sphere,
Fills it more fully than the water did;
Holds thrice the weight of water in itself
Resolved into a subtler element.
And yet the vulgar call the sphere first full
110 Up to the visible height—and after, void;
Not knowing air's more hidden properties.

And thus our soul, misknown, cries out to Zeus
To vindicate his purpose in our life:
Why stay we on the earth unless to grow?
115 Long since, I imaged, wrote the fiction out,
That he or other god descended here
And, once for all, showed simultaneously
What, in its nature, never can be shown,
Piecemeal or in succession;—showed, I say,
120 The worth both absolute and relative
Of all his children from the birth of time,
His instruments for all appointed work.
I now go on to image,—might we hear
The judgement which should give the due to each,
125 Show where the labour lay and where the ease,
And prove Zeus' self, the latent everywhere!
This is a dream:—but no dream, let us hope,
That years and days, the summers and the springs,
Follow each other with unwaning powers.
130 The grapes which dye thy wine are richer far,
Through culture, than the wild wealth of the rock;
The suave plum than the savage-tasted drupe;[4]
The pastured honey-bee drops choicer sweet;
The flowers turn double, and the leaves turn flowers;
135 That young and tender crescent-moon, thy slave,
Sleeping above her robe as buoyed by clouds,
Refines upon the women of my youth.
What, and the soul[5] alone deteriorates?
I have not chanted verse like Homer, no—
140 Nor swept string like Terpander,[6] no—nor carved
And painted men like Phidias and his friend:[7]
I am not great as they are, point by point.
But I have entered into sympathy
With these four, running these into one soul,
145 Who, separate, ignored each other's art.
Say, is it nothing that I know them all?

---

[1] rhombus, equilateral parallelogram.

[2] diamond-shaped figure.

[3] four-sided figure with two parallel sides.

[4] wild plum.

[5] in the non-Christian sense, "inner essence" or "consciousness."

[6] seventh-century BC founder of Greek music.

[7] the Greek sculptor of the fifth-century BC, and probably Pericles, the great Athenian statesman.

The wild flower was the larger; I have dashed
Rose-blood upon its petals, pricked its cup's
Honey with wine, and driven its seed to fruit,
150 And show a better flower if not so large:
I stand myself. Refer this to the gods
Whose gift alone it is! which, shall I dare
(All pride apart) upon the absurd pretext
That such a gift by chance lay in my hand,
155 Discourse of lightly or depreciate?
It might have fallen to another's hand: what then?
I pass too surely: let at least truth stay!

And next, of what thou followest on to ask.
This being with me as I declare, O king,
160 My works, in all these varicoloured kinds,
So done by me, accepted so by men—
Thou askest, if (my soul thus in men's hearts)
I must not be accounted to attain
The very crown and proper end of life?
165 Inquiring thence how, now life closeth up,
I face death with success in my right hand:
Whether I fear death less than dost thyself
The fortunate of men? "For" (writest thou)
"Thou leavest much behind, while I leave naught.
170 Thy life stays in the poems men shall sing,
The pictures men shall study; while my life,
Complete and whole now in its power and joy,
Dies altogether with my brain and arm,
Is lost indeed; since, what survives myself?
175 The brazen statue to o'erlook my grave,
Set on the promontory which I named.
And that—some supple courtier of my heir
Shall use its robed and sceptred arm, perhaps,
To fix the rope to, which best drags it down.
180 I go then: triumph thou, who dost not go!"

Nay, thou art worthy of hearing my whole mind.
Is this apparent, when thou turn'st to muse
Upon the scheme of earth and man in chief,
That admiration grows as knowledge grows?
185 That imperfection means perfection hid,

Reserved in part, to grace the after-time?
If, in the morning of philosophy,
Ere aught had been recorded, nay perceived,
Thou, with the light now in thee, couldst have
looked
190 On all earth's tenantry, from worm to bird,
Ere man, her last, appeared upon the stage—
Thou wouldst have seen them perfect, and deduced
The perfectness of others yet unseen.
Conceding which,—had Zeus then questioned thee
195 "Shall I go on a step, improve on this,
Do more for visible creatures than is done?"
Thou wouldst have answered, "Ay, by making each
Grow conscious in himself—by that alone.
All's perfect else: the shell sucks fast the rock,
200 The fish strikes through the sea, the snake both
swims
And slides, forth range the beasts, the birds take
flight,
Till life's mechanics can no further go—
And all this joy in natural life is put
Like fire from off thy finger into each,
205 So exquisitely perfect is the same.
But 'tis pure fire, and they mere matter are;
It has them, not they it: and so I choose
For man, thy last premeditated work
(If I might add a glory to the scheme)
210 That a third thing should stand apart from both,
A quality arise within his soul,
Which, intro-active,[1] made to supervise
And feel the force it has, may view itself,
And so be happy." Man might live at first
215 The animal life: but is there nothing more?
In due time, let him critically learn
How he lives; and, the more he gets to know
Of his own life's adaptabilities,
The more joy-giving will his life become.
220 Thus man, who hath this quality, is best.

---

[1] internally active.

But thou, king, hadst more reasonably said:
"Let progress end at once,—man make no step
Beyond the natural man, the better beast,
Using his senses, not the sense of sense."
225 In man there's failure, only since he left
The lower and inconscious forms of life.
We called it an advance, the rendering plain
Man's spirit might grow conscious of man's life,
And, by new lore so added to the old,
230 Take each step higher over the brute's head.
This grew the only life, the pleasure-house,
Watch-tower and treasure-fortress of the soul,
Which whole surrounding flats of natural life
Seemed only fit to yield subsistence to;
235 A tower that crowns a country. But alas,
The soul now climbs it just to perish there!
For thence we have discovered ('tis no dream—
We know this, which we had not else perceived)
That there's a world of capability
240 For joy, spread round about us, meant for us,
Inviting us; and still the soul craves all,
And still the flesh replies, "Take no jot more
Than ere thou clombst the tower to look abroad!
Nay, so much less as that fatigue has brought
245 Deduction to it." We struggle, fain to enlarge
Our bounded physical recipiency,[1]
Increase our power, supply fresh oil to life,
Repair the waste of age and sickness: no,
It skills not! life's inadequate to joy,
250 As the soul sees joy, tempting life to take.
They praise a fountain in my garden here
Wherein a Naiad[2] sends the water-bow
Thin from her tube; she smiles to see it rise.
What if I told her, it is just a thread
255 From that great river which the hills shut up,
And mock her with my leave to take the same?
The artificer has given her one small tube

Past power to widen or exchange—what boots[3]
To know she might spout oceans if she could?
260 She cannot lift beyond her first thin thread:
And so a man can use but a man's joy
While he sees God's. Is it for Zeus to boast,
"See, man, how happy I live, and despair—
That I may be still happier—for thy use!"
265 If this were so, we could not thank our lord,
As hearts beat on to doing; 'tis not so—
Malice it is not. Is it carelessness?
Still, no. If care—where is the sign? I ask,
And get no answer, and agree in sum,
270 O king, with thy profound discouragement,
Who seest the wider but to sigh the more.
Most progress is most failure: thou sayest well.

    The last point now:—thou dost except a case—
Holding joy not impossible to one
275 With artist-gifts—to such a man as I
Who leave behind me living works indeed;
For, such a poem, such a painting lives.
What? dost thou verily trip upon a word,
Confound the accurate view of what joy is
280 (Caught somewhat clearer by my eyes than thine)
With feeling joy? confound the knowing how
And showing how to live (my faculty)
With actually living?—Otherwise
Where is the artist's vantage o'er the king?
285 Because in my great epos I display
How divers men young, strong, fair, wise, can act—
Is this as though I acted? if I paint,
Carve the young Phoebus,[4] am I therefore young?
Methinks I'm older that I bowed myself
290 The many years of pain that taught me art!
Indeed, to know is something, and to prove
How all this beauty might be enjoyed, is more:
But, knowing naught, to enjoy is something too.
Yon rower, with the moulded muscles there,

---

[1] receptivity.

[2] (statue of a) water-nymph.

---

[3] use.

[4] Apollo, god of sun and poetry.

295 Lowering the sail, is nearer it than I.
I can write love-odes: thy fair slave's an ode.
I get to sing of love, when grown too grey
For being beloved: she turns to that young man,
The muscles all a-ripple on his back.
300 I know the joy of kingship: well, thou art king!

"But," sayest thou—(and I marvel, I repeat
To find thee trip on such a mere word) "what
Thou writest, paintest, stays; that does not die:
Sappho[1] survives, because we sing her songs,
305 And Aeschylus, because we read his plays!"
Why, if they live still, let them come and take
Thy slave in my despite, drink from thy cup,
Speak in my place. Thou diest while I survive?
Say rather that my fate is deadlier still,
310 In this, that every day my sense of joy
Grows more acute, my soul (intensified
By power and insight) more enlarged, more keen;
While every day my hairs fall more and more,
My hand shakes, and the heavy years increase—
315 The horror quickening still from year to year,
The consummation coming past escape
When I shall know most, and yet least enjoy—
When all my works wherein I prove my worth,
Being present still to mock me in men's mouths,
320 Alive still, in the praise of such as thou,
I, I the feeling, thinking, acting man,
The man who loved his life so over-much,
Sleep in my urn. It is so horrible,
I dare at times imagine to my need
325 Some future state revealed to us by Zeus,
Unlimited in capability
For joy, as this is in desire for joy,
—To seek which, the joy-hunger forces us:
That, stung by straitness of our life, made strait
330 On purpose to make prized the life at large—
Freed by the throbbing impulse we call death,

We burst there as the worm into the fly,[2]
Who, while a worm still, wants his wings. But no!
Zeus has not yet revealed it; and alas,
335 He must have done so, were it possible!

Live long and happy, and in that thought die:
Glad for what was! Farewell. And for the rest,
I cannot tell thy messenger aright
Where to deliver what he bears of thine
340 To one called Paulus;[3] we have heard his fame
Indeed, if Christus be not one with him—
I know not, nor am troubled much to know.
Thou canst not think a mere barbarian Jew,
As Paulus proves to be, one circumcised,
345 Hath access to a secret shut from us?
Thou wrongest our philosophy, O king,
In stooping to inquire of such an one,
As if his answer could impose at all!
He writeth, doth he? well, and he may write.
350 Oh, the Jew findeth scholars! certain slaves
Who touched on this same isle, preached him and
        Christ;
And (as I gathered from a bystander)
Their doctrine could be held by no sane man.
—1855

Abt Vogler [4]

(After he has been extemporizing upon the musical
instrument of his invention) [5]

I

Would that the structure brave,[6] the manifold
    music I build,

---

[1] Greek lyric poet of the seventh-century BC.

[2] butterfly (emblem of the soul).

[3] St. Paul.

[4] Abbé Georg Joseph Vogler (1749–1814), German composer, organist,
theorist, teacher and noted extemporizer, had been the master of John
Relfe, Browning's music teacher.

[5] the orchestrion, a kind of large organ.

[6] splendid.

Bidding my organ obey, calling its keys to their
    work,
Claiming each slave of the sound, at a touch, as
    when Solomon[1] willed
Armies of angels that soar, legions of demons
    that lurk,
5 Man, brute, reptile, fly,—alien of end and of aim,
    Adverse, each from the other heaven-high, hell-
    deep removed,—
Should rush into sight at once as he named the
    ineffable Name,
And pile him a palace straight, to pleasure the
    princess he loved!

II

Would it might tarry like his, the beautiful
    building of mine,
10   This which my keys in a crowd pressed and
    importuned to raise!
Ah, one and all, how they helped, would dispart
    now and now combine,
    Zealous to hasten the work, heighten their
    master his praise!
And one would bury his brow with a blind plunge
    down to hell,
    Burrow awhile and build, broad on the roots of
    things,
15 Then up again swim into sight, having based me
    my palace well,
    Founded it, fearless of flame, flat on the nether
    springs.[2]

III

And another would mount and march, like the
    excellent minion he was,
    Ay, another and yet another, one crowd but
    with many a crest,

Raising my rampired[3] walls of gold as transparent
    as glass,
20   Eager to do and die, yield each his place to the
    rest:
For higher still and higher (as a runner tips with fire,
    When a great illumination surprises a festal
    night—
Outlining round and round Rome's dome[4] from
    space to spire)
    Up, the pinnacled glory reached, and the pride
    of my soul was in sight.

IV

25 In sight? Not half? for it seemed, it was certain, to
    match man's birth,
    Nature in turn conceived, obeying an impulse
    as I;
And the emulous heaven yearned down, made
    effort to reach the earth,
    As the earth had done her best, in my passion,
    to scale the sky:
Novel splendours burst forth, grew familiar and
    dwelt with mine,
30   Not a point nor peak but found and fixed its
    wandering star;
Meteor-moons, balls of blaze: and they did not pale
    nor pine,
    For earth had attained to heaven, there was no
    more near nor far.

V

Nay more; for there wanted not who walked in the
    glare and glow,
    Presences plain in the place; or, fresh from the
    Protoplast,[5]
35 Furnished for ages to come, when a kindlier wind
    should blow,

---

[1] Solomon was reputed to be able to control spirits with a seal that bore God's "ineffable name" (l. 7).

[2] perhaps referring to the belief that the earth rested on a great deep.

---

[3] strengthened against attack, ramparted.

[4] St. Peter's was lighted on special occasions.

[5] just created.

Lured now to begin and live, in a house to their
liking at last;
Or else the wonderful Dead who have passed
through the body and gone,
But were back once more to breathe in an old
world worth their new:
What never had been, was now; what was, as it
shall be anon;
40   And what is,—shall I say, matched both? for I
was made perfect too.

VI

All through my keys that gave their sounds to a
wish of my soul,
All through my soul that praised as its wish
flowed visibly forth,
All through music and me! For think, had I painted
the whole,
Why, there it had stood, to see, nor the process
so wonder-worth:
45   Had I written the same, made verse—still, effect
proceeds from cause,
Ye know why the forms are fair, ye hear how
the tale is told;
It is all triumphant art, but art in obedience to laws,
Painter and poet are proud in the artist-list
enrolled:—

VII

But here is the finger of God, a flash of the will
that can,
50   Existent behind all laws, that made them and,
lo, they are!
And I know not if, save in this, such gift be allowed
to man,
That out of three sounds he frame, not a fourth
sound, but a star.
Consider it well: each tone of our scale in itself is
naught;
It is everywhere in the world—loud, soft, and
all is said:

55   Give it to me to use! I mix it with two in my
thought:
And, there! Ye have heard and seen: consider
and bow the head!

VIII

Well, it is gone at last, the palace of music I reared;
Gone! and the good tears start, the praises that
come too slow;
For one is assured at first, one scarce can say that he
feared,
60   That he even gave it a thought, the gone thing
was to go.
Never to be again! But many more of the kind
As good, nay, better perchance: is this your
comfort to me?
To me, who must be saved because I cling with my
mind
To the same, same self, same love, same God:
ay, what was, shall be.

IX

65   Therefore to whom turn I but to thee, the ineffable
Name?
Builder and maker, thou, of houses not made
with hands!
What, have fear of change from thee who art ever
the same?
Doubt that thy power can fill the heart that thy
power expands?
There shall never be one lost good! What was, shall
live as before;
70   The evil is null, is naught, is silence implying
sound;
What was good shall be good, with, for evil, so
much good more;
On the earth the broken arcs; in the heaven, a
perfect round.

X

All we have willed or hoped or dreamed of good
    shall exist;
  Not its semblance, but itself; no beauty, nor
    good, nor power
75 Whose voice has gone forth, but each survives for
    the melodist
  When eternity affirms the conception of an
    hour.
The high that proved too high, the heroic for earth
    too hard,
  The passion that left the ground to lose itself in
    the sky,
Are music sent up to God by the lover and the bard;
80   Enough that he heard it once: we shall hear it
    by-and-by.

XI

And what is our failure here but a triumph's
    evidence
  For the fulness of the days? Have we withered
    or agonized?
Why else was the pause prolonged but that singing
    might issue thence?
  Why rushed the discords in but that harmony
    should be prized?
85 Sorrow is hard to bear, and doubt is slow to clear,
    Each sufferer says his say, his scheme of the weal
    and woe:
But God has a few of us whom he whispers in the
    ear;
  The rest may reason and welcome: 'tis we
    musicians know.

XII

Well, it is earth with me; silence resumes her reign:
90   I will be patient and proud, and soberly
    acquiesce.

Give me the keys. I feel for the common chord[1]
    again,
  Sliding by semitones, till I sink to the minor,[2]
    —yes,
And I blunt[3] it into a ninth,[4] and I stand on alien
    ground,[5]
  Surveying awhile the heights I rolled from into
    the deep;
95 Which, hark, I have dared and done, for my
    resting-place is found,
  The C Major of this life:[6] so, now I will try to
    sleep.
—1864

Rabbi Ben Ezra [7]

I

Grow old along with me!
  The best is yet to be,
The last of life, for which the first was made:
  Our times are in His hand
5   Who saith "A whole I planned,
Youth shows but half; trust God: see all nor be
    afraid!"

II

---

1 three-note chord made up of the first, third, and fifth notes in the scale.

2 modulating from the key of the "common chord" to its relative minor key.

3 flatten one note.

4 one note more than the octave.

5 the discord of the ninth. The ground is "alien" because Vogler pioneered the use of the ninth in his system of harmony.

6 the level of ordinary living. Probably Vogler is returning to the key in which his improvisation began.

7 Abraham Ibn Ezra (Abenezra) (1092–1167), a Spanish Jew, spent the better part of his life travelling in exile; he was a distinguished scholar and a man of genius in several areas. It is generally agreed that the Rabbi is a spokesman for Browning himself.

  Much in the poem suggests that Browning is replying to Edward FitzGerald's *Rubáiyát* (1859).

Not that, amassing flowers,
Youth sighed "Which rose makes ours,
Which lily leave and then as best recall?"
10   Not that, admiring stars,
It yearned "Nor Jove, nor Mars;
Mine be some figured flame which blends,
transcends them all!"

III

Not for such hopes and fears
Annulling youth's brief years,
15 Do I remonstrate: folly wide the mark!
Rather I prize the doubt
Low kinds exist without,
Finished and finite clods, untroubled by a spark.

IV

Poor vaunt of life indeed,
20 Were man but formed to feed
On joy, to solely seek and find and feast:
Such feasting ended, then
As sure an end to men;
Irks care the crop-full bird? Frets doubt the maw-
crammed beast?

V

25 Rejoice we are allied
To That which doth provide
And not partake, effect and not receive!
A spark disturbs our clod;
Nearer we hold of God
30 Who gives, than of His tribes that take, I must
believe.

VI

Then, welcome each rebuff
That turns earth's smoothness rough,
Each sting that bids nor sit nor stand but go!
Be our joys three-parts pain!
35 Strive, and hold cheap the strain;

Learn, nor account the pang; dare, never grudge
the throe!

VII

For thence,—a paradox
Which comforts while it mocks,—
Shall life succeed in that it seems to fail:
40   What I aspired to be,
And was not, comforts me:
A brute I might have been, but would not sink i'
the scale.

VIII

What is he but a brute
Whose flesh has soul to suit,
45 Whose spirit works lest arms and legs want play?
To man, propose this test—
Thy body at its best,
How far can that project thy soul on its lone way?

IX

Yet gifts should prove their use:
50   I own the Past profuse
Of power each side, perfection every turn:
Eyes, ears took in their dole,
Brain treasured up the whole;
Should not the heart beat once "How good to live
and learn"?

X

55   Not once beat "Praise be Thine!
I see the whole design,
I, who saw power, see now love perfect too:
Perfect I call Thy plan:
Thanks that I was a man!
60 Maker, remake, complete,—I trust what Thou
shalt do!"

XI

For pleasant is this flesh;
Our soul, in its rose-mesh
Pulled ever to the earth, still yearns for rest;

Would we some prize might hold
65   To match those manifold
Possessions of the brute,—gain most, as we did
        best!,

XII

Let us not always say
    "Spite of this flesh today
I strove, made head, gained ground upon the whole!"
70   As the bird wings and sings,
    Let us cry "All good things
Are ours, nor soul helps flesh more, now, than flesh
        helps soul!"

XIII

Therefore I summon age
    To grant youth's heritage,
75 Life's struggle having so far reached its term:
    Thence shall I pass, approved
    A man, for aye removed
From the developed brute; a god though in the
        germ.

XIV

And I shall thereupon
80   Take rest, ere I be gone
Once more on my adventure brave and new:
    Fearless and unperplexed,
    When I wage battle next,
What weapons to select, what armour to indue.[1]

XV

85 Youth ended, I shall try[2]
    My gain or loss thereby;
Leave the fire ashes, what survives is gold:
    And I shall weigh the same,
    Give life its praise or blame:
90 Young, all lay in dispute; I shall know, being old.

---

[1] put on.

[2] test, or try to find out.

XVI

For note, when evening shuts,
    A certain moment cuts
The deed off, calls the glory from the grey:
    A whisper from the west
95   Shoots—"Add this to the rest,
Take it and try its worth: here dies another day."

XVII

So, still within this life,
    Though lifted o'er its strife,
Let me discern, compare, pronounce at last,
100   "This rage was right i' the main,
    That acquiescence vain:
The Future I may face now I have proved[3] the
        Past."

XVIII

For more is not reserved
    To man, with soul just nerved
105 To act tomorrow what he learns today:
    Here, work enough to watch
    The Master work, and catch
Hints of the proper craft, tricks of the tool's true
        play.

XIX

As it was better, youth
110   Should strive, through acts uncouth,
Toward making, than repose on aught found made:
    So, better, age, exempt
    From strife, should know, than tempt[4]
Further. Thou waitedest age: wait death nor be
        afraid!

XX

Enough now, if the Right
115   And Good and Infinite
Be named here, as thou callest thy hand thine own,

---

[3] tested.

[4] attempt.

With knowledge absolute,
Subject to no dispute
120 From fools that crowded youth, nor let thee feel
alone.

XXI

Be there, for once and all,
Severed great minds from small,
Announced to each his station in the Past!
Was I, the world arraigned,
125 Were they, my soul disdained,
Right? Let age speak the truth and give us peace at
last!

XXII

Now, who shall arbitrate?
Ten men love what I hate,
Shun what I follow, slight what I receive;
130 Ten, who in ears and eyes
Match me: we all surmise,
They this thing, and I that: whom shall my soul
believe?

XXIII

Not on the vulgar mass
Called "work," must sentence pass,
135 Things done, that took the eye and had the price;
O'er which, from level stand,
The low world laid its hand,
Found straightway to its mind, could value in a
trice:

XXIV

But all, the world's coarse thumb
140 And finger failed to plumb,
So passed[1] in making up the main account;
All instincts immature,
All purposes unsure,
That weighed not as his work, yet swelled the
man's amount:

XXV

145 Thoughts hardly to be packed
Into a narrow act,
Fancies that broke through language and escaped;
All I could never be,
All, men ignored in me,
150 This, I was worth to God, whose wheel the pitcher
shaped.[2]

XXVI

Ay, note that Potter's wheel,
That metaphor! and feel
Why time spins fast, why passive lies our clay,—
Thou, to whom fools propound,
155 When the wine makes its round,
"Since life fleets, all is change; the Past gone, seize
today!"[3]

XXVII

Fool! All that is, at all,
Lasts ever, past recall;
Earth changes, but thy soul and God stand sure:
160 What entered into thee,
That was, is, and shall be:
Time's wheel runs back or stops: Potter and clay
endure.

XXVIII

He fixed thee 'mid this dance
Of plastic[4] circumstance,
165 This Present, thou, forsooth, wouldst fain arrest:
Machinery just meant
To give thy soul its bent,

---

[1] ignored.

---

[2] The image that begins here and dominates the conclusion of the poem
is a common one: that of God as potter and man as pot. In this version,
the wheel becomes earthly time and circumstance, and the clay is man's
spiritual being. The image occurs in FitzGerald's *Rubáiyát*.

[3] ll. 154–56 are an obvious reference to FitzGerald's *Rubáiyát*.

[4] fashioning.

Try[1] thee and turn thee forth, sufficiently
    impressed.

XXIX

170
What though the earlier grooves
  Which ran the laughing loves
Around thy base, no longer pause and press?
    What though, about thy rim,
    Skull-things in order grim
Grow out, in graver mood, obey the sterner stress?[2]

XXX

175
Look not thou down but up!
  To uses of a cup,
The festal board, lamp's flash and trumpet's peal,
    The new wine's foaming flow,
    The Master's lips a-glow!
180
Thou, heaven's consummate cup, what need'st
    thou with earth's wheel?

XXXI

But I need, now as then,
  Thee, God, who mouldest men;
And since, not even while the whirl was worst,
    Did I,—to the wheel of life
185
    With shapes and colours rife,
Bound dizzily,—mistake my end, to slake Thy
    thirst:

XXXII

So, take and use Thy work:
  Amend what flaws may lurk,
What strain o' the stuff, what warpings past the aim!
190
    My times be in Thy hand!
    Perfect the cup as planned!
Let age approve of youth, and death complete the
    same!

—1864

---

[1] test.

[2] heavier pressure.

Caliban upon Setebos; or, Natural Theology in the Island [1]

"Thou thoughtest that I was altogether such a one as thyself."

['W]ill sprawl, now that the heat of day is
    best,
Flat on his belly in the pit's much mire,
With elbows wide, fists clenched to prop his chin.
5
And, while he kicks both feet in the cool slush,
And feels about his spine small eft-things[4] course,
Run in and out each arm, and make him laugh:
And while above his head a pompion[5]-plant,
Coating the cave-top as a brow its eye,
10
Creeps down to touch and tickle hair and beard,
And now a flower drops with a bee inside,
And now a fruit to snap at, catch and crunch,—
He looks out o'er yon sea which sunbeams cross
And recross till they weave a spider-web
15
(Meshes of fire, some great fish breaks at times)
And talks to his own self, howe'er he please,

---

[3] It is generally believed that the poem was to some extent triggered by Darwin's *Origin of Species* (November, 1859). Browning was interested in the furore that followed the appearance of Darwin's book, and the topical appeal of an example of the "missing link" is evident. Browning's hero is the man-monster of *The Tempest* turned theologian—at the end of the play Caliban resolves to "seek for grace" (5.1.296), and the resolve might have sparked Browning's imagination; the original Caliban's character, situation, and pronouncements lie behind almost everything in Browning's characterization. Setebos was the god of Caliban's dam, Sycorax (1.2.373); the Quiet may derive in part from the Unitarian conception of God. The "Natural Theology" of the title is Theology based on natural evidence, without revelation. The poem has generated much excellent discussion. One topic has been the poem's use of the third person (Caliban's first word—"Will"—means "he will," which means "I will") and the shifts from the third to first person. The prevailing view is that Browning had Caliban normally use the third person essentially to stress his primitiveness. The Quiet is neuter [*it*]; Setebos is third person with a capital [*He*]; Caliban, though he sometimes uses the first person, is generally third person without the capital [*he*], and frequently without the pronoun at all [*Thinketh*].

[4] newts or similar creatures.

[5] pumpkin.

Touching that other, whom his dam[1] called God.
Because to talk about Him, vexes—ha,
Could He but know! and time to vex is now,
20 When talk is safer than in winter-time.
Moreover Prosper and Miranda[2] sleep
In confidence he drudges at their task,
And it is good to cheat the pair, and gibe,
Letting the rank[3] tongue blossom into speech.]

25 Setebos, Setebos, and Setebos!
'Thinketh, He dwelleth i' the cold o' the moon.

'Thinketh He made it, with the sun to match,
But not the stars;[4] the stars came otherwise;
Only made clouds, winds, meteors, such as that:
30 Also this isle, what lives and grows thereon,
And snaky sea which rounds and ends the same.

'Thinketh, it came of being ill at ease:
He hated that He cannot change His cold,
Nor cure its ache. 'Hath spied an icy fish
That longed to 'scape the rock-stream where she lived,
35 And thaw herself within the lukewarm brine
O' the lazy sea her stream thrusts far amid,
A crystal spike 'twixt two warm walls of wave;
Only, she ever sickened, found repulse
At the other kind of water, not her life,
40 (Green-dense and dim-delicious, bred o' the sun)
Flounced back from bliss she was not born to breathe,
And in her old bounds buried her despair,
Hating and loving warmth alike: so He.

'Thinketh, He made thereat the sun, this isle,
45 Trees and the fowls here, beast and creeping thing.
Yon otter, sleek-wet, black, lithe as a leech;
Yon auk,[5] one fire-eye in a ball of foam,
That floats and feeds; a certain badger brown
He hath watched hunt with that slant white-wedge eye
50 By moonlight; and the pie[6] with the long tongue
That pricks deep into oakwarts[7] for a worm,
And says a plain word when she finds her prize,
But will not eat the ants; the ants themselves
That build a wall of seeds and settled stalks
55 About their hole—He made all these and more,
Made all we see, and us, in spite: how else?
He could not, Himself, make a second self
To be His mate; as well have made Himself:
He would not make what he mislikes or slights,
60 An eyesore to Him, or not worth His pains:
But did, in envy, listlessness or sport,
Make what Himself would fain, in a manner, be—
Weaker in most points, stronger in a few,
Worthy, and yet mere playthings all the while,
65 Things He admires and mocks too,—that is it,
Because, so brave, so better though they be,
It nothing skills[8] if He begin to plague.
Look now, I[9] melt a gourd-fruit into mash,
Add honeycomb and pods, I have perceived,
70 Which bite like finches when they bill and kiss,—
Then, when froth rises bladdery,[10] drink up all,
Quick, quick, till maggots[11] scamper through my brain;
Last, throw me on my back i' the seeded thyme,
And wanton, wishing I were born a bird.

---

[1] Sycorax in *The Tempest* 1.2.373; there her God is Setebos.

[2] the protagonist of *The Tempest* (and Caliban's master) and his daughter. In the play Prospero naps in the afternoon.

[3] rebellious.

[4] The stars are the realm of the Quiet, we learn later.

[5] a kind of sea bird.

[6] magpie or the pied woodpecker (?).

[7] oak galls.

[8] avails.

[9] Caliban's first shift to the first person.

[10] bubbly.

[11] fancies.

75 Put case, unable to be what I wish,
I yet could make a live bird out of clay:
Would not I take clay, pinch my Caliban
Able to fly?—for, there, see, he hath wings,
And great comb like the hoopoe's[1] to admire,
80 And there, a sting to do his foes offence,
There, and I will that he begin to live,
Fly to yon rock-top, nip me off the horns
Of grigs[2] high up that make the merry din,
Saucy through their veined wings, and mind me not.
85 In which feat, if his leg snapped, brittle clay,
And he lay stupid-like,—why, I should laugh;
And if he, spying me, should fall to weep,
Beseech me to be good, repair his wrong,
Bid his poor leg smart less or grow again,—
90 Well, as the chance were, this might take or else
Not take my fancy: I might hear his cry,
And give the mankin three sound legs for one,
Or pluck the other off, leave him like an egg,
And lessoned[3] he was mine and merely clay.
95 Were this no pleasure, lying in the thyme,
Drinking the mash, with brain become alive,
Making and marring clay at will? So He.

'Thinketh, such shows nor right nor wrong in Him,
Nor kind, nor cruel: He is strong and Lord.
100 'Am strong myself compared to yonder crabs
That march now from the mountain to the sea,
'Let twenty pass, and stone the twenty-first,
Loving not, hating not, just choosing so.[4]
'Say, the first straggler that boasts purple spots
105 Shall join the file, one pincer twisted off;
'Say, this bruised fellow shall receive a worm,
And two worms he whose nippers end in red;
As it likes me each time, I do: so He.

Well then, 'supposeth He is good i' the main,
110 Placable if His mind and ways were guessed,
But rougher than His handiwork, be sure!
Oh, He hath made things worthier than Himself,
And envieth that, so helped, such things do more
Than He who made them! What consoles but this?
115 That they, unless through Him, do naught at all,
And must submit: what other use in things?
'Hath cut a pipe of pithless elder-joint
That, blown through, gives exact the scream o' the
  jay
When from her wing you twitch the feathers blue:
120 Sound this, and little birds that hate the jay
Flock within stone's throw, glad their foe is hurt:
Put case such pipe could prattle and boast forsooth
"I catch the birds, I am the crafty thing,
I make the cry my maker cannot make
125 With his great round mouth; he must blow
  through mine!"
Would not I smash it with my foot? So He.

But wherefore rough, why cold and ill at ease?
Aha, that is a question! Ask, for that,
What knows,—the something over Setebos
130 That made Him, or He, may be, found and fought,
Worsted, drove off and did to nothing, perchance.
There may be something quiet o'er His head,
Out of His reach, that feels nor joy nor grief,
Since both derive from weakness in some way.
135 I joy because the quails come; would not joy
Could I bring quails here when I have a mind:
This Quiet, all it hath a mind to, doth.
'Esteemeth stars the outposts of its couch,
But never spends much thought nor care that way.
140 It may look up, work up,—the worse for those
It works on! 'Careth but for Setebos
The many-handed as a cuttle-fish,
Who, making Himself feared through what He does,
Looks up, first, and perceives he cannot soar
145 To what is quiet and hath happy life;
Next looks down here, and out of very spite

[1] a crested colourful bird.
[2] grasshoppers or crickets.
[3] having been taught a lesson.
[4] a clear hit at doctrines of predestination.

Makes this a bauble-world to ape yon real,
These good things to match those as hips[1] do grapes.
'Tis solace making baubles, ay, and sport.
150 Himself peeped late, eyed Prosper at his books
Careless and lofty, lord now of the isle:
Vexed, 'stitched a book of broad leaves, arrow-
    shaped,
Wrote thereon, he knows what, prodigious words;
Has peeled a wand and called it by a name;
155 Weareth at whiles for an enchanter's robe
The eyed skin of a supple oncelot;[2]
And hath an ounce[3] sleeker than youngling mole,
A four-legged serpent he makes cower and couch,
Now snarl, now hold its breath and mind his eye,
160 And saith she is Miranda and my wife:
'Keeps for his Ariel[4] a tall pouch-bill crane
He bids go wade for fish and straight disgorge;
Also a sea-beast, lumpish, which he snared,
Blinded the eyes of, and brought somewhat tame,
165 And split its toe-webs, and now pens the drudge
In a hole o' the rock and calls him Caliban;
A bitter heart that bides its time and bites.
'Plays thus at being Prosper in a way,
Taketh his mirth with make-believes: so He.

170 His dam held that the Quiet made all things
Which Setebos vexed only: 'holds not so.
Who made them weak, meant weakness He might
    vex.
Had He meant other, while His hand was in,
Why not make horny eyes no thorn could prick,
175 Or plate my scalp with bone against the snow,
Or overscale my flesh 'neath joint and joint,
Like an orc's[5] armour? Ay,—so spoil His sport!
He is the One now: only He doth all.

'Saith, He may like, perchance, what profits Him.
180 Ay, himself loves what does him good; but why?
'Gets good no otherwise. This blinded beast
Loves whose places flesh-meat on his nose,
But, had he eyes, would want no help, but hate
Or love, just as it liked him: He hath eyes.
185 Also it pleaseth Setebos to work,
Use all His hands, and exercise much craft,
By no means for the love of what is worked.
'Tasteth, himself, no finer good i' the world
When all goes right, in this safe summer-time,
190 And he wants little, hungers, aches not much,
Than trying what to do with wit and strength.
'Falls to make something: 'piled yon pile of turfs,
And squared and stuck there squares of soft white
    chalk,
And, with a fish-tooth, scratched a moon on each,
195 And set up endwise certain spikes of tree,
And crowned the whole with a sloth's skull a-top,
Found dead i' the woods, too hard for one to kill.
No use at all i' the work, for work's sole sake;
'Shall some day knock it down again: so He.

200 'Saith He is terrible: watch His feats in proof!
One hurricane will spoil six good months' hope.
He hath a spite against me, that I know,
Just as He favours Prosper, who knows why?
So it is, all the same, as well I find.
205 'Wove wattles[6] half the winter, fenced them firm
With stone and stake to stop she-tortoises
Crawling to lay their eggs here: well, one wave,
Feeling the foot of Him upon its neck,
Gaped as a snake does, lolled out its large tongue,
210 And licked the whole labour flat: so much for spite.
'Saw a ball[7] flame down late (yonder it lies)
Where, half an hour before, I slept i' the shade:
Often they scatter sparkles: there is force!
'Dug up a newt He may have envied once

---

[1] fruit of the wild rose.

[2] ocelot or jaguar.

[3] lynx or snow-leopard or cheetah.

[4] Prospero's airy servant in *The Tempest*.

[5] probably sea monster.

[6] twigs.

[7] meteor (fire ball).

215 And turned to stone, shut up inside a stone.
Please Him and hinder this?—What Prosper does?
Aha, if He would tell me how! Not He!
There is the sport: discover how or die!
All need not die, for of the things o' the isle
220 Some flee afar, some dive, some run up trees;
Those at His mercy,—why, they please Him most
When...when...well, never try the same way twice!
Repeat what act has pleased, He may grow wroth.
You must not know His ways, and play Him off,
225 Sure of the issue. 'Doth the like himself:
'Spareth a squirrel that it nothing fears
But steals the nut from underneath my thumb,
And when I threat, bites stoutly in defence:
'Spareth an urchin[1] that contrariwise,
230 Curls up into a ball, pretending death
For fright at my approach: the two ways please.
But what would move my choler more than this,
That either creature counted on its life
Tomorrow and next day and all days to come,
235 Saying, forsooth, in the inmost of its heart,
"Because he did so yesterday with me,
And otherwise with such another brute,
So must he do henceforth and always."—Ay?
Would teach the reasoning couple what "must"
means!
240 'Doth as he likes, or wherefore Lord? So He.

'Conceiveth all things will continue thus,
And we shall have to live in fear of Him
So long as He lives, keeps His strength: no change,
If He have done His best, make no new world
245 To please Him more, so leave off watching this,—
If He surprise not even the Quiet's self
Some strange day,—or, suppose, grow into it
As grubs grow butterflies: else, here are we,
And there is He, and nowhere help at all.

250 'Believeth with the life, the pain shall stop.
His dam held different, that after death
He both plagued enemies and feasted friends:
Idly! He doth His worst in this our life,
Giving just respite lest we die through pain,
255 Saving last pain for worst,—with which, an end.
Meanwhile, the best way to escape His ire
Is, not to seem too happy. 'Sees, himself,
Yonder two flies, with purple films[2] and pink,
Bask on the pompion-bell above: kills both.
260 'Sees two black painful[3] beetles roll their ball
On head and tail as if to save their lives:
Moves them the stick away they strive to clear.

Even so, 'would have Him misconceive, suppose
This Caliban strives hard and ails no less,
265 And always, above all else, envies Him;
Wherefore he mainly dances on dark nights,
Moans in the sun, gets under holes to laugh,
And never speaks his mind save housed as now:
Outside, 'groans, curses. If He caught me here,
270 O'erheard this speech, and asked "What chucklest
at?"
'Would, to appease Him, cut a finger off,
Or of my three kid yearlings burn the best,
Or let the toothsome apples rot on tree,
Or push my tame beast for the orc to taste:
275 While myself lit a fire, and made a song
And sung it, *"What I hate, be consecrate*
To celebrate Thee and Thy state, no mate
For Thee; what see for envy in poor me?"
Hoping the while, since evils sometimes mend,
280 Warts rub away and sores are cured with slime,
That some strange day, will either the Quiet catch
And conquer Setebos, or likelier He
Decrepit may doze, doze, as good as die.
[What, what? A curtain[4] o'er the world at once!

---

[1] hedgehog.

[2] wings.

[3] taking pains.

[4] thundercloud.

285 Crickets stop hissing; not a bird—or, yes,
There scuds His raven that has told Him all!
It was fool's play, this prattling! Ha! The wind
Shoulders the pillared dust, death's house o' the
move,[1]
And fast invading fires begin! White blaze—
290 A tree's head snaps—and there, there, there, there,
there,

His thunder follows! Fool to gibe at Him!
Lo! 'Lieth flat and loveth Setebos!
'Maketh his teeth meet through his upper lip,
Will let those quails fly, will not eat this month
295 One little mess of whelks, so he may 'scape!]
—1864

---

[1] a whirlwind that has picked up dust.

Edward Lear
1812 – 1888

Edward Lear was an artist and poet. He is known for his landscapes and natural history drawings, as well as for his nonsense poems and limericks.

❦

The Owl and the Pussy-Cat

The Owl and the Pussy-Cat went to sea
　In a beautiful pea-green boat,
They took some honey, and plenty of money,
　Wrapped up in a five-pound note.
5 The Owl looked up to the stars above,
　And sang to a small guitar,
"O lovely Pussy! O Pussy, my love,
　What a beautiful Pussy you are,
　　You are,
10　　You are!
What a beautiful Pussy you are!"

Pussy said to the Owl, "You elegant fowl!
　How charmingly sweet you sing!
O let us be married! too long we have tarried:
15　But what shall we do for a ring?"
They sailed away for a year and a day,
　To the land where the Bong-tree grows
And there in a wood a Piggy-wig stood
　With a ring at the end of his nose,
20　　His nose,
　　His nose,
With a ring at the end of his nose.

"Dear Pig, are you willing to sell for one shilling
25　Your ring?" Said the Piggy, "I will."
So they took it away, and were married next day
　By the Turkey who lives on the hill.
They dinèd on mince, and slices of quince,

Which they ate with a runcible spoon;[1]
30 And hand in hand, on the edge of the sand,
　They danced by the light of the moon,
　　The moon,
　　The moon,
They danced by the light of the moon.
—1871

The Dong with a Luminous Nose

When awful darkness and silence reign
　Over the Great Gromboolian plain,
　　Through the long, long wintry nights;—
When the angry breakers roar
5 As they beat on the rocky shore;—
　　When Storm-clouds brood on the towering
　　　heights
Of the Hills of the Chankly Bore:—

Then, through the vast and gloomy dark,
There moves what seems a fiery spark,
10　A lonely spark with silvery rays
　　Piercing the coal-black night,—
　　A meteor strange and bright:—
Hither and thither the vision strays,
　A single lurid light.

15 Slowly it wanders,—pauses,—creeps,—
Anon it sparkles,—flashes and leaps;
And ever as onward it gleaming goes
A light on the Bong-tree stems it throws.

---

[1] as coined by Lear, a fork with three prongs, two of which are broad, the third curved and sharp-edged.

And those who watch at that midnight hour
20 From Hall or Terrace, or lofty Tower,
Cry, as the wild light passes along,—
        "The Dong!—the Dong!
        "The wandering Dong through the forest goes!
        "The Dong! the Dong!
25   "The Dong with a luminous Nose!"

        Long years ago
        The Dong was happy and gay,
Till he fell in love with a Jumbly Girl
        Who came to those shores one day.
30 For the Jumblies came in a Sieve, they did,—
Landing at eve near the Zemmery Fidd
        Where the Oblong Oysters grow,
        And the rocks are smooth and gray.
And all the woods and the valleys rang
35 With the Chorus they daily and nightly sang,—
        "Far and few, far and few,
        Are the lands where the Jumblies live;
        Their heads are green, and their hands are
            blue
        And they went to sea in a Sieve."

40 Happily, happily passed those days!
        While the cheerful Jumblies staid;
        They danced in circlets all night long,
To the plaintive pipe of the lively Dong,
        In the moonlight, shine, or shade.
45 For day and night he was always there
By the side of the Jumbly Girl so fair,
With her sky-blue hands, and her sea-green hair.
Till the morning came of that hateful day
When the Jumblies sailed in their Sieve away,
50 And the Dong was left on the cruel shore
Gazing—gazing for evermore,—
Ever keeping his weary eyes on
That pea-green sail on the far horizon,—
Singing the Jumbly Chorus still
55 As he sate all day on the grassy hill,—

"Far and few, far and few,
Are the lands where the Jumblies live;
Their heads are green, and their hands are blue
And they went to sea in a Sieve."

60 But when the sun was low in the West,
    The Dong arose and said,
"What little sense I once possessed
    Has quite gone out of my head!"
And since that day he wanders still
65 By lake and forest, marsh and hill,
Singing—"O somewhere, in valley or plain
"Might I find my Jumbly Girl again!
"For ever I'll seek by lake and shore
"Till I find my Jumbly Girl once more!"

70   Playing a pipe with silvery squeaks,
        Since then his Jumbly Girl he seeks,
        And because by night he could not see,
        He gathered the bark of the Twangum Tree
            On the flowery plain that grows.
75   And he wove him a wondrous Nose,—
        A Nose as strange as a Nose could be!
Of vast proportions and painted red,
And tied with cords to the back of his head.
        —In a hollow rounded space it ended
80   With a luminous Lamp within suspended,
            All fenced about
            With a bandage stout
            To prevent the wind from blowing it
                out;—
        And with holes all round to send the light,
85   In gleaming rays on the dismal night.

And now each night, and all night long,
Over those plains still roams the Dong;
And above the wail of the Chimp and Snipe
You may hear the squeak of his plaintive pipe
90 While ever he seeks, but seeks in vain
To meet with his Jumbly Girl again;
Lonely and wild—all night he goes,—

The Dong with a luminous Nose!
And all who watch at the midnight hour,
95 From Hall or Terrace, or lofty Tower,
Cry, as they trace the Meteor bright,
Moving along through the dreary night,—
        "This is the hour when forth he goes,
        "The Dong with the luminous Nose!
100   "Yonder—over the plain he goes;
            "He goes!
            "He goes;
        "The Dong with the luminous Nose!"
—1877

How Pleasant to Know Mr. Lear

The Self-Portrait of the Laureate of Nonsense

"How pleasant to know Mr. Lear!"
    Who has written such volumes of stuff!
Some think him ill-tempered and queer,
    But a few think him pleasant enough.

5   His mind is concrete and fastidious,
        His nose is remarkably big;
His visage is more or less hideous,
        His beard it resembles a wig.

He has ears, and two eyes, and ten fingers,
10   Leastways if you reckon two thumbs;
Long ago he was one of the singers,
        But now he is one of the dumbs.

He sits in a beautiful parlour,
        With hundreds of books on the wall;
15 He drinks a great deal of Marsala,
        But never gets tipsy at all.

He has many friends, laymen and clerical,
        Old Foss is the name of his cat:[1]
His body is perfectly spherical,
20   He weareth a runcible hat.

When he walks in a waterproof white,
        The children run after him so!
Calling out, "He's come out in his night-
        gown, that crazy old Englishman, oh!"

25 He weeps by the side of the ocean,
        He weeps on the top of the hill;
He purchases pancakes and lotion,
        And chocolate shrimps from the mill.

He reads but he cannot speak Spanish,
30   He cannot abide ginger beer:
Ere the days of his pilgrimage vanish,
        How pleasant to know Mr. Lear!
—1894 (1879)

---

[1] It was; Lear's beloved feline companion died in 1887 at the age of 17.

Charlotte Brontë
1816 – 1855

Charlotte Brontë was the third daughter of Patrick Brontë and Maria Branwell and the eldest of the three famous sisters. After the traumatic experience of the Clergy Daughters' School (fictionalized in *Jane Eyre*), Charlotte attended school at Roe Head near Mirfield and later taught there; like her sister Anne, she worked as a governess to help support the family. The sisters decided to open their own school and, hoping to increase their facility with languages, Charlotte and Emily attended the Pensionnat Heger in Brussels in 1842. While Charlotte is remembered primarily as a novelist, her poems, and especially her poems on the deaths of her sisters, have a haunting quality. Charlotte survived all of her siblings and married in 1854, but died in the winter of 1855 of consumption and complications arising from pregnancy.

❧❧❧

The Missionary

Plough, vessel, plough the British main,
Seek the free ocean's wider plain;
Leave English scenes and English skies,
Unbind, dissever English ties;
5   Bear me to climes remote and strange,
Where altered life, fast-following change,
Hot action, never-ceasing toil,
Shall stir, turn, dig, the spirit's soil;
Fresh roots shall plant, fresh seed shall sow,
10 Till a new garden there shall grow,
Cleared of the weeds that fill it now,—
Mere human love, mere selfish yearning,
Which, cherished, would arrest me yet.
I grasp the plough, there's no returning,
15 Let me, then, struggle to forget.

But England's shores are yet in view,
And England's skies of tender blue
Are arched above her guardian sea.
I cannot yet Remembrance flee;
20 I must again, then, firmly face
That task of anguish, to retrace.
Wedded to home—I home forsake;
Fearful of change—I changes make;
Too fond of ease—I plunge in toil;
25 Lover of calm—I seek turmoil:

Nature and hostile Destiny
Stir in my heart a conflict wild;
And long and fierce the war will be
Ere duty both has reconciled.

30 What other tie yet holds me fast
To the divorced, abandoned past?
Smouldering, on my heart's altar lies
The fire of some great sacrifice,
Not yet half quenched. The sacred steel
35 But lately struck my carnal will,
My life-long hope, first joy and last,
What I loved well, and clung to fast;
What I wished wildly to retain,
What I renounced with soul-felt pain;
40 What—when I saw it, axe-struck, perish—
Left me no joy on earth to cherish;
A man bereft—yet sternly now
I do confirm that Jephtha[1] vow:
Shall I retract, or fear, or flee?
45 Did Christ, when rose the fatal tree
Before Him, on Mount Calvary?[2]
'Twas a long fight, hard fought, but won,
And what I did was justly done.

---

[1] the biblical judge who killed his only daughter because he had declared to God that if he conquered in battle he would sacrifice the first thing he met on returning home: Judges 11:30–40.

[2] the mount near Jerusalem where Christ was crucified.

Yet, Helen! from thy love I turned,
50 When my heart most for thy heart burned;
I dared thy tears, I dared thy scorn—
Easier the death-pang had been borne.
Helen, thou might'st not go with me,
I could not—dared not stay for thee!
55 I heard afar, in bonds complain
The savage from beyond the main;
And that wild sound rose o'er the cry
Wrung out by passion's agony;
And even when, with the bitterest tear
60 I ever shed, mine eyes were dim,
Still, with the spirit's vision clear,
I saw Hell's empire, vast and grim,
Spread on each Indian river's shore,
Each realm of Asia covering o'er.
65 There the weak, trampled by the strong,
Live but to suffer—hopeless die;
There pagan-priests, whose creed is Wrong,
Extortion, Lust, and Cruelty,
Crush our lost race—and brimming fill
70 The bitter cup of human ill;
And I—who have the healing creed,
The faith benign of Mary's Son,
Shall I behold my brother's need,
And selfishly to aid him shun?
75 I—who upon my mother's knees,
In childhood, read Christ's written word,
Received His legacy of peace,
His holy rule of action heard;
I—in whose heart the sacred sense
80 Of Jesus' love was early felt;
Of His pure, full benevolence,
His pitying tenderness for guilt;
His shepherd-care for wandering sheep,
For all weak, sorrowing, trembling things,
85 His mercy vast, His passion deep
Of anguish for man's sufferings;
I—schooled from childhood in such lore—
Dared I draw back or hesitate,
When called to heal the sickness sore

90 Of those far off and desolate?
Dark, in the realm and shades of Death,
Nations, and tribes, and empires lie,
But even to them the light of Faith
Is breaking on their sombre sky:
95 And be it mine to bid them raise
Their drooped heads to the kindling scene,
And know and hail the sunrise blaze
Which heralds Christ the Nazarene.
I know how Hell the veil will spread
100 Over their brows and filmy eyes,
And earthward crush the lifted head
That would look up and seek the skies;
I know what war the fiend will wage
Against that soldier of the Cross,
105 Who comes to dare his demon—rage,
And work his kingdom shame and loss.
Yes, hard and terrible the toil
Of him who steps on foreign soil,
Resolved to plant the gospel vine,
110 Where tyrants rule and slaves repine;
Eager to lift Religion's light
Where thickest shades of mental night
Screen the false god and fiendish rite;
Reckless that missionary blood,
115 Shed in wild wilderness and wood,
Has left, upon the unblest air,
The man's deep moan—the martyr's prayer.
I know my lot—I only ask
Power to fulfil the glorious task;
120 Willing the spirit, may the flesh
Strength for the day receive afresh.
May burning sun or deadly wind
Prevail not o'er an earnest mind;
May torments strange or direst death
125 Nor trample truth, nor baffle faith.
Though such blood-drops should fall from me
As fell in old Gethsemane,[1]
Welcome the anguish, so it gave

---

[1] the garden outside Jerusalem where the agony, betrayal, and arrest of Christ took place: Matthew 26:36.

More strength to work—more skill to save.
130 And, oh! if brief must be my time,
If hostile hand or fatal clime
Cut short my course—still o'er my grave,
Lord, may Thy harvest whitening wave.
So I the culture may begin,
135 Let others thrust the sickle in;
If but the seed will faster grow,
May my blood water what I sow!
What! have I ever trembling stood,
And feared to give to God that blood?
140 What! has the coward love of life
Made me shrink from the righteous strife?
Have human passions, human fears
Severed me from those Pioneers
Whose task is to march first, and trace
145 Paths for the progress of our race?
It has been so; but grant me, Lord,
Now to stand steadfast by Thy word!
Protected by salvation's helm,
Shielded by faith, with truth begirt,
150 To smile when trials seek to whelm
And stand 'mid testing fires unhurt
Hurling Hell's strongest bulwarks down,
Even when the last pang thrills my breast,
When Death bestows the Martyr's crown,
155 And calls me into Jesus' rest.
Then for my ultimate reward—
Then for the world-rejoicing word—
The voice from Father—Spirit—Son:
"Servant of God, well hast thou done!"
—1846

Master and Pupil [1]

I gave, at first, attention close;
  Then interest warm ensued;

From interest, as improvement rose,
  Succeeded gratitude.

5 Obedience was no effort soon,
  And labour was no pain;
If tired, a word, a glance alone
  Would give me strength again.

From others of the studious band
10 Ere long he singled me;
But only by more close demand
  And sterner urgency.

The task he from another took,
  From me he did reject;
15 He would no slight omission brook,
  And suffer no defect.

If my companions went astray,
  He scarce their wanderings blamed;
If I but faltered in the way,
20 His anger fiercely flamed.

When sickness stayed awhile my course,
  He seemed impatient still,
Because his pupil's flagging force
  Could not obey his will.

25 One day when summoned to the bed
  Where pain and I did strive,
I heard him, as he bent his head,
  Say, "God, she must revive!"

I felt his hand, with gentle stress,
30 A moment laid on mine,
And wished to mark my consciousness
  By some responsive sign.

But powerless then to speak or move,
  I only felt, within,

[1] The original draft of the above poem is in an exercise-book used by Charlotte Brontë in Brussels, 1843.

35 The sense of Hope, the strength of Love,
    Their healing work begin.

And as he from the room withdrew,
    My heart his steps pursued;
I longed to prove, by efforts new,
40   My speechless gratitude.

When once again I took my place,
    Long vacant, in the class,
Th' unfrequent smile across his face
    Did for one moment pass.

45 The lessons done; the signal made
    Of glad release and play,
He, as he passed, an instant stayed,
    One kindly word to say.

"Jane, till to-morrow you are free
50   From tedious task and rule;
This afternoon I must not see
    That yet pale face in school.

"Seek in the garden-shades a seat,
    Far from the playground din;
55 The sun is warm, the air is sweet:
    Stay till I call you in."

A long and pleasant afternoon
    I passed in those green bowers;
All silent, tranquil, and alone
60   With birds, and bees, and flowers.

Yet, when my master's voice I heard
    Call, from the window, "Jane!"
I entered, joyful, at the word,
    The busy house again.

65 He, in the hall, paced up and down;
    He paused as I passed by;

His forehead stern relaxed its frown;
    He raised his deep-set eye.

"Not quite so pale," he murmured low.
70   "Now, Jane, go rest awhile,"
And as I smiled his smoothened brow
    Returned as glad a smile.

My perfect health restored, he took
    His mien austere again;
75 And, as before, he would not brook
    The slightest fault from Jane.

The longest task, the hardest theme
    Fell to my share as erst,
And still I toiled to place my name
80   In every study first.

He yet begrudged and stinted praise,
    But I had learnt to read
The secret meaning of his face,
    And that was my best meed.

85 Even when his hasty temper spoke
    In tones that sorrow stirred,
My grief was lulled as soon as woke
    By some relenting word.

And when he lent some precious book,
90   Or gave some fragrant flower,
I did not quail to Envy's look,
    Upheld by Pleasure's power.

At last our school ranks took their ground,
    The hard-fought field I won;
95 The prize, a laurel-wreath, was bound
    My throbbing forehead on.

Low at my master's knee I bent,
    The offered crown to meet;

Its green leaves through my temples sent
100   A thrill as wild as sweet.

The strong pulse of Ambition struck
   In every vein I owned;
At the same instant, bleeding broke
   A secret, inward wound.

105 The hour of triumph was to me
   The hour of sorrow sore;
A day hence I must cross the sea,
   Ne'er to recross it more.

An hour hence, in my master's room,
110   I with him sat alone,
And told him what a dreary gloom
   O'er joy had parting thrown.

He little said; the time was brief,
   The ship was soon to sail;
115 And while I sobbed in bitter grief
   My master but looked pale.

They called in haste: he bade me go,
   Then snatched me back again;
He held me fast and murmured low,
120   "Why will they part us, Jane?

"Were you not happy in my care?
   Did I not faithful prove?
Will others to my darling bear
   As true, as deep a love?

125 "O God, watch o'er my foster-child!
   Oh, guard her gentle head!
When winds are high and tempests wild
   Protection round her spread!

"They call again: leave then my breast;
130   Quit thy true shelter, Jane;

But when deceived, repulsed, opprest,
   Come home to me again!"
—1857 (1845?)

On the Death of Emily Jane Brontë[1]

My darling, thou wilt never know
The grinding agony of woe
   That we have borne for thee.
Thus may we consolation tear
5 E'en from the depth of our despair
   And wasting misery.

The nightly anguish thou art spared
When all the crushing truth is bared
   To the awakening mind,
10 When the galled heart is pierced with grief,
Till wildly it implores relief,
   But small relief can find.

Nor know'st thou what it is to lie
Looking forth with streaming eye
15   On life's lone wilderness.
"Weary, weary, dark and drear,
How shall I the journey bear,
   The burden and distress?"

Then since thou art spared such pain
20 We will not wish thee here again;
   He that lives must mourn.
God help us through our misery
And give us rest and joy with thee
   When we reach our bourne!
—1896 (DECEMBER 24, 1848)

---

[1] Emily Jane Brontë died on 19 December 1848.

On the Death of Anne Brontë[1]

There's little joy in life for me,
    And little terror in the grave;
I've lived the parting hour to see
    Of one I would have died to save.

5 Calmly to watch the failing breath,
    Wishing each sigh might be the last;
Longing to see the shade of death
    O'er those belovèd features cast.

The cloud, the stillness that must part
10   The darling of my life from me;
And then to thank God from my heart,
    To thank Him well and fervently;

Although I knew that we had lost
    The hope and glory of our life;
15 And now, benighted, tempest-tossed,
    Must bear alone the weary strife.
      —1896 (JUNE 21, 1849)

Reason

Unloved I love, unwept I weep,
    Grief I restrain, hope I repress;
Vain is this anguish, fixed and deep,
    Vainer desires or means of bliss.

5 My life is cold, love's fire being dead;
    That fire self-kindled, self-consumed;
What living warmth erewhile it shed,
    Now to how drear extinction doomed!

Devoid of charm how could I dream
10   My unasked love would e'er return?
What fate, what influence lit the flame
    I still feel inly, deeply burn?

Alas! there are those who should not love;
    I to this dreary band belong;
15 This knowing let me henceforth prove
    Too wise to list delusion's song.

No, Syren! Beauty is not mine;
    Affection's joy I ne'er shall know;
Lonely will be my life's decline,
20   Even as my youth is lonely now.

Come Reason—Science—Learning—Thought—
    To you my heart I dedicate;
I have a faithful subject brought:
    Faithful because most desolate.

25 Fear not a wandering, feeble mind:
    Stern Sovereign, it is all your own
To crush, to cheer, to loose, to bind;
    Unclaimed, unshared, it seeks your throne.

Soft may the breeze of summer blow,
30   Sweetly its sun in valleys shine;
All earth around with love may glow,--
    No warmth shall reach this heart of mine.

Vain boast and false! Even now the fire
    Though smothered, slacked, repelled, is burning
35 At my life's source; and stronger, higher,
    Waxes the spirit's trampled yearning.

It wakes but to be crushed again:
    Faint I will not, nor yield to sorrow;
Conflict and force will quell the brain;
40   Doubt not I shall be strong to-morrow.

Have I not fled that I may conquer?
    Crost the dark sea in firmest faith
That I at last might plant my anchor
    Where love cannot prevail to death?
      —1913 (JANUARY 1836)

---

[1] Anne Brontë died at Scarborough on 28 May 1849.

"The house was still—the room was still"

The house was still—the room was still
  'Twas eventide in June
A caged canary to the sun
Then setting—trilled a tune

5 A free bird on that lilac bush
Outside the lattice heard
He listened long—there came a hush
He dropped an answering word—

The prisoner to the free replied
—1915 (1846–47)

The Lonely Lady

She was alone that evening—and alone
  She had been all that heavenly summer day.
She scarce had seen a face, or heard a tone
  And quietly the hours had slipped away,
5 Their passage through the silence hardly known
  Save when the clock with silver chime did say
The number of the hour, and all in peace
Listened to hear its own vibration cease.

Wearied with airy task, with tracing flowers
10   Of snow on lace, with singing hymn or song
With trying all her harp's symphonious powers
  By striking full its quivering strings along,
And drawing out deep chords, and shaking showers
  Of brilliant sound, from shell and wires among,
15 Wearied with reading books, weary with weeping,
Heart-sick of Life, she sought for death in sleeping.

She lay down on her couch—but could she sleep?
  Could she forget existence in a dream
That blotting out reality might sweep
20   Over her weariness, the healing stream
Of hope and hope's fruition?—Lo the deep

And amber glow of that departing beam
Shot from that blood-red sun—points to her brow
Straight like a silent index, mark it now

25 Kindling her perfect features, bringing bloom
  Into the living marble, smooth and bright
As sculptured effigy on hallowed tomb
  Glimmering amid the dimmed and solemn light
  Native to Gothic pile—so wan, so white
30 In shadow gleamed that face, in rosy flush
Of setting sun, rich with a living blush.

Up rose the lonely lady, and her eyes
  Instinctive raised their fringe of raven shade
And fixed upon those vast and glorious skies
35   Their lustre that in death alone might fade.
Skies fired with crimson clouds, burning with dyes
  Intense as blood—they arched above and rayed
The firmament with broad and vivid beams
That seemed to bend towards her all their gleams.

40 It was the arc of battle, leagues away
  In the direction of that setting sun
An army saw that livid summer day
  Closing their serried[1] ranks and squared upon,
Saw it with awe, so deeply was the ray,
45   The last ray tinged with blood—so wild it shone,
So strange the semblance gory, burning, given
To pool and stream and sea by that red heaven.
—1934 (MAY, 1837)

"Is this my tomb, this humble stone"

Is this my tomb, this humble stone
  Above this narrow mound?
Is this my resting place, so lone,
  So green, so quiet round?
5 Not even a stately tree to shade
  The sunbeam from my bed,

—————
[1] crowded.

Not even a flower in tribute laid
  As sacred to the dead.

I look along those evening hills,
10 As mute as earth may be,
I hear not even the voice of rills—
  Not even a cloud I see.
How long is it since human tread
  Was heard on that dim track
15 Which, through the shadowy valleys led,
  Winds far, and farther back?

And was I not a lady once,
  My home a princely hall?
And did not hundreds make response
20 Whene'er I deigned to call?
Methinks, as in a doubtful dream,
  That dwelling proud I see
Where I caught first the early beam
  Of being's day's spring face.

25 Methinks the flash is round me still
  Of mirrors broad and bright;
Methinks I see the torches fill
  My chambers with their light,
And o'er my limbs the draperies flow
30 All gloss and silken shine,
On my cold brow the jewels glow
  As bright as festal wine.

Who then disrobed that worshipped form?
  Who wound this winding sheet?
35 Who turned the blood that ran so warm
  To Winter's frozen sleet?
O can it be that many a sun
  Has set, as that sets now,
Since last its fervid lustre shone
40 Upon my living brow?

Have all the wild dark clouds of night
  Each eve for years drawn on

While I interred so far from light
  Have slumbered thus alone?
45 Has this green mound been wet with rain—
  Such rain as storms distil
When the wind's high and warning strain
  Swells loud on sunless hill?

And I have slept where roughest hind
50 Had shuddered to pass by,
And no dread did my spirit find
  In all that snow-racked sky,
Though shook the iron-rails around
  As, swept by deepened breeze,
55 They gave a strange and hollow sound
  That living veins might freeze.

O was that music like my own?—
  Such as I used to play
When soft and clear and holy shone
60 The summer moon's first ray,
And saw me lingering still to feel
  The influence of that sky?
O words may not the peace reveal
  That filled its concave high,

65 As rose and bower how far beneath
  Hung down o'ercharged with dew,
And sighed their sweet and fragrant breath
  To every gale that blew
The hour for music, but in vain,
70 Each ancient stanza rose
To lips that could not with their strain
  Break Earth's and Heaven's repose.

Yet first a note and then a line
  The fettered tongue would say,
75 And then the whole rich song divine
  Found free a gushing way.
Past, lost, forgotten, I am here,
  They dug my chamber deep,

I know no hope, I feel no fear,
80   I sleep—how calm I sleep!
—1934 (JUNE 4, 1837)

"Obscure and little seen my way"

Obscure and little seen my way
Through life has ever been,
But winding from my earliest day
Through many a wondrous scene.
5   None ever asked what feelings moved
My heart, or flushed my cheek,

And if I hoped, or feared or loved
No voice was heard to speak.

I watched, I thought, I studied long,
10   The crowds I moved unmarked among,
I nought to them and they to me
But shapes of strange variety.
The Great with all the elusive shine
Of power and wealth and lofty line
15   I long have marked and well I know.
—1934 (NOVEMBER 1837)

Emily Jane Brontë
1818 – 1848

Emily Brontë was the fourth daughter of Patrick Brontë and Maria Branwell. Emily is justly considered the most intense of the sisters and expresses in her work a passionate and, at times, violent gothic sensibility. The extraordinary creative exertion, on the part of Emily, Anne, and Charlotte, that followed their unsuccessful plan to open a school, produced the enigmatic *Wuthering Heights*, which was published with Anne's *Agnes Grey* in 1847. Though Emily is best remembered for this startling novel, her poetry—honest, impassioned, and vigorous—equally declares its composer "[n]o trembler in the world's storm-troubled sphere" ("No Coward Soul is Mine"). The success, or at least notoriety, of *Wuthering Heights* was followed less than one year later by the death of Emily's brother Branwell. It is said that Emily caught a cold at Branwell's funeral and that she subsequently became consumptive. After having refused to see a doctor, Emily died at Haworth in December of 1848.

"Riches I hold in light esteem"

Riches I hold in light esteem
And Love I laugh to scorn
And lust of Fame was but a dream
That vanished with the morn—

5   And if I pray, the only prayer
That moves my lips for me
Is—"Leave the heart that now I bear
And give me liberty."

Yes, as my swift days near their goal
10 'Tis all that I implore—
Through life and death, a chainless soul
With courage to endure!
—(MARCH 1, 1841)

To Imagination

When weary with the long day's care,
And earthly change from pain to pain,
And lost, and ready to despair,
Thy kind voice calls me back again—
5   O my true friend, I am not lone
While thou canst speak with such a tone!

So hopeless is the world without,
The world within I doubly prize;
Thy world where guile and hate and doubt
10 And cold suspicion never rise;
Where thou and I and Liberty
Have undisputed sovereignty.

What matters it that all around
Danger and grief and darkness lie,
15 If but within our bosom's bound
We hold a bright unsullied sky,
Warm with ten thousand mingled rays
Of suns that know no winter days?

Reason indeed may oft complain
20 For Nature's sad reality,
And tell the suffering heart how vain
Its cherished dreams must always be;
And Truth may rudely trample down
The flowers of Fancy newly blown.

25 But thou art ever there to bring
The hovering visions back and breathe
New glories o'er the blighted spring
And call a lovelier life from death,
And whisper with a voice divine
30 Of real worlds as bright as thine.

I trust not to thy phantom bliss,
Yet still in evening's quiet hour
With never-failing thankfulness
I welcome thee, benignant power,
35 Sure solacer of human cares
And brighter hope when hope despairs.
—1846 (SEPTEMBER 3, 1844)

Plead For Me

O thy bright eyes must answer now,
When Reason, with a scornful brow,
Is mocking at my overthrow;
O thy sweet tongue must plead for me
5 And tell why I have chosen thee!

Stern Reason is to judgement come
Arrayed in all her forms of gloom:
Wilt thou my advocate be dumb?
No, radiant angel, speak and say
10 Why I did cast the world away;

Why I have persevered to shun
The common paths that others run;
And on a strange road journeyed on
Heedless alike of Wealth and Power—
15 Of Glory's wreath and Pleasure's flower.

These once indeed seemed Beings divine,
And they perchance heard vows of mine
And saw my offerings on their shrine—
But, careless gifts are seldom prized,
20 And mine were worthily despised;

So with a ready heart I swore
To seek their altar-stone no more,
And gave my spirit to adore
Thee, ever present, phantom thing—
25 My slave, my comrade, and my King!

A slave because I rule thee still;
Incline thee to my changeful will
And make thy influence good or ill—
A comrade, for by day and night
30 Thou art my intimate delight—

My Darling Pain that wounds and sears
And wrings a blessing out from tears
By deadening me to real cares;
And yet, a king—though prudence well
35 Have taught thy subject to rebel.

And am I wrong to worship where
Faith cannot doubt nor Hope despair
Since my own soul can grant my prayer?
Speak, God of Visions, plead for me
40 And tell why I have chosen thee!
—1846 (OCTOBER 14, 1844)

Remembrance

Cold in the earth, and the deep snow piled
above thee!
Far, far removed, cold in the dreary grave!
Have I forgot, my Only Love, to love thee,
Severed at last by Time's all-wearing wave?

5 Now, when alone, do my thoughts no longer hover
Over the mountains on Angora's[1] shore;
Resting their wings where heath and fern-leaves
cover
That noble heart for ever, ever more?

Cold in the earth, and fifteen wild Decembers
10 From those brown hills have melted into spring—
Faithful indeed is the spirit that remembers
After such years of change and suffering!

---

[1] Ankara, a city in Asia Minor.

Sweet Love of youth, forgive if I forget thee
While the World's tide is bearing me along:
15 Sterner desires and darker hopes beset me,
Hopes which obscure but cannot do thee wrong.

No other Sun has lightened up my heaven;
No other Star has ever shone for me:
All my life's bliss from thy dear life was given—
20 All my life's bliss is in the grave with thee.

But when the days of golden dreams had perished
And even Despair was powerless to destroy,
Then did I learn how existence could be cherished,
Strengthened and fed without the aid of joy;

25 Then did I check the tears of useless passion,
Weaned my young soul from yearning after thine;
Sternly denied its burning wish to hasten
Down to that tomb already more than mine!

And even yet, I dare not let it languish,
30 Dare not indulge in Memory's rapturous pain;
Once drinking deep of that divinest anguish,
How could I seek the empty world again?
—1846 (1845)

The Prisoner
A Fragment

In the dungeon-crypts, idly did I stray,
Reckless of the lives wasting there away;
"Draw the ponderous bars! open, Warder stern!"
He dared not say me nay—the hinges harshly turn.

5 "Our guests are darkly lodged," I whisper'd, gazing
through
The vault, whose grated eye showed heaven more
grey than blue;
(This was when glad spring laughed in awaking
pride;)

"Aye, darkly lodged enough!" returned my sullen
guide.

Then, God forgive my youth; forgive my careless
tongue;
10 I scoffed, as the chill chains on the damp
flag-stones rung:
"Confined in triple walls, art thou so much to fear,
That we must bind thee down and clench thy
fetters here?"

The captive raised her face, it was as soft and mild
As sculptured marble saint, or slumbering
unwean'd child;
15 It was so soft and mild, it was so sweet and fair,
Pain could not trace a line, nor grief a shadow
there!

The captive raised her hand and pressed it to her
brow;
"I have been struck," she said, "and I am suffering
now;
Yet these are little worth, your bolts and irons
strong,
20 And, were they forged in steel, they could not hold
me long."

Hoarse laughed the jailor grim: "Shall I be won to
hear;
Dost think, fond, dreaming wretch, that I shall
grant thy prayer?
Or, better still, wilt melt my master's heart with
groans?
Ah! sooner might the sun thaw down these granite
stones.

25 "My master's voice is low, his aspect bland and
kind,
But hard as hardest flint, the soul that lurks
behind;

And I am rough and rude, yet not more rough to
    see
Than is the hidden ghost that has its home in me."

About her lips there played a smile of almost scorn,
30 "My friend," she gently said, "you have not heard
    me mourn;
When you my kindred's lives, *my* lost life, can
    restore,
Then may I weep and sue,—but never, friend,
    before!

Still, let my tyrants know, I am not doomed to wear
Year after year in gloom, and desolate despair;
35 A messenger of Hope, comes every night to me,
And offers for short life, eternal liberty.

He comes with western winds, with evening's
    wandering airs,
With that clear dusk of heaven that brings the
    thickest stars.
Winds take a pensive tone, and stars a tender fire,
40 And visions rise, and change, that kill me with
    desire.

Desire for nothing known in my maturer years,
When Joy grew mad with awe, at counting future
    tears.
When, if my spirit's sky was full of flashes warm,
I knew not whence they came, from sun, or
    thunder storm.

45 But, first, a hush of peace—a soundless calm
    descends;
The struggle of distress, and fierce impatience ends.
Mute music soothes my breast, unuttered harmony,
That I could never dream, till Earth was lost to me.

Then dawns the Invisible; the Unseen its truth
    reveals;
50 My outward sense is gone, my inward essence feels:

Its wings are almost free—its home, its harbour
    found,
Measuring the gulf, it stoops, and dares the final
    bound.

Oh, dreadful is the check—intense the agony—
When the ear begins to hear, and the eye begins to
    see;
55 When the pulse begins to throb, the brain to think
    again,
The soul to feel the flesh, and the flesh to feel the
    chain.

Yet I would lose no sting, would wish no torture
    less,
The more that anguish racks, the earlier it will bless;
And robed in fires of hell, or bright with heavenly
    shine,
60 If it but herald death, the vision is divine!"

She ceased to speak, and we, unanswering, turned
    to go—
We had no further power to work the captive woe:
Her cheek, her gleaming eye, declared that man
    had given
A sentence, unapproved, and overruled by Heaven.
—1846 (1845)

"No coward soul is mine" [1]

No coward soul is mine
  No trembler in the world's storm-troubled
    sphere
I see Heaven's glories shine
And Faith shines equal arming me from Fear

5 O God within my breast
Almighty ever-present Deity

---

[1] "The following are the last lines my sister Emily ever wrote."
(Charlotte Brontë's note.)

Life, that in me hast rest
As I Undying Life, have power in Thee

Vain are the thousand creeds
10 That move men's hearts, unutterably vain,
Worthless as withered weeds
Or idlest froth amid the boundless main

To waken doubt in one
Holding so fast by thy infinity
15 So surely anchored on
The steadfast rock of Immortality

With wide-embracing love
Thy spirit animates eternal years
Pervades and broods above,
20 Changes, sustains, dissolves, creates and rears

Though Earth and moon were gone
And suns and universes ceased to be
And thou wert left alone
Every Existence would exist in thee

25 There is not room for Death
Nor atom that his might could render void
Since thou art Being and Breath
And what thou art may never be destroyed.
—1850 (JANUARY 2, 1846)

Stanzas—"Often rebuked, yet always back returning"[1]

Often rebuked, yet always back returning
To those first feelings that were born with me,
And leaving busy chase of wealth and learning
For idle dreams of things which cannot be:

5 To-day, I will seek not the shadowy region;
Its unsustaining vastness waxes drear;
And visions rising, legion after legion,
Bring the unreal world too strangely near.

I'll walk, but not in old heroic traces,
10 And not in paths of high morality,
And not among the half-distinguished faces,
The clouded forms of long-past history.

I'll walk where my own nature would be leading:
It vexes me to choose another guide:
15 Where the gray flocks in ferny glens are feeding;
Where the wild wind blows on the mountain
side.

What have those lonely mountains worth revealing?
More glory and more grief than I can tell:
The earth that wakes *one* human heart to feeling
20 Can centre both the worlds of Heaven and Hell.
—1850

A Farewell to Alexandria[2]

I've seen this dell in July's shine
As lovely as an angel's dream;
Above, heaven's depth of blue divine;
Around, the evening's golden beam.

5 I've seen the purple heather-bell
Look out by many a storm-worn stone;
And oh, I've seen such music swell,
Such wild notes wake these passes lone—

So soft, yet so intensely felt,
10 So low, yet so distinctly heard,
My breath would pause, my eyes would melt,
And my tears dew the green heath-sward.

---

[1] The authorship of this poem has alternately been credited to Charlotte and Emily Brontë; there is no firm evidence for either claim.

[2] This poem was given the title of "The Outcast Mother" in *The Cornhill Magazine*, May, 1860, where it was initially published.

I'd linger here a summer day,
Nor care how fast the hours flew by,
15 Nor mark the sun's departing ray
Smile sadly glorious from the sky.

Then, then I might have laid thee down
And deemed thy sleep would gentle be;
I might have left thee, darling one,
20 And thought thy God was guarding thee!

But now there is no wandering glow,
No gleam to say that God is nigh;
And coldly spreads thy couch of snow,
And harshly sounds thy lullaby.

25 Forests of heather, dark and long,
Wave their brown, branching arms above,
And they must soothe thee with their song,
And they must shield my child of love!

Alas, the flakes are heavily falling;
30 They cover fast each guardian crest;
And chilly white their shroud is palling
Thy frozen limbs and freezing breast.

Wakes up the storm more madly wild,
The mountain drifts are tossed on high—
35 Farewell, unblessed, unfriended child,
I cannot bear to watch thee die!
—1860 (JULY 12, 1839)

"Long neglect has worn away"

Long neglect has worn away
Half the sweet enchanting smile;
Time has turned the bloom to grey;
Mould and damp the face defile.

5 But that lock of silky hair,
Still beneath the picture twined,

Tells what once those features were,
Paints their image on the mind.

Fair the hand that traced that line,
10 "Dearest, ever deem me true";
Swiftly flew the fingers fine
When the pen that motto drew.
—1902 (1837)

"The night is darkening round me"

The night is darkening round me,
The wild winds coldly blow;
But a tyrant spell has bound me
And I cannot, cannot go.

5 The giant trees are bending
Their bare boughs weighed with snow,
And the storm is fast descending
And yet I cannot go.

Clouds beyond clouds above me,
10 Wastes beyond wastes below
But nothing drear can move me;
I will not, cannot go.
—1902 (1837)

"What winter floods, what showers of spring"

What winter floods, what showers of spring
Have drenched the grass by night and day;
And yet, beneath, that spectre ring,
Unmoved and undiscovered lay

5 A mute remembrancer of crime,
Long lost, concealed, forgot for years,
It comes at last to cancel time,
And waken unavailing tears.
—1910 (1839)

"She dried her tears, and they did smile"

She dried her tears, and they did smile
To see her cheeks' returning glow;
Nor did discern how all the while
That full heart throbbed to overflow.

5   With that sweet look and lively tone,
And bright eye shining all the day,
They could not guess, at midnight lone
How she would weep the time away.
—1910 (1839?)

Eliza Cook
1818 – 1889

First publishing at the age of seventeen, Eliza Cook gained an early reputation for unpretentiously moral and humane verse, focussing on domesticity and social issues concerning women and children. Prolific in her personal publications (*Lays of the Wild Harp* [1835], *Melaia and Other Poems* [1838], *Poems, Second Series* [1845], and *New Echoes, and Other Poems* [1864]), Cook also contributed to London periodicals such as *The Weekly Dispatch*, and edited and contributed to her biweekly periodical, *Eliza Cook's Journal* (1849–54).

❧❧❧

The Waters

What was it that I loved so well about my
    childhood's home?
It was the wide and wave-lashed shore, the black
    rocks, crowned with foam
It was the sea-gull's flapping wing, all trackless in
    its flight;
Its screaming note that welcomed on the fierce and
    stormy night.
5 The wild heath had its flowers and moss, the forest
    had its trees,
Which, bending to the evening wind, made music
    in the breeze:
But earth, ha! ha! I laugh e'en now, earth had no
    charms for *me*;
No scene half bright enough to win my young
    heart from the sea!
No! 'twas the ocean, vast and deep, the fathomless,
    the free!
10 The mighty, rushing waters that were ever dear to
    me!

My earliest steps would wander, from the green
    and fertile land,
Down where the clear, blue ocean rolled, to pace
    the rugged strand;
I'd proudly fling the proffered bribe and gilded toy
    away,
To gather up the salt sea weeds, or dabble in the
    spray!
15 I shouted to the distant crew, or launched my
    mimic bark;
I met the morning's freshness there, and lingered
    till the dark:
When dark, I climbed, with bounding step, the
    steep and jutting cliff,
To see them trim the beacon-light to guide the
    fisher's skiff!
Oh! how I loved the Waters, and even longed to be
20 A bird, or boat, or anything that dwelt upon the
    Sea.

The moon! the moon! oh, tell me, do ye love her
    placid ray?
Do ye love the shining, starry train that gathers
    round her way?
Oh! if ye do, go watch her when she climbs above
    the main,
While her full transcript lives below, upon the
    crystal plain.
25 While her soft light serenely falls; and rising billows
    seem
Like sheets of silver spreading forth to meet her
    hallowed beam;
Look! and thy soul will own the spell; thou'lt feel as
    I have felt;
Thou'lt love the waves as I have loved, and kneel as
    I have knelt;

And, well I know, the prayer of saint or martyr
    ne'er could be
30 More fervent in its faith than mine, beside the
    moon-lit Sea.

I liked not those who nurtured me; they gave my
    bosom pain;
They strove to fix their shackles on a soul that
    spurned the chain:
I grew rebellious to their hope, disdainful of their
    care;
And all they dreaded most, my spirit loved the
    most to dare.
35 And am I changed? have I become a tame and
    fashioned thing?
Have I yet learned to sing the joys that Pleasure's
    minions sing?
Is there a smile upon my brow, when mixed with
    Folly's crowd?
Is the false whisper dearer than the storm-wail,
    shrill and loud?
No! no! my soul is as it was, and as it e'er will be—
40 Loving, and free as what it loves, the curbless,
    mighty Sea.
    —1835

The Ploughshare of Old England

The sailor boasts his stately ship, the bulwark of
    the isle;
The soldier loves his sword, and sings of tented
    plains the while;
But we will hang the ploughshare up within our
    fathers' halls,
And guard it as the deity of plenteous festivals.
5 We'll pluck the brilliant poppies, and the far-famed
    barley-corn,
To wreathe with bursting wheat-ears that outshine
    the saffron morn;
We'll crown it with a glowing heart, and pledge
    our fertile land:

The Ploughshare of Old England, and the sturdy
    peasant band.

The work it does is good and blest, and may be
    proudly told;
10 We see it in the teeming barns, and fields of waving
    gold;
Its metal is unsullied, no blood-stain lingers there:
God speed it well, and let it thrive unshackled
    everywhere.
The bark may rest upon the wave, the spear may
    gather dust,
But never may the prow that cuts the furrow lie
    and rust.
15 Fill up, fill up, with glowing heart, and pledge our
    fertile land:
The Ploughshare of Old England, and the sturdy
    peasant band.
    —1838

Song of the Red Indian

Oh! why does the white man hang on my path,
    Like the hound on the tiger's track?
Does the flush of my dark skin awaken his wrath?
    Does he covet the bow at my back?
5 He has rivers and seas where the billow and breeze
    Bear riches for him alone;
And the sons of the wood never plunge in the flood
    That the white man calls his own.
Then why should he covet the streams where none
10   But the red-skin dare to swim?
Oh! why should he wrong the hunter one
    Who never did harm to him?

The Father above thought fit to give
    To the white man corn and wine;
15 There are golden fields where he may live,
    But the forest shades are mine.
The eagle has its place of rest,
    The wild horse where to dwell;

And the Spirit who gave the bird its nest,
20   Made me a home as well.
Then back, go back from the red-skin's track
        For the hunter's eyes grow dim,
To find the white man wrongs the one
        Who never did harm to him.

25 Oh! why does the pale-face always call
        The red man "heathen brute?"
He does not bend where the dark knees fall,
        But the tawny lip is mute.
We cast no blame on his creed or name,
30   Or his temples, fine and high;
But he mocks at us with a laughing word
        When we worship a star-lit sky.
Yet, white man, what has thy good faith done
        And where can its mercy be,
35 If it teach thee to hate the hunter one
        Who never did harm to thee?

We need no book to tell us how
        Our lives shall pass away;
For we see the onward torrent flow,
40   And the mighty tree decay.
"Let thy tongue be true and thy heart be brave,"
        Is among the red-skins' lore;
We can bring down the swift wing and dive in the
            wave,
        And we seek to know no more.
45 Then back, go back, and let us run
        With strong, unfettered limb;
For why should the white man wrong the one
        Who never did harm to him?

We know there's a hand that has fixed the hill
50   And planted the prairie plain;
That can fling the lightnings when it will,
        And pour out the torrent rain.
Far away and alone, where the headlong tide
        Dashes on with our bold canoe.
55 We ask and trust that hand to guide

And carry us safely through.
The Great Spirit dwells in the beautiful sun,
        And while we kneel in its light,
Who will not own that the hunter one
60   Has an altar pure and bright?

The painted streak on a warrior's cheek
        Appears a wondrous thing;
The white man stares at a wampum[1] belt,
        And a plume from the heron's wing.
65 But the red man wins the panthers' skins
        To cover his dauntless form;
While the pale-face hides his breast in a garb
        That he takes from the crawling worm.
And your lady fair, with her gems so rare,
70   Her ruby, gold, and pearl,
Would be as strange to other eyes
        As the bone-decked Indian girl.

Then why does the cruel, white man come
        With the war-whoop's yelling sound?
75 Oh! why does he take our wigwam home,
        And the jungled hunting-ground?
The wolf-cub has its lair of rest,
        And the wild horse where to dwell,
And the Spirit who gave the bird its nest
80   Made me a place as well.
Then back, go back, from the red-skin's track;
        For the hunter's eyes grow dim,
To find that the white man wrongs the one
        Who never did harm to him.
—1845

Song of the Ugly Maiden

Oh! the world gives little of love or light,
        Though my spirit pants for much;
For I have no beauty for the sight,

---
[1] small beads made of shells, used by North American Indians for ornament, money, etc.

329

No riches for the touch.
5 I hear men sing o'er the flowing cup
    Of woman's magic spell;
And vows of zeal they offer up,
    And eloquent tales they tell.
They bravely swear to guard the fair
10   With strong, protecting arms;
But will they worship woman's worth
    Unblent with woman's charms?
No! ah, no! 'tis little they prize
Crookbacked forms and rayless eyes.

15 Oh! 'tis a saddening thing to be
    A poor and Ugly one;
In the sand Time puts in his glass for me,
    Few sparkling atoms run.
For my drawn lids bear no shadowing fringe,
20   My locks are thin and dry;
My teeth wear not the rich pearl tinge,
    Nor my lips the henna dye.
I know full well I have naught of grace
    That maketh woman "divine;"
25 The wooer's praise and doting gaze
    Have never yet been mine.
Where'er I go all eyes will shun
The loveless mien of the Ugly one.

I join the crowd where merry feet
30   Keep pace with the merry strain;
I note the earnest words that greet
    The fair ones in the train.
The stripling youth has passed me by;
    He leads another out!
35 She has a light and laughing eye,
    Like sunshine playing about.
The wise man scanneth calmly round,
    But his gaze stops not with me;
It has fixed on a head whose curls, unbound,
40   Are bright as curls can be;
And he watches her through the winding dance
With smiling care and tender glance.

The gay cavalier has thrust me aside;
    Whom does he hurry to seek?
45 One with a curving lip of pride,
    And a forehead white and sleek.
The grey-haired veteran, young with wine,
    Would head the dance once more;
He looks for a hand, but passes mine.
50   As all have passed before.
The pale, scarred face may sit alone,
    The unsightly brow may mope;
There cometh no tongue with winning tone
    To flatter Affection's hope.
55 O Ugliness! thy desolate pain
Had served to set the stamp on Cain.[1]

My quick brain hears the thoughtless jeers
    That are whispered with laughing grin;
As though I had fashioned my own dull orbs,
60   And chosen my own seared skin.
Who shall dream of the withering pang,
    As I find myself forlorn—
Sitting apart, with lonely heart,
    'Mid cold neglect and scorn?
65 I could be glad as others are,
    For my soul is young and warm;
And kind it had been to darken and mar
    My feelings with my form;
For fondly and strong as my spirit may yearn,
70 It gains no sweet love in return.

Man, just Man! I know thine eye
    Delighteth to dwell on those
Whose tresses shade, with curl or braid,
    Cheeks soft and round as the rose.
75 I know thou wilt ever gladly turn
    To the beautiful and bright;
But is it well that thou shouldst spurn
    The one GOD chose to blight?
Oh! why shouldst thou trace my shrinking face

---

[1] the oldest son of Adam and Eve, who killed his brother Abel: Genesis 4.

80   With coarse, deriding jest?
    Oh! why forget that a charmless brow
       May abide with a gentle breast?
    Oh! why forget that gold is found
    Hidden beneath the roughest ground?

85   Would that I had passed away
       Ere I knew that I was born;
    For I stand in the blessed light of day
       Like a weed among the corn,—
    The black rock in the wide, blue sea—
90   The snake in the jungle green,
    Oh! who will stay in the fearful way
       Where such ugly things are seen?
    Yet mine is the fate of lonelier state
       Than that of the snake or rock;
95   For those who behold me in their path
       Not only shun, but mock.
    O Ugliness! thy desolate pain
    Had served to set the stamp on Cain.
    —1845

A Song For The Workers

Written for the Early Closing Movement

Let man toil to win his living,
    Work is not a task to spurn:
Poor is gold of others' giving,
    To the silver that we earn.

5   Let Man proudly take his station
       At the smithy, loom, or plough;
    The richest crown-pearls in a nation
       Hang from Labor's reeking brow.

    Though her hand grows hard with duty,
10   Filling up the common Fate;
    Let fair Woman's cheek of beauty
       Never blush to own its state.

    Let fond Woman's heart of feeling
       Never be ashamed to spread
15   Industry and honest dealing
       As a barter for her bread.

    Work on bravely, GOD's own daughters!
       Work on stanchly, GOD's own sons!
    But when Life has too rough waters,
20   Truth must fire her minute guns.

    Shall ye be *unceasing* drudges?
       Shall the cry upon your lips
    Never make your selfish judges
       Less severe with Despot-whips?

25   Shall the mercy that we cherish,
       As old England's primest boast,
    See no slaves but those who perish
       On a far and foreign coast?

    When we reckon hives of money,
30   Owned by Luxury and Ease,
    Is it just to grasp the honey
       While Oppression chokes the bees?

    Is it just the poor the lowly
       Should be held as soulless things?
35   Have they not a claim as holy
       As rich men, to angel's wings?

    Shall we burden boyhood's muscle?
       Shall the young girl mope and lean,
    Till we hear the dead leaves rustle
40   On a tree that should be green?

    Shall we bar the brain from thinking
       Of aught else than work and woe?
    Shall we keep parched lips from drinking
       Where refreshing waters flow?

45   Shall we strive to shut out Reason

Knowledge, Liberty, and Health?
Shall all Spirit-light be treason
  To the mighty King of Wealth?

Shall we stint with niggard measure,
50   Human joy, and human rest?
Leave no profit—give no pleasure
  To the toiler's human breast?

Shall our men, fatigued to loathing,
  Plod on sickly, worn, and bowed?
55 Shall our maidens sew fine clothing,
  Dreaming of their own white shroud?

  No! for Right is up and asking
Loudly for a juster lot;
  And Commerce must not let her tasking
60 Form a nation's canker-spot.

  Work on bravely, GOD's own daughters!
    Work on stanchly, GOD's own sons!
But, till ye have smoother waters,
  Let Truth fire her minute guns!
—1853

Arthur Hugh Clough
1819 — 1861

Arthur Hugh Clough was educated at Rugby and Balliol College, Oxford. He became a fellow of Oriel and then principal of University Hall, London. His poems appeared in *Ambarvalia* (1849), *Dipsychus* (1850), *Amours de Voyage* (1858), and *Mari Magno or Tales On Board* (1861). Clough and Matthew Arnold were friends and poetic rivals; after Clough's premature death in 1861 Arnold wrote the problematic elegy "Thyrsis" in his memory. Clough's short verse reveals his clear-sighted cynicism about social conventions; his longer works, such as the novel-in-verse *Amours de Voyage*, combine social commentary with ambitious formal experimentation.

Duty—that's to say complying

Duty—that's to say complying
  With whate'er's expected here;
On your unknown cousin's dying,
  Straight be ready with the tear;
5 Upon etiquette relying,
Unto usage naught denying,
Lend your waist to be embraced,
  Blush not even, never fear;
Claims of kith and kin connection,
10   Claims of manners honour still,
Ready money of affection
    Pay, whoever drew the bill.
With the form conforming duly,
Senseless what it meaneth truly,
15 Go to church—the world require you,
    To balls—the world require you too,
And marry—papa and mamma desire you,
    And your sisters and schoolfellows do.
Duty—'tis to take on trust
20 What things are good, and right, and just;
    And whether indeed they be or be not,
    Try not, test not, feel not, see not:
'Tis walk and dance, sit down and rise
By leading, opening ne'er your eyes;
25 Stunt sturdy limbs that Nature gave,
And be drawn in a Bath chair[1] along to the grave.

'Tis the stern and prompt suppressing,
    As an obvious deadly sin,
All the questing and the guessing
30   Of the soul's own soul within:
    'Tis the coward acquiescence
      In a destiny's behest,
    To a shade by terror made
    Sacrificing aye the essence
35   Of all that's truest, noblest, best;
    'Tis the blind non-recognition
      Or of goodness, truth, or beauty,
    Save by precept and submission;
      Moral blank, and moral void,
40   Life at very birth destroyed,
Atrophy, exinanition![2]
Duty!—
Yea, by duty's prime condition,
    Pure nonentity of duty!
—1849

Qui Laborat, Orat [3]

Oonly Source of all our light and life,
  Whom as our truth, our strength, we see and
    feel,

---

[1] a wheeled chair first used at Bath, a city popular with invalids because of its hot springs.

[2] utter emptiness.

[3] This poem is dated Oxford, 1845, in *Poems* (Norton, 1862), but Thomas Arnold dated it 1847. Published 1849. "He who works, prays."

But whom the hours of mortal moral strife
    Alone aright reveal!

5   Mine inmost soul, before Thee inly brought,
    Thy presence owns ineffable, divine;
Chastised each rebel self-encentered thought,
    My will adoreth Thine.

With eye down-dropt, if then this earthly mind
10   Speechless remain, or speechless e'en depart,
Nor seek to see (for what of earthly kind
    Can see Thee as Thou art?)—

If sure assured 'tis but profanely bold
    In thought's abstractest forms to seem to see,
15 It dare not dare thee dread communion hold
    In ways unworthy Thee,—

O not unowned, Thou shalt unnamed forgive,
    In worldly walks the prayerless heart prepare,
And if in work its life it seem to live,
20   Shalt make that work be prayer.

Nor times shall lack, when, while the work it plies,
    Unsummoned powers the blinding film shall
        part,
And scarce by happy tears made dim, the eyes
    In recognition start.

25 As wills Thy will, or give or e'en forbear
    The beatific supersensual sight,
So, with Thy blessing blest, that humbler prayer
    Approach Thee morn and night.
    —1849

The Latest Decalogue [1]

Thou shalt have one God only; who
    Would be at the expense of two?
No graven images may be
Worshipped, except the currency:
5   Swear not at all; for thy curse
Thine enemy is none the worse:
At church on Sunday to attend
Will serve to keep the world thy friend:
Honour thy parents; that is, all
10 From whom advancement may befall:
Thou shalt not kill; but need'st not strive
Officiously to keep alive:
Do not adultery commit;
Advantage rarely comes of it:
15 Thou shalt not steal; an empty feat,
When it's so lucrative to cheat:
Bear not false witness; let the lie
Have time on its own wings to fly:
Thou shalt not covet; but tradition
20 Approves all forms of competition.

The sum of all is, thou shalt love,
If any body, God above:
At any rate shall never labour
More than thyself to love thy neighbour. [2]
—1850

"Say not the struggle nought availeth"

Say not the struggle nought availeth,
    The labour and the wounds are vain,
The enemy faints not, nor faileth,
    And as things have been, things remain.

---

[1] The original decalogue was the ten commandments given to Moses by God on Mount Sinai.

[2] These last four lines were not originally published with the poem. Discovered in one of the poet's manuscripts, they were appended to the poem in 1951.

5   If hopes were dupes, fears may be liars;
    It may be, in yon smoke concealed,
  Your comrades chase e'en now the fliers,
    And, but for you, possess the field.

  For while the tired waves, vainly breaking,
10   Seem here no painful inch to gain,
  Far back through creeks and inlets making
    Came, silent, flooding in, the main,

  And not by eastern windows only,
    When daylight comes, comes in the light,
15   In front the sun climbs slow, how slowly,
    But westward, look, the land is bright.
  —1855 (1849)

Speranza (Lady Wilde)
1821? – 1896

The writer known as Speranza was born Jane Francesca (or possibly just Frances) Elgee in Wexford to Charles Elgee and Sarah Kingsbury. A titanic personality herself, she begat another in the form of her son, Oscar Wilde. She was highly politicized and given, in the name of Irish independence, to anti-British, sometimes incendiary rhetoric in her writing (an Irish periodical to which she contributed was suppressed for sedition in 1848). In 1864 Speranza published a collection of verse entitled *Poems*, and in 1867 she published *Poems: Second Series: Translations*. In 1851 she married an Irish surgeon, antiquary, and nationalist. Together they collected ancient Irish myths and legends, participating (with friend W. B. Yeats) in the Celtic cultural renaissance of the late nineteenth and early twentieth centuries. When her husband died in 1876, Speranza relocated to London and became there, as in Dublin, the centre of a devoted artistic salon. She continued to write, and the influence of the women's movement is evident in her collections of essays, *Notes on Men, Women, and Books* (1891) and *Social Studies* (1893).

❧❧❧

The Voice of the Poor

I

Was sorrow ever like to our sorrow?
    Oh, God above!
Will our night never change into a morrow
    Of joy and love?
5 A deadly gloom is on us waking, sleeping,
    Like the darkness at noontide,
That fell upon the pallid mother, weeping
    By the Crucified.

II

Before us die our brothers of starvation:
10   Around are cries of famine and despair
Where is hope for us, or comfort, or salvation—
    Where—oh! where?
If the angels ever hearken, downward bending,
    They are weeping, we are sure,
15 At the litanies of human groans ascending
    From the crushed hearts of the poor.

III

When the human rests in love upon the human,
    All grief is light;

But who bends one kind glance to illumine
20   Our life-long night?
The air around is ringing with their laughter—
    God has only made the rich to smile;
But we—in our rags, and want, and woe—we
    follow after,
25   Weeping the while.

IV

And the laughter seems but uttered to deride us.
    When—oh! when
Will fall the frozen barriers that divide us
    From other men?
30 Will ignorance for ever thus enslave us?
    Will misery for ever lay us low?
All are eager with their insults, but to save us,
    None, none, we know.

V

We never knew a childhood's mirth and gladness,
35   Nor the proud heart of youth, free and brave;
Oh! a deathlike dream of wretchedness and sadness,
    Is life's weary journey to the grave.
Day by day we lower sink and lower,
    Till the Godlike soul within,

40 Falls crushed, beneath the fearful demon power
    Of poverty and sin.

VI

So we toil on, on with fever burning
    In heart and brain;
So we toil on, on through bitter scorning,
45   Want, woe, and pain:
We dare not raise our eyes to the blue heaven,
    Or the toil must cease—
We dare not breathe the fresh air God has given
    One hour in peace.

VII

50 We must toil, though the light of life is burning,
    Oh, how dim!
We must toil on our sick bed, feebly turning
    Our eyes to Him,
Who alone can hear the pale lip faintly saying,
55   With scarce moved breath
While the paler hands, uplifted, aid the praying—
    "Lord, grant us *Death!*"
—1864

A Lament For the Potato

A.D. 1739.
(From the Irish)

There is woe, there is clamour, in our desolated land,
And wailing lamentation from a famine-stricken band;
And weeping are the multitudes in sorrow and despair,
For the green fields of Munster[1] lying desolate and bare.

5 Woe for Lorc's[2] ancient kingdom, sunk in slavery and grief;
Plundered, ruined, are our gentry, our people, and their Chief;
For the harvest lieth scattered, more worth to us than gold,
All the kindly food that nourished both the young and the old.

Well I mind me of the cosherings,[3] where princes might dine,
10 And we drank until nightfall the best seven sorts of wine;
Yet was ever the Potato our old, familiar dish,
And the best of all sauces with the beeves and the fish.

But the harp now is silent, no one careth for the sound;
No flowers, no sweet honey, and no beauty can be found;
15 Not a bird its music thrilling though the leaves of the wood,
Nought but weeping and hands wringing in despair for our food.

And the Heavens, all in darkness, seem lamenting our doom,
No brightness in the sunlight, not a ray to pierce the gloom;
The cataract comes rushing with a fearful deepened roar,
20 And ocean bursts its boundaries, dashing wildly on the shore.

Yet, in misery and want, we have one protecting man,

[1] a south-western province of Ireland.

[2] "Lorc, or Lorcan, an ancient King of Munster, the grandfather of the great King Brian Boru." (Speranza's note.) Brian Boru (c. 941–1014 AD), hero and high-king of Ireland from 1002 until his death.

[3] rich banquets and feasts.

Kindly Barry,[1] of Fitzstephen's old hospitable clan;
By mount and river working deeds of charity and
    grace:
Blessings ever on our champion, best hero of his
    race!

25 Save us, God! In Thy mercy bend to hear the
    people's cry,
From the famine-stricken fields, rising bitterly on
    high;
Let the mourning and the clamour cease in Lorc's
    ancient land,
And shield us in the death-hour by Thy strong,
    protecting hand![2]
—1864

Tristan and Isolde [3]

The Love Sin.

None, unless the saints above,
  Knew the secret of their love;
For with calm and stately grace
Isolde held her queenly place,
5 Tho' the courtiers' hundred eyes
Sought the lovers to surprise,
Or to read the mysteries
Of a love—so rumour said—
By a magic philtre fed,

10 Which for ever in their veins
Burn'd with love's consuming pains.

Yet their hands would twine unseen,
  In a clasp 'twere hard to sever;
And whoso watched their glances meet,
15   Gazing as they'd gaze for ever,
Might have marked the sudden heat
Crims'ning on each flushing cheek,
As the tell-tale blood would speak
Of love that never should have been—
20 The love of Tristan and his Queen.

But, what hinders that the two,
  In the spring of their young life,
Love each other as they do?
Thus the tempting thoughts begin—
25 Little recked they of the sin;
Nature joined them hand in hand,
Is not that a truer band
  Than the formal name of wife?

Ah! what happy hours were theirs!
30   One might note them at the feast
Laughing low to loving airs,
  Loving airs that pleased them best;
Or interchanging the swift glance
In the mazes of the dance.
35 So the sunny moments rolled,
And they wove bright threads of gold
  Through the common web of life;
Never dreaming of annoy,
  Or the wild world's wicked strife;
40 Painting earth and heaven above
  In the light of their own joy,
In the purple light of love.

Happy moments, which again
Brought sweet torments in their train:
45 All love's petulance and fears,
Wayward doubts and tender tears;

---

[1] not identified.

[2] "This Irish poem, so pathetic and expressive in its simplicity, first appeared in the *Dublin University Magazine*, in the Essay on 'The Food of the Irish,' by Sir William Wilde. It is quoted by him as 'highly characteristic both of the feelings of the people and the extent of the calamity of that time; besides being a good specimen of the native poetry of the Irish more than a hundred years ago.'" (Speranza's note.)

[3] a medieval legend in which Tristan is sent to Ireland by king Mark of Cornwall to bring back the princess Isolde to become the king's bride. Unbeknownst to either of them, Tristan and Isolde drink a love potion and eventually die together.

Little jealousies and pride,
That can loving hearts divide:
Murmured vow and clinging kiss,
50 Working often bane as bliss;
All the wild, capricious changes
Through which lovers' passion ranges.

Yet would love, in every mood,
Find Heaven's manna for its food;
55 For love will grow wan and cold,
And die ere ever it is old,
That is never assailed by fears,
Or steeped in repentant tears,
Or passed through the fire like gold.

60 So loved Tristan and Isolde,
In youth's sunny, golden time,
In the brightness of their prime;
Little dreaming hours would come,
Like pale shadows from the tomb,
65 When an open death of doom
Had been still less hard to bear,
Than the ghastly, cold despair
Of those hidden vows, whose smart
Pale the cheek, and break the heart.
—1864

Matthew Arnold
1822 – 1888

Matthew Arnold, son of Thomas Arnold, headmaster of the famous public school Rugby from 1828 to 1842, was a poet and prose writer, traditionally ranked with Browning and Tennyson as one of the most important poets of the Victorian age. But unlike Browning and Tennyson, Arnold could not sustain his poetic impulse. His poetry, which he began publishing early in his career, reflected a deep sense of personal insecurity, barrenness, and even a note of resigned despair. These traits are evi-

dent in *The Strayed Reveller and Other Poems* (1849), *Empedocles on Etna and Other Poems* (1852), and "Thyrsis" (1866), an elegy on the death of his friend Arthur Hugh Clough. After 1855 Arnold wrote very little poetry, turning instead to the production of a great deal of high quality prose including literary criticism, political and cultural commentary, and religious writings. His most important work in cultural commentary is *Culture and Anarchy* (1869).

❧

To a Gipsy Child by the Sea-Shore

Douglas, Isle of Man[1]

Who taught this pleading to unpractised eyes?
Who hid such import in an infant's gloom?
Who lent thee, child, this meditative guise?
Who massed, round that slight brow, these clouds of doom?

5 Lo! sails that gleam a moment and are gone;
The swinging waters, and the clustered pier.
Not idly Earth and Ocean labour on,
Nor idly do these sea-birds hover near.

But thou, whom superfluity of joy[2]
10 Wafts not from thine own thoughts, nor longings vain,
Nor weariness, the full-fed soul's annoy—
Remaining in thy hunger and thy pain;

Thou, drugging pain by patience; half averse
From thine own mother's breast, that knows not thee;

15 With eyes which sought thine eyes thou didst converse,
And that soul-searching vision fell on me.

Glooms that go deep as thine I have not known:
Moods of fantastic sadness, nothing worth.
Thy sorrow and thy calmness are thine own:
20 Glooms that enhance and glorify this earth.

What mood wears like complexion to thy woe?
His, who in mountain glens, at noon of day,
Sits rapt, and hears the battle break below?
—Ah! thine was not the shelter, but the fray.

25 Some exile's, mindful how the past was glad?
Some angel's, in an alien planet born?
—No exile's dream was ever half so sad,
Not any angel's sorrow so forlorn.

Is the calm thine of stoic souls, who weigh
30 Life well, and find it wanting, nor deplore;
But in disdainful silence turn away,
Stand mute, self-centred, stern, and dream no more?

Or do I wait, to hear some gray-haired king
Unravel all his many-coloured lore;

---

[1] probably written August 1843 or 1844, after the Arnold family passed part of the long vacation at Douglas on the Isle of Man.

[2] Cf. stanza 3 and 4 of Wordsworth's "Immortality Ode."

35 Whose mind hath known all arts of governing,
Mused much, loved life a little, loathed it more?

Down the pale cheek long lines of shadow slope,
Which years, and curious thought, and suffering
give.
—Thou hast foreknown the vanity of hope,
40 Foreseen thy harvest—yet proceed'st to live.

O meek anticipant of that sure pain
Whose sureness gray-haired scholars hardly learn!
What wonder shall time breed, to swell thy strain?
What heavens, what earth, what sun shalt thou
discern?

45 Ere the long night, whose stillness brooks no star,
Match that funereal aspect with her pall,
I think thou wilt have fathomed life too far,
Have known too much—or else forgotten all.

The Guide of our dark steps a triple veil
50 Betwixt our senses and our sorrow keeps;
Hath sown with cloudless passages the tale
Of grief, and eased us with a thousand sleeps.

Ah! not the nectarous poppy lovers use,
Not daily labour's dull, Lethæan spring,
55 Oblivion in lost angels can infuse
Of the soiled glory and the trailing wing.

And though thou glean, what strenuous gleaners
may,
In the thronged fields where winning comes by
strife;
And though the just sun gild, as mortals pray,
60 Some reaches of thy storm-vext stream of life;[1]

Though that blank sunshine blind thee; though the
cloud

That severed the world's march and thine be gone;
Though ease dulls grace, and Wisdom be too proud
To halve a lodging that was all her own—

65 Once, ere the day decline, thou shalt discern,
Oh once, ere night, in thy success, thy chain!
Ere the long evening close, thou shalt return,
And wear this majesty of grief again.
—1849[2]

The Strayed Reveller

THE PORTICO OF CIRCE'S PALACE, EVENING

A Youth. Circe.

THE YOUTH

Faster, faster,
O Circe, Goddess,
Let the wild, thronging train,
The bright procession
5 Of eddying forms,
Sweep through my soul!

Thou standest, smiling
Down on me! thy right arm,
Leaned up against the column there,
10 Props thy soft cheek;
Thy left holds, hanging loosely,
The deep cup, ivy-cinctured,
I held but now.

Is it, then, evening
15 So soon? I see the night-dews,
Clustered in thick beads, dim
The agate brooch-stones
On thy white shoulder;
The cool night-wind, too,

---

[1] a figure favoured by Romantic poets, and Arnold.

[2] We are following Kenneth and Miriam Allott in arranging the poems by date of composition as far as that can be determined. For a detailed presentation of materials related to Arnold's poems, sources, annotations, textual variants, etc., see *The Poems of Matthew Arnold*, ed. Kenneth and Miriam Allott, 2nd ed. (London: Longmans, 1979).

20 Blows through the portico,
Stirs thy hair, Goddess,
Waves thy white robe!

CIRCE

Whence art thou, sleeper?

THE YOUTH

When the white dawn first
25 Through the rough fir-planks
Of my hut, by the chestnuts,
Up at the valley-head,
Came breaking. Goddess!
I sprang up, I threw round me
30 My dappled fawn-skin;
Passing out, from the wet turf,
Where they lay, by the hut door,
I snatched up my vine-crown, my fir-staff,
All drenched in dew—
35 Came swift down to join
The rout early gathered
In the town, round the temple,
Iacchus'[1] white fane
On yonder hill.

40 Quick I passed, following
The wood-cutters' cart-track
Down the dark valley; I saw
On my left, through the beeches,
Thy palace, Goddess,
45 Smokeless, empty!
Trembling, I entered; beheld
The court all silent,
The lions sleeping,
On the altar this bowl.
50 I drank, Goddess!
And sank down here, sleeping,
On the steps of thy portico.

CIRCE

Foolish boy! Why tremblest thou?
Thou lovest it, then, my wine?
55 Wouldst more of it? See, how glows.
Through the delicate, flushed marble,
The red, creaming liquor,
Strown with dark seeds!
Drink, then! I chide thee not,
60 Deny thee not my bowl.
Come, stretch forth thy hand, then—so!
Drink—drink again!

THE YOUTH

Thanks, gracious one!
Ah, the sweet fumes again!
65 More soft, ah me,
More subtle-winding
Than Pan's flute-music!
Faint—faint! Ah me,
Again the sweet sleep!

CIRCE

70 Hist! Thou—within there!
Come forth, Ulysses!
Art tired with hunting?
While we range the woodland,
See what the day brings.

ULYSSES

75 Ever new magic!
Hast thou then lured hither,
Wonderful Goddess, by thy art,
The young, languid-eyed Ampelus,[2]
Iacchus' darling—
80 Or some youth beloved of Pan,
Of Pan and the Nymphs?
That he sits, bending downward
His white, delicate neck
To the ivy-wreathed marge
85 Of thy cup; the bright, glancing vine-leaves

---

[1] a minor deity identified with Dionysus.

[2] son of a nymph and satyr.

That crown his hair,
Falling forward, mingling
With the dark ivy-plants—
His fawn-skin, half untied,
90 Smeared with red wine-stains? Who is he,
That he sits, overweighed
By fumes of wine and sleep,
So late, in thy portico?
What youth, Goddess, what guest
95 Of Gods or mortals?

CIRCE

Hist! he wakes!
I lured him not hither, Ulysses.
Nay, ask him!

THE YOUTH

Who speaks? Ah, who comes forth
100 To thy side, Goddess, from within?
How shall I name him?
This spare, dark-featured,
Quick-eyed stranger?
Ah, and I see too
105 His sailor's bonnet,
His short-coat, travel-tarnished,
With one arm bare!—
Art thou not he, whom fame
This long time rumours
110 The favoured guest of Circe, brought by the waves?
Art thou he, stranger?
The wise Ulysses,
Laertes' son?

ULYSSES

I am Ulysses.
115 And thou, too, sleeper?
Thy voice is sweet.
It may be thou hast followed
Through the islands some divine bard,
By age taught many things,
120 Age and the Muses;

And heard him delighting
The chiefs and people
In the banquet, and learned his songs,
Of Gods and Heroes,
125 Of war and arts,
And peopled cities,
Inland, or built
By the grey sea.—If so, then hail!
I honour and welcome thee.

THE YOUTH

130 The Gods are happy.
They turn on all sides
Their shining eyes,
And see below them
The earth and men.

135 They see Tiresias[1]
Sitting, staff in hand,
On the warm, grassy
Asopus bank,
His robe drawn over
140 His old, sightless head,
Revolving inly
The doom of Thebes.

They see the Centaurs[2]
In the upper glens
145 Of Pelion, in the streams,
Where red-berried ashes fringe
The clear-brown shallow pools,
With streaming flanks, and heads
Reared proudly, snuffing
150 The mountain wind.

They see the Indian
Drifting, knife in hand,
His frail boat moored to

---

[1] the blind soothsayer who foresaw the "doom of Thebes."

[2] savage inhabitants of Mt. Pelion in Thessaly, often depicted as half man, half horse.

A floating isle thick-matted
155 With large-leaved, low-creeping melon-plants,
And the dark cucumber.
He reaps, and stows them,
Drifting—drifting; round him,
Round his green harvest-plot,
160 Flow the cool lake-waves,
The mountains ring them.

They see the Scythian[1]
On the wide steppe, unharnessing
His wheeled house at noon.
165 He tethers his beast down, and makes his meal—
Mares' milk, and bread
Baked on the embers: all around
The boundless, waving grass-plains stretch, thick-
starred
With saffron and the yellow hollyhock
170 And flag-leaved iris-flowers.
Sitting in his cart
He makes his meal; before him, for long miles,
Alive with bright green lizards,
And the springing bustard-fowl,
175 The track, a straight black line,
Furrows the rich soil; here and there
Clusters of lonely mounds
Topped with rough-hewn,
Grey, rain-bleared statues, overpeer
180 The sunny waste.

They see the ferry
On the broad, clay-laden
Lone Chorasmian stream;[2] thereon,
With snort and strain,
185 Two horses, strongly swimming, tow
The ferry-boat, with woven ropes
To either bow
Firm harnessed by the mane; a chief,

With shout and shaken spear,
190 Stands at the prow, and guides them; but astern
The cowering merchants, in long robes,
Sit pale beside their wealth
Of silk-bales, and of balsam-drops,
Of gold and ivory,
195 Of turquoise-earth and amethyst,
Jasper and chalcedony,
And milk-barred onyx-stones.
The loaded boat swings groaning
In the yellow eddies;
200 The Gods behold them.

They see the Heroes
Sitting in the dark ship
On the foamless, long-heaving.
Violet sea,
205 At sunset nearing
The Happy Islands.[3]

These things, Ulysses,
The wise bards also
Behold and sing.
210 But oh, what labour!
O prince, what pain!
They too can see
Tiresias; but the Gods,
Who give them vision,
215 Added this law:
That they should bear too
His groping blindness,
His dark foreboding,
His scorned white hairs;
220 Bear Hera's anger
Through a life lengthened
To seven ages.[4]

[1] nomadic northern tribe.

[2] the river Oxus.

[3] Greek paradise for heroes.

[4] Tiresias was blinded by Hera as a result of a dispute, and Zeus lengthened his life to seven generations.

They see the Centaurs
On Pelion; then they feel,
225 They too, the maddening wine
Swell their large veins to bursting; in wild pain
They feel the biting spears
Of the grim Lapithæ, and Theseus, drive,
Drive crashing through their bones; they feel
230 High on a jutting rock in the red stream
Alcmena's dreadful son[1]
Ply his bow; such a price
The Gods exact for song:
To become what we sing.

235 They see the Indian
On his mountain lake; but squalls
Make their skiff reel, and worms
In the unkind spring have gnawn
Their melon-harvest to the heart.—They see
240 The Scythian; but long frosts
Parch them in winter-time on the bare steppe,
Till they too fade like grass; they crawl
Like shadows forth in spring.

They see the merchants
245 On the Oxus stream; but care
Must visit first them too, and make them pale.
Whether, through whirling sand,
A cloud of desert robber-horse have burst
Upon their caravan; or greedy kings,
250 In the walled cities the way passes through,
Crushed them with tolls; or fever-airs,
On some great river's marge,
Mown them down, far from home.

They see the Heroes
255 Near harbour; but they share
Their lives, and former violent toil in Thebes,
Seven-gated Thebes, or Troy;
Or where the echoing oars

Of Argo first
260 Startled the unknown sea.

The old Silenus[2]
Came, lolling in the sunshine,
From the dewy forest-coverts,
This way, at noon.
265 Sitting by me, while his Fauns
Down at the water-side
Sprinkled and smoothed
His drooping garland,
He told me these things.

270 But I, Ulysses,
Sitting on the warm steps,
Looking over the valley,
All day long, have seen,
Without pain, without labour,
275 Sometimes a wild-haired Mænad—[3]
Sometimes a Faun with torches—
And sometimes, for a moment,
Passing through the dark stems
Flowing-robed, the beloved,
280 The desired, the divine,
Beloved Iacchus.

Ah, cool night-wind, tremulous stars!
Ah, glimmering water,
Fitful earth-murmur,
285 Dreaming woods!
Ah, golden-haired, strangely smiling Goddess,
And thou, proved, much enduring,
Wave-tossed Wanderer!
Who can stand still?
290 Ye fade, ye swim, ye waver before me—
The cup again!

[1] Hercules also fought the Centaurs.

[2] Silenus, satyr teacher and companion of the youthful Dionysus.

[3] female worshipper of Iacchus.

Faster, faster,
O Circe, Goddess,
Let the wild, thronging train,
295 The bright procession
Of eddying forms,
Sweep through my soul!
—1849 (1847–48?)

Resignation

To Fausta[1]

To die be given us, or attain!
   Fierce work it were, to do again.
So pilgrims, bound for Mecca, prayed
At burning noon; so warriors said,
5 Scarfed with the cross, who watched the miles
Of dust which wreathed their struggling files
Down Lydian mountains; so, when snows
Round Alpine summits, eddying, rose,
The Goth, bound Rome-wards; so the Hun,
10 Crouched on his saddle, while the sun
Went lurid down o'er flooded plains
Through which the groaning Danube strains
To the drear Euxine;—so pray all,
Whom labours, self-ordained, enthrall;
15 Because they to themselves propose
On this side the all-common close
A goal which, gained, may give repose.
So pray they; and to stand again
Where they stood once, to them were pain;
20 Pain to thread back and to renew
Past straits, and currents long steered through.

But milder natures, and more free—
Whom an unblamed serenity
Hath freed from passions, and the state
25 Of struggle these necessitate;

Whom schooling of the stubborn mind
Hath made, or birth hath found, resigned—
These mourn not, that their goings pay
Obedience to the passing day.
30 These claim not every laughing Hour
For handmaid to their striding power;
Each in her turn, with torch upreared,
To await their march; and when appeared,
Through the cold gloom, with measured race,
35 To usher for a destined space
(Her own sweet errands all foregone)
The too imperious traveller on.
These, Fausta, ask not this; nor thou,
Time's chafing prisoner, ask it now!

40 We left, just ten years since, you say,
That wayside inn we left to-day.[2]
Our jovial host, as forth we fare,
Shouts greeting from his easy chair.
High on a bank our leader stands,
45 Reviews and ranks his motley bands,
Makes clear our goal to every eye—
The valley's western boundary.
A gate swings to! our tide hath flowed
Already from the silent road.
50 The valley-pastures, one by one,
Are threaded, quiet in the sun;
And now beyond the rude stone bridge
Slopes gracious up the western ridge.
Its woody border, and the last
55 Of its dark upland farms is past—
Cool farms, with open-lying stores,
Under their burnish'd sycamores;
All past! and through the trees we glide,
Emerging on the green hill-side.
60 There climbing hangs, a far-seen sign,
Our wavering, many-coloured line;
There winds, upstreaming slowly still
Over the summit of the hill.

---

[1] Arnold's elder sister Jane with whom he walked in the Lake District in the period 1847–49. She is named a female Faust because she is uneasy with inaction and desires a life of accomplishment.

---

[2] the inn at Wythburn, Cumberland.

And now, in front, behold outspread
65 Those upper regions we must tread!
Mild hollows, and clear heathy swells,
The cheerful silence of the fells.
Some two hours' march with serious air,
Through the deep noontide heats we fare;
70 The red-grouse, springing at our sound,
Skims, now and then, the shining ground;
No life, save his and ours, intrudes
Upon these breathless solitudes.
O joy! again the farms appear.
75 Cool shade is there, and rustic cheer;
There springs the brook will guide us down,
Bright comrade, to the noisy town.
Lingering, we follow down; we gain
The town, the highway, and the plain.
80 And many a mile of dusty way,
Parched and road-worn, we made that day;
But, Fausta, I remember well,
That as the balmy darkness fell
We bathed our hands with speechless glee,
85 That night, in the wide-glimmering sea.

Once more we tread this self-same road,
Fausta, which ten years since we trod;
Alone we tread it, you and I,
Ghosts of that boisterous company.
90 Here, where the brook shines, near its head,
In its clear, shallow, turf-fringed bed;
Here, whence the eye first sees, far down,
Capped with faint smoke, the noisy town;
Here sit we, and again unroll,
95 Though slowly, the familiar whole.
The solemn wastes of healthy hill
Sleep in the July sunshine still;
The self-same shadows now, as then,
Play through this grassy upland glen;
100 The loose dark stones on the green way
Lie strewn, it seems, where then they lay;
On this mild bank above the stream,
(You crush them!) the blue gentians gleam.

Still this wild brook, the rushes cool,
105 The sailing foam, the shining pool!
These are not changed; and we, you say,
Are scarce more changed, in truth, than they.

The gipsies, whom we met below,
They, too, have long roamed to and fro;
110 They ramble, leaving, where they pass,
Their fragments on the cumbered grass.
And often to some kindly place
Chance guides the migratory race,
Where, though long wanderings intervene,
115 They recognise a former scene.
The dingy tents are pitched; the fires
Give to the wind their wavering spires;
In dark knots crouch round the wild flame
Their children, as when first they came;
120 They see their shackled beasts again
Move, browsing, up the gray-walled lane.
Signs are not wanting, which might raise
The ghost in them of former days—
Signs are not wanting, if they would;
125 Suggestions to disquietude.
For them, for all, time's busy touch,
While it mends little, troubles much.
Their joints grow stiffer—but the year
Runs his old round of dubious cheer;
130 Chilly they grow—yet winds in March,
Still, sharp as ever, freeze and parch;
They must live still—and yet, God knows,
Crowded and keen the country grows;
It seems as if, in their decay,
135 The law grew stronger every day.[1]
So might they reason, so compare,
Fausta, times past with times that are.
But no!—they rubbed through yesterday
In their hereditary way,
140 And they will rub through, if they can,
To-morrow on the self-same plan,

---

[1] laws against trespassing become more strictly enforced.

Till death arrive to supersede,
For them, vicissitude and need.

The poet, to whose mighty heart
145 Heaven doth a quicker pulse impart,
Subdues that energy to scan
Not his own course, but that of man.
Though he move mountains, though his day
Be passed on the proud heights of sway,
150 Though he hath loosed a thousand chains,
Though he hath borne immortal pains,
Action and suffering though he know—
He hath not lived, if he lives so.
He sees, in some great-historied land,
155 A ruler of the people stand,
Sees his strong thought in fiery flood
Roll through the heaving multitude;
Exults—yet for no moment's space
Envies the all-regarded place.
160 Beautiful eyes meet his—and he
Bears to admire uncravingly;[1]
They pass—he, mingled with the crowd,
Is in their far-off triumphs proud.
From some high station he looks down,
165 At sunset, on a populous town;
Surveys each happy group which fleets,
Toil ended, through the shining streets,
Each with some errand of its own—
And does not say: *I am alone.*
170 He sees the gentle stir of birth
When morning purifies the earth;
He leans upon a gate and sees
The pastures, and the quiet trees.
Low, woody hill, with gracious bound,
175 Folds the still valley almost round;
The cuckoo, loud on some high lawn,
Is answered from the depth of dawn;
In the hedge straggling to the stream,
Pale, dew-drenched, half-shut roses gleam;

180 But, where the farther side slopes down,
He sees the drowsy new-waked clown
In his white quaint-embroidered frock
Make, whistling, tow'rd his mist-wreathed flock—
Slowly, behind his heavy tread,
185 The wet, flowered grass heaves up its head.
Leaned on his gate, he gazes—tears
Are in his eyes, and in his ears
The murmur of a thousand years.
Before him he sees life unroll,
190 A placid and continuous whole—
That general life, which does not cease,
Whose secret is not joy, but peace;
That life, whose dumb wish is not missed
If birth proceeds, if things subsist;
195 The life of plants, and stones, and rain,
The life he craves—if not in vain
Fate gave, what chance shall not control,
His sad lucidity of soul.

You listen—but that wandering smile,
200 Fausta, betrays you cold the while!
Your eyes pursue the bells of foam
Washed, eddying, from this bank, their home.
Those gipsies, so your thoughts I scan,
Are less, the poet more, than man.
205 *They feel not, though they move and see;*
Deeper the poet feels; but he
Breathes, when he will, immortal air,
Where Orpheus and where Homer are.
In the day's life, whose iron round
210 *Hems us all in, he is not bound;*
He leaves his kind, o'erleaps their pen,
And flees the common life of men.
He escapes thence, but we abide—
Not deep the poet sees, but wide.
215 The world in which we live and move
Outlasts aversion, outlasts love,
Outlasts each effort, interest, hope,
Remorse, grief, joy;—and were the scope
Of these affections wider made,

---

[1] emotionally detached.

220 Man still would see, and see dismayed,
Beyond his passion's widest range,
Far regions of eternal change.
Nay, and since death, which wipes out man,
Finds him with many an unsolved plan,
225 With much unknown, and much untried,
Wonder not dead, and thirst not dried,
Still gazing on the ever full
Eternal mundane spectacle—
This world in which we draw our breath,
230 In some sense, Fausta, outlasts death.

Blame thou not, therefore, him who dares
Judge vain beforehand human cares;
Whose natural insight can discern
What through experience others learn;
235 Who needs not love and power, to know
Love transient, power an unreal show;
Who treads at ease life's uncheered ways—
Him blame not, Fausta, rather praise!
Rather thyself for some aim pray
240 Nobler than this, to fill the day;
Rather that heart, which burns in thee,
Ask, not to amuse, but to set free;
Be passionate hopes not ill resigned
For quiet, and a fearless mind.
245 And though fate grudge to thee and me
The poet's rapt security,
Yet they, believe me, who await
No gifts from chance, have conquered fate.
They, winning room to see and hear,
250 And to men's business not too near,
Through clouds of individual strife
Draw homeward to the general life.
Like leaves by suns not yet uncurled;
To the wise, foolish; to the world,
255 Weak; yet not weak, I might reply,
Not foolish, Fausta, in His eye,
To whom each moment in its race,
Crowd as we will its neutral space,

Is but a quiet watershed
260 Whence, equally, the seas of life and death are fed.

Enough, we live!—and if a life,
With large results so little rife,
Though bearable, seem hardly worth
This pomp of words, this pain of birth;
265 Yet, Fausta, the mute turf we tread,
The solemn hills around us spread,
This stream which falls incessantly,
The strange-scrawled rocks,[1] the lonely sky,
If I might lend their life a voice,
270 Seem to bear rather than rejoice.
And even could the intemperate prayer
Man iterates, while these forbear,
For movement, for an ampler sphere,
Pierce Fate's impenetrable ear;
275 Not milder is the general lot
Because our spirits have forgot,
In action's dizzying eddy whirled,
The something that infects the world.
—1849 (1843–48?)

The Forsaken Merman

Come, dear children, let us away;
Down and away below!
Now my brothers call from the bay,
Now the great winds shoreward blow,
5 Now the salt tides seaward flow;
Now the wild white horses play,
Champ and chafe and toss in the spray.
Children dear, let us away!
This way, this way!

10 Call her once before you go—
Call once yet!
In a voice that she will know:

---

[1] striations on boulders transported by glacial action in the Lake District.

"Margaret! Margaret!"
Children's voices should be dear
15 (Call once more) to a mother's ear;
Children's voices, wild with pain—
Surely she will come again!
Call her once and come away;
This way, this way!
20 "Mother dear, we cannot stay!
The wild white horses foam and fret."
Margaret! Margaret!

Come, dear children, come away down;
Call no more!
25 One last look at the white-walled town,
And the little grey church on the windy shore,
Then come down!
She will not come though you call all day;
Come away, come away!
30 Children dear, was it yesterday
We heard the sweet bells over the bay?
In the caverns where we lay,
Through the surf and through the swell,
The far-off sound of a silver bell?
35 Sand-strewn caverns, cool and deep,
Where the winds are all asleep;
Where the spent lights quiver and gleam,
Where the salt weed sways in the stream,
Where the sea-beasts, ranged all round,
40 Feed in the ooze of their pasture-ground;
Where the sea-snakes coil and twine,
Dry their mail and and bask in the brine;
Where great whales come sailing by,
Sail and sail, with unshut eye,
45 Round the world for ever and aye?
When did music come this way?
Children dear, was it yesterday?
Children dear, was it yesterday
(Call yet once) that she went away?
50 Once she sate with you and me,
On a red gold throne in the heart of the sea,
And the youngest sate on her knee.

She combed its bright hair, and she tended it well,
When down swung the sound of a far-off bell.
55 She sighed, she looked up through the clear green
sea;
She said: "I must go, for my kinfolk pray
In the little grey church on the shore to-day.
'Twill be Easter-time in the world—ah me!
And I lose my poor soul, Merman! here with thee."
60 I said: "Go up, dear heart, through the waves;
Say thy prayer, and come back to the kind
sea-caves!"
She smiled, she went up through the surf in the bay.
Children dear, was it yesterday?

Children dear, were we long alone?
65 "The sea grows stormy, the little ones moan;
Long prayers," I said, "in the world they say;
Come!" I said; and we rose through the surf in the
bay.
We went up the beach, by the sandy down
Where the sea-stocks bloom, to the white-walled
town;
70 Through the narrow paved streets, where all was
still,
To the little grey church on the windy hill.
From the church came a murmur of folk at their
prayers,
But we stood without in the cold blowing airs.
We climbed on the graves, on the stones worn with
rains,
75 And we gazed up the aisle through the small leaded
panes.
She sate by the pillar; we saw her clear:
"Margaret, hist! come quick, we are here!
Dear heart," I said, "we are long alone;
The sea grows stormy, the little ones moan."
80 But, ah, she gave me never a look,
For her eyes were sealed to the holy book!
Loud prays the priest; shut stands the door.
Come away, children, call no more!
Come away, come down, call no more!

85 Down, down, down!
Down to the depths of the sea!
She sits at her wheel in the humming town,
Singing most joyfully.
Hark what she sings: "O joy, O joy,
90 For the humming street, and the child with its toy!
For the priest, and the bell, and the holy well;[1]
For the wheel where I spun,
And the blessed light of the sun!"
And so she sings her fill,
95 Singing most joyfully,
Till the spindle drops from her hand,
And the whizzing wheel stands still.
She steals to the window, and looks at the sand,
And over the sand at the sea;
100 And her eyes are set in a stare;
And anon there breaks a sigh,
And anon there drops a tear,
From a sorrow-clouded eye,
And a heart sorrow-laden,
105 A long, long sigh;
For the cold strange eyes of a little Mermaiden
And the gleam of her golden hair.

 Come away, away children:
Come children, come down!
110 The hoarse wind blows coldly;
Lights shine in the town.
She will start from her slumber
When gusts shake the door;
She will hear the winds howling,
115 Will hear the waves roar.
We shall see, while above us
The waves roar and whirl,
A ceiling of amber,
A pavement of pearl.
120 Singing: "Here came a mortal,
But faithless was she!

And alone dwell for ever
The kings of the sea."

But, children, at midnight,
125 When soft the winds blow,
When clear falls the moonlight,
When spring-tides are low;
When sweet airs come seaward
From heaths starred with broom,
130 And high rocks throw mildly
On the blanched sands a gloom;
Up the still, glistening beaches,
Up the creeks we will hie,
Over banks of bright seaweed
135 The ebb-tide leaves dry.
We will gaze, from the sand-hills,
At the white, sleeping town;
At the church on the hill-side—
And then come back down.
140 Singing: "There dwells a loved one,
But cruel is she!
She left lonely for ever
The kings of the sea."
 —1849 (1847–49?)

To Marguerite—Continued

Yes! in the sea of life enisled,
 With echoing[2] straits between us thrown,
Dotting the shoreless watery wild,
We mortal millions live *alone*.
5 The islands feel the enclasping flow,
And then their endless bounds they know.

But when the moon their hollows lights,
And they are swept by balms of spring,
And in their glens, on starry nights,
10 The nightingales divinely sing;

---

[1] holy water font.

[2] to make communication difficult.

And lovely notes, from shore to shore,
Across the sounds and channels pour—

Oh! then a longing like despair
Is to their farthest caverns sent;
15 For surely once, they feel, we were
Parts of a single continent!
Now round us spreads the watery plain—
Oh might our marges meet again!

Who ordered, that their longing's fire
20 Should be, as soon as kindled, cooled?
Who renders vain their deep desire?—
A God, a God their severance ruled!
And bade betwixt their shores to be
The unplumbed, salt, estranging sea.
—1852 (1849)

Stanzas in Memory
of the Author of "Obermann"[1]

November, 1849

In front the awful Alpine track
Crawls up its rocky stair;

The autumn storm-winds drive the rack,
Close o'er it, in the air.

5 Behind are the abandon'd baths[2]
Mute in their meadows lone;
The leaves are on the valley paths,
The mists are on the Rhone—

The white mists rolling like a sea!
10 I hear the torrents roar.
—Yes, Obermann, all speaks of thee;
I feel thee near once more!

I turn thy leaves! I feel their breath
Once more upon me roll;
15 That air of languor, cold, and death,
Which brooded o'er thy soul.

Fly hence, poor wretch, whoe'er thou art,
Condemned to cast about,[3]
All shipwreck in thy own weak heart,
20 For comfort from without!

---

[1] The following note on Senancour was first attached to the poem in 1869: "The author of *Obermann*, Étienne Pivert de Senancour, has little celebrity in France, his own country; and out of France he is almost unknown. But the profound inwardness, the austere sincerity, of his principal work, *Obermann*, the delicate feeling for nature which it exhibits, and the melancholy eloquence of many passages of it, have attracted and charmed some of the most remarkable spirits of this century, such as George Sand and Sainte-Beuve, and will probably always find a certain number of spirits whom they touch and interest.

Senancour was born in 1770. He was educated for the priesthood, and passed some time in the seminary of St. Sulpice; broke away from the Seminary and from France itself, and passed some years in Switzerland, where he married; returned to France in middle life, and followed thenceforward the career of a man of letters, but with hardly any fame or success. He died an old man in 1846, desiring that on his grave might be placed these words only: *Éternité, deviens mon asile!*

The influence of Rousseau, and certain affinities with more famous and fortunate authors of his own day,—Chateaubriand and Madame de Staël,—are everywhere visible in Senancour. But though, like these eminent personages, he may be called a sentimental writer, and though

Obermann, a collection of letters from Switzerland treating almost entirely of nature and of the human soul, may be called a work of sentiment, Senancour has a gravity and severity which distinguish him from all other writers of the sentimental school. The world is with him in his solitude far less than it is with them; of all writers he is the most perfectly isolated and the least attitudinising. His chief work, too, has a value and power of its own, apart from these merits of its author. The stir of all the main forces, by which modern life is and has been impelled, lives in the letters of *Obermann*; the dissolving agencies of the eighteenth century, the fiery storm of the French Revolution, the first faint promise and dawn of that new world which our own time is but now more fully bringing to light—all these are to be felt, almost to be touched, there. To me, indeed, it will always seems that the impressiveness of this production can hardly be rated too high.

Besides *Obermann* there is one other of Senancour's works which, for those spirits who feel his attraction, is very interesting; its title is *Libres Méditations d'un Solitaire Inconnu*."

[2] "The baths of Leuk. This poem was conceived, and partly composed, in the valley going down from the foot of the Gemmi Pass towards the Rhone." (Arnold's note, first added in 1869.)

[3] turning the ship away from the wind to ease its passage.

A fever in these pages burns
Beneath the calm they feign;
A wounded human spirit turns,
Here, on its bed of pain.

25 Yes, though the virgin mountain-air
Fresh through these pages blows;
Though to these leaves the glaciers spare
The soul of their white snows;

Though here a mountain-murmur swells
30 Of many a dark-boughed pine;
Though, as you read, you hear the bells
Of the high-pasturing kine—

Yet, through the hum of torrent lone,
And brooding mountain-bee,
35 There sobs I know not what ground-tone
Of human agony.

Is it for this, because the sound
Is fraught too deep with pain,
That Obermann! the world around
40 So little loves thy strain?

Some secrets may the poet tell,
For the world loves new ways;
To tell too deep ones is not well—
It knows not what he says.

45 Yet, of the spirits who have reigned
In this our troubled day,
I know but two,[1] who have attained,
Save thee, to see their way.

By England's lakes, in grey old age,
50 His quiet home one keeps;
And one, the strong much-toiling sage,
In German Weimar sleeps.

But Wordsworth's eyes avert their ken
From half of human fate;
55 And Goethe's course few sons of men
May think to emulate.

For he pursued a lonely road,
His eyes on Nature's plan;
Neither made man too much a God,
60 Nor God too much a man.

Strong was he, with a spirit free
From mists, and sane, and clear;
Clearer, how much! than ours—yet we
Have a worse course to steer.

65 For though his manhood bore the blast
Of a tremendous time,
Yet in a tranquil world was passed
His tenderer youthful prime.

But we, brought forth and reared in hours
70 Of change, alarm, surprise—
What shelter to grow ripe is ours?
What leisure to grow wise?

Like children bathing on the shore,
Buried a wave beneath,
75 The second wave succeeds, before
We have had time to breathe.

Too fast we live, too much are tried,
Too harassed, to attain
Wordsworth's sweet calm, or Goethe's wide
80 And luminous view to gain.

And then we turn, thou sadder sage,
To thee! we feel thy spell!
—The hopeless tangle of our age,
Thou too hast scanned it well!

[1] Wordsworth died in 1850 and Goethe in 1832 (see ll. 49–56).

85 Immoveable thou sittest, still
As death, composed to bear!
Thy head is clear, thy feeling chill,
And icy thy despair.

Yes, as the son of Thetis said,
90 I hear thee saying now:
Greater by far than thou are dead;
Strive not! die also thou!

Ah! two desires toss about
The poet's feverish blood.
95 One drives him to the world without,
And one to solitude.

The glow, he cries, *the thrill of life,*
Where, where do these abound?
Not in the world, not in the strife
100 Of men, shall they be found.

He who hath watched, not shared, the strife,
Knows how the day hath gone.
He only lives with the world's life,
Who hath renounced his own.

105 To thee we come, then! Clouds are rolled
Where thou, O seer! art set;
Thy realm of thought is drear and cold—
The world is colder yet!

And thou hast pleasures, too, to share
110 With those who come to thee—
Balms floating on thy mountain-air,
And healing sights to see.

How often, where the slopes are green
On Jaman,[1] has thou sate
115 By some high chalet-door, and seen
The summer-day grow late;

And darkness steal o'er the wet grass
With the pale crocus starred,

And reach that glimmering sheet of glass
120 Beneath the piny sward,

Lake Leman's[2] waters, far below!
And watched the rosy light
Fade from the distant peaks of snow;
And on the air of night

125 Heard accents of the eternal tongue
Through the pine branches play—
Listened, and felt thyself grow young!
Listened and wept—Away!

Away the dreams that but deceive
130 And thou, sad guide, adieu!
I go, fate drives me; but I leave
Half of my life with you.

We, in some unknown Power's employ,
Move on a rigorous line;
135 Can neither, when we will, enjoy,
Nor, when we will, resign.

I in the world must live; but thou,
Thou melancholy shade!
Wilt not, if thou canst see me now,
140 Condemn me, nor upbraid.

For thou art gone away from earth,
And place with those dost claim,
The Children of the Second Birth,
Whom the world could not tame;

145 And with that small, transfigured band,
Whom many a different way
Conducted to their common land,
Thou learn'st to think as they.

Christian and pagan, king and slave,
150 Soldier and anchorite,

---

[1] overlooking Vevey on the Lake of Geneva.

[2] Lake Geneva.

Distinctions we esteem so grave,
Are nothing in their sight.

They do not ask, who pined unseen,
Who was on action hurled,
155   Whose one bond is, that all have been
Unspotted by the world.

There without anger thou wilt see
Him who obeys thy spell
No more, so he but rest, like thee,
160   Unsoiled!—and so, farewell.

Farewell!—Whether thou now liest near
That much-loved inland sea,
The ripples of whose blue waves cheer
Vevey and Meillerie;

165   And in that gracious region bland,
Where with clear-rustling wave
The scented pines of Switzerland
Stand dark round thy green grave,

Between the dusty vineyard-walls
170   Issuing on that green place
The early peasant still recalls
The pensive stranger's face,

And stoops to clear thy moss-grown date
Ere he plods on again;
175   Or whether, by maligner fate,
Among the swarms of men,

Where between granite terraces
The blue Seine rolls her wave,
The Capital of Pleasure sees
180   The hardly-heard-of grave;

Farewell! Under the sky we part,
In this stern Alpine dell.
O unstrung will! O broken heart!
A last, a last farewell!
—1852 (1849)

Empedocles on Etna[1]

A DRAMATIC POEM

PERSONS

EMPEDOCLES
PAUSANIAS, *a Physician.*
CALLICLES, *a young Harp-player.*

The Scene of the Poem is on Mount Etna; at first in the forest region, afterwards on the summit of the mountain.

ACT 1. SCENE 1

Morning. A Pass in the forest region of Etna.

---

[1] See the opening paragraphs of Arnold's "Preface to *Poems*, 1853" for the poet's (after) thoughts on the poem. The following are Arnold's notes on the poem, preserved in the Yale MS:

"He is a philosopher.

He has not the religious consolation of other men, facile because adapted to their weaknesses, or because shared by all around and charging the atmosphere they breathe.

He sees things as they are—the world as it is—God as he is: in their stern simplicity.

The sight is a severe and mind-tasking one: to know the mysteries which are communicated to others by fragments, in parables.

But he started towards it in hope: his first glimpses of it filled him with joy; he had friends who shared his hope and joy and communicated to him theirs: even now he does not deny that the sight is capable of affording rapture and the purest peace.

But his friends are dead: the world is all against him, and incredulous of the truth: his mind is overtasked by the effort to hold fast so great and severe a truth in solitude: the atmosphere he breathes not being modified by the presence of human life, is too rare for him. He perceives still the truth of the truth, but cannot be transported and rapturously agitated by his [*for* its] grandeur: his spring and elasticity of mind are gone: he is clouded, oppressed, dispirited, without hope and energy.

Before he becomes the victim of depression and overtension of mind, to the utter deadness to joy, grandeur, spirit, and animated life, he desires to die; to be reunited with the universe, before by exaggerating his human side he has become utterly estranged from it."

Act I concerns "modern thought"—essentially Stoic and empty of meaningful ethical values—and Act II presents "modern feelings"—depression and ennui ("Preface").

CALLICLES

(Alone, resting on a rock by the path.)

The mules, I think, will not be here this hour;
They feel the cool wet turf under their feet
By the stream-side, after the dusty lanes
In which they have toiled all night from Catana,[1]
5 And scarcely will they budge a yard. O Pan,
How gracious is the mountain at this hour!
A thousand times have I been here alone,
Or with the revellers from the mountain-towns,
But never on so fair a morn; the sun
10 Is shining on the brilliant mountain-crests,
And on the highest pines; but farther down,
Here in the valley, is in shade; the sward
Is dark, and on the stream the mist still hangs;
One sees one's footprints crushed in the wet grass,
15 One's breath curls in the air; and on these pines
That climb from the stream's edge, the long grey
    tufts,
Which the goats love, are jewelled thick with dew.
Here will I stay till the slow litter comes.
I have my harp too—that is well. Apollo!
20 What mortal could be sick or sorry here?
I know not in what mind Empedocles,
Whose mules I followed, may be coming up,
But if, as most men say, he is half mad
With exile, and with brooding on his wrongs,
25 Pausanias, his sage friend, who mounts with him,
Could scarce have lighted on a lovelier cure.
The mules must be below, far down. I hear
Their tinkling bells, mixed with the song of birds,
Rise faintly to me—now it stops! Who's here?
30 Pausanias! and on foot? alone?

PAUSANIAS

                    And thou, then?
I left thee supping with Peisianax,
With thy head full of wine, and thy hair crowned,
Touching thy harp as the whim came on thee,
And praised and spoiled by master and by guests

35 Almost as much as the new dancing-girl.
Why hast thou followed us?

CALLICLES

                    The night was hot,
And the feast past its prime; so we slipped out
Some of us, to the portico to breathe—
Peisianax, thou know'st, drinks late; and then,
40 As I was lifting my soiled garland off,
I saw the mules and litter in the court,
And in the litter sate Empedocles;
Thou, too, wast with him. Straightway I sped home;
I saddled my white mule, and all night long
45 Through the cool lovely country followed you,
Passed you a little since as morning dawned,
And have this hour sate by the torrent here,
Till the slow mules should climb in sight again.
And now?

PAUSANIAS

        And now, back to the town with speed!
50 Crouch in the wood first, till the mules have passed;
They do but halt, they will be here anon.
Thou must be viewless to Empedocles;
Save mine, he must not meet a human eye.
One of his moods is on him that thou know'st;
55 I think, thou wouldst not vex him.

CALLICLES

                    No—and yet
I would fain stay, and help thee tend him. Once
He knew me well, and would oft notice me;
And still, I know not how, he draws me to him,
And I could watch him with his proud sad face,
60 His flowing locks and gold-encircled brow
And kingly gait, for ever; such a spell
In his severe looks, such a majesty
As drew of old the people after him,
In Agrigentum and Olympia,
65 When his star reigned, before his banishment,
Is potent still on me in his decline.

---

[1] town at the foot of Mt. Etna.

356

But oh! Pausanias, he is changed of late;
There is a settled trouble in his air
Admits no momentary brightening now,
70 And when he comes among his friends at feasts,
'Tis as an orphan among prosperous boys.
Thou know'st of old he loved this harp of mine,
When first he sojourned with Peisianax;
He is now always moody, and I fear him;
75 But I would serve him, soothe him, if I could,
Dared one but try.

PAUSANIAS
            Thou wast a kind child ever!
He loves thee, but he must not see thee now.
Thou hast indeed a rare touch on thy harp,
He loves that in thee, too; there was a time
80 (But that is passed), he would have paid[1] thy strain
With music to have drawn the stars from heaven.
He hath his harp and laurel with him still,
But he has laid the use of music by,
And all which might relax his settled gloom.
85 Yet thou may'st try thy playing, if thou wilt—
But thou must keep unseen; follow us on,
But at a distance! in these solitudes,
In this clear mountain-air, a voice will rise,
Though from afar, distinctly; it may soothe him.
90 Play when we halt, and, when the evening comes
And I must leave him (for his pleasure is
To be left musing these soft nights alone
In the high unfrequented mountain-spots),
Then watch him, for he ranges swift and far,
95 Sometimes to Etna's top, and to the cone;
But hide thee in the rocks a great way down,
And try thy noblest strains, my Callicles,
With the sweet night to help thy harmony!
Thou wilt earn my thanks sure, and perhaps his.

CALLICLES
100 More than a day and night, Pausanias,
Of this fair summer-weather, on these hills,

Would I bestow to help Empedocles.
That needs no thanks; one is far better here
Than in the broiling city in these heats.
105 But tell me, how hast thou persuaded him
In this his present fierce, man-hating mood,
To bring thee out with him alone on Etna?

PAUSANIAS
Thou hast heard all men speaking of Pantheia,
The woman who at Agrigentum lay
110 Thirty long days in a cold trance of death,
And whom Empedocles called back to life.
Thou art too young to note it, but his power
Swells with the swelling evil of this time,
And holds men mute to see where it will rise.
115 He could stay swift diseases in old days,
Chain madmen by the music of his lyre,
Cleanse to sweet airs the breath of poisonous
      streams,
And in the mountain-chinks inter the winds.
This he could do of old; but now, since all
120 Clouds and grows daily worse in Sicily,
Since broils tear us in twain, since this new swarm
Of sophists[2] has got empire in our schools
Where he was paramount, since he is banished
And lives a lonely man in triple gloom—
125 He grasps the very reins of life and death.
I asked him of Pantheia yesterday,
When we were gathered with Peisianax,
And he made answer, I should come at night
On Etna here, and be alone with him,
130 And he would tell me, as his old, tried friend,
Who still was faithful, what might profit me;
That is, the secret of this miracle.

CALLICLES
Bah! Thou a doctor! Thou art superstitious.
Simple Pausanias, 'twas no miracle!
135 Pantheia, for I know her kinsmen well,
Was subject to these trances from a girl.

---

[1] rewarded.

[2] the proponents of specious (sophistical) reasoning.

Empedocles would say so, did he deign;
But he still lets the people, whom he scorns,
Gape and cry *wizard* at him, if they list.
140 But thou, thou art no company for him!
Thou art as cross, as soured as himself!
Thou hast some wrong from thine own citizens,
And then thy friend is banished, and on that,
Straightway thou fallest to arraign the times,
145 As if the sky was impious not to fall.
The sophists are no enemies of his;
I hear, Gorgias, their chief, speaks nobly of him,
As of his gifted master, and once friend.
He is too scornful, too high-wrought, too bitter.
150 'Tis not the times, 'tis not the sophists vex him;
There is some root of suffering in himself,
Some secret and unfollowed vein of woe,
Which makes the time look black and sad to him.
Pester him not in this his sombre mood
155 With questionings about an idle tale,
But lead him through the lovely mountain-paths,
And keep his mind from preying on itself,
And talk to him of things at hand and common,
Not miracles! thou art a learned man,
160 But credulous of fables as a girl.

PAUSANIAS

And thou, a boy whose tongue outruns his
    knowledge,
And on whose lightness blame is thrown away.
Enough of this! I see the litter wind
Up by the torrent-side, under the pines.
165 I must rejoin Empedocles. Do thou
Crouch in the brushwood till the mules have passed;
Then play thy kind part well. Farewell till night!

SCENE II
*Noon. A Glen on the highest skirts of the woody region
of Etna.*
EMPEDOCLES — PAUSANIAS

PAUSANIAS

The noon is hot. When we have crossed the stream,
We shall have left the woody tract, and come
Upon the open shoulder of the hill.
See how the giant spires of yellow bloom
5 Of the sun-loving gentian, in the heat,
Are shining on those naked slopes like flame!
Let us rest here; and now, Empedocles,
Pantheia's history!
                    [*A harp-note below is heard.*

EMPEDOCLES
                    Hark! what sound was that
Rose from below? If it were possible,
10 And we were not so far from human haunt,
I should have said that some one touched a harp.
Hark! there again!

PAUSANIAS
                    'Tis the boy Callicles,
The sweetest harp-player in Cantana.
He is for ever coming on these hills,
15 In summer, to all country-festivals,
With a gay revelling band; he breaks from them
Sometimes, and wanders far among the glens.
But heed him not, he will not mount to us;
I spoke with him this morning. Once more,
    therefore,
20 Instruct me of Pantheia's story, Master,
As I have prayed thee.

EMPEDOCLES
                    That? and to what end?

PAUSANIAS

It is enough that all men speak of it.
But I will also say, that when the Gods
Visit us as they do with sign and plague,
25 To know those spells of thine which stay their hand
Were to live free from terror.

EMPEDOCLES

        Spells? Mistrust them!
Mind is the spell which governs earth and heaven.
Man has a mind with which to plan his safety;
Know that, and help thyself!

PAUSANIAS

        But thine own words?
30 "The wit and counsel of man was never clear,
Troubles confound the little wit he has."
Mind is a light which the Gods mock us with,
To lead those false who trust it.
        [*The harp sounds again.*

EMPEDOCLES

        Hist! once more!
Listen, Pausanias! —Ay, 'tis Callicles;
35 I know these notes among a thousand. Hark!

CALLICLES

(*Sings unseen, from below*)
The track winds down to the clear stream,
To cross the sparkling shallows; there
The cattle love to gather, on their way
To the high mountain-pastures, and to stay,
40 Till the rough cow-herds drive them past,
Knee-deep in the cool ford; for 'tis the last
Of all the woody, high, well-watered dells
On Etna; and the beam
Of noon is broken there by chestnut-boughs
45 Down its steep verdant sides; the air
Is freshened by the leaping stream, which throws
Eternal showers of spray on the mossed roots
Of trees, and veins of turf, and long dark shoots

Of ivy-plants, and fragrant hanging bells
50 Of hyacinths, and on late anemones,
That muffle its wet banks; but glade,
And stream, and sward, and chestnut-trees,
End here; Etna beyond, in the broad glare
Of the hot noon, without a shade,
55 Slope beyond slope, up to the peak, lies bare;
The peak, round which the white clouds play.

In such a glen, on such a day,
On Pelion, on the grassy ground,
Chiron, the aged Centaur lay,
60 The young Achilles standing by.
The Centaur taught him to explore
The mountains; where the glens are dry
And the tired Centaurs come to rest,
And where the soaking springs abound
65 And the straight ashes grow for spears,
And where the hill-goats come to feed,
And the sea-eagles build their nest.
He showed him Phthia far away,
And said: O boy, I taught this lore
70 To Peleus, in long distant years!
He told him of the Gods, the stars,
The tides; and then of mortal wars,
And of the life which heroes lead
Before they reach the Elysian place
75 And rest in the immortal mead;
And all the wisdom of his race.

The music below ceases, and EMPEDOCLES *speaks,
accompanying himself in a solemn manner on his
harp.*

The out-spread world to span
A cord the Gods first slung,
And then the soul of man
80 There, like a mirror, hung,
And bade the winds through space impel the gusty
toy.

Hither and thither spins
The wind-borne, mirroring soul,
A thousand glimpses wins,
85 And never sees a whole;
Looks once, and drives elsewhere, and leaves its last
employ.

The Gods laugh in their sleeve
To watch man doubt and fear,
Who knows not what to believe
90 Since he sees nothing clear,
And dares stamp nothing false where he finds
nothing sure.

Is this, Pausanias, so?
And can our souls not strive,
But with the winds must go,
95 And hurry where they drive?
Is fate indeed so strong, man's strength indeed so
poor?

I will not judge. That man,
Howbeit, I judge as lost,
Whose mind allows a plan,
100 Which would degrade it most;
And he treats doubt the best who tries to see least
ill.

Be not, then, fear's blind slave!
Thou art my friend; to thee,
All knowledge that I have,
105 All skill I wield, are free.
Ask not the latest news of the last miracle.

Ask not what days and nights
In trance Pantheia lay,
But ask how thou such sights
110 May'st see without dismay;
Ask what most helps when known, thou son of
Anchitus!

What? hate, and awe, and shame
Fill thee to see our time;
Thou feelest thy soul's frame
115 Shaken and out of chime?
What? life and chance go hard with thee too, as
with us;

Thy citizens, 'tis said,
Envy thee and oppress,
Thy goodness no men aid,
120 All strive to make it less;
Tyranny, pride, and lust, fill Sicily's abodes;

Heaven is with earth at strife,
Signs make thy soul afraid,
The dead return to life,
125 Rivers are dried, winds stayed;
Scarce can one think in calm, so threatening are the
Gods;

And we feel, day and night,
The burden of ourselves—
Well, then, the wiser wight
130 In his own bosom delves,
And asks what ails him so, and gets what cure he
can.

The sophist sneers: Fool, take
Thy pleasure, right or wrong.
The pious wail: Forsake
135 A world these sophists throng.
Be neither saint nor sophist-led, but be a man!

These hundred doctors try
To preach thee to their school.
We have the truth! they cry;
140 And yet their oracle,
Trumpet it as they will, is but the same as thine.

Once read thy own breast right,
And thou hast done with fears;

Man gets no other light,
145   Search he a thousand years.
Sink in thyself! there ask what ails thee, at that
    shrine!

What makes thee struggle and rave?
    Why are men ill at ease?
    'Tis that the lot they have
150   Fails their own will to please;
For man would make no murmuring, were his will
    obeyed.

And why is it, that still
    Man with his lot thus fights?
    'Tis that he makes this *will*
155   The measure of his *rights*,
And believes Nature outraged if his will's gainsaid.

Couldst thou, Pausanias, learn
    How deep a fault is this;
    Couldst thou but once discern
160   Thou hast no *right* to bliss,
No title from the Gods to welfare and repose;

Then thou wouldst look less mazed
    Whene'er of bliss debarred,
    Nor think the Gods were crazed
165   When thy own lot went hard.
But we are all the same—the fools of our own
    woes!

For, from the first faint morn
    Of life, the thirst for bliss
    Deep in man's heart is born;
170   And, sceptic as he is,
He fails not to judge clear if this be quenched or
    no.

Nor is the thirst to blame.
    Man errs not that he deems
    His welfare his true aim,

175 He errs because he dreams
The world does but exist that welfare to bestow.

We mortals are no kings
    For each of whom to sway
    A new-made world up-springs,
180   Meant merely for his play;
No, we are strangers here; the world is from of old.

In vain our pent wills fret,
    And would the world subdue,
    Limits we did not set
185   Condition we all do;
Born into life we are, and life must be our mould.

Born into life! man grows
    Forth from his parents' stem,
    And blends their bloods, as those
190   Of theirs are blent in them;
So each new man strikes root into a far fore-time.

Born into life! we bring
    A bias with us here,
    And, when here, each new thing
195   Affects us we come near;
To tunes we did not call our being must keep
    chime.

Born into life! in vain,
    Opinions, those or these,
    Unaltered to retain
200   The obstinate mind decrees;
Experience, like a sea, soaks all-effacing in.

Born into life! who lists
    May what is false hold dear,
    And for himself make mists
205   Through which to see less clear;
The world is what it is, for all our dust and din.

Born into life! 'tis we,
And not the world, are new;
Our cry for bliss, our plea,
210 Others have urged it too—
Our wants have all been felt, our errors made
before.

No eye could be too sound
To observe a world so vast,
No patience too profound
215 To sort what's here amassed;
How man may here best live no care too great to
explore.

But we—as some rude guest
Would change, where'er he roam,
The manners there professed
220 To those he brings from home—
We mark not the world's course, but would have *it*
take *ours*.

The world's course proves the terms
On which man wins content;
Reason the proof confirms—
225 We spurn it, and invent
A false course for the world, and for ourselves, false
powers.

Riches we wish to get,
Yet remain spendthrifts still;
We would have health, and yet
230 Still use our bodies ill;
Bafflers of our own prayers, from youth to life's last
scenes.

We would have inward peace,
Yet will not look within;
We would have misery cease,
235 Yet will not cease from sin;
We want all pleasant ends, but will use no harsh
means;

We do not what we ought,
What we ought not, we do,
And lean upon the thought
240 That chance will bring us through;
But our own acts, for good or ill, are mightier
powers.

Yet, even when man forsakes
All sin—is just, is pure,
Abandons all which makes
245 His welfare insecure—
Other existences there are, that clash with ours.

Like us, the lightning-fires
Love to have scope and play;
The stream, like us, desires
250 An unimpeded way;
Like us, the Libyan wind delights to roam at large.

Streams will not curb their pride
The just man not to entomb,
Nor lightnings go aside
255 To give his virtues room;
Now is that wind less rough which blows a good
man's barge.

Nature, with equal mind,
Sees all her sons at play;
Sees man control the wind,
260 The wind sweep man away;
Allows the proudly-riding and the foundering bark.

And, lastly, though of ours
No weakness spoil our lot,
Though the non-human powers
265 Of Nature harm us not,
The ill deeds of other men make often *our* life dark.

What were the wise man's plan?
Through this sharp, toil-set life,
To work as best he can,

270 And win what's won by strife.
But we an easier way to cheat our pains have
found.

Scratched by a fall, with moans
As children of weak age
Lend life to the dumb stones
275 Whereon to vent their rage,
And bend their little fists, and rate the senseless
ground;

So, loth to suffer mute,
We, peopling the void air,
Make Gods to whom to impute
280 The ills we ought to bear;
With God and Fate to rail at, suffering easily.

Yet grant—as sense long missed
Things that are now perceived,
And much may still exist
285 Which is not yet believed—
Grant that the world were full of Gods we cannot
see;

All things the world which fill
Of but one stuff are spun,
That we who rail are still,
290 With what we rail at, one;
One with the o'erlaboured Power that through the
breadth and length

Of earth, and air, and sea,
In men, and plants, and stones,
Hath toil perpetually,
295 And travails, pants, and moans
Fain would do all things well, but sometimes fails
in strength.

And patiently exact
This universal God
Alike to any act

300 Proceeds at any nod,
And quietly declaims the cursings of himself.

This is not what man hates,
Yet he can curse but this.
Harsh Gods and hostile Fates
305 Are dreams! this only *is*—
Is everywhere; sustains the wise, the foolish elf.

Nor only, in the intent
To attach blame elsewhere,
Do we at will invent
310 Stern Powers who make their care
To embitter human life, malignant Deities;

But, next, we would reverse
The scheme ourselves have spun,
And what we made to curse
315 We now would lean upon,
And feign kind Gods who perfect what man vainly
tries.

Look, the world tempts our eye,
And we would know it all!
We map the starry sky,
320 We mine this earthen ball,
We measure the sea-tides, we number the sea-
sands;

We scrutinise the dates
Of long-past human things,
The bounds of effaced states,
325 The lines of deceased kings;
We search out dead men's words, and works of
dead men's hands;

We shut our eyes, and muse
How our own minds are made.
What springs of thought they use,
330 How rightened, how betrayed—

And spend our wit to name what most employ
  unnamed.

But still, as we proceed
The mass swells more and more
Of volumes yet to read,
335   Of secrets yet to explore.
Our hair grows grey, our eyes are dimmed, our heat
  is tamed;

We rest our faculties,
And thus address the Gods:
"True science if there is,
340   It stays in your abodes!
Man's measures cannot mete the immeasurable All.

"You only can take in
The world's immense design.
Our desperate search was sin,
345   Which henceforth we resign,
Sure only that your mind sees all things which
  befall."

Fools! That in man's brief term
He cannot all things view,
Affords no ground to affirm
350   That there are Gods who do;
Nor does being weary prove that he has where to
  rest.

Again. Our youthful blood
Claims rapture as its right;
The world, a rolling flood
355   Of newness and delight,
Draws in the enamoured gazer to its shining breast;

Pleasure, to our hot grasp,
Gives flowers after flowers;
With passionate warmth we clasp
360   Hand after hand in ours;

Nor do we soon perceive how fast our youth is
  spent.

At once our eyes grow clear!
We see, in blank dismay,
Year posting after year,
365   Sense after sense decay;
Our shivering heart is mined by secret discontent;

Yet still, in spite of truth,
In spite of hopes entombed,
That longing of our youth
370   Burns ever unconsumed,
Still hungrier for delight as delights grow more
  rare.

We pause; we hush our heart,
And thus address the Gods:
"The world hath failed to impart
375   The joy our youth forebodes,
Failed to fill up the void which in our breasts we
  bear.

"Changeful till now, we still
Looked on to something new;
Let us, with changeless will,
380   Henceforth look on to you,
To find with you the joy we in vain here require!"

Fools! That so often here
Happiness mocked our prayer,
I think, might make us fear
385   A like event elsewhere;
Make us, not fly to dreams, but moderate desire.

And yet, for those who know
Themselves, who wisely take
Their way through life, and bow
390   To what they cannot break,
Why should I say that life need yield but *moderate*
  bliss?

Shall we, with temper spoiled,
Health sapped by living ill,
And judgment all embroiled
395 By sadness and self-will
Shall *we* judge what for man is not true bliss or is?

Is it so small a thing
To have enjoyed the sun,
To have lived light in the spring,
400 To have loved, to have thought, to have done;
To have advanced true friends, and beat down
baffling foes—

That we must feign a bliss
Of doubtful future date,
And, while we dream on this,
405 Lose all our present state,
And relegate to worlds yet distant our repose?

Not much, I know, you prize
What pleasures may be had,
Who look on life with eyes
410 Estranged, like mine, and sad;
And yet the village-churl feels the truth more than
you,

Who's loth to leave this life
Which to him little yields—
His hard-tasked sunburnt wife,
415 His often-laboured fields,
The boors with whom he talked, the country-spots
he knew.

But thou, because thou hear'st
Men scoff at Heaven and Fate,
Because the Gods thou fear'st
420 Fail to make blest thy state,
Tremblest, and wilt not dare to trust the joys there
are!

I say: Fear not! Life still
Leaves human effort scope.
But, since life teems with ill,
425 Nurse no extravagant hope;
Because thou must not dream, thou need'st not
then despair!

*A long pause. At the end of it the notes of a harp
below are again heard, and* CALLICLES *sings:—*

Far, far from here,
The Adriatic breaks in a warm bay
Among the green Illyrian hills; and there
430 The sunshine in the happy glens is fair,
And by the sea, and in the brakes.
The grass is cool, the sea-side air
Buoyant and fresh, the mountain flowers
More virginal and sweet than ours.
435 And there, they say, two bright and aged snakes,
Who once were Cadmus and Harmonia,[1]
Bask in the glens or on the warm sea-shore,
In breathless quiet, after all their ills;
Nor do they see their country, nor the place
440 Where the Sphinx lived among the frowning hills,
Nor the unhappy palace of their race,
Nor Thebes, nor the Ismenus, any more.

There those two live, far in the Illyrian brakes!
They had stayed long enough to see,
445 In Thebes, the billow of calamity
Over their own dear children rolled,
Curse upon curse, pang upon pang,
For years, they sitting helpless in their home,
A grey old man and woman; yet of old
450 The Gods had to their marriage come,
And at the banquet all the Muses sang.

Therefore they did not end their days
In sight of blood; but were rapt, far away,

---

[1] Cadmus, the founder of Thebes, and Harmonia, his wife.

To where the west-wind plays,
455 And murmurs of the Adriatic come
To those untrodden mountain-lawns; and there
Placed safely in changed forms, the pair
Wholly forget their first sad life, and home,
And all that Theban woe, and stray
460 For ever through the glens, placid and dumb.

EMPEDOCLES

That was my harp-player again! —where is he?
Down by the stream?

PAUSANIAS

Yes, Master, in the wood.

EMPEDOCLES

He ever loved the Theban story well!
But the day wears. Go now, Pausanias,
465 For I must be alone. Leave me one mule;
Take down with thee the rest to Catana.
And for young Callicles, thank him from me;
Tell him, I never failed to love his lyre—
But he must follow me no more to-night.

PAUSANIAS

470 Thou wilt return to-morrow to the city?

EMPEDOCLES

Either to-morrow or some other day,
In the sure revolutions of the world,
Good friend, I shall revisit Catana.
I have seen many cities in my time,
475 Till mine eyes ache with the long spectacle,
And I shall doubtless see them all again;
Thou know'st me for a wanderer from of old.
Meanwhile, stay me not now. Farewell, Pausanias!
He departs on his way up the mountain.

PAUSANIAS (*alone*)

I dare not urge him further—he must go;
480 But he is strangely wrought! I will speed back

And bring Peisianax to him from the city;
His counsel could once soothe him. But, Apollo!
How his brow lightened as the music rose!
Callicles must wait here, and play to him;
485 I saw him through the chestnuts far below,
Just since, down at the stream. Ho! Callicles!
He descends, calling.

ACT II
Evening. The Summit of Etna.

EMPEDOCLES

Alone!—
On this charred, blackened, melancholy waste,
Crowned by the awful peak, Etna's great mouth,
Round which the sullen vapour rolls—alone!
5 Pausanias is far hence, and that is well,
For I must henceforth speak no more with man.
He hath his lesson too, and that debt's paid;
And the good, learned, friendly, quiet man
May bravelier front his life, and in himself
10 Find henceforth energy and heart. But I—
The weary man, the banished citizen,
Whose banishment is not his greatest ill,
Whose weariness no energy can reach,
And for whose hurt courage is not the cure—
15 What should I do with life and living more?

No, thou art come too late, Empedocles!
And the world hath the day, and must break thee,
Not thou the world. With men thou canst not live,
Their thoughts, their ways, their wishes, are not
thine;
20 And being lonely thou art miserable,
For something has impaired thy spirit's strength,
And dried its self-sufficing fount of joy.
Thou canst not live with men nor with thyself—
O sage! O sage! Take then the one way left;
25 And turn thee to the elements, thy friends,
Thy well-tried friends, thy willing ministers,

And say: Ye helpers, hear Empedocles,
Who asks this final service at your hands!
Before the sophist-brood hath overlaid
30 The last spark of man's consciousness with words—
Ere quite the being of man, ere quite the world
Be disarrayed of their divinity—
Before the soul lose all her solemn joys,
And awe be dead, and hope impossible,
35 And the soul's deep eternal night come on—
Receive me, hide me, quench me, take me home!

*He advances to the edge of the crater. Smoke and fire
break forth with a loud noise, and* CALLICLES *is heard
below singing:—*

The lyre's voice is lovely everywhere;
In the court of Gods, in the city of men,
And in the lonely rock-strewn mountain-glen,
40 In the still mountain air.
Only to Typho[1] it sounds hatefully;
To Typho only, the rebel o'erthrown,
Through whose heart Etna drives her roots of stone
To imbed them in the sea.

45 Wherefore dost thou groan so loud?
Wherefore do thy nostrils flash,
Through the dark night, suddenly,
Typho, such red jets of flame?
Is thy tortured heart still proud?
50 Is thy fire-scathed arm still rash?
Still alert thy stone-crushed frame?
Doth thy fierce soul still deplore
Thine ancient rout by the Cilician hills,
And that cursed treachery on the Mount of Gore?[2]
55 Do thy bloodshot eyes still weep
The fight which crowned thine ills,
Thy last mischance on this Sicilian deep?

Hast thou sworn, in thy sad lair,
Where erst the strong sea-currents sucked thee
    down,
60 Never to cease to writhe, and try to rest,
Letting the sea-stream wander through thy hair?
That thy groans, like thunder pressed,
Begin to roll, and almost drown
The sweet notes whose lulling spell
65 Gods and the race of mortals love so well,
When through thy caves thou hearest music swell?

But an awful pleasure bland
Spreading o'er the Thunderer's face,
When the sound climbs near his seat,
70 The Olympian council sees;
As he lets his lax right hand,
Which the lightnings doth embrace,
Sink upon his mighty knees.
And the eagle, at the beck
75 Of the appeasing, gracious harmony,
Droops all his sheeny, brown, deep-feathered neck,
Nestling nearer to Jove's feet;
While o'er his sovran eye
The curtains of the blue films slowly meet.

80 And the white Olympus-peaks
Rosily brighten, and the soothed Gods smile
At one another from their golden chairs,
And no one round the charméd circle speaks.
Only the loved Hebe bears
85 The cup about, whose draughts beguile
Pain and care, with a dark store
Of fresh-pulled violets wreathed and nodding o'er;
And her flushed feet glow on the marble floor.

EMPEDOCLES

He fables, yet speaks truth!
90 The brave, impetuous heart yields everywhere
To the subtle, contriving head;
Great qualities are trodden down,
And littleness united

---

[1] Typho, one of the giants who warred on the Olympian gods, was pinned by Jove under Mt. Etna, from where he spews lava and fire.

[2] Mt. Haemus, so called, from Typho's blood spilt on it in his last battle with Zeus.

Is become invincible.
95 These rumblings are not Typho's groans, I know!
These angry smoke-bursts
Are not the passionate breath
Of the mountain-crushed, tortured, intractable
    Titan king—
But over all the world
100 What suffering is there not seen
Of plainness oppressed by cunning,
As the well-counselled Zeus oppressed
That self-helping son of earth!
What anguish of greatness,
105 Railed and hunted from the world,
Because its simplicity rebukes
This envious, miserable age!

I am weary of it.
—Lie there, ye ensigns
110 Of my unloved preëminence
In an age like this!
Among a people of children,
Who thronged me in their cities,
Who worshipped me in their houses,
115 And asked, not wisdom,
But drugs to charm with,
But spells to mutter—
All the fool's-armoury of magic! Lie there,
My golden circlet,
120 My purple robe![1]

CALLICLES (*from below*)
As the sky-brightening south-wind clears the day,
And makes the massed clouds roll,
The music of the lyre blows away
The clouds which wrap the soul.
125 Oh! that Fate had let me see
That triumph of the sweet persuasive lyre,

That famous, final victory,
When jealous Pan with Marsyas did conspire;[2]

When, from far Parnassus' side,
130 Young Apollo, all the pride
Of the Phrygian flutes to tame,
To the Phrygian highlands came;
Where the long green reed-beds sway
In the rippled waters grey
135 Of that solitary lake
Where Mæander's springs are born;
Whence the ridged pine-wooded roots
Of Messogis westward break,
Mounting westward, high and higher.
140 There was held the famous strife;
There the Phyrgian brought his flutes,
And Apollo brought his lyre;
And, when now the westering sun
Touched the hills, the strife was done,
145 And the attentive Muses said:
"Marsyas, thou art vanquishéd!"
Then Apollo's minister
Hanged upon a branching fir
Marsyas, that unhappy Faun,
150 And began to whet his knife.
But the Mænads,[3] who were there,
Left their friend, and with robes flowing
In the wind, and loose dark hair
O'er their polished bosoms blowing,
155 Each her ribboned tambourine
Flinging on the mountain-sod,
With a lovely frightened mien
Came about the youthful God.
But he turned his beauteous face
160 Haughtily another way,
From the grassy sun-warmed place
Where in proud repose he lay,

[1] symbols of civic power.

[2] Marsyas, a satyr, foolishly challenged Apollo to a musical contest. The winner could do as he wished with the vanquished. Apollo won and had Marsyas flayed alive.

[3] female followers of Bacchus.

With one arm over his head,
Watching how the whetting sped.

165   But aloof, on the lake-strand,
Did the young Olympus stand,
Weeping at his master's end;
For the Faun had been his friend.
For he taught him how to sing,
170 And he taught him flute-playing.
Many a morning had they gone
To the glimmering mountain-lakes,
And had torn up by the roots
The tall crested water-reeds
175 With long plumes and soft brown seeds,
And had carved them into flutes,
Sitting on a tabled stone
Where the shoreward ripple breaks.
And he taught him how to please
180 The red-snooded Phrygian girls,
Whom the summer evening sees
Flashing in the dance's whirls
Underneath the starlit trees
In the mountain-villages.
185 Therefore now Olympus stands,
At his master's piteous cries
Pressing fast with both his hands
His white garment to his eyes,
Not to see Apollo's scorn;
190 Ah, poor Faun, poor Faun! ah, poor Faun!

EMPEDOCLES

And lie thou there,
My laurel bough!¹
Scornful Apollo's ensign, lie thou there!
Though thou hast been my shade in the world's
    heat—
195 Though I have loved thee, lived in honouring
    thee—
Yet lie thou there,
My laurel bough!

I am weary of thee.
I am weary of the solitude
200 Where he who bears thee must abide—
Of the rocks of Parnassus,
Of the gorge of Delphi,
Of the moonlit peaks, and the caves.
Thou guardest them, Apollo!
205 Over the grave of the slain Pytho,²
Though young, intolerably severe!
Thou keepest aloof the profane,
But the solitude oppresses thy votary!
The jars of men reach him not in thy valley—
210 But can life reach him?
Thou fencest him from the multitude—
Who will fence him from himself?
He hears nothing but the cry of the torrents,
And the beating of his own heart.
215 The air is thin, the veins swell,
The temples tighten and throb there—
Air! air!

Take thy bough, set me free from my solitude;
I have been enough alone!

220 Where shall thy votary fly them? back to men?
But they will gladly welcome him once more,
And help him to unbend his too tense thought,
And rid him of the presence of himself,
And keep their friendly chatter at his ear,
225 And haunt him, till the absence from himself,
That other torment, grow unbearable;
And he will fly to solitude again,
And he will find its air too keen for him,
And so change back; and many thousand times
230 Be miserably bandied to and fro
Like a sea-wave, betwixt the world and thee,
Thou young, implacable God! and only death
Can cut his oscillations short, and so
Bring him to poise. There is no other way.

¹ sign of his poetic life.

² serpent which guarded Delphi, slain by Apollo.

235 And yet what days were those, Parmenides!
When we were young, when we could number
    friends
In all the Italian cities like ourselves,
When with elated hearts we joined your train,
Ye Sun-born Virgins! on the road of truth.
240 Then we could still enjoy, then neither thought
Nor outward things were closed and dead to us;
But we received the shock of mighty thoughts
On simple minds with a pure natural joy;
And if the sacred load oppressed our brain,
245 We had the power to feel the pressure eased,
The brow unbound, the thoughts flow free again,
In the delightful commerce of the world.
We had not lost our balance then, nor grown
Thought's slaves, and dead to every natural joy.
250 The smallest thing could give us pleasure then—
The sports of the country-people,
A flute-note from the woods,
Sunset over the sea;
Seed-time and harvest,
255 The reapers in the corn,
The vinedresser in his vineyard,
The village-girl at her wheel.

Fullness of life and power of feeling, ye
Are for the happy, for the souls at ease,
260 Who dwell on a firm basis of content!
But he, who has outlived his prosperous days—
But he, whose youth fell on a different world
From that on which his exiled age is thrown—
Whose mind was fed on other food, was trained
265 By other rules than are in vogue to-day—
Whose habit of thought is fixed, who will not
    change,
But, in a world he loves not, must subsist
In ceaseless opposition, be the guard
Of his own breast, fettered to what he guards,
270 That the world win no mastery over him—
Who has no friend, no fellow left, not one;
Who has no minute's breathing space allowed

To nurse his dwindling faculty of joy—
Joy and the outward world must die to him,
275 As they are dead to me.

A long pause, during which EMPEDOCLES *remains
motionless, plunged in thought. The night deepens. He
moves forward and gazes round him, and proceeds:—*

And you, ye stars,
Who slowly begin to marshal,
As of old, the fields of heaven,
Your distant, melancholy lines!
280 Have you, too, survived yourselves?
Are you, too, what I fear to become?
You, too, once lived;
You, too, moved joyfully
Among august companions,
285 In an older world, peopled by Gods,
In a mightier order,
The radiant, rejoicing, intelligent Sons of Heaven.
But now, ye kindle
Your lonely, cold-shining lights,
290 Unwilling lingerers
In the heavenly wilderness,
For a younger, ignoble world;
And renew, by necessity,
Night after night your courses,
295 In echoing, unneared silence,
Above a race you know not—
Uncaring and undelighted,
Without friend and without home;
Weary like us, though not
300 Weary with our weariness.

No, no, ye stars! there is no death with you,
No languor, no decay! languor and death,
They are with me, not you! ye are alive—
Ye, and the pure dark ether where ye ride
305 Brilliant above me! And thou, fiery world.
That sapp'st the vitals of this terrible mount
Upon whose charred and quaking crust I stand—

Thou, too, brimmest with life! —the sea of cloud,
That heaves its white and billowy vapours up
310 To moat this isle of ashes from the world,
Lives; and that other fainter sea, far down,
O'er whose lit floor a road of moonbeams leads
To Etna's Liparëan sister-fires
And the long dusky line of Italy—
315 That mild and luminous floor of waters lives,
With held-in joy swelling its heart; I only,
Whose spring of hope is dried, whose spirit has
      failed,
I, who have not, like these, in solitude
Maintained courage and force, and in myself
320 Nursed an immortal vigour—I alone
Am dead to life and joy, therefore I read
In all things my own deadness.
                    A long silence. He continues:—

Oh, that I could glow like this mountain!
Oh, that my heart bounded with the swell of the
      sea!
325 Oh, that my soul were full of light as the stars!
Oh, that it brooded over the world like the air!

But no, this heart will glow no more; thou art
A living man no more, Empedocles!
Nothing but a devouring flame of thought—
330 But a naked, eternally restless mind!
                    After a pause:—

To the elements it came from
Everything will return—
Our bodies to earth,
Our blood to water,
335 Heat to fire,
Breath to air,
They were well born, they will be well entombed—
But mind?...

And we might gladly share the fruitful stir
340 Down in our mother earth's miraculous womb;

Well would it be
With what rolled of us in the stormy main;
We might have joy, blent with the all-bathing air,
Or with the nimble, radiant life of fire.

345 But mind, but thought—
If these have been the master part of us—
Where will *they* find their parent element?
What will receive *them*, who will call *them* home?
But we shall still be in them, and they in us,
350 And we shall be the strangers of the world,
And they will be our lords, as they are now;
And keep us prisoners of our consciousness,
And never let us clasp and feel the All
But through their forms, and modes, and stifling
      veils.
355 And we shall be unsatisfied as now;
And we shall feel the agony of thirst,
The ineffable longing for the life of life
Baffled for ever; and still thought and mind
Will hurry us with them on their homeless march,
360 Over the unallied unopening earth,
Over the unrecognising sea; while air
Will blow us fiercely back to sea and earth,
And fire repel us from its living waves.
And then we shall unwillingly return
365 Back to this meadow of calamity,
This uncongenial place, this human life;
And in our individual human state
Go through the sad probation all again,
To see if we will poise our life at last,
370 To see if we will now at last be true
To our own only true, deep-buried selves,
Being one with which we are one with the whole
      world;
Or whether we will once more fall away
Into some bondage of the flesh or mind,
375 Some slough of sense, or some fantastic maze
Forged by the imperious lonely thinking-power.
And each succeeding age in which we are born
Will have more peril for us than the last;

Will goad our senses with a sharper spur,
380 Will fret our minds to an intenser play,
Will make ourselves harder to be discerned.
And we shall struggle awhile, gasp and rebel—
And we shall fly for refuge to past times,
Their soul of unworn youth, their breath of
    greatness;
385 And the reality will pluck us back,
Knead us in its hot hand, and change our nature.
And we shall feel our powers of effort flag,
And rally them for one last fight—and fail;
And we shall sink in the impossible strife,
390 And be astray for ever.

        Slave of sense
I have in no wise been; but slave of thought?...
And who can say: I have been always free,
Lived ever in the light of my own soul?—
I cannot; I have lived in wrath and gloom,
395 Fierce, disputatious, ever at war with man,
Far from my own soul, far from warmth and light.
But I have not grown easy in these bonds—
But I have not denied what bonds these were.
Yea, I take myself to witness,
400 That I have loved no darkness,
Sophisticated no truth,
Nursed no delusion,
Allowed no fear!

    And therefore, O ye elements! I know—
405 Ye know it too—it hath been granted me
Not to die wholly, not to be all enslaved.
I feel it in this hour. The numbing cloud
Mounts off my soul; I feel it, I breathe free.

Is it but for a moment?
410 —Ah, boil up, ye vapours!
Leap and roar, thou sea of fire!
My soul glows to meet you.
Ere it flag, ere the mists
Of despondency and gloom

415 Rush over it again,
Receive me, save me!

                [He plunges into the crater.

      CALLICLES (*from below*)
Through the black, rushing smoke-bursts,
Thick breaks the red flame;
All Etna heaves fiercely
420 Her forest-clothed frame.

Not here, O Apollo!
Are haunts meet for thee.
But, where Helicon breaks down
In cliff to the sea,

425 Where the moon-silvered inlets
Send far their light voice
Up the still vale of Thisbe,[1]
O speed, and rejoice!

On the sward at the cliff-top
430 Lie strewn the white flocks,
On the cliff-sides the pigeons
Roost deep in the rocks.

In the moonlight the shepherds,
Soft lulled by the rills,
435 Lie wrapped in their blankets
Asleep on the hills.

—What forms are these coming
So white through the gloom?
What garments out-glistening
440 The gold-flowered broom?

What sweet-breathing presence
Out-perfumes the thyme?
What voice enrapture
The night's balmy prime?

---

[1] a village in the valley below Mt. Helicon, the mountain of the muses ("the Nine" of l. 446).

445 'Tis Apollo comes leading
His choir, the Nine.
—The leader is fairest,
But all are divine.

They are lost in the hollows!
450 They stream up again!
What seeks on this mountain
The glorified train?

They bathe on this mountain,
In the spring by their road;
455 Then on to Olympus,
Their endless abode.

—What praise do they mention?
Of what is it told?
What will be for ever;
460 That was from of old.

First hymn they the Father
Of all things; and then,
The rest of immortals,
The action of men.

465 The day in his hotness,
The strife with the palm;
The night in her silence,
The stars in their calm.
—1852 (1849–52)

Memorial Verses

April, 1850

Goethe in Weimer sleeps, and Greece,
Long since, saw Byron's struggle cease.[1]
But one such death remained to come;
The last poetic voice is dumb—
5 We stand to-day by Wordsworth's tomb.

---

[1] Goethe died in 1832, Byron in Greece in 1824.

When Byron's eyes were shut in death,
We bowed our head and held our breath.
He taught us little; but our soul
Had *felt* him like the thunder's roll.
10 With shivering heart the strife we saw
Of passion with eternal law;
And yet with reverential awe
We watched the fount of fiery life
Which served for that Titanic strife.

15 When Goethe's death was told, we said:
Sunk, then, is Europe's sagest head.
Physician of the iron age,
Goethe has done his pilgrimage.
He took the suffering human race,
20 He read each wound, each weakness clear;
And struck his finger on the place,
And said: *Thou ailest here, and here!*
He looked on Europe's dying hour[2]
Of fitful dream and feverish power;
25 His eye plunged down the weltering strife,
The turmoil of expiring life—
He said: *The end is everywhere,*
Art still has truth, take refuge there!
And he was happy, if to know
30 Causes of things, and far below
His feet to see the lurid flow
Of terror, and insane distress,
And headlong fate, be happiness.

And Wordsworth!—Ah, pale ghosts, rejoice!
35 For never has such soothing voice
Been to your shadowy world conveyed,
Since erst, at morn, some wandering shade
Heard the clear song of Orpheus come
Through Hades, and the mournful gloom.
40 Wordsworth has gone from us—and ye,
Ah, may ye feel his voice as we!
He too upon a wintry clime

---

[2] the industrial and political revolutions of the eighteenth and nineteenth centuries, undermining basic Christian values.

Had fallen—on this iron time
Of doubts, disputes, distractions, fears.
45   He found us when the age had bound
Our souls in its benumbing round;
He spoke, and loosed our heart in tears.
He laid us as we lay at birth
On the cool flowery lap of earth,
50   Smiles broke from us and we had ease;
The hills were round us, and the breeze
Went o'er the sun-lit fields again;
Our foreheads felt the wind and rain.
Our youth returned; for there was shed
55   On spirits that had long been dead,
Spirits dried up and closely furled,
The freshness of the early world.

Ah! since dark days still bring to light
Man's prudence and man's fiery might,
60   Time may restore us in his course
Goethe's sage mind and Byron's force;
But where will Europe's latter hour
Again find Wordsworth's healing power?
Others will teach us how to dare,
65   And against fear our breast to steel;
Others will strengthen us to bear—
But who, ah! who, will make us feel?
The cloud of mortal destiny,
Others will front it fearlessly—
70   But who, like him, will put it by?

Keep fresh the grass upon his grave,
O Rotha,[1] with thy living wave!
Sing him thy best! For few or none
Hears thy voice right, now he is gone.
—1852 (1850)

Dover Beach

The sea is calm to-night.
The tide is full, the moon lies fair
Upon the straits; on the French coast the light
Gleams and is gone; the cliffs of England stand,
5   Glimmering and vast, out in the tranquil bay.
Come to the window, sweet is the night-air!
Only, from the long line of spray
Where the sea meets the moon-blanched land,
Listen! you hear the grating roar
10   Of pebbles which the waves draw back, and fling,
At their return, up the high strand,
Begin, and cease, and then again begin,
With tremulous cadence slow, and bring
The eternal note of sadness in.

15   Sophocles long ago
Heard it on the Ægæan, and it brought
Into his mind the turbid ebb and flow
Of human misery; we
Find also in the sound a thought,
20   Hearing it by this distant northern sea.

The Sea of Faith
Was once, too, at the full, and round earth's shore
Lay like the folds of a bright girdle furled.
But now I only hear
25   Its melancholy, long, withdrawing roar,
Retreating, to the breath
Of the night-wind, down the vast edges drear
And naked shingles[2] of the world.

Ah, love, let us be true
30   To one another! for the world, which seems
To lie before us like a land of dreams,
So various, so beautiful, so new,
Hath really neither joy, nor love, nor light,
Nor certitude, nor peace, nor help for pain;

---

[1] stream near Grasmere, Wordsworth's burial site.

[2] pebbled beaches.

35 And we are here as on a darkling plain
Swept with confused alarms of struggle and flight,
Where ignorant armies clash by night.
—1867 (1851)

The Buried Life

Light flows our war of mocking words, and yet,
  Behold, with tears mine eyes are wet!
I feel a nameless sadness o'er me roll.
Yes, yes, we know that we can jest,
5 We know, we know that we can smile!
But there's a something in this breast,
To which thy light words bring no rest,
And thy gay smiles no anodyne.[1]
Give me thy hand, and hush awhile,
10 And turn those limpid eyes on mine,
And let me read there, love! thy inmost soul.

Alas! is even love too weak
To unlock the heart, and let it speak?
Are even lovers powerless to reveal
15 To one another what indeed they feel?
I knew the mass of men concealed
Their thoughts, for fear that if revealed
They would by other men be met
With blank indifference, or with blame reproved;
20 I knew they lived and moved
Tricked in disguises, alien to the rest
Of men, and alien to themselves—and yet
The same heart beats in every human breast!

But we, my love!—doth a like spell benumb
25 Our hearts, our voices? must we too be dumb?

Ah! well for us, if even we,
Even for a moment, can get free
Our heart, and have our lips unchained;
For that which seals them hath been deep-ordained!

30 Fate, which foresaw
How frivolous a baby man would be—
By what distractions he would be possessed,
How he would pour himself in every strife,
And well-nigh change his own identity—
35 That it might keep from his capricious play
His genuine self, and force him to obey

Even in his own despite his being's law,
Bade through the deep recesses of our breast
The unregarded river of our life
40 Pursue with indiscernible flow its way;
And that we should not see
The buried stream, and seem to be
Eddying at large in blind uncertainty,
Though driving on with it eternally.

45 But often, in the world's most crowded streets,
But often, in the din of strife,
There rises an unspeakable desire
After the knowledge of our buried life;
A thirst to spend our fire and restless force
50 In tracking out our true, original course;

A longing to inquire
Into the mystery of this heart which beats
So wild, so deep in us—to know
Whence our lives come and where they go.
55 And many a man in his own breast then delves,
But deep enough, alas! none ever mines.
And we have been on many thousand lines,[2]
And we have shown, on each, spirit and power;
But hardly have we, for one little hour,
60 Been on our own line, have we been ourselves—
Hardly had skill to utter one of all
The nameless feelings that course through our
    breast,

---

[1] that which relieves pain.

[2] Arnold's note on ll. 57–60 in the Yale MS: "We have been on a thousand lines and on each have shown spirit talent even geniality but hardly for an hour between birth and death have we been on our own one natural line, have we been ourselves, have we breathed freely."

But they course on for ever unexpressed.
And long we try in vain to speak and act
65 Our hidden self, and what we say and do
Is eloquent, is well—but 'tis not true!
And then we will no more be racked
With inward striving, and demand
Of all the thousand nothings of the hour
70 Their stupefying power;
Ah yes, and they benumb us at our call!
Yet still, from time to time, vague and forlorn,
From the soul's subterranean depth upborne
As from an infinitely distant land,
75 Come airs, and floating echoes, and convey
A melancholy into all our day.
Only—but this is rare—
When a belovéd hand is laid in ours,
When, jaded with the rush and glare
80 Of the interminable hours,
Our eyes can in another's eyes read clear,
When our world-deafened ear
Is by the tones of a loved voice caressed—
A bolt is shot back somewhere in our breast,
85 And a lost pulse of feeling stirs again.
The eye sinks inward, and the heart lies plain,
And what we mean, we say, and what we would,
    we know.
A man becomes aware of his life's flow,
And hears its winding murmur; and he sees
90 The meadows where it glides, the sun, the breeze.

And there arrives a lull in the hot race
Wherein he doth for ever chase
That flying and elusive shadow, rest.
An air of coolness plays upon his face,
95 And an unwonted calm pervades his breast.
And then he thinks he knows
The hills where his life rose,
And the sea where it goes.
—1852 (1849–52)

Stanzas from the Grande Chartreuse [1]

Through Alpine meadows soft-suffused
With rain, where thick the crocus blows,
Past the dark forges long disused,
The mule-track from Saint Laurent[2] goes.
5 The bridge is crossed, and slow we ride,
Through forest, up the mountain-side.

The autumnal evening darkens round,
The wind is up, and drives the rain;
While, hark! far down, with strangled sound
10 Doth the Dead Guier's stream[3] complain,
Where that wet smoke, among the woods,
Over his boiling cauldron broods.

Swift rush the spectral vapours white
Past limestone scars with ragged pines,
15 Showing—then blotting from our sight!
Halt—through the cloud-drift something shines!
High in the valley, wet and drear,
The huts of Courrerie[4] appear.

Strike leftward! cries our guide; and higher
20 Mounts up the stony forest-way.
At last the encircling trees retire;
Look! through the showery twilight grey
What pointed roofs are these advance?
A palace of the Kings of France?

25 Approach, for what we seek is here!
Alight, and sparely sup, and wait
For rest in this outbuilding near;
Then cross the sward and reach that gate.

---

[1] Carthusian monastery in the French Alps which Arnold visited in 1851 on his way from Grenoble to Chambéry.

[2] a village near the monastery.

[3] a river near the monastery.

[4] another nearby village.

Knock; pass the wicket! Thou art come
30   To the Carthusians' world-famed home.

The silent courts, where night and day
Into their stone-carved basins cold
The splashing icy fountains play—
The humid corridors behold!
35   Where, ghostlike in the deepening night,
Cowled forms brush by in gleaming white.

The chapel, where no organ's peal
Invests the stern and naked prayer—
With penitential cries they kneel
40   And wrestle; rising then, with bare
And white uplifted faces stand,
Passing the Host from hand to hand;[1]

Each takes, and then his visage wan
Is buried in his cowl once more.
45   The cells! —the suffering Son of Man
Upon the wall—the knee-worn floor—
And where they sleep, that wooden bed,
Which shall their coffin be, when dead!

The library, where tract and tome
50   Not to feed priestly pride are there,
To hymn the conquering march of Rome,
Nor yet to amuse, as ours are!
They paint of souls the inner strife,
Their drops of blood, their death in life.

55   The garden, overgrown—yet mild,
See, fragrant herbs are flowering there!
Strong children of the Alpine wild
Whose culture is the brethren's care;
Of human tasks their only one,
60   And cheerful works beneath the sun.

Those halls, too, destined to contain
Each its own pilgrim-host of old,
From England, Germany, or Spain—
All are before me! I behold
65   The House, the Brotherhood austere!
—And what am I, that I am here?

For rigorous teachers seized my youth,
And purged its faith, and trimmed its fire,
Showed me the high, white star of Truth,
70   There bade me gaze, and there aspire.
Even now their whispers pierce the gloom
What dost thou in this living tomb?

Forgive me, masters of the mind!
At whose behest I long ago
75   So much unlearnt, so much resigned—
I come not here to be your foe!
I seek these anchorites, not in ruth,
To curse and to deny your truth;

Not as their friend, or child, I speak!
80   But as, on some far northern strand,
Thinking of his own Gods, a Greek
In pity and mournful awe might stand
Before some fallen Runic stone—[2]
For both were faiths, and both are gone.

85   Wandering between two worlds, one dead,
The other powerless to be born,
With nowhere yet to rest my head,
Like these, on earth I wait forlorn.
Their faith, my tears, the world deride—
90   I come to shed them at their side.

Oh, hide me in your gloom profound,
Ye solemn seats of holy pain!
Take me, cowled forms, and fence me round,
Till I possess my soul again;

[1] The host (the consecrated bread) is not passed from hand to hand during mass. Arnold is probably referring to the Pax (a small tablet), which was kissed by the priest and then passed through the congregation.

[2] an inscribed religious tablet.

95 Till free my thoughts before me roll,
Not chafed by hourly false control!

For the world cries your faith is now
But a dead time's exploded dream;
My melancholy, sciolists say,
100 Is a past mode, an outworn theme—
As if the world had ever had
A faith, or sciolists[1] been sad!

Ah, if it *be* passed, take away,
At least, the restlessness, the pain;
105 Be man henceforth no more a prey
To these out-dated stings again!
The nobleness of grief is gone—
Ah, leave us not the fret alone!

But—if you cannot give us ease—
110 Last of the race of them who grieve,
Here leave us to die out with these
Last of the people who believe!
Silent, while years engrave the brow;
Silent—the best are silent now.

115 Achilles[2] ponders in his tent,
The kings of modern thought are dumb;
Silent they are, though not content,
And wait to see the future come.
They have the grief men had of yore,
120 But they contend and cry no more.

Our fathers watered with their tears
This sea of time whereon we sail,
Their voices were in all men's ears
Who passed within their puissant hail.
125 Still the same ocean round us raves,
But we stand mute, and watch the waves.

For what availed it, all the noise
And outcry of the former men?
Say, have their sons achieved more joys,
130 Say, is life lighter now than then?
The sufferers died, they left their pain—
The pangs which tortured them remain.

What helps it now, that Byron bore,
With haughty scorn which mocked the smart,
135 Through Europe to the Ætolian shore[3]
The pageant of his bleeding heart?
That thousands counted every groan,
And Europe made his woe her own?

What boots it, Shelley! that the breeze
140 Carried thy lovely wail away,
Musical through Italian trees
Which fringe thy soft blue Spezzian bay?[4]
Inheritors of thy distress
Have restless hearts one throb the less?

145 Or are we easier, to have read,
O Obermann![5] the sad, stern page,
Which tells us how thou hidd'st thy head
From the fierce tempest of thine age
In the lone brakes of Fontainebleau
150 Or chalets near the Alpine snow?

Ye slumber in your silent grave!
The world, which for an idle day
Grace to your mood of sadness gave,
Long since hath flung her weeds away.
155 The eternal trifler breaks your spell;
But we—we learnt your lore too well!

Years hence, perhaps, may dawn an age,
More fortunate, alas! than we,

[1] a pretender to knowledge.

[2] the hero whose potential is thwarted by indecision.

[3] the Greek province where Byron died.

[4] on the Gulf of Spezia, where Shelley spent his final days.

[5] an imaginary recluse created by Étienne Pivert de Senancour (1770–1846).

Which without hardness will be sage,
160 And gay without frivolity.
Sons of the world, oh, speed those years;
But, while we wait, allow our tears!

Allow them! We admire with awe
The exulting thunder of your race;
165 You give the universe your law,
You triumph over time and space!
Your pride of life, your tireless powers,
We laud them, but they are not ours.

We are like children reared in shade
170 Beneath some old-world abbey wall,
Forgotten in a forest-glade,
And secret from the eyes of all.
Deep, deep the greenwood round them waves,
Their abbey, and its close of graves!

175 But, where the road runs near the stream,
Oft through the trees they catch a glance
Of passing troops in the sun's beam—
Pennon, and plume, and flashing lance!
Forth to the world those soldiers fare,
180 To life, to cities, and to war!

And through the wood, another way,
Faint bugle-notes from far are borne,
Where hunters gather, staghounds bay,
Round some fair forest-lodge at morn.
185 Gay dames are there, in sylvan green;
Laughter and cries—those notes between!

The banners flashing through the trees
Make their blood dance and chain their eyes;
That bugle-music on the breeze
190 Arrests them with a charmed surprise.
Banner by turns and bugle woo:
Ye shy recluses, follow too!

O children, what do ye reply?—
"Action and pleasure, will ye roam

195 Through these secluded dells to cry
And call us?—but too late ye come!
Too late for us your call ye blow,
Whose bent was taken long ago.

"Long since we pace this shadowed nave;
200 We watch those yellow tapers shine,
Emblems of hope over the grave,
In the high altar's depth divine;
The organ carries to our ear
Its accents of another sphere.

205 "Fenced early in this cloistral round
Of reverie, of shade, of prayer,
How should we grow in other ground?
How can we flower in foreign air?
—Pass, banners, pass, and bugles, cease;
210 And leave our desert to its peace!"
—1855 (1851–55)

The Scholar-Gipsy [1]

Go, for they call you, shepherd, from the hill;
Go, shepherd, and untie the wattled cotes! [2]
No longer leave thy wistful flock unfed,

[1] The tale of the Scholar-Gipsy is from Joseph Glanvill's *The Vanity of Dogmatizing* (1661). Arnold's note to the poem is a collection of sentences from Glanvill: "There was very lately a lad in the University at Oxford, who was by his poverty forced to leave his studies there; and at last to join himself to a company of vagabond gipsies. Among these extravagant people, by the insinuating subtilty of his carriage, he quickly got so much of their love and esteem as that they discovered to him their mystery. After he had been a pretty while well exercised in the trade, there chanced to ride by a couple of scholars, who had formerly been of his acquaintance. They quickly spied out their old friend among the gipsies; and he gave them an account of the necessity which drove him to that kind of life, and told them that the people he went with were not such imposters as they were taken for, but that they had a traditional kind of learning among them, and could do wonders by the power of imagination, their fancy binding that of others; that himself had learned much of their art, and when he had compassed the whole secret, he intended, he said, to leave their company, and give the world an account of what he had learned."

[2] sheepfolds made of interwoven twigs.

379

Nor let thy bawling fellows rack their throats,
    Nor the cropped herbage shoot another head.
      But when the fields are still,
    And the tired men and dogs all gone to rest,
    And only the white sheep are sometimes
        seen
      Cross and recross the strips of moon-
        blanched green,
Come, shepherd, and again begin the quest![1]

Here, where the reaper was at work of late—
    In this high field's dark corner, where he leaves
      His coat, his basket, and his earthen cruse,
    And in the sun all morning binds the sheaves,
      Then here, at noon, comes back his stores to
        use—
      Here will I sit and wait,
    While to my ear from uplands far away
      The bleating of the folded flocks is borne,
      With distant cries of reapers in the corn—
All the live murmur of a summer's day.

Screened is this nook o'er the high, half-reaped
    field,
    And here till sun-down, shepherd! will I be.
      Through the thick corn the scarlet poppies
        peep,
    And round green roots and yellowing stalks I
        see
      Pale pink convolvulus in tendrils creep;
      And air-swept lindens yield
    Their scent, and rustle down their perfumed
        showers
      Of bloom on the bent grass where I am laid,
    And bower me from the August sun with
        shade;
And the eye travels down to Oxford's towers.

And near me on the grass lies Glanvil's book—
    Come, let me read the oft-read tale again!

The story of the Oxford scholar poor,
    Of pregnant parts and quick inventive brain,
      Who, tired of knocking at preferment's door,
        One summer-morn forsook
    His friends, and went to learn the gipsy-lore,
      And roamed the world with that wild
        brotherhood,
    And came, as most men deemed, to little
        good,
But came to Oxford and his friends no more.

But once, years after, in the country-lanes,
    Two scholars, whom at college erst he knew,
      Met him, and of his way of life enquired;
    Whereat he answered, that the gipsy-crew,
      His mates, had arts to rule as they desired
        The workings of men's brains,
    And they can bind them to what thoughts they
        will.[2]
      "And I," he said, "the secret of their art,
      When fully learned, will to the world impart;
    But it needs heaven-sent moments for this
        skill."

This said, he left them, and returned no more.
    But rumours hung about the country-side,
      That the lost Scholar long was seen to stray,
    Seen by rare glimpses, pensive and tongue-tied,
      In hat of antique shape, and cloak of grey,
        The same the gipsies wore.
    Shepherds had met him on the Hurst[3] in spring;
    At some lone alehouse in the Berkshire
        moors,
      On the warm ingle-bench,[4] the smock-
        frocked boors[5]
Had found him seated at their entering,

---

[1] for the Scholar-Gipsy.

[2] in Glanvill, by hypnotism.

[3] hill outside Oxford.

[4] bench by a fireplace.

[5] peasants.

But, 'mid their drink and clatter, he would fly.
And I myself seem half to know thy looks,
And put the shepherds, wanderer! on thy
trace;
And boys who in lone wheatfields scare the
rooks
65 I ask if thou hast passed their quiet place;
Or in my boat I lie
Moored to the cool bank in the summer-heats,
'Mid wide grass meadows which the
sunshine fills,
And watch the warm, green-muffled
Cumner hills,
70 And wonder if thou haunt'st their shy retreats.

For most, I know, thou lov'st retiréd ground!
Thee at the ferry Oxford riders blithe,
Returning home on summer-nights, have
met
Crossing the stripling Thames at Bab-lock-
hithe,
75 Trailing in the cool stream thy fingers wet,
As the punt's rope chops round;
And leaning backward in a pensive dream,
And fostering in thy lap a heap of flowers
Plucked in shy fields and distant Wychwood
bowers,
80 And thine eyes resting on the moonlit stream.

And then they land, and thou art seen no more!
Maidens, who from the distant hamlets come
To dance around the Fyfield elm in May,
Oft through the darkening fields have seen thee
roam,
85 Or cross a stile into the public way.
Oft thou hast given them store
Of flowers—the frail-leafed, white anemone,
Dark bluebells drenched with dews of
summer eves,
And purple orchises with spotted leaves—
90 But none hath words she can report of thee.

And, above Godstow Bridge, when hay-time's here
In June, and many a scythe in sunshine flames,
Men who through those wide fields of
breezy grass
Where black-winged swallows haunt the
glittering Thames,
95 To bathe in the abandoned lasher pass,[1]
Have often passed thee near
Sitting upon the river bank o'ergrown;
Marked thine outlandish garb, thy figure
spare,
Thy dark vague eyes, and soft abstracted
air—
100 But, when they came from bathing, thou wast
gone!

At some lone homestead in the Cumner hills,
Where at her open door the housewife darns,
Thou hast been seen, or hanging on a gate
To watch the threshers in the mossy barns.
105 Children, who early range these slopes and
late
For cresses from the rills,
Have known thee eying, all an April-day,
The springing pastures and the feeding kine;
And marked thee, when the stars come out
and shine,
110 Through the long dewy grass move slow away.

In autumn, on the skirts of Bagley Wood—
Where most the gipsies by the turf-edged way
Pitch their smoked tents, and every bush
you see
With scarlet patches tagged and shreds of grey,
115 Above the forest-ground called Thessaly—
The blackbird, picking food,
Sees thee, nor stops his meal, nor fears at all;
So often has he known thee past him stray,

---
[1] pool below a dam.

Rapt, twirling in thy hand a withered spray,
120 And waiting for the spark from heaven to fall.

And once, in winter, on the causeway chill
Where home through flooded fields foot-
travellers go,
Have I not passed thee on the wooden
bridge,
Wrapped in thy cloak and battling with the
snow,
125 Thy face tow'rd Hinksey and its wintry
ridge?
And thou hast climbed the hill,
And gained the white brow of the Cumner
range;
Turned once to watch, while thick the
snowflakes fall,
The line of festal light in Christ-Church
hall—
130 Then sought thy straw in some sequestered
grange.

But what—I dream! Two hundred years are flown
Since first thy story ran through Oxford halls,
And the grave Glanvil did the tale inscribe
That thou wert wandered from the studious
walls
135 To learn strange arts, and join a gipsy-tribe;
And thou from earth art gone
Long since, and in some quiet churchyard laid—
Some country-nook, where o'er thy
unknown grave
Tall grasses and white flowering nettles wave,
140 Under a dark, red-fruited yew-tree's shade.

—No, no, thou hast not felt the lapse of hours!
For what wears out the life of mortal men?
'Tis that from change to change their being
rolls;
'Tis that repeated shocks, again, again,
145 Exhaust the energy of strongest souls

And numb the elastic powers.
Till having used our nerves with bliss and teen,[1]
And tired upon a thousand schemes our wit,
To the just-pausing Genius we remit
150 Our worn-out life, and are—what we have
been.

Thou hast not lived, why should'st thou perish, so?
Thou hadst *one* aim, *one* business, *one* desire;
Else wert thou long since numbered with the
dead!
Else hadst thou spent, like other men, thy fire!
155 The generations of thy peers are fled,
And we ourselves shall go;
But thou possessest an immortal lot,
And we imagine thee exempt from age
And living as thou liv'st on Glanvil's page,
160 Because thou hadst—what we, alas! have not.

For early didst thou leave the world, with powers
Fresh, undiverted to the world without,
Firm to their mark, not spent on other
things;
Free from the sick fatigue, the languid doubt,
165 Which much to have tried, in much been
baffled, brings.
O life unlike to ours!
Who fluctuate idly without term or scope,
Of whom each strives, nor knows for what
he strives,
And each half-lives a hundred different lives;
170 Who wait like thee, but not, like thee, in hope.

Thou waitest for the spark from heaven! and we,
Light half-believers of our casual creeds,
Who never deeply felt, nor clearly willed,
Whose insight never has borne fruit in deeds,
175 Whose vague resolves never have been
fulfilled;
For whom each year we see

---
[1] grief or woe.

Breeds new beginnings, disappointments new;
 Who hesitate and falter life away,
  And lose to-morrow the ground won
   to-day—
180 Ah! do not we, wanderer! await it too?

Yes, we await it!—but it still delays,
 And then we suffer! and amongst us one,
  Who most has suffered, takes dejectedly
  His seat upon the intellectual throne;
185   And all his store of sad experience he
   Lays bare of wretched days;
 Tells us his misery's birth and growth and signs,
  And how the dying spark of hope was fed,
  And how the breast was soothed, and how
   the head,
190 And all his hourly varied anodynes.[1]

This for our wisest! and we others pine,
 And wish the long unhappy dream would end,
  And waive all claim to bliss, and try to bear;
 With close-lipped patience for our only friend,
195   Sad patience, too near neighbour to despair—
   But none has hope like thine!
 Thou through the fields and through the woods
   dost stray,
  Roaming the country-side, a truant boy,
  Nursing thy project in unclouded joy,
200 And every doubt long blown by time away.

O born in days when wits were fresh and clear,
 And life ran gaily as the sparkling Thames;
  Before this strange disease of modern life,
 With its sick hurry, its divided aims,
205   Its heads o'ertaxed, its palsied hearts, was
   rife—
   Fly hence, our contact fear!
 Still fly, plunge deeper in the bowering wood!
  Averse, as Dido did with gesture stern

From her false friend's approach in Hades
   turn,[2]
210 Wave us away, and keep thy solitude!

Still nursing the unconquerable hope,
 Still clutching the inviolable shade,
  With a free, onward impulse brushing
   through,
 By night, the silvered branches of the glade—
215   Far on the forest-skirts, where none pursue,
   On some mild pastoral slope
 Emerge, and resting on the moonlit pales
  Freshen thy flowers as in former years
  With dew, or listen with enchanted ears,
220 From the dark dingles,[3] to the nightingales!

But fly our paths, our feverish contact fly!
 For strong the infection of our mental strife,
  Which, though it gives no bliss, yet spoils
   for rest;
 And we should win thee from thy own fair life,
225   Like us distracted, and like us unblest.
   Soon, soon thy cheer would die,
 Thy hopes grow timorous, and unfixed thy
   powers,
  And thy clear aims be cross and shifting
   made;
  And then thy glad perennial youth would
   fade,
230 Fade, and grow old at last, and die like ours.

Then fly our greetings, fly our speech and smiles!
 —As some grave Tyrian[4] trader, from the sea,
  Descried at sunrise an emerging prow
 Lifting the cool-haired creepers stealthily,
235   The fringes of a southward-facing brow

---

[1] relieving pain.

[2] Dido killed herself when Aeneas deserted her, and she turned away
from him "with gesture stern" when he visited Hades.

[3] wooded dells.

[4] traders from Tyre, in Asia Minor, who fled from the aggressive Greeks.

Among the Ægean isles;
And saw the merry Grecian coaster come,
 Freighted with amber grapes, and Chian
  wine,
 Green, bursting figs, and tunnies[1] steeped in
  brine—
240 And knew the intruders on his ancient home,

The young light-hearted masters of the waves—
 And snatched his rudder, and shook out more
  sail;
 And day and night held on indignantly
O'er the blue Midland waters with the gale,
245 Betwixt the Syrtes[2] and soft Sicily,
  To where the Atlantic raves[3]
Outside the western straits; and unbent sails
 There, where down cloudy cliffs, through
  sheets of foam,
 Shy traffickers, the dark Iberians come;
250 And on the beach undid his corded bales.
 —1853 (1852–53)

Thyrsis [4]

A MONODY, to commemorate the author's friend, ARTHUR
HUGH CLOUGH, who died at Florence, 1861

How changed is here each spot man makes or
  fills!
In the two Hinkseys[5] nothing keeps the same;
 The village street its haunted mansion lacks,
 And from the sign is gone Sibylla's[6] name,

5 And from the roofs the twisted chimney-
  stacks—
 Are ye too changed, ye hills?
See, 'tis no foot of unfamiliar men
 To-night from Oxford up your pathway
  strays!
 Here came I often, often, in old days—
10 Thyrsis and I; we still had Thyrsis then.

Runs it not here, the track by Childsworth Farm,
 Past the high wood, to where the elm-tree
  crowns
  The hill behind whose ridge the sunset
   flames?
The signal-elm, that looks on Ilsley Downs,
15 The Vale, the three lone weirs, the youthful
   Thames?[7]
  This winter-eve is warm,
 Humid the air! leafless, yet soft as spring,
  The tender purple spray on copse and briers!
  And that sweet city with her dreaming spires,
20 She needs not June for beauty's heightening,

Lovely all times she lies, lovely to-night!—
 Only, methinks, some loss of habit's power
  Befalls me wandering through this upland
   dim.
 Once passed I blindfold here, at any hour;
25 Now seldom come I, since I came with him.
  That single elm-tree bright
 Against the west—I miss it! is it gone?
  We prized it dearly; while it stood, we said,
  Our friend, the Gipsy-Scholar, was not dead;
30 While the tree lived, he in these fields lived on.

Too rare, too rare, grow now my visits here,
 But once I knew each field, each flower, each
  stick;
  And with the country-folk acquaintance
  made

---

1. fish.

2. Gulf of Sidra on the northern coast of Africa.

3. beyond the Straits of Gibraltar.

4. modelled on the form of the pastoral elegy originally written in Greek by Theocritus. Especially appropriate for this poem because Arnold and Clough had spent much time walking in the Cumner countryside near Oxford as undergraduates.

5. villages of North and South Hinksey.

6. Sybella Curr, keeper of an inn in South Hinksey, who died in 1860.

7. that is, near its source.

By barn in threshing time, by new-built rick.
35   Here, too, our shepherd-pipes we first
          assayed.
          Ah me! this many a year
     My pipe is lost, my shepherd's holiday!
          Needs must I lose them, needs with heavy
          heart
40   Into the world and wave of men depart;
     But Thyrsis of his own will went away.[1]

     It irked him to be here, he could not rest.
          He loved each simple joy the country yields,
               He loved his mates; but yet he could not
               keep,[2]
     For that a shadow loured on the fields,
45   Here with the shepherds and the silly[3] sheep.
          Some life of men unblest
     He knew, which made him droop, and filled his
     head.
          He went; his piping took a troubled sound
          Of storms that rage outside our happy
          ground;
50   He could not wait their passing, he is dead.

     So, some tempestuous morn in early June,
          When the year's primal burst of bloom is o'er,
               Before the roses and the longest day—
     When garden-walks and all the grassy floor
55   With blossoms red and white of fallen May
               And chestnut-flowers are strewn—
     So have I heard the cuckoo's parting cry,
          From the wet field, through the vexed
          garden-trees,
               Come with the volleying rain and tossing
               breeze;
60   *The bloom is gone, and with the bloom go I!*

Too quick despairer, wherefore wilt thou go?
     Soon will the high Midsummer pomps come on,
          Soon will the musk carnations break and
          swell,
     Soon shall we have gold-dusted snapdragon,
65   Sweet-William with his homely cottage-
          smell,
               And stocks in fragrant blow;
     Roses that down the alleys shine afar,
          And open, jasmine-muffled lattices,
          And groups under the dreaming garden-trees,
70   And the full moon, and the white evening-star.

He hearkens not! light comer, he is flown!
     What matters it? next year he will return,
          And we shall have him in the sweet spring-
          days,
     With whitening hedges, and uncrumpling fern,
75   And blue-bells trembling by the forest-ways,
               And scent of hay new-mown.
     But Thyrsis never more we swains shall see;
          See him come back and cut a smoother reed,
          And blow a strain the world at last shall
          heed—
80   For Time, not Corydon,[4] hath conquered thee!

Alack, for Corydon no rival now!
     But when Sicilian shepherds lost a mate,
          Some good survivor with his flute would go,
     Piping a ditty sad for Bion's[5] fate;
85   And cross the unpermitted ferry's flow,[6]
               And relax Pluto's[7] brow,
     And make leap up with joy the beauteous head
     Of Proserpine, among whose crownéd hair

[1]   a reference to Clough's resignation of his Oriel fellowship in 1848 and his departure from Oxford. But he did not leave, as Arnold suggests (ll. 46–47), for reasons of social conscience.

[2]   stay.

[3]   innocent.

[4]   Corydon wins over Thyrsis in a musical contest in Virgil's seventh Eclogue.

[5]   from Moschus's pastoral elegy, "Lament for Bion."

[6]   The crossing of the river Styx to the underworld could be made only by the dead.

[7]   king of the underworld and Proserpine, his queen.

Are flowers first opened on Sicilian air,
90 And flute his friend, like Orpheus,[1] from the
    dead.

O easy access to the hearer's grace
    When Dorian shepherds sang to Proserpine!
        For she herself had trod Sicilian fields,
    She knew the Dorian water's gush divine,
95   She knew each lily white which Enna yields,
            Each rose with blushing face;
    She loved the Dorian pipe, the Dorian strain.
        But ah, of our poor Thames she never heard!
        Her foot the Cumner cowslips never stirred;
100 And we should tease her with our plaint in vain!

Well! wind-dispersed and vain the words will be,
    Yet, Thyrsis, let me give my grief its hour
        In the old haunt, and find our tree-topped
            hill!
    Who, if not I, for questing here hath power?
105   I know the wood which hides the daffodil,
            I know the Fyfield tree,[2]
    I know what white, what purple fritillaries[3]
        The grassy harvest of the river-fields,
        Above by Ensham, down by Sandford,
            yields,
110 And what sedged brooks are Thames's
        tributaries;

I know these slopes; who knows them if not I?
    But many a dingle on the loved hill-side,
        With thorns once studded, old, white-
            blossomed trees,
    Where thick the cowslips grew, and far descried
115   High towered the spikes of purple orchises,
            Hath since our day put by

The coronals of that forgotten time;
    Down each green bank hath gone the
        ploughboy's team,
    And only in the hidden brookside gleam
120 Primroses, orphans of the flowery prime.

Where is the girl, who by the boatman's door,
    Above the locks, above the boating throng,
        Unmoored our skiff when through the
            Wytham flats,
    Red loosestrife and blond meadow-sweet among
125   And darting swallows and light water-gnats,
            We tracked the shy Thames shore?
    Where are the mowers, who, as the tiny swell
        Of our boat passing heaved the river-grass,
        Stood with suspended scythe to see us pass?
130 They are all gone, and thou art gone as well!

Yes, thou art gone! and round me too the night
    In ever-nearing circle weaves her shade.
        I see her veil draw soft across the day,
    I feel her slowly chilling breath invade
135   The cheek grown thin, the brown hair
            sprent[4] with grey;
            I feel her finger light
    Laid pausefully upon life's headlong train;
        The foot less prompt to meet the morning
            dew,
        The heart less bounding at emotion new,
140 And hope, once crushed, less quick to spring
        again.

And long the way appears, which seemed so short
    To the less practised eye of sanguine youth;
        And high the mountain-tops, in cloudy air,
    The mountain-tops where is the throne of
        Truth,
145   Tops in life's morning-sun so bright and
            bare!

---

[1] Orpheus won the release of his wife Eurydice with the beauty of his
playing.

[2] elm tree near the village of Fyfield.

[3] lily-like flower.

[4] sprinkled.

Unbreachable the fort
Of the long-battered world uplifts its wall;
   And strange and vain the earthly turmoil
     grows,
   And near and real the charm of thy repose,
150   And night as welcome as a friend would fall.

But hush! the upland hath a sudden loss
   Of quiet!—Look, adown the dusk hill-side,
     A troop of Oxford hunters going home,
   As in old days, jovial and talking, ride!
155   From hunting with the Berkshire hounds
       they come.
     Quick! let me fly, and cross
   Into yon farther field!—'Tis done; and see,
     Backed by the sunset, which doth glorify
     The orange and pale violet evening-sky,
160   Bare on its lonely ridge, the Tree! the Tree!

I take the omen! Eve lets down her veil,
   The white fog creeps from bush to bush about,
     The west unflushes, the high stars grow
      bright,
   And in the scattered farms the lights come out.
165   I cannot reach the signal-tree to-night,
      Yet, happy omen, hail!
   Hear it from thy broad lucent Arno-vale[1]
     (For there thine earth-forgetting eyelids keep
     The morningless and unawakening sleep
170   Under the flowery oleanders pale),

Hear it, O Thyrsis, still our tree is there!
   Ah, vain! These English fields, this upland dim,
     These brambles pale with mist engarlanded,
   That lone, sky-pointing tree, are not for him;
175   To a boon southern country he is fled,
      And now in happier air,
   Wandering with the great Mother's[2] train divine

     (And purer or more subtle soul than thee,
      I trow, the mighty Mother doth not see)
180   Within a folding of the Apennine,[3]

Thou hearest the immortal chants of old!
   Putting his sickle to the perilous grain
     In the hot cornfield of the Phrygian king,
   For thee the Lityerses-song again
185   Young Daphnis with his silver voice doth
      sing;
     Sings his Sicilian fold,
   His sheep, his hapless love, his blinded eyes—
     And how a call celestial round him rang,
     And heavenward from the fountain-brink he
      sprang,
190   And all the marvel of the golden skies.[4]

There thou art gone, and me thou leavest here
   Sole in these fields! yet will I not despair.
     Despair I will not, while I yet descry
   'Neath the mild canopy of English air
195   That lonely tree against the western sky.
     Still, still these slopes, 'tis clear,
   Our Gipsy-Scholar haunts, outliving thee!
     Fields where soft sheep from cages pull the
      hay,

---

[1] Florence, in the Arno valley, where Clough is buried.

[2] goddess of nature, Cybele.

[3] mountain range near Florence.

[4] Arnold's note to this stanza is from Servius's commentary on Virgil's *Eclogues*: "Daphnis, the ideal Sicilian shepherd of Greek pastoral poetry, was said to have followed into Phrygia his mistress Piplea, who had been carried off by robbers, and to have found her in the power of the king of Phrygia, Lityerses. Lityerses used to make strangers try a contest with him in reaping corn and to put them to death if he overcame them. Hercules arrived in time to save Daphnis, took upon himself the reaping-contest with Lityerses, overcame him, and slew him. The Lityerses-song connected with this tradition was, like the Linus-song, one of the early plaintive strains of Greek popular poetry, and used to be sung by corn-reapers. Other traditions represented Daphnis as beloved by a nymph who exacted from him an oath to love no one else. He fell in love with a princess, and was struck blind by the jealous nymph. Mercury, who was his father, raised him to heaven, and made a fountain spring up in the place from which he ascended. At this fountain the Sicilians offered yearly sacrifices."

Woods with anemones in flower till May,
200   Know him a wanderer still; then why not me?

A fugitive and gracious light he seeks,
    Shy to illumine; and I seek it too.
        This does not come with houses or with gold,
    With place, with honour, and a flattering crew;
205   'Tis not in the world's market bought and
            sold—
        But the smooth-slipping weeks
    Drop by, and leave its seeker still untired;
        Out of the heed of mortals he is gone,
    He wends unfollowed, he must house alone;
210   Yet on he fares, by his own heart inspired.

Thou too, O Thyrsis, on like quest wast bound;
    Thou wanderedst with me for a little hour!
        Men gave thee nothing; but this happy quest,
    If men esteemed thee feeble, gave thee power,
215   If men procured thee trouble, gave thee rest.
        And this rude Cumner ground,
    Its fir-topped Hurst, its farms, its quiet fields,
        Here cam'st thou in thy jocund youthful
            time,
        Here was thine height of strength, thy
            golden prime!
220   And still the haunt beloved a virtue yields.

What though the music of thy rustic flute
    Kept not for long its happy, country tone;
        Lost it too soon, and learnt a stormy note
    Of men contention-tossed, of men who groan,
225   Which tasked thy pipe too sore, and tired
            thy throat
        It failed, and thou wast mute![1]
    Yet hadst thou always visions of our light,
        And long with men of care thou couldst not
          stay,
        And soon thy foot resumed its wandering
          way,
230   Left human haunt, and on alone till night.

Too rare, too rare, grow now my visits here!
    'Mid city-noise, not, as with thee of yore,
        Thyrsis! in reach of sheep-bells is my home.
    —Then through the great town's harsh, heart-
          wearying roar,
235   Let in thy voice a whisper often come,
        To chase fatigue and fear:
    Why faintest thou? I wandered till I died.
        Roam on! The light we sought is shining
         still.
        Dost thou ask proof? Our tree yet crowns
         the hill,
240   *Our Scholar travels yet the loved hill-side.*
    —1866 (1864–65)

---

[1] Clough published no new poems in England after 1849.

Dante Gabriel Rossetti
1828 — 1882

Although he was the son of an Italian political refugee, Dante Gabriel Rossetti (born Gabriel Charles) never pursued a political life, preferring instead to concentrate on artistic endeavours. Rossetti demonstrated extraordinary talent in both painting and poetry. His interest in art developed, in part, from his study of Keats's poems and letters, in which a sensuous response to beauty, through colour, texture, words, and women, functioned as a source of inspiration. With Ford Madox Brown, John Everett Millais, and William Holman Hunt, Rossetti formed the Pre-Raphaelite Brotherhood in 1848 in a concerted effort to reject neoclassical conventions in favour of the simplicity and purity of pre-Renaissance art. While the diverse interests of each artist led to the break-up of the circle within a few years, the group's presence and ideas aroused immense interest and opposition during its formation and after its dissolution. Rossetti's personal view of art is one that connects the heavenly with the earthly and implicitly earthly, an artistic approach which is reflected in his poetry. "The Blessed Damozel" was first published in the Pre-Raphaelite journal *The Germ* in 1850. *Poems by D.G. Rossetti*, containing the original version of *The House of Life* sonnet sequence, was published in 1871.

§§§

The Blessed Damozel [1]

The blessed damozel leaned out
    From the gold bar of Heaven;
Her eyes were deeper than the depth
    Of waters stilled at even;
5 She had three lilies in her hand,
    And the stars in her hair were seven.

Her robe, ungirt from clasp to hem,
    No wrought flowers did adorn,
But a white rose of Mary's gift,
10   For service meetly worn;
Her hair that lay along her back
    Was yellow like ripe corn.

Herseemed[2] she scarce had been a day
    One of God's choristers;
15 The wonder was not yet quite gone
    From that still look of hers;

Albeit, to them she left, her day
    Had counted as ten years.

(To one, it is ten years of years.
20   …Yet now, and in this place,
Surely she leaned o'er me—her hair
    Fell all about my face…
Nothing: the autumn-fall of leaves.
    The whole years sets apace.)

25 It was the rampart of God's house
    That she was standing on;
By God built over the sheer depth
    The which is Space begun;
So high, that looking downward thence
30   She scarce could see the sun.

It lies in Heaven, across the flood
    Of ether,[3] as a bridge.
Beneath, the tides of day and night
    With flame and darkness ridge

---

[1] the Anglo-Norman form of damsel—a young unmarried woman, a maiden, a virgin.

[2] it seemed to her.

[3] hypothetical substance which was supposed to be diffused in space beyond the earth's atmosphere.

35 The void, as low as where this earth
        Spins like a fretful midge.[1]

    Around her, lovers, newly met
        'Mid deathless love's acclaims,
    Spoke evermore among themselves
40   Their heart-remembered names;
    And the souls mounting up to God
        Went by her like thin flames.

    And still she bowed herself and stooped
        Out of the circling charm;
45 Until her bosom must have made
        The bar she leaned on warm,
    And the lilies lay as if asleep
        Along her bended arm.

    From the fixed place of Heaven she saw
50   Time like a pulse shake fierce
    Through all the worlds. Her gaze still strove
        Within the gulf to pierce
    Its path; and now she spoke as when
        The stars sang in their spheres.

55 The sun was gone now; the curled moon
        Was like a little feather
    Fluttering far down the gulf; and now
        She spoke through the still weather.
    Her voice was like the voice the stars
60   Had when they sang together.[2]

    (Ah sweet! Even now, in that bird's song,
        Strove not her accents there,
    Fain to be hearkened? When those bells
        Possessed the mid-day air,
65 Strove not her steps to reach my side
        Down all the echoing stair?)

    "I wish that he were come to me,
        For he will come," she said.
    "Have I not prayed in Heaven?—on earth,
70   Lord, Lord, has he not pray'd?
    Are not two prayers a perfect strength?
        And shall I feel afraid?

    "When round his head the aureole clings,
        And he is clothed in white,
75 I'll take his hand and go with him
        To the deep wells of light;
    As unto a stream we will step down,
        And bathe there in God's sight.

    "We two will stand beside that shrine,
80   Occult, withheld, untrod,
    Whose lamps are stirred continually
        With prayer sent up to God;
    And see our old prayers, granted, melt
        Each like a little cloud.

85 "We two will lie i' the shadow of
        That living mystic tree[3]
    Within whose secret growth the Dove[4]
        Is sometimes felt to be,
    While every leaf that His plumes touch
90   Saith His Name audibly.

    "And I myself will teach to him,
        I myself, lying so,
    The songs I sing here; which his voice
        Shall pause in, hushed and slow,
95 And find some knowledge at each pause,
        Or some new thing to know."

    (Alas! we two, we two, thou say'st!
        Yea, one wast thou with me
    That once of old. But shall God lift

---

[1] common name for a variety of small flies and insects.

[2] See Job 38.7: "When the morning stars sang together, and all the sons of God shouted for joy."

---

[3] See Revelation 22.2: "the tree of life" in Heaven.

[4] the Holy Spirit, Holy Ghost.

100   To endless unity
The soul whose likeness with thy soul
      Was but its love for thee?)

"We two," she said, "will seek the groves
      Where the lady Mary is,
105 With her five handmaidens, whose names
      Are five sweet symphonies,
Cecily, Gertrude, Magdalen,
      Margaret and Rosalys.

"Circlewise sit they, with bound locks
110   And foreheads garlanded;
Into the fine cloth white like flame
      Weaving the golden thread,
To fashion the birth-robes for them
      Who are just born, being dead.

115 "He shall fear, haply, and be dumb:
      Then will I lay my cheek
To his, and tell about our love,
      Not once abashed or weak:
And the dear Mother will approve
120   My pride, and let me speak.

"Herself shall bring us, hand in hand,
      To Him round whom all souls
Kneel, the clear-ranged unnumbered heads
      Bowed with their aureoles:
125 And angels meeting us shall sing
      To their citherns and citoles.[1]

"There will I ask of Christ the Lord
      Thus much for him and me:—
Only to live as once on earth
130   With Love,—only to be,
As then awhile, for ever now
      Together, I and he."

She gazed and listened and then said,
      Less sad of speech than mild,—
135 "All this is when he comes." She ceased.
      The light thrilled towards her, fill'd
With angels in strong level flight.
      Her eyes prayed, and she smil'd.

(I saw her smile.) But soon their path
140   Was vague in distant spheres:
And then she cast her arms along
      The golden barriers,
And laid her face between her hands,
      And wept. (I heard her tears.)
—1850 (1847)

My Sister's Sleep [2]

She fell asleep on Christmas Eve:
      At length the long-ungranted shade
      Of weary eyelids overweigh'd
The pain nought else might yet relieve.

5 Our mother, who had leaned all day
      Over the bed from chime to chime,
      Then raised herself for the first time,
And as she sat her down, did pray.

Her little work-table was spread
10   With work to finish. For the glare
      Made by her candle, she had care
To work some distance from the bed.

Without, there was a cold moon up,
      Of winter radiance sheer and thin;

---

[1] antique stringed instruments.

[2] The Margaret of the poem is fictive; neither of Rossetti's two sisters had died when the poem was first written and published.

15 The hollow halo it was in
Was like an icy crystal cup.[1]

Through the small room, with subtle sound
    Of flame, by vents the fireshine drove[2]
    And reddened. In its dim alcove
20 The mirror shed a clearness round.

I had been sitting up some nights,
    And my tired mind felt weak and blank;
    Like a sharp strengthening wine it drank
The stillness and the broken lights.

25 Twelve struck. That sound, by dwindling years
    Heard in each hour, crept off; and then
    The ruffled silence spread again,
Like water that a pebble stirs.

Our mother rose from where she sat:
30   Her needles, as she laid them down,
    Met lightly, and her silken gown
Settled: no other noise than that.

"Glory unto the Newly Born!"[3]
    So, as said angels, she did say;
35   Because we were in Christmas Day,
Though it would still be long till morn.

Just then in the room over us
    There was a pushing back of chairs,
    As some who had sat unawares
40 So late, now heard the hour, and rose.

With anxious softly-stepping haste
    Our mother went where Margaret lay,
    Fearing the sounds o'erhead—should they
Have broken her long watched-for rest!

45 She stooped an instant, calm, and turned;
    But suddenly turned back again;
    And all her features seemed in pain
With woe, and her eyes gazed and yearned.

For my part, I but hid my face,
50   And held my breath, and spoke no word:
    There was none spoken; but I heard
The silence for a little space.

Our mother bowed herself and wept:
    And both my arms fell, and I said,
55   "God knows I knew that she was dead."
And there, all white, my sister slept.

Then kneeling, upon Christmas morn
    A little after twelve o'clock,
    We said, ere the first quarter struck,
60 "Christ's blessing on the newly born!"
        —1850; 1870 (1847; 1869)

Jenny

*Vengeance of Jenny's case! Fie on her! Never name
her, child!*—(Mrs. Quickly)

Lazy laughing languid Jenny,
Fond of a kiss and fond of a guinea,
Whose head upon my knee to-night
Rests for while, as if grown light
5 With all our dances and the sound
To which the wild tunes spun you round:
Fair Jenny mine, the thoughtless queen
Of kisses which the blush between
Could hardly make much daintier;
10 Whose eyes are as blue skies, whose hair

---

[1] In early versions of the poem, the moon is "hollow, like an altar cup." This and other revisions were made to the poem in 1869 in an attempt, as Rossetti said in a letter, to "eliminate the religious element altogether" from the poem.

[2] was fanned.

[3] a reference, perhaps, to the Christmas hymn "Hark, the Herald Angels Sing."

Is countless gold incomparable:
Fresh flower, scarce touched with signs that tell
Of Love's exuberant hotbed:—Nay,
Poor flower left torn since yesterday
15   Until to-morrow leave you bare;
Poor handful of bright spring-water
Flung in the whirlpool's shrieking face;
Poor shameful Jenny, full of grace
Thus with your head upon my knee;—
20   Whose person or whose purse may be
The lodestar of your reverie?

This room of yours, my Jenny, looks
A change from mine so full of books,
Whose serried ranks hold fast, forsooth,
25   So many captive hours of youth,—
The hours they thieve from day and night
To make one's cherished work come right,
And leave it wrong for all their theft,
Even as to-night my work was left:
30   Until I vowed that since my brain
And eyes of dancing seemed so fain,
My feet should have some dancing too:—
And thus it was I met with you.
Well, I suppose 'twas hard to part,
35   For here I am. And now, sweetheart,
You seem too tired to get to bed.

It was a careless life I led
When rooms like this were scarce so strange
Not long ago. What breeds the change,—
40   The many aims or the few years?
Because to-night it all appears
Something I do not know again.

The cloud's not danced out of my brain,—
The cloud that made it turn and swim
45   While hour by hour the books grew dim.
Why, Jenny, as I watch you there,—
For all your wealth of loosened hair,
Your silk ungirdled and unlac'd

And warm sweets open to the waist,
50   All golden in the lamplight's gleam,—
You know not what a book you seem,
Half-read by lightning in a dream!
How should you know, my Jenny? Nay,
And I should be ashamed to say:—
55   Poor beauty, so well worth a kiss!
But while my thought runs on like this
With wasteful whims more than enough,
I wonder what you're thinking of.

If of myself you think at all,
60   What is the thought?—conjectural
On sorry matters best unsolved?—
Or inly is each grace revolved
To fit me with a lure?—or (sad
To think!) perhaps you're merely glad
65   That I'm not drunk or ruffianly
And let you rest upon my knee.

For sometimes, were the truth confess'd,
You're thankful for a little rest,—
Glad from the crush to rest within,
70   From the heart-sickness and the din
Where envy's voice at virtue's pitch
Mocks you because your gown is rich;
And from the pale girl's dumb rebuke,
Whose ill-clad grace and toil-worn look
75   Proclaim the strength that keeps her weak,
And other nights than yours bespeak;
And from the wise unchildish elf,
To schoolmate lesser than himself
Pointing you out, what thing you are:—
80   Yes, from the daily jeer and jar,
From shame and shame's outbraving too,
Is rest not sometimes sweet to you?—
But most from the hatefulness of man,
Who spares not to end what he began,
85   Whose acts are ill and his speech ill,
Who, having used you at his will,

Thrusts you aside, as when I dine
I serve the dishes and the wine.

Well, handsome Jenny mine, sit up:
90 I've filled our glasses, let us sup,
And do not let me think of you,
Lest shame of yours suffice for two.
What, still so tired? Well, well then, keep
Your head there, so you do not sleep;
95 But that the weariness may pass
And leave you merry, take this glass.
Ah! lazy lily hand, more bless'd
If ne'er in rings it had been dress'd
Nor ever by a glove conceal'd!

100 Behold the lilies of the field,
They toil not neither do they spin;
(So doth the ancient text[1] begin,—
Not of such rest as one of these
Can share.) Another rest and ease
105 Along each summer-sated hath
From its new lord the garden hath
Than that whose spring in blessings ran
Which praised the bounteous husbandman,
Ere yet, in days of hankering breath,
110 The lilies sickened unto death.

What, Jenny, are your lilies dead?
Aye, and the snow-white leaves are spread
Like winter on the garden-bed.
But you had roses left in May,—
115 They were not gone too. Jenny, nay,
But must your roses die, and those
Their purfled buds that should unclose?
Even so; the leaves are curled apart,
Still red as from the broken heart,
120 And here's the naked stem of thorns.

Nay, nay, mere words. Here nothing warns
As yet of winter. Sickness here
Or want alone could waken fear,—
Nothing but passion wrings a tear.
125 Except when there may rise unsought
Haply at times a passing thought
Of the old days which seem to be
Much older than any history
That is written in any book;
130 When she would lie in fields and look
Along the ground through the blown grass,
And wonder where the city was,
Far out of sight, whose broil and bale
They told her then for a child's tale.

135 Jenny, you know the city now.
A child can tell the tale there, how
Some things which are not yet enroll'd
In market-lists are bought and sold
Even till the early Sunday light,
140 When Saturday night is market-night
Everywhere, be it dry or wet,
And market-night in the Haymarket.[2]
Our learned London children know,
Poor Jenny, all your pride and woe;
145 Have seen your lifted silken skirt
Advertise dainties through the dirt;
Have seen your coach-wheels splash rebuke
On virtue; and have learned your look
When, wealth and health slipped past, you stare
150 Along the streets alone, and there,
Round the long park, across the bridge,
The cold lamps at the pavement's edge
Wind on together and apart,
A fiery serpent for your heart.

155 Let the thoughts pass, an empty cloud!
Suppose I were to think aloud,—
What if to her all this were said?

---

[1] Matthew 6:28–9.

[2] a street in the theatre district of London, in this period a notorious haunt of prostitutes.

Why, as a volume seldom read
Being opened halfway shuts again,
160 So might the pages of her brain
Be parted at such words, and thence
Close back upon the dusty sense.
For is there hue or shape defin'd
In Jenny's desecrated mind,
165 Where all contagious currents meet,
A Lethe of the middle street?[1]
Nay, it reflects not any face,
Nor sound is in its sluggish pace,
But as they coil those eddies clot,
170 And night and day remember not.

Why, Jenny, you're asleep at last!—
Asleep, poor Jenny, hard and fast,—
So young and soft and tired; so fair,
With chin thus nestled in your hair,
175 Mouth quiet, eyelids almost blue
As if some sky of dreams shone through!

Just as another woman sleeps!
Enough to throw one's thoughts in heaps
Of doubt and horror,—what to say
180 Or think,—this awful secret sway,
The potter's power over the clay![2]
Of the same lump (it has been said)
For honour and dishonour made,
Two sister vessels. Here is one.

185 My cousin Nell is fond of fun,
And fond of dress, and change, and praise,
So mere a woman in her ways:
And if her sweet eyes rich in youth
Are like her lips that tell the truth,
190 My cousin Nell is fond of love.
And she's the girl I'm proudest of.
Who does not prize her, guard her well?

The love of change, in cousin Nell,
Shall find the best and hold it dear:
195 The unconquered mirth turn quieter
Not through her own, through others' woe:
The conscious pride of beauty glow
Beside another's pride in her,
One little part of all they share.
200 For Love himself shall ripen these
In a kind soil to just increase
Through years of fertilizing peace.

Of the same lump (as it is said)
For honour and dishonour made,
205 Two sister vessels. Here is one.

It makes a goblin of the sun.

So pure,—so fall'n! How dare to think
Of the first common kindred link?
Yet, Jenny, till the world shall burn
210 It seems that all things take their turn;
And who shall say but this fair tree
May need, in changes that may be,
Your children's children's charity?
Scorned then, no doubt, as you are scorn'd!
215 Shall no man hold his pride forewarn'd
Till in the end, the Day of Days,
At Judgment, one of his own race,
As frail and lost as you, shall rise,—
His daughter, with his mother's eyes?

220 How Jenny's clock ticks on the shelf!
Might not the dial scorn itself
That has such hours to register?
Yet as to me, even so to her
Are golden sun and silver moon,
225 In daily largesse of earth's boon,
Counted for life-coins to one tune.
And if, as blindfold fates are toss'd,
Through some one man this life be lost,
Shall soul not somehow pay for soul?

[1] Gutters—often containing sewage—used to flow down the middle of the street. Lethe is the river of forgetfulness in Hades.

[2] Romans 9:21.

230   Fair shines the gilded aureole
In which our highest painters place
Some living woman's simple face.
And the stilled features thus descried
As Jenny's long throat droops aside,—
235 The shadows where the cheeks are thin,
And pure wide curve from ear to chin,—
With Raffael's, Leonardo's hand[1]
To show them to men's souls, might stand,
Whole ages long, the whole world through,
240 For preachings of what God can do.
What has man done here? How atone,
Great God, for this which man has done?
And for the body and soul which by
Man's pitiless doom must now comply
245 With lifelong hell, what lullaby
Of sweet forgetful second birth
Remains? All dark. No sign on earth
What measure of God's rest endows
The many mansions of his house.[2]

250   If but a woman's heart might see
Such erring heart unerringly
For once! But that can never be.

    Like a rose shut in a book
In which pure women may not look,
255 For its base pages claim control
To crush the flower within the soul;
Where through each dead rose-leaf that clings,
Pale as transparent Psyche-wings,[3]
To the vile text, are traced such things
260 As might make lady's cheek indeed
More than a living rose to read;
So nought save foolish foulness may
Watch with hard eyes the sure decay;

And so the life-blood of this rose,
265 Puddled with shameful knowledge, flows
Through leaves no chaste hand may unclose:
Yet still it keeps such faded show
Of when 'twas gathered long ago,
That the crushed petals' lovely grain,
270 The sweetness of the sanguine stain,
Seen of a woman's eyes, must make
Her pitiful heart, so prone to ache,
Love roses better for its sake:—
Only that this can never be:—
275 Even so unto her sex is she.

    Yet, Jenny, looking long at you,
The woman almost fades from view.
A cipher of man's changeless sum
Of lust, past, present, and to come,
280 Is left. A riddle that one shrinks
To challenge from the scornful sphinx.[4]

    Like a toad within a stone[5]
Seated while Time crumbles on;
Which sits there since the earth was curs'd
285 For Man's transgression at the first;
Which, living through all centuries,
Not once has seen the sun arise;
Whose life, to its cold circle charmed,
The earth's whole summers have not warmed;
290 Which always—whitherso the stone
Be flung—sits there, deaf, blind, alone;—
Aye, and shall not be driven out
Till that which shuts him round about
Break at the very Master's stroke,
295 And the dust thereof vanish as smoke,

[1] the painters Raphael (1483–1520) and Leonardo da Vinci (1452–1519).

[2] John 14:2.

[3] Psyche means the soul; Psyche was also a beautiful maiden beloved but then spurned by Cupid.

[4] in Greek mythology, a monster with the head and breasts of a woman, the body of a lion, the wings of a bird, and the tail of a serpent. The sphinx spoke in a human voice, setting riddles and devouring those who could not find answers.

[5] It was thought that a toad confined within a cave or rock could live indefinitely without sustenance.

And the seed of Man vanish as dust:—
Even so within this world is Lust.

   Come, come, what use in thoughts like this?
Poor little Jenny, good to kiss,—
300 You'd not believe by what strange roads
Thought travels, when your beauty goads
A man to-night to think of toads!
Jenny, wake up…Why, there's the dawn!

   And there's an early waggon drawn
305 To market, and some sheep that jog
Bleating before a barking dog;
And the old streets come peering through
Another night that London knew;
And all as ghostlike as the lamps.

310   So on the wings of day decamps
My last night's frolic. Glooms begin
To shiver off as lights creep in
Past the gauze curtains half drawn-to,
And the lamp's doubled shade grows blue,—
315 Your lamp, my Jenny, kept alight,
Like a wise virgin's, all one night!
And in the alcove coolly spread
Glimmers with dawn your empty bed;
And yonder your fair face I see
320 Reflected lying on my knee,
Where teems with first foreshadowings
Your pier-glass scrawled with diamond rings:[1]
And on your bosom all night worn
Yesterday's rose now droops forlorn,
325 But dies not yet this summer morn.

   And now without, as if some word
Had called upon them that they heard,
The London sparrows far and nigh
Clamour together suddenly;
330 And Jenny's cage-bird grown awake

Here in their song his part must take,
Because here too the day doth break.

   And somehow in myself the dawn
Among stirred clouds and veils withdrawn
335 Strikes greyly on her. Let her sleep.
But will I wake her if I heap
These cushions thus beneath her head
Where my knee was? No,—there's your bed,
My Jenny, while you dream. And there
340 I lay among your golden hair
Perhaps the subject of your dreams,
These golden coins.
           For still one deems
That Jenny's flattering sleep confers
New magic on the magic purse,—
345 Grim web, how clogged with shrivelled flies!
Between the threads fine fumes arise
And shape their pictures in the brain.
There roll no streets in glare and rain,
Nor flagrant man-swine whets his tusk;
350 But delicately sighs in musk
The homage of the dim boudoir;
Or like a palpitating star
Thrilled into song, the opera-night
Breathes faint in the quick pulse of light;
355 Or at the carriage-window shine
Rich wares for choice; or, free to dine,
Whirls through its hour of health (divine
For her) the concourse of the Park.
And though in the discounted dark
360 Her functions there and here are one,
Beneath the lamps and in the sun
There reigns at least the acknowledged belle
Apparelled beyond parallel.
Ah Jenny, yes, we know your dreams.

---

[1] A pier-glass is a mirror; the names of Jenny's lovers have been scratched on the mirror with a diamond ring.

365   For even the Paphian Venus[1] seems
A goddess o'er the realms of love,
When silver-shrined in shadowy grove:
Aye, or let offerings nicely plac'd
But hide Priapus[2] to the waist,
370 And whoso looks on him shall see
An eligible deity.

   Why, Jenny, waking here alone
May help you to remember one,
Though all the memory's long outworn
375 Of many a double-pillowed morn.
I think I see you when you wake,
And rub your eyes for me, and shake
My gold, in rising, from your hair,
A Danaë[3] for a moment there.

380   Jenny, my love rang true! for still
Love at first sight is vague, until
That tinkling makes him audible.

   And must I mock you to the last,
Ashamed of my own shame,—aghast
385 Because some thoughts not born amiss
Rose at a poor fair face like this?
Well, of such thoughts so much I know:
In my life, as in hers, they show,
By a far gleam which I may near,
390 A dark path I can strive to clear.

   Only one kiss. Good-bye, my dear.
—1870 (1848–50; 1869–70)

The House of Life:

A Sonnet-Sequence [4]

"A Sonnet is a moment's monument,—"
INTRODUCTORY SONNET

A Sonnet is a moment's monument,—
   Memorial from the Soul's eternity
    To one dead deathless hour. Look that it be,
Whether for lustral[5] rite or dire portent,
5 *Of its own arduous fulness reverent:*
   Carve it in ivory or in ebony,
    As Day or Night may rule; and let Time see
Its flowering crest impearled and orient.[6]

A Sonnet is a coin: its face reveals
10   *The soul,—its converse, to what Power 'tis due:—*
Whether for tribute to the august appeals
   Of Life, or dower in Love's high retinue,
It serve; or, 'mid the dark wharf's cavernous breath,
In Charon's palm it pay the toll to Death.[7]
—1881 (1880)

---

[1] Paphos is a city on Cyprus where Venus was worshipped in orgiastic rites. The Paphian Venus represents sexual love, and "Paphian" can mean prostitute.

[2] in Greek mythology, the god of reproductive power, fertility, and gardens, represented by a phallic statue.

[3] daughter of Acrisius, King of Argos, who locked her up in a tower to prevent her marrying. In order to seduce Danae, Zeus transformed himself into a shower of gold.

---

[4] The work is a collection of sonnets which were composed from 1848–81, and published from 1863–81. The number of sonnets is 102 (if the "Introductory Sonnet" is included) or 103 (if "Nuptial Sleep" is included). Rossetti first published 50 sonnets in *Poems* (1870), with his final version appearing in *Ballads and Sonnets* (1881).

[5] cleansing, purificatory.

[6] precious, shining.

[7] In Greek myth, Charon was the ferryman who conveyed the dead in his boat across the river Styx to Hades, a task for which each passenger paid him a coin. The dead were buried with a coin in their mouths to pay Charon's fee.

Nuptial Sleep
SONNET VI[a] [1]

At length their long kiss severed, with sweet
    smart:
    And as the last slow sudden drops are shed
    From sparkling eaves when all the storm has fled,
So singly flagged the pulses of each heart.
5 Their bosoms sundered, with the opening start
    Of married flowers to either side outspread
    From the knit stem; yet still their mouths, burnt
      red,
Fawned on each other where they lay apart.

Sleep sank them lower than the tide of dreams,
10 And their dreams watched them sink, and slid
      away.
Slowly their souls swam up again, through gleams
    Of watered light and dull drowned waifs of day;
Till from some wonder of new woods and streams
    He woke, and wondered more: for there she lay.
—1870

The Portrait
SONNET X

O Lord of all compassionate control,
  O Love! let this my lady's picture glow
  Under my hand to praise her name, and show
Even of her inner self the perfect whole:
5 That he who seeks her beauty's furthest goal,
  Beyond the light that the sweet glances throw
  And refluent wave of the sweet smile, may know
The very sky and sea-line of her soul.

Lo! it is done. Above the enthroning throat
10 The mouth's mould testifies of voice and kiss,

[1] Distressed by Robert Buchanan's criticism in "The Fleshly School of Poetry," Rossetti removed "Nuptial Sleep" from the sequence after its initial publication in 1870.

The shadowed eyes remember and foresee.
Her face is made her shrine. Let all men note
  That in all years (O Love, thy gift is this!)
    They that would look on her must come to
    me.
—1870 (1869)

Silent Noon
SONNET XIX

Your hands lie open in the long fresh grass,—
  The finger-points look through like rosy
    blooms:
    Your eyes smile peace. The pasture gleams and
    glooms
'Neath billowing skies that scatter and amass.
All round our nest, far as the eye can pass,
  Are golden kingcup-fields with silver edge
  Where the cow-parsley skirts the hawthorn-
    hedge.
5 'Tis visible silence, still as the hour-glass.

Deep in the sun-searched growths the dragon-fly
Hangs like a blue thread loosened from the sky:—
  So this wing'd hour is dropt to us from above.
Oh! clasp we to our hearts, for deathless dower,
This close-companioned inarticulate hour
  When twofold silence was the song of love.
—1870

Willowwood
SONNETS XLIX, L, LI, LII

I

I sat with Love upon a woodside well,
  Leaning across the water, I and he;
  Nor ever did he speak nor looked at me,
But touched his lute wherein was audible
5 The certain secret thing he had to tell:
  Only our mirrored eyes met silently

In the low wave; and that sound came to be
The passionate voice I knew; and my tears fell.

And at their fall, his eyes beneath grew hers;
10 And with his foot and with his wing-feathers
      He swept the spring that watered my heart's
         drouth.
Then the dark ripples spread to waving hair,
And as I stooped, her own lips rising there
      Bubbled with brimming kisses at my mouth.

II

And now Love sang: but his was such a song,
So meshed with half-remembrance hard to free,
      As souls disused in death's sterility
May sing when the new birthday tarries long.
5 And I was made aware of dumb throng
      That stood aloof, one form by every tree,
      All mournful forms, for each was I or she,
The shades of those our days that had no tongue.

They looked on us, and knew us and were known;
10   While fast together, alive from the abyss,
      Clung the soul-wrung implacable close kiss;
And pity of self through all made broken moan
Which said, "For once, for once, for once alone!"
      And still Love sang, and what he sang was
         this:—

III

"O YE, all ye that walk in Willowwood,
That walk with hollow faces burning white;
What fathom-depth of soul-struck widowhood,
      What long, what longer hours, one lifelong
         night,
5 Ere ye again, who so in vain have wooed
      Your last hope lost, who so in vain invite
Your lips to that their unforgotten food,
      Ere ye, ere ye again shall see the light!

Alas! the bitter banks in Willowwood,
10   With tear-spurge wan, with blood-wort burning
         red:
Alas! if ever such a pillow could
      Steep deep the soul in sleep till she were dead,—
Better all life forget her than this thing,
That Willowwood should hold her wandering!"

IV

So sang he: and as meeting rose and rose
      Together cling through the wind's wellaway
      Nor change at once, yet near the end of day
The leaves drop loosened where the heart-stain
         glows,—
5 So when the song died did the kiss unclose;
      And her face fell back drowned, and was as grey
      As its grey eyes; and if it ever may
Meet mine again I know not if Love knows.

Only I know that I leaned low and drank
10 A long draught from the water where she sank,
      Her breath and all her tears and all her soul:
And as I leaned, I know I felt Love's face
Pressed on my neck with moan of pity and grace,
      Till both our heads were in his aureole.
—1869 (1869)

The Soul's Sphere
SONNET LXII

Some prisoned moon in steep cloud-fastnesses,—
    Throned queen and thralled; some dying sun
         whose pyre
      Blazed with momentous memorable fire;—
Who hath not yearned and fed his heart with these?
5 Who, sleepless, hath not anguished to appease
      Tragical shadow's realm of sound and sight
      Conjectured in the lamentable night?…
Lo! the soul's sphere of infinite images!

What sense shall count them? Whether it forecast
10   The rose-winged hours that flutter in the van
   Of Love's unquestioning unrevealèd span,—
Visions of golden futures: or that last
Wild pageant of the accumulated past
   That clangs and flashes for a drowning man.
—1881 (1873)

The Landmark
SONNET LXVII

Was *that* the landmark? What,—the foolish well
   Whose wave, low down, I did not stoop to drink,
   But sat and flung the pebbles from its brink
In sport to send its imaged skies pell-mell,
5 (And mine own image, had I noted well!)—
   Was that my point of turning?—I had thought
   The stations of my course should rise unsought,
As altar-stone or ensigned citadel.

But lo! the path is missed, I must go back,
10   And thirst to drink when next I reach the spring
Which once I stained, which since may have grown
     black.
   Yet though no light be left nor bird now sing
   As here I turn, I'll thank God, hastening,
That the same goal is still on the same track.
—1869 (1854)

Autumn Idleness
SONNET LXIX

This sunlight shames November where he grieves
   In dead red leaves, and will not let him shun
   The day, though bough with bough be over-run.
But with a blessing every glade receives
5 High salutation; while from hillock-eaves
   The deer gaze calling, dappled white and dun,

As if, being foresters of old, the sun
Had marked them with the shade of forest-leaves.

Here dawn to-day unveiled her magic glass;
10   Here noon now gives the thirst and takes the
     dew;
Till eve bring rest when other good things pass.
   And here the lost hours the lost hours renew
While I still lead my shadow o'er the grass,
   Nor know, for longing, that which I should do.
—1870 (1850)

The Hill Summit
SONNET LXX

This feast-day of the sun, his altar there
   In the broad west has blazed for vesper-song;
   And I have loitered in the vale too long
And gaze now a belated worshiper.
5 Yet may I not forget that I was 'ware,
   So journeying, of his face at intervals
   Transfigured where the fringed horizon falls,—
A fiery bush with coruscating hair.

And not that I have climbed and won this height,
10   I must tread downward through the sloping
     shade
And travel the bewildered tracks till night.
   Yet for this hour I still may here be stayed
   And see the gold air and the silver fade
And the last bird fly into the last light.
—1870 (1853)

Old and New Art

SONNETS LXXIV, LXXV, LXXVI

I. ST. LUKE THE PAINTER [1]

Give honour unto Luke Evangelist;
For he it was (the aged legends say)
Who first taught Art to fold her hands and pray.
Scarcely at once she dared to rend the mist
5 Of devious symbols: but soon having wist
How sky-breadth and field-silence and this day
Are symbols also in some deeper way,
She looked through these to God and was God's
priest.

And if, past noon, her toil began to irk,
10 And she sought talismans, and turned in vain
To soulless self-reflections of man's skill,—
Yet now, in this the twilight, she might still
Kneel in the latter grass to pray again,
Ere the night cometh and she may not work. [2]

II. NOT AS THESE

"I am not as these are," the poet saith
In youth's pride, and the painter, among men
At bay, where never pencil comes nor pen,
And shut about with his own frozen breath.
5 To others, for whom only rhyme wins faith
As poets,—only paint as painters,—then
He turns in the cold silence; and again
Shrinking, "I am not as these are," he saith.

And say that this is so, what follows it?
10 For were thine eyes set backwards in thine head,
Such words were well; but they see on, and
far.

Unto the lights of the great Past, new-lit
Fair for the Future's track, look thou instead,—
Say thou instead, "I am not as *these* are."

III. THE HUSBANDMEN

Though God, as one that is an householder,
Called these to labour in His vineyard first,
Before the husk of darkness was well burst
Bidding them grope their way out and bestir,
5 (Who, questioned of their wages, answered, "Sir,
Unto each man a penny:") though the worst
Burthen of heat was theirs and the dry thirst:
Though God has since found none such as these
were
To do their work like them:—Because of this
10 Stand not ye idle in the market-place.
Which of ye knoweth *he* is not that last
Who may be first by faith and will?—yea, his
The hand which after the appointed days
And hours shall give a Future to their Past?
—1870 (1849)

Soul's Beauty

SONNET LXXVII

Under the arch of Life, where love and death,
Terror and mystery, guard her shrine, I saw
Beauty enthroned; and though her gaze struck
awe,
I drew it in as simply as my breath.
5 Hers are the eyes which, over and beneath,
The sky and sea bend on thee,—which can draw,
By sea or sky or woman, to one law,
The allotted bondman of her palm and wreath.

This is that Lady Beauty, in whose praise
10 Thy voice and hand shake still,—long known to
thee
By flying hair and fluttering hem,—the beat
Following her daily of thy heart and feet,

---

[1] Luke, the Evangelist, is also the patron saint of artists (and physicians). Tradition says that he painted a portrait of the Virgin Mary.

[2] John 9:4.

402

How passionately and irretrievably,
In what fond flight, how many ways and days!
—1868 (1867)

Body's Beauty
SONNET LXXVIII

Of Adam's first wife, Lilith,[1] it is told
(The witch he loved before the gift of Eve,)
That, ere the snake's, her sweet tongue could
    deceive,
And her enchanted hair was the first gold.
5 And still she sits, young while the earth is old,
    And, subtly of herself contemplative,
    Draws men to watch the bright web she can
        weave,
Till heart and body and life are in its hold.

The rose and poppy are her flowers; for where
10   Is he not found, O Lilith, whom shed scent
And soft-shed kisses and soft sleep shall snare?
    Lo! as that youth's eyes burned at thine, so went
    Thy spell through him, and left his straight
        neck bent
And round his heart one strangling golden hair.
—1868 (1867)

A Superscription
SONNET XCVII

Look in my face; my name is Might-have-been;
    I am also called No-more, Too-late, Farewell;
    Unto thine ear I hold the dead-sea shell
Cast up thy Life's foam-fretted feet between;

5 Unto thine eyes the glass where that is seen
    Which had Life's form and Love's, but by my
        spell
    Is now a shaken shadow intolerable,
Of ultimate things unuttered the frail screen.

Mark me, how still I am! But should there dart
10   One moment through thy soul the soft surprise
    Of that winged Peace which lulls the breath of
        sighs,—
Then shalt thou see me smile, and turn apart
Thy visage to mine ambush at thy heart
    Sleepless with cold commemorative eyes.
—1869 (1868)

The One Hope
SONNET CI

When vain desire at last and vain regret
    Go hand in hand to death, and all is vain,
    What shall assuage the unforgotten pain
And teach the unforgetful to forget?
5 Shall Peace be still a sunk stream long unmet,—
    Or may the soul at once in a green plain
    Stoop through the spray of some sweet life-
        fountain
And cull the dew-drenched flowering amulet?

10 Ah! when the wan soul in that golden air
    Between the scriptured petals softly blown
    Peers breathless for the gift of grace unknown,—
Ah! let none other alien spell soe'er
But only the one Hope's one name be there,—
    Not less nor more, but even that word alone.
—1870 (1870)

---

[1] In Rabbinical writings, Lilith is said to have been the first wife of Adam.

Arthur Munby
1828 – 1910

Arthur Munby was a civil servant, diarist, and minor poet. He was obsessed with working-class women, and his verse concerns that group and country life. Munby's diaries reveal that his obsession was partly sexual in nature, and his interest in working-class women led him to pursue, interview, record, and photograph them. In 1873 he secretly married his maidservant, Hannah Cullwick (1833–1909).

cɔcɔ

The Serving Maid

When you go out at early morn,
    Your busy hands, sweet drudge, are bare;
    For you must work, and none are there
To see with scorn—to feel with scorn.

5   And when the weekly wars begin,
    Your arms are naked to the hilt,
    And many a sturdy pail's a-tilt
To sheathe them in—to plunge them in.

For you at least can understand
10   That daily work is hard and stern,
    That those who toil for bread must learn
To bare the hand—to spoil the hand.

But in the evening, when they dine,
    And you behind each frequent chair
15   Are flitting lightly here and there
To bring them wine—to pour them wine;

Oh then, from every dainty eye
    That may not so be shock'd or grieved,
    Your hands are hid, your arms are sleeved:
20 We ask not why—we tell not why.

Ah fools! Though you for workday scours,
    And they for show, unveil their charms,
    Love is not bound to snowy arms,
He thinks of yours—he speaks of yours:

25 To me his weighted shaft has come;
    Though hand and arm are both unseen,
    Your rosy wrist peeps out between
And sends it home—and speeds it home.
—1865

Woman's Rights

One must take the rough with the smooth.
Nec crimen duras esset habere manus.

Some say, that women should be weak;
    That sunburnt throat and roughen'd cheek
        Are wholly out of place
For that sweet sex, whose duty lies
5   In having lovely lips and eyes,
        And attitudes all grace.

And some, with difference, are agreed
That women should be weak, indeed,
        Of body and of limb;
10 But, *en revanche,*[1] in brain and mind
They may and ought to be a kind
        Of stronger seraphim.

Weak? cries another; why, they are!
No talk of 'should be:' you're aware
15   That much diversity
Of ways, of frame, and, in a word,

---

[1] in return; as a retaliation. The term was introduced into English in the nineteenth century.

Of nature, makes it quite absurd
    For them to work as we.

"Of course!" says one; "it's not our trade:
20 Our little hands were never made
    To wipe another's dust;
So here's the formula I use:
'Let women work because they choose,
    And men because they must.'

25 "That is, at handiwork. But brains!
I shall not waste (says she) much pains
    To prove and prove again
That women needn't stay at home
To use them; they may go and come,
30   A better sort of men,

"At mart and meeting, church and bar:
Wherever fame and fortune are
    There I (she says) believe
That woman shortly will resort;
35 Till every Adam finds in court
    An opposition Eve."

Alas, my lively learned friends!
This child but feebly comprehends
    The meaning of it all:
40 What with your speeches and your sections,
Your arguments and grave objections,
    Your—well, I won't say gall;

Your pamphlets, letters to the *Times*,
Smart magazines, and ready rhymes
45   On everything but love;
And papers too by high-soul'd men,
Whose bosoms bleed for Lydia, when
    She soils her dainty glove;

I tell you, what with this and that,
50 We plain ones can't think what you're at;
    Indeed we really can't:

And therefore, in the name of sense,
Eschew negation and pretence,
    And say the thing you want!

55 Look here: you strive, and nobly too,
To find employment for that crew
    Of hapless imbeciles
(Excuse the word) whose lot in life
Lies 'twixt the needle and the knife,
60   Unless they sell their smiles:

You trust them with a watch's works;
You make them prentices and clerks;
    Put pens behind their ears;
Or bid them tell the feeling cords,
65 In vivid music of dumb words,
    Our triumphs and our fears:

'Tis new; but who will interfere?
For me, I trust that every year
    Your telegraphic maids,
70 Your girls who copy briefs and wills
Or set up circulars and bills,
    May flourish in their trades.

Et puis, mesdames?[1] These quiet duties
May do for sedentary beauties;
75   But, you yourselves must own,
All women don't like sitting still;
All are not competent to fill
    A clerkly seat in town.

Some lasses, neither slim nor fair,
80 Live mostly in the open air,
    And rather like it, too:
Their faces and their hands are brown;
Their fists, perchance, might knock you down,
    If they were minded to!

---

[1] "And then, ladies?"

85 What say you then of such as these?
 May they continue, if they please,
  To swing the pail, to scrub,
 To make the cheese, to warm the cruds,
 And lash the storm of steaming suds
90 Within the washing-tub?

 "Well, yes," say you; "undoubtedly:
 We meddle not with them; you see
  Our business is with wrong:
 We wish to set the balance straight,
95 And somewhat equalize in fate
  The feeble and the strong.

 "We seek the *middle* classes' good:
 Their overflowing womanhood
  Exactly suits our plan;
100 Which is, to prove the latent might
 Of women, and assert their right
  To work abreast of man."

 Good: and a blessing on the deed!
 Since then you're anxious to succeed,
105 I gladly make it known
 That Nature, in her wiser hours,
 Has seconded this plan of yours
  By teachings of her own.

 "Whene'er you take your walks abroad,"
110 You'll haply see along the road,
  In field, or yard, or farm,
 Those girls of whom I spoke just now:
 You'll see them lift a sweating brow,
  Or bare a rough red arm

115 Right up through all its brawny length;
 And do with ease such feats of strength
  As make you ladies stare;
 Or, pausing in their toil, they'll stand
 And hold you out a harden'd hand,
120 And ask you how you are.

 Is it not comfort, then, to know
 These wenches have such thews to show,
  And work with such a will?
 What health there is in every face!
125 And, if with a Herculean grace,[1]
  Are they not graceful still?

 "Oh no!" you scream, "good gracious, no!
 You *wicked* man! How dare you so
  Distort our publish'd views?
130 We *hate* what is unfeminine;
 We can't see anything divine
  In muscles or in thews!

 "Hard hands! and oh, a dirty face!
 What sad indelible disgrace
135 For this soft sex of ours!
 We want them to be nice and clean;
 With tasteful dress and gentle mien,
  Like nymphs among the flowers!

 "If these poor souls are so degraded
140 They fancy they can work, unaided
  By our wise counsellings,
 We must, we really must, present
 And pass a Bill through Parliament
  To stop such dreadful things!

145 "Why were they never, never taught
 To scorn their labour as they ought,
  And feel that it is wrong
 Thus to use strength and gain by it?
 It doesn't signify one bit
150 That they *are* well and strong:

 "We're bound to *show* them what they want;
 To say they mustn't and they shan't
  Destroy their fair complexions
 By doing work that *men* should do:

---

[1] In Greek mythology, Hercules was a hero of superhuman physical strength, the son of Zeus and Alcmene.

155   Great, big, ungrateful men like you,
     Who raise these weak objections!"

I raise objections? Nay, my dears:
  'Tis true, I've watch'd their work for years
     With no unfriendly eye;
160   Because, alas! in every point
  My facts are somewhat out of joint
     With half your theory.

But now, you see, you're caught at last:
  Women, whose powers are so vast,
165   Are *children*, after all!
  They mustn't give, as men may give,
  Their sweat and brains, nor freely live
     In great things and in small:

They must be guided from above,
170   By quips of patronizing love,
     To do or not to do:
  Though they be made of stalwart stuff,
  Buxom and brave and stout enough,
     And full of spirit too,

175   Yet they may never seek, forsooth,
  To enterprize their lusty youth
     In labours or commands
  Which, while they leave unfetter'd course
  To native energy and force,
180   Might spoil their pretty hands!

"Nay, spoil their woman's heart," say you.
  What! Then you think it isn't true
     That every woman dims
  The moon-like lustre of her kind
185   As much by manliness of mind
     As manliness of limbs?

Or else—and this is what you mean—
  You simply seek a grander scene,
     A more sublime display,

190   For female talents of the brain:
  You strive (I hope 'tis not in vain)
     To find your sex a way

To share our honours and our fame—
  The civic or forensic name
195   On which your fancy lingers;
  But, when it comes to rough hard work,
  You will not help us with a fork—
     Much less with your white fingers.

There is a game that schoolboys use,
200   Called "Heads I win, and tails you lose";
     And this smart game of shares,
  Wherein we men are to be drudges,
  And you both *élégantes*[1] and Judges,
     Seems very much like theirs.

205   Why don't you drop it, and be frank?
  For our part, we must say point-blank,
     With much respectful moan,
  That we'll oppose you tooth and nail,
  Unless you'll swallow *all* the whale,
210   Or let the beast alone.

Either agree, you stand apart,
  As much by nature as by art,
     In power of the mind—
  In grasp of knowledge—in the right
215   Of work—in such inferior might
     As differs kind from kind;

Either confess (and Truth forbid
  We should allow it, if you did)
     That you are born to serve:
220   Slight creatures, only fit to stand
  The smaller tasks of head and hand:
     Weaklings in every nerve:

---

[1] elegant women.

Or else, take heart of grace, and say,
"You men, we'll meet you any day
225   On all the field of life;
Save only to our bounded sex
The matron care that guards and checks
    A mother, or a wife."

Since there is work for all and each,
230 Rough or refined in frame and speech,
    Rudely or gently nurst,—
Take it; and if you need defence,
Cry, *Honi soit qui mal y pense,*[1]
    And let them think their worst.

235 But don't come forth, with hand on hip
And such grand airs of championship
    To battle for your right,
And then turn round on half your troops
With these terrific howls and whoops,
240   Because they love to fight

In ways less ladylike than yours:
Don't say your Amazons[2] are boors,
    And mustn't seek to ride,
Because, when they have tighten'd girth,
245 Like half the women of the earth
    They choose to mount astride.

Don't practise, in your noble rage,
To stint an honest maiden's wage
    And dwarf her vigour too,
250 Whene'er her daily labours fall
'Mid scenes which you think bad for all,
    Because they startle *you.*

Weaklings, indeed! Yon stunted girl
Who minds the bobbins as they twirl
255   Or plies the flashing loom,

She is a weakling, if you will:
And yet, because she works on still
    Shut up inside a room,

You let her work; you don't pretend
260 That *that* degrades her in the end:
    But, if she dares to go
And brace her muscles in the fields,
Till with a sinewy arm she wields
    The hayfork or the hoe,

265 Straight you lift up your prudish eyes,
Affect a feminine surprise,
    And do your best to spoil
The hearty health, the bluff content,
That Nature's righteous self hath sent
270   To bless her sunburnt toil!

Weaklings? I chanced to be of late
Where young Tom Prentiss and his mate
    Were working side by side:
Who was his mate? A *woman*, dears!
275 A lass whom he has loved for years;
    His sweetheart, Ellen Hyde.

Ah, Ellen is a girl to see;
She has not sacrificed—not she—
    Her massive breadth of limb:
280 If any lad less kind and good
Than Tom, should happen to be rude,
    She'd make short work of him!

Yet with her strength she is most fair;
Fairest of all the women there,
285   When summer morns are rathe
She seeks her labour, and her large
Lithe form is hail'd by every barge
    That lies along the staith.

Save the red beads about her neck
290 (Tom's gift) her beauty has no speck

---

[1] literally, "evil to him who evil thinks." The motto of the "Most Noble Order of the Garter," the highest order of knighthood in Great Britain.

[2] in Greek mythology, a race of female warriors living in Scythia.

Of gawds and coquetries:
Her bonnet tilted o'er her brow
Is set there, not to guard its snow,
    But just to shade her eyes.

295 Beneath a sleeveless vest of say
Her ample shoulders freely play,
    Her bosom beats at ease;
And, veil'd by half her kilted gown,
The lindsey kirtle[1] loiters down
300   Not far below her knees.

Her hosen? Yes, their warm grey strands
Were knitted by her own true hands
    Beside the cottage fire;
And ankle-boots of size and weight,
305 Nail-studded, shoed with iron plate,
    Complete her brave attire.

Thus have I seen her ply her trade,
With Tom at hand to cheer and aid—
    Though aid she needed none:
310 Who should compare her frame with his
Might fairly doubt, if that or this
    Could better work alone:

And sometimes, when a pause was made,
Leaning on pickaxe or on spade
315   She smiled and whisper'd low,
Whilst, with long labour grown too warm
She drew her firm and freckled arm
    Across her beaded brow.

Thus too, within her mother's home
320 I've seen her frankly go and come—
    So bonny, and so tall;
And seen her sleek her chestnut hair,
And mend her things of workday wear,
    And smooth her Sunday shawl,

325 And sew, in hope of leisure hours,
Her bonnet with the wee bit flowers
    That Tom would most approve;
And in her broken looking-glass
Behold unmoved as sweet a lass
330   As man could wish to love.

Ah Virtue, what a sight was here!
A sight for those to whom is dear
    The substance, not the show:
A woman strong to dare and do,
335 Yet soft towards suffering, and true
    In welfare and in woe:

Whose woman's nature is not lost,
Nor marr'd, nor even tempest-tost,
    But strengthen'd and controll'd:
340 Who, working thus with sinewy hands,
Grows deaf to Folly's fond commands,
    Grows calm and solemn-soul'd.

Yes, ladies of the Yankee creed,[2]
We scruple not to see you bleed—
345   With lancets—if you will,
Or show the pulpit and the bar
How worthy of ourselves you are
    In subtlety and skill;

But, leave your stronger mates alone:
350 They, tense of thews and stout of bone,
    Rejoice to work amain;
And so they shall, in breadth and length:
As free to use their woman's strength
    As you your woman's brain.
—1865

---

[1] "Kilted" means "tucked up"; "kirtle" is a woman's gown or outer petticoat. The term was archaic in the nineteenth century.

[2] Yankee refers to a citizen of the U.S.A.; to be precise, of New England.

Elizabeth Siddal
1829 – 1862

Elizabeth Siddal met one of the young Pre-Raphaelites, Walter Deverell, when she was working in a milliner's shop near Leicester Square in London when she was about twenty. Attracted by her unusual beauty, Deverell asked her to model for one of his pictures. She later modelled for Holman Hunt, Dante Gabriel Rossetti, and Millais— for whom she posed, in one of the most popular of Victorian depictions, as the drowned Ophelia (in a bath of cooling water, as a result of which she caught a bad cold). In 1852 she became exclusively Rossetti's model; they were married in May 1860. On 10 February, 1862, she took an overdose of laudanum, whether accidentally or intentionally, and died the next morning. Her poems invite interesting comparison with the lyrics of Christina Rossetti.

❦

The Lust of the Eyes

I care not for my Lady's soul
    Though I worship before her smile;
I care not where be my Lady's goal
    When her beauty shall lose its wile.

5 Low sit I down at my Lady's feet
    Gazing through her wild eyes
Smiling to think how my love will fleet
    When their starlike beauty dies.

I care not if my Lady pray
10   To our Father which is in Heaven
But for joy my heart's quick pulses play
    For to me her love is given.

Then who shall close my Lady's eyes
    And who shall fold her hands?
15 Will any hearken if she cries
    Up to the unknown lands?
    —1899

Worn Out

Thy strong arms are around me, love,
    My head is on thy breast:

Though words of comfort come from thee,
    My soul is not at rest:

5 For I am but a startled thing,
    Nor can I ever be
Aught save a bird whose broken wing
    Must fly away from thee.

I cannot give to thee the love
10   I gave so long ago—
The love that turned and struck me down
    Amid the blinding snow.

I can but give a sinking heart
    And weary eyes of pain,
15 A faded mouth that cannot smile
    And may not laugh again.

Yet keep thine arms around me, love,
    Until I drop to sleep:
Then leave me—saying no good-bye,
20   Lest I might fall and weep.
    —1899 (1856)

At Last

O mother, open the window wide
 And let the daylight in;
The hills grow darker to my sight
 And thoughts begin to swim.

5 And mother dear, take my young son,
 (Since I was born of thee)
And care for all his little ways
 And nurse him on thy knee.

And mother, wash my pale pale hands
10 And then bind up my feet;
My body may no longer rest
 Out of its winding sheet.

And mother dear, take a sapling twig
 And green grass newly mown,
15 And lay them on my empty bed
 That my sorrow be not known.

And mother, find three berries red
 And pluck them from the stalk,
And burn them at the first cockcrow
20 That my spirit may not walk.

And mother dear, break a willow wand,
 And if the sap be even,
Then save it for sweet Robert's sake
 And he'll know my soul's in heaven.

25 And mother, when the big tears fall,
 (And fall, God knows, they may)
Tell him I died of my great love
 And my dying heart was gay.

And mother dear, when the sun has set
30 And the pale kirk grass waves,
Then carry me through the dim twilight
 And hide me among the graves.
—1899 (1861)

Love and Hate

O pe not thy lips, thou foolish one,
 Nor turn to me thy face:
The blasts of heaven shall strike me down
 Ere I will give thee grace.

5 Take thou thy shadow from my path,
 Nor turn to me and pray:
The wild, wild winds thy dirge may sing
 Ere I will bid thee stay.

Lift up thy false brow from the dust,
10 Nor wild thine hands entwine
Among the golden summer-leaves
 To mock the gay sunshine.

And turn away thy false dark eyes,
 Nor gaze into my face:
15 Great love I bore thee; now great hate
 Sits grimly in its place.

All changes pass me like a dream,
 I neither sing nor pray;
And thou art like the poisonous tree
20 That stole my life away.
—1906 (1857)

Christina Rossetti
1830 – 1894

The youngest child in the Rossetti family, Christina Georgina Rossetti was educated at home, in an environment where the men were political, academic, and artistic, and the women were intensely religious. Her father, Gabriele, was an Italian political refugee; her brothers were the poet, painter, and critic, Dante Gabriel, and the critic, William Michael; her sister, Maria Francesca, was a nun. Christina herself was a devout Anglo-Catholic, influenced by the Oxford Movement which attempted to bring early Catholic doctrines and rites into the Anglican church. Associated with the Pre-Raphaelite Brotherhood, Christina contributed to its journal, *The Germ*, and published works which reflected both her devout religiosity and the artistic and poetic influences of the PRB. Gaining immediate recognition with *Goblin Market and Other Poems* (1862) and continued praise with *The Prince's Progress and Other Poems* (1866), Rossetti's works are distinctive in their remarkably simple diction and beautiful, languid imagery.

༄

Goblin Market

Morning and evening
Maids heard the goblins cry:
"Come buy our orchard fruits,
Come buy, come buy:
5   Apples and quinces,
Lemons and oranges,
Plump unpecked cherries,
Melons and raspberries,
Bloom-down-cheeked peaches,
10 Swart-headed mulberries,
Wild free-born cranberries,
Crab-apples, dewberries,
Pine-apples, blackberries,
Apricots, strawberries;—
15 All ripe together
In summer weather,—
Morns that pass by,
Fair eves that fly;
Come buy, come buy:
20 Our grapes fresh from the vine,
Pomegranates full and fine,
Dates and sharp bullaces,
Rare pears and greengages,
Damsons[1] and bilberries,
25 Taste them and try:
Currants and gooseberries,
Bright-fire-like barberries,
Figs to fill your mouth,
Citrons from the South,
30 Sweet to tongue and sound to eye;
Come buy, come buy."

Evening by evening
Among the brookside rushes,
Laura bowed her head to hear,
35 Lizzie veiled her blushes:
Crouching close together
In the cooling weather,
With clasping arms and cautioning lips,
With tingling cheeks and finger tips.
40 "Lie close," Laura said,
Pricking up her golden head:
"We must not look at goblin men,
We must not buy their fruits:
Who knows upon what soil they fed
45 Their hungry thirsty roots?"
"Come buy," call the goblins

---

[1] a variety of plum, as are bullaces and greengages.

Hobbling down the glen.
"Oh," cried Lizzie, "Laura, Laura,
You should not peep at goblin men."
50 Lizzie covered up her eyes,
Covered close lest they should look;
Laura reared her glossy head,
And whispered like the restless brook:
"Look, Lizzie, look, Lizzie,
55 Down the glen tramp little men.
One hauls a basket,
One bears a plate,
One lugs a golden dish
Of many pounds' weight.
60 How fair the vine must grow
Whose grapes are so luscious;
How warm the wind must blow
Through those fruit bushes."
"No," said Lizzie: "No, no, no;
65 Their offers should not charm us,
Their evil gifts would harm us."
She thrust a dimpled finger
In each ear, shut eyes and ran:
Curious Laura chose to linger
70 Wondering at each merchant man.
One had a cat's face,
One whisked a tail,
One tramped at a rat's pace,
One crawled like a snail,
75 One like a wombat prowled obtuse and furry,
One like a ratel[1] tumbled hurry skurry.
She heard a voice like voice of doves
Cooing all together:
They sounded kind and full of loves
80 In the pleasant weather.

Laura stretched her gleaming neck
Like a rush-imbedded swan,
Like a lily from the beck,[2]

Like a moonlit poplar branch,
85 Like a vessel at the launch
When its last restraint is gone.

Backwards up the mossy glen
Turned and trooped the goblin men,
With their shrill repeated cry,
90 "Come buy, come buy."
When they reached where Laura was
They stood stock still upon the moss,
Leering at each other,
Brother with queer brother;
95 Signalling each other,
Brother with sly brother.
One set his basket down,
One reared his plate;
One began to weave a crown
100 Of tendrils, leaves, and rough nuts brown
(Men sell not such in any town);
One heaved the golden weight
Of dish and fruit to offer her:
"Come buy, come buy," was still their cry.

105 Laura stared but did not stir,
Longed but had no money.
The whisk-tailed merchant bade her taste
In tones as smooth as honey,
The cat-faced purr'd,
110 The rat-paced spoke a word
Of welcome, and the snail-paced even was heard;
One parrot-voiced and jolly
Cried "Pretty Goblin" still for "Pretty Polly";
One whistled like a bird.

115 But sweet-tooth Laura spoke in haste:
"Good Folk, I have no coin;
To take were to purloin:
I have no copper in my purse,
I have no silver either,

---

[1] South African animal, much like a badger.

[2] small brook.

120 And all my gold is on the furze[1]
That shakes in windy weather
Above the rusty heather."
"You have much gold upon your head,"
They answered all together:
125 "Buy from us with a golden curl."
She clipped a precious golden lock,
She dropped a tear more rare than pearl,
Then sucked their fruit globes fair or red.
Sweeter than honey from the rock,
130 Stronger than man-rejoicing wine,
Clearer than water flowed that juice;
She never tasted such before,
How should it cloy with length of use?
She sucked and sucked and sucked the more
135 Fruits which that unknown orchard bore;
She sucked until her lips were sore;
Then flung the emptied rinds away
But gathered up one kernel stone,
And knew not was it night or day
140 As she turned home alone.

Lizzie met her at the gate
Full of wise upbraidings:
"Dear, you should not stay so late,
Twilight is not good for maidens;
145 Should not loiter in the glen
In the haunts of goblin men.
Do you not remember Jeanie,
How she met them in the moonlight,
Took their gifts both choice and many,
150 Ate their fruits and wore their flowers
Plucked from bowers
Where summer ripens at all hours?
But ever in the noonlight
She pined and pined away;
155 Sought them by night and day,
Found them no more but dwindled and grew grey;
Then fell with the first snow,

While to this day no grass will grow
Where she lies low:
160 I planted daisies there a year ago
That never blow.
You should not loiter so."
"Nay, hush," said Laura:
"Nay, hush, my sister:
165 I ate and ate my fill,
Yet my mouth waters still;
Tomorrow night I will
Buy more:" and kissed her:
"Have done with sorrow;
170 I'll bring you plums tomorrow
Fresh on their mother twigs,
Cherries worth getting;
You cannot think what figs
My teeth have met in,
175 What melons icy-cold
Piled on a dish of gold
Too huge for me to hold,
What peaches with a velvet nap,
Pellucid[2] grapes without one seed:
180 Odorous indeed must be the mead
Whereon they grow, and pure the wave they drink
With lilies at the brink,
And sugar-sweet their sap."

Golden head by golden head,
185 Like two pigeons in one nest
Folded in each other's wings,
They lay down in their curtained bed:
Like two blossoms on one stem,
Like two flakes of new-fall'n snow,
190 Like two wands of ivory
Tipped with gold for awful kings.
Moon and stars gazed in at them,
Wind sang to them lullaby,
Lumbering owls forbore to fly,
195 Not a bat flapped to and fro

---

[1] a prickly evergreen shrub with dark-green spines and yellow flowers.

[2] translucent.

Round their nest:
Cheek to cheek and breast to breast
Locked together in one nest.

Early in the morning
200 When the first cock crowed his warning,
Neat like bees, as sweet and busy,
Laura rose with Lizzie:
Fetched in honey, milked the cows,
Aired and set to rights the house,
205 Kneaded cakes of whitest wheat,
Cakes for dainty mouths to eat,
Next churned butter, whipped up cream,
Fed their poultry, sat and sewed;
Talked as modest maidens should:
210 Lizzie with an open heart,
Laura in an absent dream,
One content, one sick in part;
One warbling for the mere bright day's delight,
One longing for the night.

215 At length slow evening came:
They went with pitchers to the reedy brooks;
Lizzie most placid in her look,
Laura most like a leaping flame.
They drew the gurgling water from its deep.
220 Lizzie plucked purple and rich golden flags,
Then turning homeward said: "The sunset flushes
Those furthest loftiest crags;
Come Laura, not another maiden lags.
No wilful squirrel wags,
225 The beasts and birds are fast asleep."
But Laura loitered still among the rushes,
And said the bank was steep.

And said the hour was early still,
The dew not fall'n, the wind not chill;
230 Listening ever, but not catching
The customary cry,
"Come buy, come buy,"
With its iterated jingle

Of sugar-baited words:
235 Not for all her watching
Once discerning even one goblin
Racing, whisking, tumbling, hobbling—
Let alone the herds
That used to tramp along the glen,
240 In groups or single,
Of brisk fruit-merchant men.

Till Lizzie urged, "O Laura, come;
I hear the fruit-call, but I dare not look:
You should not loiter longer at this brook:
245 Come with me home.
The stars rise, the moon bends her arc,
Each glow-worm winks her spark,
Let us get home before the night grows dark:
For clouds may gather
250 Though this is summer weather,
Put out the lights and drench us through;
Then if we lost our way what should we do?"

Laura turned cold as stone
To find her sister heard that cry alone,
255 That goblin cry,
"Come buy our fruits, come buy."
Must she then buy no more such dainty fruit?
Must she no more such succous[1] pasture find,
Gone deaf and blind?
260 Her tree of life drooped from the root:
She said not one word in her heart's sore ache:
But peering thro' the dimness, nought discerning,
Trudged home, her pitcher dripping all the way;
So crept to bed, and lay
265 Silent till Lizzie slept;
Then sat up in a passionate yearning,
And gnashed her teeth for baulked desire, and wept
As if her heart would break.

---

[1] succulent.

Day after day, night after night,
270 Laura kept watch in vain
In sullen silence of exceeding pain.
She never caught again the goblin cry,
"Come buy, come buy;"—
She never spied the goblin men
275 Hawking their fruits along the glen:
But when the noon waxed bright
Her hair grew thin and grey;
She dwindled, as the fair full moon doth turn
To swift decay and burn
280 Her fire away.

One day remembering her kernel-stone
She set it by a wall that faced the south;
Dewed it with tears, hoped for a root,
Watched for a waxing shoot,
285 But there came none.
It never saw the sun,
It never felt the trickling moisture run:
While with sunk eyes and faded mouth
She dreamed of melons, as a traveller sees
290 False waves in desert drouth
With shade of leaf-crowned trees,
And burns the thirstier in the sandful breeze.

She no more swept the house,
Tended the fowl or cows,
295 Fetched honey, kneaded cakes of wheat,
Brought water from the brook:
But sat down listless in the chimney-nook
And would not eat.

Tender Lizzie could not bear
300 To watch her sister's cankerous care,
Yet not to share.
She night and morning
Caught the goblins' cry:
"Come buy our orchard fruits,
305 Come buy, come buy;"—
Beside the brook, along the glen,

She heard the tramp of goblin men,
The voice and stir
Poor Laura could not hear;
310 Longed to buy fruit to comfort her,
But feared to pay too dear.
She thought of Jeanie in her grave,
Who should have been a bride;
But who for joys brides hope to have
315 Fell sick and died
In her gay prime,
In earliest winter time,
With the first glazing rime,
With the first snow-fall of crisp winter time.

320 Till Laura dwindling
Seemed knocking at Death's door.
Then Lizzie weighed no more
Better and worse;
But put a silver penny in her purse,
325 Kissed Laura, crossed the heath with clumps of furze
At twilight, halted by the brook:
And for the first time in her life
Began to listen and look.

Laughed every goblin
330 When they spied her peeping:
Came towards her hobbling,
Flying, running, leaping,
Puffing and blowing,
Chuckling, clapping, crowing.

335 Clucking and gobbling,
Mopping and mowing,
Full of airs and graces,
Pulling wry faces,
Demure grimaces,
340 Cat-like and rat-like,
Ratel- and wombat-like,
Snail-paced in a hurry,
Parrot-voiced and whistler,
Helter skelter, hurry skurry,

345 Chattering like magpies,
Fluttering like pigeons,
Gliding like fishes,—
Hugged her and kissed her:
Squeezed and caressed her:
350 Stretched up their dishes,
Panniers,[1] and plates:
"Look at our apples
Russet and dun,
Bob at our cherries,
355 Bite at our peaches,
Citrons and dates,
Grapes for the asking,
Pears red with basking
Out in the sun,
360 Plums on their twigs;
Pluck them and suck them,—
Pomegranates, figs."

"Good folk," said Lizzie,
Mindful of Jeanie:
365 "Give me much and many:"
Held out her apron,
Tossed them her penny.
"Nay, take a seat with us,
Honour and eat with us,"
370 They answered grinning:
"Our feast is but beginning.
Night yet is early,
Warm and dew-pearly,
Wakeful and starry:
375 Such fruits as these
No man can carry;
Half their bloom would fly,
Half their dew would dry,
Half their flavour would pass by.
380 Sit down and feast with us,
Be welcome guest with us,
Cheer you and rest with us."—

"Thank you," said Lizzie: "But one waits
At home alone for me:
385 So without further parleying,
If you will not sell me any
Of your fruits though much and many,
Give me back my silver penny
I tossed you for a fee."—
390 They began to scratch their pates,
No longer wagging, purring,
But visibly demurring,
Grunting and snarling.
One called her proud,
395 Cross-grained, uncivil;
Their tones waxed loud,
Their looks were evil.
Lashing their tails
They trod and hustled her,
400 Elbowed and jostled her,
Clawed with their nails,
Barking, mewing, hissing, mocking,
Tore her gown and soiled her stocking,
Twitched her hair out by the roots,
405 Stamped upon her tender feet,
Held her hands and squeezed their fruits
Against her mouth to make her eat.

White and golden Lizzie stood,
Like a lily in a flood,—
410 Like a rock of blue-veined stone
Lashed by tides obstreperously,—
Like a beacon left alone
In a hoary roaring sea,
Sending up a golden fire,—
415 Like a fruit-crowned orange-tree
White with blossoms honey-sweet
Sore beset by wasp and bee,—
Like a royal virgin town
Topped with gilded dome and spire
420 Close beleaguered by a fleet
Mad to tug her standard down.

---

[1] large wicker baskets.

One may lead a horse to water,
Twenty cannot make him drink.
Though the goblins cuffed and caught her,
425 Coaxed and fought her,
Bullied and besought her,
Scratched her, pinched her black as ink,
Kicked and knocked her,
Mauled and mocked her,
430 Lizzie uttered not a word;
Would not open lip from lip
Lest they should cram a mouthful in:
But laughed in heart to feel the drip
Of juice that syruped all her face,
435 And lodged in dimples of her chin,
And streaked her neck which quaked like curd.
At last the evil people,
Worn out by her resistance,
Flung back her penny, kicked their fruit
440 Along whichever road they took,
Not leaving root or stone or shoot;
Some writhed into the ground,
Some dived into the brook
With ring and ripple,
445 Some scudded on the gale without a sound,
Some vanished in the distance.

In a smart, ache, tingle,
Lizzie went her way;
Knew not was it night or day;
450 Sprang up the bank, tore thro' the furze,
Threaded copse and dingle,
And heard her penny jingle
Bouncing in her purse,—
Its bounce was music to her ear.
455 She ran and ran
As if she feared some goblin man
Dogged her with gibe or curse
Or something worse:
But not one goblin skurried after,
460 Nor was she pricked by fear;
The kind heart made her windy-paced

That urged her home quite out of breath with haste
And inward laughter.

She cried, "Laura," up the garden,
465 "Did you miss me?
Come and kiss me.
Never mind my bruises,
Hug me, kiss me, suck my juices
Squeezed from goblin fruits for you,
470 Goblin pulp and goblin dew.
Eat me, drink me, love me;
Laura, make much of me;
For your sake I have braved the glen
And had to do with goblin merchant men."

475 Laura started from her chair,
Flung her arms up in the air,
Clutched her hair:
"Lizzie, Lizzie, have you tasted
For my sake the fruit forbidden?
480 Must your light like mine be hidden,
Your young life like mine be wasted,
Undone in mine undoing,
And ruined in my ruin,
Thirsty, cankered, goblin-ridden?"—
485 She clung about her sister,
Kissed and kissed and kissed her:
Tears once again
Refreshed her shrunken eyes,
Dropping like rain
490 After long sultry drouth;
Shaking with aguish fear, and pain,
She kissed and kissed her with a hungry mouth.

Her lips began to scorch,
That juice was wormwood to her tongue,
495 She loathed the feast:
Writhing as one possessed she leaped and sung,
Rent all her robe, and wrung
Her hands in lamentable haste,
And beat her breast.

500 Her locks streamed like the torch
Borne by a racer at full speed,
Or like the mane of horses in their flight,
Or like an eagle when she stems[1] the light
Straight toward the sun,
505 Or like a caged thing freed,
Or like a flying flag when armies run.

Swift fire spread through her veins, knocked at her
heart,
Met the fire smouldering there
510 And overbore its lesser flame;
She gorged on bitterness without a name:
Ah fool, to choose such part
510 Of soul-consuming care!
Sense failed in the mortal strife:
Like the watch-tower of a town
Which an earthquake shatters down,
Like a lightning-stricken mast,
515 Like a wind-uprooted tree
Spun about,
Like a foam-topped waterspout
Cast down headlong in the sea,
She fell at last;
520 Pleasure past and anguish past,
Is it death or is it life?

Life out of death.
That night long Lizzie watched by her,
Counted her pulse's flagging stir,
525 Felt for her breath,
Held water to her lips, and cooled her face
With tears and fanning leaves.
But when the first birds chirped about their eaves,
And early reapers plodded to the place
530 Of golden sheaves,
And dew-wet grass
Bowed in the morning winds so brisk to pass,
And new buds with new day
Opened of cup-like lilies on the stream,

535 Laura awoke as from a dream,
Laughed in the innocent old way,
Hugged Lizzie but not twice or thrice;
Her gleaming locks showed not one thread of grey,
Her breath was sweet as May,
540 And light danced in her eyes.

Days, weeks, months, years
Afterwards, when both were wives
With children of their own;
Their mother-hearts beset with fears,
545 Their lives bound up in tender lives;
Laura would call the little ones
And tell them of her early prime,
Those pleasant days long gone
Of not-returning time:
550 Would talk about the haunted glen,
The wicked quaint fruit-merchant men,
Their fruits like honey to the throat
But poison in the blood
(Men sell not such in any town):
555 Would tell them how her sister stood
In deadly peril to do her good,
And win the fiery antidote:
Then joining hands to little hands
Would bid them cling together,—
560 "For there is no friend like a sister
In calm or stormy weather;
To cheer one on the tedious way,
To fetch one if one goes astray,
To lift one if one totters down,
565 To strengthen whilst one stands."
—1862 (APRIL 27, 1859)

A Birthday

My heart is like a singing bird
Whose nest is in a watered shoot:
My heart is like an apple tree
Whose boughs are bent with thickset fruit;
5 My heart is like a rainbow shell

---
[1] makes headway against.

That paddles in a halcyon[1] sea;
My heart is gladder than all these
   Because my love is come to me.

Raise me a dais of silk and down;
10   Hang it with vair[2] and purple dyes;
Carve it in doves and pomegranates,
   And peacocks with a hundred eyes;
Work it in gold and silver grapes,
   In leaves and silver fleurs-de-lys;
15 Because the birthday of my life
   Is come, my love is come to me.
—1862

After Death

The curtains were half drawn; the floor was
      swept
   And strewn with rushes; rosemary and may[3]
Lay thick upon the bed on which I lay,
Where, through the lattice, ivy-shadows crept.
5 He leaned above me, thinking that I slept
   And could not hear him; but I heard him say,
   "Poor child, poor child"; and as he turned away
Came a deep silence, and I knew he wept.
He did not touch the shroud, or raise the fold
10   That hid my face, or take my hand in his,
      Or ruffle the smooth pillows for my head.
      He did not love me living; but once dead
   He pitied me; and very sweet it is
To know he still is warm though I am cold.
—1862

An Apple Gathering

I plucked pink blossoms from mine apple tree
   And wore them all that evening in my hair:
Then in due season when I went to see
   I found no apples there.

5 With dangling basket all along the grass
   As I had come I went the selfsame track:
My neighbors mocked me while they saw me pass
   So empty-handed back.

Lilian and Lilias smiled in trudging by,
10   Their heaped-up basket teased me like a jeer;
Sweet-voiced they sang beneath the sunset sky,
   Their mother's home was near.

Plump Gertrude passed me with her basket full,
   A stronger hand than hers helped it along;
15 A voice talked with her through the shadows cool
   More sweet to me than song.

Ah Willie, Willie, was my love less worth
   Than apples with their green leaves piled above?
I counted rosiest apples on the earth
20   Of far less worth than love.

So once it was with me you stooped to talk
   Laughing and listening in this very lane;
To think that by this way we used to walk
   We shall not walk again!

25 I let my neighbors pass me, ones and twos
   And groups; the latest said the night grew chill,
And hastened: but I loitered; while the dews
   Fell fast I loitered still.
—1862

---

[1] tranquil.

[2] a kind of squirrel fur, bluish-grey and white, represented heraldically by rows of blue and white shields or bells.

[3] hawthorn flowers.

Echo [1]

Come to me in the silence of the night;
  Come in the speaking silence of a dream;
Come with soft rounded cheeks and eyes as bright
    As sunlight on a stream;
5   Come back in tears,
O memory, hope, love of finished years.

Oh dream how sweet, too sweet, too bitter sweet,
  Whose wakening should have been in Paradise,
Where souls brimfull of love abide and meet;
10   Where thirsting longing eyes
      Watch the slow door
That opening, letting in, lets out no more.

Yet come to me in dreams, that I may live
  My very life again tho' cold in death:
15 Come back to me in dreams, that I may give
    Pulse for pulse, breath for breath:
      Speak low, lean low,
As long ago, my love, how long ago.
—1862

"No, Thank you, John"

I never said I loved you, John:
  Why will you teaze me day by day,
And wax a weariness to think upon
    With always "do" and "pray"?

5 You know I never loved you, John;
    No fault of mine made me your toast:
Why will you haunt me with a face as wan
    As shows an hour-old ghost?

I dare say Meg or Moll would take
10   Pity upon you, if you'd ask:

And pray don't remain single for my sake
  Who can't perform that task.

I have no heart?—Perhaps I have not;
  But then you're mad to take offence
15 That I don't give you what I have not got:
  Use your own common sense.

Let bygones be bygones:
  Don't call me false, who owed not to be true:
I'd rather answer "No" to fifty Johns
20   Than answer "Yes" to you.

Let's mar our pleasant days no more,
  Song-birds of passage, days of youth:
Catch at today, forget the days before:
  I'll wink at your untruth.

25 Let us strike hands as hearty friends;
  No more, no less; and friendship's good:
Only don't keep in view ulterior ends,
  And points not understood

In open treaty. Rise above
30   Quibbles and shuffling off and on:
Here's friendship for you if you like; but love,—
  No, thank you, John.
—1862

Song

When I am dead, my dearest,
  Sing no sad songs for me;
Plant thou no roses at my head,
  Nor shady cypress tree.
5 Be the green grass above me
  With showers and dewdrops wet;
And if thou wilt, remember,
  And if thou wilt, forget.

---

[1] the nymph who, because of her unrequited lover for Narcissus, pined away until only her voice remained.

I shall not see the shadows,
10   I shall not feel the rain;
I shall not hear the nightingale
    Sing on as if in pain.[1]
And dreaming through the twilight
    That doth not rise nor set,
15 Haply I may remember,
    And haply may forget.
—1862

Uphill

Does the road wind uphill all the way?
    Yes, to the very end.
Will the day's journey take the whole long day?
    From morn to night, my friend.

5 But is there for the night a resting place?
    A roof for when the slow dark hours begin.
May not the darkness hide it from my face?
    You cannot miss that inn.

Shall I meet other wayfarers at night?
10   Those who have gone before.
Then must I knock, or call when just in sight?
    They will not keep you standing at that door.

Shall I find comfort, travel-sore and weak?
    Of labor you shall find the sum.
15 Will there be beds for me and all who seek?
    Yea, beds for all who come.
—1862

---

[1] Tereus, a Thracian king, husband of Procne, fell in love with and raped Philomela, Procne's sister. To conceal his conduct he cut out her tongue. But Philomela communicated with Procne via a piece of embroidery. Procne killed the king's son Itys, and the two sisters fled. As a result of their prayer to the gods to be changed into birds, Philomela became a nightingale and Procne a swallow.

A Better Resurrection

I have no wit, no words, no tears;
  My heart within me like a stone
Is numbed too much for hopes or fears;
    Look right, look left, I dwell alone;
5 I lift mine eyes, but dimmed with grief
    No everlasting hills I see;
My life is in the falling leaf:
    O Jesus, quicken me.

My life is like a faded leaf,
10   My harvest dwindled to a husk;
Truly my life is void and brief
    And tedious in the barren dusk;
My life is like a frozen thing,
    No bud nor greenness can I see:
15 Yet rise it shall—the sap of Spring;
    O Jesus, rise in me.

My life is like a broken bowl,
    A broken bowl that cannot hold
One drop of water for my soul
    Or cordial in the searching cold;
20 Cast in the fire the perished thing,
    Melt and remould it, till it be
A royal cup for Him my King:
    O Jesus, drink of me.
—1862

"The Iniquity of the Fathers Upon the Children"

Oh the rose of keenest thorn!
One hidden summer morn
Under the rose I was born.

I do not guess his name
5 Who wrought my Mother's shame,
And gave me life forlorn,

But my Mother, Mother, Mother,
I know her from all other.
My Mother pale and mild,
10 Fair as ever was seen,
She was but scarce sixteen,
Little more than a child,
When I was born
To work her scorn.
15 With secret bitter throes,
In a passion of secret woes,
She bore me under the rose.

One who my Mother nursed
Took me from the first:—
20 "O nurse, let me look upon
This babe that costs so dear;
Tomorrow she will be gone:
Other mothers may keep
Their babes awake and asleep,
25 But I must not keep her here."—
Whether I know or guess,
I know this not the less.

So I was sent away
That none might spy the truth:
30 And my childhood waxed to youth
And I left off childish play.
I never cared to play
With the village boys and girls;
And I think they thought me proud,
35 I found so little to say
And kept so from the crowd:
But I had the longest curls
And I had the largest eyes,
And my teeth were small like pearls;
40 The girls might flout and scout me,
But the boys would hang about me
In sheepish mooning wise.

Our one-street village stood
A long mile from the town,

45 A mile of windy down
And bleak one-sided wood,
With not a single house.
Our town itself was small,
With just the common shops,
50 And throve in its small way.
Our neighbouring gentry reared
The good old-fashioned crops,
And made old-fashioned boasts
Of what John Bull would do
55 If Frenchman Frog appeared,
And drank old-fashioned toasts,
And made old-fashioned bows
To my Lady at the Hall.

My Lady at the Hall
60 Is grander than they all:
Hers is the oldest name
In all the neighbourhood;
But the race must die with her
Tho' she's a lofty dame,
65 For she's unmarried still.

Poor people say she's good
And has an open hand
As any in the land,
And she's the comforter
70 Of many sick and sad;
My nurse once said to me
That everything she had
Came of my Lady's bounty:
"Tho' she's greatest in the county
75 She's humble to the poor,
No beggar seeks her door
But finds help presently.
I pray both night and day
For her, and you must pray:
80 But she'll never feel distress
If needy folk can bless."

I was a little maid
When here we came to live
From somewhere by the sea.
85 Men spoke a foreign tongue
There where we used to be
When I was merry and young,
Too young to feel afraid;
The fisher-folk would give
90 A kind strange word to me,
There by the foreign sea:
I don't know where it was,
But I remember still
Our cottage on a hill,
95 And fields of flowering grass
On that fair foreign shore.

I like my old home best,
But this was pleasant too:
So here we made our nest
100 And here I grew.
And now and then my Lady
In riding past our door
Would nod to Nurse and speak,
Or stoop and pat my cheek;
105 And I was always ready
To hold the field-gate wide
For my Lady to go thro';
My Lady in her veil
So seldom put aside,
110 My Lady grave and pale.

I often sat to wonder
Who might my parents be,
For I knew of something under
My simple-seeming state.
115 Nurse never talked to me
Of mother or of father,
But watched me early and late
With kind suspicious cares:
Or not suspicious, rather
120 Anxious, as if she knew

Some secret I might gather
And smart for unawares.
Thus I grew.

But Nurse waxed old and grey,
125 Bent and weak with years.
There came a certain day
That she lay upon her bed
Shaking her palsied head,
With words she gasped to say
130 Which had to stay unsaid.
Then with a jerking hand
Held out so piteously
She gave a ring to me
Of gold wrought curiously,
135 A ring which she had worn
Since the day that I was born,
She once had said to me:
I slipped it on my finger;
Her eyes were keen to linger
140 On my hand that slipped it on;
Then she sighed one rattling sigh
And stared on with sightless eyes:—
The one who loved me was gone.

How long I stayed alone
145 With the corpse, I never knew,
For I fainted dead as stone:
When I came to life once more
I was down upon the floor,
With neighbours making ado
150 To bring me back to life.
I heard the sexton's wife
Say: "Up, my lad, and run
To tell it at the Hall;
She was my Lady's nurse,
155 And done can't be undone.
I'll watch by this poor lamb.
I guess my Lady's purse
Is always open to such:
I'd run up on my crutch

160   A cripple as I am,"
(For cramps had vexed her much)
"Rather than this dear heart
Lack one to take her part."

For days day after day
165   On my weary bed I lay
Wishing the time would pass;
Oh, so wishing that I was
Likely to pass away:
For the one friend whom I knew
170   Was dead, I knew no other,
Neither father nor mother;
And I, what should I do?

One day the sexton's wife
Said: "Rouse yourself, my dear:
175   My Lady has driven down
From the Hall into the town,
And we think she's coming here.
Cheer up, for life is life."

But I would not look or speak,
180   Would not cheer up at all.
My tears were like to fall,
So I turned round to the wall
And hid my hollow cheek
Making as if I slept,
185   As silent as a stone,
And no one knew I wept.
What was my Lady to me,
The grand lady from the Hall?
She might come, or stay away,
190   I was sick at heart that day:
The whole world seemed to be
Nothing, just nothing to me,
For aught that I could see.

Yet I listened where I lay:
195   A bustle came below,
A clear voice said: "I know;

I will see her first alone,
It may be less of a shock
If she's so weak today:"—
200   A light hand turned the lock,
A light step crossed the floor,
One sat beside my bed:
But never a word she said.

For me, my shyness grew
205   Each moment more and more:
So I said never a word
And neither looked nor stirred;
I think she must have heard
My heart go pit-a-pat:
210   Thus I lay, my Lady sat,
More than a mortal hour—
(I counted one and two
By the house-clock while I lay):
I seemed to have no power
215   To think of a thing to say,
Or do what I ought to do,
Or rouse myself to a choice.

At last she said: "Margaret,
Won't you even look at me?"
220   A something in her voice
Forced my tears to fall at last,
Forced sobs from me thick and fast;
Something not of the past,
Yet stirring memory;
225   A something new, and yet
Not new, too sweet to last,
Which I never can forget.

I turned and stared at her:
Her cheek showed hollow-pale;
230   Her hair like mine was fair,
A wonderful fall of hair
That screened her like a veil;
But her height was statelier,
Her eyes had depth more deep;

235 I think they must have had
Always a something sad,
Unless they were asleep.

While I stared, my Lady took
My hand in her spare hand
240 Jewelled and soft and grand,
And looked with a long long look
Of hunger in my face;
As if she tried to trace
Features she ought to know,
245 And half hoped, half feared, to find.
Whatever was in her mind
She heaved a sigh at last,
And began to talk to me.

"Your nurse was my dear nurse,
250 And her nursling's dear," said she:
"No one told me a word
Of her getting worse and worse,
Till her poor life was past"
(Here my Lady's tears dropped fast):
255 "I might have been with her,
I might have promised and heard,
But she had no comforter.
She might have told me much
Which now I shall never know,
260 Never never shall know."
She sat by me sobbing so,
And seemed so woe-begone,
That I laid one hand upon
Hers with a timid touch,
265 Scarce thinking what I did,
Not knowing what to say:
That moment her face was hid
In the pillow close by mine,
Her arm was flung over me,
270 She hugged me, sobbing so
As if her heart would break,
And kissed me where I lay.

After this she often came
To bring me fruit or wine,
275 Or sometimes hothouse flowers.
And at nights I lay awake
Often and often thinking
What to do for her sake.
Wet or dry it was the same:
280 She would come in at all hours,
Set me eating and drinking
And say I must grow strong;
At last the day seemed long
And home seemed scarcely home
285 If she did not come.

Well, I grew strong again:
In time of primroses,
I went to pluck them in the lane;
In time of nestling birds,
290 I heard them chirping round the house;
And all the herds
Were out at grass when I grew strong,
And days were waxen long,
And there was work for bees
295 Among the May-bush boughs,
And I had shot up tall,
And life felt after all
Pleasant, and not so long
When I grew strong.

300 I was going to the Hall
To be my Lady's maid:
"Her little friend," she said to me,
"Almost her child,"
She said and smiled
305 Sighing painfully;
Blushing, with a second flush
As if she blushed to blush.

Friend, servant, child: just this
My standing at the Hall;
310 The other servants call me "Miss,"

My Lady calls me "Margaret,"
With her clear voice musical.
She never chides when I forget
This or that; she never chides.
315 Except when people come to stay,
(And that's not often) at the Hall,
I sit with her all day
And ride out when she rides.
She sings to me and makes me sing;
320 Sometimes I read to her,
Sometimes we merely sit and talk.
She noticed once my ring
And made me tell its history:
That evening in our garden walk
325 She said she should infer
The ring had been my father's first,
Then my mother's, given for me
To the nurse who nursed
My mother in her misery,
330 That so quite certainly
Some one might know me, who…
Then she was silent, and I too.

I hate when people come:
The women speak and stare
335 And mean to be so civil.
This one will stroke my hair,
That one will pat my cheek
And praise my Lady's kindness,
Expecting me to speak;
340 I like the proud ones best
Who sit as struck with blindness,
As if I wasn't there.
But if any gentleman
Is staying at the Hall
345 (Tho' few come prying here),
My Lady seems to fear
Some downright dreadful evil,
And makes me keep my room
As closely as she can:
350 So I hate when people come,

It is so troublesome.
In spite of all her care,
Sometimes to keep alive
I sometimes do contrive
355 To get out in the grounds
For a whiff of wholesome air,
Under the rose you know:
It's charming to break bounds,
Stolen waters are sweet,
360 And what's the good of feet
If for days they mustn't go?
Give me a longer tether,
Or I may break from it.

Now I have eyes and ears
365 And just some little wit:
"Almost my Lady's child;"
I recollect she smiled,
Sighed and blushed together;
Then her story of the ring
370 Sounds not improbable,
She told it me so well
It seemed the actual thing:—
Oh, keep your counsel close,
But I guess under the rose,
375 In long past summer weather
When the world was blossoming,
And the rose upon its thorn:
I guess not who he was
Flawed honour like a glass
380 And made my life forlorn,
But my Mother, Mother, Mother,
Oh, I know her from all other.

My Lady, you might trust
Your daughter with your fame.
385 Trust me, I would not shame
Our honourable name,
For I have noble blood
Tho' I was bred in dust
And brought up in the mud.

390 I will not press my claim,
Just leave me where you will:
But you might trust your daughter,
For blood is thicker than water
And you're my mother still.

395 So my Lady holds her own
With condescending grace,
And fills her lofty place
With an untroubled face
As a queen may fill a throne.
400 While I could hint a tale—
(But then I am her child)—
Would make her quail;
Would set her in the dust,
Lorn with no comforter,
405 Her glorious hair defiled
And ashes on her cheek:
The decent world would thrust
Its finger out at her,
Not much displeased I think
410 To make a nine days' stir;
The decent world would sink
Its voice to speak of her.

Now this is what I mean
To do, no more, no less:
415 Never to speak, or show
Bare sign of what I know.
Let the blot pass unseen;
Yea, let her never guess
I hold the tangled clue
420 She huddles out of view.
Friend, servant, almost child,
So be it and nothing more
On this side of the grave.
Mother, in Paradise,
425 You'll see with clearer eyes;
Perhaps in this world even
When you are like to die
And face to face with Heaven

You'll drop for once the lie:
430 But you must drop the mask, not I.

My Lady promises
Two hundred pounds with me
Whenever I may wed
A man she can approve:
435 And since besides her bounty
I'm fairest in the county
(For so I've heard it said,
Tho' I don't vouch for this),
Her promised pounds may move
440 Some honest man to see
My virtues and my beauties;
Perhaps the rising grazier,
Or temperance publican,
May claim my wifely duties.
445 Meanwhile I wait their leisure
And grace-bestowing pleasure,
I wait the happy man;
But if I hold my head
And pitch my expectations
450 Just higher than their level,
They must fall back on patience:
I may not mean to wed,
Yet I'll be civil.

Now sometimes in a dream
455 My heart goes out of me
To build and scheme,
Till I sob after things that seem
So pleasant in a dream:
A home such as I see
460 My blessed neighbours live in
With father and with mother,
All proud of one another,
Named by one common name
From baby in the bud
465 To full-blown workman father;
It's little short of Heaven.
I'd give my gentle blood

To wash my special shame
And drown my private grudge;
470 I'd toil and moil much rather
The dingiest cottage drudge
Whose mother need not blush,
Than live here like a lady
And see my Mother flush
475 And hear her voice unsteady
Sometimes, yet never dare
Ask to share her care.

Of course the servants sneer
Behind my back at me;
480 Of course the village girls,
Who envy me my curls
And gowns and idleness,
Take comfort in a jeer;
Of course the ladies guess
485 Just so much of my history
As points the emphatic stress
With which they laud my Lady;
The gentlemen who catch
A casual glimpse of me
490 And turn again to see,
Their valets on the watch
To speak a word with me,
All know and sting me wild;
Till I am almost ready
495 To wish that I were dead,
No faces more to see,
No more words to be said,
My Mother safe at last
Disburdened of her child,
500 And the past past.

"All equal before God"—
Our Rector has it so,
And sundry sleepers nod:
It may be so; I know
505 All are not equal here,
And when the sleepers wake

They make a difference.
"All equal in the grave"—
That shows an obvious sense:
510 Yet something which I crave
Not death itself brings near;
How should death half atone
For all my past; or make
The name I bear my own?

515 I love my dear old Nurse
Who loved me without gains;
I love my mistress even,
Friend, Mother, what you will:
But I could almost curse
520 My Father for his pains;
And sometimes at my prayer
Kneeling in sight of Heaven
I almost curse him still:
Why did he set his snare
525 To catch at unaware
My Mother's foolish youth;
Load me with shame that's hers,
And her with something worse,
A lifelong lie for truth?

530 I think my mind is fixed
On one point and made up:
To accept my lot unmixed;
Never to drug the cup
But drink it by myself.
535 I'll not be wooed for pelf;[1]
I'll not blot out my shame
With any man's good name;
But nameless as I stand,
My hand is my own hand,
540 And nameless as I came
I go to the dark land.

---

[1] money, wealth.

"All equal in the grave"—
I bide my time till then:
"All equal before God"—
545 Today I feel His rod,
Tomorrow He may save:
      Amen.
—1866

Monna Innominata

A Sonnet of Sonnets

Beatrice, immortalized by "altissimo poeta…cotanto amante"; Laura, celebrated by a great though an inferior bard,—have alike paid the exceptional penalty of exceptional honour, and have come down to us resplendent with charms, but (at least, to my apprehension) scant of attractiveness.

These heroines of world-wide fame were preceded by a bevy of unnamed ladies, "donne innominate," sung by a school of less conspicuous poets; and in that land and that period which gave simultaneous birth to Catholics, to Albigenses, and to Troubadours, one can imagine many a lady as sharing her lover's poetic aptitude, while the barrier between them might be one held sacred by both, yet not such as to render mutual love incompatible with mutual honour.

Had such a lady spoken for herself, the portrait left us might have appeared more tender, if less dignified, than any drawn even by a devoted friend. Or had the Great Poetess of our own day and nation only been unhappy instead of happy, her circumstances would have invited her to bequeath to us, in lieu of the "Portuguese Sonnets," an inimitable "donna innominata" drawn not from fancy but from feeling, and worthy to occupy a niche beside Beatrice and Laura.

1

Lo dì che han detto a' dolci amici addio.[1]—DANTE.
Amor, con quanto sforzo oggi mi vinci![2]—PETRARCA.

Come back to me, who wait and watch for
    you:—
  Or come not yet, for it is over then,
  And long it is before you come again,
So far between my pleasures are and few.
5 While, when you come not, what I do I do
    Thinking "Now when he comes," my sweetest
      "when":
  For one man is my world of all the men
This wide world holds; O love, my world is you.
Howbeit, to meet you grows almost a pang
10   Because the pang of parting comes so soon;
    My hope hangs waning, waxing, like a moon
      Between the heavenly days on which we meet:
Ah me, but where are now the songs I sang
    When life was sweet because you called them
      sweet?

2

Era già l'ora che volge il desio.[3]—DANTE.
Ricorro al tempo ch' io vi vidi prima.[4]—PETRARCA.

I wish I could remember that first day,
  First hour, first moment of your meeting me,
  If bright or dim the season, it might be
Summer or Winter for aught I can say;
5 So unrecorded did it slip away,
    So blind was I to see and to foresee,
    So dull to mark the budding of my tree
That would not blossom yet for many a May.
If only I could recollect it, such
10   A day of days! I let it come and go
    As traceless as a thaw of bygone snow;

---

[1] "The day they have said to their sweet friends farewell." Translations by Emilia Spoldi.

[2] "Love, today with great effort you have overcome me!"

[3] "It was now the hour that turneth back desire."

[4] "I have recourse to the time when I first saw you."

It seemed to mean so little, meant so much;
If only now I could recall that touch,
    First touch of hand in hand—Did one but
        know!

3

O ombre vane, fuor che ne l'aspetto![1]—DANTE.
Immaginata guida la conduce.[2]—PETRARCA.

I dream of you to wake: would that I might
  Dream of you and not wake but slumber on;
    Nor find with dreams the dear companion gone,
As Summer ended Summer birds take flight.
5 In happy dreams I hold you full in sight,
    I blush again who waking look so wan;
    Brighter than sunniest day that ever shone,
In happy dreams your smile makes day of night.
Thus only in a dream we are at one,
10   Thus only in a dream we give and take
      The faith that maketh rich who take or give;
    If thus to sleep is sweeter than to wake,
      To die were surely sweeter than to live,
Though there be nothing new beneath the sun.

4

Poca favilla gran fiamma seconda.[3]—DANTE.
Ogni altra cosa, ogni pensier va fore,
E sol ivi con voi rimansi amore.[4]—PETRARCA.

I loved you first: but afterwards your love,
  Outsoaring mine, sang such a loftier song
As drowned the friendly cooings of my dove.
    Which owes the other most? My love was long,
5   And yours one moment seemed to wax more
      strong;
I loved and guessed at you, you construed me
And loved me for what might or might not be—

---

[1] "O empty shadows, save in aspect only!"

[2] "Imaginary guide leads her."

[3] "A little spark is followed by great flame."

[4] "Every other thing, every thought disappears
    And here alone with you I stay."

Nay, weights and measures do us both a wrong.
For verily love knows not "mine" or "thine";
10   With separate "I" and "thou" free love has done,
      For one is both and both are one in love:
Rich love knows nought of "thine that is not mine";
    Both have the strength and both the length
      thereof,
  Both of us, of the love which makes us one.

5

Amor che a nullo amato amar perdona.[5]—DANTE.
Amor m'addusse in sì gioiosa spene.[6]—PETRARCA.

O my heart's heart, and you who are to me
  More than myself myself, God be with you,
    Keep you in strong obedience leal[7] and true
To Him whose noble service setteth free;
5 Give you all good we see or can foresee,
    Make your joys many and your sorrows few,
    Bless you in what you bear and what you do,
Yea, perfect you as He would have you be.
So much for you; but what for me, dear friend?
10   To love you without stint and all I can
Today, tomorrow, world without an end;
    To love you much and yet to love you more,
      As Jordan[8] at his flood sweeps either shore;
Since woman is the helpmeet made for man.

6

Or puoi la quantitate
Comprender de l'amor che a te mi scalda.[9]—DANTE.
Non vo'che da tal nodo amor mi scioglia.[10]—PETRARCA.

Trust me, I have not earned your dear rebuke,—
  I love, as you would have me, God the most;

---

[5] "Love which exempts no one beloved from loving."

[6] "Love roused in me such joyful hope."

[7] loyal.

[8] a river flowing into the Dead Sea.

[9] "Now canst thou the sum of love which
    Warms me to thee comprehend."

[10] "I don't want love to release me from such knot."

Would lose not Him, but you, must one be lost,
Nor with Lot's wife[1] cast back a faithless look,
5   Unready to forego what I forsook;
   This say I, having counted up the cost,
   This, though I be the feeblest of God's host,
The sorriest sheep Christ shepherds with His crook.
Yet while I love my God the most, I deem
10   That I can never love you overmuch;
      I love Him more, so let me love you too;
Yea, as I apprehend it, love is such
I cannot love you if I love not Him,
      I cannot love Him if I love not you.

7

Qui primavera sempre ed ogni frutto.[2]—DANTE.
Ragionando con meco ed io con lui.[3]—PETRARCA.

"Love me, for I love you"—and answer me,
   "Love me, for I love you": so shall we stand
   As happy equals in the flowering land
Of love, that knows not a dividing sea.
5   Love builds the house on rock and not on sand,
      Love laughs what while the winds rave
         desperately;
And who hath found love's citadel unmanned?
      And who hath held in bonds love's liberty?—
My heart's a coward though my words are brave—
10   We meet so seldom, yet we surely part
      So often; there's a problem for your art!
         Still I find comfort in his Book, who saith,
Though jealousy be cruel as the grave,
      And death be strong, yet love is strong as
         death.

8

Come dicesse a Dio, D'altro non calme.[4]—DANTE.
Spero trovar pietà non che perdono.[5]—PETRARCA.

"I, if I perish, perish"—Esther[6] spake:
   And bride of life or death she made her fair
   In all the lustre of her perfumed hair
And smiles that kindle longing but to slake.
5   She put on pomp of loveliness, to take
      Her husband through his eyes at unaware;
      She spread abroad her beauty for a snare,
Harmless as doves and subtle as a snake.
She trapped him with one mesh of silken hair,
10   She vanquished him by wisdom of her wit,
         And built her people's house that it should
            stand:—
      If I might take my life so in my hand,
And for my love to Love put up my prayer,
      And for love's sake by Love be granted it!

9

O dignitosa coscienza e netta![7]—DANTE.
Spirto più acceso di virtuti ardenti.[8]—PETRARCA.

Thinking of you, and all that was, and all
   That might have been and now can never be,
   I feel your honoured excellence, and see
Myself unworthy of the happier call:
5   For woe is me who walk so apt to fall,
      So apt to shrink afraid, so apt to flee,
      Apt to lie down and die (ah woe is me!)
Faithless and hopeless turning to the wall.
And yet not hopeless quite nor faithless quite,
10   Because not loveless; love may toil all night,
      But take at morning; wrestle till the break

----

1   Glancing back at the doomed city of Sodom, she turned into a pillar of salt.

2   "Here evermore was Spring and every fruit."

3   "Reasoning with me and I with him."

----

4   "As if it said to God, nothing else I care for."

5   "I hope to find not only pardon, but pity."

6   the Jewish wife of the Persian King, Ahasuerus (Xerxes), who delivered her people from Haman's slaughter.

7   "O noble conscience and without a stain!"

8   "More vivid spirit of ardent virtues."

Of day, but then wield power with God and
man:—
So take I heart of grace as best I can,
Ready to spend and be spent for your sake.

10

Con miglior corso e con migliore stella.[1]—DANTE.
La vita fugge e non s'arresta un' ora.[2]—PETRARCA.

Time flies, hope flags, life plies a wearied wing;
  Death following hard on life gains ground apace;
  Faith runs with each and rears an eager face,
Outruns the rest, makes light of everything,
5 Spurns earth, and still finds breath to pray and sing;
    While love ahead of all uplifts his praise,
    Still asks for grace and still gives thanks for grace,
Content with all day brings and night will bring.
Life wanes; and when love folds his wings above
10   Tired hope, and less we feel his conscious pulse,
      Let us go fall asleep, dear friend, in peace:
      A little while, and age and sorrow cease;
    A little while, and life reborn annuls
Loss and decay and death, and all is love.

11

Vien dietro a me e lascia dir le genti.[3]—DANTE.
Contando i casi della vita nostra.[4]—PETRARCA.

Many in aftertimes will say of you
  "He loved her"—while of me what will they
say?
  Not that I loved you more than just in play,
For fashion's sake as idle women do.
5 Even let them prate; who know not what we knew
    Of love and parting in exceeding pain,
    Of parting hopeless here to meet again,
Hopeless on earth, and heaven is out of view.

But by my heart of love laid bare to you,
10 My love that you can make not void nor vain,
Love that foregoes you but to claim anew
    Beyond this passage of the gate of death,
    I charge you at the Judgment make it plain
    My love of you was life and not a breath.

12

Amor che ne la mente mi ragiona.[5]—DANTE.
Amor vien nel bel viso di costei.[6]—PETRARCA.

If there be any one can take my place
  And make you happy whom I grieve to grieve,
  Think not that I can grudge it, but believe
I do commend you to that nobler grace,
5 That readier wit than mine, that sweeter face;
    Yea, since your riches make me rich, conceive
    I too am crowned, while bridal crowns I weave,
And thread the bridal dance with jocund pace.
For if I did not love you, it might be
10   That I should grudge you some one dear delight;
      But since the heart is yours that was mine
own,
    Your pleasure is my pleasure, right my right,
Your honourable freedom makes me free,
    And you companioned I am not alone.

13

E drizzeremo gli occhi al Primo Amore.[7]—DANTE.
Ma trovo peso non da le mie braccia.[8]—PETRARCA.

If I could trust mine own self with your fate,
  Shall I not rather trust it in God's hand?
  Without Whose Will one lily doth not stand,
Nor sparrow fall at his appointed date;
5 Who numbereth the innumerable sand,
Who weighs the wind and water with a weight,

---

[1] "With better course and with a better star."

[2] "Life is flying from me, not stopping an hour."

[3] "Come after me and let the people talk."

[4] "Telling over the events of our life."

[5] "Love that within my mind discourses with me."

[6] "Love appears in her lovely face."

[7] "And unto the First Love will turn our eyes."

[8] "But I find a burden, not for my arms (to bear)."

To Whom the world is neither small nor great,
    Whose knowledge foreknew every plan we
       planned.
Searching my heart for all that touches you,
    I find there only love and love's goodwill
10 Helpless to help and impotent to do,
Of understanding dull, of sight most dim;
And therefore I commend you back to Him
    Whose love your love's capacity can fill.

14

E la Sua Volontade è nostra pace.[1]—DANTE.
Sol con questi pensier, con altre chiome.[2]—PETRARCA.

Youth gone, and beauty gone if ever there
    Dwelt beauty in so poor a face as this;
    Youth gone and beauty, what remains of bliss?
I will not bind fresh roses in my hair,
5 To shame a cheek at best but little fair,—
    Leave youth his roses, who can bear a thorn,—
I will not seek for blossoms anywhere,
    Except such common flowers as blow with corn.
Youth gone and beauty gone, what doth remain?
10   The longing of a heart pent up forlorn,
        A silent heart whose silence loves and longs;
        The silence of a heart which sang its songs
    While youth and beauty made a summer morn,
Silence of love that cannot sing again.
—1881

"For Thine Own Sake, O My God"

Wearied of sinning, wearied of repentance,
    Wearied of self, I turn, my God, to Thee;
To Thee, my Judge, on Whose all-righteous
       sentence

Hangs mine eternity:
5 I turn to Thee, I plead Thyself with Thee,—
    Be pitiful to me.

Wearied I loathe myself, I loathe my sinning,
    My stains, my festering sores, my misery:
Thou the Beginning, Thou ere my beginning
10   Didst see and didst foresee
Me miserable, me sinful, ruined me,—
    I plead Thyself with Thee.

I plead Thyself with Thee Who art my Maker,
    Regard Thy handiwork that cries to Thee;
15 I plead Thyself with Thee Who wast partaker
    Of mine infirmity,
Love made Thee what Thou art, the love of me,—
    I plead Thyself with Thee.
—1882

In an Artist's Studio

One face looks out from all his canvasses,
    One selfsame figure sits or walks or leans;
    We found her hidden just behind those screens,
That mirror gave back all her loveliness.
5 A queen in opal or in ruby dress,
    A nameless girl in freshest summer greens,
    A saint, an angel;—every canvass means
The same one meaning, neither more nor less.
He feeds upon her face by day and night,
10   And she with true kind eyes looks back on him
Fair as the moon and joyful as the light:
    Not wan with waiting, not with sorrow dim;
Not as she is, but was when hope shone bright;
    Not as she is, but as she fills his dream.
—1896

---

[1] "And his will is our peace."

[2] "Alone with these thoughts, with different tresses."

Lewis Carroll
1832 – 1898

Lewis Carroll was the pseudonym of Charles Lutwidge Dodgson, a professor of mathematics at Oxford. His major achievements are the famous works of fantasy, *Alice's Adventures in Wonderland* (1865), and its sequel, *Through the Looking Glass* (1872). Carroll was also the author of many humorous poems, most notably *The Hunting of the Snark* (1876). Some of his best poems, "Jabberwocky" and "The Walrus and the Carpenter," were included in the Alice books.

❧❧❧

Jabberwocky

'Twas brillig and the slithy toves
    Did gyre and gimble in the wabe;
All mimsy were the borogroves,
    And the mome raths outgrabe.

5 "Beware the Jabberwock, my son!
    The jaws that bite, the claws that catch!
Beware the Jubjub bird, and shun
    The frumious Bandersnatch!"

He took his vorpal sword in hand:
10   Long time the manxome foe he sought—
So rested he by the Tumtum tree.
    And stood awhile in thought.

And as in uffish thought he stood,
    The Jabberwock, with eyes of flame,
15 Came whiffling through the tulgey wood,
    And burbled as it came!

One, two! One, two! And though and through
    The vorpal blade went snicker-snack!
He left it dead, and with its head
20   He went galumphing back.

"And hast thou slain the Jabberwock?
    Come to my arms, my beamish boy!
O frabjous day! Callooh! Callay!"
    He chortled in his joy.

25 "Twas brillig and the slithy toves
    Did gyre and gimble in the wabe;
All mimsy were the borogroves,
    And the mome raths outgrabe.
—1872 (1855)

The Walrus and the Carpenter

The sun was shining on the sea,
    Shining with all his might:
He did his very best to make
    The billows smooth and bright—
5 And this was odd, because it was
    The middle of the night.

The moon was shining sulkily,
    Because she thought the sun
Had got no business to be there
10   After the day was done—
"It's very rude of him," she said,
    "To come and spoil the fun!"

The sea was wet as wet could be,
    The sands were dry as dry.
15 You could not see a cloud, because
    No cloud was in the sky:

No birds were flying overhead—
  There were no birds to fly.

The Walrus and the Carpenter
20   Were walking close at hand:
They wept like anything to see
  Such quantities of sand:
"If this were only cleared away,"
  They said, "it would be grand!"

25 "If seven maids with seven mops
  Swept it for half a year,
Do you suppose," the Walrus said,
  "That they could get it clear?"
"I doubt it," said the Carpenter,
30 And shed a bitter tear.

"O Oysters, come and walk with us!"
  The Walrus did beseech.
"A pleasant walk, a pleasant talk,
  Along the briny beach:
35 We cannot do with more than four,
  To give a hand to each."

The eldest Oyster looked at him,
  But never a word he said:
The eldest Oyster winked his eye,
40 And shook his heavy head—
Meaning to say he did not choose
  To leave the oyster-bed.

But four young Oysters hurried up,
  All eager for the treat:
45 Their coats were brushed, their faces washed,
  Their shoes were clean and neat—
And this was odd, because you know,
  They hadn't any feet.

Four other Oysters followed them,
50 And yet another four;
And thick and fast they came at last,

And more, and more, and more—
  All hopping through the frothy waves,
  And scrambling to the shore.

55 The Walrus and the Carpenter
  Walked on a mile or so,
And then they rested on a rock
  Conveniently low:
And all the little Oysters stood
60 And waited in a row.

"The time has come," the Walrus said,
  "To talk of many things:
Of shoes—and ships—and sealing wax—
  Of cabbages—and kings—
65 And why the sea is boiling hot—
  And whether pigs have wings."

"But wait a bit," the Oysters cried,
  "Before we have our chat;
For some of us are out of breath,
70 And all of us are fat!"
"No hurry!" said the Carpenter.
  They thanked him much for that.

"A loaf of bread," the Walrus said,
  "Is what we chiefly need:
75 Pepper and vinegar besides
  Are very good indeed—
Now, if you're ready, Oysters dear,
  We can begin to feed."

"But not on us!" the Oysters cried,
80 Turning a little blue.
"After such kindness, that would be
  A dismal thing to do!"
"The night is fine," the Walrus said.
  "Do you admire the view?

85 "It was so kind of you to come!
  And you are very nice!"

The carpenter said nothing but
  "Cut us another slice.
I wish you were not quite so deaf—
90   I've had to ask you twice!"

"It seems a shame," the Walrus said,
  "To play them such a trick.
After we've brought them out so far,
  And made them trot so quick!"
95 The Carpenter said nothing but
  "The butter's spread too thick!"

"I weep for you," the Walrus said:
  "I deeply sympathize."

With sobs and tears he sorted out
100 Those of the largest size,
Holding his pocket-handkerchief
  Before his streaming eyes.

"O Oysters," said the Carpenter,
  "You've had a pleasant run!
105 Shall we be trotting home again?"
  But answer came there none—
And this was scarcely odd, because
  They'd eaten every one.
  —1872 (1869)

William Morris
1834 – 1896

Educated at Marlborough College (1848–51), and Exeter College, Oxford (1853–56), Morris was the author of prose romances and verse narratives. In addition, he was a pioneering designer, a translator, and a leader of the early British socialist movement. Morris's major works include a volume of lyric and dramatic verse, *The Defence of Guenevere and other Poems* (1858), and *The Earthly Paradise* (1868–70), twenty-four verse narratives derived from classical and medieval tales.

❧❧❧

The Defence of Guenevere [1]

But, knowing now that they would have her
   speak,
She threw her wet hair backward from her brow,
Her hand close to her mouth touching her cheek,

As though she had had there a shameful blow,
5 And feeling it shameful to feel aught but shame
All through her heart, yet felt her cheek burned so,

She must a little touch it; like one lame
She walked away from Gauwaine,[2] with her head
Still lifted up; and on her cheek of flame

10 The tears dried quick; she stopped at last and said:
"O knights and lords, it seems but little skill
To talk of well-known things past now and dead.

"God wot[3] I ought to say, I have done ill,
And pray you all forgiveness heartily!
15 Because you must be right, such great lords—still

"Listen, suppose your time were come to die,
And you were quite alone and very weak;
Yea, laid a dying while very mightily

"The wind was ruffling up the narrow streak
20 Of river through your broad lands running well:
Suppose a hush should come, then some one speak:

"'One of these cloths is heaven, and one is hell,
Now choose one cloth for ever; which they be,
I will not tell you, you must somehow tell

25 "'Of your own strength and mightiness; here, see!'
Yea, yea, my lord, and you to ope your eyes,
At foot of your familiar bed to see

"A great God's angel standing, with such dyes,
Not known on earth, on his great wings, and hands
30 Held out two ways, light from the inner skies

"Showing him well, and making his commands
Seem to be God's commands, moreover, too,
Holding within his hands the cloths on wands;

"And one of these strange choosing cloths was blue,
35 Wavy and long, and one cut short and red;
No man could tell the better of the two.

---

[1] Guenevere, the wife of King Arthur, was accused of adultery with the knight Sir Lancelot. In this dramatic monologue she speaks in self-defence at her trial. The story is recounted in Malory's *Morte d'Arthur*.

[2] a knight of Arthur's Round Table, and Guenevere's chief accuser.

[3] God knows.

"After a shivering half-hour you said:
'God help! heaven's colour, the blue'; and he said,
   'hell.'
Perhaps you then would roll upon your bed,

40 "And cry to all good men that loved you well,
'Ah Christ! if only I had known, known, known;'
Launcelot went away, then I could tell,

"Like wisest man how all things would be, moan,
And roll and hurt myself, and long to die,
45 And yet fear much to die for what was sown.

"Nevertheless you, O Sir Gauwaine, lie,
Whatever may have happened through these years,
God knows I speak truth, saying that you lie."

Her voice was low at first, being full of tears,
50 But as it cleared, it grew full loud and shrill,
Growing a windy shriek in all men's ears,

A ringing in their startled brains, until
She said that Gauwaine lied, then her voice sunk,
And her great eyes began again to fill,

55 Though still she stood right up, and never shrunk,
But spoke on bravely, glorious lady fair!
Whatever tears her full lips may have drunk,

She stood, and seemed to think, and wrung her hair,
Spoke out at last with no more trace of shame,
60 With passionate twisting of her body there:

"It chanced upon a day that Launcelot came
To dwell at Arthur's court: at Christmas-time
This happened; when the heralds sung his name,

"'Son of King Ban of Benwick,' seemed to chime
65 Along with all the bells that rang that day,
O'er the white roofs, with little change of rhyme.

"Christmas and whitened winter passed away,
And over me the April sunshine came,
Made very awful with black hail-clouds, yea

70 "And in the Summer I grew white with flame,
And bowed my head down—Autumn, and the sick
Sure knowledge things would never be the same,

"However often Spring might be most thick
Of blossoms and buds, smote on me, and I grew
75 Careless of most things, let the clock tick, tick,

"To my unhappy pulse, that beat right through
My eager body; while I laughed out loud,
And let my lips curl up at false or true,

"Seemed cold and shallow without any cloud.
80 Behold my judges, then the cloths were brought:
While I was dizzied thus, old thoughts would
   crowd,

"Belonging to the time ere I was bought
By Arthur's great name and his little love;
Must I give up for ever then, I thought,

85 "That which I deemed would ever round me move
Glorifying all things; for a little word,
Scarce ever meant at all, must I now prove

"Stone-cold for ever? Pray you, does the Lord
Will that all folks should be quite happy and good?
90 I love God now a little, if this cord

"Were broken, once for all what striving could
Make me love anything in earth or heaven?
So day by day it grew, as if one should

"Slip slowly down some path worn smooth and
   even,
95 Down to a cool sea on a summer day;
Yet still in slipping there was some small leaven

"Of stretched hands catching small stones by the
    way,
Until one surely reached the sea at last,
And felt strange new joy as the worn head lay

100 "Back, with the hair like sea-weed; yea all past
Sweat of the forehead, dryness of the lips,
Washed utterly out by the dear waves o'ercast

"In the lone sea, far off from any ships!
Do I not know now of a day in Spring?
105 No minute of that wild day ever slips

"From out my memory; I hear thrushes sing,
And wheresoever I may be, straightway
Thoughts of it all come up with the most fresh
    sting;

"I was half mad with beauty on that day,
110 And went without my ladies all alone,
In a quiet garden walled round every way;

"I was right joyful of that wall of stone,
That shut the flowers and trees up with the sky,
And trebled all the beauty: to the bone,

115 "Yea right through to my heart, grown very shy
With weary thoughts, it pierced, and made me glad;
Exceedingly glad, and I knew verily,

"A little thing just then had made me mad;
I dared not think, as I was wont to do,
120 Sometimes, upon my beauty; if I had

"Held out my long hand up against the blue,
And, looking on the tenderly darken'd fingers,
Thought that by rights one ought to see quite
    through,

"There, see you, where the soft still light yet lingers,
125 Round by the edges; what should I have done,
If this had joined with yellow spotted singers,

"And startling green drawn upward by the sun?
But shouting, loosed out, see now! all my hair,
And trancedly stood watching the west wind run

130 "With faintest half-heard breathing sound—why
    there
I lose my head e'en now in doing this;
But shortly listen—In that garden fair

"Came Launcelot walking; this is true, the kiss
Wherewith we kissed in meeting that spring day,
135 I scarce dare talk of the remember'd bliss,

"When both our mouths went wandering in one
    way,
And aching sorely, met among the leaves;
Our hands being left behind strained far away.

"Never within a yard of my bright sleeves
140 Had Launcelot come before—and now, so nigh!
After that day why is it Guenevere grieves?

"Nevertheless you, O Sir Gauwaine, lie,
Whatever happened on through all those years,
God knows I speak truth, saying that you lie.

145 "Being such a lady could I weep these tears
If this were true? A great queen such as I
Having sinn'd this way, straight her conscience
    sears;

"And afterwards she liveth hatefully,
Slaying and poisoning, certes never weeps,—
150 Gauwaine be friends now, speak me lovingly.

"Do I not see how God's dear pity creeps
All through your frame, and trembles in your
    mouth?
Remember in what grave your mother sleeps,

"Buried in some place far down in the south,
155 Men are forgetting as I speak to you;
By her head sever'd in that awful drouth

"Of pity that drew Agravaine's[1] fell blow,
I pray your pity! let me not scream out
For ever after, when the shrill winds blow

160 "Through half your castle-locks! let me not shout
For ever after in the winter night
When you ride out alone! in battle-rout

"Let not my rusting tears make your sword light!
Ah! God of mercy, how he turns away!
165 So, ever must I dress me to the fight;

"So—let God's justice work! Gauwaine, I say,
See me hew down your proofs: yea, all men know
Even as you said how Mellyagraunce[2] one day,

"One bitter day in *la Fausse Garde*,[3] for so
170 All good knights held it after, saw—
Yea, sirs, by cursed unknightly outrage; though

"You, Gauwaine, held his word without a flaw,
This Mellyagraunce saw blood upon my bed—
Whose blood then pray you? is there any law

175 "To make a queen say why some spots of red
Lie on her coverlet? or will you say,
'Your hands are white, lady, as when you wed,

"'Where did you bleed?' and must I stammer
    out—'Nay,
I blush indeed, fair lord, only to rend
180 My sleeve up to my shoulder, where there lay

"'A knife-point last night': so must I defend
The honour of the lady Guenevere?
Not so, fair lords, even if the world should end

"This very day, and you were judges here
185 Instead of God. Did you see Mellyagraunce
When Launcelot stood by him? what white fear

"Curdled his blood, and how his teeth did dance,
His side sink in? as my knight cried and said,
'Slayer of unarm'd men, here is a chance!

190 "'Setter of traps,[4] I pray you guard your head,
By God I am so glad to fight with you,
Stripper of ladies, that my hand feels lead

"'For driving weight; hurrah now! draw and do,
For all my wounds are moving in my breast,
195 And I am getting mad with waiting so.'

"He struck his hands together o'er the beast,
Who fell down flat, and grovell'd at his feet,
And groan'd at being slain so young—'at least.'

"My knight said: 'Rise you, sir, who are so fleet
200 At catching ladies, half-arm'd will I fight,
My left side all uncovered!' then I weet,

---

[1] Gauwaine's brother, who accused his mother of infidelity and murdered her.

[2] Mellyagraunce had charged Guenevere with adultery after he found blood on her sheets while she was staying at his castle. The blood was actually Lancelot's, who had cut his arm climbing through Guenevere's window, but Lancelot defended her honour, saying that it came from wounded knights who had been placed in her rooms.

[3] the False Castle, the phrase expressing Guenevere's contempt.

[4] Mellyagraunce attempted to prevent Lancelot from defending Guenevere's honour in a duel by making him fall through a trapdoor into a dungeon.

"Up sprang Sir Mellyagraunce with great delight
Upon his knave's face; not until just then
Did I quite hate him, as I saw my knight

205 "Along the lists look to my stake and pen
With such a joyous smile, it made me sigh
From agony beneath my waist-chain,[1] when

"The fight began, and to me they drew nigh;
Ever Sir Launcelot kept him on the right,
210 And traversed warily, and ever high

"And fast leapt caitiff's sword, until my knight
Sudden threw up his sword to his left hand,
Caught it, and swung it; that was all the fight.

"Except a spout of blood on the hot land;
215 For it was hottest summer; and I know
I wonder'd how the fire, while I should stand,

"And burn, against the heat, would quiver so,
Yards above my head; thus these matters went;
Which things were only warnings of the woe

220 "That fell on me. Yet Mellyagraunce was shent,[2]
For Mellyagraunce had fought against the Lord;
Therefore, my lords, take heed lest you be blent[3]

"With all this wickedness; say no rash word
Against me, being so beautiful; my eyes,
225 Wept all away to grey, may bring some sword

"To drown you in your blood; see my breast rise,
Like waves of purple sea, as here I stand;
And how my arms are moved in wonderful wise,

"Yea also at my full heart's strong command,
230 See through my long throat how the words go up
In ripples to my mouth; how in my hand

"The shadow lies like wine within a cup
Of marvellously colour'd gold; yea now
This little wind is rising, look you up,

235 "And wonder how the light is falling so
Within my moving tresses: will you dare,
When you have looked a little on my brow,

"To say this thing is vile? or will you care
For any plausible lies of cunning woof,
240 When you can see my face with no lie there

"For ever? am I not a gracious proof—
'But in your chamber Launcelot was found'—
Is there a good knight then would stand aloof,

"When a queen says with gentle queenly sound:
245 'O true as steel, come now and talk with me,
I love to see your step upon the ground

"'Unwavering, also well I love to see
That gracious smile light up your face, and hear
Your wonderful words, that all mean verily

250 "'The thing they seem to mean: good friend, so dear
To me in everything, come here to-night,
Or else the hours will pass most dull and drear;

"'If you come not, I fear this time I might
Get thinking over much of times gone by,
255 When I was young, and green hope was in sight:

"'For no man cares now to know why I sigh;
And no man comes to sing me pleasant songs,
Nor any brings me the sweet flowers that lie

---

[1] Guenevere is chained to a stake where she will be burned.

[2] disgraced, ruined.

[3] blended with or blinded by.

"'So thick in the gardens; therefore one so longs
260 To see you, Launcelot; that we may be
Like children once again, free from all wrongs

"'Just for one night.' Did he not come to me?
What thing could keep true Launcelot away
If I said 'Come'? there was one less than three

265 "In my quiet room that night, and we were gay;
Till sudden I rose up, weak, pale, and sick,
Because a bawling broke our dream up, yea

"I looked at Launcelot's face and could not speak,
For he looked helpless too, for a little while;
270 Then I remember how I tried to shriek,

"And could not, but fell down; from tile to tile
The stones they threw up rattled o'er my head
And made me dizzier; till within a while

"My maids were all about me, and my head
275 On Launcelot's breast was being soothed away
From its white chattering, until Launcelot said—

"By God! I will not tell you more to-day,
Judge any way you will—what matters it?
You know quite well the story of that fray,

280 "How Launcelot still'd their bawling, the mad fit
That caught up Gauwaine—all, all, verily,
But just that which would save me; these things
    flit.

"Nevertheless you, O Sir Gauwaine, lie,
Whatever may have happen'd these long years,
285 God knows I speak truth, saying that you lie!

"All I have said is truth, by Christ's dear tears."
She would not speak another word, but stood
Turn'd sideways; listening, like a man who hears

His brother's trumpet sounding through the wood
290 Of his foes' lances. She lean'd eagerly,
And gave a slight spring sometimes, as she could

At last hear something really; joyfully
Her cheek grew crimson, as the headlong speed
Of the roan charger drew all men to see,
295 The knight who came was Launcelot at good need.
—1858

The Haystack in the Floods [1]

Had she come all the way for this,
To part at last without a kiss?
Yea, had she borne the dirt and rain
That her own eyes might see him slain
5 Beside the haystack in the floods?

Along the dripping leafless woods,
The stirrup touching either shoe,
She rode astride as troopers do;
With kirtle kilted[2] to her knee,
10 To which the mud splash'd wretchedly;
And the wet dripp'd from every tree
Upon her head and heavy hair,
And on her eyelids broad and fair;
The tears and rain ran down her face.
15 By fits and starts they rode apace,
And very often was his place
Far off from her; he had to ride
Ahead, to see what might betide
When the roads cross'd; and sometimes, when
20 There rose a murmuring from his men,
Had to turn back with promises;
Ah me! she had but little ease;

---

[1] After the defeat of the French at Poitiers in 1356, Sir Robert de Marny, an English knight, and his mistress Jehane are travelling through France, intent on reaching the frontier of Gascony, which is in English hands. They are confronted by a traitorous French knight, Godmar, who intends to murder Robert and seize Jehane.

[2] skirt tucked up.

And often for pure doubt and dread
She sobb'd, made giddy in the head
25 By the swift riding; while, for cold,
Her slender fingers scarce could hold
The wet reins; yea, and scarcely, too,
She felt the foot within her shoe
Against the stirrup: all for this,
30 To part at last without a kiss
Beside the haystack in the floods.

For when they near'd that old soak'd hay,
They saw across the only way
That Judas, Godmar, and the three
35 Red running lions dismally
Grinn'd from his pennon,[1] under which,
In one straight line along the ditch,
The counted thirty heads.
                              So then,
While Robert turn'd round to his men,
40 She saw at once the wretched end,
And, stooping down, tried hard to rend
Her coif the wrong way from her head,
And hid her eyes; while Robert said:
"Nay, love, 'tis scarcely two to one,
45 At Poictiers where we made them run[2]
So fast—why, sweet my love, good cheer.
The Gascon frontier is so near,
Nought after this."

                    But, "O," she said,
"My God! my God! I have to tread
50 The long way back without you; then
The court at Paris;[3] those six men;
The gratings of the Chatelet;

The swift Seine on some rainy day
Like this, and people standing by,
55 And laughing, while my weak hands try
To recollect how strong men swim.
All this, or else a life with him,
For which I should be damned at last,
Would God that this next hour were past!"

60 He answer'd not, but cried his cry,
"St. George for Marny!"[4] cheerily;
And laid his hand upon her rein.
Alas! no man of all his train
Gave back that cheery cry again;
65 And, while for rage his thumb beat fast
Upon his sword-hilt, some one cast
About his neck a kerchief long,
And bound him.

                    Then they went along
To Godmar; who said: "Now, Jehane,
70 Your lover's life is on the wane
So fast, that, if this very hour
You yield not as my paramour,
He will not see the rain leave off—
Nay, keep your tongue from gibe and scoff,
75 Sir Robert, or I slay you now."

She laid her hand upon her brow,
Then gazed upon the palm, as though
She thought her forehead bled, and—"No!"
She said, and turn'd her head away,
80 As there were nothing else to say,
And everything were settled: red
Grew Godmar's face from chin to head:
"Jehane, on yonder hill there stands
My castle, guarding well my lands:
85 What hinders me from taking you,
And doing that I list to do
To your fair wilful body, while

---

[1] pennant or banner.

[2] The English won the Battle of Poitiers despite being outnumbered five to one; Gascony was English territory at this time.

[3] Jehane fears being tried as a witch and imprisoned in the Grand Chatelet prison. Women accused of being witches were thrown into a river as a test of their innocence: if they sank and drowned they were deemed innocent, but if they swam they were found guilty.

[4] Robert calls on St. George, the patron saint of England.

Your knight lies dead?"
                            A wicked smile
Wrinkled her face, her lips grew thin,
90 A long way out she thrust her chin:
"You know that I should strangle you
While you were sleeping; or bite through
Your throat, by God's help—ah!" she said,
"Lord Jesus, pity your poor maid!
95 For in such wise they hem me in,
I cannot choose but sin and sin,
Whatever happens: yet I think
They could not make me eat or drink,
And so should I just reach my rest."
100 "Nay, if you do not my behest,
O Jehane! though I love you well,"
Said Godmar, "would I fail to tell
All that I know?" "Foul lies," she said.
"Eh? lies, my Jehane? by God's head,
105 At Paris folks would deem them true!
Do you know, Jehane, they cry for you,
'Jehane the brown! Jehane the brown!
Give us Jehane to burn or drown!'—
Eh—gag me Robert!—sweet my friend,
110 This were indeed a piteous end
For those long fingers, and long feet,
And long neck, and smooth shoulders sweet;
An end that few men would forget
That saw it—So, an hour yet:
115 Consider, Jehane, which to take
Of life or death!"
                            So, scarce awake,
Dismounting, did she leave that place,
And totter some yards: with her face
Turn'd upward to the sky she lay,
120 Her head on a wet heap of hay,
And fell asleep: and while she slept,
And did not dream, the minutes crept
Round to the twelve again; but she,
Being waked at last, sigh'd quietly,
125 And strangely childlike came, and said:
"I will not." Straightway Godmar's head,

As though it hung on strong wires, turn'd
Most sharply round, and his face burn'd.

For Robert—both his eyes were dry,
130 He could not weep, but gloomily
He seem'd to watch the rain; yea, too,
His lips were firm; he tried once more
To touch her lips, she reach'd out, sore
And vain desire so tortured them,
135 The poor grey lips, and now the hem
Of his sleeve brush'd them.
                            With a start
Up Godmar rose, thrust them apart;
From Robert's throat he loosed the bands
Of silk and mail; with empty hands
140 Held out, she stood and gazed, and saw,
The long bright blade without a flaw
Glide out from Godmar's sheath, his hand
In Robert's hair; she saw him bend
Back Robert's head; she saw him send
145 The thin steel down; the blow told well,
Right backward the knight Robert fell,
And moan'd as dogs do, being half dead,
Unwitting, as I deem: so then
Godmar turn'd grinning to his men,
150 Who ran, some five or six, and beat
His head to pieces at their feet.

Then Godmar turn'd again and said:
"So, Jehane, the first fitte[1] is read!
Take note, my lady, that your way
155 Lies backward to the Chatelet!"
She shook her head and gazed awhile
At her cold hands with a rueful smile,
As though this thing had made her mad.

This was the parting that they had
160 Beside the haystack in the floods.
—1858

------

[1] section or canto of a poem.

Algernon Charles Swinburne
1837 – 1909

Algernon Charles Swinburne's family background was aristocratic (his father was an admiral and his grandfather a baronet), and his education was privileged—he was educated at Eton and Oxford. Beginning his writing at Oxford (1856–60), he met Dante Gabriel Rossetti and was briefly associated with the Pre-Raphaelite circle. Swinburne led a dissolute, wild life (his predilection for flagellation pornography is infamous), attaining literary notoriety with *Atalanta in Calydon* (1865) and *Poems and Ballads, First Series #1* (1866). In an age that prided itself on middle-class values and religiosity, Swinburne's works were blasphemous, erotic, and subversive, rebelling against the moral repressiveness of his time as he asserted a doctrine of "l'art pour l'art." Engaged in literary debates with Thomas Carlyle, John Ruskin, and Ralph Waldo Emerson over the value of morality in art, his essay "Under the Microscope" (1872) is a response, parodic as it is, to Robert Buchanan's "The Fleshly School of Poetry" (1871), which attacked both Swinburne and Rossetti's sensuous, poetic impulses. A liberal republican, in the *Song of Italy* (1867) and *Songs before Sunrise* (1871) he sided with Italian political revolt against oppression. Swinburne was also a respected scholar, publishing studies of William Blake (1868), William Shakespeare (1880), and essays on French and English contemporaries. With an aesthetic vision that influenced younger generations, Swinburne was a poet who drew on a wide range of interests, and was willing to pursue his own beliefs against the prejudices of his time.

❧❧❧

The Triumph of Time

Before our lives divide for ever,
While time is with us and hands are free
(Time, swift to fasten and swift to sever
    Hand from hand, as we stand by the sea),
5 I will say no word that a man might say
Whose whole life's love goes down in a day;
For this could never have been; and never,
    Though the gods and the years relent, shall be.

Is it worth a tear, is it worth an hour
10   To think of things that are well outworn?
Of fruitless husk and fugitive flower,
    The dream foregone and the deed forborne?
Though joy be done with and grief be vain,
Time shall not sever us wholly in twain;
15 Earth is not spoilt for a single shower;
    But the rain has ruined the ungrown corn.

It will grow not again, this fruit of my heart,
    Smitten with sunbeams, ruined with rain.
The singing seasons divide and depart,
20   Winter and summer depart in twain.
It will grow not again, it is ruined at root,
The bloodlike blossom, the dull red fruit;
Though the heart yet sickens, the lips yet smart,
    With sullen savour of poisonous pain.

25 I have given no man of my fruit to eat;
    I trod the grapes, I have drunken the wine.
Had you eaten and drunken and found it sweet,
    This wild new growth of the corn and vine,
This wine and bread without lees or leaven,
30 We had grown as gods, as the gods in heaven,
Souls fair to look upon, goodly to greet,
    One splendid spirit, your soul and mine.

In the change of years, in the coil of things,
    In the clamour and rumour of life to be,
35 We, drinking love at the furthest springs,

446

Covered with love as a covering tree,
We had grown as gods, as the gods above,
Filled from the heart to the lips with love,
Held fast in his hands, clothed warm with his wings,
40   O love, my love, had you loved but me!

We had stood as the sure stars stand, and moved
    As the moon moves, loving the world; and seen
Grief collapse as a thing disproved,
    Death consume as a thing unclean.
45 Twain halves of a perfect heart, made fast
Soul to soul while the years fell past;
Had you loved me once, as you have not loved;
    Had the chance been with us that has not been.

I have put my days and dreams out of mind,
50   Days that are over, dreams that are done.
Though we seek life through, we shall surely find
    There is none of them clear to us now, not one.
But clear are these things; the grass and the sand,
Where, sure as the eyes reach, ever at hand,
55 With lips wide open and face burnt blind,
    The strong sea-daisies feast on the sun.

The low downs lean to the sea; the stream,
    One loose thin pulseless tremulous vein,
Rapid and vivid and dumb as a dream,
60   Works downward, sick of the sun and the rain;
No wind is rough with the rank rare flowers;
The sweet sea, mother of loves and hours,
Shudders and shines as the grey winds gleam,
    Turning her smile to a fugitive pain.

65 Mother of loves that are swift to fade,
    Mother of mutable winds and hours.
A barren mother, a mother-maid,
    Cold and clean as her faint salt flowers.
I would we twain were even as she,
70 Lost in the night and the light of the sea,
Where faint sounds falter and wan beams wade,
    Break, and are broken, and shed into showers.

The loves and hours of the life of a man,
    They are swift and sad, being born of the sea,
75 Hours that rejoice and regret for a span,
    Born with a man's breath, mortal as he;
Loves that are lost ere they come to birth,
Weeds of the wave, without fruit upon earth.
I lose what I long for, save what I can,
80   My love, my love, and no love for me!

It is not much that a man can save
    On the sands of life, in the straits of time,
Who swims in sight of the great third wave
    That never a swimmer shall cross or climb.
85 Some waif washed up with the strays and spars
That ebb-tide shows to the shore and the stars;
Weed from the water, grass from a grave,
    A broken blossom, a ruined rhyme.

There will no man do for your sake, I think,
90   What I would have done for the least word said.
I had wrung life dry for your lips to drink,
    Broken it up for your daily bread:
Body for body and blood for blood,
As the flow of the full sea risen to flood
95 That yearns and trembles before it sink,
    I had given, and lain down for you, glad and
        dead.

Yea, hope at highest and all her fruit,
    And time at fullest and all his dower,
I had given you surely, and life to boot,
100   Were we once made one for a single hour.
But now, you are twain, you are cloven apart,
Flesh of his flesh, but heart of my heart;
And deep in one is the bitter root,
    And sweet for one is the lifelong flower.

105 To have died if you cared I should die for you,
        clung
    To my life if you bade me, played my part

447

As it pleased you—these were the thoughts that
 stung,
 The dreams that smote with a keener dart
Than shafts of love or arrows of death;
110 These were but as fire is, dust, or breath,
Or poisonous foam on the tender tongue
 Of the little snakes that eat my heart.

I wish we were dead together to-day,
 Lost sight of, hidden away out of sight,
115 Clasped and clothed in the cloven clay,
 Out of the world's way, out of the light,
Out of the ages of worldly weather,
Forgotten of all men altogether,
As the world's first dead, taken wholly away,
120 Made one with death, filled full of the night.

How we should slumber, how we should sleep,
 Far in the dark with the dreams and the dews!
And dreaming, grow to each other, and weep,
 Laugh low, live softly, murmur and muse;
125 Yea, and it may be, struck through by the dream,
Feel the dust quicken and quiver, and seem
Alive as of old to the lips, and leap
 Spirit to spirit as lovers use.

Sick dreams and sad of a dull delight;
130 For what shall it profit when men are dead
To have dreamed, to have loved with the whole
 soul's might,
 To have looked for day when the day was fled?
Let come what will, there is one thing worth,
To have had fair love in the life upon earth:
135 To have held love safe till the day grew night,
 While skies had colour and lips were red.

Would I lose you now? would I take you then,
 If I lose you now that my heart has need?
And come what may after death to men,
140 What thing worth this will the dead years breed?
Lose life, lose all; but at least I know,

O sweet life's love, having loved you so,
 Had I reached you on earth, I should lose not again,
 In death nor life, nor in dream or deed.

145 Yea, I know this well: were you once sealed mine,
 Mine in the blood's beat, mine in the breath,
Mixed into me as honey in wine,
 Not time, that sayeth and gainsayeth,
Nor all strong things had severed us then;
150 Not wrath of gods, nor wisdom of men,
Nor all things earthly, nor all divine,
 Nor joy nor sorrow, nor life nor death.

I had grown pure as the dawn and the dew,
 You had grown strong as the sun or the sea,
155 But none shall triumph a whole life through:
 For death is one, and the fates are three.[1]
At the door of life, by the gate of breath,
There are worse things waiting for men than death;
Death could not sever my soul and you,
160 As these have severed your soul from me.

You have chosen and clung to the chance they sent
 you,
 Life sweet as perfume and pure as prayer.
But will it not one day in heaven repent you?
 Will they solace you wholly, the days that were?
165 Will you lift up your eyes between sadness and bliss,
Meet mine, and see where the great love is,
And tremble and turn and be changed? Content you;
 The gate is strait; I shall not be there.

But you, had you chosen, had you stretched hand,
170 Had you seen good such a thing were done,
I too might have stood with the souls that stand
 In the sun's sight, clothed with the light of the
 sun;
But who now on earth need care how I live?

---

[1] in Greek mythology, the goddesses Clotho, Lachesis, and Atropos.
Clotho spins the thread of life, Lachesis determines the length of life,
and Atropos cuts the thread of life.

Have the high gods anything left to give,
175 Save dust and laurels and gold and sand?
 Which gifts are goodly; but I will none.

O all fair lovers about the world,
 There is none of you, none, that shall comfort
  me.
My thoughts are as dead things, wrecked and
  whirled
180 Round and round in a gulf of the sea;
And still, through the sound and the straining stream,
Through the coil and chafe, they gleam in a dream,
The bright fine lips so cruelly curled,
 And strange swift eyes where the soul sits free.

185 Free, without pity, withheld from woe,
 Ignorant; fair as the eyes are fair.
Would I have you change now, change at a blow,
 Startled and stricken, awake and aware?
Yea, if I could, would I have you see
190 My very love of you filling me,
And know my soul to the quick, as I know
 The likeness and look of your throat and hair?

I shall not change you. Nay, though I might,
 Would I change my sweet one love with a word?
195 I had rather your hair should change in a night,
 Clear now as the plume of a black bright bird;
Your face fail suddenly, cease, turn grey,
Die as a leaf that dies in a day.
I will keep my soul in a place out of sight,
200 Far off, where the pulse of it is not heard.

Far off it walks, in a bleak blown space,
 Full of the sound of the sorrow of years.
I have woven a veil for the weeping face,
 Whose lips have drunken the wine of tears;
205 I have found a way for the failing feet,
A place for slumber and sorrow to meet;
There is no rumour about the place,
 Nor light, nor any that sees or hears.

I have hidden my soul out of sight, and said
210 "Let none take pity upon thee, none
Comfort thy crying: for lo, thou art dead,
 Lie still now, safe out of sight of the sun.
Have I not built thee a grave, and wrought
Thy grave-clothes on thee of grievous thought
215 With soft spun verses and tears unshed,
 And sweet light visions of things undone?

"I have given thee garments and balm and myrrh,
 And gold, and beautiful burial things.
But thou, be at peace now, make no stir;
220 Is not thy grave as a royal king's?
Fret not thyself though the end were sore;
Sleep, be patient, vex me no more.
Sleep; what hast thou to do with her?
 The eyes that weep, with the mouth that sings?"

225 Where the dead red leaves of the years lie rotten,
 The cold old crimes and the deeds thrown by,
The misconceived and the misbegotten,
 I would find a sin to do ere I die,
Sure to dissolve and destroy me all through,
230 That would set you higher in heaven, serve you
And leave you happy, when clean forgotten,
 As a dead man out of mind, am I.

Your lithe hands draw me, your face burns through
  me,
 I am swift to follow you, keen to see;
235 But love lacks might to redeem or undo me;
 As I have been, I know I shall surely be;
"What should such fellows as I do?"[1] Nay,
My part were worse if I chose to play;
For the worst is this after all; if they knew me,
240 Not a soul upon earth would pity me.

And I play not for pity of these; but you,
 If you saw with your soul what man am I,

---

[1] *Hamlet* 3.1.128–29.

You would praise me at least that my soul all
    through
    Clove to you, loathing the lives that lie;
245 The souls and lips that are bought and sold,
The smiles of silver and kisses of gold,
The lapdog loves that whine as they chew,
    The little lovers that curse and cry.

There are fairer women, I hear; that may be;
250   But I, that I love you and find you fair,
Who are more than fair in my eyes if they be,
    Do the high gods know or the great gods care?
Though the swords in my heart for one were
    seven,[1]
Would the iron hollow of doubtful heaven,
255 That knows not itself whether night-time or day be,
    Reverberate words and a foolish prayer?

I will go back to the great sweet mother,
    Mother and lover of men, the sea.
I will go down to her, I and none other,
260   Close with her, kiss her and mix her with me;
Cling to her, strive with her, hold her fast:
O fair white mother, in days long past
Born without sister, born without brother,
    Set free my soul as thy soul is free.

265 O fair green-girdled mother of mine,
    Sea, that art clothed with the sun and the rain,
Thy sweet hard kisses are strong like wine,
    Thy large embraces are keen like pain.
Save me and hide me with all thy waves,
270 Find me one grave of thy thousand graves,
Those pure cold populous graves of thine
    Wrought without hand in a world without
    stain.

I shall sleep, and move with the moving ships,
    Change as the winds change, veer in the tide;

275 My lips will feast on the foam of thy lips,
    I shall rise with thy rising, with thee subside;
Sleep, and not know if she be, if she were,
Filled full with life to the eyes and hair,
As a rose is fulfilled to the roseleaf tips
280   With splendid summer and perfume and pride.

This woven raiment of nights and days,
    Were it once cast off and unwound from me,
Naked and glad would I walk in thy ways,
    Alive and aware of thy ways and thee;
285 Clear of the whole world, hidden at home,
Clothed with the green and crowned with the foam,
A pulse of the life of thy straits and bays,
    A vein in the heart of the streams of the sea.

Fair mother, fed with the lives of men,
290   Thou art subtle and cruel of heart, men say.
Thou hast taken, and shalt not render again;
    Thou art full of thy dead, and cold as they.
But death is the worst that comes of thee;
Thou art fed with our dead, O mother, O sea,
295 But when hast thou fed on our hearts? or when,
    Having given us love, hast thou taken away?

O tender-hearted, O perfect lover,
    Thy lips are bitter, and sweet thine heart.
The hopes that hurt and the dreams that hover,
300   Shall they not vanish away and apart?
But thou, thou art sure, thou art older than earth;
Thou art strong for death and fruitful of birth;
Thy depths conceal and thy gulfs discover;
    From the first thou wert; in the end thou art.

305 And grief shall endure not for ever, I know.
    As things that are not shall these things be;
We shall live through seasons of sun and of snow,
    And none be grievous as this to me.
We shall hear, as one in a trance that hears,
310 The sound of time, the rhyme of the years;

[1] the Seven Sorrows of Mary.

Wrecked hope and passionate pain will grow
    As tender things of a spring-tide sea.

Sea-fruit that swings in the waves that hiss,
    Drowned gold and purple and royal rings.
315 And all time past, was it all for this?
    Times unforgotten, and treasures of things?
Swift years of liking and sweet long laughter,
That wist not well of the years thereafter
Till love woke, smitten at heart by a kiss,
320   With lips that trembled and trailing wings?

There lived a singer in France of old
    By the tideless dolorous midland sea.
In a land of sand and ruin and gold
    There shone one woman, and none but she.
325 And finding life for her love's sake fail,
Being fain to see her, he bade set sail,
Touched land, and saw her as life grew cold,
    And praised God, seeing; and so died he.

Died, praising God for his gift and grace:
330   For she bowed down to him weeping, and said
"Live"; and her tears were shed on his face
    Or ever the life in his face was shed.
The sharp tears fell through her hair, and stung
Once, and her close lips touched him and clung
335 Once, and grew one with his lips for a space;
    And so drew back, and the man was dead.[1]

O brother, the gods were good to you.
    Sleep, and be glad while the world endures.
Be well content as the years wear through;
340   Give thanks for life, and the loves and lures;
Give thanks for life, O brother, and death,
For the sweet last sound of her feet, her breath,

For gifts she gave you, gracious and few,
    Tears and kisses, that lady of yours.

345 Rest, and be glad of the gods; but I,
    How shall I praise them, or how take rest?
There is not room under all the sky
    For me that knows not of worst or best,
Dream or desire of the days before,
350 Sweet things or bitterness, any more.
Love will not come to me now though I die,
    As love came close to you, breast to breast.

I shall never be friends again with roses;
    I shall loathe sweet tunes, where a note grown
      strong
355 Relents and recoils, and climbs and closes,
    As a wave of the sea turned back by song.
There are sounds where the soul's delight takes fire,
Face to face with its own desire;
A delight that rebels, a desire that reposes;
360   I shall hate sweet music my whole life long.

The pulse of war and passion of wonder,
    The heavens that murmur, the sounds that shine,
The stars that sing and the loves that thunder,
    The music burning at heart like wine,
365 An armed archangel whose hands raise up
All senses mixed in the spirit's cup
Till flesh and spirit are molten in sunder—
    These things are over, and no more mine.

These were a part of the playing I heard
370   Once, ere my love and my heart were at strife:
Love that sings and hath wings as a bird,
    Balm of the wound and heft of the knife.
Fairer than earth is the sea, and sleep
Than overwatching of eyes that weep,
375 Now time has done with his one sweet word,
    The wine and leaven of lovely life.

---

[1] The legend of Geoffrey Rudel, a twelfth-century troubadour of Provence, who fell in love with the princess of Tripoli, whom he had never seen. He sailed across the Mediterranean Sea to visit her but fell ill on the voyage and was believed dead when the ship arrived. The princess came to see his body; Rudel revived for a few moments and then died.

I shall go my ways, tread out my measure,
  Fill the days of my daily breath
With fugitive things not good to treasure,
380   Do as the world doth, say as it saith;
But if we had loved each other—O sweet,
Had you felt, lying under the palms of your feet,
The heart of my heart, beating harder with pleasure
  To feel you tread it to dust and death—

385 Ah, had I not taken my life up and given
  All that life gives and the years let go,
The wine and honey, the balm and leaven,
  The dreams reared high and the hopes brought
    low?
Come life, come death, not a word be said;
390 Should I lose you living, and vex you dead?
I never shall tell you on earth; and in heaven,
  If I cry to you then, will you hear or know?
    —1866

Itylus [1]

Swallow, my sister, O sister swallow,
  How can thine heart be full of the spring?
    A thousand summers are over and dead.
What hast thou found in the spring to follow?
5   What hast thou found in thine heart to sing?
    What wilt thou do when the summer is
      shed?

O swallow, sister, O fair swift swallow,
  Why wilt thou fly after spring to the south,
    The soft south whither thine heart is set?
10 Shall not the grief of the old time follow?

Shall not the song thereof cleave to thy mouth?
  Hast thou forgotten ere I forget?

Sister, my sister, O fleet sweet swallow,
  Thy way is long to the sun and the south;
15   But I, fulfilled of my heart's desire,
Shedding my song upon height, upon hollow,
  From tawny body and sweet small mouth
    Feed the heart of the night with fire.

I the nightingale all spring through,
20 O swallow, sister, O changing swallow,
    All spring through till the spring be done,
Clothed with the light of the night on the dew,
  Sing, while the hours and the wild birds follow,
    Take flight and follow and find the sun.

25 Sister, my sister, O soft light swallow,
  Though all things feast in the spring's
    guest-chamber,
    How hast thou heart to be glad thereof yet?
For where thou fliest I shall not follow,
  Till life forget and death remember,
30   Till thou remember and I forget.

Swallow, my sister, O singing swallow,
  I know not how thou hast heart to sing.
    Hast thou the heart? is it all past over?
Thy lord the summer is good to follow,
35 And fair the feet of thy lover the spring:
    But what wilt thou say to the spring thy
      lover?

O swallow, sister, O fleeting swallow,
  My heart in me is a molten ember
    And over my head the waves have met.
40 But thou wouldst tarry or I would follow,
  Could I forget or thou remember,
    Couldst thou remember and I forget.

---

[1] Tereus, king of Thrace, raped his sister-in-law Philomela and cut out her tongue to prevent her from accusing him. Philomela wove the story into a tapestry which she gave to her sister, Tereus's wife Procne. In revenge, Procne killed her son Itylus (or Itys) and fed his body to Tereus. The sisters then fled, transformed into birds: Philomela into a nightingale and Procne into a swallow. Cf. Arnold's "Philomela."

O sweet stray sister, O shifting swallow,
  The heart's division divideth us.
45   Thy heart is light as a leaf of a tree;
But mine goes forth among sea-gulfs hollow
To the place of the slaying of Itylus,
  The feast of Daulis,[1] the Thracian sea.

O swallow, sister, O rapid swallow,
50   I pray thee sing not a little space.
    Are not the roofs and the lintels wet?
The woven web that was plain to follow,
  The small slain body, the flowerlike face,
    Can I remember if thou forget?

55 O sister, sister, thy first-begotten!
  The hands that cling and the feet that follow,
    The voice of the child's blood crying yet
Who hath remembered me? who hath forgotten?
    Thou hast forgotten, O summer swallow,
60   But the world shall end when I forget.
    —1866

Anactoria

τίνος αὖ τὺ πειθοῖ
μὰψ σαγηνεύσας φιλότατα[2]—SAPPHO.[3]

My life is bitter with thy love; thine eyes
  Blind me, thy tresses burn me, thy sharp sighs
Divide my flesh and spirit with soft sound,
And my blood strengthens, and my veins abound.
5 I pray thee sigh not, speak not, draw not breath;
Let life burn down, and dream it is not death.
I would the sea had hidden us, the fire

(Wilt thou fear that, and fear not my desire?)
Severed the bones that bleach, the flesh that cleaves,
10 And let our sifted ashes drop like leaves.
I feel thy blood against my blood: my pain
Pains thee, and lips bruise lips, and vein stings vein.
Let fruit be crushed on fruit, let flower on flower,
Breast kindle breast, and either burn one hour.
15 Why wilt thou follow lesser loves? are thine
Too weak to bear these hands and lips of mine?
I charge thee for my life's sake, O too sweet
To crush love with thy cruel faultless feet,
I charge thee keep thy lips from hers or his,
20 Sweetest, till theirs be sweeter than my kiss:
Lest I too lure, a swallow for a dove,
Erotion or Erinna[4] to my love.
I would my love could kill thee; I am satiated
With seeing thee live, and fain would have thee
    dead.
25 I would earth had thy body as fruit to eat,
And no mouth but some serpent's found thee sweet.
I would find grievous ways to have thee slain,
Intense device, and superflux of pain;
Vex thee with amorous agonies, and shake
30 Life at thy lips, and leave it there to ache;
Strain out thy soul with pangs too soft to kill,
Intolerable interludes, and infinite ill;
Relapse and reluctation of the breath,
Dumb tunes and shuddering semitones of death.
35 I am weary of all thy words and soft strange ways,
Of all love's fiery nights and all his days,
And all the broken kisses salt as brine
That shuddering lips make moist with waterish
    wine,
And eyes the bluer for all those hidden hours
40 That pleasure fills with tears and feeds from flowers,
Fierce at the heart with fire that half comes through,
But all the flowerlike white stained round with blue;
The fervent underlid, and that above
Lifted with laughter or abashed with love;

---

[1] the feast in the city of Daulis, Greece, at which Tereus ate the flesh of his son Itys.

[2] "Of whom by persuasion hast thou vainly caught love?" A mistranslation of Sappho's "Ode to Aphrodite," ll. 18–19. The correct version is "Whom shall I make to give thee room in her heart's love?"

[3] Sappho of Lesbos was a Greek lyric poet of the seventh-century BC. Anactoria was one of her lovers.

[4] Erotion is a Greek male name. Erinna was another of Sappho's lovers.

45   Thine amorous girdle, full of thee and fair,
     And leavings of the lilies in thine hair.
     Yea, all sweet words of thine and all thy ways,
     And all the fruit of nights and flower of days,
     And stinging lips wherein the hot sweet brine
50   That Love was born of burns and foams like wine,
     And eyes insatiable of amorous hours,
     Fervent as fire and delicate as flowers,
     Coloured like night at heart, but cloven through
     Like night with flame, dyed round like night with
          blue,
55   Clothed with deep eyelids under and above—
     Yea, all thy beauty sickens me with love;
     Thy girdle empty of thee and now not fair,
     And ruinous lilies in thy languid hair.
     Ah, take no thought for Love's sake; shall this be,
60   And she who loves thy lover not love thee?
     Sweet soul, sweet mouth of all that laughs and lives,
     Mine is she, very mine; and she forgives.
     For I beheld in sleep the light that is
     In her high place in Paphos,[1] heard the kiss
65   Of body and soul that mix with eager tears
     And laughter stinging through the eyes and ears;
     Saw Love, as burning flame from crown to feet,
     Imperishable, upon her storied seat;
     Clear eyelids lifted toward the north and south,
70   A mind of many colours, and a mouth
     Of many tunes and kisses; and she bowed,
     With all her subtle face laughing aloud,
     Bowed down upon me, saying, "Who doth thee
          wrong,
     Sappho?" but thou—thy body is the song,
75   Thy mouth the music; thou art more than I,
     Though my voice die not till the whole world die;
     Though men that hear it madden; though love
          weep,
     Though nature change, though shame be charmed
          to sleep.
     Ah, wilt thou slay me lest I kiss thee dead?

80   Yet the queen laughed from her sweet heart and said:
     "Even she that flies shall follow for thy sake,
     And she shall give thee gifts that would not take,
     Shall kiss that would not kiss thee" (yea, kiss me)
     "When thou wouldst not"—when I would not kiss
          thee!
85   Ah, more to me than all men as thou art,
     Shall not my songs assuage her at the heart?
     Ah, sweet to me as life seems sweet to death,
     Why should her wrath fill thee with fearful breath?
     Nay, sweet, for is she God alone? hath she
90   Made earth and all the centuries of the sea,
     Taught the sun ways to travel, woven most fine
     The moonbeams, shed the starbeams forth as wine,
     Bound with her myrtles, beaten with her rods,
     The young men and the maidens and the gods?
95   Have we not lips to love with, eyes for tears,
     And summer and flower of women and of years?
     Stars for the foot of morning, and for noon
     Sunlight, and exaltation of the moon;
     Waters that answer waters, fields that wear
100 Lilies, and languor of the Lesbian[2] air?
     Beyond those flying feet of fluttered doves,
     Are there not other gods for other loves?
     Yea, though she scourge thee, sweetest, for my sake,
     Blossom not thorns and flowers not blood should
          break.
105 Ah that my lips were tuneless lips, but pressed
     To the bruised blossom of thy scourged white
          breast!
     Ah that my mouth for Muses'[3] milk were fed
     On the sweet blood thy sweet small wounds had
          bled!
     That with my tongue I felt them, and could taste
110 The faint flakes from thy bosom to the waist!
     That I could drink thy veins as wine, and eat
     Thy breasts like honey! that from face to feet
     Thy body were abolished and consumed,

----

[1]   Cyprus, a centre for the worship of Aphrodite.

[2]   from Lesbos.

[3]   goddesses of poetry and the other arts.

And in my flesh thy very flesh entombed!
115 Ah, ah, thy beauty! like a beast it bites,
Stings like an adder, like an arrow smites.
Ah sweet, and sweet again, and seven times sweet
The paces and the pauses of thy feet!
Ah sweeter than all sleep or summer air
120 The fallen fillets fragrant from thine hair!
Yea, though their alien kisses do me wrong,
Sweeter thy lips than mine with all their song;
Thy shoulders whiter than a fleece of white,
And flower-sweet fingers, good to bruise or bite
125 As honeycomb of the inmost honey-cells,
With almond-shaped and roseleaf-coloured shells,
And blood like purple blossom at the tips
Quivering; and pain made perfect in thy lips
For my sake when I hurt thee; O that I
130 Durst crush thee out of life with love, and die,
Die of thy pain and my delight, and be
Mixed with thy blood and molten into thee!
Would I not plague thee dying overmuch?
Would I not hurt thee perfectly? not touch
135 Thy pores of sense with torture, and make bright,
Thine eyes with bloodlike tears and grievous light
Strike pang from pang as note is struck from note,
Catch the sob's middle music in thy throat,
Take thy limbs living, and new-mould with these
140 A lyre of many faultless agonies?
Feed thee with fever and famine and fine drouth,
With perfect pangs convulse thy perfect mouth,
Make thy life shudder in thee and burn afresh,
And wring thy very spirit through the flesh?
145 Cruel? but love makes all that love him well
As wise as heaven and crueller than hell.
Me hath love made more bitter toward thee
Than death toward man; but were I made as he
Who hath made all things to break them one by one,
150 If my feet trod upon the stars and sun
And souls of men as his have always trod,
God knows I might be crueller than God.
For who shall change with prayers or thanksgivings

The mystery of the cruelty of things?
155 Or say what God above all gods and years
With offering and blood-sacrifice of tears,
With lamentation from strange lands, from graves
Where the snake pastures, from scarred mouth of slaves
From prison, and from plunging prows of ships
160 Through flamelike foam of the sea's closing lips—
With thwartings of strange signs, and wind-blown hair
Of comets, desolating the dim air,
When darkness is made fast with seals and bars,
And fierce reluctance of disastrous stars,
165 Eclipse, and sound of shaken hills, and wings
Darkening, and blind inexpiable things—
With sorrow of labouring moons, and altering light
And travail of the planets of the night,
And weeping of the weary Pleiads seven,[1]
170 Feeds the mute melancholy lust of heaven?
Is not his incense bitterness, his meat
Murder? his hidden face and iron feet
Hath not man known, and felt them on their way
Threaten and trample all things and every day?
175 Hath he not sent us hunger? who hath cursed
Spirit and flesh with longing? filled with thirst
Their lips who cried unto him? who bade exceed
The fervid will, fall short the feeble deed,
Bade sink the spirit and the flesh aspire,
180 Pain animate the dust of dead desire,
And life yield up her flower to violent fate?
Him would I reach, him smite, him desecrate,
Pierce the cold lips of God with human breath,
And mix his immortality with death.
185 Why hath he made us? what had all we done
That we should live and loathe the sterile sun,
And with the moon wax paler as she wanes,
And pulse by pulse feel time grow through our veins?
Thee too the years shall cover; thou shalt be

---

[1] in Greek mythology, the seven daughters of Atlas and Pleione who were transformed into stars when Orion pursued them.

190 As the rose born of one same blood with thee,
As a song sung, as a word said, and fall
Flower-wise, and be not any more at all,
Nor any memory of thee anywhere;
For never Muse has bound above thine hair
195 The high Pierian flower[1] whose graft outgrows
All summer kinship of the mortal rose
And colour of deciduous days, nor shed
Reflex and flush of heaven about thine head,
Nor reddened brows made pale by floral grief
200 With splendid shadow from that lordlier leaf.
Yea, thou shalt be forgotten like spilt wine,
Except these kisses of my lips on thine
Brand them with immortality; but me—
Men shall not see bright fire nor hear the sea,
205 Nor mix their hearts with music, nor behold
Cast forth of heaven, with feet of awful gold
And plumeless wings that make the bright air blind,
Lightning, with thunder for a hound behind
Hunting through fields unfurrowed and unsown,
210 But in the light and laughter, in the moan
And music, and in grasp of lip and hand
And shudder of water that makes felt on land
The immeasurable tremor of all the sea,
Memories shall mix and metaphors of me.
215 Like me shall be the shuddering calm of night,
When all the winds of the world for pure delight
Close lips that quiver and fold up wings that ache;
When nightingales are louder for love's sake,
And leaves tremble like lute-strings or like fire;
220 Like me the one star swooning with desire
Even at the cold lips of the sleepless moon,
As I at thine; like me the waste white noon,
Burnt through with barren sunlight; and like me
The land-stream and the tide-stream in the sea.
225 I am sick with time as these with ebb and flow,
And by the yearning in my veins I know
The yearning sound of waters; and mine eyes
Burn as that beamless fire which fills the skies

---

[1] Pieria was a region on the slopes of Mt. Olympus where the Muses lived and were worshipped.

With troubled stars and travailing things of flame;
230 And in my heart the grief consuming them
Labours, and in my veins the thirst of these,
And all the summer travail of the trees
And all the winter sickness; and the earth,
Filled full with deadly works of death and birth,
235 Sore spent with hungry lusts of birth and death,
Has pain like mine in her divided breath;
Her spring of leaves is barren, and her fruit
Ashes; her boughs are burdened, and her root
Fibrous and gnarled with poison; underneath
240 Serpents have gnawn it through with tortuous teeth
Made sharp upon the bones of all the dead,
And wild birds rend her branches overhead.
These, woven as raiment for his word and thought,
These hath God made, and me as these, and
    wrought
245 Song, and hath lit it at my lips; and me
Earth shall not gather though she feed on thee.
As a shed tear shalt thou be shed; but I—
Lo, earth may labour, men live long and die,
Years change and stars, and the high God devise
250 New things, and old things wane before his eyes
Who wields and wrecks them, being more strong
    than they—
But, having made me, me he shall not slay.
Nor slay nor satiate, like those herds of his
Who laugh and live a little, and their kiss
255 Contents them, and their loves are swift and sweet,
And sure death grasps and gains them with slow
    feet,
Love they or hate they, strive or bow their knees—
And all these ends he hath his will of these.
Yea, but albeit he slay me, hating me—
260 Albeit he hide me in the deep dear sea
And cover me with cool wan foam, and ease
This soul of mine as any soul of these,
And give me water and great sweet waves, and make
The very sea's name lordlier for my sake,
265 The whole sea sweeter—albeit I die indeed
And hide myself and sleep and no man heed,

Of me the high God hath not all his will.
Blossom of branches, and on each high hill
Clear air and wind, and under in clamorous vales
270 Fierce noises of the fiery nightingales,
Buds burning in the sudden spring like fire,
The wan washed sand and the waves' vain desire,
Sails seen like blown white flowers at sea, and words
That bring tears swiftest, and long notes of birds
275 Violently singing till the whole world sings—
I Sappho shall be one with all these things,
With all high things for ever; and my face
Seen once, my songs once heard in a strange place,
Cleave to men's lives, and waste the days thereof
280 With gladness and much sadness and long love.
Yea, they shall say, earth's womb has borne in vain
New things, and never this best thing again;
Borne days and men, borne fruits and wars and
        wine,
Seasons and songs, but no song more like mine.
285 And they shall know me as ye who have known me
        here,
Last year when I loved Atthis, and this year
When I love thee; and they shall praise me, and say
"She hath all time as all we have our day,
Shall she not live and have her will"—even I?
290 Yea, though thou diest, I say I shall not die.
For these shall give me of their souls, shall give
Life, and the days and loves wherewith I live,
Shall quicken me with loving, fill with breath,
Save me and serve me, strive for me with death.
295 Alas, that neither moon nor snow nor dew
Nor all cold things can purge me wholly through,
Assuage me nor allay me nor appease,
Till supreme sleep shall bring me bloodless ease;
Till time wax faint in all his periods;
300 Till fate undo the bondage of the gods,
And lay, to slake and satiate me all through,
Lotus[1] and Lethe[2] on my lips like dew,

And shed around and over and under me
Thick darkness and the insuperable sea.
—1866

Hymn to Proserpine [3]

(After the Proclamation in Rome
of the Christian Faith) [4]

Vicisti, Galilæe [5]

I have lived long enough, having seen one thing,
        that love hath an end;
Goddess and maiden and queen, be near me now
        and befriend.
Thou art more than the day or the morrow, the
        seasons that laugh or that weep;
For these give joy and sorrow; but thou,
        Proserpina, sleep.
5 Sweet is the treading of wine, and sweet the feet of
        the dove;
But a goodlier gift is thine than foam of the grapes
        or love.
Yea, is not even Apollo, with hair and harpstring of
        gold,
A bitter God to follow, a beautiful God to behold?
I am sick of singing: the bays burn deep and chafe:
        I am fain
10 To rest a little from praise and grievous pleasure
        and pain.
For the Gods we know not of, who give us our
        daily breath,
We know they are cruel as love or life, and lovely as
        death.
O Gods dethroned and deceased, cast forth, wiped
        out in a day!

---

[1] The lotus is said to induce forgetfulness.

[2] Lethe is the river of forgetfulness in Hades.

[3] the Roman counterpart of the Greek goddess Persephone, Queen of the underworld.

[4] the Edict of Milan, passed by Constantine in 313 AD, which officially recognized Christianity.

[5] "Thou hast conquered, Galilean": reported to be the dying words of the Emperor Julian (331–63 AD), who had renounced Christianity during his lifetime.

From your wrath is the world released, redeemed
from your chains, men say.
15 New Gods are crowned in the city; their flowers
have broken your rods;
They are merciful, clothed with pity, the young
compassionate Gods.
But for me their new device is barren, the days are
bare;
Things long past over suffice, and men forgotten
that were.
Time and the Gods are at strife; ye dwell in the
midst thereof,
20 Draining a little life from the barren breasts of love.
I say to you, cease, take rest; yea, I say to you all, be
at peace,
Till the bitter milk of her breast and the barren
bosom shall cease.
Wilt thou yet take all, Galilean? but these thou
shalt not take,
The laurel, the palms and the pæan, the breast of
the nymphs in the brake;
25 Breasts more soft than a dove's that tremble with
tenderer breath;
And all the wings of the Loves, and all the joy
before death;
All the feet of the hours that sound as a single lyre,
Dropped and deep in the flowers, with strings that
flicker like fire.
More than these wilt thou give, things fairer than
all these things?
30 Nay, for a little we live, and life hath mutable
wings.
A little while and we die; shall life not thrive as it
may?
For no man under the sky lives twice, outliving his
day.
And grief is a grievous thing, and a man hath
enough of his tears:
Why should he labour, and bring fresh grief to
blacken his years?

35 Thou hast conquered, O pale Galilean; the world
has grown grey from thy breath;
We have drunken of things Lethean, and fed on
the fulness of death.
Laurel is green for a season, and love is sweet for a
day;
But love grows bitter with treason, and laurel
outlives not May.
Sleep, shall we sleep after all? for the world is not
sweet in the end;
40 For the old faiths loosen and fall, the new years
ruin and rend.
Fate is a sea without shore, and the soul is a rock
that abides;
But her ears are vexed with the roar and her face
with the foam of the tides.
O lips that the live blood faints in, the leavings of
racks and rods!
O ghastly glories of saints, dead limbs of gibbeted
Gods!
45 Though all men abase them before you in spirit,
and all knees bend,
I kneel not neither adore you, but standing, look to
the end.
All delicate days and pleasant, all spirits and
sorrows are cast
Far out with the foam of the present that sweeps to
the surf of the past:
Where beyond the extreme sea-wall, and between
the remote sea-gates,
50 Waste water washes, and tall ships founder, and
deep death waits:
Where, mighty with deepening sides, clad about
with the seas as with wings,
And impelled of invisible tides, and fulfilled of
unspeakable things,
White-eyed and poisonous-finned, shark-toothed
and serpentine-curled,
Rolls, under the whitening wind of the future, the
wave of the world.

55 The depths stand naked in sunder behind it, the
    storms flee away;
In the hollow before it the thunder is taken and
    snared as a prey;
In its sides is the north-wind bound; and its salt is
    of all men's tears;
With light of ruin, and sound of changes, and pulse
    of years:
With travail of day after day, and with trouble of
    hour upon hour;
60 And bitter as blood is the spray; and the crests are
    as fangs that devour:
And its vapour and storm of its steam as the
    sighing of spirits to be;
And its noise as the noise in a dream; and its depth
    as the roots of the sea:
And the height of its heads as the height of the
    utmost stars of the air:
And the ends of the earth at the might thereof
    tremble, and time is made bare.
65 Will ye bridle the deep sea with reins, will ye
    chasten the high sea with rods?
Will ye take her to chain her with chains, who is
    older than all ye Gods? [1]
All ye as a wind shall go by, as a fire shall ye pass
    and be past;
Ye are Gods, and behold, ye shall die, and the
    waves be upon you at last.
In the darkness of time, in the deeps of the years, in
    the changes of things,
70 Ye shall sleep as a slain man sleeps, and the world
    shall forget you for kings.
Though the feet of thine high priests tread where
    thy lords and our forefathers trod,
Though these that were Gods are dead, and thou
    being dead art a God,
Though before thee the throned Cytherean [5] be
    fallen, and hidden her head,

Yet thy kingdom shall pass, Galilean, thy dead shall
    go down to thee dead.
75 Of the maiden thy mother men sing as a goddess
    with grace clad around;
Thou art throned where another was king; where
    another was queen she is crowned.
Yea, once we had sight of another: but now she is
    queen, say these.
Not as thine, not as thine was our mother, a
    blossom of flowering seas,
Clothed round with the world's desire as with
    raiment, and fair as the foam,
80 And fleeter than kindled fire, and a goddess, and
    mother of Rome. [6]
For thine came pale and a maiden, and sister to
    sorrow; but ours,
Her deep hair heavily laden with odour and colour
    of flowers,
White rose of the rose-white water, a silver
    splendour, a flame,
Bent down unto us that besought her, and earth
    grew sweet with her name.
85 For thine came weeping, a slave among slaves, and
    rejected; but she
Came flushed from the full-flushed wave, and
    imperial, her foot on the sea.
And the wonderful waters knew her, the winds and
    the viewless ways,
And the roses grew rosier, and bluer the sea-blue
    stream of the bays.
Ye are fallen, our lords, by what token? we wist that
    ye should not fall.
90 Ye were all so fair that are broken; and one more
    fair than ye all.
But I turn to her still, having seen she shall surely
    abide in the end;
Goddess and maiden and queen, be near me now
    and befriend.

---

[1] Cf. Job 38–41.

[5] Aphrodite, who came ashore at Cythera after her birth in the sea.

[6] Aeneas, the founder of Rome, was protected by his mother Venus.

O daughter of earth, of my mother, her crown and
blossom of birth,
I am also, I also, thy brother; I go as I came unto
earth.
95   In the night where thine eyes are as moons are in
heaven, the night where thou art,
Where the silence is more than all tunes, where
sleep overflows from the heart,
Where the poppies¹ are sweet as the rose in our
world, and the red rose is white,
And the wind falls faint as it blows with the fume
of the flowers of the night.
And the murmur of spirits that sleep in the shadow
of Gods from afar
100 Grows dim in thine ears and deep as the deep dim
soul of a star,
In the sweet low light of thy face, under heavens
untrod by the sun,
Let my soul with their souls find place, and forget
what is done and undone.
Thou art more than the Gods who number the
days of our temporal breath;
For these give labour and slumber; but thou,
Proserpina, death.
105 Therefore now at thy feet I abide for a season in
silence. I know
I shall die as my fathers died, and sleep as they
sleep; even so.
For the glass of the years is brittle wherein we gaze
for a span;
A little soul for a little bears up this corpse which is
man.
So long I endure, no longer; and laugh not again,
neither weep.
110 For there is no God found stronger than death; and
death is a sleep.
—1866

¹ the flowers of sleep and oblivion, traditionally associated with
Proserpine.

The Leper ²

Nothing is better, I well think,
  Than love; the hidden well-water
Is not so delicate to drink:
  This was well seen of me and her.

5 I served her in a royal house;
  I served her wine and curious meat.
For will to kiss between her brows,
  I had no heart to sleep or eat.

Mere scorn God knows she had of me,
10 A poor scribe, nowise great or fair,
Who plucked his clerk's hood back to see
  Her curled-up lips and amorous hair.

I vex my head with thinking this.
  Yea, though God always hated me,
15 And hates me now that I can kiss
  Her eyes, plait up her hair to see

² Swinburne appended a fraudulent note, purporting to be from the
Grandes Chroniques de France (1505) but actually in his own approx-
imation of sixteenth-century French, to *The Leper*; it translates as follows:
"In those days the country was full of unclean persons and lepers. This
caused the King great dismay, seeing that God must be greatly offended.
Now it came to pass that a noble woman, Yolande de Sallières by name,
was afflicted and sorely wasted by this ugly disease; all her friends and
relations having before their very eyes the anger of God thrust her forth
from their homes, resolving never to shelter or succour a body cursed by
God and an abomination to all men. In former days, this lady had been
a beauty most pleasing to behold, generous with her body and of easy
virtue. However, none of those lovers who had frequently embraced and
tenderly kissed her wanted now to shelter so hideous a woman and so
detestable a sinner. A clerk who had once served her in the office of
lackey and go-between in matters venereal took her in and hid her in a
little hut. There the poor woman died a cruel and wretched death; and
after her died the said clerk who had cared for her out of true love for six
months, washing her, clothing her, and unclothing her every day with his
own hands. They even say that the naughty man, the cursed clerk,
remembering the great former loveliness of this ruined beauty pleasured
himself aplenty in kissing her on her dreadful, leprous lips and pressing
her gently to him with lover's hands. Wherefore, he died of the same
awful disease. This took place in Gastinois near Fontainebellant. And
when King Philippe heard of this happening he was greatly amazed by
it" (trans. Robin F. Jones).

How she then wore it on the brows,
    Yet am I glad to have her dead
Here in this wretched wattled house
20   Where I can kiss her eyes and head.

Nothing is better, I well know,
    Than love; no amber in cold sea
Or gathered berries under snow:
    That is well seen of her and me.

25 Three thoughts I make my pleasure of:
    First I take heart and think of this:
That knight's gold hair she chose to love,
    His mouth she had such will to kiss.

Then I remember that sundawn
30   I brought him by a privy way
Out at her lattice, and thereon
    What gracious words she found to say.

(Cold rushes for such little feet—
    Both feet could lie into my hand.
35 A marvel was it of my sweet
    Her upright body could so stand.)

"Sweet friend, God give you thank and grace;
    Now am I clean and whole of shame,
Nor shall men burn me in the face
40   For my sweet fault that scandals them."

I tell you over word by word.
    She, sitting edgewise on her bed,
Holding her feet, said thus. The third,
    A sweeter thing than these, I said.

45 God, that makes time and ruins it
    And alters not, abiding God,
Changed with disease her body sweet,
    The body of love wherein she abode.

Love is more sweet and comelier
50   Than a dove's throat strained out to sing.
All they spat out and cursed at her
    And cast her forth for a base thing.

They cursed her, seeing how God had wrought
    This curse to plague her, a curse of his.
55 Fools were they surely, seeing not
    How sweeter than all sweet she is.

He that had held her by the hair,
    With kissing lips blinding her eyes,
Felt her bright bosom, strained and bare,
60   Sigh under him, with short mad cries

Out of her throat and sobbing mouth
    And body broken up with love,
With sweet hot tears his lips were loth
    Her own should taste the savour of,

65 Yea, he inside whose grasp all night
    Her fervent body leapt or lay,
Stained with sharp kisses red and white,
    Found her a plague to spurn away.

I hid her in this wattled house,
70   I served her water and poor bread.
For joy to kiss between her brows
    Time upon time I was nigh dead.

Bread failed; we got but well-water
    And gathered grass with dropping seed;
75 I had such joy of kissing her,
    I had small care to sleep or feed.

Sometimes when service made me glad
    The sharp tears leapt between my lids,
Falling on her, such joy I had
80   To do the service God forbids.

"I pray you let me be at peace,
    Get hence, make room for me to die."

She said that: her poor lip would cease,
    Put up to mine, and turn to cry.

85 I said, "Bethink yourself how love
    Fared in us twain, what either did;
Shall I unclothe my soul thereof?
    That I should do this, God forbid."

Yea, though God hateth us, he knows
90   That hardly in a little thing
Love faileth of the work it does
    Till it grow ripe for gathering.

Six months, and now my sweet is dead
    A trouble takes me; I know not
95 If all were done well, all well said,
    No word or tender deed forgot.

Too sweet, for the least part in her,
    To have shed life out by fragments; yet,
Could the close mouth catch breath and stir,
100   I might see something I forget.

Six months, and I sit still and hold
    In two cold palms her cold two feet.
Her hair, half grey half ruined gold,
    Thrills me and burns me in kissing it.

105 Love bites and stings me through, to see
    Her keen face made of sunken bones.
Her worn-off eyelids madden me,
    That were shot through with purple once.

She said, "Be good with me; I grow
110   So tired for shame's sake, I shall die
If you say nothing": even so.
    And she is dead now, and shame put by.

Yea, and the scorn she had of me
    In the old time, doubtless vexed her then.

115 I never should have kissed her. See
    What fools God's anger makes of men!

She might have loved me a little too,
    Had I been humbler for her sake.
But that new shame could make love new
120   She saw not—yet her shame did make.

I took too much upon my love,
    Having for such mean service done
Her beauty and all the ways thereof,
    Her face and all the sweet thereon.

125 Yea, all this while I tended her,
    I know the old love held fast his part,
I know the old scorn waxed heavier,
    Mixed with sad wonder, in her heart.

It may be all my love went wrong—
130   A scribe's work writ awry and blurred,
Scrawled after the blind evensong—
    Spoilt music with no perfect word.

But surely I would fain have done
    All things the best I could. Perchance
135 Because I failed, came short of one,
    She kept at heart that other man's.

I am grown blind with all these things:
    It may be now she hath in sight
Some better knowledge; still there clings
140   The old question. Will not God do right?
—1866

The Garden of Proserpine [1]

Here, where the world is quiet;
Here, where all trouble seems

---

[1] The garden is the underworld, ruled by Proserpine, daughter of Ceres
(or Demeter) the Earth Mother.

Dead winds' and spent waves' riot
   In doubtful dreams of dreams;
5 I watch the green field growing
For reaping folk and sowing,
For harvest-time and mowing,
   A sleepy world of streams.

I am tired of tears and laughter,
10   And men that laugh and weep;
Of what may come hereafter
   For men that sow to reap:
I am weary of days and hours,
Blown buds of barren flowers,
15 Desires and dreams and powers
   And everything but sleep.

Here life has death for neighbour,
   And far from eye or ear
Wan waves and wet winds labour,
20   Weak ships and spirits steer;
They drive adrift, and whither
They wot not who make thither;
But no such winds blow hither,
   And no such things grow here.

25 No growth of moor or coppice,
   No heather-flower or vine,
But bloomless buds of poppies,
   Green grapes of Proserpine,
Pale beds of blowing rushes
30 Where no leaf blooms or blushes
Save this whereout she crushes
   For dead men deadly wine.

Pale, without name or number,
   In fruitless fields of corn,
35 They bow themselves and slumber
   All night till light is born;
And like a soul belated,
In hell and heaven unmated,

By cloud and mist abated
40   Comes out of darkness morn.

Though one were strong as seven,
   He too with death shall dwell,
Nor wake with wings in heaven,
   Nor weep for pains in hell;
45 Though one were fair as roses,
His beauty clouds and closes;
And well though love reposes,
   In the end it is not well.

Pale, beyond porch and portal,
50   Crowned with calm leaves, she stands
Who gathers all things mortal
   With cold immortal hands;
Her languid lips are sweeter
Than love's who fears to greet her
55 To men that mix and meet her
   From many times and lands.

She waits for each and other,
   She waits for all men born;
Forgets the earth her mother,
60   The life of fruits and corn;
And spring and seed and swallow
Take wing for her and follow
Where summer song rings hollow
   And flowers are put to scorn.

65 There go the loves that wither,
   The old loves with wearier wings;
And all dead years draw thither,
   And all disastrous things;
Dead dreams of days forsaken,
70 Blind buds that snows have shaken,
Wild leaves that winds have taken,
   Red strays of ruined springs.

We are not sure of sorrow,
   And joy was never sure;

75 To-day will die to-morrow;
    Time stoops to no man's lure;
And love, grown faint and fretful,
With lips but half regretful
Sighs, and with eyes forgetful
80   Weeps that no loves endure.

From too much love of living,
    From hope and fear set free,
We thank with brief thanksgiving
    Whatever gods may be
85 That no life lives for ever;
That dead men rise up never;
That even the weariest river
    Winds somewhere safe to sea.

Then star nor sun shall waken,
90   Nor any change of light:
Nor sound of waters shaken,
    Nor any sound or sight:
Nor wintry leaves or vernal,
Nor days nor things diurnal;
95 Only the sleep eternal
    In an eternal night.
—1866

A Forsaken Garden

In a coign of the cliff between lowland and
    highland,
    At the sea-down's edge between windward and
      lee,
Walled round with rocks as an inland island,
    The ghost of a garden fronts the sea.
5 A girdle of brushwood and thorn encloses
    The steep square slope of the blossomless bed
Where the weeds that grew green from the graves
    of its roses
      Now lie dead.

The fields fall southward, abrupt and broken,
10   To the low last edge of the long lone land.
If a step should sound or a word be spoken,
    Would a ghost not rise at the strange guest's
      hand?
So long have the grey bare walks lain guestless,
    Through branches and briars if a man make way,
15 He shall find no life but the sea-wind's, restless
      Night and day.

The dense hard passage is blind and stifled
    That crawls by a track none turn to climb
To the strait waste place that the years have rifled
20   Of all but the thorns that are touched not of time.
The thorns he spares when the rose is taken;
    The rocks are left when he wastes the plain.
The wind that wanders, the weeds wind-shaken,
      These remain.

25 Not a flower to be pressed of the foot that falls not;
    As the heart of a dead man the seed-plots are dry;
From the thicket of thorns whence the nightingale
    calls not,
    Could she call, there were never a rose to reply.
Over the meadows that blossom and wither
30   Rings but the note of a sea-bird's song;
Only the sun and the rain come hither
      All year long.

The sun burns sere and the rain dishevels
    One gaunt bleak blossom of scentless breath.
35 Only the wind here hovers and revels
    In a round where life seems barren as death.
Here there was laughing of old, there was weeping,
    Haply, of lovers none ever will know,
Whose eyes went seaward a hundred sleeping
40   Years ago.

Heart handfast in heart as they stood, "Look thither,"
    Did he whisper? "look forth from the flowers to
      the sea;

For the foam-flowers endure when the rose-
blossoms wither,
And men that love lightly may die—but we?"
45 And the same wind sang and the same waves
whitened,
And or ever the garden's last petals were shed,
In the lips that had whispered, the eyes that had
lightened,
Love was dead.

Or they loved their life through, and then went
whither?
50 And were one to the end—but what end who
knows?
Love deep as the sea as a rose must wither,
As the rose-red seaweed that mocks the rose.
Shall the dead take thought for the dead to love
them?
What love was ever as deep as a grave?
55 They are loveless now as the grass above them
Or the wave.

All are at one now, roses and lovers,
Not known of the cliffs and the fields and the
sea.
Not a breath of the time that has been hovers
60 In the air now soft with a summer to be.
Not a breath shall there sweeten the seasons
hereafter
Of the flowers or the lovers that laugh now or
weep,
When as they that are free now of weeping and
laughter
We shall sleep.

65 Here death may deal not again for ever;
Here change may come not till all change end.
From the graves they have made they shall rise up
never,
Who have left nought living to ravage and rend.

Earth, stones, and thorns of the wild ground
growing,
70 While the sun and the rain live, these shall be;
Till a last wind's breath upon all these blowing
Roll the sea.

Till the slow sea rise and the sheer cliff crumble,
Till terrace and meadow the deep gulfs drink,
75 Till the strength of the waves of the high tides
humble
The fields that lessen, the rocks that shrink,
Here now in his triumph where all things falter,
Stretched out on the spoils that his own hand
spread,
As a god self-slain on his own strange altar,
80 Death lies dead.
—1878

At A Month's End

The night last night was strange and shaken:
More strange the change of you and me.
Once more, for the old love's love forsaken,
We went out once more toward the sea.

5 For the old love's love-sake dead and buried,
One last time, one more and no more,
We watched the waves set in, the serried
Spears of the tide storming the shore.

Hardly we saw the high moon hanging,
10 Heard hardly through the windy night
Far waters ringing, low reefs clanging,
Under wan skies and waste white light.

With chafe and change of surges chiming,
The clashing channels rocked and rang
15 Large music, wave to wild wave timing,
And all the choral water sang.

Faint lights fell this way, that way floated,
    Quick sparks of sea-fire keen like eyes
From the rolled surf that flashed, and noted
20   Shores and faint cliffs and bays and skies.

The ghost of sea that shrank up sighing
    At the sand's edge, a short sad breath
Trembling to touch the goal, and dying
    With weak heart heaved up once in death—

25 The rustling sand and shingle shaken
    With light sweet touches and small sound—
These could not move us, could not waken
    Hearts to look forth, eyes to look round.

Silent we went an hour together,
30   Under grey skies by waters white.
Our hearts were full of windy weather,
    Clouds and blown stars and broken light.

Full of cold clouds and moonbeams drifted
    And streaming storms and straying fires,
35 Our souls in us were stirred and shifted
    By doubts and dreams and foiled desires.

Across, aslant, a scudding sea-mew
    Swam, dipped, and dropped, and grazed the sea:
And one with me I could not dream you;
40   And one with you I could not be.

As the white wing the white wave's fringes
    Touched and slid over and flashed past—
As a pale cloud a pale flame tinges
    From the moon's lowest light and last—

45 As a star feels the sun and falters,
    Touched to death by diviner eyes—
As on the old gods' untended altars
    The old fire of withered worship dies—

(Once only, once the shrine relighted
50   Sees the last fiery shadow shine,
Last shadow of flame and faith benighted,
    Sees falter and flutter and fail the shrine)

So once with fiery breath and flying
    Your winged heart touched mine and went,
55 And the swift spirits kissed, and sighing,
    Sundered and smiled and were content.

That only touch, that feeling only,
    Enough we found, we found too much;
For the unlit shrine is hardly lonely
60   As one the old fire forgets to touch.

Slight as the sea's sight of the sea-mew,
    Slight as the sun's sight of the star:
Enough to show one must not deem you
    For love's sake other than you are.

65 Who snares and tames with fear and danger
    A bright beast of a fiery kin,
Only to mar, only to change her
    Sleek supple soul and splendid skin?

Easy with blows to mar and maim her,
70   Easy with bonds to bind and bruise;
What profit, if she yield her tamer
    The limbs to mar, the soul to lose?

Best leave or take the perfect creature,
    Take all she is or leave complete;
75 Transmute you will not form or feature,
    Change feet for wings or wings for feet.

Strange eyes, new limbs, can no man give her;
    Sweet is the sweet thing as it is.
No soul she hath, we see, to outlive her;
80   Hath she for that no lips to kiss?

So may one read his weird, and reason,
    And with vain drugs assuage no pain.
For each man in his loving season
    Fools and is fooled of these in vain.

85   Charms that allay not any longing,
    Spells that appease not any grief,
Time brings us all by handfuls, wronging
    All hurts with nothing of relief.

Ah, too soon shot, the fool's bolt misses!
90   What help? the world is full of loves;
Night after night of running kisses,
    Chirp after chirp of changing doves.

Should Love disown or disesteem you
    For loving one man more or less?
95   You could not tame your light white sea-mew,
    Nor I my sleek black pantheress.

For a new soul let whoso please pray,
    We are what life made us, and shall be.
For you the jungle and me the sea-spray,
100   And south for you and north for me.

But this one broken foam-white feather
    I throw you off the hither wing,
Splashed stiff with sea-scurf and salt weather,
    This song for sleep to learn and sing—

105 Sing in your ear when, daytime over,
    You, couched at long length on hot sand
With some sleek sun-discoloured lover,
    Wince from his breath as from a brand:

Till the acrid hour aches out and ceases,
110   And the sheathed eyeball sleepier swims,
The deep flank smoothes its dimpling creases,
    And passion loosens all the limbs:

Till dreams of sharp grey north-sea weather
    Fall faint upon your fiery sleep,

115 As on strange sands a strayed bird's feather
    The wind may choose to lose or keep.

But I, who leave my queen of panthers,
    As a tired honey-heavy bee
Gilt with sweet dust from gold-grained anthers
120   Leaves the rose-chalice, what for me?

From the ardours of the chaliced centre,
    From the amorous anthers' golden grime,
That scorch and smutch all wings that enter,
    I fly forth hot from honey-time.

125 But as to a bee's gilt thighs and winglets
    The flower-dust with the flower-smell clings;
As a snake's mobile rampant ringlets
    Leave the sand marked with print of rings;

So to my soul in surer fashion
130   Your savage stamp and savour hangs;
The print and perfume of old passion,
    The wild-beast mark of panther's fangs.
—1878

Ave Atque Vale [1]

In Memory of Charles Baudelaire [2]

Nous devrions pourtant lui porter quelques fleurs;
Les morts, les pauvres morts, ont de grandes douleurs,
Et quand Octobre souffle, émondeur des vieux arbres,
Son vent mélancolique à l'entour de leurs marbres,
Certe, ils doivent trouver les vivants bien ingrats.
             —"Les Fleurs du Mal."

---

[1] "Hail and Farewell." From Catullus's lament for his dead brother, "Frater ave atque vale."

[2] The French poet Charles Baudelaire (1821–67) was enormously admired by Swinburne, who wrote this elegy on receiving an account of Baudelaire's death. The report was untrue.

I

Shall I strew on thee rose or rue or laurel,
  Brother, on this that was the veil of thee?
  Or quiet sea-flower moulded by the sea,
Or simplest growth of meadow-sweet or sorrel,
5   Such as the summer-sleepy Dryads[1] weave,
    Waked up by snow-soft sudden rains at eve?
Or wilt thou rather, as on earth before,
    Half-faded fiery blossoms, pale with heat
    And full of bitter summer, but more sweet
10 To thee than gleanings of a northern shore
    Trod by no tropic feet?

II

For always thee the fervid languid glories
    Allured of heavier suns in mightier skies;
    Thine ears knew all the wandering watery sighs
15 Where the sea sobs round Lesbian promontories,
    The barren kiss of piteous wave to wave
    That knows not where is that Leucadian grave
Which hides too deep the supreme head of song.
    Ah, salt and sterile as her kisses were,
20   The wild sea winds her and the green gulfs bear
Hither and thither, and vex and work her wrong,
    Blind gods that cannot spare.[2]

III

Thou sawest, in thine old singing season, brother,
    Secrets and sorrows unbeheld of us:
25   Fierce loves, and lovely leaf-buds poisonous,
Bare to thy subtler eye, but for none other
    Blowing by night in some unbreathed-in clime;
    The hidden harvest of luxurious time,
Sin without shape, and pleasure without speech;
30   And where strange dreams in a tumultuous sleep
    Make the shut eyes of stricken spirits weep;

And with each face thou sawest the shadow on each,
    Seeing as men sow men reap.[3]

IV

O sleepless heart and sombre soul unsleeping,
35   That were athirst for sleep and no more life
    And no more love, for peace and no more strife!
Now the dim gods of death have in their keeping
    Spirit and body and all the springs of song,
    Is it well now where love can do no wrong,
40 Where stingless pleasure has no foam or fang
    Behind the unopening closure of her lips?
    Is it not well where soul from body slips
And flesh from bone divides without a pang
    As dew from flower-bell drips?

V

45 It is enough; the end and the beginning
    Are one thing to thee, who art past the end.
    O hand unclasped of unbeholden friend,
For thee no fruits to pluck, no palms for winning,
    No triumph and no labour and no lust,
50   Only dead yew-leaves and a little dust.
O quiet eyes wherein the light saith nought,
    Whereto the day is dumb, nor any night
    With obscure finger silences your sight,
Nor in your speech the sudden soul speaks thought,
55   Sleep, and have sleep for light.

VI

Now all strange hours and all strange loves are over,
    Dreams and desires and sombre songs and sweet,
    Hast thou found place at the great knees and feet
Of some pale Titan-woman[4] like a lover,
60   Such as thy vision here solicited,
    Under the shadow of her fair vast head,
The deep division of prodigious breasts,
    The solemn slope of mighty limbs asleep,

---

[1] tree-nymphs.

[2] Lines 14–22 refer to the tradition that the Greek poet Sappho of Lesbos was supposed to have drowned herself off the island of Leucas. Baudelaire refers to Sappho in his poem "Lesbos."

---

[3] Cf. Galatians 6:7.

[4] a reference to Baudelaire's poem "La Géante" ("The Giantess"). In Greek mythology the Titans were giants.

The weight of awful tresses that still keep
65 The savour and shade of old-world pine-forests
　　Where the wet hill-winds weep?

VII

Hast thou found any likeness for thy vision?
　　O gardener of strange flowers, what bud, what
　　　bloom,
　　Hast thou found sown, what gathered in the
　　　gloom?
70 What of despair, of rapture, of derision,
　　What of life is there, what of ill or good?
　　Are the fruits grey like dust or bright like blood?
Does the dim ground grow any seed of ours,
　　The faint fields quicken any terrene root,
75 　　In low lands where the sun and moon are mute
And all the stars keep silence? Are there flowers
　　At all, or any fruit?

VIII

Alas, but though my flying song flies after,
　　O sweet strange elder singer, thy more fleet
80 　　Singing, and footprints of thy fleeter feet,
Some dim derision of mysterious laughter
　　From the blind tongueless warders of the dead,
　　Some gainless glimpse of Proserpine's[1] veiled
　　　head,
Some little sound of unregarded tears
85 　　Wept by effaced unprofitable eyes,
　　And from pale mouths some cadence of dead
　　　sighs—
These only, these the hearkening spirit hears,
　　Sees only such things rise.

IX

Thou art far too far for wings of words to follow,
90 　　Far too far off for thought or any prayer.
　　What ails us with thee, who art wind and air?
What ails us gazing where all seen is hollow?
　　Yet with some fancy, yet with some desire,

---

[1] queen of the underworld.

Dreams pursue death as winds a flying fire,
95 Our dreams pursue our dead and do not find.
　　Still, and more swift than they, the thin flame
　　　flies,
　　The low light fails us in elusive skies,
Still the foiled earnest ear is deaf, and blind
　　Are still the eluded eyes.

X

100 Not thee, O never thee, in all time's changes,
　　Not thee, but this the sound of thy sad soul,
　　The shadow of thy swift spirit, this shut scroll
I lay my hand on, and not death estranges
　　My spirit from communion of thy song—
105 These memories and these melodies that throng
Veiled porches of a Muse funereal—[2]
　　These I salute, these touch, these clasp and fold
　　As though a hand were in my hand to hold,
Or through mine ears a mourning musical
110 　　Of many mourners rolled.

XI

I among these, I also, in such station
　　As when the pyre was charred, and piled the sods,
　　And offering to the dead made, and their gods,
The old mourners had, standing to make libation,
115 　　I stand, and to the gods and to the dead
　　Do reverence without prayer or praise, and shed
Offering to these unknown, the gods of gloom,
　　And what of honey and spice my seedlands bear,
　　And what I may of fruits in this chilled air,
120 And lay, Orestes-like, across the tomb
　　A curl of severed hair.[3]

---

[2] Melpomene, the muse of tragedy.

[3] King Agamemnon (l. 123) was murdered by his wife and her lover. After a long absence from home, Orestes returns and lays a lock of his hair on his father's tomb as a sacrifice. Orestes meets his sister, Electra, at Agamemnon's tomb. The story is recounted in Aeschylus's (525–456 BC) drama the *Choëphori*.

XII

But by no hand nor any treason stricken,
    Not like the low-lying head of Him, the King,
    The flame that made of Troy a ruinous thing,
125 Thou liest, and on this dust no tears could quicken
    There fall no tears like theirs that all men hear
    Fall tear by sweet imperishable tear
Down the opening leaves of holy poets' pages.
    Thee not Orestes, not Electra mourns;
130   But bending us-ward with memorial urns
The most high Muses that fulfil all ages
    Weep, and our God's heart yearns.

XIII

For, sparing of his sacred strength, not often
    Among us darkling here the lord of light[1]
135   Makes manifest his music and his might
In hearts that open and in lips that soften
    With the soft flame and heat of songs that shine.
    Thy lips indeed he touched with bitter wine,
And nourished them indeed with bitter bread;
140   Yet surely from his hand thy soul's food came,
    The fire that scarred thy spirit at his flame
Was lighted, and thine hungering heart he fed
    Who feeds our hearts with fame.

XIV

Therefore he too now at thy soul's sunsetting,
145   God of all suns and songs, he too bends down
    To mix his laurel with thy cypress crown,
And save thy dust from blame and from forgetting.
    Therefore he too, seeing all thou wert and art,
    Compassionate, with sad and sacred heart,
150 Mourns thee of many his children the last dead,
    And hallows with strange tears and alien sighs
    Thine unmelodious mouth and sunless eyes,
And over thine irrevocable head
    Sheds light from the under skies.

XV

155 And one weeps with him in the ways Lethean,
    And stains with tears her changing bosom chill:
    That obscure Venus of the hollow hill,[2]
That thing transformed which was the Cytherean,
    With lips that lost their Grecian laugh divine
160   Long since, and face no more called Erycine;
A ghost, a bitter and luxurious god.
    Thee also with fair flesh and singing spell
    Did she, a sad and second prey, compel
Into the footless places once more trod,
165   And shadows hot from hell.

XVI

And now no sacred staff shall break in blossom,
    No choral salutation lure to light
    A spirit sick with perfume and sweet night
And love's tired eyes and hands and barren bosom.
170   There is no help for these things; none to mend
    And none to mar; not all our songs, O friend,
Will make death clear or make life durable.
    Howbeit with rose and ivy and wild vine
    And with wild notes about this dust of thine
175 At least I fill the place where white dreams dwell
    And wreathe an unseen shrine.

XVII

Sleep; and if life was bitter to thee, pardon,
    If sweet, give thanks; thou hast no more to live;
    And to give thanks is good, and to forgive.
180 Out of the mystic and the mournful garden
    Where all day through thine hands in barren
        braid
    Wove the sick flowers of secrecy and shade,
Green buds of sorrow and sin, and remnants grey,
    Sweet-smelling, pale with poison, sanguine-
        hearted,
185   Passions that sprang from sleep and thoughts
        that started,

---

[1] Apollo, god of the sun and of poetry.

[2] In the legend of Tannhäuser, Venus the Cytherean, or Erycine, appears as an enchantress who entices victims into the caverns of Horselberg, the Mountain of Venus.

Shall death not bring us all as thee one day
   Among the days departed?

XVIII

For thee, O now a silent soul, my brother,
   Take at my hands this garland, and farewell.
190   Thin is the leaf, and chill the wintry smell,
And chill the solemn earth, a fatal mother,
   With sadder than the Niobean womb,[1]

And in the hollow of her breasts a tomb.
Content thee, howsoe'er, whose days are done;
195   There lies not any troublous thing before,
   Nor sight nor sound to war against thee more,
For whom all winds are quiet as the sun,
   All waters as the shore.
—1878 (1868)

---

[1] Niobe's excessive pride in the number of children that she had led her to boast of them to Leto, the mother of Artemis and Apollo. Subsequently seven of her children were killed by Artemis and seven by Apollo.

Augusta Webster
1837 – 1894

Augusta Webster is remembered as a poet, dramatist, and essayist. She published a three-volume novel in 1864 under the name of Cecil Home; her first volume of poetry, *Blanche Lisle and Other Poems*, was also issued under this pen-name. Her dramatic works are *The Auspicious Day* (1872), *Disguises* (1879), *In a Day* (1882), and *The Sentence* (1887). The first volume of poetry to be published under Webster's own name was *Dramatic Studies* in 1866. This volume was followed by *A Woman Sold and Other Poems* in 1867, *Portraits* in 1870, *A Book of Rhyme* in 1881, and *Mother and Daughter* in 1895. The latter volume contains an unfinished and unsentimentalized sonnet cycle on the experience of motherhood. Webster advocated women's suffrage and offered her thoughts on topics relevant to married women in a collection of essays called *A Housewife's Opinions* (1878). Webster was sometimes accused of indelicacy, perhaps never more intensely than when she published her poetic consideration of the lot of the "fallen woman" in "A Castaway" (1870), but she never compromised her imaginative vision and energy.

Circe [1]

The sun drops luridly into the west;
Darkness has raised her arms to draw him down
Before the time, not waiting as of wont
Till he has come to her behind the sea;
5   And the smooth waves grow sullen in the gloom
And wear their threatening purple; more and more
The plain of waters sways and seems to rise
Convexly from its level of the shores;
And low dull thunder rolls along the beach:
10   There will be storm at last, storm, glorious storm!

Oh welcome, welcome, though it rend my
        bowers,
Scattering my blossomed roses like the dust,
Splitting the shrieking branches, tossing down
My riotous vines with their young half-tinged
        grapes
15   Like small round amethysts or beryls strung
Tumultuously in clusters; though it sate
Its ravenous spite among my goodliest pines
Standing there round and still against the sky
That makes blue lakes between their sombre tufts,

20   Or harry from my silvery olive slopes
Some hoary king whose gnarled fantastic limbs
Wear rugged armour of a thousand years;
Though it will hurl high on my flowery shores
The hostile wave that rives [2] at the poor sward [3]
25   And drags it down the slants, that swirls its foam
Over my terraces, shakes their firm blocks
Of great bright marbles into tumbled heaps,
And makes my pleached [4] and mossy labyrinths,
Where the small odorous blossoms grow like stars
30   Strewn in the milky way, a briny marsh.
What matter? let it come and bring me change,
Breaking the sickly sweet monotony.

I am too weary of this long bright calm;
Always the same blue sky, always the sea
35   The same blue perfect likeness of the sky,
One rose to match the other that has waned,
To-morrow's dawn the twin of yesterday's;
And every night the ceaseless crickets chirp
The same long joy and the late strain of birds
40   Repeats their strain of all the even month;

---

[1] the enchantress in Homer's *Odyssey*, who turned men into swine.

[2] to split or tear apart.

[3] turf.

[4] plaited.

And changelessly the petty plashing surfs
Bubble their chiming burden round the stones;
Dusk after dusk brings the same languid trance
Upon the shadowy hills, and in the fields
45 The waves of fireflies come and go the same,
Making the very flash of light and stir
Vex one like dronings of the shuttles at task.

Give me some change. Must life be only sweet,
All honey-pap as babes would have their food?
50 And, if my heart must always be adrowse
In a hush of stagnant sunshine, give me, then,
Something outside me stirring; let the storm
Break up the sluggish beauty, let it fall
Beaten below the feet of passionate winds,
55 And then to-morrow waken jubilant
In a new birth; let me see subtle joy
Of anguish and of hopes, of change and growth.

What fate is mine, who, far apart from pains
And fears and turmoils of the cross-grained world,
60 Dwell like a lonely god in a charmed isle
Where I am first and only, and, like one
Who should love poisonous savours more than
    mead,
Long for a tempest on me and grow sick
Of rest and of divine free carelessness!
65 Oh me, I am a woman, not a god;
Yea, those who tend me, even, are more than I,
My nymphs[1] who have the souls of flowers and
    birds
Singing and blossoming immortally.

Ah me! these love a day and laugh again,
70 And loving, laughing, find a full content;
But I know nought of peace, and have not loved.

Where is my love? Does someone cry for me
Not knowing whom he calls? Does his soul cry
For mine to grow beside it, grow in it?

75 Does he beseech the gods to give him me,
The one unknown rare woman by whose side
No other woman thrice as beautiful
Could once seem fair to him; to whose voice heard
In any common tones no sweetest sound
80 Of love made melody on silver lutes,
Or singing like Apollo's[2] when the gods
Grow pale with happy listening, might be peered
For making music to him; whom once found
There will be no more seeking anything?

85 Oh love, oh love, oh love, art not yet come
Out of the waiting shadows into life?
Art not yet come after so many years
That I have longed for thee? Come! I am here.

Not yet. For surely I should feel a sound
90 Of his far answer if now in the world
He sought me who will seek me—Oh, ye gods,
Will he not seek me? Is it all a dream?
Will there be only these, these bestial things
Who wallow in their styes, or mop and mow
95 Among the trees, or munch in pens and byres,
Or snarl and filch behind their wattled coops;
These things who had believed that they were men?

Nay, but he *will* come. Why am I so fair,
And marvellously minded, and with sight
100 Which flashes suddenly on hidden things,
As the gods see, who do not need to look?
Why wear I in my eyes that stronger power
Than basilisks,[3] whose gaze can only kill,
To draw men's souls to me to live or die
105 As I would have them? Why am I given pride
Which yet longs to be broken, and this scorn,
Cruel and vengeful, for the lesser men
Who meet the smiles I waste for lack of him,
And grow too glad? Why am I who I am?

[1] any of a group of minor nature goddesses in Greek mythology.

[2] the Greek and Roman sun-god, patron of music and poetry.

[3] a mythical reptile with a lethal breath and look, supposedly hatched from a cock's egg.

110 But for the sake of him whom fate will send
One day to be my master utterly,
That he should take me, the desire of all,
Whom only he in the world could bow to him.

Oh, sunlike glory of pale glittering hairs,
115 Bright as the filmy wires my weavers take
To make me golden gauzes—Oh, deep eyes,
Darker and softer than the bluest dusk
Of August violets, darker and deep
Like crystal fathomless lakes in summer noons—
120 Oh, sad sweet longing smile—Oh, lips that tempt
My very self to kisses—oh, round cheeks
Tenderly radiant with the even flush
Of pale smoothed coral—perfect lovely face
Answering my gaze from out this fleckless pool—
125 Wonder of glossy shoulders, chiselled limbs—
Should I be so your lover as I am,
Drinking an exquisite joy to watch you thus
In all a hundred changes through the day,
But that I love you for him till he comes,
130 But that my beauty means his loving it?

Oh, look! a speck on this side of the sun,
Coming—yes, coming with the rising wind
That frays the darkening cloud-wrack on the verge
And in a little while will leap abroad,
135 Spattering the sky with rushing blacknesses,
Dashing the hissing mountainous waves at the stars.
'Twill drive me that black speck a shuddering hulk
Caught in the buffeting waves, dashed impotent
From ridge to ridge, will drive it in the night
140 With that dull jarring crash upon the beach,
And the cries for help and the cries of fear and
     hope.

And then to-morrow they will thoughtfully,
With grave low voices, count their perils up,
And thank the gods for having let them live
145 And tell of wives and mothers in their homes,
And children, who would have such loss in them
That they must weep (and maybe I weep too)

With fancy of the weepings had they died.
And the next morrow they will feel their ease
150 And sigh with sleek content, or laugh elate,
Tasting delight of rest and revelling,
Music and perfumes, joyaunce for the eyes
Of rosy faces and luxurious pomps,
The savour of the banquet and the glow
155 And fragrance of the wine-cup; and they'll talk
How good it is to house in palaces
Out of the storms and struggles, and what luck
Strewed their good ship on our accessless coast.
Then the next day the beast in them will wake,
160 And one will strike and bicker, and one swell
With puffed-up greatness, and one gibe and strut
In apish pranks, and one will line his sleeve
With pilfered booties, and one snatch the gems
Out of the carven goblets as they pass,
165 One will grow mad with fever of the wine,
And one will sluggishly besot himself,
And one be lewd, and one be gluttonous;
And I shall sickly look and loathe them all.

Oh my rare cup! my pure and crystal cup,
170 With not one speck of colour to make false
The entering lights, or flaw to make them swerve!
My cup of Truth! How the lost fools will laugh
And thank me for my boon, as if I gave
Some momentary flash of the gods' joy,
175 To drink where *I* have drunk and touch the touch
Of *my* lips with their own! Aye, let them touch.

Too cruel, am I? And the silly beasts,
Crowding around me when I pass their way,
Glower on me and, although they love me still,
180 (With their poor sorts of love such as they could)
Call wrath and vengeance to their humid eyes
To scare me into mercy, or creep near
With piteous fawnings, supplicating bleats.
Too cruel? Did I choose them what they are?
185 Or change them from themselves by poisonous
     charms?

But any draught, pure water, natural wine,
Out of my cup, revealed them to themselves
And to each other. Change? there was no change;
Only disguise gone from them unawares:
190 And had there been one true right man of them
He would have drunk the draught as I had drunk,
And stood unharmed and looked me in the eyes,
Abashing me before him. But these things—
Why, which of them has even shown the kind
195 Of some one nobler beast? Pah! yapping wolves,
And pitiless stealthy wild-cats, curs, and apes,
And gorging swine, and slinking venomous snakes—
All false and ravenous and sensual brutes
That shame the Earth that bore them, these they
        are.

200   Lo, lo! the shivering blueness darting forth
On half the heavens, and the forked thin fire
Strikes to the sea: and hark, the sudden voice
That rushes through the trees before the storm,
And shuddering of the branches. Yet the sky
205 Is blue against them still, and early stars
Sparkle above the pine-tops; and the air
Clings faint and motionless around me here.

      Another burst of flame—and the black speck
210 Shows in the glare, lashed onwards. It were well
I bade make ready for our guests to-night.
—1870

A Castaway

Poor little diary, with its simple thoughts,
   Its good resolves, its "Studied French an hour,"
"Read Modern History," "Trimmed up my grey
      hat,"
"Darned stockings," "Tatted," "Practised my new
      song,"
5 "Went to the daily service," "Took Bess soup,"
"Went out to tea." Poor simple diary!
And did *I* write it? Was I this good girl,

This budding colourless young rose of home?
Did I so live content in such a life,
10 Seeing no larger scope, nor asking it,
Than this small constant round—old clothes to
      mend,
New clothes to make, then go and say my prayers,
Or carry soup, or take a little walk
And pick the ragged-robins in the hedge?
15 Then, for ambition, (was there ever life
That could forego that?) to improve my mind
And know French better and sing harder songs;
For gaiety, to go, in my best white
Well washed and starched and freshened with new
      bows,
20 And take tea out to meet the clergyman.
No wishes and no cares, almost no hopes,
Only the young girl's hazed and golden dreams
That veil the Future from her.

                        So long since:
And now it seems a jest to talk of me
25 As if I could be one with her, of me
Who am…me.

                  And what is that? My looking-glass
Answers it passably; a woman sure,
No fiend, no slimy thing out of the pools,
A woman with a ripe and smiling lip
30 That has no venom in its touch I think,
With a white brow on which there is no brand;
A woman none dare call not beautiful,
Not womanly in every woman's grace.

Aye, let me feed upon my beauty thus,
35 Be glad in it like painters when they see
At last the face they dreamed but could not find
Look from their canvas on them, triumph in it,
The dearest thing I have. Why, 'tis my all,
Let me make much of it: is it not this,
40 This beauty, my own curse at once and tool
To snare men's souls, (I know what the good say

475

Of beauty in such creatures) is it not this
That makes me feel myself a woman still,
With still some little pride, some little—

                         Stop!
45 "Some little pride, some little"—Here's a jest!
What word will fit the sense but modesty?
A wanton I, but modest!

                   Modest, true;
I'm not drunk in the streets, ply not for hire
At infamous corners with my likenesses
50 Of the humbler kind; yes, modesty's my word—
'Twould shape my mouth well too, I think I'll try:
"Sir, Mr What-you-will, Lord Who-knows-what,
My present lover or my next to come,
Value me at my worth, fill your purse full,
55 For I am modest; yes, and honour me
As though your schoolgirl sister or your wife
Could let her skirts brush mine or talk of me;
For I am modest."

              Well, I flout myself:
But yet, but yet—

                 Fie, poor fantastic fool,
60 Why do I play the hypocrite alone,
Who am no hypocrite with others by?
Where should be my "But yet"? I am that thing
Called half a dozen dainty names, and none
Dainty enough to serve the turn and hide
65 The one coarse English worst that lurks beneath:
Just that, no worse, no better.

                  And, for me,
I say let no one be above her trade;
I own my kindredship with any drab
Who sells herself as I, although she crouch
70 In fetid garrets and I have a home
All velvet and marqueterie[1] and pastilles,[2]
Although she hide her skeleton in rags

And I set fashions and wear cobweb lace:
The difference lies but in my choicer ware,
75 That I sell beauty and she ugliness;
Our traffic's one—I'm no sweet slaver-tongue
To gloze[3] upon it and explain myself
A sort of fractious angel misconceived—
Our traffic's one: I own it. And what then?
80 I know of worse that are called honourable.
Our lawyers, who with noble eloquence
And virtuous outbursts lie to hang a man,
Or lie to save him, which way goes the fee:
Our preachers, gloating on your future hell
85 For not believing what they doubt themselves:
Our doctors, who sort poisons out by chance
And wonder how they'll answer, and grow rich:
Our journalists, whose business is to fib
And juggle truths and falsehoods to and fro:
90 Our tradesmen, who must keep unspotted names
And cheat the least like stealing that they can:
Our—all of them, the virtuous worthy men
Who feed on the world's follies, vices, wants,
And do their businesses of lies and shams
95 Honestly, reputably, while the world
Claps hands and cried "good luck," which of their
     trades,
Their honourable trades, barefaced like mine,
All secrets brazened out, would shew more white?

        And whom do I hurt more than they? as much?
100 The wives? Poor fools, what do I take from them
Worth crying for or keeping? If they knew
What their fine husbands look like seen by eyes
That may perceive there are more men than one!
But, if they can, let them just take the pains
105 To keep them: 'tis not such a mighty task
To pin an idiot to your apron-string;
And wives have an advantage over us,
(The good and blind ones have) the smile or pout
Leaves them no secret nausea at odd times.

---

[1] ornamental inlaid work of wood or ivory, most often used in furniture and flooring.

[2] French from Latin *pastillus* "little loaf, lozenge."

[3] to fawn over.

110 Oh, they could keep their husbands if they cared,
But 'tis an easier life to let them go,
And whimper at it for morality.

  Oh! those shrill carping virtues, safely housed
From reach of even a smile that should put red
115 On a decorous cheek, who rail at us
With such a spiteful scorn and rancorousness,
(Which maybe is half envy at the heart)
And boast themselves so measurelessly good
And us so measurelessly unlike them,
120 What is their wondrous merit that they stay
In comfortable homes whence not a soul
Has ever thought of tempting them, and wear
No kisses but a husband's upon lips
There is no other man desires to kiss—
125 Refrain in fact from sin impossible?
How dare they hate us so? what have they done,
What borne, to prove them other than we are?
What right have they to scorn us—glass-case saints,
Dianas[1] under lock and key—what right
130 More than the well-fed helpless barn-door fowl
To scorn the larcenous wild-birds?

                              Pshaw, let be!
Scorn or no scorn, what matter for their scorn?
I have outfaced my own—that's harder work.
Aye, let their virtuous malice dribble on—
135 Mock snowstorms on the stage—I'm proof long
        since:
I have looked coolly on my what and why,
And I accept myself.

                    Oh I'll endorse
The shamefullest revilings mouthed at me,
Cry "True! Oh perfect picture! Yes, that's I!"
140 And add a telling blackness here and there,
And then dare swear you, every nine of ten,
My judges and accusers, I'd not change

My conscience against yours, you who tread out
Your devil's pilgrimage along the roads
145 That take in church and chapel, and arrange
A roundabout and decent way to hell.

  Well, mine's a short way and a merry one:
So says my pious hash of ohs and ahs,
Choice texts and choicer threats, appropriate names,
150 (Rahabs[2] and Jezebels[3]) some fierce Tartuffe[4]
Hurled at me through the post. We had rare fun
Over that tract digested with champagne.
Where is it? where's my rich repertory
Of insults Biblical? "*I prey on souls*"—
155 Only my men have oftenest none I think:
"*I snare the simple ones*"—but in these days
There seem to be none simple and none snared
And most men have their favourite sinnings planned
To do them civilly and sensibly:
160 "*I braid my hair*"—but braids are out of date:
"*I paint my cheeks*"—I always wear them pale:
"*I—*"

        Pshaw! the trash is savourless to-day:
One cannot laugh alone. There, let it burn.
What, does the windy dullard think one needs
165 His wisdom dove-tailed on to Solomon's,[5]
His threats out-threatening God's, to teach the news
That those who need not sin have safer souls?
We know it, but we've bodies to save too;
And so we earn our living.

                        Well lit, tract!
170 At least you've made me a good leaping blaze.
Up, up, how the flame shoots! and now 'tis dead.

---

[1] the Roman goddess of the moon, hunting, and virginity.

[2] a prostitute who played an important role in the Israelites' success in the battle for Jericho.

[3] the shameless and wicked woman who married Ahab, king of Israel: 1 Kings 16, 19; 2 Kings 9:7–10, 30–37.

[4] the titular hero of Molière's satirical comedy; he was a religious hypocrite.

[5] the son of David and King of Israel, famed for his wisdom.

Oh proper finish, preaching to the last—
No such bad omen either; sudden end,
And no sad withering horrible old age.
175 How one would clutch at youth to hold it tight!
And then to know it gone, to see it gone,
Be taught its absence by harsh careless looks,
To live forgotten, solitary, old—
The cruellest word that ever woman learns.
180 Old—that's to be nothing, or to be at best
A blurred memorial that in better days
There was a woman once with such a name.
No, no, I could not bear it: death itself
Shows kinder promise…even death itself,
185 Since it must come one day—

                              Oh this grey gloom!
This rain, rain, rain, what wretched thoughts it
        brings!
Death: I'll not think of it.

                          Will no one come?
'Tis dreary work alone.

                      Why did I read
That silly diary? Now, sing-song, ding-dong,
190 Come the old vexing echoes back again,
Church bells and nursery good-books, back again
Upon my shrinking ears that had forgotten—
I hate the useless memories: 'tis fools' work
Singing the hacknied dirge of "better days":
195 Best take Now kindly, give the past good-bye,
Whether it were a better or a worse.

    Yes, yes, I listened to the echoes once,
The echoes and the thoughts from the old days.
The worse for me: I lost my richest friend,
200 And that was all the difference. For the world,
I would not have that flight known. How they'd
        roar:
"What! Eulalie, when she refused us all,

'Ill' and 'away,' was doing Magdalene,[1]
Tears, ashes, and her Bible, and then off
205 To hide her in a Refuge…for a week!"

    A wild whim that, to fancy I could change
My new self for my old because I wished!
Since then, when in my languid days there comes
That craving, like homesickness, to go back
210 To the good days, the dear old stupid days,
To the quiet and the innocence, I know
'Tis a sick fancy and try palliatives.[2]

    What is it? You go back to the old home,
And 'tis not *your* home, has no place for you,
215 And, if it had, you could not fit you in it.
And could I fit me to my former self?
If I had had the wit, like some of us,
To sow my wild-oats into three per cents,
Could I not find me shelter in the peace
220 Of some far nook where none of them would come,
Nor whisper travel from this scurrilous world
(That gloats, and moralizes through its leers)
To blast me with my fashionable shame?
There I might—oh my castle in the clouds!
225 And where's its rent?—but there, were there a there,
I might again live the grave blameless life
Among such simple pleasures, simple cares:
But could they be my pleasures, be my cares?
The blameless life, but never the content—
230 Never. How could I henceforth be content
With any life but one that sets the brain
In a hot merry fever with its stir?
What would there be in quiet rustic days,
Each like the other, full of time to think,
235 To keep one bold enough to live at all?
Quiet is hell, I say—as if a woman
Could bear to sit alone, quiet all day,
And loathe herself and sicken on her thoughts.

---

[1] Mary Magdalene: Luke 8:2, and also identified with the repentant woman in Luke 7:37—commonly regarded as the reformed prostitute.

[2] used to alleviate pain or anxiety.

They tried it at the Refuge,[1] and I failed:
240 I could not bear it. Dreary hideous room,
Coarse pittance, prison rules, one might bear these
And keep one's purpose; but so much alone,
And then made faint and weak and fanciful
By change from pampering to half-famishing—
245 Good God, what thoughts come! Only one week
    more
And 'twould have ended: but in one day more
I must have killed myself. And I loathe death,
The dreadful foul corruption with who knows
What future after it.

                    Well, I came back,
250 Back to my slough. Who says I had my choice?
Could I stay there to die of some mad death?
And if I rambled out into the world
Sinless but penniless, what else were that
But slower death, slow pining shivering death
255 By misery and hunger? Choice! What choice
Of living well or ill? could I have that?
And who would give it me? I think indeed
If some kind hand, a woman's—I hate men—
Had stretched itself to help me to firm ground,
260 Taken a chance and risked my falling back,
I could have gone my way not falling back:
But, let her be all brave, all charitable,
How could she do it? Such a trifling boon—
A little work to live by, 'tis not much—
265 And I might have found will enough to last:
But where's the work? More sempstresses[2] than
    shirts;
And defter hands at white work than are mine
Drop starved at last: dressmakers, milliners,
Too many too they say; and then their trades
270 Need skill, apprenticeship. And why so bold
As hire me for their humblest drudgery?
Not even for scullery slut; not even, I think,

For governess although they'd get me cheap.
And after all it would be something hard,
275 With the marts for decent women overfull,
If I could elbow in and snatch a chance
And oust some good girl so, who then perforce
Must come and snatch her chance among our
    crowd.

Why, if the worthy men who think all's done
280 If we'll but come where we can hear them preach,
Could bring us all, or any half of us,
Into their fold, teach all us wandering sheep,
Or only half of us, to stand in rows
And baa them hymns and moral songs, good lack,
285 What would they do with us? what could they do?
Just think! with were't but half of us on hand
To find work for…or husbands. Would they try
To ship us to the colonies for wives?

Well, well, I know the wise ones talk and talk:
290 "Here's cause, here's cure:" "No, here it is, and here:"
And find society to blame, or law,
The Church, the men, the women, too few schools,
Too many schools, too much, too little taught:
Somewhere or somehow someone is to blame:
295 But I say all the fault's with God himself
Who puts too many women in the world.
We ought to die off reasonably and leave
As many as the men want, none to waste.
Here's cause; the woman's superfluity:
300 And for the cure, why, if it were the law,
Say, every year, in due percentages,
Balancing them with males as the times need,
To kill off female infants, 'twould make room;
And some of us would not have lost too much,
305 Losing life ere we know what it *can* mean.

The other day I saw a woman weep
Beside her dead child's bed: the little thing
Lay smiling, and the mother wailed half mad,
Shrieking to God to give it back again.

---

[1] usually, shelters set up for "fallen women" and prostitutes who wished
to reform.

[2] variation of "seamstress."

310 I could have laughed aloud: the little girl
Living had but her mother's life to live;
There she lay smiling, and her mother wept
To know her gone!

              My mother would have wept.

     Oh, mother, mother, did you ever dream,
315 You good grave simple mother, you pure soul
No evil could come nigh, did you once dream
In all your dying cares for your lone girl
Left to fight out her fortune helplessly
That there would be *this* danger?—for *your* girl,
320 Taught by you, lapped in a sweet ignorance,
Scarcely more wise of what things sin could be
Than some young child a summer six months old,
Where in the north the summer makes a day,
Of what is darkness…darkness that will come
325 To-morrow suddenly. Thank God at least
For this much of my life, that when you died,
That when you kissed me dying, not a thought
Of this made sorrow for you, that I too
Was pure of even fear.

                Oh yes, I thought,
330 Still new in my insipid treadmill life,
(My father so late dead), and hopeful still,
There might be something pleasant somewhere in
    it,
Some sudden fairy come, no doubt, to turn
My pumpkin to a chariot, I thought then
335 That I might plod and plod and drum the sounds
Of useless facts into unwilling ears,
Tease children with dull questions half the day
Then con dull answers in my room at night
Ready for next day's questions, mend quill pens
340 And cut my fingers, add up sums done wrong
And never get them right; teach, teach, and teach—
What I half knew, or not at all—teach, teach
For years, a lifetime—*I!*

             And yet, who knows?
It might have been, for I was patient once,
345 And willing, and meant well; it might have been
Had I but still clung on in my first place—
A safe dull place, where mostly there were smiles
But never merry-makings; where all days
Jogged on sedately busy, with no haste;
350 Where all seemed measured out, but margins broad:
A dull home but a peaceful, where I felt
My pupils would be dear young sisters soon,
And felt their mother take me to her heart,
Motherly to all lonely harmless things.
355 But I must have a conscience, must blurt out
My great discovery of my ignorance!
And who required it of me? And who gained?
What did it matter for a more or less
The girls learnt in their schoolbooks, to forget
360 In their first season? We did well together:
They loved me and I them: but I went off
To housemaid's pay, six crossgrained brats to teach,
Wrangles and jangles, doubts, disgráce…then this;
And they had a perfection found for them,
365 Who has all ladies' learning in her head
Abridged and scheduled, speaks five languages,
Knows botany and conchology[1] and globes,
Draws, paints, plays, sings, embroiders, teaches all
On a patent method never known to fail:
370 And now they're finished and, I hear, poor things,
Are the worst dancers and worst dressers out.
And where's their profit of those prison years
All gone to make them wise in lesson-books?
Who wants his wife to know weeds' Latin names?
375 Who ever chose a girl for saying dates?
Or asked if she had learned to trace a map?

    Well, well, the silly rules this silly world
Makes about women! This is one of them.
Why must there be pretence of teaching them
380 What no one ever cares that they should know,

---

[1] a branch of zoology that centres on mollusks and shells.

What, grown out of the schoolroom, they cast off
Like the schoolroom pinafore,[1] no better fit
For any use of real grown-up life,
For any use to her who seeks or waits
385 The husband and the home, for any use,
For any shallowest pretence of use,
To her who has them? Do I not know this,
I, like my betters, that a woman's life,
Her natural life, her good life, her one life,
390 Is in her husband, God on earth to her,
And what she knows, and what she can and is
Is only good as it brings good to him?

    Oh God, do I not know it? I the thing
Of shame and rottenness, the animal
395 That feed men's lusts and prey on them, I, I,
Who should not dare to take the name of wife
On my polluted lips, who in the word
Hear but my own reviling, I know that.
I could have lived by that rule, how content:
400 My pleasure to make him some pleasure, pride
To be as he would have me, duty, care,
To fit all to his taste, rule my small sphere
To his intention; then to lean on him,
Be guided, tutored, loved—no, not that word,
405 That *loved* which between men and women means
All selfishness, all cloying talk, all lust,
All vanity, all idiocy—not loved,
But cared for. I've been loved myself, I think,
Some once or twice since my poor mother died,
410 But *cared for*, never:—that's a word for homes,
Kind homes, good homes, where simple children
    come
And ask their mother is this right or wrong,
Because they know she's perfect, cannot err;
Their father told them so, and he knows all,
415 Being so wise and good and wonderful,
Even enough to scold even her at times

And tell her everything she does not know.
Ah the sweet nursery logic!

            Fool! thrice fool!
Do I hanker after that too? Fancy me
420 Infallible nursery saint, live code of law!
Me preaching! teaching innocence to be good!—
A mother!

        Yet the baby thing that woke
And wailed an hour or two, and then was dead,
Was mine, and had he lived…why then my name
425 Would have been mother. But 'twas well he died:
I could have been no mother, I, lost then
Beyond his saving. Had he come before
And lived, come to me in the doubtful days
When shame and boldness had not grown one sense,
430 For his sake, with the courage come of him,
I might have struggled back.

          But how? But how?
His father would not then have let me go:
His time had not yet come to make an end
Of my "for ever" with a hireling's fee
435 And civil light dismissal. None but him
To claim a bit of bread of if I went,
Child or no child: would he have given it me?
He! no; he had not done with me. No help,
No help, no help. Some ways can be trodden back,
440 But never our way, we who one wild day
Have given goodbye to what in our deep hearts
The lowest woman still holds best in life,
Good name—good name though given by the
    world
That mouths and garbles with its decent prate,
445 And wraps it in respectable grave shams,
And patches conscience partly by the rule
Of what one's neighbour thinks, but something
    more
By what his eyes are sharp enough to see.

---

[1] a sleeveless apron-like garment worn primarily by girls.

How I could scorn it with its Pharisees,[1]
450   If it could not scorn me: but yet, but yet—
Oh God, if I could look it in the face!

Oh I am wild, am ill, I think, to-night:
Will no one come and laugh with me? No feast,
No merriment to-night. So long alone!
455   Will no one come?

At least there's a new dress
To try, and grumble at—they never fit
To one's ideal. Yes, a new rich dress,
With lace like this too, that's a soothing balm
For any fretting woman, cannot fail;
460   I've heard men say it…and they know so well
What's in all women's hearts, especially
Women like me.

No help! no help! no help!
How could it be? It was too late long since—
Even at the first too late. Whose blame is that?
465   There are some kindly people in the world,
But what can *they* do? If one hurls oneself
Into a quicksand, what can be the end,
But that one sinks and sinks? Cry out for help?
Ah yes, and, if it came, who is so strong
470   To strain from the firm ground and lift one out?
And how, so firmly clutching the stretched hand
As death's pursuing terror bids, even so,
How can one reach firm land, having to foot
The treacherous crumbling soil that slides and gives
475   And sucks one in again? Impossible path!
No, why waste struggles, I or any one?
What is must be. What then? I where I am,
Sinking and sinking; let the wise pass by
And keep their wisdom for an apter use,
480   Let me sink merrily as I best may.

Only, I think my brother—I forgot;
He stopped his brotherhood some years ago—
But if he had been just so much less good
As to remember mercy. Did he think
485   How once I was his sister, prizing him
As sisters do, content to learn for him
The lesson girls with brothers all must learn,
To do without?

I have heard girls lament
That doing so without all things one would,
490   But I saw never aught to murmur at,
For men must be made ready for their work
And women all have more or less their chance
Of husbands to work for them, keep them safe
Like summer roses in soft greenhouse air
495   That never guess 'tis winter out of doors:
No, I saw never aught to murmur at,
Content with stinted fare and shabby clothes
And cloistered silent life to save expense,
Teaching myself out of my borrowed books,
500   While he for some one pastime, (needful, true,
To keep him of his rank; 'twas not his fault)
Spent in a month what could have given me
My teachers for a year.

'Twas no one's fault:
For could he be launched forth on the rude sea
505   Of this contentious world and left to find
Oars and the boatman's skill by some good chance?
'Twas no one's fault: yet still he might have thought
Of our so different youths and owned at least
'Tis pitiful when a mere nerveless girl
510   Untutored must put forth upon that sea,
Not in the woman's true place, the wife's place,
To trust a husband and be borne along,
But impotent blind pilot to herself.

Merciless, merciless—like the prudent world
515   That will not have the flawed soul prank itself
With a hoped second virtue, will not have

---

[1] an ancient Jewish sect that strictly observed the written law, but simultaneously insisted on the importance of the oral law that had evolved out of common usage. In this modern context, the term is a negative epithet: self-serving hypocrites.

The woman fallen once lift up herself…
Lest she should fall again. Oh how his taunts,
His loathing fierce reproaches, scarred and seared
520 Like branding iron hissing in a wound!
And it was true—*that* killed me: and I felt
A hideous hopeless shame burn out my heart,
And knew myself for ever that he said,
That which I was—Oh it was true, true, true.

525   No, not true then. I was not all that then.
Oh, I have drifted on before mad winds
And made ignoble shipwreck; not to-day
Could any breeze of heaven prosper me
Into the track again, nor any hand
530 Snatch me out of the whirlpool I have reached;
But then?

            Nay, he judged very well: he knew
Repentance was too dear a luxury
For a beggar's buying, knew it earns no bread—
And knew me a too base and nerveless thing
535 To bear my first fault's sequel and just die.
And how could he have helped me? Held my hand,
Owned me for his, fronted the angry world
Clothed with my ignominy? Or maybe
Taken me to his home to damn him worse?
540 What did I look for? for what less would serve
That he could do, a man without a purse?
He meant me well, he sent me that five pounds,
Much to him then; and, if he bade me work
And never vex him more with news of me,
545 We both knew him too poor for pensioners.
I see he did his best; I could wish now
Sending it back I had professed some thanks.

    But there! I was too wretched to be meek:
It seemed to me as if he, every one,
550 The whole great world, were guilty of my guilt,
Abettors and avengers: in my heart
I gibed them back their gibings; I was wild.

I see clear now and know one has one's life
In hand at first to spend or spare or give
555 Like any other coin; spend it, or give,
Or drop it in the mire, can the world see
You get your value for it, or bar off
The hurrying of its marts to grope it up
And give it back to you for better use?
560 And if you spend or give, that is your choice;
And if you let it slip, that's your choice too,
You should have held it firmer. Yours the blame,
And not another's, not the indifferent world's
Which goes on steadily, statistically,
565 And count by censuses not separate souls—
And if it somehow needs to its worst use
So many lives of women, useless else,
It buys us of ourselves; we could hold back,
Free all of us to starve, and some of us,
570 (Those who have done no ill, and are in luck)
To slave their lives out and have food and clothes
Until they grow unserviceably old.

    Oh, I blame no one—scarcely even myself.
It was to be: the very good in me
575 Has always turned to hurt; all I thought right
At the hot moment, judged of afterwards,
Shows reckless.

            Why, look at it, had I taken
The pay my dead child's father offered me
For having been its mother, I could then
580 Have kept life in me—many have to do it,
That swarm in the back alleys, on no more,
Cold sometimes, mostly hungry, but they live—
I could have gained a respite trying it,
And maybe found at last some humble work
585 To eke the pittance out. Not I, forsooth,
I must have spirit, must have womanly pride,
Must dash back his contemptuous wages, I
Who had not scorned to earn them, dash them back
The fiercer that he dared to count our boy
590 In my appraising: and yet now I think

I might have taken it for my dead boy's sake;
It would have been *his* gift.

           But I went forth
With my fine scorn, and whither did it lead?
Money's the root of evil do they say?
595 Money is virtue, strength: money to me
Would then have been repentance: could I live
Upon my idiot's pride?

           Well, it fell soon.
I had prayed Clement might believe me dead,
And yet I begged of him—That's like me too,
600 Beg of him and then send him back his alms!
What if he gave as to a whining wretch
That holds her hand and lies? I am less to him
Than such a one; her rags do him no wrong,
But I, I wrong him merely that I live,
605 Being his sister. Could I not at least
Have still let him forget me? But 'tis past:
And naturally he may hope I am long dead.

     Good God! to think that we were what we were
One to the other…and now!

           He has done well;
610 Married a sort of heiress, I have heard,
A dapper little madam dimple cheeked
And dimple brained, who makes him a good wife—
No doubt she'd never own but just to him,
And in a whisper, she can even suspect
615 That we exist, we other women things:
What would she say if she could learn one day
She has a sister-in-law? So he and I
Must stand apart till doomsday.

           But the jest,
To think how she would look!—Her fright, poor
    thing!
620 The notion!—I could laugh outright…or else,
For I feel near it, roll on the ground and sob.

Well, after all, there's not much difference
Between the two sometimes.

           Was that the bell?
Someone at last, thank goodness. There's a voice,
625 And that's a pleasure. Whose though? Ah, I know.
Why did she come alone, the cackling goose?
Why not have brought her sister?—she tells more
And titters less. No matter; half a loaf
Is better than no bread.

           Oh, is it you?
630 Most welcome, dear: one gets so moped alone.
—1870

Mother and Daughter Sonnets

VI

Sometimes, as young things will, she vexes me,
  Wayward, or too unheeding, or too blind.
   Like aimless birds that, flying on a wind,
Strike slant against their own familiar tree;
5 Like venturous children pacing with the sea,
    That turn but when the breaker spurts behind
    Outreaching them with spray: she in such kind
Is borne against some fault, or does not flee.

And so, may be, I blame her for her wrong,
10   And she will frown and lightly plead her part,
And then I bid her go. But 'tis not long:
   Then comes she lip to ear and heart to heart.
And thus forgiven her love seems newly strong,
And, oh my penitent, how dear thou art!
—1895

VII

Her father lessons me I at times am hard,
  Chiding a moment's fault as too grave ill,
   And let some little blot my vision fill,
Scanning her with a narrow near regard.

5 True. Love's unresting gaze is self-debarred
    From all sweet ignorance, and learns a skill,
    Not painless, of such signs as hurt love's will,
That would not have its prize one tittle[1] marred.

Alas! Who rears and loves a dawning rose
10   Starts at a speck upon one petal's rim:
Who sees a dusk creep in the shrined pearl's glows,
    Is ruined at once: "My jewel growing dim!"
I watch one bud that on my bosom blows,
    I watch one treasured pearl for me and him.
—1895

IX

Oh weary hearts! Poor mothers that look back!
    So outcasts from the vale where they were
        born
    Turn on their road and, with a joy forlorn,
See the far roofs below their arid track:
5 So in chill buffets while the sea grows black
    And windy skies, once blue, are tost and torn,
    We are not yet forgetful of the morn,
And praise anew the sunshine that we lack.

Oh, sadder than pale sufferers by a tomb
10   That say "My dead is happier, and is more,"
    Are they who dare no "is" but tell what's o'er—
Thus the frank childhood, those the lovable
        ways—
    Stirring the ashes of remembered days
For yet some sparks to warm the livelong gloom.
—1895

XII

She has made me wayside posies: here they stand,
  Bringing fresh memories of where they grew.
    As new-come travellers from a world we knew
Wake every while some image of their land,

---
[1] iota.

5 So these whose buds our woodland breezes fanned
    Bring to my room the meadow where they blew,
    The brook-side cliff, the elms where wood-
        doves coo—
And every flower is dearer for her hand.

Oh blossoms of the paths she loves to tread,
10   Some grace of her is in all thoughts you bear:
    For in my memories of your homes that were,
The old sweet loneliness they kept is fled,
And would I think it back I find instead
    A presence of my darling mingling there.
—1895

XIII

My darling scarce thinks music sweet save
    mine:
    'Tis that she does but love me more than hear.
    She'll not believe my voice to stranger ear
Is merely measure to the note and line;
5 "Not so," she says; "Thou hast a secret thine:
    The others' singing's only rich, or clear,
    But something in thy tones brings music near;
As though thy song could search me and divine."

Oh voice of mine that in some day not far
10   Time, the strong creditor, will call his debt,
Will dull—and even to her—will rasp and mar,
    Sing Time asleep because of her regret,
Be twice thy life the thing her fancies are,
    Thou echo to the self she knows not yet.
—1895

XIV

To love her as to-day is so great bliss
    I needs must think of morrows almost loth,
    Morrows wherein the flower's unclosing growth
Shall make my darling other than she is.
5 The breathing rose excels the bud I wis,
    Yet bud that will be rose is sweet for both;

And by-and-by seems like some later troth
Named in the moment of a lover's kiss.

Yes, I am jealous, as of one now strange
    That shall instead of her possess my thought,
10 Of her own self made new by any change,
    Of her to be by ripening morrows brought.
My rose of women under later skies!
Yet, ah! my child with the child's trustful eyes!
—1895

XV

That some day Death who has us all for jest
    Shall hide me in the dark and voiceless mould,
    And him whose living hand has mine in hold,
Where loving comes not nor the looks that rest,
5 Shall make us nought where we are known the best,
    Forgotten things that leave their track untold
    As in the August night the sky's dropped gold—
This seems no strangeness, but Death's natural
    hest.

But looking on the dawn that is her face
10   To know she too is Death's seems misbelief;
She should not find decay, but, as the sun
Moves mightier from the veil that hides his place,
Keep ceaseless radiance. Life is Death begun:
    But Death and her! That's strangeness passing
      grief.
—1895

XVI

She will not have it that my day wanes low,
    Poor of the fire its drooping sun denies,
    That on my brow the thin lines write good-byes

Which soon may be read plain for all to know,
5 Telling that I have done with youth's brave show;
    Alas! and done with youth in heart and eyes,
    With wonder and with far expectancies,
Save but to say "I knew such long ago."

She will not have it. Loverlike to me,
10   She with her happy gaze finds all that's best,
She sees this fair and that unfretted still,
    And her own sunshine over all the rest:
So she half keeps me as she'd have me be,
And I forget to age, through her sweet will.
—1895

XVII

And how could I grow old while she's so young?
    Methinks her heart sets time for mine to beat,
    We are so near; her new thoughts, incomplete,
Find their shaped wording happen on my tongue;
5 Like bloom on last year's winterings newly sprung
    My youth upflowers with hers, and must repeat
    Old joyaunces in me nigh obsolete.
Could I grow older while my child's so young?

And there are tales how youthful blood instilled
10   Thawing frore[1] Age's veins gave life new course,
And quavering limbs and eyes made indolent
    Grew freshly eager with beginning force:
She so breathes impulse. Were my years twice spent,
Not burdening Age, with her, could make me
    chilled.
—1870

---

[1] frozen.

Thomas Hardy
1840 – 1928

Thomas Hardy was born and lived most of his life in rural Dorsetshire. Although now best known for his fiction (e.g. *The Return of the Native* [1878], *The Mayor of Casterbridge* [1886], *Tess of the d'Urbervilles* [1891], and *Jude the Obscure* [1895]), Hardy began and ended his career as a poet. His early poetry and some new works were published in *Wessex Poems* (1898), followed over the years by seven volumes of lyrics and narratives.

☙❧

Hap

If but some vengeful god would call to me
From up the sky, and laugh: "Thou suffering
    thing,
Know that thy sorrow is my ecstasy,
That thy love's loss is my hate's profiting!"

5 Then would I bear it, clench myself, and die,
Steeled by the sense of ire unmerited;
Half-eased in that a Powerfuller than I
Had willed and meted me the tears I shed.

But not so. How arrives it joy lies slain,
10 And why unblooms the best hope ever sown?
—Crass Casualty obstructs the sun and rain,
And dicing Time for gladness casts a moan....
These purblind Doomsters had as readily strown
Blisses about my pilgrimage as pain.
—(1866)[1]

Neutral Tones

We stood by a pond that winter day,
  And the sun was white, as though chidden of
    God,
And a few leaves lay on the starving sod;
  —They had fallen from an ash, and were gray.

5 Your eyes on me were as eyes that rove
Over tedious riddles of years ago;
And some words played between us to and fro
  On which lost the more by our love.

The smile on your mouth was the deadest thing
10 Alive enough to have strength to die;
And a grin of bitterness swept thereby
  Like an ominous bird a-wing...

Since then, keen lessons that love deceives,
And wrings with wrong, have shaped to me
15 Your face, and the God-curst sun, and a tree,
  And a pond edged with grayish leaves.
—(1867)

A Broken Appointment

You did not come,
And marching Time drew on, and wore me
  numb.—
Yet less for loss of your dear presence there
Than that I thus found lacking in your make
5 That high compassion which can overbear
Reluctance for pure lovingkindness' sake
Grieved I, when, as the hope-hour stroked its sum,
  You did not come.

You love not me,
10 And love alone can lend you loyalty;

---

[1] dates of composition given, if known. The order is that of *Collected Poems* (1926).

487

—I know and knew it. But, unto the store
Of human deeds divine in all but name,
Was it not worth a little hour or more
To add yet this: Once you, a woman, came
15   To soothe a time-torn man; even though it be
        You love not me?

The Darkling Thrush

I leant upon a coppice gate
    When Frost was spectre-gray,
And Winter's dregs made desolate
    The weakening eye of day.
5   The tangled bine-stems scored the sky
        Like strings of broken lyres,
And all mankind that haunted nigh
        Had sought their household fires.

The land's sharp features seemed to be
10   The Century's corpse outleant,
His crypt the cloudy canopy,
        The wind his death-lament.
The ancient pulse of germ and birth
        Was shrunken hard and dry,
15   And every spirit upon earth
        Seemed fervourless as I.

At once a voice arose among
        The bleak twigs overhead
In a full-hearted evensong
20   Of joy illimited;
An aged thrush, frail, gaunt, and small,
        In blast-beruffled plume,
Had chosen thus to fling his soul
        Upon the growing gloom.

25   So little cause for carolings
        Of such ecstatic sound
Was written on terrestrial things
        Afar or nigh around,

That I could think there trembled through
30   His happy good-night air
Some blessed Hope, whereof he knew
        And I was unaware.
—(1900)

The Self-Unseeing

Here is the ancient floor,
    Footworn and hollowed and thin,
Here was the former door
Where the dead feet walked in.

5   She sat here in her chair,
Smiling into the fire;
He who played stood there,
Bowing it higher and higher.

Childlike, I danced in a dream;
10   Blessings emblazoned that day;
Everything glowed with a gleam;
Yet we were looking away!

In Tenebris [1]

II

*Considerabam ad dexteram, et videbam; et non erat
qui cognosceret me....Non est qui requirat animam
meam.*—Ps. CXLI. [2]

When the clouds' swoln bosoms echo back the
    shouts of the many and strong
That things are all as they best may be, save a few
        to be right ere long,

---

[1] "In darkness" or "in gloom." Vulgate version, Psalm 141.

[2] "I looked on my right hand, and beheld, but there was no man that
would know me...no man cared for my soul." King James version, Psalm
142.

And my eyes have not the vision in them to discern
    what to these is so clear,
The blot seems straightway in me alone; one better
    he were not here.

5 The stout upstanders say, All's well with us: ruers
    have nought to rue!
And what the potent say so oft, can it fail to be
    somewhat true?
Breezily go they, breezily come; their dust smokes
    around their career,
Till I think I am one born out of due time, who
    has no calling here.

Their dawns bring lusty joys, it seems; their
    evenings all that is sweet;
10 Our times are blessed times, they cry: Life shapes it
    as is most meet,
And nothing is much the matter; there are many
    smiles to a tear;
Then what is the matter is I, I say. Why should
    such an one be here?…

Let him in whose ears the low-voiced Best is killed
    by the clash of the First,
Who holds that if way to the Better there be, it
    exacts a full look at the Worst,
15 Who feels that delight is a delicate growth cramped
    by crookedness, custom, and fear,
Get him up and be gone as one shaped awry; he
    disturbs the order here.
—(1895–96)

The Minute Before Meeting

The grey gaunt days dividing us in twain
    Seemed hopeless hills my strength must faint
    to climb,
But they are gone; and now I would detain
The few clock-beats that part us; rein back Time,

5 And live in close expectance never closed
In change for far expectance closed at last,
So harshly has expectance been imposed
On my long need while these slow blank months
    passed.

And knowing that what is now about to be
10 Will all *have been* in O, so short a space!
I read beyond it my despondency
When more dividing months shall take its place,
Thereby denying to this hour of grace
A full-up measure of felicity.
—(1871)

Night in the Old Home

When the wasting embers redden the chimney-
    breast,
And Life's bare pathway looms like a desert track to
    me,
And from hall and parlour the living have gone to
    their rest,
My perished people who housed them here come
    back to me.

5 They come and seat them around in their mouldy
    places,
Now and then bending towards me a glance of
    wistfulness,
A strange upbraiding smile upon all their faces,
And in the bearing of each a passive tristfulness.

"Do you uphold me, lingering and languishing here,
A pale late plant of your once strong stock?" I say
    to them;
"A thinker of crooked thoughts upon Life in the
    sere,
And on That which consigns men to night after
    showing the day to them?"

"—O let be the Wherefore! We fevered our years
    not thus:
Take of Life what it grants, without question!" they
    answer me seemingly.
15 "Enjoy, suffer, wait: spread the table here freely like
    us,
And, satisfied, placid, unfretting, watch Time away
    beamingly!"

The Something that Saved Him

It was when
Whirls of thick waters laved me
    Again and again,
That something arose and saved me;
5   Yea, it was then.

    In that day
Unseeing the azure went I
    On my way,
And to white winter bent I,
10   Knowing no May.

    Reft of renown,
Under the night clouds beating
    Up and down,
In my needfulness greeting
15   Cit and clown.

    Long there had been
Much of a murky colour
    In the scene,
Dull prospects meeting duller;
20   Nought between.

    Last, there loomed
A closing-in blind alley,
    Though there boomed

A feeble summons to rally
25   Where it gloomed.

    The clock rang;
The hour brought a hand to deliver;
    I upsprang,
And looked back at den, ditch and river,
30   And sang.

Afterwards

When the Present has latched its postern
    behind my tremulous stay,
    And the May month flaps its glad green leaves
      like wings,
Delicate-filmed as new-spun silk, will the
    neighbours say,
    "He was a man who used to notice such
      things"?

5 If it be in the dusk when, like an eyelid's soundless
    blink,
    The dewfall-hawk comes crossing the shades to
      alight
Upon the wind-warped upland thorn, a gazer may
    think,
    "To him this must have been a familiar sight."

If I pass during some nocturnal blackness, mothy
    and warm,
10   When the hedgehog travels furtively over the
      lawn,
One may say, "He strove that such innocent
    creatures should come to no harm,
    But he could do little for them; and now he is
      gone."

If, when hearing that I have been stilled at last, they
    stand at the door,

Watching the full-starred heavens that winter
  sees,
15 Will this thought rise on those who will meet my
      face no more,
    "He was one who had an eye for such
      mysteries"?

And will any say when my bell of quittance is heard
    in the gloom,
  And a crossing breeze cuts a pause in its
    outrollings,
Till they rise again, as they were a new bell's boom,
20   "He hears it not now, but used to notice such
      things"?

A Young Man's Exhortation

Call off your eyes from care
By some determined deftness; put forth joys
Dear as excess without the core that cloys,
  And charm Life's lourings fair.

5   Exalt and crown the hour
That girdles us, and fill it full with glee,
Blind glee, excelling aught could ever be
  Were heedfulness in power.

    Send up such touching strains
10 That limitless recruits from Fancy's pack
Shall rush upon your tongue, and tender back
  All that your soul contains.

    For what do we know best?
That a fresh love-leaf crumpled soon will dry,
15 And that men moment after moment die,
  Of all scope dispossest.

    If I have seen one thing
It is the passing preciousness of dreams;

That aspects are within us; and who seems
20   Most kingly is the King.
  —(1867)

Snow in the Suburbs

Every branch big with it,
  Bent every twig with it;
Every fork like a white web-foot;
Every street and pavement mute:
5 Some flakes have lost their way, and grope back
    upward, when
Meeting those meandering down they turn and
    descend again.
  The palings are glued together like a wall,
  And there is no waft of wind with the
    fleecy fall.

    A sparrow enters the tree,
10   Whereon immediately
A snow-lump thrice his own slight size
Descends on him and showers his head and eyes,
    And overturns him,
    And near inurns him,
15   And lights on a nether twig, when its brush
Starts off a volley of other lodging lumps with a
    rush.

    The steps are a blanched slope,
    Up which, with feeble hope,
A black cat comes, wide-eyed and thin;
20   And we take him in.

In a Wood

From *The Woodlanders*

Pale beech and pine so blue,
  Set in one clay,
Bough to bough cannot you

Live out your day?
5 When the rains skim and skip,
Why mar sweet comradeship,
Blighting with poison-drip
    Neighbourly spray?

Heart-halt and spirit-lame,
10   City-opprest,
Unto this wood I came
    As to a nest;
Dreaming that sylvan peace
Offered the harrowed ease—
15 Nature a soft release
    From men's unrest.

But, having entered in,
    Great growths and small
Show them to men akin—
20   Combatants all!
Sycamore shoulders oak,
Bines the slim sapling yoke,
Ivy-spun halters choke
    Elms stout and tall.

25 Touches from ash, O wych,
    Sting you like scorn!
You, too, brave hollies, twitch
    Sidelong from thorn.
Even the rank poplars bear
30 Lothly a rival's air,
Cankering in blank despair
    If overborne.

Since, then, no grace I find
    Taught me of trees,
35 Turn I back to my kind,
    Worthy as these.
These at least smiles abound,
There discourse trills around,
There, now and then, are found
40   Life-loyalties.
    —1877

Gerard Manley Hopkins
1844 – 1889

Gerard Manley Hopkins, the Oxford-educated English poet and Roman Catholic priest, was an innovative technician who applied his art to the dual themes of nature and religion. Converting to Catholicism in 1866 under the guidance of the Tractarians, Hopkins joined the Society of Jesus in 1868. Encouraged to eulogize the loss of five nuns at sea, Hopkins wrote *The Wreck of the Deutschland* (1875–76). Representing Hopkins's first successful experiment with "sprung rhythm," the poem eschews the accentual-syllabic measures conventionally associated with modern English verse. Poems such as "The Windhover" (1877) and the "terrible sonnets" (1885–89) have garnered Hopkins recognition as a poet of stunning originality.

୧ଓ୧

The Wreck of the Deutschland

*To the
happy memory of five Franciscan nuns
exiles by the Falck Laws*[1]
*drowned between midnight and morning of
Dec. 7th, 1875*

PART THE FIRST

1

THOU mastering me
    God! giver of breath and bread;
World's strand, sway of the sea;
    Lord of living and dead;
5 Thou hast bound bones and veins in me,
        fastened me flesh,
And after it is almost unmade, what with dread,
    Thy doing: and dost thou touch me afresh?
Over again I feel thy finger and find thee.

2

        I did say yes
10 O at lightning and lashed rod;
    Thou heardst me truer than tongue confess
        Thy terror, O Christ, O God;

Thou knowest the walls, altar and hour and night:
The swoon of a heart that the sweep and the
        hurl of thee trod
15 Hard down with a horror of height:
And the midriff astrain with leaning of, laced with
        fire of stress.

3

        The frown of his face
    Before me, the hurtle of hell
Behind, where, where was a, where was a place?
20 I whirled out wings that spell
And fled with a fling of the heart to the heart of
        the Host.
My heart, but you were dovewinged, I can tell,
        Carrier-witted, I am bold to boast,
To flash from the flame to the flame then, tower
        from the grace to the grace.

4

        I am soft sift
25 In an hourglass—at the wall
Fast, but mined with a motion, a drift,
    And it crowds and it combs to the fall;
I steady as a water in a well, to a poise, to a pane,
30 But roped with, always, all the way down from
        the tall
    Fells or flanks of the voel,[2] a vein

---

[1] The Falk Laws, so-called after the Prussian minister of education, Adalbert Falk, were a series of anti-Catholic decrees passed in Germany in 1873. The *Deutschland* sank in the mouth of the Thames as over 200 German Catholics were attempting to find refuge in America.

---

[2] a Welsh word meaning a bare hill or mountain.

Of the gospel proffer, a pressure, a principle,
    Christ's gift.

5

    I kiss my hand
      To the stars, lovely-asunder
35   Starlight, wafting him out of it; and
        Glow, glory in thunder;
    Kiss my hand to the dappled-with-damson west:
    Since, tho' he is under the world's splendour
      and wonder,
      His mystery must be instressed, stressed;
40 For I greet him the days I meet him, and bless
      when I understand.

6

    Not out of his bliss
      Springs the stress felt
    Nor first from heaven (and few know this)
      Swings the stroke dealt—
45 Stroke and a stress that stars and storms deliver,
    That guilt is hushed by, hearts are flushed by
      and melt—
    But it rides time like riding a river
    (And here the faithful waver, the faithless fable and
      miss).

7

    It dates from day
      Of his going in Galilee;[1]
50 Warm-laid grave of a womb-life grey;
      Manger, maiden's knee;
    The dense and the driven Passion,[2] and frightful
      sweat:
    Thence the discharge of it, there its swelling to
      be,
55   Though felt before, though in high flood
      yet—

What none would have known of it, only the heart,
    being hard at bay.

8

    Is out with it! Oh,
      We lash with the best or worst
    Word last! How a lush-kept plush-capped sloe
60   Will, mouthed to flesh-burst,
    Gush!—flush the man, the being with it, sour
      or sweet,
    Brim, in a flash, full!—Hither then, last or first,
      To hero of Calvary,[3] Christ,'s feet—
    Never ask if meaning it, wanting it, warned of
      it—men go.

9

65   Be adored among men,
      God, three-numberèd form;
    Wring thy rebel, dogged in den,
      Man's malice, with wrecking and storm.
    Beyond saying sweet, past telling of tongue,
70   Thou art lightning and love, I found it, a winter
      and warm;
    Farther and fondler of heart thou hast wrung:
Hast thy dark descending and most art merciful
    then.

10

    With an anvil-ding
      And with fire in him forge thy will
    Or rather, rather then, stealing as Spring
75   Through him, melt him but master him
      still:
    Whether at once, as once at a crash Paul,[4]
    Or as Austin, a lingering-out swéet skíll,
      Make mercy in all of us, out of us all
80 Mastery, but be adored, but be adored King.

---

[1] the homeland of Christ, who was called "The Galilean."

[2] the sufferings of Christ.

---

[3] the place of Christ's crucifixion.

[4] The sudden conversion of St. Paul: Acts 22:6–16; "Austin" is St. Augustine of Hippo (354–430), whose conversion, described in his *Confessions*, was gradual.

PART THE SECOND

11

"Some find me a sword; some
   The flange and the rail; flame,
Fang, or flood" goes Death on drum,
   And storms bugle his fame.
85 But wé dream we are rooted in earth—Dust!
Flesh falls within sight of us, we, though our
      flower the same,
   Wave with the meadow, forget that there must
The sour scythe cringe, and the blear share come.

12

   On Saturday sailed from Bremen,[1]
90   American-outward-bound,
   Take settler and seamen, tell men with
      women,
      Two hundred souls in the round—
O Father, not under thy feathers nor ever as
      guessing
The goal was a shoal, of a fourth the doom to
      be drowned;
95   Yet did the dark side of the bay of thy blessing
Not vault them, the million of rounds of thy mercy
      not reeve even them in?

13

   Into the snow she sweeps,
      Hurling the haven behind,
   The Deutschland, on Sunday; and so the sky
      keeps,
      For the infinite air is unkind,
100 And the sea flint-flake, black-backed in the
      regular blow,
Sitting Eastnortheast, in cursed quarter, the wind;
   Wiry and white-fiery and whirlwind-
      swivellèd snow
Spins to the widow-making unchilding unfathering
      deeps.

14

105   She drove in the dark to leeward,
      She struck—not a reef or a rock
   But the combs[2] of a smother of sand: night
      drew her
      Dead to the Kentish Knock;[3]
And she beat the bank down with her bows and
      the ride of her keel:
110   The breakers rolled on her beam with ruinous
      shock;
   And canvas and compass, the whorl and the
      wheel
Idle for ever to waft her or wind her with, these she
endured.

15

   Hope had grown grey hairs,
      Hope had mourning on,
115   Trenched with tears, carved with cares,
      Hope was twelve hours gone;
And frightful a nightfall folded rueful a day
Nor rescue, only rocket and lightship, shone,
      And lives at last were washing away:
120 To the shrouds they took,—they shook in the
hurling and horrible airs.

16

   One stirred from the rigging to save
      The wild woman-kind below,
   With a rope's end round the man, handy
      and brave—
      He was pitched to his death at a blow,
125 For all his dreadnought breast and braids of thew:
   They could tell him for hours, dandled the to
      and fro
      Through the cobbled foam-fleece. What
      could he do
With the burl of the fountains of air, buck and the
      flood of the wave?

17

They fought with God's cold—
130   And they could not and fell to the deck
        (Crushed them) or water (and drowned
            them) or rolled
        With the sea-romp over the wreck,
    Night roared, with the heart-break hearing a
        heart-broke rabble,
    The woman's wailing, the crying of child
        without check—
135   Till a lioness arose breasting the babble,
    A prophetess towered in the tumult, a virginal
        tongue told.

18

        Ah, touched in your bower of bone,
        Are you! turned for an exquisite smart,
        Have you! make words break from me here
            all alone,
140   Do you!—mother of being in me, heart.
    O unteachably after evil, but uttering truth,
    Why, tears! is it? tears; such a melting, a
        madrigal start!
    Never-eldering revel and river of youth,
    What can it be, this glee? the good you have there
        of your own?

19

145   Sister, a sister calling
        A master, her master and mine!—
    And the inboard seas run swirling and
        hawling;
    The rash smart sloggering brine
    Blinds her; but she that weather sees one thing,
        one;
150   Has one fetch in her: she rears herself to divine
        Ears, and the call of the tall nun
    To the men in the tops and the tackle rode over the
        storm's brawling.

20

        She was first of a five and came
        Of a coifèd sisterhood.
155   (O Deutschland, double a desperate name!
        O world wide of its good!
    But Gertrude,[1] lily, and Luther, are two of a town,
    Christ's lily and beast of the waste wood:
        From life's dawn it is drawn down,
160   Abel is Cain's brother[2] and the breasts they have
        sucked the same.)

21

        Loathed for a love men knew in them,
        Banned by the land of their birth,
    Rhine refused them, Thames would ruin them;
        Surf, snow, river and earth
165   Gnashed: but thou art above, thou Orion[3] of light;
    Thy unchancelling poising palms were weighing
        the worth,
        Thou martyr-master: in thy sight
    Storm flakes were scroll-leaved flowers, lily
        showers—sweet heaven was astrew in them.

22

        Five! the finding and sake
170   And cipher of suffering Christ.
        Mark, the mark is of man's make
        And the word of it Sacrificed.
    But he scores it in scarlet himself on his own
        bespoken,
    Before-time-taken, dearest prizèd and priced—
175   Stigma, signal, cinquefoil token
    For lettering of the lamb's fleece, ruddying of the
        rose-flake.

_____

[1] St. Gertrude (1256–1302), lived near Eisleben, Germany, the birth-place of Martin Luther.

[2] Cain, the first-born son of Adam and Eve, murdered his brother Abel.

[3] the constellation named after the giant hunter of Greek mythology.

23

Joy fall to thee, father Francis,
    Drawn to the Life that died;
With the gnarl of the nails in thee, niche of
    the lance, his
180   Lovescape crucified[1]
And seal of his seraph-arrival! and these thy
    daughters
And five-livèd and leavèd favour and pride,
    Are sisterly sealed in wild waters,
To bathe in his fall-gold mercies, to breathe in his
    all-fire glances.

24

185   Away in the loveable west,
    On a pastoral forehead of Wales,[2]
I was under a roof here, I was at rest,
    And they the prey of the gales;
She to the black-about air, to the breaker, the
    thickly
190 Falling flakes, to the throng that catches and
    quails
    Was calling "O Christ, Christ, come
    quickly":[3]
The cross to her she calls Christ to her, christens
    her wild-worst Best.

25

    The majesty! what did she mean?
    Breathe, arch and original Breath.[4]
195 Is it love in her of the being as her lover had
    been?
    Breathe, body of lovely Death.
They were else-minded then, altogether, the men

---

[1] Christ's five wounds, described as the Lovescape, are reproduced in the stigmata received by St. Francis.

[2] Hopkins was studying theology at St. Beuno's College in Wales.

[3] *The Times* of London reported that these were the last words of one of the nuns.

[4] the Holy Spirit.

Woke thee with a *We are perishing* in the
    weather of Gennesareth.[5]
    Or is it that she cried for the crown then,
200 The keener to come at the comfort for feeling the
    combating keen?

26

    For how to the heart's cheering
    The down-dugged ground-hugged grey
Hovers off, the jay-blue heavens appearing
    Of pied and peeled May!
205 Blue-beating and hoary-glow height; or night,
    still higher,
    With belled fire and the moth-soft Milky Way,
    What by your measure is the heaven of desire,
The treasure never eyesight got, nor was ever
    guessed what for the hearing?

27

    No, but it was not these.
    The jading and jar of the cart,
210 Time's tasking, it is fathers that asking for ease
    Of the sodden-with-its-sorrowing heart,
Not danger, electrical horror; then further it finds
The appealing of the Passion is tenderer in
    prayer apart:
215   Other, I gather, in measure her mind's
Burden, in wind's burly and beat of endragonèd
    seas.

28

    But how shall I...make me room there:
    Reach me a...Fancy, come faster—
    Strike you the sight of it? look at it loom there,
220   Thing that she...There then! the Master,
    Ipse,[6] the only one, Christ, King, Head:
He was to cure the extremity where he had cast
    her;
    Do, deal, lord it with living and dead;

---

[5] See Matthew 14:22–23.

[6] "He himself."

497

Let him ride, her pride, in his triumph, despatch
and have done with his doom there.

29

225   Ah! there was a heart right!
           There was single eye!
      Read the unshapeable shock night
          And knew the who and the why;
Wording it how but by him that present and
    past,
230 Heaven and earth are word of, worded by?—
      The Simon Peter[1] of a soul! to the blast
Tarpeïan-fast,[2] but a blown beacon of light.

30

           Jesu, heart's light,
           Jesu, maid's son,
235   What was the feast followed the night
          Thou hadst glory of this nun?—
Feast of the one woman without stain.[3]
For so conceivèd, so to conceive thee is done;
         But here was heart-throe, birth of a brain,
240 Word, that heard and kept thee and uttered thee
    outright.

31

         Well, she has thee for the pain, for the
         Patience; but pity of the rest of them!
      Heart, go and bleed at a bitterer vein for the
         Comfortless unconfessed of them—
245 No not uncomforted: lovely felicitous
    Providence
Finger of a tender of, O of a feathery delicacy,
    the breast of the
      Maiden could obey so, be a bell to, ring of
      it, and

Startle the poor sheep back! is the shipwrack then a
    harvest, does tempest carry the grain for thee?

32

         I admire thee, master of the tides,
250   Of the Yore-flood,[4] of the year's fall;
    The recurb and the recovery of the gulf's sides,
      The girth of it and the wharf of it and
      the wall;
  Stanching, quenching ocean of a motionable
    mind;
  Ground of being, and granite of it: past all
255   Grasp God, throned behind
Death with a sovereignty that heeds but hides,
    bodes but abides;

33

         With a mercy that outrides
         The all of water, an ark
    For the listener; for the lingerer with a love
      glides
260   Lower than death and the dark;
A vein for the visiting of the past-prayer, pent in
    prison,
The-last-breath penitent spirits—the uttermost
    mark
    Our passion-plungèd giant risen,
The Christ of the Father compassionate, fetched in
    the storm of his strides.

34

265   Now burn, new born to the world,
         Double-natured name,
    The heaven-flung, heart-fleshed, maiden-
      furled
      Miracle-in-Mary-of-flame,
Mid-numberèd he in three of the thunder-throne!
270 Not a dooms-day dazzle in his coming nor dark
    as he came;
      Kind, but royally reclaiming his own;

---

[1] See Matthew 14:28.

[2] possibly a reference to the Tarpeian women, warlike female attendants in Virgil's *Aeneid* 11.

[3] the Feast of the Immaculate Conception of the Virgin Mary, December 8.

[4] Genesis 1.1–10: the primordial waters; Genesis 6–8: Noah's flood:

A released shower, let flash to the shire, not a
lightning of fire hard-hurled.

35

Dame, at our door
Drowned, and among our shoals,
275   Remember us in the roads, the heaven-haven
of the reward:
Our King back, Oh, upon English souls!
Let him easter in us, be a dayspring to the
dimness of us, be a crimson-cresseted east,
More brightening her, rare-dear Britain, as his
reign rolls,
Pride, rose, prince, hero of us, high-priest,
280   Our hearts' charity's hearth's fire, our thoughts'
chivalry's throng's Lord.
—1918 (1876)

God's Grandeur

The world is charged with the grandeur of God.
    It will flame out, like shining from shook foil;
    It gathers to a greatness, like the ooze of oil
Crushed. Why do men then now not reck his rod?
5 Generations have trod, have trod, have trod;
    And all is seared with trade; bleared, smeared
with toil;
    And wears man's smudge and shares man's
smell: the soil
Is bare now, nor can foot feel, being shod.

And for all this, nature is never spent;
10   There lives the dearest freshness deep down
things;
And though the last lights off the black West went
    Oh, morning, at the brown brink eastward,
springs—
Because the Holy Ghost[1] over the bent
    World broods with warm breast and with ah!
bright wings.
—1895 (1877)

---

[1] the third person of the Christian Trinity; the Divine or Holy Spirit.

The Windhover

To Christ our Lord

I caught this morning morning's minion, king-
   dom of daylight's dauphin, dapple-dawn-
drawn Falcon, in his riding
Of the rolling level underneath him steady air,
and striding
High there, how he rung upon the rein of a
wimpling wing
5 In his ecstasy! then off, off forth on swing,
    As a skate's heel sweeps smooth on a bow-bend:
the hurl and gliding
    Rebuffed the big wind. My heart in hiding
Stirred for a bird,—the achieve of, the mastery of
the thing!

Brute beauty and valour and act, oh, air, pride,
plume, here
10   Buckle! AND the fire that breaks from thee then,
a billion
Times told lovelier, more dangerous, O my
chevalier!

    No wonder of it: shéer plód makes plough
down sillion
Shine, and blue-bleak embers, ah my dear,
    Fall, gall themselves, and gash gold-vermilion.
—1918 (1877)

Felix Randal

Felix Randal the farrier, O is he dead then? my
  duty all ended,
Who have watched his mould of man, big-boned
and hardy-handsome
Pining, pining, till time when reason rambled in it
and some
Fatal four disorders, fleshed there, all contended?

499

5 Sickness broke him. Impatient, he cursed at first,
      but mended
   Being anointed and all; though a heavenlier heart
      began some
   Months earlier, since I had our sweet reprieve and
      ransom
   Tendered to him. Ah well, God rest him all road
      ever he offended!

   This seeing the sick endears them to us, us too it
      endears.
10 My tongue had taught thee comfort, touch had
      quenched thy tears,
   Thy tears that touched my heart, child, Felix, poor
      Felix Randal;

   How far from then forethought of, all thy more
      boisterous years,
   When thou at the random grim forge, powerful
      amidst peers,
   Didst fettle for the great grey drayhorse his bright
      and battering sandal!
   —1918 (1880)

"As kingfishers catch fire, dragonflies draw flame"

   As kingfishers catch fire, dragonflies draw flame;
      As tumbled over rim in roundy wells
      Stones ring; like each tucked string tells, each
         hung bell's
   Bow swung finds tongue to fling out broad its
      name;
5 Each mortal thing does one thing and the same:
      Deals out that being indoors each one dwells;
      Selves—goes itself; *myself* it speaks and spells,
   Crying *What I do is me: for that I came.*

   Í say more: the just man justices;
10   Keeps gráce: thát keeps all his goings graces;
   Acts in God's eye what in God's eye he is—

Chríst. For Christ plays in ten thousand places,
Lovely in limbs, and lovely in eyes not his
   To the Father through the features of men's
      faces.
—1918 (1881 OR 1882)

The Leaden Echo and the Golden Echo

(*Maidens' song from St. Winefred's Well*) [1]

THE LEADEN ECHO

   How to kéep—is there ány any, is there none
   such, nowhere known some, bow or brooch
      or braid or brace, láce, latch or catch or key to
         keep
   Back beauty, keep it, beauty, beauty, beauty,...from
      vanishing away?
   Ó is there no frowning of these wrinkles, rankèd
      wrinkles deep,
   Down? no waving off of these most mournful
      messengers, still messengers, sad and stealing
      messengers of grey?—
   No there 's none, there 's none, O no there 's none,
5 Nor can you long be, what you now are, called fair,
   Do what you may do, what, do what you may,
   And wisdom is early to despair:
   Be beginning; since, no, nothing can be done
   To keep at bay
10 Age and age's evils, hoar hair,
   Ruck and wrinkle, drooping, dying, death's worst,
      winding sheets, tombs and worms and tumbling
      to decay;
   So be beginning, be beginning to despair.
   O there 's none; no no no there 's none:
   Be beginning to despair, to despair,
   Despair, despair, despair, despair.

---

[1] St. Winifred, a virgin martyr, is the patron saint of North Wales.
Prince Caradoc made violent advances to her and struck off her head,
but it was replaced by St. Beuno who brought her back to life. On the
spot where her head had lain, the healing spring of Holywell gushed
forth.

THE GOLDEN ECHO

                                        Spare!
There ís one, yes I have one (Hush there!),
Only not within seeing of the sun.
Not within the singeing of the strong sun,
5 Tall sun's tingeing, or treacherous the tainting of
        the earth's air,
Somewhere elsewhere there is ah well where! one,
Ońe. Yes I cán tell such a key, I dó know such a place,
Where whatever's prizèd and passes of us,
        everything that's fresh and fast flying of us,
        seems to us sweet of us and swiftly away with,
        done away with, undone,
Undone, done with, soon done with, and yet dearly
        and dangerously sweet
10 Of us, the wimpled-water-dimpled, not-by-
        morning-matchèd face,
The flower of beauty, fleece of beauty, too too apt
        to, ah! to fleet,
Never fleets móre, fastened with the tenderest truth
To its own best being and its loveliness of youth: it
        is an ever-lastingness of, O it is an all youth!
Come then, your ways and airs and looks, locks,
        maidengear, gallantry and gaiety and grace,
15 Winning ways, airs innocent, maiden manners,
        sweet looks, loose locks, long locks, lovelocks,
        gaygear, going gallant, girlgrace—
Resign them, sign them, seal them, send them,
        motion them with breath,
And with sighs soaring, soaring síghs, deliver
Them; beauty-in-the-ghost, deliver it, early now,
        long before death
Give beauty back, beauty, beauty, beauty, back to
        God, beauty's self and beauty's giver.
20 See; not a hair is, not an eyelash, not the least lash
        lost; every hair
Is, hair of the head, numbered.
Nay, what we had lighthanded left in surly the
        mere mould
Will have waked and have waxed and have walked
        with the wind what while we slept,

This side, that side hurling a heavyheaded
        hundredfold
25 What while we, while we slumbered.
O then, weary then whý should we tread? O why
        are we so haggard at the heart, so care-coiled,
        care-killed, so fagged, so fashed, so cogged, so
        cumbered,
When the thing we freely fórfeit is kept with fonder
        a care,
Fonder a care kept than we could have kept it, kept
Far with fonder a care (and we, we should have lost
        it) finer, fonder
30 A care kept.—What kept? do but tell us where
        kept, where.—
Yonder.—What high as that! We follow, now we
        follow.—Yonder, yes yonder, yonder,
Yonder.
—1918 (1882)

Carrion Comfort

Not, I'll not, carrion comfort, Despair, not feast
        on thee;
Not untwist—slack they may be—these last strands
        of man
In me ór, most weary, cry I can no more. I can;
Can something, hope, wish day come, not choose
        not to be.

5 But ah, but O thou terrible, why wouldst thou
        rude on me
Thy wring-world right foot rock? lay a lionlimb
        against me? scan
With darksome devouring eyes my bruisèd bones?
        and fan,
O in turns of tempest, me heaped there; me frantic
        to avoid thee and flee?

Why? That my chaff might fly; my grain lie, sheer
        and clear.

10 Nay in all that toil, that coil, since (seems) I kissed
    the rod,
Hand rather, my heart lo! lapped strength, stole
    joy, would laugh, chéer.
Cheer whom though? The hero whose heaven-
    handling flung me, fóot tród
Me? or me that fought him? O which one? is it
    each one? That night, that year
Of now done darkness I wretch lay wrestling with
    (my God!) my God.
—1918 (1855)

"No worst, there is none"

No worst, there is none. Pitched past pitch of
    grief,
More pangs will, schooled at forepangs, wilder wring.
Comforter, where, where is your comforting?
5 Mary,[1] mother of us, where is your relief?
My cries heave, herds-long; huddle in a main; a
    chief-
woe, world-sorrow; on an age-old anvil wince and
    sing—
Then lull, then leave off. Fury[2] had shrieked "No
    ling-
ering! Let me be fell: force I must be brief."
O the mind, mind has mountains; cliffs of fall
10 Frightful, sheer, no-man-fathomed. Hold them
    cheap
May who ne'er hung there. Nor does long our small
Durance deal with that steep or deep. Here! creep,
Wretch, under a comfort serves in a whirlwind: all
Life death does end and each day dies with sleep.
—1918 (1885?)

Tom's Garland

upon the Unemployed

Tom—garlanded with squat and surly steel
    Tom; then Tom's fallowbootfellow piles pick
By him and rips out rockfire homeforth—sturdy
    Dick;
Tom Heart-at-ease, Tom Navvy: he is all for his
    meal
5 Sure, 's bed now. Low be it: lustily he his low lot
    (feel
That ne'er need hunger, Tom; Tom seldom sick,
Seldomer heartsore; that treads through,
    prickproof, thick
Thousands of thorns, thoughts) swings though.
    Commonweal
Little Í reck ho! lacklevel in, if all had bread:
10 What! Country is honour enough in all us—lordly
    head,
With heaven's lights high hung round, or,
    mother-ground
That mammocks, might foot. But nó way sped,
Nor mind nor mainstrength; gold go garlanded
With, perilous, O nó; nor yet plod safe shod sound;
15   Undenizened, beyond bound
Of earth's glory, earth's ease, all; no one, nowhere,
In wide the world's weal; rare gold, bold steel, bare
        In both; care, but share care—
This, by Despair, bred Hangdog dull; by Rage,
20 Manwolf, worse; and their packs infest the age.
—1918 (1887)

Harry Ploughman

Hard as hurdle arms, with a broth of goldish
    flue
Breathed round; the rack of ribs; the scooped flank;
    lank
Rope-over thigh; knee-nave; and barrelled shank—
    Head and foot, shoulder and shank—

---

1 the Virgin Mary, mother of Christ.

2 The Roman Furies were merciless goddesses of vengeance whose
punishments continued after death.

5   By a grey eye's heed steered well, one crew, fall to;
Stand at stress. Each limb's barrowy brawn, his thew
That onewhere curded, onewhere sucked or sank—
          Soared ór sánk—,
Though as a beechbole firm, find his, as at a
    rollcall, rank
10 And features, in flesh, what deed he each must do—
          His sinew-service where do.

He leans to it, Harry bends, look. Back, elbow, and
    liquid waist
In him, all quail to the wallowing o' the plough. 'S

    cheek crimsons; curls
Wag or crossbridle, in a wind lifted, windlaced—
15   See his wind- lilylocks -laced;
Churlsgrace, too, child of Amansstrength, how it
    hangs or hurls
Them—broad in bluff hide his frowning feet
    lashed! raced
With, along them, cragiron under and cold furls—
      With-a-fountain's shining-shot
      furls.

—1918 (1887)

Michael Field
1846 – 1914 (Katherine Bradley) and 1862 – 1913 (Edith Cooper)

Katherine Bradley and her niece, Edith Cooper, formed one of the most remarkable relationships in the history of English letters. Enjoying a common passion for classical art, they developed a strong emotional and intellectual bond. Bradley and Cooper first collaborated under the names Arran and Isla Leigh; together they produced a volume of poetry entitled *Bellerophon and Other Poems* (1881). Their first efforts under the masculine pseudonym Michael Field were two tragic dramas published in 1884 entitled *Callirrhoe* and *Fair Rosamund*. The former was extremely well received until the true identity of Michael Field was revealed. They produced, over the course of their lives, 27 verse tragedies and numerous volumes of poems, among them *Long Ago* (1889), *Sight and Song* (1892), and *Underneath the Bough* (1893). Bradley and Cooper converted to Roman Catholicism near the end of their lives; they died of the same disease (cancer) within nine months of one another.

☙☙☙

Preface

The aim of this little volume is, as far as may be, to translate into verse what the lines and colours of certain chosen pictures sing in themselves; to express not so much what these pictures are to the poet, but rather what poetry they objectively incarnate. Such an attempt demands patient, continuous sight as pure as the gazer can refine it of theory, fancies, or his mere subjective enjoyment.

"Il faut, par un effort d'esprit, se transporter dans les personnages et non les attirer à soi."[1] For *personnages* substitute *peintures*,[2] and this sentence from Gustave Flaubert's "Correspondence" resumes the method of art-study from which these poems arose.

Not even "le grand Gustave" could ultimately illude himself as a formative power in his work—not after the pain of a lifetime directed to no other end. Yet the effort to see things from their own centre, by suppressing the habitual centralisation of the visible in ourselves, is a process by which we eliminate our idiosyncrasies and obtain an impression clearer, less passive, more intimate.

When such effort has been made, honestly and with persistence, even then the inevitable force of individuality must still have play and a temperament mould the purified impression:—

> "When your eyes have done their part,
> Thought must length it in the heart."

M. F.

—(FEBRUARY 15, 1892)

La Gioconda [3]

Leonardo Da Vinci

The Louvre

Historic, side-long, implicating eyes;
A smile of velvet's lustre on the cheek;
Calm lips the smile leads upward; hand that lies
Glowing and soft, the patience in its rest
5 Of cruelty that waits and doth not seek
For prey; a dusky forehead and a breast
Where twilight touches ripeness amorously:
Behind her, crystal rocks, a sea and skies
Of evanescent blue on cloud and creek;

---

[1] "It is necessary, by an effort of spirit, to transport oneself into the personages and not to draw them to oneself."

[2] paintings.

[3] the portrait by Leonardo da Vinci, also known as the *Mona Lisa*.

10 Landscape that shines suppressive of its zest
For those vicissitudes by which men die.
—1892

The Birth of Venus

Sandro Botticelli[1]

The Uffizi

Frills of brimming wavelets lap
Round a shell that is a boat;
Roses fly like birds and float
Down the crisp air; garments flap:
5 Midmost of the breeze, with locks
In possession of the wind,
Coiling hair in loosened shocks,
Sways a girl who seeks to bind
New-born beauty with a tress
10 Gold about her nakedness.

And her chilled, wan body sweet
Greets the ruffled cloak of rose,
Daisy-stitched, that Flora[2] throws
Toward her ere she set her feet
15 On the green verge of the world:
Flora, with the corn-flower dressed,
Round her neck a rose-spray curled
Flowerless, wild-rose at her breast,
To her goddess hastes to bring
20 The wide chiton[3] of the spring.

While from ocean, breathing hard,
With sole pressure toward the bay,—
Olive raiment, pinions grey
By clipt rose-stems thinly starred,

25 Zephyrus[4] and Boreas[5] pass,
One in wonder, one desire:
And the cool sea's dawnlit mass
Boreas' foot has lifted higher,
As he blows the shell to land,
30 Where the reed invades the sand.

She who treads the rocking shell—
Tearful shadow in her eyes
Of reluctant sympathies,
On her mouth a pause, a spell,
35 Candour far too lone to speak
And no knowledge on her brows;
Virgin stranger, come to seek
Covert of strong orange-boughs
By the sea-wind scarcely moved,—
40 She is Love that hath not loved.
—1892

"Death, men say, is like a sea"

Death, men say, is like a sea
That engulfs mortality,
Treacherous, dreadful, blindingly
    Full of storm and terror.

5 Death is like the deep, warm sand
Pleasant when we come to land,
Covering up with tender hand
    The wave's drifted error.

Life's a tortured, booming gurge
10 Winds of passion strike and urge,
And transmute to broken surge
    Foam-crests of ambition.

[1] Italian Renaissance painter (1444?–1510).

[2] the Roman goddess of flowers.

[3] a loose garment of varied length, worn by both men and women in ancient Greece.

[4] the personification of the west wind in Greek mythology. Zephyrus was perceived as the most gentle and warming of all sylvan deities.

[5] in Greek myth, the god of the north wind.

Death's a couch of golden ground,
Warm, soft, permeable mound,
15 Where from even memory's sound
    We shall have remission.
—1893

"Ah, Eros doth not always smite"

Ah, Eros[1] doth not always smite
    With cruel, shining dart,
Whose bitter point with sudden might
    Rends the unhappy heart—
5 Not thus forever purple-stained,
    And sore with steely touch,
Else were its living fountain drained
    Too oft and overmuch.
O'er it sometimes the boy will deign
10   Sweep the shaft's feathered end;
And friendship rises without pain
    Where the white plumes descend.
—1893

"Sometimes I do despatch my heart"

Sometimes I do despatch my heart
    Among the graves to dwell apart:
On some the tablets are erased,
Some earthquake-tumbled, some defaced,
5 And some that have forgotten lain
A fall of tears makes green again;
And my brave heart can overtread
Her brood of hopes, her infant dead,
And pass with quickened footsteps by
10 The headstone of hoar memory,
    Till she hath found
    One swelling mound
With just her name writ and *beloved*;
From that she cannot be removed.
—1893

"Solitary Death, make me thine own"

Solitary Death, make me thine own,
    And let us wander the bare fields together;
        Yea, thou and I alone,
Roving in unembittered unison forever.

5   I will not harry thy treasure-graves,
    I do not ask at thy still hands a lover;
        My heart within me craves
    To travel till we twain Time's wilderness discover.

    To sojourn with thee my soul was bred,
10 And I, the courtly sights of life refusing,
        To the wide shadows fled,
    And mused upon thee often as I fell a-musing.

    Escaped from chaos, thy mother Night,
    In her maiden breast a burthen that awed her,
15   By cavern waters white
    Drew thee her first-born, her unfathered off-spring,
        toward her.

    On dewy plats, near twilight dingle,
    She oft, to still thee from men's sobs and curses
        In thine ears a-tingle,
20   Pours her cool charms, her weird, reviving chaunt
        rehearses.

    Though mortals menace thee or elude,
    And from thy confines break in swift transgression.
        Thou for thyself art sued
    Of me, I claim thy cloudy purlieus[2] my possession.

25   To a lone freshwater, where the sea
    Stirs the silver flux of the reeds and willows,
        Come thou, and beckon me
    To lie in the lull of the sand-sequestered billows:

---

[1] the god of love, and son of Aphrodite.

[2] environs.

Then take the life I have called my own
30 And to the liquid universe deliver;
  Loosening my spirit's zone,
Wrap round me as thy limbs the wind, the light,
 the river.
—1893

Love's Sour Leisure

As a poem in my mind
 Thy sweet lineaments are shrined:
From the memory, alas!
Sweetest, sweetest verse will pass;
5 And the fragments I must piece
Lest the fair tradition cease.
There is balmy air I trow
On the uplands of thy brow,
But the temple's veinèd mound
10 Is the Muses' sacred ground;
While the tresses pale are groves
That the laurelled godhead loves.
There is something in the cheek
Like a dimple still to seek,
15 As my poet timidly
Love's incarnate kiss would flee.
But the mouth! That land to own
Long did Aphroditè[1] moan,
Ere the virgin goddess grave
20 From the temptress of the wave
That most noble clime did win;
Who, retreating to the chin,
Took her boy's bow for a line,
The sweet boundary to define,
25 And about the beauteous bays
Still in orbèd queenship plays.
I have all the charact'ry
Of thy features, yet lack thee;
And by couplets to confess
30 What I wholly would possess

Doth but whet the appetite
Of my too long-famished sight:
Vainly if my eyes entreat,
Tears will be their daily meat.
—1893

"It was deep April, and the morn"

It was deep April, and the morn
 Shakspere was born;
The world was on us, pressing sore;
My Love and I took hands and swore,
5 Against the world, to be
Poets and lovers evermore,
To laugh and dream on Lethe's[2] shore,
To sing to Charon[3] in his boat,
Heartening the timid souls afloat;
10 Of judgment never to take heed,
But to those fast-locked souls to speed,
Who never from Apollo[4] fled,
Who spent no hour among the dead;
  Continually
15   With them to dwell,
Indifferent to heaven and hell.
—1893

An Aeolian Harp

Dost thou not hear? Amid dun, lonely hills
 Far off a melancholy music shrills,
As for a joy that no fruition fills.

Who live in that far country of the wind?
5 The unclaimed hopes, the powers but half-divined,
The shy, heroic passions of mankind.

---

[1] Greek goddess of love.

[2] the river of forgetfulness in Hades.

[3] the boatman who ferries dead souls across the river Styx to Hades.

[4] in Greek and Roman myth, the god of poetry, music, prophecy, and medicine. Epitomizing manly beauty and youth, Apollo is also associated with Helios, the sun god.

And all are young in those reverberant bands;
None marshalls them, no mellow voice commands;
They whirl and eddy as the shifting sands.

10 There, there is ruin, and no ivy clings;
There pass the mourners for untimely things,
There breaks the stricken cry of crownless kings.

But ever and anon there spreads a boom
Of wonder through the air, arraigning doom
15 With ineffectual plaint as from a tomb.
—1893

Alice Meynell
1847 – 1922

Alice Meynell was a poet, journalist, and political activist, particularly in support of the non-militant suffragists. Her first volume of poetry, *Preludes* (1875), was admired by Tennyson and Ruskin, and through her later work she became friends with fellow-poets Francis Thompson, Coventry Patmore, and George Meredith. Her best poems, reflecting the Victorian themes of the ambiguity of motherhood, the fallen woman, and the social and political ramifications of motherhood (she bore eight children), are personal lyrics.

A Letter from a Girl to Her Own Old Age

Listen, and when thy hand this paper presses,
O time-worn woman, think of her who blesses
What thy thin fingers touch, with her caresses.

O mother, for the weight of years that break thee!
5 O daughter, for slow time must yet awake thee,
And from the changes of my heart must make thee!

O fainting traveler, morn is gray in heaven.
Dost thou remember how the clouds were driven?
And are they calm about the fall of even?

10 Pause near the ending of thy long migration,
For this one sudden hour of desolation
Appeals to one hour of thy meditation.

Suffer, O silent one, that I remind thee
Of the great hills that stormed the sky behind thee,
15 Of the wild winds of power that have resigned
    thee.

Know that the mournful plain where thou must
    wander
Is but a gray and silent world, but ponder
The misty mountains of the morning yonder.

Listen:—the mountain winds with rain were
    fretting,

20 And sudden gleams the mountain-tops besetting.
I cannot let thee fade to death, forgetting.

What part of this wild heart of mine, I know not,
Will follow with thee where the great winds blow
    not,
And where the young flowers of the mountain
    grow not.

25 Yet let my letter with my lost thoughts in it
Tell what the way was when thou didst begin it
And win with thee the goal when thou shalt win it.

Oh, in some hour of thine, my thoughts shall guide
    thee.
Suddenly, though time, darkness, silence, hide thee,
30 This wind from thy lost country flits beside thee,—

Telling thee: all thy memories moved the maiden,
With thy regrets was morning overshaden;
With sorrow, thou hast left, her life was laden.

But whether shall my thoughts turn to pursue thee?
35 Life changes, and the years and days renew thee.
Oh, Nature brings my straying heart unto thee.

Her winds will join us, with their constant kisses
Upon the evening as the morning tresses,
Her summers breathe the same unchanging blisses.

40 And we, so altered in our shifting phases,
Track one another 'mid the many mazes
By the eternal child-breath of the daisies.

I have not writ this letter of divining
To make a glory of thy silent pining,
45 A triumph of thy mute and strange declining.

Only one youth, and the bright life was shrouded.
Only one morning, and the day was clouded.
And one old age with regrets is crowded.

O hush, O hush! Thy tears my words are steeping.
50 O hush, hush, hush! So full, the fount of weeping?
Poor eyes, so quickly moved, so near to sleeping?

Pardon the girl; such strange desires beset her.
Poor woman, lay aside the mournful letter
That breaks thy heart; the one who wrote, forget
her:

55 The one who now thy faded features guesses,
With filial fingers thy gray hair caresses,
With morning tears thy mournful twilight blesses.
—1875

In February

Rich meanings of the prophet-Spring adorn,
Unseen, this colourless sky of folded showers,
And folded winds; no blossom in the bowers;
A poet's face asleep in this grey morn.

5 Now in the midst of the old world forlorn
A mystic child is set in these still hours.
I keep this time, even before the flowers,
Sacred to all the young and the unborn:

To all the miles and miles of unsprung wheat,
10 And to the Spring waiting beyond the portal,
And to the future of my own young art,

And, among all these things, to you, my sweet,
My friend, to your calm face and the immortal
Child tarrying all your life-time in your heart.
—1875

A Father of Women

AD SOROREM E.B. [1]
"Thy father was transfused into thy blood."
Dryden: Ode to Mrs. Killigrew [2]

Our father works in us,
The daughters of his manhood. Not undone
Is he, not wasted, though transmuted thus,
And though he left no son.

5 Therefore on him I cry
To arm me: "For my delicate mind a casque,
A breastplate for my heart, courage to die,
Of thee, captain, I ask.

"Nor strengthen only; press
10 A finger on this violent blood and pale,
Over this rash will let thy tenderness
A while pause, and prevail.

"And shepherd-father, thou
Whose staff folded my thoughts before my birth,
15 Control them now I am of earth, and now
Thou art no more of earth.

----

[1] "To my sister."

[2] Dryden's "Ode to Anne Killigrew" is not an expression of his private grief, but an extremely ornate gesture which raises the deceased poet artist to the heights of symbolism, in which she comes to embody the arts themselves.

"O liberal, constant, dear,
Crush in my nature the ungenerous art
Of the inferior; set me high, and here,
20   Here garner up thy heart!"

Like to him now are they,
The million living fathers of the War—
Mourning the crippled world, the bitter day—
    Whose striplings are no more.

25   The crippled world! Come then,
Fathers of women with your honour in trust;
Approve, accept, know them daughters of men,
    Now that your sons are dust.
    —1917

The Threshing Machine

No "fan is in his hand" for these
    Young villagers beneath the trees,
Watching the wheels. But I recall
The rhythm of rods that rise and fall,
5   Purging the harvest, over-seas.

No fan, no flail, no threshing-floor!
And all their symbols evermore
    Forgone in England now—the sign,
    The visible pledge, the threat divine,
10   The chaff dispersed, the wheat in store.

The unbreathing engine marks no tune,
Steady at sunrise, steady at noon,
    Inhuman, perfect, saving time,
    And saving measure, and saving rhyme—
15   And did our Ruskin[1] speak too soon?

"No noble strength on earth" he sees
"Save Hercules'[2] arm"; his grave decrees
    Curse wheel and steam. As the wheels ran
    I saw the other strength of man,
20   I knew the brain of Hercules.
    —1923

Reflections

(I) In Ireland

A mirror faced a mirror: ire and hate
Opposite ire and hate; the multiplied,
The complex charge rejected, intricate,
    From side to sullen side;

5   One plot, one crime, one treachery, nay, one name,
    Assumed, denounced, in echoes of replies.
The doubt, exchanged, lit thousands of one flame
    Within those mutual eyes.

(II) In "Othello"[3]

A mirror faced a mirror: in sweet pain
    His dangers with her pity did she track,
Received her pity with his love again,
    And these she wafted back.

5   That masculine passion in her little breast
    She bandied with him; her compassion he
Bandied with her. What tender sport! No rest
    Had love's infinity.

---

[1] John Ruskin (1819–1900), English writer, art critic, and social reformer.

[2] in Greek and Roman myth, the son of Zeus and the mortal, Alcmene, lauded and immortalized for feats of strength, especially the twelve labours imposed on him by Hera, Zeus's wife.

[3] a Shakespearean tragedy in which the title character, a noble and celebrated Moor, is made madly jealous by Iago. Duped, Othello kills his faithful and beloved wife, Desdemona.

(III) *In Two Poets*

A mirror faced a mirror: O thy word,
Thou lord of images, did lodge in me,
Locked to my heart, homing from home, a bird,
A carrier, bound for thee.

5 Thy migratory greatness, greater far
For that return, returns; now grow divine
By endlessness my visiting thoughts, that are
Those visiting thoughts of thine.
—1923

Oscar Wilde
1854 – 1900

Oscar Wilde was born in Ireland, attended Trinity College, Dublin, and graduated from Oxford in 1878. Wilde was an adherent of the "art for art's sake" movement (see Walter Pater), a position articulated in the essay, "The Critic as Artist" (1890). His major works include *The Picture of Dorian Gray* (1890), essays such as

"The Soul of Man Under Socialism" (1891), and a number of plays such as *Lady Windermere's Fan* (1892), *Salomé* (1894), and *The Importance of Being Earnest* (1895). Wilde's homosexuality led to a series of trials and in 1895 he was sentenced to two years in jail. He died in Paris.

❧❧❧

Requiescat [1]

Tread lightly, she is near
    Under the snow,
Speak gently, she can hear
    The daisies grow.

5 All her bright golden hair
    Tarnished with rust,
She that was young and fair
    Fallen to dust.

Lily-like, white as snow,
10   She hardly knew
She was a woman, so
    Sweetly she grew.

Coffin-board, heavy stone,
    Lie on her breast,
15 I vex my heart alone,
    She is at rest.

Peace, Peace, she cannot hear
    Lyre or sonnet,
All my life's buried here,
20   Heap earth upon it.

AVIGNON
—1881, REV. 1882

Hélas! [2]

To drift with every passion till my soul
  Is a stringed lute on which all winds can play,
Is it for this that I have given away
Mine ancient wisdom, and austere control?
5 Methinks my life is a twice-written scroll
Scrawled over on some boyish holiday
With idle songs for pipe and virelay,
Which do but mar the secret of the whole.
Surely there was a time I might have trod
10 The sunlight heights, and from life's dissonance
Struck one clear chord to reach the ears of God:
Is that time dead? lo! with a little rod
I did but touch the honey of romance—
And must I lose a soul's inheritance?
—1881

---

[1] "May s/he rest." The expression "R.I.P." means rest in peace, or *requiescat in pace*.

[2] "Alas."

Impressions

I
LE JARDIN [1]

The lily's withered chalice falls
  Around its rod of dusty gold,
  And from the beech-trees on the wold
The last wood-pigeon coos and calls.

5 The gaudy leonine sunflower
    Hangs black and barren on its stalk,
    And down the windy garden walk
The dead leaves scatter,—hour by hour.

Pale privet-petals white as milk
10 Are blown into a snowy mass:
    The roses lie upon the grass
Like little shreds of crimson silk.

II
LA MER [2]

A white mist drifts across the shrouds,
  A wild moon in this wintry sky
  Gleams like an angry lion's eye
Out of a mane of tawny clouds.

5 The muffled steersman at the wheel
    Is but a shadow in the gloom;—

And in the throbbing engine-room
Leap the long rods of polished steel.

The shattered storm has left its trace
10 Upon this huge and heaving dome,
    For the thin threads of yellow foam
Float on the waves like ravelled lace.
—1882

Symphony in Yellow

An omnibus across the bridge
  Crawls like a yellow butterfly,
  And, here and there, a passer-by
Shows like a little restless midge.

5 Big barges full of yellow hay
    Are moved against the shadowy wharf,
    And, like a yellow silken scarf,
The thick fog hangs along the quay.

The yellow leaves begin to fade
10 And flutter from the Temple elms,[3]
    And at my feet the pale green Thames
Lies like a rod of rippled jade.
—1889

---

[1] the garden.

[2] the sea.

[3] the part of London known as the Temple lies between Fleet Street and the Thames River. Originally the site of the Templar's headquarters, the area is now given over to law courts and offices.

Rudyard Kipling
1865 – 1936

Rudyard Kipling was a poet, novelist, and short story writer. He was born in Bombay, but was placed in a foster home in England in 1871. He returned to live in India in 1882, then settled in England in 1889. Kipling's work includes a volume of poetry, *Departmental Ditties* (1886), short stories, *Plain Tales From The Hills* (1888), and his masterpiece based on his Indian experience, the novel *Kim* (1901).

⁓⁓⁓

Gentlemen-Rankers

To the legion of the lost ones, to the cohort of
    the damned,
  To my brethren in their sorrow overseas,
Sings a gentleman of England cleanly bred,
    machinely crammed,
  And a trooper of the Empress, if you please.
5 Yes, a trooper of the forces who has run his own six
    horses,
  And faith he went the pace and went it blind,
And the world was more than kin while he held the
    ready tin,
  But to-day the Sergeant's something less than
    kind.
    We're poor little lambs who've lost our way,
      Baa! Baa! Baa!
10   We're little black sheep who've gone astray,
      Baa—aa—aa!
    Gentlemen-rankers out on the spree,
    Damned from here to Eternity,
    God ha' mercy on such as we,
15   Baa! Yah! Bah!

Oh, it's sweet to sweat through stables, sweet to
    empty kitchen slops,
  And it's sweet to hear the tales the troopers tell,
To dance with blowzy housemaids at the
    regimental hops
20 And thrash the cad who says you waltz too well.

Yes, it makes you cock-a-hoop to be "Rider" to
    your troop,
  And branded with a blasted worsted spur,
When you envy, O how keenly, one poor Tommy[1]
    living cleanly
  Who blacks your boots and sometimes calls you
    "Sir."

25 If the home we never write to, and the oaths we
    never keep,
  And all we know most distant and most dear,
Across the snoring barrack-room return to break
    our sleep,
  Can you blame us if we soak ourselves in beer?
When the drunken comrade mutters and the great
    guard-lantern gutters
30 And the horror of our fall is written plain,
Every secret, self-revealing on the aching
    whitewashed ceiling,
  Do you wonder that we drug ourselves from
    pain?

We have done with Hope and Honour, we are lost
    to Love and Truth,
  We are dropping down the ladder rung by
    rung,
35 And the measure of our torment is the measure of
    our youth.
    God help us, for we knew the worst too young!

---

[1] a British soldier.

Our shame is clean repentance for the crime that
    brought the sentence,
  Our pride it is to know no spur of pride,
And the Curse of Reuben holds us till an alien turf
    enfolds us
40   And we die, and none can tell Them where we
    died.
    We're poor little lambs who've lost our way,
    Baa! Baa! Baa!
    We're little black sheep who've gone astray,
    Baa—aa—aa!
45   Gentlemen-rankers out on the spree,
    Damned from here to Eternity,
    God ha' mercy on such as we,
    Baa! Yah! Bah!

—1892

In the Neolithic Age [1]

In the Neolithic Age savage warfare did I wage
  For food and fame and woolly horses' pelt.
I was singer to my clan in that dim, red Dawn of
  Man,
  And I sang of all we fought and feared and felt.

5 Yea, I sang as now I sing, when the Prehistoric
    spring
  Made the piled Biscayan ice-pack split and shove;
And the troll and gnome and dwerg, and the Gods
  of Cliff and Berg
  Were about me and beneath me and above.

But a rival of Solutré, told the tribe my style was
  outré [2]—
10 'Neath a tomahawk, of diorite, he fell.

And I left my views on Art, barbed and tanged,
    below the heart
  Of a mammothistic etcher at Grenelle. [3]

Then I stripped them, scalp from skull, and my
    hunting-dogs fed full,
  And their teeth I threaded neatly on a thong;
15 And I wiped my mouth and said, "It is well that
    they are dead,
  "For I know my work is right and theirs was
    wrong."

But my Totem [4] saw the shame; from his ridgepole-
    shrine he came,
  And he told me in a vision of the night:—
"There are nine and sixty ways of constructing
    tribal lays,
20 "And every single one of them is right!"

. . . .

Then the silence closed upon me till They put new
    clothing on me
  Of whiter, weaker flesh and bone more frail;
And I stepped beneath Time's finger, once again a
    tribal singer,
  And a minor poet certified by Traill! [5]

25 Still they skirmish to and fro, men my messmates
    on the snow,
  When we headed off the aurochs [6] turn for turn;
When the rich Allobrogenses never kept
    amanuenses,
  And our only plots were piled in lakes at Berne. [7]

---

[1] the later stone age.

[2] outside the bounds of propriety.

[3] a district of Paris, on the left band of the Seine.

[4] A totem is a natural object, usually an animal, taken as the emblem of a person or clan.

[5] Henry Duff Traill (1842–1900).

[6] extinct wild ox.

[7] city in Switzerland, founded in the twelfth century.

Still a cultured Christian age sees us scuffle, squeak,
and rage,
30   Still we pinch and slap and jabber, scratch and
dirk;
Still we let our business slide—as we dropped the
half-dressed hide—
To show a fellow-savage how to work.

Still the world is wondrous large,—seven seas from
marge to marge—
And it holds a vast of various kinds of man;
35 And the wildest dreams of Kew[1] are the facts of
Khatmandhu,[2]
And the crimes of Clapham[3] chaste in
Martaban.[4]

Here's my wisdom for your use, as I learned it
when the moose
And the reindeer roared where Paris roars
to-night:—
*"There are nine and sixty ways of constructing tribal
lays,*
40   *"And—every—single—one—of—them—is—
right!"*
—1892

Recessional[5]
1897

God of our fathers, known of old,
Lord of our far-flung battle-line,

Beneath whose awful Hand we hold
    Dominion over palm and pine—
5 Lord God of Hosts, be with us yet,
Lest we forget—lest we forget![6]

The tumult and the shouting dies;
    The Captains and the Kings depart:
Still stands Thine ancient sacrifice,
10   An humble and a contrite heart.[7]
Lord God of Hosts, be with us yet,
Lest we forget—lest we forget!

Far-called, our navies melt away;
    On dune and headland sinks the fire:
15 Lo, all our pomp of yesterday
    Is one with Nineveh and Tyre![8]
Judge of the Nations, spare us yet,
Lest we forget—lest we forget!

If, drunk with sight of power, we loose
20   Wild tongues that have not Thee in awe,
Such boastings as the Gentiles[9] use,
    Or lesser breeds without the Law—
Lord God of Hosts, be with us yet,
Lest we forget—lest we forget!

25 For heathen heart that puts her trust
    In reeking tube and iron shard,
All valiant dust that builds on dust,
    And guarding, calls not Thee to guard,
For frantic boast and foolish word—
30 Thy mercy on Thy People, Lord!
—1897 (1897)

---

[1] an affluent district of Richmond, west of London.

[2] Katmandu or Kathmandu, the capital city of Nepal.

[3] a residential district of London.

[4] a village in Lower Burma, invaded by British troops during the Anglo-Burmese wars of 1824 and 1852.

[5] A recessional is a hymn sung while the clergy and the choir leave the church in procession at the end of a service. Kipling's poem was written as the year of Queen Victoria's Diamond Jubilee, celebrating her sixtieth year on the throne, was ending.

[6] Deuteronomy 6:12.

[7] Psalms 51:17.

[8] Nineveh was the capital of ancient Assyria, now buried under sand. Tyre, in Phoenicia, was once an important maritime city but has fallen from greatness.

[9] Romans 2:14.

The White Man's Burden [1]

Take up the White Man's burden—
    Send forth the best ye breed—
Go bind your sons to exile
    To serve your captives' need;
5 To wait in heavy harness,
    On fluttered folk and wild—
Your new-caught, sullen peoples,
    Half-devil and half-child.

Take up the White Man's burden—
10   In patience to abide,
To veil the threat of terror
    And check the show of pride;
By open speech and simple,
    An hundred times made plain,
15 To seek another's profit,
    And work another's gain.

Take up the White Man's burden—
    The savage wars of peace—
Fill full the mouth of Famine
20   And bid the sickness cease;
And when your goal is nearest
    The end for others sought,
Watch Sloth and heathen Folly
    Bring all your hope to nought.

25 Take up the White Man's burden—
    No tawdry rule of kings,
But toil of serf and sweeper—
    The tale of common things.
The ports ye shall not enter,
30   The roads ye shall not tread,
Go make them with your living,
    And mark them with your dead!

Take up the White Man's burden—
    And reap his old reward:
35 The blame of those ye better,
    The hate of those ye guard—
The cry of hosts ye humour
    (Ah, slowly!) toward the light:—
"Why brought ye us from bondage,
40   "Our loved Egyptian night?" [2]

Take up the White Man's burden—
    Ye dare not stoop to less—
Nor call too loud on Freedom
    To cloak your weariness;
45 By all ye cry or whisper,
    By all ye leave or do,
The silent, sullen peoples
    Shall weigh your Gods and you.

Take up the White Man's burden—
50   Have done with childish days—
The lightly proffered laurel.
    The easy, ungrudged praise.
Comes now, to search your manhood
    Through all the thankless years,
55 Cold, edged with dear-bought wisdom,
    The judgment of your peers!
—1899

If

If you can keep your head when all about you
    Are losing theirs and blaming it on you,
If you can trust yourself when all men doubt you,
    But make allowance for their doubting too;
5 If you can wait and not be tired by waiting,
    Or being lied about, don't deal in lies,

---

[1] This phrase, used to describe the United States's responsibility for Cuba and the Philippines, became popular towards the end of the Spanish-American War in 1898.

[2] Exodus 16:2–3: when the Israelites were hungry in the wilderness, journeying from Egypt, they cried against Moses and Aaron: "Would to God we had died by the hand of the Lord in the land of Egypt, where we sat by the flesh pots, and when we did eat bread to the full."

Or being hated, don't give way to hating,
    And yet don't look too good, nor talk too wise:

If you can dream—and not make dreams your
    master;
10   If you can think—and not make thoughts your
    aim;
If you can meet with Triumph and Disaster
    And treat those two impostors just the same;
If you can bear to hear the truth you've spoken
    Twisted by knaves to make a trap for fools,
15 Or watch the things you gave your life to, broken,
    And stoop and build 'em up with worn-out
    tools:

If you can make one heap of all your winnings
    And risk it on one turn of pitch-and-toss,

And lose, and start again at your beginnings
20   And never breath a word about your loss;
If you can force your heart and nerve and sinew
    To serve your turn long after they are gone,
And so hold on when there is nothing in you
    Except the Will which says to them: "Hold on!"

25 If you can talk with crowds and keep your virtue,
    Or walk with Kings—nor lose the common touch,
If neither foes nor loving friends can hurt you,
    If all men count with you, but none too much;
If you can fill the unforgiving minute
30   With sixty seconds' worth of distance run,
Yours is the Earth and everything that's in it,
    And—which is more—you'll be a Man, my son!
—1910

Lionel Johnson
1867 – 1902

Lionel Johnson was a participant in the so-called "Aesthetic" or "Decadent Movement" (or "art for art's sake" movement), with Walter Pater, Oscar Wilde, and Ernest Dowson.

 espe

The Dark Angel

Dark Angel, with thine aching lust
To rid the world of penitence:
Malicious Angel, who still dost
My soul such subtile violence!

5 Because of thee, no thought, no thing,
Abides for me undesecrate:
Dark Angel, ever on the wing,
Who never reachest me too late!

When music sounds, then changest thou
10 Its silvery to a sultry fire:
Nor will thine envious heart allow
Delight untortured by desire.

Through thee, the gracious Muses[1] turn
To Furies,[2] O mine Enemy!
15 And all the things of beauty burn
With flames of evil ecstasy.

Because of thee, the land of dreams
Becomes a gathering place of fears:
Until tormented slumber seems
20 One vehemence of useless tears.

When sunlight glows upon the flowers,
Or ripples down the dancing sea:
Thou, with thy troop of passionate powers,
Beleaguerest, bewilderest, me.

25 Within the breath of autumn woods,
Within the winter silences:
Thy venomous spirit stirs and broods,
O Master of impieties!

The ardour of red flame is thine,
30 And thine the steely soul of ice:
Thou poisonest the fair design
Of nature, with unfair device.

Apples of ashes, golden bright;
Waters of bitterness, how sweet!
35 O banquet of a foul delight,
Prepared by thee, dark Paraclete![3]

Thou art the whisper in the gloom,
The hinting tone, the haunting laugh:
Thou art the adorner of my tomb,
40 The minstrel of mine epitaph.

I fight thee, in the Holy Name!
Yet, what thou dost, is what God saith:
Tempter! should I escape thy flame,
Thou wilt have helped my soul from Death:

45 The second Death, that never dies,
That cannot die, when time is dead:

---

[1] in Greek mythology, the nine daughters of Zeus and Mnemosyne. Originally goddesses of memory, the Muses were later identified with individual arts and sciences.

[2] the Roman name for the Greek *erinyes*, three goddesses. Accounts of their origin vary; they were said to be the daughters of night, or of Earth and Darkness. They were merciless goddesses of vengeance who punished all transgressors, especially those who neglected filial duty or the claims of kinship.

[3] a title of the Holy Spirit; literally, "the advocate" or comforter.

Live Death, wherein the lost soul cries,
Eternally uncomforted.

Dark Angel, with thine aching lust!
50   Of two defeats, of two despairs:
Less dread, a change to drifting dust,
Than thine eternity of cares.

Do what thou wilt, thou shalt not so,
Dark Angel! triumph over me:
Lonely, unto the Lone I go;
Divine, to the Divinity.
—1894 (1893)

Summer Storm

To Harold Child

The wind, hark! the wind in the angry woods:
  And how clouds purple the west: there broods
    Thunder, thunder; and rain will fall;
  Fresh fragrance cling to the wind from all
5   Roses holding water wells,
  Laurels gleaming to the gusty air;
      Wilding mosses of the dells,
  Drenched hayfields, and dripping hedgerows fair.

The wind, hark! the wind dying again:
10   The wind's voice matches the far-off main,
    In sighing cadences: Pan[1] will wake,
  Pan in the forest, whose rich pipes make
      Music to the folding flowers,
  In the pure eve, where no hot spells are:
15   Those be favourable hours
  Hymned by Pan beneath the shepherd star.
—1895 (1887)

Dead

To Olivier Georges Destrée

In Merioneth,[2] over the sad moor
  Drives the rain, the cold wind blows:
    Past the ruinous church door,
The poor procession without music goes.

5 Lonely she wandered out her hour, and died.
    Now the mournful curlew cries
    Over her, laid down beside
Death's lonely people: lightly down she lies.

In Merioneth, the wind lives and wails,
10   On from hill to lonely hill:
    Down the loud, triumphant gales,
A spirit cries *Be strong!* and cries *Be still!*
—1895 (1887)

The End

To Austin Ferrand

I gave you more than love: many times more:
  I gave mine honour into your fair keeping.
You lost mine honour: wherefore now restore
The love, I gave; not dead, but cold and sleeping.
5 You loveless, I dishonoured, go our ways:
Dead is the past: dead must be all my days.

Death and the shadows tarry not: fulfil
Your years with folly and love's imitation.
You had mine all: mine only now, to kill
10 All trembling memories of mine adoration.
That done, to lie me down, and die, and dream,
What once, I thought you were: what still, you seem.
—1897 (1887)

---

[1] Greek "all" or "everything." In Greek mythology, the god of pastures, forests, flocks, and herds; the universal deity, Pan, had the torso of a man and the body and legs of a goat. Legend has it that the cry "Great Pan is dead" was heard at the moment of Christ's crucifixion.

---

[2] English for Meirionnydd, a region of Wales. It was the territory of Meirion, grandson of Cunedda, who conquered northern and western Wales in the fifth century AD.

Nihilism

To Samuel Smith

Among immortal things not made with hands;
Among immortal things, dead hands have made:
Under the Heavens, upon the Earth, there stands
Man's life, my life: of life I am afraid.

5 Where silent things, and unimpassioned things,
Where things of nought, and things decaying, are:
I shall be calm soon, with the calm, death brings.
The skies are gray there, without any star.

Only the rest! the rest! Only the gloom,
10 Soft and long gloom! The pausing from all thought!
My life, I cannot taste: the eternal tomb
Brings me the peace, which life has never brought.

For all the things I do, and do not well;
All the forced drawings of a mortal breath:
15 Are as the hollow music of a bell,
That times the slow approach of perfect death.
—1897 (1888)

The Darkness

To the Rev. Fr. Dover, S.J.

Master of spirits! hear me: King of souls!
I kneel before Thine altar, the long night,
Besieging Thee with penetrable prayers;
And all I ask, light from the Face of God.
5 Thy darkness Thou hast given me enough,
The dark clouds of Thine angry majesty:
Now give me light! I cannot always walk
Surely beneath the full and starless night.
Lighten me, fallen down, I know not where,
10 Save, to the shadows and the fear of death.
Thy Saints in light see light, and sing for joy:
Safe from the dark, safe from the dark and cold.
But from my dark comes only doubt of light:

Disloyalty, that trembles to despair.
15 Now bring me out of night, and with the sun
Clothe me, and crown me with Thy seven stars,[1]
Thy spirits in the hollow of Thine hand.
Thou from the still throne of Thy tabernacle
Wilt come to me in glory, O Lord God!
20 Thou wilt, I doubt Thee not: I worship Thee
Before Thine holy altar, the long night.
Else have I nothing in the world, but death:
Thine hounding winds rush by me day and night,
Thy seas roar in mine ears: I have no rest,
25 No peace, but am afflicted constantly,
Driven from wilderness to wilderness.
And yet Thou hast a perfect house of light,
Above the four great winds, an house of peace:
Its beauty of the crystal and the dew,
30 Guard Angels and Archangels, in their hands
The blade of a sword shaken. Thither bring
Thy servant: when the black night falls on me,
With bitter voices tempting in the gloom,
Send out Thine armies, flaming ministers,
35 And shine upon the night: for what I would,
I cannot, save these help me. O Lord God!
Now, when my prayers upon Thine altar lie,
When Thy dark anger is too hard for me:
Through vision of Thyself, through flying fire,
40 Have mercy, and give light, and stablish me!
—1897 (1889)

In a Workhouse

To Hartley Withers

Old hopes I saw there: and perchance I saw
Other old passions in their trembling age,
Withered, and desolate, but not yet dead:
And I had rather seen an house of death,
5 Than those live men, unmanned, wasted, forlorn,
Looking toward death out of their empty lives.

---

[1] the planets, or the constellation of the Pleiades or the Great Bear; see *King Lear* 1.5.1605.

They could not with the sad comfort of thought
Fill up the miserable day; nor muse
Upon the shadowy nature of the world,
10 And on that meditation stay themselves.
Nor wisdom of bright dreaming came there back
To these dulled minds, that never had the time,
The hard day's labour done, to do with dreams.
Nought theirs, but sullen waiting for no end;
15 Nought, but surrender to necessity.
No solemn faith, nor no impassioned trust,
Mastered their wills: here were no pagan souls,
Grandly enduring dooms, mighty to bear
Stern visitation of majestic fates,
20 Proudly alone and strong: these had no wills,
These were none else, than worn and haggard things,
Nor men, nor brutes, nor shades: and yet alive.
Bruised victims of the trampling years, hurt souls,
They fell before the march of their own kind:
25 Now, scarred memorials of laborious war,
Tragic and monumental live these men.
—1897 (1889)

Bagley Wood

To Percy Addleshaw

The night is full of stars, full of magnificence:
Nightingales hold the wood, and fragrance
    loads the dark.
Behold, what fires august, what lights eternal! Hark,
What passionate music poured in passionate love's
    defence!
5 Breathe but the wafting wind's nocturnal
    frankincense!
Only to feel this night's great heart, only to mark
The splendours and the glooms, brings back the
    patriarch,
Who on Chaldæan wastes found God through
    reverence.

Could we but live at will upon this perfect height,
10 Could we but always keep the passion of this peace,
Could we but face unshamed the look of this pure
    light,
Could we but win earth's heart, and give desire
    release:
Then were we all divine, and then were ours by
    right
These stars, these nightingales, these scents: then
    shame would cease.
—(1890)

The Destroyer of a Soul

I hate you with a necessary hate.
First, I sought patience: passionate was she:
My patience turned in very scorn of me,
That I should dare forgive a sin so great,
5 As this, through which I sit disconsolate;
Mourning for that live soul, I used to see;
Soul of a saint, whose friend I used to be:
Till you came by! a cold, corrupting, fate.

Why come you now? You, whom I cannot cease
10 With pure and perfect hate to hate? Go, ring
The death-bell with a deep, triumphant toll!
Say you, my friend sits by me still? Ah, peace!
Call you this thing my friend? this nameless thing?
This living body, hiding its dead soul?
—(1892)

The Precept of Silence

I know you: solitary griefs,
Desolate passions, aching hours!
I know you: tremulous beliefs,
Agonized hopes, and ashen flowers!

5 The winds are sometimes sad to me;
The starry spaces, full of fear:

Mine is the sorrow on the sea,
And mine the sigh of places drear.

Some players upon plaintive strings
10 Publish their wistfulness abroad:
I have not spoken of these things,
Save to one man, and unto God.
—(1893)

A Proselyte

Heart of magnificent desire:
O equal of the lordly sun!
Since thou hast cast on me thy fire,
My cloistral peace, so hardly won,
5   Breaks from its trance:
      One glance
From thee hath all its joy undone.

Of lonely quiet was my dream;
Day gliding into fellow day,
10 With the mere motion of a stream:
But now in vehement disarray

Go time and thought,
    Distraught
With passion kindled at thy ray.

15 Heart of tumultuary might,
O greater than the mountain flame,
That leaps upon the fearful night!
On me thy devastation came,
    Sudden and swift;
20   A gift
Of joyous torment without name.

Thy spirit stings my spirit: thou
Takest by storm and ecstasy
The cloister of my soul. And now,
25 With ardour that is agony,
    I do thy will;
      Yet still
Hear voices of calm memory.
—(1894)

Charlotte Mew
1869 – 1928

Charlotte Mew was born in London into a middle-class family that witnessed the early death of three children and the institutionalization of two others due to insanity. Mew's first publication, a short story, appeared in *The Yellow Book* in 1894. Her first collection of poetry was not published until 1916. *The Farmer's Bride*, as the collection was called, did not sell well, but it was well-received in literary circles. Eschewing marriage, Mew formed a pas-sionate yet unrequited regard for her friend May Sinclair. Mew wrote very little after 1916, producing one volume of poetry entitled *Saturday Market* in 1921 and producing another entitled *The Rambling Sailor*, which was post-humously published in 1929. Suffering from what was diagnosed as neurasthenia, she was admitted in 1928 to a nursing home, where she ultimately ended her own life.

The Farmer's Bride

To—
He asked life of thee, and thou gavest him a long life:
even for ever and ever…

Three Summers since I chose a maid,
   Too young maybe—but more's to do
At harvest-time than bide and woo.
   When us was wed she turned afraid
5 Of love and me and all things human;
   Like the shut of a winter's day.
Her smile went out, and 'twasn't a woman—
     More like a little frightened fay.[1]
       One night, in the Fall, she runned away.

10 "Out 'mong the sheep, her be," they said,
   'Should properly have been abed;
But sure enough she wasn't there
   Lying awake with her wide brown stare.
So over seven-acre field and up-along across the
   down
15 We chased her, flying like a hare
Before our lanterns. To Church-Town
     All in a shiver and a scare
We caught her, fetched her home at last
     And turned the key upon her, fast.

20 She does the work about the house
   As well as most, but like a mouse:
     Happy enough to chat and play
     With birds and rabbits and such as they,
     So long as men-folk keep away.
25 "Not near, not near!" her eyes beseech
When one of us comes within reach.
     The women say that beasts in stall
     Look round like children at her call.
     I've hardly heard her speak at all.

30 Shy as a leveret,[2] swift as he,
Straight and slight as a young larch tree,
Sweet as the first wild violets, she,
To her wild self. But what to me?

The short days shorten and the oaks are brown,
35   The blue smoke rises to the low grey sky,
One leaf in the still air falls slowly down,
    A magpie's spotted feathers lie
On the black earth spread white with rime,
The berries redden up to Christmas-time.
40   What's Christmas-time without there be
    Some other in the house than we!

   She sleeps up in the attic there
   Alone, poor maid. 'Tis but a stair

---

[1] fairy.

[2] a hare during its first year.

Betwixt us. Oh! my God! the down,
45 The soft young down of her, the brown,
The brown of her—her eyes, her hair, her hair!
—1916

In Nunhead Cemetery

It is the clay that makes the earth stick to his
        spade;
    He fills in holes like this year after year;
The others have gone; they were tired, and half afraid
    But I would rather be standing here;

5   There is nowhere else to go. I have seen this place
        From the windows of the train that's going past
    Against the sky. This is rain on my face—
        It was raining here when I saw it last.

There is something horrible about a flower;
10   This, broken in my hand, is one of those
    He threw in just now: it will not live another hour;
        There are thousands more: you do not miss a
            rose.

One of the children hanging about
        Pointed at the whole dreadful heap and smiled
15 This morning, after THAT was carried out;
        There is something terrible about a child.

We were like children, last week, in the Strand;
        That was the day you laughed at me
    Because I tried to make you understand
20   The cheap, stale chap I used to be
        Before I saw the things you make me see.

This is not a real place; perhaps by-and-by
        I shall wake—I am getting drenched with all
            this rain:
    To-morrow I will tell you about the eyes of the
        Crystal Palace train

25 Looking down on us, and you will laugh and I
        shall see what you see again.

    Not here, not now. We said "Not yet
    Across our low stone parapet
Will the quick shadows of the sparrows fall."

30 But still it was a lovely thing
        Through the grey months to wait for Spring
    With the birds that go a-gypsying
In the parks till the blue seas call.
        And next to these, you used to care
35   For the lions in Trafalgar Square,
Who'll stand and speak for London when her bell
        of Judgment tolls—
    And the gulls at Westminster that were
        The old sea-captains' souls.
40 To-day again the brown tide splashes, step by step,
        the river stair,
        And the gulls are there!

By a month we have missed our Day:
    The children would have hung about
Round the carriage and over the way
45   As you and I came out.

We should have stood on the gulls' black cliffs and
        heard the sea
    And seen the moon's white track,
I would have called, you would have come to me
        And kissed me back.

50 You have never done that: I do not know
        Why I stood staring at your bed
And heard you, though you spoke so low,
        But could not reach your hands, your little head.
    There was nothing we could not do, you said,
55   And you went, and I let you go!

Now I will burn you back, I will burn you through,
    Though I am damned for it we two will lie

And burn, here where the starlings fly
    To these white stones from the wet sky—;
60   Dear, you will say this is not I—
It would not be you, it would not be you!

If for only a little while
    You will think of it you will understand,
      If you will touch my sleeve and smile
65   As you did that morning in the Strand
        I can wait quietly with you
        Or go away if you want me to—
      God! What is God? but you face has gone and
        your hand!
        Let me stay here too.

70   When I was quite a little lad
      At Christmas time we went half mad
      For joy of all the toys we had,
And then we used to sing about the sheep
    The shepherds watched by night;
75 We used to pray to Christ to keep
    Our small souls safe till morning light—;
I am scared, I am staying with you to-night—
        Put me to sleep.

I shall stay here: here you can see the sky;
80 The houses in the streets are much too high;
    There is no one left to speak to there;
    Here they are everywhere,
And just above them fields and fields of roses lie—
If he would dig it all up again they would not die.
—1916

The Road To Kérity

Do you remember the two old people we passed
    on the road to Kérity,
Resting their sack on the stones, by the drenched
    wayside,
Looking at us with their lightless eyes through the
    driving rain, and then out again

To the rocks, and the long white line of the tide:
5 Frozen ghosts that were children once, husband
    and wife, father, and mother,
Looking at us with those frozen eyes; have you ever
      seen anything quite so chilled or
      so old?
      But we—with our arms about each
      other,
      We did not feel the cold!
—1916

I Have Been Through The Gates

His heart, to me, was a place of palaces and
    pinnacles and shining towers;
I saw it then as we see things in dreams,—I do not
    remember how long I slept;
I remember the trees, and the high, white walls,
    and how the sun was always on the towers;
The walls are standing to-day, and the gates: I have
    been through the gates, I have groped, I have
    crept
5 Back, back. There is dust in the streets, and blood;
    they are empty; darkness is over them;
His heart is a place with the lights gone out,
    forsaken by great winds and the heavenly rain,
    unclean and unswept,
Like the heart of the holy city, old, blind, beautiful
    Jerusalem,
      Over which Christ wept.
—1916

The Cenotaph [1]

Not yet will those measureless fields be green
    again
Where only yesterday the wild, sweet, blood of
    wonderful youth was shed;

---

[1] an empty tomb or monument honouring someone whose body is elsewhere.

527

There is a grave whose earth must hold too long,
    too deep a stain,
Though for ever over it we may speak as proudly as
    we may tread.
5 But here, where the watchers by lonely hearths
    from the thrust of an inward sword have more
    slowly bled,
We shall build the Cenotaph: Victory, winged,
    with Peace, winged too, at the column's head.
And over the stairway, at the foot—oh! here, leave
    desolate, passionate hands to spread
Violets, roses, and laurel, with the small, sweet,
    twinkling country things
Speaking so wistfully of other Springs,
10 From the little gardens of little places where son or
    sweetheart was born and bred.
In splendid sleep, with a thousand brothers
        To lovers—to mothers
        Here, too, lies he:
Under the purple, the green, the red,
15 It is all young life: it must break some women's
    hearts to see
Such a brave, gay coverlet to such a bed!
Only, when all is done and said,
God is not mocked and neither are the dead.

For this will stand in our Market-place—
20   Who'll sell, who'll buy
        (Will you or I
Lie each to each with the better grace)?
While looking into every busy whore's and
    huckster's face
As they drive their bargains, is the Face
25 Of God: and some young, piteous, murdered face.
    —1916

V. R. I. [1]

I. *January 22ⁿᵈ, 1901* [2]

"A Nation's Sorrow." No. In that strange hour
    We did but note the flagging pulse of day,
The sudden pause of Time, and turn away
Incredulous of grief; beyond the power
5 Of question or of tears. Thy people's pain
    Was their perplexity: Thou could'st not be
God's and not England's. Let Thy spirit reign,
    For England is not England without Thee.
Still Thine, Immortal Dead, she still shall stake
10   Thy fame against the world, and hold supreme
Thy unsuspended sway. Then lay not down
    Thy sceptre, lest her Empire prove a dream
Of Thine, great, gentle Sleeper, who shalt wake
    When God doth please, to claim another
    crown.

II. *February 2ⁿᵈ, 1901* [3]

When, wrapped in the calm majesty of sleep,
    She passes through her people to her rest,
    Has she no smile in slumber? Is her breast,
Even to their sorrow, pulseless? Shall they weep
5 And She not with them? Nothing is so strange
    As this, that England's passion, be it pain,
    Or joy, or triumph, never shall again
Find voice in her. No change is like this change.
For all this mute indifference of death,
10   More dear She is than She has ever been.
    The dark crowd gathers: not "The Queen! The
    Queen!"
Upon its lips to-day. A quickened breath—
    She passes—through the hush, the straining
    gaze,
    The vast, sweet silence of its love and praise.
—1916

---

[1] "Victoria Regina Imperatrix."

[2] the date of Queen Victoria's death.

[3] the date of Queen Victoria's funeral.

POETIC THEORY

ოჯი

William Johnson Fox
1786 – 1864

William J. Fox was a Unitarian minister, a man of letters, and a politician. He already had some reputation as a drama critic when, with the establishment of the *Westminster Review* in 1824, he published his first article. By 1830 he was co-editor of the *Monthly Repository*, the leading organ of the Unitarians. In 1831 he purchased the journal's copyright and made it an organ of social reform and literary criticism. Fox's astute interest in promising young authors is demonstrated in his 1831 Tennyson article printed here, as well as in his 1833 review of Robert Browning's first published work, *Pauline*. Fox subsequently established a life-long friendship with Browning.

⸙⸙⸙

Tennyson ~ Poems, Chiefly Lyrical ~ 1830

It would be a pity that poetry should be an exception to the great law of progression that obtains in human affairs; and it is not. The machinery of a poem is not less susceptible of improvement than the machinery of a cotton-mill; nor is there any better reason why the one should retrograde from the days of Milton, than the other from those of Arkwright. Of course we do not mean that the cases are precisely parallel, but the difference is not so much in favour of the perfectibility of the cotton-mill as is often imagined. Man cannot be less progressive than his own works and contrivances; in fact it is by his improvement that they are improved; and the mechanical arts are continually becoming superior to what they were, just because the men who are occupied in or about those arts have grown wiser than their predecessors, and have the advantage of a clearer knowledge of principles, an experience more extended or more accurately recorded, and perhaps a stronger stimulus to invention. Their progressiveness is merely a consequence from, a sort of reflection of, the progressiveness of his nature; but poetry is far nearer and dearer; it is essential to that nature itself; it is part and parcel of his constitution; and can only retrograde in the retrogradation of humanity.

There is nothing mysterious, or anomalous, in the power of producing poetry, or in that of its enjoyment; neither the one nor the other is a supernatural gift bestowed capriciously nobody knows how, when, or why. It may be a compound, but it is not incapable of analysis; and although our detection of the component parts may not enable us to effect their combination at pleasure, it may yet guide us to many useful conclusions and well-grounded anticipations. The elements of poetry are universal. The exercise of the organs of sight and sense stimulates man to some degree of descriptive poetry; wherever there is passion, there is dramatic poetry; wherever enthusiasm, there is lyric poetry; wherever reflection, there is metaphysical poetry. It is as widely diffused as the electric fluid.[1] It may be seen flashing out by fits and starts all the world over. The most ignorant talk poetry when they are in a state of excitement, the firmly-organized think and feel poetry with every breeze of sensation that sweeps over their well-tuned nerves. There is an unfathomable store of it in human nature; the species must fail before that can be exhausted; the only question is, whether there be any reason why these permanent elements should not be wrought into their combined form, in the future, with a facility and power which bear some direct ratio to the progress of society.

---

[1] a reference to the widely held nineteenth-century theory that an electric fluid pervaded the entire universe and was present in all material bodies.

So far as poetry is dependent upon physical organization; and doubtless it is to some extent so dependent; there is no reason why it should deteriorate. Eyes and ears are organs which nature finishes off with very different gradations of excellence. Nervous systems vary from the finest degree of susceptibility down to the toughness of a coil of hempen cable. *Poeta nascitur*[1] in a frame the most favourable to acute perception and intense enjoyment of the objects of sense; and it would be difficult to show that poets are not, and will not continue to be, produced as excellent as they have been, and as frequently. Why, then, should not those species of poetry which may be termed its music and its painting, which spring from, and appeal to, our sense of the beautiful in form or colour and of harmonious modulation, abound as much as heretofore? He is no lover of nature who has any notion that the half of her loveliness has ever yet been told. Descriptive poetry is the most exhaustible; but our coal mines will fail us much sooner. No man ever yet saw all the beauty of a landscape. He may have watched it from the rising to the setting sun, and through the twilight, and the moonlight, and the starlight, and all round the seasons, but he is deceived if he thinks then that it has nothing more for him. Indeed it is not he who ever will think so, but the man who drove down one day and back the next because he found the place so dull. The world has tired of descriptive poetry because it has been deluged with what was neither poetical nor descriptive. The world was quite right to be no longer tolerant of the repetition of conventional, traditionary, unfelt, and unmeaning phrases. But Cowper[2] did not find the ground preoccupied. Bucolics, and Georgics, and Eclogues, and Pastorals, all made reverential room for his honest verses; and the shelf on which they took their stand is far from crowded. Nature will never cease to be poetical, nor society either. Spears and shields; gods, goddesses, and muses; and all the old scenery and machinery may indeed wear out. That is of little consequence. The age of chivalry was but one, and poetry has many ages. The classical and romantic schools are both but sects of a religion which is universal. Even the fields which have been most frequently reaped will still bear harvests; and rich ones too. Bards began with battles some thousands of years ago, and yet nobody ever wrote the Fight of Flodden field till it was indited by Scott,[3] nor did any one anticipate Campbell's glorious ballad of the battle of Hohenlinden.[4] Genius is never anticipated. No wit ever complained that all the good things had been said; nor will any poet, to the world's end, find that all worthy themes have been sung. Is not the French Revolution as good as the siege of Troy? And the landing of the Pilgrim Fathers on the shores of America, as that of the Trojan fugitives on the coast of Italy? The world has never been more disposed to make the want of a hero "an uncommon want" than in these supposed unpoetical days on which we are fallen. And were they not provided, poetry might do without them. The old epics will probably never be surpassed, any more than the old coats of mail; and for the same reason; nobody wants the article; its object is accomplished by other means; they are become mere curiosities. A long story, with a plot to be ravelled and unravelled, and characters to be developed, and descriptions to be introduced, and a great moral lesson at the end of it, is now always done, and best done, in prose. A large portion always was prose in fact, and necessarily so; but literary superstition kept up the old forms after every body felt them intolerably wearisome and soporific, though few dared be so heretical as to say so, until the utili-

---

[1] "a poet is born."

[2] William Cowper (1731–1800), an important pastoral poet of the second half of the eighteenth century.

[3] Sir Walter Scott (1771–1832), poet and novelist, author of *The Waverly Novels*. His highly successful poem, *Marmion* (1808), featured the historical battle of Flodden field.

[4] Thomas Campbell (1777–1844), author of martial lyrics, and poems expressing both the heroism and futility of battle, such as *Hohenlinden*.

tarian spirit showed itself even in poetical criticism, and then the dull farce ended. This we take to be a great reformation. We have left off singing what ought only to be said, but the singing is neither the less nor the worse on that account. Nor will it be. The great principle of human improvement is at work in poetry as well as everywhere else. What is it that is reforming our criminal jurisprudence? What is shedding its lights over legislation? What purifies religions? What makes all arts and sciences more available for human comfort and enjoyment? Even that which will secure a succession of creations out of the unbounded and everlasting materials of poetry, our ever-growing acquaintance with the philosophy of mind and of man, and the increasing facility with which that philosophy is applied. This is the essence of poetic power, and he who possesses it never need furbish up ancient armour, or go to the East Kehama-hunting, or bulbul-catching.[1] Poetry, like charity, begins at home. Poetry, like morality, is founded on the precept, know thyself. Poetry, like happiness, is in the human heart. Its inspiration is of that which is in man, and it will never fail because there are changes in costume and grouping. What is the vitality of the *Iliad*? Character; nothing else. All the rest is only read either out of antiquarianism or of affectation. Why is Shakespeare the greatest of poets? Because he was one of the greatest of philosophers. We reason on the conduct of his characters with as little hesitation as if they were real living human beings. Extent of observation, accuracy of thought, and depth of reflection, were the qualities which won the prize of sovereignty for his imagination, and the effect of these qualities was practically to anticipate, so far as was needful for his purposes, the mental philosophy of a future age. Metaphysics must be the stem of poetry for the plant to thrive; but if the stem flourishes we are not likely to be at a loss for leaves, flowers, and fruit. Now whatever theories may have come into fashion, and gone out of fashion, the real science of mind advances with the progress of society like all other sciences. The poetry of the last forty years already shows symptoms of life in exact proportion as it is imbued with this science. There is least of it in the exotic legends of Southey,[2] and the feudal romances of Scott. More of it, though in different ways, in Byron and Campbell. In Shelley there would have been more still, had he not devoted himself to unsound and mystical theories. Most of all in Coleridge and Wordsworth. They are all going or gone; but here is a little book as thoroughly and unitedly metaphysical and poetical in its spirit as any of them; and sorely shall we be disappointed in its author if it be not the precursor of a series of productions which shall beautifully illustrate our speculations, and convincingly prove their soundness.

Do not let our readers be alarmed. These poems are any thing but heavy; anything but stiff and pedantic, except in one particular, which shall be noticed before we conclude; anything but cold and logical. They are graceful, very graceful; they are animated, touching, and impassioned. And they are so, precisely because they are philosophical; because they are not made up of metrical cant and conventional phraseology; because there is sincerity where the author writes from experience, and accuracy whether he writes from experience or observation; and he only writes from experience or observation, because he has felt and thought, and learned to analyze thought and feeling; because his own mind is rich in poetical associations, and he has wisely been content with its riches; and because, in his composition, he has not sought to construct an elaborate and artificial harmony, but only to pour forth his thoughts in those expressive and simple melodies whose meaning, truth, and power, are the soonest recognized and the longest felt.

---

[1] animal and song-bird of Persia.

[2] the poet Robert Southey (1774–1843).

The most important department in which metaphysical science has been a pioneer for poetry is in the analysis of particular states of mind; a work which is now performed with ease, power, and utility as much increased, as in the grosser dissections of the anatomical lecturer. Hence the poet, more fortunate than the physician, has provision made for an inexhaustible supply of subjects. A new world is discovered for him to conquer. The poets of antiquity rarely did more than incidentally touch this class of topics; the external world had not yet lost its freshness; situations, and the outward expression of the thoughts, feelings and passions generated by those situations, were a province so much nearer at hand, and presented so much to be done and enjoyed, that they rested there content, like the two tribes and a half of Israel, who sought not to cross the narrow boundary that separated them from a better and richer country.[1] Nor let them be blamed; it was for the philosophers to be the first discoverers and settlers, and for poetry afterwards to reap the advantage of their labours. This has only been done recently, or rather is only beginning to be done at all. Metaphysical systems and discussions in verse, there have been indeed, from Lucretius down to Akenside.[2] But they have generally had just argument enough to spoil the poetry, and just poetry enough to spoil the argument. They resembled paintings of the bones, arteries, veins, and muscles; very bad as a substitute to the anatomist for the real substances in the human body, and still worse for the artist as the materials for a pleasant picture. Science, mental or physical, cannot be taught poetically; but the power derived from science may be used poetically; and metaphysics may do as much for the poet as anatomy has done for the painter, in truth, more, for the painter's knowledge of the human frame does not furnish him with distinct subjects for the exercise of his art; we have

just remarked the unfitness. The benefit which the painter derives is that of being able to delineate the external appearances of the living body with greater truth and effect. And while the poet has an analogous advantage from mental science in the greater truth and effect of his delineations of external action, character, passion, and all that belongs to situation and grouping; he also finds in the phenomena exhibited in moral dissection (though not in the operation itself, in the application of the logical scalpel) some of the finest originals for his pictures; and they exist in infinite variety.

Mr Tennyson has some excellent specimens of this class. He seems to obtain entrance into a mind as he would make his way into a landscape; he climbs the pineal gland as if it were a hill in the centre of the scene; looks around on all objects with their varieties of form, their movements, their shades of colour, and their mutual relations and influences; and forthwith produces as graphic a delineation in the one case as Wilson or Gainsborough[3] could have done in the other, to the great enrichment of our gallery of intellectual scenery. In the "Supposed Confessions of a second-rate sensitive mind not in unity with itself," there is an extraordinary combination of deep reflection, metaphysical analysis, picturesque description, dramatic transition, and strong emotion. The author personates (he can personate anything he pleases from an angel to a grasshopper) a timid sceptic, but who must evidently always remain such, and yet be miserable in his scepticism; whose early associations, and whose sympathies, make religion a necessity to his heart; yet who has not lost his pride in the prowess of his youthful infidelity; who is tossed hither and thither on the conflicting currents of feeling and doubt, without that vigorous intellectual decision which alone could "ride in the whirlwind and direct the storm," until at last he disappears with an exclamation which remains on the ear like

[1] a reference to the flight of the Jews from Egypt: Exodus 14:5–30.

[2] from the ancients (Lucretius, Roman poet and philosopher [96?–55 BC]), to the moderns (Mark Akenside, poet [1721–70]).

[3] eighteenth-century English painters.

the bubbling cry
Of some strong swimmer in his agony.

Now without intruding any irreverent comparison or critical profanity we do honestly think this state of mind as good a subject for poetical description as even the shield of Achilles itself. Such topics are more in accordance with the spirit and intellect of the age than those about which poetry has been accustomed to be conversant; their adoption will effectually redeem it from the reproach of being frivolous and enervating; and of their affinity with the best pictorial qualities of poetry we have conclusive evidence in this very composition. The delineations of the trustful infant, the praying mother, the dying lamb, are as good as anything of the kind can be; while those of the supposed author's emotions as he gazes on "Christians with happy countenances," or stands by the Christian grave, or realizes again, with a mixture of self-admiration and self-reproach, "the unsunned freshness of his strength," when he "went forth in quest of truth," are of a higher order, and are more powerfully, though not less gracefully finished.

Our author has the secret of the transmigration of the soul. He can cast his own spirit into any living thing, real or imaginary. Scarcely Vishnu[1] himself becomes incarnate more easily, frequently, or perfectly. And there is singular refinement, as well as solid truth, in his impersonations, whether they be of inferior creatures or of such elemental beings as Syrens, as mermen and mermaidens. He does not merely assume their external shape, and exhibit his own mind masquerading. He takes their senses, feelings, nerves, and brain, along with their names and local habitations; still it is himself in them, modified but not absorbed by their peculiar constitution and mode of being. In "The Merman" one seems to feel the principle of thought injected by a strong volition into the cranium of the finny worthy,

and coming under all the influences, as thinking principles do, of the physical organization to which it is for the time allied: for a moment the identification is complete; and then a consciousness of contrast springs up between the reports of external objects brought to the mind by the senses and those which it has been accustomed to receive; and this consciousness gives to the description a most poetical colouring:

> There would be neither moon nor star;
> But the wave would make music above us afar—
> Low thunder and light in the magic night—
>   Neither moon nor star.
> We would call aloud in the dreary dells, &c.

The Mermaid is beautifully discriminated, and most delicately drawn. She is the younger sister of Undine; or Undine herself before she had a soul.[2] And the Syrens, who could resist these Sea Fairies, as the author prefers calling them? We must introduce a fragment of their song, though it is barbarous to break such a piece of coral for a specimen:

> Day and night to the billow the fountain calls
> …
> Whither away, whither away, whither away with
>   the sail and the oar?

The poet has here done, in the character of the Sea-Fairies, that which he has several times done in his own person, and always admirably; he has created a scene out of the character, and made the feeling within generate an appropriate assemblage of external objects. Every mood of the mind has its own outward world, or rather makes its own outward world. But it is not always, perhaps with sensitive and imaginative minds it is seldom, that the external objects, and their qualities will be seen through the medium of congeniality. It is thus in "L'Allegro" and "Il Penseroso";

---

[1] the second member of the trinity in Hindu theology, popularly believed to have had several human incarnations.

[2] a female water spirit who could acquire a soul by marrying, and having a child by, a mortal.

but Milton was a happy man; the visions of both those poems were seen with the eyes of happiness, the only difference being that the one depicts a state of light-hearted, and the other of sober-minded enjoyment. There is not less truth, perhaps a more refined observation, in the opposite course which our author has taken in the two poems "Nothing Will Die," and "All Things Will Die." The outward objects, at the commencement of each, are precisely the same; the states of mind, are in contrast; and each seizes with avidity on some appearance which is uncongenial with itself. He who thinks that nothing will die, yet looks with wondering, and almost wearied eye on the ever-flowing stream, &c.; and he, who feels that all things must die, gazes mournfully on those same objects in the "gayest, happiest attitude," which his own fancy has unconsciously compelled them to assume. There is this difference, however, that the felicitous conviction, in the first poem, enables the mind to recover itself with a sort of elastic bound; while in the second the external beauty and enjoyment, being at permanent variance with the tone of feeling, the mind after a melancholy recognition of their loveliness sinks into unmixed gloom, and surrounds itself with objects of deeper and darker shade. We shall be better understood by quoting the commencement of each.

NOTHING WILL DIE

ALL THINGS WILL DIE

Both poems conclude nearly in the same terms, with the exception of a discriminative epithet or two; but expressing in the one case an exulting joyousness, "So let the wind range"; and in the other a reckless and desperate gaiety, just as religion and infidelity sometimes approximate, in terms, to the inculcation of the same moral; and while the preacher of immortality cries "rejoice evermore," the expectant of annihilation shouts, "Let us eat and drink, for tomorrow we die."

"Mariana" is, we are disposed to think, although there are several poems which rise up reproachfully in our recollection as we say so, altogether, the most perfect composition in the volume. The whole of this poem, of eighty-four lines, is generated by the legitimate process of poetical creation, as that process is conducted in a philosophical mind, from a half sentence in Shakespeare. There is no mere amplification; it is all production; and production from that single germ. That must be a rich intellect, in which thoughts thus take root and grow. Mariana, the forsaken betrothed of Angelo, is described in *Measure for Measure*, as living in seclusion at "the moated grange." Mr Tennyson knows the place well; the ruinous, old, lonely house, the neglected garden, the forlorn stagnation of the locality.

> About a stonecast from the wall
> …
> The level waste, the rounding grey.

And here it was, that the deserted one lingered day after day in that "hope deferred which maketh the heart sick." The dreariness of the abode and the surrounding scenery was nothing to her;

> She only said, "My life is dreary,
>   He cometh not," she said;
> She said, "I am aweary, aweary,
>   I would that I were dead!"

The poem takes us through the circuit of four-and-twenty hours of this dreary life. Through all the changes of the night and day she has but one feeling, the variation of which is only by different degrees of acuteness and intensity in the misery it produces; and again and again we feel, before its repetition, the coming of the melancholy burthen,

> And ever when the moon was low
> …
> I would that I were dead.

The day, by its keener expectancy, was more harassing and agitating than the night; and by its sights and sounds, in that lonely place, and under the strange interpretations of a morbid fancy and a breaking heart, did yet more "confound her sense." Her deserted parents, the greyheaded domestics that had nursed her infancy in her father's house, seemed to be there; she recognized them, and what would they with her?

> Old faces glimmered through the doors,
> Old footsteps trod the upper floors,
> Old voices called her from without.

Again the hour passed at which Angelo used to arrive; again the evening is come when he used to be there, where he never would be again; the bright sunshiny evening, blazing and fading; and

> —most she loathed the hour
> …
> Oh God, that I were dead!"

A considerable number of the poems are amatory; they are the expression not of heartless sensuality, nor of a sickly refinement, nor of fantastic devotion, but of manly love; and they illustrate the philosophy of the passion while they exhibit the various phases of its existence, and embody its power. An arrangement of them might be made which should depict the whole history of passion from its birth to its apotheosis, or its death. We have seen

THE BURIAL OF LOVE

Had we space we should discuss this topic. It is of incalculable importance to society. Upon what love is, depends what woman is, and upon what woman is, depends what the world is, both in the present and the future. There is not a greater moral necessity in England than that of a reformation in female education. The boy is a son; the youth is a lover; and the man who thinks lightly of the elevation of character and the extension of happiness which woman's influence is capable of producing, and ought to be directed to the production of, in society, is neither the wisest of philosophers nor the best of patriots. How long will it be before we shall have read to better purpose the eloquent lessons, and the yet more eloquent history, of that gifted and glorious being, Mary Wollstonecraft?[1]

Mr Tennyson sketches females as well as ever did Sir Thomas Lawrence.[2] His portraits are delicate, his likenesses (we will answer for them) perfect, and they have life, character, and individuality. They are nicely assorted also to all the different gradations of emotion and passion which are expressed in common with the descriptions of them. There is an appropriate object for every shade of feeling, from the light touch of a passing admiration, to the triumphant madness of soul and sense, or the deep and everlasting anguish of survivorship.

Lilian is the heroine of the first stage:

> Airy, fairy Lilian,
> …
> Cruel little Lilian.

Madeline indicates that another degree has been taken in the freemasonry of love, "smiling frowning evermore." And so we are conducted, through various gradations, to Isabel, "the stately flower of female fortitude, and perfect wifehood," to the intense and splendid passion of "Hero," and to the deep pathos of the ballad and dirge of "Oriana."

We had noted many other passages for extract or remark, but our limits are prescribed and almost arrived at. We should also have illustrated the felicitous effect often produced by the iteration of a word

---

[1] Mary Wollstonecraft (1759–97), author of *A Vindication of the Rights of Women* (1792).

[2] (1769–1830), English portrait painter, successor to Sir Joshua Reynolds as principal painter to the King in 1792.

or sentence so posited that it conveys a different meaning or shade of meaning, excites a varied kind of emotion, and is involuntarily uttered in a different tone. There are many beautiful instances of this kind. In the ballad of Oriana, and in the songs, repetition, with a slight variation of epithet, is also practised with great power. Rousseau's[1] *air des trois notes* is only a curiosity; Mr Tennyson has made some very touching, and some very animating melodies, of little more than that number of words. He is a master of musical combinations. His songs set themselves, and generate their own tunes, as all songs do which are good for anything; but they are not many. Perhaps our author is only surpassed, among recent poets, by Coleridge, in the harmony of his versification.

It would also have been pleasant to have transcribed and analyzed such pictures as those of the Dying Swan, the Sleeping Beauty, Adeline, &c.; and to have shown how the author can breathe his own spirit into unconscious things, making them instinct with life and feeling. One stanza of an autumnal song may intimate to some readers the facility and grace with which he identifies himself with nature.

> A spirit haunts the year's last hours
> ...
> Heavily hangs the tigerlily.

We must protest against the irregularities of measure, and the use of antiquated words and obsolete pronunciation, in which our author indulges so freely. He exposes himself thereby to the charge, and we think not unfairly, of indolence and affectation. There are few variations of effect which a skilful artist cannot produce, if he will but take the pains, without deviating from that regularity of measure which is one of the original elements of poetical enjoyment; made so by the tendency of the human frame to periodical movements; and the continued sacrifice of which is but ill compensated to the disappointed ear

by any occasional, and not otherwise attainable correspondence between the movement of a verse and the sense which it is intended to convey. Nor certainly is any thing gained by a song's being studded with words which to most readers may require a glossary.

Mr Tennyson has the propensity which Shelley had, to use a word or two which young ladies of the present day are not accustomed to read or sing in the parlour; in singing, we believe, the toleration is greater than in reading or conversation; sentences, avoiding the words, but meaning much worse, are not generally proscribed.

That these poems will have a very rapid and extensive popularity we do not anticipate. Their very originality will prevent their being generally appreciated for a time. But that time will come, we hope, to a not far distant end. They demonstrate the possession of powers, to the future direction of which we look with some anxiety. A genuine poet has deep responsibilities to his country and the world, to the present and future generations, to earth and heaven. He, of all men, should have distinct and worthy objects before him, and consecrate himself to their promotion. It is thus that he best consults the glory of his art, and his own lasting fame. Mr Tennyson has a dangerous quality in that facility of impersonation on which we have remarked, and by which he enters so thoroughly into the most strange and wayward idiosyncrasies of other men. It must not degrade him into a poetical harlequin. He has higher work to do than that of disporting himself amongst "mystics" and "flowing philosophers." He knows that "the poet's mind is holy ground"; he knows that the poet's portion is to be

> Dower'd with the hate of love, the scorn of scorn,
> The love of love;

he has shown, in the lines from which we quote, his own just conception of the grandeur of a poet's

---

[1] Jean Jacques Rousseau (1712–78), French philosopher and writer.

destiny; and we look to him for its fulfilment. It is not for such men to sink into mere verse-makers for the amusement of themselves or others. They can influence the associations of unnumbered minds; they can command the sympathies of unnumbered hearts; they can disseminate principles; they can give those principles power over men's imaginations; they can excite in a good cause the sustained enthusiasm that is sure to conquer; they can blast the laurels of the tyrants, and hallow the memories of the martyrs of patriotism; they can act with a force, the extent of which it is difficult to estimate, upon national feel-

ings and character, and consequently upon national happiness. If our estimate of Mr Tennyson be correct, he too is a poet; and many years hence may be read his juvenile description of that character with the proud consciousness that it has become the description and history of his own work:

> So many minds did gird their orbs with beams
> ...
> Her beautiful bold brow.

—1831

Arthur Henry Hallam
1811 – 1833

Arthur Henry Hallam, a young man of great talent and potential, entered Trinity College, Cambridge, in 1828 and became a close friend of Tennyson, probably beginning in 1829. With Tennyson, Hallam was a member of the "Cambridge Apostles," an undergraduate debating and discussion society. In August, 1831, Hallam published a review of Tennyson's 1830 *Poems, Chiefly Lyrical* in the *Englishman's Magazine*. Hallam died from a haemorrhage while visiting Vienna in September, 1833, and Tennyson began composing some sections of his elegiac *In Memoriam A.H.H.* as early as October, 1833. It was published in 1850, the year that Tennyson became Poet Laureate.

❧❧❧

On Some of the Characteristics of Modern Poetry

AND ON THE LYRICAL POEMS OF ALFRED TENNYSON [1]

So Mr. Montgomery's[2] *Oxford*, by the help of some pretty illustrations, has contrived to prolong its miserable existence to a second edition! But this is slow work, compared to that triumphant progress of the *Omnipresence,* which, we concede to the author's friends, was "truly astonishing." We understand, moreover, that a new light has broken upon this "desolator desolate;" and since the "columns" have begun to follow the example of "men and gods," by whom our poetaster has long been condemned, "it is the fate of genius," he begins to discover, "to be unpopular." Now, strongly as we protest against Mr. Montgomery's application of this maxim to his own case, we are much disposed to agree with him as to its abstract correctness. Indeed, the truth which it involves seems to afford the only solution of so curious a phenomenon as the success, partial and transient though it be, of himself, and other of his calibre.

When Mr. Wordsworth, in his celebrated Preface to the *Lyrical Ballads*, asserted that immediate or rapid popularity was not the test of poetry, great was the consternation and clamour among those farmers of public favour, the established critics. Never had so audacious an attack been made upon their undoubted privileges and hereditary charter of oppression.

"What! *The Edinburgh Review* not infallible!" shrieked the amiable petulance of Mr. Jeffrey.

"*The Gentleman's Magazine* incapable of decision!" faltered the feeble garrulity of Silvanus Urban.[3]

And straightway the whole sciolist herd, men of rank, men of letters, men of wealth, men of business, all the "mob of gentlemen who think with ease,"[4] and a terrible number of old ladies and boarding-school misses began to scream in chorus, and prolonged the notes of execration with which they overwhelmed the new doctrine, until their wits and their voices fairly gave in from exhaustion. Much, no doubt, they did, for much persons will do when they fight for their dear selves; but there was one thing they could not do, and unfortunately it was the only one of any importance. They could not put down Mr. Words-

---

[1] This review of Tennyson's *Poems, Chiefly Lyrical* (1830), appeared in *The Englishman's Magazine* in August, 1831. Because of the close friendship between Hallam and Tennyson, it is generally accepted that the essay reflects Tennyson's own view of his early work.

[2] Robert Montgomery (1807–55), a third-rate contemporary poetaster.

[3] Francis Jeffrey, the editor of *The Edinburgh Review* from 1802–29; Sylvanus Urban was the pseudonym used by successive editors of *The Gentleman's Magazine*.

[4] Pope's satiric description of the Cavalier and Court poets who "wrote with ease" in the reign of Charles I and Charles II.

worth by clamour, or prevent his doctrine, once uttered, and enforced by his example, from awakening the minds of men, and giving a fresh impulse to art. It was the truth, and it prevailed; not only against the exasperation of that hydra, the Reading Public, whose vanity was hurt, and the blustering of its keepers, whose delusion was exposed, but even against the false glosses and narrow apprehensions of the Wordsworthians themselves. It is the madness of all who loosen some great principle, long buried under a snow-heap of custom and superstition, to imagine that they can restrain its operation, or circumscribe it by their purposes. But the right of private judgment was stronger than the will of Luther; and even the genius of Wordsworth cannot expand itself to the full periphery of poetic art.

It is not true, as his exclusive admirers would have it, that the highest species of poetry is the reflective; it is a gross fallacy, that because certain opinions are acute or profound, the expression of them by the imagination must be eminently beautiful. Whenever the mind of the artist suffers itself to be occupied, during its periods of creation, by any other predominant motive than the desire of beauty, the result is false in art.

Now there is undoubtedly no reason why he may not find beauty in those moods of emotion, which arise from the combinations of reflective thought; and it is possible that he may delineate these with fidelity, and not be led astray by any suggestions of an unpoetical mood. But though possible, it is hardly probable; for a man whose reveries take a reasoning turn, and who is accustomed to measure his ideas by their logical relations rather than the congruity of the sentiments to which they refer, will be apt to mistake the pleasure he has in knowing a thing to be true, for the pleasure he would have in knowing it to be beautiful, and so will pile his thoughts in a rhetorical battery, that they may convince, instead of letting them flow in a natural course of contemplation, that they may enrapture.

It would not be difficult to shew, by reference to the most admired poems of Wordsworth, that he is frequently chargeable with this error; and that much has been said by him which is good as philosophy, powerful as rhetoric, but false as poetry. Perhaps this very distortion of the truth did more in the peculiar juncture of our literary affairs to enlarge and liberalize the genius of our age, than could have been effected by a less sectarian temper.

However this may be, a new school of reformers soon began to attract attention, who, professing the same independence of immediate favor, took their stand on a different region of Parnassus from that occupied by the Lakers,[1] and one, in our opinion, much less liable to perturbing currents of air from ungenial climates. We shall not hesitate to express our conviction, that the cockney school (as it was termed in derision from a cursory view of its accidental circumstances) contained more genuine inspiration, and adhered more steadily to that portion of truth which it embraced, than any *form* of art that has existed in this country since the days of Milton. Their *caposetta*[2] was Mr. Leigh Hunt, who did little more than point the way, and was diverted from his aim by a thousand personal predilections and political habits of thought.

But he was followed by two men of very superior make; men who were born poets, lived poets, and went poets to their untimely graves. Shelley and Keats were indeed of opposite genius; that of the one was vast, impetuous, and sublime, the other seemed to be "fed with honeydew," and to have "drunk the milk of Paradise."[3] Even the softness of Shelley

---

[1] "This cant term was justly ridiculed by Mr. Wordsworth's supporters; but it was not so easy to substitute an inoffensive denomination. We are not at all events the first who have used it without a contemptuous intention, for we remember to have heard a disciple quote Aristophanes in its behalf:—Ουτος ου τοιυ ήδαδων τωνδ 'ων όραυ' υμεις αει αλλα ΑΙΜΝΑΙΟΣ. 'This is no common, no barn-door fowl: No, but a Lakist.'" (Hallam's note.)

[2] head of a sect.

[3] from Coleridge's "Kubla Khan."

comes out in bold, rapid, comprehensive strokes; he has no patience for minute beauties, unless they can be massed into a general effect of grandeur. On the other hand, the tenderness of Keats cannot sustain a lofty flight; he does not generalize or allegorize Nature; his imagination works with few symbols, and reposes willingly on what is given freely.

Yet in this formal opposition of character there is, it seems to us, a groundwork of similarity sufficient for the purposes of classification, and constituting a remarkable point in the progress of literature. They are both poets of sensation rather than reflection. Susceptible of the slightest impulse from external nature, their fine organs trembled into emotion at colors, and sounds, and movements, unperceived or unregarded by duller temperaments. Rich and clear were their perceptions of visible forms; full and deep their feelings of music. So vivid was the delight attending the simple exertions of eye and ear, that it became mingled more and more with their trains of active thought, and tended to absorb their whole being into the energy of sense. Other poets *seek* for images to illustrate their conceptions; these men had no need to seek; they lived in a world of images; for the most important and extensive portion of their life consisted in those emotions which are immediately conversant with the sensation. Like the hero of Goethe's novel, they would hardly have been affected by what is called the pathetic parts of a book; but the *merely beautiful* passages, "those from which the spirit of the author looks clearly and mildly forth," would have melted them to tears.[1] Hence they are not descriptive, they are picturesque. They are not smooth and *negatively* harmonious; they are full of deep and varied melodies.

This powerful tendency of imagination to a life of immediate sympathy with the external universe, is not nearly so liable to false views of art as the opposite disposition of purely intellectual contemplation.

For where beauty is constantly passing before "that inward eye, which is the bliss of solitude;"[2] where the soul seeks it as a perpetual and necessary refreshment to the sources of activity and intuition; where all the other sacred ideas of our nature, the idea of good, the idea of perfection, the idea of truth, are habitually contemplated through the medium of this predominant mood, so that they assume its colour, and are subject to its peculiar laws, there is little danger that the ruling passion of the whole mind will cease to direct its creative operations, or the energetic principle of love for the beautiful sink, even for a brief period, to the level of a mere notion in the understanding.

We do not deny that it is, on other accounts, dangerous for frail humanity to linger with fond attachment in the vicinity of sense. Minds of this description are especially liable to moral temptations; and upon them, more than any, it is incumbent to remember, that their mission as men, which they share with their fellow-beings, is of infinitely higher interest than their mission as artists, which they possess by rare and exclusive privilege. But it is obvious that, critically speaking, such temptations are of slight moment. Not the gross and evident passions of our nature, but the elevated and less separable desires, are the dangerous enemies which misguide the poetic spirit in its attempts at self-cultivation. That delicate sense of fitness which grows with the growth of artist feelings, and strengthens with their strength, until it acquires a celerity and weight of decision hardly inferior to the correspondent judgments of conscience, is weakened by every indulgence of heterogeneous aspirations, however pure they may be, however lofty, however suitable to human nature.

We are therefore decidedly of opinion that the heights and depths of art are most within the reach of those who have received from nature the "fearful and wonderful" constitution we have described, whose

[1] *Wilhelm Meisters Lehrjahre* 5.6.

[2] Wordsworth, "I Wandered Lonely as a Cloud."

poetry is a sort of magic, producing a number of impressions, too multiplied, too minute, and too diversified to allow of our tracing them to their causes, because just such was the effect, even so boundless and so bewildering, produced on their imaginations by the real appearance of Nature.

These things being so, our friends of the new school had evidently much reason to recur to the maxim laid down by Mr. Wordsworth, and to appeal from the immediate judgment of lettered or unlettered contemporaries to the decision of a more equitable posterity. How should they be popular, whose senses told them a richer and ampler tale than most men could understand, and who constantly expressed, because they constantly felt, sentiments of exquisite pleasure or pain, which most men were not permitted to experience? The public very naturally derided them as visionaries, and gibbeted *in terrorem*[1] those inaccuracies of diction occasioned sometimes by the speed of their conceptions, sometimes by the inadequacy of language to their peculiar conditions of thought.

But it may be asked, does not this line of argument prove too much? Does it not prove that there is a barrier between these poets and all other persons so strong and immovable, that, as has been said of the Supreme Essence, we must be themselves before we can understand them in the least? Not only are they not liable to sudden and vulgar estimation, but the lapse of ages, it seems, will not consolidate their fame, nor the suffrages of the wise few produce any impression, however remote or slow matured, on the judgment of the incapacitated many.

We answer, this is not the import of our argument. Undoubtedly the true poet addresses himself, in all his conceptions, to the common nature of us all. Art is a lofty tree, and may shoot up far beyond our grasp, but its roots are in daily life and experience. Every bosom contains the elements of those

complex emotions which the artist feels, and every head can, to a certain extent, go over in itself the process of their combination, so as to understand his expressions and sympathize with his state. But this requires exertion; more or less, indeed, according to the difference of occasion, but always some degree of exertion. For since the emotions of the poet, during composition, follow a regular law of association, it follows that to accompany their progress up to the harmonious prospect of the whole, and to perceive the proper dependence of every step on that which preceded, it is absolutely necessary *to start from the same point,* i.e. clearly to apprehend that leading sentiment of the poet's mind, by their conformity to which the host of suggestions are arranged.

Now this requisite exertion is not willingly made by the large majority of readers. It is so easy to judge capriciously, and according to indolent impulse! For very many, therefore, it has become *morally* impossible to attain the author's point of vision, on account of their habits, or their prejudices, or their circumstances; but it is never *physically* impossible, because nature has placed in every man the simple elements, of which art is the sublimation. Since then this demand on the reader for activity, when he wants to peruse his author in a luxurious passiveness, is the very thing that moves his bile, it is obvious that those writers will be always most popular who require the least degree of exertion. Hence, whatever is mixed up with art, and appears under its semblance, is always more favorably regarded than art free and unalloyed. Hence, half the fashionable poems in the world are mere rhetoric, and half the remainder are, perhaps, not liked by the generality for their substantial merits. Hence, likewise, of the really pure compositions, those are most universally agreeable which take for their primary subject the *usual* passions of the heart, and deal with them in a simple state, without applying the transforming powers of high imagination. Love, friendship, ambition, religion, &c., are matters of daily experience even amongst unimagina-

[1] as a warning.

tive tempers. The forces of association, therefore, are ready to work in these directions, and little effort of will is necessary to follow the artist.

For the same reason, such subjects often excite a partial power of composition, which is no sign of a truly poetic organization. We are very far from wishing to depreciate this class of poems, whose influence is so extensive, and communicates so refined a pleasure. We contend only that the facility with which its impressions are communicated is no proof of its elevation as a form of art, but rather the contrary.

What, then, some may be ready to exclaim, is the pleasure derived by most men, from Shakespeare, or Dante, or Homer, entirely false and factitious? If these are really masters of their art, must not the energy required of the ordinary intelligences that come in contact with their mighty genius, be the greatest possible? How comes it then, that they are popular? Shall we not say, after all, that the difference is in the power of the author, not in the tenor of his meditations? Those eminent spirits find no difficulty in conveying to common apprehensions their lofty sense and profound observation of Nature. They keep no aristocratic state, apart from the sentiments of society at large; they speak to the hearts of all, and by the magnetic force of their conceptions, elevate inferior intellects into a higher and purer atmosphere.

The truth contained in this observation is undoubtedly important; geniuses of the most universal order, and assigned by destiny to the most propitious era of a nation's literary development, have a clearer and a larger access to the minds of their compatriots than can ever open to those who are circumscribed by less fortunate circumstances. In the youthful periods of any literature there is an expansive and communicative tendency in mind which produces unreservedness of communion, and reciprocity of vigor between different orders of intelligence.

Without abandoning the ground which has always been defended by the partizans of Mr. Words-worth, who declare with perfect truth, that the number of real admirers of what is really admirable in Shakespeare and Milton is much fewer than the number of apparent admirers might lead one to imagine, we may safely assert that the intense thoughts set in circulation by those "orbs of song" and their noble satellites "in great Eliza's golden time," did not fail to awaken a proportionable intensity of the nature of numberless auditors. Some might feel feebly, some strongly; the effect would vary according to the character of the recipient; but upon none was the stirring influence entirely unimpressive. The knowledge and power thus imbibed became a part of national existence; it was ours as Englishmen; and amid the flux of generations and customs we retain unimpaired this privilege of intercourse with greatness.

But the age in which we live comes late in our national progress. That first raciness and juvenile vigor of literature, when nature "wandered as in her prime, and played at will her virgin fancies" is gone, never to return.[1] Since that day we have undergone a period of degradation. "Every handicraftsman has worn the mask of Poesy."[2] It would be tedious to repeat the tale so often related of the French contagion and the heresies of the Popian school.

With the close of the last century came an era of reaction, an era of painful struggle to bring our over-civilised condition of thought into union with the fresh productive spirit that brightened the morning of our literature. But repentance is unlike innocence; the laborious endeavor to restore has more complicated methods of action than the freedom of untainted nature. Those different powers of poetic disposition, the energies of Sensitive,[3] of Reflective,

---

[1] Hallam's synthesis of l. 40 and l. 784 from Wordsworth's "Descriptive Sketches" (1793 ed.).

[2] Keats, "Sleep and Poetry," ll. 200–01.

[3] "We are aware that this is not the right word, being appropriated by common use to a different signification. Those who think the caution given by Caesar should not stand in the way of urgent occasion, may

of Passionate Emotion, which in former times were intermingled, and derived from mutual support an extensive empire over the feelings of men, were now restrained within separate spheres of agency. The whole system no longer worked harmoniously, and by intrinsic harmony acquired external freedom; but there arose a violent and unusual action in the several component functions, each for itself, all striving to reproduce the regular power which the whole had once enjoyed.

Hence the melancholy which so evidently characterises the spirit of modern poetry; hence that return of the mind upon itself and the habit of seeking relief in idiosyncrasies rather than community of interest. In the old times the poetic impulse went along with the general impulse of the nation; in these it is a reaction against it, a check acting for conservation against a propulsion towards change.

We have indeed seen it urged in some of our fashionable publications, that the diffusion of poetry must be in the direct ratio of the diffusion of machinery, because a highly civilized people must have new objects of interest, and thus a new field will be open to description. But this notable argument forgets that against this *objective* amelioration may be set the decrease of *subjective* power, arising from a prevalence of social activity, and a continual absorption of the higher feelings into the palpable interests of ordinary life. The French Revolution may be a finer theme than the war of Troy; but it does not so evidently follow that Homer is to find his superior.

Our inference, therefore, from this change in the relative position of artists to the rest of the community is, that modern poetry in proportion to its depth and truth is likely to have little immediate authority over public opinion. Admirers it will have; sects consequently it will form; and these strong undercurrents will in time sensibly affect the principal stream. Those writers whose genius, though great, is

not strictly and essentially poetic, become mediators between the votaries of art and the careless cravers for excitement.[1] Art herself, less manifestly glorious than in her periods of undisputed supremacy, retains her essential prerogatives, and forgets not to raise up chosen spirits who may minister to her state and vindicate her title.

One of the faithful Islâm, a poet in the truest and highest sense, we are anxious to present to our readers. He has yet written little and published less; but in these "preludes of a loftier strain"[2] we recognize the inspiring god. Mr. Tennyson belongs decidedly to the class we have already described as Poets of Sensation. He sees all the forms of nature with the "eruditus oculus," and his ear has a fairy fineness. There is a strange earnestness in his worship of beauty which throws a charm over his impassioned song, more easily felt than described, and not to be escaped by those who have once felt it. We think he has more definiteness and roundness of general conception than the late Mr. Keats, and is much more free from blemishes of diction and hasty capriccios of fancy. He has also this advantage over that poet and his friend Shelley, that he comes before the public unconnected with any political party or peculiar system of opinions. Nevertheless, true to the theory we have stated, we believe his participation in their characteristic excellences is sufficient to secure him a share of their unpopularity.

The volume of "Poems, chiefly Lyrical," does not contain above 154 pages; but it shews us much more of the character of its parent mind, than many books we have known of much larger compass and more boastful pretensions. The features of original genius are clearly and strongly marked. The author imitates

---

substitute 'sensuous'; a word in use amongst our elder divines, and revived by a few bold writers in our own time." (Hallam's note.)

[1] "May we not compare them to the bright but unsubstantial clouds which, in still evenings, girdle the side of lofty mountains, and seem to form a natural connexion between the lowly vallies spread out beneath, and those isolated peaks that hold the 'last parley with the setting sun'?" (Hallam's note.)

[2] Shelley's *The Revolt of Islam*, "Dedication" 10.83.

nobody; we recognise the spirit of his age, but not the individual form of this or that writer. His thoughts bear no more resemblance to Byron or Scott, Shelley or Coleridge, than to Homer or Calderon, Firdúsí or Calidasa.[1]

We have remarked five distinctive excellencies of his own manner. First, his luxuriance of imagination, and at the same time his control over it. Secondly his power of embodying himself in ideal characters, or rather moods of character, with such extreme accuracy of adjustment, that the circumstances of the narration seem to have a natural correspondence with the predominant feeling, and, as it were, to be evolved from it by assimilative force. Thirdly his vivid, picturesque delineation of objects, and the peculiar skill with which he holds all of them *fused*, to borrow a metaphor from science, in a medium of strong emotion. Fourthly, the variety of his lyrical measures, and exquisite modulation of harmonious words and cadences to the swell and fall of the feelings expressed. Fifthly, the elevated habits of thought, implied in these compositions, and imparting a mellow soberness of tone, more impressive, to our minds, than if the author had drawn up a set of opinions in verse, and sought to instruct the understanding rather than to communicate the love of beauty to the heart.

We shall proceed to give our readers some specimens in illustration of these remarks, and, if possible, we will give them entire; for no poet can be fairly judged of by fragments, least of all, a poet like Mr. Tennyson, whose mind conceives nothing isolated, nothing abrupt, but every part with reference to some other part, and in subservience to the idea of the whole.

Recollections of the Arabian Nights!—What a delightful, endearing title! How we pity those to whom it calls up no reminiscence of early enjoyment, no sentiment of kindliness as towards one who sings

a song they have loved, or mentions with affection a departed friend! But let nobody expect a multifarious enumeration of Viziers, Barmecides, Fireworshippers, and Cadis;[2] trees that sing, horses that fly, and Goules that eat rice-pudding!

Our author knows what he is about; he has, with great judgment, selected our old acquaintance, "the good Haroun Alraschid," as the most prominent object of our childish interest, and with him has called up one of those luxurious garden scenes, the account of which, in plain prose, used to make our mouth water for sherbet, since luckily we were too young to think much about Zobeide![3] We think this poem will be the favourite among Mr. Tennyson's admirers; perhaps upon the whole it is our own; at least we find ourselves recurring to it oftener than to any other, and every time we read it, we feel the freshness of its beauty increase, and are inclined to exclaim with Madame de Sévigné, "*à force d'être ancien, il m'est nouveau.*"[4] But let us draw the curtain.

RECOLLECTIONS OF THE ARABIAN NIGHTS

When the breeze of a joyful dawn blew free
In the silken sail of infancy,
The tide of time flow'd back with me,
    The forward-flowing tide of time;
And many a sheeny summer-morn,
Adown the Tigris I was borne,
By Bagdat's shrines of fretted gold,
High-walled gardens green and old;
True Mussulman was I and sworn,
    For it was in the golden prime
      Of good Haroun Alraschid.

---

[1] Calderón (1600–81), Spanish dramatist; Firdúsí (c. 950–1020), Persian poet; Calidasa (third century AD.?), Indian poet and dramatist.

[2] characters in the *Arabian Nights*.

[3] Haroun-al-Raschid (763–809), caliph of Baghdad, appears in many of the tales. Zobeide was his wife.

[4] "Because it is old, it is new to me." Madame de Sévigny (1626–96), famous letter-writer.

Anight my shallop, rustling thro'
The low and bloomed foliage, drove
The fragrant, glistening deeps, and clove
15   The citron-shadows in the blue;
By garden porches on the brim,
The costly doors flung open wide,
Gold glittering thro' lamplight dim,
And broider'd sofas on each side.
20   In sooth it was a goodly time,
        For it was in the golden prime
           Of good Haroun Alraschid.

Often, where clear-stemm'd platans guard
The outlet, did I turn away
25   The boat-head down a broad canal
From the main river sluiced, where all
The sloping of the moonlit sward
Was damask-work, and deep inlay
Of braided blooms unmown, which crept
30   Adown to where the water slept.
        A goodly place, a goodly time,
        For it was in the golden prime
           Of good Haroun Alraschid.

A motion from the river won
35   Ridged the smooth level, bearing on
My shallop thro' the star-strown calm,
Until another night in night
I enter'd, from the clearer light,
Imbower'd vaults of pillar'd palm,
40   Imprisoning sweets, which, as they clomb
Heavenward, were stay'd beneath the dome
        Of hollow boughs. A goodly time,
        For it was in the golden prime
           Of good Haroun Alraschid.

45   Still onward; and the clear canal
Is rounded to as clear a lake.
From the green rivage many a fall
Of diamond rillets musical,
Thro' little crystal arches low
50   Down from the central fountain's flow
Fallen silver-chiming, seemed to shake
The sparkling flints beneath the prow.

A goodly place, a goodly time,
For it was in the golden prime
55   Of good Haroun Alraschid.

Above thro' many a bowery turn
A walk with vari-colored shells
Wander'd engrain'd. On either side
All round about the fragrant marge
60   From fluted vase, and brazen urn
In order, eastern flowers large,
Some dropping low their crimson bells
Half-closed, and others studded wide
        With disks and tiars, fed the time
65   With odor in the golden prime
           Of good Haroun Alraschid.

Far off, and where the lemon grove
In closest coverture upsprung,
The living airs of middle night
70   Died round the bulbul as he sung;
Not he, but something which possess'd
The darkness of the world, delight,
Life, anguish, death, immortal love,
Ceasing not, mingled, unrepress'd,
75   Apart from place, withholding time,
        But flattering the golden prime
           Of good Haroun Alraschid.

Black the garden-bowers and grots
Slumber'd; the solemn palms were ranged
80   Above, unwoo'd of summer wind;
A sudden splendor from behind
Flush'd all the leaves with rich gold-green,
And, flowing rapidly between
Their interspaces, counterchanged
85   The level lake with diamond-plots
        Of dark and bright. A lovely time,
        For it was in the golden prime
           Of good Haroun Alraschid.

Dark-blue the deep sphere overhead,
90   Distinct with vivid stars inlaid,
Grew darker from that under-flame;
So, leaping lightly from the boat,

With silver anchor left afloat,
In marvel whence that glory came
95 Upon me, as in sleep I sank
In cool soft turf upon the bank,
   Entranced with that place and time,
   So worthy of the golden prime
     Of good Haroun Alraschid.

100 Thence thro' the garden I was drawn—
A realm of pleasance, many a mound,
And many a shadow-chequer'd lawn
Full of the city's stilly sound,
And deep myrrh-thickets blowing round
105 The stately cedar, tamarisks,
Thick rosaries of scented thorn,
Tall orient shrubs, and obelisks
   Graven with emblems of the time,
   In honor of the golden prime
110   Of good Haroun Alraschid.

With dazed vision unawares
From the long alley's latticed shade
Emerged, I came upon the great
Pavilion of the Caliphat.
115 Right to the carven cedarn doors,
Flung inward over spangled floors,
Broad-based flights of marble stairs
Ran up with golden balustrade,
   After the fashion of the time,
120   And humor of the golden prime
     Of good Haroun Alraschid.

The fourscore windows all alight
As with the quintessence of flame,
A million tapers flaring bright
125 From twisted silvers look'd to shame
The hollow-vaulted dark, and stream'd
Upon the mooned domes aloof
In inmost Bagdat, till there seem'd
Hundreds of crescents on the roof
130   Of night new-risen, that marvellous time
   To celebrate the golden prime
     Of good Haroun Alraschid.

Then stole I up, and trancedly
Gazed on the Persian girl alone,
135 Serene with argent-lidded eyes
Amorous, and lashes like to rays
Of darkness, and a brow of pearl
Tressed with redolent ebony,
In many a dark delicious curl,
140 Flowing beneath her rose-hued zone;
   The sweetest lady of the time,
   Well worthy of the golden prime
     Of good Haroun Alraschid.

Six columns, three on either side,
145 Pure silver, underpropt a rich
Throne of the massive ore, from which
Down-droop'd, in many a floating fold,
Engarlanded and diaper'd
With inwrought flowers, a cloth of gold.
150 Thereon, his deep eye laughter-stirr'd
With merriment of kingly pride,
   Sole star of all that place and time,
   I saw him—in his golden prime,
    THE GOOD HAROUN ALRASCHID

Criticism will sound but poorly after this; yet we cannot give silent votes. The first stanza, we beg leave to observe, places us at once in the position of feeling, which the poem requires. The scene is before us, around us; we cannot mistake its localities, or blind ourselves to its colours. That happy ductility of childhood returns for the moment; "true Mussulmans are we, and sworn," and yet there is a latent knowledge, which heightens the pleasure, that to our change from really childish thought we owe the capacities by which we enjoy the recollection.

As the poem proceeds, all is in perfect keeping. There is a solemn distinctness in every image, a majesty of slow motion in every cadence, that aids the illusion of thought, and steadies its contemplation of the complete picture. Originality of observation seems to cost nothing to our author's liberal genius; he lavishes images of exquisite accuracy and elaborate splendour, as a common writer throws about metaphorical truisms, and exhausted tropes. Amidst all the varied luxuriance of the sensations described, we are never permitted to lose sight of the idea which gives unity to this variety, and by the recurrence of which, as a sort of mysterious influence, at the close of every stanza, the mind is wrought up, with consummate art, to the final disclosure. This poem is a perfect gallery of pictures; and the concise boldness, with which in a few words an object is clearly painted, is sometimes (see the 6th stanza) majestic as Milton, sometimes (see the 12th) sublime as Aeschylus.

We have not, however, so far forgot our vocation as critics, that we would leave without notice the slight faults which adhere to this precious work. In the 8th stanza, we doubt the propriety of using the bold compound "black-green," at least in such close vicinity to "gold-green;" nor is it perfectly clear by the term, although indicated by the context, that "diamond plots" relates to shape rather than colour. We are perhaps very stupid, but "vivid stars unrayed" does not convey to us a very precise notion. "*Rosaries* of scented thorn," in the 10th stanza is, we believe, an entirely unauthorized use of the word. Would our author translate "*biferique rosaria Paesti*"—"And *rosaries* of Paestum, twice in bloom?[1]

To the beautiful 13th stanza we are sorry to find any objection; but even the bewitching loveliness of that "Persian girl" shall not prevent our performing the rigid duty we have undertaken, and we must hint to Mr. Tennyson that "redolent" is no synonyme for "fragrant." Bees may be redolent *of* honey; spring may be "redolent *of* youth and love;" but the absolute use of the word has, we fear, neither in Latin nor English any better authority than the monastic epitaph on Fair Rosamund: "*Hic jacet in tombâ Rosa Mundi, non Rosa Munda, non redolet, sed olet, quae redolere solet.*"[2]

We are disposed to agree with Mr. Coleridge when he says "no adequate compensation can be made for the mischief a writer does by confounding the distinct senses of words."[3] At the same time our feelings in this instance rebel strongly in behalf of "redolent;" for the melody of the passage, as it stands, is beyond the possibility of improvement, and unless he should chance to light upon a word very nearly resembling this in consonants and vowels, we can hardly quarrel with Mr. Tennyson if, in spite of our judgment, he retains the offender in his service.

Our next specimen is of a totally different character, but not less complete, we think, in its kind. Have we among our readers any who delight in the heroic poems of Old England, the inimitable ballads? Any to whom Sir Patrick Spens, and Clym of the Clough, and Glorious Robin are consecrated names? Any who sigh with disgust at the miserable abortions of simpleness mistaken for simplicity, or florid weakness substituted for plain energy which they may often have seen dignified with the title of Modern Ballads?

Let such draw near and read *The Ballad of Oriana*. We know no more happy seizure of the antique spirit in the whole compass of our literature; yet there is no foolish self-desertion, no attempt at obliterating the present, but everywhere a full discrimination of how much ought to be yielded and how much retained. The author is well aware that the art of one generation cannot *become* that of another by any will or skill; but the artist may transfer the spirit of the past, making it a temporary form for his own spirit, and so effect, by idealizing power, a new and legitimate

---

[2] Rosamund Clifford, mistress of Henry II. "Here in this tomb lies the Rose of the World, not the lovely Rosa; she is no longer fragrant as she used to be but gives forth an offensive odor." Hallam's pedantic point is that this is the only authority one could cite for using "redolent" with the proposition "of" as a synonym for "fragrant."

[3] probably not a direct quotation, but a paraphrase of a familiar Coleridgian idea. "See "Aphorism 1" in "Prudential Aphorisms," *Aids to Reflection*.

---

[1] The translation is, in fact, correct.

combination. If we were asked to name among the real antiques that which bears greatest resemblance to this gem, we should refer to the ballad of *Fair Helen of Kirkconnel Lea* in the *Minstrelsy of the Scottish Border*.[1] It is a resemblance of mood, not of execution. They are both highly wrought lyrical expressions of pathos; and it is very remarkable with what intuitive art every expression and cadence in *Fair Helen* is accorded to the main feeling.

The characters that distinguish the language of our *lyrical* from that of our *epic* ballads have never yet been examined with the accuracy they deserve. But, beyond question, the class of poems which in point of harmonious combination *Oriana* most resembles, is the Italian. Just thus the meditative tenderness of Dante and Petrarch is embodied in the clear, searching notes of Tuscan song. These mighty masters produce two-thirds of their effect by *sound*. Not that they sacrifice sense to sound, but that sound conveys their meaning where words would not. There are innumerable shades of fine emotion in the human heart, especially when the senses are keen and vigilant, which are too subtle and too rapid to admit of corresponding phrases. The understanding takes no definite note of them; how then can they leave signatures in language? Yet they exist; in plenitude of being and beauty they exist; and in music they find a medium through which they pass from heart to heart. The tone becomes the sign of the feeling; and they reciprocally suggest each other.

Analogous to this suggestive power may be reckoned, perhaps, in a sister art, the effects of Venetian colouring. Titian *explains* by tints, as Petrarch by tones. Words would not have done the business of the one, nor any groupings or *narration by form,* that of the other. But, shame upon us! we are going back to our metaphysics, when that "sweet, meek face" is waiting to be admitted.

---

[1] edited by Sir Walter Scott, 1802–03.

THE BALLAD OF ORIANA

My heart is wasted with my woe,
    Oriana.
There is no rest for me below,
    Oriana.
5 When the long dun wolds are ribb'd with snow,
And loud the Norland whirlwinds blow,
    Oriana,
Alone I wander to and fro,
    Oriana.

10 Ere the light on dark was growing,
    Oriana,
At midnight the cock was crowing,
    Oriana;
Winds were blowing, waters flowing,
15 We heard the steeds to battle going,
    Oriana,
Aloud the hollow bugle blowing,
    Oriana.

In the yew-wood black as night,
20   Oriana,
Ere I rode into the fight,
    Oriana,
While blissful tears blinded my sight
By star-shine and by moonlight,
25   Oriana,
I to thee my troth did plight,
    Oriana.

She stood upon the castle wall,
    Oriana;
30 She watch'd my crest among them all,
    Oriana;
She saw me fight, she heard me call,
When forth there stept a foeman tall,
    Oriana,
35 Atween me and the castle wall,
    Oriana.

The bitter arrow went aside,
    Oriana;

40 The false, false arrow went aside,
     Oriana;
The damned arrow glanced aside,
And pierced thy heart, my love, my bride,
     Oriana!
Thy heart, my life, my love, my bride,
45   Oriana!

O, narrow, narrow was the space,
     Oriana!
Loud, loud rung out the bugle's brays,
     Oriana.
50 O, deathful stabs were dealt apace.
The battle deepen'd in its place,
     Oriana;
But I was down upon my face,
     Oriana.

55 They should have stabb'd me where I lay,
     Oriana!
How could I rise and come away,
     Oriana?
How could I look upon the day?
60 They should have stabb'd me where I lay,
     Oriana—
They should have trod me into clay,
     Oriana.

O breaking heart that will not break,
65   Oriana!
O pale, pale face so sweet and meek,
     Oriana!
Thou smilest, but thou dost not speak,
And then the tears run down my cheek,
70   Oriana.
What wantest thou? whom dost thou seek,
     Oriana?

I cry aloud; none hear my cries,
     Oriana.
75 Thou comest atween me and the skies,
     Oriana
I feel the tears of blood arise
Up from my heart unto my eyes,

80   Oriana.
Within thy heart my arrow lies,
     Oriana!

O cursed hand! O cursed blow!
     Oriana!
O happy thou that liest low,
85   Oriana!
All night the silence seems to flow
Beside me in my utter woe,
     Oriana.
A weary, weary way I go,
90   Oriana!

When Norland winds pipe down the sea,
     Oriana,
I walk, I dare not think of thee,
     Oriana.
95 Thou liest beneath the greenwood tree,
I dare not die and come to thee,
     Oriana.
I hear the roaring of the sea,
     Oriana.

We have heard it objected to this poem that the name occurs once too often in every stanza. We have taken the plea into our judicial consideration, and the result is that we overrule it and pronounce that the proportion of the melodious cadences to the pathetic parts of the narration could not be diminished without materially affecting the rich lyrical impression of the ballad.

For what is the author's intention? To gratify our curiosity with a strange adventure? To shake our nerves with a painful story? Very far from it. Tears indeed may "blind our sight" as we read; but they are "blissful tears." The strong musical delight prevails over every painful feeling and mingles them all in its deep swell until they attain a composure of exalted sorrow, a mood in which the latest repose of agitation becomes visible, and the influence of beauty spreads like light over the surface of the mind.

The last line, with its dreamy wildness, reveals the design of the whole. It is transferred, if we mistake not, from an old ballad (a freedom of immemorial usage with ballad-mongers, as our readers doubtless know) but the merit lies in the abrupt application of it to the leading sentiment, so as to flash upon us in a few little words a world of meaning, and to consecrate the passion that was beyond cure or hope by resigning it to the accordance of inanimate Nature, who, like man, has her tempests and occasions of horror, but august in their largeness of operation, awful by their dependence on a fixed and perpetual necessity.

We must give one more extract, and we are almost tempted to choose by lot among many that crowd on our recollection, and solicit our preference with such witchery as it is not easy to withstand. The poems towards the middle of the volume seem to have been written at an earlier period than the rest. They display more unrestrained fancy and are less evidently proportioned to their ruling ideas than those which we think of later date. Yet in the *Ode to Memory*—the only one which we have the poet's authority for referring to early life—there is a majesty of expression, united to a truth of thought, which almost confounds our preconceived distinctions.

The *Confessions of a Second-rate, Sensitive Mind* are full of deep insight into human nature, and into those particular trials which are sure to beset men who think and feel for themselves at this epoch of social development. The title is perhaps ill-chosen. Not only has it an appearance of quaintness which has no sufficient reason, but it seems to us incorrect. The mood portrayed in this poem, unless the admirable skill of delineation has deceived us, is rather the clouded season of a strong mind than the habitual condition of one feeble and "second-rate." Ordinary tempers build up fortresses of opinion on one side or another; they will see only what they choose to see. The distant glimpse of such agony as is here brought out to view is sufficient to keep them for ever in illusions, voluntarily raised at first, but soon trusted in with full reliance as inseparable parts of self.

Mr. Tennyson's mode of "rating" is different from ours. He may esteem none worthy of the first order who has not attained a complete universality of thought, and such trustful reliance on a principle of repose which lies beyond the war of conflicting opinions, that the grand ideas, "*qui planent sans cesse au dessus de l'humanité,*" [1] cease to affect him with bewildering impulses of hope and fear. We have not space to enter further into this topic; but we should not despair of convincing Mr. Tennyson that such a position of intellect would not be the most elevated, nor even the most conducive to perfection of art.

The "How" and the "Why" appears to present the reverse of the same picture. It is the same mind still: the sensitive sceptic, whom we have looked upon in his hour of distress, now scoffing at his own state with an earnest mirth that borders on sorrow. It is exquisitely beautiful to see in this, as in the former portrait, how the feeling of art is kept ascendant in our minds over distressful realities, by constant reference to images of tranquil beauty, whether touched pathetically, as the Ox and the Lamb in the first piece, or with fine humour, as the "great bird" and "little bird" in the second.

The Sea Fairies is another strange title; but those who turn to it with the very natural curiosity of discovering who these new births of mythology may be, will be unpardonable if they do not linger over it with higher feelings. A stretch of lyrical power is here exhibited which we did not think the English language had possessed. The proud swell of verse as the harp tones "run up the ridged sea," and the soft and melancholy lapse as the sounds die along the widening space of water, are instances of that right imitation which is becoming to art, but which in the hands of the unskilful, or the affecters of easy popularity, is often converted into a degrading mimicry,

---

[1] ideas "which soar forever above humanity."

detrimental to the best interests of the imagination.

A considerable portion of this book is taken up with a very singular and very beautiful class of poems on which the author has evidently bestowed much thought and elaboration. We allude to the female characters, every trait of which presumes an uncommon degree of observation and reflection. Mr. Tennyson's way of proceeding seems to be this. He collects the most striking phenomena of individual minds until he arrives at some leading fact, which allows him to lay down an axiom or law; and then, working on the law thus attained, he clearly discerns the tendency of what new particulars his invention suggests, and is enabled to impress an individual freshness and unity on ideal combinations. These expressions of character are brief and coherent; nothing extraneous to the dominant fact is admitted, nothing illustrative of it, and, as it were, growing out of it, is rejected. They are like summaries of mighty dramas. We do not say this method admits of such large luxuriance of power as that of our real dramatists; but we contend that it is a new species of poetry, a graft of the lyric on the dramatic, and Mr. Tennyson deserves the laurel of an inventor, an enlarger of our modes of knowledge and power.

We must hasten to make our election; so, passing by the "airy, fairy Lilian," who "clasps her hands" in vain to retain us; the "stately flower" of matronly fortitude, "revered Isabel"; Madeline, with her voluptuous alternation of smile and frown; Mariana, last, but oh not least—we swear by the memory of Shakespeare, to whom a monument of observant love has here been raised by simply expanding all the latent meanings and beauties contained in one stray thought of his genius[1]—we shall fix on a lovely, albeit somewhat mysterious lady, who has fairly taken our "heart from out our breast."

---

[1] Tennyson's epigraph under the title of "Mariana" is from Shakespeare's *Measure for Measure* 3.1.277: "Mariana in the moated grange."

ADELINE

I

Mystery of mysteries,
　　Faintly smiling Adeline,
　　　Scarce of earth nor all divine,
Nor unhappy, nor at rest,
　　　But beyond expression fair
　　　With thy floating flaxen hair;
Thy rose-lips and full blue eyes
　　　Take the heart from out my breast.
　　Wherefore those dim looks of thine,
　　Shadowy, dreaming Adeline?

II

Whence that aery bloom of thine,
　　Like a lily which the sun
Looks thro' in his sad decline,
　　And a rose-bush leans upon,
Thou that faintly smilest still,
　　As a Naiad in a well,
　　Looking at the set of day,
Or a phantom two hours old
　　Of a maiden past away,
Ere the placid lips be cold?
　　Wherefore those faint smiles of thine,
　　　Spiritual Adeline?

III

What hope or fear or joy is thine?
Who talketh with thee, Adeline?
　　For sure thou art not all alone.
　　　Do beating hearts of salient springs
　　Keep measure with thine own?
　　　Hast thou heard the butterflies
　　　　What they say betwixt their wings?
　　　Or in stillest evenings
With what voice the violet woos
To his heart the silver dews?
　　　Or when little airs arise,
　　How the merry bluebell rings
　　To the mosses underneath?
　　Hast thou look'd upon the breath

Of the lilies at sunrise?
Wherefore that faint smile of thine,
Shadowy, dreaming Adeline?

IV

Some honey-converse feeds thy mind,
   Some spirit of a crimson rose
   In love with thee forgets to close
His curtains, wasting odorous sighs
All night long on darkness blind.
What aileth thee? whom waitest thou
With thy soften'd, shadow'd brow,
   And those dew-lit eyes of thine,
   Thou faint smiler, Adeline?

V

Lovest thou the doleful wind
   When thou gazest at the skies?
Doth the low tongued Orient
   Wander from the side of the morn
   Dripping with Sabæan spice
On thy pillow, lowly bent
   With melodious airs lovelorn,
Breathing Light against thy face,
While his locks a-drooping twined
Round thy neck in subtle ring
Make a carcanet of rays,
   And ye talk together still,
In the language wherewith Spring
   Letters cowslips on the hill?
Hence that look and smile of thine,
   Spiritual Adeline.

Is not this beautiful? When this Poet dies, will not the Graces and the Loves mourn over him, "*fortunatâque favilla nascentur violae.*[1] How original is the imagery, and how delicate! How wonderful the new world thus created for us, the region between real and unreal! The gardens of Armida[2] were but poorly musical compared with the roses and lillies

that bloom around thee, thou faint smiler, Adeline, on whom the glory of imagination reposes, endowing all thou lookest on with sudden and mysterious life. We could expatiate on the deep meaning of this poem, but it is time to twitch our critical mantles; and, as our trade is not that of mere enthusiasm, we shall take our leave with an objection (perhaps a cavil) to the language of the cowslips, which we think too ambiguously spoken of for a subject on which nobody, except Mr. Tennyson, can have any information. The "ringing bluebell," too, if it be not a pun, suggests one, and might probably be altered to advantage.

One word more before we have done, and it shall be a word of praise. The language of this book, with one or two rare exceptions, is thorough and sterling English. A little more respect, perhaps, was due to the "*jus et norma loquendi*",[3] but we are inclined to consider as venial a fault arising from generous enthusiasm for the principles of sound analogy, and for that Saxon element, which constituted the intrinsic freedom and nervousness of our native tongue. We see no signs in what Mr. Tennyson has written of the Quixotic spirit which has led some persons to desire the reduction of English to a single form, by excluding nearly the whole of Latin and Roman derivatives. Ours is necessarily a compound language; as such alone it can flourish and increase; nor will the author of the poems we have extracted be likely to barter for a barren appearance of symmetrical structure that fertility of expression and variety of harmony which "the speech that Shakspeare spoke" derived from the sources of southern phraseology.

In presenting this young poet to the public as one not studious of instant popularity, nor likely to obtain it, we may be thought to play the part of a fashionable lady who deludes her refractory mate into doing what she chooses by pretending to wish the exact contrary; or of a cunning pedagogue who

---

[1] "Violets will be born from these blest ashes": Persius, *Satires* 1. 39–40

[2] Armida, in Tasso's *Jerusalem Delivered*, lured Christians who were attacking the Holy City into gardens.

[3] "the right and rule of speech" from Horace, *Ars Poetica*, l. 72.

practises a similar manoeuvre on some self-willed Flibbertigibbet[1] of the school room. But the supposition would do us wrong. We have spoken in good faith, commending this volume to feeling hearts and imaginative tempers, not to the stupid readers, or the voracious readers, or the malignant readers, or the readers after dinner!

We confess, indeed, we never knew an instance in which the theoretical abjurers of popularity have shewn themselves very reluctant to admit its actual advances. So much virtue is not, perhaps, in human nature; and if the world should take a fancy to buy up these poems, in order to be revenged on the *Englishman's Magazine,*[2] who knows whether even we might not disappoint its malice by a cheerful adaptation of our theory to "existing circumstances?" —1831

---

[1] devil.

[2] the periodical in which this review appeared.

Letitia E. Landon
L.E.L.
1802 – 1838

Letitia Elizabeth Landon, the poet and novelist well known in her own time as L.E.L., was born in Chelsea. She wrote to support her family, producing, tirelessly, five volumes of poetry in seven years: *The Fate of Adelaide* (1821), *The Improvisatrice* (1824), *The Troubadour* (1825), *The Golden Violet* (1827), and *The Venetian Bracelet, the Lost Pleiad, A History of the Lyre, and Other Poems* (1828). Landon embraces the Romantic aesthetic of spontaneity, yet tends to elaborate typically Victorian topics (indulging at times in excesses of Victorian sentimentality). As well as poetry, she published four novels between 1831 and 1838. She married George Maclean, the colonial governor of Cape Coast Castle in Ghana, and accompanied him back to the Gold Coast despite rumours that Maclean was a bigamist. Four months later, L.E.L. was found dead in her room with a bottle of prussic acid in her hand.

℮℈℮

On the Ancient and Modern Influence of Poetry [1]

It is curious to observe how little one period resembles another. Centuries are the children of one mighty family, but there is no family-likeness between them. We ourselves are standing on the threshold of a new era, and we are already hastening to make as wide a space, mark as vast a difference as possible, between our own age and its predecessor. Whatever follies we may go back upon, whatever opinions we may re-adopt, they are never those which have gone *immediately* before us. Already there is a wide gulph between the last century and the present. In religion, in philosophy, in politics, in manners, there has passed a great change; but in none has been worked a greater change than in poetry, whether as it regards the art itself, or the general feeling towards it. The decline and fall of that Roman empire of the mind seems now advanced as an historical fact; while we are equally ready to admit that some twenty years since the republic was in its plenitude of power. In the meantime a new set of aspirants have arisen, and a new set of opinions are to be won. But it is from the past that we best judge of the present; and perhaps we shall more accurately say what poetry is by referring to what it has been.

Poetry in every country has had its origin in three sources, connected with the strongest feelings belonging to the human mind—Religion, War, and Love. The mysteries of the present; the still greater mysteries of the future; the confession of some superior power so deeply felt; higher impulses speaking so strongly of some spiritual influence of a purer order than those of our common wants and wishes;—these all found words and existence in poetry. The vainest fictions of mythology were the strongest possible evidence how necessary to the ignorance of humanity was the belief of a superior power; so entire was the interior conviction, that sooner than believe in nothing no belief was too absurd for adoption. The imagination, which is the source of poetry, has in every country been the beginning as well as the ornament of civilization. It civilizes because it refines. A general view of its influence in the various quarters of the globe will place this in the most striking point of view.

Africa is the least civilized quarter of the globe, not so much from its savage as from its apathetic

---

[1] from *New Monthly Magazine* Vol. 35, November 1832.

state; one could almost believe that it had been formed from the dregs of the other parts. Now, the distinguishing mark of its deficiency in that soil of mind wherewith the intellect works, is its total want of imagination. It is the only great portion of the world which is not emphatically made known to us by its own peculiar religion. Her mythology was the earthly immortality of Greece. Greece is indelibly linked with the idea of civilization; but all those fine and graceful beliefs which made its springs holy places, and haunted the fragrant life of every flower and leaf, were the creations of its earliest time. Look from thence to the fierce regions of the North,—how full is the Scandinavian faith of the wild and wonderful! or to the East, how gorgeous their tales of enchantment, with their delicate Peris, and the fallen and fearful spirits in their subterranean caverns! —again, the faith of Brahma, with its thousand deities. Or, to cross the wide Atlantic, there are the vestiges of a terrible creed yet touched with something of spiritual loveliness, in their singing-birds bringing tidings of the departed, and in the green hunting-grounds which made their future hope. Each and all these creeds are the work and wonder of the imagination—but in these Africa has no part. No august belief fills with beauty or terror the depths of her forests, and no fallen temple makes its site sacred though in ruins. Her creeds have neither beauty nor grandeur. The Devil is their principal Deity, and their devotion is born of physical fear. Other nations have had their various faiths, created and coloured by the scenes which gave them birth. The religion of Greece was beautiful as her own myrtle and olive groves. The Scandinavian was like its own wild mountains and snowy wastes, with just gleams of beauty from its starry nights and meteors. The Arabian was glowing and magnificent as the summer earth and radiant sky of its believers; while that of the American Indian was terrible as the huge serpents and the interminable forests which gave shelter to its mysteries. But in Africa the sunny sky, the noble

rivers, the woods, splendid in size and foliage, have been without their wonted effect. Slaves from the earliest period, the very superstitions of her sable sons are mean fears caught from their masters; all about them is earthly, utterly unredeemed by those spiritual awakenings which are as lights from another world. We might believe that some great original curse has been said over them, and that they are given over into the hand of man and not of God. And in simple truth that curse has been slavery. The Helots[1] even of Greece were uninspired. "A slave cannot be eloquent," said Longinus;[2] nor poetical either—the wells of his enthusiasm are dried up. What some ancient writer says of iron may be applied to Poetry—its use is the first step to civilization, and civilization is freedom.

Next to Religion War was the great source of poetry; and the deeds of the brave were sung in that spirit of encouragement which one man will ever receive from the praise bestowed on the deeds of another, when he meditates similar achievements of his own. And here we may be permitted a few words on what we cannot but consider an unjust and erroneous opinion, now much insisted upon,—that poets and conquerors have been equal enemies of the human race—the one but acting what the other praised; and that the sin of encouragement was equal, if not greater, than that of commission. In answer to this we must observe that it is not fair to judge of former actions by our present standard. Our first view of society is always the same: we see the human race dwelling in small dispersed sets, with rude habits, the results of hardships and of dangers. A more favourable situation, or, more commonly, the influence of some superior mind, which from the wonderful effects produced by a single man is often a nation's history: these or similar causes first placed some of the tribes in positions of comparative com-

---

[1] a member of the lowest class of serfs in ancient Sparta.

[2] Greek philosopher and rhetorician (213?–73 AD).

fort and advancement. This position would of course be envied by their savage and starving neighbours, who would consider brute force the only means of sharing their advantages. Single motives never last: ambition, aggrandisement, conquest with a view to security, soon gave a thousand motives to warfare that had originally began in want and self-defence. It has required centuries so to consolidate kingdoms that now a breathing space is allowed for reflection on the sin of sacrificing man's most valuable possession—life. But what part has the poet taken in these scenes of bloodshed? One certainly of amelioration. If he has sung of conquerors, the qualities held up to admiration were those of magnanimity and generosity. He has spoken of the love and liberty as holding light the love of life; and the highest eulogium of a warrior was that he died in defence of his native country. But to give our assertion the support of an example.—Perhaps the spirit which animates, the desire which excites, the power which supports, a conqueror, were never more entirely personified than in Xerxes.[1] He possessed to the utmost that grasping ambition, that carelessness of human blood, which characterize the mere conqueror; yet with all the purple pomp of his power, we are not aware of his having been held up otherwise than in reprobation, while the whole world has been filled with the fame of his brave opposers; and the names of those who fell at Marathon are still the watchwords of freedom. Again, in the days of chivalry, what were the qualities the minstrel lauded in the knight?—his valour, certainly, but still more his courtesy, his protection of the weak against the strong, his devotion, his truth;—till the "ungentle knight" was almost as much a phrase of disgrace as that of the "recreant."

Love was the third great fountain of poetry's inspiration; and who that has ever loved will deny the necessity of a language, beyond the working-day tongue of our ordinary run of hopes and fears, to express feelings which have so little in common with them. What has been the most popular love-poetry in all countries?—that which gave expression to its spiritual and better part—constancy kept like a holy thing—blessings on the beloved one, though in that blessing we have ourselves no share; or sad and affectionate regrets in whose communion our own nature grows more kindly from its sympathy. We are always the better for entering into other's sorrow or other's joy.

The whole origin and use of poetry may be expressed in a few brief words: it originates in that idea of superior beauty and excellence inherent in every nature—and it is employed to keep that idea alive; and the very belief in excellence is one cause of its existence. When we speak of poetry as the fountain whence youth draws enthusiasm for its hopes,— where the warrior strengthens his courage, and the lover his faith,—the treasury where the noblest thoughts are garnered,—the archives where the noblest deeds are recorded,—we but express an old belief. One of our great reviews—the "Westminster"—in speaking of the fine arts, &c. says, "The aristocracy do well to encourage poetry: it is by fiction themselves exist—and what is poetry but fiction?" We deny that poetry is fiction; its merit and its power lie alike in its truth: to one heart the aspiring and elevated will come home; to another the simple and natural: the key-note to one will be the voice of memory, which brings back young affections—early confidence,—hill and valley yet glad with the buoyant step which once past over them,—flowers thrice lovely from thoughts indelibly associated with their leaf or breath: such as these are touched by all that restores, while it recalls, days whose enjoyment would have been happiness, could they but have had the knowledge of experience without its weariness. To another, poetry will be a vision and a delight, because the virtue of which he dreams is there realized—and because the "love which his spirit has painted" is to be found in its

---

[1] king of Persia (486–65 BC).

pages. But in each and all cases the deep well of sympathy is only to be found when the hazel rod is poised by the hand of truth. And, till some moral steam is discovered as potent as that now so active in the physical world, vain will be the effort to regulate mankind like machinery: there will ever be spiritual awakenings, and deep and tender thoughts, to turn away from the hurry and highways of life, and whose place of refuge will still be the green paths and pleasant waters of poesy. That tribes of worse than idle followers have crowded the temple, and cast the dust they brought around the soiled altar,—that many have profaned their high gift to base use—that poetry has often turned aside from its divine origin and diviner end,—is what must be equally admitted and lamented; but who will deny that our best and most popular (indeed in this case best and popular are equivalent terms) poetry makes its appeal to the higher and better feelings of our nature, and not a poet but owes his fame to that which best deserves it? What a code of pure and beautiful morality, applicable to almost every circumstance, might be drawn from Shakspeare!

The influence of poetry has two eras,—first as it tends to civilize; secondly as it tends to prevent that very civilization from growing too cold and too selfish. Its first is its period of action; its second is that of feeling and reflection: it is that second period which at present exists. On the mere principle of utility, in our wide and weary world, with its many sorrows and more cares, how anxiously we ought to keep open every source of happiness! and who among us does not recollect some hour when a favourite poet spread before us a page like that of a magician's; when some expression has seemed like the very echo of our feelings; how often and with what a sensation of pleasure have long-remembered passages sprang to our lips; how every natural beauty has caught a fresh charm from being linked with some associate verse! Who that has these or similar recollections but would

keep the ear open, and the heart alive, to the "song that lightens the languid way!"

Why one age should be more productive in poetry than another is one of those questions—a calculation of the mental longitude—likely to remain unanswered. That peculiar circumstances do not create the poet is proved by the fact, that only one individual is so affected: if it were mere circumstance, it would affect alike all who are brought within its contact. What confirmation of this theory (if theory it be) is to be found in the history of all poets!—where are we to seek the cause which made them such, if not in their own minds? We daily see men living amid beautiful scenery; and scenery is much dwelt upon by the advocates of circumstance. Switzerland is a most beautiful country, yet what great poet has it ever produced? The spirit which in ancient days peopled grove and mountain with Dryad and Oread,[1] or, in modern times, with associations, must be in him who sees, not in the object seen. How many there are, leading a life of literary leisure, living in a romantic country, and writing poetry all their days, who yet go down to their unremembered graves no more poets than if they had never turned a stanza! While, on the other hand, we see men with every obstacle before them, with little leisure and less encouragement, yet force their upward way, make their voice heard, and leave their memory in imperishable song. Take Burns for an example: much stress has been laid on the legendary ballads he was accustomed to hear from infancy; but if these were so potent, why did they not inspire his brother as well as himself? Mr. Gilbert Burns is recorded, by every biographer, to have been a sensible, and even a superior man; he dwelt in the same country—he heard the same songs—why was he not a poet too? There can be but one answer, —there was not that inherent quality in his mind which there was in his brother's. Many young men are born to a higher name than fortune—many spend

---

[1] in Greek mythology, wood nymph and mountain nymph.

their youth amid the most exciting scenes—yet why do none of these turn out a Byron, but for some innate first cause? What made Milton in old age,—in sickness, in poverty—depressed by all that would have weighed to the very dust an ordinary man—without one of man's ordinary encouragements,—what could have made him turn to the future as to a home, collect his glorious energies, and finish a work, the noblest aid ever given to the immortality of a language? What, but that indefinable spirit, whose enthusiasm is nature's own gift to the poet. *Poeta nascitur non fit*[1] is, like many other old truths, the very truth after all.

We cannot but consider that, though some be still among us, our own great poets belong to another age. Their fame is established, and their horde of imitators have dispersed; those wearying followers who, to use the happy expression of a contemporary writer, "think that breaking the string is bending the bow of Ulysses." We hear the daily complaints of the want of present taste and talent for poetry: we are more prepared to admit the latter than the former. In the most sterile times of the imagination, love of poetry has never been lacking; the taste may have been bad, but still the taste existed. Wordsworth truly says, "that, with the young, poetry is a passion;" and there will always be youth in the world to indulge the hopes, and feel the warm and fresh emotions, which their fathers have found to be vain, or have utterly exhausted. To these, poetry will ever be a natural language; and it is the young who make the reputation of a poet. We soon lose that keen delight, which marvels if others share not in it: the faculty of appreciation is the first which leaves us. It is tact rather than feeling which enables experience to foresee the popularity of a new poet. As to the alleged want of taste, we only refer to the editions of established authors which still find purchasers: one has just appeared of Scott, another of Byron. With what

enthusiasm do some set up Wordsworth for an idol, and others Shelley! But this taste is quite another feeling to that which creates; and the little now written possesses beauty not originality. The writers do not set their own mark on their property: one might have put forth the work of the other, or it might be that of their predecessors. This was not the case some few years ago. Who could have mistaken the picturesque and chivalric page of Scott for the impassioned one of Byron? or who could for a moment have hesitated as to whether a poem was marked with the actual and benevolent philosophy of Wordsworth, or the beautiful but ideal theory of Shelley? We are now producing no great or original (the words are synonymous) poet. We have graceful singing in the bower, but no voice that startles us into wonder, and hurries us forth to see whose trumpet is awakening the land. We know that when the snow has long lain, warming and fertilizing the ground, and when the late summer comes, hot and clear, the rich harvest will be abundant under such genial influences. Perhaps poetry too may have its atmosphere; and a long cold winter may be needed for its glad and glorious summer. The soil of song, like that of earth, may need rest for renewal. Again we repeat, that though the taste be not, the spirit of the day is, adverse to the production of poetry. Selfishness is its principle, indifference its affectation, and ridicule its commonplace. We allow no appeals save to our reason, or to our fear of laughter. We must either be convinced or sneered into things. Neither calculation nor sarcasm are the elements for poetry. A remark made by Scott to one of his great compeers shows how he knew the age in which he was fated to end his glorious career:—"Ah—it is well that we have made our reputation!" The personal is the destroyer of the spiritual; and to the former everything is now referred. We talk of the author's self more than his works, and we know his name rather than his writings. There is a base macadamizing spirit in literature; we seek to level all the

---

[1] a poet is born, not made.

high places of old. But till we can deny that fine "farther looking hope" which gives such a charm to Shakspeare's confessional sonnets; till we can deny that "The Paradise Lost" was the work of old age, poverty, and neglect, roused into delightful exertion by a bright futurity; till we can deny the existence of those redeemers of humanity—we must admit, also, the existence of a higher, more prophetic, more devoted and self-relying spirit than is to be accounted for on the principles either of vanity or of lucre: we shall be compelled to admit that its inspiration is, indeed,

> "A heavenly breath
> Along an earthly lyre." [1]

Methinks there are some mysteries in the soul on whose precincts it were well to "tread with unsandalled foot." [2] Poetry like religion requires faith, and we are the better and happier for yielding it. The imagination is to the mind what life is to the body—its vivifying and active part. In antiquity, poetry had to create, it now has to preserve. Its first effort was against barbarism, its last is against selfishness. A world of generous emotions, of kindly awakenings, those

> "Which bid the perished pleasures move
> In mournful mockery o'er the soul of love;" [3]

a world of thought and feeling, now lies in the guardianship of the poet. These are they who sit in the gate called the beautiful, which leads to the temple. Its meanest priests should feel that their office is sacred. Enthusiasm is no passion of the drawing-room, or of the pence-table: its home is the heart, and its hope is afar. This is too little the creed of our generation; yet, without such creed, poetry has neither present life nor future immortality. As Whitehead [4] finely says in his poem of "The Solitary,"—

> "Not for herself, not for the wealth she brings,
> Is the muse wooed and won, but for the deep,
>   Occult, profound, unfathomable things,—
> The engine of our tears whene'er we weep,
> The impulse of our dreams whene'er we sleep,
>   The mysteries that our sad hearts possess,
> Which, and the keys whereof, the Muse doth keep,—
>   Oh! to kindle soft humanity, to raise,
> With gentle strength infused, the spirit bowed;
>   To pour a second sunlight on our days,
> And draw the restless lightning from our cloud;
> To cheer the humble and to dash the proud.
>   Besought in peace to live, in peace to die,—
>   The poet's task is done—Oh, Immortality!"

He is only a true poet, who can say, in the words of Coleridge, "My task has been my delight; I have not looked either to guerdon or praise, and to me Poetry is its own exceeding great reward." [5]
—1832

---

[1] not identified.

[2] not identified.

[3] not identified.

---

[4] William Whitehead (1715–85), a minor eighteenth-century poet.

[5] source in Coleridge not identified.

John Stuart Mill
1806 – 1873

John Stuart Mill was born in London and was educated at home by his father, James Mill. He began studying Greek at the age of three, and before entering his teens he was intensely involved with the study of calculus, political economy, and logic. In 1820–21 he lived in France, attending university lectures at Montpellier. When he returned to London, he joined his father in the Examiner's Office of the East India Company which, like his father, he eventually headed. Mill was one of the leading British philosophers of the nineteenth century. His works include the two-volume *System of Logic* (1843), *Principles of Political Economy* (1848), *On Liberty* (1859), *Utilitarianism* (1863), and *The Subjection of Women* (1869). Raised by his father to believe in the Benthamite principles of Utilitarianism, Mill later realized that such a rationalistic upbringing sorely neglected emotional development (see his *Autobiography* [1873]). In "What is Poetry?" (1833), Mill argues for the importance of poetry, which appeals to the senses, in contrast to science, which addresses belief.

ତ୍ତ୍ର

"What is Poetry?" [1]

It has often been asked, what is poetry? And many and various are the answers which have been returned. The vulgarest of all—one with which no person possessed of the faculties to which poetry addresses itself can ever have been satisfied—is that which confounds poetry with metrical composition: yet to this wretched mockery of a definition, many have been led back, by the failure of all their attempts to find any other that would distinguish what they have been accustomed to call poetry, from much which they have known only under other names.

That, however, the word *poetry* does import something quite peculiar in its nature, something which may exist in what is called prose as well as in verse, something which does not even require the instrument of words, but can speak, through those other audible symbols called musical sounds, and even through the visible ones, which are the language of sculpture, painting, and architecture; all this, as we believe, is and must be felt, though perhaps indistinctly, by all upon whom poetry in any of its shapes produces any impression beyond that of tickling the ear. To the mind, poetry is either nothing, or it is the better part of all art whatever, and of real life too; and the distinction between poetry and what is not poetry, whether explained or not, is felt to be fundamental.

Where everyone feels a difference, a difference there must be. All other appearance may be fallacious, but the appearance of a difference is itself a real difference. Appearances too, like other things, must have a cause, and that which can cause anything, even an illusion, must be a reality. And hence, while a half-philosophy disdains the classifications and distinctions indicated by popular language, philosophy carried to its highest point may frame new ones, but never sets aside the old, content with correcting and regularizing them. It cuts fresh channels for thought, but it does not fill up such as it finds ready-made, but traces, on the contrary, more deeply, broadly, and distinctly, those into which the current has spontaneously flowed.

Let us then attempt, in the way of modest inquiry, not to coerce and confine nature within the bounds of an arbitrary definition, but rather to find the boundaries which she herself has set, and erect a barrier round them; not calling mankind to account for having misapplied the word *poetry*, but attempt-

---

[1] first published in January 1833, in the *Monthly Repository*, signed "Antiquus."

ing to clear up to them the conception which they already attach to it, and to bring before their minds as a distinct principle that which, as a vague feeling, has really guided them in their actual employment of the term.

The object of poetry is confessedly to act upon the emotions; and therein is poetry sufficiently distinguished from what Wordsworth affirms to be its logical opposite, namely, not prose, but matter of fact or science.[1] The one addresses itself to the belief, the other to the feelings. The one does its work by convincing or persuading, the other by moving. The one acts by presenting a proposition to the understanding, the other by offering interesting objects of contemplation to the sensibilities.

This, however, leaves us very far from a definition of poetry. We have distinguished it from one thing, but we are bound to distinguish it from everything. To present thoughts or images to the mind for the purpose of acting upon the emotions, does not belong to poetry alone. It is equally the province (for example) of the novelist: and yet the faculty of the poet and the faculty of the novelist are as distinct as any other two faculties; as the faculty of the novelist and of the orator, or of the poet and the metaphysician. The two characters may be united, as characters the most disparate may; but they have no natural connection.

Many of the finest poems are in the form of novels, and in almost all good novels there is true poetry. But there is a radical distinction between the interest felt in a novel as such, and the interest excited by poetry; for the one is derived from incident, the other from the representation of feeling. In one, the source of the emotion excited is the exhibition of a state or states of human sensibility; in the other, of a series of states of mere outward circumstances. Now, all minds are capable of being affected more or less by representations of the latter kind, and all, or almost

all, by those of the former; yet the two sources of interest correspond to two distinct and (as respects their greatest development) mutually exclusive characters of mind. So much is the nature of poetry dissimilar to the nature of fictitious narrative, that to have a really strong passion for either of the two, seems to presuppose or to superinduce a comparative indifference to the other.

At what age is the passion for a story, for almost any kind of story, merely as a story, the most intense? In childhood. But that also is the age at which poetry, even of the simplest description, is least relished and least understood; because the feelings with which it is especially conversant are yet undeveloped, and not having been even in the slightest degree experienced, cannot be sympathized with. In what stage of the progress of society, again, is storytelling most valued, and the storyteller in greatest request and honor? In a rude state; like that of the Tartars and Arabs at this day, and of almost all nations in the earliest ages. But in this state of society there is little poetry except ballads, which are mostly narrative, that is, essentially stories, and derive their principal interest from the incidents. Considered as poetry, they are of the lowest and most elementary kind: the feelings depicted, or rather indicated, are the simplest our nature has; such joys and griefs as the immediate pressure of some outward event excites in rude minds, which live wholly immersed in outward things, and have never, either from choice or a force they could not resist, turned themselves to the contemplation of the world within. Passing now from childhood, and from the childhood of society, to the grown-up men and women of this most grown-up and unchildlike age—the minds and hearts of greatest depth and elevation are commonly those which take greatest delight in poetry; the shallowest and emptiest, on the contrary, are, by universal remark, the most addicted to novel reading. This accords, too, with all analogous experience of human nature. The sort of persons whom not merely in

---

[1]   in his "Preface" to the *Lyrical Ballads*.

books but in their lives, we find perpetually engaged in hunting for excitement from without, are invariably those who do not possess, either in the vigor of their intellectual powers or in the depth of their sensibilities, that which would enable them to find ample excitement nearer at home. The same persons whose time is divided between sightseeing, gossip, and fashionable dissipation, take a natural delight in fictitious narrative; the excitement it affords is of the kind which comes from without. Such persons are rarely lovers of poetry, though they may fancy themselves so, because they relish novels in verse. But poetry, which is the delineation of the deeper and more secret workings of the human heart, is interesting only to those to whom it recalls what they have felt, or whose imagination it stirs up to conceive what they could feel, or what they might have been able to feel, had their outward circumstances been different.

Poetry, when it is really such, is truth; and fiction also, if it is good for anything, is truth: but they are different truths. The truth of poetry is to paint the human soul truly: the truth of fiction is to give a true picture of life. The two kinds of knowledge are different, and come by different ways, come mostly to different persons. Great poets are often proverbially ignorant of life. What they know has come by observation of themselves; they have found there one highly delicate, and sensitive, and refined specimen of human nature, on which the laws of human emotion are written in large characters, such as can be read off without much study: and other knowledge of mankind, such as comes to men of the world by outward experience, is not indispensable to them as poets: but to the novelist such knowledge is all in all; he has to describe outward things, not the inward man; actions and events, not feelings; and it will not do for him to be numbered among those who, as Madame Roland said of Brissot,[1] know man but not men.

All this is no bar to the possibility of combining both elements, poetry and narrative or incident, in the same work, and calling it either a novel or a poem; but so may red and white combine on the same human features, or on the same canvas; and so may oil and vinegar, though opposite natures, blend together in the same composite taste. There is one order of composition which requires the union of poetry and incident, each in its highest kind—the dramatic. Even there the two elements are perfectly distinguishable, and may exist of unequal quality, and in the most various proportion. The incidents of a dramatic poem may be scant and ineffective, though the delineation of passion and character may be of the highest order; as in Goethe's glorious *Torquato Tasso*; or again, the story as a mere story may be well got up for effect, as is the case with some of the most trashy productions of the Minerva press:[2] it may even be, what those are not, a coherent and probable series of events, though there be scarcely a feeling exhibited which is not exhibited falsely, or in a manner absolutely commonplace. The combination of the two excellencies is what renders Shakespeare so generally acceptable, each sort of readers finding in him what is suitable to their faculties. To the many he is great as a storyteller, to the few as a poet.

In limiting poetry to the delineation of states of feeling, and denying the name where nothing is delineated but outward objects, we may be thought to have done what we promised to avoid—to have not found, but made a definition, in opposition to the usage of the English language, since it is established by common consent that there is a poetry called descriptive. We deny the charge. Description is not poetry because there is descriptive poetry, no more than science is poetry because there is such a thing as a didactic poem; no more, we might almost say, than Greek or Latin is poetry because there are Greek and Latin poems. But an object which admits

---

[1] Marie Jeanne Phlipon Roland de la Platière, in *Appel à l'impartiale postérité*, 1795.

[2] publishing house, from 1790 to 1820, of William Lane, a busy caterer to popular taste.

of being described, or a truth which may fill a place in a scientific treatise, may also furnish an occasion for the generation of poetry, which we thereupon choose to call descriptive or didactic. The poetry is not in the object itself, nor in the scientific truth itself, but in the state of mind in which the one and the other may be contemplated. The mere delineation of the dimensions and colors of external objects is not poetry, no more than a geometrical ground plan of St. Peter's or Westminster Abbey is painting. Descriptive poetry consists, no doubt, in description, but in description of things as they appear, not as they are; and it paints them not in their bare and natural lineaments, but arranged in the colors and seen through the medium of the imagination set in action by the feelings. If a poet is to describe a lion, he will not set about describing him as a naturalist would, nor even as a traveler would, who was intent upon stating the truth, the whole truth, and nothing but the truth. He will describe him by imagery, that is, by suggesting the most striking likenesses and contrasts which might occur to a mind contemplating the lion, in the state of awe, wonder, or terror, which the spectacle naturally excites, or is, on the occasion, supposed to excite. Now this is describing the lion professedly, but the state of excitement of the spectator really. The lion may be described falsely or in exaggerated colors, and the poetry be all the better; but if the human emotion be not painted with the most scrupulous truth, the poetry is bad poetry, i.e., is not poetry at all, but a failure.

Thus far our progress towards a clear view of the essentials of poetry has brought us very close to the last two attempts at a definition of poetry which we happen to have seen in print, both of them by poets and men of genius. The one is by Ebenezer Elliott,[1] the author of *Corn-Law Rhymes*, and other poems of still greater merit. "Poetry," says he, "is impassioned truth." The other is by a writer in *Blackwood's Maga-*

zine, and comes, we think, still nearer the mark. We forget his exact words, but in substance he defined poetry as "man's thoughts tinged by his feelings." There is in either definition a near approximation to what we are in search of. Every truth which man can announce, every thought, even every outward impression, which can enter into his consciousness, may become poetry when shown through any impassioned medium, when invested with the coloring of joy, or grief, or pity, or affection, or admiration, or reverence, or awe, or even hatred or terror: and, unless so colored, nothing, be it as interesting as it may, is poetry. But both these definitions fail to discriminate between poetry and eloquence. Eloquence, as well as poetry, is impassioned truth; eloquence, as well as poetry, is thoughts colored by the feelings. Yet common apprehension and philosophic criticism alike recognize a distinction between the two: there is much that everyone would call eloquence, which no one would think of classing as poetry. A question will sometimes arise, whether some particular author is a poet; and those who maintain the negative commonly allow, that though not a poet, he is a highly eloquent writer.

The distinction between poetry and eloquence appears to us to be equally fundamental with the distinction between poetry and narrative, or between poetry and description. It is still farther from having been satisfactorily cleared up than either of the others, unless, which is highly probable, the German artists and critics have thrown some light upon it which has not yet reached us. Without a perfect knowledge of what they have written, it is something like presumption to write upon such subjects at all, and we shall be the foremost to urge that, whatever we may be about to submit, may be received, subject to correction from them.

Poetry and eloquence are both alike the expression or uttering forth of feeling. But if we may be excused the seeming affectation of the antithesis, we should say that eloquence is *heard*, poetry is *over-*

---

[1] (1781–1849), working-class poet.

heard. Eloquence supposes an audience; the peculiarity of poetry appears to us to lie in the poet's utter unconsciousness of a listener. Poetry is feeling confessing itself to itself, in moments of solitude, and bodying itself forth in symbols which are the nearest possible representations of the feeling in the exact shape in which it exists in the poet's mind. Eloquence is feeling pouring itself forth to other minds, courting their sympathy, or endeavoring to influence their belief, or move them to passion or to action.

All poetry is of the nature of soliloquy. It may be said that poetry, which is printed on hot-pressed paper, and sold at a bookseller's shop, is a soliloquy in full dress, and upon the stage. But there is nothing absurd in the idea of such a mode of soliloquizing. What we have said to ourselves, we may tell to others afterwards; what we have said or done in solitude, we may voluntarily reproduce when we know that other eyes are upon us. But no trace of consciousness that any eyes are upon us must be visible in the work itself. The actor knows that there is an audience present; but if he act as though he knew it, he acts ill. A poet may write poetry with the intention of publishing it; he may write it even for the express purpose of being paid for it; that it should be poetry, being written under any such influences, is far less probable; not, however, impossible; but not otherwise possible than if he can succeed in excluding from his work every vestige of such lookings-forth into the outward and everyday world, and can express his feelings exactly as he has felt them in solitude, or as he feels that he should feel them, though they were to remain forever unuttered. But when he turns round and addresses himself to another person; when the act of utterance is not itself the end, but a means to an end—viz., by the feelings he himself expresses to work upon the feelings, or upon the belief, or the will of another—when the expression of his emotions, or of his thoughts, tinged by his emotions, is tinged also by that purpose, by that desire of making

an impression upon another mind, then it ceases to be poetry, and becomes eloquence.

Poetry, accordingly, is the natural fruit of solitude and meditation; eloquence, of intercourse with the world. The persons who have most feeling of their own, if intellectual culture have given them a language in which to express it, have the highest faculty of poetry; those who best understand the feelings of others, are the most eloquent. The persons, and the nations, who commonly excel in poetry, are those whose character and tastes render them least dependent for their happiness upon the applause, or sympathy, or concurrence of the world in general. Those to whom that applause, that sympathy, that concurrence are most necessary, generally excel most in eloquence. And hence, perhaps, the French, who are the least poetical of all great and refined nations, are among the most eloquent: the French, also, being the most sociable, the vainest, and the least self-dependent.

If the above be, as we believe, the true theory of the distinction commonly admitted between eloquence and poetry; or though it be not that, yet if, as we cannot doubt, the distinction above stated be a real bona fide distinction, it will be found to hold, not merely in the language of words, but in all other language, and to intersect the whole domain of art.

Take, for example, music: we shall find in that art, so peculiarly the expression of passion, two perfectly distinct styles; one of which may be called the poetry, the other the oratory of music. This difference being seized would put an end to much musical sectarianism. There has been much contention whether the character of Rossini's music—the music, we mean, which is characteristic of that composer—is compatible with the expression of passion. Without doubt, the passion it expresses is not the musing, meditative tenderness, or pathos, or grief of Mozart, the great poet of his art. Yet it is passion, but garrulous passion—the passion which pours itself into other ears; and therein the better calculated for dramatic effect, having a natural adaptation for dialogue. Mozart also is great in musical oratory; but his most touching compositions are in the opposite style—that of soliloquy. Who can imagine *"Dove sono"*[1] *heard?* We imagine it *over-heard.* The same is the case with many of the finest national airs. Who can hear those words, which speak so touchingly the sorrows of a mountaineer in exile:

My heart's in the Highlands—my heart is not
   here;
My heart's in the Highlands, a-chasing the deer,
A-chasing the wild-deer, and following the roe—
My heart's in the Highlands, wherever I go.

Who can hear those affecting words, married to as affecting an air, and fancy that he sees the singer? That song has always seemed to us like the lament of a prisoner in a solitary cell, ourselves listening, unseen, in the next. As the direct opposite of this, take "Scots wha hae wi' Wallace bled,"[2] where the music is as oratorical as the poetry.

Purely pathetic music commonly partakes of soliloquy. The soul is absorbed in its distress, and though there may be bystanders, it is not thinking of them. When the mind is looking within and not without, its state does not often or rapidly vary; and hence the even, uninterrupted flow, approaching almost to monotony, which a good reader, or a good singer, will give to words or music of a pensive or melancholy cast. But grief, taking the form of a prayer, or of a complaint becomes oratorical; no longer low, and even, and subdued, it assumes a more emphatic rhythm, a more rapidly returning accent; instead of a few slow, equal notes, following one after another at regular intervals, it crowds note upon note, and ofttimes assumes a hurry and bustle like joy. Those who are familiar with some of the best of Rossini's serious compositions, such as the air *"Tu che i miseri conforti,"* in the opera of *Tancredi,* or the

duet *"Ebben per mia memoria,"* in *La Gazza Ladra,* will at once understand and feel our meaning. Both are highly tragic and passionate; the passion of both is that of oratory, not poetry. The like may be said of that most moving prayer in Beethoven's *Fidelio* "*Komm, Hoffnung, lass das letzte Stern/Der Müde nicht erbleichen*";[3] in which Madam Devrient, last summer, exhibited such consummate powers of pathetic expression. How different from Winter's beautiful *"Paga pii,"* the very soul of melancholy exhaling itself in solitude; fuller of meaning, and, therefore, more profoundly poetical than the words for which it was composed—for it seems to express not simply melancholy, but the melancholy of remorse.

If, from vocal music, we now pass to instrumental, we may have a specimen of musical oratory in any fine military symphony or march: while the poetry of music seems to have attained its consummation in Beethoven's Overture to *Egmont.* We question whether so deep an expression of mixed grandeur and melancholy was ever in any other instance produced by mere sounds.

In the arts which speak to the eye, the same distinctions will be found to hold, not only between poetry and oratory, but between poetry, oratory, narrative, and simple imitation or description.

Pure description is exemplified in a mere portrait or a mere landscape—productions of art, it is true, but of the mechanical rather than of the fine arts, being works of simple imitation, not creation. We say, a mere portrait, or a mere landscape, because it is possible for a portrait or a landscape, without ceasing to be such, to be also a picture. A portrait by Lawrence, or one of Turner's views, is not a mere copy from nature: the one combines with the given features that particular expression (among all good and pleasing ones) which those features are most capable of wearing, and which, therefore, in combination with them, is capable of producing the great-

---

[1] Wolfgang Amadeus Mozart, *Le Nozze di Figaro.*

[2] two songs by Robert Burns.

[3] "Come, Hope, do not let the last star of the tired ones fade away."

est positive beauty. Turner, again, unites the objects of the given landscape with whatever sky, and whatever light and shade, enable those particular objects to impress the imagination most strongly. In both, there is creative art—not working after an actual model, but realizing an idea.

Whatever in painting or sculpture expresses human feeling, or character, which is only a certain state of feeling grown habitual, may be called, according to circumstances, the poetry or the eloquence of the painter's or the sculptor's art; the poetry, if the feeling declares itself by such signs as escape from us when we are unconscious of being seen; the oratory, if the signs are those we use for the purpose of voluntary communication.

The poetry of painting seems to be carried to its highest perfection in the *Peasant Girl* of Rembrandt, or in any Madonna or Magdalen of Guido;[1] that of sculpture, in almost any of the Greek statues of the gods; not considering these in respect to the mere physical beauty, of which they are such perfect models, not undertaking either to vindicate or to contest the opinion of philosophers, that even physical beauty is ultimately resolvable into expression; we may safely affirm, that in no other of man's works did so much of soul ever shine through mere inanimate matter.

The narrative style answers to what is called historical painting, which it is the fashion among connoisseurs to treat as the climax of the pictorial art. That it is the most difficult branch of the art, we do not doubt, because, in its perfection, it includes the perfection of all the other branches: as in like manner an epic poem, though, insofar as it is epic (i.e., narrative), it is not poetry at all, is yet esteemed the greatest effort of poetic genius, because there is no kind whatever of poetry which may not appropriately find a place in it. But a historical picture, as such, that is, as the representation of an incident, must

necessarily, as it seems to us, be poor and ineffective. The narrative powers of painting are extremely limited. Scarcely any picture, scarcely any series even of pictures, which we know of, tells its own story without the aid of an interpreter; you must know the story beforehand; then, indeed, you may see great beauty and appropriateness in the painting. But it is the single figures which, to us, are the great charm even of a historical picture. It is in these that the power of the art is really seen: in the attempt to narrate, visible and permanent signs are far behind the fugitive audible ones which follow so fast one after another, while the faces and figures in a narrative picture, even though they be Titian's, stand still. Who would not prefer one *Virgin and Child* of Raphael, to all the pictures which Rubens, with his fat, frowzy Dutch Venuses, ever painted? Though Rubens, besides excelling almost everyone in his mastery over all the mechanical parts of his art, often shows real genius in grouping his figures, the peculiar problem of historical painting. But, then, who, except a mere student of drawing and coloring, ever cared to look twice at any of the figures themselves? The power of painting lies in poetry, of which Rubens had not the slightest tincture—not in narrative, where he might have excelled.

The single figures, however, in an historical picture, are rather the eloquence of painting than the poetry: they mostly (unless they are quite out of place in the picture) express the feelings of one person as modified by the presence of others. Accordingly the minds whose bent leads them rather to eloquence than to poetry, rush to historical painting. The French painters, for instance, seldom attempt, because they could make nothing of, single heads, like those glorious ones of the Italian masters, with which they might glut themselves day after day in their own Louvre. They must all be historical; and they are, almost to a man, attitudinizers. If we wished to give to any young artist the most impressive warning our imaginations could devise, against that kind of vice in

---

[1] Guido Reni (1575–1642), Italian painter of sacred objects.

the pictorial, which corresponds to rant in the histrionic art, we would advise him to walk once up and once down the gallery of the Luxembourg; even now when David, the great corrupter of taste, has been translated from this world to the next, and from the Luxembourg, consequently, into the more elevated sphere of the Louvre. Every figure in French painting or statuary seems to be showing itself off before spectators: they are in the worst style of corrupted eloquence, but in no style of poetry at all. The best are stiff and unnatural; the worst resemble figures of cataleptic patients. The French artists fancy themselves imitators of the classics, yet they seem to have no understanding and no feeling of that repose which was the peculiar and pervading character of Grecian art, until it began to decline: a repose tenfold more indicative of strength than all their stretching and straining; for strength, as Thomas Carlyle says, does not manifest itself in spasms.

There are some productions of art which it seems at first difficult to arrange in any of the classes above illustrated. The direct aim of art as such, is the production of the beautiful; and as there are other things beautiful besides states of mind, there is much of art which may seem to have nothing to do with either poetry or eloquence as we have defined them. Take for instance a composition of Claude, or Salvator Rosa.[1] There is here creation of new beauty: by the grouping of natural scenery, conformably indeed to the laws of outward nature, but not after any actual model; the result being a beauty more perfect and faultless than is perhaps to be found in any actual landscape. Yet there is a character of poetry even in these, without which they could not be so beautiful. The unity, and wholeness, and aesthetic congruity of the picture still lies in singleness of expression; but it is expression in a different sense from that in which we have hitherto employed

---

[1] Claude (le) Lorrain (1604–05[?]–82), French painter, draughtsman, and etcher, noted as an ideal landscape artist, and Salvator Rosa (1615–72), Italian landscape painter.

the term. The objects in an imaginary landscape cannot be said, like the words of a poem or the notes of a melody, to be the actual utterance of a feeling; but there must be some feeling with which they harmonize, and which they have a tendency to raise up in the spectator's mind. They must inspire a feeling of grandeur, a loveliness, a cheerfulness, a wildness, a melancholy, a terror. The painter must surround his principal objects with such imagery as would spontaneously arise in a highly imaginative mind, when contemplating those objects under the impression of the feelings which they are intended to inspire. This, if it be not poetry, is so nearly allied to it, as scarcely to require being distinguished.

In this sense we may speak of the poetry of architecture. All architecture, to be impressive, must be the expression or symbol of some interesting idea; some thought, which has power over the emotions. The reason why modern architecture is so paltry, is simply that it is not the expression of any idea; it is a mere parroting of the architectural tongue of the Greeks, or of our Teutonic ancestors, without any conception of a meaning.

To confine ourselves, for the present, to religious edifices: these partake of poetry, in proportion as they express, or harmonize with, the feelings of devotion. But those feelings are different according to the conception entertained of the beings, by whose supposed nature they are called forth. To the Greek, these beings were incarnations of the greatest conceivable physical beauty, combined with supernatural power: and the Greek temples express this, their predominant character being graceful strength; in other words, solidity, which is power, and lightness which is also power, accomplishing with small means what seemed to require great; to combine all in one word, *majesty*. To the Catholic, again, the Deity was something far less clear and definite; a being of still more resistless power than the heathen divinities; greatly to be loved; still more greatly to be feared; and wrapped up in vagueness, mystery, and incomprehensibility. A certain solemnity, a feeling of doubting and trembling hope, like that of one lost in a boundless forest who thinks he knows his way but is not sure, mixes in all the genuine expressions of Catholic devotion. This is eminently the expression of the pure Gothic cathedral; conspicuous equally in the mingled majesty and gloom of its vaulted roofs and stately aisles, and in the "dim religious light"[1] which steals through its painted windows.

There is no generic distinction between the imagery which is the expression of feeling and the imagery which is felt to harmonize with feeling. They are identical. The imagery in which feeling utters itself forth from within, is also that in which it delights when presented to it from without. All art, therefore, in proportion as it produces its effects by an appeal to the emotions partakes of poetry, unless it partakes of oratory, or of narrative. And the distinction which these three words indicate, runs through the whole field of the fine arts.

The above hints have no pretension to the character of a theory. They are merely thrown out for the consideration of thinkers, in the hope that if they do not contain the truth, they may do somewhat to suggest it. Nor would they, crude as they are, have been deemed worthy of publication, in any country but one in which the philosophy of art is so completely neglected, that whatever may serve to put any inquiring mind upon this kind of investigation, cannot well, however imperfect in itself, fail altogether to be of use.

—JANUARY 1833

---

[1] from Milton's "Il Penseroso."

Robert Browning
1812 – 1889

Robert Browning is recognized for his poetic achievement in the dramatic monologue, especially those poems in the volumes published in 1855, *Men and Women*, and 1864, *Dramatis Personae*. Browning received little formal education—six years of schooling from the ages of nine to fourteen, and part of one year at London University. His home education was the result of his immersion in his bank-clerk father's large and esoteric library, and the influence of his nonconformist mother's religion and her interest in nature and music. Browning's depth of learning and interest in poetic experimentation is evident in his early work—*Pauline* (1833), *Paracelsus* (1835), and *Sordello* (1840), as well as in the series *Bells and Pomegranates* (1841–46). This series also contained *Dramatic Lyrics* (1842), and *Dramatic Romances and Lyrics* (1845), the former of which included his famous "My Last Duchess," and the latter his first blank-verse dramatic monologue, "The Bishop Orders His Tomb at St. Praxed's Church." Browning met Elizabeth Barrett, whose contemporary reputation as a poet exceeded his, in 1845, and they married on 12 May 1846, after which they immediately took up residence in Italy. Browning returned to England in 1861 after Elizabeth's death, and worked on his complex multinarrative poem *The Ring and the Book* (1868–69). His poetic experimentation continued until his death in 1889.

❧❧❧

"Introductory Essay" ["Essay on Shelley"] [1]

An opportunity having presented itself for the acquisition of a series of unedited letters by Shelley, all more or less directly supplementary to and illustrative of the collection already published by Mr. Moxon, that gentleman has decided on securing them. They will prove an acceptable addition to a body of correspondence, the value of which towards a right understanding of its author's purpose and work, may be said to exceed that of any similar contribution exhibiting the worldly relations of a poet whose genius has operated by a different law.

Doubtless we accept gladly the biography of an objective poet, as the phrase now goes; one whose endeavour has been to reproduce things external (whether the phenomena of the scenic universe, or the manifested action of the human heart and brain) with an immediate reference, in every case, to the common eye and apprehension of his fellow men, assumed capable of receiving and profiting by this reproduction. It has been obtained through the poet's double faculty of seeing external objects more clearly, widely, and deeply, than is possible to the average mind, at the same time that he is so acquainted and in sympathy with its narrower comprehension as to be careful to supply it with no other materials than it can combine into an intelligible whole. The auditory of such a poet will include, not only the intelligences which, save for such assistance, would have missed the deeper meaning and enjoyment of the original objects, but also the spirits of a like endowment with his own, who, by means of his abstract, can forthwith pass to the reality it was made from, and either corroborate their impressions of things known already, or supply themselves with new from whatever shows in the inexhaustible variety of existence may have hitherto escaped their knowledge. Such a poet is properly the ποιητης, the fashioner; and the thing fashioned, his poetry, will of necessity be substantive, projected from himself and distinct. We

---

[1] The "Introductory Essay" to the *Letters of Percy Bysshe Shelley* was published early in 1852 by Edward Moxon, Browning's friend and the publisher of the *Bells and Pomegranates* (1841–46) series. The letters were found to be spurious before the book was distributed, and it was immediately withdrawn from circulation.

are ignorant what the inventor of *Othello* conceived of that fact as he beheld it in completeness, how he accounted for it, under what known law he registered its nature, or to what unknown law he traced its coincidence. We learn only what he intended we should learn by that particular exercise of his power,—the fact itself,—which, with its infinite significances, each of us receives for the first time as a creation, and is hereafter left to deal with, as, in proportion to his own intelligence, he best may. We are ignorant, and would fain be otherwise.

Doubtless, with respect to such a poet, we covet his biography. We desire to look back upon the process of gathering together in a lifetime, the materials of the work we behold entire; of elaborating, perhaps under difficulty and with hindrance, all that is familiar to our admiration in the apparent facility of success. And the inner impulse of this effort and operation, what induced it? Did a soul's delight in its own extended sphere of vision set it, for the gratification of an insuppressible power, on labour, as other men are set on rest? Or did a sense of duty or of love lead it to communicate its own sensations to mankind? Did an irresistible sympathy with men compel it to bring down and suit its own provision of knowledge and beauty to their narrow scope? Did the personality of such an one stand like an open watchtower in the midst of the territory it is erected to gaze on, and were the storms and calms, the stars and meteors, its watchman was wont to report of, the habitual variegation of his every-day life, as they glanced across its open roof or lay reflected on its four-square parapet? Or did some sunken and darkened chamber of imagery witness, in the artificial illumination of every storied compartment we are permitted to contemplate, how rare and precious were the outlooks through here and there an embrasure upon a world beyond, and how blankly would have pressed on the artificer the boundary of his daily life, except for the amorous diligence with which he had rendered permanent by art whatever came to

diversify the gloom? Still, fraught with instruction and interest as such details undoubtedly are, we can, if needs be, dispense with them. The man passes, the work remains. The work speaks for itself, as we say: and the biography of the worker is no more necessary to an understanding or enjoyment of it, than is a model or anatomy of some tropical tree, to the right tasting of the fruit we are familiar with on the market-stall,—or a geologist's map and stratification, to the prompt recognition of the hill-top, our landmark of every day.

We turn with stronger needs to the genius of an opposite tendency—the subjective poet of modern classification. He, gifted like the objective poet with the fuller perception of nature and man, is impelled to embody the thing he perceives, not so much with reference to the many below as to the one above him, the supreme Intelligence which apprehends all things in their absolute truth,—an ultimate view ever aspired to, if but partially attained, by the poet's own soul. Not what man sees, but what God sees—the *Ideas* of Plato, seeds of creation lying burningly on the Divine Hand—it is toward these that he struggles. Not with the combination of humanity in action, but with the primal elements of humanity he has to do; and he digs where he stands,—preferring to seek them in his own soul as the nearest reflex of that absolute Mind, according to the intuitions of which he desires to perceive and speak. Such a poet does not deal habitually with the picturesque groupings and tempestuous tossings of the forest-trees, but with their roots and fibres naked to the chalk and stone. He does not paint pictures and hang them on the walls, but rather carries them on the retina of his own eyes: we must look deep into his human eyes, to see those pictures on them. He is rather a seer, accordingly, than a fashioner, and what he produces will be less a work than an effluence. That effluence cannot be easily considered in abstraction from his personality,—being indeed the very radiance and aroma of his personality, projected from it but not separated. Therefore, in our approach to the poetry, we necessarily approach the personality of the poet; in apprehending it we apprehend him, and certainly we cannot love it without loving him. Both for love's and for understanding's sake we desire to know him, and as readers of his poetry must be readers of his biography also.

I shall observe, in passing, that it seems not so much from any essential distinction in the faculty of the two poets or in the nature of the objects contemplated by either, as in the more immediate adaptability of these objects to the distinct purpose of each, that the objective poet, in his appeal to the aggregate human mind, chooses to deal with the doings of men, (the result of which dealing, in its pure form, when even description, as suggesting a describer, is dispensed with, is what we call dramatic poetry), while the subjective poet, whose study has been himself, appealing through himself to the absolute Divine mind, prefers to dwell upon those external scenic appearances which strike out most abundantly and uninterruptedly his inner light and power, selects that silence of the earth and sea in which he can best hear the beating of his individual heart, and leaves the noisy, complex, yet imperfect exhibitions of nature in the manifold experience of man around him, which serve only to distract and suppress the working of his brain. These opposite tendencies of genius will be more readily descried in their artistic effect than in their moral spring and cause. Pushed to an extreme and manifested as a deformity, they will be seen plainest of all in the fault of either artist, when subsidiarily to the human interest of his work his occasional illustrations from scenic nature are introduced as in the earlier works of the originative painters—men and women filling the foreground with consummate mastery, while mountain, grove and rivulet show like an anticipatory revenge on that succeeding race of landscape-painters whose "figures" disturb the perfection of their earth and sky. It would be idle to inquire, of these two kinds of poetic faculty

in operation, which is the higher or even rarer endowment. If the subjective might seem to be the ultimate requirement of every age, the objective, in the strictest state, must still retain its original value. For it is with this world, as starting point and basis alike, that we shall always have to concern ourselves: the world is not to be learned and thrown aside, but reverted to and relearned. The spiritual comprehension may be infinitely subtilized, but the raw material it operates upon, must remain. There may be no end of the poets who communicate to us what they see in an object with reference to their own individuality; what it was before they saw it, in reference to the aggregate human mind, will be as desirable to know as ever. Nor is there any reason why these two modes of poetic faculty may not issue hereafter from the same poet in successive perfect works, examples of which, according to what are now considered the exigences of art, we have hitherto possessed in distinct individuals only. A mere running-in of the one faculty upon the other, is, of course, the ordinary circumstance. Far more rarely it happens that either is found so decidedly prominent and superior, as to be pronounced comparatively pure: while of the perfect shield, with the gold and the silver side set up for all comers to challenge, there has yet been no instance. Either faculty in its eminent state is doubtless conceded by Providence as a best gift to men, according to their especial want. There is a time when the general eye has, so to speak, absorbed its fill of the phenomena around it, whether spiritual or material, and desires rather to learn the exacter significance of what it possesses, than to receive any augmentation of what is possessed. Then is the opportunity for the poet of loftier vision, to lift his fellows, with their half-apprehensions, up to his own sphere, by intensifying the import of details and rounding the universal meaning. The influence of such an achievement will not soon die out. A tribe of successors (Homerides) working more or less in the same spirit, dwell on his discoveries and reinforce his doctrine; till, at unawares, the world is found to be subsisting wholly on the shadow of a reality, on sentiments diluted from passions, on the tradition of a fact, the convention of a moral, the straw of last year's harvest. Then is the imperative call for the appearance of another sort of poet, who shall at once replace this intellectual rumination of food swallowed long ago, by a supply of the fresh and living swathe; getting at new substance by breaking up the assumed wholes into parts of independent and unclassed value, careless of the unknown laws for re-combining them (it will be the business of yet another poet to suggest those hereafter), prodigal of objects for men's outer and not inner sight, shaping for their uses a new and different creation from the last, which it displaces by the right of life over death,—to endure until, in the inevitable process, its very sufficiency to itself shall require, at length, an exposition of its affinity to something higher,—when the positive yet conflicting facts shall again precipitate themselves under a harmonizing law, and one more degree will be apparent for a poet to climb in that mighty ladder, of which, however cloud-involved and undefined may glimmer the topmost step, the world dares no longer doubt that its gradations ascend.

Such being the two kinds of artists, it is naturally, as I have shown, with the biography of the subjective poet that we have the deeper concern. Apart from his recorded life altogether, we might fail to determine with satisfactory precision to what class his productions belong, and what amount of praise is assignable to the producer. Certainly, in the face of any conspicuous achievement of genius, philosophy, no less than sympathetic instinct, warrants our belief in a great moral purpose having mainly inspired even where it does not visibly look out of the same. Greatness in a work suggests an adequate instrumentality; and none of the lower incitements, however they may avail to initiate or even effect many considerable displays of power, simulating the nobler inspiration to which they are mistakenly referred, have been found able,

under the ordinary conditions of humanity, to task themselves to the end of so exacting a performance as a poet's complete work. As soon will the galvanism that provokes to violent action the muscles of a corpse, induce it to cross the chamber steadily: sooner. The love of displaying power for the display's sake, the love of riches, of distinction, of notoriety,—the desire of a triumph over rivals, and the vanity in the applause of friends,—each and all of such whetted appetites grow intenser by exercise and increasingly sagacious as to the best and readiest means of self-appeasement,—while for any of their ends, whether the money or the pointed finger of the crowd, or the flattery and hate to heart's content, there are cheaper prices to pay, they will all find soon enough, than the bestowment of a life upon a labour, hard, slow, and not sure. Also, assuming the proper moral aim to have produced a work, there are many and various states of an aim: it may be more intense than clear-sighted, or too easily satisfied with a lower field of activity than a steadier aspiration would reach. All the bad poetry in the world (accounted poetry, that is, by its affinities) will be found to result from some one of the infinite degrees of discrepancy between the attributes of the poet's soul, occasioning a want of correspondency between his work and the verities of nature,—issuing in poetry, false under whatever form, which shows a thing not as it is to mankind generally, nor as it is to the particular describer, but as it is supposed to be for some unreal neutral mood, midway between both and of value to neither, and living its brief minute simply through the indolence of whatever accepts it or his incapacity to denounce a cheat. Although of such depths of failure there can be no question here we must in every case betake ourselves to the review of a poet's life ere we determine some of the nicer questions concerning his poetry,—more especially if the performance we seek to estimate aright, has been obstructed and cut short of completion by circumstances,—a disastrous youth or a premature death. We may learn from the biography whether his spirit invariably saw and spoke from the last height to which it had attained. An absolute vision is not for this world, but we are permitted a continual approximation to it, every degree of which in the individual, provided it exceed the attainment of the masses, must procure him a clear advantage. Did the poet ever attain to a higher platform than where he rested and exhibited a result? Did he know more than he spoke of?

I concede however, in respect to the subject of our study as well as some few other illustrious examples, that the unmistakable quality of the verse would be evidence enough, under usual circumstances, not only of the kind and degree of the intellectual but of the moral constitution of Shelley: the whole personality of the poet shining forward from the poems, without much need of going further to seek it. The "Remains"—produced within a period of ten years, and at a season of life when other men of at all comparable genius have hardly done more than prepare the eye for future sight and the tongue for speech—present us with the complete enginery of a poet, as signal in the excellence of its several adaptitudes as transcendent in the combination of effects,—examples, in fact, of the whole poet's function of beholding with an understanding keenness the universe, nature and man, in their actual state of perfection in imperfection,—of the whole poet's virtue of being untempted by the manifold partial developments of beauty and good on every side, into leaving them the ultimates he found them,—induced by the facility of the gratification of his own sense of those qualities, or by the pleasure of acquiescence in the shortcomings of his predecessors in art, and the pain of disturbing their conventionalisms,—the whole poet's virtue, I repeat, of looking higher than any manifestation yet made of both beauty and good, in order to suggest from the utmost actual realization of the one a corresponding capability in the other, and out of the calm, purity and energy of nature, to reconstitute and store up for the forthcoming stage of

man's being, a gift in repayment of that former gift, in which man's own thought and passion had been lavished by the poet on the else-incompleted magnificence of the sunrise, the else-uninterpreted mystery of the lake,—so drawing out, lifting up, and assimilating this ideal of a future man, thus descried as possible, to the present reality of the poet's soul already arrived at the higher state of development, and still aspirant to elevate and extend itself in conformity with its still-improving perceptions of, no longer the eventual Human, but the actual Divine. In conjunction with which noble and rare powers, came the subordinate power of delivering these attained results to the world in an embodiment of verse more closely answering to and indicative of the process of the informing spirit, (failing as it occasionally does, in art, only to succeed in highest art),—with a diction more adequate to the task in its natural and acquired richness, its material colour and spiritual transparency,—the whole being moved by and suffused with a music at once of the soul and the sense, expressive both of an external might of sincere passion and an internal fitness and consonancy,—than can be attributed to any other writer whose record is among us. Such was the spheric poetical faculty of Shelley, as its own self-sufficing central light, radiating equally through immaturity and accomplishment, through many fragments and occasional completion, reveals it to a competent judgement.

But the acceptance of this truth by the public, has been retarded by certain objections which cast us back on the evidence of biography, even with Shelley's poetry in our hands. Except for the particular character of these objections, indeed, the non-appreciation of his contemporaries would simply class, now that it is over, with a series of experiences which have necessarily happened and needlessly been wondered at, ever since the world began, and concerning which any present anger may well be moderated, no less in justice to our forerunners than in policy to ourselves. For the misapprehensiveness of his age is exactly what a poet is sent to remedy; and the interval between his operation and the generally perceptibly effect of it, is no greater, less indeed, than in many other departments of the great human effort. The *E pur si muove*[1] of the astronomer was as bitter a word as any uttered before or since by a poet over his rejected living work, in that depth of conviction which is so like despair.

But in this respect was the experience of Shelley peculiarly unfortunate—that the disbelief in him as a man, even preceded the disbelief in him as a writer; the misconstruction of his moral nature preparing the way for the misappreciation of his intellectual labours. There existed from the beginning,—simultaneous with, indeed anterior to his earliest noticeable works, and not brought forward to counteract any impression they had succeeded in making, —certain charges against his private character and life, which, if substantiated to their whole breadth, would materially disturb, I do not attempt to deny, our reception and enjoyment of his works, however wonderful the artistic qualities of these. For we are not sufficiently supplied with instances of genius of his order, to be able to pronounce certainly how many of its constituent parts have been tasked and strained to the production of a given lie, and how high and pure a mood of the creative mind may be dramatically simulated as the poet's habitual and exclusive one. The doubts, therefore, arising from such a question, required to be set at rest, as they were effectually, by those early authentic notices of Shelley's career and the corroborative accompaniment of his letters, in which not only the main tenor and principal result of his life, but the purity and beauty of many of the processes which had conduced to them, were made apparent enough for the general reader's purpose,—whoever lightly condemned Shelley first, on the evidence of reviews and gossip, as lightly acquitting him now, on that of memoirs and

correspondence. Still, it is advisable to lose no opportunity of strengthening and completing the chain of biographical testimony; much more, of course, for the sake of the poet's original lovers, whose volunteered sacrifice of particular principle in favour of absorbing sympathy we might desire to dispense with, than for the sake of his foolish haters, who have long since diverted upon other objects their obtuseness or malignancy. A full life of Shelley should be written at once, while the materials for it continue in reach; not to minister to the curiosity of the public, but to obliterate the last stain of that false life which was forced on the public's attention before it had any curiosity on the matter,—a biography, composed in harmony with the present general disposition to have faith in him, yet not shrinking from a candid statement of all ambiguous passages, through a reasonable confidence that the most doubtful of them will be found consistent with a belief in the eventual perfection of his character, according to the poor limits of our humanity. Nor will men persist in confounding, any more than God confounds, with genuine infidelity and an atheism of the heart, those passionate, impatient struggles of a boy towards distant truth and love, made in the dark, and ended by one sweep of the natural seas before the full moral sunrise could shine out on him. Crude convictions of boyhood, conveyed in imperfect and inapt forms of speech,— for such things all boys have been pardoned. There are growing-pains, accompanied by temporary distortion, of the soul also. And it would be hard indeed upon this young Titan of genius, murmuring in divine music his human ignorances, through his very thirst for knowledge, and his rebellion, in mere aspiration to law, if the melody itself substantiated the error, and the tragic cutting short of life perpetuated into sins, such faults as, under happier circumstances, would have been left behind by the consent of the most arrogant moralist, forgotten on the lowest steps of youth.

[1] the words of Galileo, spoken (quietly?) after recanting his assertion of the earth's movement: "And yet it does move."

The responsibility of presenting to the public a biography of Shelley, does not, however, lie with me: I have only to make it a little easier by arranging these few supplementary letters, with a recognition of the value of the whole collection. This value I take to consist in a most truthful conformity of the Correspondence, in its limited degree, with the moral and intellectual character of the writer as displayed in the highest manifestations of his genius. Letters and poems are obviously an act of the same mind, produced by the same law, only differing in the application to the individual or collective understanding. Letters and poems may be used indifferently as the basement of our opinion upon the writer's character; the finished expression of a sentiment in the poems, giving light and significance to the rudiments of the same in the letters, and these, again, in their incipiency and unripeness, authenticating the exalted mood and reattaching it to the personality of the writer. The musician speaks on the note he sings with; there is no change in the scale, as he diminishes the volume into familiar intercourse. There is nothing of that jarring between the man and the author, which has been found so amusing or so melancholy; no dropping of the tragic mask, as the crowd melts away; no mean discovery of the real motives of a life's achievement, often, in other lives, laid bare as pitifully as when, at the close of a holiday, we catch sight of the internal lead-pipes and wood-valves, to which, and not to the ostensible conch and dominant Triton of the fountain, we have owed our admired water-work. No breaking out, in household privacy, of hatred, anger and scorn, incongruous with the higher mood and suppressed artistically in the book: no brutal return to self-delighting, when the audience of philanthropic schemes is out of hearing: no indecent stripping off the grander feeling and rule of life as too costly and cumbrous for every-day wear. Whatever Shelley was, he was with an admirable sincerity. It was not always truth that he thought and spoke; but in the purity of truth he spoke and thought always.

Everywhere is apparent his belief in the existence of Good, to which Evil is an accident; his faithful holding by what he assumed to be the former, going everywhere in company with the tenderest pity for those acting or suffering on the opposite hypothesis. For he was tender, though tenderness is not always the characteristic of very sincere natures; he was eminently both tender and sincere. And not only do the same affection and yearning after the well-being of his kind, appear in the letters as in the poems, but they express themselves by the same theories and plans, however crude and unsound. There is no reservation of a subtler, less costly, more serviceable remedy for his own ill, than he has proposed for the general one; nor does he ever contemplate an object on his own account, from a less elevation than he uses in exhibiting it to the world. How shall we help believing Shelley to have been, in his ultimate attainment, the splendid spirit of his own best poetry, when we find even his carnal speech to agree faithfully, at faintest as at strongest, with the tone and rhythm of his most oracular utterances?

For the rest, these new letters are not offered as presenting any new feature of the poet's character. Regarded in themselves, and as the substantive productions of a man, their importance would be slight. But they possess interest beyond their limits, in confirming the evidence just dwelt on, of the poetical mood of Shelley being only the intensification of his habitual mood; the same tongue only speaking, for want of the special excitement to sing. The very first letter, as one instance for all, strikes the key-note of the predominating sentiment of Shelley throughout his whole life—his sympathy with the oppressed. And when we see him at so early an age, casting out, under the influence of such a sympathy, letters and pamphlets on every side, we accept it as the simple exemplification of the sincerity, with which, at the close of his life, he spoke of himself, as—

One whose heart a stranger's tear might wear
As water-drops the sandy fountain stone;
Who loved and pitied all things, and could moan
For woes which others hear not, and could see
The absent with the glass of phantasy,
And near the poor and trampled sit and weep,
Following the captive to his dungeon deep—
One who was as a nerve o'er which do creep
The else-unfelt oppressions of this earth. [1]

Such sympathy with his kind was evidently developed in him to an extraordinary and even morbid degree, at a period when the general intellectual powers it was impatient to put in motion, were immature or deficient.

I conjecture, from a review of the various publications of Shelley's youth, that one of the causes of his failure at the outset, was the peculiar *practicalness* of his mind, which was not without a determinate effect on his progress in theorizing. An ordinary youth, who turns his attention to similar subjects, discovers falsities, incongruities, and various points for amendment, and, in the natural advance of the purely critical spirit unchecked by considerations of remedy, keeps up before his young eyes so many instances of the same error and wrong, that he finds himself unawares arrived at the startling conclusion that all must be changed—or nothing: in the face of which plainly impossible achievement, he is apt (looking perhaps a little more serious by the time he touches at the decisive issue), to feel, either carelessly or considerately, that his own attempting a single piece of service would be worse than useless even, and to refer the whole task to another age and person—safe in proportion to his incapacity. Wanting words to speak, he has never made a fool of himself by speaking. But, in Shelley's case, the early fervour and power to *see*, was accompanied by as precocious a fertility to *contrive*: he endeavoured to realize as he went on idealizing; every wrong had simultaneously

its remedy, and, out of the strength of his hatred for the former, he took the strength of his confidence in the latter—till suddenly he stood pledged to the defence of a set of miserable little expedients, just as if they represented great principles, and to an attack upon various great principles, really so, without leaving himself time to examine whether, because they were antagonistical to the remedy he had suggested, they must therefore be identical or even essentially connected with the wrong he sought to cure,—playing with blind passion into the hands of his enemies, and dashing at whatever red cloak was held forth to him, as the cause of the fireball he had last been stung with—mistaking Churchdom for Christianity, and for marriage, "the sale of love" and the law of sexual oppression.

Gradually, however he was leaving behind him this low practical dexterity, unable to keep up with his widening intellectual perception; and, in exact proportion as he did so, his true power strengthened and proved itself. Gradually he was raised above the contemplation of spots and the attempt at effacing them, to the great Abstract Light, and, through the discrepancy of the creation, to the sufficiency of the First Cause. Gradually he was learning that the best way of removing abuses is to stand fast by truth. Truth is one, as they are manifold; and innumerable negative effects are produced by the upholding of one positive principle. I shall say what I think,—had Shelley lived he would have finally ranged himself with the Christians; his very instinct for helping the weaker side (if numbers make strength), his very "hate of hate," which at first mistranslated itself into delirious Queen Mab notes and the like, would have got clearer-sighted by exercise. The preliminary step to following Christ, is the leaving the dead to bury their dead—not clamouring on His doctrine for an especial solution of difficulties which are referable to the general problem of the universe. Already he had attained to a profession of "a worship to the Spirit of good within, which requires (before it sends that

---

inspiration forth, which impresses its likeness upon all it creates) devoted and disinterested homage, *as Coleridge says,*"—and Paul likewise. And we find in one of his last exquisite fragments, avowedly a record of one of his own mornings and its experience, as it dawned on him at his soul and body's best in his boat on the Serchio—that as surely as

> The stars burnt out in the pale blue air,
> And the thin white moon lay withering there—
> Day had kindled the dewy woods,
> And the rocks above, and the stream below,
> And the vapours in their multitudes,
> And the Apennine's shroud of summer snow—
> Day had awakened all things that be; [1]

just so surely, he tells us (stepping forward from this delicious dance-music, choragus-like, into the grander measure befitting the final enunciation),

> All rose to do the task He set to each,
> Who shaped us to his ends and not our own;
> The million rose to learn, and One to teach
> What none yet ever knew or can be known. [2]

No more difference than this, from David's pregnant conclusion so long ago!

Meantime, as I call Shelley a moral man, because he was true, simple-hearted, and brave, and because what he acted corresponded to what he knew, so I call him a man of religious mind, because every audacious negative cast up by him against the Divine, was interpenetrated with a mood of reverence and adoration,—and because I find him everywhere taking for granted some of the capital dogmas of Christianity, while most vehemently denying their historical basement. There is such a thing as an efficacious knowledge of and belief in the politics of Junius, or the poetry of Rowley, though a man

should at the same time dispute the title of Chatterton to the one, and consider the author of the other, as Byron wittily did, "really, truly, nobody at all."[3] There is even such a thing, we come to learn wonderingly in these very letters, as a profound sensibility and adaptitude for art, while the science of the percipient is so little advanced as to admit of his stronger admiration for Guido (and Carlo Dolce!) than for Michael Angelo. A Divine Being has Himself said, that "a word against the Son of man shall be forgiven to a man," while "a word against the Spirit of God" (implying a general deliberate preference of perceived evil to perceived good) "shall not be forgiven to a man." Also, in religion, one earnest and unextorted assertion of belief should outweigh, as a matter of testimony, many assertions of unbelief. The fact that there is a gold-region is established by the finding of one lump, though you miss the vein never so often.

He died before his youth ended. In taking the measure of him as a man, he must be considered on the whole and at his ultimate spiritual stature, and not be judged of at the immaturity and by the mistakes of ten years before: that, indeed, would be to judge of the author of "Julian and Maddalo" by "Zastrozzi." Let the whole truth be told of his worst mistake. I believe, for my own part, that if anything could now shame or grieve Shelley, it would be an attempt to vindicate him at the expense of another.

In forming a judgement, I would, however, press on the reader the simple justice of considering tenderly his constitution of body as well as mind, and

---

[1] "The Boat on the Serchio," ll. 7–13.

[2] ll. 30–33.

[3] "Or, to take our illustrations from the writings of Shelley himself, there is such a thing as admirably appreciating a work by Andrea Verocchio,—and fancifully characterising the Pisan Torre Guelfa by the Ponte a Mare, black against the sunsets,—and consummately painting the islet of San Clemente with its penitentiary for rebellious priests, to the west between Venice and the Lido—while you believe the first to be a fragment of an antique sarcophagus,—the second, Ugolino's Tower of Famine (the vestiges of which should be sought for in the Piazza de' Cavalieri)—and the third (as I convinced myself last summer at Venice), San Servolo with its madhouse—which, far from being "windowless," is as full of windows as a barrack." (Browning's note.)

how unfavourable it was to the steady symmetries of conventional life; the body, in the torture of incurable disease, refusing to give repose to the bewildered soul, tossing in its hot fever of the fancy,—and the laudanum-bottle making but a perilous and pitiful truce between these two. He was constantly subject to "that state of mind" (I quote his own note to "Hellas") "in which ideas may be supposed to assume the force of sensation, through the confusion of thought with the objects of thought, and excess of passion animating the creations of the imagination": in other words, he was liable to remarkable delusions and hallucinations. The nocturnal attack in Wales, for instance, was assuredly a delusion; and I venture to express my own conviction derived from a little attention to the circumstances of either story, that the idea of the enamoured lady following him to Naples, and of the "man in the cloak" who struck him at the Pisan post-office, were equally illusory,—the mere projection, in fact, from himself, of the image of his own love and hate.

> To thirst and find no fill—to wail and wander
> With short unsteady steps—to pause and ponder—
> To feel the blood run through the veins and tingle
> When busy thought and blind sensation mingle,—
> To nurse the image of *unfelt caresses*
> Till dim imagination just possesses
> The half-created shadow— [1]

of unfelt caresses,—and of unfelt blows as well: to such conditions was his genius subject. It was not at Rome only (where he heard a mystic voice exclaiming, "Cenci, Cenci," in reference to the tragic theme which occupied him at the time),—it was not at Rome only that he mistook the cry of "old rags." The habit of somnambulism is said to have extended to the very last days of his life.

Let me conclude with a thought of Shelley as a poet. In the hierarchy of creative minds, it is the presence of the highest faculty that gives first rank, in virtue of its kind, not degree; no pretension of a lower nature, whatever the completeness of development or variety of effect, impeding the precedency of the rarer endowment though only in the germ. The contrary is sometimes maintained; it is attempted to make the lower gifts (which are potentially included in the higher faculty) of independent value, and equal to some exercise of the special function. For instance, should not a poet possess common sense? Then the possession of abundant common sense implies a step towards becoming a poet. Yes; such a step as the lapidary's, when, strong in the fact of carbon entering largely into the composition of the diamond, he heaps up a sack of charcoal in order to compete with the Koh-i-noor. I pass at once, therefore, from Shelley's minor excellencies to his noblest and predominating characteristics.

This I call his simultaneous perception of Power and Love in the absolute, and of Beauty and Good in the concrete, while he throws, from his poet's station between both, swifter, subtler, and more numerous films for the connexion of each with each, than have been thrown by any modern artificer of whom I have knowledge; proving how, as he says,

> The spirit of the worm within the sod,
> In love and worship blends itself with God. [2]

I would rather consider Shelley's poetry as a sublime fragmentary essay towards a presentment of the correspondency of the universe to Deity, of the natural to the spiritual, and of the actual to the ideal, than I would isolate and separately appraise the worth of many detachable portions which might be acknowledged as utterly perfect in a lower moral point of view, under the mere conditions of art. It would be easy to take my stand on successful instances of objectivity in Shelley: there is the unri-

---

[1] "To thirst and find no fill," ll. 1–7.

[2] *Epipsychidion*, ll. 128–29.

valled "Cenci"; there is the "Julian and Maddalo" too; there is the magnificent "Ode to Naples": why not regard, it may be said, the less organized matter as the radiant elemental foam and solution, out of which would have been evolved, eventually, creations as perfect even as those? But I prefer to look for the highest attainment, not simply the high,—and, seeing it, I hold by it. There is surely enough of the work "Shelley" to be known enduringly among men, and, I believe, to be accepted of God, as human work may; and around the imperfect proportions of such, the most elaborated productions of ordinary art must arrange themselves as inferior illustrations.

It is because I have long held these opinions in assurance and gratitude, that I catch at the opportunity offered to me of expressing them here; knowing that the alacrity to fulfil an humble office conveys more love than the acceptance of the honour of a higher one, and that better, therefore, than the signal service it was the dream of my boyhood to render to his fame and memory, may be the saying of a few, inadequate words upon these scarcely more important supplementary letters of SHELLEY.
—PARIS, DECEMBER 4, 1851.

Arthur Hugh Clough
1819 – 1861

Arthur Hugh Clough was educated at Rugby and Balliol College, Oxford. He became a fellow of Oriel and then principal of University Hall, London. His poems appeared in *Ambarvalia* (1849), *Amours de Voyage* (1849), *Dipsychus* (1850), and *Mari Magno or Tales On Board* (1861). Clough and Matthew Arnold were friends and poetic rivals; after Clough's premature death in 1861 Arnold wrote the problematic elegy "Thyrsis" in his memory. Clough's short verse reveals his clear-sighted cynicism about social conventions; his longer works, such as the novel-in-verse *Amours de Voyage*, combine social commentary with ambitious formal experimentation.

e/3e/3

Recent English Poetry: A Review of Several Volumes of Poems by Alexander Smith, Matthew Arnold, and Others [1]

Poems by Alexander Smith,[2] a volume recently published in London, and by this time reprinted in Boston, deserve attention. They have obtained in England a good deal more notice than is usually accorded there to first volumes of verse; nor is this by any means to be ascribed to the mere fact that the writer is, as we are told, a mechanic; though undoubtedly that does add to their external interest, and perhaps also enhances their intrinsic merit. It is to this, perhaps, that they owe a force of purpose and character which makes them a grateful contrast to the ordinary languid collectanea published by young men of literary habits; and which, on the whole, may be accepted as more than compensation for many imperfections of style and taste.

The models, whom this young poet has followed, have been, it would appear, predominantly, if not exclusively, the writers of his own immediate time, *plus* Shakspeare. The antecedents of the Life-Drama, the one long poem which occupies almost the whole of his volume, are to be found in the Princess, in parts of Mrs. Browning, in the love of Keats, and the *habit* of Shakspeare. There is no Pope, or Dryden,[3] or even Milton; no Wordsworth, Scott, or even Byron to speak of. We have before us, we may say, the latest disciple of the school of Keats, who was indeed no well of English undefiled, though doubtless the fountain-head of a true poetic stream. Alexander Smith is young enough to free himself from his present manner, which does not seem his simple and natural own. He has given us, so to say, his Endymion; it is certainly as imperfect, and as mere a promise of something wholly different as was that of the master he has followed.

We are not sorry, in the mean time, that this Endymion is not upon Mount Latmos.[4] The natural man does pant within us after *flumina silvasque;*[5] yet really, and truth to tell, is it not, upon the whole, an easy matter to sit under a green tree by a purling brook, and indite pleasing stanzas on the beauties of Nature and fresh air? Or is it, we incline to ask, so very great an exploit to wander out into the pleasant field of Greek or Latin mythology, and reproduce, with more or less of modern adaptation,—

---

[1] first published in the *North American Review*, July, 1853.

[2] Smith (1830–67), whose first book of poems was published in 1853, was a member of the so-called Spasmodic School.

[3] "The word *spoom*, which Dryden uses as the verb of the substantive *spume*, occurs also in Beaumont and Fletcher. Has Keats employed it? It seems hardly to deserve reimpatriation." (Clough's note.)

[4] frequented by the mythological Endymion.

[5] streams and woods.

the shadows
Faded and pale, yet immortal, of Faunus, the
Nymphs, and the Graces? [1]

Studies of the literature of any distant age, or country; all the imitations and *quasi*-translations which help to bring together into a single focus, the scattered rays of human intelligence; poems after classical models, poems from Oriental sources, and the like, have undoubtedly a great literary value. Yet there is no question, it is plain and patent enough, that people much prefer Vanity Fair and Bleak House. Why so? Is it simply because we have grown prudent and prosaic, and should not welcome, as our fathers did, the Marmions and the Rokebys, the Childe Harolds, and the Corsairs? [2] Or is it, that to be wildly popular, to gain the ear of multitudes, to shake the hearts of men, poetry should deal more than at present it usually does, with general wants, ordinary feelings, the obvious rather than the rare facts of human nature? Could it not attempt to convert into beauty and thankfulness, or at least into some form and shape, some feeling, at any rate, of content—the actual, palpable things with which our every-day life is concerned; introduce into business and weary task-work a character and a soul of purpose and reality; intimate to us relations which, in our unchosen, peremptorily-appointed posts, in our grievously narrow and limited spheres of action, we still, in and through all, retain to some central, celestial fact? Could it not console us with a sense of significance, if not of dignity, in that often dirty, or at least dingy, work which it is the lot of so many of us to have to do, and which some one or other, after all, must do? Might it not divinely condescend to all infirmities; be in all points tempted as we are; exclude nothing, least of all guilt and distress, from its wide fraternization; not content itself merely with talking of what may be

better elsewhere, but seek also to deal with what *is* here? We could each one of us, alas, be so much that somehow we find we are not; we have all of us fallen away from so much that we still long to call ours. Cannot the Divine Song in some way indicate to us our unity, though from a great way off, with those happier things; inform us, and prove to us, that though we are what we are, we may yet, in some way, even in our abasement, even by and through our daily work, be related to the purer existence.

The modern novel is preferred to the modern poem, because we do here feel an attempt to include these indispensable latest addenda—these phenomena which, if we forget on Sunday, we must remember on Monday—these positive matters of fact, which people, who are not verse-writers, are obliged to have to do with.

Et fortasse cupressum
Scis simulare; quid hoc, si fractis enatat expes
Navibus, aere dato qui pingitur? [3]

The novelist does try to build us a real house to be lived in; and this common builder, with no notion of the orders, is more to our purpose than the student of ancient art who proposes to lodge us under an Ionic portico. We are, unhappily, not gods, nor even marble statues. While the poets, like the architects, are—a good thing enough in its way—studying ancient art, comparing, thinking, theorizing, the common novelist tells a plain tale, often trivial enough, about this, that, and the other, and obtains one reading at any rate; is thrown away indeed tomorrow, but is devoured to-day.

We do not at all mean to prepare the reader for finding the great poetic desideratum in this present Life-Drama. But it has at least the advantage, such as it is, of not showing much of the *littérateur* or con-

---

[1] from Clough's *Amours de Voyage* 3.225–26.

[2] heroes of poetic romances by Scott and Byron.

[3] Horace, *Ars Poetica*, ll. 19–21: "Perhaps you know how to draw a cypress; but what good is that if you are hired by a sailor to paint his portrait struggling to shore after a wreck?"

noisseur, or indeed the student; nor is it, as we have said, mere pastoral sweet piping from the country. These poems were not written among books and busts, nor yet

> By shallow rivers, to whose falls
> Melodious birds sing madrigals.[1]

They have something substantive and lifelike, immediate and firsthand, about them. There is a charm, for example, in finding, as we do, continual images drawn from the busy seats of industry; it seems to satisfy a want that we have long been conscious of, when we see the black streams that welter out of factories, the dreary lengths of urban and suburban dustiness,

> the squares and streets,
> And the faces that one meets,[2]

irradiated with a gleam of divine purity. There are moods when one is prone to believe that, in these last days, no longer by "clear spring or shady grove," no more upon any Pindus or Parnassus, or by the side of any Castaly,[3] are the true and lawful haunts of the poetic powers: but, we could believe it, if anywhere, in the blank and desolate streets, and upon the solitary bridges of the midnight city, where Guilt is, and wild Temptation, and the dire Compulsion of what has once been done—there, with these tragic sisters around him, and with Pity also, and pure Compassion, and pale Hope, that looks like Despair, and Faith in the garb of Doubt, there walks the discrowned Apollo, with unstrung lyre; nay, and could he sound it, those mournful Muses would

scarcely be able as of old, to respond and "sing in turn with their beautiful voices."[4]

To such moods, and in such states of feeling, this Life-Drama will be an acceptable poem. Under the guise of a different story, a story unskilful enough in its construction, we have seemed continually to recognize the ingenuous, yet passionate, youthful spirit, struggling after something like right and purity amidst the unnumbered difficulties, contradictions, and corruptions of the heated and crowded, busy, vicious, and inhuman town. Eager for action, incapable of action without some support, yet knowing not on what arm to dare lean; not untainted; hard-pressed; in some sort, at times, overcome,—still we seem to see the young combatant, half combatant half martyr, resolute to fight it out, and not to quit this for some easier field of battle,—one way or other to make something of it.

The story, such as we have it, is inartificial enough. Walter, a boy of poetic temperament and endowment, has, it appears, in the society of a poet friend now deceased, grown up with the ambition of achieving something great in the highest form of human speech. Unable to find or make a way, he is diverted from his lofty purposes by a romantic love-adventure, obscurely told, with a "Lady" who finds him asleep, Endymion-like, under a tree. The fervor and force of youth wastes itself here in vain; a quick disappointment,—for the lady is betrothed to another,—sends him back enfeebled, exhausted, and embittered, to essay once again his task. Disappointed affections, and baffled ambition, contending henceforward in unequal strife with the temptations of scepticism, indifference, apathetic submission, base indulgence, and the like;—the sickened, and defeated, yet only too strong, too powerful man, turning desperately off, and recklessly at last plunging in mid-unbelief into joys to which only belief and moral purpose can give reality;—out of horror-stricken

---

[1] from Christopher Marlowe's "The Passionate Shepherd to His Love," ll. 7–8.

[2] from Tennyson's *Maud* 2.4.232–33. *Maud* was first published in 1855, but these lines appeared in an annual in 1834.

[3] two mountains and a fountain sacred to Apollo and the Muses.

[4] not identified.

guilt, the new birth of clearer and surer, though humbler, conviction, trust, resolution;—these happy changes met, perhaps a little prematurely and almost more than halfway, by success in the aims of a purified ambition, and crowned too, at last, by the blessings of a regenerate affection,—such is the argument of the latter half of the poem; and there is something of a current and tide, so to say, of poetic intention in it, which carries on the reader, (after the first few scenes,) perforce, in spite of criticism and himself, through faulty imagery, turgid periods, occasional bad versification and even grammar, to the close. Certainly, there is something of a real flesh-and-blood heart and soul in the case, or this could not be so.

Of the first four or five scenes, perhaps the less said the better. There are frequent fine lines, occasional beautiful passages; but the tenor of the narrative is impeded and obstructed to the last degree, not only by accumulations of imagery, but by episode, and episode within episode, of the most embarrassing form. It is really discouraging to turn page upon page, while Walter is quoting the poems of his lost friend, and wooing the unknown lady of the wood with a story of another lady and an Indian page. We could almost recommend the reader to begin with the close of scene IV., where the hero's first love-disappointment is decided, and the lady quits her young poet.

> "I must go,
> Nay, nay, I go alone! Yet one word more.
> Strive for the Poet's crown, but ne'er forget,
> How poor are fancy's blooms to thoughtful fruits:
> That gold and crimson mornings, though more bright
> Than soft blue days, are scarcely half their worth.
> Walter 'farewell,' the world shall hear of thee.
> [She still lingers.
> "I have a strange sweet thought. I do believe
> I shall be dead in spring, and that the soul
> Which animates and doth inform these limbs,
> Will pass into the daisies of my grave:

> If memory shall ever lead thee there,
> Through daisies I'll look up into thy face,
> And feel a dim sweet joy; and if they move
> As in a little wind, thou'lt know 'tis I."

The ensuing scene, between Walter and a Peasant, is also obscurely and indecisively given; and before Part VI., it would have been well, we think, to place some mark of the lapse of time. The second division of the poem here commences. We are reintroduced to the hero in a room in London, reading a poetical manuscript. Edward, a friend, enters and interrupts. We quote from a speech of Walter's.

> "Thou mock'st at much;
> And he who sneers at any living hope,
> Or aspiration of a human heart,
> Is just so many stages less than God,
> That universal and all-sided Love.
> I'm wretched, Edward, to the very heart:
> I see an unreached heaven of young desire
> Shine through my hopeless tears. My drooping sails
> Flap idly 'gainst the mast of my intent.
> I rot upon the waters, when my prow
> Should grate the golden isles.
> *Edward.* What wouldst thou do?
> Thy train did teem with vapors wild and vast.
> *Walter.* But since my younger and my hotter days,
> (As nebula condenses to an orb,)
> These vapors gathered to one shining hope
> Sole hanging in my sky.
> *Edward.* What hope is that?
> *Walter.* To set this age to music—the great work
> Before the poet now—I do believe
> When it is fully sung, its great complaint,
> Its hope, its yearning, told to earth and heaven,
> Our troubled age shall pass, as doth a day
> That leaves the west all crimson with the promise
> Of the diviner morrow, which even then
> Is hurrying up the great world's side with light."

Two scenes of conversation are given between Walter and this friend, Edward, cold, clear-sighted, a little cynical, but patient, calm, resigned, and moral. He as it happens is going on the morrow to Bedfordshire to visit

"Old Mr. Wilmott, nothing in himself,
But rich as ocean. He has in his hand
Sea-marge and moor, and miles of stream and grove,
Dull flats, scream-startled, as the exulting train
Streams like a meteor through the frighted night,
Wind-billowed plains of wheat, and marshy fens,
Unto whose reeds on midnights blue and cold,
Long strings of geese come clanging from the stars,
Yet wealthier in one child than all of these."

Thither Walter accompanies him. We subjoin part of a dialogue between him and the "one child," in whom, more than in all his land, old Mr. Wilmott was blest. Walter had been describing his own story under the name of another person.

"*Violet.* Did you know well that youth of whom you
    spake?
Walter. Know him! Oh yes; I knew him as myself,—
Two passions dwelt at once within his soul,

.   .   .   .

The dead was Love, the living, Poetry.
Violet. Alas! if Love rose never from the dead.
Walter. Between him and the lady of his love
There stood a wrinkled worldling.

.   .   .   .   .   .

                        And when she died,
The rivers of his heart ran all to waste;
They found no ocean; dry sands sucked them up.
Lady! he was a fool, a pitiful fool!
She said she loved him, would be dead in spring—
She asked him but to stand beside her grave—
She said she would be daisies—and she thought
'T would give her joy to feel that he was near.
She died, like music; and would you believe it?
He kept her foolish words within his heart,
As ceremonious as a chapel keeps
A relic of a saint. And in the spring

The doting idiot went.
Violet. What found he there?
Walter. Laugh till your sides ache! oh, he went, poor
    fool,
But he found nothing, save red-trampled clay,
And a dull, sobbing rain. Do you not laugh?
Amid the comfortless rain he stood and wept;
Bareheaded in the mocking, pelting rain.
He might have known 't was ever so on earth.
Violet. You cannot laugh yourself, sir, nor can I.
Her unpolluted corse[1] doth sleep in earth
Like a pure thought within a sinful soul.
Dearer is Earth to God for her sweet sake.["]

The issue and catastrophe of a new love-adventure here, in this unhappy and distempered period of baffled and disappointed ambition, and power struggling vainly for a vent, may be conjectured from the commencement of a scene, which perhaps might be more distinctly marked as the opening of the third part.

[*A bridge in a City. Midnight. Walter alone.*]
"Adam lost Paradise—eternal tale,
Repeated in the lives of all his sons.
I had a shining orb of happiness,—
God gave it me, but sin passed over it
As smallpox passes o'er a lovely face,
Leaving it hideous. I have lost for ever
The paradise of young and happy thoughts,
And now stand in the middle of my life
Looking back through my tears, ne'er to return.
I've a stern tryst with death, and must go on,
Though with slow steps and oft-reverted eyes.
'Tis a thick, rich-hazed, sumptuous autumn night;
The moon grows like a white flower in the sky;
The stars are dim. The tired year rests content
Among her sheaves, as a fond mother rests
Among her children—all her work is done,
There is a weight of peace upon the world;
It sleeps; God's blessing on it. Not on me.

.   .   .   .

---

[1] archaic form of corpse.

Good men have said,
That sometimes God leaves sinners to their sin,—
He has left me to mine, and I am changed;
My worst part is insurgent, and my will
Is weak and powerless as a trembling king
When millions rise up hungry. Woe is me!
My soul breeds sins as a dead body worms,—
They swarm and feed upon me.["]

Three years appear to have gone by, when Walter, like a stag sorehunted, returns to the home of his childhood.

"'Twas here I spent my youth, as far removed
From the great heavings, hopes and fears of man,
As unknown isle asleep in unknown seas.
Gone my pure heart, and with it happy days;
No manna falls around me from on high,
Barely from off the desert of my life
I gather patience and severe content.
God is a worker. He has thickly strewn
Infinity with grandeur. God is Love;
He yet shall wipe away creation's tears,
And all the worlds shall summer in his smile.
Why work I not. The veriest mote that sports
Its one-day life within the sunny beam,
Has its stern duties. Wherefore have I none?
I will throw off this dead and useless past,
As a strong runner, straining for his life,
Unclasps a mantle to the hungry winds.
A mighty purpose rises large and slow
From out the fluctuations of my soul,
As ghostlike from the dim and trembling sea
Starts the completed moon.["]

Here, in this determination, he writes his poem, —attains in this spirit the object which had formerly been his ambition. And here, in the last scene, we find him happy, or peaceful at least, with Violet.

"*Violet.* I always pictured you in such a place
Writing your book, and hurrying on, as if
You had a long and wondrous tale to tell,

And felt Death's cold hand closing round your heart.
Walter. Have you read my book?
Violet. I have.
Walter. It is enough.
The book was only written for two souls,
And they are thine and mine.
Violet. For many weeks,
When I was dwelling by the moaning sea,
Your name was blown to me on every wind,
And I was glad; for by that sign I knew
You had fulfilled your heart, and hoped you would
Put off the robes of sorrow, and put on
The singing crown of Fame."

Again, below, she resumes,—

"Walter! dost thou believe
Love will redeem all errors? Oh, my friend,
This gospel saves you! doubt it, you are lost.
Deep in the mists of sorrow long I lay,
Hopeless and still, when suddenly this truth
Like a slant sunbeam quivered through the mist,
And turned it into radiance. In the light
I wrote these words, while you were far away,
Fighting with shadows. Oh, Walter, in one boat
We floated o'er the smooth, moon-silvered sea;
The sky was smiling with its orbs of bliss;
And while we lived within each other's eyes,
We struck and split, and all the world was lost
In one wild whirl of horror darkening down.
At last I gained a deep and silent isle,
Moaned on by a dim sea, and wandered round,
Week after week, the happy-mournful shore,
Wondering if you had 'scaped.
Walter. Thou noble soul,
Teach me, if thou art nearer God than I!
My life was one long dream; when I awoke,
Duty stood like an angel in my path,
And seemed so terrible, I could have turned
Into my yesterdays, and wandered back
To distant childhood, and gone out to God
By the gate of birth, not death. Life, lift me up
By thy sweet inspiration, as the tide
Lifts up a stranded boat upon the beach.

I will go forth 'mong men, not mailed in scorn,
But in the armor of a pure intent.
Great duties are before me, and great songs,
And whether crowned or crownless, when I fall,
It matters not, so as God's work is done.
I've learned to prize the quiet lightning deed,
Not the applauding thunder at its heels,
Which men call Fame. Our night is past;
We stand in precious sunrise; and beyond,
A long day stretches to the very end."

So be it, O young Poet; Poet, perhaps it is early to affirm; but so be it, at any rate, O young man. While you go forth in that "armor of pure intent," the hearts of some readers, be assured, will go with you.

Empedocles on Etna and other Poems, with its earlier companion volume, The Strayed Reveller and other Poems, are, it would seem, the productions (as is, or was, the English phrase) of a scholar and a gentleman; a man who has received a refined education, seen refined "society," and been more, we dare say, in the world, which is called the world, than in all likelihood has a Glasgow mechanic. More refined, therefore, and more highly educated sensibilities,—too delicate, are they, for common service?—a calmer judgment also, a more poised and steady intellect, the *siccum lumen* of the soul; a finer and rarer aim perhaps, and certainly a keener sense of difficulty, in life;—these are the characteristics of him whom we are to call "A." Empedocles, the sublime Sicilian philosopher, the fragments of whose moral and philosophic poems testify to his genius and character,—Empedocles, in the Poem before us, weary of misdirected effort, weary of imperfect thought, impatient of a life which appears to him a miserable failure, and incapable, as he conceives, of doing any thing that shall be true to that proper interior self,

"Being one with which we are one with the whole
world,"

wandering forth, with no determined purpose, into the mountain solitudes, followed for a while by Pausanias, the eager and laborious physician, and at a distance by Callicles, the boy-musician, flings himself at last, upon a sudden impulse and apparent inspiration of the intellect, into the boiling crater of Etna; rejoins there the elements. "Slave of sense," he was saying, pondering near the verge,

"Slave of sense
I have in no wise been: but slave of thought?
And who can say, he has been always free,
Lived ever in the light of his own soul?
I cannot:—

. . . .

But I have not grown easy in these bonds,
But I have not denied what bonds these were.
Yea, I take myself to witness
That I have loved no darkness,
Sophisticated no truth,
Nursed no delusion,
Allowed no fear.
And therefore, O ye Elements, I know—
Ye know it too—it hath been granted me,
Not to die wholly, not to be all enslaved.
I feel it in this hour. The numbing cloud
Mounts off my soul: I feel it, I breathe free.

Is it but for a moment?
Ah, boil up, ye vapors!
Leap and roar, thou sea of Fire!
My soul glows to meet you.
Ere it flag, ere the mists
Of despondency and gloom
Rush over it again,
Receive me! save me!["]
[*He plunges into the crater.*]

The music of the boy Callicles, to which he chants his happy mythic stories, somewhat frigidly perhaps, relieves, as it sounds in the distance, the gloomy catastrophe.

Tristram and Iseult (these names form the title of the next and only other considerable poem) are, in the old romantic cycle of North-France and Germany, the hero and the heroine of a mournful tale. Tristram of Lyonness[e], the famed companion of King Arthur, received in youth a commission to bring from across the sea the Princess Iseult of Ireland, the destined bride of the King of Cornwall. The mother of the beautiful princess gave her, as a parting gift, a cup of a magic wine, which she and her royal husband should drink together on their marriage-day in their palace at Tyntagil; so they should love each other perfectly and forever. But on the voyage it befell—

> The calm sea shines, loose hang the vessel's sails,
> Before us are the sweet green fields of Wales,
> And overhead the cloudless sky of May.
> 'Ah, would I were'—

(saith Iseult)

> "Ah, would I were in those green fields at play,
> Not pent on shipboard this delicious day.
> Tristram, I pray thee of thy courtesy,
> Reach me my golden cup that stands by thee,
> And pledge me in it first for courtesy.'

On the dreamy seas it so befell, that Iseult and Tristram drank together of the golden cup. Tristram, therefore, and Iseult should love each other perfectly and for ever. Yet nothing the less for this must Iseult be wedded to the King of Cornwall; and Tristram, vainly lingering, fly and go forth upon his way.

But it so chanced that, after long and weary years of passion vainly contended with, years of travel and hard fighting, Tristram, lying wounded in Brittany, was tended by another, a youthful, innocent Iseult, in whose face he seemed to see the look of that Iseult of the past, that was, and yet could not be, his. Weary, and in his sad despondency, Tristram wedded Iseult of Brittany, whose heart, in his stately deep distress, he had moved to a sweet and tender affection. The modern poem opens with the wedded knight come home again, after other long years, and other wars, in which he had fought at King Arthur's side with the Roman emperor, and subdued the heathen Saxons on the Rhine, lying once more sick and sad at heart, upon what ere long he feels shall be his deathbed. Ere he die, he would see, once yet again, her with whom in his youth he drank of that fatal cup.

> *Tristram.* Is she not come? the messenger was sure.
> Prop me upon the pillows once again—
> Raise me, my page: this cannot long endure.
> Christ! what a night! how the sleet whips the pane!
> What lights will those out to the northward be?
> *The Page.* The lanterns of the fishing-boats at sea.

And so through the whole of Part I. of our poem, lies the sick and weary knight upon his bed, reviewing sadly, while sadly near him stands his timid and loving younger Iseult, reviewing, half sleeping, half awake, those old times, that hapless voyage, and all that thence ensued; and still in all his thought recurring to the proud Cornish Queen, who, it seems, will let him die unsolaced. He speaks again, now broad awake.

> Is my page here? Come turn me to the fire.
> Upon the window panes the moon shines bright;
> The wind is down; but she'll not come to-night.
> Ah no,—she is asleep in Tyntagil—
>
> . . . .
>
> My princess, art thou there? Sweet, 'tis too late.
> To bed and sleep; my fever is gone by;
> To-night my page shall keep me company.
> Where do the children sleep? kiss them for me.
> Poor child, thou art almost as pale as I;
> This comes of nursing long and watching late.
> To bed—good night.

And so, (our poet passing without notice from Tristram's semi-dramatic musings and talkings, to his own not more coherent narrative)—

> She left the gleam-lit fireplace,
> She came to the bed-side;
> She took his hands in hers; her tears
> Down on her slender fingers rained.
> She raised her eyes upon his face—
> Not with a look of wounded pride—
> A look as if the heart complained;—
> Her look was like a sad embrace;
> The gaze of one who can divine
> A grief, and sympathize.
> Sweet flower, thy children's eyes
> Are not more innocent than thine.

Sleeping with her little ones, and, it may be, dreaming too, though less happily than they, lies Iseult of Brittany. And now—

> What voices are those on the clear night air?
> What lights in the courts? what steps on the stair?

PART II

> *Tristram.* Raise the light, my page, that I may see her.
> —Thou art come at last, then, haughty Queen!
> Long I've waited, long have fought my fever,
> Late thou comest, cruel thou hast been.
> *Iseult.* Blame me not, poor sufferer, that I tarried.
> I was bound; I could not break the band,
> Chide not with the past, but feel the present;
> I am here—we meet—I hold thy hand.

Yes, the Queen Iseult of Cornwall, Iseult that was of Ireland, Iseult of the ship upon the dreamy seas long since, has crossed these stormy seas to-night, is here, holds his hand. And so proceeds, through some six or seven pages of Part II., the fine colloquy of the two sad, world-worn, late-reunited lovers. When we open upon Part III.,

> A year had flown, and in the chapel old
> Lay Tristram and Queen Iseult dead and cold.

Beautiful, simple old mediaeval story! We have followed it, led on as much by its own intrinsic charm as by the form and coloring—beautiful too, but indistinct—which our modern poet has given it. He is obscure at times, and hesitates and falters in it; the knights and dames, we fear, of old North-France and Western Germany would have been grievously put to it to make him out. Only upon a fourth re-reading, and by the grace of a happy moment, did we satisfy our critical conscience that, when the two lovers have sunk together in death, the knight on his pillows, and Queen Iseult kneeling at his side, the poet, after passing to the Cornish court where she was yesternight, returns to address himself to a hunter with his dogs, worked in the tapestry of the chamber here, whom he conceives to be pausing in the pictured chase, and staring, with eyes of wonder, on the real scene of the pale knight on the pillows and the kneeling lady fair. But

> Cheer, cheer thy dogs into the brake,
> O hunter! and without a fear
> Thy golden-tasselled bugle blow,
> And through the glade thy pastime take!
> For thou wilt rouse no sleepers here,
> For these thou seest are unmoved;
> Cold, cold as those who lived and loved
> A thousand years ago."

Fortunately, indeed, with the commencement of Part III., the most matter-of-fact quarterly conscience may feel itself pretty well set at ease by the unusually explicit statements that

> A year had fled; and in the chapel old
> Lay Tristram and Queen Iseult dead and cold.
> The young surviving Iseult, one bright day
> Had wandered forth; her children were at play
> In a green circular hollow in the heath

Which borders the sea shore; a country path
Creeps over it from the tilled fields behind.

Yet anon, again and thicker now perhaps than ever, the mist of more than poetic dubiousness closes over and around us. And as he sings to us about the widowed lady Iseult, sitting upon the sea-banks of Brittany, watching her bright-eyed children, talking with them and telling them old Breton stories, while still, in all her talk and her story, her own dreamy memories of the past, and perplexed thought of the present, mournfully mingle, it is really all but impossible to ascertain her, or rather his, real meanings. We listen, indeed, not quite unpleased, to a sort of faint musical mumble, conveying at times a kind of subdued half-sense, or intimating, perhaps, a three-quarters-implied question; Is any thing real?—is love any thing?—what is any thing?—is there substance enough even in sorrow to mark the lapse of time?—is not passion a diseased unrest?—did not the fairy Vivian, when the wise Merlin forgot his craft to fall in love with her, wave her wimple over her sleeping adorer?

> Nine times she waved the fluttering wimple round,
> And made a little plot of magic ground;
> And in that daisied circle, as men say,
> Is Merlin prisoner to the judgment day,
> But she herself whither she will can rove,
> For she was passing weary of his love.

Why or wherefore, or with what purport, who will venture exactly to say?—but such, however, was the tale which, while Tristram and his first Iseult lay in their graves, the second Iseult, on the sea-banks of Brittany, told her little ones.

And yet, dim and faint as is the sound of it, we still prefer this dreamy patience, the soft submissive endurance of the Breton lady, and the human passions and sorrows of the Knight and the Queen, to the high, and shall we say, pseudo-Greek inflation of

the philosopher musing above the crater, and the boy Callicles, singing myths upon the mountain.

Does the reader require morals and meanings to these stories? What shall they be, then?—the deceitfulness of knowledge, and the illusiveness of the affections, the hardiness and roughness and contrariousness of the world, the difficulty of living at all, the impossibility of doing any thing,—*voilà tout?* A charitable and patient reader, we believe, (such as is the present reviewer.) will find in the minor poems that accompany these pieces, intimations—what more can reader or reviewer ask?—of some better and further thing than these; some approximations to a kind of confidence, some incipiences of a degree of hope, some roots, retaining some vitality, of conviction and moral purpose.

> And though we wear out life, alas,
> Distracted as a homeless wind,
> In beating where we must not pass,
> And seeking what we shall not find,
>
> Yet shall we one day gain, life past,
> Clear prospect o'er our being's whole
> Shall we ourselves, and learn at last
> Our true affinities of soul.
>
> We shall not then deny a course
> To every thought the mass ignore,
> We shall not then call hardness force,
> Nor lightness wisdom any more.[1]

In the future, it seems, there is something for us; and for the present also, which is more germane to our matter, we have discovered some precepts about "hope, light and *persistence,*"[2] which we intend to make the most of. Meantime, it is one promising point in our author of the initial, that his second is certainly on the whole an improvement upon his first

---

[1] from "A Farewell," ll. 49–60.

[2] from "The Second Best," l. 23. Emphasis added by Clough.

volume. There is less obvious study of effect; upon the whole, a plainer and simpler and less factitious manner and method of treatment. This, he may be sure, is the only safe course. Not by turning and twisting his eyes, in the hope of seeing things as Homer, Sophocles, Virgil, or Milton saw them; but by seeing them, by accepting them as he sees them, and faithfully depicting accordingly, will he attain the object he desires.

In the earlier volume, one of the most generally admired pieces was "The Forsaken Merman."

> Come, dear children, let us away
> Down, and away below,

says the Merman, standing upon the sea-shore, whither he and his children came up to call back the human Margaret, their mother, who had left them to go, for one day—for Easterday—to say her prayers with her kinsfolk in the little gray church on the shore:

> ' 'Twill be Easter-time in the world—ah me,
> And I lose my poor soul, Merman, here with thee.'

And when she staid, and staid on, and it seemed a long while, and the little ones began to moan, at last, up went the Merman with the little ones to the shore, and so on into the town, and to the little gray church, and there looked in through the small leaded panes of the window. There she sits in the aisle; but she does not look up, her eyes are fixed upon the holy page; it is in vain we try to catch her attention.

> Come away, children, call no more,
> Come away, come down, call no more.

Down, down to the depths of the sea. She will live up there and be happy, among the things she had known before. Yet sometimes a thought will come across her; there will be times when she will

> Steal to the window and look at the sand;
> And over the sand at the sea;
> And anon there breaks a sigh,
> And anon there drops a tear,
> From a sorrow-clouded eye,
> And a heart sorrow-laden,
>   A long, long sigh,
> For the cold strange eyes of a little mermaiden,
> And the gleam of her golden hair.

Come away, children, come down. We will be happy in our bright home under the sea—happy, though the cruel one leaves us lonely for ever. Yet we too, sometimes at midnight, when winds blow softly, and the moonlight falls clear,

> Up the still glistening beaches,
> Up the creeks we will hie,
> Over banks of bright sea-weed
> The ebb-tide leaves dry.
> We will gaze from the sand hills
> At the white sleeping town,
> At the church on the hill side;
>   And then come back down,—
> Singing, 'there dwells a loved one,
> But cruel is she,
> She left lonely for ever
> The Kings of the Sea.'

It is a beautiful poem, certainly; and deserves to have been given at full length. "The Strayed Reveller" itself is more ambitious, perhaps a little strained. It is a pleasing and significant imagination, however, to present to us Circe and Ulysses in colloquy with a stray youth from the train of Bacchus, who drinks eagerly the cup of the enchantress, not as did the sailors of the Ithacan king, for gross pleasure, but for the sake of the glorious and superhuman vision and knowledge it imparts.

> 'But I, Ulysses,
> Sitting on the warm steps,
> Looking over the valley,

All day long have seen,
Without pain, without labor,
Sometimes a wild-haired maenad,
Sometimes a Faun with torches."

But now, we are fain to ask, where are we, and whither are we unconsciously come? Were we not going forth to battle in the armor of a righteous purpose, with our first friend, with Alexander Smith? How is it we find ourselves here, reflecting, pondering, hesitating, musing, complaining, with "A." As the wanderer at night, standing under a stormy sky, listening to the wild harmonies of winds, and watching the wild movements of the clouds, the tree-tops, or possibly the waves, may, with a few steps, very likely, pass into a lighted sitting-room, and a family circle, with pictures and books, and literary leisure, and ornaments, and elegant small employments,—a scene how dissimilar to that other, and yet how entirely natural also;—so it often happens too with books. You have been reading Burns, and you take up Cowper. You feel at home, how strangely! in both of them. Can both be the true thing? and if so, in what new form can we express the relation, the harmony, between them? Such a discrepancy there certainly does exist between the two books that have been before us here. We close the one and open the other, and feel ourselves moving to and fro between two totally different, repugnant, and hostile theories of life. Are we to try and reconcile them, or judge between them?

May we escape from all the difficulty by a mere quotation, and pronounce with the shepherd of Virgil,

"Non nostrum inter vos tantas componere lites
Et vitulâ tu dignus, et hic." [1]

Or will the reader be content to bow down with us in this place, and acknowledge the presence of that highest object of worship among the modern Germans, an *antinomy*.[2] (That is, O unlearned reader, ignorant, not impossibly, of Kant and the modern German religion,—in brief, a contradiction in terms, the ordinary *phenomenal* form of a *noumenal*[3] Verity; as, for example, *the world must have had a beginning,* and, *the world cannot have had a beginning,* in the transcendental fusion or confusion of which consists the Intelligible or unintelligible truth.) Will you be content, O reader, to plod in German manner over miles of a straight road, that seems to lead somewhere, with the prospect of arriving at last at some point where it will divide at equal angles, and lead equally in two opposite directions, where you may therefore safely pause, and thankfully set up your rest, and adore in sacred doubt the Supreme Bifurcation? Or do you hold, with Voltaire, who said (*apropos* of the question then debated among the French wits, whether there were or were not a God) that "after all, one must take a side"?

With all respect for the Antinomies and Germans, and "most distinguished consideration" for Voltaire and Parisian persiflage, still, it may not be quite necessary for us, on the present occasion, either to stand still in transcendental doubt, or toss up, as it were, for our side. Individuals differ in character, capacity, and positions; and, according to their circumstances, will combine, in every possible variety of degree, the two elements of thoughtful discriminating selection and rejection, and frank and bold acceptance of what lies around them. Between the extremes of ascetic and timid self-culture, and of unquestioning, unhesitating confidence, we may

---

[1] *Eclogues* 3.108–09: "It is not within our power to determine the strife between you: you are both worthy of the heifer."

[2] a contradiction or inconsistency between two apparently reasonable principles or laws.

[3] In the transcendental philosophy of Immanuel Kant (1724–1804), the noumenon is essence beyond human comprehension; the phenomenon is the form of the noumenon apprehensible to humans through the senses and reason.

consent to see and tolerate every kind and gradation of intermixture. Nevertheless, upon the whole, for the present age, the lessons of reflectiveness and the maxims of caution do not appear to be more needful or more appropriate than exhortations to steady courage and calls to action. There is something certainly of an over-educated weakness of purpose in Western Europe—not in Germany only, or France, but also in more busy England. There is a disposition to press too far the finer and subtler intellectual and moral susceptibilities; to insist upon following out, as they say, to their logical consequences, the notices of some single organ of the spiritual nature; a proceeding which perhaps is hardly more sensible in the grown man than it would be in the infant to refuse to correct the sensations of sight by those of the touch. Upon the whole, we are disposed to follow out, if we must follow out at all, the analogy of the bodily senses; we are inclined to accept rather than investigate; and to put our confidence less in arithmetic and antinomies, than in

A few strong instincts and a few plain rules.[1]

Let us remark also in the minor Poems, which accompany Empedocles, a disposition, perhaps, to assign too high a place to what is called Nature. It may indeed be true, as the astronomers say, though after all it is no very great piece of knowledge, that the heavenly bodies describe ellipses; and go on, from and to all the ages, performing that self-repeating, unattaining curve. But does it, therefore, of necessity follow that human souls do something analogous in the spiritual spaces? Number is a wonderful thing, and the laws of nature sublime; nevertheless, have we not a sort of intuition of the existence, even in our own poor human selves, of something akin to a Power superior to, and transcending, all manifestations of Nature, all intelligible forms of Number and

---

[1] from Wordsworth's sonnet, "Alas, what boots the long laborious quest."

Law. We quote one set of verses, in which our author does appear to have escaped for once from the dismal cycle of his rehabilitated Hindoo-Greek theosophy—

MORALITY.

We cannot kindle when we will
The fire that in the heart resides,
The spirit bloweth and is still,
In mystery our soul abides;—
    But tasks, in hours of insight willed,
Can be through hours of gloom fulfilled.

With aching hands and bleeding feet
We dig and heap, lay stone on stone;
We bear the burden and the heat
Of the long day, and wish 'twere done.
    Not till the hours of light return,
All we have built do we discern.

Then when the clouds are off the soul,
When thou dost look in Nature's eye,
Ask how *she* viewed thy self-control,
Thy struggling tasked morality—
    Nature whose free, light, cheerful air,
Oft made thee, in thy gloom despair.

And she, whose censure thou dost dread,
Whose eye thou wert afraid to seek,—
See, on her face a glow is spread,
A strong emotion on her cheek.
    'Ah child,' she cries, 'that strife divine,
Whence was it, for it is not mine?

There is no effort on my brow—
I do not strive, I do not weep;
I rush with the swift spheres, and glow
In joy, and when I will, I sleep,—
    Yet that severe, that earnest air,
I saw, I felt it once more, but where?

I knew not yet the gauge of Time,
Nor wore the manacles of space,—
I felt it in some other clime,

I saw it in some other place.
    'T was when the heavenly house I trod,
And lay upon the breast of God.'

In youth from rock to rock I went
    With pleasure high and turbulent,—
        Most pleased, when most uneasy.[2]

It is wonderful what stores of really valuable thought may lie neglected in a book, simply because they are not put in that form which serves our present occasions. But if we have been inclined to yield to a preference for the picture of simple, strong, and certain, rather than of subtle, shifting, and dubious feelings, and in point of tone and matter to go along with the young mechanic, in point of diction and manner, we must certainly assign the palm to "A," in spite of a straining after the rounded Greek form, such as, to some extent, vitiates even the style of Milton. Alexander Smith lies open to much graver critical carping. He writes, it would almost seem, under the impression that the one business of the poet is to coin metaphors and similes. He tells them out as a clerk might sovereigns at the Bank of England. So many comparisons, so much poetry; it is the sterling currency of the realm. Yet he is most pleased, perhaps, when he can double or treble a similitude; speaking of A, he will call it a B, which is, as it were, the C of a D. By some maturer effort we may expect to be thus conducted even to Z. But simile within simile, after the manner of Chinese boxes, are more curious than beautiful; nor is it the true aim of the poet, as of the Italian boy in the street, to poise upon his head, for public exhibition, a board crowded as thick as they can stand with images, big and little, black and white, of anybody and everybody, in any possible order of disorder, as they happen to pack. *Tanquam scopulum, insolens verbum,*[1] says the precept of ancient taste, which our author seems to accept freely, with the modern comment of—

The movement of his poem is indeed rapid enough; there is a sufficient impetus to carry us over a good deal of rough and "rocky" ground; there is a real continuity of poetic purpose;—but it is so perpetually presumed upon; the attention, which the reader desires to devote to the pursuit of the main drift of what calls itself a single poem, *simplex et unum,* is so incessantly called off to look at this [and look at] that; when, for example, we would fain follow the thought and feeling of Violet and Walter, we are with such peremptory and frequent eagerness summoned to observe how like the sky is to *x* and the stars are to *y*, that on the whole, though there is a real continuity of purpose, we cannot be surprised that the critic of the London Examiner failed to detect it. Keats and Shelley, and Coleridge, perhaps, before them, with their extravagant love for Elizabethan phraseology, have led to this mischief. Has not Tennyson followed a little too much in their train? Coleridge, we suppose, would have maintained it to be an excellence in the "myriad-minded" dramatist, that he so often diverts us from the natural course of thought, feeling, and narrative, to see how curiously two trifles resemble each other, or that, in a passage of deep pathos, he still finds time to apprise us of a paronomasia.[3] But faults which disfigure Shakespeare are not beauties in a modern volume.

I rot upon the waters when my prow
    Should *grate* the golden isles

may be a very Elizabethan, but is certainly rather a vicious expression. Force and condensation are good, but it is possible to combine them with purity of phrase. One of the most successful delineations in the

---

[1] a saying of Julius Caesar: "Avoid an unusual word as a pilot would a dangerous rock."

[2] from Wordsworth's "To a Daisy."

[3] the act of punning.

whole poem is contained in the following passage, which introduces scene VII.

> [A balcony overlooking the sea.]
> The lark is singing in the blinding sky,—
> Hedges are white with May. The bridegroom sea
> Is toying with the shore, his wedded bride,
> And in the fulness of his marriage joy,
> He decorates her tawny front with shells—
> Retires a space to see how fair she looks,
> Then proud, runs up to kiss her. All is fair,—
> All glad, from grass to sun. Yet more I love
> Than this, the shrinking day that sometimes comes
> In winter's front, so fair 'mongst its dark peers,
> It seems a straggler from the files of June,
> Which in its wanderings had lost its wits,
> And half its beauty, and when it returned,
> Finding its old companions gone away,
> It joined November's troop, then marching past;
> And so the frail thing comes, and greets the world
> With a thin crazy smile, then bursts in tears—
> And all the while it holds within its hand
> A few half-withered flowers;—I love and pity it.

It may be the fault of our point of view; but certainly we do not find even here that happy, unimpeded sequence which is the charm of really good writers. Is there not something incongruous in the effect of the immediate juxtaposition of these two images? We have lost, it may be, that impetuosity, that *élan*, which lifts the young reader over hedge and ditch at flying leaps, across country,—or we should not perhaps entertain any offence, or even surprise, at being transferred *per saltum*[1] from the one field to the other. But we could almost ask, was the passage, so beautiful, though perhaps a little prolonged, about the June day in November, written consecutively, and in one flow, with the previous, and also beautiful one about ocean and his bride. We dare say it was; but it does not read, somehow, in the same straight line with it,—

---

[1] at a bound.

Tantum series juncturaque pollet.[2]

We venture, too, to record a perhaps hypercritical objection to "the *blinding* sky" in this particular collocation. Perhaps in the first line of a scene, while the reader has not yet warmed to his duty, simplicity should be especially observed;—a single image, without any repeated reflection, so to speak, in a second mirror, should suffice. The following, which open scene XI., are better.

> "Summer hath murmured with her leafy lips
> Around my home, and I have heard her not;
> I've missed the process of three several years
> From shaking wind flowers to the tarnished gold
> That rustles sere on Autumn's aged limbs."

Except the last two lines. Our author will not keep his eye steady upon the thing before him; he goes off, and distracts us, and breaks the impression he had begun to succeed in giving, by bidding us look now at something else. Some simpler epithets that *shaking*, and some plainer language than *tarnished gold* or *aged limbs*, would have done the work better. We are quite prepared to believe that these faults and these *disagreeables* have personally been necessities to the writer, are awkwardnesses of growth, of which the full stature may show no trace. He should be assured, however, that though the rude vigor of the style of his Life-Drama may attract upon the first reading, yet in any case, it is not the sort of writing which people recur to with pleasure and fall back upon with satisfaction. It may be a groundless fancy, yet we do fancy, that there is a whole hemisphere, so to say, of the English language which he has left unvisited. His diction feels to us, as if between Milton and Burns he had not read, and between Shakespeare and Keats had seldom admired. Certainly there is but little inspiration in the compositions of the last century;

---

[2] Horace, *Ars Poetica*, l. 242: Clough's point is that everything must be part of a simple whole.

yet English was really best and most naturally written, when there was, perhaps, least to write about. To obtain a real command of the language, some familiarity with the prose writers, at any rate, of that period, is almost essential; and to write out, as a mere daily task, passages, for example, of Goldsmith, would do a verse-composer of the nineteenth century as much good, we believe, as the study of Beaumont and Fletcher.[1]

—1855

---

[1] Clough's concluding remarks on two minor poets are omitted here.

Matthew Arnold
1822 – 1888

Matthew Arnold, son of Thomas Arnold, headmaster of the famous public school Rugby from 1828 to 1842, was a poet and prose writer, traditionally ranked with Browning and Tennyson as one of the most important poets of the Victorian age. But unlike Browning and Tennyson, Arnold could not sustain his poetic impulse. His poetry, which he began publishing early in his career, reflected a deep sense of personal insecurity, barrenness, and even a note of resigned despair. These traits are evident in *The Strayed Reveller and Other Poems* (1849), *Empedocles on Etna and Other Poems* (1852), and "Thyrsis" (1866), an elegy on the death of his friend Arthur Hugh Clough. After 1855 Arnold wrote very little poetry, turning instead to the production of a great deal of high quality prose including literary criticism, political and cultural commentary, and religious writings. His most important work in cultural commentary is *Culture and Anarchy* (1869).

❧

Preface to the First Edition of Poems

(1853)

In two small volumes of Poems, published anonymously, one in 1849, the other in 1852, many of the Poems which compose the present volume have already appeared. The rest are now published for the first time.

I have, in the present collection, omitted the Poem from which the volume published in 1852 took its title.[1] I have done so, not because the subject of it was a Sicilian Greek born between two and three thousand years ago, although many persons would think this a sufficient reason. Neither have I done so because I had, in my own opinion, failed in the delineation which I intended to effect. I intended to delineate the feelings of one of the last of the Greek religious philosophers, one of the family of Orpheus and Musaeus,[2] having survived his fellows, living on into a time when the habits of Greek thought and feeling had begun fast to change, character to dwindle, the influence of the Sophists[3] to prevail. Into the feelings of a man so situated there entered much that we are accustomed to consider as exclusively modern; how much, the fragments of Empedocles himself which remain to us are sufficient at least to indicate. What those who are familiar only with the great monuments of early Greek genius suppose to be its exclusive characteristics, have disappeared; the calm, the cheerfulness, the disinterested objectivity have disappeared; the dialogue of the mind with itself has commenced; modern problems have presented themselves; we hear already the doubts, we witness the discouragement, of Hamlet and of Faust.

The representations of such a man's feelings must be interesting, if consistently drawn. We all naturally take pleasure, says Aristotle,[4] in any imitation or representation whatever: this is the basis of our love of Poetry: and we take pleasure in them, he adds, because all knowledge is naturally agreeable to us; not to the philosopher only, but to mankind at large. Every representation therefore which is consistently drawn may be supposed to be interesting, inasmuch as it gratifies this natural interest in knowledge of all kinds. What is *not* interesting, is that which does not

---

[1] "Empedocles on Etna." Arnold's "Preface" is extremely important and self-revealing, as Arnold uses it to rationalize his exclusion of his most important poem from the 1853 volume.

[2] legendary Greek poets and musicians. Orpheus was the father of Musaeus.

[3] Greek teachers of philosophy who were masters of sophistical reasoning.

[4] *Poetics* 4.2–5.

add to our knowledge of any kind; that which is vaguely conceived and loosely drawn; a representation which is general, indeterminate, and faint, instead of being particular, precise, and firm.

Any accurate representation may therefore be expected to be interesting; but, if the representation be a poetical one, more than this is demanded. It is demanded, not only that it shall interest, but also that it shall inspirit and rejoice the reader: that it shall convey a charm, and infuse delight. For the Muses, as Hesiod says,[1] were born that they might be "a forget-fulness of evils, and a truce from cares": and it is not enough that the Poet should add to the knowledge of men, it is required of him also that he should add to their happiness. "All Art," says Schiller,[2] "is dedicated to Joy, and there is no higher and no more serious problem, than how to make men happy. The right Art is that alone, which creates the highest enjoyment."

A poetical work, therefore, is not yet justified when it has been shown to be an accurate, and therefore interesting representation; it has to be shown also that it is a representation from which men can derive enjoyment. In presence of the most tragic circumstances, represented in a work of Art, the feeling of enjoyment, as is well known, may still subsist: the representation of the most utter calamity, of the liveliest anguish, is not sufficient to destroy it: the more tragic the situation, the deeper becomes the enjoyment; and the situation is more tragic in proportion as it becomes more terrible.

What then are the situations, from the representation of which, though accurate, no poetical enjoyment can be derived? They are those in which the suffering finds no vent in action; in which a continuous state of mental distress is prolonged, unrelieved by incident, hope, or resistance; in which there is everything to be endured, nothing to be done. In such situations there is inevitably something morbid, in the description of them something monotonous. When they occur in actual life, they are painful, not tragic; the representation of them in poetry is painful also.

To this class of situations, poetically faulty as it appears to me, that of Empedocles, as I have endeavored to represent him, belongs; and I have therefore excluded the Poem from the present collection.

And why, it may be asked, have I entered into this explanation respecting a matter so unimportant as the admission or exclusion of the Poem in question? I have done so, because I was anxious to avow that the sole reason for its exclusion was that which has been stated above; and that it has not been excluded in deference to the opinion which many critics of the present day appear to entertain against subjects chosen from distant times and countries: against the choice, in short, of any subjects but modern ones.

"The Poet," it is said,[3] and by an intelligent critic, "the Poet who would really fix the public attention must leave the exhausted past, and draw his subjects from matters of present import, and *therefore* both of interest and novelty."

Now this view I believe to be completely false. It is worth examining, inasmuch as it is a fair sample of a class of critical dicta everywhere current at the present day, having a philosophical form and air, but no real basis in fact; and which are calculated to vitiate the judgment of readers of poetry, while they exert, so far as they are adopted, a misleading influence on the practice of those who make it.

What are the eternal objects of Poetry, among all nations and at all times? They are actions; human actions; possessing an inherent interest in themselves, and which are to be communicated in an interesting manner by the art of the Poet. Vainly will the latter imagine that he has everything in his own power; that

---

[1] early Greek poet in his *Theogony*, ll. 54–56.

[2] German poet and critic of the Romantic period.

[3] "In *The Spectator* of April 2nd, 1853. The words quoted were not used with reference to poems of mine." (Arnold's note.) The critic was R.S. Rintoul, the editor of the magazine.

he can make an intrinsically inferior action equally delightful with a more excellent one by his treatment of it; he may indeed compel us to admire his skill, but his work will possess, within itself, an incurable defect.

The Poet, then, has in the first place to select an excellent action; and what actions are the most excellent? Those, certainly, which most powerfully appeal to the great primary human affections: to those elementary feelings which subsist permanently in the race, and which are independent of time. These feelings are permanent and the same; that which interests them is permanent and the same also. The modernness or antiquity of an action, therefore, has nothing to do with its fitness for poetical representation; this depends upon its inherent qualities. To the elementary part of our nature, to our passions, that which is great and passionate is eternally interesting; and interesting solely in proportion to its greatness and to its passion. A great human action of a thousand years ago is more interesting to it than a smaller human action of to-day, even though upon the representation of this last the most consummate skill may have been expended, and though it has the advantage of appealing by its modern language, familiar manners, and contemporary allusions, to all our transient feelings and interests. These, however, have no right to demand of a poetical work that it shall satisfy them; their claims are to be directed elsewhere. Poetical works belong to the domain of our permanent passions: let them interest these, and the voice of all subordinate claims upon them is at once silenced.

Achilles, Prometheus, Clytemnestra, Dido—what modern poem presents personages as interesting, even to us moderns, as these personages of an "exhausted past"? We have the domestic epic dealing with the details of modern life which pass daily under our eyes; we have poems representing modern personages in contact with the problems of modern life, moral, intellectual, and social; these works have been pro-

duced by poets the most distinguished of their nation and time; yet I fearlessly assert that *Hermann and Dorothea, Childe Harold, Jocelyn,* the *Excursion,*[1] leave the reader cold in comparison with the effect produced upon him by the later books of the *Iliad,* by the *Oresteia,* or by the episode of Dido.[2] And why is this? Simply because in the three last-named cases the action is greater, the personages nobler, the situations more intense: and this is the true basis of the interest in a poetical work, and this alone.

It may be urged, however, that past actions may be interesting in themselves, but that they are not to be adopted by the modern Poet, because it is impossible for him to have them clearly present to his own mind, and he cannot therefore feel them deeply, nor represent them forcibly. But this is not necessarily the case. The externals of a past action, indeed, he cannot know with the precision of a contemporary; but his business is with its essentials. The outward man of Oedipus[3] or of Macbeth, the houses in which they lived, the ceremonies of their courts, he cannot accurately figure to himself; but neither do they essentially concern him. His business is with their inward man; with their feelings and behaviour in certain tragic situations, which engage their passions as men; these have in them nothing local and casual; they are as accessible to the modern Poet as to a contemporary.

The date of an action, then, signifies nothing: the action itself, its selection and construction, this is what is all-important. This the Greeks understood far more clearly than we do. The radical difference between their poetical theory and ours consists, as it appears to me, in this: that, with them, the poetical character of the action in itself, and the conduct of it, was the first consideration; with us, attention is fixed

---

[1] narrative and philosophical poems by Goethe, Byron, Lamartine, and Wordsworth.

[2] Clytemnestra, the wife of Agamemnon, is in Aeschylus's *Oresteia*; Dido in Virgil's *Aeneid,* Book 4.

[3] king of Thebes and hero of Sophocles's *Oedipus Tyrannus.*

mainly on the value of the separate thoughts and images which occur in the treatment of an action. They regarded the whole; we regard the parts. With them, the action predominated over the expression of it; with us, the expression predominates over the action. Not that they failed in expression or were inattentive to it; on the contrary, they are the highest models of expression, the unapproached masters of the *grand style*:[1] but their expression is so excellent because it is so admirably kept in its right degree of prominence; because it is so simple and so well subordinated; because it draws its force directly from the pregnancy of the matter which it conveys. For what reason was the Greek tragic poet confined to so limited a range of subjects? Because there are so few actions which unite in themselves, in the highest degree, the conditions of excellence: and it was not thought that on any but an excellent subject could an excellent Poem be constructed. A few actions, therefore, eminently adapted for tragedy, maintained almost exclusive possession of the Greek tragic stage; their significance appeared inexhaustible; they were as permanent problems, perpetually offered to the genius of every fresh poet. This too is the reason of what appears to us moderns a certain baldness of expression in Greek tragedy; of the triviality with which we often reproach the remarks of the chorus, where it takes part in the dialogue: that the action itself, the situation of Orestes, or Merope, or Alcmaeon,[2] was to stand the central point of interest, unforgotten, absorbing, principal; that no accessories were for a moment to distract the spectator's attention from this; that the tone of the parts was to be perpetually kept down, in order not to impair the grandiose effect of the whole. The terrible old mythic story on which the drama was founded stood, before he entered the theatre, traced in its bare outlines upon the spectator's mind; it stood in his memory, as

a group of statuary, faintly seen, at the end of a long and dark vista: then came the Poet, embodying outlines, developing situations, not a word wasted, not a sentiment capriciously thrown in: stroke upon stroke, the drama proceeded: the light deepened upon the group; more and more it revealed itself to the rivetted gaze of the spectator: until at last, when the final words were spoken, it stood before him in broad sunlight, a model of immortal beauty.

This was what a Greek critic demanded; this was what a Greek poet endeavored to effect. It signified nothing to what time an action belonged; we do not find that the *Persae*[3] occupied a particularly high rank among the dramas of Aeschylus because it represented a matter of contemporary interest: this was not what a cultivated Athenian required; he required that the permanent elements of his nature should be moved; and dramas of which the action, though taken from a long-distant mythic time, yet was calculated to accomplish this in a higher degree than that of the *Persae*, stood higher in his estimation accordingly. The Greeks felt, no doubt, with their exquisite sagacity of taste, that an action of present times was too near them, too much mixed up with what was accidental and passing, to form a sufficiently grand, detached, and self-subsistent object for a tragic poem: such objects belonged to the domain of the comic poet, and of the lighter kinds of poetry. For the more serious kinds, for *pragmatic* poetry, to use an excellent expression of Polybius,[4] they were more difficult and severe in the range of subjects which they permitted. Their theory and practice alike, the admirable treatise of Aristotle, and the unrivalled works of their poets, exclaim with a thousand tongues—"All depends upon the subject; choose a fitting action, penetrate yourself with the

---

[1]   noble, heroic, or great.

[2]   three heroic characters in Greek tragedies, each of whom avenged the murder of some member of his family.

[3]   a tragedy written by Aeschylus, produced in 472 BC.

[4]   Greek historian. Pragmatic poetry is poetry concerned with matters of everyday life.

feeling of its situations; this done, everything else will follow."

But for all kinds of poetry alike there was one point on which they were rigidly exacting; the adaptability of the subject to the kind of poetry selected, and the careful construction of the poem.

How different a way of thinking from this is ours! We can hardly at the present day understand what Menander [1] meant, when he told a man who inquired as to the progress of his comedy that he had finished it, not having yet written a single line, because he had constructed the action of it in his mind. A modern critic would have assured him that the merit of his piece depended on the brilliant things which arose under his pen as he went along. We have poems which seem to exist merely for the sake of single lines and passages; not for the sake of producing any total-impression. We have critics who seem to direct their attention merely to detached expressions, to the language about the action, not to the action itself. I verily think that the majority of them do not in their hearts believe that there is such a thing as a total-impression to be derived from a poem at all, or to be demanded from a poet; they think the term a common-place of metaphysical criticism. They will permit the Poet to select any action he pleases, and to suffer that action to go as it will, provided he gratifies them with occasional bursts of fine writing, and with a shower of isolated thoughts and images. That is, they permit him to leave their poetical sense ungratified, provided that he gratifies their rhetorical sense and their curiosity. Of his neglecting to gratify these, there is little danger; he needs rather to be warned against the danger of attempting to gratify these alone; he needs rather to be perpetually reminded to prefer his action to everything else; so to treat this, as to permit its inherent excellences to develop themselves, without interruption from the intrusion of his personal peculiarities: most fortunate, when he most

entirely succeeds in effacing himself, and in enabling a noble action to subsist as it did in nature.

But the modern critic not only permits a false practice; he absolutely prescribes false aims.—"A true allegory of the state of one's own mind in a representative history," the Poet is told, "is perhaps the highest thing that one can attempt in the way of poetry."[2]—And accordingly he attempts it. An allegory of the state of one's own mind, the highest problem of an art which imitates actions! No assuredly, it is not, it never can be so: no great poetical work has ever been produced with such an aim. *Faust* itself, in which something of the kind is attempted, wonderful passages as it contains, and in spite of the unsurpassed beauty of the scenes which relate to Margaret, *Faust* itself, judged as a whole, and judged strictly as a poetical work, is defective: its illustrious author, the greatest poet of modern times, the greatest critic of all times, would have been the first to acknowledge it; he only defended his work, indeed, by asserting it to be "something incommensurable."

The confusion of the present times is great, the multitude of voices counselling different things bewildering, the number of existing works capable of attracting a young writer's attention and of becoming his models, immense: what he wants is a hand to guide him through the confusion, a voice to prescribe to him the aim which he should keep in view, and to explain to him that the value of the literary works which offer themselves to his attention is relative to their power of helping him forward on his road towards this aim. Such a guide the English writer at the present day will nowhere find. Failing this, all that can be looked for, all indeed that can be desired, is, that his attention should be fixed on excellent models; that he may reproduce, at any rate, something of their excellence, by penetrating himself with their works and by catching their spirit, if he cannot be taught to produce what is excellent independently.

---

[1] Greek comic dramatist (342?–292 BC).

[2] David Masson, in the *North British Review*, August, 1853.

Foremost among these models for the English writer stands Shakespeare: a name the greatest perhaps of all poetical names; a name never to be mentioned without reverence. I will venture, however, to express a doubt whether the influence of his works, excellent and fruitful for the readers of poetry, for the great majority, has been of unmixed advantage to the writers of it. Shakespeare indeed chose excellent subjects—the world could afford no better than *Macbeth*, or *Romeo and Juliet*, or *Othello*: he had no theory respecting the necessity of choosing subjects of present import, or the paramount interest attaching to allegories of the state of one's own mind; like all great poets, he knew well what constituted a poetical action; like them, wherever he found such an action, he took it; like them, too, he found his best in past times. But to these general characteristics of all great poets he added a special one of his own; a gift, namely, of happy, abundant, and ingenious expression, eminent and unrivalled: so eminent as irresistibly to strike the attention first in him, and even to throw into comparative shade his other excellences as a poet. Here has been the mischief. These other excellences were his fundamental excellences *as a poet*; what distinguishes the artist from the mere amateur, says Goethe, is *Architectonicè* in the highest sense; that power of execution, which creates, forms, and constitutes: not the profoundness of single thoughts, not the richness of imagery, not the abundance of illustration. But these attractive accessories of a poetical work being more easily seized than the spirit of the whole, and these accessories being possessed by Shakespeare in an unequalled degree, a young writer having recourse to Shakespeare as his model runs great risk of being vanquished and absorbed by them, and, in consequence, of reproducing, according to the measure of his power, these, and these alone. Of this preponderating quality of Shakespeare's genius, accordingly, almost the whole of modern English poetry has, it appears to me, felt the influence. To the exclusive attention on the part of his imitators to this

it is in a great degree owing, that of the majority of modern poetical works the details alone are valuable, the composition worthless. In reading them one is perpetually reminded of that terrible sentence on a modern French poet—*il dit tout ce qu'il veut, mais malheureusement il n'a rien à dire.*[1]

Let me give an instance of what I mean. I will take it from the works of the very chief among those who seem to have been formed in the school of Shakespeare: of one whose exquisite genius and pathetic death render him for ever interesting. I will take the poem of *Isabella, or the Pot of Basil*, by Keats. I choose this rather than the *Endymion*, because the latter work (which a modern critic has classed with the *Fairy Queen!*), although undoubtedly there blows through it the breath of genius, is yet as a whole so utterly incoherent, as not strictly to merit the name of a poem at all. The poem of *Isabella*, then, is a perfect treasure-house of graceful and felicitous words and images: almost in every stanza there occurs one of those vivid and picturesque turns of expression, by which the object is made to flash upon the eye of the mind, and which thrill the reader with a sudden delight. This one short poem contains, perhaps, a greater number of happy single expressions which one could quote than all the extant tragedies of Sophocles. But the action, the story? The action in itself is an excellent one; but so feebly is it conceived by the Poet, so loosely constructed, that the effect produced by it, in and for itself, is absolutely null. Let the reader, after he has finished the poem of Keats, turn to the same story in the *Decameron*:[2] he will then feel how pregnant and interesting the same action has become in the hands of a great artist, who above all things delineates his object; who subordinates expression to that which it is designed to express.

---

[1] "He says all he wishes to, but unfortunately he has nothing to say." The poet referred to is Théophile Gautier, the leader of the French school of Art for Art's Sake.

[2] by Boccaccio.

I have said that the imitators of Shakespeare, fixing their attention on his wonderful gift of expression, have directed their imitation to this, neglecting his other excellences. These excellences, the fundamental excellences of poetical art, Shakespeare no doubt possessed them—possessed many of them in a splendid degree; but it may perhaps be doubted whether even he himself did not sometimes give scope to his faculty of expression to the prejudice of a higher poetical duty. For we must never forget that Shakespeare is the great poet he is from his skill in discerning and firmly conceiving an excellent action, from his power of intensely feeling a situation, of intimately associating himself with a character; not from his gift of expression, which rather even leads him astray, degenerating sometimes into a fondness for curiosity of expression, into an irritability of fancy, which seems to make it impossible for him to say a thing plainly, even when the press of the action demands the very directest language, or its level character the very simplest. Mr. Hallam,[1] than whom it is impossible to find a saner and more judicious critic, has had the courage (for at the present day it needs courage) to remark, how extremely and faultily difficult Shakespeare's language often is. It is so: you may find main scenes in some of his greatest tragedies, *King Lear* for instance, where the language is so artificial, so curiously tortured, and so difficult, that every speech has to be read two or three times before its meaning can be comprehended. This over-curiousness of expression is indeed but the excessive employment of a wonderful gift—of the power of saying a thing in a happier way than any other man; nevertheless, it is carried so far that one understands what M. Guizot[2] meant, when he said that Shakespeare appears in his language to have tried all styles except that of simplicity. He has not the severe and

scrupulous self-restraint of the ancients, partly no doubt, because he had a far less cultivated and exacting audience: he has indeed a far wider range than they had, a far richer fertility of thought; in this respect he rises above them: in his strong conception of his subject, in the genuine way in which he is penetrated with it, he resembles them, and is unlike the moderns: but in the accurate limitation of it, the conscientious rejection of superfluities, the simple and rigorous development of it from the first line of his work to the last, he falls below them, and comes nearer to the moderns. In his chief works, besides what he has of his own, he has the elementary soundness of the ancients; he has their important action and their large and broad manner: but he has not their purity of method. He is therefore a less safe model; for what he has of his own is personal, and inseparable from his own rich nature; it may be imitated and exaggerated, it cannot be learned or applied as an art; he is above all suggestive; more valuable, therefore, to young writers as men than as artists. But clearness of arrangement, rigour of development, simplicity of style—these may to a certain extent be learned: and these may, I am convinced, be learned best from the ancients, who although infinitely less suggestive than Shakespeare, are thus, to the artist, more instructive.

What then, it will be asked, are the ancients to be our sole models? the ancients with their comparatively narrow range of experience, and their widely different circumstances? Not, certainly, that which is narrow in the ancients, nor that in which we can no longer sympathize. An action like the action of the *Antigone* of Sophocles, which turns upon the conflict between the heroine's duty to her brother's corpse and that to the laws of her country, is no longer one in which it is possible that we should feel a deep interest. I am speaking too, it will be remembered, not of the best sources of intellectual stimulus for the general reader, but of the best models of instruction for the individual writer. This last may certainly learn

---

[1] Henry Hallam (1777–1859), in his *Introduction to the Literature of Europe in the Fifteenth, Sixteenth, and Seventeenth Centuries.*

[2] French historian (1787–1874), in his preface to *Shakespeare and His Time.*

of the ancients, better than anywhere else, three things which it is vitally important for him to know:—the all-importance of the choice of a subject; the necessity of accurate construction; and the subordinate character of expression. He will learn from them how unspeakably superior is the effect of the one moral impression left by a great action treated as a whole, to the effect produced by the most striking single thought or by the happiest image. As he penetrates into the spirit of the great classical works, as he becomes gradually aware of their intense significance, their noble simplicity, and their calm pathos, he will be convinced that it is this effect, unity and profoundness of moral impression, at which the ancient Poets aimed; that it is this which constitutes the grandeur of their works, and which makes them immortal. He will desire to direct his own efforts towards producing the same effect. Above all, he will deliver himself from the jargon of modern criticism, and escape the danger of producing poetical works conceived in the spirit of the passing time, and which partake of its transitoriness.

The present age makes great claims upon us: we owe it service, it will not be satisfied without our admiration. I know not how it is, but their commerce with the ancients appears to me to produce, in those who constantly practise it, a steadying and composing effect upon their judgment, not of literary works only, but of men and events in general. They are like persons who have had a very weighty and impressive experience; they are more truly than others under the empire of facts, and more independent of the language current among those with whom they live. They wish neither to applaud nor to revile their age: they wish to know what it is, what it can give them, and whether this is what they want. What they want, they know very well; they want to educe and cultivate what is best and noblest in themselves: they know, too, that this is no easy task—χαλεπὸν as Pittacus

said, χαλεπὸν ἐσθλὸν ἔμμεαι[1]—and they ask themselves sincerely whether their age and its literature can assist them in the attempt. If they are endeavouring to practise any art, they remember the plain and simple proceedings of the old artists, who attained their grand results by penetrating themselves with some noble and significant action, not by inflating themselves with a belief in the pre-eminent importance and greatness of their own times. They do not talk of their mission, nor of interpreting their age, nor of the coming Poet; all this, they know, is the mere delirium of vanity; their business is not to praise their age, but to afford to the men who live in it the highest pleasure which they are capable of feeling. If asked to afford this by means of subjects drawn from the age itself, they ask what special fitness the present age has for supplying them: they are told that it is an era of progress, an age commissioned to carry out the great ideas of industrial development and social amelioration. They reply that with all this they can do nothing; that the elements they need for the exercise of their art are great actions, calculated powerfully and delightfully to affect what is permanent in the human soul; that so far as the present age can supply such actions, they will gladly make use of them; but that an age wanting in moral grandeur can with difficulty supply such, and an age of spiritual discomfort with difficulty be powerfully and delightfully affected by them.

A host of voices will indignantly rejoin that the present age is inferior to the past neither in moral grandeur nor in spiritual health. He who possesses the discipline I speak of will content himself with remembering the judgements passed upon the present age, in this respect, by the two men, the one of strongest head, the other of widest culture, whom it has produced; by Goethe and by Niebuhr.[2] It will be sufficient for him that he knows the opinions held by

---

[1] "It is hard to be excellent." Pittacus (seventh century BC) was one of the so-called Seven Sages of Greece.

[2] the German historian of Rome (1776–1831).

these two great men respecting the present age and its literature; and that he feels assured in his own mind that their aims and demands upon life were such as he would wish, at any rate, his own to be; and their judgement as to what is impeding and disabling such as he may safely follow. He will not, however, maintain a hostile attitude towards the false pretensions of his age; he will content himself with not being overwhelmed by them. He will esteem himself fortunate if he can succeed in banishing from his mind all feelings of contradiction, and irritation, and impatience; in order to delight himself with the contemplation of some noble action of a heroic time, and to enable others, through his representation of it, to delight in it also.

I am far indeed from making any claim, for myself, that I possess this discipline; or for the following Poems, that they breathe its spirit. But I say, that in the sincere endeavour to learn and practise, amid the bewildering confusion of our times, what is sound and true in poetical art, I seemed to myself to find the only sure guidance, the only solid footing, among the ancients. They, at any rate, knew what they wanted in Art, and we do not. It is this uncertainty which is disheartening, and not hostile criticism. How often have I felt this when reading words of disparagement or of cavil: that it is the uncertainty as to what is really to be aimed at which makes our difficulty, not the dissatisfaction of

the critic, who himself suffers from the same uncertainty. *Non me tua fervida terrent Dicta: Dii me terrent, et Jupiter hostis.* [1]

Two kinds of *dilettanti*, says Goethe, there are in poetry: he who neglects the indispensable mechanical part, and thinks he has done enough if he shows spirituality and feeling; and he who seeks to arrive at poetry merely by mechanism, in which he can acquire an artisan's readiness, and is without soul and matter. And he adds, that the first does most harm to Art, and the last to himself. If we must be *dilettanti*: if it is impossible for us, under the circumstances amidst which we live, to think clearly, to feel nobly, and to delineate firmly: if we cannot attain to the mastery of the great artists—let us, at least, have so much respect for our Art as to prefer it to ourselves: let us not bewilder our successors: let us transmit to them the practice of Poetry, with its boundaries and wholesome regulative laws, under which excellent works may again, perhaps, at some future time, be produced, not yet fallen into oblivion through our neglect, not yet condemned and cancelled by the influence of their eternal enemy, Caprice.

—1853

---

[1] "Your hot words do not frighten me....The gods frighten me, and Jupiter as my enemy": *Aeneid* 12.894–95.

John Ruskin
1819 – 1900

John Ruskin was one of the most prolific and important social and aesthetic theorists and critics of the Victorian period. His major early interests were painting and architecture, in part inspired by his youthful travels and his encounters with Italian painting and Gothic architecture. Ruskin's first major work, *Modern Painters* (in five volumes [1834–60]), began as a defence of J.M.W. Turner (1775–1851), the only "Modern" painter, Ruskin believed, who accurately depicted nature in terms of the energy infusing natural form. "Of the Pathetic Fallacy" offers examples of those who deviate from such accuracy. His work on architecture, *The Seven Lamps of Architecture* (1849) and *The Stones of Venice* (1851–53), and his wide-ranging social commentary, e.g. *Unto This Last* (1862) and *Fors Clavigera* (1871–84), continued to articulate his aesthetic and moral concerns.

cↄcↄ

Of the Pathetic Fallacy [1]

1. German dullness and English affectation, have of late much multiplied among us the use of two of the most objectionable words that were ever coined by the troublesomeness of metaphysicians—namely, *objective,* and *subjective.*

No words can be more exquisitely, and in all points, useless; and I merely speak of them that I may, at once and for ever, get them out of my way and out of my readers's. But to get that done, they must be explained.

The word *blue,* say certain philosophers, means the sensation of color which the human eye receives in looking at the open sky, or at a bell gentian.

Now, say they farther, as this sensation can only be felt when the eye is turned to the object, and as, therefore, no such sensation is produced by the object when nobody looks at it, therefore the thing, when it is not looked at, is not blue; and thus (say they) there are many qualities of things which depend as much on something else as on themselves. To be sweet, a thing must have a taster; it is only sweet while it is being tasted, and if the tongue had not capacity of taste, then the sugar would not have the quality of sweetness.

And then they agree that the qualities of things which thus depend upon our perception of them, and upon our human nature as affected by them, shall be called subjective; and the qualities of things which they always have, irrespective of any other nature, as roundness or squareness, shall be called objective.

From these ingenious views the step is very easy to a farther opinion, that it does not much matter what things are in themselves, but only what they are to us; and that the only real truth of them is their appearance to, or effect upon, us. From which position, with a hearty desire for mystification, and much egotism, selfishness, shallowness, and impertinence, a philosopher may easily go so far as to believe, and say, that everything in the world depends upon his seeing or thinking of it, and that nothing, therefore, exists, but what he sees or thinks of.

2. Now, to get rid of all these ambiguities and troublesome words at once, be it observed that the word *blue* does *not* mean the *sensation* caused by a gentian on the human eye; but it means the *power* of producing that sensation: and this power is always there, in the thing, whether we are there to experience it or not, and would remain there though there were not left a man on the face of the earth. Precisely

---

[1] Ruskin's "Of the Pathetic Fallacy" was first published in 1856 in his *Modern Painters*, Vol. 3, Part 4, Chapter 12.

in the same way gunpowder has a power of exploding. It will not explode if you put no match to it. But it has always the power of so exploding, and is therefore called an explosive compound, which it very positively and assuredly is, whatever philosophy may say to the contrary.

In like manner, a gentian does not produce the sensation of blueness if you don't look at it. But it has always the power of doing so; its particles being everlastingly so arranged by its Maker. And, therefore, the gentian and the sky are always verily blue, whatever philosophy may say to the contrary; and if you do not see them blue when you look at them, it is not their fault, but yours.[1]

3. Hence I would say to these philosophers: If, instead of using the sonorous phrase, *It is objectively so,* you will use the plain old phrase, *It is so,* and if instead of the sonorous phrase, *It is subjectively so,* you will say, in plain old English, *It does so,* or *It seems so to me,* you will, on the whole, be more intelligible to your fellow creatures; and besides, if you find that a thing which generally *does so* to other people (as a gentian looks blue to most men) does *not* so to you, on any particular occasion, you will not fall into the impertinence of saying, that the thing is not so, or did not so, but you will say simply (what you will be all the better for speedily finding out), that something is the matter with you. If you find that you cannot explode the gunpowder, you will not declare that all gunpowder is subjective, and all explosion imaginary, but you will simply suspect and declare yourself to be an ill-made match. Which, on the whole, though there may be a distant chance of a mistake about it, is, nevertheless, the wisest conclusion you can come to until further experiment.[2]

4. Now, therefore, putting these tiresome and absurd words quite out of our way, we may go on at our ease to examine the point in question—namely, the difference between the ordinary, proper, and true appearances of things to us; and the extraordinary, or false appearances, when we are under the influence of emotion, or contemplative fancy;[3] false appearances, I say, as being entirely unconnected with any real power or character in the object, and only imputed to it by us.

For instance, "The spendthrift crocus, bursting through the mold/Naked and shivering, with his cup of gold."[4]

This is very beautiful and yet very untrue. The crocus is not a spendthrift, but a hardy plant; its yellow is not gold, but saffron. How is it that we enjoy so much the having it put into our heads that it is anything else than a plain crocus?

---

[1] "It is quite true, that in all qualities involving sensation, there may be a doubt whether different people receive the same sensation from the same thing (compare [*Modern Painters*] Part 2, Section 1, Chapter 5); but, though this makes such facts not distinctly explicable, it does not alter the facts themselves. I derive a certain sensation, which I call sweetness, from sugar. That is a fact. Another person feels a sensation, which *he* also calls sweetness, from sugar. That is also a fact. The sugar's power to produce these two sensations, which we suppose to be, and which are, in all probability, very nearly the same in both of us, and, on the whole, in the human race, is its sweetness." (Ruskin's note.)

[2] "In fact (for I may as well, for once, meet our German friends in their own style), all that has been subjected to us on the subject seems object to this great objection; that the subjection of all things (subject to no exceptions) to senses which are, in us, both subject and object, and objects of perpetual contempt, cannot but make it our ultimate object to subject ourselves to the sense, and to remove whatever objections existed to such subjection. So that, finally, that which is the subject of examination or object of attention, uniting thus in itself the characters of subness and obness (so that, that which has no obness in it should be subsubjective, or a subsubject, and that which has no subness in it should be called upper or oberobjective, or an obobject); and we also, who suppose ourselves the objects of every arrangement, and are certainly the subjects of every sensual impression, thus uniting in ourselves, in an obverse or adverse manner, the characters of obness and subness, must both become metaphysically dejected or rejected, nothing remaining in *us* objective, but subjectivity, and the very objectivity of the object being lost in the abyss of this subjectivity of the human.

There is, however, some meaning in the above sentence, if the reader cares to make it out; but in a pure German sentence of the highest style there is often none whatever." (Ruskin's note.)

[3] "Contemplative, in the sense explained in [*Modern Painters*] Part 3, Section 2, Chapter 4." (Ruskin's note.)

[4] "Holmes (Oliver Wendell), quoted by Miss Mitford in her *Recollections of a Literary Life*." (Ruskin's note.)

It is an important question. For, throughout our past reasonings about art, we have always found that nothing could be good or useful, or ultimately pleasurable, which was untrue. But here is something pleasurable in written poetry, which is nevertheless *un*true. And what is more, if we think over our favorite poetry, we shall find it full of this kind of fallacy, and that we like it all the more for being so.

5. It will appear also, on consideration of the matter, that this fallacy is of two principal kinds. Either, as in this case of the crocus, it is the fallacy of willful fancy, which involves no real expectation that it will be believed; or else it is a fallacy caused by an excited state of the feelings, making us, for the time, more or less irrational. Of the cheating of the fancy we shall have to speak presently; but in this chapter, I want to examine the nature of the other error, that which the mind admits when affected strongly by emotion. Thus, for instance, in *Alton Locke*,[1] "They rowed her in across the rolling foam—/The cruel, crawling foam."

The foam is not cruel, neither does it crawl. The state of mind which attributes to it these characters of a living creature is one in which the reason is unhinged by grief. All violent feelings have the same effect. They produce in us a falseness in all our impressions of external things, which I would generally characterize as the "pathetic fallacy."

6. Now we are in the habit of considering this fallacy as eminently a character of poetical description, and the temper of mind in which we allow it, as one eminently poetical, because passionate. But I believe, if we look well into the matter, that we shall find the greatest poets do not often admit this kind of falseness—that it is only the second order of poets who much delight in it.[2]

Thus, when Dante describes the spirits falling from the bank of Acheron "as dead leaves flutter from a bough,"[3] he gives the most perfect image possible of their utter lightness, feebleness, passiveness, and scattering agony of despair, without, however, for an instant losing his own clear perception that *these* are souls, and *those* are leaves; he makes no confusion of one with the other. But when Coleridge speaks of "the one red leaf, the last of its clan,/That dances as often as dance it can,"[4] he has a morbid, that is to say, a so far false, idea about the leaf; he fancies a life in it, and will, which there are not; confuses its powerlessness with choice, its fading death with merriment, and the wind that shakes it with music. Here, however, there is some beauty, even in the morbid passage; but take an instance in Homer and Pope. Without the knowledge of Ulysses, Elpenor, his youngest follower, has fallen from an upper chamber in the Circean palace, and has been left dead, unmissed by his leader or companions, in the

---

[1] by Charles Kingsley (1819–75).

[2] "I admit two orders of poets, but no third; and by these two orders I mean the creative (Shakespeare, Homer, Dante), and reflective or perceptive (Wordsworth, Keats, Tennyson). But both of these must be *first*-rate in their range, though their range is different; and with poetry second-rate in *quality* no one ought to be allowed to trouble mankind. There is quite enough of the best—much more than we can ever read or enjoy in the length of a life; and it is a literal wrong or sin in any person to encumber us with inferior work. I have no patience with apologies made by young pseudopoets, "that they believe there is *some* good in what they have written: that they hope to do better in time," etc. *Some* good! If there is not *all* good, there is no good. If they ever hope to do better, why do they trouble us now? Let them rather courageously burn all they have done, and wait for the better days. There are few men, ordinarily educated, who in moments of strong feeling could not strike out a poetical thought, and afterwards polish it so as to be presentable. But men of sense know better than so to waste their time; and those who sincerely love poetry, know the touch of the master's hand on the chords too well to fumble among them after him. Nay, more than this, all inferior poetry is an injury to the good, inasmuch as it takes away the freshness of rhymes, blunders upon and gives a wretched commonalty to good thoughts; and, in general, adds to the weight of human weariness in a most woeful and culpable manner. There are few thoughts likely to come across ordinary men, which have not already been expressed by greater men in the best possible way; and it is a wiser, more generous, more noble thing to remember and point out the perfect words, than to invent poorer ones, wherewith to encumber temporarily the world." (Ruskin's note.)

[3] *The Divine Comedy*, "Inferno" 3.112.

[4] *Christabel* 1.49–50.

haste of their departure. They cross the sea to the Cimmerian land; and Ulysses summons the shades from Tartarus. The first which appears is that of the lost Elpenor. Ulysses, amazed, and in exactly the spirit of bitter and terrified lightness which is seen in Hamlet,[1] addresses the spirit with the simple, startled words: "Elpenor! How camest thou under the shadowy darkness? Hast thou come faster on foot than I in my black ship?"[2] Which Pope renders thus:

O, say, what angry power Elpenor led
To glide in shades, and wander with the dead?
How could thy soul, by realms and seas disjoined,
Outfly the nimble sail, and leave the lagging wind?

I sincerely hope the reader finds no pleasure here, either in the nimbleness of the sail, or the laziness of the wind! And yet how is it that these conceits are so painful now, when they have been pleasant to us in the other instances?

7. For a very simple reason. They are not a *pathetic* fallacy at all, for they are put into the mouth of the wrong passion—a passion which never could possibly have spoken them—agonized curiosity. Ulysses wants to know the facts of the matter; and the very last thing his mind could do at the moment would be to pause, or suggest in any wise what was *not* a fact. The delay in the first three lines, and conceit in the last, jar upon us instantly like the most frightful discord in music. No poet of true imaginative power could possibly have written the passage.[3]

---

[1] "Well said, old mole! canst work i' the ground so fast?" [*Hamlet* 1.5.162.] (Ruskin's note.)

[2] *Odyssey* 11.56–57.

[3] "It is worth while comparing the way a similar question is put by the exquisite sincerity of Keats:

'He wept, and his bright tears
Went trickling down the golden bow he held.
Thus, with half-shut, suffused eyes, he stood;
While from beneath some cumbrous boughs hard by
With a solemn step an awful goddess came,
And there was purport in her looks for him,

Therefore, we see that the spirit of truth must guide us in some sort, even in our enjoyment of fallacy. Coleridge's fallacy has no discord in it, but Pope's has set our teeth on edge. Without farther questioning, I will endeavor to state the main bearings of this matter.

8. The temperament which admits the pathetic fallacy, is, as I said above, that of a mind and body in some sort too weak to deal fully with what is before them or upon them; borne away, or overclouded, or overdazzled by emotion; and it is a more or less noble state, according to the force of the emotion which had induced it. For it is no credit to a man that he is not morbid or inaccurate in his perceptions, when he has no strength of feeling to warp them; and it is in general a sign of higher capacity and stand in the ranks of being, that the emotions should be strong enough to vanquish, partly, the intellect, and make it believe what they choose. But it is still a grander condition when the intellect also rises, till it is strong enough to assert its rule against, or together with, the utmost efforts of the passions; and the whole man stands in an iron glow, white hot, perhaps, but still strong, and in no wise evaporating; even if he melts, losing none of his weight.

So, then, we have the three ranks: the man who perceives rightly, because he does not feel, and to whom the primrose is very accurately the primrose, because he does not love it. Then, secondly, the man who perceives wrongly, because he feels, and to whom the primrose is anything else than a primrose: a star, or a sun, or a fairy's shield, or a forsaken maiden. And then, lastly, there is the man who perceives rightly in spite of his feelings, and to whom the primrose is forever nothing else than itself—a little flower, apprehended in the very plain and leafy

---

Which he with eager guess began to read
Perplexed, the while melodiously he said,
"How camest thou over the unfooted sea?"
[*Hyperion* 3.42–50.]"
(Ruskin's note.)

fact of it, whatever and how many soever the associations and passions may be that crowd around it. And, in general, these three classes may be rated in comparative order, as the men who are not poets at all, and the poets of the second order, and the poets of the first; only however great a man may be, there are always some subjects which *ought* to throw him off his balance; some, by which his poor human capacity of thought should be conquered, and brought into the inaccurate and vague state of perception, so that the language of the highest inspiration becomes broken, obscure, and wild in metaphor, resembling that of the weaker man, overborne by weaker things.

9. And thus, in full, there are four classes: the men who feel nothing, and therefore see truly; the men who feel strongly, think weakly, and see untruly (second order of poets); the men who feel strongly, think strongly, and see truly (first order of poets); and the men who, strong as human creatures can be, are yet submitted to influences stronger than they, and see in a sort untruly, because what they see is inconceivably above them. This last is the usual condition of prophetic inspiration.

10. I separate these classes, in order that their character may be clearly understood; but of course they are united each to the other by imperceptible transitions, and the same mind, according to the influences to which it is subjected, passes at different times into the various states. Still, the difference between the great and less man is, on the whole, chiefly is the point of *alterability*. That is to say, the one knows too much, and perceives and feels too much of the past and future, and of all things beside and around that which immediately affects him, to be in any wise shaken by it. His mind is made up; his thoughts have an accustomed current; his ways are steadfast; it is not this or that new sight which will at once unbalance him. He is tender to impression at the surface, like a rock with deep moss upon it; but there is too much mass of him to be moved. The smaller man, with the same degree of sensibility, is at

once carried off his feet; he wants to do something he did not want to do before; he views all the universe in a new light through his tears; he is gay or enthusiastic, melancholy or passionate, as things come and go to him. Therefore the high creative poet might even be thought, to a great extent, impassive (as shallow people think Dante stern), receiving indeed all feelings to the full, but having a great center of reflection and knowledge in which he stands serene, and watches the feeling, as it were, from far off.

Dante, in his most intense moods, has entire command of himself, and can look around calmly, at all moments, for the image or the word that will best tell what he sees to the upper or lower world. But Keats and Tennyson, and the poets of the second order, are generally themselves subdued by the feelings under which they write, or, at least, write as choosing to be so; and therefore admit certain expressions and modes of thought which are in some sort diseased or false.

11. Now so long as we see that the *feeling* is true, we pardon, or are even pleased by, the confessed fallacy of sight which it induces: we are pleased, for instance, with those lines of Kingsley's above quoted, not because they fallaciously describe foam, but because they faithfully describe sorrow. But the moment the mind of the speaker becomes cold, that moment every such expression becomes untrue, as being forever untrue in the external facts. And there is no greater baseness in literature than the habit of using these metaphorical expressions in cold blood. An inspired writer, in full impetuosity of passion, may speak wisely and truly of "raging waves of the sea foaming out their own shame"; but it is only the basest writer who cannot speak of the sea without talking of "raging waves," "remorseless floods," "ravenous billows," etc.; and it is one of the signs of the highest power in a writer to check all such habits of thought, and to keep his eyes fixed firmly on the *pure fact*, out of which if any feeling comes to him or his reader, he knows it must be a true one.

To keep to the waves, I forget who it is who represents a man in despair desiring that his body may be cast into the sea, "Whose changing mound, and foam that passed away,/Might mock the eyes that questioned where I lay."

Observe, there is not a single false, or even overcharged, expression. *Mound* of the sea wave is perfectly simply and true; *changing* is as familiar as may be; *foam that passed away,* strictly literal; and the whole line descriptive of the reality with a degree of accuracy which I know not any other verse, in the range of poetry, that altogether equals. For most people have not a distinct idea of the clumsiness and massiveness of a large wave. The word *wave* is used too generally of ripples and breakers, and bendings in light drapery or grass: it does not by itself convey a perfect image. But the word *mound* is heavy, large, dark, definite; there is no mistaking the kind of wave meant, nor missing the sight of it. Then the term *changing* has a peculiar force also. Most people think of waves as rising and falling. But if they look at the sea carefully, they will perceive that the waves do not rise and fall. They change. Change both place and form, but they do not fall; one wave goes on, and on, and still on; now lower, now higher, now tossing its mane like a horse, now building itself together like a wall, now shaking, now steady, but still the same wave, till at last it seems struck by something, and changes, one knows not how—becomes another wave.

The close of the line insists on this image, and paints it still more perfectly—*foam that passed away.* Not merely melting, disappearing, but passing on, out of sight, on the career of the wave. Then, having put the absolute ocean fact as far as he may before our eyes, the poet leaves us to feel about it as we may, and to trace for ourselves the opposite fact—the image of the green mounds that do not change, and the white and written stones that do not pass away; and thence to follow out also the associated images of the calm life with the quiet grave, and the despairing life with the fading foam—"Let no man move his bones."[1] "As for Samaria, her king is cut off like the foam upon the water."[2]

But nothing of this is actually told or pointed out, and the expressions, as they stand, are perfectly severe and accurate, utterly uninfluenced by the firmly governed emotion of the writer. Even the word *mock* is hardly an exception, as it may stand merely for *deceive* or *defeat,* without implying any impersonation of the waves.

12. It may be well, perhaps, to give one or two more instances to show the peculiar dignity possessed by all passages, which thus limit their expression to the pure fact, and leave the hearer to gather what he can from it. Here is a notable one from the *Iliad.* Helen, looking from the Scaean gate of Troy over the Grecian host, and telling Priam the names of its captains, says at last:

> I see all the other dark-eyed Greeks; but two I cannot see—Castor and Pollux—whom one mother bore with me. Have they not followed from fair Lacedaemon, or have they indeed come in their sea-wandering ships, but now will not enter into the battle of men, fearing the shame and the scorn that is in me?

Then Homer: "So she spoke. But them, already, the life-giving earth possessed, there in Lacedaemon, in the dear fatherland."[3]

Note, here, the high poetical truth carried to the extreme. The poet has to speak of the earth in sadness, but he will not let that sadness affect or change his thoughts of it. No; though Castor and Pollux be dead, yet the earth is our mother still, fruitful, life-giving. These are the facts of the thing. I see nothing else than these. Make what you will of them.

---

[1] 2 Kings 23:18.

[2] Hosea 10:7.

[3] *Iliad* 3.243–44.

13. Take another very notable instance from Casimir de la Vigne's terrible ballad, *La Toilette de Constance.* I must quote a few lines out of it here and there, to enable the reader who has not the book by him, to understand its close.[1]

> *Adieu, bal, plaisir, amour!*
> *On disait, Pauvre Constance!*
> *Et on dansait, jusqu'au jour,*
> *Chez l'ambassadeur de France.*

Yes, that is the fact of it. Right or wrong, the poet does not say. What you may think about it, he does not know. He has nothing to do with that. There lie the ashes of the dead girl in her chamber. There they danced, till the morning, at the Ambassador's of France. Make what you will of it.

If the reader will look through the ballad, of which I have quoted only about the third part, he will find that there is not, from beginning to end of it, a single poetical (so called) expression, except in one stanza. The girl speaks as simple prose as may be; there is not a word she would not have actually used as she was dressing. The poet stands by, impassive as a statue, recording her words just as they come. At last the doom seizes her, and in the very presence of death, for an instant, his own emotions conquer him. He records no longer the facts only, but the facts as they seem to him. The fire gnaws with *voluptuousness—without pity.* It is soon past. The fate is fixed forever; and he retires into his pale and crystalline atmosphere of truth. He closes all with the calm veracity, "They said, 'Poor Constance!'"

14. Now in this there is the exact type of the consummate poetical temperament. For, be it clearly and constantly remembered, that the greatness of a poet depends upon the two facilities, acuteness of feeling, and command of it. A poet is great, first in proportion to the strength of his passion, and then,

that strength being granted, in proportion to his government of it; there being, however, always a point beyond which it would be inhuman and monstrous if he pushed this government, and, therefore, a point at which all feverish and wild fancy becomes just and true. Thus the destruction of the kingdom of Assyria cannot be contemplated firmly by a prophet of Israel. The fact is too great, too wonderful. It overthrows him, dashes him into a confused element of dreams. All the world is to his stunned thought, full of strange voices. "Yea, the fir trees rejoice at thee, and the cedars of Lebanon, saying, 'Since thou art gone down to the grave, no feller is come up against us.'"[2] So, still more, the thought of the presence of deity cannot be borne without this great astonishment. "The mountains and the hills shall break forth before you into singing, and all the trees of the fields shall clap their hands."[3]

15. But by how much this feeling is noble when it is justified by the strength of its cause, by so much it is ignoble when there is not cause enough for it; and beyond all other ignobleness is the mere affectation of it, in hardness of heart. Simply bad writing may almost always, as above noticed, be known by its adoption of these fanciful metaphorical expressions as a sort of current coin; yet there is even a worse, at least a more harmful condition of writing than this, in which such expressions are not ignorantly and feelinglessly caught up, but, by some master, skillful in handling, yet insincere, deliberately wrought out with chill and studied fancy; as if we should try to make an old lava stream look red-hot again, by covering it with dead leaves, or white-hot, with hoarfrost.

When Young is lost in veneration, as he dwells on the character of truly good and holy man, he permits himself for a moment to be overborne by the feeling so far as to exclaim—

---

[1] Here Ruskin quotes part of the poem; the last four lines of the quote are included here.

[2] Isaiah 14:8.

[3] Isaiah 55:12.

Where shall I find him? Angels, tell me where.
You know him; he is near you; point him out.
Shall I see glories beaming from his brow,
Or trace his footsteps by the rising flowers? [1]

This emotion has a worthy cause, and is thus true and right. But now hear the coldhearted Pope say to a shepherd girl—

Where'er you walk, cool gales shall fan the glade;
Trees, where you sit, shall crowd into a shade;
Your praise the birds shall chant in every grove,
And winds shall waft it to the powers above.
But would you sing, and rival Orpheus' strain,
The wondering forests soon should dance again;
The moving mountains hear the powerful call,
And headlong streams hang, listening, in their fall. [2]

This is not, nor could it for a moment be mistaken for, the language of passion. It is simple falsehood, uttered by hypocrisy in definite absurdity, rooted in affectation, and coldly asserted in the teeth of nature and fact. Passion will indeed go far in deceiving itself; but it must be a strong passion, not the simple wish of a lover to tempt his mistress to sing. Compare a very closely parallel passage in Wordsworth, in which the lover has lost his mistress:

Three years had Barbara in her grave been laid,
When thus his moan he made:

"Oh, move, thou cottage, from beyond yon oak,
   Or let the ancient tree uprooted lie,
That in some other way yon smoke
   May mount into the sky.

If still behind yon pine tree's ragged bough,
   Headlong, the waterfall must come,
   Oh, let it, then, be dumb—

Be anything, sweet stream, but that which thou art now." [3]

Here is a cottage to be moved, if not a mountain, and a waterfall to be silent, if it is not to hang listening: but with what different relation to the mind that contemplates them! Here, in the extremity of its agony, the soul cries out wildly for relief, which at the same moment it partly knows to be impossible, but partly believes possible, in a vague impression that a miracle *might* be wrought to give relief even to a less sore distress—that nature is kind, and God is kind, and that grief is strong: it knows not well what *is* possible to such grief. To silence a stream, to move a cottage wall—one might think it could do as much as that!

16. I believe these instances are enough to illustrate the main point I insist upon respecting the pathetic fallacy—that so far as it *is* a fallacy, it is always the sign of a morbid state of mind, and comparatively of a weak one. Even in the most inspired prophet it is a sign of the incapacity of his human sight or thought to bear what has been revealed to it. In ordinary poetry, if it is found in the thoughts of the poet himself, it is at once a sign of his belonging to the inferior school; if in the thoughts of the characters imagined by him, it is right or wrong according to the genuineness of the emotion from which it springs; always, however, implying necessarily *some* degree of weakness in the character.

Take two most exquisite instances from master hands. The Jessy of Shenstone, and the Ellen of Wordsworth, have both been betrayed and deserted. Jessy, in the course of her most touching complaint, says:

If through the garden's flowery tribes I stray,
   Where bloom the jasmines that could once allure,

---

[1] *Night Thoughts* 2.345.

[2] *Summer: The Second Pastoral, or Alexis*, ll. 78–84. Ruskin has omitted four lines following the first couplet.

---

[3] *'Tis Said, that Some Have Died for Love*, but somewhat misquoted.

"Hope not to find delight in us," they say,
  "For we are spotless, Jessy; we are pure."[1]

Compare this with some of the words of Ellen:

"Ah, why," said Ellen, sighing to herself,
"Why do not words, and kiss, and solemn pledge,
And nature, that is kind in woman's breast,
And reason, that in man is wise and good,
And fear of Him who is a righteous Judge,
Why do not these prevail for human life,
To keep two hearts together, that began
Their springtime with one love, and that have need
Of mutual pity and forgiveness sweet
To grant, or be received; while that poor bird—
O, come and hear him! Thou who hast to me
Been faithless, hear him—though a lowly creature,
One of God's simple children, that yet know not
The Universal Parent, *how* he sings!
As if he wished the firmament of heaven
Should listen, and give back to him the voice
Of his triumphant constancy and love;
The proclamation that he makes, how far
His darkness doth transcend our fickle light."[2]

The perfection of both these passages, as far as regards truth and tenderness of imagination in the two poets, is quite insuperable. But of the two characters imagined, Jessy is weaker than Ellen, exactly in so far as something appears to her to be in nature which is not. The flowers do not really reproach her. God meant them to comfort her, not to taunt her; they would do so if she saw them rightly.

Ellen, on the other hand, is quite above the slightest erring emotion. There is not the barest film of fallacy in all her thoughts. She reasons as calmly as if she did not feel. And, although the singing of the bird suggests to her the idea of its desiring to be heard in heaven, she does not for an instant admit any veracity in the thought. "As if," she says, "I know he means nothing of the kind; but it does verily seem as if." The reader will find, by examining the rest of the poem, that Ellen's character is throughout consistent in this clear though passionate strength.

It then being, I hope, now made clear to the reader in all respects that the pathetic fallacy is powerful only so far as it is pathetic, feeble so far as it is fallacious, and, therefore, that the dominion of truth is entire, over this, as over every other natural and just state of the human mind, we may go on to the subject for the dealing with which this prefatory inquiry became necessary; and why necessary, we shall see forthwith.[3]

—1856

---

[1] *Elegy* 26.

[2] *The Excursion* 6.869–87.

[3] "I cannot quit this subject without giving two more instances, both exquisite, of the pathetic fallacy, which I have just come upon, in *Maud*:

'For a great speculation had failed;
  And ever he muttered and maddened, and ever wanned with despair;
And out he walked when the wind like a broken worlding wailed,
  And the *flying gold of the ruined woodlands drove through the air.*

There has fallen a splendid tear
  From the passion-flower at the gate.

. . .

The red rose cries, "She is near, she is near";
  And the white rose weeps, "She is late."
The larkspur listens, "I hear, I hear";
  And the lily whispers, "I wait."'"

(Ruskin's note.)
Tennyson 1.9–12, 908–09, and 912–15, but l. 9 is misquoted.

Matthew Arnold
1822 – 1888

(See previous biographical note on page 598.)

❧❧❧

The Function of Criticism at the Present Time [1]

Many objections have been made to a proposition which, in some remarks of mine on translating Homer, I ventured to put forth; a proposition about criticism, and its importance at the present day. I said: "Of the literature of France and Germany, as of the intellect of Europe in general, the main effort, for now many years, has been a critical effort; the endeavour, in all branches of knowledge, theology, philosophy, history, art, science, to see the object as in itself it really is." I added, that owing to the operation in English literature of certain causes, "almost the last thing for which one would come to English literature is just that very thing which now Europe most desires,—criticism;" [2] and that the power and value of English literature was thereby impaired. More than one rejoinder declared that the importance I here assigned to criticism was excessive, and asserted the inherent superiority of the creative effort of the human spirit over its critical effort. And the other day, having been led by a Mr. Shairp's excellent notice of Wordsworth [3] to turn again to his biogra-

phy, I found, in the words of this great man, whom I, for one, must always listen to with the profoundest respect, a sentence passed on the critic's business, which seems to justify every possible disparagement of it. Wordsworth says in one of his letters:

"The writers in these publications" (the Reviews), "while they prosecute their inglorious employment, can not be supposed to be in a state of mind very favourable for being affected by the finer influences of a thing so pure as genuine poetry." [4]

And a trustworthy reporter of his conversation quotes a more elaborate judgment to the same effect:

"Wordsworth holds the critical power very low, infinitely lower than the inventive; and he said to-day that if the quantity of time consumed in writing critiques on the works of others were given to original composition, of whatever kind it might be, it would be much better employed; it would make a man find out sooner his own level, and it would do infinitely less mischief. A false or malicious criticism may do much injury to the minds of others, a stupid invention, either in prose or verse, is quite harmless." [5]

It is almost too much to expect of poor human nature, that a man capable of producing some effect in one line of literature, should, for the greater good of society, voluntarily doom himself to impotence

---

[1] published in November, 1864.

[2] in "On Translating Homer," lectures given at Oxford 1860–61.

[3] J.C. Shairp, Scots critic, wrote "Wordsworth: The Man and Poet" which appeared in *North British Review* 61 (1864), pp. 1–54. Arnold inserted the following footnote: " I cannot help thinking that a practice, common in England during the last century, and still followed in France, of printing a notice of this kind,—a notice by a competent critic,—to serve as an introduction to an eminent author's works, might be revived among us with advantage. To introduce all succeeding editions of Wordsworth, Mr. Shairp's notice might, it seems to me, excellently serve; it is written from the point of view of an admirer, nay, of a

disciple, and that is right; but then the disciple must be also, as in this case he is, a critic, a man of letters, not, as too often happens, some relation or friend with no qualification for his task except affection for his author."

[4] letter to Bernard Barton (1816) in Christopher Wordsworth, *Memoirs of William Wordsworth* (1851), 2.53.

[5] William Knight, *The Life of Wordsworth* (1880), 3.438.

and obscurity in another. Still less is this to be expected from men addicted to the composition of the "false or malicious criticism" of which Wordsworth speaks. However, everybody would admit that a false or malicious criticism had better never been written. Everybody, too, would be willing to admit, as a general proposition, that the critical faculty is lower than the inventive. But is it true that criticism is really, in itself, a baneful and injurious employment; is it true that all time given to writing critiques on the works of others would be much better employed if it were given to original composition of whatever kind this may be? Is it true Johnson had better have gone on producing more *Irenes*[1] instead of writing his *Lives of the Poets*; nay, is it certain that Wordsworth himself was better employed in making his Ecclesiastical Sonnets than when he made his celebrated Preface, so full of criticism, and criticism of the works of others?[2] Wordsworth was himself a great critic, and it is to be sincerely regretted that he has not left us more criticism; Goethe was one of the greatest of critics, and we may sincerely congratulate ourselves that he has left us so much criticism. Without wasting time over the exaggeration which Wordsworth's judgment on criticism clearly contains, or over an attempt to trace the causes,—not difficult, I think, to be traced,—which may have led Wordsworth to this exaggeration, a critic may with advantage seize an occasion for trying his own conscience, and for asking himself of what real service at any given moment the practice of criticism either is or may be made to his own mind and spirit, and to the minds and spirits of others.

The critical power is of lower rank than the creative. True; but in assenting to this proposition, one or two things are to be kept in mind. It is undeniable that the exercise of a creative power, that a free creative activity, is the highest function of man; it is

proved to be so by man's finding in it his true happiness. But it is undeniable, also, that men may have the sense of exercising this free creative activity in other ways than in producing great words of literature or art; if it were not so, all but a very few men would be shut out from the true happiness of all men. They may have it in well-doing, they may have it in learning, they may have it even in criticising. This is one thing to be kept in mind. Another is, that the exercise of the creative power in the production of great works of literature or art, however high this exercise of it may rank, is not at all epochs and under all conditions possible; and that therefore labour may be vainly spent in attempting it, which might with more fruit be used in preparing for it, in rendering it possible. This creative power works with elements, with materials; what if it has not those materials, those elements, ready for its use? In that case it must surely wait till they are ready. Now in literature,—I will limit myself to literature, for it is about literature that the question arises,—the elements with which the creative power works are ideas; the best ideas, on every matter which literature touches, current at the time. At any rate we may lay it down as certain that in modern literature no manifestation of the creative power not working with these can be very important or fruitful. And I say *current* at the time, not merely accessible at the time; for creative literary genius does not principally show itself in discovering new ideas; that is rather the business of the philosopher. The grand work of literary genius is a work of synthesis and exposition, not of analysis and discovery; its gift lies in the faculty of being happily inspired by a certain intellectual and spiritual atmosphere, by a certain order of ideas, when it finds itself in them; of dealing divinely with these ideas, presenting them in the most effective and attractive combinations,—making beautiful works with them, in short. But it must have the atmosphere, it must find itself amidst the order of ideas, in order to work freely; and these it is not so easy to command. This is why great

---

[1] *Irene* (1749), an unsuccessful play by Samuel Johnson.

[2] "Preface" to the second edition (1800) of the *Lyrical Ballads*.

creative epochs in literature are so rare, this is why there is so much that is unsatisfactory in the productions of many men of real genius; because, for the creation of a masterwork of literature two powers must concur, the power of the man and the power of the moment, and the man is not enough without the moment; the creative power has, for its happy exercise, appointed elements, and those elements are not in its own control.

Nay, they are more within the control of the critical power. It is the business of the critical power, as I said in the words already quoted, "in all branches of knowledge, theology, philosophy, history, art, science, to see the object as in itself it really is." Thus it tends, at last, to make an intellectual situation of which the creative power can profitably avail itself. It tends to establish an order of ideas, if not absolutely true, yet true by comparison with that which it displaces; to make the best ideas prevail. Presently these new ideas reach society, the touch of truth is the touch of life, and there is a stir and growth everywhere; out of this stir and growth come the creative epochs of literature.

Or, to narrow our range, and quit these considerations of the general march of genius and of society—considerations which are apt to become too abstract and impalpable,—every one can see that a poet, for instance, ought to know life and the world before dealing with them in poetry; and life and the world being in modern times very complex things, the creation of a modern poet, to be worth much, implies a great critical effort behind it; else it must be a comparatively poor, barren, and short-lived affair. This is why Byron's poetry had so little endurance in it, and Goethe's so much; both Byron and Goethe had a great productive power, but Goethe's was nourished by a great critical effort providing the true materials for it, and Byron's was not; Goethe knew life and the world, the poet's necessary subjects, much more comprehensively and thoroughly than

Byron. He knew a great deal more of them, and he knew them much more as they really are.

It has long seemed to me that the burst of creative activity in our literature, through the first quarter of this century, had about it in fact something premature; and that from this cause its productions are doomed, most of them, in spite of the sanguine hopes which accompanied and do still accompany them, to prove hardly more lasting than the productions of far less splendid epochs. And this prematureness comes from its having proceeded without having its proper data, without sufficient materials to work with. In other words, the English poetry of the first quarter of this century, with plenty of energy, plenty of creative force, did not know enough. This makes Byron so empty of matter, Shelley so incoherent, Wordsworth even, profound as he is, yet so wanting in completeness and variety. Wordsworth cared little for books, and disparaged Goethe. I admire Wordsworth, as he is, so much that I cannot wish him different; and it is vain, no doubt, to imagine such a man different from what he is, to suppose that he *could* have been different. But surely the one thing wanting to make Wordsworth an even greater poet than he is,—his thought richer, and his influence of wider application,—was that he should have read more books, among them, no doubt, those of that Goethe whom he disparaged without reading him.

But to speak of books and reading may easily lead to a misunderstanding here. It was not really books and reading that lacked to our poetry at this epoch; Shelley had plenty of reading, Coleridge had immense reading. Pindar and Sophocles—as we all say so glibly, and often with so little discernment of the real import of what we are saying—had not many books; Shakspeare was no deep reader. True; but in the Greece of Pindar and Sophocles, in the England of Shakspeare, the poet lived in a current of ideas in the highest degree animating and nourishing to the creative power; society was, in the fullest measure, permeated by fresh thought, intelligent and alive.

And this state of things is the true basis for the creative power's exercise, in this it finds its data, its materials, truly ready for its hand; all the books and reading in the world are only valuable as they are helps to this. Even when this does not actually exist, books and reading may enable a man to construct a kind of semblance of it in his own mind, a world of knowledge and intelligence in which he may live and work. This is by no means an equivalent to the artist for the nationally diffused life and thought of the epochs of Sophocles or Shakspeare; but, besides that it may be a means of preparation for such epochs, it does really constitute, if many share in it, a quickening and sustaining atmosphere of great value. Such an atmosphere the many-sided learning and the long and widely combined critical effort of Germany formed for Goethe, when he lived and worked. There was no national glow of life and thought there, as in the Athens of Pericles or the England of Elizabeth. That was the poet's weakness. But there was a sort of equivalent for it in the complete culture and unfettered thinking of a large body of Germans. That was his strength. In the England of the first quarter of this century there was neither a national glow of life and thought, such as we had in the age of Elizabeth, nor yet a culture and a force of learning and criticism such as were to be found in Germany. Therefore the creative power of poetry wanted, for success in the highest sense, materials and a basis; a thorough interpretation of the world was necessarily denied to it.

At first sight it seems strange that out of the immense stir of the French Revolution and its age should not have come a crop of works of genius equal to that which came out of the stir of the great productive time of Greece, or out of that of the Renascence, with its powerful episode the Reformation. But the truth is that the stir of the French Revolution took a character which essentially distinguished it from such movements as these. These were, in the main, disinterestedly intellectual and spiritual movements; movements in which the human spirit looked for its satisfaction in itself and in the increased play of its own activity. The French Revolution took a political, practical character. The movement which went on in France under the old *régime,* from 1700 to 1789, was far more really akin than that of the Revolution itself to the movement of the Renascence; the France of Voltaire and Rousseau told far more powerfully upon the mind of Europe than the France of the Revolution. Goethe reproached this last expressly with having "thrown quiet culture back." [1] Nay, and the true key to how much in our Byron, even in our Wordsworth, is this!—that they had their source in a great movement of feeling, not in a great movement of mind. The French Revolution, however,—that object of so much blind love and so much blind hatred,—found undoubtedly its motive-power in the intelligence of men, and not in their practical sense; this is what distinguishes it from the English Revolution of Charles the First's time. This is what makes it a more spiritual event than our Revolution, an event of much more powerful and worldwide interest, though practically less successful; it appeals to an order of ideas which are universal, certain, permanent. 1789 asked of a thing, Is it rational? 1642 asked of a thing, Is it legal? or, when it went furthest, Is it according to conscience? This is the English fashion, a fashion to be treated, within its own sphere, with the highest respect; for its success, within its own sphere, has been prodigious. But what is law in one place is not law in another; what is law here to-day is not law even here to-morrow; and as for conscience, what is binding on one man's conscience is not binding on another's. The old woman who threw her stool at the head of the surpliced minister in St. Giles's Church at Edinburgh[2] obeyed an impulse to which millions of the human race may be permitted to remain strangers. But the prescriptions of reason are absolute, unchanging, of universal

---

[1] in "The Four Seasons: Spring."

[2] Janet Geddes threw the stool on July 25, 1637, in protest against the effort by Charles I to impose the English liturgy on the Scottish Church.

validity; *to count by tens is the easiest way of count-ing*—that is a proposition of which every one, from here to the Antipodes, feels the force; at least I should say so if we did not live in a country where it is not impossible that any morning we may find a letter in *The Times* declaring that a decimal coinage is an absurdity.[1] That a whole nation should have been penetrated with an enthusiasm for pure reason, and with an ardent zeal for making its prescriptions triumph, is a very remarkable thing, when we consider how little of mind or anything so worthy and quickening as mind, comes into the motives which alone, in general, impel great masses of men. In spite of the extravagant direction given to this enthusiasm, in spite of the crimes and follies in which it lost itself, the French Revolution derives from the force, truth, and universality of the ideas which it took for its law, and from the passion with which it could inspire a multitude for these ideas, a unique and still living power; it is—it will probably long remain—the greatest, the most animating event in history. And as no sincere passion for the things of the mind, even though it turn out in many respects an unfortunate passion, is ever quite thrown away and quite barren of good, France has reaped from hers one fruit—the natural and legitimate fruit, though not precisely the grand fruit she expected: she is the country in Europe where *the people* is most alive.

But the mania for giving an immediate political and practical application to all these fine ideas of the reason was fatal. Here an Englishman is in his element: on this theme we can all go on for hours. And all we are in the habit of saying on it has undoubtedly a great deal of truth. Ideas cannot be too much prized in and for themselves, cannot be too much lived with; but to transport them abruptly into the world of politics and practice, violently to revolutionise this world to their bidding—that is quite another thing. There is the world of ideas and there is the world of

practice; the French are often for suppressing the one and the English the other; but neither is to be suppressed. A member of the House of Commons said to me the other day: "That a thing is an anomaly, I consider to be no objection to whatever." I venture to think he was wrong; that a thing is an anomaly *is* an objection to it, but absolutely and in the sphere of ideas: it is not necessarily, under such and such circumstances, or at such and such a moment, an objection to it in the sphere of politics and practice. Joubert has said beautifully: "C'est la force et la droit qui règlent toutes choses dans le monde; la force en attendant le droit."[2] (Force and right are the governors of the this world; force till right is ready.) *Force till right is ready*; and till right is ready, force, the existing order of things, is justified, is the legitimate ruler. But right is something moral, and implies inward recognition, free assent of the will; we are not ready for right,—*right*, so far as we are concerned, *is not ready*,—until we have attained this sense of seeing it and willing it. The way in which for us it may change and transform force, the existing order of things, and become, in its turn, the legitimate ruler of the world, should depend on the way in which, when our time comes, we see it and will it. Therefore for other people enamoured of their own newly discerned right, to attempt to impose it upon us as ours, and violently to substitute their right for our force, is an act of tyranny, and to be resisted. It sets at nought the second great half of our maxim, *force till right is ready*. This was the grand error of the French Revolution; and its movement of ideas, by quitting the intellectual sphere and rushing furiously into the political sphere, ran, indeed, a prodigious and memorable course, but produced no such intellectual fruit as the movement of ideas of the Renascence, and created, in opposition to itself, what I may call an *epoch of concentration*. The great force of that epoch of concentration was England; and the great voice of

---

[1] A decimal coinage bill was introduced and withdrawn in 1863.

[2] Joseph Joubert (1754–1824), *Pensées* (Paris, 1874).

that epoch of concentration was Burke. It is the fashion to treat Burke's writings on the French Revolution as superannuated and conquered by the event; as the eloquent but unphilosophical tirades of bigotry and prejudice. I will not deny that they are often disfigured by the violence and passion of the moment, and that in some directions Burke's view was bounded, and his observation therefore at fault. But on the whole, and for those who can make the needful corrections, what distinguishes these writings is their profound, permanent, fruitful, philosophical truth. They contain the true philosophy of an epoch of concentration, dissipate the heavy atmosphere which its own nature is apt to engender round it, and make its resistance rational instead of mechanical.

But Burke is so great because, almost alone in England, he brings thought to bear upon politics, he saturates politics with thought. It is his accident that his ideas were at the service of an epoch of concentration, not of an epoch of expansion; it is his characteristic that he so lived by ideas, and had such a source of them welling up within him, that he could float even an epoch of concentration and English Tory politics with them. It does not hurt him that Dr. Price[1] and the Liberals were enraged with him; it does not even hurt him that George the Third and the Tories were enchanted with him. His greatness is that he lived in a world which neither English Liberalism nor English Toryism is apt to enter;—the world of ideas, not the world of catchwords and party habits. So far is it from being really true of him that he "to party gave up what was meant for mankind,"[2] that at the very end of his fierce struggle with the French Revolution, after all his invectives against its false pretensions, hollowness, and madness, with his sincere conviction of its mischievousness, he can close a memorandum on the best means of combating it,

some of the last pages he ever wrote,—the *Thoughts on French Affairs*, in December 1791,—with these striking words:

"The evil is stated, in my opinion, as it exists. The remedy must be where power, wisdom, and information, I hope, are more united with good intentions than they can be with me. I have done with this subject, I believe, for ever. It has given me many anxious moments for the last two years. *If a great change is to be made in human affairs, the minds of men will be fitted to it; the general opinions and feelings will draw that way. Every fear, every hope will forward it; and then they who persist in opposing this mighty current in human affairs, will appear rather to resist the decrees of Providence itself, than the mere designs of men. They will not be resolute and firm, but perverse and obstinate.*"

That return of Burke upon himself has always seemed to me one of the finest things in English literature, or indeed in any literature. That is what I call living by ideas; when one side of a question has long had your earnest support, when all your feelings are engaged, when you hear all round you no language but one, when your party talks this language like a steam-engine and can imagine no other,—still to be able to think, still to be irresistibly carried, if so it be, by the current of thought to the opposite side of the question, and, like Balaam, to be unable to speak anything *but what the Lord has put in your mouth*.[3] I know nothing more striking, and I must add that I know nothing more un-English.

For the Englishman in general is like my friend the Member of Parliament, and believes, point-blank, that for a thing to be an anomaly is absolutely no objection to it whatever. He is like the Lord Auckland of Burke's day, who, in a memorandum on the French Revolution, talks of "certain miscreants, assuming the name of philosophers, who have presumed themselves capable of establishing a new

---

[1] Richard Price (1723–91), a Nonconformist minister, preached a sermon in praise of the French Revolution which Burke attacked in his *Reflections on the French Revolution* (1790).

[2] Goldsmith in his "Retaliation."

[3] Numbers 22:35,38.

system of society."[1] The Englishman has been called a political animal, and he values what is political and practical so much that ideas easily become objects of dislike in his eyes, and thinkers "miscreants," because ideas and thinkers have rashly meddled with politics and practice. This would be all very well if the dislike and neglect confined themselves to ideas transported out of their own sphere, and meddling rashly with practice; but they are inevitably extended to ideas as such, and to the whole life of intelligence; practice is everything, a free play of the mind is nothing. The notion of the free play of the mind upon all subjects being a pleasure in itself, being an object of desire, being an essential provider of elements without which a nation's spirit, whatever compensations it may have for them, must, in the long run, die of inanition,[2] hardly enters into an Englishman's thoughts. It is noticeable that the word *curiosity*, which in other languages is used in a good sense, to mean, as a high and fine quality of man's nature, just this disinterested love of a free play of the mind on all subjects, for its own sake,—it is noticeable, I say, that this word has in our language no sense of the kind, no sense but a rather bad and disparaging one. But criticism, real criticism, is essentially the exercise of this very quality. It obeys an instinct prompting it to try to know the best that is known and thought in the world, irrespectively of practice, politics, and everything of the kind; and to value knowledge and thought as they approach this best, without the intrusion of any other considerations whatever. This is an instinct for which there is, I think, little original sympathy in the practical English nature, and what there was of it had undergone a long benumbing period of blight and suppression in the epoch of concentration which followed the French Revolution.

But epochs of concentration cannot well endure for ever; epochs of expansion, in the due course of things, follow them. Such an epoch of expansion seems to be opening in this country. In the first place all danger of a hostile forcible pressure of foreign ideas upon our practice has long disappeared; like the traveller in the fable,[3] therefore, we begin to wear our cloak a little more loosely. Then, with a long peace, the ideas of Europe steal gradually and amicably in, and mingle, though in infinitesimally small quantities at a time, with our own notions. Then, too, in spite of all that is said about the absorbing and brutalising influence of our passionate material progress, it seems to me indisputable that this progress is likely, though not certain, to lead in the end to an apparition of intellectual life; and that man, after he has made himself perfectly comfortable and has now to determine what to do with himself next, may begin to remember that he has a mind, and that the mind may be made the source of great pleasure. I grant it is mainly the privilege of faith, at present, to discern this end to our railways, our business, and our fortune-making; but we shall see if, here as elsewhere, faith is not in the end the true prophet. Our ease, our travelling, and our unbounded liberty to hold just as hard and securely as we please to the practice to which our notions have given birth, all tend to beget an inclination to deal a little more freely with these notions themselves, to canvass them a little, to penetrate a little into their real nature. Flutterings of curiosity, in the foreign sense of the word, appear amongst us, and it is in these that criticism must look to find its account. Criticism first; a time of true creative activity, perhaps,—which, as I have said, must inevitably be preceded amongst us by a time of criticism,—hereafter, when criticism has done its work.

It is of the last importance that English criticism should clearly discern what rule for its course, in

---

[1] William Eden, Lord Auckland (1744–1814), English diplomat.

[2] emptiness.

[3] in Aesop's fable of the wind and the sun.

order to avail itself of the field now opening to it, and to produce fruit for the future, it ought to take. The rule may be summed up in one word,—*disinterestedness*. And how is criticism to show disinterestedness? By keeping aloof from what is called "the practical view of things;" by resolutely following the law of its own nature, which is to be a free play of the mind on all subjects which it touches. By steadily refusing to lend itself to any of those ulterior, political, practical considerations about ideas, which plenty of people will be sure to attach to them, which perhaps ought often to be attached to them, which in this country at any rate are certain to be attached to them quite sufficiently, but which criticism has really nothing to do with. Its business is, as I have said, simply to know the best that is known and thought in the world, and by in its turn making this known, to create a current of true and fresh ideas. Its business is to do this with inflexible honesty, with due ability; but its business is to do no more, and to leave alone all questions of practical consequences and applications, questions which will never fail to have due prominence given to them. Else criticism, besides being really false to its own nature, merely continues in the old rut which it has hitherto followed in this country, and will certainly miss the chance now given to it.

For what is at present the bane of criticism in this country? It is that practical considerations cling to it and stifle it. It subserves interests not its own. Our organs of criticism are organs of men and parties having practical ends to serve, and with them those practical ends are the first thing and the play of the mind the second; so much play of mind as is compatible with the prosecution of those practical ends is all that is wanted. An organ like the *Revue des Deux Mondes*, having for its main function to understand and utter the best that is known and thought in the world, existing, it may be said, as just an organ for a free play of the mind, we have not. But we have the *Edinburgh Review*, existing as an organ of the old Whigs, and for as much play of the mind as may suit its being that; we have the *Quarterly Review*, existing as an organ of the Tories, and for as much play of mind as may suit its being that; we have the *British Quarterly Review*, existing as an organ of the political Dissenters, and for as much play of mind as may suit its being that; we have *The Times*, existing as an organ of the common, satisfied, well-to-do Englishman, and for as much play of mind as may suit its being that. And so on through all the various fractions, political and religious, of our society; every fraction has, as such, its organ of criticism, but the notion of combining all fractions in the common pleasure of a free disinterested play of mind meets with no favour. Directly this play of mind wants to have more scope, and to forget the pressure of practical considerations a little, it is checked, it is made to feel the chain. We saw this the other day in the extinction, so much to be regretted, of the *Home and Foreign Review*. Perhaps in no organ of criticism in this country was there so much knowledge, so much play of mind; but these could not save it. The *Dublin Review* subordinates play of mind to the practical business of English and Irish Catholicism, and lives. It must needs be that men should act in sects and parties, that each of these sects and parties should have its organ, and should make this organ subserve the interests of its action; but it would be well, too, that there should be a criticism, not the minister of these interests, not their enemy, but absolutely and entirely independent of them. No other criticism will ever attain any real authority or make any real way towards its end,—the creating a current of true and fresh ideas.

It is because criticism has so little kept in the pure intellectual sphere, has so little detached itself from practice, has been so directly polemical and controversial, that it has so ill accomplished, in this country, its best spiritual work; which is to keep man from a self-satisfaction which is retarding and vulgarizing, to lead him towards perfection, by making his mind dwell upon what is excellent in itself, and the absolute beauty and fitness of things. A polemical practical criticism makes men blind even to the ideal imperfection of their practice, makes them willingly assert its ideal perfection, in order the better to secure it against attack; and clearly this is narrowing and baneful for them. If they were reassured on the practical side, speculative considerations of ideal perfection they might be brought to entertain, and their spiritual horizon would thus gradually widen. Sir Charles Adderley[1] says to the Warwickshire farmers:—

"Talk of the improvement of breed! Why, the race we ourselves represent, the men and women, the old Anglo-Saxon race, are the best breed in the whole world…The absence of a too enervating climate, too unclouded skies, and a too luxurious nature, has produced so vigorous a race of people, and has rendered us so superior to all the world."

Mr. Roebuck[2] says to the Sheffeld cutlers:—

"I look around me and ask what is the state of England? Is not property safe? Is not every man able to say what he likes? Can you not walk from one end of England to the other in perfect security? I ask you whether, the world over or in past history, there in anything like it? Nothing. I pray that our unrivaled happiness may last."[3]

Now obviously there is a peril for poor human nature in words and thoughts of such exuberant self-satisfaction, until we find ourselves safe in the streets of the Celestial City.

Das wenige verschwindet leicht dem Blicke
Der vorwärts sieht, wie viel noch übrig bleibt—

says Goethe; "the little that is done seems nothing when we look forward and see how much we have yet to do."[4] Clearly this is a better line of reflection for weak humanity, so long as it remains on this earthly field of labour and trial.

But neither Sir Charles Adderley nor Mr. Roebuck is by nature inaccessible to considerations of this sort. They only lose sight of them owing to the controversial life we all lead, and the practical from which all speculation takes with us. They have in view opponents whose aim is not ideal, but practical; and in their zeal to uphold their own practice against these innovators, they go so far as even to attribute to this practice an ideal perfection. Somebody has been wanting to introduce a six-pound franchise, or to abolish church-rates, or to collect agricultural statistics by force, or to diminish local self-government. How natural, in reply to such proposals, very likely improper or ill-timed, to go a little beyond the mark and to say stoutly, "such a race of people as we stand, so superior to all the world! The Old Anglo-Saxon race, the best breed in the whole world! I pray that our unrivaled happiness may last! I ask you whether, the world over or in past history, there is anything like it?" And so long as criticism answers this dithyramb by insisting that the old Anglo-Saxon race would be still more superior to all others if it had no church-rates, or that our unrivalled happiness would last yet longer with a six-pound franchise, so long will the strain, "The best breed in the whole world!" swell louder and louder, everything ideal and refining will be lost out of sight, and both the assailed and their critics will remain in a sphere, to say the truth, perfectly unvital, a sphere in which spiritual progression is impossible. But let criticism leave church-rates and the franchise alone, and in the most candid spirit, without a single lurking thought of practical innovation, confront with our dithyramb this para-

---

[1] Conservative statesman (1814–1905).

[2] John Arthur Roebuck (1801–79), was a Benthamite and member of Parliament from Sheffield.

[3] speeches reported in the London *Times* on 17 September 1863, and 19 August 1864.

[4] in *Iphigenia in Tauris* 1.2.91–92.

graph on which I stumbled in a newspaper immediately after reading Mr. Roebuck:—

"A shocking child murder has just been committed at Nottingham. A girl named Wragg left the workhouse there on Saturday morning with her young illegitimate child. The child was soon afterwards found dead on Mapperly Hills, having been strangled. Wragg is in custody."

Nothing but that; but, in juxtaposition with the absolute eulogies of Sir Charles Adderley and Mr. Roebuck, how eloquent, how suggestive are those few lines! "Our old Anglo-Saxon breed, the best in the whole world!"—how much that is harsh and ill-favoured there is in this best! *Wragg!* If we are to talk of ideal perfection of "the best in the whole world," has any one reflected what a touch of grossness in our race, what an original shortcoming in the more delicate spiritual perceptions, is shown by the natural growth amongst us of such hideous names—Higginbottom, Stiggins, Bugg! In Ionia and Attica they were luckier in this respect that "the best race in the world;" by the Ilissus there was no Wragg, poor thing![1] And "our unrivaled happiness";—what an element of grimness, bareness, and hideousness mixes with it and blurs it; the workhouse, the dismal Mapperly Hills,—how dismal those who have seen them will remember;—the gloom, the smoke, the cold, the strangled illegitimate child! "I ask you whether, the world over or in past history, there is anything like it?" Perhaps not, one is inclined to answer; but at any rate, in that case, the world is very much to be pitied. And the final touch,—short, bleak, and inhuman: *Wragg is in custody.* The sex lost in the confusion of our unrivalled happiness; or (shall I say?) the superfluous Christian name lopped off by the straightforward vigour of our old Anglo-Saxon breed! There is profit for the spirit in such contrasts as this; criticism serves the cause of perfection by establishing them. By eluding sterile conflict, by refusing to remain in the sphere where alone narrow and relative conceptions have any worth and validity, criticism may diminish its momentary importance, but only in this way has it a chance of gaining admittance for those wider and more perfect conceptions to which all its duty is really owed. Mr. Roebuck will have a poor opinion of an adversary who replies to his defiant songs of triumph only by murmuring under his breath, *Wragg is in custody;* but in no other way will these songs of triumph be induced gradually to moderate themselves, to get rid of what in them is excessive and offensive, and to fall into a softer and truer key.

It will be said that it is a very subtle and indirect action which I am thus prescribing for criticism, and that, by embracing in this manner the Indian virtue of detachment and abandoning the sphere of practical life, it condemns itself to a slow and obscure work. Slow and obscure it may be, but it is the only proper work of criticism. The mass of mankind will never have any ardent zeal for seeing things as they are; very inadequate ideas will always satisfy them. On these inadequate ideas reposes, and must repose, the general practice of the world. That is as much as saying that whoever sets himself to see things as they are will find himself one of a very small circle; but it is only by this small circle resolutely doing its own work that adequate ideas will ever get current at all. The rush and roar of practical life will always have a dizzying and attracting effect upon the most collected spectator, and tend to draw him into its vortex; most of all will this be the case where that life is so powerful as it is in England. But it is only by remaining collected, and refusing to lend himself to the point of view of the practical man, that the critic can do the practical man any service; and it is only by the greatest sincerity in pursuing his own course, and by at last convincing even the practical man of his sincerity, that he can escape misunderstandings which perpetually threaten him.

---

[1] a famous river near Athens.

For the practical man is not apt for fine distinctions, and yet in these distinctions truth and the highest culture greatly find their account. But it is not easy to lead a practical man,—unless you reassure him as to your practical intentions, you have no chance of leading him,—to see a thing which he has always been used to look at from one side only, which he greatly values, and which, looked at from that side, quite deserves, perhaps, all the prizing and admiring which he bestows upon it,—that this thing, looked at from another side, may appear much less beneficent and beautiful, and yet retain all its claims to our practical allegiance. Where shall we find language innocent enough, how shall we make the spotless purity of our intentions evident enough, to enable us to say to the political Englishman that the British Constitution itself, which, seen from the practical side, looks such a magnificent organ of progress and virtue, seen from the speculative side,—with its compromises, its love of facts, its horror of theory, its studied avoidance of clear thoughts,—that, seen from this side, our august Constitution sometimes looks,—forgive me, shade of Lord Somers!¹—a colossal machine for the manufacture of Philistines? How is Cobbett² to say this and not be misunderstood, blackened as he is with the smoke of a lifelong conflict in the field of political practice? How is Mr. Carlyle to say it and not be misunderstood, after his furious raid into this field with his *Latter-day Pamphlets?* how is Mr. Ruskin, after his pugnacious political economy? I say, the critic must keep out of the region of immediate practice in the political, social, humanitarian sphere, if he wants to make a beginning for that more free speculative treatment of things, which may perhaps one day make its benefits felt even in this sphere, but in a natural and thence irresistible manner.

Do what he will, however, the critic will still remain exposed to frequent misunderstandings, and nowhere so much as in this country. For here people are particularly indisposed even to comprehend that without this free disinterested treatment of things, truth and the highest culture are out of the question. So immersed are they in practical life, so accustomed to take all their notions from this life and its processes, that they are apt to think that truth and culture themselves can be reached by the processes of this life, and that it is an impertinent singularity to think of reaching them in any other. "We are all *terrae filii*,"³ cries their eloquent advocate; "all Philistines together. Away with the notion of proceeding by any other course than the course dear to the Philistines; let us have a social movement, let us organise and combine a party to pursue truth and new thought, let us call it *the liberal party,* and let us all stick to each other, and back each other up. Let us have no nonsense about independent criticism, and intellectual delicacy, and the few and the many. Don't let us trouble ourselves about foreign thought; we shall invent the whole thing for ourselves as we go along. If one of us speaks well, applaud him; if one of us speaks ill, applaud him too; we are all in the same movement, we are all liberals, we are all in pursuit of truth." In this way the pursuit of truth becomes really a social, practical, pleasurable affair, almost requiring a chairman, a secretary, and advertisements; with the excitement of an occasional scandal, a little resistance, to give the happy sense of difficulty overcome; but, in general, plenty of bustle and very little thought. To act is so easy, as Goethe says: to think is so hard! It is true that the critic has many temptations to go with the stream, to make one of the party movement, one of these *terrae filii*; it seems ungracious to refuse to be a *terrae filius*, when so many excellent people are; but

---

¹ chair of the committee which drew up the *Declaration of Rights* in 1689.

² William Cobbett (1762–1835), a radical journalist with an abrasive style.

³ "sons of the earth."

the critic's duty is to refuse, or, if resistance is vain, at least to cry with Obermann: "*Périssons en résistant.*"[1]

How serious a matter it is to try and resist, I had ample opportunity of experiencing when I ventured some time ago to criticise the celebrated first volume of Bishop Colenso.[2] The echoes of the storm which was then raised I still, from time to time, hear grumbling around me. That storm arose out of a misunderstanding almost inevitable. It is result of no little culture to attain to a clear perception that science and religion are two wholly different things. The multitude will for ever confuse them; but happily that is of no great real importance, for while the multitude imagines itself to live by its false science, it does really live by its true religion. Dr. Colenso, however, in his first volume did all he could to strengthen the confusion,[3] and to make it dangerous. He did this with the best intentions, I freely admit, and with the most candid ignorance that this was the natural effect of what he was doing; but, says Joubert, "Ignorance, which in matters of morals extenuates the crime, is itself, in intellectual matters, a crime of the first order."[4] I criticised Bishop Colenso's speculative confusion. Immediately there was a cry raised: "What is this? here is a liberal attacking a liberal. Do you not belong to the movement? are not you a friend of truth? Is not Bishop Colenso in pursuit of truth? then speak with proper respect of his book. Dr. Stanley[5] is another friend of truth, and you speak with proper respect of his book; why make these invidious differences? both books are excellent, admirable, liberal; Bishop Colenso's perhaps the most so, because it is the boldest, and will have the best practical consequences for the liberal cause. Do you want to encourage to the attack of a brother liberal his, and your, and our implacable enemies, the *Church and State Review* or the *Record*,—the High Church rhinoceros and the Evangelical hyæna? Be silent, therefore; or rather speak, speak as loud as ever you can! and go into ecstacies over the eighty and odd pigeons."

But criticism cannot follow this coarse and indiscriminate method. It is unfortunately possible for a man in pursuit of truth to write a book which reposes upon a false conception. Even the practical consequences of a book are to genuine criticism no recommendation of it, if the book is, in the highest sense, blundering. I see that a lady who herself, too, is in pursuit of truth, and who writes with great ability, but a little too much, perhaps, under the influence of the practical spirit of the English liberal movement, classes Bishop Colenso's book and M. Renan's together, in her survey of the religious state of Europe, as facts of the same order, works, both of them, of "great importance"; "great ability, power, and skill;" Bishop Colenso's, perhaps, the most powerful; at least, Miss Cobbe gives special expression to her gratitude that to Bishop Colenso "has been given the strength to grasp, and the courage to teach, truths of such deep import."[6] In the same way, more than one popular writer has compared him to

---

[1] "Let us perish resisting," from Senancour's *Obermann*.

[2] "So sincere is my dislike to all personal attack and controversy, that I abstain from reprinting, at this distance of time form the occasion which called them forth, the essays in which I criticised Dr. Colenso's book; I feel bound, however, after all that has passed, to make here a final declaration, of my sincere impenitence for having published them. Nay, I cannot forbear repeating yet once more, for his benefit and that of his readers, this sentence from my original remarks upon him: 'There is truth of science and truth of religion; truth of science does not become truth of religion till it is made religious.' And I will add: Let us have all the science there is from the men of science; from the men of religion let us have religion." (Arnold's note.) Arnold thought that John William Colenso's (1814-83) *The Pentateuch and Book of Joshua Critically Examined* (1862), was superficial.

[3] "It has been said I make it 'a crime against literary criticism and the higher culture to attempt to inform the ignorant.' Need I point out that the ignorant are not informed by being confirmed in a confusion?" (Arnold's note.)

[4] *Pensées.*

[5] Arthur P. Stanley. Arnold had compared his *The Bible: Its Form and Substance* (1863), favorably to Colenso's.

[6] Frances Power Cobbe, *Broken Lights* (1864). Ernest Renan's the *Vie de Jésus* (1863), and D.F. Strauss's book, mentioned below, was *Das Leben Jesu* (1835).

Luther. Now it is just this kind of false estimate which the critical spirit is, it seems to me, bound to resist. It is really the strongest possible proof of the low ebb at which, in England, the critical spirit is, that while the critical hit in the religious literature of Germany is Dr. Strauss's book, in that of France M. Renan's book, the book of Bishop Colenso is the critical hit in the religious literature of England. Bishop Colenso's book reposes on a total misconception of the essential elements of the religious problem, as that problem is now presented for solution. To criticism, therefore, which seeks to have the best that is known and thought on this problem, it is, however well meant, of no importance whatever. M. Renan's book attempts a new synthesis of the elements furnished to us by the Four Gospels. It attempts, in my opinion, a synthesis, perhaps premature, perhaps impossible, certainly not successful. Up to the present time, at any rate, we must acquiesce in Fleury's sentence on such recastings of the Gospel-story: "*Quiconque s'imagine la pouvoir mieux écrire, ne l'entend pas.*"[1] M. Renan had himself passed by anticipation a like sentence on his own work, when he said: "If a new presentation of the character of Jesus were offered to me, I would not have it; its very clearness would be, in my opinion, the best proof of its insufficiency." His friends may with perfect justice rejoin that at the sight of the Holy Land, and of the actual scene of the Gospel-story, all the current of M. Renan's thoughts may have naturally changed, and a new casting of that story irresistibly suggested itself to him; and that this is just a case for applying Cicero's maxim: Change of mind is not inconsistency—*nemo doctus unquam mutationem consilii inconstantiam dixit esse.*"[2] Nevertheless, for criticism, M. Renan's first thought must still be the truer one, as long as his new casting so fails more fully to commend itself, more

fully (to use Coleridge's happy phrase about the Bible) to *find* us.[3] Still M. Renan's attempt is, for criticism, of the most real interest and importance, since, with all its difficulty, a fresh synthesis of the New Testament *data*,—not a making war on them, in Voltaire's fashion, not a leaving them out of mind, in the world's fashion, but the putting a new construction upon them, the taking them from under the old, traditional, conventional point of view and placing them under a new one,—is the very essence of the religious problem, as now presented; and only by efforts in this direction can it receive a solution.

Again, in the same spirit in which she judges Bishop Colenso, Miss Cobbe, like so many earnest liberals of our practical race, both here and in America, herself sets vigorously about a positive re-construction of religion, about making a religion of the future out of hand, or at least setting about making it. We must not rest, she and they are always thinking and saying, in negative criticism, we must be creative and constructive; hence we have such works as her recent *Religious Duty*, and works still more considerable, perhaps, by others, which will be in every one's mind. These works often have much ability; they often spring out of sincere convictions, and a sincere wish to do good; and they sometimes, perhaps, do good. Their fault is (if I may be permitted to say so) one which they have in common with the British College of Health, in the New Road. Everyone knows the British College of Health; it is that building with the lion and the statue of the Goddess Hygeia before it; at least I am sure about the lion, though I am not absolutely certain about the Goddess Hygeia. This building does credit, perhaps, to the resources of Dr. Morrison[4] and his disciples; but it falls a good deal short of one's idea of what a British College of Health ought to be. In England,

---

[1] "Whoever imagines that he can write it better, does not understand it," from Claude Fleury's *Discours sur l'histoire ecclésiastique* (1691–1720).

[2] *Letters to Atticus* 15.7: "No learned man has said it to be inconsistent to change his mind."

[3] in his *Confessions of an Inquiring Spirit.*

[4] James Morrison, a self-styled "Hygeist" who sold "Morrison's Pills" as a universal cure-all. The British College of Health was the name of his pharmacy.

where we hate public interference and love individual enterprise, we have a whole crop of places like the British College of Health; the grand name without the grand thing. Unluckily, creditable to individual enterprise as they are, they tend to impair our taste by making us forget what more grandiose, noble, or beautiful character properly belongs to a public institution. The same may be said of the religions of the future of Miss Cobbe and others. Creditable, like the British College of Health, to the resources of their authors, they yet tend to make us forget what more grandiose, noble, or beautiful character properly belongs to religious constructions. The historic religions, with all their faults, have had this; it certainly belongs to the religious sentiment, when it truly flowers, to have this; and we impoverish our spirit if we allow a religion of the future without it. What then is the duty of criticism here? To take the practical point of view, to applaud the liberal movement and all its works,—its New Road religions of the future into the bargain,—for their general utility's sake? By no means; but to be perpetually dissatisfied with these works, while they perpetually fall short of a high and perfect ideal.

In criticism, these are elementary laws; but they never can be popular, and in this country they have been very little followed, and one meets with immense obstacles in following them. That is a reason for asserting them again and again. Criticism must maintain its independence of the practical spirit and its aims. Even with well-meant efforts of the practical spirit it must express dissatisfaction, if in the sphere of the ideal they seem impoverishing and limiting. It must not hurry on to the goal because of its practical importance. It must be patient, and know how to wait; and flexible, and know how to attach itself to things and how to withdraw from them. It must be apt to study and praise elements that for the fulness of spiritual perfection are wanted, even though they belong to a power which in the practical sphere may be maleficent. It must be apt to discern the spiritual shortcomings or illusions of powers that in the practical sphere may be beneficent. And this without any notion of favouring or injuring, in the practical sphere, one power or the other; without any notion of playing off, in this sphere, one power against the other. When one looks, for instance, at the English Divorce Court,—an institution which perhaps has its practical conveniences, but which in the ideal sphere is so hideous; an institution which neither makes divorce impossible nor makes it decent, which allows a man to get rid of his wife, or a wife of her husband, but makes them drag one another first, for the public edification, through a mire of unutterable infamy,—when one looks at this charming institution, I say, with its crowded trials, its newspaper reports, and its money compensations, this institution in which the gross unregenerate British Philistine has indeed stamped an image of himself,—one may be permitted to find the marriage theory of Catholicism refreshing and elevating. Or when Protestantism, in virtue of its supposed rational and intellectual origin, gives the law to criticism too magisterially, criticism may and must remind it that its pretensions, in this respect, are illusive and do it harm; that the Reformation was a moral rather than an intellectual event; that Luther's theory of grace no more exactly reflects the mind of the spirit than Bossuet's philosophy of history reflects it;[1] and that there is no more antecedent probability of the Bishop of Durham's stock of ideas being agreeable to perfect reason than of Pope Pius the Ninth's. But criticism will not on that account forget the achievements of Protestantism in the practical and moral sphere; nor that, even in the intellectual sphere, Protestantism, though in a blind and stumbling manner, carried forward the Renascence, while Catholicism threw itself violently across its path.

I lately heard a man of thought and energy contrasting the want of ardour and movement which he

---

[1] In his *Discourse on Universal History* (1681), Jacques Bossuet explains history as divinely guided for the benefit of Catholicism.

now found amongst young men in this country with what he remembered in his own youth, twenty years ago. "What reformers we were then!" he exclaimed; "what a zeal we had! how we canvassed every institution in Church and State, and were prepared to remodel them all on first principles!" He was inclined to regret, as a spiritual flagging, the lull which he saw. I am disposed rather to regard it as a pause in which the turn to a new mode of spiritual progress is being accomplished. Everything was long seen, by the young and ardent amongst us, in inseparable connection with politics and practical life. We have pretty well exhausted the benefits of seeing things in this connection, we have got all that can be got by so seeing them. Let us try a more disinterested mode of seeing them; let us betake ourselves more to the serener life of the mind and spirit. This life too, may have its excesses and dangers; but they are not for us at present. Let us think of quietly enlarging our stock of true and fresh ideas, and not, as soon as we get an idea or half an idea, be running out with it into the street, and trying to make it rule there. Our ideas will, in the end, shape the world all the better for maturing a little. Perhaps in fifty years' time it will in the English House of Commons be an objection to an institution that it is an anomaly, and my friend the Member of Parliament will shudder in his grave. But let us in the meanwhile rather endeavour that in twenty years' time it may, in English literature, be an objection to a proposition that it is absurd. That will be a change so vast, that the imagination almost fails to grasp it. *Ab integro saeclorum nascitur ordo.*[1]

If I have insisted so much on the course which criticism must take where politics and religion are concerned, it is because, where these burning matters are in question, it is most likely to go astray. I have wished, above all, to insist on the attitude which criticism should adopt towards things in general; on its right tone and temper of mind. But then comes

another question as to the subject-matter which literary criticism should most seek. Here, in general, its course is determined for it by the idea which is the law of its being; the idea of a disinterested endeavour to learn and propagate the best that is known and thought in the world, and thus to establish a current of fresh and true ideas. By the very nature of things, as England is not all the world, much of the best that is known and thought in the world cannot be of English growth, must be foreign; by the nature of things, again, it is just this that we are least likely to know, while English thought is streaming in upon us from all sides, and takes excellent care that we shall not be ignorant of its existence. The English critic of literature, therefore, must dwell much on foreign thought, and with particular heed on any part of it, which, while significant and fruitful in itself, is for any reason specially likely to escape him. Again, judging is often spoken of as the critic's one business, and so in some sense it is; but the judgment which almost insensibly forms itself in a fair and clear mind, along with fresh knowledge, is the valuable one; and thus knowledge, and ever fresh knowledge, must be the critic's great concern for himself. And it is by communicating fresh knowledge, and letting his own judgment pass along with it,—but insensibly, and in the second place, not the first, as a sort of companion and clue, not as an abstract lawgiver,—that the critic will generally do most good to his readers. Sometimes, no doubt, for the sake of establishing an author's place in literature, and his relation to a central standard (and if this is not done, how are we to get at our *best in the world?*) criticism may have to deal with a subject-matter so familiar that fresh knowledge is out of the question, and then it must be all judgment; an enunciation and detailed application of principles. Here the great safeguard is never to let oneself become abstract, always to retain an intimate and lively consciousness of the truth of what one is saying, and, the moment this fails us, to be sure that something is wrong. Still, under all circumstances,

---

[1] "Order is born from the renewal of generations": Virgil, *Eclogues* 4.5.

this mere judgment and application of principles is, in itself, not the most satisfactory work to the critic; like mathematics, it is tautological, and cannot well give us, like fresh learning, the sense of creative activity.

But stop, someone will say; all this talk is of no practical use to us whatever; this criticism of yours is not what we have in our minds when we speak of criticism; when we speak of critics and criticism, we mean critics and criticism of the current English literature of the day; when you offer to tell criticism of its function, it is to this criticism that we expect you to address yourself. I am sorry for it, for I am afraid I must disappoint these expectations. I am bound by my own definition of criticism: *a disinterested endeavour to learn and propagate the best that is known and thought in the world.* How much of current English literature comes into this "best that is known and thought in the world"? Not very much, I fear; certainly less, at this moment, than of the current literature of France or Germany. Well, then, am I to alter my definition of criticism, in order to meet the requirements of a number of practising English critics, who, after all, are free in their choice of a business? That would be making criticism lend itself just to one of those alien practical considerations, which, I have said, are so fatal to it. One may say, indeed, to those who have to deal with the mass—so much better disregarded—of current English literature, that they may at all events endeavour, in dealing with this, to try it, so far as they can, by the standard of the best that is known and thought in the world; one may say, that to get anywhere near this standard, every critic should try and possess one great literature, at least, besides his own; and the more unlike his own, the better. But, after all, the criticism I am really concerned with,—the criticism which alone can much help us for the future, the criticism which, throughout Europe, is at the present day meant, when so much stress is laid on the importance of criticism and the critical spirit,—is

a criticism which regards Europe as being, for intellectual and spiritual purposes, one great confederation, bound to a joint action and working to a common result; and whose members have, for their proper outfit, a knowledge of Greek, Roman, and Eastern antiquity, and of one another. Special, local, and temporary advantages being put out of account, that modern nation will in the intellectual and spiritual sphere make most progress, which most thoroughly carries out this programme. And what is that but saying that we too, all of us, as individuals, the more thoroughly we carry it out, shall make the more progress?

There is so much inviting us!—what are we to take? what will nourish us in growth towards perfection? That is the question which, with the immense field of life and of literature lying before him, the critic has to answer; for himself first, and afterwards for others. In this idea of the critic's business the essays brought together in the following pages have had their origin; in this idea, widely different as are their subjects, they have, perhaps, their unity.

I conclude with what I said at the beginning: to have the sense of creative activity is the great happiness and the great proof of being alive, and it is not denied to criticism to have it; but then criticism must be sincere, simple, flexible, ardent, ever widening its knowledge. Then it may have, in no contemptible measure, a joyful sense of creative activity; a sense which a man of insight and conscience will prefer to what he might derive from a poor, starved, fragmentary, inadequate creation. And at some epochs no other creation is possible.

Still, in full measure, the sense of creative activity belongs only to genuine creation; in literature we must never forget that. But what true man of letters ever can forget it? It is no such common matter for a gifted nature to come into possession of a current of true and living ideas, and to produce amidst the inspiration of them, that we are likely to underrate it. The epochs of Aeschylus and Shakespeare make us feel their pre-eminence. In an epoch like those is, no doubt, the true life of literature; there is the promised land, towards which criticism can only beckon. That promised land it will not be ours to enter, and we shall die in the wilderness: but to have desired to enter it, to have saluted it from afar, is already, perhaps, the best distinction among contemporaries; it will certainly be the best title to esteem with posterity.

—1864

Walter Bagehot
1826 – 1877

Walter Bagehot was a businessman, economist, historian, and literary critic. Among Bagehot's literary studies, his essay "Wordsworth, Tennyson and Browning; or Pure, Ornate, and Grotesque Art in English Poetry" relates the poetry of Milton and Wordsworth to "Pure" or classical art, that of Tennyson to "Ornate" or Romantic art, and the poetry of Browning to "Grotesque" (i.e. ugly) or medieval art.

❧❧❧

Wordsworth, Tennyson, and Browning; or, Pure, Ornate, and Grotesque Art in English Poetry [1]

We couple these two books together, not because of their likeness, for they are as dissimilar as books can be; nor on account of the eminence of their authors, for in general two great authors are too much for one essay; but because they are the best possible illustration of something we have to say upon poetical art—because they may give to it life and freshness. The accident of contemporaneous publication has here brought together two books very characteristic of modern art, and we want to show how they are characteristic.

Neither English poetry nor English criticism have ever recovered the *eruption* which they both made at the beginning of this century into the fashionable world. The poems of Lord Byron were received with an avidity that resembles our present avidity for sensation novels, and were read by a class which at present reads little but such novels. Old men who remember those days may be heard to say, "We hear nothing of poetry now-a-days; it seems quite down." And "down" it certainly is, if for poetry it be a descent to be no longer the favourite excitement of the more frivolous part of the "upper" world. That stimulating poetry is now little read. A stray school-boy may still be detected in a wild admiration for the *Giaour* or the *Corsair* (and it is suitable to his age, and he should not be reproached for it), but the *real* posterity—the quiet students of a past literature—never read them or think of them. A line or two linger on the memory; a few telling strokes of occasional and felicitous energy are quoted, but this is all. As wholes, these exaggerated stories were worthless; they taught nothing, and, therefore, they are forgotten. If now-a-days a dismal poet were, like Byron, to lament the fact of his birth, and to hint that he was too good for the world, the *Saturday Review* would say that "they doubted if he *was* too good; that a sulky poet was a questionable addition to a tolerable world; that he need not have been born, as far as they were concerned." Doubtless, there is much in Byron besides his dismal exaggeration, but it was that exaggeration which made "the sensation," which gave him a wild moment of dangerous fame. As so often happens, the cause of his momentary fashion is the cause also of his lasting oblivion. Moore's[2] former reputation was less excessive, yet it has not been more permanent. The prettiness of a few songs preserves the memory of his name, but as a poet to *read* he is forgotten. There is nothing to read in him; no exquisite thought, no sublime feeling, no consummate description of true character. Almost the sole result of the poetry of that time is the harm which it has done. It degraded for a time the whole character of the art. It said by practice, by a most efficient and

[1] This essay first appeared in the *National Review*, November 1864, Vol. 1 (New Series), pp. 27–66, prompted by the publication of Tennyson's *Enoch Arden* volume and Browning's *Dramatis Personae*.

[2] Thomas Moore (1779–1852), Irish poet and friend of Byron.

successful practice, that it was the aim, the *duty* of poets, to catch the attention of the passing, the fashionable, the busy world. If a poem "fell dead," it was nothing; it was composed to please the "London" of the year, and if that London did not like it, why, it had failed. It fixed upon the minds of a whole generation, it engraved in popular memory and tradition, a vague conviction that poetry is but one of the many *amusements* for the light classes, for the lighter hours of all classes. The mere notion, the bare idea, that poetry is a deep thing, a teaching thing, the most surely and wisely elevating of human things, is even now to the coarse public mind nearly unknown.

As was the fate of poetry, so inevitably was that of criticism. The science that expounds which poetry is good and which is bad is dependent for its popular reputation on the popular estimate of poetry itself. The critics of that day had *a* day, which is more than can be said for some since; they professed to tell the fashionable world in what books it would find new pleasure, and therefore they were read by the fashionable world. Byron counted the critic and poet equal. The *Edinburgh Review* penetrated among the young, and into places of female resort where it does not go now. As people ask, "Have you read *Henry Dunbar*? and what do you think of it?" so they then asked, "Have you read the *Giaour*? and what do you think of it?" Lord Jeffrey, a shrewd judge of the world, employed himself in telling it what to think; not so much what it ought to think, as what at bottom it did think; and so by dexterous sympathy with current society he gained contemporary fame and power. Such fame no critic must hope for now. His articles will not penetrate where the poems themselves do not penetrate. When poetry was noisy, criticism was loud; now poetry is a still small voice, and criticism must be smaller and stiller. As the function of such criticism was limited, so was its subject. For the great and (as time now proves) the *permanent* part of the poetry of his time—for Shelley and for Words-

worth—Lord Jeffrey had but one word. He said[1] "It won't do." And it will not do to amuse a drawing-room.

The doctrine that poetry is a light amusement for idle hours, a metrical species of sensational novel, has not indeed been without gainsayers wildly popular. Thirty years ago, Mr. Carlyle most rudely contradicted it. But perhaps this is about all that he has done. He has denied, but he has not disproved. He has contradicted the floating paganism, but he has not founded the deep religion. All about and around us a *faith* in poetry struggles to be extricated, but it is not extricated. Some day, at the touch of the true word, the whole confusion will by magic cease; the broken and shapeless notions cohere and crystallise into a bright and true theory. But this cannot be yet.

But though no complete theory of the poetic art as yet be possible for us, though perhaps only our children's children will be able to speak on this subject with the assured confidence which belongs to accepted truth, yet something of some certainty may be stated on the easier elements, and something that will throw light on these two new books. But it will be necessary to assign reasons, and the assigning of reasons is a dry task. Years ago, when criticism only tried to show how poetry could be made a *good* amusement, it was not impossible that criticism itself should be amusing. But now it must at least be serious, for we believe that poetry is a serious and a deep thing.

There should be a word in the language of literary art to express what the word "picturesque" expresses for the fine arts. *Picturesque* means fit to be put into a picture; we want a word *literatesque*, "fit to be put into a book."

.   .   .   .

There are an infinite number of classes of human beings, but in each of these classes there is a distinc-

---

[1] The first words in Lord Jeffrey's celebrated review of "The Excursion" were "This will never do."

tive type which, if we could expand it out in words, would define the class. We cannot expand it in formal terms any more than a landscape, or a species of landscapes; but we have an art, an art of words, which can draw it. Travellers and others often bring home, in addition to their long journals—which, though so living to them, are so dead, so inanimate, so undescriptive to all else—a pen-and-ink sketch, rudely done very likely, but which, perhaps, even the more for the blots and strokes, gives a distinct notion, an emphatic image, to all who see it. They say at once, *now* we know the sort of thing. The sketch has *hit* the mind. True literature does the same. It describes sorts, varieties, and permutations, by delineating the type of each sort, the ideal of each variety, the central, the marking trait of each permutation.

On this account, the greatest artists of the world have ever shown an enthusiasm for reality. To care for notions and abstractions; to philosophise; to reason out conclusions; to care for schemes of thought, are signs in the artistic mind of secondary excellence. A Schiller, an Euripides,[1] a Ben Jonson cares for *ideas*—for the parings of the intellect, and the distillation of the mind; a Shakespeare, a Homer, a Goethe finds his mental occupation, the true home of his natural thoughts, in the real world—"which is the world of all of us"—where the face of nature, the moving masses of men and women, are ever changing, ever multiplying, ever mixing one with the other. The reason is plain—the business of the poet, of the artist, is with *types*; and those types are mirrored in reality. As a painter must not only have a hand to execute, but an eye to distinguish—as he must go here and then there through the real world to catch the picturesque man, the picturesque scene, which are to live on his canvas—so the poet must find in that reality, the *literatesque* man, the *literatesque* scene which nature intends for him, and which will live in

his page. Even in reality he will not find this type complete, or the characteristics perfect; but there, he will find at least *something*, some hint, some intimation, some suggestion; whereas, in the stagnant home of his own thoughts he will find nothing pure, nothing *as it is,* nothing which does not bear his own mark, which is not somehow altered by a mixture with himself.

.   .   .   .

But in these delicate matters, it is easy to misapprehend. There is, undoubtedly, a sort of poetry which is produced as it were out of the author's mind. The description of the poet's own moods and feelings is a common sort of poetry—perhaps the commonest sort. But the peculiarity of such cases is that the poet does not describe himself *as* himself: autobiography is not his subject; he takes himself as a specimen of human nature; he describes, not himself, but a distillation of himself : he takes such of his moods as are most characteristic, as most typify certain moods of certain men, or certain moods of all men; he chooses preponderant feelings of special sorts of men, or occasional feelings of men of all sorts; but with whatever other difference and diversity, the essence is that such self-describing poets describe what is *in* them, but not *peculiar* to them,—what is generic, not what is special and individual. Gray's *Elegy* describes a mood which Gray felt more than other men, but which most others, perhaps all others, feel too. It is more popular, perhaps, than any English poem, because that sort of feeling is the most diffused of high feelings, and because Gray added to a singular nicety of fancy an habitual proneness to a *contemplative*—a discerning but unbiased—meditation on death and on life. Other poets cannot hope for such success: a subject, so popular, so grave, so wise, and yet so suitable to the writer's nature, is hardly to be found. But the same ideal, the same unautobiographical character, is to be found in the

---

[1] Johann Cristoph Friedrich von Schiller (1759–1805), German philosopher. Euripedes (480–406 BC), Greek tragedian.

writings of meaner men. Take sonnets of Hartley Coleridge, for example:—

I
To A Friend

When we were idlers with the loitering rills,
The need of human love we little noted:
Our love was nature; and the peace that floated
On the white mist, and dwelt upon the hills,
To sweet accord subdued our wayward wills:
One soul was ours, one mind, one heart devoted,
That, wisely doating, ask'd not why it doated,
And ours the unknown joy, which knowing kills.
But now I find, how dear thou wert to me;
That man is more than half of nature's treasure,
Of that fair Beauty which no eye can see,
Of that sweet music which no ear can measure;
And now the streams may sing for others' pleasure,
The hills sleep on in their eternity.

II
To The Same

In the great city we are met again,
Where many souls there are, that breathe and die,
Scarce knowing more of nature's potency,
Than what they learn from heat, or cold, or rain,
The sad vicissitude of weary pain:
For busy man is lord of ear and eye,
And what hath nature, but the vast, void sky,
And the throng'd river toiling to the main?
Oh! say not so, for she shall have her part
In every smile, in every tear that falls;
And she shall hide her in the secret heart,
Where love persuades, and sterner duty calls:
But worse it were than death, or sorrow's smart
To live without a friend within these walls.

III
To The Same

We part'd on the mountains, as two streams
From one clear spring pursue their several ways;
And thy fleet course hath been through many a maze
In foreign lands, where silvery Padus gleams
To that delicious sky, whose glowing beams
Brighten'd the tresses that old Poets praise;
Where Petrarch's patient love, and artful lays,
And Ariosto's song of many themes,
Moved the soft air. But I, a lazy brook,
As close pent up within my native dell,
Have crept along from nook to shady nook,
Where flowrets blow, and whispering Naiads dwell.
Yet now we meet, that parted were so wide,
O'er rough and smooth to travel side by side.

The contrast of instructive and enviable locomotion with refining but instructive meditation is not special and peculiar to these two, but general and universal. It was set down by Hartley Coleridge because he was the most meditative and refining of men.

What sort of literatesque types are fit to be described in the sort of literature called poetry, is a matter on which much might be written. Mr. Arnold, some years since, put forth a theory that the art of poetry could only delineate *great actions*. But though, rightly interpreted and understood—using the word action so as to include high and sound activity in contemplation—this definition may suit the highest poetry, it certainly cannot be stretched to include many inferior sorts and even many good sorts. Nobody in their senses would describe Gray's *Elegy* as the delineation of a "great action;" some kinds of mental contemplation may be energetic enough to deserve this name, but Gray would have been frightened at the very word. He loved scholarlike calm and quiet inaction; his very greatness depended on his *not* acting, on his "wise passiveness," on his indulging the grave idleness which so well appreciates so much of human life. But the best answer—the *reductio ad absurdum*—of Mr. Arnold's doctrine, is the mutilation which it has caused him to make of his own writings. It has forbidden him, he tells us, to reprint *Empedocles*—a poem undoubtedly containing defects and even excesses, but containing also these lines:—

> And yet what days were those, Parmenides!
> When we were young, when we could number friends
> In all the Italian cities like ourselves,
> When with elated hearts we join'd your train,
> Ye Sun-born virgins! on the road of truth.
> Then we could still enjoy, then neither thought
> Nor outward things were clos'd and dead to us,
> But we received the shock of mighty thoughts
> On simple minds with a pure natural joy;
> And if the sacred load oppress'd our brain,
> We had the power to feel the pressure eased,
> The brow unbound, the thoughts flow free again,
> In the delightful commerce of the world.
> We had not lost our balance then, nor grown
> Thought's slaves, and dead to every natural joy.
> The smallest thing could give us pleasure then—
> The sports of the country—people,
> A flute note from the woods,
> Sunset over the sea;
> Seed-time and harvest,
> The reapers in the corn,
> The vinedresser in his vineyard,
> The village-girl at her wheel.
> Fullness of life and power of feeling, ye
> Are for the happy, for the souls at ease,
> Who dwell on a firm basis of content!
> But he, who has outlived his prosperous days—
> But he, whose youth fell on a different world
> From that on which his exiled age is thrown—
> Whose mind was fed on other food, was train'd
> By other rules than are in vogue to-day—
> Whose habit of thought is fix'd, who will not change,
> But in a world he loves not, must subsist
> In ceaseless opposition, be the guard

> Of his own breast, fetter'd to what he guards,
> That the world win no mastery over him—
> Who has no friend, no fellow left, not one;
> Who has no minute's breathing space allow'd
> To nurse his dwindling faculty of joy—
> Joy and the outward world must die to him,
> As they are dead to me.

> (235–75)

What freak of criticism can induce a man who has written such poetry as this, to discard it, and say it is not poetry? Mr. Arnold is privileged to speak of his own poems, but no other critic could speak so and not be laughed at.

We are disposed to believe that no very sharp definition can be given—at least in the present state of the critical art—of the boundary line between poetry and other sorts of imaginative delineation. Between the undoubted dominions of the two kinds there is a debateable land; everybody is agreed that the *Œdipus at Colonus is* poetry: everyone is agreed that the wonderful appearance of Mrs. Veal is *not* poetry. But the exact line which separates grave novels in verse, like *Aylmer's Field* or *Enoch Arden*, from grave novels not in verse, like *Silas Marner* or *Adam Bede*, we own we cannot draw with any confidence. Nor, perhaps, is it very important; whether a narrative is thrown into verse or not certainly depends in part on the taste of the age, and in part on its mechanical helps. Verse is the only mechanical help to the memory in rude times, and there is little writing till a cheap something is found to write upon, and a cheap something to write with. Poetry—verse, at least—is the literature of *all work* in early ages; it is only later ages which write in what *they* think a natural and simple prose. There are other casual influences in the matter too; but they are not material now. We need only say here that poetry, because it has a more marked rhythm than prose, must be more intense in meaning and more concise in style than prose. People expect a "marked rhythm" to imply something worth marking; if it fails to do so they are disappointed. They are displeased at the visible waste of a powerful instrument; they call it "doggerel," and rightly call it, for the metrical expression of full thought and eager feeling—the burst of metre—incident to high imagination, should not be wasted on petty matters which prose does as well,—which it does better—which it suits by its very limpness and weakness, whose small changes it follows more easily, and to whose lowest details it can fully and without effort degrade itself. Verse, too, should be *more concise*, for long continued rhythm tends to jade the mind, just as brief rhythm tends to attract the attention. Poetry should be memorable and emphatic, intense, and *soon over*.

The great divisions of poetry, and of all other literary art, arise from the different modes in which these *types*—these characteristic men, these characteristic feelings—may be variously described. There are three principal modes which we shall attempt to describe—the *pure*, which is sometimes, but not very wisely, called the classical; the *ornate*, which is also unwisely called romantic; and the *grotesque*, which might be called the mediæval. We will describe the nature of these a little. Criticism, we know, must be brief—not, like poetry, because its charm is too intense to be sustained—but on the contrary, because its interest is too weak to be prolonged; but elementary criticism, if an evil, is a necessary evil; a little while spent among the simple principles of art is the first condition, the absolute pre-requisite, for surely apprehending and wisely judging the complete embodiments and miscellaneous forms of actual literature.

The definition of *pure* literature is that it describes the type in its simplicity; we mean, with the exact amount of accessory circumstance which is necessary to bring it before the mind in finished perfection, and *no more* than that amount. The *type* needs some accessories from its nature—a picturesque landscape does not consist wholly of picturesque features. There

is a setting of surroundings—as the Americans would say, of *fixings*—without which the reality is not itself. By a traditional mode of speech, as soon as we see a picture in which a complete effect is produced by detail so rare and so harmonised as to escape us, we say how "classical." The whole which is to be seen appears at once and through the detail, but the detail itself is not seen: we do not think of that which gives us the idea; we are absorbed in the idea itself. Just so in literature, the pure art is that which works with the fewest strokes; the fewest, that is, for its purpose, for its aim is to call up and bring home to men an idea, a form, a character; and if that idea be twisted, that form be involved, that character perplexed, many strokes of literary art will be needful. Pure art does not mutilate its object: it represents it as fully as is possible with the slightest effort which is possible: it shrinks from no needful circumstances, as little as it inserts any which are needless. The precise peculiarity is not merely that no incidental circumstance is inserted which does not tell on the main design:—no art is fit to be called *art* which permits a stroke to be put in without an object;—but that only the minimum of such circumstance is inserted at all. The form is sometimes said to be bare, the accessories are sometimes said to be invisible, because the appendages are so choice that the shape only is perceived.

· · · · · · · · · ·

The extreme opposite to this pure art is what may be called ornate art. This species of art aims also at giving a delineation of the typical idea in its perfection and its fulness, but it aims at so doing in a manner most different. It wishes to surround the type with the greatest number of circumstances which it will *bear*. It works not by choice and selection, but by accumulation and aggregation. The idea is not, as in the pure style, presented with the least clothing which it will endure, but with the richest and most involved clothing that it will admit.

We are fortunate in not having to hunt out of past literature an illustrative specimen of the ornate style. Mr. Tennyson has just given one, admirable in itself, and most characteristic of the defects and the merits of this style. The story of *Enoch Arden*, as he has enhanced and presented it, is a rich and splendid composite of imagery and illustration. Yet how simple that story is in itself. A sailor who sells fish, breaks his leg, gets dismal, gives up selling fish, goes to sea, is wrecked on a desert island, stays there some years, on his return finds his wife married to a miller, speaks to a landlady on the subject, and dies. Told in the pure and simple, the unadorned and classical style, this story would not have taken three pages, but Mr. Tennyson has been able to make it the principal, the largest, tale in his new volume. He has done so only by giving to every event and incident in the volume an accompanying commentary. He tells a great deal about the torrid zone which a rough sailor like Enoch Arden certainly would not have perceived; and he gives to the fishing village, to which all the characters belong, a softness and a fascination which such villages scarcely possess in reality.

The description of the tropical island, on which the sailor is thrown, is an absolute model of adorned art:—

> This mountain wooded to the peak, the lawns
> And winding glades high up like ways to Heaven,
> The slender coco's drooping crown of plumes,
> The lightning flash of insect and of bird,
> The lustre of the long convolvuluses
> That coil'd around the stately stems, and ran
> Ev'n to the limit of the land, the glows
> And glories of the broad belt of the world,
> All these he saw; but what he fain had seen
> He could not see, the kindly human face,
> Nor ever hear a kindly voice, but heard
> The myriad shriek of wheeling ocean-fowl,
> The league-long roller thundering on the reef,
> The moving whisper of huge trees that branch'd
> And blossom'd in the zenith, or the sweep

> Of some precipitous rivulet to the wave,
> As down the shore he ranged, or all day long
> Sat often in the seaward-gazing gorge,
> A shipwreck'd sailor, waiting for a sail:
> No sail from day to day, but every day
> The sunrise broken into scarlet shafts
> Among the palms and ferns and precipices;
> The blaze upon the waters to the east;
> The blaze upon his island overhead;
> The blaze upon the waters to the west;
> Then the great stars that globed themselves in Heaven,
> The hollower-bellowing ocean, and again
> The scarlet shafts of sunrise—but no sail.
>
> (568–95)

No expressive circumstance can be added to this description, no enhancing detail suggested. A much less happy instance is the description of Enoch's life before he sailed:—

> While Enoch was abroad on wrathful seas,
> Or often journeying landward; for in truth
> Enoch's white horse, and Enoch's ocean spoil
> In ocean-smelling osier, and his face,
> Rough-redden'd with a thousand winter gales,
> Not only to the market-cross were known,
> But in the leafy lanes behind the down,
> Far as the portal-warding lion-whelp,
> And peacock yew-tree of the lonely Hall,
> Whose Friday fare was Enoch's ministering.
>
> (90–100)

So much has not often been made of selling fish.

The essence of ornate art is in this manner to accumulate round the typical object, everything which can be said about it, every associated thought that can be connected with it, without impairing the essence of the delineation.

The first defect which strikes a student of ornate art—the first which arrests the mere reader of it—is what is called a want of simplicity. Nothing is described as it is, everything has about it an atmosphere of *something else*. The combined and associated thoughts, though they set off and heighten particular ideas and aspects of the central and typical conception, yet complicate it: a simple thing—"a daisy by the river's brim"—is never left by itself, something else is put with it; something not more connected with it than "lion-whelp" and the "peacock yew-tree" are with the "fresh fish for sale" the Enoch carries past them. Even in the highest cases, ornate art leaves upon a cultured and delicate taste the conviction that it is not the highest art, that it is somehow excessive and overrich, that it is not chaste in itself or chastening to the mind that sees it—that it is in an unexplained manner unsatisfactory, "a thing in which we feel there is some hidden want!"

That want is a want of "definition." We must all know landscapes, river landscapes especially, which are in the highest sense beautiful, which when we first see them give us a delicate pleasure; which in some—and these the best cases—give even a gentle sense of surprise that such things should be so beautiful, and yet when we come to live in them, to spend even a few hours in them, we seem stifled and oppressed. On the other hand, there are people to whom the sea-shore is a companion, an exhilaration; and not so much for the brawl of the shore as for the *limited* vastness, the finite infinite, of the ocean as they see it. Such people often come home braced and nerved, and if they spoke out the truth, would have only to say "We have seen the horizon line;" if they were let alone, indeed, they would gaze on it hour after hour, so great to them is the fascination, so full the sustaining calm, which they gain from that union of form and greatness. To a very inferior extent, but still, perhaps, to an extent which most people understand better, a common arch will have the same effect. A bridge completes a river landscape; if of the old and many-arched sort, it regulates by a long series of defined forms the vague outline of wood and river which before had nothing to measure it; if of the new scientific sort, it introduces still more strictly a geometrical element; it stiffens the scenery which was

before too soft, too delicate, too vegetable. Just such is the effect of pure style in literary art. It calms by conciseness; while the ornate style leaves on the mind a mist of beauty, an excess of fascination, a complication of charm, the pure style leaves behind it the simple, defined, measured idea, as it is, and by itself. That which is chaste chastens; there is a poised energy—a state half thrill, and half tranquillity —which pure art gives; which no other can give; a pleasure justified as well as felt; an ennobled satisfaction at what ought to satisfy us, and must ennoble us.

Ornate art is to pure art what a painted statue is to an unpainted. It is impossible to deny that a touch of colour *does* bring out certain parts, does convey certain expressions, does heighten certain features, but it leaves on the work as a whole, a want, as we say, "of something;" a want of that inseparable chasteness which clings to simple sculpture, an impairing predominance of alluring details which impairs our satisfaction with our own satisfaction; which makes us doubt whether a higher being than ourselves will be satisfied even though we are so. In the very same manner, though the *rouge* of ornate literature excites our eye, it also impairs our confidence.

. . . .

It will be said, if ornate art be, as you say, an inferior species of art, why should it ever be used? If pure art be the best sort of art, why should it not always be used?

The reason is this: literary art, as we just now explained, is concerned with literatesque characters in literatesque situations; and the *best* art is concerned with the *most* literatesque characters in the *most* literatesque situations. Such are the subjects of pure art; it embodies with the fewest touches, and under the most select and choice circumstances, the highest conceptions; but it does not follow that only the best subjects are to be treated by art, and then only in the very best way. Human nature could not endure such a critical commandment as that, and it would be an erroneous criticism which gave it. *Any* literatesque character may be described in literature under *any* circumstances which exhibit its literatesqueness.

. . . .

For these reasons ornate art is within the limits as legitimate as pure art. It does what pure art could not do. The very excellence of pure art confines its employment. Precisely because it gives the best things by themselves and exactly as they are, it fails when it is necessary to describe inferior things among other things, with a list of enhancements and a crowd of accompaniments that in reality do not belong to it. Illusion, half belief, unpleasant types, imperfect types, are as much the proper sphere of ornate art, as an inferior landscape is the proper sphere for the true efficacy of moonlight. A really great landscape needs sunlight and bears sunlight; but moonlight is an equaliser of beauties; it gives a romantic unreality to what will not stand the bare truth. And just so does romantic art.

There is, however, a third kind of art which differs from these on the point in which they most resemble one another. Ornate art and pure art have this in common, that they paint the types of literature in as good perfection as they can. Ornate art, indeed, uses undue disguises and unreal enhancements; it does not confine itself to the best types; on the contrary it is its office to make the best of imperfect types and lame approximations; but ornate art, as much as pure art, catches its subject in the best light it can, takes the most developed aspect of it which it can find, and throws upon it the most congruous colours it can use. But grotesque art does just the contrary. It takes the type, so to say, *in difficulties*. It gives a representation of it in its minimum development, amid the circumstances least favourable to it, just while it is struggling with obstacles, just where it is encumbered with incongruities. It deals, to use the language of science, not with normal types but with abnormal specimens; to use the language of old philosophy, not with what nature is striving to be, but with what by some lapse she has happened to become.

This art works by contrast. It enables you to see, it makes you see, the perfect type by painting the opposite deviation. It shows you what ought to be by what ought not to be; when complete, it reminds you of the perfect image by showing you the distorted and imperfect image. Of this art we possess in the present generation one prolific master. Mr. Browning is an artist working by incongruity. Possibly hardly one of his most considerable efforts can be found which is not great because of its odd mixture. He puts together things which no one else would have put together, and produces on our minds a result which no one else would have produced, or tried to produce. His admirers may not like all we may have to say of him. But in our way we too are among his admirers. No one ever read him without seeing not only his great ability but his great *mind*. He not only possesses superficial useable talents, but the strong something, the inner secret something, which uses them and controls them; he is great, not in mere accomplishments, but in himself. He has applied a hard strong intellect to real life; he has applied the same intellect to the problems of his age. He has striven to know what *is*: he has endeavoured not to be cheated by counterfeits, not to be infatuated with illusions. His heart is in what he says. He has battered his brain against his creed till he believes it. He has accomplishments too, the more effective because they are mixed. He is at once a student of mysticism and a citizen of the world. He brings to the club sofa distinct visions of old creeds, intense images of strange thoughts: he takes to the bookish student tidings of wild Bohemia, and little traces of the *demi-monde*. He puts down what is good for the naughty and what is naughty for the good. Over women his easier writings exercise that imperious power which belongs to the writings of a great man of the world upon such matters. He knows women, and therefore they wish to know him. If we blame many of Browning's efforts, it is in the interest of art, and not from a wish to hurt or degrade him.

If we wanted to illustrate the nature of grotesque art by an exaggerated instance, we should have selected a poem which the chance of late publication brings us in this new volume. Mr. Browning has undertaken to describe what may be called *mind in difficulties*—mind set to make out the universe under the worst and hardest circumstances. He takes "Caliban," not perhaps exactly Shakespeare's Caliban, but an analogous and worse creature; a strong thinking power, but a nasty creature—a gross animal, uncontrolled and unelevated by any feeling of religion or duty. The delineation of him will show that Mr. Browning does not wish to take undue advantage of his readers by a choice of nice subjects.

> 'Will sprawl, now that the heat of day is best,
> Flat on his belly in the pit's much mire,
> With elbows wide, fists clenched to prop his chin.
> And, while he kicks both feet in the cool slush,
> And feels about his spine small eft-things course,
> Run in and out each arm, and make him laugh;
> And while above his head a pompion-plant,
> Coating the cave-top as a brow its eye,
> Creeps down to touch and tickle hair and beard,
> And now a flower drops with a bee inside,
> And now a fruit to snap at, catch and crunch,—
>
> (1–11)

This pleasant creature proceeds to give his idea of the origin of the universe, and it is as follows. Caliban speaks in the third person, and is of opinion that the maker of the universe took to making it on account of his personal discomfort:—

> Setebos, Setebos, and Setebos!
> 'Thinketh, He dwelleth i' the cold o' the moon.
> 'Thinketh He made it, with the sun to match,
> But not the stars; the stars came otherwise;

> Only made clouds, winds, meteors, such as that;
> Also this isle, what lives and grows thereon,
> And snaky sea which rounds and ends the same.
>
> 'Thinketh, it came of being ill at ease:
> He hated that He cannot change His cold,
> Nor cure its ache. 'Hath spied an icy fish
> That longed to 'scape the rock-stream where she lived,
> And thaw herself within the lukewarm brine
> O' the lazy sea her stream thrusts far amid,
> A crystal spike 'twixt two warm walls of wave;
> Only she ever sickened, found repulse
> At the other kind of water, not her life,
> (Green-dense and dim-delicious, bred o' the sun)
> Flounced back from bliss she was not born to breathe,
> And in her old bounds buried her despair,
> Hating and loving warmth alike: so He.
>
> 'Thinketh, He made thereat the sun, this isle,
> Trees and the fowls here, beast and creeping thing.
> Yon otter, sleek-wet, black, lithe as a leech;
> Yon auk, one fire-eye, in a ball of foam,
> That floats and feeds; a certain badger brown
> He hath watched hunt with that slant white-wedge eye
> By moonlight; and the pie with the long tongue
> That pricks deep into oakwarts for a worm,
> And says a plain word when she finds her prize,
> But will not eat the ants; the ants themselves
> That build a wall of seeds and settled stalks
> About their hole—He made all these and more,
> Made all we see, and us, in spite: how else?
>
> (24–56)

It may seem perhaps to most readers that these lines are very difficult, and that they are unpleasant. And so they are. We quote them to illustrate, not the *success* of grotesque art, but the *nature* of grotesque art. It shows the end at which this species of art aims, and if it fails it is from over-boldness in the choice of a subject by the artist, or from the defects of its execution. A thinking faculty more in difficulties—a great type—an inquisitive, searching intellect under more disagreeable conditions, with worse helps, more likely to find falsehood, less likely to find truth, can scarcely be imagined. Nor is the mere description of the thought at all bad: on the contrary, if we closely examine it, it is very clever. Hardly anyone could have amassed so many ideas at once nasty and suitable. But scarcely any readers—any casual readers—who are not of the sect of Mr. Browning's admirers will be able to examine it enough to appreciate it. From a defect, partly of subject, and partly of style, many of Mr. Browning's works make a demand upon the reader's zeal and sense of duty to which the nature of most readers is unequal. They have on the turf the convenient expression "staying power": some horses can hold on and others cannot. But hardly any reader not of especial and peculiar nature can hold on through such composition. There is not enough of "staying power" in human nature. One of his greatest admirers once owned to us that he seldom or never began a new poem without looking on in advance, and foreseeing with caution what length of intellectual adventure he was about to commence. Whoever will work hard at such poems will find much mind in them: they are a sort of quarry of ideas, but whoever goes there will find these ideas in such a jagged, ugly, useless shape that he can hardly bear them.

. . . .

It is very natural that a poet whose wishes incline, or whose genius conducts him, to a grotesque art, should be attracted towards mediæval subjects. There is no age whose legends are so full of grotesque subjects, and no age where real life was so fit to suggest them. Then, more than at any other time, good principles have been under great hardships. The vestiges of ancient civilisation, the germs of modern civilisation, the little remains of what had been, the small beginnings of what is, were buried under a cumbrous mass of barbarism and cruelty. Good elements hidden in horrid accompaniments are the special theme of grotesque art, and these mediæval life and legends afford more copiously than could

have been furnished before Christianity gave its new elements of good, or since modern civilisation has removed some few at least of the old elements of destruction. A *buried* life like the spiritual mediæval was Mr. Browning's natural element, and he was right to be attracted by it. His mistake has been, that he has not made it pleasant; that he has forced his art to topics on which no one could charm, or on which he, at any rate, could not; that on these occasions and in these poems he has failed in fascinating men and women of sane taste.

. . . .

Something more we had to say of Mr. Browning, but we must stop. It is singularly characteristic of this age that the poems which rise to the surface should be examples of ornate art and grotesque art, not of pure art. We live in the realm of the *half* educated. The number of readers grows daily, but the quality of readers does not improve rapidly. The middle class is scattered, headless; it is well-meaning, but aimless; wishing to be wise, but ignorant how to be wise. The aristocracy of England never was a literary aristocracy, never even in the days of its full power, of its unquestioned predominance, did it guide—did it even seriously try to guide—the taste of England. Without guidance young men, and tired men, are thrown amongst a mass of books; they have to choose which they like; many of them would much like to improve their culture, to chasten their taste, if they knew how. But left to themselves they take, not pure art, but showy art; not that which permanently relieves the eye and makes it happy whenever it looks, and as long as it looks, but *glaring* art which catches and arrests the eye for a moment, but which in the end fatigues it. But before the wholesome remedy of nature—the fatigue—arrives, the hasty reader has passed on to some new excitement, which in its turn stimulates for an instant, and then is passed by for ever. These conditions are not favourable to the due appreciation of pure art—of that art which must be known before it is admired—which must have fastened irrevocably on the brain before you appreciate it—which you must love ere it will seem worthy of your love. Women, too, whose voice in literature counts as well as that of men—and in a light literature counts for more than that of men—women, such as we know them, such as they are likely to be, ever prefer a delicate unreality to a true or firm art. A dressy literature, an exaggerated literature, seem to be fated to us. These are our curses, as other times had theirs.

.   .   .   .

—1864

Robert Buchanan
1841 – 1901

"The Fleshly School of Poetry: Mr. D.G. Rossetti," signed "Thomas Maitland" (published in the *Contemporary Review* for October, 1871), was a review of the fifth edition of Rossetti's *Poems*. Buchanan was a minor poet, critic, and novelist. He took sides in the literary squabbles of the 1860s against Swinburne and the Rossettis, and his attack in this essay reflects his personal as well as his literary animosity. Rossetti answered him in "The Stealthy School of Criticism" and Swinburne in *Under the Microscope*, both of which follow.

ↄ℈ↄ

The Fleshly School of Poetry: Mr. D.G. Rossetti

If, on the occasion of any public performance of Shakespeare's great tragedy, the actors who perform the parts of Rosencranz and Guildenstern were, by a preconcerted arrangement and by means of what is technically known as "gagging," to make themselves fully as prominent as the leading character, and to indulge in soliloquies and business strictly belonging to Hamlet himself, the result would be, to say the least of it, astonishing; yet a very similar effect is produced on the unprejudiced mind when the "walking gentlemen"[1] of the fleshly school of poetry, who bear precisely the same relation to Mr. Tennyson as Rosencranz and Guildenstern do to the prince of Denmark in the play, obtrude their lesser identities and parade their smaller idiosyncrasies in the front rank of leading performers. In their own place, the gentlemen are interesting and useful. Pursuing still the theatrical analogy, the present drama of poetry might be cast as follows: Mr. Tennyson supporting the part of Hamlet, Mr. Matthew Arnold that of Horatio, Mr. Bailey that of Voltimand, Mr. Buchanan that of Cornelius, Messrs. Swinburne and Morris the parts of Rosencranz and Guildenstern, Mr. Rossetti that of Osric, and Mr. Robert Lytton that of "A Gentleman."[2] It will be seen that we have left no place for Mr. Browning, who may be said, however, to play the leading character in his own peculiar fashion on alternate nights.

This may seem a frivolous and inadequate way of opening our remarks on a school of verse-writers which some people regard as possessing great merits; but in good truth, it is scarcely possible to discuss with any seriousness the pretensions with which foolish friends and small critics have surrounded the fleshly school, which, in spite of its spasmodic[3] ramifications in the erotic direction, is merely one of the many sub-Tennysonian schools expanded to supernatural dimensions, and endeavouring by affectations all its own to overshadow its connection with the great original. In the sweep of one single poem, the weird and doubtful "Vivien,"[4] Mr. Tennyson has concentrated all the epicene force which, wearisomely expanded, constitutes the characteristic of the writers at present under consideration; and if in "Vivien" he has indicated for them the bounds of sensualism in art, he has in *Maud*, in the dramatic person of the hero, afforded distinct precedent for the hysteric tone and overloaded style which is now so familiar to readers of Mr. Swinburne. The fleshliness of "Vivien" may indeed be described as the distinct quality held in common by all the members of the

---

[1] actors who simply walk on and off stage.

[2] Philip Bailey, founder of the Spasmodic School, and author of *Festus*

(1830 and 1845). Lytton was the son of Edward Bulwer-Lytton (1803–73), novelist.

[3] "by fits and starts," and as related to the Spasmodic School.

[4] later called "Merlin and Vivien," one of the *Idylls of the King*.

last sub-Tennysonian school, and it is a quality which becomes unwholesome when there is no moral or intellectual quality to temper and control it. Fully conscious of this themselves, the fleshly gentlemen have bound themselves by solemn league and covenant to extol fleshliness as the distinct and supreme end of poetic and pictorial art; to aver that poetic expression is greater than poetic thought, and by inference that the body is greater than the soul, and sound superior to sense; and that the poet, properly to develop his poetic faculty, must be an intellectual hermaphrodite, to whom the very facts of day and night are lost in a whirl of aesthetic terminology. After Mr. Tennyson has probed the depths of modern speculation in a series of commanding moods, all right and interesting in him as the reigning personage, the walking gentlemen, knowing that something of the sort is expected from all leading performers, bare their roseate bosoms and aver that *they* are creedless; the only possible question here being, if any disinterested person cares twopence whether Rosencranz, Guildenstern, and Osric are creedless or not—their self-revelation on that score being so perfectly gratuitous? But having gone so far, it was and is too late to retreat. Rosencranz, Guildenstern, and Osric, finding it impossible to risk an individual bid for the leading business, have arranged all to play leading business together, and mutually to praise, extol, and imitate each other; and although by these measures they have fairly earned for themselves the title of the Mutual Admiration School, they have in a great measure succeeded in their object—to the general stupefaction of a British audience. It is time, therefore, to ascertain whether any of these gentlemen has actually in himself the making of a leading performer. When the *Athenæum*—once more cautious in such matters—advertised nearly every week some interesting particular about Mr. Swinburne's health, Mr. Morris's holiday-making, or Mr. Rossetti's genealogy, varied with such startling statements as "We are informed that Mr. Swinburne dashed off

his noble ode *at a sitting*," or "Mr. Swinburne's songs have already reached a second edition," or "Good poetry seems to be in demand; the first edition of Mr. O'Shaughnessy's[1] poems is exhausted;" when the *Academy* informed us that "During the past year or two Mr. Swinburne has written several novels" (!), and that some review or other is to be praised for giving Mr. Rossetti's poems "the attentive study which they demand"—when we read these things we might or might not know pretty well how and where they originated; but to a provincial eye, perhaps, the whole thing really looked like leading business. It would be scarcely worth while, however, to inquire into the pretensions of the writers on merely literary grounds, because sooner or later all literature finds its own level, whatever criticism may say or do in the matter; but it unfortunately happens in the present case that the fleshly school of verse-writers are, so to speak, public offenders, because they are diligently spreading the seeds of disease broadcast wherever they are read and understood. Their complaint too is catching, and carries off many young persons. What the complaint is, and how it works, may be seen on a very slight examination of the works of Mr. Dante Gabriel Rossetti, to whom we shall confine our attention in the present article.

Mr. Rossetti has been known for many years as a painter of exceptional powers, who, for reasons best known to himself, has shrunk from publicly exhibiting his pictures, and from allowing anything like a popular estimate to be formed of their qualities. He belongs, or is said to belong, to the so-called Pre-Raphaelite school, a school which is generally considered to exhibit much genius for colour, and great indifference to perspective. It would be unfair to judge the painter by the glimpses we have had of his works, or by the photographs which are sold of the principal paintings. Judged by the photographs, he is an artist who conceives unpleasantly, and draws ill.

---

[1] Arthur William O'Shaughnessy (1844–81), a minor poet related to the Pre-Raphaelite circle.

Like Mr. Simeon Solomon,[1] however, with whom he seems to have many points in common, he is distinctively a colourist, and of his capabilities in colour we cannot speak, though we should guess that they are great; for if there is any good quality by which his poems are specially marked, it is a great sensitiveness to hues and tints as conveyed in poetic epithet. These qualities, which impress the casual spectator of the photographs from his pictures, are to be found abundantly among his verses. There is the same thinness and transparence of design, the same combination of the simple and the grotesque, the same morbid deviation from healthy forms of life, the same sense of weary, wasting, yet exquisite sensuality; nothing virile, nothing tender, nothing completely sane; a superfluity of extreme sensibility, of delight in beautiful forms, hues, and tints, and a deep-seated indifference to all agitating forces and agencies, all tumultuous griefs and sorrows, all the thunderous stress of life, and all the straining storm of speculation. Mr. Morris is often pure, fresh, and wholesome as his own great model; Mr. Swinburne startles us more than once by some fine flash of insight; but the mind of Mr. Rossetti is like a glassy mere, broken only by the dive of some water-bird or the hum of winged insects, and brooded over by an atmosphere of insufferable closeness, with a light blue sky above it, sultry depths mirrored within it, and a surface so thickly sown with waterlilies that it retains its glassy smoothness even in the strongest wind. Judged relatively to his poetic associates, Mr. Rossetti must be pronounced inferior to either. He cannot tell a pleasant story like Mr. Morris, nor forge alliterative thunderbolts like Mr. Swinburne. It must be conceded, nevertheless, that he is neither so glibly imitative as the one, nor so transcendently superficial as the other.

Although he has been known for many years as a poet as well as a painter—as a painter and poet idolized by his own family and personal associates—and although he has once or twice appeared in print as a contributor to magazines, Mr. Rossetti did not formally appeal to the public until rather more than a year ago, when he published a copious volume of poems, with the announcement that the book, although it contained pieces composed at intervals during a period of many years, "included nothing which the author believes to be immature." This work was inscribed to his brother, Mr. William Rossetti, who, having written much both in poetry and criticism, will perhaps be known to bibliographers as the editor of the worst edition of Shelley which has yet seen the light. No sooner had the work appeared than the chorus of eulogy began. "The book is satisfactory from end to end," wrote Mr. Morris in the *Academy*; "I think these lyrics, with all their other merits, the most complete of their time; nor do I know what lyrics of any time are to be called *great*, if we are to deny the title to these." On the same subject Mr. Swinburne went into a hysteria of admiration: "golden affluence," "jewel-coloured words," "chastity of form," "harmonious nakedness," "consummate fleshly sculpture," and so on in Mr. Swinburne's well-known manner when reviewing his friends.[2] Other critics, with a singular similarity of phrase, followed suit. Strange to say, moreover, no one accused Mr. Rossetti of naughtiness. What had been heinous in Mr. Swinburne was majestic exquisiteness in Mr. Rossetti. Yet we question if there is anything in the unfortunate *Poems and Ballads* quite so questionable on the score of thorough naughtiness as many pieces in Mr. Rossetti's collection. Mr. Swinburne was wilder, more outrageous, more blasphemous, and his subjects were more atrocious in themselves; yet the hysterical tone slew the animalism, the furiousness of epithet lowered the sensation; and the first feeling of disgust at such themes as "Laus Veneris" and "Anactoria," faded away into

---

[1] Pre-Raphaelite painter.

[2] a reference to Swinburne's 1870 *Fortnightly Review* article on Rossetti's poems.

comic amazement. It was only a little mad boy letting off squibs; not a great strong man, who might be really dangerous to society. "I *will* be naughty!" screamed the little boy; but, after all, what did it matter? It is quite different, however, when a grown man, with the self-control and easy audacity of actual experience, comes forward to chronicle his amorous sensations, and, first proclaiming in a loud voice his literary maturity, and consequent responsibility, shamelessly prints and publishes such a piece of writing as this sonnet on "Nuptial Sleep;"—

At length their long kiss severed, with sweet smart:
    And as the last slow sudden drops are shed
    From sparkling eaves when all the storm has fled,
So singly flagged the pulses of each heart.
Their bosoms sundered, with the opening start
    Of married flowers to either side outspread
    From the knit stem; yet still their mouths, burnt red,
Fawned on each other where they lay apart.
Sleep sank them lower than the tide of dreams,
    And their dreams watched them sink, and slid away.
Slowly their souls swam up again, through gleams
    Of watered light and dull drowned waifs of day;
Till from some wonder of new woods and streams
    He woke, and wondered more: for there she lay.

This, then, is "the golden affluence of words, the firm outline, the justice and chastity of form." Here is a full-grown man, presumably intelligent and cultivated, putting on record for other full-grown men to read, the most secret mysteries of sexual connection, and that with so sickening a desire to reproduce the sensual mood, so careful a choice of epithet to convey mere animal sensations, that we merely shudder at the shameless nakedness. We are no purists in such matters. We hold the sensual part of our nature to be as holy as the spiritual or intellectual part, and we believe that such things must find their equivalent in all; but it is neither poetic, nor manly, nor even human, to obtrude such things as the themes of whole poems. It is simply nasty. Nasty as it is, we are

very mistaken if many readers do not think it nice. English society of one kind purchases the *Day's Doings*.[1] English society of another kind goes into ecstasy over Mr. Solomon's pictures—pretty pieces of morality, such as "Love dying by the breath of Lust." There is not much to choose between the two objects of admiration, except that painters like Mr. Solomon lend actual genius to worthless subjects, and thereby produce veritable monsters—like the lovely devils that danced round Saint Anthony.[2] Mr. Rossetti owes his so-called success to the same causes. In poems like "Nuptial Sleep," the man who is too sensitive to exhibit his pictures, and so modest that it takes him years to make up his mind to publish his poems, parades his private sensations before a coarse public, and is gratified by their applause.

It must not be supposed that all Mr. Rossetti's poems are made up of trash like this. Some of them are as noteworthy for delicacy of touch as others are for shamelessness of exposition. They contain some exquisite pictures of nature, occasional passages of real meaning, much beautiful phraseology, lines of peculiar sweetness, and epithets chosen with true literary cunning. But the fleshly feeling is everywhere. Sometimes, as in "The Stream's Secret," it is deliciously modulated, and adds greatly to our emotion of pleasure at perusing a finely-wrought poem; at other times, as in the "Last Confession," it is fiercely held in check by the exigencies of a powerful situation and the strength of a dramatic speaker; but it is generally in the foreground, flushing the whole poem with unhealthy rose-colour, stifling the senses with overpowering sickliness, as of too much civet. Mr. Rossetti is never dramatic, never impersonal—always attitudinizing, posturing, and describing his own exquisite emotions. He is the Blessed Damozel, leaning over the "gold bar of heaven," and seeing

---

[1] a popular *Illustrated Journal* of daily events.

[2] a reference to the temptations of St. Anthony depicted in the painting by Joachim Patinir (1485–1524).

Time like a pulse shake fierce
  Thro' all the worlds.

he is "heaven-born Helen, Sparta's queen," whose "each twin breast is an apple sweet;" he is Lilith the first wife of Adam; he is the rosy Virgin of the poem called "Ave," and the Queen in the "Staff and Scrip;" he is "Sister Helen" melting her waxen man; he is all these, just as surely as he is Mr. Rossetti soliloquizing over Jenny in her London lodging, or the very nuptial person writing erotic sonnets to his wife.[1] In petticoats or pantaloons, in modern times or in the middle ages, he is just Mr. Rossetti, a fleshly person, with nothing particular to tell us or teach us, with extreme self-control, a strong sense of colour, and a careful choice of diction. Amid all his "affluence of jewel-coloured words," he has not given us one rounded and noteworthy piece of art, though his verses are all art; not one poem which is memorable for its own sake, and quite separate from the displeasing identity of the composer. The nearest approach to a perfect whole is the "Blessed Damozel," a peculiar poem, placed first in the book, perhaps by accident, perhaps because it is a key to the poems which follow. This poem appeared in a rough shape many years ago in the *Germ,* an unwholesome periodical started by the Pre-Raphaelites, and suffered, after gasping through a few feeble numbers, to die the death of all such publications. In spite of its affected title, and of numberless affectations throughout the text, the "Blessed Damozel" has great merits of its own, and a few lines of real genius. We have heard it described as the record of actual grief and love, or, in simple words, the apotheosis of one actually lost by the writer; but, without having any private knowledge of the circumstance of its composition, we feel that such an account of the poem is inadmissible. It does not contain one single note of sorrow. It is a "composition," and a clever one. Read the opening stanzas:—

The blessed damozel leaned out
  From the gold bar of Heaven;
Her eyes were deeper than the depth
  Of water stilled at even;
She had three lilies in her hand,
  And the stars in her hair were seven.

Her robe, ungirt from clasp to hem,
  No wrought flowers did adorn,
But a white rose of Mary's gift,
  For service meetly worn;
Her hair that lay along her back
  Was yellow like ripe corn.

This is a careful sketch for a picture, which, worked into actual colour by a master, might have been worth seeing. The steadiness of hand lessens as the poem proceeds, and although there are several passages of considerable power,—such as that where, far down the void,

        this earth
  Spins like a fretful midge

or that other, describing how

      the curled moon
  Was like a little feather
  Fluttering far down the gulf—

the general effect is that of a queer old painting in a missal, very affected and very odd. What moved the British critic to ecstacy in this poem seems to us very sad nonsense indeed, or, if not sad nonsense, very meretricious affectation. Thus, we have seen the following verses quoted with enthusiasm, as italicized—

And still she bowed herself and stooped
  Out of the circling charm;
Until her bosom must have made
The bar she leaned on warm,

---

[1] his sonnet sequence "The House of Life."

And the lilies lay as if asleep
    Along her bended arm.

From the fixed place of Heaven she saw
    Time like a pulse shake fierce
Thro' all the worlds. Her gaze still strove
    Within the gulf to pierce
Its path; and now she spoke as when
    The stars sang in their spheres.

It seems to us that all these lines are very bad, with the exception of the two admirable lines ending the first verse, and that the italicized portions are quite without merit, and almost without meaning. On the whole, one feels disheartened and amazed at the poet who, in the nineteenth century, talks about "damozels," "citherns," and "citoles," and addresses the mother of Christ as the "Lady Mary,"—

With her five handmaidens, whose names
    Are five sweet symphonies,
Cecily, Gertrude, Magdalen,
    Margaret and Rosalys.

A suspicion is awakened that the writer is laughing at us. We hover uncertainly between picturesqueness and namby-pamby, and the effect, as Artemus Ward[1] would express it, is "weakening to the intellect." The thing would have been almost too much in the shape of a picture, though the workmanship might have made amends. The truth is that literature, and more particularly poetry, is in a very bad way when one art gets hold of another, and imposes upon it its conditions and limitations. In the first few verses of the "Damozel" we have the subject, or part of the subject, of a picture, and the inventor should either have painted it or left it alone altogether; and, had he done the latter, the world would have lost nothing. Poetry is something more than painting; and an idea will not become a poem, because it is too smudgy for a picture.

In a short notice from a well-known pen, giving the best estimate we have seen of Mr. Rossetti's powers as a poet, the *North American Review* offers a certain explanation for affectation such as that of Mr. Rossetti. The writer suggests that "it may probably be the expression of genuine moods of mind in natures too little comprehensive."[2] We would rather believe that Mr. Rossetti lacks comprehension than that he is deficient in sincerity; yet really, to paraphrase the words which Johnson applied to Thomas Sheridan, Mr. Rossetti is affected, naturally affected, but it must have taken him a great deal of trouble to become what we now see him—such an excess of affectation is not in nature.[3] There is very little writing in the volume spontaneous in the sense that some of Swinburne's verses are spontaneous; the poems all look as if they had taken a great deal of trouble. The grotesque mediævalism of "Stratton Water" and "Sister Helen," the mediaeval classicism of "Troy Town," the false and shallow mysticism of "Eden Bower," are one and all essentially imitative, and must have cost the writer much pains. It is time, indeed, to point out that Mr. Rossetti is a poet possessing great powers of assimilation and some faculty for concealing the nutriment on which he feeds. Setting aside the *Vita Nuova* and the early Italian poems, which are familiar to many readers by his own excellent translations,[4] Mr. Rossetti may be described as a writer who has yielded to an unusual extent to the complex influences of the literature surrounding him at the present moment. He has the painter's imitative power developed in proportion to his lack of the poet's conceiving imagination. He

---

[1] American humorist Charles F. Browne, who wrote under this pseudonym for *Punch*.

[2] J.R. Dennett, "Rossetti's Poems," *North American Review* (October, 1870), 473.

[3] "Why, sir, Sherry is dull, *naturally* dull; but it must have taken him a *great deal of trouble* to become what we now see him—such an excess of stupidity is not in nature.—*Boswell's Life*." (Buchanan's note.)

[4] *The Early Italian Poets* (1861).

reproduces to a nicety the manner of an old ballad, a trick in which Mr. Swinburne is also an adept. Cultivated readers, moreover, will recognise in every one of these poems the tone of Mr. Tennyson broken up by the style of Mr. and Mrs. Browning, and disguised here and there by the eccentricities of the pre-Raphaelites. The "Burden of Nineveh" is a philosophical edition of "Recollections of the Arabian Nights;" "A Last Confession" and "Dante at Verona" are, in the minutest trick and form of thought, suggestive of Mr. Browning; and that the sonnets have been largely moulded and inspired by Mrs. Browning can be ascertained by any critic who will compare them with the *Sonnets from the Portuguese*. Much remains, nevertheless, that is Mr. Rossetti's own. We at once recognise as his own property such passages as this:—

>   I looked up
> And saw where a brown-shouldered harlot leaned
> Half through a tavern window thick with vine.
> Some man had come behind her in the room
> And caught her by her arms, and she had turned
> With that coarse empty laugh on him, as now
> *He munched her neck with kisses, while the vine*
> *Crawled in her back.*

Or this:—

> As I stooped, her own lips rising there
> *Bubbled with brimming kisses at my mouth*

Or this:—

> Have seen your lifted silken skirt
> Advertise dainties through the dirt!

Or this:—

> What more prize than love to impel thee,
> *Grip* and *lip* my limbs as I tell thee. [1]

Passages like these are the common stock of the walking gentlemen of the fleshly school. We cannot forbear expressing our wonder, by the way, at the kind of women whom it seems the unhappy lot of these gentlemen to encounter. We have lived as long in the world as they have, but never yet came across persons of the other sex who conduct themselves in the manner described. Females who bite, scratch, scream, bubble, munch, sweat, writhe, twist, wriggle, foam, and in a general way slaver over their lovers, must surely possess some extraordinary qualities to counteract their otherwise most offensive mode of conducting themselves. It appears, however, on examination, that their poet-lovers conduct themselves in a similar manner. They, too, bite, scratch, scream, bubble, munch, sweat, writhe, twist, wriggle, foam, and slaver, in a style frightful to hear of. Let us hope that it is only their fun, and that they don't mean half they say. At times, in reading such books as this, one cannot help wishing that things had remained for ever in the asexual state described in Mr. Darwin's great chapter on Palingenesis.[2] We get very weary of this protracted hankering after a person of the other sex; it seems meat, drink, thought, sinew, religion for the fleshly school. There is no limit to the fleshliness, and Mr. Rossetti finds in it its own religious justification much in the same way as Holy Willie:—

> Maybe thou let'st this fleshly thorn
> Perplex thy servant night and morn,
>   'Cause he's so gifted.
> If so, thy hand must e'en be borne,
>   Until thou lift it. [3]

---

[1] quotations from "A Last Confession," "The House of Life," "Jenny," and "Eden Bower."

[2] probably a reference to *The Descent of Man* (1871).

[3] incorrectly quoted stanza from Burns's "Holy Willie's Prayer."

Whether he is writing of the holy Damozel, or of the Virgin herself, or of Lilith, or Helen, or of Dante, or of Jenny the street-walker, he is fleshly all over, from the roots of his hair to the tip of his toes; never a true lover merging his identity into that of the beloved one; never spiritual, never tender; always self-conscious and aesthetic. "Nothing," says a modern writer, "in human life is so utterly remorseless—not love, not hate, not ambition, not vanity—as the artistic or æsthetic instinct morbidly developed to the suppression of conscience and feeling;" and at no time do we feel more fully impressed with this truth than after the perusal of "Jenny," in some respects the finest poem in the volume, and in all respects the poem best indicative of the true quality of the writer's humanity. It is a production which bears signs of having been suggested by Mr. Buchanan's quasi-lyrical poems, which it copies in the style of title, and particularly by "Artist and Model;" but certainly Mr. Rossetti cannot be accused, as the Scottish writer has been accused, of maudlin sentiment and affected tenderness. The first two lines are perfect:—

Lazy laughing languid Jenny,
Fond of a kiss and fond of a guinea;

And the poem is a soliloquy of the poet—who has been spending the evening in dancing at a casino—over his partner, whom he has accompanied home to the usual style of lodgings occupied by such ladies, and who has fallen asleep with her head upon his knee, while he wonders, in a wretched pun—

Whose person or whose purse may be
The lodestar of your reverie?

The soliloquy is long, and in some parts beautiful, despite a very constant suspicion that we are listening to an emasculated Mr. Browning, whose whole tone and gesture, so to speak, is occasionally introduced with startling fidelity; and there are here and there glimpses of actual thought and insight, over and above the picturesque touches which belong to the writer's true profession, such as that where, at daybreak—

lights creep in
Past the gauze curtains half drawn to,
And *the Lamp's doubled shade grows blue.*

What we object to in this poem is not the subject, which any writer may be fairly left to choose for himself; nor anything particularly vicious in the poetic treatment of it; nor any bad blood bursting through in special passages. But the whole tone, without being more than usually coarse, seems heartless. There is not a drop of piteousness in Mr. Rossetti. He is just to the outcast, even generous; severe to the seducer; sad even at the spectacle of lust in dimity and fine ribbons. Notwithstanding all this, and a certain delicacy and refinement of treatment unusual with this poet, the poem repels and revolts us, and we like Mr. Rossetti least after its perusal. We are angry with the fleshly person at last. The "Blessed Damozel" puzzled us, the "Song of the Bower" amused us, the love-sonnet depressed and sickened us, but "Jenny," though distinguished by less special viciousness of thought and style than any of these, fairly makes us lose patience. We detect its fleshliness at a glance; we perceive that the scene was fascinating less through its human tenderness than because it, like all the others, possessed an inherent quality of animalism. "The whole work" ("Jenny,") writes Mr. Swinburne, "is worthy to fill its place for ever as one of the most perfect poems of an age or generation. There is just the same life-blood and breadth of poetic interest in this episode of a London street and lodging as in the song of 'Troy Town' and the song of 'Eden Bower;' just as much, and no jot more,"— to which last statement we cordially assent; for there is bad blood in all, and breadth of poetic interest in none. "Vengeance of Jenny's case," indeed!—when such a poet as this comes fawning over her, with tender compassion in one eye and aesthetic enjoyment in the other!

It is time that we permitted Mr. Rossetti to speak for himself, which we will do by quoting a fairly representative poem entire:—

LOVE-LILY.

Between the hands, between the brows,
    Between the lips of Love-Lily,
A spirit is born whose birth endows
    My blood with fire to burn through me;
Who breathes upon my gazing eyes,
    Who laughs and murmurs in mine ear,
At whose least touch my colour flies,
    And whom my life grows faint to hear.

Within the voice, within the heart,
    Within the mind of Love-Lily,
A spirit is born who lifts apart
    His tremulous wings and looks at me;
Who on my mouth his finger lays,
    And shows, while whispering lutes confer,
That Eden of Love's watered ways
    Whose winds and spirits worship her.

Brows, hands, and lips, heart, mind, and voice,
    Kisses and words of Love-Lily,—
Oh! bid me with your joy rejoice
    Till *riotous longing rest in me!*
Ah! let not hope be still distraught,
    But find in her its gracious goal,
Whose speech Truth knows not from her thought,
    Nor Love her body from her soul.

With the exception of the usual "riotous longing," which seems to make Mr. Rossetti a burthen to himself, there is nothing to find fault with in the extreme fleshliness of these verses, and to many people who live in the country they may even appear beautiful. Without pausing to criticise a thing so trifling—as well might we dissect a cobweb or anatomize a medusa—let us ask the reader's attention to a peculiarity to which all the students of the fleshly

school must sooner or later give their attention—we mean the habit of accenting the last syllable in words which in ordinary speech are accentuated on the penultimate:—

Between the hands, between the brows,
    Between the lips of Love-Lil*ee!*

which may be said to give to the speaker's voice a sort of cooing tenderness just bordering on a loving whistle. Still better as an illustration are the lines:—

Saturday night is market night
Everywhere, be it dry or wet,
And market night in the Haymar-*ket!*

which the reader may advantageously compare with Mr. Morris's

        Then said the king
Thanked be thou; *neither for nothing*
Shalt thou this good deed do to me;

or Mr. Swinburne's

    In either of the twain
    Red roses full of rain;
    She hath for bond*women*
    All kinds of flowers. [1]

It is unnecessary to multiply examples of an affectation which disfigures all these writers—Guildenstern, Rosencranz, and Osric; who, in the same spirit which prompts the ambitious nobodies that rent London theatres in the "empty" season to make up for their dullness by fearfully original "new readings," distinguish their attempt at leading business by affecting the construction of their grandfathers and great-grandfathers, and the accentuation of the poets of the court of James I. It is in all respects a sign of remarkable genius, from this point of view, to rhyme "was" with "grass," "death" with "lièth," "love" with "of," "once" with "suns," and so on *ad nauseam*. We are far from disputing the value of bad rhymes used

---

[1] "Madonna Mia," ll. 5–8.

occasionally to break up the monotony of verse, but the case is hard when such blunders become the rule and not the exception, when writers deliberately lay themselves out to be as archaic and affected as possible. Poetry is perfect human speech, and these archaisms are the mere fiddlededeeing of empty heads and hollow hearts. Bad as they are, they are the true indication of falser tricks and affectations which lie far deeper. They are trifles, light as air, showing how the wind blows. The soul's speech and the heart's speech are clear, simple, natural, and beautiful, and reject the meretricious tricks to which we have drawn attention.

It is on the score that these tricks and affectations have procured the professors a number of imitators, that the fleshly school deliver their formula that great poets are always to be known because their manner is immediately reproduced by small poets, and that a poet who finds few imitators is probably of inferior rank—by which they mean to infer that they themselves are very great poets indeed. It is quite true that they are imitated. On the stage, twenty provincial "stars" copy Charles Kean, while not one copies his father; there are dozens of actors who reproduce Mr. Charles Dillon, and not one who attempts to reproduce Macready.[1] When we take up the poems of Mr. O'Shaughnessy, we are face to face with a second-hand Mr. Swinburne; when we read Mr. Payne's queer allegories, we remember Mr. Morris's early stage; and every poem of Mr. Marston's reminds us of Mr. Rossetti.[2] But what is really most droll and puzzling in the matter is, that these imitators seem to have no difficulty whatever in writing nearly, if not quite, as well as their masters. It is not bad imitations they offer us, but poems which read just like the originals; the fact being that it is easy to reproduce

sound when it has no strict connection with sense, and simple enough to cull phraseology not hopelessly interwoven with thought and spirit. The fact that these gentlemen are so easily imitated is the most damning proof of their inferiority. What merits they have lie with their faults on the surface, and can be caught by any young gentleman as easily as the measles, only they are rather more difficult to get rid of. All young gentlemen have animal faculties, though few have brains; and if animal faculties without brains will make poems, nothing is easier in the world. A great and good poet, however, is great and good irrespective of manner, and often in spite of manner; he is great because he brings great ideas and new light, because his thought is a revelation; and, although it is true that a great manner generally accompanies great matter, the manner of great matter is almost inimitable. The great poet is not Cowley,[3] imitated and idolized and reproduced by every scribbler of his time; nor Pope, whose trick of style was so easily copied that to this day we cannot trace his own hand with any certainty in the *Iliad*; nor Donne, nor Sylvester,[4] nor the Della Cruscans.[5] Shakespeare's blank verse is the most difficult and Jonson's the most easy to imitate, of all the Elizabethan stock and Shakespeare's verse is the best verse, because it combines the great qualities of all contemporary verse, with no individual affectations; and so perfectly does this verse, with all its splendour, intersect with the style of contemporaries *at their best*, that we would undertake to select passage after passage which would puzzle a good judge to tell which of the Elizabethans was the author—Marlowe, Beaumont, Dekker, Marston, Webster, or Shakespeare himself. The great poet is Dante, full of the thunder of a great Idea; and Milton, unapproachable in the serene white light of thought and sumptuous

---

[1] Charles Kean, actor son of the famous Edmund Kean, Charles Dixon, Victorian actor, and W.C. Macready, another actor of great stature.

[2] Buchanan refers to Arthur W.E. O'Shaughnessy's *An Epic of Women* (1820), John Payne's *The Masque of Shadows* (1870), and Philip B. Marston's *Songtide and Other Poems* (1871).

[3] Abraham Cowley (1618–87).

[4] Joshua Sylvester (1563–1618), translator.

[5] a group of pretentious later eighteenth-century English poets.

wealth of style; and Shakespeare, all poets by turns, and all men in succession; and Goethe, always innovating, and ever indifferent to innovation for its own sake; and Wordsworth, clear as crystal and deep as the sea; and Tennyson, with his vivid range, far-piercing sight, and perfect speech; and Browning, great, not by virtue of his eccentricities, but because of his close intellectual grasp. Tell *Paradise Lost*, the *Divine Comedy*, in naked prose; so the same by *Hamlet*, *Macbeth*, and *Lear*; read Mr. Hayward's translation of *Faust*; take up the *Excursion*, a great poem, though its speech is nearly prose already; turn the "Guinevere" into a mere story; reproduce Pompilia's last dying speech without a line of rhythm. Reduced to bald English, all these poems, and all great poems, lose much; but how much do they not retain? They are poems to the very roots and depths of being, poems born and delivered from the soul, and treat them as cruelly as you may, poems they will remain. So it is with all good and thorough creations, however low in their rank; so it is with the "Ballot in a Wedding" and "Clever Tom Clinch," just as much as with the "Epistle of Karsheesh," or Goethe's torso of "Prometheus;" with Shelley's "Skylark," or Alfred de Musset's "A la Lune," as well as Racine's "Athalie," Victor Hugo's "Parricide," or Hood's "Last Man." A poem is a poem, first as to the soul, next as to the form. The fleshly persons who wish to create form for its own sake are merely pronouncing their own doom. But *such* form! If the Pre-Raphaelite fervour gains ground, we shall soon have popular songs like this:—

> When winds do roar, and rains do pour,
> Hard is the life of the sail*or*;
> He scarcely as he reels can tell
> The side-lights from the binn*acle*;
> He looketh on the wild wa*ter*, &c.,

and so on, till the English speech seems the speech of raving madmen. Of a piece with other affectations is the device of a burthen, of which the fleshly persons

are very fond for its own sake, quite apart from its relevancy. Thus Mr. Rossetti sings:—

> Why did you melt your waxen man,
>   Sister Helen?
> To-day is the third since you began.
> The time was long, yet the time ran,
>   Little brother.
> (*O mother, Mary mother,*
> *Three days to-day between Heaven and Hell*)

This burthen is repeated, with little or no alteration, through thirty-four verses, and might with as much music, and far more point, run as follows:—

> Why did you melt your waxen man,
>   Sister Helen?
> To-day is the third since you began.
> The time was long, yet the time ran,
>   Little brother.
> (*O Mr. Dante Rossetti,*
> *What stuff is this about Heaven and Hell?*)

About as much to the point is a burthen of Mr. Swinburne's, something to the following effect:—

> We were three maidens in the green corn,
> *Hey chickaleerie, the red cock and gray,*
> Fairer maidens were never born,
> *One o'clock, two o'clock, off and away.* [1]

We are not quite certain of the words, as we quote from memory, but we are sure our version fairly represents the original, and is quite as expressive. Productions of this sort are "silly sooth" in good earnest, though they delight some newspaper critics of the day, and are copied by young gentlemen with animal faculties morbidly developed by too much tobacco and too little exercise. Such indulgence, however, would ruin the strongest poetical constitution; and it unfortunately happens that neither masters nor pupils were naturally very healthy. In such a poem as "Eden Bower" there is not one scrap

---

[1] Buchanan's parody of "The King's Daughter," opening lines.

of imagination, properly so-called. It is a clever grotesque in the worst manner of Callot,[1] unredeemed by a gleam of true poetry or humour. No good poet would have wrought into a poem the absurd tradition about Lilith; Goethe was content to glance at it merely, with a grim smile, in the great scene in the Brocken.[2] We may remark here that poems of this unnatural and morbid kind are only tolerable when they embody a profound meaning, as do Coleridge's "Ancient Mariner" and "Cristabel." Not that we would insult the memory of Coleridge by comparing his exquisitely conscientious work with this affected rubbish about "Eden Bower" and "Sister Helen," though his influence in their composition is unmistakable. Still more unmistakable is the influence of that most unwholesome poet, Beddoes,[3] who, with all his great powers, treated his subjects in a thoroughly insincere manner, and is now justly forgotten.

The great strong current of English poetry rolls on, ever mirroring in its bosom new prospects of fair and wholesome thought. Morbid deviations are endless and inevitable; there must be marsh and stagnant mere as well as mountain and wood. Glancing backward into the shady places of the obscure, we see the once prosperous nonsense-writers each now consigned to his own little limbo—Skelton and Gower still playing fantastic tricks with the mother-tongue; Gascoigne outlasting the applause of all, and living to see his own works buried before him; Sylvester doomed to oblivion by his own fame as a

translator; Carew the idol of the courts, and Donne the beloved of the schoolmen, both buried in the same oblivion; the fantastic Fletchers winning the wonder of collegians, and fading out through sheer poetic impotence; Cowley shaking all England with his pindarics, and perishing with them; Waller,[4] the famous, saved from oblivion by the natural note of one single song—and so on, through league after league of a flat and desolate country which once was prosperous, till we come again to these fantastic figures of the fleshly school, with their droll mediaeval garments, their funny archaic speech, and the fatal marks of literary consumption in every pale and delicate visage. Our judgment on Mr. Rossetti, to whom we in the meantime confine our judgment, is substantially that of the *North American Reviewer*, who believes that "we have in him another poetical man, and a man markedly poetical, and of a kind apparently, though not radically, different from any of our secondary writers of poetry, but that we have not in him a new poet of any weight;" and that he is "so affected, sentimental, and painfully self-conscious, that the best to be done in his case is to hope that this book of his, having unpacked his bosom of so much that is unhealthy, may have done him more good than it has given others pleasure." Such, we say, is our opinion, which might very well be wrong, and have to undergo modification, if Mr. Rossetti was younger and less self-possessed. His "maturity" is fatal.

—1871

---

[1] Jacques Callot (1592–1635), French painter and engraver.

[2] the scene called "Walpurgis Night," the night of the witches.

[3] Thomas Lovell Beddoes (1803–49), late Romantic poet.

---

[4] fifteenth-, sixteenth-, and seventeenth-century English poets.

Dante Gabriel Rossetti
1828 – 1882

Although he was the son of an Italian political refugee, Dante Gabriel Rossetti (born Gabriel Charles) never pursued a political life, preferring instead to concentrate on artistic endeavours. Demonstrating extraordinary talent in both painting and poetry, Rossetti's interest in art developed, in part, from his study of Keats' poems and letters, in which a sensuous response to beauty, through colour, texture, words, and women, functioned as a source of inspiration. With Ford Madox Brown, John Everett Millais, and William Holman Hunt, Rossetti formed the Pre-Raphaelite Brotherhood in 1848 in a concerted effort to reject neoclassical conventions in favour of the simpli-city and purity of pre-Renaissance art. While the diverse interests of each artist led to the break-up of the circle within a few years, the group's presence and ideas aroused immense interest and opposition during its formation and after its dissolution. Rossetti's personal view of art is one that connects the heavenly with the earthly and implicitly earthly, an artistic approach which is reflected in his poetry. Initially better known for his paintings, his poem "The Blessed Damozel" was published in the Pre-Raphaelite journal *The Germ* in 1850. *Poems by D.G. Rossetti*, containing the original version of *The House of Life* sonnet sequence, was published in 1871.

❧❧❧

The Stealthy School Of Criticism

Your paragraph, a fortnight ago, relating to the pseudonymous authorship of an article, violently assailing myself and other writers of poetry, in the *Contemporary Review* for October last, reveals a species of critical masquerade which I have expressed in the heading given to this letter. Since then, Mr. Sidney Colvin's note, qualifying the report that he intends to "answer" that article, has appeared in your pages; and my own view as to the absolute forfeit, under such conditions, of all claim to honourable reply, is precisely the same as Mr. Colvin's. For here a critical organ, professedly adopting the principle of open signature, would seem, in reality, to assert (by silent practice, however, not by enunciation,) that if the anonymous in criticism was—as itself originally inculcated—but an early caterpillar stage, the nominate too is found to be no better than a homely transitional chrysalis, and that the ultimate butterfly form for a critic who likes to sport in sunlight and yet to elude the grasp, is after all the pseudonymous. But, indeed, what I may call the "Siamese" aspect of the entertainment provided by the *Review* will elicit but one verdict. Yet I may, perhaps, as the individual chiefly attacked, be excused for asking your assistance now in giving a specific denial to specific charges which, if unrefuted, may still continue, in spite of their author's strategic *fiasco*, to serve his purpose against me to some extent.

The primary accusation, on which this writer grounds all the rest, seems to be that others and myself "extol fleshliness as the distinct and supreme end of poetic and pictorial art; aver that poetic expression is greater than poetic thought; and, by inference, that the body is greater than the soul, and sound superior to sense."

As my own writings are alone formally dealt with in the article, I shall confine my answer to myself; and this must first take unavoidably the form of a challenge to prove so broad a statement. It is true, some fragmentary pretence at proof is put in here and there throughout the attack, and thus far an opportunity is given of contesting the assertion.

A Sonnet entitled *Nuptial Sleep* is quoted and abused at page 338 of the *Review*, and is there dwelt upon as a "whole poem," describing "merely animal sensations." It is no more a whole poem, in reality, than is any single stanza of any poem throughout the book. The poem, written chiefly in sonnets, and of which this is one sonnet-stanza, is entitled *The House of Life*; and even in my first published instalment of the whole work (as contained in the volume under notice) ample evidence is included that no such passing phase of description as the one headed *Nuptial Sleep* could possibly be put forward by the author of *The House of Life* as his own representative view of the subject of love. In proof of this, I will direct attention (among the love-sonnets of this poem) to Nos. 2, 8, 11, 17, 28, and more especially 13, which, indeed, I had better print here.

LOVE-SWEETNESS

"Sweet dimness of her loosened hair's downfall
    About thy face; her sweet hands round thy head
    In gracious fostering union garlanded;
Her tremulous smiles; her glances' sweet recall
Of love; her murmuring sighs memorial;
    Her mouth's culled sweetness by thy kisses shed
    On cheeks and neck and eyelids, and so led
Back to her mouth which answers there for all:—

"What sweeter than these things, except the thing
    In lacking which all these would lose their sweet:—
    The confident heart's still fervour; the swift beat
And soft subsidence of the spirit's wing
Then when it feels, in cloud-girt wayfaring,
    The breath of kindred plumes against its feet?"

Any reader may bring any artistic charge he pleases against the above sonnet; but one charge it would be impossible to maintain against the writer of the series in which it occurs, and that is, the wish on his part to assert that the body is greater than the soul. For here all the passionate and just delights of the body are declared—somewhat figuratively, it is true, but unmistakably—to be as naught if not ennobled by the concurrence of the soul at all times. Moreover, nearly one half of this series of sonnets has

nothing to do with love, but treats of quite other life-influences. I would defy any one to couple with fair quotation of Sonnets 29, 30, 31, 39, 40, 41, 43, or others, the slander that their author was not impressed, like all other thinking men, with the responsibilities and higher mysteries of life; while Sonnets 35, 36, and 37, entitled *The Choice*, sum up the general view taken in a manner only to be evaded by conscious insincerity. Thus much for *The House of Life*, of which the sonnet *Nuptial Sleep* is one stanza, embodying, for its small constituent share, a beauty of natural universal function, only to be reprobated in art if dwelt on (as I have shown that it is not here) to the exclusion of those other highest things of which it is the harmonious concomitant.

At page 342, an attempt is made to stigmatize four short quotations as being specially "my own property," that is, (for the context shows the meaning,) as being grossly sensual; though all guiding reference to any precise page or poem in my book is avoided here. The first of these unspecified quotations is from the *Last Confession*; and is the description referring to the harlot's laugh, the hideous character of which, together with its real or imagined resemblance to the laugh heard soon afterwards from the lips of one long cherished as an ideal, is the immediate cause which makes the maddened hero of the poem a murderer. Assailants may say what they please; but no poet or poetic reader will blame me for making the incident recorded in these seven lines as repulsive to the reader as it was to the hearer and beholder. Without this, the chain of motive and result would remain obviously incomplete. Observe also that these are but seven lines in a poem of some five hundred, not one other of which could be classed with them.

A second quotation gives the last two lines *only* of the following sonnet, which is the first of four sonnets in *The House Of Life* jointly entitled *Willow-wood*:—

"I sat with Love upon a woodside well,
  Leaning across the water, I and he;
  Nor ever did he speak nor looked at me,
But touched his lute wherein was audible
The certain secret thing he had to tell:
  Only our mirrored eyes met silently
  In the low wave; and that sound seemed to be
The passionate voice I knew; and my tears fell.

"And at their fall, his eyes beneath grew hers;
And with his foot and with his wing-feathers
  He swept the spring that watered my heart's drouth.
Then the dark ripples spread to waving hair,
And as I stooped, her own lips rising there
  Bubbled with brimming kisses at my mouth."

The critic has quoted (as I said) only the last two lines, and he has italicized the second as something unbearable and ridiculous. Of course the inference would be that this was really my own absurd bubble-and-squeak notion of an actual kiss. The reader will perceive at once, from the whole sonnet transcribed above, how untrue such an inference would be. The sonnet describes a dream or trance of divided love momentarily re-united by the longing fancy; and in the imagery of the dream, the face of the beloved rises through deep dark waters to kiss the lover. Thus the phrase, "Bubbled with brimming kisses," etc., bears purely on the special symbolism employed, and from that point of view will be found, I believe, perfectly simple and just.

A third quotation is from *Eden Bower*, and says,

"What more prize than love to impel thee?
  Grip and lip my limbs as I tell thee!"

Here again no reference is given, and naturally the reader would suppose that a human embrace is described. The embrace, on the contrary, is that of a fabled snake-woman and a snake. It would be possible still, no doubt, to object on other grounds to this conception; but the ground inferred and relied on for

full effect by the critic is none the less an absolute misrepresentation. These three extracts, it will be admitted, are virtually, though not verbally, garbled with malicious intention; and the same is the case, as I have shown, with the sonnet called *Nuptial Sleep* when purposely treated as a "whole poem."

The last of the four quotations grouped by the critic as conclusive examples consists of two lines from *Jenny*. Neither some thirteen years ago, when I wrote this poem, nor last year when I published it, did I fail to foresee impending charges of recklessness and aggressiveness, or to perceive that even some among those who could really *read* the poem, and acquit me on these grounds, might still hold that the thought in it had better have dispensed with the situation which serves it for framework. Nor did I omit to consider how far a treatment from without might here be possible. But the motive powers of art reverse the requirement of science, and demand first of all an *inner* standing-point. The heart of such a mystery as this must be plucked from the very world in which it beats or bleeds; and the beauty and pity, the self-questionings and all-questionings which it brings with it, can come with full force only from the mouth of one alive to its whole appeal, such as the speaker put forward in the poem,—that is, of a young and thoughtful man of the world. To such a speaker, many half-cynical revulsions of feeling and reverie, and a recurrent presence of the impressions of beauty (however artificial) which first brought him within such a circle of influence, would be inevitable features of the dramatic relations portrayed. Here again I can give the lie, in hearing of honest readers, to the base or trivial ideas which my critic labours to connect with the poem. There is another little charge, however, which this minstrel in mufti brings against *Jenny*, namely, one of plagiarism from that very poetic self of his which the tutelary prose does but enshroud for the moment. This question can, fortunately, be settled with ease by others who have read my critic's poems; and thus I need the less regret that, not happening myself to be in that position, I must be content to rank with those who cannot pretend to an opinion on the subject.

It would be humiliating, need one come to serious detail, to have to refute such an accusation as that of "binding oneself by solemn league and covenant to extol fleshliness as the distinct and supreme end of poetic and pictorial art"; and one cannot but feel that here every one will think it allowable merely to pass by with a smile the foolish fellow who has brought a charge thus framed against any reasonable man. Indeed, what I have said already is substantially enough to refute it, even did I not feel sure that a fair balance of my poetry must, of itself, do so in the eyes of every candid reader. I say nothing of my pictures; but those who know them will laugh at the idea. That I may, nevertheless, take a wider view than some poets or critics, of how much, in the material conditions absolutely given to man to deal with as distinct from his spiritual aspirations, is admissible within the limits of Art,—this, I say, is possible enough; nor do I wish to shrink from such responsibility. But to state that I do so to the ignoring or overshadowing of spiritual beauty, is an absolute falsehood, impossible to be put forward except in the indulgence of prejudice or rancour.

I have selected, amid much railing on my critic's part, what seemed the most representative indictment against me, and have, so far, answered it. Its remaining clauses set forth how others and myself "aver that poetic expression is greater than poetic thought... and sound superior to sense"—an accusation elsewhere, I observe, expressed by saying that we "wish to create form for its own sake." If writers of verse are to be listened to in such arraignment of each other, it might be quite competent of me to prove, from the works of my friends in question, that no such thing is the case with them; but my present function is to confine myself to my own defence. This, again, it is difficult to do quite seriously. It is no part of my undertaking to dispute the verdict of any "contemporary," however contemptuous or contemptible, on my own measure of executive success; but the accusation cited above is not against the poetic value of certain work, but against its primary and (by assumption) its admitted aim. And to this I must reply that so far, assuredly, not even Shakespeare himself could desire more arduous human tragedy for development in Art than belongs to the themes I venture to embody, however incalculably higher might be his power of dealing with them. What more inspiring for poetic effort than the terrible Love turned to Hate,—perhaps the deadliest of all passion-woven complexities,—which is the theme of *Sister Helen*, and, in a more fantastic form, of *Eden Bower*—the surroundings of both poems being the mere machinery of a central universal meaning? What, again, more so than the savage penalty exacted for a lost ideal, as expressed in the *Last Confession*;—than the outraged love for man and burning compensations in art and memory of *Dante at Verona*;—than the baffling problems which the face of *Jenny* conjures up;—or than the analysis of passion and feeling attempted in *The House of Life*, and others among the more purely lyrical poems? I speak here, as does my critic in the clause adduced, of *aim*, not of *achievement*; and so far, the mere summary is instantly subversive of the preposterous imputation. To assert that the poet whose matter is such as this aims chiefly at "creating form for its own sake," is, in fact, almost an ingenuous kind of dishonesty; for surely it delivers up the asserter at once, bound hand and foot, to the tender mercies of contradictory proof. Yet this may fairly be taken as an example of the spirit in which a constant effort is here made against me to appeal to those who either are ignorant of what I write, or else belong to the large class too easily influenced by an assumption of authority in addressing them. The false name appended to the article must, as is evident, aid this position vastly; for who, after all, would not be apt to laugh at seeing one poet confessedly come forward as aggressor against another in the field of criticism?

It would not be worth while to lose time and patience in noticing minutely how the system of misrepresentation is carried into points of artistic detail,—giving us, for example, such statements as that the burthen employed in the ballad of *Sister Helen* "is repeated with little or no alteration through thirty-four verses," whereas the fact is, that the alteration of it in every verse is the very scheme of the poem. But these are minor matters quite thrown into the shade by the critic's more daring sallies. In addition to the class of attack I have answered above, the article contains, of course, an immense amount of personal paltriness; as, for instance, attributions of my work to this, that, or the other absurd derivative source; or again, pure nonsense (which can have no real meaning even to the writer) about "one art getting hold of another, and imposing on it its conditions and limitations"; or, indeed, what not besides? However, to such antics as this, no more attention is possible than that which Virgil enjoined Dante to bestow on the meaner phenomena of his pilgrimage.

Thus far, then, let me thank you for the opportunity afforded me to join issue with the Stealthy School of Criticism. As for any literary justice to be done on this particular Mr. Robert-Thomas, I will merely ask the reader whether, once identified, he does not become manifestly his own best "sworn tormentor"? For who will then fail to discern all the palpitations which preceded his final resolve in the great question whether to be or not to be his acknowledged self when he became an assailant? And yet this is he who, from behind his mask, ventures to charge another with "bad blood," with "insincerity," and the rest of it (and that where poetic fancies are alone in question); while every word on his own tongue is covert rancour, and every stroke from his pen perversion of truth. Yet, after all, there is nothing wonderful in the lengths to which a fretful poet-critic will carry such grudges as he may bear, while publisher and editor can both be found who are willing to consider such means admissible, even to the clear subversion of first professed tenets in the *Review* which they conduct.

In many phases of outward nature, the principle of chaff and grain holds good,—the base enveloping the precious continually; but an untruth was never yet the husk of a truth. Thresh and riddle and winnow it as you may,—let it fly in shreds to the four winds,—falsehood only will be that which flies and that which stays. And thus the sheath of deceit which this pseudonymous undertaking presents at the outset insures in fact what will be found to be its real character to the core.

—1871

Algernon Charles Swinburne
1837 – 1909

Algernon Charles Swinburne's family background was aristocratic (his father was an admiral and his grandfather a baronet), and his education was privileged—he was educated at Eton and Oxford. Beginning his writing at Oxford (1856–60), he met Dante Gabriel Rossetti and was briefly associated with the Pre-Raphaelite circle. Swinburne led a dissolute, wild life (his predilection for flagellation pornography is infamous), attaining literary notoriety with *Atalanta in Calydon* (1865), and *Poems and Ballads, Series #1* (1866). In an age that prided itself on middle-class values and religiosity, Swinburne's works were blasphemous, erotic, and subversive, rebelling against the moral repressiveness of his time as he asserted a doctrine of "l'art pour l'art." Engaged in literary debates with Thomas Carlyle, John Ruskin, and Ralph Waldo Emerson over the value of morality in art, his essay "Under the Microscope" (1872), is a response, parodic as it is, to Robert Buchanan's "The Fleshly School of Poetry" (1871), which attacked both Swinburne's and Rossetti's sensuous, poetic impulses. A liberal republican, in the *Song of Italy* (1867) and *Songs before Sunrise* (1871) he sided with Italian political revolt against oppression. Swinburne was also a respected scholar, publishing studies of William Blake (1868), William Shakespeare (1880), and essays on French and English contemporaries. With an aesthetic vision that influenced younger generations, Swinburne was a poet who drew on a wide range of interests, and was willing to pursue his own beliefs against the prejudices of his time.

⁊⊙⊱

From *Under The Microscope*

It seems to me that the moral tone of the Arthurian story has been on the whole lowered and degraded by Mr. Tennyson's mode of treatment.[1] Wishing to make his central figure the noble and perfect symbol of an ideal man, he has removed not merely the excuse but the explanation of the fatal and tragic loves of Launcelot and Guenevere. The hinge of the whole legend of the Round Table, from its first glory to its final fall, is the incestuous birth of Mordred from the connexion of Arthur with his half-sister, unknowing and unknown; as surely as the hinge of the Oresteia[2] from first to last is the sacrifice at Aulis. From the immolation of Iphigenia springs the wrath of Clytæmnestra, with all its train of evils ensuing; from the sin of Arthur's youth proceeds the ruin of his reign and realm through the falsehood of his wife, a wife unloving and unloved. Remove in either case the plea which leaves the heroine less sinned against indeed than sinning, but yet not too base for tragic compassion and interest, and there remains merely the presentation of a vulgar adulteress. From the background of the one story the ignoble figure of Ægisthus starts into the foreground, and we see in place of the terrible and patient mother, perilous and piteous as a lioness bereaved, the congenial harlot of a coward and traitor. A poet undertaking to rewrite the Agamemnon, who should open his poem with some scene of dalliance or conspiracy between Ægisthus and Clytæmnestra and proceed to make of their common household intrigue the mainspring of his plan, would not more depress the design and lower the keynote of the Æschylean drama, than Mr. Tennyson has lowered the note and deformed the outline of the Arthurian story, by reducing Arthur to the level of a wittol, Guenevere to the level of a woman of intrigue, and Launcelot to the level of a "co-respondent." Treated as he has

---

[1] Swinburne refers to Alfred Lord Tennyson's *Idylls of the King* (1869).

[2] The *Oresteia* trilogy by the ancient Greek dramatist Aeschylus (525–456 BC), consists of *Agamemnon*, *Choephori*, and *Eumenides*.

treated it, the story is rather a case for the divorce-court than for poetry. At the utmost it might serve the recent censor of his countrymen, the champion of morals so dear to President Thiers[1] and the virtuous journalist[2] who draws a contrast in favour of his chastity between him and other French or English authors, for a new study of the worn and wearisome old topic of domestic intrigue; but such "camelias" should be left to blow in the common hotbeds of the lower kind of novelist. Adultery must be tragic and exceptional to afford stuff for art to work upon; and the debased preference of Mr. Tennyson's heroine for a lover so much beneath her noble and faithful husband is as mean an instance as any day can show in its newspaper reports of a common woman's common sin. In the old story, the king, with the doom denounced in the beginning by Merlin hanging over all his toils and triumphs as a tragic shadow, stands apart in no undignified patience to await the end in its own good time of all his work and glory, with no eye for the pain and passion of the woman who sits beside him as queen rather than as wife. Such a figure is not unfit for the centre of a tragic action; it is neither ignoble nor inconceivable; but the besotted blindness of Mr. Tennyson's "blameless king" to the treason of a woman who has had the first and last of his love and the whole devotion of his blameless life is nothing more or less than pitiful and ridiculous. All the studious care and exquisite eloquence of the poet can throw no genuine halo round the sprouting brows of a royal husband who remains to the very last the one man in his kingdom insensible of his disgrace. The unclean taunt of the hateful Vivien is simply the expression in vile language of an undeniable truth; such a man as this king is indeed hardly "man at all;" either fool or coward he must surely be. Thus it is that by the very excision of what may have seemed in his eyes a moral blemish Mr. Tennyson has blemished the whole story; by the very exaltation of his hero as something more than man he has left him in the end something less. The keystone of the whole building is removed, and in place of a tragic house of song where even sin had all the dignity and beauty that sin can retain, and without which it can afford no fit material for tragedy, we find an incongruous edifice of tradition and invention where even virtue is made to seem either imbecile or vile. The story as it stood of old had in it something almost of Hellenic dignity and significance; in it as in the great Greek legends we could trace from a seemingly small root of evil the birth and growth of a calamitous fate, not sent by mere malevolence of heaven, yet in its awful weight and mystery of darkness apparently out of all due retributive proportion to the careless sin or folly of presumptuous weakness which first incurred its infliction; so that by mere hasty resistance and return of violence for violence a noble man may unwittingly bring on himself and all his house the curse denounced on parricide, by mere casual indulgence of light love and passing wantonness a hero king may unknowingly bring on himself and all his kingdom the doom imposed on incest. This presence and imminence of Fate inevitable as invisible throughout the tragic course of action can alone confer on such a story the proper significance and the necessary dignity; without it the action would want meaning and the passion would want nobility; with it, we may hear in the high funereal homily which concludes as with dirge-music the great old book of Sir Thomas Mallory some echo not utterly unworthy of that supreme lament of wondering and wailing spirits—

ποῖ δῆτα κρανεῖ, ποῖ καταλήξει
μετακοιμισθὲν μένος ἄτης;[3]

---

[1] Louis Adolphe Thiers (1797–1877), French historian and statesman, first president of the Third Republic.

[2] Robert Buchanan (1841–1901), poet, novelist, and dramatist; anonymous author of "The Fleshly School of Poetry" (1872).

---

[3] "Where will the doom come to fulfillment?
Where will the rage of calamity be lulled to rest and cease?"

The fatal consequence or corollary of this original flaw in his scheme is that the modern poet has been obliged to degrade all the other figures of the legend in order to bring them into due harmony with the degraded figures of Arthur and Guenevere. The courteous and loyal Gawain of the old romancers, already deformed and maligned in the version of Mallory himself, is here a vulgar traitor; the benignant Lady of the Lake, foster-mother of Launcelot, redeemer and comforter of Pelleas, becomes the very vilest figure in all that cycle of more or less symbolic agents and patients which Mr. Tennyson has set revolving round the figure of his central wittol. I certainly do not share the objection of the virtuous journalist to the presentation in art of an unchaste woman; but I certainly desire that the creature presented should retain some trace of human or if need be of devilish dignity. The Vivien of Mr. Tennyson's idyl seems to me, to speak frankly, about the most base and repulsive person ever set forth in serious literature. Her impurity is actually eclipsed by her incredible and incomparable vulgarity—("*O ay,*" *said Vivien, "that were likely too*"). She is such a sordid creature as plucks men passing by the sleeve. I am of course aware that this figure appears the very type and model of a beautiful and fearful temptress of the flesh, the very embodied and ennobled ideal of danger and desire, in the chaster eyes of the virtuous journalist who grows sick with horror and disgust at the license of other French and English writers; but I have yet to find the French or English contempo-

rary poem containing a passage that can be matched against the loathsome dialogue in which Merlin and Vivien discuss the nightly transgressions against chastity, within doors and without, of the various knights of Arthur's court. I do not remember that any modern poet whose fame has been assailed on the score of sensual immorality—say for instance the author of "Mademoiselle de Maupin" or the author of the "Fleurs du Mal"[1]—has ever devoted an elaborate poem to describing the erotic fluctuations and vacillations of a dotard under the moral and physical manipulation of a prostitute. The conversation of Vivien is exactly described in the poet's own phrase—it is "as the poached filth that floods the middle street." Nothing like it can be cited from the verse which embodies other poetic personations of unchaste women. From the Cleopatra of Shakespeare and the Dalilah of Milton to the Phraxanor of Wells, a figure worthy to be ranked not far in design below the highest of theirs, we may pass without fear of finding any such pollution. Those heroines of sin are evil, but noble in their evil way; it is the utterly ignoble quality of Vivien which makes her so unspeakably repulsive and unfit for artistic treatment. "Smiling saucily," she is simply a subject for the police-court.

—1872

---

[1] Théophile Gautier published *Mademoiselle de Maupin* in 1835–36, and Charles Baudelaire published *Les Fleurs du mal* in 1857.

Walter Pater
1839 – 1894

Walter Pater was educated at King's School, Canterbury, and Queen's College, Oxford. After receiving a fellowship at Oxford in 1865, he established himself in rooms at Brasenose College and devoted himself to his lectures, particularly on Plato and Platonics, and the study of art. In his influential *Studies in the History of the Renaissance* (1873), he argues for the concept of nondiscursive, nonutilitarian art, epitomized by his phrase, "art for art's sake," which became a slogan for the aesthetic movement of the 1870s and 1880s and the subsequent "decadence" of the 1890s.

❧❧❧

Preface and Conclusion to
The Renaissance: Studies in Art and Poetry

PREFACE

Many attempts have been made by writers on art and poetry to define beauty in the abstract, to express it in the most general terms, to find some universal formula for it. The value of these attempts has most often been in the suggestive and penetrating things said by the way. Such discussions help us very little to enjoy what has been well done in art or poetry, to discriminate between what is more and what is less excellent in them, or to use words like beauty, excellence, art, poetry, with a more precise meaning than they would otherwise have. Beauty, like all other qualities presented to human experience, is relative; and the definition of it becomes unmeaning and useless in proportion to its abstractness. To define beauty, not in the most abstract but in the most concrete terms possible, to find not its universal formula, but the formula which expresses most adequately this or that special manifestation of it, is the aim of the true student of aesthetics.

"To see the object as in itself it really is," has been justly said to be the aim of all true criticism whatever; and in aesthetic criticism the first step towards seeing one's object as it really is, is to know one's own impression as it really is, to discriminate it, to realise it distinctly. The objects with which aesthetic criticism deals—music, poetry, artistic and accomplished forms of human life—are indeed receptacles of so many powers or forces: they possess, like the products of nature, so many virtues or qualities. What is this song or picture, this engaging personality presented in life or in a book, to *me*? What effect does it really produce on me? Does it give me pleasure? and if so, what sort or degree of pleasure? How is my nature modified by its presence, and under its influence? The answers to these questions are the original facts with which the aesthetic critic has to do; and, as in the study of light, of morals, of number, one must realise such primary data for one's self, or not at all. And he who experiences these impressions strongly, and drives directly at the discrimination and analysis of them, has no need to trouble himself with the abstract question what beauty is in itself, or what its exact relation to truth or experience—metaphysical questions, as unprofitable as metaphysical questions elsewhere. He may pass them all by as being, answerable or not, of no interest to him.

The aesthetic critic, then, regards all the objects with which he has to do, all works of art, and the fairer forms of nature and human life, as powers or forces producing pleasurable sensations, each of a more or less peculiar or unique kind. This influence he feels, and wishes to explain, by analysing and reducing it to its elements. To him, the picture, the landscape, the engaging personality in life or in a book, *La Gioconda*, the hills of Carrara, Pico of

Mirandola,[1] are valuable for their virtues, as we say, in speaking of a herb, a wine, a gem; for the property each has of affecting one with a special, a unique, impression of pleasure. Our education becomes complete in proportion as our susceptibility to these impressions increases in depth and variety. And the function of the aesthetic critic is to distinguish, to analyse, and separate from its adjuncts, the virtue by which a picture, a landscape, a fair personality in life or in a book, produces this special impression of beauty or pleasure, to indicate what the source of that impression is, and under what conditions it is experienced. His end is reached when he has disengaged that virtue, and noted it, as a chemist notes some natural element, for himself and others; and the rule for those who would reach this end is stated with great exactness in the words of a recent critic of Sainte-Beuve;—*De se borner à connaître de près les belles choses, et à s'en nourrir en exquis amateurs, en humanistes accomplis.*[2]

What is important, then, is not that the critic should possess a correct abstract definition of beauty for the intellect, but a certain kind of temperament, the power of being deeply moved by the presence of beautiful objects. He will remember always that beauty exists in many forms. To him all periods, types, schools of taste, are in themselves equal. In all ages there have been some excellent workmen, and some excellent work done. The question he asks is always:—in whom did the stir, the genius, the sentiment of the period find itself? where was the receptacle of its refinement, its elevation, its taste?

"The ages are all equal," says William Blake, "but genius is always above its age."[3]

Often it will require great nicety to disengage this virtue from the commoner elements with which it may be found in combination. Few artists, not Goethe or Byron even, work quite cleanly, casting off all *débris*, and leaving us only what the heat of their imagination has wholly fused and transformed. Take, for instance, the writings of Wordsworth. The heat of his genius, entering into the substance of his work, has crystallised a part, but only a part, of it; and in that great mass of verse there is much which might well be forgotten. But scattered up and down it, sometimes fusing and transforming entire compositions, like the Stanzas on *Resolution and Independence*, or the *Ode on the Recollections of Childhood*, sometimes, as if at random, depositing a fine crystal here or there, in a matter it does not wholly search through and transmute, we trace the action of his unique, incommunicable faculty, that strange, mystical sense of a life in natural things, and of man's life as a part of nature, drawing strength and colour and character from local influences, from the hills and streams, and from natural sights and sounds. Well! that is the *virtue*, the active principle in Wordsworth's poetry, and then the function of the critic of Wordsworth is to follow up that active principle, to disengage it, to mark the degree in which it penetrates his verse.

The subjects of the following studies are taken from the history of the *Renaissance*, and touch what I think the chief points in that complex, many-sided movement. I have explained in the first of them what I understand by the word, giving it a much wider scope than was intended by those who originally used it to denote that revival of classical antiquity in the fifteenth century which was only one of many results of a general excitement and enlightening of the human mind, but of which the great aim and

---

[1] "La Gioconda" refers to Leonardo da Vinci's Mona Lisa; marble is quarried from the "hills of Carrara"; Pico of Mirandola (1463–94) was an Italian philosopher about whom Pater wrote an essay included in *The Renaissance*.

[2] "To confine themselves to knowing beautiful things intimately, and to sustain themselves by these, as sensitive amateurs and accomplished humanists do."

[3] Blake makes this comment in an annotation of *The Works of Sir Joshua Reynolds*.

achievements of what, as Christian art, is often falsely opposed to the Renaissance, were another result. This outbreak of the human spirit may be traced far into the middle age itself, with its motives already clearly pronounced, the care for physical beauty, the worship of the body, the breaking down of those limits which the religious system of the middle age imposed on the heart and the imagination. I have taken as an example of this movement, this earlier Renaissance within the middle age itself, and as an expression of its qualities, two little compositions in early French; not because they constitute the best possible expression of them, but because they help the unity of my series, inasmuch as the Renaissance ends also in France, in French poetry, in a phase of which the writings of Joachim du Bellay[1] are in many ways the most perfect illustration. The Renaissance, in truth, put forth in France an aftermath, a wonderful later growth, the products of which have to the full that subtle and delicate sweetness which belongs to a refined and comely decadence, just as its earliest phases have the freshness which belongs to all periods of growth in art, the charm of *ascêsis*,[2] of the austere and serious girding of the loins in youth.

But it is in Italy, in the fifteenth century, that the interest of the Renaissance mainly lies,—in that solemn fifteenth century which can hardly be studied too much, not merely for its positive results in the things of the intellect and the imagination, its concrete works of art, its special and prominent personalities, with their profound aesthetic charm, but for its general spirit and character, for the ethical qualities of which it is a consummate type.

The various forms of intellectual activity which together make up the culture of an age, move for the most part from different starting points, and by unconnected roads. As products of the same genera-

tion they partake indeed of a common character, and unconsciously illustrate each other; but of the producers themselves, each group is solitary, gaining what advantage or disadvantage there may be in intellectual isolation. Art and poetry, philosophy and the religious life, and that other life of refined pleasure and action in the conspicuous places of the world, are each of them confined to its own circle of ideas, and those who prosecute either of them are generally little curious of the thoughts of others. There come, however, from time to time, eras of more favourable conditions, in which the thoughts of men draw nearer together than is their wont, and the many interests of the intellectual world combine in one complete type of general culture. The fifteenth century in Italy is one of these happier eras, and what is sometimes said of the age of Pericles is true of that of Lorenzo:—it is an age productive in personalities, many-sided, centralised, complete. Here, artists and philosophers and those whom the action of the world has elevated and made keen, do not live in isolation, but breathe a common air, and catch light and heat from each other's thoughts. There is a spirit of general elevation and enlightenment in which all alike communicate. The unity of this spirit gives unity to all the various products of the Renaissance; and it is to this intimate alliance with mind, this participation in the best thoughts which that age produced, that the art of Italy in the fifteenth century owes much of its grave dignity and influence.

I have added an essay on Winckelmann,[3] as not incongruous with the studies which precede it, because Winckelmann, coming in the eighteenth century, really belongs in spirit to an earlier age. By his enthusiasm for the things of the intellect and the imagination for their own sake, by his Hellenism, his life-long struggle to attain to the Greek spirit, he is in sympathy with the humanists of a previous century.

---

[1] du Bellay (1524–60), a French poet about whom Pater wrote an essay in *The Renaissance*.

[2] asceticism.

[3] Johann Joachim Winckelmann (1717–68), a German classical scholar.

He is the last fruit of the Renaissance, and explains in a striking way its motive and tendencies.

CONCLUSION

To regard all things and principles of things as inconstant modes or fashions has more and more become the tendency of modern thought. Let us begin with that which is without—our physical life. Fix upon it in one of its more exquisite intervals, the moment, for instance, of delicious recoil from the flood of water in summer heat. What is the whole physical life in that moment but a combination of natural elements to which science gives their names? But those elements, phosphorus and lime and delicate fibres, are present not in the human body alone: we detect them in places most remote from it. Our physical life in perpetual motion of them—the passage of the blood, the waste and repairing of the lenses of the eye, the modification of the tissues of the brain under every ray of light and sound—processes which science reduces to simpler and more elementary forces. Like the elements of which we are composed, the action of these forces extends beyond us: it rusts iron and ripens corn. Far out on every side of us those elements are broadcast, driven in many currents; and birth and gesture and death and the springing of violets from the grave are but a few out of ten thousand resultant combinations. That clear, perpetual outline of face and limb is but an image of ours, under which we group them—a design in a web, the actual threads of which pass out beyond it. This at least of flame-like our life has, that it is but the concurrence, renewed from moment to moment, of forces parting sooner or later on their ways.

Or, if we begin with the inward world of thought and feeling, the whirlpool is still more rapid, the flame more eager and devouring. There it is no longer the gradual darkening of the eye, the gradual fading of colour from the wall—movements of the shoreside, where the water flows down indeed, though in apparent rest—but the race of the midstream, a drift of momentary acts of sight and passion and thought. At first sight experience seems to bury us under a flood of external objects, pressing upon us with a sharp and importunate reality, calling us out of ourselves in a thousand forms of action. But when reflexion begins to play upon those objects they are dissipated under its influence; the cohesive force seems suspended like some trick of magic; each object is loosed into a group of impressions—colour, odour, texture—in the mind of the observer. And if we continue to dwell in thought on this world, not of objects in the solidity with which language invests them, but of impressions, unstable, flickering, inconsistent, which burn and are extinguished with our consciousness of them, it contracts still further: the whole scope of observation is dwarfed into the narrow chamber of the individual mind. Experience, already reduced to a group of impressions, is ringed round for each one of us by that thick wall of personality through which no real voice has ever pierced on its way to us, or from us to that which we can only conjecture to be without. Every one of those impressions is the impression of the individual in his isolation, each mind keeping as a solitary prisoner its own dream of a world. Analysis goes a step farther still, and assures us that those impressions of the individual mind to which, for each one of us, experience dwindles down, are in perpetual flight; that each of them is limited by time, and that as time is infinitely divisible, each of them is infinitely divisible also; all that is actual in it being a single moment, gone while we try to apprehend it, of which it may ever be more truly said that it has ceased to be than that it is. To such a tremulous wisp constantly reforming itself on the stream, to a single sharp impression, with a sense in it, a relic more or less fleeting, of such moments gone by, what is real in our life fines itself down. It is with this movement, with the passage and dissolution of impressions, images, sensations, that analysis leaves off—that continual vanishing away, that strange, perpetual weaving and unweaving of ourselves.

Philosophiren, says Novalis, *ist dephlegmatisiren, vivificiren.*[1] The service of philosophy, of speculative culture, towards the human spirit, is to rouse, to startle it to a life of constant and eager observation. Every moment some form grows perfect in hand or face; some tone on the hills or the sea is choicer than the rest; some mood of passion or insight or intellectual excitement is irresistibly real and attractive to us,—for that moment only. Not the fruit of experience, but experience itself, is the end. A counted number of pulses only is given to us of a variegated, dramatic life. How may we see in them all that is to be seen in them by the finest senses? How shall we pass most swiftly from point to point, and be present always at the focus where the greatest number of vital forces unite in their purest energy?

To burn always with this hard, gemlike flame, to maintain this ecstasy, is success in life. In a sense it might even be said that our failure is to form habits: for, after all, habit is relative to a stereotyped world, and meantime it is only the roughness of the eye that makes any two persons, things, situations, seem alike. While all melts under our feet, we may well grasp at any exquisite passion, or any contribution to knowledge that seems by a lifted horizon to set the spirit free for a moment, or any stirring of the senses, strange dyes, strange colours, and curious odours, or work of the artist's hands, or the face of one's friend. Not to discriminate every moment some passionate attitude in those about us, and in the very brilliancy of their gifts some tragic dividing of forces on their ways, is, on this short day of frost and sun, to sleep before evening. With this sense of the splendour of our experience and of its awful brevity, gathering all we are into one desperate effort to see and touch, we shall hardly have time to make theories about the things we see and touch. What we have to do is to be for ever curiously testing new opinions and courting new impressions, never acquiescing in a facile orthodoxy of Comte,[2] or of Hegel,[3] or of our own. Philosophical theories or ideas, as points of view, instruments of criticism, may help us to gather up what might otherwise pass unregarded by us. "Philosophy is the microscope of thought." The theory or idea or system which requires of us the sacrifice of any part of this experience, in consideration of some interest into which we cannot enter, or some abstract theory we have not identified with ourselves, or of what is only conventional, has no real claim upon us.

One of the most beautiful passages of Rousseau[4] is that in the sixth book of the *Confessions*, where he describes the awakening in him of the literary sense. An undefinable taint of death had clung always about him, and now in early manhood he believed himself smitten by mortal disease. He asked himself how he might make as much as possible of the interval that remained; and he was not biassed by anything in his previous life when he decided that it must be by intellectual excitement, which he found just then in the clear, fresh writings of Voltaire. Well! we are all *condamnés*[5] as Victor Hugo says: we are all under sentence of death but with a sort of indefinite reprieve—*les hommes sont tous condamnés à mort avec des sursis indéfinis*: we have an interval and then our place knows us no more. Some spend this interval in listlessness, some in high passions, the wisest, at least among "the children of this world,"[6] in art and song. For our one chance lies in expanding that interval, in getting as many pulsations as possible into the given time. Great passions may give us this quickened sense of life, ecstasy and sorrow of love, the various forms

---

[1] "To philosophize is to cast off inertia, to make oneself alive."
Novalis (Friedrich von Hardenberg [1772–1801]) was a German Romantic.

[2] Auguste Compte (1798–1857), French Positivist.

[3] Georg W.F. Hegel (1770–1831), German Idealist.

[4] Jean-Jacques Rousseau (1712–78), French philosopher and writer.

[5] condemned.

[6] Luke 16:8.

of enthusiastic activity, disinterested or otherwise, which come naturally to many of us. Only be sure it is passion—that it does yield you this fruit of a quickened, multiplied consciousness. Of such wisdom, the poetic passion, the desire of beauty, the love of art for its own sake, has most. For art comes to you proposing frankly to give nothing but the highest quality to your moments as they pass, and simply for those moments' sake.

—1873

Gerard Manley Hopkins
1844 – 1889

Gerard Manley Hopkins, the Oxford-educated English poet and Roman Catholic priest, was an innovative technician who applied his art to the dual themes of nature and religion. Converting to Catholicism in 1866 under the guidance of the Tractarians, Hopkins joined the Society of Jesus in 1868. Encouraged to eulogize the loss of five nuns at sea, Hopkins wrote *The Wreck of the Deutschland* (1875–76). Representing Hopkins's first successful experiment with "sprung rhythm," the poem eschews the accentual-syllabic measures conventionally associated with modern English verse. Poems such as "The Windhover" (1877) and the "terrible sonnets" (1885–89) have garnered Hopkins recognition as a poet of stunning originality.

ⵏⵏⵏ

Author's Preface [1]

The poems in this book are written some in Running Rhythm, the common rhythm in English use, some in Sprung Rhythm, and some in a mixture of the two. And those in the common rhythm are some counterpointed, some not.

Common English rhythm, called Running Rhythm above, is measured by feet of either two or three syllables and (putting aside the imperfect feet at the beginning and end of lines and also some unusual measures in which feet seem to be paired together and double or composite feet to arise) never more or less.

Every foot has one principal stress or accent, and this or the syllable it falls on may be called the Stress of the foot and the other part, the one or two unaccented syllables, the Slack. Feet (and the rhythms made out of them) in which the stress comes first are called Falling Feet and Falling Rhythms, feet and rhythm in which the slack comes first are called Rising Feet and Rhythms, and if the stress is between two slacks there will be Rocking Feet and Rhythms. These distinctions are real and true to nature; but for purposes of scanning it is a great convenience to follow the example of music and take the stress always first, as the accent or the chief accent always comes first in a musical bar. If this is done there will be in common English verse only two possible feet—the so-called accentual Trochee and Dactyl, and correspondingly only two possible uniform rhythms, the so-called Trochaic and Dactylic. But they may be mixed and then what the Greeks called a Logaoedic Rhythm arises. These are the facts and according to these the scanning of ordinary regularly-written English verse is very simple indeed and to bring in other principles is here unnecessary.

But because verse written strictly in these feet and by these principles will become same and tame the poets have brought in licences and departures from rule to give variety, and especially when the natural rhythm is rising, as in the common ten- syllable or five-foot verse, rhymed or blank. These irregularities are chiefly Reversed Feet and Reversed or Counterpoint Rhythm, which two things are two steps or degrees of licence in the same kind. By a reversed foot I mean the putting the stress where, to judge by the rest of the measure, the slack should be and the slack where the stress, and this is done freely at the beginning of a line and, in the course of a line, after a pause; only scarcely ever in the second foot or place and never in the last, unless when the poet designs some extraordinary effect; for these places are characteristic and sensitive and cannot well be touched. But the reversal of the first foot and of some middle foot

---

[1] written about 1883, prefatory to Hopkins's manuscript poems kept by Robert Bridges.

after a strong pause is a thing so natural that our poets have generally done it, from Chaucer down, without remark and it commonly passes unnoticed and cannot be said to amount to a formal change of rhythm, but rather is that irregularity which all natural growth and motion shews. If however the reversal is repeated in two feet running, especially so as to include the sensitive second foot, it must be due either to great want of ear or else is a calculated effect, the super-inducing or *mounting* of a new rhythm upon the old; and since the new or mounted rhythm is actually heard and at the same time the mind naturally supplies the natural or standard foregoing rhythm, for we do not forget what the rhythm is that by rights we should be hearing, two rhythms are in some manner running at once and we have something answerable to counterpoint in music, which is two or more strains of tune going on together, and this is Counterpoint Rhythm. Of this kind of verse Milton is the great master and the choruses of *Samson Agonistes* are written throughout in it—but with the disadvantage that he does not let the reader clearly know what the ground-rhythm is meant to be and so they have struck most readers as merely irregular. And in fact if you counterpoint throughout, since only one of the counter rhythms is actually heard, the other is really destroyed or cannot come to exist, and what is written is one rhythm only and probably Sprung Rhythm, of which I now speak.

Sprung Rhythm, as used in this book, is measured by feet of from one to four syllables, regularly, and for particular effects any number of weak or slack syllables may be used. It has one stress, which falls on the only syllable, if there is only one, or, if there are more, then scanning as above, on the first, and so gives rise to four sorts of feet, a monosyllable and the so-called accentual Trochee, Dactyl, and the First Paeon. And there will be four corresponding natural rhythms; but nominally the feet are mixed and any one may follow any other. And hence Sprung Rhythm differs from Running Rhythm in having or

being only one nominal rhythm, a mixed or "loga-oedic" one, instead of three, but on the other hand in having twice the flexibility of foot, so that any two stresses may either follow one another running or be divided by one, two, or three slack syllables. But strict Sprung Rhythm cannot be counterpointed. In Sprung Rhythm, as in logaoedic rhythm generally, the feet are assumed to be equally long or strong and their seeming inequality is made up by pause or stressing.

Remark also that it is natural in Sprung Rhythm for the lines to be *rove over*, that is for the scanning of each line immediately to take up that of the one before, so that if the first has one or more syllables at its end the other must have so many the less at its beginning; and in fact the scanning runs on without break from the beginning, say, of a stanza to the end and all the stanza is one long strain, though written in lines asunder.

Two licences are natural to Sprung Rhythm. The one is rests, as in music; but of this an example is scarcely to be found in this book, unless in the *Echos*, second line. The other is *hangers* or *outrides*, that is one, two, or three slack syllables added to a foot and not counting in the nominal scanning. They are so called because they seem to hang below the line or ride forward or backward from it in another dimension than the line itself, according to a principle needless to explain here. These outriding half feet or hangers are marked by a loop underneath them, and plenty of them will be found.

The other marks are easily understood, namely accents, where the reader might be in doubt which syllable should have the stress; slurs, that is loops *over* syllables, to tie them together into the time of one; little loops at the end of a line to shew that the rhyme goes on to the first letter of the next line; what in music are called pauses ⌒, to shew that the syllable should be dwelt on; and twirls ~, to mark reversed or counterpointed rhythm.

Note on the nature and history of Sprung Rhythm—Sprung Rhythm is the most natural of things. For (1) it is the rhythm of common speech and of written prose, when rhythm is perceived in them. (2) It is the rhythm of all but the most monotonously regular music, so that in the words of choruses and refrains and in songs written closely to music it arises. (3) It is found in nursery rhymes, weather saws, and so on; because, however these may have been once made in running rhythm, the terminations having dropped off by the change of language, the stresses come together and so the rhythm is sprung. (4) It arises in common verse when reversed or counterpointed, for the same reason.

But nevertheless in spite of all this and though Greek and Latin lyric verse, which is well known, and the old English verse seen in "Pierce Ploughman" are in sprung rhythm, it has in fact ceased to be used since the Elizabethan age, Greene being the last writer who can be said to have recognized it. For perhaps there was not, down to our days, a single, even short, poem in English in which sprung rhythm is employed—not for single effects or in fixed places—but as the governing principle of the scansion. I say this because the contrary has been asserted: if it is otherwise the poem should be cited.

Some of the sonnets in this book are in five -foot, some in six-foot or Alexandrine lines.

Nos. 13 and 22 are Curtal-Sonnets, that is they are constructed in proportions resembling those of the sonnet proper, namely, 6 + 4 instead of 8 + 6, with however a half-line tailpiece (so that the equation is rather $\frac{12}{2} + \frac{9}{2} = \frac{21}{2} = 10\frac{1}{2}$).

—1883

Alice Meynell
1847 – 1922

Alice Meynell was a poet, journalist, and political activist, particularly in support of the non-militant suffragists. Her first volume of poetry, *Preludes* (1875), was admired by Tennyson and Ruskin, and through her later work she became friends with fellow-poets Francis Thompson, Coventry Patmore, and George Meredith. Her best poems, reflecting the Victorian themes of the ambiguity of motherhood, the fallen woman, and the social and political ramifications of motherhood (she bore eight children), are personal and lyrical.

ↄ⁊ↄↄ

Tennyson [1]

Fifty years after Tennyson's birth he was saluted a great poet by that unanimous acclamation which includes mere clamour. Fifty further years, and his centenary was marked by a new detraction. It is sometimes difficult to distinguish the obscure but not unmajestic law of change from the sorry custom of reaction. Change hastes not and rests not, reaction beats to and fro, flickering about the moving mind of the world. Reaction—the paltry precipitancy of the multitude—rather than the novelty of change, has brought about a ferment and corruption of opinion on Tennyson's poetry. It may be said that opinion is the same now as it was in the middle of the nineteenth century—the same, but turned. All that was not worth having of admiration then has soured into detraction now. It is of no more significance, acrid, than it was, sweet. What the herding of opinion gave yesterday it is able to take away to-day, that and no more.

But besides the common favour-disfavour of the day, there is the tendency of educated opinion, once disposed to accept the whole of Tennyson's poetry as though he could not be "parted from himself," and now disposed to reject the whole, on the same plea. But if ever there was a poet who needed to be thus "parted"—the word is his own—it is he who wrote both narrowly for his time and liberally for all time, and who—this is the more important character of his poetry—had both a style and a manner: a masterly style, a magical style, a too dainty manner, nearly a trick; a noble landscape and in it figures something ready-made. He is a subject for our alternatives of feeling, nay, our conflicts, as is hardly another poet. We may deeply admire and wonder, and, in another line or hemistich, grow indifferent or slightly averse. He sheds the luminous suns of dreams upon men and women who would do well with footlights; waters their way with rushing streams of Paradise and cataracts from visionary hills; laps them in divine darkness; leads them into those touching landscapes, "the lovely that are not beloved," long grey fields, cool sombre summers, and meadows thronged with unnoticeable flowers; speeds his carpet knight—or is that hardly a just name for one whose sword "smites" so well?—upon a carpet of authentic wild flowers; pushes his rovers, in costume, from off blossoming shores, on the keels of old romance. The style and the manner, I have said, run side by side. If we may take one poet's too violent phrase, and consider poets to be "damned to poetry," why, then, Tennyson is condemned by a couple of sentences, "to run concurrently." We have the style and the manner locked together at times in a single stanza, locked and yet not mingled. There should be no danger for the more judicious reader lest impatience at the peculiar Tennyson trick should involve the great Tennyson style in a sweep of protest. Yet the danger has in fact proved real within the present and recent years, and

---

[1] first published in *Hearts of Controversy*, 1917.

seems about to threaten still more among the less judicious. But it will not long prevail. The vigorous little nation of lovers of poetry, alive one by one within the vague multitude of the nation of England, cannot remain finally insensible to what is at once majestic and magical in Tennyson. For those are not qualities they neglect in their other masters. How, valuing singleness of heart in the sixteenth century, splendour in the seventeenth, composure in the eighteenth; how, with a spiritual ear for the note—commonly called Celtic, albeit it is the most English thing in the world—the wild wood note of the remoter song; how, with the educated sense of style, the liberal sense of ease; how, in a word, fostering Letters and loving Nature, shall that choice nation within England long disregard these virtues in the nineteenth-century master? How disregard him, for more than the few years of reaction, for the insignificant reasons of his bygone taste, his insipid courtliness, his prettiness, or what not? It is no dishonour to Tennyson, for it is a dishonour to our education, to disparage a poet who wrote but the two—had he written no more of their kind—lines of "The Passing of Arthur," of which, before I quote them, I will permit myself the personal remembrance of a great contemporary author's opinion. Meredith, speaking to me of the high-water mark of English style in poetry and prose, cited those lines as topmost in poetry:

> On one side lay the ocean, and on one
> Lay a great water, and the moon was full.[1]

Here is no taint of manner, no pretty posture or habit, but the simplicity of poetry and the simplicity of Nature, something on the yonder side of imagery. It is to be noted that this noble passage is from Tennyson's generally weakest kind of work—blank verse; and should thus be a sign that the laxity of so many parts of the "Idylls" and other blank verse

poems was a kind of unnecessary fault. Lax this form of poetry undoubtedly is with Tennyson. His blank verse is often too easy; it cannot be said to fly, for the paradoxical reason that it has no weight; it slips by, without halting or tripping indeed, but also without the friction of the movement of vitality. This quality, which is so near to a fault, this quality of ease, has come to be disregarded in our day. That Horace Walpole overpraised this virtue is not good reason that we should hold it for a vice. Yet we do more than undervalue it; and several of our authors, in prose and poetry, seem to find much merit in the manifest difficulty; they will not have a key to turn, though closely and tightly, in oiled wards; let the reluctant iron catch and grind, or they would even prefer to pick you the lock.

But though we may think it time that the quality once overprized should be restored to a more proportionate honour, our great poet Tennyson shows us that of all merits ease is, unexpectedly enough, the most dangerous. It is not only, with him, that the wards are oiled, it is also that the key turns loosely. This is true of much of the beautiful "Idylls," but not of their best passages, nor of such magnificent blank verse as that of the close of "A Vision of Sin," or of "Lucretius." As to the question of ease, we cannot have a better maxim than Coventry Patmore's saying that poetry "should confess, but not suffer from, its difficulties."[2] Tennyson is always an artist, and the finish of his work is one of the principal notes of his versification. How this finish comports with the excessive ease of his prosody remains his own peculiar secret. Ease, in him, does not mean that he has any unhandsome slovenly ways. On the contrary, he resembles rather the warrior with the pouncet box.[3] Tennyson certainly *worked*, and the exceeding ease of his blank verse comes perhaps of this little para-

---

[1] *Idylls of the King*, "The Passing of Arthur," ll. 170–80.

[2] not identified.

[3] a small box with a perforated lid for perfumes. For "the warrior with the pouncet box" see *1 Henry IV*. 1.3.36–41.

dox—that he makes somewhat too much show of the hiding of his art.

In the first place the poet with the great welcome style and the little unwelcome manner, Tennyson is, in the second place, the modern poet who withstood France. (That is, of course, modern France—France since the Renaissance. From medieval Provence there is not an English poet who does not own inheritance.) It was some time about the date of the Restoration that modern France began to be modish in England. A ruffle at the court of Charles, a couplet in the ear of Pope, a *tour de phrase* from Mme de Sévigné[1] much to the taste of Walpole, later the good example of French painting—rich interest paid for the loan of our Constable's initiative—later still a scattering of French taste, French critical business, over all the shallow places of our literature—these have all been phases of a national vanity of ours, an eager and anxious fluttering or jostling to be foremost and French. Matthew Arnold's essay on criticism fostered this anxiety, and yet I find in this work of his a lack of easy French knowledge, such as his misunderstanding of the word *brutalité*, which means no more, or little more, than roughness. Matthew Arnold, by the way, knew so little of the French character as to altogether ignorant of French provincialism, French practical sense, and French "convenience." "Convenience" is his dearest word of contempt, "practical sense" his next dearest, and he throws them a score of times in the teeth of the English. Strange is the irony of truth. For he bestows those withering words on the nation that has the fifty religions, and attributes "ideas"—as the antithesis of "convenience" and "practical sense"—to the nation that has the fifty sauces. And not for a moment does he suspect himself of this blunder, so manifest as to be disconcerting to his reader. One seems to hear an incurably English accent in all this, which indeed is reported, by his acquaintance, of Matthew Arnold's

actual speaking of French. It is certain that he has not the interest of familiarity with the language, but only the interest of strangeness. Now, while we meet the effect of the French coat in our seventeenth century, of the French light verse in our earlier eighteenth century, and of French philosophy in our later, of the French revolution in our Wordsworth, of the French painting in our nineteenth-century studios, of French fiction—and the dregs are still running—in our libraries, of French poetry in our Swinburne, of French criticism in our Arnold, Tennyson shows the effect of nothing French whatever. Not the Elizabethans, not Shakespeare, not Jeremy Taylor,[2] not Milton, not Shelley were (in their art, not in their matter) more insular in their time. France, by the way, has more than appreciated the homage of Tennyson's contemporaries; Victor Hugo avers, in *Les Misérables*, that our people imitate his people in all things, and in particular he rouses in us a delighted laughter of surprises by asserting that the London street-boy imitates the Parisian street-boy. There is, in fact, something of a street-boy in some of our late more literary mimicries.

We are apt to judge a poet too exclusively by his imagery. Tennyson is hardly a great master of imagery. He has more imagination than imagery. He sees the thing, with so luminous a mind's eye, that it is sufficient to him; he needs not to see it more beautifully by a similitude. "A clear-walled city" is enough; "meadows" are enough—indeed Tennyson reigns for ever over all meadows; "the happy birds that change their sky"; "Bright Phosphor, fresher for the night"; "Twilight and evening bell"; "the stillness of the central sea"; "that friend of mine who lives in God"; "the solitary morning"; "Four grey walls and four grey towers"; "Watched by weeping queens"; these are enough, illustrious, and needing not illustration.

If we do not see Tennyson to be the lonely, the first, the *one* that he is, this is because of the throng

---

[1] Marie de Rabutin-Chantel Sévigné (1626–96), French letter-writer and Salonist.

[2] Jeremy Taylor (1613–67), Anglican clergyman and religious writer.

of his following, though a number that are of that throng hardly know, or else would deny, their flocking. But he added to our literature not only in the way of cumulation, but by the advent of his single genius. He is one of the few fountain-head poets of the world. The new landscape which was his—the lovely unbeloved—is, it need hardly be said, the matter of his poetry and not its inspiration. It may have seemed to some readers that it is the novelty, in poetry, of this homely unscenic scenery—this Lincolnshire quality—that accounts for Tennyson's freshness of vision. But it is not so. Tennyson is fresh also in scenic scenery; he is fresh with the things that others have outworn; mountains, desert islands, castles, elves, what you will that is conventional. Where are there more divinely poetic lines than those, which will never be wearied with quotation, beginning, "A splendour falls"? What castle walls have stood in such a light of old romance, where in all poetry is there a sound wilder than that of those faint "horns of elfland"? Here is the remoteness, the beyond, the light delirium, not of disease but of more rapturous and delicate health, the closer secret of poetry. This most English of modern poets has been taunted with his mere gardens. He loved, indeed, the "lazy lilies,"[1] of the exquisite garden of "The Gardener's Daughter," but he betook his ecstatic English spirit also far afield and overseas; to the winter places of his familiar nightingale:

> When first the liquid note beloved of men
> Comes flying over many a windy wave;[2]

to the lotus-eaters' shore; to the outland landscapes of "The Palace of Art"—the "clear-walled city by the sea," the "pillared town," the "full-fed river";[3] to the "pencilled valleys" of Monte Rosa;[4] to the "vale in Ida,"[5] to that tremendous upland in the "Vision of Sin":

> At last I heard a voice upon the slope
> Cry to the summit, Is there any hope?
> To which an answer pealed from that high land,
> But in a tongue no man could understand.[6]

The Cleopatra of "The Dream of Fair Women" is but a ready-made Cleopatra, but when in the shades of her forest she remembers the sun of the world, she leaves the page of Tennyson's poorest manner and becomes one with Shakespeare's queen:

> We drank the Libyan sun to sleep.[7]

Nay, there is never a passage of manner but a great passage of style rebukes our dislike and recalls our heart again. The dramas, less than the lyrics, and even less than the "Idylls," are matter for the true Tennysonian. Their action is, at its liveliest, rather vivacious than vital, and the sentiment, whether in "Becket" or in "Harold," is not only modern, it is fixed within Tennyson's own peculiar score or so of years. But that he might have answered, in drama, to a stronger stimulus, a sharper spur, than his time administered, may be guessed from a few passages of "Queen Mary," and from the dramatic terror of the arrow in "Harold." The line has appeared in prophetic fragments in earlier scenes, and at the moment of doom it is the outcry of unquestionable tragedy:

> Sanguelac—Sanguelac—the arrow—
> the arrow!—Away![8]

---

[1] l. 42.

[2] *Idylls of the King*, "The Marriage of Geraint," ll. 336–37.

[3] l. 97, l. 124, l. 73.

[4] "The Daisy," l. 67.

[5] "Œnone," l. 1.

[6] ll. 219–22.

[7] l. 145.

[8] *Harold* 3.1.402.

Tennyson is also an eminently all-intelligible poet. Those whom he puzzles or confounds must be a flock with an incalculable liability to go wide of any road—"down all manner of streets," as the desperate drover cries in the anecdote. But what are streets, however various, to the ways of error that a great flock will take in open country—minutely, individually wrong, making mistakes upon hardly perceptible occasions, or none—"minute fortuitous variations in any possible direction," as used to be said in exposition of the Darwinian theory? A vast outlying public, like that of Tennyson, may make you as many blunders as it has heads; but the accurate clear poet proved his meaning to all accurate perceptions. Where he hesitates, his is the sincere pause of process and uncertainty. It has been said that Tennyson, midway between the student of material science and the mystic, wrote and thought according to an age that wavered, with him, between the two minds, and that men have now taken one way or the other. Is this indeed true, and are men so divided and so sure? Or have they not rather already turned, in numbers, back to the parting, or meeting, of eternal roads? The religious question that arises upon experience of death has never been asked with more sincerity and attention than by him. If "In Memoriam" represents the mind of yesterday it represents no less the mind of to-morrow. It is true that pessimism and insurrection in their ignobler forms—nay, in the ignoblest form of a fashion—have, or had but yesterday, the control of the popular pen. Trivial pessimism or trivial optimism, it matters little which prevails. For those who follow the one habit to-day would have followed the other in a past generation. Fleeting as they are, it cannot be within their competence to neglect or reject the philosophy of "In Memoriam." To the dainty stanzas of that poem, it is true, no great struggle of reasoning was to be committed, nor would any such dispute be judiciously entrusted to the rhymes of a song of sorrow. Tennyson here proposes, rather than closes with, the ultimate question of our destiny. The conflict, for which he proves himself strong enough, is in that magnificent poem of a thinker, "Lucretius." But so far as "In Memoriam" attempts, weighs, falters, and confides, it is true to the experience of human anguish and intellect.

I say intellect advisedly. Not for him such blunders of thought as Coleridge's in "The Ancient Mariner" or Wordsworth's in "Hartleap Well." Coleridge names the sun, moon, and stars as when, in a dream, the sleeping imagination is threatened with some significant illness. We see them in his great poem as apparitions. Coleridge's senses are infinitely and transcendently spiritual. But a candid reader must be permitted to think the mere story silly. The wedding-guest might rise the morrow morn a sadder but he assuredly did not rise a wiser man.

As for Wordsworth, the most beautiful stanzas of "Hartleap Well" are fatally rebuked by the truths of Nature. He shows us the ruins of an aspen wood, a blighted hollow, a dreary place, forlorn because an innocent stag, hunted, had there broken his heart in a leap from the rocks above; grass would not grow there.

> This beast not unobserved by Nature fell,
> His death was mourned by sympathy divine.[1]

And the signs of that sympathy are cruelly asserted by the poet to be these woodland ruins—cruelly, because the daily sight of the world blossoming over the agonies of beast and bird is made less tolerable to us by such a fiction.

> The Being that is in the clouds and air
>
> .   .   .   .   .   .
>
> Maintains a deep and reverential care
> For the unoffending creature whom He loves.[2]

---

[1] ll. 163–64.

[2] l. 165, ll. 167–68.

The poet offers us as a proof of that "reverential care," the visible alteration of Nature at the scene of suffering—an alteration we have to dispense with every day we pass in the woods. We are tempted to ask whether Wordsworth himself believed in the sympathy he asks us—on such grounds!—to believe in? Did he think his faith to be worthy of no more than a fictitious sign and a false proof?

Nowhere in the whole of Tennyson's thought is there such an attack upon our reason and our heart. He is more serious than the solemn Wordsworth.

And this poem, with all else that Tennyson wrote, tutors, with here and there a subtle word, this nature-loving nation to perceive land, light, sky, and ocean, as he perceived. To this we return, upon this we dwell. He has been to us, firstly, the poet of two geniuses—a small and an immense; secondly, the modern poet who answered in the negative that most significant modern question, French or not French? But he was, before the outset of all our study of him, of all our love of him, the poet of landscape, and this he is more dearly than pen can describe him. This eternal character of his is keen in the verse that is winged to meet a homeward ship with her "dewy decks," and in the sudden island landscape,

> The clover sod,
> That takes the sunshine and the rains,
> Or where the kneeling hamlet drains
> The chalice of the grapes of God.

It is poignant in the garden-night:

> A breeze began to tremble o'er
> The large leaves of the sycamore,
>
> .   .   .   .
>
> And gathering freshlier overhead,
> Rocked the full-foliaged elm, and swung
> The heavy-folded rose, and flung

The lilies to and fro, and said
"The dawn, the dawn," and died away.[1]

His are the exalted senses that sensual poets know nothing of. I think the sense of hearing as well as the sense of sight, has never been more greatly exalted than by Tennyson:

> As from beyond the limit of the world,
> Like the last echo born of a great cry.[2]

As to this garden-character so much decried I confess that the "lawn" does not generally delight me, the word nor the thing. But in Tennyson's page the word is wonderful, as though it had never been dull: "The mountain lawn was dewy-dark."[3] It is not that he brings the mountains too near or ranks them in his own peculiar garden-plot, but that the word withdraws to summits, withdraws into dreams; the lawn is aloft, alone, and as wild as ancient snow. It is the same with many another word or phrase changed, by passing into his vocabulary, into something rich and strange. His own especially is the March month—his "roaring moon." His is the spirit of the dawning month of flowers and storms; the golden, soft names of daffodil and crocus are caught by the gale as you speak them in his verse, in a fine disproportion with the energy and gloom. His was a new apprehension of nature, an increase in the number, and not only in the sum, of our national apprehensions of poetry in nature. Unaware of a separate angel of modern poetry is he who is insensible to the Tennyson note—the new note that we reaffirm even with the notes of Vaughan, Traherne,[4] Wordsworth, Coleridge, Blake well in our ears—the Tennyson note of splendour, all-distinct. He showed the perpet-

---

[1] *In Memoriam*, 1.10.12, ll. 13–16, ll. 54–61.

[2] *Idylls of the King*, "The Passing of Arthur," ll. 458–59.

[3] "Œnone," l. 48.

[4] Henry Vaughan (1622–95), Welsh poet; Thomas Traherne (c.1638–74), poet and religious writer.

ually transfigured landscape in transfiguring words. He is the captain of our dreams. Others have lighted a candle in England, he lit a sun. Through him our daily suns, and also the backward and historic suns long since set, which he did not sing, are magnified; and he bestows upon us an exalted retrospection. Through him Napoleon's sun of Austerlitz rises, for us, with a more brilliant menace upon arms and the plain; through him Fielding's "most melancholy sun" lights the dying man to the setting-forth on that last voyage of his with such an immortal gleam, denying hope, as would not have lighted, for us, the memory of that seaward morning, had our poetry not undergone the illumination, the transcendent sunrise, of Tennyson's genius.

Emerson knew that the poet speaks adequately then only when he speaks "a little wildly, or with the flower of the mind." Tennyson, the clearest-headed of poets, is our wild poet; wild, notwithstanding that little foppery we know of in him—that walking delicately, like Agag;[1] wild, notwithstanding the work, the ease, the neatness, the finish; notwithstanding the assertion of manliness which, in asserting, somewhat misses the mark; a wilder poet than the rough, than the sensual, than the defiant, than the accuser, than the denouncer. Wild flowers are his—great poet—wild winds, wild lights, wild heart, wild eyes!

—1917

Robert Browning [2]

It says much for the power of Browning that he was able to leaven the mass of cultivated people by means of a comparatively little knot of readers. That he should be popular in any literal sense of the word had always been an impossibility which Browning very frankly accepted. Too obscure to be understood

without unusual power of thought and especially without unusual mobility of mind, on the part of his reader, his work is also seldom musical enough to haunt the memory; and these two defects, if defects they be, have become proverbial with regard to him, and inseparable from his name. Yet he has, now and then, written verse in which a difficult thought has been expressed pellucidly, and verse ringing with true significant music, and occasionally even with a too obvious and insistent tune; but these exceptions are very naturally lost sight of in his prevailing practice. Now, in our opinion no author should be blamed for obscurity, nor should any pains be grudged in the effort to understand him, provided that he has done his best to be intelligible. Difficult thoughts are quite distinct from difficult words. Difficulty of thought is the very heart of poetry. Those who complain of it would restrict poetry to literal narrative for its epics, to unanalysed—and therefore ultimately to unrealized and conventional—passion for its drama, and to songs for its lyrics. Doubtless narrative, dramas of primary passion, and singable songs are all excellent things; masterpieces have been done in these ways— but in the past—in a fresher, broader, and simpler time than ours. Those masterpieces bring their own age with them, as it were, into our hearts; we ourselves assume a singleness of mind as we read them; they are neither too obvious nor too unthoughtful to interest us; but it is far otherwise with modern work which is laid upon the same lines.

Our age is not simple—we inherit so much from other ages; and our language has lost the freshness of its early literature—reasons why the poetry of our time should be complex in thought and should depend upon something more mental than the charm of form sufficient in the lyrics of the Elizabethans. The English language was once so beautiful, so fresh and free, that any well-composed group of English words would make a poem. But some of the vitality has been written out of the language since then; it is richer now than ever, but it has lost that youthfulness

---

[1] King of the Amalekites, 1 Samuel 15:32.

[2] first published in *The Pen*, 1880.

of form; and though the poems of those other times cannot themselves cease to be fresh to us, nothing can now be written of exactly their character. Beauty of manner must therefore be secondary in modern poetry to importance of thought; and no true thinking is altogether easy. Granted that modern poetry must be thoughtful or nothing, and that thought is difficult, we shall here have a sufficient apology for more than half Browning's obscurity. The rest must, as usual, be ascribed to the mere construction of his phrases; he has his own way of dropping out articles and other little words, which leads to grammatical ambiguities never, perhaps, suspected by the author himself and greatly to be lamented; grammatical obscurity is, perhaps, the one obscurity of which a reader has a right to complain. The same habit of contraction adds greatly to the tenseness of the verse, and it is this tenseness which we might wish to see relaxed. Even when his thought is closest, the words might fit it a little less tightly, we think; but Browning's mannerisms are not, as mannerisms, displeasing, for they are full of himself—of one of the most original personalities of contemporary literature. He, like Tennyson, is essential, not accidental, in English poetry.

Browning is, as a poet, distinctively a man of the world; we use the term in the sense in which it is employed by men when they intend praise; he is keenly interested in things as they are; he is impartial and has a masculine tolerance and patience which belong essentially to the dramatic genius; he prefers to be shrewd rather than profound in the mental analysis which delights him; there are heights in the human soul that tempt this explorer less than level ways—provided these are intricate enough. Browning is distinctively human, but not in the sense which the word generally bears; he is not exactly gentle or sympathetic, or penetrated with the pathos of the human tragedy; he is curious in human things, interested, experimental, and he preserves a sane cheerfulness altogether characteristic of himself. This

last, which supports him through pages upon pages of inquiries and experiments as to the mental processes of a spirit-rapping cheat also inspires him with poems on death, now heroically grotesque, now ecstatic.

> I would hate that death bandaged my eyes, and
> forebore,
>   And bade me creep past,
> No! Let me taste the whole of it, fare like my peers,
>   The heroes of old,
> Bear the brunt, in a minute pay glad life's arrears
>   Of pain, darkness, and cold.
>
> .   .   .   .   .   .
>
> The fiend-voices that rave
>   Shall dwindle, shall blend,
> Shall change, shall become first a peace out of pain,
>   Then a light, then thy breast,
> O thou soul of my soul! I shall clasp thee again,
>   And with God be the rest![1]

In the following the "little minute's sleep" is past:

> "What! and is it you again?" quoth I.
> "I again; whom else did you expect?" quoth
>   she.

Then he tells her how much relieved he is to be rid of life and he sketches his own epitaph:

> "Afflictions sore long time be bore; do end," quoth
>   I.
> I end with "Love is all and death is nought," quoth
>   she.[2]

He carries this same temper of mind through his study of Bishop Blougram's sophistries, and through the resignation of *Any Wife to Any Husband*. And surely Browning's work loses something by this

---

[1] "Prospice," ll. 15–28.

[2] a series of somewhat misquoted lines from the "Epilogue" of *Fifine at the Fair* (ll. 7–8, 30–31).

equanimity, this large tolerance of his. A mind less serene, whole, scientific, and independent might of-tener be touched, or hurt, or discouraged into seeking a lofty and lovely ideal which is rare in his poetry. Not that Browning cannot conceive it, but that he is too closely and intently at work with things as they are to attend to it.

But no one who has not followed him through his labours of analysis, can understand the pleasure of the more studious reader at hearing Browning's cool, strong, argumentative voice break in the rare note of emotion, caused by his own sudden rise to a higher moral and mental beauty than lies in the path of a man of the world. When this happens, not the feeling only, but the verse softens and relaxes; for his style, like his thought, is knotted—is as knotty, indeed, as a fugue. But when that higher, fresher thought comes, it brings with it its own inevitable music. No poet has written fuller, more important, and more significant music than Browning at these rare mo-ments. For instance, in that fine drama, *The Return of the Druses*, there is some difficulty in the character of Anael with her double love and her half-deliberate delusion, so that much of the verse allotted to her is intricate enough; but where strong single feeling rises in the heart of this exiled Druse girl, what exquisite music sweeps out indeliberately!—

Dost thou snow-swathe thee kinglier, Lebanon,
Than in my dreams? [1]

English poetry might in vain be searched for a nobler cadence. In *Pippa Passes* (to our mind the most beautiful, though not therefore necessarily the most intellectual, of all Browning's works) such music is too frequent to allow us to choose examples; it occurs in *Balaustion's Adventure*, now and then, and less frequently elsewhere. Far more strongly accented musical pieces occur now and then in his work; *Evelyn Hope* and *A Lover's Quarrel* are as melodi-

ous—except for an occasional jerk—as the warmest admirers of insistently rhythmic verse could possibly require; but these bear the same relation to the higher music of which we have just spoken, as is borne by a tune of Rossini's [2] to one of Schumann's [3] significant sentences of notes.

—1913

from *The Rhythm of Life*

If life is not always poetical, it is at least metrical. Periodicity rules over the mental experience of man, according to the path of the orbit of his thoughts. Distances are not gauged, ellipses not measured, velocities not ascertained, times not known. Nevertheless, the recurrence is sure. What the mind suffered last week, or last year, it does not suffer now; but it will suffer again next week or next year. Happiness is not a matter of events; it depends upon the tides of the mind. Disease is metrical, closing in at shorter and shorter periods towards death, sweeping abroad at longer and longer intervals towards recovery. Sorrow for one cause was intolera-ble yesterday, and will be intolerable to-morrow; to-day it is easy to bear, but the cause has not passed. Even the burden of a spiritual distress unsolved is bound to leave the heart to a temporary peace; and remorse itself does not remain—it returns. Gaiety takes us by a dear surprise. If we had made a course of notes of its visits, we might have been on the watch, and would have had an expectation instead of a discovery. No one makes such observations; in all the diaries of students of the interior world, there have never come to light the records of the Kepler [4] of

[1] 2.179–80.

[2] Gioachino Antonio Rossini (1792–1868), Italian composer.

[3] Robert Schumann (1810–56), German composer, pianist, and con-ductor.

[4] Johann Kepler (1571–1630), German mathematician who proposed early laws of planetary motion.

such cycles. But Thomas à Kempis[1] knew of the recurrences, if he did not measure them. In his cell alone with the elements—"What wouldst thou more than these? for out of these were all things made"— he learnt the stay to be found in the depth of the hour of bitterness, and the remembrance that restrains the soul at the coming of the moment of delight, giving it a more conscious welcome, but presaging for it an inexorable flight. And "rarely, rarely comest thou,"[2] sighed Shelley, not to Delight merely, but to the Spirit of Delight. Delight can be compelled beforehand, called, and constrained to our service—Ariel can be bound to a daily task; but such artificial violence throws life out of metre, and it is not the spirit that is thus compelled. *That* flits upon an orbit elliptically or parabolically or hyperbolically curved, keeping no man knows what trysts with Time.

It seems fit that Shelley and the author of the "Imitation"[3] should both have been keen and simple enough to perceive these flights, and to guess at the order of this periodicity. Both souls were in close touch with the spirits of their several worlds, and no deliberate human rules, no infractions of the liberty and law of the universal movement, kept from them the knowledge of recurrences. *Eppur si muove.*[4] They knew that presence does not exist without absence; they knew that what is just upon its flight of farewell is already on its long path of return. They knew that what is approaching to the very touch is hastening towards departure. "O wind," cried Shelley, in autumn,

> O wind,
> If winter comes can spring be far behind?[5]

They knew that the flux is equal to the reflux; that to interrupt with unlawful recurrences, out of time, is to weaken the impulse of onset and retreat; the sweep and impetus of movement. To live in constant efforts after an equal life, whether the equality be sought in mental production, or in spiritual sweetness, or in the joy of the senses, is to live without either rest or full activity. The souls of certain of the saints, being singularly simple and single, have been in the most complete subjection to the law of periodicity. Ecstasy and desolation visited them by seasons. They endured, during spaces of vacant time, the interior loss of all for which they had sacrificed the world. They rejoiced in the uncovenanted beatitude of sweetness alighting in their hearts. Like them are the poets whom, three times or ten times in the course of a long life, the Muse has approached, touched, and forsaken. And yet hardly like them; not always so docile, nor so wholly prepared for the departure, the brevity, of the golden and irrevocable hour. Few poets have fully recognized the metrical absence of their Muse. For full recognition is expressed in one only way—silence.

It has been found that several tribes in Africa and in America worship the moon, and not the sun; a great number worship both; but no tribes are known to adore the sun, and not the moon. On her depend the tides; and she is Selene, mother of Herse, bringer of the dews that recurrently irrigate lands where rain is rare. More than any other companion of earth is she the Measurer. Early Indo-Germanic languages knew her by that name. Her metrical phases are the symbol of the order of recurrence. Constancy in approach and in departure is the reason of her inconstancies. Juliet[6] will not receive a vow spoken in

---

1 Thomas à Kempis (c. 1380–1471), German mystic.

2 "Song" 1.

3 Thomas à Kempis's "Of the Imitation of Christ."

4 a version of the words spoken (quietly?) by Galileo following his recantation of his theory of the earth's movement: "And yet, it moves."

5 "Ode to the West Wind" (1820), ll. 69–70.

6 *Romeo and Juliet* 2.2.109–11: "O! swear not by the moon, the inconstant moon, / That monthly changes in her circled orb, / Lest that

invocation of the moon; but Juliet did not live to know that love itself has tidal times—lapses and ebbs which are due to the metrical rule of the interior heart, but which the lover vainly and unkindly attributes to some outward alteration in the beloved. For man—except those elect already named—is hardly aware of periodicity. The individual man either never learns it fully, or learns it late. And he learns it so late, because it is a matter of cumulative experience upon which cumulative evidence is long lacking. It is in the after-part of each life that the law is learnt so definitely as to do away with the hope or fear of continuance. That young sorrow comes so near to despair is a result of this young ignorance. So is the early hope of great achievement. Life seems so long, and its capacity so great, to one who knows nothing of all the intervals it needs must hold—intervals between aspirations, between actions, pauses as inevitable as the pauses of sleep. And life looks impossible to the young unfortunate, unaware of the inevitable and unfailing refreshment. It would be for their peace to learn that there is a tide in the affairs of men, in a sense more subtle—if it is not too audacious to add a meaning to Shakespeare—than the phrase was meant to contain. Their joy is flying away from them on its way home; their life will wax and wane; and if they would be wise, they must wake and rest in its phases, knowing that they are ruled by the law that commands all things—a sun's revolutions and the rhythmic pangs of maternity.

—1913

thy love prove likewise variable."

Index of First Lines

Index of Authors and Titles